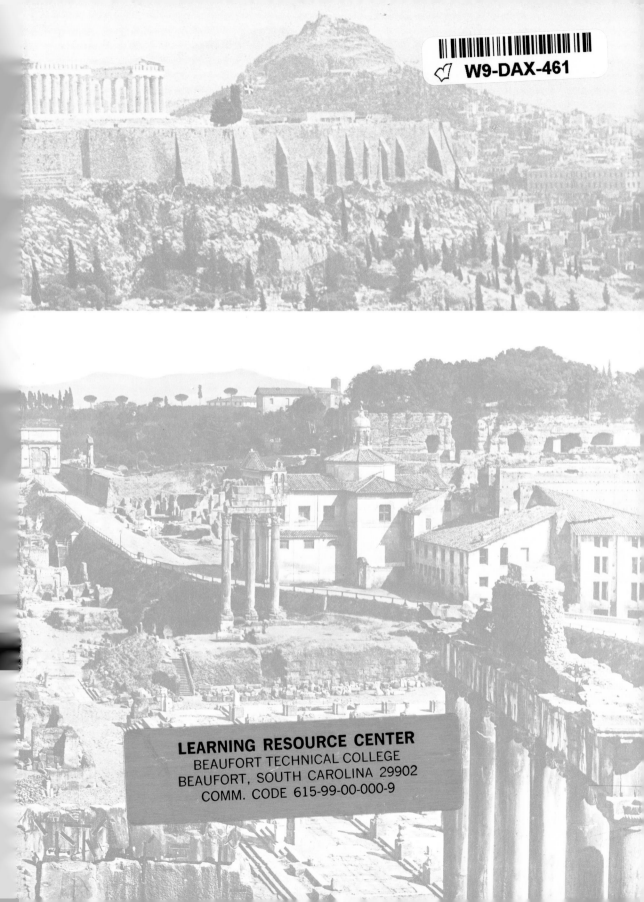

W9-DAX-461

ILLUSTRATED ENCYCLOPAEDIA OF THE CLASSICAL WORLD

In memory of my mother Deborah Shatzman

I.S.

ILLUSTRATED ENCYCLOPAEDIA OF THE CLASSICAL WORLD

Michael Avi Yonah and Israel Shatzman

FOREWORD by F. W. WALBANK

Rathbone Professor of Ancient History and Classical
Archaeology, University of Liverpool

Harper & Row, Publishers
New York, Evanston, San Francisco, London

ILLUSTRATED ENCYCLOPAEDIA
OF THE CLASSICAL WORLD

Designed by OFRA KAMAR

39, Tchernichovski St., P.O. Box 7147, Jerusalem.

For information address Harper & Row, Publishers, Inc., 10 East 53rd Street, New York, N.Y. 10022

FIRST U.S. EDITION

ISBN: 0–06–010178–4

LIBRARY OF CONGRESS CATALOG CARD
NUMBER: 73–14245

Set by Isratypeset Ltd., Jerusalem
Plates by Printone Ltd., Jerusalem
Printed by Central Press, Jerusalem
Bound by Keter, Jerusalem
Colour pages and jacket printed by Japhet Press, Givataim

PRINTED IN ISRAEL

CONTENTS

FOREWORD 6

NOTES ON THE USE OF THE ENCYCLOPAEDIA 8

LIST OF ABBREVIATIONS 9

ENCYCLOPAEDIA OF THE CLASSICAL WORLD 13

MAPS 489

TABLES 494

SELECT BIBLIOGRAPHY 501

INDEX 504

ACKNOWLEDGMENTS 510

FOREWORD

The civilisation of Greece and Rome has deep roots in English-speaking lands all over the world, and especially in Britain and the United States. Until a few decades ago the study of Greek and Latin was a major element in the education provided in the British public and grammar schools, Horace was quoted, recognised — and even understood! — in the House of Commons, and Demosthenes and Cicero were thought of affectionately, almost as if they were contemporaries. Indeed, so blurred was the difference that it was a common practice to put up statues of kings and statesmen clad in Roman togas. Similarly, across the Atlantic the Founding Fathers of the new American republic turned eagerly to the classics for counsel in devising their constitution, classical placenames such as Syracuse, Utica, Rome, Carthage, Athens or Ithaca proliferated across the American countryside, and George Washington was seen as a modern Cincinnatus, called from the farm to lead his country's armies.

Very little of all this survives today. The modern school curriculum now takes in a whole range of new subjects; but comparatively few still learn to read the classical authors in the original. Yet, paradoxically, interest in the achievements and everyday life of Greece and Rome has never been greater among the educated public. For this there are several obvious reasons. In the first place, far more people than ever before now have the chance to visit classical lands — not merely the parts of Italy which made up the Grand Tour for eighteenth century gentlemen, but in addition the remoter sites of Greece, Sicily, Turkey, North Africa, Egypt and Palestine, not to mention France and Spain, where the Greeks and Romans left so many impressive marks of their occupation.

Secondly, there are the many recent additions to our knowledge of the classical world which make it a lively and exciting field to work in or to study. As examples one may take the new discoveries which archaeology has made and continues to make as a result of chance or systematic excavation, the tangible evidence of newly found inscriptions on stone or of papyri unearthed in Egypt or in caves along the banks of the Dead Sea, and the deciphering of the Linear B script on Minoan and Mycenaean tablets as an early form of Greek, which can throw light on the social organisation of Greece and Crete in the second millenium BC. Such things as these have sparked off an interest among the general public in a society which at certain times in its evolution and in certain respects is so closely related to our own — indeed we are sprung from it — but is at the same time strikingly different both in its beliefs and values and in its level of technology and its social structure.

Finally, no one can interest himself to a more than superficial level in English literature or, for that matter, in any other modern literature without being constantly reminded of the debt which so many writers of our own past owe to Greek and Roman literature for the themes and indeed the very structure of their work, not to mention the myths and legends to which we so frequently find reference being made.

Faced with this intrusion of the ancient world into our own lives at various points, we inevitably ask questions; and to answer these there is a traditional standby — the encyclopaedia. Classical encyclopaedias have a long and honourable record as the quick guide to the various facets of Greek and Roman life and thought. Over recent centuries such works have appeared in a variety of shapes and sizes, from the single slim volume to the vast German *Real—Encyclopädie* of Paully and Wissowa, begun in 1893 and now at last reaching completion in over 80 volumes. Whatever their size, the general purpose of such works conforms to the summing-up which Lemprière made in his preface to the new and expanded edition of his *Classical Dictionary* in 1839, when he offered his readers "a judicious selection of whatever was grand striking and interesting in the annals of nations, in the fleeting revolutions of communities and empires, and in the character of men, who have rendered themselves illustrious in the walks either of Science, Philosophy, Arts or Arms, and who have commanded the notice or the admiration of posterity".

That is also the aim of the present work — though nowadays we might not, perhaps, phrase it so grandiloquently. It has been designed to satisfy the requirements of those who have no direct training in the classical disciplines, but who, for one reason or another, are interested in the classical world, and want clear, concise and reliable information about it. It was planned originally by the late Professor M. Avi-Yonah of the Hebrew University in Jerusalem, a scholar widely known for his work on classical art, late Roman and Byzantine history and ancient topography; his large model of Jerusalem at the time of Herod the Great will be familiar to most visitors to that city. However, the illness which eventually resulted in his death in 1974 compelled him to relinquish his direction of the project before it had got very far, and in 1973, by arrangement with the publishers, the editorship was transferred to Dr. Israel Shatzman, also of the Hebrew University. Dr. Shatzman is a scholar with a long list of published work dealing especially with problems of Roman wealth and politics, but also with Roman religion and Roman historiography. His wide interests made him an eminently suitable choice to take over the Encyclopaedia, and under his editorship it has assumed a rather different shape from the one originally planned.

To the original list of persons and places envisaged by the first editor, Dr. Shatzman has added articles to cover general terms, ancient institutions, branches of classical literature, and the main facets of social and religious life. Thus increased in scope and depth, the work now contains some 2,300 articles in all, most written or revised by the new editor, and comprehending the main themes, persons and places of Greek and Roman history, classical mythology and religion, philosophy and thought, together with the most important writers, artists and statesmen, the chief sites, the topography and the social background of the ancient world. In it the student of other disciplines as well as the general reader will find briefly set out, without any assumptions of previous specialised knowledge, the basic facts on each of these topics. Whether he is interested in Virgil or Mycenaean palaces, the Roman constitution or the role of slavery in the ancient world, the procedures in the Athenian law-courts or the structure and strategy of the Roman army, the legends illustrated on Attic vases of the conditions in which Greek tragedies were performed, he (or she) will find the information he requires. Illustrations have been widely used to supplement the text and there are six maps and many tables. Finally, bibliographies have been added after the various articles, to enable the reader to pursue further any special interest.

It is the hope of all who have been concerned in the production of this book that it may help to keep alive a consciousness and understanding of the classical heritage which, after many centuries, is still in so many ways at the roots of our whole way of life.

F. W. Walbank

NOTES ON THE USE OF THE ENCYCLOPAEDIA

An asterisk marks articles appearing in this work where further relevent information can be found. There are many names, institutions and terms which do not have separate articles but are explained in other articles. These appear in the index and it is always advisable to consult it.

Many articles are accompanied by short bibliographies listing texts, translations or modern works. In many cases a bibliographical reference is to a book with the addition (s.v.), which refers to the index of the book where the reader is advised to consult the appropriate name or term. As far as possible only works in English have been given. In addition, there is a classified Select Bibliography on page 501 which covers all the subjects treated in this encyclopaedia. Many of the works listed have good bibliographies.

Roman persons are listed by their more familiar names (e.g. Cicero rather than Tullius). The spelling of the names is generally in the latinized form, but the uniformity has not been imposed throughout the Encyclopaedia.

The abbreviations used in both the entries and the bibliographies are listed on page 9.

I would like to take this opportunity to thank the staff of the Jerusalem Publishing House for their consideration and helpful cooperation. Special thanks are due to Dr. Raphael Posner and Mr. Alec Israel, whose help has been most valuable in the preparation of the text.

I.S.

LIST OF ABBREVIATIONS

ABSA	*Annual of the British School at Athens.*
AJA	*American Journal of Archeology.*
AJP	*American Journal of Philology.*
Alföldi, *Early Rome*	A. Alföldi, *Early Rome and the Latins,* 1965.
Altheim, *Rom. Rel.*	F. Altheim, *A History of Roman Religion,* 1938.
Apollod.	Apollodorus, *Bibliotheca.*
Apol.Rhod.	Apollonius Rhodius, *Argonautica.*
Appian, *BC*	Appian, *Civil Wars.*
Ib.	*Iberian Wars.*
Arist. *Athen.Pol.*	Aristotle, *Constitution of Athens.*
Poet.	*Poetica.*
Arnim, *St.Vet.Fr.*	H. von Arnim (ed.), *Stoicorum Veterum Fragmenta,* 1903.
Athen.	Athenaeus.
Badian, *Studies*	E. Badian, *Studies in Greek and Roman History,* 1964.
Beare, *Rome. St.*	W. Beare, *The Roman Stage*[3], 1965.
Bowra, *Gr.Lyr.Poet.*	C.M. Bowra, *Greek Lyric Poetry from Alcman to Simonides*[2], 1961.
E.Gr.El.	*Early Greek Elegists,* 1938.
Budé	Collection des Univ. de France, publiée sous le patronage de l'Assoc.
	G. Budé. (texts and French translations).
	ICIL Corpus Inscriptionum Latinarum.
ClP	*Classical Philology.*
ClQ	*Classical Quarterly.*
Caesar, *Bell.Gall.*	Caesar, *Gallic Wars.*
Bell. Civ.	*Civil Wars.*
Cary, *Geographical Background*	M. Cary, *The Geographical Background of Greek and Roman History,* 1949.
Cic. *Amic.*	Cicero, *De Amicitia.*
Div.	*De Divinatione.*
Fin.	*De Finibus Bonorum et Malorum.*
Nat. De.	*De Natura Deorum.*
Leg.	*De Legibus*
Off.	*De Officiis.*
Rep.	*De Republica.*
Verr.	*In Verrem.*
Cymunt, *Oriental Religions*	F. Cymont, *Oriental Religions in Roman Paganism* (En. tr.), 1956.
Diehl, *An.Lyr.Gr.*	E. Diehl (ed.), *Anthologia Lyrica Graeca*[3], 1951–4.
Diels, *Fr. Vor.*	H. Diels (ed.), *Die Fragmente der Vorsokratiker*[3], 1954.
Dill, *Roman Society*	S. Dill, *Roman Society in the Last Century of the Western Empire,* 1898.
Dio	Cassius Dio.
Diod. Sic.	Diodorus Siculus.
Diog.Laert.	Diogenes Laertius.
Dion. Hal.·	Dionysius of Halicarnassus, *Antiquitates Romanae.*
Dudley, *Cynicism*	D.R. Dudley, *A History of Cynicism,* 1937.
Duff, *Min.Lat.Poets,*	J.W. and A.M. Duff, *Minor Latin Poets* (Loeb), 1934.
Dunbabin, *Western Greeks,*	T.J. Dunbabin, *The Western Greeks,* 1948.
ESAR	T. Frank (ed.), *An Economic Survey of Ancient Rome,* 1933–1940.
Edmonds, *Fr.At.Com.*	J.M. Edmonds, *The Fragments of Attic Comedy,* 1957–61.

Eur. *Alc.*   Euripides, *Alcestis.*
   Bacch.   *Bacchae.*
   El.   *Electra.*
   Hec.   *Hecuba.*
   Med.   *Medea.*
   Or.   *Orestes.*

Farnell, *Cults*   L.R. Farnell, *The Cults of the Greek States,* 1896—1909.

Frazer, *Alexandria*   P.M. Frazer, *Ptolemaic Alexandria,* 1972.

Frere, *Britannia*   S.S. Frere, *Britannia,* 1967.

Gaius, *Inst.*   Gaius, *Institutiones.*

Gell.   Aulus Gellius, *Noctes Atticae.*

Graham, *Col.Moth.Cit.*   A.J. Graham, *Colony and Mother City in Ancient Greece,* 1964.

Guthrie, *Gr.Gods.*   W.K.C. Guthrie, *The Greeks and their Gods*[3], 1950.

Hammond, *Epirus*   N.G.L. Hammond, *Epirus,* 1967.

Hansen, *Attalids*   C.V. Hansen, *The Attalids of Pergamum*[2], 1971.

Hdt.   Herodotus.

Hesiod *Theog.*   *Theogonia.*
   Erg.   *Erga.*

Hignett, *Athen.Const.*   C. Hignett, *A History of the Athenian Constitutions,* 1952.

Hom. *Il.*   Homer, *Iliad.*
   Od.   *Odyssey*

Hor. *Epist.*   Horace, *Epistulae.*
   Carm.   *Carmina* (Odes).
   Sat.   *Satirae.*

Il.   *Iliad.*

JHS   *Journal of Hellenic Studies.*

JRS   *Journal of Roman Studies.*

Jacoby, *Fr. Gr. Hist.*   F. Jacoby (ed.), *Die Fragmente der griechischen Historiker,* 1923–

Jolowicz, *Roman Law*[3]   F.H. Jolowicz and B. Nichols, *Historical Introduction to the Study of Roman Law*[3], 1972.

Jones, *Cities*   A.H.M. Jones, *The Cities of the Eastern Roman Provinces*[2], 1972.
   Studies   *Studies in Roman Government and Law,* 1960.
   Lat.Rom.Emp.   *The Later Roman Empire 284–602,* 1964.

Joseph., *BJ*   Josephus, *Jewish Wars.*
   AJ   *Jewish Antiquities.*

Keil, *Gr.Lat.*   H. Keil (ed.), *Grammatici Latini,* 1855–1923.

Kennedy, *Persuasion*   G.A. Kennedy, *The Art of Persuasion in Greece,* 1963.

Kerényi, *Heroes*   C. Kerényi, *The Heroes of the Greeks,* 1959.
   Gods   *The Gods of the Greeks,* 1951.

Kirk–Raven, *Presocratic Philosophers*   G.S. Kirk and J.E. Raven, *The Presocratic Philosophers,* 1957.

Larsen, *Gr.Fed.St.*   J.A.O. Larsen, *Greek Federal States,* 1968.

Latt, *R.Rel.*   K. Latte, *Römische Religionsgeschichte,* 1968.

Liv.   Livy.

Loeb   Loeb Classical Library.

Macrob. *Sat.*   Macrobius, *Saturnalia.*

Malcovati, *Or.Rom.Fr.*   E. Malcovati (ed.), *Oratorum Romanorum Fragmenta*[3], 1965.

Mon. Anc.   *Monumentum Ancyranum.*

Min.At.Or.   K.J. Maidment and J.O. Burtt, *Minor Attic Orators* (Loeb), 1941.

Morel, *Fr.Poet.Lat.*   W. Morel, *Fragmenta Poetarum Latinorum,* 1927.

Nash, *Pict.Dict.Rome*   E. Nash, *Pictorial Dictionary of Ancient Rome,* 1961–2.

Nilsson, *Religion*   M.P. Nilsson, *The Minoan-Mycenaean Religion and its Survival in Greek Religion*[2], 1950.

OCT   *Oxford Classical Texts.*

Ogilvie, *Livy*   R.M. Ogilvie, *Commentary on Livy, Books 1–5,* 1965.

Ov. *Am.*   Ovid, *Amores.*
   Met.   *Metamorphoses.*
   Pont.   *Epistulae ex Ponto.*
   Tr.   *Tristia.*

PBSR   *Papers of the British School at Rome.*

Page, *Poet.Mel.Gr.*   D.L. Page, *Poetae Melicai Graeci,* 1962.

Palmer, *Archaic Community*   R.E.A. Palmer, *The Archaic Community of the Romans,* 1970.

Parker, *Roman Legions*   H.M.D. Parker, *The Roman Legions*[2], 1958.

Pausan.   Pausanias.

Pearson, *His.Al.Gr.*   L. Pearson, *The Lost Histories of Alexander the Great,* 1960.

Peter, *Hist.Rom.Rel.*	H. Peter (ed.), *Historicorum Romanorum Reliquiae,* 1906–1914.
Phil. *Leg.*	Philo Judaeus, *Legatio ad Gaium.*
Philostr. *Vit.Soph.*	Philostratus, *Vitae Sophistarum.*
Pickard–Cambridge, *Dithyramb*[2]	A.W. Pickard–Cambridge, *Dithyramb, Tragedy and Comedy*[2], (rev. by T.B.L. Webster), 1962.
Dramatic Festivals	*The Dramatic Festivals of Athens,* 1953.
Pind. *Nem.*	Pindar, *Nemean Odes.*
Ol.	*Olympian Odes.*
Pyth.	*Pythian Odes.*
Platner–Ashby, *Top.Dict.Rome*	S.B. Platner and T. Ashby, *A Topographical Dictionary of Ancient Rome,* 1929.
Plin. *NH*	Pliny the Elder, *Naturalis Historia.*
Plin. *Ep.*	Pliny the Younger, *Epistulae.*
Plut. *Anton*	Plutarch, *Antonius.*
Brut.	*Brutus.*
Caes.	*Caesar.*
Lyc.	*Lycurgus.*
Per.	*Pericles.*
Philop.	*Philopoemen.*
Pol., Polyb.	Polybius.
Quint. *Inst.*	Quintilian, *Institutio Oratoria.*
Rostovtzeff, *Hellenistic World*	M.I. Rostovtzeff, *The Social and Economic History of the Hellenistic World,* 1941.
Roman Empire	*The Social and Economic History of the Roman Empire*[2], 1957.
S.H.A.	*Scriptores Historiae Augustae.*
Sall. *Cat.*	Sallust, *Bellum Catilinae.*
Iug., B.G.	*Bellum Jugurthinum.*
Scullard, *Etruscan Cities*	H.H. Scullard, *The Etruscan Cities and Rome,* 1967.
Rom.Pol.[2]	*Roman Politics*[2], 1973.
Sen. *Ep.*	Seneca the Younger, *Epistulae.*
Shackleton Bailey, *Cicero's Letters*	D. R. Shackleton Bailey, *Cicero's Letters to Atticus,* 1965–1970.
Sherwin–White, *Rom.Cit.*	A.N. Sherwin–White, *The Roman Citizenship*[2], 1973.
Suet. *Aug.*	Suetonius, *Divus Augustus.*
Calig.	*Gaius Caligula.*
Claud.	*Divus Claudius.*
Dom.	*Domitianus.*
Iul.	*Divus Iulius.*
Syme, *Rom.Rev.*	R. Syme, *The Roman Revolution,* 1939.
Tacitus	*Tacitus,* 1958.
Tac. *Agr.*	Tacitus, *Agricola.*
Ann.	*Annales.*
Hist.	*Historiae.*
TAPA	*Transactions of the American Philological Association.*
Thomson, *Ancient Geography*	J.C. Thomson, *A History of Ancient Geography,* 1948.
Thuc.	Thucydides.
Tyrrel–Purser	R.Y. Tyrrell and L.C. Purser, *The Correspondence of Cicero,* 1904–1933.
Val.Max.	Valerius Maximus.
Varro, *Lin.Lat.*	Varro, *De Lingua Latina.*
Ver. *Aen.*	Virgil, *Aeneid.*
Ecl.	*Eclogues.*
Georg.	*Georgics.*
Warmington, *Rem.Ol.Lat.*	E.H. Warmington, *Remains of Old Latin,* 1935–1940.
Webster, *Lat.Gr.Com.*	T.B.L. Webster, *Studies in Later Greek Comedy,* 1953.
Will. *Hist.Pol.*	E. Will, *Histoire politique du Mond hellenistique,* 1966–
Xenophon, *Hell.*	Xenophon, *Hellenica.*

A

ABACUS Counting-frame used in Egypt, Greece and Rome, with vertical columns of units, tens, hundreds, etc., and with movable markers.

ABDERA Greek city on the southern coast of *Thrace, founded in 656 BC by the Ionians of *Clazomenae, destroyed by the Thracians and refounded by settlers from *Teos, c. 543 BC (Hdt.1.168). A prosperous trading city, A. was a member of the Delian League in the 5th century BC. It lost its independence to Macedonia in the 4th century. A. was the home of many profound thinkers; *Democritus, the founder of the atomic theory; *Protagoras, the Sophist friend of Pericles; and Anaxarchus, who accompanied Alexander the Great on his Asian campaigns. The fact that such eminent philosophers left their native town to find more fertile fields abroad, engendered the idea, first found in a story by *Machon, that the Abderites were impossibly stupid, which gave their city a reputation similar to that of Gotham in England.
J. M. F. May, *The Coinage of Abdera*, 1966.

ABYDOS Greek colony at the narrowest point of the Hellespont, on the Asiatic coast, founded by *Miletus. From here, the Persian army under Xerxes crossed to Europe in 480 BC. A. joined the Delian League in 477 BC, remaining under Athenian control until 412 BC when, for a time, it belonged to Sparta. In 200 BC, A. was occupied by *Philip V and after his defeat by Rome, in 197 BC, it fell to *Antiochus III; later on it appears to have regained its autonomy.

ACADEMY A grove near Athens named after the hero Academus. Plato founded a school there, c. 385 BC, which was an association for the cult of Apollo and the Muses. The communal life and education of the A. aimed at bettering the moral disposition and conduct of its members, besides training them for active politics. Philosophy and the natural sciences were given first priority, and the importance Plato ascribed to mathematics is reflected in the story that the inscription "Let no one enter in who does not know geometry" was placed on the entrance to the A. When Plato died, the pupils chose his nephew, *Speusippus, as their head. Under him and his successors (*Xenocrates, Crates, etc.) the main disciplines were ethics and the natural sciences. When *Arcesilaus became head in the beginning of the so-called Middle Academy, c. 265 BC, the main subject was scepticism. This tendency continued under *Carneades in the 2nd century, and in the 1st century BC, *Antiochus of Ascalon reverted to the teachings of the old A. Little is known about the A. during the period of the Roman Empire. The last prominent head was *Proclus in the 5th century AD. The school was closed by order of Justinian in AD 529.
H. Cherniss, *The Riddle of the First Academy*, 1942.

ACARNANIA Region north of the western end of the Gulf of Corinth, regarded as part of Middle Greece. A. was inhabited by old-fashioned, honest peasants and horse-breeders who served as lightly-armed slingers and javelin throwers. Corinthian colonization in A. drove the local population to seek the aid of Athens, their former enemy. A. was allied to Athens throughout the Peloponnesian War, and the alliance survived the defeat of an A. force at Aegitium and of the Athenians under *Demosthenes (1) (426 BC). Forced to join the Peloponnesian League under Sparta, A. left it at the first opportunity, rejoining the Second Attic League (375 BC). In the Hellenistic period, A. formed a confederation of cities, with the worship of Zeus Stratos and an autonomous coinage. In that period, A. allied itself with Macedonia against Epirus and its rapacious Aetolian neighbours. It managed to retain its independence until 30 BC when its cities were depopulated by Augustus, who moved the inhabitants to his town of Nicopolis near the battlefield of Actium.
Larsen, *Gr. Fed. St.*, 89—95, 264—273.

ACCA LARENTIA Roman goddess whose festival was celebrated annually on 23 December. A. was said to be the wife of *Faustulus who raised *Romulus and Remus; she had twelve sons, said to be the first *Fratres Arvales. In another tale, A. was a rich prostitute who left her fortune to the Roman people; her festival was instituted in gratitude. She was probably connected with Larunda, a goddess of Sabine origin to whom an annual sacrifice had been made on 23 December.

ACCIUS, Lucius Tragedian, poet and historian, c. 170—86 BC; son of a freedman of Pisaurum in Umbria, A. lived in Rome and travelled in Asia in 140 BC and again in 104 BC. Of the 46 tragedies he wrote, several had Roman subjects such as Brutus the liberator (one of his patrons was D. Junius Brutus, consul in 138 BC), and *Decius

Mus. The others dealt with Greek legends, such as the Trojan War, and many were imitations of Greek tragedies. A. was among the first to discuss Latin orthography and grammar, under the influence of Hellenistic philology. His *Annales*, written in rather heavy hexameter, gave an account of the yearly festivals. Though of humble descent, A. was known for his forcefulness and wrote his tragedies in a vigorous, dignified style, giving his characters a melodramatic touch. He was highly esteemed by Cicero and Virgil and was considered by some authorities to be the best Roman tragedian. 700 verses of his have survived, including such well-known sayings as *oderint dum metuant*, "Let them hate me, provided they fear me", which has been attributed to several Roman emperors.
E. H. Warmington, *Remains of Old Latin*[2] (Loeb), 1936; Morel, *Fr. Poet Lat.*

ACHAEA, ACHAEANS General appelation of the Greeks in the Mycenaean period, which probably appeared first in a Hittite text (*Achiyyawa*), wherein the city of Miletus (*Milatawa*) is the bone of contention between the Hittite king and the king of A. The use of the collective appelation A. for all Greeks continued in Homer and in later poetic usage. In Classical Greece the name was reserved

Achaean coin of 370–360 BC; reverse: Zeus enthroned, and obverse: Artemis

for two areas: southeastern Thessaly and a region on the northern coast of the Peloponnese. The two areas were linked by a common worship of Zeus Amarios at Aigion. Like the rest of the Peloponnese, A. was under Spartan hegemony from at least 417 BC. It was 2,325 sq km in area and could provide 36,000 soldiers. The first A. League, which was in existence by the early 4th century and which issued coins from 360, was dissolved in 324 BC. Renewed in 280 BC, the League became the strongest power in Greece, admitting even non-Achaean cities like the Dorian *Sicyon (252 BC) and the Arcadian *Megalopolis (235 BC). Led by *Aratus of Sicyon, the League managed to expel the Macedonians from Corinth, and then expanded into Arcadia. In the ensuing conflict with Sparta, A. was defeated by *Cleomenes III of Sparta, and forced to appeal to Macedonia. *Philopoemen of Megalopolis reorganized the army in 208 BC. From 198 BC on, A. was allied to Rome against Macedonia. Corinth was added in 194 BC and Sparta in 192 BC, and from 191 to 146 BC, the A. League consisted of about 60 cities, and was the closest approach to a federal state ever achieved by the Greeks. Citizenship in any city of the league conferred federal citizenship, although voting in the federal assemblies was by city. There were two assemblies: the *synodoi* met several times a year and were mainly elective; the *syncletoi* held extraordinary meetings to decide upon vital matters. The League controlled foreign affairs, the waging of war and the making of peace, as well as the right of coinage. There was a federal court, the *nomographoi*, mainly to arbitrate between the cities and their citizens; its officials were ten *demiourgoi* and two *strategoi* (after 255 BC, only one). The armed forces were composed of a standing army of 3,000 *epilectoi* (infantry), 300 cavalry, and a general levy of 30,000 (the latter of limited fighting value). From 217 BC on, the League also employed mercenaries. After the final defeat of Macedonia by Rome, in 168 BC, Rome came to suspect the A. League, and forced it to provide 1,000 hostages (among them the historian *Polybius) who were deported to Italy. The war with Sparta, in 146 BC, was followed by Roman intervention, resulting in the sacking of Corinth and the dissolution of the League. After 27 BC, A. was the name of the Roman province including Greece, with its capital at Corinth.
Larsen, *Gr. Fed. St.*, 80–89, 215–240;
Larsen, *ESAR*, 4, 436–496.

ACHAEUS (1) Athenian tragedian of the 5th century BC, native of Eretria. A.'s first play was presented in 447 BC, and one of his plays won a victory. Though he was much esteemed, only a few fragments of his works, of which 19 titles are known, have survived.

ACHAEUS (2) Seleucid general; son of Andromachus and cousin or uncle of *Antiochus III. In the early years of the latter's reign, A. was regent in Asia Minor. He defeated *Attalus I of Pergamum, regaining former Seleucid territories (223–222 BC), and in 220 BC, had himself proclaimed king in *Laodicea. Antiochus III retaliated in 216 BC, and from 215 to 213 BC, A. was besieged in the citadel of Sardis. He was persuaded to attempt an escape, but was betrayed by his companions and handed over to Antiochus III, bound hand and foot. A. was executed by dismemberment and decapitation and his body was sewn up in an ass' skin and crucified.

ACHARNAE Populous deme of Attica, producing oil and wine. The Acharnians were known as coal-burners and in *Aristophanes' comedy, *The Acharnians*, they appear as such.

ACHATES Companion and friend of *Aeneas, whose fidelity became proverbial ("*fidus Achates*", Ver. *Aen.* 1.888, etc.).

ACHELOUS ("The White One") The longest river in Greece, originating in Epirus and flowing into the Ionian Sea. A.'s clear waters (Hesiod calls them "silver waved") made it the symbol of all sweet-water rivers. In myth, A. was the eldest son of *Oceanus, who fought with *Heracles for the hand of the fair *Deianira. Although the river-god confused his adversary by repeatedly changing guise (a reflection of the changing aspect of a flowing surface), Heracles overcame him in his bull-guise, and broke off one of his horns. In return for the horn, A. gave Heracles the *Cornucopiae* of *Amalthea.

ACHERON River in Epirus, feared because of its swampy surroundings and occasional disappearance underground. In legend, A. was the main river of *Hades, and it served as the entrance to the nether regions; its name was interpreted as the "sighs" of the dead; in Virgil it represents the nether world as a whole (*Acheronta movebo, Aen.* 7.312).

ACHILLAS Ptolemaic general. A. organized the assassination of Pompey (48 BC) after his defeat at Pharsalus. When Caesar refused to countenance the deed and reward its perpetrator, A. turned against Rome and led an Egyptian army in the Alexandrian War of 48–47 BC. Arsinoë, sister of *Cleopatra VII, had him assassinated, after she had fled from Caesar.

ACHILLES Strongest, swiftest and most beautiful of the Homeric heroes; son of *Peleus, king of the Myrmidons in Thessaly, and hence a descendant of Zeus and *Thetis. To make him invulnerable, his mother dipped him into the river Styx (or into fire or boiling water, having first anointed him with *Ambrosia); the heel she held him by remained his weak spot. A. was educated by the centaur *Chiron.

When the Trojan War was about to commence, A.'s mother took fright at the prophecy that he would meet his death under the walls of Troy, and she disguised him under the name Pyrrha ("The Flaming One", an allusion to his red hair) amongst the daughters of King Lycomedes of Scyrus. There, A. begot his son *Neoptolemus (or Pyrrhus) with Deidameia. Since another oracle had stated that Troy could not be vanquished without A., *Odysseus and *Diomedes sought him out among the maidens, by the simple ruse of blowing a trumpet in the palace court, ostensibly offering a mixture of feminine ornaments and weapons for sale. All the maidens disappeared, but A. seized a sword and shield, thus revealing himself.

A. went off to Troy, accompanied by his friend

Achilles handing over Briseis to Agamemnon's men

*Patroclus, his mentor Phoenix and 50 ships. He camped on the extreme right wing of the Greek force. Quarrels with *Agamemnon caused A. to retire to his tent (at this point in the tale, the *Iliad* of Homer begins); the Trojans were thereupon victorious. After his friend Patroclus, equipped with A.'s armour, was killed by Hector, A. abandoned his seclusion. Equipped with new armour, made by Hephaestus at Thetis' request, A. slew Hector, dragged his body around the walls of Troy seven times, and only then reluctantly allowed *Priam to ransom the remains. A. held sumptuous funeral games for Patroclus (bringing the tale in the *Iliad* to a close). In later traditions, A. is represented as defeating the Amazon *Penthesilea and the hero *Memnon. A. was slain by *Paris, whose arrow pierced him in the heel, and his body and armour were retrieved by *Ajax and Odysseus.

A. is represented as having chosen a short, glorious life rather than a long, inglorious one. However, in the *Nekyia* ("Underworld") book of the *Odyssey*, A. is supposed to have changed his mind thinking it better to be the lowliest shepherd on earth than king in the underworld (*Od.* 11, 489–91). Greek youths of an idealistic bent regarded A. as an heroic prototype, and he was a particular favourite of Alexander the Great. As posterity could not support the thought of A. lingering in Hades, he was placed either in Elysium or on Leuce, the island of the blessed (in the mouth of the Danube), where he was supposed to reign.
D. L. Page, *History and the Homeric Iliad* (1959), 197ff.

ACHILLES TATIUS Greek writer of the 2nd century AD at Alexandria. A.'s exant work is an eight-book romance called *Leucippe and Cleitophon*, which describes the love of two heroes, who are kidnapped and separated, but who, in the end, overcome all dangers. Fond of detail, A. occasionally inserts tedious, irrelevant treatises on various subjects and lengthy secondary tales.
S. Gaselee, *Achilles Tatius* (Loeb), 1947 (1917).

ACRAGAS (modern Agrigento) Important Dorian city on the southwestern coast of Sicily, also known by the Latin name Agrigentum, founded by colonists from *Gela and *Rhodes (581 BC), A. was a large city (with a 350 m acropolis) on the Acragas and Hypsas rivers. The city prospered under the tyrant *Pharlaris, and became the second city in Sicily after Syracuse. This prosperity continued during the 5th century BC under the tyrant *Theron, and under the subsequent democratic regime. In 406 BC, it was captured and pillaged by the Carthaginians.

A. was resettled in the second half of the 4th century BC, and recovered to some extent. During the First Punic War, it was sacked by the Romans (261 BC) and later by the Carthaginians (255 BC). In the Second Punic War, it was conquered by the Romans and its population was sold into slavery. Shortly thereafter, new settlers arrived and in the 1st century BC it was again a prosperous city. In 43 BC it received Roman citizenship. The remains of A.'s beautiful temples can still be seen even after the recent earthquake.
Dunbabin, *Western Greeks*, 305–324 (s.v.);
P. Griffo, *Agrigento – a Guide*[2], 1956.

ACRON, Helenius Grammarian of the 2nd century AD, whose commentaries on Terence and Horace have not survived. There are extant scholia on Horace, spuriously attributed to A. in the Renaissance period, which have come to be known as Pseudo-A.; some of them may, however, rely on A.'s commentaries.
O. Keller (ed.), *Acron*, 1902–4.

ACROPOLIS ("topmost" or "high town") The usual appellation for the citadel in Greek cities, though it was sometimes given a special name, like the Cadmeia in Thebes or Acrocorinth in Corinth. The A. is found in Greek cities wherever the topography permitted, as in Priene, Pergamon, etc.

Usually, A. denotes the citadel of Athens, a 300 foot rock at the southern end of the ancient city. The A. of Athens was already inhabited in Neolithic times, and in the 14th/13th centuries BC, it served as the palace-citadel of the Mycenaean kings of Athens. Owing to its strength, the Ionians of Athens survived the Doric invasions. In Mycenaean times, it was surrounded by a "cyclopic" wall and a source near the gate (Enneakrounos) assured its water supply. In the 6th century BC, Athena's holy olive and the rock fault caused by Poseidon's trident were shown there. The Peisistratids erected the Hecatompedon (100 foot) temple 530–520 BC, with six columns in the front and 13 on the sides.

In 480 BC, the A. of Athens was utterly destroyed by the Persians. Themistocles refortified the walls with various materials and Cimon provided the south side with a straight wall. The space between the wall and rock was filled with debris, a valuable findspot for Archaic sculpture. Pericles provided the A. with splendid buildings and sculpture. The Propylea built by Mnesicles in 437–432 BC were planned with a false south front, leaving space for the Temple of Nike. The sacred way of the processions wound through the Propylea, and around the west and north sides of the Parthenon (built 447–432 BC), passing the gigantic statue of Athena Promachos, and affording successive views of the Parthenon, and the south side of the Erechtheum (421–406 BC), each building visible at a time.

The architectural glories of the classical period in Athens are manifest in the A. In later times, various additions were made, such as the temple of Rome and Augustus. In the Byzantine period, the Parthenon became a church, which the Turks later used as a powder magazine, and which was blown up by a Venetian bomb in 1687. The main sculptures of the Parthenon were carried to London by Lord Elgin in 1814. After the liberation of Greece, Turkish additions were dismantled, and the A. was excavated and restored as far as possible.
J. T. Hill, *The Ancient City of Athens*, 1953.

ACTA Administrative regulations and proceedings of Roman emperors, magistrates, and official bodies. Under the Republic, the A. of magistrates were not legally binding on subsequent office-holders unless endorsed by the Senate. Pompey's provincial arrangements in the East were not ratified by the Senate until 59 BC. The first time magistrates took an oath to observe the A. of a particular person was in 45 BC – for Caesar. Oaths to uphold the A. of the living emperor became normative. Only a *damnatio memoriae* could abolish A. The proceedings of the Senate were known as *A. senatus* (or *commentarii senatus*). In 59 BC, Caesar initiated the daily publication of A. (*A. diurna*), a sort of gazette.

ACTAEON Boeotian hunter, son of *Aristaeus and Autonoë. In the best-known version of his myth, A. came upon Artemis while she bathed. As punishment, she transformed him into a stag, and he was torn to pieces by his own hounds. There are numerous representations of this myth in ancient art. A.'s metamorphosis into a stag is often indicated by two antlers sprouting from his head.

ACTE, Claudia Freedwoman, from Asia Minor, who was

The Acropolis of Athens; Lycabettus in the background

*Nero's mistress until his marriage to Poppaea. Bitterly opposed by Nero's mother *Agrippina (3), A. remained faithful to him, and assisted at his burial in the family tomb of the Domitii, after his suicide in AD 68.

ACTIUM Promontory on the Ambracian Gulf, on the western coast of Greece, famous as the site of Octavian's decisive battle with Antony (2 September, 31 BC). Octavian commemorated his victory with the Actian games in honour of Apollo held every four years, and by the foundation of Nicopolis, "City of Victory", near the scene of the battle.

ADHERBAL (1) Important commander of the Carthaginians in Sicily during the First Punic War. A. defeated the Romans at Drepanum in 249 BC in the one and only Carthaginian naval victory.

(2) Carthaginian admiral of the Second Punic War, defeated by Gaius *Laelius (1) in the Straits of Gibraltar in 206 BC.

(3) Numidian king, eldest son of King Micipsa and grandson of *Massinissa. Upon the death of his father (118 BC), the Numidian kingdom was divided equally between A., his brother Hiempsal and his nephew *Jugurtha. Weak and irresolute, A. was unable to maintain rule in Eastern Numidia, even though he was confirmed by the Roman Senate. A. was besieged by Jugurtha at Cirta in 112 BC, and tortured to death.

ADIABENE Country on the two Zab rivers in northern Mesopotamia. The kings of A. were dependent on *Parthia, and were involved in her wars with Rome. Queen Helene of A. converted to Judaism and went to live in Jerusalem in the 1st century AD. The country was conquered by Trajan (AD 116), and reconquered by Septimus Severus (AD 196), who took the title *Adiabenus*. Subsequently, A. became part of the Sassanid Empire.

ADMETUS Greek mythological hero, son of Pheres, king of Pherae in Thessaly. Apollo served a one-year term as A.'s herdsman in punishment for killing the cyclopes. His presence caused unnatural fertility within the herd, and as a final service, the god aided A. in harnessing a boar and a lion to his chariot, thereby enabling him to gain the hand of *Alcestis, the fair daughter of Pelias. When A. failed to sacrifice to Artemis at his marriage, the Fates decreed his death, but later agreed to the death of another member of his family in his stead. When A.'s parents refused to sacrifice themselves, Alcestis offered herself. Heracles, however, who came on the scene by chance, wrestled with Death, and freed the devoted wife. This myth was made famous in a play by Euripides.

ADONIS Eastern god of fertility (Babylonian *Dumuzi*; Syrian *Tammuz*), adopted into the Greek pantheon as a minor deity. A.'s death and resurrection symbolized the cycle of winter and spring. Greek women preserved his memory by tending special Gardens of Adonis in their homes, and by participating in mourning rites. In his best-known myth, A. is the offspring of Cinyras (a priest-king of Cyprus) and his daughter Myrrha (who upon giving birth was transformed into a tree — the myrrh). Aphrodite saved the infant, and turned him over to Persephone's care. The mature A. became Aphrodite's lover and the two goddesses became rivals for the youth until, finally, Zeus allowed each of them to have him for a part of the year. A. was killed by a wild boar, and his departure for the chase despite the entreaties of his mistress, and her mourning afterwards, are frequently portrayed in ancient art.

ADRASTUS In Greek mythology, son of Talaus, king of Argos. A. was compelled to leave Argos at a young age, and he went to his grandfather Polybus in Sicyon, married his daughter, and succeeded to the throne after Polybus' death. A. was later reconciled with *Amphiaraus, gave him his sister Eriphyle in marriage and returned to rule Argos. A. married his daughters Argeia and Deipyle to the exiles *Polynices, son of *Oedipus, and *Tydeus of Calydon, whom he promised to restore. Thus, A., together with his sons-in-law, his brother-in-law Amphiaraus, and three others set out on an expedition — the "Seven against Thebes". On their way they stopped at Nemea, where the king's son was killed by a serpent; funeral games were held in his honour (the initiation of the Nemean games). In the attack on Thebes, all were killed except for A., whose excellent horse *Arion (1) saved him. A., however, kept his promise, and ten years later, together with the Epigoni, the sons of the Seven, he captured Thebes. His son had been killed during the battle, however, and, overcome with grief, A. died in Megara on his way home. Megara, Sicyon and Athens had cults for A. Aeschylus' tragedy, *The Seven Against Thebes*, deals with the subject.

AEDILES Roman magistrates. In the early Republic, there were two plebeian A., responsible for the *aedes Cereris* (the temple of *Ceres) and the related cult. In 367 BC, two A. *curules* were instituted, patrician in odd years and plebeian in even years. The A. *curules* were elected in the *comitia tributa*, while the original A. *plebeii* were elected in the *concilium plebis*. The jurisdiction of the A. was *cura urbis*, "care for the city", which included the supervision of streets, markets, weights and measures, and public order. The task of the *cura annonae*, to ensure the supply of corn and its orderly distribution in Rome, proved too difficult during the late Republic, and from Caesar on, special officials were given this task. The *cura ludorum* included the various public games, and the A. were given an allocation for this purpose by the Senate, although they were expected to use their own funds as well. This non-compulsory office enhanced a candidate's chances for higher magistracies but in the late Republic, only wealthy persons could afford it. Under the Empire, the A. lost power and their duties were transferred to other officials. A. was also the title of certain local officials in *municipia*.
Jolowicz, *Roman Law*[3], 49—50, 329—330.

AEDUI Gallic tribe which allegedly took part in the invasion of Italy in the 6th century BC (Liv. 5.34). The A. lived in the region of Burgundy, and allied themselves with Rome in 121 BC. They assisted Caesar in subdueing Gaul, and their chieftains were the first Gauls to become senators, under Claudius. The main town of the A. was Augustodunum (modern Autun).

King Aegeus consulting the Pythia of Delphi

AEGEUS King of Athens, son of Pandion. A. and his brothers reconquered *Attica, and A. received Athens as his share. Returning from the oracle at Delphi, A. visited Pittheus of Troezen, by whose daughter *Aethra he begat *Theseus. Back in Athens, A. married Medea, who fled after her unsuccessful attempt to poison Theseus. Theseus routed his cousins, the fifty children of Pallas, and volunteered to leave for Crete as a sacrifice to the Minotaur. Theseus promised A. that his ship would hoist a white sail if he had returned alive, and a black one if he had died. In the excitement of coming home, Theseus forgot to change sails, and A. threw himself into the sea in despair. The Aegean Sea henceforth bore his name. Modern scholarship regards A. as a local incarnation of Poseidon, who was also thought to be Theseus' father.
Plutarch, *Theseus*.

AEGINA Large island (85 sq km) in the Saronic Gulf, strategically located between Corinth and Athens. Minoan and Mycenaean ceramics were discovered on the island which was conquered by the Dorians of *Epidaurus in the 11th century BC. In the first part of the seventh century it was under the control of *Pheidon, the Argive tyrant. A. issued some of the earliest silver coins in Greece (*c.* 650 BC). They bore the symbol of a sea-turtle. The Aeginetic standard of coinage was one of the two accepted in the Archaic Greek world — the other was the Euboic standard. A. developed early maritime trade extending as far as Spain. It was the only city of Greece proper that secured commercial rights in Naucratis, but it never founded colonies.

A.'s decline began with its long conflict with Athens. First hostilities were in 506 BC. Some years later, A. allegedly sympathized with Persia and only the intervention of *Demaratus in 491 BC prevented the Spartan king *Cleomenes (1) from waging war on it. Yet its sailors and soldiers fought with distinction at Artemesium, Salamis, and Plataea, and Pindar praises their valour at Salamis in his 5th Isthmian ode.

The growth of Athenian naval power following the Persian Wars threatened A.'s security. In 459 BC, a war broke out in which A. was defeated. It was compelled to join the Delian League, and its annual payment was 30 talents. Following the outbreak of the Peloponnesian War in 431 BC, the Aeginetans were expelled from their island, which was given to Athenian settlers. At the end of the war, they were restored by *Lysander, but the island never regained its former importance and prosperity, and was frequently controlled by foreign powers. In the 6th century BC, a school of sculptors working in bronze and marble developed at A. The pediment sculptures of the temple of Athena Aphaia (western pediment, c. 510 BC; eastern pediment, c. 490 BC) are among the masterpieces of Archaic sculpture. They depict the battle between the Greeks and Trojans, with Athena assisting the Greeks. The stylistic developments between the two pediments are significant in the evolution of the Archaic style. The sculptures are presently located in Munich. In addition to the temple of Aphaia, which was excavated by German archaeologists, the remains include ancient quays and a temple of Zeus Hellenios.

AEGISTHUS Son of Thyestes, paramour of *Clytemnestra during *Agamemnon's absence at the Trojan War. A. and Clytemnestra murdered her husband when he returned from Troy. A. ruled at Mycenae for seven years, till he was slain by Orestes, Agamemnon's son. The story was dramatized by Aeschylus (*Agamemnon*) and Sophocles; the former represents A. as a coward, dominated by a strong-willed queen.

AEGOSPOTAMOI ("The Goat Rivers") River and region on the eastern coast of the Thracian Chersonnesus (the Gallipoli peninsula). Here in 405 BC *Lysander, the Spartan admiral, caught the Athenian fleet unmanned — 160 Athenian ships were destroyed, and only twelve escaped to Salamis in Cyprus. This was the decisive battle of the Peloponnesian War.

AELIUS Roman plebeian clan. Its first member held the consulate in 337 BC. Its most important branches were the Paeti and the Tuberones. The name A. became very common after Hadrian's time. (See *Antoninus, *Commodus, *Hadrian, *Stilo, *Verus.)

AEMILIANUS, Marcus Aemilius Governor of *Moesia in AD 252/3. After successfully fighting the Goths, A. was proclaimed emperor by his army, in AD 253. His rivals *Gallus and Volusianus were murdered by rebellious soldiers and soon afterwards A. suffered the same fate.

AEMILIANUS, Lucius Mussius Prefect of Egypt in AD 257–9, where he persecuted Christians by order of the Emperor *Valerianus, who had been captured by the Persians. A. had himself proclaimed emperor, but was defeated and executed by Theodotus, general of *Gallienus.

AEMILIUS Roman patrician clan. Its first member was consul in 484 BC. The main subbranches of the family were the Lepidi, Paulli, Regilli and Scaurii. (See *Lepidus, *Papinianus, *Paullus, *Scaurus.)

AENEAS Trojan hero, son of *Anchises and Aphrodite. A. saved his father and his son from the flames of Troy, together with the sacred *Palladium. After a long sea-voyage, he reached Carthage where Queen *Dido fell in love with him, tried to detain him, and when he escaped,

committed suicide. Then he sailed to Latium where he duelled with and defeated Turnus, the betrothed of Lavinia, daughter of King *Latinus; A. married her, and together they founded the city of Lavinium. A.'s son Iulus founded *Alba Longa, mother city of Rome. A. was thus the ancestor of the Iulian family, which through him claimed to be descendants of Venus (Aphrodite). During a battle, A. disappeared and became a god. This legend, connecting Rome with Troy and Greek mythology, was the subject of Virgil's *Aeneid*, the national epic poem of the Romans.
H. Boas, *Aeneas' Arrival in Latium*, 1938;
Ogilvie, *Livy*, 33–5.

AENEAS "Tacticus" Author of several military works, one of which, about the defence of cities, is extant. A. is the earliest known writer of this sort of literature. His work reflects social conflict and fears of revolution prevalent in Greek states in the mid-4th century BC. A. is probably to be identified with A. of Stymphalus, who was the commander of the Arcadian League in 367 BC.
L. W. Hunter — S. A. Hadford, *Aineiou Poliorketika*, 1927.

AENUS Greek city of Aeolic origin (Hdt. 7.58), at the mouth of the river Hebrus on the Thracian coast. A. owed its prosperity to its location on the trade routes to the Black Sea and the Hebrus valley. It is mentioned by Homer (*Il.* 4.520). In the 5th century BC, A. was a member of the Delian League. It fell to the Macedonians in the 4th century BC, and belonged to the Ptolemaic empire in later times.
J. M. F. May, *Ainos, its History and Coinage*, 1950.

AEOLIANS Greek tribal group said to have inhabited various parts of Greece, especially the regions of Thessaly and Boeotia, before the Dorians arrived. The A. migrated to the western coast of Asia Minor and occupied the northern part up to the Hellespont, along with several adjacent islands. There were several stages in the A.'s expansion in this region, from the 11th century BC to the 7th century BC. Mitylene in *Lesbos, Cyme, *Ilium and *Smyrna were among the larger towns of the A., but most of them never rose to real importance. Several of the southern A. cities formed a league. In some cities the A. mixed with Ionians and other native population. They lived mainly from agriculture.

Aeolic was a separate dialect in the Greek language, and was spoken with some elements of West Greek in Thessaly and Boeotia. There are Aeolic elements in Greek epic poetry. Aeolic Smyrna claimed Homer as a native son, and *Sappho and *Alcaeus, natives of Lesbos, wrote their poetry in the Aeolic dialect.
J. M. Cook, *The Greeks in Ionia and the East*, 1962

AEOLUS (1) Son of Hellen and brother of Dorus and Xuthus. The eponym of the Aeolians.

AEOLUS (2) Homeric ruler of the Winds, who resided on a floating island called Aeolia in the far west, with his six sons and six daughters. A. received *Odysseus and kept him as his guest for a whole month. He gave Odysseus the stormy winds in a leather bag, thus assuring him of a peaceful voyage to Ithaca; but when he had almost reached home safely, his companions suspected that the bag contained treasure, and opened it. The escaping winds blew Odysseus' ship back to Aeolia, and A. refused to receive him a second time. In later periods A. was thought to rule the winds in a cave on the island of Lipara though the decision to unleash them rested with Poseidon or Zeus. The most dreaded of A.'s charges was Boreas, the North Wind; Zephyrus, the West Wind, Notus, the South Wind and Eurus, the East Wind, were considered much milder. A. has been identified with A. (1).

AEQUI Italian tribe living in the mountainous central area of the peninsula. From the early 5th century BC, the A. pressed toward the Latin plains, penetrating as far as the Alban hills. Only in 431 BC did Rome defeat them — at the battle of Mount Algidus. Thereafter the A. were confined to their original area, which was conquered by Rome in 304 BC, and colonized at Alba Fucens and Carsioli. The remaining A. received Roman citizenship without political rights (*civitas sine suffragio*).

AERARIUM The treasury of the Roman people, located in the temple of Saturn at the Capitol, hence, *A. Saturni*. The urban *quaestors, under the direction of the Senate, were responsible for its administration. The A. also served as an archive for all state documents (laws, public contracts and lists of booty). Caesar appointed two aediles to administer it and these were later replaced by two *praefecti* and then by two praetors (under Augustus). In AD 56, Nero placed the A. under the *praefecti*, and this arrangement lasted into the 4th century AD. Under the Republic, the A. received all state revenues, with a special department (*A. sanctius*) for the 5% tax on manumission. Augustus organized the *A. militare* (AD 6), which received the new 1% tax on sales and the 5% tax on inheritances, in addition to Augustus' initial donation of 170 million sesterces. Pensions to discharged soldiers were paid out of these revenues. The A. declined under the Empire, with the development of the *Fiscus.
Jones, *Studies*;
F. Miller, *JRS*, 1964, 33ff.

AESCHINES Athenian orator and politician, who was a bitter enemy of Demosthenes; born at the beginning of the 4th century BC. His father, a humble man, served some time as a mercenary soldier, and then opened a school in Athens assisted by A. Although A. did not receive the appropriate education for a political career and had to earn his living, he knew the techniques of rhetoric well without formal study. For a time he was an actor. In 357 BC he served as assistant to the politician Aristophon and was then employed by *Eubulus. He also served as a secretary of the *Ekklesia.

A. made his first public appearance in 348, when he delivered an attack against Philip of Macedonia on account of the destruction of *Olynthus. Shortly thereafter, upon the initiative of Eubulus, he went to the Peloponnesus in an attempt to unite the Greeks against Philip, but the mission failed. In 347/6, A. was a member of the Boule and took part in the embassy that went to negotiate with Philip. After the first round of negotiations, A. still advocated a general treaty of all the Greek states. In the meanwhile Philip took control of Thermopylae and Phocis. The peace, named after *Philocrates, the leading member of the embassy, was nevertheless defended by A., who henceforth preferred peace to war. This attitude led to his enmity with Demosthenes, who accused him of taking bribes from Macedonia. In 345, Timarchus, a henchman of Demosthenes, brought charges against A. in connection with the peace, but was counter-charged by A. and convicted. Demosthenes renewed the attack in 343 by prosecuting him as if he had been responsible for the conclusion of the peace. A., helped by Eubulus and *Phocion, successfully defended his policy, though he was acquitted by a very small majority. His speech reveals him to be an opportunist. He argued that both states and individuals have to shift their attitudes according to circumstance. He also openly admitted that he strove for peace which he regarded as far more honourable than war.

In 339, A. represented Athens in the Amphictionic council at Delphi, and unwisely brought about the war against Amphissa, which gave Philip another opportunity for expansion. In 336, when Ctesiphon proposed to give a crown to Demosthenes for his excellent service to Athens, A. thought the time was appropriate for an attack on Demosthenes and brought in a charge of *graphe paranomon*. Meanwhile Philip was murdered and he withdrew the charge. In 330, he renewed the attack. The formal charge was against Ctesiphon, but in fact he tried to condemn Demosthenes' policy. Demosthenes replied in his masterpiece *De Corona* and the result was that not even a fifth of the jury members voted for A. Instead of paying the fine necessary in such cases, A. left Athens and is said to have spent the rest of his life in Rhodes, where he taught rhetoric. The date of his death is not known.

In their duel for winning the support of the Athenian public, Demosthenes was triumphant over A. Demosthenes also won the sympathy and admiration of many generations to come for his gallantry in defending the freedom of the Greek states against Macedonian imperialism. But A.'s opportunism seems no less patriotic. His judgement of the political forces may have been unimaginative, but it was more realistic, aiming to do the best for Athens in a given situation. He did make mistakes, and on two occasions these proved fatal. When the legates of Amphissa proposed to fine Athens in 339, he counter-charged them with sacrilege on account of their cultivation of the sacred land of Crisa. His speech so inflamed the Delphinians that next morning they attacked the Amphissians in Crisa. This was typical of his oratory — which strove for influence over the audience, rather than the appreciation of literary experts. His extant speeches, *Against Timarchus, On the Embassy*, and *Against Ctesiphon*, show that he could use ordinary words with vigour and dignity, and his vivid descriptions are usually lucid. Unlike Demosthenes he had a powerful voice and a natural sense for witticism. As an orator he disliked gestures (hence called by Demosthenes "noble statue"), preferring the dignity of appearance. He was proud of the education he had acquired and would quote verses in his speeches. He was indeed a self-made man in this respect. He ruined himself, eventually, by misjudging public feeling in his attack on Demosthenes in 330 BC.
C.D. Adams (Loeb), 1919;
U. Martin — G. de Budé (Budé), 1952;
Kennedy, *Persuasion*.

AESCHYLUS Reputedly the creator of tragedy, born in 525 BC, of a noble family of Eleusis. When he was 14 years old, the tyrant *Hippias was expelled from Athens, which was soon to have a democratic constitution. These events evidently made a profound impression on A., who is one of the earliest authors to portray the traditional tyrant and to praise the rule of law and freedom as mainstays of democracy. His first play was produced soon after 500 BC. In 490 BC he fought at the battle of Marathon, where his brother was killed trying to capture a Persian boat. In 484, A. won his first victory in the *Dionysia with a play that is no longer extant. In 480 he fought at Salamis and is also said to have fought at Artemisium and Plataea. Shortly after 472 he visited Syracuse where he wrote *The Women of Aetna* in honour of the foundation of that city by *Hieron in 476. *Persae* was written in 472. In 468, he was defeated at the

Dionysia by Sophocles but the following year he produced and was victorious with the *Septem contra Thebas*. In 458 the *Oresteia*, A.'s only extant trilogy, was awarded the first prize. He visited Sicily in 456, and died there in Gela. A. had won 12 victories, and after his death his plays won still more victories when a special enactment allowed all to compete with his plays. Descendants of A.'s sister were successful tragedians well into the 4th century.

According to one source, A. wrote 90 plays. More than 80 titles are known. Their subject matter was the usual in Greek tragedy: traditional mythology, the Trojan War, the Argonautic saga, the fate of the Theban royal house, the Danaids etc. The *Persae* was an exception in that it dealt with contemporary events. Of all his work, only seven plays are extant, in addition to some 400 fragments, which are known from papyri dating from the 3rd century BC. The order of several tetralogies is known, such as: a) *Phineus, Persae, Glaucus Potnieus*, and the satyr-play *Prometheus*; b) *Laius, Oedipus, Septem contra Thebas*, and the satyr-play *Sphinx*; c) *Agamemnon, Choephoroe, Eumenides* and the satyr-play *Proteus*; d) *Supplices, Aegyptii, Danaides*; satyr-play *Amymone*.

The extant plays are:

1) *Persae*. This play deals with the victory of the Greeks over the Persians at Salamis. It takes place at Susa where the Persian elders discuss the prolonged stay of Xerxes in Greece. The King's mother appears after having had a portentous dream, and soon a messenger comes to tell of the defeat. The Queen then prays to Darius who comes from the nether world and advises the Persians to evacuate Greece because otherwise they will suffer a devastating defeat. Xerxes soon arrives but disregards the warning; the way for the destruction of the Persian army is open. The moral lesson of the play is that excessive human pride (*hybris*) is punished by heaven; a general law which is applied to the particular case of the rise and fall of Xerxes in his attack on Greece. A question arises: did Xerxes act out of free will, or was he impelled by the god, because whatever happens is in accordance with divine purpose? The answer is that the Persians were doomed in Greece, but Xerxes himself brought about the disaster. Interestingly, this play about the great Greek victory is not nationalistic, though it does express pride in the independence of the Athenians.

2) *Septem contra Thebas*. This is the third play of the trilogy that treated the fate of Laius, king of Thebes, and his descendants. In the first two, Laius is told by the Delphic Oracle that in order to secure Thebes, he must not have children. He does not obey, and is killed by his son Oedipus who marries the widow without knowing she is his mother. When the truth emerges, the Queen kills herself, and Oedipus ceases to reign (the precise version of A. is not known). Oedipus curses his sons. The extant play is concerned with the destruction of the third generation. Polynices with the help of *Adrastas and others (the Famous Seven) attacks Thebes which is defended by his brother Eteocles. Both brothers are driven by an irresistible force, the result of the curse. The inevitable end is that they kill one another, thus atoning for the old sin.

3) *Supplices*. This is the first play of the trilogy that dealt with the *Danaids. Here they flee from Egypt to Argos in order to avoid marriage with their cousins. Their reason is not clear, perhaps an inborn aversion to men.

4) *Oresteia*. This trilogy expounds the fate of the house of Agamemnon. In the first play, *Agamemnon*, the great king returns from the Trojan War to be murdered by his wife *Clytemnestra and her lover *Aegisthus. This is the Queen's revenge for Agamemnon's sacrifice of their daughter Iphigenia to Artemis. The second play, *Choephoroe*, takes place seven years later. Orestes takes revenge for the murder of his father. In the third play, *Eumenides*, Orestes is purified at Delphi and told by Apollo to appear at the court of the Areopagus and answer the charges of the Erinyes. Orestes, defended by Apollo, is narrowly acquitted. The angered Erinyes, the Furies who avenge murders, are appeased by Athena who offers them a cult in Athens under the name Eumenides ("the Kindly Ones"). The theme of the trilogy is again crime and punishment. This is in fact a vicious circle because murder is punished by murder, which in turn calls for punishment and so forth. The Greek idea of blood feud is at the background of this cycle. However, it was the goddess' will that Iphigenia should be sacrificed; Agamemnon was driven by powers beyond his control. It is also possible that he had to pay for the crime of his father, *Atreus. On the other hand, the chorus in *Agamemnon* blames Agamemnon because he was not justified in going to war for the sake of a woman. The problem of blood feud is solved in the trilogy by reconciliation, and this fits in with the Athenian view that the court of the Areopagus was the first one established to try cases of murder, and dispense with the custom of private vengeance. The *Oresteia* is considered a masterpiece of Greek tragedy for its majestic treatment of the problems of justice and divine providence, and for its passages of great lyric poetry.

5) *Prometheus Bound*. If there was a trilogy that treated the myth of Prometheus, it can hardly be reconstructed. Evidently, *Prometheus Unbound* followed *Prometheus Bound*. Prometheus helped Zeus conquer his brothers the Titans, who were then relegated to Tartarus. But when Zeus wanted to destroy mankind, Prometheus saved them with the gift of fire. In punishment, he was nailed to a rock at the end of the world. The extant play concentrates on the tyrannical behavior of Zeus, a harsh, cruel and ungrateful ruler. Prometheus knows that Zeus, too, might be overthrown, and refuses to reveal the secret to Hermes, Zeus' herald. Consequently at the end of the play he is thrown to Tartarus.

A.'s tragedies seek the reasons for the laws of heaven and earth. He believes that there is a universal order which can be understood: suffering and experience bring knowledge and wisdom. While accepting the traditional idea of inherited crime, and the sin of pride and excessiveness, he emphasizes the concept that man brings about his own downfall by his own deeds. And since A. aims mainly at revealing the universal order and man's place in it, he is less concerned with portraying the characters of his heroes and the development of their thoughts and emotions.

Tragedies were produced in the *Dionysia before A., but he was considered the creator of tragedy probably because his plays were the first to portray heroic struggles in a solemn manner. He also introduced the second actor, and bold scenic effects, later generally discontinued, like gods flying on a *mechane* (hence *deus ex machina*). In contrast to later poets, like Euripides, his figures are majestic heroes whose thoughts and actions are extraordinary, and accordingly, A.'s language is rich, sublime, and highly metaphorical. Aristophanes said that he was the first Greek to build towering structures out of majestic words.

G. Murray, *Aeschylus the Creator of Tragedy,* 1940;
P. Vellacott, *Aeschylus* (Penguin), 1956;
H. W. Smyth – H. Lloyd Jones (Loeb), 1922–1957.

Aesopus talking to a fox; 5th century BC cup

AESOP The most famous fabulist in all history. He lived in the first half of the 6th century BC, and though Thrace was probably his place of origin, he was a slave on the island of *Samos. In extant literature he is mentioned by *Herodotus, *Aristophanes, *Plato, *Aristotle and many others. He was considered one of the Seven Wise Men of Greece, and there are legends that he served as a diplomat for *Croesus, and that he was killed as a scapegoat by the Delphians. As early as the 5th century BC, fables were ascribed to A. The first collection of Aesopic fables (which has not survived) was made by *Demetrius of Phalerum. The earliest extant collection was made by Babrius, c. AD 100. These are written in metre, while earlier popular fables were probably in prose form. Over the centuries various collections of fables have been ascribed to A.

B. E. Perry, *Babrius and Phaedrus*.

AETHIOPIA, AETHIOPIANS In Homer, a nation in the extreme east, bordering on the Ocean. The A. were dark-skinned because *Helios began his daily journey across the sky from their land. Their king, Memnon, came to the aid of Troy, but was slain by Achilles. Like all remote (and hence little known) nations, the A. were endowed by the Greeks with legendary qualities, such as longevity, strict morality, strength and wealth. They were also said to have a fountain of youth. In the Hellenistic period, the dark-skinned Nubians living south of Egypt were identified with the A. The Ptolemies sent many expeditions to Nubia, to capture elephants for use in warfare. In the 4th century BC, the capital of A. was transferred southward, from Napata to Meroë on the Nile. In the 3rd century BC, the kings of Napata (especially Ergamenes, c. 240 BC) exerted a strong influence on the priests of Thebes and rivalled the Ptolemies for rule over southern Egypt. In 23 BC, the Romans destroyed Napata and extended their influence over Meroë (where a marble head of Augustus has been found in excavations). In AD 320, the kings of Axum conquered the country and, having adopted Christianity, they were visited by Byzantine traders, one of whom, Cosmas Indicopleustes, has left a description of the country, including the text of a then extant Ptolemaic inscription at Adulis. The A. were valuable allies of the Byzantines in their struggle for the domination of the Red Sea.

AETHRA Daughter of Pitheus, king of Troezen, and mother of Theseus. Because both Poseidon and *Aegeus are said to have visited her on the same night, Theseus is sometimes denoted son of Poseidon. In Homer, A. is a handmaiden of Helen. Her grandsons *Demophon and Acamas were believed to have rescued her during the fall of *Troy, a scene which is depicted on Greek vases.

AETIUS, Flavius Important Roman general. A. was born near Silistria on the Danube, c. AD 390, to a cavalry commander, Gaudentius. From the age of 15 to 18, he was a hostage, first with Alaric and then with the Huns, which led to his good relations with Hun rulers, and his understanding of their ways of warfare. In AD 425, A. was appointed second-in-command in Gaul. He removed his commander-in-chief, Felix, and his successor Bonifatius, in AD 432, and with the aid of the Huns, obtained command of the entire army of the Western Empire. He was elevated to the rank of Patrician, and was four times consul (in AD 432, 437, 446, and 454). During his period of office, the Romans lost Britain and Africa, but A. was successful in defending Gaul. In alliance with the *Visigoths, he defeated the dreaded Attila at the Catalaunian fields, in AD 451. All-powerful at the court of *Galla Placidia and *Valentinian III at Ravenna, A. betrothed his son to the daughter of Valentinian III. A.'s relations with the senatorial aristocracy aroused the suspicions of Valentinian who allowed A. the honour of committing suicide during an audience at the Palatine palace in Rome on 21 September AD 454.

AETNA Extant Latin poem, seeking to explain the phenomenon of the volcano of the same name, in Sicily. Its author is unknown — it has spuriously been ascribed to Virgil — and it was probably composed in the 1st century AD.

Duff, *Minor Latin Poets*.

AETOLIA, AETOLIANS A country in the west part of central Greece, separated from Acarnania by the river Achelous, and from Malis by Mount Oxya. The country is generally mountainous, with plains in the central area, and the southwest shore is devoid of good harbours. Though mentioned by Homer, the A. were nevertheless considered semi-barbarous, probably because of some mixture with the Illyrians, and for many centuries they maintained a tribal organization, did not develop cities and did not participate in the main currents of Greek politics. Some Aetolian figures are found in Greek mythology, such as *Meleager and *Deinaria.

Soon after 370 BC, a few Aetolian towns and the tribe formed a confederacy. The state institutions included a general assembly which held biennial meetings, in which citizens of the constituent cities of the confederacy could participate; a council (*synedrion*) in which each city was represented according to population; a standing committee of state; a general (*strategos*) chosen for one year. The central institutions had control of foreign affairs, state finances, and the army. The cities remained autonomous in matters of internal affairs and thus each Aetolian had a double citizenship: that of the confederacy and that of his local city. New communities that attached themselves to the A. confederation in later times did not share equally in the political rights. At the end of the 4th century the A. became notorious as robbers because of their raids on the countries of central Greece. But it was mainly due to the A. that in 279 BC, the invading Celts were driven from Delphi. They expanded their territory and controlled the Delphic Amphictiony. They embarked on several wars, mainly against Macedonia. Philip V defeated them, and in 212 they allied themselves with Rome against him. This cooperation lasted to the Second Macedonian War. However, they did not receive the reward they expected and therefore allied themselves with *Antiochus III. They were defeated by Rome in 189 and lost *Ambracia, and later, other territory as well. In their treaty with Rome they had to recognize its superiority. In 27 BC A. became part of the province Achaea.

Larsen, *Gr. Fed. St.*, 78–80, 195–215.

AFRANIUS, Lucius Commander under *Pompey against *Sertorius and *Mithridates VI. Although of low birth, A.'s military prowess won the favour of his commander, who assisted him in becoming consul in 60 BC. In 55 BC, A. was sent to Spain as Pompey's representative and governor of the province. At the beginning of the Civil War between Pompey and Caesar, A. was outmanoeuvred by Caesar and forced to surrender at Ilerda, in August 49 BC. Released by Caesar, he rejoined Pompey and after the defeat at *Pharsalus, he fled to Africa. A. was captured after *Thapsus (46 BC), and killed by rioting soldiers in Caesar's camp.

AFRICA In antiquity the term A. referred only to the northern part of that continent, which faces the Mediterranean Sea. More narrowly, it meant the area ruled by Carthage which was annexed by Rome (as the province of *Africa proconsularis*), in 146 BC. Later annexations to the province included the territory of Numidia (46 BC) and Mauretania (AD 40). The A. provinces were among the richest of the Roman Empire, producing wheat and oil for the Italian market. In the 2nd–3rd centuries AD, it became an important centre of literature (*Apuleius) and of Christianity (Tertullian, Augustine). Byzantine A. was conquered by the Vandals (AD 429), but reconquered (AD 533) under Belisarius and held until the Moslem Conquest (AD 670). Several important battles of antiquity took place in A. (*Zama, *Thapsus). Roman villas dotted the land, and the ruins of legionary camps (Timgad, Lambaesis) are found along the A. *limes*. Especially remarkable are the thousands of mosaic pavements in private houses and baths which reveal an evolution in the particularly vivid multihued style of figurative art. The counterpart of the the modern term A. was, in antiquity, "Libya", which together with Asia and Europe formed the known world of the ancients.

T. R. S. Broughton, *The Romanization of Africa Proconsularis*, 1929; R. M. Haywood, *ESAR*, 4, 1–119.

AGAMEMNON In Greek mythology, king of Mycenae and overlord of the *Achaeans who participated in the Trojan War. A. was the son of *Atreus and brother of *Menelaus. In one version, he succeeded to the throne after compelling his uncle Thyestes to leave Mycenae. A. married *Clytemnestra after killing her first husband in battle. He organized the expedition against Troy for the sake of his brother, whose wife Helen had been carried off by *Paris. While A. was at Troy, *Aegisthus became his wife's paramour and, on his return from Troy, A. was killed by the lovers, along with *Cassandra, daughter of Priam. A post-Homeric version relates that this was Clytemnestra's revenge for A.'s sacrifice of their daughter *Iphigenia at Aulis, as a means of appeasing Artemis.

Greek poets and tragedians exploited and elaborated upon the myth of A., who may have been a real king of Mycenae, but certainly not of all Achaea. A. had a hero-cult at various sites in the Peloponessus, Boeotia and elsewhere and in later times his grave was shown at Mycenae. A.'s myth was often depicted on Greek vases.

AGATHARCHIDES Greek scholar of the 2nd century BC at Cnidos. A. wrote historical, ethnographical and geographical works and extracts from his *On the Red Sea* (five books) are preserved by *Diodorus Siculus and *Photius. He also wrote a voluminous *History of Europe, History of Asia*, and a work *On Wonders*, as well as a philosophical work.

Thomson, *Ancient Geography* (s.v.).

AGATHOCLES Tyrant of Syracuse, born in 360 BC. At an early age he migrated to Syracuse and became wealthy through his paternal inheritance and a good marriage. A. showed his military ability under *Timoleon, and later fought with distinction against the *Brutii in southern Italy. He was twice exiled from Syracuse but, in 317 BC, he managed to seize power, being *strategos autocrator* in name, and tyrant in fact. He achieved this by using mercenaries and advocating an anti-oligarchic policy which won him the support of the masses. A. pursued a vigorous foreign policy and brought eastern Sicily under his control. Carthage, with some assistance from the Greek oligarchs, defeated him at Licata (311 BC) and Syracuse itself came under siege. The next year, A. landed an army in Africa and defeated the Carthaginians. He was aided by Ophellas, Ptolemaic governor of Cyrene, but in 309 BC, he procured Ophellas' murder and seized his army. Meanwhile, the Carthaginian blockade of Syracuse failed, and A. returned to Sicily in 308 BC, to defeat an attack led by *Acragas. In the following year, however, he lost his army in Africa. Subsequently, A. controlled all Greek Sicily, the river Halycus forming his boundary with the limited area left to Carthage. A. took the royal title in 304 BC, following the example of the *Diadochi, and later expanded his control over southern Italy, conquering even Corcyra. Unable to found a dynasty, A. restored democratic government before he died in 289 BC.

AGATHON The most prominent Athenian tragedian after *Aeschylus, *Sophocles and *Euripides. Born c. 446 BC, A. was influenced by the Sophists (*Protagoras and *Gorgias), and was famous for his beauty. A. probably had oligarchic inclinations and, in 411 BC, congratulated *Antiphon for his trial speech. A. left Athens c. 407 BC, going to the court of the Macedonian king *Archelaus (1), where he died sometime before 400 BC. A.'s first victory was at the *Lenaea in 416 BC; the celebration of the occasion is the scene of Plato's *Symposium*, and A. is made to deliver a speech in praise of Eros. A.'s tragedies are innovatory. *Antheus* had no relation to any myth, his choral songs were not connected to the plot, and his music was novel. His innovations were noted and criticized by Aristotle. None of A.'s plays has survived, and the fragments amount to scarcely 40 lines.

AGELADES Argive sculptor in the late 6th or 5th century BC. The great sculptors *Phidias, *Myron and *Polyclitus were his pupils. He worked in bronze, and the coins of *Messene are thought to represent his famous statue of Zeus, made for the temple on Mount Ithome.

AGER PUBLICUS Public land of the Roman people. Within the Roman state, land with no owner, and land confiscated from private owners, became AP. During the conquest of Italy, Rome confiscated much land from opposing states; thus the entire area of *Veii became AP. The proportion of land confiscated, however, generally varied according to circumstances. AP. was treated in several ways: distributed to individuals (*ager viritim assignatus*); used to establish *coloniae*, Roman or Latin (*ager colonicus*); sold by the quaestors (*ager quaestorius*); leased by the censors (*ager a censoribus locatus*); rented by individuals in devastated areas (*ager occupatorius*), though the rent was not vigorously collected. In the *ager occupatorius*, a maximum 500 *iugera* — about 300 acres — was allowed per individual by the Licinio-Sextian laws of 367 BC; pasture land used exclusively by individual herders (*ager compascuus*); and land open to the public as pasture. The first two categories ceased to be AP. and, in time, categories of a semi-public nature came about.

The use of AP. was a source of conflict throughout almost the entire period of the Republic. The wealthy favoured modes of disposal which enabled them to exploit the AP. whereas the common people agitated for the distribution of AP. to the needy. This problem became acute in the second half of the 2nd century BC. After the Second Punic War and the subjugation of Cisalpine Gaul, large tracts of land were confiscated in southern Italy and the Po valley. In the first decades of the 2nd century BC, the Senate conducted a programme of colonization and individual assignation of AP. which ceased in the 60s of that century, when the number of small farmers who lost their plots of land was increasing because of long service in Rome's foreign wars and the ensuing prosperity among Roman businessmen and senators. The agrarian bill of Tiberius *Gracchus sought to enforce the Licinio-Sextian law and to assist needy citizens by the distribution of small holdings. Despite strong opposition, the bill was passed and much public land was distributed, until 119 BC. In 111 BC, a new law gave private ownership to old *possessores* of lawful sizes of the *ager occupatorius* and to several other holders of AP. After this, not much AP. remained in Italy, but in the 1st century BC confiscations by *Sulla, Caesar, the triumvirs and Augustus made extensive additions, which were soon utilized for the settlement of discharged veterans. In the provinces, too, much AP. accumulated, being mostly former royal land and the territories of penalized cities, such as Carthage and Corinth (there were precedents in Italy, for example, *Capua). From Caesar's time on, provincial AP. was used extensively for the colonization of veterans. Under the Empire, AP. came to be included in the Imperial domains.
G. Tibiletti, *Athenaeum*, 1948, 173ff., 1949, 3ff., 1950, 245ff.; Badian, *Historia*, 1962, 209ff.

AGESILAUS Spartan king of the Eurypontid dynasty, born in 444 BC. When his half-brother *Agis II died (399 BC), A. succeeded to the throne with the aid of *Lysander, his nephew being passed over because of suspected illegitimacy. In 396 BC, A. became commander-in-chief of the Spartan army operating against Persia in Asia Minor. Though he defeated the satrap Tissaphernes, and won other victories, the naval battle of *Conon and Pharnabazus off Cnidos in 394 BC shattered the Spartan empire overseas. The same year, A. was recalled to strengthen Sparta in the Corinthian War. At the battle of Coronea (in *Boeotia), A. achieved a hard-won victory over *Thebes and its allies, yet this was insufficient to secure Sparta's position in central Greece. He continued to command the Spartan armies in the following years with some success, but it was through diplomacy and the intervention of Persia that Spartan supremacy was restored with the peace of *Antalcidas in 386 BC. The new alliance between Athens and Thebes in 378 BC led A. to bring a Spartan expedition into Boeotia, but he was unsuccessful. A.'s stubborn refusal to let Thebes represent Boeotia undermined the peace congress of 371 BC, and resulted in the crushing defeat of Sparta at the battle of Leuctra. A., who did not take part in the battle, defended Sparta against the invasions of *Epaminondas. A. went abroad twice in his old age as a mercenary, to gain needed funds for his country; he died on his way back from Egypt in 360 BC.

A. was a leading Spartan personality in the first half of the 4th century BC. Though devoted to his country and persistent in his efforts to secure its hegemony, he lacked an understanding of the true needs of Sparta and the proper judgement to deal with its allies and subjects adequately.
Xenophon, *Agesilaus; Hellenica*; Plutarch, *Agesilaus*; Nepos, *Agesilaus*.

AGILO Alamannic warrior in Roman service who gained the favour of *Constantius II while commanding the Imperial equerries (AD 354), and was promoted commander of the foot-guards (AD 359). In AD 360, he served on the Mesopotamian front. When the Emperor began to campaign against *Julianus, A. followed him till his death (AD 363). A.'s loyalty was appreciated by Julianus, but A. preferred to resign from the army. In AD 360, he married the daughter of Araxius, a friend of both Julianus and *Libanius. A.'s last service post was general to *Procopius, pretender to the Imperial throne (AD 365). A. ensured the victory of *Valens by deserting Procopius during the decisive battle at Naceleia (AD 366).

AGIS (1) II Eurypontid king of Sparta, who succeeded to the throne after his father's death in 427 BC. In 418, A. won a great victory at Mantinea, thus firmly establishing Spartan rule in the Peloponnesus. In 413 BC, he occupied Decelea in Attica, using it as a base against Athens, till the end of the Peloponnesian War. In 402—400 BC, he subjugated *Elis, and died shortly thereafter.

AGIS (2) III Eurypontid king of Sparta, 338—331 BC. Supported by Persia and with a following of many cities of the Peloponnesus, A. fought Macedonia in 333 BC. He was defeated by *Antipater (1) at *Megalopolis.
Badian, *Hermes*, 1967, 172ff.

AGIS (3) IV Eurypontid king of Sparta, born c. 262 BC. On his accession to the throne in 244 BC. A. sought to introduce social and economic reform. The lands of Sparta were controlled by a hundred families; the number of citizens had decreased to 700, and many persons were suffering from heavy debt. In 243 BC, the ephor Lysander, A.'s supporter, initiated bills for cancellation of debts and enlargement of the citizen-body. Resistance to these reforms was overcome initially, but the support of A.'s wealthy and influential uncle, Agesilaus, was lost after the cancellation of mortgages. In A.'s absence, the other king, Leonidas, returned to Sparta, and when A. returned he was captured and put to death. A.'s wife married *Cleomenes III (Leonidas' son), who later realized A.'s ideal of a return to the Lycurgan constitution.
Plutarch, *Agis*; A. Fuks, *CPh*, 1962, 161—5.

AGONES Competitions for prizes, at Greek public festivals, including athletic competitions of various sorts (wrestling, boxing, discus throwing, javelin throwing, foot-races and jumping), chariot- and horse-races, and musical and dramatic contests (tragedies and comedies),

Runner, wrestlers and spear-thrower on an archaic statue-base

dances, instrumental music, recitations and singing. The origins of the A. were the funeral competitions in honour of deceased heroes, such as those for Patroclus in the *Iliad*. The competitors aimed at distinction in physical or spiritual achievements. Such festivals were held in many Greek cities at fixed times and they were of a religious character, being associated with local or broader cults. There were A. that attracted competitors and spectators from the entire Greek world. During these pan-Hellenic A., it was customary to suspend all inter-Greek hostilities. The most famous A. were the Olympic (for Zeus), the Pythian (for Apollo), the Isthmian (for Poseidon) and the Nemean (for Zeus). Each festival had its own programme, some giving preference to musical contests (Pythian), others to athletics (Olympic). The Athenian *Dionysia consisted of dramatic competitions only. The A. remained typical of the Greek way of life. At Rome, they were first held in 186 BC and several regular A. were later established there. With the rise of Christianity, the A. gradually disappeared, and the Olympic A. were terminated in AD 393.

E. N. Gardiner, *Greek Athletic Sports and Festivals*, 1910; H. A. Harris, *Greek Athletes and Athletics*, 1964.

AGORA In Greek cities, the assembly of the people, its meeting-place and, consequently, the market place. The A. was the centre of public life in the *polis. See also *Apella, *Ekklesia.

AGORACRITUS Greek sculptor of the 5th century BC at Paros, a pupil of *Phidias. Fragments of A.'s statue of Nemesis (Pausan. 1.33,3), originally made as an Aphrodite (Plin. *NH* 36.17), were found at Rhamnus in Attica. Copies of A.'s colossal marble statue of the Mother of the Gods for the Athenian *Agora, have been found.

AGORANOMOI Officials supervising the *Agora in Greek cities. Their numbers and methods of election varied, but they were always responsible for the maintenance of order and honesty in trade, as well as for the collection of market taxes. They had authority to fine persons who disturbed the peace.

Jones, *The Greek City* (s.v.).

AGRICOLA, Gnaeus Julius Son of the senator Lucius Julius Graecinus, born at Forum Iulii (Frejus), Provence, in AD 40, and educated at Massilia. In AD 59–60, A.

served in Britain; returning to Rome, he married the daughter of a senator from Narbonne. A. continued his career as quaestor in Asia (AD 64) and was praetor in AD 68 when the revolt against Nero broke out. In AD 70, he joined Vespasian, who appointed him commander of the XXX Legion (Valeria Victrix) and granted him patrician status (AD 73). From AD 74 to 76, he served as governor of Aquitania, and in AD 77 he was suffect consul. From AD 77 to 84, A. was governor of *Britannia; in seven campaigns his troops reached the Firth of Forth-Clyde line, advancing as far north as the river Tay. He defeated Calgacus in AD 83, at Mons Graupius in the Highlands. A.'s fleet also circumnavigated the British Isles. As governor, he devoted himself to furthering the Romanization of southern Britain. He was recalled in AD 84, and honoured with triumphal ornaments. Fearing the suspicions of *Domitian, he lived thereafter in retirement, till his death in AD 93. A. was immortalized in a biography by his son-in-law, the historian *Tacitus.

R. M. Ogilvie – I. A. Richmond (ed.), *Agricola*, 1967; A. R. Burn, *Agricola and the Roman Britain*, 1953.

AGRIGENTUM *See* **ACRAGAS**.

AGRIPPA (1), Marcus Vipsanius Roman statesman and general, born of an obscure family in 63 BC. His friendship with *Octavian influenced his whole life. A. accompanied Octavian to Apollonia, met him in Rome after the death of Caesar and helped him organize a private army. In the Perusine War, A. rendered yeoman service by preventing the relieving army from reaching the city besieged by Octavian. As urban prefect, A. was in charge of the protection of Italy against Sextus *Pompeius. He negotiated with Antony on Octavian's behalf at Brundisium (39 BC) and became governor of Gaul. During his governorship, A. defeated the Aquitanians, crossed the Rhine and settled the Germanic *Ubii beyond the river.

Convinced that the struggle for the Empire would be decided at sea, A. set out to build a fleet for his friend and patron, and reconstructed the harbour of Baiae near Naples. After his first consulate in 37 BC, A.'s fleet attacked Sextus Pompeius. In 36 BC, he won the battle at Naulochus, in honour of which he was granted the *corona navalis* (though he declined the triumph, as he again did in 31 BC). In 35/34 BC, he was with his fleet in Illyrium. As

Marcus Vipsanius Agrippa

aedile in 33 BC, he began to reorganize the water supply of Rome and opened the first public bath. With the approaching conflict against Antony and Cleopatra, A. built more ships, and was in charge of Octavian's forces at Actium. He served as joint consul with Octavian in 28 BC and again in 27 BC, during the establishment of the Principate, and in 28 BC was also joint censor. From 24 BC on, A. developed the *Campus Martius in Rome, which culminated in the dedication of the *Pantheon. A. represented Augustus in Rome during the latter's absence and in 23 BC, when the Emperor was critically ill, he was practically designated successor.

From 23 to 18 BC, A. administered the East from Mitylene, and fought with the Cantabri in Spain during a similar tour of duty in Gaul and Spain (20–18 BC). In his last years, A. was invested with the tribunician authority and became thus officially co-ruler. In 17 BC he returned to the East in an attempt to install Polemon I as King of *Bosporus (2). In 15 BC, he visited Judaea and became friendly with *Herod. A. died in Campania in 12 BC. He had married three times, Caecilia Attica, *Atticus' daughter (37 BC), Claudia Marcella, a niece of Augustus (28 BC), and *Julia, daughter of Augustus (21 BC). This last dynastic marriage produced three sons, Gaius, Lucius Caesar and Agrippa who was born after the death of his father, and two daughters, Julia and Agrippina the Elder (who married *Germanicus). A. acquired large estates in Sicily, the Chersonese and Egypt. His death was deeply mourned by Augustus, and he was buried in the Imperial mausoleum. A. is traditionally represented as a dour Roman of the old school, an efficient administrator

and able general, adhering strictly to his duties. Dio rightly observed that he helped Augustus establish a monarchy at Rome (54.29).

M. Reinhold, *Marcus Agrippa,* 1933;
F. W. Shipley, *Agrippa's Building Activities in Rome,* 1933.

AGRIPPA (2) POSTUMUS, Marcus Vipsanius Third son of *Agrippa (1) and *Julia, born after the death of his father (hence "Postumus") in 12 BC. As sole surviving grandchild of Augustus, A. was adopted by the Emperor at the age of 16. Later he was banished to the island of Planasia (AD 7), and was murdered there, upon the accession of Tiberius (AD 14).

AGRIPPA (3) I, Marcus Julius King of the Jews, grandson of *Herod and *Mariamme the Hasmonean, son of Aristobulus; born in 10 BC. When A. was 3 years old, his father was executed by Herod (as his grandmother had been in 29 BC). A. was educated in Rome, together with *Drusus (4), son of Tiberius. He left Rome in AD 23, to serve under his uncle *Herod Antipas. After many adventures, he returned to Rome in AD 36, where he became friendly with *Caligula. The suspicious Emperor Tiberius, however, had him put in chains. After Caligula's accession, A. was endowed with the lands of his uncle Herod Phillip, and in AD 39 with those of Herod Antipas. In return for supporting *Claudius in the crisis after Caligula's assassination, A. received Judaea and Samaria (AD 41). He gained the favour of his Jewish subjects, but was disliked by Gentiles and Christians. He died suddenly at Caesarea in AD 44.

Josephus, *BJ,* 2; *AJ,* 18–19; Philo, *Leg;* Jones, *Herods,* 184–216.

AGRIPPA (4) II, Marcus Julius Son of *Agrippa I, born in AD 28. After his father's death, A. was considered too young to rule the kingdom, but in AD 48 he was given the Kingdom of Chalcis in the Lebanon. In AD 53, he received the tetrarchy of Herod Philip and in AD 61 Nero added eastern Galilee and parts of Trans-Jordan. In the Jewish War, he supported the Romans. He died in AD 95, the last of his dynasty.

Josephus, *BJ,* 2; *AJ,* 20; Jones, *Herods,* 217–261.

AGRIPPINA (1), Vipsania Daughter of *Agrippa (1) and his first wife, Caecilia Attica. A. married Tiberius, who divorced her by order of Augustus, in order to marry Julia, the Emperor's daughter. Afterwards A. married Gaius Asinius Gallus, for whom Tiberius henceforth nursed a deep hatred. She died in AD 20.

AGRIPPINA (2) the Elder, Vipsania Daughter of *Agrippa (1) and *Julia, born in 14 BC. In AD 5, A. married *Germanicus, grandson of *Livia, and bore him nine children, among them Nero (not the emperor), Drusus, Caligula, Agrippina, Drusilla and Julia Livilla. She accompanied her husband to Germany and to the East. When Germanicus died at Antioch, A. accused *Piso (4), governor of Syria (and indirectly Tiberius), of poisoning him. She was exiled to the island of Pandateria in AD 29, and died there in AD 33. Tiberius accorded her the honour of a burial in the mausoleum of Augustus.

AGRIPPINA (3) the Younger, Julia Daughter of *Agrippina (2) the Elder. Born in AD 15 at Colonia Agrippinensis (Köln), A. married Cn. *Domitius Ahenobarbus in AD 28, and in AD 37 bore him a son, the future Emperor *Nero. A. was exiled by Caligula to the Pontian islands, but a year later she was recalled by her uncle Claudius. In AD 49, she married Claudius, and a year later persuaded him to adopt her son Nero, giving him preference over

Bust of Agrippina the Younger

Claudius' own son *Britannicus. A. is purported to have poisoned Claudius in AD 54, in order to ensure Nero's succession. She dominated Nero during his minority, up to AD 58, when he came under the influence of his mistress (later his wife), *Poppaea Sabina. Roman scandal mongers accused A. of having had incestuous relations with her son. In AD 59, Nero decided to eliminate her. An attempt to drown her miscarried, but she was finally assassinated by two soldiers, under the orders of *Anicetus, at her villa at Baiae.

J. P. V. D. Balsdon, *Roman Women*, 1962.

AHALA, Gaius Servilius In Roman legend, *magister equitum* (commander of the cavalry) under *Cincinnatus. Presumably on the orders of the Senate, A. killed Spurius *Maelius, who was suspected of tyrannic intentions. The story was later embellished to justify the Senate proceedings against the *Gracchi.

Ogilvie, *Livy*, 550—555.

AIAS (1) (Ajax) Telemonius Known as "the Great", to distinguish him from A. (2), his name means "son of Telamon, king of Salamis". Described as enormous and powerful, A. was the strongest Greek in the Trojan War after *Achilles. He fought *Hector in a duel that ended in an exchange of gifts. He was one of the envoys who persuaded Achilles to resume fighting and he distinguished himself in the defence of the Greek camp, during which he struck Hector down with a stone. In the funeral games for *Patroclus, A. had an even wrestling-match with *Odysseus. After Achilles' death, A. was one of those who fought to recover his body. It was Odysseus, however, who won the

arms of Achilles. This drove A. mad, and he slaughtered a herd of cattle and sheep, mistaking them for the hated Agamemnon and Odysseus. When he regained his senses, he committed suicide by throwing himself on a sword. There are several versions of A.'s death: that being invulnerable, he was killed by the Trojans, who threw lumps of clay over him; or that he died after being pierced by *Paris' arrow. A. had a hero-cult at several sites: Salamis, Attica, the Troad and Byzantium. A.'s story served playwrights; the trilogy of Aeschylus dealing with it is now lost, but Sophocles' *Ajax* is extant. A.'s duel with Hector, the competition with Odysseus for Achilles' armour and, in particular, his suicide (as well as other themes) were extensively depicted by Greek artists.

AIAS (2) Son of Oïleus king of Locris (known as "the Lesser"). A. led the Locrian contingent of 40 ships to Troy, where he showed his courage on several occasions. A. often fought alongside A. Telemonius, and was known as a good runner. Quarrelsome and mean, he was hated by Athena. When Troy was captured A. maltreated *Cassandra, dragging her from the altar of Athena. In punishment, he was drowned on the voyage home. To atone for A.'s deed, the Locrians used to send two virgins to serve in Athena's temple in *Ilium, and if they were caught outside the temple, they were killed. This practice continued till the 2nd century BC, when the 1,000-year punishment came to its completion. The theme of A. and Cassandra was a favourite among Greek artists.

ALAE Originally, in military terminology, A. denoted the two units of Italian allies attached to a Roman legion. From the 1st century BC on, A. denoted a cavalry unit. Under the Empire an A. numbered 500 or 1,000 horsemen of the *auxilia*, commanded by an equestrian prefect.

ALAMANNI Germanic tribal group established in southwestern Germany by the beginning of the 3rd century AD. The early movements and origins of the A. are obscure; in later times they invaded Gaul, reaching even into Italy. Soon after AD 260, the A. stormed the Roman frontiers and occupied the area between the Main and the Rhine. Despite defeats, they continued to harass the western Roman provinces till the 5th century AD. Towards the end of the 5th century AD, the A. were defeated and annexed by the Franks.

ALANI Nomadic people in southeastern Russia, who ranged from the Aral Sea to the Don in the first three centuries AD. Their attempts to expand south into the Caucasus were checked by the Romans. Driven by the Huns in the 4th century AD, they pushed into the west, reaching Gaul in AD 406 and then Spain, where they joined the Vandals.

B. S. Bachrach, *A History of the Alans*, 1973.

ALARIC King of the Visigoths, born *c.* AD 370. In AD 391, he became chieftain of his tribe in Thrace, and served under *Theodosius I against *Eugenius (AD 394). After the death of Theodosius (AD 395), A. manoeuvered the leaders of the Eastern empire (*Arcadius and his minister Rufinus) against *Honorius and his minister *Stilicho, who ruled in the West. A. attacked Greece and obtained from Arcadius nomination as Imperial general for *Illyricum; as such, he attacked Venetia, in AD 401. In AD 403, he was defeated by Stilicho at Milan, and retreated to the region of the Save. After the death of Stilicho (AD 408), he resumed his attacks against Rome, and obtained a huge ransom as well as rule of Venetia, Noricum and Dalmatia. In AD 409, he was even able to establish a rival emperor to Honorius, the urban prefect

*Attalus. Continued resistance to A.'s demands led to a final assault upon Rome, and in August AD 410, the capital fell to the Goths, an event of tremendous moral impact on the entire Roman world, and viewed by pagans as a sign of divine wrath. The same year, A. attempted to cross over to Africa but he died on the way, at Cosenza in southern Italy. A.'s body was buried, with great treasure, in the bed of the river Busento, which had been diverted for this purpose.

ALASTOR In Greek mythology, a powerful demon invoked to take vengeance upon criminals, especially those like *Oedipus and the descendants of *Atreus. The criminal himself could be referred to by this appellative; it was also an appellative of the *Erinyes.

ALBA LONGA Ancient city in the Alban Hills in Latium, approx. 18 km southeast of Rome (near Castel Gondolfo). Greek and Roman traditions ascribed its foundations to *Ascanius, c. 1125 BC. This date is supported by excavated tombs. AL.'s antiquity presumably gave rise to the legend that it founded all the cities in Latium. The Roman king *Servius Tullius destroyed it in the 6th century BC, but the inhabitants were given Roman citizenship. Some of the leading Roman families, notably the Iulii Caesares and the Servilii, boasted of Alban origin, and *Romulus was considered a descendant of Alban kings. In later times it was a place of fashionable villas, notably the magnificent one of *Domitian.

ALBAN HILLS (modern Monte Cavo) Range in Latium, approx. 20 km southeast of Rome, rising to 950 m. A temple of Jupiter Latiaris, common to the Latins, was located in the AH., and the Latin festival (*Feriae Latinae*) was held here. Several Roman generals celebrated private triumphs in the AH., after their applications for public triumphs had been rejected.

ALBINUS Platonist philosopher of the 2nd century AD who taught at Smyrna. Two of A.'s works are extant: *Prologus*, an introduction to the dialogues of Plato; and *Didaskalikos* (or *Epitome*), an outline of Plato's theories. In fact, A. confused Aristotelian concepts with Platonic doctrines.
R. E. Witt, *Albinus and the History of Middle Platonism*, 1937.

ALBUCIUS, Titus Roman politician, praetor in 105 BC. A. failed in his accusation of extortion against *Scaevola (3). He was propraetor in Sicily, where he had some success and arranged a self-made triumph, but was accused of extortion and condemned to exile (103 BC). A convinced Epicurean and fanatic Hellenist, A. went off contentedly to live in Athens.

ALCAEUS (1) Lyric poet, native of Mytilene in *Lesbos, born c. 620 BC, a contemporary of *Sappho. A. was active in politics, opposing the tyrants of his city, as did his elder brothers; his aim was to restore an aristocratic regime. A.'s brothers succeeded in eliminating the tyrant Melanchros, who was succeeded by Myrsilus. The latter was killed and *Pittacus was elected *aisymnetes* (that is, arbitrator and sole ruler). A., who had fought against Athens with Pittacus at Sigeum, now bitterly attacked him, ridiculing his personal manners and bodily appearance. He was forced to leave his native city for the second time, going first to Egypt and later to Thrace. Before Pittacus ended his ten-year rule, he proclaimed an amnesty and A. and his brother Antimenidas, who served as a mercenary in Babylon, were allowed to return (prior to 580 BC). There are no further data on his life, nor on the date and manner of his death.

A.'s poems were studied and arranged in ten books by the Alexandrian scholars, *Aristophanes of Byzantium and *Aristarchus. Of these poems, only fragments have survived. Subject matter was often A.'s own participation in politics, and thus the fragments reflect many events and A.'s reactions to them: Myrsilus' murder; Pittachus' character; A.'s fight at Sigeum (where he lost his shield). One part of the poems, in which he describes the state as a ship, was called *Stasiotica* ("Civil Strife"). He also wrote hymns to the gods as well as erotic drinking songs. He used a wide variety of metres, and invented some stanza forms of his own (hence the "alcaic").
E. Lobel – D. L. Page, *Poetarum Lesbiorum Fragmenta*, 1955; D. L. Page, *Sappho and Alcaeus*, 1955.

ALCAEUS (2) Greek poet of Messene, contemporary of *Philip V. About 20 of his epigrams are extant, some of them abusive attacks on the Macedonian king.
Bowra, *Gr. Lyr. Poet.*, 130ff.

ALCAMENES Prominent Greek sculptor, probably a native of Athens (or Lemnos) who flourished in the second half of the 5th century BC. A. was said to have been the pupil and rival of *Phidias. Of the many works he made for Athens, only a few have survived in later copies. Among the famous works mentioned by *Pausanias (3) are the "Aphrodite of the Gardens", and a seated figure in the temple of Dionysus represented on Roman coins, as well as a statue of "Hermes Propylaeus", of which there are late copies. A. worked in gold, bronze, marble and ivory.

ALCATHOUS Son of *Pelops and Hippodameia. After the murder of his brother, Chrysippus, A. was compelled to leave *Elis. He killed the lion of Cithaeron, married the daughter of the king of Megara and succeeded him after his death. A. restored the walls of Megara, and built temples to Apollo and Artemis. He had a hero-cult at Megara, and a festival (*Alcathoia*).

ALCESTIS In Greek mythology, daughter of Pelias and wife of *Admetus who volunteered to die in place of her husband, but returned from the nether world. In one version *Persephone, impressed by A.'s devotion to her husband, returned her; in another version, she was rescued by *Heracles, who fought Hades (or Thanatos). The myth was depicted by various artists, and *Euripides' *Alcestis* is extant.

ALCIBIADES Athenian politician and general, born c. 450 BC, son of Cleinias, and, on his mother's side, from the *Alcmaeonidae family. A.'s uncle *Pericles became his guardian after his father's death. He was the pupil and friend of Socrates, but developed some of the worse aspects of Sophistic training, unscrupulous ambition and a cynical attitude to morals.

He was the leader of the radical democrats in 420 BC, his aim being to resume the war against Sparta and to expand the Athenian empire. It was mainly through A.'s intrigues that *Argos, *Elis and *Mantinea became allies. This success was shortlived, for Athens sent only a token force to help her Peloponnesian allies, and Sparta won a decisive victory at Mantinea in 418 BC. The next year, he made an alliance with his opponent, *Nicias, to defeat *Hyperbolus' attempts to ostracize him. Though opposed by Nicias, A. was largely responsible for the Athenian decision to despatch a military expedition against Syracuse in 415 BC. He was made general, along with Nicias and Lammachus. However, after the expedition left for Sicily, A. was accused of the mutilation of the statues of Hermes and the profanation of the mysteries of *Eleusis.

Rather than stand trial, he fled to Sparta and was condemned to death *in absentia*.

On A.'s advice, the Spartans sent an able commander, Gylippus, to Syracuse and later permanently occupied *Decelea, thus helping to defeat the Sicilian enterprise and creating a permanent menace to Athens for the remainder of the war. Sparta became active in the Aegean Sea with the help of A., and, in 412 BC, many Ionian states revolted against Athens. A. did not feel secure, however, and he went over to the Persian satrap Tissaphernes. He failed to draw him into cooperation with Athens, and turned to the Athenians at Samos. Under his command, victories were gained for Athens in the Hellespont and Ionia (411–408 BC), the Bosporan food supply was secured, and many of the rebellious allies were subdued.

Pardoned for his former crimes, A. returned to Athens and was elected extraordinary commander in 407 BC. The defeat of one of his officers in 406 gave rise to demagogic attacks on A. and he fled to Phrygia. Pharnabazus, at the request of *Lysander and the *Thirty Tyrants of Athens, procured A.'s murder in 404 BC.

Thucydides, 5–8; Xenophon, *Hellenica*, 1;
Plutarch, *Alcibiades*; G. Hatzfeld, *Alcibiade*[2], 1951.

ALCIDAMAS Greek rhetorician and Sophist of the 4th century BC, native of Elaea in Aeolis. A. was a pupil of *Gorgias, and taught rhetoric at Athens. In contrast to Isocrates, he insisted on practical training for improvisatory speech. His work *On Sophists* is extant.

ALCINOUS In Homer, son of Nausithous (*Od.* 7.63) and grandson of Poseidon. A. married his cousin Arete and had a daughter, *Nausicaa, and five sons. He was king of the Phaeacians in Scheria, where Odysseus arrived after being shipwrecked. A. entertained Odysseus lavishly, providing him with the ship that took him home. In the myth of the Argonauts, A.'s grandmother was Cercyra. A. had a hero-cult at Corcyra, which is identified with the land of the Phaeacians. After his wife's intervention in the dispute between the Argonauts and the Colchians, A. adjudged Medea to *Jason (1).

ALCMAEON In Greek mythology, son of *Amphiaraus and Eriphyle. Fulfilling his father's orders, A. killed his mother – in one version, before he captured Thebes as leader of the Epigoni, and in another version, after the expedition. Persecuted by the *Erinyes, he wandered over the land until he was purified by King Phegeus of Psophis, whose daughter he then married. The Erinyes, however, still pursued him and he continued to wander until he arrived at the mouth of the river *Achelous and married the river-god's daughter, Callirhoë. Phegeus' sons then killed him in revenge. His grave was shown in ancient times at Psophis in *Arcadia. A. is depicted occasionally on Greek vases. Euripides wrote a play, *Alcmaeon in Corinth*.

ALCMAEONIDAE A very powerful aristocratic family in Athens, reputedly descended from *Alcmaeon. *Megacles of the A. put down an attempt by *Cylon to establish tyranny at Athens; his son Alcmaeon commanded an Athenian army in the sacred war against Crisa, and won a chariot-race in the Olympic games. Alcmaeon's son Megacles married Agariste, daughter of Sicyon's tyrant *Cleisthenes. Under *Pisistratus and his sons, the family was periodically exiled. It finally brought about the fall of the Pisistratids and returned to Athens permanently. *Cleisthenes (2) was of the A., and *Pericles and *Alcibiades had A. mothers. Under democratic Athens, the family no longer played an important role in politics.

ALCMAN Greek lyric poet – the first, according to Alexandrian scholars. He flourished in the second half of the 7th century BC, but details of his life are obscure. He may have been from Sardis, but is also said to have been a Laconian by birth. A. is also supposed to have been freed from slavery thanks to his poetical talents. It is certain that he worked at Sparta, and his grave was shown there in the 2nd century AD.

A.'s lyrical poems were edited by Alexandrian scholars in six books; the surviving fragments are known from papyri. Many of the poems were written for Spartan festivals, to be sung by male and female choruses. He also wrote hymns for Hera, Athena, Aphrodite, and Apollo and for the Dioscuri. The 120 extant fragments hardly support the tradition that A. invented the love-song. Much of a choral poem for maidens is extant (*Partheneion*), including a description of the relations between the maidens of the chorus. A.'s language is derived from the Dorian and Aeolic dialects. He uses a variety of metres, and the structure of his *Partheneion* is elaborate. His poems were studied and commented on by various scholars in antiquity.

Bowra, *Gr. Lyr. Poet.*, 16ff.; Page, *Poet. Mel. Gr.*;
D. L. Page, *Alcman, the Partheneion*, 1951.

ALCMENE In Greek mythology, daughter of Electrion, king of Mycenae. A. married her uncle *Amphitryon, who then accidentally killed her father and fled with her to Thebes. A. refused to sleep with her husband until he had avenged the murder of her eight brothers by the Teleboans and Taphians. While her husband was absent in the war of revenge, she was visited by Zeus and bore twins: Heracles (from Zeus) and Ipicles (from her husband). When she died *Hermes took her body to the Islands of the Blessed. She had cults at Thebes, Attica and Megara.

ALESIA (modern Alise-Ste Reine) Fortress town of the Gallic Mandubii, famous for Caesar's siege of *Vercingetorix which took place there in 52 BC. Remains of the Caesarean circumvallation have been found.
G. Le Gall, *Alésie*, 1963.

ALEUADAE Thessalian aristocratic family, most powerful at *Larissa. Traditionally, the political organization of Thessaly was established by one of the A., Aleuas the Red. A.'s cooperation with the Persians led to their decline, after the failure of Xerxes' expedition to Greece. From the end of the 5th century on, they opposed the tyrants of Pherae, but lost influence with the ascendancy of Macedonia.
H. D. Westlake, *Thessaly in the Fourth Century*, 1965.

ALEXANDER (1) I Son of Amyntas, king of Macedonia, c. 494–450 BC. During the invasion of *Xerxes, A. was compelled to cooperate with the Persians, though he rendered significant assistance to the Greeks and acted as mediator. A. exploited the Persian defeat, and extended his kingdom to the Strymon valley. Further expansion was limited by the vigorous policy of Athens.

A. was the first Macedonian king to issue coins, and it was he who began the Hellenization of Macedonia, inviting the poets *Pindar and *Bacchylides to his court. Because A. claimed an Argive origin and because of his services to the Greeks, he was allowed to take part in the Olympic games, where he won a victory.

ALEXANDER (2) of Pherae Tyrant, who seized power in 369 BC, seeking to rule Thessaly under the title *Tagus, though he never achieved complete control. The *Aleuadae opposed him, and *Pelopidas of Thebes brought about the formation of a Thessalian League,

Alexander the Great at battle; a mosaic from Pompeii

which defeated him. Pherae subsequently entered into an alliance with Boeotia. He was murdered in 358 BC by the sons of *Jason (2), a former tyrant of Pherae.
H. D. Westlake, *Thessaly in the Fourth Century*, 1965.

ALEXANDER (3) I of Molossia Brother of *Olympias, he was supported by his brother-in-law *Philip II. A. became king of Molossia in Epirus in 342 BC, and he united the other Epirote tribes into a league, with himself as leader (*hegemon*). At Tarentum's request, A. went to Italy in 334 BC, defeated Tarentum's enemies, the Lucanians, and made an alliance with Rome. He quarreled with the Tarantines and was murdered in 330 BC. A.'s wife Cleopatra was the sister of Alexander the Great.
Hammond, *Epirus*, 534ff.

ALEXANDER (4) III, the Great Son of *Philip II of Macedonia and *Olympias of Epirus, born in 356 BC. When A. was 13 years old, *Aristotle became his tutor, instructing him in poetry, drama and politics. The period of instruction ended in 340 BC when A. was appointed regent for his father.

At the battle of *Chaeronea (338 BC), A. fought with distinction as a cavalry leader. His passionate character, and his father's subsequent marriages, led to friction between father and son, as he was not assured of his succession to the throne. When Philip was murdered (336 BC), A. secured the crown and quickly disposed of all rivals. He renewed the so-called League of Corinth, and was elected its general to conduct the war against Persia.

His first campaigns, however, were waged to secure Macedonia; he got as far as the Danube, and penetrated into Illyria. During his absence, Thebes revolted, and he quickly returned to destroy the city, and sold its inhabitants into slavery (335 BC).

A. had inherited the war against Persia from Philip who had organized a capable army to avenge the destruction wrought by *Xerxes' invasion of Greece, almost 150 years previously, and to free the Greeks then subject to Persia. For A. the war was the way to grand exploits and expansion; for his men it was an opportunity to gain riches and power. Apparently there were no precise geo-

graphical aims set for A.'s expedition, which numbered some 40,000 Macedonian and Greek troops. A. crossed the Hellespont in 334 BC, winning his first victory at the battle of Granicus, which enabled him to free the Greek cities in Ionia. He then proceeded to complete the conquest of Asia Minor. Meanwhile, *Darius III concentrated his forces and advanced into Syria. A. won a great victory over him at Issus, in November 333 BC. At this point, A. rejected the peace offers of the Persian king, and turned to the conquest of *Phoenicia. *Tyre fell after a prolonged siege, and A. had it destroyed. He then proceeded into Palestine and put Gaza to siege. The conquest of Egypt was easily achieved and here A. founded his new city, *Alexandria. He went to the Oasis of Siwa, to consult the famous oracle of Amnon, whereupon the high priest there hailed him as the son of Amnon, as was the custom with a Pharaoh. This tactic was employed — for instance, by *Callisthenes — to spread the belief that A. was the son of Zeus.

During this time, Darius gained a much needed respite for mustering his forces. The next decisive battle took place at Gaugamela, between the Tigris and Zab rivers, in October 331 BC. Once again, A. won a brilliant victory, all Persia subsequently lying at his mercy. He took the satrapies of Babylonia, Elam and Persia, and pursued Darius into Media. Darius was murdered by his own men in 330 BC.

A. now regarded himself as the legitimate ruler of the Persian Empire. He punished Darius' murderers and established control over the entire empire. In the next three years, A. carried operations into Bactria and Sogdiana, where he faced national opposition and irregular warfare. A. fought hard, employing new tactics, such as the subdivision of his army, and pacified the country. During this phase, he married Roxana, daughter of a local chieftain.

By now, a rift had developed between him and his veteran Macedonian commanders who opposed his increasingly autocratic tendencies and philo-Persian policies. In 330 BC, A. executed *Philotas, after a trial before the army and brought about the murder of Philotas' father

*Parmenion, his senior general. In 327 BC, A. killed
*Cleitus — who'had saved his life at the battle of Granicus
— during a drunken quarrel about A.'s oriental tendencies.
A.'s attempt to introduce the Persian custom of
proskynesis, "prostration", was resented and led to the
execution of Callisthenes. Nonetheless, the army remained loyal to him.

In 327 BC, A. advanced into India. Taxiles, king of the
land between the Indus and the Jhelum, submitted. Porus,
king of the land between the Jhelum and the Chenab, was
defeated at a great battle on the Hydaspes (Beas). But A.'s
army refused to continue the unending advance to the
East. A.'s entreaties were of no avail, and he had to accede
to the soldiers' demands. They began to return in 325 BC,
along a new route. A. went down the Indus to its delta,
and then split his forces: the army crossed the desert of
Gedrosia, while the fleet, under the command of *Nearchus, set sail on an unknown course to the Persian Gulf.
After many hardships both Nearchus and A. reached
Persia (324 BC).

A. began at once to supervise the administration of his
empire. His autocracy became more pronounced as he
executed governors and officials accused of misconduct.
Despite opposition, he pursued a policy of cooperation
with the Iranians and had 30,000 of them trained in the
Macedonian manner of war. He married the daughter of
Darius, encouraged his officers to marry Iranian women,
and held a mass wedding for 10,000 soldiers at Susa. He
adopted the court ceremony of the Persian kings. When
he sought to incorporate oriental soldiers within his army
by forming new, mixed units, the Macedonians revolted.
There was a reconciliation and a feast was celebrated at
Opis in the summer of 324 BC. Veterans who wished to
return to Macedonia were allowed to do so, but this hardly settled the matter as A. adhered to his new ideals of
government.

His relations with the Greek states were aggravated by
his order to restore exiles — this violated the autonomy of
the cities.

In his last months, A. was occupied with plans for
further explorations, and an expedition into Arabia. A
severe attack of fever brought his life to an end in June
323 BC. Ptolemy I buried him in a great tomb in Alexandria.

A.'s conquests opened a new period in history, and led
to profound changes in the vast area from Greece to
India. Greek traders and settlers came in the wake of his
army, and A. laid the foundations for the hellenization of
the conquered lands by founding tens of new cities with
Greek constitutions and Macedonian-Greek populations.
For A., the conquests had been an opportunity to advance science. Many scholars accompanied him, various
explorations — for instance, to the Caspian Sea — were
undertaken, and he is said to have ordered that all scientifically important phenomena observed in the new countries
were to be reported to his former tutor, Aristotle. His outstanding achievements were ascribable to his individual
personality and to the Macedonian army which his father
had bequeathed to him. He was versatile in war, seeking
new solutions to new conditions, and he was able to with-
stand severe and prolonged hardship. In the art of siege
warfare, A. surpassed the other generals of antiquity. An
excellent fighter, he personally led his cavalry into battle,
and was often wounded. This won him the almost unlimited devotion of his soldiers. The character and
achievements of A. form an abundant source for legends,
which exist to this day in both Asia and Europe.
Arrian, Anabasis; Diod. Sic. 17; Plutarch, Alexander;
L. Pearson, The Lost Histories of Alexander the Great,
1960; P. Green, Alexander of Macedon, 1970.

ALEXANDER (5) Aetolus The only known Aetolian
poet. Native of Pleuron, born in 315 BC. A. was commissioned by *Ptolemy Philadelphus c. 285 BC to arrange
a collection of plays for the Alexandrian library. From c.
276 BC on, he was at the court of *Antigonus (2) Gonatas,
where he met *Aratus of Soli. Several fragments of poems
— among them, Apollo, a poem about ill-fated love, and
Musae, a poem on poets — and the title of one tragedy are
extant.

ALEXANDER (6) Balas Native of Smyrna. Supported
by *Attalus II, A. claimed to be the son of *Antiochus
IV. A. defeated *Demetrius I Soter in 150 BC with the
support of Egypt and Rome. He was a poor ruler, however, and Demetrius' son defeated him in 146 BC. He was
murdered the following year.

Coin of Alexander Balas

ALEXANDER (7) Polyhistor Native of Miletus, born in the late 2nd century BC. A. was sold into slavery in the Mithridatic War, brought to Rome, where *Sulla set him free, and renamed L. Cornelius Alexander. He was burnt to death in his house at Laurentum.

A.'s numerous books on history, geography and literature were compilations of earlier works; extant fragments of them come from later writers who used his works.

ALEXANDER (8) of Aphrodisias Peripatetic philosopher who was active at the end of the 2nd century and the early 3rd century AD. A. taught at Athens from AD 198 on, and dedicated one of his works to *Septimius Severus and his son *Caracalla. He won fame for his commentaries on Aristotle; of these, *Prior Analytics*, *De sensu*, *Topics*, *Meteorologica* and *Metaphysica* are extant. Several of his own works have also survived.

ALEXANDER (9), Severus (Gessius Bassianus Alexianus) Roman emperor who ruled under the title Marcus Aurelius Severus Alexander, born of a noble Phoenician family at Acre in AD 208. A. was the grandson of *Julia Maesa (sister of *Julia Domna, wife of *Septimius Severus). His mother, *Julia Mammaea, was a forceful personality. She had her son proclaimed emperor in AD 222. A. abolished the excesses of his predecessor *Elagabalus, and effected a compromise with the Senate without radically changing the character of the Severan domination. He was a youth of unblemished character, deeply religious although eclectic in belief. According to his biographer, A. kept statues of Abraham and Jesus in his Palatine chapel. His great weakness was his inability to handle the army, and he failed to protect the eminent jurist *Ulpian who, as prefect of the Praetorians, was killed by his own men. The situation on the frontiers grew dangerous when the Sassanid dynasty replaced the Parthians in AD 224, and Ardashir I began a vigorous offensive against Rome. A. led an unsuccessful expedition to the East in AD 232, and in AD 233 was forced to withdraw troops to Germany, where a barbarian invasion was threatening. In AD 234, he attempted to negotiate with the *Alamanni; he and his mother were killed by rebellious soldiers near

Portrait of Alexander Severus

Moguntiacum in AD 235. A. was succeeded by the brutal but energetic *Maximinus Thrax.
Herodian, 6; Dio, 79–80.

ALEXANDER (10) JANNAEUS Hasmonaean king and High Priest, son of John *Hyrcanus (1). He succeeded to the throne in 103 BC after the death of his brother Aristobulus I, whose widow Alexandra Salome he married. In a series of wars, not always successful, he extended his rule over the entire coast of Palestine, the Jordan valley, the Galilee (already attacked by his brother), and much of Transjordan. He forced the conquered Ituraeans to convert to Judaism. But the quarrel with the Pharisees, already begun under his father, developed into a civil war which lasted six years. Before he died in 76 BC, while besieging Ragaba, east of the Jordan, he advised his wife and successor to become reconciled with the Pharisees.

ALEXANDRIA Many cities named after *Alexander the Great were founded by him or by his successors; the more important are A. ad Issum (modern Alexandretta), A. of the Arii (modern Herat), and A. of the Arachosii, at Kandahar, Afghanistan.

The most important A. is at the western end of the Nile delta in Egypt. This metropolis, located west of the Canopic arm of the Nile, was founded by Alexander in 331 BC. A. was given a Greek constitution as an autonomous polis. The city consisted of five quarters and was originally Hippodamic in plan. The city proper was connected with the adjacent islet of Pharos by a 1,200 m long mole where the famous lighthouse was built in 279 BC. Flanking the mole were an eastern and a western harbour, the former being the best harbour on the Mediterranean coast of Egypt. A. attracted Greeks, Macedonians, and other peoples, especially Jews. When *Ptolemy I gained control of Egypt, A. became the

Anchor on a coin of Alexander Janaeus who conquered the whole seacoast of Palestine

Dying soldier from the temple of Aphaea at Aegina

A vase-painting by the Brygus-painter

administrative centre of the land. Under him and his son, Ptolemy Philadelphus, A. became the centre of scientific and literary activity in the Hellenistic world. The Alexandrian Library was the largest in the world, reputedly containing some 700,000 volumes. Famous scholars such as *Eratosthenes, *Aristarchus, *Callimachus and *Apollonius Rhodius worked there. The famous *Museum of A. was apparently founded by Ptolemy I as an institution of research and learning. Other' famous buildings in the city included the Ptolemaic palace, the temple of *Sarapis, the Gymnasium and the Caesareum. The city's prosperity came mainly from commerce, gaining impetus from the centralized and monopolistic system of the Ptolemaic economy. A. was connected to the Red Sea by the Nile and a system of canals, making it an outlet for Oriental trade. Industry, too, was developed, A. being a major centre of papyrus manufacture.

The city lost its position as a centre of learning in 145 BC, when Ptolemy Physcon expelled the scholars, notably *Aristarchus. The Ptolemies rescinded its autonomous status at some uncertain date, and this situation did not change with the Roman conquest. Anti-Roman sentiments smouldered in A. throughout the Roman period with occasional rioting. Hostilities between the Greeks and Jews caused frequent disturbances until the Jews revolted under Trajan, and their quarter was destroyed. The Alexandrians vigorously maintained their citizenship rights and Egyptians could become Roman citizens once they became Alexandrians.

A. was occupied by *Zenobia in the 3rd century AD, captured by the Persians in 618, and regained by *Heraclius in AD 629. It was conquered by the *Arabs in AD 642.

Tarn, *Alexander the Great*, 1948, 2, 232–259; Frazer, *Alexandria*.

ALEXIS Writer of Middle and New Comedy, born at *Thurii *c.* 375 BC and died at an old age (perhaps 106). A. lived and wrote in Athens. He is said to have been *Menander's teacher (in another source, his uncle). He is credited with 245 plays, and several victories at the *Dionysia and the *Lenaea. No complete play has survived, but 136 titles and 340 fragments have come down to us. A. introduced the parasite type into comedy, and burlesqued mythological subjects. The chorus in his comedies sometimes kept to its traditional role of addressing the actors, and at other times broke out of the plot altogether. The fragments indicate A.'s thematic ingenuity. The *Poenulus* of *Plautus is probably based on A.'s *Carchedonius*.

Webster, *Later Greek Comedy* (s.v.).

ALFENUS VARUS, Publius Roman politician under the Second Triumvirate. As a member of a commission to distribute land amongst veterans, A. confiscated the territory of Mantua, where Virgil's estate was located. A. was suffect consul in 39 BC. He studied law under the jurist Servius Sulpicius Rufus, and wrote a *digesta* in forty books, later epitomes of which were excerpted by the compilers of the *Digesta* of Justinian.

ALGIDUS The eastern part of the *Alban hills, dominating the route leading southeast from Rome toward the Trerus valley (the later *via Latina*). In the 5th century BC, A. was occupied by the *Aequi, who were dislodged by Rome in 431 BC. There were temples to Diana and Fortuna at A.

ALIMENTA Roman funds for the support of poor children, originating in private endowments and, after *Nerva, contributed to by emperors as well. The A. gave mortgage loans to landowners, and moneys from the interest were distributed to needy children. The system was developed by the state both out of charity and also to encourage a high birthrate to counter a decline in Italian manpower. Many inscriptions testify to the spread of the system throughout Italy in the 2nd century AD.

Hands, *Charities and Social Aid in Greece and Rome*, 1968, 108–114.

ALLOBROGES Gallic tribe occupying the region between the lake of Geneva and the Graiae Alps (St. Bernard) and bordering on the Rhone. Rome conquered the A. in 121 BC, and they were later included in the province of Gallia Narbonensis. The A. were often exploited by Roman officials and merchants; they refused to cooperate with *Catiline, and tried to revolt in 61 BC, but were promptly defeated.

ALLECTUS *Praefectus praetorio* and finance minister of *Carausius in Britain (AD 293). A. slew his master and had himself proclaimed emperor, maintaining his rule over *Brittania for three years (AD 293–6). When Asclepiodotus, admiral of *Constantius I Chlorus, landed in Britain and marched against London, A. opposed him but fell in battle.

ALPHEUS Largest river in the Peloponnesus, rising in *Arcadia and flowing into the Ionian Sea. In mythology, A., son of Thetis, pursued the nymph Arethusa to the island of Ortygia at Syracuse where she turned into a spring (in one version, she later turned into a river). This led to the belief that the water of A. flowed under the sea to Arethusa in Syracuse. A. was also said to have fallen in love with Artemis, who eluded him. A. had a cult at Olympia and at other sites.

ALYATTES King of Lydia, son of Sadyattes, who ruled from 619 BC (according to Herodotus). A. expelled the Cimmerians and gained control over Asia as far as the river Halys, which later became the border with Persia. He expanded his kingdom into Ionia, and in 560 BC was succeeded by his son, *Croesus.

ALYPIUS (1) Author of a comprehensive, extant work on Greek musical theory. Nothing is known of his life, except that he worked in the 3rd or 4th century AD.

ALYPIUS (2) Born in Antioch, A. was appointed governor of Britain during his friend *Julian's rule over Gaul and the West. A noted geographer, he prepared a map of the British Isles. During Julian's war with *Constantius II, A. supported his patron. In AD 363, he was appointed to supervise the rebuilding of the Temple in Jerusalem, but, being a cautious pagan, he halted all work after an earthquake on 27 May of that year. After Julian's death, he fulfilled important official functions under *Valens.

AMAFINUS, Gaius Contemporary of *Cicero (1), a writer who popularized Epicurean philosophy in his works. His style was regarded as uncouth.

AMALTHEA Nymph, daughter of Oceanus (or Melisseus), who nursed the infant Zeus when he was hidden from his father Cronus. When Zeus took control of the universe, he rewarded A. by setting her among the stars as Capella. A. was described as a she-goat, with a splendid pair of horns, the "cornucopiae". Whoever owned one of her horns could eat or drink whatever he wished. A broken horn appears often in ancient art.

AMASEIA Capital of the kings of *Pontus, situated in a narrow part of the Iris valley. *Strabo, a native of A., gives a detailed description of its location. Pompey annexed A. to the Roman Empire, upon the conquest of

Pontus, and it became the metropolis of the western part of the region (Pontus Galaticus).

AMASIS King of Egypt from 570 BC, after a revolt against King Apries which was initially directed against his foreign mercenaries. A. pursued a phil-Hellenic policy, giving commercial concessions to Greeks at *Naucratis, employing Greek mercenaries, and cultivating good relations with the Greek states. Under A.'s rule, Egypt enjoyed a long period of economic prosperity and peace. He died in 526 BC, one year before the conquest of Egypt by *Cambyses.

AMAZONS Legendary warlike race of women from somewhere in Central Asia, southern Russia or northeastern Asia Minor. Their legends were apparently so popular that new ones were continually added.

The A. appear as early as the *Iliad: *Bellorphon defeated them in Lycia, and Priam also fought them, though in another myth they came to the aid of Priam, and their queen, Penthesilea, was killed by *Achilles (who had fallen in love with her). Theseus visited the land of the A. and abducted Antiope (or Hyppolyta), whose sister Oreithyia led an avenging expedition. The A. passed

The War of the Amazons on a Roman sarcophagus found near Caesarea

through Scythia, the Danube and Thrace, and arrived in Attica. They were defeated in a decisive battle at Athens. Evacuating Attica, the A. then settled in Scythia.

Theseus had a son, *Hippolytus, by his A. The ninth labour of *Heracles was to obtain the golden girdle of Ares, worn by the Queen of the A. *Jason, too, fought them, and one legend describes *Dionysus' victory over the A. According to a late legend, Alexander met them in his campaigns in Central Asia. The A. were supposed to have extended their empire to Thrace, and penetrated into Asia Minor and' Syria where they founded many cities, including Ephesus, Smyrna, Sinope and Cyrene.

The A. had peculiar customs — killing or mutilating their male infants so that they would grow up to perform the womanly duties. The A. were good hunters and among the first to fight on horseback. They used brass bows, axes and crescent-shaped shields. To facilitate the drawing of the bow, right breasts were amputated, hence the popular etymology of their name, a-mazos ("breast-less"). They worshipped Ares and Artemis. It is possible that the myth of the A. represents an encounter with matriarchal tribes. Motifs from A. legends (their battles with Heracles, Theseus, Achilles) were used extensively in ancient art.

AMBARVALIA An annual rite performed at Rome to lustrate the fields of the Roman territory.
Latte, *R. Rel.*, 41f., 65.

AMBITUS The "walking about" of Roman candidates for office, in an attempt to win voters' support. A. acquired the sense of election campaigning and, when bribery became involved, laws were passed against illegal canvassing (*de ambitu*) — this probably as early as 358 BC. The severe penalties of the laws passed in the later Republic, however, did little to stop this practice.

AMBIVIUS TURPIO, Lucius Actor and director, who appeared in the plays of *Terence and *Caecilius. A.'s performance in the *Hecyra* of Terence assured the success of this comedy and was long remembered.

AMBRACIA (modern Arta) Greek city on the Gulf of A. (Latin Actium), on the western coast of Greece. A. was founded by Corinth in the 7th century BC. In the Peloponnesian War, A. sided with Sparta, and suffered a defeat by *Acarnania and Athens (426 BC). *Philip II conquered it and it later became *Pyrrhus' capital. From 230 BC on, A. was under Aetolian control; Rome conquered it in 189 BC.
Hammond, *Epirus*, 140ff.

AMBROSIA and NECTAR Originally the stuff the gods ate and drank, which gave them immortality. In time, however, A. was actually thought of as the food, and N. the drink, of the gods. Though reserved for the gods, some mortals, too, enjoyed A. and N. The horns of *Amalthea flowed with A. and N., their sweet smell perhaps being associated with honey and mead.

AMICITIA ("friendship") In Rome, besides the notion of personal intimate relationship, it denoted political and social cooperation between persons or bodies with common interest. *Amici* ("friends"), however, kept their political independence, especially if of the same social position and prestige. In the relations of Rome with foreign states and rulers, A. denoted a friendly relationship without formal obligation. But it did imply moral responsibility for the security of the foreign party who, in turn, was expected to assist Rome. As the Roman party, both state and individual, became more powerful, the relationship came to resemble that of *client and patron.

Under the Empire, the *amici Caesaris*, "friends of Caesar", were those summoned by the emperor for consultation, thus forming the *consilium Caesaris*.
M. Gelzer, *The Roman Nobility*, 1969, 86—110; Badian, *Clientelae*, 12ff.; P. A. Brunt, *Crisis of the Roman Republic* (ed. R. Seager), 199—218.

AMISUS (modern Samsun) Greek city on the southern coast of the Black Sea, founded in the 6th century BC, probably by *Miletus. In the 5th century BC, A. received Athenian settlers and was renamed Piraeus. In the first half of the 3rd century BC, it became the seat of the kings of Pontus. Situated on a major route, A. was a centre of trade. *Lucullus freed it from the Pontic kings in 71 BC.
Magie, *Asia* (s.v.).

AMMIANUS MARCELLINUS Roman historian. Born at Antioch *c.* AD 330, descendant of an educated Greek family, A. joined the Imperial Guards (as *protector domesticus*) and from AD 353 served on the staff of Ursicinus, following him to Gaul against Silvanus. In AD 356—7, A. campaigned with *Julian against the Alamanni. He followed the army to Amida, and lived through the Persian siege in AD 359. When the city fell, he made an adventurous escape to *Antioch. A. also took part in Julian's Persian campaign of AD 363 (probably with the Euphrates fleet), after which he left the service. He lived at Antioch till at least AD 371, and later visited Egypt, Greece and even Thrace (in order to see the battlefield of Adrianople). In AD 380, he settled in Rome, where he developed close relations with the pagan aristocracy, particularly the circle of *Symmachus. He died there about AD 395.

A. wrote a history of Rome in 31 books, continuing the *Historiae* of *Tacitus from the accession of *Nerva to the battle of Adrianople (AD 96 to 378). Books 14 to 31 (on AD 353—78) are extant. His original plan was to write his history down to the death of Julian (AD 363). Occasionally, he speaks of the Christian clergy with irony, but he respects the Christian belief. Though a great believer in oracles, premonitions and the like, he is generally regarded as an impartial historian — the last great historian of antiquity. His Latin style was somewhat artificial.
E. A. Thomson, *The Historical Work of Ammianus Marcelinus*, 1947; J. C. Rolfe (Loeb), 1935—7; *Latin Historians* (ed. T. A. Dorey), 1966.

AMPHIARAUS In Greek mythology, A. is connected with *Argos and *Boeotia, and is said to be the son of Oeclus (or Apollo). He married Eriphyle, sister of the Argive king, *Adrastus, and once quarrelled with his brother-in-law — the two men would have killed each other had not Eriphyle intervened and made them swear to obey her in any future differences. Endowed with powers of foresight, A. refused to take part in the expedition against Thebes. But his wife was bribed by Polynices, son of Oedipus, and he was forced to follow her decision in his dispute with Adrastus. A. directed his son *Alcmaeon to avenge his death. The attack on Thebes was a complete disaster. A. tried to escape in his chariot, but Zeus sent a thunderbolt, and A. and his chariot vanished into a cleft (on the bank of the river Ismenus). A. had an oracular sanctuary at *Oropus, at the spot where he was believed to have vanished. The myth alludes to the chtonic character of A. the god. His name, meaning "most sacred", is found in early Mycenaean documents. A mythological hero may have become assimilated in time with some local Boeotian god. Some motifs of his myth appear in Greek vase-painting.

AMPHICTIONIES Probably from *amphictiones*, "neighbouring inhabitants", people living in the same vicinity. The A. were leagues of tribes and states concerned with the administration of temples. The most famous was that associated with the temple of Demeter near Thermopylae, and hence called *Pylaea*.

According to Herodotus, the A. took its name from Amphictyon, son or grandson of *Deucalion (2), who founded the league. Other A. centred around Delos, with its temple of Apollo; Calaureia (an island in the Saronic Gulf), with its temple of Poseidon; and Onchestos in Boeotia, with its temple of Poseidon.

By the 8th century BC, the A. of Anthela (near Thermopylae) shifted its centre to the temple of Apollo at Delphi. The original members of the Delphic A. were tribes of Thessalians, Boeotians, Dorians, Ionians, Perrhaebians, Dolopians, Magnetes, Locrians, Aenianes, Achaeans (from Phtiotis in Thessaly), Malians and Phocians. Each tribe had two votes in the *synedrion*, which met regularly in spring and autumn. In the course of time, however, certain states replaced tribes — thus, Athens represented the Ionians; the votes of the Phocians were held by Philip II; and Delphi itself obtained two votes. The *synedrion* supervised operation of the Delphic temple and was responsible for the celebration of the Pythian games. Members were forbidden by oath to block wells and springs, and destroy other Amphictionic cities. The A. could declare sacred war against violators of its decisions or property.

Three such wars were conducted, the first against Crisa, which was destroyed at the beginning of the 6th century, the second and third against *Phocis. Powerful states sought to dominate the decisions of the A. Thessaly did so in the 6th century BC, and Philip II and the Aetolian League had control in the third century BC. The Delphic A. still existed under the Roman Empire, but it had long lost its political significance.
Ehrenberg, *Greek State*, 108–110.

AMPHILOCHUS Son of *Amphiaraus and, like him, a seer. A. participated with his brother *Alcmaeon in the expedition against Thebes, and in the murder of their mother. He fought at Troy, and went to Claros with *Calchas, who died there. A. continued his wanderings with *Mopsus the seer, and they founded Mallus in Cilicia, where an oracular sanctuary was later devoted to them. A. was credited with other foundations, and had cults in Athens, Sparta, and Aetolia.

AMPHION and ZETHUS Twin sons of Antiope and Zeus (or Epopeus of Sicyon). Their mother was incarcerated by her uncle Lycus, and A. and Z. were raised by a shepherd. When their mother escaped, A. and Z. recognized her, and the two then killed Lycus and his wife Dirce. A. and Z. built the walls of Thebes and gave the city the name of Z.'s wife, Thebe (A.'s wife was *Niobe). A. was such an excellent musician that the stones of the city walls were said to have moved into place when A. played the lyre (an instrument Hermes gave him). He was killed by Apollo.

AMPHIPOLIS Greek city situated on a hill, surrounded on three sides by the river Strymon. An earlier Thracian city named Ennea Hodoi, "the nine roads", had stood here on the conjunction of many important highways. The first two settlements had failed and it was not until 437 BC that Athens established it as a successful colony. Owing to its position, A. commanded the routes to inner Thrace and the Hellespont. One reason for its foundation was its proximity to the silver and gold mines of Mount

Pangaeus. A. also benefited from the fertile land and the abundant ship-timber in its vicinity. The Spartan general *Brasidas captured A. in 424 BC, and *Cleon found his death there when he tried to recapture the city, in 422 BC. *Philip II took A. in 357 BC, and it remained under Macedonian rule until 186 BC.
G. Papastavru, *Amphipolis*, 1936.

AMPHISSA City of the Ozolian Locrians, situated in a plain about 15 km northwest of Delphi, commanding the road from Doris to the Gulf of Corinth. In the third sacred war, A. cooperated with Thebes against *Phocis, but was subdued in 353 BC. In 339 BC, *Aeschines turned the scales against A. in the Amphictionic *synedrion*, by accusing it of unlawful cultivation of Crisaean lands; war was declared against A., and it was captured and partially destroyed by *Philip II, in 338 BC.
L. Lerart, *Les Locriens de l'ouest*, 1952.

AMPHITHEATRES Buildings for gladiatorial contests and beast-baiting, with elliptical arenas surrounded by seats for spectators. The performances had long been carried out before permanent buildings were constructed. The earliest extant A. (*c.* 80–70 BC) is at *Pompeii. In Rome the first permanent A. was built by *Statilius Taurus in 29 BC. The arena was equipped with substructures which gave access to men and beasts and facilitated drainage. The best known A. is the *Colosseum.
Platner-Ashby, *Top. Dict. Rome* (s.v.).

AMPHITRYON Son of *Alcaeus and husband of *Alcmene, his niece. A. accidentally killed Electryon, his brother-in-law, while assisting him in the war against Pterelaus and his sons. He fled to Thebes, to be purified by *Creon, whose aid against Pterelaus he received after he had rid Creon of the terrible vixen Teumessus. A. killed Pterelaus and captured his city, Thaphos, with the help of the latter's daughter, Comaetho, who loved him. A.'s wife, Alcmene, bore Heracles to Zeus, who had impersonated her absent husband. This affiliation was a Theban attempt to connect their local hero A. with Heracles.

The amphitheatre in Pompeii

AMYCLAE Ancient pre-Hellenic town on the river *Eurotas, approx. 5 km south of Sparta, mentioned by Homer as being under the control of *Menelaus. By the 8th century BC, it was subdued by Sparta. There is evidence that A. was independent in the 1st century BC. The A. cult for the ancient god *Hyacinthus was superseded by Apollo Amyclaeus after the Spartan conquest. *Pausanias (3.8) gives a detailed account of the sanctuary and the throne of Apollo at A., remains of which have been found.

AMYNTAS (2) Commander of the Galatian troops of *Brutus (2) and *Cassius (2). A. took part in the battle of Philippi in 42 BC, but changed sides in time to be pardoned by the triumvirs. After the Galatian king *Deiotarus died in 40 BC, Antony allowed A. to rule much of Asia Minor, including Galatia and Lycaonia. Though present with Antony at Actium, A. opportunely shifted allegiance to Octavian, who confirmed his position. He was killed in 25 BC, and part of his kingdom was organized as the Roman province of Galatia. A. was a very wealthy man and left a large inheritance to Augustus.

AMYNTAS (1) III King of Macedonia, who ascended to the throne in 393 BC, after slaying Amyntas II. With Thessalian aid, A. repulsed the Illyrians. Through opportune alliances with various powers (the League of Chalcidice, Sparta, Athens and Iason of Pherae), he succeeded in securing his kingdom against external foes and imposing his will within Macedonia. He died in 370 BC. He was the father of *Philip II.

ANACHARSIS Scythian of the royal line who, according to Herodotus (4.76–7), visited Greece and other lands. A. had come to know the cult of Magna Mater in *Cyzicus and attempted to introduce it in Scythia for which attempt the Scythians killed him. From the 4th century BC on, more details were added to his tale, making him the ideal of the uncorrupt, wise barbarian, especially in Cynic writings. He was considered one of the ancient Seven Sages, and various sayings and letters were attributed to him.

ANACREON Lyric poet, native of the Ionian *Teos, born in the first half of the 6th century BC. A. was one of the Teans who left their home city in 545 BC, after the Persian conquest of Lydia and Ionia, to settle in *Abdera. Some fragments of his works contain allusions to events during his stay there. Later he was invited to the court of *Polycrates of Samos, where he wrote some love-songs and is said to have mentioned his patron in his poems. A. stayed in Samos until 522 BC, when Polycrates was executed by the Persian satrap Oroetes. His next patron was the Athenian tyrant *Hipparchus. After Hipparchus' murder in 514 BC, A. went to Thessaly, but probably returned to Athens where he won much esteem at a later time. A statue in his honour was erected on the Acropolis. *Critias, one of whose ancestors was close to A., paid him honour in his poetry.

A. lived to an old age. His grave was said to be in Teos, where, according to *Theocritus, his statue stood. He was accused of drinking and lust, but this was probably an inference from his songs of wine and love. A.'s poems were arranged by the Alexandrian scholar *Aristarchus in three groups: lyric poetry, iambic poetry and elegiacs. The lyric poems included hymns and love-songs; the iambic included satyrical poems (and his attack on the poet Artemon), and the elegiacs were dedications and epitaphs. In his symposiac love- and drinking-songs, written for amusement, A. uses a peculiar verse style,

named after him – *Anacreontea*. Fragments of his poems are known mainly from citations by grammarians and from a few papyri. His poetry was admired for its elegance, simplicity and clarity.
Bowra, *Gr. Lyr. Poet.*, 269ff.; Page, *Poet. Mel. Gr.*

ANACTORIUM Greek city on the southern shore of the Gulf of *Ambracia, founded by *Cypselus with settlers from Corinth and Corcyra. A contingent from A. fought at *Plataea (479 BC). The Acarnanians captured A. in 425 BC, and resettled it.

ANAGNIA (modern Anagni) Important and prosperous town of the *Hernici in the Trerus valley. With the defeat of the Hernici in 306 BC, A. became a *civitas sine suffragio*, receiving full Roman citizenship in the 2nd century BC. It was renowned for its many temples.

ANAXAGORAS Greek philosopher, son of Hegesibulus, born in *Clazomenae at the beginning of the 5th century BC. A. moved to Athens in 480 BC where he became close to Pericles and is said to have been also associated with Socrates and Euripides. After long activity in Athens he was accused of impiety by the enemies of Pericles, probably in 450 BC (or 430 BC, the date in some accounts). Leaving Athens, he settled in Lampsacus, where he died in 428 BC.

In his one work, of which only fragments have survived, A. develops his theory of the nature and origins of the universe but the fragmentary nature of the evidence makes it difficult to reconstruct his views, and several points are obscure and disputed. A. surely took account of former schools, notably the problems raised by the Eleatic school of *Parmenides, whose theory that there is no coming-into-being but composition, no perishing but dissolution A. accepted. A. assumed an original, primeval mixed substance at the beginning of the world which consisted of innumerable "seeds", which could be split off infinitely into elements resembling the whole and one another. It is difficult to reconcile this fundamental idea with A.'s other concept, that "in everything is a portion of everything". Only the mind (*nous*) is unmixed and hence it governs substance and causes motion. The resulting rotary motion forces the "seeds" to separate – light, hot and dry, going out and their opposites, dark, cold and wet, entering. A. also studied astronomy and held that the moon received its light from the sun.
Kirk-Raven, *Presocratic Philosophers*, 362–394.

ANAXILAS Native of *Rhegium who overthrew the oligarchic regime there in 494 BC and became tyrant. A. sought control of Zancle with the aid of refugees from Miletus and Samos, but they preferred to cooperate with *Hippocrates, tyrant of *Gela. A. captured Zancle in 490 BC, colonized it with other Greeks and renamed it *Messena, as many of the settlers came from *Messenia, and his own family originated there. He opposed the tyrants *Gelon of Syracuse and *Theron of Acragas, and cooperated with their enemy Carthage. After Carthage's defeat at Himera, in 480 BC, brought hostilities to an end, *Hieron I married A.'s daughter. A. died in 476 BC.
Dunbabin, *Western Greeks*, 387–394 (s.v.).

ANAXIMANDER Greek philosopher, son of Praxiades, born in *Miletus c. 610 BC; he was said to be a pupil, companion and kinsman of *Thales. A. was the first to write a philosophical work in prose (perhaps entitled *On Nature*). He died c. 546 BC.

According to A.'s cosmology, the primary material, the beginning of all things, is neither air, fire, water, earth nor any of the so-called elements, but rather something infinite which A. called the Infinite (*apeiron*). This was divine, imperishable, eternal and timeless. The *apeiron* contains everything, and from it come the innumerable worlds (successive rather than coexistent), which it surrounds. Worlds are created by pairs of opposed substances, which "pay penalty to each other according to the assessment of time for their injustice". The earth, in A.'s cosmology, is cylindrical and its depth is a third of its width; it is stationed in the centre, held by nothing and, because it is equidistant from the extremes, it cannot move. Thus, A. was the first to introduce the idea that the earth floats without support.

A. held an interesting view of evolution: fish developed out of heated water and earth, in which they grew until puberty; from the fishlike creatures men and women ultimately grew. A. is credited with several scientific inventions; he probably introduced the *gnomon* (a rod indicating the sun's direction and height by its shadow), drew a map of the world and perhaps one of the heavens. An imaginative and ingenious thinker, A. was the. first to produce a rational explanation of the universe and man.

ANAXIMENES Greek philosopher of the 6th century BC, son of Eurystratus, native of *Miletus, died *c.* 526 BC. Probably a pupil of *Anaximander. A.'s cosmogony, like that of Anaximander, presumed the existence of primeval substance, out of which all other materials came. For A. this was air — probably the invisible atmospheric air and not mist as in Homer — which is vast in extent and surrounds all other things. According to its density in a particular place, it produces fire, wind, vapour, water, earth or stone and from these basic forms all other material is compounded. The divine air is always in motion, producing worlds which constantly form and disintegrate. A.'s conception of the earth is primitive; it is a shallow, table-like surface floating on air. Moist vapour is exhaled from the earth and, by rarefaction, becomes leaves of fire. These are the heavenly bodies, which also float on air and revolve around the earth.

Kirk-Raven, *Presocratic Philosophers*, 143—162.

ANCHISES Trojan hero, son of Capys, of the royal family of Troy. Aphrodite fell in love with A. and bore him a son, *Aeneas. Aphrodite forbade A. to reveal her identity and, because he once boasted of his love affair with her, Zeus punished him by blinding (or laming) him. A.'s son carried him from burning Troy on his shoulders. The location of A.'s grave was variously related, Drepanum in Sicily being preferred by Virgil. The theme of the rescue of A. from Troy appears in Archaic vase-painting and is found in Etruria in the 6th century BC.

ANCONA Italian coastal town, on the Adriatic Sea, possessing a good natural harbour. A. was founded by colonists from Syracuse, at the beginning of the 4th century BC; in the 3rd century BC it was already under Roman control. A. served several times as a naval base for Roman armies departing to Dalmatia and the East. Its harbour was improved by Trajan, and an arch was erected there to commemorate the work.

ANCUS MARCIUS Reputedly fourth king of Rome (642—617 BC), the grandson of *Numa Pompilius. A. expanded Roman territory, allegedly settling a colony at *Ostia that ensured access to the sea. He also built fortifications and the first bridge over the Tiber (Pons Sublicius).

Ogilvie, *Livy*, 125—6.

ANDOCIDES Athenian politician and orator, third in the canon of the ten Attic orators. Born *c.* 400 BC to Leogoras, he was a member of an aristocratic club, and was active against the extreme democrats. He was involved in the scandal of the mutilation of the Hermes in 415 BC, a sacrilege probably perpetrated to delay the military expedition under *Alcibiades and *Nicias against Syracuse. A. admitted his part in the affair and received immunity but, as his freedom of activity was curtailed, he preferred to go into exile. He made two attempts to return — in 411 and 408 BC — and it was only with the general amnesty of 403 BC that he was able to come home. He then resumed political activities and in 399 BC was charged with the sacrilege of 415 BC, but his speech won his acquittal. In 391 BC, A. went to Sparta as a

Anchises carried off from Troy by Aenear; Attic jug (c. 530 BC).

member of an embassy, in an attempt to terminate the so-called Corinthian War. On its return to Athens, the embassy failed to persuade the Athenians to accept the peace terms which it had negotiated and its members were prosecuted. Rather than wait to be condemned, A. went into exile once again. No further details of his life are known.

A. was not a professional orator, and only three of his speeches are extant: *On His Return,* delivered in 408 BC, in an unsuccessful attempt to secure his return; *On The Mysteries,* delivered during his trial in 399 BC; and *On Peace,* delivered in 391 BC, a vain attempt to win the approval of the Athenians. The first two are indicative of A.'s lack of training in the conventional techniques of his day. A. was considered the poorest orator by ancient critics.
K. J. Maidment, *Minor Attic Orators* (Loeb), 1941.1; Kennedy, *Persuasion,* 145–9.

ANDRISCUS Native of Andramyttium in northwestern Asia Minor. A. impersonated Philip, son of the last Macedonian king *Perseus. Though he was turned over to the Romans, he managed to escape and, in 149 BC, invaded Macedonia, winning a victory over the Roman praetor there. A. established his rule as a Macedonian king and entered into connections with Carthage. In 148 BC, the Roman general Q. Caecilius Metellus defeated him, after which Macedonia was made a Roman province.

ANDROMACHE Wife of *Hector, daughter of Eëtion, king of Thebes. *Achilles slew her father, seven brothers and husband. A.'s son Astynax was killed at the capture of Troy. A. was given to *Neoptolemus and bore him a son, Molossus, ancestor of the Epirote Molossians. Neoptolemus, however, was killed at Delphi, and A. married *Helenus, another of Priam's sons; they settled in Epirus, where they founded Buthrotum and were visited by *Aeneas. Euripides' tragedy *Andromache* is extant.

ANDROMEDA Daughter of the Ethiopian king, Cepheus. A.'s beautiful mother Cassiepeia (or Cassiope) boasted that she and her daughter surpassed the Nereids in beauty and as punishment, Poseidon sent a sea-monster to devastate the country. Cepheus was told by the oracle of Ammon that, to save his country, he had to sacrifice his daughter to the monster. A. was chained to a rock near Joppa. *Perseus arrived and fell in love with her and Cepheus promised to give him A. in marriage if he could save her. Perseus killed the monster but then Phineus claimed A. for himself. Perseus showed Phineus the head of the Medusa and he and all his followers were turned to stone. Perseus took A. with him to Argos, where he had several children by her. The figures in this myth appear as heavenly constellations.

ANDROS The northernmost of the Cycladic group, an island of approx. 390 sq km. A. was forced to cooperate with Xerxes in his invasion of Greece. Later, it joined the Athenian empire, paying tribute and Pericles established a *cleruchy here. A. revolted against Athens in 410 BC, but it was a member of the Second Athenian League. In the Hellenistic period, A. was mainly under Macedonian control and, in 200 BC, it was given to Pergamum. With the death of *Attalus III, A. came to form part of the Roman province of Asia.

ANDROTION Athenian politician and historian, born c. 410 BC to a wealthy family. A. entered politics c. 387 and was a member of the *Boule. He served as ambassador and commander on various occasions. As a pupil of *Isocrates, A. pursued an anti-Persian policy; in 353 BC, he was prosecuted on a charge of *graphe paranomon.

The speech against him on that occasion was written by *Demosthenes. Several years later, he was in exile at *Megara, where he wrote his history of Attica, *Atthis, the main source for *Philochorus' Atthis, and which was utilized by Aristotle for his Constitution of Athens. Of its eight books, reaching 343 BC, only fragments have survived. A. died in 340 BC.
F. Jacoby, *Atthis,* 1949, 95ff.

ANICETUS Teacher and freedman of *Nero. A. was prefect of the fleet at Misenum in AD 59; he planned and supervised the murder of *Agrippina (3), Nero's mother, and he supplied the pretext for the murder of the Emperor's wife, *Octavia. In AD 62, A. was banished to Sardinia.

ANNA PERENNA Roman goddess of uncertain character, either a year-goddess or a goddess of vegetation, associated with *Ceres. *Ovid relates several tales of A., in one of which she is identified with Anna, sister of *Dido. A.'s annual festival was celebrated on 15 March – the first month according to the older Roman calendar – in a grove near Rome.

ANNALS The Roman *Pontifex Maximus would annually set up a whitened board (*tabula dealbata*) before his official residence, the *Regia, on which he recorded important events connected with the activity of the *Pontifices – festivals, triumphs, prodigies, famines, etc. These tables reputedly dated from the early history of Rome, but they suffered much damage in the Gallic conquest of 390 BC. P. Mucius Scaevola, Pontifex Maximus in 130–115 BC, published the *Annales Maximi* in eight books, reproducing the contents of the tables in yearly arrangement and thus providing an official narrative of Roman history. Whether the documents really dated from the 5th century BC, and to what extent they were preserved prior to the 3rd century BC, are disputed points. It is certain that they had decisive influence on Roman historians, and they served as sources for the early history of Rome, setting an example for the arrangement of historical works in annual cycles.

The A. of the poet *Ennius was an historical narrative of Rome in epic form. The first Roman historians, such as *Fabius Pictor and *Cincius Alimentus (who wrote in Greek), were thought to have employed annalistic treatment but, probably, under the influence of Hellenistic examples, they did not follow a yearly framework. However, in the course of the 2nd century BC, the annalistic style came to be adopted by Roman historians. The term A. was given to historical works dealing with past events whereas *historia* referred to treatises on contemporaneous history. This distinction, however, was not strictly adhered to and there were A. which treated contemporaneous history as well. Following the conventions of Greek historiography, Roman historians tended to include speeches in their works, usually fictitious or elaborated, and not as delivered by the historical figures.

ANNONA Literally "the yearly produce", A. came to denote the corn supply of the city of Rome. The *cura A.* ("Supervision of the A.") was placed under the *aediles but was always the concern of the Roman Senate. With the growth of the population of the city, and in view of fluctuations in the production of corn, the securing of a constant supply of corn became a most serious problem. Gaius *Gracchus passed a law (*lex frumentaria*) to assure regular corn supplies and to secure a steady stock of corn from which the state could distribute grain at relatively low prices. From the law of *Clodius in 58 BC on, grain

was distributed *gratis,* and the number of recipients fluctuated between 150,000 and 320,000. The ordinary aediles could no longer cope with this matter and, after various experiments, Augustus instituted a *praefectus annonae,* a high official of equestrian status to deal specifically with the corn supply. Under the Republic, most of the grain came from Sicily and Sardinia; the Empire, however, derived most of its corn from Egypt and Africa. A large organization grew up around the collection of the necessary corn, its transport to Rome and its distribution there. To facilitate the importation, the Emperor Claudius built a new harbour at *Ostia, and granted privileges to shipowners (*navicularii*) who transported foodstuffs. The corn supply was largely based on the provincials' *decuma,* a tithe of the grain harvest. Under the Severi, an additional tax, the *A. militaris,* was introduced in Italy and in all provinces, consisting of payments in kind for the maintenance of the army.
D. Van Berchem, *Les Distributions de blé,* 1939.

ANTALCIDAS Spartan diplomat and general, active in the first half of the 4th century BC. From 393 BC on, A. made overtures to Persia, trying to win support against Athens for which he was willing to recognize Persian hegemony over all Asia Minor. A. first won the backing of the satrap Tiribazuz and, in 388 BC, *Artaxerxes II himself agreed to cooperate with Sparta. With support from both Persia and *Dionysius I, A. cut the corn supply from the Black Sea to Athens and her allies, in 388 BC. Peace was finally arranged in 386 BC, variously named the Peace of A. or the King's Peace. Its two main terms were that the authority of the Persian king over the Greek cities of Asia Minor was recognized, as was the autonomy of the other Greek states. The second provision aimed at securing the Spartan domination of Greece. In 372 BC, *Thebes refused to accept these conditions, claiming to represent the whole of Boeotia. The next year, Thebes defeated Sparta at the battle of Leuctra. In 367 BC, A. went again on a diplomatic mission to renew Persian support. He failed and committed suicide soon after.

ANTENOR (1) Noble Trojan who entertained *Menelaus and *Odysseus before the Trojan War. During the war, in which seven of his eleven sons fell, A. urged the Trojans to give Helen up to the Greeks. In recognition for this, he was not slain when the city was captured. In one version of the story, A. went to Cyrene; in the Roman version, he led the Eneti, allies of Troy, and founded Patavium in Venetia.

ANTENOR (2) Athenian sculptor of the second part of the 6th century BC. A. made the famous statues of *Harmodius and *Aristogeiton, which were carried off by the Persians in 480 BC. They were later recovered and placed alongside the new statues made by *Critias. Two bases of his statues have been found.

ANTHESTERIA Festival celebrated in Athens and many other Ionian cities during the 11th—13th of Anthesterion (February/March). A. was associated with Dionysius and with the souls of the dead. On its first day, the *pithoegia,* wine-jars, were opened. On the following day, contests of wine-drinking were held, with even children taking part in the festivities. A holy marriage between Dionysus, carried in on a ship, and the wife of the *archon basileus* then took place, and in the evening of the same day, the souls of the dead, and their patron Hermes Chtonius, were presented with cooked fruits. The festival ended with 'the expulsion of the souls from the city.
Pickard-Cambridge, *Dramatic Festivals*[2], 1ff.

ANTHOLOGIA PALATINA Collection of Greek poems gathered at the end of the 10th century AD; known from a single manuscript found in the library of the Count Palatine (Heidelberg). The AP. consists of 15 books, based mainly on the non-extant anthology of the Byzantine scholar Cephalus. In the early 10th century AD, the latter collected poems from earlier *anthologiai* ("garlands"), the earliest of which was that of *Meleager (2), who lived in the 2nd century BC. As a result, the AP. preserves numerous ancient Greek poems, as well as later material of various sorts. Another collection, made late in the 13th century AD by the monk Planudes, contains many epigrams which are not in the AP. It is added as Book 16 to the AP. in editions of the Greek Anthology.
A. S. F. Gow — D. L. Page, *The Greek Anthology,* 1965—1968; W. R. Paton (Loeb), 1916—18.

ANTIGONE Daughter of *Oedipus and Iocasta whose other children were Eteocles, Polynices and Ismene. A. and Ismene appear in the legend of Oedipus only in a relatively late version (from the late 7th century BC), and are not mentioned by Homer or in the other epics. Ismene was probably originally a Theban heroine having no connection with Oedipus; she was said to have been killed by *Tydeus, and her name appears in the river Ismenus, in a hill named Ismenion, and in the temple and oracle of Apollo Ismenius. Traces of early tales can be seen in the version that A. and her sister were burnt to death by Laodamas, son of Eteocles. The myths concerning the fate of Oedipus and his descendants were utilized and elaborated by the Athenian tragedians, and the story of A. is best known from the tragedies of *Sophocles and *Euripides. A. went into exile with her father, taking care of him in Colonus. She could not persuade her brother Polynices to forgo his attack on Thebes. In *Antigone,* by Sophocles, A. disobeyed *Creon's orders and buried her dead brother Polynices (an act in which Ismene refused to take part). Creon then ordered A. to be buried alive in a tomb, though she was betrothed to his son Haemon, and though Tiresias the seer had warned him that he would offend the gods. A. committed suicide, as did Haemon and, subsequently, Creon's wife. In another version, used by Euripides, A. was turned over to Haemon to be executed for her disobedience. He, however, hid her and she bore him a son. Later, Creon recognized the lad, for he bore the particular sign of all the descendants of *Cadmus on his body, and ordered him to be put to death. A. and Haemon then committed suicide. There is one version in which Creon made his peace with A., through the intervention of Dionysius (or Theseus).

ANTIGONUS (1) I Monophthalmus Macedonian noble, born *c.* 382 BC. A. served under *Philip II, participated in *Alexander's expedition and was appointed satrap of Phrygia in 333 BC, remaining in that office until Alexander's death. Supported by *Antipater (1), A. seized control of Pamphylia and Lycia. He alone of the *Diadochi sought to preserve the unity of Alexander's empire. In 319 BC, A. defeated Alcetas, brother of *Perdicas, in Pisidia. Until 316 BC, A.'s main campaigns were directed against *Eumenes of Cardia who was executed after the battle of Gabiene. A. then had most of the Asiatic empire of Alexander under his control. A. organized a League of the Islands and sought to further his influence in Greece; yet his rivals, notably *Cassander, *Ptolemy I and *Lysimachus, maintained their positions. In 312 BC, A.'s son *Demetrius I was defeated at Gaza, and in the same year *Seleucus I regained Babylonia, which he had lost in 316 BC. Seleucus then took control of the eastern satrapies. A peace was concluded in 311 BC, but A. did not despair of achieving the reunification of the empire. He renewed his attack on Seleucus in 310 BC, and in 307 BC Demetrius occupied Athens, the next year defeating the Ptolemaic fleet off Salamis in Cyprus. In the same year, A. and his son assumed the royal title. In 302 BC, A. renewed the League of Corinth; his enemies, however, united against him, and the final battle was fought at Ipsus in 301 BC, with Lysimachus and Seleucus emerging victorious. A. himself fell while waiting the return of his son Demetrius, who had vainly pursued part of the enemy forces.

Diod. Sic. 18–20; Plutarch, *Eumenes*; *Demetrius.*

ANTIGONUS (2) II Gonatas Son of *Demetrius I and grandson of *Antigonus (1) I Monophthalmus, born *c.* 320 BC. When his father left for Asia in 287 BC, A. was left as viceroy in Greece. In 285 BC he concluded a peace with *Pyrrhus against *Lysimachus. A. took the royal title in 283 BC, after the death of his father. His first attempt to occupy Macedonia failed, in 280 BC, but in 278 BC, *Antiochus I signed a treaty with him forgoing his claims to Macedonia. The next year, A. crushed a Gallic horde at Lysimacheia, and soon occupied Macedonia. But in 274 BC, *Pyrrhus defeated him, conquering Thessaly and part of Macedonia. Instead of pursuing his success, Pyrrhus turned to the Peloponnesus; A. joined forces with Sparta, and Pyrrhus was slain in Argos. A.'s control of Greece was secured by Macedonian garrisons in key locations and through his support of tyrants in several cities; still, he was forced into the Chremonidean War (*Chremonides), which ended in the capitulation of Athens. A. won a decisive naval victory at Cos then, or in 255 BC, the year he concluded a peace with *Ptolemy II. In 250 BC, he lost Corinth, whose governor had revolted. He regained it in 245 BC, only to lose it again to *Aratus (2), in 243 BC. Aratus defeated the Aetolians, A.'s allies, in 241 BC, and A. subsequently concluded a peace with the Achaean League. He died in 239 BC.

In contrast to his father, A. was cautious but persistent, and in the long run he succeeded where the brilliant Demetrius failed. Through him Macedonia was secured for the Antigonid dynasty.

W. W. Tarn, *Antigonos Gonatas*, 1913.

ANTIGONUS (3) III Doson Son of Demetrius the Fair, half-brother of *Antigonus (2) II Gonatas, born *c.* 263 BC. When *Demetrius (2) died in 229 BC, his son *Philip V was only nine years old, and A. became his guardian, regent and step-father by marrying his mother. A. soon repelled the Dardanians, regained Thessaly and, in 227 BC, assumed the royal title. In the same year, he went on an expedition to Caria, establishing his influence there, and to some extent, in the Aegean. In response to overtures from *Aratus (2), A. consented to cooperate with the Achaeans against *Cleomenes III of Sparta. In 224 BC, he occupied Arcadia and organized a Hellenic League (with himself as leader), which included Achaea, Thessaly, Boeotia, Acarnania, Phocis and Locris. A. took Corinth, destroyed Mantinea and, in 222 BC, completely defeated Cleomenes at Sellasia, as a result of which Sparta was forced to join the league. A. was soon called to repel an Illyrian invasion of Macedonia. Shortly after the battle, he died, leaving the throne to *Philip V.

Polybius, 2; Plutarch, *Cleom.*; *Aratus.*

ANTIGONUS (4) Mathathias Youngest son of the Judaean king Aristobulus II. In 56 BC, A. escaped from Rome with his father who, however, was later captured and returned. Supported by the Parthians, A. became king in Jerusalem in 40 BC, while *Herod made good his escape to Rome. After the Romans had expelled the Parthians, he was captured and executed at Antioch (37 BC). He was the last of the Hasmonean dynasty.

ANTILOCHUS Elder son of *Nestor, who fought with distinction in the Trojan War. A. was a favourite of *Achilles, and it was he who informed Achilles of the death of Patroclus. A. took part in the chariot-race in Patroclus' funeral games. He was slain defending his father from Memnon and Achilles avenged his death.

ANTIMACHUS Greek poet of the late 5th and early 4th centuries BC, native of Colophon. Of A.'s poems only fragments have survived. He wrote *Thebais, Lyde, Deltoi* and *Artemis*: the first was an epic and its theme was the expedition of the Seven against Thebes; the second, written in elegiacs, described various legends, such as those of *Oedipus and *Bellerophon. A. was moved to write it after the loss of his beloved Lyde. It is said that Plato was interested in A.'s poetry, but there were conflicting views on the value of his work. A. wrote scholarly poetry and in this respect was ahead of his times, for this style became dominant only with the Alexandrian school of the 3rd century BC.

Diehl, *An. Lyr. Gr.*, 1.

ANTINOUPOLIS (modern Sheikh Abadeh) City in Middle Egypt, founded in AD 130 by Hadrian, to commemorate his favourite, Antinous, who was drowned in the Nile. A. was given a Greek constitution and special privileges; it later became the centre of the district of *Thebes (2). Its theatre, hippodrome and other public buildings were still extant at the beginning of the 19th century, but subsequently were utilized as quarries for modern construction.

ANTIOCH Several cities founded by Seleucid rulers were named A., the more important of which were: (1) A. in Margiana (modern Merv), founded by *Antiochus I after a city founded by *Alexander (4) on the same site had been destroyed by natives; three important trade routes joined here, leading to Central Asia and India; (2) A. "of Pisidia" (near modern Yalvac), situated in Phrygia, became a free city by Rome in 188 BC, and colonized in 25 BC (a copy of Augustus' *Monumentum Ancyranum* was found there); and (3) A. on the Orontes in Syria (modern Antakya), the most important city bearing this name.

The last named Hellenistic city, some 25 km from the sea, was founded by *Seleucus I in 300 BC, after his victory over *Antigonus (1) I at Ipsus; he named it after his father, Antiochus. Due to its position, it became the capital of the Seleucids, who facilitated its development, lavishing money upon it in extensive building. *Seleucia (2), at the mouth of the Orontes, founded at the same time, was its port. The original population consisted of Macedonian and Athenian settlers. Economically, A.'s prosperity was based on its fertile agricultural hinterland and on commerce; it rose to be the third great city of the Hellenistic world, after Alexandria and Seleucia on the Tigris. With the disintegration of the Seleucid empire, A. was taken by the Armenian king *Tigranes (83 BC). Pompey made it capital of the new province of Syria, in 64 BC. The Jewish community of A. claimed to have originated in the time of Seleucus I. Christianity made progress in A. quite early, and Paul and Peter both stayed there and the bishop of A. later ranked equal with those of Alexandria and Rome. *Libanius lived there almost all

Tyche goddess of Antioch, a Roman copy. Note the river god at the base

of his life, and *Ammianus Marcellinus was a native of A. The city was captured by the Arabs in AD 637.

G. Downey, *History of Antioch,* 1961.

ANTIOCHUS (1) I Soter Son of *Seleucus I and the Bactrian princess Apama, born in 324 BC. From 293 on, A.'s father appointed him viceroy of the eastern provinces, and permitted him to marry his own younger wife, Stratonice. A. succeeded to the throne upon his father's death, in 281 BC. He concluded a treaty with *Antigonus (2) II Gonatas in 278 BC, and from that time till the beginning of the 2nd century BC, good relations between the Seleucids and the Macedonian kings were maintained. About 275 BC, A. crushed the Celts in an important battle known as the "Battle of the Elephants" (hence his surname, *Soter*, "Saviour"). A. settled the survivors in Phrygia. In the First Syrian War (274–271), A. lost much territory to *Ptolemy II in Asia Minor and Syria. A.'s elder son Seleucus, co-regent from 280 BC on, was suspected of treason and executed. In 262 BC, A. was defeated by *Eumenes I of Pergamum, and he died the next year. Under A., the ruler-cult of the Seleucid kings was developed. He founded many Hellenistic cities, especially in the eastern provinces of his empire.

Will, *His. Pol.* (s.v.).

ANTIOCHUS (2) II Theos Second son of *Antiochus (1) I, born *c.* 287 BC, who succeeded to the throne upon his father's death, in 261 BC. During the Second Syrian War (260–253 BC), against *Ptolemy II, and in cooperation with *Antigonus (2) II Gonatas, A. regained much of the Seleucid territory in Syria and southern and western Asia Minor. On conclusion of the war, A. married *Berenice, Ptolemy's daughter (252 BC). On his death in 246 BC, however, A. was succeeded by *Seleucus II, his son from his first wife; Berenice was subsequently murdered.

Will, *His. Pol.* (s.v.)..

ANTIOCHUS (3) III, "the Great" The second son of *Seleucus II, born *c.* 242 BC, and succeeded to the throne in 223 BC. A.'s general, *Achaeus, who had regained the Seleucid territory lost to Pergamum in Asia Minor, revolted in 220 BC. In that year, A. was forced to deal with Molon, governor of Media, who had declared independence in 222 BC. A. defeated him, and he committed suicide. Then A. attacked the Ptolemaic Empire (the Fourth Syrian War 219–216 BC). After initial successes, he lost a decisive battle at Raphia (217 BC) and was forced to sue Ptolemy IV for peace, though he still controlled Seleucia in Pieria. Next, he turned against Achaeus, whose own men betrayed him in 213 BC. He then set out on his famous expedition to the East (212–206). He occupied Armenia and the rulers of Bactria and Parthia recognized him as their overlord. He reached India and also operated in "Arabia". On his return A. was recognized as "the Great". In 203–202 BC, he made a secret alliance with Philip V against the child-king *Ptolemy V. In the Fifth Syrian War (*c.* 202–198 BC), A. conquered Phoenicia and Palestine, the decisive battle taking place at Panion. His ambitions in the West drove him across the Hellespont to occupy Thrace (196 BC). Rome decided to intervene in the matter, and, after prolonged negotiations, war broke out. A. invaded Greece in 192 BC. After being defeated at Thermopylae (191 BC), he retreated into Asia Minor. In 189 BC, he lost a decisive battle at Magnesia, and was forced to agree to Roman terms (the treaty of Apamea, 188 ·BC). He lost all his territories in Asia Minor west of the Taurus. He was killed in 187 BC, while pillaging a temple in an attempt to raise reparation money for Rome.

Will, *His. Pol.* (s.v.).

ANTIOCHUS (4) IV Epiphanes Third son of *Antiochus (3), born *c.* 215 BC and a hostage at Rome after 188 BC. A. ascended to the Seleucid throne upon the murder of his brother, *Seleucus IV. In the Sixth Syrian War (170–168 BC), A. occupied Egypt, but Roman intervention forced him to evacuate that country. Upon his return from the Egyptian war, he founded a Greek city in Jerusalem and attempted to Hellenize the Jews – this, and the suppression of the cult of Yahweh, led to the revolt of Judas Maccabaeus. A. died in 164 BC while on a tour designed to bolster his authority in the Eastern provinces.

ANTIOCHUS (5) VII Sidetes Second son of *Demetrius I, ascended to the Seleucid throne in 138 BC, after his elder brother *Demetrius II was captured by the Parthians. A. soon defeated and killed the usurper Tryphon, and restored his authority over *Judaea. He next turned against Parthia and, after some success, recovered Media and Babylonia (130 BC). In 129 BC, however, he was defeated and slain by the Parthians. A. was the last powerful king of the Seleucid line, and after his defeat the empire rapidly disintegrated.

Coin of Antiochus III with Apollo on the reverse

ANTIOCHUS (6) of Ascalon Greek philosopher, born *c.*
120 BC. Known as the founder of the Fifth Academy, A.
studied philosophy at Athens under Philo of Larissa. As a
result of the Mithridatic War he came to Rome where he
met L. *Lucullus with whom he became friendly. A.
abandoned Scepticism, which had been dominant at the
Academy since the time of *Arcesilaus. By 80 BC he was
the head of the Academy, and Cicero heard his lectures
there. Though A. revived many of the views of the Old
Academy, his philosophy was mainly eclectic, adopting
Stoic and Peripatetic doctrines.
Bréhier, *Philosophy*, 143–5.

ANTIPATER (1) Son of Iolaus, a Macedonian noble,
born *c.* 398 BC. A. was one of *Philip II's best officers,
and represented him in diplomatic affairs. He took part in
the negotiations which led to the peace of *Philocrates
(346 BC). After Philip's murder, A. supported Alexander in
securing the throne. When Alexander left for Asia (334 BC),
A. remained as his viceroy in Macedonia and Greece. In 331
BC, he suppressed the Spartan revolt of *Agis III (who fell
at Megalopolis). On poor terms with Alexander's mother,
Olympias, he was summoned by Alexander in 324 BC.
Alexander's death intervened, and A. was involved in a
revolt in Thessaly, Athens and Aetolia. Besieged in Lamia
(323–322 BC), he was later able to unite with *Craterus,
and he crushed the Greeks at the battle of Crannon. Joining the other Macedonian generals against *Perdicoas (2),
A. was recognized as regent after Perdicoas' death in 321
BC. He died in 319 BC, leaving Alexander's empire without a leader able to forestall its disintegration.

ANTIPATER (2) Father of *Herod the Great, of
Idumean stock, son of the homonymous governor of
Idumea under Alexander Janneus. A. married a
Nabatean princess and was on good terms with the
Nabatean king *Aretas III. In the struggle between Hyrcanus II and his brother Aristobulus, A. supported the
former. In the following years, he was consistently loyal
to whichever Roman general happened to be in power,
and he was rewarded accordingly. In 55 BC, he assisted
*Gabinius in restoring Ptolemy Auletes to the throne of
Egypt, and in 49 BC he followed Pompey, though he
changed sides after Pharsalus. A. gave valuable assistance
to Caesar in the Alexandrian War in 47 BC, and he was
subsequently made *epitropos* of the Jews. His sons Herod
and Phasael were installed as governors of Galilee and
Judaea, respectively. He was murdered in 43 BC while
collecting money for *Cassius.

ANTIPHANES Prominent Athenian poet of the Middle
Comedy, born *c.* 405 BC. A. produced his first play *c.*
385 BC. He was a prolific writer and is said to have written 260 or more comedies; of these, 134 titles, and more
than 300 fragments are extant. A considerable number of
the latter deal with mythological themes, and others with
professions and types (flute-player, painter, parasite). A.
died at the age of 74.

ANTIPHON Earliest Attic orator, son of Sophilos, born
in 480 BC. A. taught rhetoric and was a *logographos*, one
who composed court speeches for others. He was apparently not active in politics for most of his life, though in
411 BC he did play a leading part in the oligarchic revolution in Athens, seeking to end the war with Sparta.
When the regime of the Four Hundred collapsed, A. was
tried, and despite an excellent speech in his own defence
(Thuc. 8.68), he was condemned and executed.

Sixty speeches — many of them spurious — went under A.'s name in antiquity. Of these, three speeches for actual cases, three *tetralogies*, and some fragments of other speeches are extant. The *tetralogies* were exercises to show how the prosecution and defence ought to present their cases. Each *tetralogy* consists of 4 alternating speeches of attack and defence, and all are cases of accidental or deliberate murder. During his time, Greek theory of rhetoric was in its initial stages, and A. set the pattern for organizing court speeches. His invention of models was the beginning of a long tradition. As was common in Greek rhetoric, antithetic constructions of words and thoughts often appear in A.'s speeches; for persuasion, he relied extensively on arguments of probability, and often used poetical diction.

K. J. Maidment, *Attic Minor Orators* (Loeb), 1941.1;
H. N. Fowler, *Plutarch's Moralia* (Loeb), 1936.10;
Kennedy, *Persuasion,* 129—133.

ANTISTHENES Influential Greek philosopher, son of the Athenian Antisthenes and a Thracian slave-girl, born *c.* 450 BC. A. studied under *Gorgias, but was primarily a pupil and follower of Socrates. After Socrates' death (399 BC), A. opened a school of his own at the gymnasium of Cynosarges, near Athens. The *Cynics regarded him as the founder of their sect, and he was probably the teacher of *Diogenes of Sinope. The Stoics claimed A. for themselves in order to establish a link with Socrates. A. died in 360 BC.

Concerned mainly with ethics, A. believed man's aim in life should be *eudaimonia*, "happiness", through *arete*, "virtue", reached by learning and knowledge. Earthly possessions and conventional pleasures, he argued, do not produce happiness. These doctrines were adopted by the early Stoics. His criticism of conventional views on religion and the state was adopted by the Cynics. He emphasized the importance of knowing the precise meaning of words if one wanted to understand the things represented by them. Fragments of A.'s dialogues (*Heracles, Cyrus, Protrepticus*) and commentaries on Homer have survived. Two fictional orations (for Odysseus and Aias) are also extant.

Diog. Laert. 6. 1—19; Dudley, *Cynicism,* 1—16.

ANTIUM (modern Anzio) Coastal town in southern Latium. This very ancient Latin town (Dion. Hal. 1.72) was taken by the *Volsci (*c.* 500 BC) who made it their centre. According to legend, it was from A. that *Coriolanus set out for his war against Rome. It is doubtful that it was colonized by the Latin League in 467 BC. In the 4th century BC, it fought several times against Rome, until its conquest in 338 BC, when a Roman colony was founded there (Liv. 8.14). The prows of the captured Antiate ships decorated the *rostra at Rome, and the Antiates had a bad reputation as pirates, even after 338 BC. Under the late Republic, A. became a place of luxury villas, and the Emperors Caligula and Gaius were born there.

ANTONIA (1) Elder daughter of Marcus *Antonius (4) (Mark Antony) and Octavia, Octavian's sister. Born in 39 BC, A. married L. *Domitius (4) Ahenobarbus; their son was the father of the Emperor Nero, and their daughter was the mother of *Messalina.

ANTONIA (2) The younger daughter of Marcus *Antonius (4) (Mark Antony) and Octavia, born in 36 BC. A. married *Drusus (3), brother of the Emperor Tiberius, and *Germanicus and the Emperor Claudius were her sons. A. assisted Tiberius in discovering the conspiracy of Sejanus in

AD 31. When her grandson Caligula became emperor, in AD 37, he gave A. the title Augusta, but shortly thereafter compelled her to commit suicide.

ANTONINUS PIUS, T. Aelius Hadrianus Roman emperor, born 19 September AD 86, at Lanuvium in Latium. A.'s father, T. Aurelius Fulvus, consul in AD 89, was of a provincial family from Nîmes; his mother, Arria Fadilla, was also from a consular family. After his father's early death, A. was raised by his maternal grandfather. In due course, he became quaestor, praetor, and consul in AD 120. He was appointed one of four consular judges introduced by Hadrian to administer law in Italy, his territory being Etruria and Umbria. Later, *c.* AD 135, he became governor of Asia and a member of Hadrian's *consilium principis*. In AD 138, Hadrian adopted him, made him his successor, and conferred on him the *imperium proconsulare* and the *tribunicia potestas*. In deference to Hadrian, A. adopted M. Annius Verus (the future Emperor *Marcus Aurelius), nephew of his wife *Faustina (1), as well as L. *Verus. When A. succeeded to the throne (10 July AD 138), the Senate gave him the title *Pius* ("dutiful"). He made the Senate consecrate Hadrian, and completed the mausoleum for him — the modern Sant'Angelo fortress — in Rome. Marcus Aurelius was betrothed to A.'s daughter *Faustina, and served with him as consul in AD 140. In AD 139, A. received the title *pater patria*, "father of the fatherland".

In the provinces, A. had to contend with several disturbances. The marauding attacks of the *Brigantes led to the extension of the northern frontier in Britain to the Clyde-Forth line where a wall (the "Antonine Wall") was built. The Germanic frontier was further fortified, and, late in his reign, the restiveness in Dacia was dealt with (in AD 158) by partitioning the province into three sections. There were some military operations against Parthia in connection with Armenia, and a revolt in Maretania was quelled. But all these events on the fringe of the empire did not disturb the general prosperity of the provinces. Administration was generally good, and more provincials entered the Senate and the imperial bureaucracy. Under A., the government of the empire became still more centralized. Though there was extensive public building, and financial support to distressed cities, the relative peace and controlled public expenditure facilitated the accumulation of huge reserves, and the treasury held 675 million *denarii* on A.'s death. It was under the benevolent rule of A. that Aelius *Aristides delivered his oration *To Rome*, in which the empire appears as a democratic framework for flourishing cities, while everyone — subject and ruler alike — enjoys life under the protection of the Caesar. In contrast to Hadrian, A. cultivated good relations with the senatorial aristocracy, though he usually used his *consilium* for questions of government. Much esteemed, A. died on 7 March AD 161, and was immediately deified. He was buried in the mausoleum of Hadrian.

M. Hammond, *The Antonine Monarchy,* 1959.

ANTONIUS (1), Marcus Roman statesman and famous orator, of a plebeian family, born in 143 BC. He was quaestor in 113 BC and as praetor, in 102 BC, he fought against the pirates of Cilicia, returning in 100 BC to celebrate a triumph. When A. became consul, in 99 BC, he was the first in his family to hold this office. As censor, in 97 BC, he registered many Italians as citizens. In 95 BC, he defended his former quaestor, Norbanus, in court. A. was killed in 87 BC, after the capture of Rome by

*Marius. A. and L. *Crassus were the most prominent
orators of the age, but A. never published his speeches. He
appears as one of the interlocutors in the rhetorical works
of Cicero (*De Oratore, Brutus*), and he himself wrote a
work on rhetoric, no longer extant.

ANTONIUS (2), Marcus, "Creticus" Son of M. *Antonius (1). While praetor in 74 BC, he was given a special
command to fight the pirates. Though he exploited the
provinces, he was a complete failure as commander. He
suffered a naval defeat at Crete, and died in 72 BC.

ANTONIUS (3), Gaius, "Hybrida" Son of M. *Antonius
(1). A. served with *Sulla and profitted during the
proscriptions. Prosecuted for extortion, he obtained the
protection of the tribunes, but was expelled from the
Senate by the censors in 70 BC. Probably regaining his
seat in the Senate as praetor in 66 BC, A. allied himself
with *Catiline for the consulate of 63 BC, and won the
elections with Cicero. Though A. commanded the army
against his former ally, Catiline, he did not take part in
the decisive battle, allowing his legate Petreius to lead the
attack. Through a pact with Cicero, he received the province of Macedonia, which he governed from 62 to 60 BC.
On his return, he was prosecuted and convicted in 59 BC
(Cicero spoke in his defence). He went into exile in
Cephallenia but Caesar permitted him to return. A. was
censor in 42 BC.

ANTONIUS (4), Marcus (Mark Antony) Born *c.* 82 BC,
the eldest son of M. Antonius (2) "Creticus". A. had led
an extravagant youth, but with the help of his friend
*Curio (2), and by marrying well, he improved his uncertain
finances. He held his first military position in 57—55 BC,
as cavalry officer under *Gabinius. He served with distinction in the operations in Palestine and Egypt, and
went to Caesar in Gaul, in 54 BC. Caesar helped him win
the election for quaestor in 52 BC, and for the next two
years he continued his service in Gaul. As tribune in 49
BC, he was one of the few magistrates who backed
Caesar's interests, but he was forced to leave Rome when
the Senate voted a state of emergency. After the conquest
of Italy, Caesar went to Spain, leaving A. behind to take
care of various problems. He commanded the left wing of
Caesar's army in 48 BC, at the Battle of Pharsalus. As
Caesar's *magister equitum*, he bought much auctioned
property from the estates of Pompey and his followers.
After an estrangement from Caesar, A. was reconciled
with him, and served with him as consul in 44 BC.

After Caesar's murder, A. rose to dominance in Rome.
He took possession of public money, and money and
papers belonging to Caesar, and passed various laws to gain
personal support. After a short, conciliatory phase with
the tyrannicides, A. agitated against them and enlisted
veteran Caesarian soldiers. He made himself governor of
the provinces of Gallia Cisalpina and Gallia Transalpina
and for a while had Rome under his control. *Brutus (2)
and *Cassius (2) left for the East, but the appearance of
Octavian complicated his situation, and soon thereafter
*Cicero began to attack him.

In 43 BC, A. besieged D. *Brutus at Mutina, and was
declared a public enemy by the Senate. Losing the Battle
of Forum Gallorum to the consuls *Hirtius and *Pansa,
A. crossed the Alps into Gallia, where he soon gained
support from the old Caesarian generals, *Lepidus (3),
*Polio and *Plancus. In the meantime, Octavian had taken
control of Rome, after the death of the consuls. A., Lepidus
and Octavian reached an agreement and, on 27 November
43 BC, a law was passed giving them absolute power as

tresviri rei publicae constituendae for five years. The so-
called Second Triumvirate now proscribed their personal
enemies and Caesar's murderers, and A. took revenge on
Cicero.

In 42 BC, it was mainly due to A. that Cassius and
Brutus were defeated at Philippi. While Octavian returned
to Italy to take care of the settlement of the veteran
soldiers, A. took control of the eastern part of the empire.
He vigorously collected money for his soldiers, made
administrative arrangements, and became closely associated with *Cleopatra. In Italy, A.'s second wife, Fulvia,
and his brother began a war against Octavian, but were
besieged and captured at Perusia in 41 BC. The following
year, A. and Octavian came to an agreement at Brundisium, and A. married Octavian's sister (Fulvia had died
in Greece). A second treaty was made at Misenum, in 39
BC, with Sextus *Pompeius. Subsequently, A. went to
Athens.

The Parthian invasion of Asia Minor and Syria was
brought to an end by A.'s officer *Ventidius, in 38 BC.
Once again, A. returned to Italy (37 BC), and a new agreement was made with Octavian, the Triumvirate being renewed for another five years. A. left for the East without
Octavia, and in the following years his relations with
Octavian deteriorated. While Octavian succeeded in defeating Sextus Pompeius, setting Lepidus aside in 36 BC,
and thereby establishing his control over Italy and the
entire West, A. suffered defeat by the Parthians. At this
time, A. was living with Cleopatra. In 34 BC, she was
proclaimed Queen of Queens, and her son (by Caesar)
King of Kings. Her children by A. were made king and
queen of particular territories, and her own territories
were extended. A propaganda war commenced between
A. and Octavian. In 32 BC, A.'s supporters fled Italy, and
he formally divorced Octavia. Octavian marred A.'s reputation by publishing his will, in which A. had left inheritances to Cleopatra's children and asked to be buried in
Alexandria. War was formally declared against Cleopatra;
before the decisive battle took place, A. lost the support
of some of his men, who detested Cleopatra. He lost the
Battle of *Actium and retreated to Egypt, where he killed
himself, on 1 August 30 BC.

A. was a good commander and he won the loyalty of
his soldiers with his courage and power of endurance. In
politics, he was outmanoeuvred by Octavian and, in the
end, his personal attachment to Cleopatra proved fatal.
Cicero, *Philippics, Letters* (s.v.); Plut. *Anton.*;
Suet, *Jul., Aug.*; App. *BC*, 2–5; Dio, 41–51;
Syme, *Rom. Rev.*

ANYTOS Well-to-do Athenian politician, prominent in
the late 5th century BC. In 409 BC, A. was prosecuted for
his failure to secure Pylos, but acquitted, allegedly
through bribery. After 403 BC, he was strategos several
times, and took a leading part in the restoration of
Athenian democracy. A. is known mainly for his prosecution of Socrates in 399 BC.

APAMEA The name of several Hellenistic cities: (1) A.
in Bithynia, made a *colonia* by Augustus; (2) A. on the
Orontes, in Syria, founded by *Seleucus I or his son
*Antiochus I — the prosperous city where *Posidonius was
born; (3) A. in Phrygia, where *Antiochus III signed a
peace treaty with Rome, in 188 BC.

APATURIA Three-day Ionian festival for the phratries,
the descendants of a single father. Under the protection
of Zeus *Phratrios* and Apollo *Patroos*, the A. was held in
the month of Pyanospion (October/November). On the

last day of the A., new members were admitted to the phratries — children, ephebes and young wives. The ceremony included sacrifices.

APELLA The Sparta assembly, which derived its name from the *Apellai* festival held for Apollo, in which new members were admitted to the phratries (cf. *Apaturia). The institution of the A. was ascribed to *Lycurgus (1), but a popular assembly probably existed earlier (*Ekklesia). Unlike assemblies in democratic constitutions, the A. could only confirm or reject motions put before it. It elected the ordinary officials of Sparta, notably the members of the *gerousia and the *ephors, and the generals. It also decided on major questions of foreign policy (treaties, war and peace), and confirmed succession to the throne when this was in doubt. In the Archaic period, the king and the *gerousia* controlled the A. From the 5th century BC on, the meetings were presided over by the ephors. Voting was usually by acclamation, but if the result was unclear, a division would take place.
Thuc. 1. 79—87; Arist. *Pol.*, 1273a;
Plut. *Lyc.*, 6; Forrest, *Sparta*, 47—53.

APELLES Prominent 4th century BC Greek painter from Colophon. A. made portraits of *Philip II and *Alexander the Great. He was considered the greatest painter of his day. Among his well-known works were: an Aphrodite made for Cos, Alexander with the thunderbolt, and Calumny (none of which has survived).

APHRODITE Greek goddess of love, beauty and fertility. According to myth, she was born of sea foam (the etymology of her name is *aphros*, "foam") and rode on a shell to the island of *Cythera, thence to the Peloponnesus, and finally to *Paphos in Cyprus (Hesiod *Theog.* 188—200). Another version (at least as early as Homer), makes her the daughter of Zeus and *Dione. A.'s cult probably originated with the Semitic goddess Astarte, and she was associated with *Adonis, another divinity of Oriental origin. But she was admitted to the Greek pantheon in very remote times, much earlier than Adonis. She was worshipped nearly everywhere in the Greek world, especially at *Paphos, at *Cythera and at Corinth.

A.'s various titles reveal the functions and ideas with which she came to be associated: goddess of the sea (*Pontia*), of the sky (*Ourania* — a name reflecting her Oriental origin), of prostitutes (*Porne*), and of the people (*Pandemos*). She was also associated with *Hermes and *Eros. She had love affairs with *Ares (*Od.* 8.266—367), Hermes (their offspring was *Hermaphroditus), Poseidon and Dionysus, and with the mortal *Anchises (by whom she conceived *Aeneas). Her magic girdle enabled her to seduce anyone she chose. Her cuckold husband was *Hephaestus. *Paris awarded her the golden apple in the beauty contest with Hera and Athena, and A. promised him that he would be loved by *Helen. During the Trojan War, she sided with the Trojans, and was even wounded by *Diomedes. Occasionally evident in myth are her powers of fertility and procreation.

There are statues of A. by almost all the Greek masters (e.g. Phidias, Alcamenes). The one by Praxiteles, in Cnidos, of which later Roman copies are extant, was considered a masterpiece. Famous extant A.'s modelled on the Cnidian are the A. of Cyrene and the Venus de Milo. She is generally represented nude, semi-nude or clothed, in either a standing or a bathing position, in her aspect of the goddess of beauty or as the victorious goddess in arms.
Kerényi, *Gods*, 67—81.

Aphrodite, commonly called Venus de Milo. A late 2nd century BC copy of Aphrodite of Cnidos by Praxiteles

APICIUS, M. Gavius Famous Roman gourmet of the Augustan era. He took his surname from an earlier gourmet of the late 2nd century BC. A. wrote several culinary treatises (Plin. *NH*, 10.133), but the extant *De Re Coquinaria*, "On Cooking", ascribed to him during the Renaissance, was composed in the 4th century AD.
B. Flower – E. Rosenbaum, *The Roman Cookery Book*, 1958.

APION Greek Alexandrian scholar during the early Principate. Son of Posidonius. A.'s teacher was the Alexandrian scholar *Didymus. A. headed the anti-Jewish delegation from Alexandria, which appeared before Caligula in Rome. He died during the reign of Claudius. (*Josephus Flavius used "Against Apion" as the title for an apologetic book aimed at anti-Jewish authors.) A. wrote prolifically, producing among other things a work on Egypt (in five books) and a Homeric glossary. The latter was used by Apollonius Sophista (of the late 1st century AD) for his *lexicon Homerium*, of which an abridgement is extant. A. himself (as well as Apollonius) followed *Aristarchus.
Jacoby, *Fr. Gr. Hist.*, 616.

APOIKIA (pl. apoikiai) A Greek city founded by settlers from a mother city; in contrast to Roman *coloniae* (whose settlers remained Roman citizens, subject to the laws and magistrates of Rome). The A. was a politically independent city-state, a new *polis. It generally stood on good terms with its mother-city, although this was not always the case (for instance, in the relations between *Corcyra and *Corinth). By establishing A., the Greeks expanded from Greece proper, and in the first period of expansion – from the end of the Mycenean period into the early 1st millennium BC – they colonized the Aegean islands and the western coast of Asia Minor. The 8th–6th centuries BC were the great period of Greek colonization, and A. were established along the coasts leading to the Black Sea, on the Dalmatian coast, in Sicily, in southern Italy, and on the Mediterranean coasts of Spain and Gaul. A new burst of colonization opened with the conquests of Alexander the Great.

Each A. had its own constitution, given to it on its foundation. In early times, the founder (*oikistes*) usually consulted the Delphic Oracle prior to actual settlement. Each colonist received a plot of land in the territory of the A. A later addition of settlers to an A. was known as *epoikia*.
J. Boardman, *The Greeks Overseas*, 1964;
A. J. Graham, *Colony and Mother City in Ancient Greece*, 1964.

APOLLO Greek god of prophecy, music, medicine, etc. There are various interpretations of the etymology of his name: "the destroyer", "the splendid", "the mighty", etc. The origins of his cult are obscure, though he probably came from the north rather than from Asia Minor, despite some evidence that would connect him with Lycia. The *Hyperboreans, a legendary people living somewhere in the north, were believed to be A.'s special worshippers, and (according to Herodotus 4.33) they used to send offerings to the Delian temple of A. At any rate, A. was a typical Greek god as early as Homer; his name has not yet been found in the Mycenaean documents.

In Greek mythology, A. was the son of Zeus and *Leto, who bore him and his twin Artemis on the Delian Mount Cynthus (there exist other accounts of his place of birth). In a later version, Leto disguises herself as a she-wolf in order to hide from Hera, and goes to Delos from

the land of the Hyperboreans. Another cycle of legends connects A. with Delphi. Armed with his typical weapon, the bow and arrow, A. goes to Mount Parnassus, where he wounds the dragon *Python and then kills him. After performing a ceremony of purification, he takes possession of the Delphic oracular sanctuary. While there, he is visited by Leto and Artemis. A formidable giant, Tityus, son of Earth, tries to violate Leto, but A. and Artemis kill him, and he is sent to *Tartarus, where two vultures eat his liver. In another myth, he defeats the

Statue of Apollo from the west pediment of the temple of Zeus at Olympia

satyr *Marsyas and flays him alive. Pan, too, is defeated by him in a musical contest. It was A. who killed the Aloadae (Ephialtes and Otus, sons of Poseidon and the wife of Aloeus) when they tried to conquer Olympus, and he and Artemis killed the children of *Niobe, wife of *Amphion. He had many love-affairs with women and nymphs. The nymph Dryope bore him Amphissus, who founded the city of Oeta and built a temple for A. Coronis, daughter of the Lapith Phlegyas, bore him *Asclepius, but she was unfaithful and A. sent Artemis to kill her. This son was given to *Chiron to raise and tutor. Cyrene, daughter of the Lapith king Hypseus, bore him *Aristaeus. But A. was not always successful—*Daphne managed to elude him, Marpessa preferred *Idas to A., and *Cassandra deceived him, though he took his revenge by making her prophecies disbelieved. Once A. quarrelled with Zeus and killed Cyclopes; as punishment, he had to serve under the mortal *Admetus for a year.

A. was worshipped throughout the Greek world. His most famous sanctuary was at *Delphi, and his oracular shrine there was the most influential in Greek history. Other important temples of A. were at Delos (where he was honoured by a pan-Ionian festival), *Didyma, and Claros (in Ionia). With the Greek colonization of the West, the cult of A. spread to Italy. He was known quite early in Etruria, and he had a temple in Rome in the late 5th century BC.

A.'s titles reveal some of his functions: as A. Lyceus, he was protector of herds and flocks, the one who guarded them from the wolf; as A. Archegetes, "leader", he was consulted before the foundation of an *apoikia (the questions were usually directed to the Delphic shrine), or before the establishment of new institutions and constitutions (*Lycurgus consulted him in Sparta). A. was said to have given Arcadia its laws, and was especially associated with civilization and advanced culture — hence he was the patron of mathematics, medicine, astronomy, poetry, music and philosophy, and, naturally, he was as-associated with the *Muses. His manifestation as sun-god was a late development.

A. was a favourite subject in Greek art from the Archaic period on. Numerous statues of him are extant (Greek, Etruscan and Roman), usually depicting him as the perfect youth. Occasionally, he appears grouped with other figures — Artemis, the Muses, etc. One of the best preserved Greek statues is that of A. in the west pediment of the temple of Zeus at Olympia.
Guthrie, Greek Gods, 73—87, 183—204.

APOLLODORUS (1) Greek comedy writer of the first half of the 3rd century BC, native of Carystus. A. wrote 47 plays, five of which won victories. *Terence's Hecyra and Phormio are Latin reproductions of original plays by A. (Hecyra and Epidicazomenos).
Webster, Later Greek Comedy, 225—252.

APOLLODORUS (2) Greek scholar of the 2nd century BC; died after 120 BC. *Aristarchus was A.'s teacher in Alexandria, which he left, in 145 BC, with the expulsion of scholars by *Ptolemy Physcon. A. may have stayed with *Attalus II in Pergamum for a time, later living in Athens. His interests included religion, mythology, history, biography, geography. His four-book Chronica covered the period from the end of the Trojan War to 144 BC; his Peri Theon, "On Gods", treated Greek religion, probably in rationalistic terms, and his Bibliotheca dealt with Greek mythology. A. also wrote a very erudite commentary on Homer's "Catalogue of Ships", of which

many citations are extant in *Strabo's Geographica, as well as commentaries on *Epicharmus and Sophron, Sicilian comedy writers of the 5th century BC. A.'s Etymologiai was a glossary work.
J. G. Frazer, Apollodorus, The Library (Loeb), 1921.

APOLLODORUS (3) of Pergamum Very prominent Greek teacher of rhetoric in the 1st century BC. A.'s most famous pupil at Rome was Octavian. His rhetorical work, Techne, now lost, was translated into Latin. He strongly advocated a four-part composition of speeches: introduction, narration, argumentation and peroration.

APOLLODORUS (4) of Damascus Prominent architect of the first half of the 2nd century AD. During Trajan's campaigns against the Dacians, A. built a bridge across the Danube. In Rome, he planned and built several buildings for Trajan: the Forum, Basilica, Column, an odeon and a circus. Some parts of his work on engines of war, Poliorcetica, are extant. A.'s criticism of Hadrian's building plans led to his expulsion from Rome in AD 129, and he was later put to death.

APOLLONIA Greek city on the southern coast of Illyria, founded by settlers from Corinth and Corcyra early in the 6th century BC. Its good location on the route west contributed to its prosperity. From 229 BC on, A. adhered to Rome, thereby gaining various benefits. One of two branches of the Via Egnatia, Rome's main artery to Asia, started at A. Octavian was studying there, in 44 BC, when he received news of Caesar's death.

APOLLONIUS (1) Financial administrator (dioicetes) of *Ptolemy II and Ptolemy III, c. 260—240 BC. A very wealthy man, A. had a large estate in the Fayoum, as well as other properties in Egypt. The papers of his secretary, *Zeno, are known from papyri. A. also had extensive commercial interests outside Egypt.

APOLLONIUS (2) Rhodius Greek poet and scholar, probably a native of Alexandria, born early in the 3rd century BC. A. acquired his surname from his stay in Rhodes, late in his life. He studied under *Callimachus and became the second Head of the Alexandrian Library, after the death of *Zenodotus (c. 260 BC). A literary dispute arose between A. and his former teacher, Callimachus, who held a minor position in the Library. Callimachus strongly condemned the writing of long, epic poetry, while A. held that there was room for this genre. The literary dispute developed into a fierce personal quarrel, which Callimachus won. A. was forced to leave Alexandria after the succession of Ptolemy III Euergetes, in 247 BC. He settled in Rhodes, and was said later to have become reconciled with Callimachus.

A.'s main work is the extant Argonautica, an epic in four books describing the voyage of *Jason and his comrades to Cholchis to fetch the Golden Fleece. It was of the genre that Callimachus criticized for its repetition of old material and freely invented heroic deeds. In doing this, A. had nonetheless mastered the old myths concerning the Argonauts, and his scholarly exposition was characteristic of Alexandrian poetry. The Argonautica is full of scholarly aetiologies of various customs, institutions and names. The poem suffers primarily from a lack of proportion in its treatment of vast material and a resulting lack of unity. The heroic portrait of Jason, the main hero of the epic, is far less successful than his description of Medea's growing love for Jason, which conflicts with her filial duty. The elaboration of the love theme was A.'s contribution to the epic genre. True to the tendency of the period, A. humanizes his gods. He was

Above: Porphyry statue of a Roman emperor, of the 3rd century AD. It was found propped up in the town square of Byzantine Caesarea, which served as an open-air museum

Overleaf: Dionysian mystery scene in Pompeian fresco

The basilica of Trajan at Rome (planned by Apollodorus (4)) — a reconstruction

influenced by Homer in style, metre and vocabulary. Despite its defects, the *Argonautica* became a popular example of the Hellenistic literature of its kind. Virgil was influenced by it, and the extant *Scholia depend on commentaries written on it. The poem is known from a large number of papyri and manuscripts. Only a few fragments of A.'s other poems and philological writings, including stories on the foundation of cities, are known. One of his epigrams, directed against Callimachus, is extant.
R. C. Seaton, *Apollonius Rhodius* (Loeb), 1912.

APOLLONIUS (3) of Perge An outstanding Greek mathematician, native of Perge in Pamphylia. Few details of his life are known. Born *c.* 260 BC, A. came to Alexandria where he studied and worked under Ptolemy III and Ptolemy IV. He visited Asia Minor and stayed for a time in Pergamum. The manner, place and date of his death are not known.

As a scientist, A.'s main interest was to understand forms and situations, as is plainly manifest in his outstanding work, *Conica*, on conics. Of its eight books, books 1–4 are extant in the original Greek, and books 5–7 in Arabic translation; book 8 has not survived. A. was not satisfied with the first edition, which he had hurriedly completed. He revised the work and dedicated the first three books to Eudemus of Pergamum. After Eudemus' death, A. dedicated books 4–8 to Attalus. He obviously knew the works of his predecessors and drew upon them. Though he states that his first four books are elementary, he introduces even here many new theorems and matters not discussed by earlier mathematicians. Books 5–8 are detailed investigations of specific topics (maxima and minima, similarity of conics, determination of limits, etc.). By his new approach, A. proved that the three types of conics could be generated from the same general type of cone. He thereby introduced and defined the terms *elleipsis, parabole* and *hyperbole.* Thanks to its logical, systematic, and highly advanced exposition of conics, this work became a standard textbook, superseding all previous works on the subject by Menaichmus, Aristaeus, Euclid, and Archimedes.

Of his other works, one, "Cutting Off of a Ratio" (*logou apotome*) is extant in Arabic translation. *Pappus gives a short account of five others: "Cutting Off of an Area" (*choriou apotome*), "Determinate Section" (*diorismene tome*), "Tangencies" (*epaphai*), "Plane Loci" (*topoi epipedoi*) and "Inclinations" (*neuseis*). To astronomy, he contributed his important elaboration upon the theory of epicycles, showing its relationship to the eccentric theory, and thereby accounting for the motion of the moon and the retrogradation of the planets. A.'s theories were used by *Hipparchus (2) and Claudius *Ptolemy.
T. L. Heath, *Apollonius of Perga*, 1961 (1896).

APOLLONIUS (4) of Tyana (in Cappadocia) A philosopher, known mainly from an untrustworthy biography by

Left: Bust portrait of Julius Caesar

*Philostratus in the early 3rd century AD. A. lived in the 1st century AD and died under *Nerva. He tried to imitate the life of Pythagoras, wandering from place to place, teaching and preaching, and was said to perform miracles and see into the future. Hierocles, governor of Bithynia under Diocletian (known for his persecutions of Christians), compared him with Christ, which provoked a reply from Eusebius. Caracalla and Alexander Severus were apparently impressed by A. and adored him, but *Lucian regarded him as a charlatan.

APOLLONIUS (5), Dyscolus Prominent Greek grammarian of the 2nd century AD, son of Mnesitheus, native of Alexandria. Apart from a short stay in Rome, A. lived his entire life in Alexandria. Of his numerous works, some twenty titles are known. He treated almost all aspects of Greek grammar. Four works are extant: "On Syntax" (peri syntaxeos), "On Pronouns" (peri antonymias), "On Conjunctions" (peri syndesmon), and "On Adverbs" (peri epirematon). In the first, he treats parts of speech (the article, pronoun, verb, preposition) and their correct order in the sentence, but his rules are sometimes the result of a rigid application of his theories. A. makes extensive use of analogy to establish correct forms. He greatly influenced later grammarians and was regarded as a master of this science. His work is particularly important for its comprehensive outline of ancient grammatical scholarship.

R. Schneider – G. Uhlig, Grammatici Graeci, 2.

APPENDIX VERGILIANA Collection of Latin poems, attributed to Virgil; some were believed to be Virgilian as early as the 1st century AD, but it seems sufficiently clear that they were not written by Virgil. The AV. includes the following poems: Catalepton, Ciris, Copa, Culex Dirae and Lydia, Elegiae in Maecenatum, Moretum, Priapea and *Aetna.

H. R. Fairclough, Vergil (Loeb), 2.

APPIANUS Greek historian, born in Alexandria at the end of the 1st century AD. A. was in Alexandria during the Jewish revolt of AD 116. Under Hadrian, he received Roman citizenship, settled in Rome and became friendly with *Fronto, who helped him obtain the office of procurator Augusti. A. lived into the days of *Marcus Aurelius.

In his Romaika, a history of the Roman wars in 24 books, each book or group of books treats the wars of a particular period or country: Book 1, Wars of the Kings; Book 2, Italian Wars; Book 3, Samnite Wars; Book 4, Celtic Wars; Book 5, Sicilian Wars; Book 6, Hispanic Wars; Book 7, Hannibalic War; Book 8, Libyan (African) Wars; Book 9, Macedonian and Illyrian Wars; Book 10, Hellenic and Asian Wars; Book 11, Syrian Wars; Book 12, Mithridatic Wars; Books 13–17, Civil Wars; Books 18–21, Egyptian Wars; Book 22, Wars of the Caesars until Trajan; Book 23, Dacian Wars; Book 24, Arabian Wars. Books 6–8 and 11–17 are extant in full, and there are fragments of Books 1–5, 9 and 24. Since A. rarely mentions his authorities, it is not always clear whether he is following a historian of the Republic or a later source. His narrative, although succinct at times, is at other times expansive, and, occasionally, sensational or dramatic. Some sections of A.'s work are particularly important, being the principal extant source on the Hispanic Wars after 154 BC, and the Civil Wars, between 133 and 70 BC.

H. E. White, Appian's Roman History (Loeb), 1912–13.

APULEIUS Latin rhetorician and writer, born of a wealthy family c. AD 125, in Madaurus (Numidia). Edu-cated at Carthage and Athens, A. travelled to various places, spending some time in Rome, and later living in Africa. After exhausting his patrimony, he consented to marry the rich, widowed mother of his friend Sicinius. Sicinius' uncle accused A. of practising witchcraft on the widow, and he was tried at Sabratha (in Tripoli) in AD 158. He was acquitted, and, shortly thereafter, he settled in Carthage, where he became famous and honoured, and was appointed priest of the emperor-cult. The date of his death is unknown.

A.'s most famous work, the Metamorphoses (11 books), relates the adventures of a certain Lucius who witnessed various marvels after being transformed into an ass (the work is usually referred to as "The Golden Ass"). In this framework, as he himself notes, A. recounts the Milesian fables (see *Aristides (2)). "Cupid and Psyche" is the best known of these secondary tales. In the 11th book, the goddess Isis transforms Lucius into a human being. (The framework story, "Lucius or Ass", is included in a manuscript of *Lucian, and was also told by Lucius of Patras, perhaps its original author.) This is the only complete extant romance in Latin.

A.'s Apologia is the speech he delivered in his own defence when charged with witchcraft. In it, he shows his wit and power of rhetoric as he demonstrates the ridiculousness of the charge. His Florida is a selection of 23 excerpts from his declamations. De Deo Socratis is a discourse on the divine nature of Socrates. De Dogmate Platonis is a description in 2 books of Plato's theories of ethics and physics. And De Mundo is a translation of the treatise peri cosmou ("On Universe"), falsely attributed to Aristotle. According to many scholars, the last two were not written by A. None of A.'s other poems, speeches, astronomical and biological works, etc., has survived. His style is colourful, his narrative is rich in imagination, and his vocabulary is diversified.

R. Graves, The Transformations of Lucius (Penguin), 1950; E. H. Haight, Apuleius and his Influence, 1927.

APULIA (modern Puglia) Region in southeastern Italy, deriving its name from the Apuli who lived in the vicinity of Mount Garganus, though the name A. came to cover the area up to *Calabria. The Daunii and Peucetii also lived here, and the population as a whole came under Greek influence. By 317 BC, Rome had taken control of the area (Liv. 9.20). A. was known as a breeding land for horses and sheep, and was famous for its wool. It also produced wine and oil. It was devastated during the Hannibalic War and again in the revolt of the Italian allies of Rome, in 90 BC. This, and the spread of malaria, led to its decline.

AQUAE Many towns developed under the Roman Empire around thermal springs, including: 1) A. Sextiae (modern Aix-en-Provence), founded by Sextius Calvinus in 122 BC, where the Teutones were defeated by *Marius in 102 BC; 2) A. Sulis (modern Bath in Britain), where the springs were exploited from the 1st century AD on; 3) A. Mattiacae (modern Wiesbaden), occupied by the Romans from Augustus's time on; 4) A. Grani (modern Aachen/Aix-la-Chapelle), developed from the 1st century AD on.

AQUEDUCTS and CANALS Canals for irrigation and drainage and navigation were used in Mesopotamia and Egypt from times immemorial. Indeed, only by canalization could the population of these two countries secure their subsistence. In Greece and Italy life did not depend to such an extent on control of the water sources. Still

Roman aqueduct at Caesarea Maritima in Palestine

there were some regions where agriculture and healthy life could be developed or maintained only by careful attention to water problems. An attempt to drain Lake Copais in Greece was already made in Mycenaean times but evidently not with much success. In Italy the Etruscans attained high achievements in this respect, both by tunnels and canals in Etruria and the Po valley. The Romans inherited their techniques, though these were not adequate enough to drain the Pompetine marshes in south Latium. The rich aristocrats of the late Republic used to cut canals to the sea to supply sea water for their fish ponds. Much work was done to secure water communications at the mouths of rivers, notably the Po and the Tiber. Outside Italy, Roman generals executed similar projects: by digging a canal, *Drussus (3) connected the lower Rhine to the North Sea. The plans, however, to dig a "Corinth Canal" and a "Suez Canal" did not materialize, though under the Ptolemies the Nile was connected to Alexandria (the Canopic Canal) and the Bitter Lakes.

One of the great achievements of the Romans was the A., the purpose of which was to supply water for domestic use and for irrigation. The first Roman A. was built by the censor *Claudius (2) Caecus in 312 BC, and his Aqua Appia was followed by the Annio Vetus in 272 BC. But the growth of the population of Rome required larger quantities of water and in 144 BC the Senate allocated 180 million sesterces for a new A., the Aqua Marcia. By sophisticated engineering techniques, the Romans were able to secure the flow of water by gravitation alone for ten kilometres, cutting tunnels in mountains and constructing bridges and arched structures over valleys. Italian towns had their own A. and later some of the finest A.

were constructed in the provinces. In Rome itself *Agrippa (1) did much to rebuild the old A. and constructed new ones. After his death in 12 BC his special staff was left to the state and in later time it numbered 240 men. Under the Republic there were no special magistrates to take care of A.; usually censors and aediles undertook that duty. Augustus introduced a three-member board (*Curatores aquarum*) to maintain the A. of the city.
Frontinus, *De Aquis Urbis Romae*; Platner-Ashby, *Top. Dict. Rome* (s.v.); E. B. Van Deman, *The Building of the Roman Aqueducts*, 1934.

AQUILEIA City in northeastern Italy, *c.* 10 km from the Adriatic Sea, founded by Rome as a Latin *colonia* in 181 BC in an effort to check the Celts (Liv. 39.22,54). A.'s good communications across the Alps to central Europe, as well as with the rest of Italy, and the exploitation of nearby gold mines, gave the city its wealth. Besides being a centre of trade and commerce, A. served as a base for the advance of Roman power into the Balkans and central Europe. It flourished until its devastation by *Attila, in AD 452.(Amm. Marc. 21.11).

AQUINCUM Roman military fortress on the Danube at Budapest. Nearby, *canabae* and a town developed, the town receiving colonial status under Septimius Severus. A. was the residence of the governor of Lower Pannonia. Remains of various public buildings have been uncovered on the site.

AQUITANIA Land of the Aquitani, between the Pyrenees, the Atlantic coast and the Garonne. Initial Roman operations here under Pompey were followed up by *Caesar, who subjected A. to Roman rule, though the final subjugation was made by *Agrippa (38 BC) and

*Messala Corvinus (27 BC). The Roman province was extended to the Loire under Augustus, with its capital at Burdigala (Bordeaux).

ARABIA Knowledge of A. had reached Greece by the 5th century BC, and Herodotus knew of Persian contacts with the Arabs in the days of *Darius I. It was only with *Alexander (4), however, and during the Hellenistic period, that more concrete knowledge was acquired and direct relations were established. Despite several Greek passages along the coasts of A., and those of the Seleucids to India from the Persian Gulf (until the rise of Parthia), the Arabs of the southern peninsula virtually controlled Indian trade, and Ptolemaic attempts to oust the Arabs failed. Rome first encountered Arabs in 66 BC, when *Scaurus the Younger, acting on behalf of Pompey, ordered the Nabataean king *Aretas III to withdraw from Judaea. After the Roman conquest of Egypt, Augustus sought to establish control over southern A., but this effort fell short of success. Under the protection of the Roman navy in the Red Sea, direct travel from Egypt to India was maintained, and the importance of the Arab traders declined. Under Trajan, the client kingdom of the Nabataeans was annexed in AD 106 and organized as a province of A. In the 2nd century AD, A. was known to consist of *A. petraea* (the northern part), *A. deserta* (the desert interior) and *A. felix* (the south).
Cary, *Geography*, 183–188.

ARA PACIS AUGUSTAE Altar dedicated by the Senate on 30 January 9 BC on the occasion of Augustus' return from his tour of Spain and Gaul. It was situated on the eastern side of the *Campus Martius, and its reliefs depicted various mythological and official scenes, including portraits of the family of Augustus. It was probably meant to represent the prosperity of the Roman people which resulted from the achievements of Augustus. From the 16th century on, various fragments of the monument have been found on the site. The monument in its entirety was reconstructed in 1938.
G. M. C. Toynbee, *JRS*, 1961, 153ff.

ARATUS (1) Greek poet and scholar, native of Soli in Cilicia, born shortly after 315 BC. A. studied under the poet Menecrates of Ephesus and was much influenced in Athens by *Zeno, the founder of Stoicism. He was invited to the court of *Antigonus II Gonatas, in 277 BC, where he composed several poems in honour of his patron. A. stayed with *Antiochus I for some time, but later returned to Macedonia. The date of his death is not known.

A.'s only extant work is his famous *Phaenomena*. His other "scientific" and non-scientific poems – elegies, hymns, epigrams, etc. – have not survived. Of the 1,154 verses of the *Phaenomena*, the first 752 describe the heavenly bodies, while the rest, entitled *Prognoseis kata semeion*, deal with meteorological signs. There is a purely poetical passage within his scientific accounts. The philosophical views expressed in the poem are essentially Stoic, but A. actually followed the descriptions of the constellations as given in *Eudoxus' *Phaenomena*.

A.'s work was very successful. Many commentaries were written on it, and it was translated into Latin several times. The commentary by *Hipparchus (2) is extant, as are large portions of the translations made by Cicero, *Germanicus and *Avienus.
G. R. Mair, *Callimachus, Lycophron and Aratus* (Loeb), 1921.

ARATUS (2) Achaean statesman, native of *Sicyon, born in 271 BC. After A.'s father was murdered in a political disturbance in 264 BC, he fled to Argos. In 251 BC, A. freed Sicyon from its tyrant and the city was admitted to the Achaean League. Within several years, he became the leading statesman of the League. His aim was to fight tyrannies and reduce Macedonian control over Greece, and to extend the power of the League. A.'s anti-Macedonian policy won him financial support from *Ptolemy III. From 245 to 213 BC, he served as general (strategos) of the League on alternating years. A. captured Corinth from the Macedonians by a surprise attack in 243 BC. In 241 BC, he defeated the Aetolians, who became allies in 239 BC. After his defeat by *Cleomenes IV of Sparta, in 228 BC, A. changed his anti-Roman policy. He sought help from *Antigonus III Doson, with whose approval Achaea joined Antigonus' Hellenic League, in 224 BC. After *Philip V's succession to the throne, A. fought with him against Aetolia, Sparta and Elis (220–219 BC). He helped rid Philip of his powerful minister, Apelles (218 BC), but refused to follow Macedonia's anti-Roman policy. He died in 213 BC. It was mainly due to A.'s policy and opportune decisions that the Achaean League was able to expand and keep its unity and influence.
Polyb. 2. 37–71; 4–5; Plut. *Aratus*;
F. W. Walbank, *Aratos of Sicyon*, 1933.

ARAUSIO (modern Orange) Town in Gallia Narbonensis, famous for the great victory of the Cimbri over Rome in 105 BC. A colony of veterans was founded here under Augustus.

ARCADIA Central part of the Peloponnesus, bordered by *Messenia and *Laconia in the south, *Elis in the west, *Achaea in the north, and Argolis in the east, with a southwest outlet to the sea. A mountainous country, some of A.'s summits rise to more than 2,200 m. The river Alpheus, originating in southern Arcadia, drains most of the country. Being mountainous, it consisted mainly of numerous villages, though the cities of *Mantinea, *Tegea and Orchomenus developed in the eastern plains. The population spoke a distinct Greek dialect, related to the Cyprian. A. was known as a land of shepherds, famous for its primitive cults, and the human sacrifices said to have been offered at the temple of Zeus on Mount Lycaeon. Anyone entering the sanctuary was punished by death. *Pan, god of shepherds and flocks, was considered an Arcadian deity. The gloomy character of *Demeter was prominent in her Arcadian cult. She was called Erinys at Thelpusa and "Black" at Phigalia, where she was horse-headed (Poseidon was said to have mated with her in the form of a horse). A. remained in political disunion almost until the end of the Classical period. From the 6th century BC on, it was under Spartan control, but after the Spartan defeat at Leuctra (371 BC) *Epaminondas' invasion of the Peloponnesus enabled the Arcadians to assert their independence. A new town, *Megalopolis, was founded. It incorporated the inhabitants of forty villages and became the centre of the new Arcadian League. The old Arcadian cities, however, were jealous and this unity did not last for long. From the mid-3rd century BC on, the Arcadian cities joined the *Achaean League. Under the Roman Empire, A. was desolated. In literature A. came to be seen as the ideal rustic paradise.
Pausan. 8; Larsen, *Gr. Fed. St.*, 180–195.

ARCADIUS, Flavius Son of *Theodosius I, born AD 377. Became emperor of the Eastern Roman Empire in AD 383. A. had little effective power and the empire was actually governed by his ministers, notably *Stilicho. He died in AD 408.

ARCAS In Greek mythology, son of Zeus and Callisto. A.'s grandfather, Lycaeon, killed him, offering the meat to Zeus. The god, however, turned Lycaeon into a wolf and revived A. Later, A. encountered his mother, who appeared in the form of a she-bear. As A. was about to kill her, Zeus transferred them both to the heavens as constellations, she as The Great Bear and he as Arctophylax. A. was believed to be the ancestor of the Arcadians.

ARCESILAUS Greek philosopher, native of Pitane in Aeolia. Born in 316 BC, A. came to Athens, where he first studied under the Peripatetic *Theophratus, and was later "converted" to the Academy by Crantor. He was influenced by Polemo and Crates. After the death of Crates, A. became head of the Academy (c. 268 BC), and with him began the so-called Middle Academy, during which sceptical doctrines were taught. A. himself did not write, but his views are known to some extent from later authors. He believed himself a loyal follower of Socrates and Plato, avoiding positive doctrines and conclusions. When discussing a proposition, one must take into consideration the arguments for and against it; at the end of such a discussion, no conclusion should be made, the right attitude being to refrain from judgement (*epoche*). A.'s refusal to assert any positive statement went so far, according to Cicero, that he said he knew nothing, not even his own ignorance (Socrates had said that he knew of his own ignorance). A. severely attacked the Stoic theory of knowledge, stressing that the unreliability of the senses made it impossible for positive truth to be ascertained. In ethics, he held the principle of *eulogon*, whereby moral questions should be decided by the criterion of reasonableness. This line of Scepticism was maintained in the Academy until the time of *Antiochus of Ascalon.
Cicero, *Acad. Pr.*; *Lucullus*; Diog. Laert. 4.28–45; Sextus Empiricus; *Pyr.* 1.232–4; Bréhier, *Philosophy*, 112–7.

ARCHELAUS (1) Illegitimate son of the Macedonian king *Perdiccas II. A. eliminated his rivals and secured his succession to the throne on Perdiccas' death in 413 BC. He did much to assert his authority against the separatist tendencies of the cantons of Upper Macedonia, and it was under him that *Pella replaced *Aegaea as the Macedonian capital. A. reorganized the Macedonian army, built roads and constructed fortresses. In foreign policy, he cultivated good relations with Athens, and supplied her timber for ship-building. A. invited Greek poets — notably Euripides — to his court. He ended his life during a conspiracy, in 399 BC.

ARCHELAUS (2) Greek general of *Mithridates VI. In 88 BC, A. conquered Bithynia, proceeded to the Aegean Sea and occupied Greece. He was defeated by *Sulla in the battles of Chaeronea and Orchomenus (86 BC). A. helped bring about the peace treaty of Dardanus between the king and Sulla. But Mithridates was suspicious of him and he transferred his allegiance to Rome in 83 BC. A. later supported *Lucullus in the war against Mithridates.

ARCHIDAMUS II Spartan king of the Eurypontid dynasty. It is likely that he ascended to the throne in 476 BC. It was mainly due to A. that Sparta suppressed the revolt of the Messenians, who sought to take advantage of the losses Sparta suffered in the earthquake of 465/464 BC. A. spoke out against declaring war on Athens in 431 BC, but he commanded the Spartan armies that invaded Attica in the first years of the Peloponnesian War, and

hence the first part of that war was named after him. He died in 427 BC.

ARCHIDAMUS III Son of *Agesilaus II, born c. 400 BC. A. succeeded his father in 361/360 BC. In 371 BC he rescued and led home those Spartans who had survived the battle of *Leuctra (in which he had no part). He twice commanded the Spartan army against Arcadia, and took a leading part in the war against *Epaminondas (362 BC). He apparently impressed *Isocrates, who composed a speech, *Archidamus*, in which the future king opposed the plans of Thebes (366 BC). A. was probably considered by Isocrates as a possible leader of the Greeks against Persia. In 343 BC, A. went to Italy to assist Terentum against the Lucanians, and he was killed in battle in 338 BC.

ARCHILOCHUS Greek poet, one of the first to write elegiac and iambic poetry. A. was born in Paros, one of the Cycladic islands, probably early in the 7th century BC (though some ancient writers date him in the second half of the 8th century BC). A.'s father was Telesicles, his mother was a slave-girl named Enipo. Because A. was poor, when he fell in love with a girl named Neobule, her father Lycambes would not accept him as a son-in-law. A. took revenge by composing slanderous poems against them, on account of which, it was later said, Neobule hanged herself. Becoming a mercenary soldier, A. went to Thassos with settlers from Paros, fought against the Thracians, and died in the battle against the Naxians. A monument was later dedicated to him at Paros; its inscription has been found.

Only fragments of A.'s poems have survived (many in citations by grammarians), others are known from papyri. A. employed new metres: iambic trimeters, trochaic tetrameters, and some mixed metres of his own. He also wrote dactylic hexameters and elegiacs. A.'s poems were later arranged according to rhythmic forms. In both form and content, his writing was personal. He wrote about love and hate, his experiences in war, his relations with other people, his poverty and his misfortunes. A.'s strong, individualistic character is indicated by his disregard for conventions, and he was not ashamed to write that he had lost his shield in battle — he would obtain another as good as the one lost. In one poem, occasioned by the loss of many of his compatriots in a shipwreck, A. expressed the idea that, as tears did not heal his sorrow, enjoyment would not be a bad pursuit. He was proud of his art of taking revenge upon whoever maltreated him. He used popular fables in his poems (in one, Lycambes was the eagle and he himself the fox). A poet of much originality, A. was considered as great as Homer, Pindar and Sophocles.
Diehl, *An. Lyr. Gr.*;
A. R. Burn, *The Lyric Age of Greece*, 1960, 159–170.

ARCHIMEDES One of the greatest mathematicians of all times, most famous for his original contributions to theoretical mathematics and for his mechanical inventions. A. was born c. 287 BC in Syracuse; his father was the astronomer Pheidias. He was a friend of the Syracusan king, *Hieron II and his son Gelon. Although he lived for a time in Egypt where he came to know the scholars Dositheus, Conon of Samos, and Eratosthenes, he spent most of his life in his native city.

A popular story has it that Hieron asked A. to verify whether a crown he had had made was of pure gold. While taking a bath, A. noticed that the deeper his body sank the more water was displaced. He thus discovered the principle of specific gravity by which each element displaces a certain volume of water. In his excitement he ran naked through the streets shouting *"Heureca"* ("I have found it"). His inventions included the hydraulic screw ("Archimedes' screw"), an orrery, and compound pulleys. His famous statement, "Give me a place to stand and I can move the earth", was made when he showed Hieron how little force was needed to move a ship by means of his pulleys. When the Romans besieged Syracuse, A. is said to have invented various machines for use in its defence, among them catapults and a system of concave mirrors which harnessed the sun's rays to ignite the sails of the Roman ships. The city was taken in 211 BC and A. was killed while working on problems in geometry. He had asked that his tombstone be inscribed with a diagram of a sphere within a cylinder.

Although his inventions were considered marvels, A. did not write about them. He did however leave several works on geometry, arithmetic, mechanics, optics and astronomy. He was the creator of hydrostatics and statics, two branches of mechanics. In geometry his main interest was measurements. A considerable number of his works are extant, including:

1. *On Quadrature of the Parabola* which gives two methods — one mechanical and one geometrical — for determining the area of a parabola.

2. *On the Sphere and Cylinder*, a two-book treatise which expounds theorems about the measurement of the surface and volume of a sphere, or any segment thereof, e.g., the surface of a sphere is 4 times that of its great circle, i.e., surface = $4\pi r^2$.

3. *On Spirals* which gives the properties and measurements of the Archimedes spiral.

4. *On Conoids and Spheroids*, on the determination of the volumes of paraboloids and ellipsoids.

5. *Measurement of the Circle,* in which A. demonstrates the value of π.

6. *Book of Lemmas*, problems in plane geometry.

7. *On the Heptagon.* Nos. 6 and 7 are known only through Arabic translations.

8. *On Equilibrium of Planes*, a two-book treatise discussing the theory of centres of gravity and the principle of levers.

9. *On Floating Bodies*, in which, *inter alia*, A. establishes the theory of hydrostatics.

10. *The Sand Reckoner*, which, on the basis of assumed givens, calculates the number of grains of sand in the universe. His aim in this work was to show how to deal with great numbers and for this purpose he devised the notation 100,000,000. His calculation was that the number of grains of sand was not more than 10^{63}.

11. *On the Method*, in which A. shows how he arrived at geometrical theorems after studying the properties of various figures by mechanical methods. This work was first discovered in 1906.

Th. Heath, *The Works of Archimedes*, 1897;
E. J. Dijkstehuis, *Archimedes*, 1956.

ARCHITECTURE Greek A. presented one of the finest artistic achievements of that people; it is a sad memorial to the destructive tendency of mankind that so little has survived the passing of time. However, enough has remained to bear testimony to the genius of the Greeks in this field. What is known about Greek A. is based on painstaking study of the extant remains, more often than not known by archaeological excavations, and some literary sources. These include the works of the Roman writers *Vitruvius (1st century AD) and *Pliny the Elder (1st century AD), and that of the Greek *Pausanias (3).

A crane operated by a tread-mill — a detail of a Roman sepulchral monument

The great architectural achievements of the Mycenaean civilization were the royal palaces and citadels, city walls, and tholos tombs. The main unit of the great palaces, known from Mycenae, *Tiryns and *Pylos, was the *Megaron. These were not only the residence of the king and his family but also the industrial, administrative and storage centres of the kingdom; hence the Megaron was surrounded by other structures which had rooms for the other purposes. The Treasury of Atreus and Tomb of Clytemnestra in Mycenae and the Treasury of Minyas at Orchomenos are the best known of the tholos tombs. The main feature of the tholos was a circular domed chamber: that of the Treasury of Atreus is 14 m high and has a diameter of 16 m. It is approached through a long passage, and the whole structure is covered with earth. These, as well as the palaces, were built of huge blocks of stone. The techniques used included the post and lintel for gates (the famous Lion Gate of Mycenae), the corbel vault in the tholos tombs, and the inverted arch. The citadels were fortified by Cyclopean walls, made of irregular, massive polygonal blocks. In all these there was nothing to indicate the subsequent development of Greek A.

After the collapse of the Mycenaean civilization and with the decline of the monarchy and of material conditions in the Dark Age there was no room for the great palaces. It was in the building of *temples, houses for the gods, that the Greeks attained their highest level of A. Other characteristic Greek buildings were the *theatre, the *Gymnasium, the *Stoa, and the *Stadium. Both the plans and the materials used until the 7th century BC were simple, even poor. Stone was used only for the foundations, walls were made of unbaked bricks and the roofing was based on wooden beams and pillars. From the late 7th century on bricks were replaced by stone, and later by marble, in the building of the temples and other buildings. Stone was carefully cut into sharp edged blocks often with polished surfaces; only clamps and dowels, of wood or bronze, were used for holding the stones together. Private houses remained simple in plan and material until the Hellenistic times. They consisted of a main dining room, a women's quarter (gynaikon), bedrooms, a kitchen and a bath, all arranged around a courtyard. Furniture and decoration were very modest. The peristyle courtyard came into fashion only in the Hellenistic period.

While keeping to the traditional technique of the post and lintel as the basic device of construction, the Greeks developed the so-called Orders, distinct styles of buildings according to the different types of columns. The two main Orders, Doric and Ionic, were well established in the Greek world by the end of the 6th century BC. It is difficult to determine precisely how they resemble their proto-type wooden constructions. Functionally the columns were posts for supporting the beams of the buildings. The great achievement of the Greek architects was that they used these functional elements of beams and posts to attain unsurpassed decorations both in forms and proportions.

The earliest temples in the Doric Order date from the end of the 7th century BC. The Doric column rose from the stylobate, the three-step floor; it had a massive, tapered shaft with usually 20 shallow flutes. Its height increased from over four times the lower diameter to about 5½ times in the 5th century. The shafts supported the capital, made of the round echinus and square abacus, on which rested the architrave – a horizontal, bare beam. It served as a basis for the roof construction and directly supported

the frieze which consisted of alternating triglyphs and metops, one of the typical characteristics of the Order. On top of it came the cornice from which sprang the roof. The whole impression is of solidity and majesty, and some of the best Greek sculptures were to be found in the friezes and pediments of the Doric temple.

The Ionic Order developed in the Greek cities of western Asia Minor and in the adjacent islands. Compared to the Doric, the Ionic column was slender and the whole style was more ornate. It had a base from which sprang the shaft with its 24 deep flutes, and volute-shaped capital. The frieze above the architrave consisted of a continuous strip around the building, usually decorated with reliefs. This Order came to be used in Greece proper in the 5th century BC, mainly mixed with the Doric Order in the same temples. The Corinthian Order, invented traditionally by the sculptor Callimachus in the late 5th century BC, was a form developed from the Ionic Order; its main characteristic was the capital with acanthus leaves. This Order was popular in the Hellenistic times and especially with the Romans.

Roman A. began with very simple, even primitive, buildings. Temples for gods were first built under foreign influence, Etruscan and Greek. Characteristic public buildings were the *basilica, *amphitheatre, arch, *circus, and *forum (1). Private houses developed from the primitive urn-shaped huts on the Palatine through the *atrium-type house to the magnificent *villas of the late Republic and the Empire. In the crowded cities the dominant type of building was the insula, a several-storied block of flats, usually with shops facing the street or inward courtyard on the first floor. Overcrowded and built with cheap materials (timber and sun-dried bricks), they suffered from frequent fires and collapses despite the effort of Augustus to improve security. In the more affluent parts of the cities there were comfortable apartments even in insulae, as is evident from the extant buildings of *Ostia. In the cities, only the well-to-do could afford to have a detached house, domus. The material used included thatch, puddled rubble, timber, bricks (sun-dried and baked), stone, marble and granite. The usual type of stone used in Rome during the late Republic was the Traventine, which was to be found near Tivoli. Yet Augustus "found Rome built with bricks and left it covered with marble". Indeed the use of bricks was widespread to the late Roman Empire. It was the use of concrete, made of volcanic ash and first used at Puteoli, which was peculiar to Roman buildings and gave them strength and hardness. For decoration the outside bricks were arranged in regular patterns and often covered with layers of marble veneer, fine stucco, mosaic or painted plaster.

While the essential element of Greek A. was the post and lintel, by which the Greeks always remained limited, the Romans developed the arch and vault systems. The extensive and skillful use of concrete made possible the building of vaulted halls and it was by these devices that Roman A. successfully coped with problems of interior space. The great achievement of the Romans in this respect can be seen in the huge imperial baths, all based on the concrete-vaulted system. Another excellent example is the dome of the *Pantheon. Mainly for decorative purposes the Romans received from the Greeks the three great Orders, but usually preferred the Corinthian. They were mainly employed in temples, basilicas and porticos.

The rich aristocracy in the late Republic and under the Empire and the Roman emperors often built extravagant

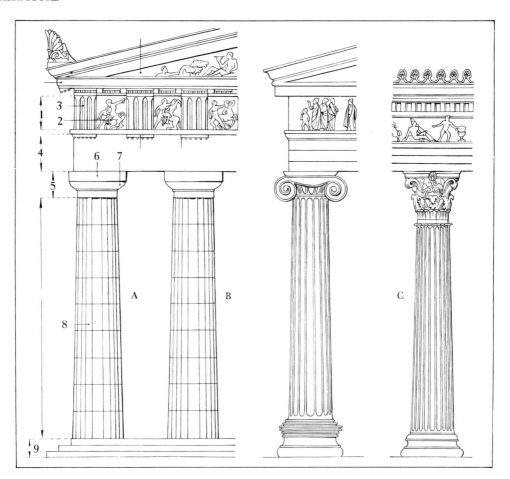

The three Orders: Doric, Ionic, Corinthian   A— Doric, B— Ionic, C— Corinthian

1— frieze. 2— metope. 3— triglyph. 4— architrave. 5— capital 6— abacus. 7— echinus. 8— fluting. 9— stylobate.

buildings. These were multi-roomed complexes, lavishly decorated with wall-paintings, mosaics and sculptures, and included pools, peristyles, gardens etc. The Palatine Hill at Rome from the times of Augustus on was covered by imperial palaces. Of the more extravagant examples the *Domus Aurea* of Nero, the palace of Domitian on the Palatine and the villa of Hadrian at Tibur (Tivoli) are noteworthy.
A. Boethius, *Roman and Greek Architecture*, 1948;
W. B. Dinsmoor, *The Architecture of Ancient Greece*, 1950; A. Boethius — J. B. Ward — Perkins, *Etruscan and Roman Architecture*, 1969.

ARCHONTES Title of high officials in many Greek states, best known at Athens. The first A. appeared when the powers of the kings began to be limited and during the transition to the aristocratic form of government. The three ancient A. at Athens were the *basileus* (king), the *polemarchos* (army commander), and the *archon eponymos* (by whose name the year was designated). Until the 8th century BC the *A. basileus* were descendants of *Codrus. In the 8th century the three A. held office for ten years, and from 683 BC on they were elected annually. Some time later the newly instituted *thesmothetai* raised the number of the A. to nine. Until the beginning of the 5th century the A. were the highest officials of the Athenian state. On finishing their term of office the A. became members of the *Areopagus for life.

Following the reforms of *Cleisthenes (2) each new tribe chose an archon, the tenth being elected as secretary of the *thesmothetai*. But the development of democracy at Athens brought about a decline in the prestige and powers of the A. From 487 BC, they were elected by lot. From 457 BC *zeugitai* were allowed to be chosen, not only citizens of the two upper classes of *Solon's system. Actually *thetes* also were elected. The A. lost much of their power (e.g., the command of the army), retaining some jurisdiction, however (e.g. the *basileus* presided over inheritance cases; see also *Thesmothetai) and religious duties.
Hignett, *Athenian Constitution*;
Ehrenberg, *The Greek State* (s.v.).

ARDEA An old town in Latium inhabited by the Rutuli. According to legend, Turnus, its king, fought and was killed by *Aeneas (Virgil, *Aeneid*, bks. 7—12). It was probably under Roman control by the end of the 6th century BC (Polyb. 3.22,11). A Latin *colonia* was established here in 442 BC. A. retained its loyalty to Rome and was severely damaged by the Samnites. By the early 2nd century BC it was a state prison. As a consequence of a malaria epidemic A. was already in decline during the latter part of the Roman Republic.
A. Alföldi, *Early Rome* (s.v.).

ARELATE (modern Arles) A town of the powerful Gallic tribe of Salluvii on the Rhone. Greeks established trading centres there. Its port was improved at the end of the 2nd century BC. Caesar sent a colony of veterans to A. in 46 BC, and under the Empire it prospered as a centre of trade. From the time of Constantine, emperors resided here occasionally. The Visigoths took control of A. in AD 476. Considerable remains of the amphitheatre, forum, theatre and baths are extant.
L. A. Constans, *Arles Antique*, 1921.

AREOPAGUS The "hill of Ares" situated west of the Athenian *Acropolis. Inasmuch as the ancient State Council (Boule) of Athens met here, it was subsequently called the Boule of A. It dates back to the time of the monarchy and in mythology the A. was a court of homicide even for

Aphrodite of Arles. A Roman copy of Praxiteles' famous original

gods (Pausan 1.21,7). In early times it consisted of the aristocracy, but by the early 6th century BC all ex-*Archontes* became life members, which means that it numbered about 200–250. Under the aristocracy the A. probably controlled the government of the state (Arist. *Athen. Pol.* 3.6). It certainly had extensive judicial functions, notably in cases of deliberate homicide, arson, and the infliction of personal injury. The court is also said to have been responsible for the guarding of the laws (*nomophylakia*), which is understood to mean that it had the powers to prosecute state officials and others who acted against the laws. It had the power to fine, to exile and to pass death sentences without appeal. However, it is far from clear what other functions the A. had and some authorities have denied that it had any. The A. lost much of its power and influence with the development of the democracy in the 5th century BC, though it is possible that due to its important role in the wars against the Persian invasion, it enjoyed prestige for a while after 480 BC (Aris. *Athen. Pol.* 23; 25). However, in 462/1, it lost the function of "guarding of the laws" by the reforms of *Ephialetes. From 457, *zeugitai*, and virtually all citizens, could be elected *Archontes*, and as a result the prestige of the A. rapidly declined. From then on it remained only a court without political importance, and appeals could be made against its decisions. The A. lasted till the late Roman Empire when it numbered thirty-one members.
Aristotle, *Athen. Pol.*; Hignett, *Athenian Constitution.*

ARES The Greek god of war. According to one view, he had been originally a god of vegetation. His name possibly means "the harmful, the revengeful". The unclear reference to A. in Linear B documents from Cnossus does not shed light on his character at that stage. As from Homer he is associated with battles, murders, and bloodshed, that is, he was not a national war-god of the type that could be found amongst other peoples. In fact, his name is occasionally used as a synonym for war and murder (*Il.* 17.490). Significantly, his sister was *Eris, who personified rivalry and discord. This warlike, violent god did not enjoy popularity with the Greeks. Homer evidently detested him, describing him as impetuous, treacherous and murderous, and ascribing his origin to barbarous Thrace (*Il.* 13.298–301), and this tradition is also found in Herodotus (5.7). Probably due to his unpleasant character, the cult of A. was not popular in the Greek world, though he was worshipped in Aetolia, Thessaly, Thebes, Athens, and the Peloponnesus. In some places women were the main participants in his cult. A peculiar characteristic of his cult was that, in several states, dogs were sacrificed to him. On these occasions he had the title *Enylaios*, probably the name of a Bronze-Age god with whom A. was identified by the Greeks.

As early as in Homer's time, A. is a member of the Olympian family; his parents were Zeus and Hera. Many tales were told of his love-affairs. Perhaps the most famous concerns that with Aphrodite. Homer describes in detail how Hephaestus, Aphrodite's husband, caught the lovers in their bed (*Od.* 8.266–367). Phobus, Deimus and Harmonia were children that Aphrodite bore him. He had other sons who resembled him in their quarrelsome spirit and savage character. He killed Halirrhothius, Poseidon's son, who tried to rape his daughter, Alcippe. He was charged with murder, and the hill on which the proceedings took place was henceforth termed the *Areopagus. A. appears in works of art associated with various themes since early times. His love-affair with

Aphrodite was apparently a popular theme.
Farnell, *Cults,* 5, 396–417.

ARETAS The name of several Nabataean kings:
1. A. II (110–96 BC) was defeated by Alexander Jannaeus in 96 in his attempt to save Gaza.
2. A. III (87–62 BC) took control of Damascus in 85 and defeated Alexander Jannaeus. Subsequently, he had to turn it over to *Tigranes. In the Jewish civil war between Aristobulus II and Hyrcanus, he supported the latter but had to stop the siege of Jerusalem in 66 because of the intervention of *Scaurus (2).
3. A. IV (9 BC–AD 39) helped the Roman governor of Syria in his operations against Judaea after the death of *Herod the Great. He defeated *Herodes Antipas in AD 37, after the latter divorced his wife, the daughter of A. The timely death of the Emperor Tiberius saved him from Roman punishment and he was soon given Damascus by *Caligula. When St. Paul fled from that city it was ruled by a governor of A.

ARETHUSA See **ALPHEUS.**

AREUS Spartan king (309–265 BC). He fought *Antigonus Gonatas in 280 BC. In 272 BC he helped save Sparta from the attack of *Pyrrhus. He failed to help Athens in the Chremonidean War and was killed in battle at Corinth in 265 BC.

ARGEI Twenty-seven *sacraria* (chapels) of A. were visited in a yearly religious procession at Rome held on 16–17 March. On 14 May, 27 effigies of men called A. were thrown from the Pons Sublicius into the Tiber by the Vestals. The meaning of the ceremony is disputed; it may have been a ritual of purification.
R. E. A. Palmer, *Archaic Community,* 84–97.

ARGENTORATE (modern Strasbourg) Originally a town of the Gallic Triboci, it was a legionary camp and gradually *canabae* developed here, beginning in the time of Augustus.
R. Forrer, *Strasbourg – Argentorate,* 1927.

ARGONAUTS The myth of the A. describes the voyage of those Greek heroes who took part in the expedition of *Jason on the ship Argo to bring the Golden Fleece from Colchis. The legend is possibly based on a real exploration of the Black Sea made by the Minyans who lived in Boeotia and Thessaly. According to the legend not only Minyans but heroes from all over Greece accepted Jason's invitation to the adventure. The enlarged list included such famous names as *Castor and Polydeucus, *Idas and Lynceus, *Meleager, *Heracles, *Amphiarus, *Atalanta, *Admetus, and *Orpheus. Several of the A. were endowed with special powers: Euphemus with extraordinary speed, Lynceus with amazing sight, and Calais and Zetes with the power to fly. It was Argos the Thespian who built the ship Argo with the help of Athena. The ship was built for fifty oarsmen, and so there was room for that number of heroes to participate. On their way to Colchis, the A. had several adventures. They stayed a long time with the women of Lemnos who had killed all the men on their island. As a result of this visit the island was repopulated. They visited Samothrace and were initiated into its mysteries. They received a friendly reception at Cyzicus but killed its eponymous king at night by mistake. Later Heracles left them to search for his beautiful page, Hylas, who was taken away by water-nymphs. On their way Polydeucus killed Amycus. They delivered the Thracian king *Phineus from the *Harpies and in return he taught them the route to Colchis. Upon his advice they followed a dove in order to pass through the Clashing

Air view of Oboda, a Nabataean city in the Negev (southern Palestine) rebuilt by Aretas IV

Rocks (Symplegades). They passed through other islands and countries until their arrival at Colchis. Here Jason took possession of the Golden Fleece with the help of Medea. The story of their return voyage, on which they were pursued by the Colchian king or his son, has many versions. According to some accounts they travelled up the Danube and returned by way of the Po. Other accounts relate that they arrived at the North Sea and came back through the Straits of Gibraltar. They were also said to have arrived at Libya and to have returned by the route on which they originally sailed to Colchis.

The myth of the A. is one of the oldest in Greek mythology. In Homer it is briefly mentioned to *Circe to Odysseus (*Od.* 13.69–72). The story is referred to by many authors and is the subject of several extant poems: the 4th Pythian Ode of *Pindar, the *Argonautica* of *Apollonius Rhodius, and the *Argonautica* of *Valerius Flaccus. Various themes of the myth were used by artists beginning in the 6th century BC.

J. R. Bacon, *The Voyage of the Argonauts,* 1925.

ARGOS (1) Several figures in Greek mythology.

1. An argonaut who built the Argo.

2. A giant with many eyes (the number varies). After *Io was turned into a heifer, A. was assigned the task of watching her by Hera. Hermes made him sleep by playing the flute and then killed him. He turned into a peacock. His name became proverbial for a diligent watchman.

3. The legendary hero-founder of the city Argos.

ARGOS (2) The main city in the eastern Peloponnesus, inhabited from the Bronze Age to the present, bearing the same name. The city is situated 5 km from the sea in the south of the plain which bore its name. The settlement spread to the hills, Larissa and Aspis. The human habitation of the site probably dates back to the end of the 3rd millenium BC. There was a sizeable settlement there from at least the middle of the 2nd millenium. To judge from the remains found in the excavations, A. was dependent on one of its powerful neighbour cities, *Mycenae or *Tiryns in the Mycenaean period. There are no traces of a palace or fortifications. In Homer and in many myths it was one of the important cities of that age. Indeed, in poetry *Argeioi* is a name for all the Greeks, and Agamemnon is sometimes called king of A. instead of Mycenae. One of the main Greek heroes in the Trojan War was the Argive king, *Diomedes.

With the rest of the Peloponnesus A. was taken by the Dorians at the close of the 2nd millenium. It was under the new invaders that A. rose to power, taking control of the eastern part of the Peloponnesus (Argolis). Temenus, the Dorian conqueror of A., probably took Corinth as well. A. presumably acquired its prominent place in Greek mythology during this Archaic period. A. maintained its dominant position up to the time of King *Pheidon in the 7th century BC. This king, sometimes referred to as a tyrant, took control of the Olympic games, won a victory over Sparta and is said to have struck coins in *Aegina.

In the following century the power of A. declined as Sparta rose to be the leading state in the Peloponnesus. In 494 BC A. suffered a heavy defeat at the hands of the Spartan king *Cleomenes I. It was able, however, to destroy Mycenae and Tiryns c. 470–468 and thus to rule almost the whole of the Argive plain. About the same time democracy replaced monarchy at A. In the Peloponnesian War it sided with Athens and was defeated by Sparta in 418. It fought again with Athens against Sparta in 395 and later joined *Phillip II. In the first part of the 3rd

century it was ruled by tyrants, and in 229 BC became a member of the Achaean League. A. survived the two destructions inflicted on her by the Goths (AD 267 and 395).

The main and best-known cult of A. was that of Hera, whose temple was situated about 10 km to the north. In fact, she was the city-goddess, hence, her title *Argeia.* Other important deities here were Apollo and Athena. Two Argive sculptors, *Ageladas and *Polyclitus, gained fame.

ARIADNE In Greek mythology the daughter of *Minos, king of Crete and Pasiphae. In love with *Theseus, she gave him a ball of thread with which he found his way out of the *Labyrinth after killing the Minotaur. He took her from Crete but abandoned her on the island of Dia, usually identified with Naxos. According to one version she died there, but, according to most accounts, she married *Dionysus. It seems that originally she was a Minoan goddess. At Cyprus she was worshipped as Aphrodite A. Her name means "very holy"; she was also called *Aridela,* meaning "very bright". Her adventure with Theseus was a favourite theme with artists dating from the 5th century BC.

ARIARAMNES Son of Ariarathes II. Ruler of Cappadocia, *c.* 280–230 BC.

ARIARATHES The name of several rulers of Cappadocia, descendants of A. I, the Persian satrap of the country at the time of Alexander the Great.

1. A. II took control of the country *c.* 301 BC but recognized Seleucus I as his overlord.

2. A. III, son of Ariaramnes, ruled, initially with his father, as from *c.* 250 until 220 BC. He married the daughter of *Antiochus II, and was the first of his dynasty to be called king.

3. A. IV, 220–163 BC, married the daughter of *Antiochus III. After the defeat of Antiochus III by Rome he became her loyal ally.

4. A. V succeeded his father A. IV in 163 BC. He aided in the Hellenization of his country. Like his father, he was a loyal supporter of Rome and helped her in the war against *Aristonicus. He died in 130 BC.

5. A. VI succeeded his father A. V in 130 BC and received Lycaonia from Rome after the final suppression of Aristonicus. He married the daughter of *Mithridates V, and was murdered *c.* 116 BC.

6. A. VII succeeded his father A. VI in 116 BC. He was killed by his uncle *Mithridates VI, in 101 BC.

7. A. IX, son of Mithridates VI, proclaimed king of Cappadocia in 101 by his father. He was hated by the Cappadocians, and consequently, Rome intervened and proclaimed a new king, Ariobarzanes, in 95 BC. He was restored by Tigranes, expelled again in 89, and returned in 88. A. probably died in late 87 BC.

Magie, *Asia* (s.v.).

ARICIA (modern Ariccia) An old, prominent Latin city, situated about 25 km southeast of Rome. According to legend it was founded by *Alba Longa. In the 6th century it was a centre of a Latin League. It played an important role in resisting the Etruscans at the end of that century and in the battle at Lake Regillus against Rome in 496 BC. After the Latin War of 340–338 BC it was granted Roman citizenship. Nearby was the famous sanctuary of Diana Nemorensis. Augustus' mother, Atia, was a native of A.

Alföldi, *Early Rome,* 15–6, 48–56.

ARIMASPOI A mythical one-eyed people reputedly living in north Scythia and neighbours of the *Hyperboreans. They fought griffins who guarded a hoard of gold (Herodotus 3.116; 4.13 and 27).

ARIMINUM (modern Rimini) An Umbrian town on the Adriatic coast. A Latin *colonia* was established there in 268 BC, and it served as an important base for the Roman advance to and control of *Gallia Cisalpina. With the construction of the *Via Flaminia in 220 BC a direct connection was established with Rome. It received Roman citizenship in 89 BC and suffered damages and confiscations under Sulla and the triumvirs. In the Civil War of AD 69 it suffered under the Flavian army.

ARIOBARZANES The name of three kings of Cappadocia:
1. A. I was declared king by Sulla in 95 BC. He was expelled three times by *Mithridates VI and *Tigranes of Armenia but time and again was restored by Rome. In 63 BC he gave up the throne to his son.
2. A. II ascended to the throne upon the abdication of his father in 63 BC. He was killed in 52 BC.
3. A. III succeeded his father, A. II, in 52 BC. He supported *Pompey, to whom he was heavily indebted, in the civil war against Caesar. Caesar pardoned him and even gave him Armenia Minor. He was killed by *Cassius in 42 BC.
Magie, *Asia* (s.v.); Badian, *Rom. Imp.* (s.v.).

ARION (1) The excellent horse of *Adrastus, born to *Demeter, disguised as a mare, after Poseidon, in the shape of a stallion, coupled with her.

ARION (2) A Greek poet, native of Methymne in Lesbos, lived in the second part of the 7th century BC. The Corinthian tyrant, *Periander (625–585 BC), at whose court A. stayed for many years, was his patron. He visited Italy and Sicily, and on the return voyage was thrown to sea. A dolphin saved him and carried him to shore. He was the first to create the dithyramb – a choral song in honour of Dionysus – as a literary genre (Herodotus 1.23). He was said to have taught choirs to perform his dithyrambs. Of his poetry nothing has survived.
Lesky, *Greek Tragedy*, 32–4.

ARIOVISTUS King of the Suebi who invaded Gaul in *c.* 72 BC. He defeated the powerful Gallic tribe of the Aedui. Though the Roman Senate recognized him as "king and friend of the Roman people", Caesar roundly defeated him in 58 BC (Caesar. *BG* 1.31–33). A. left Gallia and died before 54 BC.

ARISTAEUS A Greek minor god or hero, son of Apollo and Cyrene, daughter of king of the Lapiths. He was first brought up by the Centaur *Chiron and subsequently was taught the arts of healing and sooth-saying by the Muses. The myth was related in the 9th Pythian Ode of *Pindar. Virgil recounts how A. pursued Eurydice, Orpheus' wife, who was bitten by a snake and died. The punishment he received was that all his bees died. Upon the advice of his mother he sacrificed cattle to the nymphs; nine days later he found swarms of bees in the carcasses (*Georg.* 4. 315–558). In one version A. was the father of *Actaeon. He was worshipped in Thessaly, Boeotia, Cyrene, and elsewhere.

ARISTAGORAS Son of Molpagoras, ruled Miletus in the absence of the tyrant *Histaeus, his father-in-law. Following the failure of the Persian expedition which he had recommended against Naxos, he instigated the Ionian revolt in 499 BC. He was denied help at Sparta, but, at his request, Athens and *Eretria sent 20 and 5 ships, respectively, for the war against Persia. In this respect he was responsible for the great wars between the Persians and

the Greeks. Before the collapse of the revolt he left for Thrace where he fell in battle (Herodotus 5).

ARISTARCHUS (1) A Greek astronomer and mathematician, native of Samos, pupil of *Straton of Lampsacus who lived *c.* 310–230 BC. A. is famous as "the ancient Copernicus". He accepted the view that the earth rotates on its own axis and he proposed the hypothesis that the sun rests unmoved while the earth, Mercury, Venus, and other planets revolve in circles about it. The treatise in which he put forward his heliocentric theory is not extant and, in fact, the theory is known because of its chance mention by Archimedes (*Sand Reckoner*, 4–5). The only extant work of A. is *On the Sizes and Distances of the Sun and Moon*. On the basis of certain hypotheses he calculates by trigonometrical ratios the sizes and distances of the moon and sun. But there are errors in the hypotheses and the results are wrong, e.g. the diameter of the sun is found to be between 18–20 times that of the moon.
T. L. Heath, *Aristrachus of Samos,* 1913.

ARISTARCHUS (2) A prominent Greek scholar, native of Samothrace, lived *c.* 217–145 BC. *Aristophanes of Byzantium was his teacher. Subsequently he was tutor of *Ptolemy VII Eupator, and became head of the Alexandrian Library *c.* 153 BC. He left Alexandria in 145 upon the return of *Ptolemy VIII Physcon. He died soon after in Cyprus. As a scholar A. was interested in grammatical matters and especially in literary and textual criticism. Among his pupils were *Apollodorus (6) and *Dionysius Thrax. Though A. was mainly interested in Homer, he also dealt with a considerable number of other poets: Hesiod, Archilochus, Alcaeus, Anacreon, Pindar, Aeschylus, Sophocles, and Aristophanes. A. prepared editions of the texts of the ancient poets and wrote commentaries. Specific problems were dealt with in special treatises. For his textual criticism A. used special critical signs, still known, to note spurious verses, confused passages, etc. His main principle was that only a careful study of the usage of Homer in matters of forms, metre and language could serve as a safe guide for criticism. The extant Scholia of Homer depend largely on his work.
M. Frazer, *Alexandria,* 1, 462–7, 2, 667–675.

ARISTEAS A native of the island Proconnesus in the Marmora, said to be a servant of Apollo and author of a poem on the *Arimaspoi. Herodotus is the first to mention him (4.13). He was able to separate the soul from the body and to appear in two places at the same time; he accompanied Apollo in the shape of a raven.
J. P. D. Bolton, *Aristeas of Proconnesus,* 1962.

ARISTIDES (1) Son of Lysimachus, a prominent Athenian statesman during the first half of the 5th century. He supported *Cleisthenes (2) and in 490 BC took part in the battle of Marathon. Next year he was eponymous *archon. He apparently opposed the plan of Themistocles for Athenian naval expansion and was ostracized in 482. After the decree of general amnesty he returned in 480, took part in the battle of Salamis and as *strategos* commanded the Athenian contingent at Plataea in 479. He subsequently played a leading role in the building of the Athenian empire. As commander of the Athenian fleet in 478, he established good relations with the Ionian cities against the Spartan king, *Pausanias (1). The following year he was chosen to determine the yearly contributions of the members of the newly instituted Delian League. He died *c.* 467 BC. A. gained fame as an honest and just man in contrast to the cunning Themistocles.
Plutarch, *Aristides.*

ARISTIDES (2) Native of Miletus, lived c. 100 BC, known as the author of a collection of stories, under the title *Milesika*. The work, containing strong erotic elements, was used by later writers (e.g.. *Petronius, *Apuleius). It was translated into Latin by *Sisenna, but neither the source nor the translation has survived. *Milesia fabula* became a name for erotic stories.

S. Trenkner, *The Greek Novella in the Classical Period*, 1958, 172–7.

ARISTIDES (3), P. Aelius A Greek rhetor and writer, born in AD 117 in Mysia in Asia Minor. He studied under *Herodes Atticus in Athens. During a visit to Rome in 143 he was attacked by an illness from which he suffered periodically for the rest of his life. Consequently, he used to seek a cure at the temple of Asclepius in Pergamum and usually lived in Smyrna. Through his public lectures and speeches as well as his writings he gained extensive fame. He probably died c. 187. His extant works include 55 speeches, two treatises on rhetoric, and Sacred Teachings (*ieroi logoi*) in 6 books. His address *To Rome* is a laudatory speech for the achievement of the Roman Empire. His writings are important for the study of social conditions in his time, as well as for his personal religious experience.

C. A. Behr, *Aelius Aristides*, 1968.

ARISTIDES (4) QUINTILIANUS The author of à three book work *Peri mousikes* ("On Music"). A Neoplatonist, he probably lived in the late 3rd or 4th century AD, but no details of his life are known. His work is theoretical and deals with harmonics, rhythms and metres (1st book), the role of music in education (2nd book) and the connection between music and the physical world (3rd book).

ARISTOBULUS Greek historian, citizen of *Cassandreia. His work, whose title is not known, dealt with Alexander the Great in whose expedition against Persia he took part as a technician. *Strabo and *Arrian used his work, which is not extant.

L. Pearson, *The Lost Histories of Alexander the Great*, 1960, 150–187.

ARISTODEMUS Son of Aristocrates, nicknamed *Malacos* ("the Effeminate"), native of *Cumae who checked the advance of the Etruscans in Campania in 524 BC. He helped the Latins defeat the Etruscans at Aricia c. 505 BC. He used his popularity with the army and the people to overthrow the aristocrats and become tyrant of Cumae (Dion. Hal. 7.2–11). But c. 492 BC the aristocrats returned to power and killed him.

Alföldi, *Early Rome*, 50ff.

ARISTOGEITON and HARMODIUS Two young Athenians of an old family who conspired to kill the tyrants *Hippias and Hipparchus in 514 BC for personal reasons. They succeeded in killing Hipparchus only; Harmodius was killed instantly by Hippias' bodyguards, and his companion was tortured and executed (Herodotus 5.55; Thuc. 6.54–7). Later, after the overthrow of the tyrants in 511/10, the sculptor *Antenor was commissioned to make bronze statues of A. and H. and after these were carried away by the Persians in 480, a second group was made by *Critius and Nesiotes. Roman copies of their statues are extant. At Athens they were also honoured by annual sacrifices and were considered as liberators.

T. R. Fitzgerald, *Historia*, 1957, 275–286.

ARISTONICUS Illegitimate son of Eumenes II, king of Pergamum. After Attalus III willed his kingdom to Rome upon his death in 133 BC, A. organized a popular revolt against the new masters. His revolutionary social program appealed to the lower classes, the "have-nots", the native population and the slaves, against the well-to-do classes of the cities. The name of the new state was to be *Heliopolis* ("Sun City"). After initial successes against the Romans he was defeated and put to death at Rome.

Magie, *Asia*, 150–159.

ARISTOPHANES The greatest Greek comic poet. Only few biographical details are known about him. Born c. 450 BC he wrote his first comedy in 427. He was in Athens during the Peloponnesian War and although his plays reacted to contemporary politics, it is not known whether he took active part in the war. It is difficult to form a clear idea of his political convictions on the basis of remarks and attacks upon the politicians of his day in his extant plays. Apparently the constitutional revolutions of the time, oligarchic and democratic, did not affect him adversely. He died c. 385 BC.

A. is the only writer of the Old Comedy from whom some plays have survived. Eleven plays are extant and, in addition, over thirty titles of other plays are known. Due to his popularity, some hundreds of quotations are extant from the plays that have not survived. The extant plays are the following:

Acharnians, produced in 425, won first prize in the *Lenaea. It concerns the private peace treaty that the hero concludes with Sparta in opposition to public opinion.

Knights, produced in 424, won first prize at the Lenaea. It is a savage attack on *Cleon who loses his popularity in the Demos to a man who defeats him in his own vices.

Clouds, produced in 423, placed third in the *Dionysia. It deals with the differences between a father and his son who adopts new ideas. These ideas are represented by Socrates, who is ridiculed and to whom all the absurdities of the Sophists are ascribed.

Wasps, produced in 422, won second prize in the Lenaea. It takes its theme from – and ridicules – the avidity of the Athenians to serve in the jury-courts.

Peace, produced in 421, won second prize in the Dionysia. The hero flies to Olympus where he rescues the girl, Peace, from War and marries her.

Birds, produced in 414, won second prize in the Dionysia. Two Athenians, disgusted with their city, convince the birds to build a new city in the air, and one of them becomes its king.

Lysistrate, produced in 411. The Athenian and Spartan women decide to compel their husbands to restore peace by refusing to have sexual relations with them.

Thesmophoriazousai, produced in 411. The Athenian women, while celebrating the *Thesmophoria*, are preparing to attack Euripides, who manages to escape with his friend.

Frogs, produced in 405, won first prize in the Lenaea. Inasmuch as Athens is short of poets, Dionysius descends to Hades to bring Euripides back, but finds Aeschylus to be a better poet and fetches him instead.

Ecclesiazousai, produced probably in 391. The women take over the government of the city and replace private property by communal ownership.

Plutus, produced in 388. The blind, and hence erring, Plutus ("Wealth") is cured and as a result, just and unjust people get what they deserve.

As a playwright A. has a genius for creating fantastic scenes and an outstanding talent in parody and satire. He is a master of language and composes passages of all types: comic, serious, absurd, real, solemn and trivial. He

aims at amusing the spectators and to this end employs every means at his disposal. The subjects of his plays are based on actual life but set in an imaginary world. He depicts and ridicules the politics, social attitudes, philosophy and poetry of Athens of his time. All kinds of men are his victims: prominent figures, politicians, poets, philosophers (e.g. Cleon, Euripides and Socrates), and ordinary people. The Athenians apparently enjoyed his plays, which does not mean that they seriously accepted A.'s social and political criticism. In structure and choice of topics A.'s plays are representative of the Old Comedy. Later plays herald the transition to the Middle Comedy which is manifested in the decline of choral songs.
G. Murray, *Aristophanes*, 1933;
V. Ehrenberg, *The People of Aristophanes*[2], 1951.

ARISTOPHANES of Byzantium   Son of Apelles, a prominent Alexandrian scholar, born *c.* 257 BC. He studied in Alexandria and became Head of the Library *c.* 195 BC following the death of Eratosthenes. He died in 180 BC. His scholarship was very extensive and included textual criticism, grammar, linguistics, literature, and comprehensive studies of accentuation. His edition of the works of Homer was by far superior to the work of his predecessors but was eclipsed by that of his pupil, *Aristarchus (2). He also edited the works of Hesiod, Alcaeus and Alcman, and was the first to collect and publish — in 17 books — the poems of Pindar. He also worked on the tragedians, preparing an edition of Euripides and writing introductions, of which there are extant some short versions, to plays of Aeschylus, Sophocles, and Euripides. In the sphere of comedy, he prepared an edition of Aristophanes and wrote a treatise on Menander. The arrangement of the dialogues of Plato in trilogies is also ascribed to him. In his grammatical work he introduced the accents and breathings, and used the principle of analogy to establish the Greek declensions. His *glossai* (or *lexeis*) were studies of certain terms in Greek dialects with examples of their usage in literature. Of his works only fragments are extant.

ARISTOTLE   The outstanding Greek philosopher and scholar, son of Nicomachus, native of Stagira in Chalcidice; born 384 BC, died 322 BC. His father, a physician, had friendly relations with the Macedonian king, Amyntas II. In 367, at the age of 17, A. joined the Academy of Plato in Athens where he studied for almost twenty years. In his later years he was able to work independently on his research. Following the death of Plato in 347, A., who could not agree with the predominance of mathematics in the school, went to stay with Hermias, who ruled *Assos and Atarneus in Mysia. There he married Pythias, Hermias' niece, and upon the death of Hermias went to Mytilene, where his friend and pupil *Theophrastus lived. In 343/2 he was invited by Philip II to educate his son, Alexander. Literature and politics were probably the main subjects. A.'s tutorship ended in 340 when Alexander became regent for his father.

In 335 A. came to Athens and founded his own school there. It was near Mt. Lycabettus in a grove of Apollo Lyceius. The *Peripatetic School, as it was known, was primarily a research institution. Under A. and his prominent pupils (Theophrastus, Aristoxenus, Eudemus), research work was done in various fields: politics, astronomy, botany, physics, music, mathematics etc. The school had a large library. Alexander contributed financial support to it. He also helped A. by ordering that all interesting natural phenomena observed by hunters and fishermen throughout his empire should be forwarded to A. In 323 A. was accused of *asebeia* (impiety) and left Athens for Chalcis where he died the following year. After the death of his wife he had lived with Herpylis, who bore him a son, Nicomachus, and in his will — given by Diogenes Laertius (5.11.21) — provided for both of them and his daughter, as well as for his slaves.

The extant works of A. were not written for publication, but rather as an aid in his lectures and teaching. Therefore, important points are not always fully developed. On the other hand the published works of A. have all been lost. Also lost are the collections of materials A. used as preparation for his systematic treatments of various subjects — except for the *Athenaion Politeia*. These collections included records of victories at Olympia and Delphi (*Olympionicai, Pythionicai*), outlines of the constitutions of 158 Greek states (*Politeiai*), barbaric customs (*Nomima*), details of the dramatic performances at Athens (*Didascaliai*), etc. There is a tradition that A.'s writings, left to Theophrastus, were hidden by Neleus of Scepsis, and it was only in the early 1st century BC that they were edited (Strabo 13.54). The manuscripts were brought to Rome by *Sulla in 84 BC, and at some time later new editions were prepared.

A.'s curiosity drove him to extend his philosophical and scientific studies over various and numerous fields. His works in logic include the following: *Prior Analytics, Posterior Analytics, Topics, Sophistici Elenchi, De Interpretatione,* and *Categories* (certainly not written by A.). A. claims that he was the first to begin the systematic study of argumentation. He dealt with definitions and proofs, deductions and judgement and introduced the study of logical propositions. His main achievement here was the development of the system of syllogism.

His ethical works include the following: *Ethica Eudemeia, Ethica Megala, Ethica Nicomacheia.* The list of his works in natural science is lengthy: *Physics, De Caelo, De Generatione et Corruptione, Meteorologica, De Anima,* a collection of small treatises known as *Parva Naturalia, Historia Animalia* (not all books are by A.), *On Parts of Animals, On Generation of Animals, Metaphysics.* In these studies A. laid the foundation for the sciences of zoology, anatomy, and physiology. How many facts of natural history were known before his research and how much he discovered by his own observations cannot be known. But his precise, minute and comprehensive descriptions and the systematic treatment of the subjects transformed mere information into science. And yet errors do appear in his works: the salamander that walks through fire, goats that breathe through the ears, etc. Of his work in politics, the systematic treatment *Politica* and the *Athenaion Politeia* are extant. His earlier works, *About Colonists, On Monarchy, Politicus,* are not extant. In the *Politica,* based on historical studies of constitutions, A. examines the various forms of government and political education. Here he also treats the institution of slavery, finding it to be natural for certain people, namely, the barbarians. The earlier rhetorical works of A. were lost but his main work *Rhetoric* is extant. It deals with argumentation, persuasion and questions of style. Only part of A.'s *Poetics* is extant. Here, too, the theoretical section was based on studies of samples of poetry. Most famous is the conception of tragedy as based on imitation and associated with a catharsis of feelings of fear and pity.

Although A. was a pupil of Plato, he developed views and ideas in opposition to those of his teacher, even during the time he studied in the Academy. Generally speaking it may be said that his aversion to mathematics and preference for biology symbolized the broad and profound differences between his philosophical and scientific studies and those of Plato. Influenced by Ionian science, his interest lay in the study of the natural world surrounding him. As a result he made little contribution to the sciences of mathematics, physics, and astronomy. His sensitivity to realities possibly restricted his imaginative power. In his attempt to learn about the natural world, A. established the scientific method: first, to collect the data by careful observation and meticulous work, then to arrange and classify them according to rational criteria. Only by so doing can one learn and understand natural phenomena. This method of work characterizes his work in political science, in drama and, of course, in biology. His sense of order, common sense and reality did not call on him to adopt extreme views, thus he was able to adopt positive elements from conflicting theories.

A.'s serinal contribution to and influence upon scientific thought and scholarship was immense and manifold. It was said of him that "he set in order all parts of philosophy". It was he who laid the foundation for research work, and its exposition in the framework of defined branches of science. He established the model for the correct treatment of a scientific subject: by definitions and assumptions, by classification and orderly arrangement of the material, and by careful progress from one theme to its successor. The terminology in philosophy is to a large extent that invented by A. The separation of mathematics from philosophy, which occurred after his time, is frequently attributed to his negative influence. Concerning style, his earlier works, which were written as dialogues of set speeches, served as the model for the philosophical treatises of Cicero. Concerning drama, the rule of the unities of time, place and action erroneously ascribed to A. persists in modern times. His works on zoology, anatomy and physiology were canonized during the Middle Ages and thus prevented advancement in these sciences up to the beginning of the modern era.

D. J. Allan, *The Philosophy of Aristotle*, 1952; W. D. Ross, *Aristotle*[3], 1955; I. Düring, *Aristotle*, 1966.

ARISTOXENUS Important Greek musicologist and philosopher, native of Tarentum, born before 360 BC. His father gave him his initial musical education. He left his home city, lived for some time in Mantinea and Corinth and later came to Athens. There he studied under the Pythagorean Xenophilus and subsequently became a pupil of Aristotle in the Lyceum, who helped him to continue his studies in music. Though A. was much appreciated, Aristotle preferred to appoint Theophrastus to succeed him as the Head of the Peripatetic School. No details are known of his later life, not even the date of his death.

A. is said to have written an enormous number of books (453), all of which except for two have been lost. The titles of many of the works are known and include a variety of subjects: history, politics, education, biography, etc. But his main subject was music and more than half a dozen titles are known. The two extant works are: *Elements of Harmonics* in three books. In fact it consists of part of two works: *Principles* and *Elements*. Among the questions that are discussed in the book are: intervals and combination of intervals, modulation, and composition of melody; and *Elements of Rhythm* of which only the second book of the original work is preserved. For the understanding of A.'s theory of music, the extant works

of Plutarch (*On Music*), Cleonides (lived 2nd century AD and wrote *Introduction to Harmonics*) and *Aristides Quintilianus are important. A. describes systems (scales) that are based on tetrachords, differentiated keys and types of octaves, and recognizes *genera* and colours of tetrachords. There are deficiencies, and at times the descriptions are not clear, but it seems that A.'s system, though not perfect, presented a competent account of Greek music.

H. Macran, *Aristoxenus,* 1902; E. A. Lippman, *Musical Thought in Ancient Greece,* 1964.

ARMENIA A country east of Asia Minor bordering on Media in the east, Mesopotamia in the south, Cappadocia in the west, and Colchis and Iberia in the north. The Tigris and Euphrates draw their sources from A., where the ancient kingdom of Urartu (Ararat) was located. The Armenians are first mentioned by Herodotus (3.93). The country is described by Xenophon (*Anab.* 4.2–3) and more fully by Strabo (11.14). It was under Median and Persian rule and formed a separate satrapy. In the Hellenistic period it belonged to the Seleucid Empire, but after the defeat of *Antiochus III by Rome in 189 BC the native king Artaxias asserted his independence. He built the capital city Artaxata (modern Artashat) and ruled what was to be known as Armenia Maior, the area east of the Euphrates. The aggressive policy of his descendant, *Tigranes, led to Roman intervention in the persons of *Lucullus and *Pompey. From that time on, Rome fought Parthia first and later the Sassanid kings over the suzerainty of the country. The area west of the Euphrates, bordering on Pontus in the west, was known to the Romans as Armenia Minor. From the time of Pompey it was governed by client-kings until Vespasian annexed it to the province Cappadocia.

ARMIES, GREEK The earliest Greek A. known to us is that described by Homer, purported to be that of Mycenaean times but surely including elements of later times. Under the general command of Agamemnon, a poetical image rather than historical reality, each of the Greek leaders brought his own troops to the war against Troy. The army seems to have consisted of two elements: the kings and their vassals and the masses of soldiers, who depended on the former for social and economic reasons. Obviously only the former were fully armoured; the main parts of the armour were a long sword, a spear, a shield shaped like a figure eight and a helmet. The chieftains would come to the battlefield in chariots but fight on foot.

A characteristic feature of the classical *polis was that it had a citizen-army. Physically able citizens of over 18 (but under 60) were liable for military service with their own equipment. This meant that the rich served in the cavalry and as *hoplites, others as lightly armed soldiers. Until the rise of the *Peltasts in the 4th century BC, and the development of the cavalry by *Philip II and Alexander, Greek A. were to all intents and purposes hoplite armies. Military training attained high standards in *Sparta. The Spartan army consisted of Spartan citizens, *perioekoi*, and helots who were enlisted only in exceptional circumstances. In the early 5th century BC Sparta could send to the battlefield several thousand Spartan hoplites who were organized in territorial units (first five, later seven). But as the numbers dwindled in the course of the Peloponnesian War and thereafter, Sparta had to depend more and more on the *perioekoi* and helots. The army was usually commanded by the kings. Military training and

Above: Wall painting of a bull fighter — Cnossos.
Below: The "Throne of Minos" — Cnossos

The "Lily Prince" — stucco relief Cnossos

Above: Wall painting of a bull fighter — Cnossos.
Below: The "Throne of Minos" — Cnossos

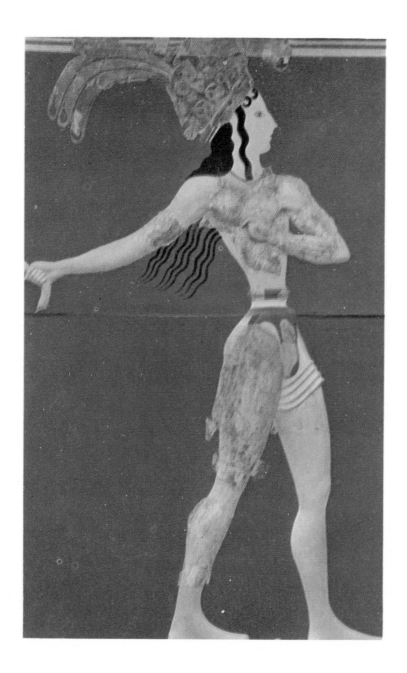

The "Lily Prince" — stucco relief Cnossos

service began at Athens at the age of 18, later developed into the system of the *Epheboi. The infantry consisted of ten units, one to each of the ten tribes established by *Cleisthenes (2) and the cavalry of two units, each one to five tribes. In the early 5th century BC the command of the army passed from the *Polemarchus to the *Strategoi. Both in Sparta and in Athens, as well as in other Greek cities, permanent armies were too expensive to be constantly maintained; hence the size of the actual army varied according to the actual needs.

The heavy hoplites of Classical Greece knew only one kind of fighting — shock tactics. If more troops were available, the line of the battle was extended or given more depth. There was no use of reserve forces. The side which could persist in fighting more than the other would win the battle. As long as fighting went on casualties were relatively low, the main losses were incurred when one side broke and fled in an unorganised retreat. However, the heavy armour and lack of cavalry limited the number of casualties.

The 4th century BC witnessed important changes in the Greek A. as well as in their methods of war. The deterioration of economic conditions and decline of the Greek cities brought about the ever increasing use of mercenaries. *Iphicrates showed that *Peltasts could match hoplites in certain conditions. *Epaminondas introduced new tactics, the central idea of which was to concentrate the main offensive effort in one wing (the left in his case) while the other one held back. This was followed by Philip II and *Alexander (4) under whom the *phalanx became fully developed. But the main novelty was the use of cavalry. In several of Alexander's battles the phalanx sustained or pushed back the attack of the enemy while the cavalry played a decisive role by developing its attack from the flank and thus led to the general rout. It was also these two who developed siegecraft which until then had relied heavily on blockades or surprises. Siege techniques now included artillery machines, mining, scaling ladders, siege-towers, and mobile sheds.

The armies of the *Diadochi and the Hellenistic kingdoms were mainly mercenary armies. Training was thorough and specialized. Armies now consisted of heavy infantry in the phalanx, lightly armed infantry, slingers, archers, and lightly and heavily armed cavalry. Elephants, encountered by Alexander in India, were a new element, first introduced by *Seleucus I. Peculiar conditions influenced the military systems of the three great Hellenistic kingdoms. The Macedonian army was mainly based on national service, though manpower shortage led to the employment of mercenaries. The Ptolemaic army consisted of "Macedonian" soldiers, who received plots of land from the king and were called to military service as and when the need rose (*Cleruchy); of mercenaries and, from the battle of Raphia (217 BC), of native Egyptians. The Seleucid kings depended more heavily on native soldiers from their various provinces. Here, too, the military settlers were the backbone of the phalanx, and of course use was made of mercenaries. Indeed, even the Greek cities and the main leagues, of *Achaea and *Aetolia, had to resort to mercenaries. However no new tactics were developed and the lack of flexibility, from which the Hellenistic phalanx suffered, proved disastrous in encounter with Rome. See *Hoplites, *Peltasts, *Phalanx.

H. W. Parke, Greek Mercenary Soldiers, 1933;
F. E. Adcock, The Greek and Macedonian Art of War, 1957;
A. M. Snodgrass, Arms and Armour of the Greeks, 1967.

ARMIES, ROMAN Rome had a citizen-army from early times. All physically able citizens over 17 were liable for military service based on their property qualification. The wealthier, registered in upper classes (*Census), served as heavy infantry with full armour, which included a thrusting spear (hasta), a round shield (clipeus), a helmet (galea), a coat of armour and greaves. Those in the lower classes served as lightly armed troops, while *Proletarii were not normally recruited. Traditionally, the army numbered 6,000 at the end of the early Monarchy as well as 1,800 cavalry. This force was divided into two units with the establishment of the Republic: each to one of the two consuls who thus commanded one *legion. With the growth of the Roman state and population in the 4th century BC, a consular army normally consisted of two legions. Roman allies, the Latins and the Italian socii, had to contribute contingents whose number was fixed in their treaties with Rome. At the early 4th century pay was introduced to the Roman army, and at the same time the well-to-do could serve as horsemen (*Equites).

The archaic Roman army fought in close ranks like the Greek phalanx. In the course of the 4th century, and in consequence of the encounter with the Gauls and the *Samnites, the Romans developed the manipular system, which was more flexible than the older system. The army was organized now for battle in three lines, the first of the hastati, the second of the principes, the third of the triarii, and each line consisted of small units, company-sized (manipuli), of which there were thirty to the legion. In addition there were the velites, lightly armed troops, who normally would open the battle. The maniples in the second line were stationed behind the gaps between the maniples of the first line, and those of the third line behind the gaps in the second line. Each man in the first two lines had a throwing spear (pilum), a long shield, oval or rectangular (scutum) and a double-edged sword for close fighting (gladius). The gaps between the lines and within the lines between the maniples made the Roman legion better fitted to fight in difficult terrain than the phalanx. But it was not flexible enough for rapid manoeuvres as was proved in the Second Punic War. This led to the emergence of the *Cohors as a tactical unit within the legion in the course of the 2nd century BC. After *Marius it became a standard unit, and Roman commanders, notably Caesar, showed great skill and tactical talent in adapting their order of the battle to topographical conditions.

The impoverishment of the small farmers in the 2nd century BC caused a shortage in military manpower. The agrarian law of Tiberius *Gracchus (2) and the lowering of the minimum census qualification for military service were not enough to cope with the problem. *Marius was the first to accept proletarian volunteers, and this became the main method of securing manpower in the 1st century BC; still conscription was occasionally used. Theoretically, the principle was to raise an army only to meet specific needs; practically, the establishment of provinces since the second half of the 3rd century resulted in keeping standing armies in several areas, notably Spain and Macedonia. A distinct characteristic of the last half century of the Republic was the armies of Roman statesmen, mainly composed of volunteers, nominally state armies, but practically private ones, as the soldiers were attached to the general from whom they expected to receive donatives, bounties, and plots of land on their discharge.

The military reforms of *Augustus consolidated the

Roman battering-ram to breach walls

changes that had taken place in the last century of the Republic. The army consisted now of 28 legions (25 after the destruction of 3 legions by *Arminius in AD 9), whose soldiers were Roman citizens, and of a corresponding number of troops recruited from the non-citizen population of the Empire, the *Auxilia. The nine cohorts of the *Praetorians formed a special force, concentrated at Rome by *Sejanus. The standing armies in the provinces were stationed in permanent camps. Legionaries served 16 years and, from AD 6, 20 years, Praetorians 12 years and, from AD 6, 16 years; and those in the *Auxilia* 20 years and, from AD 6, 25 years. Legionaries had an annual pay of 225 denarii (fixed by Caesar), which was raised to 300 by Domitian, to 500 by Septimius Severus and 750 by Caracalla. The annual pay of the Praetorians of 375 denarii was raised by Augustus to 750, and by Domitian to 1,000. The minimum pay of the infantry in the *Auxilia* was 75 denarii, raised to 100 by Domitian.

In the early Principate, Italy — mainly Cisalpine Gaul — was still an important recruiting area; later, however, the bulk of the army was recruited in the provinces. The extension of Roman citizenship, which eventually was conferred on all the provincials by *Caracalla, made the distinction between the legions and the *Auxilia* obsolete; the latter disappeared in the 3rd century AD. The system established by Augustus worked well in the 1st and 2nd centuries AD. But the lack of imperial reserve, in addition to the provincial armies stationed close to the frontiers, was felt already in the 2nd century and proved fatal in the 3rd century. *Diocletian sought to solve the difficulties by increasing the number of legions to sixty. *Constantine worked out a better solution by establishing a standing army near the frontiers and a separate mobile army which could be used wherever and whenever the need arose. See *Auxilia, *Cohors, *Equites, *Legio, *Praetorians, *Tribuni Militum.

H. M. D. Parker, *The Roman Legions*[2], 1958; R. E. Smith, *Service in the Post-Marian Roman Army*, 1958; G. Webster, *The Roman Imperial Army*, 1969; P. A. Brunt, *Italian Manpower*, 1971.

ARMINIUS Son of Segimer, chieftain of the *Cherusci, born *c*. 18 BC. A. was educated at Rome, served in the army, fought under Tiberius in Germany, and received Roman citizenship. However in AD 9 he annihilated the three legions of P. Quinctilius Varus at the Saltus Teutoburgiensis. This defeat led Augustus to abandon the conquest of Germany to the Elba. From AD 15 A. fought the attempts of *Germanicus to renew the conquest. Subsequently his own men killed him (AD 19).

ARPINUM (modern Arpino) A town of the *Volscians in the Liris valley, situated on a hill. Rome took it from the *Samnites in 305 BC and gave it *civitas sine suffragio*. It received full citizenship in 188. Cicero and Marius were natives of A.

ARRETIUM (modern Arrezo) Etruscan town at the higher part of the Arno valley. At least from the 3rd century BC on it was under Roman control. It received Roman citizenship in 89 BC and Sulla established a *colonia* there. It had a thriving bronze industry and was famous as a centre of pottery manufacture.
Scullard, *Etruscan Cities,* 165—7.

ARRIANUS, Flavius Greek historian, native of Nicomedeia in Bithynia, lived in the 2nd century AD. A. studied under *Epictetus whose lectures he preserved. He embarked on a senatorial career and was suffect consul in AD 130. As governor of Cappadocia he repelled the invasion of the *Alani. Later he lived in Athens and died after 170. His military treatises and histories of Bithynia, Parthia, and the *Diadochi have been lost. His main extant work is the history of Alexander in 7 books known as *Anabasis*. His main source was *Ptolemy I but he also used *Aristobulus. It is a plain account free from sensational and romantic stories, and is the best source for Alexander's achievement. His *Indica* is a description of India based on *Megasthenes and *Nearchus.

ARRUNTIUS, Lucius Wealthy Roman statesman, consul in AD 6, said by Augustus to be capable of governing the Empire. Though appointed governor of Nearer Spain, he was kept by Tiberius in Rome for many years. He committed suicide in AD 37 when charged with high treason and adultery.
Syme, *Tacitus,* 380—2, 442—4.

ARSACES I The founder of the Parthian empire. He established his kingdom in opposition to the Seleucid empire in 247 BC, and ruled until 210 BC. The Parthian kings used his name as a title.

ARSINOE (1) The name of several Hellenistic queens.
1. A. I, daughter of *Lysimachus and Nicaea and wife of Ptolemy II. Ptolemy III and Berenice, wife of *Antiochus II, were her children. She was banished to Coptus in 279 BC because of a conspiracy against her husband.
2. A. II, daughter of Ptolemy I and Berenice I, born *c.* 316 BC. She was married to *Lysimachus *c.* 299 BC. After her husband's death in 281 she married her half-brother Ptolemy Ceraunus. When he killed her sons she escaped to Egypt in 279, and about two years later married her younger brother, *Ptolemy II. She wielded a great deal of power and during her time the Ptolemaic empire expanded at the expense of the Macedonian and Seleucid kingdoms. By 272 BC she and her husband were deified as *theoi adelphoi*, and after her death a cult was instituted for her. The Fayûm was named Arsinoites after her.
3. A. III, daughter of Ptolemy III, married her brother, Ptolemy IV, and took part in the campaign of Raphia (217 BC). She was murdered about the time of her husband's death in 205 BC.

ARSINOE (2) The name of several Hellenistic cities.
1. The main city of the Fayûm, known as Crocodilopolis. There are still considerable extant remains, and many papyri of the Ptolemaic and Roman periods have been found there.
2. An important port city on the Gulf of Suez, founded by Ptolemy II.

Mould for Arretine vases of the late 1st century BC with a signature of Pilemo

ARTABANUS The name of several Parthian kings.
1. A. III ascended to the throne in AD 12 after a revolt against the former king, Vonones. He tried to take control of Armenia by putting his son on the Armenian throne *c.* AD 34, which led to Roman counter-measures. Subsequently he had to flee twice from his kingdom. He died *c.* AD 39.
2. A. V., the last Parthian king *c.* AD 213—27. He was defeated and killed by the Sassanid *Artaxerxes (2) I.

ARTABAZUS Son of Pharnabazus, the Persian satrap of Hellespontine Phrygia at the time of *Artaxerxes II. He revolted against Artaxerxes III and had to flee to Macedonia in 352 BC. Later he returned and served *Darius III well, but after the latter's death he was reconciled with Alexander, who appointed him satrap of Bactria. He died *c.* 325.

ARTAVASDES I Son of Tigranes, king of Armenia, who cooperated with the Parthians against Crassus in 53 BC. In 36 Antony invaded his kingdom and captured the king in 34. A. was brought to Alexandria and was executed in 31 BC by Cleopatra.

ARTAXERXES (1) The name of several Persian kings.
1. A. I, son of Xerxes and Amestris, ascended the throne after the murder of his father in 464 BC. He gave shelter to *Themistocles and under A. the Athenian intervention in Egypt ended in complete defeat. In 449 the peace of *Callias was concluded with Athens. He died in 424 BC.
2. A. II, son of *Darius II and Parysatis, succeeded his father in 404 BC. During his time there was a marked decline of central power in the empire despite some military success. He defeated the revolt of his brother *Cyrus (2) in 401 and drove back the Spartans from Asia Minor where his authority was established by the peace of *Antalcidas in 386 BC (the "King's Peace"). Egypt, however, was in a state of revolt for a long period and, in addition, he faced a revolt of satraps (366—358). He died *c.* 358 BC.
3. A. III, son of A. II, succeeded to the throne in 358 BC, executed his brothers and put an end to the revolt of the satraps. He also succeeded in reconquering Egypt in 343. By his vigorous policy the power of the central government was restored. His minister, Bagoas, murdered him by poisoning in 338 BC.

ARTAXERXES (2) The name of several kings of the new Persian Empire. A. I. (AD 211/2—241), descendant of Sasan, founded the new Empire. He first established his rule in Persepolis and then increased his power by defeating the last Parthian king, *Artabanus V, and conquering the whole of Iran, Mesopotamia, Armenia and Afhganistan.

ARTEMIS Greek goddess, daughter of Zeus and Leto and sister of Apollo. Originally she was a pre-Hellenic deity, probably Minoan. The name is attested in a Mycenaean document. For the Greeks she was the everlasting virgin, an inaccessible maiden, a devoted huntress, a lady of wild animals (*Potnia Theron*), of forests, hills and beasts. Under her special protection were girls before nubility. In the myths her companions were virgins. *Actaeon, who dared look at her when she was bathing (or even tried to rape her) was torn to pieces. Another tale was that she killed *Orion, the lover of *Eos, and yet another that she killed *Niobe for her impiety. She also killed Coronis for her infidelity to *Apollo. Callisto, one of her nymphs, was seduced by Zeus in the form of a bear, and the goddess, according to one version, killed her in her wrath, though later she appeared as the Great Bear. But *Calliste* ("the most beautiful") was a title applied to

Artemis and Apollo pursuing a giant depicted as hoplite. From the Siphnian treasury house in Delphi

A. herself, and it seems that at an earlier stage she was a mother goddess. One of her functions was to help women in childbirth; thus her nature was double, giving life and taking it.

The cult of A. spread all over the Greek world, and in many places she was a city-goddess. Beasts, goats and birds were sacrificed to her. The maidens who participated in her Attic festival at Braunion were termed *arktoi* ("she-bear"), an allusion to A.'s connection with the Great Bear. In some places her cult showed traces that human sacrifices had once been made for her. It appears that the spread of her cult was carried out because of her identification with ancient local goddesses. At Sparta she was called A. Orthia (Orthia had been an ancient Dorian goddess). In Asia Minor the Great Mother Goddess was known also as Great Artemis. Her most important cult was at Ephesus with its famous Artemisium. In Greece she was sometimes identified with *Selene, a moon goddess, and *Hecate, a chthonian goddess. Outside Greece her most famous identification was with the Italian goddess *Diana. In art she frequently appears from the 7th century on often as a huntress with her bow and arrows.
Guthrie, *The Greeks and their Gods*, 99—106.

ARTEMISIA (1) I Daughter of Lygdamis of Halicarnassus. She ruled that city, and others as well, in the role of guardian of her son. She participated in Xerxes' invasion and fought at Salamis but succeeded in escaping (Hdt. 7.99; 8.68; 87—8).

ARTEMISIA (2) II Sister and wife of *Mausolus whom she succeeded on his death *c.* 353 BC. She conquered Rhodes and won everlasting fame by building the *Mausoleum.

ARVERNI A powerful Gallic tribe of Aquitania who inhabited what today is known as Auvergne. They are thought to have invaded Italy in the 6th century BC (Liv. 5.34). In the 2nd century their kingdom extended from the Rhone to the Ocean, but their king, Bituitus, was defeated by Rome in 121. It was their king Vercingetorix who led the great Gallic revolt against Caesar in 52 BC. Their main city was Augustunemetum (Clermont-Ferrand).

Fragment of votive relief showing sacrifice at an altar of Asclepius; Piraeus, 4th century BC

ASCANIUS Son of Aeneas in Greek and Roman mythology. In an early version his mother was Eurydice; according to Virgil, she was the Trojan Creusa (*Aen.* 2.666) and, in yet another version, Lavinia, Aneas' Latin wife. Latin writers also called him Ilus or Iulus and he was considered to be the ancestor of the *gens Iulia*. He succeeded his father and later founded *Alba Longa. Romulus was one of his descendants.
Ogilvie, *Livy,* 42–3.

ASCLEPIADES (1) Prominent Greek poet of the early 3rd century BC, a native of Samos. He was also called Sicelidas. A. antagonized *Callimachus by his praise for *Antimachus. He revived the love epigram. With his friends, the poets Posidippus and Hedylus, he published a book of epigrams. The Asclepiad metres (already used by Alcaeus and Sappho) are named after him. At least forty of his epigrams are preserved in the *Anthologia Palatina.
W. and M. Wallace, *Asclepiades of Samos,* 1941.

ASCLEPIADES (2) Native of Prusa in Bithynia, famous physician in Rome during the 1st century BC. In philosophy, he was a follower of Epicurus and supported the atomic theory. In his medical practice, he advocated diet and practised surgery.

ASCLEPIUS (Latin Aesculapius) Greek hero who became the god of healing and medicine. In Homer he is still regarded as a mortal physician, who was taught his art by *Chiron (*Il.* 2.732). In a myth, related by *Pindar (*Pyth.* 3), he is the son of Apollo and *Coronis. A.'s first sanctuary was at Tricca in Thessaly; from the 5th century BC on, his cult began to spread throughout the Greek world. A.'s main place of worship was at *Epidaurus but other centres were founded at Athens (420 BC), Cos and *Pergamum (4th century BC). At *Epidaurus and *Pergamum, impressive temple complexes (*aesculapia*) have been excavated. In Rome, the cult was introduced in 293 BC, on the advice of the Sybilline books. On the whole, almost 500 places where A. was worshipped are known. A.'s cult was connected with the netherworld and his sanctuaries included round structures (*tholoi*) in which sacred snakes were apparently kept. The usual method of healing consisted of the sick sleeping in the temple; the god appeared to them in their sleep and indicated the method of treat

ment, which included the use of baths, gymnastics and dietetics. The effectiveness is proved by the numerous offerings representing sick limbs, which have been discovered at Corinth and Pergamum. As the god who cared for the health of the individual, A. remained popular throughout the Hellenistic period and under the Roman Empire. The cult of A. was connected with that of his daughter, *Hygieia, goddess of health. A. was identified with many eastern gods, such as Serapis or Imuthes in Egypt, and Eshmun in Phoenicia. A. is represented as a bearded man, resting on a staff around which a snake is wound; this latter symbol has become that of the medical profession.
Guthrie, *Greek Gods,* 242–254;
Festugière, *Personal Religion,* 84–105;
C. Kerényi, *Asklepios* (Eng. trans.), 1961.

ASCONIUS PEDIANUS, Quintus A Latin scholar, native of Padua, born in 9 BC, died in AD 76. He is best known for his commentaries on Cicero's orations, part of which is extant. This includes the commentaries on some of Cicero's speeches which are not extant (*Pro Cornelio, In Toga Candida, Pro Scauro*).

ASCULUM PICENUM (modern Ascoli Piceno) The main town of Picenum, situated near the Adriatic. It was conquered by Rome in 268 BC. The revolt of Rome's Italian allies in 90 BC started there.

ASIA In Homer, A. refers to the interior of Anatolia. With the advance in the Greek knowledge of the eastern countries, A. came to designate that part of the world east of the Mediterranean, the Red Sea and the Black Sea, separated from Europe by the river Ṭanais (Don). There was no clear idea of the boundaries between the lands south and east of Egypt, and Ethiopia was believed to extend to India. More exact knowledge was acquired following the conquests of Alexander the Great.

A. was the name Rome gave to the province organized in 129 BC upon the former kingdom of Pergamum, which was bequeathed to her by the will of *Attalus III who died in 133. It consisted of almost the whole of west Asia Minor with the adjacent islands, though some modifications of territory took place in the course of time. On the east it bordered on Cilicia and Galatia, and on the north on Bithynia. A. was the richest province of the Roman Empire during the Republican period. The provincial population suffered heavily from exploitation by Roman magistrates and businessmen, especially the *Publicani* to whom the collection of the taxes was assigned by Gaius *Gracchus. Their hatred was evidenced in 88 when they took advantage of the temporary success of *Mithridates VI to kill an alleged 80,000 Romans and Italians. *Sulla imposed fines and levies which immersed the native population in debt. They suffered additional fines, confiscations and seizure of their treasures during the civil wars of the last Republic at the hands of Pompey, Caesar, Brutus, Cassius and Antony.

Peace and normal life were restored to the province only with the final victory of Augustus over Antony. According to the settlement of 27 BC, A. became a senatorial province, governed by a proconsul under whom were a quaestor and three legates. For administrative purposes it was divided into districts, but the cities, the most important of which were Ephesus and Pergamum, retained a large degree of local autonomy. The restoration of peace and the control maintained over Roman governors by the emperors (the *Publicani* were no longer employed) led to the prosperity of the province under the Empire, especially in the 2nd century. *Dio Chrysostom and Aelius *Aristides as well as numerous inscriptions supply ample evidence of the social life of the province and of the extensive participation of the citizens in municipal affairs and imperial administration. Still there was a gulf between the prosperous, Hellenized society of the cities and the native population in the country. A. suffered from the same problems that disrupted economy, culture and society throughout the Empire in the 3rd century. It ceased to exist as a province under Diocletian who divided it into seven provinces.

Magie, *Asia.*

ASPASIA Native of Miletus, famed as Pericles' mistress, or second wife, after he divorced his first wife. She bore him a son named Pericles who received Athenian citizenship (to which he had no right since she was a foreigner) by a special decree in 429 BC. In 406 he was executed as one of the commanders responsible for the failure to save the Athenian soldiers at the Battle of Arginusae. An intelligent, cultured woman, A. associated freely with intellectuals, e.g. Socrates. She apparently had influence on Pericles, and was attacked as responsible for the war against Samos (Plut. *Per.* 24—5) and for the Peloponnesian War (Aristoph. *Ach.* 516—539). To embarrass Pericles, she was charged with impiety and procuring but Pericles won her acquittal in court. After the death of Pericles in 429 she married Lysicles who was killed the following year. Socrates' pupils commemorated her name in their writings.

ASPENDUS (modern Balkesu) A Greek port city in Pamphylia on the Eurymidon, allegedly founded by Argos. It was mainly under Persian rule in the 5th—4th centuries BC; later, it came under Ptolemaic and Seleucid rulers. It became free following the defeat of *Antiochus III by Rome in 189 BC. Impressive remains of public buildings are extant.

ASSOS A Greek city on the Gulf of Adramyttium in the Troad, founded by settlers from Methymna in *Lesbos. At one time it had been an important station for those who wished to avoid the hardships of the voyage along the western Troad. From the 6th century BC on it was usually under the control of foreign rulers: Croesus, Per-

sia, Athens, Alexander and his successors and Pergamum. Aristotle stayed in A. at the court of *Hermias in 347—345. In 133 BC it came under Roman rule. Extensive excavations in 1881—3 revealed the city to have been well planned, with some fortifications.

G. M. Cook, *The Troad,* 1973, 240—250.

ASSYRIA The name of the ancient kingdom of A. in the Upper Tigris was applied by Greek and Roman writers to cover the northern part of the region today known as Iraq. Following the conquests of Persia by Alexander and the wars of the *Diadochi, it was included in the Seleucid Empire. With the disintegration of the Seleucid Empire, the kingdom of *Adiabene arose in A. It was under Parthian control. A temporary province of A. was organized by Trajan in 116 BC, but was soon evacuated by Hadrian.

A. T. E. Olmstead, *A History of Assyria,* 1923.

ASTERIA A titaness, whose name means "starry", A. was the sister of *Leto and the mother of *Hecate. During her flight from Zeus, she turned into a quail and fell into the sea, becoming the floating island Ortygia ("quail"), later Delos.

ASTRONOMY Astronomical observations and studies were first made by Greeks for practical reasons. The rising and setting of certain constellations and stars marked the various agricultural seasons, witnessed as early as Hesiod (*Erg.* 609ff.). Astronomical data were also important for the regulation of the calendar. Some astronomical knowledge was received from the Babylonians, including the notion of the Zodiac, and presumably records of eclipses. *Thales allegedly predicted a solar eclipse (of 28 May 585 BC(?)), found the pole with the help of the Little Bear and wrote works *On the Equinox* and *On the Solstice.* All these discoveries, however, are extremely dubious. Speculations and theories on the structure of the universe were proposed by several pre-Socratic philosophers. *Anaximander was the first to suggest a mechanical model of the heavenly bodies, which he envisaged as three rings of fire (for the sun, the moon and the stars), obscured by mist and seen only through apertures; the earth, a flat cylindrical surface, was at the centre of the rings. Some truer notions were shortly advanced. The sphericity of the earth was stated by the Pythagoreans, followed by *Parmenides who also noted that the moon received its light from the sun. In the 5th century BC the Athenian astronomer Meton suggested quite an accurate system to correlate the lunar month with the solar year in a 19 year cycle to which he added 7 intercalary months amounting to 6,940 days (actually one day extra in every four cycles). It was also observed that the four seasons are of unequal lengths. That the earth was not the centre of the universe was suggested by Philolaus of Croton, a Pythagorean of the late 5th century; according to him the earth, the sun, the moon and the planets were circling round a central fire, Hestia.

Important advances were made by astronomers of the 4th century. It was Plato who defined the aim of A. as to give a mathematical account of the motions of the planets. The assumption was that the irregularities of the movements of the heavenly bodies were only apparent, while in reality the movements were regular and circular. In other words, the problem was to find out how the regular, circular movements of the planets combined to give the observer on earth the impression of irregularities. Indeed to explain the "*phaenomena*" remained the essential problem of A. for many generations down to the 17th century AD. The problem was complicated by the assumption that the earth was in the centre of the world. The solution of *Eudoxus of Cnidos was that the stations and retrogradations of the planets were the result of the circular movements of concentric spheres (four to each of the five planets: Venus, Mercury, Mars, Saturn, and Jupiter, three to the sun and the moon, and one to the fixed stars). However, his theory of "homocentric spheres" failed to give an account of the retrogradations of Venus and Mars and other phenomena. Callipus of Cyzicus (second half of the 4th century BC) tried to save the theory by adding two more spheres to the sun and moon and one more sphere to Venus, Mercury and Mars. He also corrected the 19 year cycle of Meton by proposing a 76 year cycle of 940 months with 27,759 days. Aristotle accepted the corrections of Callipus and sought to work out a mechanical model with continuous spheres (47 or 56).

In contrast to the prevailing theories, *Heraclides Ponticus developed the doctrine that the earth rotates round its axis and, probably, that Venus and Mercury circle round the sun and the earth. More important was the theory of *Aristarchus of Samos who suggested the heliocentric theory. Though the evidence is meagre, it seems that he suggested that all the planets (including earth which rotates on its axis in 24 hours) move round the sun which remains at rest at the centre of the universe. However, the theory was probably not based on mathematical calculations and seemed to be contradicted by the astronomical observations. As a result it had no adherents.

A more successful attempt to explain the apparent irregularities of the heavenly bodies was made by *Apollonius of Perge in the late 3rd century BC. He did not differ from Eudoxus in the two main notions: that of regular circular movements of the stars and that of the earth resting at the centre. His theory assumed movements in eccentric circles or epicycles of the sun, moon and planets. The first hypothesis suggested that the planets moved round circles whose centre was at some distance from the earth (hence eccentric), and thus accounted for the inequality of the seasons and for variations in what seemed the distance of the sun. The retrogradation and stations of the planets were explained by the epicyclic hypothesis: each planet revolved round a circle the centre of which moved round the circumference of a different circle in the centre of which rested the earth. In principle *Hipparchus of Nicaea followed him; he accepted his account of the sun, gave himself more precise account of the moon's movement, yet felt the need of more precise information on the movements of the planets. Indeed he devoted himself to astronomical observations which to some extent had been done by Eudoxus and *Autolycus (1). He prepared a catalogue of stars (over 800) and discovered the precession of the equinoxes. Though Claudius *Ptolemy followed his predecessors by accepting the geocentric theory, he used the epicyclic accounts to produce satisfactory, practical exposition of the movements of the heavenly bodies. His work represents the essence of ancient A.: the prediction of the positions of the heavenly bodies at a given time, including retrogradations and other phenomena. His system, expounded in his *Almagest*, was to dominate astronomical science throughout the Middle Ages.

While A. sought to give a mathematical account of the movements of the heavenly bodies, its corollary astrology sought to discover the influence of the celestial phenomena on happenings on earth. In particular it attempted to predict the fate of the individual according to the position of the stars when he was born or conceived. It had its origin in Mesopotamia and it was only in the Hellenistic period, with the influx of the Greeks to the East, that it was introduced into Greek science. The belief in astrology spread quite rapidly and was very popular under the Roman Empire. It was not only the common people who accepted it; scholars, scientists and philosophers, not to mention Roman emperors, considered astrology to be a valid science. Ptolemy wrote a four-book work on the subject, *Tetrabiblos*, still extant, and even physicians used it for practical purposes. Still, some astrological activities, as the prediction of someone's death, were forbidden by Roman emperors. The triumph of Christianity soon led to the outlaw of all divination.

O. Neugebauer, *The Exact Sciences in Antiquity*[2], 1957; D. R. Dicks, *Early Greek Astronomy to Aristotle*, 1970; C. E. R. Lloyd, *Greek Science after Aristotle*, 1973; F. H. Cramer, *Astrology in Roman Law and Politics*, 1954; O. Neugebauer — H. B. Van Hoesen, *Greek Horoscopes*, 1959.

ASTURES The tribes inhabiting the northwestern part of the Iberian peninsula who were conquered by Augustus in 26—19 BC. The A. owned many gold mines and horses. Their main city was Asturica Augusta (modern Astorga).

ASTYANAX A. ("protector of the city") was the other name given to Scamander, Hector's and Andromache's younger son (*Il.* 6.402—3). He was killed by *Neoptolemus or Odysseus. The scene of his death was depicted from the Archaic period on.

ASTYNOMOI Officials in Greek cities who were responsible for order in the streets and had general control of public and private buildings (Arist. *Pol.* 1321 b). Ten A. were elected annually in Athens. They had the power to impose fines and, in some states, they participated in the administration of festivals, harbours and markets.

ASYLIA A citizen of a Greek city who was wronged by a citizen of a second city might seek remedy by seizing the property of any other citizen of the second city. Greek cities at times legitimized this method of seeking remedy against each other. An exemption from such a seizure of property, given to individuals or to an entire state, was called A. A. was also the right of inviolability conferred on sanctuaries. People could seek "asylum" in such sanctuaries.

ATALANTA An Arcadian heroine, daughter of Iasios and Clymene. A.'s father, who wanted a son, abandoned her on a mountain. She was protected by a she-bear until she was found by hunters who raised her to be a formidable huntress. Skilful in the use of the bow, A. once killed two Centaurs who attacked her. She took part in the voyage of the *Argonauts and in the Calydonian boar-hunt. She also wrestled with Peleus. A. refused to marry — being the best runner, she offered potential suitors the opportunity of beating her in a foot-race. If she won, she would kill them with her arrows or spears. All failed and died until her cousin Melanion — who was given three golden apples by Aphrodite — made her stop to pick up the apples during a race and beat her. They coupled in a place sacred to Artemis who punished them by turning them into a lion and a lioness. In another famous version, *Meleager (1) was her lover and she bore him Parthenopaeus. The same myth was related in Boeotia, with Schoenus as her father and Hippomenes as the winner. It appears that A. was, in fact, a twin of Artemis, the great virgin huntress. As a huntress with great athletic prowess, A. began to appear on works of art during the Archaic period.

Kerényi, *Heroes*, 116—120.

ATARGATIS The goddess of Hierapolis Bambyce in Syria, known in the Greek-Roman world as *Dea Syria* (the "Syrian Goddess"). Other centres of her cult were in Baalbeck, Damascus, Palmyra and Dura Europus, but the one in Hierapolis was the wealthiest and most famous. It was pillaged by *Antiochus IV and *Crassus (4). *Lucianus described A.'s cult in the 2nd century AD, in his *dea Syria*. From the 3rd century BC on, her cult spread to the Hellenistic world and was found in Greece, Macedonia, and Egypt, and, later, in a few places in the Balkans and in Italy. Hadad was her consort and at Hierapolis they were known as Zeus and Hera; A. was identified with Aphrodite.

ATE In Homer, the daughter of Zeus who was thrown from Olympus to earth and sought to cause damage to mankind (*Il.* 19—90ff.). In Hesiod, she is the daughter of *Eris and Dysnomia (*Theog.* 230). In her original form, she personified infatuation.

ATELLANA FABULA A popular farce of Oscan origin, named after Atella, a Campanian town near Capua. A. was introduced to Rome, perhaps at the beginning of the 3rd century BC, and it developed into a literary genre by the end of the 2nd century BC. The A. had stereotyped characters, such as *Maccus* and *Bucco* (fools), *Pappus,* and *Manducius.* There was much room for improvisation by the actors. Grotesque situations and obscene language characterized the A. The literary genre came under the influence of the Greek New Comedy.

W. Beare, *The Roman Stage*[3], 1964, 137—142.

ATESTE (modern Este) A city of the *Veneti in the Po valley. It dates from the early 1st millenium BC. Rome took control of the area in 184 BC and Augustus' veterans settled here. It was the most important centre of trade and commerce in Venetia and its products were marketed across the Alps.

ATHAMAS Son of *Aeolus (1), brother of *Salmoneus and *Sisyphus. His tale was told in various versions, e.g. he founded Halos in Thessaly and was also a king in Boeotia. His first wife, the goddess Nephele, "the cloud", bore him two children, Phrixus and Helle. When A. left her and took Ino, daughter of *Cadmus, as his second wife, Nephele punished the country with a drought, but according to another version it was Ino — moved by jealousy of her step-children — who moved the women to roast the seed-corn. When it consequently failed to grow, A. consulted the Delphic Oracle which was persuaded by Ino to say that the children of Nephele were to be sacrificed. But Zeus, or Nephele, sent the marvellous golden-fleeced ram to save Phrixus and Helle from A. They flew on the ram's back, but Helle fell into the strait thenceforth named *Hellespont. Phrixus arrived at Colchis where he married Chalciope, the daughter of King Aietes (*Medea was a second daughter). He sacrificed the ram to Zeus Phryxios and gave the fleece to Aietes. Later, A. was driven mad by Hera because Ino reared Dionysus, and he killed his own son, Learchus. Ino fled with her second son, Melicertes. She leapt into the sea and became the goddess Leucathea. In addition to the motif of the wicked stepmother, the tale alludes to a ram being sacrificed as a substitute for a human. At Halos, the eldest members of the family claiming descent from A. were sacrificed to Zeus Laphystios if caught trespassing in a certain sacred building.

ATHENA The Greek goddess of war, personification of wisdom, and patroness of the arts and crafts. There is much evidence, philological, mythological and other, to show that she was originally a pre-Hellenic deity. Some would attribute Oriental origin to her. The name *a-ta-na-po-ti-ni-ja* is attested to in a tablet from Cnossos written in Linear B (*JHS* 1953, 95). The Acropolises of many cities — including those at Argos, Troy, Troezen, and Epidauros — were sacred to her. Citadels had been the place of abode of the rulers in the Bronze Age, and it appears that A. was the Mycenaean goddess who protected them.

A. was the subject of various myths, several of which concern her birth. Hesiod (*Theog.* 886—900) tells that Zeus took Metis ("wise council"), daughter of Oceanus and Tethys, as his first wife. She bore him the owl-eyed girl Tritogeneia. But he was told that the boy she was to bear would be the king of gods and men alike. Therefore Zeus seized Metis, who was then pregnant with A., and swallowed her. As a result, he suffered from a terrible headache; he gave birth to A. when Hephaestus, or Prometheus, smote his skull with a double axe. A. is said to have sprung forth from his forehead wearing golden armour, and shouting a battle cry. In another tale, her father Pallas, a winged goat-like giant, wanted to violate her but she defeated him and stripped off his skin, which she wore. According to another tale, she once played the war game with Pallas, daughter of the river Triton. To help her, Zeus gave her his fearful goatskin, the Aegis, and A. indeed killed her play-mate. A. then erected a statue to her victim — the Palladion — around which she put the Aegis. Some stories connected A. with Hephaestus, who wanted her to be his wife. But when he tried to couple with her, she vanished and his semen fell to the earth. From this semen, Earth (otherwise called Chthon) gave birth to Erichthonies (*eris* means strife). A. took care of the infant, who later became king of Athens and established the cult of A. there. In one tale, she contested the possession of Attica with Poseidon. She gave the country the olive-tree, and a divine court supported her claim.

One of the many surnames of A. was *Pallas*, which could mean either a strong young man or a maiden (cf. the myths above). She was regarded as virgin and was hence styled *Parthenos*, but curiously she was also called *Meter* ("mother"), probably in reference to the goddess of mothers. The various epithets expressed her qualities: *Glaucopis*, "owl-eyed", *Gorgopis*, "gorgon faced", *Hygieia*, "health", *Pronoia*, "providence", etc. War was one of A.'s most important functions, as was proper for one who was born armed. Homer makes her take an active part on the side of the Greeks in the Trojan War. She was in a special sense a city goddess who protected her people; hence, her names *Polias* and *Poliouchos*. A. also gave ample protection to her favourite heroes — Odysseus, Diomedes and Perseus. Her epithet, *Ergane*, emphasized her function as protectress of crafts and craftsmen, especially smiths, spinners and weavers. In many Greek cities, A. was, if not the main, at least an important deity, though her position at Athens is the best known one. Her sacred bird, the owl, became a symbol for the city. Among other goddesses with whom she was identified, Minerva is the best known.

A. frequently appears on artifacts from the 7th century on, usually in character as a war-goddess, fully armoured. Favourite themes depict the manner of her birth and her part in the battle against the Gigantes.

Nillson, *Religion*, 485—500; C. J. Herington, *Athena Parthenos and Athena Polias*, 1955.

Stele of Athena, a relief of the mid-5th century BC

ATHENAEUS (1) A physician who attended the lectures of *Posidonius and founded a Pneumatic school of medicine in Rome during the 1st century AD. Well versed in philosophy, he was imbued with Stoic ideas. According to his view, the *pneuma*, one of the basic qualities, governs the body whose main organ is the heart. He advocated dietetics for curing disease. Of his extensive work, a considerable number of fragments are extant.

ATHENAEUS (2) A native of *Naucratis, the author of a work entitled *deipnosophistai*, "the banquet of the learned". The work describes a symposium at which the participants discuss literature, philosophy, history, medicine and other subjects. The host is a Roman knight, Larensis, who was presumably A.'s patron. Fifteen books of this work, which probably numbered considerably more, are extant, as is an Epitome. The work is important because of its numerous references to works which have not survived.

ATHENS (Athenai) The city-state of the district of Attica. The city itself is situated at the southwestern part of the Attic plain, about 5 km from the Saronic Gulf. The Athenians regarded themselves as autochthonous and claimed that the colonization of Ionia had been carried out by their city. Athenian myths commemorated the times when A. was only one of the communities of Attica, and attributed their union (*synoecismus*) into one city-state to *Theseus. Yet it seems that *Eleusis was incorporated as late as the 6th century BC. Archaeological evidence confirms that the *Acropolis of A. was a centre

of Mycenaean civilization, and tradition and philological evidence support the view that A., as a centre of united Attica, successfully survived the political upheavals of the late Bronze Age and the invasions of the Dorians. It also seems probable that A. was an important centre for the Ionian emigration dating from the end of the 2nd millenium BC.

What happened in A., and elsewhere in Greece, up to the end of the Dark Age (8th century BC), is scarcely known. A. was ruled by kings, traditionally the descendants of the legendary *Codrus. At the close of this period, the power of the kings declined and the monarchy was replaced by an aristocracy, whose members became the chief new magistrates (*Archontes). Social and economic problems led to attempts to seize power and to reforms dating from the latter half of the 7th century BC. The failure of *Cylon to seize power *c.* 632 was followed by the "constitution" of *Draco which did not introduce significant changes. Civil strife led to the election of *Solon as archon and law-giver in 594. His measures included cancellation of debts, release of peasants from serfdom, redemption of those serfs sold abroad, and prohibition of loans involving the person of the debtor as security.

He also established the popular court of *Heliaea and gave further powers to the *Ekklesia. Although his measures were later considered as the beginnings of democracy in A., they were not at the time extensive enough to end the social agitation which was used by *Pisistratus to re-establish tyranny *c.* 545. The tyranny of Pisistratus and his sons lasted until 510 BC when they were expelled by a revolution of the aristocrats supported by Sparta.

The overthrow of the Pisistratids was followed by an internal struggle for power from which *Cleisthenes (2) emerged victorious. In his reforms, he ensured the development of democracy in A. His new tribes served as the basis for the administrative and political system under which the power of the aristocrats rapidly declined; at the same time, the sovereignty of the people became manifest through the rise of Cleisthenes' *Boule, the Ekklesia, the *Strategoi and the institution of *Ostracism. The *Areopagus and the Archontes lost power and influence. And after the reform of *Ephialtes, democracy was fully developed in A. The main democratic principle was the sovereignty of the Ekklesia, which not only discussed and decided on all questions but also controlled the execution of its decisions by the state officials. A corollary characteristic was the right of every citizen to speak and propose motions in the Assembly (*parhesia*), to be elected to virtually any state office, and to serve in the courts. Election was in most cases by lot. Democracy in A. meant that the people were the true rulers of the state and each citizen had a share in the government of the state; it was thus that freedom and equality were established in the city.

The rise of this democracy continued with the growth of the state as an imperial power. A beginning had been made by the conquest of *Salamis in the early 6th century and the occupation of some areas abroad under *Pisistratus. In 498 BC, A. sent a fleet of twenty ships to support the unsuccessful Ionian revolt. This led to invasions of Greece by the Persians, in whose defeats A. played a decisive role at the battles of Marathon (490), Salamis (480), Palataea and Mycale (479). A. profited from the unpopularity of *Pausanias (1), and from Sparta's unwillingness to commit herself in wars abroad, to establish

Air view of the city of Athens with the Acropolis in the upper part and the temple of Zeus (Olympieum) in the front

the Delian League in 478–477. Its aims were to liberate the Greek cities from Persian rule and to seek reparations for the damage done by the enemy. The League had its centre at Delos and, at its meetings, each member had one vote. It comprised the Greek cities of Ionia, the Hellespont, the Propontis and the Aegean islands. Each member contributed a certain number of ships or an annual tribute. From the beginning, however, A. played a leading role. The ten treasurers (*hellenotamiai*) and the commander of the league's forces were from A. Under Athenian leadership, the League drove the Persians from Europe and from the west coast of Asia Minor to Caria. The Athenian commander, *Cimon, who frequently commanded the forces, won a crushing defeat over the Persian forces on land and sea at the mouth of the Eurymedon *c.* 467 BC. In 460, A. sent an expedition to Cyprus and then to Egypt in order to support the revolt of the native prince, Inarus, against Persia. The Athenians, however, did not succeed in following up their initial successes; more Persian forces arrived, and finally, in 454, the entire force in Egypt was captured by the enemy. In 450, Cimon sailed again with a strong force to recapture Cyprus, but he died, and the following year *Callias concluded a peace with Persia.

According to the terms of this peace, Persian forces were not to operate in the western part of Asia Minor from *Phaselis to the Black Sea, and the Greek

cities there were to be autonomous. The settlement brought about a profound change in the relations between A. and her allies, which in the past had been typified by ominous events. A. forced Carystus in Euboea to join the League *c.* 472, and Naxos to remain in it *c.* 467. In 463, she severely punished Thasos following the failure of its revolt. These incidents showed that the allies were not free to leave the League. After 449, A. pursued the same policy, though the main aims of the League were achieved by the peace of Callias. In 454–453, following the Egyptian disaster, the treasury of the League was transferred to A. Under the leadership of Pericles, A. used the surplus money for her public building. All the allies, except for Samos, Chios and Lesbos, now paid tribute without contributing ships. *Cleruchies were founded on lands confiscated in allied territories. The allies had to use Athenian coins, measures and weights and to apply to courts in A. in cases involving death, exile and loss of rights.

In 440 BC, Samos, who dared to oppose A., was subdued after a long siege. A. took Samos' fleet, razed its walls to the ground and forced it to pay a heavy fine. The Attic-Delian League became an Athenian empire.

For some years A. also held a land empire in Greece proper following her war with Corinth and Aegina which began in 459 BC. A.'s defeat by Sparta at *Tanagra in 457 was followed, a few months later, by victory over Boeotia at

Oinophyta. Aegina was forced to join in the Delian League, Phocis was won and Euboea, too, came under A.'s hegemony. In 450, Cimon arranged a five-year truce with Sparta. But in 447 the Boeotians freed themselves by defeating an Athenian army at Coronea; this led to the revolts of Megara and Euboea and to the invasion of Attica by Sparta. Pericles succeeded in negotiating the evacuation of Attica and the conclusion of a thirty-year peace with Sparta in 446—445. A. had to give up her expansionist ambitions in central Greece, but she re-imposed her control over Euboea. The peace lasted until 431 BC when the apprehensions of Sparta and her allies regarding the ever-increasing power of A. caused the outbreak of the *Peloponnesian War. The period represented the zenith of A.'s power. After twenty-seven years, the war ended with the complete defeat of A., who lost her empire and a substantial part of her population. She had to demolish the *LongWalls and to maintain a fleet of no more than twelve ships; a narrow oligarchy, known as the Thirty Tyrants, was imposed on her.

But A. showed remarkable vitality. In 403 BC, the democracy was restored. With the help of Persia, *Conon defeated the Spartans at *Cnidos. And by 393, A. had rebuilt the Long Walls and her fleet. A. recovered her independence and, joined by other Greek cities, went to war against Sparta. This ended with the Peace of *Antalcidas. Opposition to the tyrannical behaviour of Sparta helped lay the foundation of a Second Athenian League with A.'s former allies in 377. This time A. undertook not to send garrisons and *cleruchies and not to interfere with the internal affairs of her allies. Generally, A.'s policy now aimed at maintaining a balance of power, and for several years she opposed Sparta. The latter was defeated at Leuctra (371) and later at Thebes. But in 358—356 many of A.'s allies seceded, and soon thereafter A. faced the rise to power of Philip II of Macedonia. The Athenian statesmen disagreed on the right policy to pursue with regard to the Macedonian king, and A. lost her positions one by one. The final attempt to check the king, made under Demosthenes' leadership, was crushed at the battle of Chaeronea (338). A. was now forced to join the Hellenic League by Philip at Corinth. After the death of Alexander, A. tried again to oust the Macedonians from Greece; the Lamian War of 323—322 ended in A.'s complete defeat. Thenceforth, A. could not only not maintain a dominant place in the Greek world, but was in fact under foreign control. There was a Macedonian garrison in *Munichia from 322 to 229 BC when A. regained her freedom. She was no longer politically important. In 87 BC, A. made the mistake of supporting *Mithridates VI and, after a siege, was captured by Sulla.

With the extensive excavations and the evidence from available literary sources, it is possible to trace part of the material development of A. Except for the few remains of some settlement, dating from late Neolithic times (c. 3000 BC), clearer evidence dates from the Mycenaean period. The Acropolis was the centre of life for the rulers of the city and the population which was concentrated around it. The natural citadel was strengthened by massive walls as early as the 14th—13th century BC. The chamber graves found at the *Areopagus apparently served the rulers. Pottery seems to have been a successful trade. There are finds of the protogeometric style (12th century), and in the 9th and 8th centuries A. was a prosperous centre for the manufacture of geometric pottery. In the 7th century, it was replaced by the proto-Attic

style. In the 6th century, the black-figured style appeared, and it was followed by the red-figured style. In the late 7th century, A. began to produce her first coins. She was the only state of mainland Greece to possess silver mines in her territory. The change from simple barter to a monetary economy was too rapid, and was in all probability a major factor in the dispossession of the peasants, their indebtedness and enslavement. This was the background for the reforms of *Solon and the rise of *Pisistratus, both of whom contributed to a remarkable development of the Athenian economy. Foreign traders and artisans were encouraged to settle in A., and peasants were helped by easy loans to cultivate new land. Attic pottery now monopolized the foreign markets. Under the Pisistratids, many public buildings were erected, especially in the *Agora and on the Acropolis, and tremendous advances were also made in sculpture.

The period of extraordinary prosperity which A. enjoyed in the 5th century BC was ushered in by the discovery of a rich silver vein in Laurion. But it was mainly during A.'s political supremacy that her manufacture and trade flourished (although she depended on a foreign supply of corn, mainly from the Black Sea region). Her coins, measures and weights were used everywhere. It was the great period — especially under Pericles — of Athenian sculpture, painting and architecture. Soon after the expulsion of the Persians, Themistocles fortified A. with strong walls (parts of which remain), and communications with Piraeus were later secured by the building of the *Long Walls. The Acropolis and the Agora were the main areas for the new public buildings: the *Parthenon, the *Erechtheum, the *Propylaea, and the temple of *Athena Nike stood in the first area; in the second, the Theseum, the Tholos, the Stoa Poicile, and the Old Bouleuterion were built. These were the more important ones among the numerous public buildings that were erected. A.'s material prosperity was paralleled by the growth of her population which numbered more than 40,000 citizens prior to the Peloponnesian War. Despite the loss of the empire, A. still prospered in the 4th century BC. The state was able to pay citizens for participation in the meetings of the Ekklesia, in the courts and in the theatre (*Theorika). Considerable public building was still undertaken — for example, the massive rebuilding of the old theatre of Dionysus by *Lycurgus (2). To a large extent this was made possible by the efficient financial administration of *Eubulus.

A. was a cultural centre dating from the 6th century BC. Solon himself was a poet. Attic pottery flourished due in large degree to its superiority in artistic design and painting. Tragedy developed with the organization of the *Dionysia by Pisistratus, who also helped with the publication of a definitive written text of the *Iliad* and the *Odyssey*. In the 5th century BC, A. became the main centre of cultural life. The advance of tragedy and comedy, philosophy and historiography, architecture and sculpture, is marked by the great names of Aeschylus, Sophocles, Euripides Aristophanes, Thucydides, Socrates and Phidias. Important thinkers and writers — like Herodotus and Anaxagoras — were encouraged to visit or reside in A. Pericles spoke proudly of A. as the school of Greece (Thuc. 2.41). Philosophy and oratory rose to their highest peaks in the 4th century BC, as is shown by the works of Plato, Aristotle, and Demosthenes, and their schools.

The political fall of A. in the Hellenistic period was reflected in the decline of her letters and arts. A. was still considered as the centre of Greek culture, and the great schools of philosophy continued to function. But except for Epicurus and Zenon (the latter a foreigner), and Menander, who belong to the beginning of the period, no great names can be cited. Because of A.'s fame, foreign rulers — for instance, the kings of Pergamum and the Ptolemies — erected public buildings here. Roman emperors and wealthy persons (e.g. *Herodes Atticus) carried on this tradition under the Roman Empire. Hadrian enlarged the city by building his Hadrianopolis in the southeast of the Acropolis. Although A. suffered at the hands of the Germanic Heruli in AD 267, she subsequently recovered.

W. G. Forrest, *The Emergence of Greek Democracy*, 1966;
V. Ehrenberg, *From Solon to Socrates*, 0000;
Hignett, *Athenian Constitution*,
A. French, *The Growth of the Athenian Economy*, 1964;
I. T. Hill, *The Ancient City of Athens*, 1953.

ATHOS The highest (1,950 m), easternmost mount of the *Chalcidice promontories. The first Persian fleet which came to attack Athens under *Mardonius was destroyed here in a storm in 492 BC. Xerxes dug a canal at the isthmus of A. In 411, a Spartan fleet was destroyed at A.

ATIMIA A Greek term which first denoted general outlawry; it later came to mean the total or partial loss of civil rights in a Greek city. In some cases it was a legal penalty (e.g. for treason and bribery of state officials); in other cases it was a temporary measure. State-debtors recovered their rights with the payment of their debt.

ATLANTIS A very large island which, so the Greeks believed, once existed beyond the Straits of Gibraltar and ruled over much of the western part of Europe and Africa. The ancient Athenians allegedly defeated the attempt of A.'s kings to extend their rule; subsequently A. was destroyed by a terrible eruption of the sea. The story is told by Plato in his *Timaeus* and may have originated in the volcanic eruption on Thera (Santorini) in the 15th century BC. The tale of the lost A. inspired many popular beliefs and stories.

ATLAS In Greek mythology, the Titan who led his brothers in the war against Zeus. His punishment lay in having to carry the sky on his shoulders (the name probably means "one who suffers much"). In the old story (Hesiod, *Theog.* 516–9), A. continued his task in the far west. In one version, *Perseus visits him and turns him into a stone with *Medusa's head; thus he is identified with the high Mount Atlas in northwest Africa. Another tale connected him with Heracles who asked A. to help him fetch the golden apples of the *Hesperides. While Heracles held the sky up, A. got the apples. He then refused to take over the burden again, whereupon Heracles asked him to carry the sky for only a little while, until he could put a cushion on his head. A. agreed, and Heracles took the apples and went away; or else he simply forced A. to take back the sky. A. was said to be the father of *Calypso (*Od.* 1.52), and, more often, of the *Pleiades. The theme of A. supporting the sky was a favourite among artists from early times. In Hellenistic sculpture, A. is depicted on supporting pillars.

ATREBATES The Gallic tribe that lived in *Belgica and was subdued by Caesar in 57 BC and again after a revolt in 51 BC. Their main town was Nemetacum (modern Arras). Part of the tribe migrated to Britain and founded a kingdom whose main city was at Cavella (Chichester).

ATREUS and THYESTES Sons of *Pelops and Hippodameia. They carried a curse either because they had killed Chryssipus, the favourite son of their father, or be-

Atlas carrying the globe above which Victory is standing

Gold mask found in 1876 by H. Schliemann in shaft-grave A at Mycenae

cause Hermes sought to avenge the murder of his son Myrtilus by Pelops. The story has many versions. Aerope, A.'s wife, deceives him by taking T. as her lover. Hermes sends a golden ram on which the kingship depended, and A. keeps it, or its golden fleece. But Aerope secretly gives it to her lover. Then the Mycenaeans are told to take a son of Pelops as their king. T. shows that the ram is in his possession. On the advice of Hermes, A. induces T. to renounce his claim to the throne if the sun turns back on its course. The sun is commanded by Zeus to turn back, and A. succeeds to the throne and sends his brother into exile. Soon thereafter, A. discovers his wife's infidelity. He invites his brother to a reconciliatory banquet, and serves him the flesh of his own children from his incestuous union with Aerope. This makes the sun turn back in horror. When T. realizes what he has eaten, he vomits, and curses his brother's family. In one version, he again succeeds to the throne, and is later exiled by Agamemnon and Menelaus, A.'s sons. In some versions, *Aegisthus is T.'s son and avenger. The "Treasury of Atreus" is the name given to the great tholos tomb discovered in Mycenae, dating from the 14th century BC.

ATRIUM The central area of an Italian house. Archaeological evidence dates the earliest one to *c.* the 3rd century BC. Many A.-type houses have been discovered in *Pompei. The A. opened onto two entrance rooms (*alae*) and gave light to the other rooms about it. When roofed, it had an opening for rain water (*compluvium*) and a basin for collecting the water in the floor (*impluvium*). The latest extant examples of A.-houses date from the 3rd century AD. The name A. was given to several public buildings of which the better known are *A. Vestae* and *A. Libertatis*.

ATTALUS (1) I Son of Attalus, born 269 BC, succeeded his cousin Eumenes I as ruler of Pergamum in 241 BC. He stopped paying the Galatians the usual tribute and, for his victory over them, he received the title *soter*, "saviour". He erected a triumphal monument in Pergamum which included the famous "Dying Gaul". A. followed a vigorous policy against the Seleucid ruler of Asia Minor,

Antiochus Hierax, and for several years (229–222 BC) he controlled most of Asia Minor. In Greece, he supported the enemies of Philip V and warred against him with the Aeolians (in 211–207 BC), and with Rhodes (from 201 BC). In 201 BC, A. also helped Rome to intervene in the Hellenistic world by inviting her to act against Philip V. As a diplomat and a soldier, A. surpassed most of his antagonists. Pergamum became one of the leading Hellenistic states during his time, though it soon became totally dependent on Rome. As a patron of arts and letters, A. helped many Greek cities, notably Athens. He died in 197 BC.

Hansen, *Attalids²*, 26–69 (s.v.).

ATTALUS (2) II Second son of Attalus (1) I, king of Pergamum, born 220 BC, succeeded his brother Eumenes II in 160 BC. Having served his brother faithfully, A. continued a pro-Roman policy. He supported *Alexander Balas against *Demetrius (4) I. For this loyalty, he was given support by Rome in his wars against Bithynia. He was a patron of letters and arts and built the Stoa of Attalus at the Athenian Agora (destroyed in AD 267 and reconstructed in 1956). A. died in 138 BC.

Hansen, *Attalids²*, 130–142 (s.v.).

ATTALUS (3) III Son of Eumenes II, king of Pergamum, born *c.* 170 BC, succeeded his uncle Attalus II (2) in 138

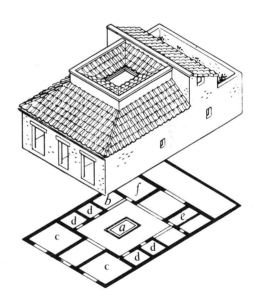

a) *impluvium*
b) *ala*
c) *taberna*
d) *cubiculum*
e) *andron*
f) *triclinium*

Plan of Atrium type house

BC. A. was a man of letters, and wrote on botanical subjects and gardening. He bequeathed his kingdom to Rome. His testament is known from literary and epigraphical evidence. He died in 133 BC.

Hansen, *Attalids²*, 142–150 (s.v.).

ATTHIS This name was applied to works which dealt with the local history of Athens. The name A. was established by the Alexandrian scholars. The forerunner of atthidographers (writers of A.) was *Hellanicus of Lesbos, in the 5th century BC. This kind of literature was in vogue around the 4th and 3rd centuries BC, and was employed by *Androtion, *Phanodemus and *Philochorus *inter alia*. The atthidographers began with the mythological origins of Athens and surveyed the development of religious customs and political institutions. For the Archaic period, they relied on oral traditions.

F. Jacoby, *Atthis*, 1949.

ATTICA The triangular southeastern part of central Greece, bordering on Boeotia in the north, Megrara in the west, the Saronic Gulf in the south, and the Aegean Sea in the east. It formed quite a natural geographical unit as it was closed by Mounts Parnes and Cithaeron on the north and on the west by Mount Cerata. The area of A. was about 2,600 sq km. The plain of A. is dissected by mountains into the Thriasian plain in the west, the plain extending from Mount Parnes to Mounts Hymettus and Pentelicus (*pedion*), the Mesogeia ("central land") in the east, and the plain of Marathon in the north. Its soil was barely arable; in several parts it was suitable for the cultivation of olives, vines and figs. In the south, around Mount Laurium, there were rich silver mines, and good marble and clay were found in the Pentelicus and Hymettus. For the political history of A. see *Athens.

Cary, *Geographic Background*, 75–000.

ATTICUS, Titus Pomponius A Roman businessman and man of letters, born in 110 BC. His father, a rich Eques and a man of culture, gave him a good education. In his early years, A. began a friendship with Cicero that lasted to the latter's death. Cicero's brother Quintus married A.'s sister. To avoid the hazards of the civil wars, A. left Rome in 85 BC, and settled in Athens, where he stayed for about twenty years. His financial affairs prospered and he found time for studies, adopting the philosophical doctrine of Epicurus. His long stay in Athens earned him the surname A. (*c*. 65 BC) and, with other Equites in 63 BC he supported his friend Cicero against *Cataline. This was the only occasion that A. ever took an active part in politics. He helped many leading statesmen, from Marius to Octavian, both financially and by carrying out various transactions. He managed in this

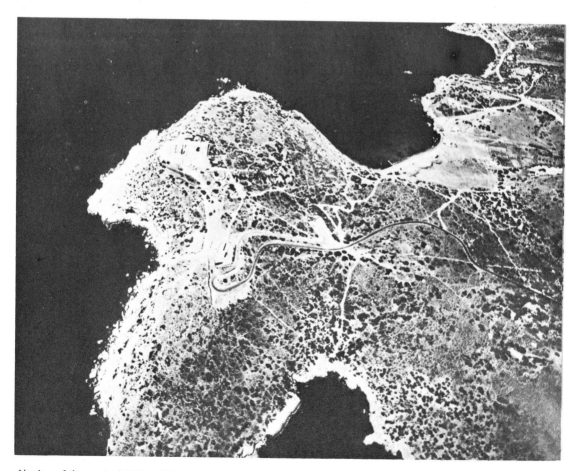

Air view of the coast of Attica with the temple of Poseidon on Cape Sunium in the foreground

Head of Attalus I

way to remain neutral throughout his life. In 58 BC, he was adopted by his very rich uncle Caecilius, from whom he received an inheritance. A.'s best known friend was Cicero, whose banker, administrator and publisher he was. (The extant *Letters to Atticus* of Cicero are the main source for facts on A.'s life.) Other men of note with whom A. had close relations include Hortensius, Lucullus, Caesar, Pompeius, Clodius, Brutus and Cato. A. wrote historical works, among them a *Liber Annalis* — a short chronological account of general and Roman history, and a *commentarius* about Cicero's consulate. None of these is extant. *Agrippa married A.'s daughter. He killed himself in 32 BC.

Shackleton Bailey, *Cicero's Letters*, 1, 3—59.

ATTILA King of the Huns AD 434—53, known as the "Scourge of God". The empire of the Huns extended in his time from the Rhine to the Don, and after A. killed his brother Bleda in AD 445, he was its sole ruler. A. invaded Gaul in AD 451 and was defeated at the battle of the Catalaunian Plains (Châlons) by *Aetius and the Visigoths. The following year, he ravaged Italy, but at the request of an embassy led by Pope Leo the Great, he agreed to withdraw, taking Princess Honoria as his prize. He died in AD 453.

E. A. Thompson, *A History of Attila and the Huns*, 1948.

ATTIS The young consort of the Asian goddess *Cybele. A Phrygian myth tells that the monstrous, androgynous Agdistis murdered and destroyed whatever it liked. At a council of the gods, Dionysus undertook to tame it. He turned a spring into wine, and when Agdistis drank the wine, he fell asleep and castrated himself. An almond tree arose from the torn genitalia. Nana plucked its fruit, put it in her lap, and gave birth to a boy who was named A. Agdistis fell in love with him and drove him mad when he decided to marry. A. thereupon castrated himself and died. Agdistis is in fact Cybele, the Great Mother, and A. is an aetiological figure for her eunuchs. The story was told in many versions. Originally, A. may have been a vegetation god. The death of A. was mourned by the devotees of Cybele. He received official recognition in Rome in Claudius' time, and later changed into a solar god whose followers were assured immortality.

Cumont, *Oriental Religions*.

AUGEIAS Son of Helios, king of Elis, who possessed large herds of cattle. The sixth labour of Heracles was to clear away the filth from his stables in one day. A. agreed to give Heracles his daughter and a tenth of his cattle if he accomplished the task. Heracles did it by diverting the river Alpheus through the stable walls. But A. refused to fulfil his promise and drove Heracles away. Later Heracles returned and killed him.

AUGURES One of the four major priestly *collegia* of the Roman state. Etymologically, the name seems to indicate that they were originally connected with rites of "increasing", or fertility. From the beginning, they were said to be responsible for the interpretation of the will of the gods. To discover the disposition of the gods towards a proposed action, they watched for signs (*auguria impetratiua*) or were told of signs known incidentally (*augurai oblatiue*) Usually, they observed the eating and drinking of the sacred chicken, or the flight of birds in a particular defined area (*templum*), or the running of animals. Thunder or the rustling of a mouse during an observation was considered an ominous sign. The A. were consulted by Roman magistrates before any important public action was undertaken. They gave their interpretation, but it was the magistrates who had to decide whether to proceed with or abandon the action. In early times, private persons could also consult the A. The institution of the A. was attributed to Romulus (Cic. *Rep.* 2.16) or Numa (Liv. 4.4). They at first numbered three Patricians. From 300 BC, there were nine, of which five were Plebeians. Sulla and Caesar increased their number to fifteen and sixteen, respectively.

AUGUSTA Colonies founded by Augustus and other emperors, or cities which received the status of colonies from them.

AUGUSTA (1) RAURICA (modern Augst) A colony founded by L. Munatius *Plancus on the territory of the Raurici in 44 BC, near modern Basel. A. received its title after Augustus had reinforced it. The prosperity of the colony in the 2nd and 3rd centuries AD declined with the destruction wrought by the *Alamanni in AD 259/60 Considerable remains of a theatre, amphitheatre, forum, basilica, temples and dwelling houses are extant.

AUGUSTA (2) EMERITA (modern Merida) A colony for veterans founded by Augustus in the Anas valley. It gained extensive territory, and became the seat of a bishop in the 3rd century AD.

AUGUSTA (3) TAURINORUM (modern Torino) Originally the main town of the Ligurian tribe of the Taurini on the conflux of the Duria Minor and the Po, which became navigable at this point. It was a *municipium* during the late Republic, but Augustus made it a colony.

AUGUSTA (4) TREVERORUM Originally a town of the Gallic *Treveri, later established by Augustus who probably made it a *colonia*. The *colonia* grew and prospered due mainly to its location as a centre of trade. It was the capital of the Emperor *Postumus and remained so under *Maximian and *Constantius Chlorus. In the 4th and 5th centuries AD, it was the residence of the Prefect of Gaul until *c.* AD 430, when it fell to the Franks. The considerable remains include a city gate (*Porta Nigra*), an amphitheatre and baths.

AUGUSTA (5) VINDELICORUM (modern Augsburg) Settlement probably began in the early 1st century AD. As a good centre of trade and communication with Italy, the Rhine and the Danube, it became the main city of *Raetia and the residence of the governor.

AUGUSTALES Officials, in Italian cities and provincial colonies, who were responsible for the performance of the cult of the living emperor. They are first attested to under Augustus. Office was for one year and could be held more than once. Freedmen − to whom other public offices were closed − could win a name by holding this office. They were forced to spend their money on games and rites connected with the cult. There was probably no essential difference between the A. and the *seviri Augustales*.

AUGUSTINUS, Aurelius (Saint Augustine) AD 354−430. Famous Christian writer and thinker, born in Thagaste (Numidia), to Monica, a devoted Catholic. A. studied in his native town and in Carthage, and in AD 373, began teaching rhetoric. He read the *Hortensius* of Cicero in AD 373, and was attracted to the study of philosophy. For nine years, he followed the Gnostic doctrines of the Manichees. Moving to Milan in AD 384, A. was much influenced by Bishop Ambrose. He converted to Catholicism and was baptized in AD 387. He returned to Africa the following year, became bishop of *Hippo (Bône) in AD 355.

A. was a prolific writer and preacher. Several of his works were directed against his former sect, the Manichees. Other works attacked the Donatists, and the views of the Christian thinker Pelagius. He also attacked Scepticism. His *De Trinitate* gives a thorough philosophical exposition of the doctrine of the Trinity. *De Doctrina Christiana* combines Christian learning with the study of the Bible. His best known writings are the *Confessions*, a moving autobiography and a chronicle of his changing convictions before he became Christian, and the *City of God* − occasioned by the capture of Rome by *Alaric − which gave force to the argument that Christianity brought disaster to the Empire. Here he describes the heavenly city as opposed to the earthly one, and gives a theological account of history. In AD 427 he stated that he had written 93 works, 83 of which are extant. For Christianity and western culture, his thinking and writings on philosophical and theological matters are a source of inspiration and significance.

In the Ancient Christian Writers Series there are translations of: *On the Greatness of the Soul* (1950); *Against the Academics* (1951); *On Free Will* (1955); *Sermons on the Psalms* (1960−1).
Note also R. S. Pine-Coffin, *Confessions* (Penguin) 1961; M. Dods, *City of God* (1934); M. Dods, *On Grace and Free Will* (1934); P. Brown, *Augustine of Hippo*, 1967.

AUGUSTODUNUM (modern Autun) The main city of the Gallic *Haedui, founded *c.* 12 BC to replace Bibracte. It had an important school in the 3rd century AD, and was destroyed in AD 269/70 when it revolted in favour of *Claudius Gothicus. The remains include city gates, a theatre and a temple.

Head of a statue of the Emperor Augustus

AUGUSTUS First Roman emperor, born as Gaius Octavius on 23 September 63 BC, adopted by Caesar as C. Iulius Caesar in 44 BC, and given the title A. by the Senate, on 16 January 27 BC. His father C. Octavius, of a wealthy Equestrian family, attained the praetorship, and died in 59 BC. Caesar, the uncle of his mother Atia, had him appointed Pontifex. A. was with Caesar in Spain in 45 BC, and in 44 BC, while studying at Apollonia, he was informed that Caesar had been murdered and that he had been adopted as the main heir in Caesar's testament.

His decision to accept the inheritance, despite the apparent dangers and later warnings and advice of relatives, shows that he was firm in his decision to avenge Caesar, and to secure a dominant political position for himself. He was supported by able friends, *Agrippa (1), *Salvidienus Rufus and *Maecenas, to mention the more prominent, and by the numerous clients of Caesar who were prepared to help the heir. Although only nineteen years old, A. showed himself an excellent politician, capable of conducting negotiations in complicated situations, and of making bold decisions. He was deceptive and knew how to conceal his intentions, and how to use propaganda and other means to gain popularity. Rebuffed by *Antonius (4), he organized a private army by offering large sums of money. With the help of Cicero, he was given the rank of senator and a propraetorian command, in January 43 BC, which legitimized his private army. He fought Antonius at the war of Mutina in which two unfriendly consuls died. In August 43 BC, A. took Rome by force and was made consul. His adoption by Caesar was now officially recognized. He soon made an alliance with *Lepidus (3) and Antonius which (by a law passed on 27 November 43 BC) established the triumvirate. The triumvirs were given extraordinary powers to govern the state for five years.

On 1 January 42 BC, Caesar was officially deified and A. duly became a god's son. In the proscriptions, A. took his revenge on Caesar's enemies, but at the battle of *Philippi, he played an insignificant role. After the battle, he took Spain and Sardinia, and was faced with the task of finding lands for the veterans. This caused much embitterment in Italy and led to the revolt of L. Antonius (Antony's brother) and the Perusine War of 41 BC, which A. cruelly subdued, though he spared *Fulvia and L. Antonius. To better his relations with Sextius *Pompeius, A. married the latter's relative Scribonia, and in 40 BC he made a new agreement with Antony, who married his sister Octavia. In 39 BC, he divorced Scribonia and shortly thereafter married *Livia.

A. now stood in open war with Pompeius who tried to block the corn supply to Rome from his base at Sicily. The triumvirs prolonged their powers for five more years in 37 BC. During the following year, A. defeated Pompeius and Lepidus, thereby taking Sicily and Africa. In the ensuing years, A. established his position in Italy and tried to eradicate bitter memories of his revolutionary appearance in Roman politics, of his cruelty in the proscriptions, and of the Perusine War. The restoration of the regular corn supply and of law and order, his extensive and generous approach to public building (in which he was immensely helped by Agrippa), and the opportunities he gave new men to advance to high offices won A. the support of the population of Rome and of the local aristocracy of the Italian towns. Through moderation and consideration he also won over many of the old Roman aristocracy. Meanwhile, it became apparent that a war with Antony was imminent. A. began a propaganda war, associating Antony with Cleopatra and with all the oriental vices. Antony's testament, in which he left inheritances to Cleopatra's children and asked to be buried in Alexandria, was published in 32 BC. Italy and the western provinces swore personal allegiance to A. in late 32 BC, thereby becoming his clients. And although many senators and consuls left Italy in 32 BC to join Antony, during the following year many of them deserted and went over to A. who was then consul. In September 31 BC, Antony was defeated at the battle of *Actium. He committed suicide before A. had completed his conquest of Egypt in 30 BC. A. was now the sole ruler of the Roman Empire.

After addressing himself to more urgent problems in 30–28 BC (discharge of veterans, distribution of lands, purge of the Senate, registration of citizens), A. made the first settlement of his constitutional position in the state in January 27 BC. Caesar's experience had taught him that it was necessary to find an adjustment between effective personal rule and the old institutions and traditions of Rome. A. formally transferred his authority over the state to the Senate and the people on 13 January 27 BC (*Mon. Anc.* 34). He received for a period of ten years a large province which consisted of Syria, Gaul and Spain. This gave him command of most of the army. In Italy his power was based on his being a consul. On 16 January he received the title A. which had a religious connotation and elevated him above the rest of humanity. Other honours were given to him, and the month Sextilis was named A. in his honour. Experience led A. to make changes in his constitutional powers. In 23 BC, he gave up the consulate and received instead the *tribunicia potestas* for life. He had already received the *sacrosanctitas* of the tribunes in 36 BC, but now his legal authority in Rome was based on the powers of the tribunes. He also received *imperium proconsulare maius* over the senatorial provinces. Subsequently, he received more privileges and his powers were renewed every five or ten years (18, 13, 8 BC, AD 3, 13). In 12 BC he became Pontifex Maximus on the death of Lepidus, and in 2 BC he received the title *Pater Patriae*. It appears that A.'s legal powers had accumulated during the years, and that no single title could designate his position; the name Princeps (not to be confused with *princeps senatus*, a position which he had held since 28 BC) was an unofficial designation. The legal position of A. expressed only one aspect of his rule. He himself chose to emphasize his *auctoritas*. This stressed his social position, the ties of allegiance between him and his clients, those he had inherited from Caesar, and those who had taken the oath of allegiance with him. He thus commanded the loyalty of a large segment of the population as well as the army. In his religious office, as Pontifex Maximus, he was head of Roman religion and the title Augustus gave him an aura of divinity. His *genius* was worshipped at Rome and in the towns of Italy, and in the provinces, especially the eastern ones, he had a cult as divine ruler, usually together with Roma.

A.'s provincial and foreign policy led to the final pacification of certain provinces and the creation of several new ones. In the years 26–19 BC, he reorganized Spain and Gaul (A. was abroad 27–25 BC). Several wars secured the southern frontiers of Egypt and Africa (29, 25, 19 BC), and in the east, he used diplomacy rather than war. An agreement with Parthia over Armenia made it a Roman protectorate, and Tiberius brought back the standards lost by *Crassus (4) (A. was in the East 22–19 BC). The most considerable advance was made in the northern frontiers from the Balkan to the Rhine. In 16–15 BC, Raetia and Noricum were organized as imperial provinces (A. was in Gaul, 15–13 BC) and in 16–9 BC, the frontier in the Balkan was pushed to the Danube; three provinces, Moesia, Pannonia and Dalmatia were organized. In a series of wars (11–7 BC) Roman armies advanced to the Elbe. But the Pannonian revolt of AD 6, and the annihilation of the army of Varus in AD 9 compelled A. to abandon Germany, and the frontiers were fixed on the lines of the Danube and Rhine.

A. sought to remedy long standing problems of Roman society and the state. By a series of laws, he tried to revive Roman morals, encourage marriage, increase the birth rate and reduce luxury. Several laws were passed to legalize the position of freed slaves and to reduce the number of manumitted slaves. The corn supply of Rome was reorganized and ensured. For administrative purposes, Rome was divided into fourteen *regiones*, Italy into eleven *regiones*. A. instituted boards of *curatores* to take charge of the administration of the Tiber and of roads. Seven *cohorts* of *vigiles* (one for every two *regiones*) were in charge of fire-fighting and security in Rome. The three *cohortes urbanae* under the *Praefectus Urbi were created by A. as a regular police force. The Ordo Equester was reorganized and rules for promotion in senatorial and equestrian careers were regularized. Close supervision reduced maladministration by Roman officials in the provinces. Military reforms consolidated developments of the late Republic. There was now a standing professional army consisting first of twenty-eight legions and after AD 9 of twenty-five (apart from the *Auxilia). Legionaries served for sixteen years, and from AD 6 for twenty years. The praetorians served sixteen years from AD 5 and the auxiliary forces twenty-five years. Discharged soldiers received payment from the aerarium militare (*Aerarium) which was founded in AD 6. A. also sought to revive Roman religion. He reconstructed old temples, built new ones, filled vacant offices and, in 17 BC, celebrated the ludi saeculari.

The restoration of internal peace, law, and security brought relief and prosperity to Roman citizens and provincials alike. Pax Augusta was the most valuable gift A. presented to his contemporaries, and their feelings of gratitude are echoed in the works of Virgil and Horace, as well as in inscriptions. But despite his general success, A.'s last years were unhappy. The relatives to whom he had given special honours and power to succeed him, died one by one: his friend and son-in-law Agrippa (12 BC), his grandsons Lucius (AD 2), and Gaius (AD 4). He banished his only daughter Julia (2 BC) and her daughter Julia (AD 8) — both for adultery. A. died on 19 August AD 14 and was deified on 17 September. Ten years earlier, he had arranged for a safe succession by adopting Tiberius and giving him tribunicia potestas and imperium proconsulare. His own summary of his achievements (Res Gestae) which had been deposited with his will at the Vestals in AD 13 was inscribed on two bronze tablets outside his Mausoleum. It is known from provincial copies (*Monumentum Ancyranum).
Syme, Rom. Rev.;
Hammond, The Augustan Principate², 1968;
A. H. M. Jones, Augustus, 1970.

AULIS A place in Boeotia where Greek ships assembled before setting out on their expedition against Troy. Famed also for its connection with *Iphigenia. A. was of no importance in historical times.

AURELIANUS, Lucius Domitius Roman emperor of humble origin, born AD 214 in Dacia Ripensis or in Sirmium. He took a leading part in the conspiracy against *Gallienus in AD 268, and, after the death of *Claudius Gothicus, was proclaimed emperor by the soldiers at Sirmium. During his five year reign he was almost constantly fighting. In AD 270, he won a victory over the Vandals in Pannonia and expelled the Juthungi and Alani from Italy. He suppressed revolts and then marched to the East to fight *Zenobia who controlled Asia Minor and Egypt. He defeated Zenobia's army and captured the queen and her city Palmyra. He returned to the Balkan to defeat the Carpi. In AD 273, Palmyra revolted, but A. swiftly sacked it. He had time to suppress a revolt in Egypt and in the same year he won a victory in Gaul over the army of *Tetricius, who surrendered before battle. Early in AD 275, while on his way to fight Persia, A. fell victim to a conspiracy initiated by his secretary, Eros. A. was called restitutor orbis, "restorer of the world", and he fully deserved that title. He eliminated rival emperors, united the empire that had been torn by civil wars for almost forty years, and secured the frontiers by successful wars. In the Danube zone, he evacuated Dacia to facilitate defence. He encircled Rome with walls (AD 271–5) to secure it against sudden inroads by barbarians. He sought to restore discipline in the army, to reform a worthless

coinage by issuing new coins, and to establish a common religion for the whole empire by introducing the cult of Sol invictus.

AURELIUS The name of a Roman plebeian clan, the first member of which became consul in 252 BC. The important families of the clan were the Cottae and the Orestae. Many Roman emperors bore the name after M. Aurelius — for example, Commodus, Caracalla, Diocletianus.

AURELIUS MARCUS Roman emperor, born M. Annius Verus in Rome on 26 April AD 121, son of Annius Verus and nephew of *Faustina the Elder. His father was of a Spanish family that rose to the highest offices in Rome. On the death of his father, he was adopted by his consular grandfather and was already a favourite of Hadrian. He received the best education in grammar, rhetoric and philosophy. Hadrian called him Verissimus and in AD 136, betrothed him to the daughter of L. Aelius, his successor. But Aelius died and Hadrian induced *Antoninus Pius, now his designated successor, to adopt A. and L. *Verus (Aelius' son). In AD 140, A. was consul with Pius, and in AD 145 he married Faustina the Younger (Pius' daughter and his own cousin). The following year he received the tribunicia potestas and imperium proconsulare, which clearly marked him as the successor of Pius.

Second century AD equestrian statue of the Emperor Marcus Aurelius

The ruins of Thamugadi, a Roman provincial town, one of the many which prospered in the 2nd century AD

He succeeded Pius on 7 March AD 161 and was known as M. Aurelius Antoninus. He made Verus joint-emperor with all titles (including *Augustus*) and powers, excepting the office of Pontifex Maximus. Verus was also betrothed to A.'s daughter. During most of his reign, A. was engaged in wars. War was conducted in the East against the Persians, and in AD 163–6 Armenia and Mesopotamia were occupied. The second war was in central Europe, where German tribes invaded the empire in AD 166, reaching as far as Italy. A. recruited more legions, raised funds, and by negotiations and extensive operations, repelled the invaders (Marcomani and Quadi) from the provinces by AD 170. He now sought to consolidate Roman power across the Danube. He conducted a series of wars against the Marcomani and Quadi in AD 170–4, and compelled them to seek peace. Further operations were postponed by the revolt of *Avidius Cassius in AD 175. Though Avidius was murdered by his own men, A. found it wise to visit Egypt and Syria. In AD 176, A. was back in Rome to celebrate a triumph. In AD 177, the second series of the Marcomanic wars began. A. himself conducted the operations and was able to occupy the territory of the Marcomani, the Quadi and the Sarmatian Iazyges. He died on 17 March AD 180, but his son and successor, *Commodus, preferred to conclude peace rather than to consolidate his achievements.

During A.'s reign, several ominous signs of the decline of the Roman Empire became apparent. The expenditure of the government was increasing due to long wars, and the rise of the imperial bureaucracy, resulting to a large extent from the albeit well-intentioned tendency of the state to take more and more matters under control, had grave long-term results. Thus more and more cities came under the control of state officials (*curatores*). The administrative staffs of the *annona, alimenta*, and other government departments were enlarged. Bureaucracy was rigidly hierarchic. The decline of free activity and civic spirit in the economy and social life, which beset the later Roman Empire, can be dated to A.'s time. The Empire also suffered from the plague which Verus' army had brought back from the East in AD 166. Finally, A. made the serious blunder of appointing his unsuitable son as his successor.

A. was the only emperor who was a philosopher. In AD 146, he abandoned rhetoric, which he had studied with his friend *Fronto, and adopted the Stoic philosophy. He wrote his reflections during the long years of war. His notes, "To Himself", written in Greek, are known as the *Meditations*, and consist of twelve books. This work reveals his personality and his loneliness. Also extant are letters he wrote to Fronto. A column to commemorate him was erected and still stands at Rome's Piazza Colonna; there is a bronze equestrian statue of him on the Capitoline hill.

A. Birley, *Marcus Aurelius*, 1966.

AURELIUS VICTOR, Sextus Of African origin, A. lived in the 4th century AD. He was *Praefectus Urbi* in AD 389. He is the author of *Caesares*, a collection of short biographies of the emperors, from Augustus to Constantinus. He did not write *Origo Gentis Romanae* and *De Viris Illustribus* which are together with his *Caesares.*

AURORA The Latin counterpart of Greek *Eos.

AURUM CORONARIUM ("gold crown") The offering of a gold crown to victorious rulers, which was an Oriental custom upheld by Hellenistic rulers from the 2nd century BC. Roman commanders benefited from it, and Roman emperors reserved this right for themselves. It was in fact demanded on various occasions, not only for triumphs, but also as an important source of income.

AUSONIUS, Decimus Magnus Roman statesman and poet, born at Burdigala (Bordeaux) at the beginning of the 4th century AD. He received a good education and was given the position of *grammaticus* and then of *rhetor* at Bordeaux. After long years of teaching, he was summoned by *Valentian I, c. AD 365, to teach his son *Gratian at *Trier. The Emperor appointed him to various offices and Gratian made him governor of the Gallic provinces in AD 378, and consul in AD 379. After Gratian's murder in AD 383, he returned to his native town, where he died c. AD 394.

A. was a prolific poet. His best known work, the *Mosella*, was written in hexameters and describes the river Moselle, the fish that inhabit it, and some of its surroundings. His *Ordo Nobilium Urbium* gives an account of important cities. There are many other extant works, including epigrams and letters. Christianity had little effect on A.'s poetry. Virgil was his favourite poet, and his influence on A.'s work is conspicuous.

Dill, *Roman Society,* 167–177.

AUSPICIUM A religious ceremony practised in Rome to divine the attitude of the gods towards proposed courses of action. *Auspicia* were very much akin to *auguria* (*Augures). An A. was taken before all the important proceedings of public life. Magistrates had the right to conduct an A. (*ius auspiciorum*), and only magistrates who acted under their own auspices could be awarded a triumph if they won a victory.

AUTOLYCUS (1) The maternal grandfather of Odysseus who, under the tutelage of Hermes, outdid all men in thievery and trickery (*Od.* 19.394–5).

AUTOLYCUS (2) Greek astronomer and mathematician of Pitane in Aeolia, said to have been a teacher of *Arcesilaus, active in the late 4th century BC. Two of his works are extant: *On the Moving Sphere*, and *On Risings and Settings*. These are the earliest Greek works of their kind still extant.

AUXILIA Auxiliary forces of foreign peoples who, from the 2nd century BC on, occasionally served with the Roman army as archers, slingers and cavalrymen. Reorganized by Augustus, they formed a standing part of the Roman army, numbering about 130,000. Their units were first recruited on a tribal and later on a local basis.

The infantry was organized in *cohortes*, consisting of 1,000 or 500 men, and the cavalry in *alae*. Their commanders were *praefecti* or *tribuni*. The infantrymen were paid 75 denarii (a third of the legionary payment) under Augustus. On completing their twenty-five year service, they received Roman citizenship. With the extension of Roman citizenship, culminating in the *constitutio Antoniniana* of *Caracalla, the distinction between the A. and the legions diminished. The A. virtually disappeared during the 3rd century AD, later A. being special infantry units, 500 strong.

G. Webster, *The Roman Imperial Army*, 1964; G. L. Cheesman, *The Auxilia of the Imperial Roman Army*, 1914.

AVENTINE (Aventinus Mons) A hill over the Tiber considered to be one of the seven hills of ancient Rome. The Plebs went in a *Secessio* to the A. It was an early centre of plebian activity. Here stood the ancient temples of Diana and Juno, and later that of Jupiter Liber (238 BC). *Ennius lived on the A.

AVERNUS (modern Lago Averno) A lake near *Puteoli, reputedly leading to the underworld and therefore visited by Odysseus and Aeneas in their descent to the realm of the dead. It was believed that birds who flew over it died.

AVIANUS A Roman poet, active probably in the first part of the 5th century AD. His forty-two elegiac fables (which may have been dedicated to Macrobius) are extant. The fables are of the Aesopic type and are based on those of Babrius (*Aesop).

A. Cameron, *ClQ* (1967), 385–396.

AVIDIUS NIGRINUS, Gaius Of a consular family, began his career under Trajan and was suffect consul in AD 110. A. governed Achaea and Dacia, and Hadrian probably considered him a suitable successor. But he was suspected of conspiracy and the Senate had him executed in AD 118.

AVIDIUS CASSIUS, Gaius Of an Equestrian family from Syria. He advanced in office under M. *Aurelius and was suffect consul after AD 161. Commanding the army of L. *Verus against Parthia in AD 164–6, he occupied Mesopotamia, and remained in the East first as governor of Syria and later of all the eastern provinces. In AD 172, he subdued a revolt in Egypt. A. proclaimed himself emperor in AD 175, but after three months, he was killed by his own soldiers.

AVIENUS Roman poet and statesman, native of Volsinii, lived in the second half of the 4th century AD. Three of his extant works are adaptations in Latin of Greek works and lore: *Descriptio Orbis Terrae*, written in hexameters and based on *Dionysius (6) Periegetes; *Ora Maritima*, written in iambics and based on various sources, some of which date from the 6th century BC; *Aratea Phaeromena* and *Aratea Prognostica*, written in hexameters and based on the work of *Aratus (1).

A. Cameron, *ClQ* (1967), 392–4.

B

BACCHUS, BACCHANALIA The Greek god *Dionysus was also called Bacchus and his mysteries Bacchanalia. His cult spread to south Italy, apparently from the Greek colonies there, from the 5th century BC on. His popularity, mainly with the low classes, and the disorder occasioned by the Bacchanalia, led the Senate to take suppressive measures in 186 BC (Liv. 39.8–18); an inscription also attests to this fact. The cult remained widespread until the late Roman Empire.

M. P. Nilsson, *The Dionysiac Mysteries of the Hellenistic and Roman Age,* 1957.

BACCHYLIDES Greek lyric poet, native of Iulis in Ceos, nephew of *Simonides. Many details of his life are only conjectural. B. was born *c.* 520 BC. He is said to have visited Macedonia, Thessaly, Athens and Aegina. B. accompanied his uncle to Sicily *c.* 476 BC, where they were guests of *Hieron (1). B. was expelled from his native city, probably for political reasons and according to Plutarch went in exile to the Peloponnesus. There is no record of the date of his death. Only a few fragments of B.'s poetry were known until, in 1896, fragmentary papyri were found in Egypt, consisting of fourteen epinician odes and six dithyrambs. The former were composed in honour of victors at Olympian, Nemean, Isthmian and Pythian games. Thus, ode No. 5 was written in celebration of Hieron's victory in the horse race at the Olympian games of 476 BC, and ode No. 4 for his victory in the Pythian horse race in 470 BC. These odes, like those of *Pindar, consist of three elements — an encomium of the victor, a mythical story, and maxims of wisdom. Compared to Pindar, B. seems to give fuller narratives of the victories and myths. B. wrote his dithyrambs for the competitions at Athens. Ode No. 18 is a dialogue between *Aegeus and the chorus, the only completely extant dramatic *dithyramb; ode No. 17 tells of the voyage of Minos and Theseus to Crete, in which Theseus dived into the sea to recover Minos' ring. In another vivid poem, B. describes the influence of wine drinking on the imagination. Of B.'s poetry, hymns, paeans, encomic and other forms, very little has survived.

Edition, translation and commentary by R. C. Jebb, 1905.

BACTRIA Country in central Asia, roughly corresponding to northern Afghanistan, extending along the middle Oxus (modern Amu Darya), with B. as its capital. A satrapy within the Persian empire, the Bactrians submitted to Alexander only after long resistance. B. formed part of the Seleucid empire, but local Greek rulers asserted their independence from *c.* the middle of the 3rd century BC (*Diodotus), and even *Antiochus III could not regain effective control (*Euthydemus I). In the first half of the 2nd century, the kings of B. extended their rule over most of Afghanistan and the western part of India. B. came under pressure from the tribes of central Asia after *c.* 140 BC; shortly afterwards, the kingdom was taken by foreign invaders (the Yueh-Chih).

A. K. Narain, *The Indo-Greeks,* 1957.

BAETICA Roman province in Spain, the Baetis (modern Guadalquivir) valley, from which it took its name, being its richest part. The river Anas (modern Guadiana) formed its western and northern borders, and the territory stretched to the Mediterranean Sea, delimited by *Carthago Nova in the north. In 27 BC this part of the Iberian peninsula, long-settled and peaceful, was assigned to the Senate as *Hispania Ulterior Baetica, soon shortened to Baetica. According to Pliny, it was divided into four juridical regions, *Gades, *Corduba, Astigi and *Hispalis, and it contained some 175 towns.

J. J. Van Nostrand in *ESAR,* 3.

BALBUS, Lucius Cornelius Native of *Gades, and probably of Phoenician stock, B. received Roman citizenship from *Pompey for service in the war against *Sertorius. After emigrating to Rome, B. was adopted by the wealthy Theophanes of Mitylene. B. was *praefectus fabrum* ("Prefect of Engineers") of *Caesar in 62 and 59 BC, and supported the formation of the triumvirate in 60 BC. While Caesar was in Gaul (58–50 BC), B. looked after and represented his financial and political interests. B. was successfully defended by Cicero in 56 BC when prosecuted for illegal acquisition of Roman citizenship. In the Civil War of 49 BC, B. followed Caesar, forsaking Pompey, his former patron. He soon became Caesar's chief assistant. After Caesar's death B. gave his support to Octavian. The circumstances of his election as consul in 40 BC, the first non-Italian in this office, are not known; it was probably a reward for his correct political choice. B. edited the commentaries of *Hirtius. B. died some time after 32 BC, leaving 25 denarii to each Roman Plebeian.

Syme, *RR* (s.v.).

The temple façade on a tetradrachm of Bar-Cochba

BAR-COCHBA, Simon Leader of the Jewish revolt in AD 132–5. His real name was Shimon Ben (son of) Cosiba. Rabbi Akiba applied to him the saying in *Num.* 24.17 "There shall come a star (*cochba* in Aramaic) out of Jacob". Sporadic references in Talmudic sources and by Greek writers give meagre information of the revolt. Some evidence comes also from coins and from the recently discovered letters of B. in the Dead Sea caves. B. was able to establish his rule in Judaea as "Nasi (prince) of Israel", and organized a regular civil administration. It was only by the concentration of large forces and a wholly destructive war that the Romans managed to suppress the revolt. B. was killed during the capture of his fortress at Bethar, southwest of Jerusalem.

BASILICA The name given to various Roman public buildings, the main characteristic of which was a large, rectangular hall. These halls were commonly timber-roofed, with galleries, colonnades, and light openings in the upper parts of the side walls. They were used for various purposes: commercial, military, religious and also as courts of justice. The B. Porcia, built by *Cato (1) in Rome in 184 BC, is the first known. Later, many others were built — often as part of a *Forum — in Rome, in Italy and in the western provinces of the Roman Empire. Noteworthy B.s in Rome include the B. Iulia (built by Augustus), the B. Ulpia (built by Trajan) and the B. Nova (built by Maxentius). The *Stoa provided the Greeks with similar facilities. The architectural design of later Chris-

Remains of a basilica in Pompeii

tian churches was influenced by the type represented in Trajan's B.

Platner-Ashby, *Top. Dict. Rome* (s.v.);
J. B. Ward-Perkins, *PBSR*, 1954, 69ff.

BASSAE Town in southwest *Arcadia, famous for its temple of Apollo, built by the architect *Ictinus in the second half of the 5th century BC. Discovered in 1765 and excavated early in the 19th century, this is one of the best-preserved Greek temples. Its sculpture has been removed to the British Museum. Several of its features are unusual. It was oriented northward (rather than eastward), and had ten engaged columns with peculiar Ionic capitals and a single, free Corinthian column, one of the earliest examples of that sort.

BELGICA Northern part of Gaul, delimited by the North Sea, and the Marne, Seine and Rhine rivers. Its name is derived from its inhabitants, the Belgae, a warlike tribal group of Celtic stock with German admixture. The formation of this group took place in the 3rd century BC. A considerable immigration from this region into southern Britain occurred *c.* 75 BC. *Caesar subdued the Belgae in 57 BC and under Augustus, B. was organized as a separate province.

C. F. C. Hawkes – G. C. Dunney, *Ar. Jour.*, 1930, 150ff.

BELLEROPHON (or Bellerophontes) Greek mythological hero, son of *Glaucus (1) and Eurymede, grandson of *Sisyphus. B. fled from Corinth and came as a suppliant to King Proetus of Tiryns. Proetus' wife fell in love with him but, after being rejected, told her husband that B.

Bellerophon in a 4th-century mosaic from Olynthus

had tried to seduce her. Proetus sent B. to Iobates, his father-in-law, king of Lycia, with instructions to kill him. Iobates asked B. to kill the Chimaera, which he succeeded in doing after taming the winged horse Pegasus. He performed other feats ordered by Iobates, who at last learned the truth and gave his daughter to B. in marriage. When B. undertook a flight on Pegasus to Olympus, Zeus seized the horse and B. fell down. From then on, lame, blind and accursed, B. wandered until his death. There are several versions of the myth.

BELLONA The old Roman goddess of war. B. had a small cult, and her temple, built soon after 296 BC in the *Campus Martius, was used by the Senate for their meetings outside the *Pomerium.

Platner-Ashby, *Top. Dict. Rome*, 82; Latte, *R. Rel.*, 235.

BELLUM SOCIALE ("Social War") The name given to the war of the Italian allies (*socii*) of Rome (91–87 BC), as a result of which Roman citizenship was given to all in Italy.

BENEVENTUM Samnite town which was made a Latin colony in 268 BC. Loyal to Rome in the Hannibalic War, it later enjoyed prosperity. *Municipium* since 89 BC, it received veterans in 42 and was a prosperous *colonia* under the Empire. Trajan's arch, the starting point of the Via Traiana leading to Brundisium, is well preserved.

E. T. Salmon, *Samnium* (s.v.).

BERENICE (1) I Daughter of Lagus (father of *Ptolemy I), born *c.* 340 BC. Magas, B.'s son from her first marriage, became king of Cyrene; her daughter, Antigone, married *Pyrrhus of Epirus. B. became mistress of Ptolemy I (*c.* 317 BC), and later married him after he divorced his wife, Eurydice (no later than 287 BC). Their son ascended the throne of Egypt as Ptolemy II, in 283 BC. B. died *c.* 279 BC. She had a joint cult with Ptolemy I, and several cities were named after her.

BERENICE (2) II Daughter of Magas, king of Cyrene, born *c.* 273 BC. In 246 BC, she married Ptolemy II, after having brought about her first husband's death. As commemorated in poetry by *Callimachus and *Catullus, B. consecrated a lock of her hair for the safe return of her husband from his Syrian War. B. and her husband had a joint cult during their lifetime. After her husband's death in 221 BC, B. ruled together with her son *Ptolemy IV, who subsequently had her murdered.

BERENICE (3) Daughter of *Agrippa I, and great-granddaughter of *Herod the Great, born in AD 28. B. was married thrice, initially to Marcus Alexander, brother of *Tiberius Alexander, in AD 41; then to her uncle, Herod, king of Chalcis, in AD 46; and finally to Polemon, king of Olba, in Cilicia, in AD 54. She later divorced the last. With her brother *Agrippa II, she made a vain effort to persuade the Jews to refrain from revolting in AD 66. B. was *Titus' mistress while he was in Judaea (AD 67–70), and then lived with him for some time in Rome (*c.* AD 75).

BERYTUS (modern Beirut) Very ancient port-city in Phoenicia, renamed Laodicea in Phoenice, probably by *Seleucus IV. With the decline of the Seleucid dynasty, B. obtained formal recognition of its freedom (81 BC). Augustus founded a Roman colony there (*c.* 16 BC), assigning it an extensive territory stretching as far as the source of the Orontes. Named "Colonia Iulia Augusta Felix Berytus", it was a great centre of trade. In the 3rd century AD, B. was famous for its School of Law, Rhetoric and Medicine.

Jones, *Cities*[2] (s.v.).

BIBULUS, Marcus Calpurnius Of a noble plebeian family. Born c. 102 BC, B. served with *Caesar as aedile in 65 BC, and as praetor in 62 BC. As an opponent of the triumvirate, B. was elected consul for 59 BC, alongside Caesar. B. was supported by his father-in-law, *Cato Uticensis, an opponent of Caesar. Shutting himself up at home, B. tried in vain to invalidate Caesar's legislation by his edicts, thus actually giving his opponent a free hand. B. governed Syria in 51–50 BC, successfully repulsing a Parthian invasion. He commanded Pompey's fleet in the Civil War of 49 BC, but failed to prevent Caesar's crossing the Adriatic Sea. B. died in 48 BC.

Syme, *RR* (s.v.).

BIOGRAPHY The development of the B. as a literary genre became feasible only with the increasingly conscious appreciation of the importance of the individual. Even before B.s proper appeared, short or long portrayals of individuals had been given in Greek epics, dirges and funeral eulogies. Historians from *Thucydides on included accounts of historical characters in their works. Indeed, one type of B. is the historical monograph dealing with an important personality. Greek literature of the 4th century presents the first works approaching B.: the *Cyropaedia, Memorabilia* and *Agesilaus* of *Xenophon, and the *Evagoras* of *Isocrates. Mention may also be made of the portrayal of Socrates in the Platonic dialogues. Here, as elsewhere, Aristotle played an important role by taking an interest in the ethical problems of human personality. His successor *Theophrastus composed the famous *Characters*, a description of stock figures. But it was *Aristoxenus who gave the accepted Peripatetic type of B. in which the individual exposed his character by his actions. This led to the emphasis on sensational stories and a disregard for historical truth. However, neither Aristoxenus' *Lives of Men* (including Pythagoras and Plato), nor the work of any of the other Greek writers of the Hellenistic period, is extant. The Alexandrian scholars who dealt with Greek authors included biographical accounts in their works. They were mainly interested in factual, biographical data, not in character portrayal. The only surviving Greek B.s are the *Parallel Lives of Illustrious Greeks and Romans* by Plutarch, the *Lives of the Philosophers* by *Diogenes Laertius, and the *Lives of Sophists* by *Philostratus.

Roman B. had native roots, though it later developed under Greek influence. Cicero tells us that it was customary to commemorate the achievements of distinguished men (*Tusc. Disp.* 4.3). The private life and public career of a man were celebrated in the *Laudatio funebris*. Short accounts of the political careers of aristocrats were given in inscriptions attached to their *Imagines* or to their sepulchres. The interest in the role played by individuals in Roman history was largely due to the tendency of Roman aristocratic families to glorify the achievements of their ancestors. Peculiar to the Romans was the development of the literature of memoirs and autobiography, from Gaius Gracchus on. The authors were statesmen and their works had a marked apologetic note (*Scaurus, P. *Rutilius Rufus and *Sulla). This tradition was followed by Roman emperors like Augustus, Tiberius, Claudius, Hadrian and Severus. But the earliest extant autobiography is the *Confessions* of Augustinus, an outstanding work. Also produced were polemical and encomiastic B.s like *Cato*, by *Cicero, and *Anticato*, by Caesar. The *Lives of Famous Men*, by the Roman writer Cornelius *Nepos, is the earliest extant collection of B.s It gives short and dull accounts of its subjects' actions and achievements. Next comes the *Agricola* of Tacitus, which includes an encomiastic description as well as a detailed account of the hero's career. The *Lives of the Twelve Caesars*, by *Suetonius, presents the best of Roman B. The *Historia Augusta* is a far inferior collection of B.s, both in literary and historical terms.

D. R. Stuart, *Epochs of Greek and Roman Biography*, 1928; T. A. Dorey (ed.), *Latin Biography*, 1967.

BION (1) Native of *Olbia, who lived in the 3rd century BC. Sold into slavery with his family, B. received a rhetorical education from his master, who later freed him and left him his property in inheritance. B. studied philosophy at Athens, in the various schools (mainly under *Crates the Cynic). B. became a wandering philosopher, teaching for hire. He wrote in the diatribist style, that is, short ethical discourses in popular language, dealing with such subjects as poverty, exile, death and autarky. He employed erotic and mythical examples, citations from poets, anecdotes, antitheses, puns and personification as methods. B. influenced such writers as *Horace, *Seneca and *Epictetus.

Diog. Laert. 4., Dudley, *Cynicism* (s.v.).

BION (2) Bucolic Greek poet, born near Smyrna in the late 2nd century BC. Little is known of his life but he seems to have spent it mostly in Sicily. B. is said to have died of poison. Of his poetry, only seventeen fragments have survived. The *Lament of Adonis* (included in Mss of *Theocritus) is considered to have been composed by B. His poetry has erotic elements, Eros appearing as the teacher of erotic poetry.

A. S. F. Gow, *Bucolici Graeci* (text), 1952;
A. Lang, *Theocritus, Bion and Moschus*, 1928.

BITHYNIA Land in northwestern Asia Minor, inhabited by Thracians from the Balkans. The original territory, the Bithynian peninsula, came in time to include the Sangarius valley with the mountainous lands around it. The western and northern borders were the Propontis, the Bosporus and the Black Sea. The expansion to the east was blocked by *Heraclea Pontica and the kingdoms of Paphlagonia and Pontus. B. was a fertile land, with abundant water, good pasturage, quarries and extensive forests producing timber of excellent quality.

The political history of B. was characterized by efforts to preserve its independence, to increase its territory, and to gain access to the sea. These aims brought B. into conflict with the Greeks, who occupied the few adequate harbours there. The Bithynian dynasty kept its autonomy under Persian rule, and maintained its independence against Alexander the Great and his successors. In 297 BC, Zipoites took the title of king. His successor, *Nicomedes I, brought the *Galatians into Asia Minor to protect B. against the Seleucids, and founded his capital on the coast at Nicomedia, which he had named after himself. He and his successors introduced Hellenistic civilization into B., founded Greek cities and supported commerce. However, the interior remained rural and it is not clear to what extent Greek civilization penetrated there. Though under *Prusias I there was some extension of the country at the expense of Pergamum and Heraclea Pontica, the wars of the Bithynian kings in the 2nd century BC were generally fruitless. The prosperity of the country, however, did not suffer from the political failures.

B. was bequeathed to the Roman people by Nicomedes IV, who died late in 75 BC. Rome had first to fight *Mithridates VI Eupator before B. could be organized as a province, a task accomplished by Pompey. B. and Pontus

were to be one province, Pompey distributing the territory amongst the existing cities, which were responsible for order and fiscal matters. From then on, B. was a peaceful province. Under the settlement of 27 BC, B. became a senatorial province, which status it retained until it was changed by Marcus Aurelius into an imperial province. Much of the social and economic situation of B. early in the 2nd century AD is known from the correspondence between Trajan and Pliny, his special legate there.
Magie, *Asia* (s.v.).

BOCCHUS (1) King of Mauretania, *c.* 111–80 BC. B. supported his son-in-law *Jugurtha in his war against Rome, after his proposal of alliance to her was rejected. For this support B. received western Numidia. B. was then influenced by *Sulla to betray Jugurtha. B. signed a treaty of friendship with Rome (*c.* 105 BC), and preserved good relations with Sulla.

BOCCHUS (2) King of Mauretania, *c.* 50–31 BC.

BOEOTIA Region in central Greece (approx. 2,500 sq km), bordered by Attica on the south, the Gulf of Corinth on the southwest, the region of Phocis on the northwest, Opuntian Locris on the north and the strait of Euboea on the east. The topography of the land is varied: mountainous in the south, flat in the centre and hilly in the north. B. has no favourable seaboard; the harbours on the Corinthian gulf are cut off from the interior by mountains, and *Aulis on the Euboean strait was unsuitable for sea-trade. B. was famous for its grain, horses and cattle. It was the Boeotian tribe, which came from Thessaly with the Dorian invasion, which gave the country its name. Formerly it had been known as the land of Cadmos. Archaeological excavations indicate human settlement here from the Stone Age on. B. was a centre of "Mycenaean" civilization; Boeotians took part in the expedition to Troy, and Homer mentions 29 Boeotian states, though later

Perseus cutting the head of the Gorgo. A 7th-century Boeotian work

there were only some 12. The main cities were *Thebes, *Thespiae, *Plataea, *Orchomenos, *Tanagra and *Chaeronea.

The Boeotians had a common cult of Athena Itonia with a temple and an annual, national festival. A Boeotian League existed at least from the 6th century BC on; it was a loose confederacy which lasted (though with some interruptions) for centuries. In the 5th and 4th centuries BC, Thebes attempted to seize control of the confederacy. A Boeotian League still existed under the later Roman Empire. *Hesiod, *Pindar and *Plutarch came from B.
Larsen, *Gr. Fed. St.,* 26ff., 175ff.

BOETHIUS, Anicius Manlius Severinus Born *c.* AD 480 to a noble family, B. was consul in AD 510 and in AD 522 was appointed Master of Offices by *Theodoric the Ostrogoth, moving to Ravenna. A year later, however, B. was suspected of treasonable communications with Constantinople. He was sentenced to death and executed in AD 524.

B. was a man of ample means, who studied philosophy and science. He wrote his most famous work, *On the Consolation of Philosophy,* while in prison. In the form of a dialogue between the author and Philosophy, it seeks to explain the unjust confusion existing in the world, evil winning the rewards of good. B. devoted his life to the study of Plato and Aristotle, and intended to translate their works into Latin with commentaries. He completed only the logical works of Aristotle. B. also wrote treatises on arithmetic and music, translated the Isagoge of *Porphyry with two commentaries and left an unfinished commentary on Cicero's *Topica.* He also wrote five theological treatises.
H. F. Stewart – E. K. Rand, *De Consolatione* (Loeb), 1918.

BOII Gallic tribe which invaded northern Italy *c.* 400 BC. They came via Gaul, probably through the St. Bernard pass. After defeating the Etruscans and Umbrians, the B. settled in the Po valley. The Etruscan city of Felsina, renamed by them Bononia, became their most important city. With Etruscans and other Gauls the B. fought Rome in 282 BC, but were defeated and forced to conclude a 45-year truce. At the battle at Telamon in 225 BC, the B. were almost annihilated; yet eight years later, when Hannibal came to Italy, the B. supported him. Following the conclusion of the Second Punic War, the Romans systematically subjugated their country; the B. were decisively beaten in 193 BC and Bononia was captured. Rome established colonies at Bononia, Parma and Mutina, leaving little land for the B. According to Strabo, the B. subsequently migrated to Bohemia which toponym preserved their name; their new territory was conquered by the Dacian king *Burebistas in the mid-1st century BC. Other B., probably under German pressure, joined in the migration of the Helvetii into Gaul in 58 BC, and were defeated by Caesar, who permitted them to settle in the land of Aedui. See *Gallia Cisalpina.

BONA DEA The Roman "Good Goddess", from whose cult men were excluded. She may have originally been a Greek goddess, introduced into Rome in the 3rd century BC. B. was equated with Fauna, daughter or wife of *Faunus. An annual nocturnal ceremony was held in December in her honour, at the house of a magistrate holding Imperium: the cult was conducted by the magistrate's wife, assisted by the *Vestal Virgins. The number of participants was limited, all of them of the aristocracy. Vines decorated the chamber and a sow was sacrificed. It is also related that there was music, dancing and wine. A temple to B. stood on the Aventine in imperial times. A scandal occurred in 62 BC when *Clodius (1) was caught, in female disguise, during the rites in Caesar's house with whose wife he was having an affair.

Platner-Ashby, *Top. Dict. Rome* (s.v.).

BONONIA (modern Bologna) Ancient city in Cisalpine Gaul. Originally a Villanovan site, it became the Etruscan city of Felsina in the late 6th century BC. The *Boii conquered it, and it was named after them by the Romans who occupied it in 196 BC. An important road-centre for north Italy, it prospered under the Empire when it had the status of *colonia*.

Scullard, *Etruscan Cities*, 198ff.

BOREAS The North Wind, conceived as king of the winds, possessing wild force and spreading cold, darkness and snow. The son of Astaeas and *Eos, B.'s brothers are the winds Zephyrus, Notus and Euros. The main cult of B. was in Attica. According to legend, Oreithyia, daughter of *Erechtheus, king of Athens, rejected B.'s advances. Becoming impatient, B. used his natural violence and carried off Oreithyia while she was dancing at the river Ilissus (or from the Areopagus). B. took her to Thrace where she bore him two sons and two daughters. B. was regarded as a brother-in-law of the Athenians, and was held to have assisted them against Xerxes' fleet at Artemisium, for which a temple was built to him on the banks of the Ilissus. In Athens B. was described as a winged human figure with wild beard and hair. Homer relates that B. disguised himself as a horse, and from his union with mares had twelve fillies (*Il.* 20.223).

BOSPORUS (1) The narrow, Thracian B. is a strait connecting the Sea of Marmora and the Black Sea, 27 km long and from 550 m to 3 km wide. The current reaches a speed of 9 km per hour. The B. served as a waterway and main avenue for commerce and migrations between the lands of the Black Sea and the Mediterranean basin, as well as between Asia and Europe. Several important cities developed along the shores of the B., principally *Chalcedon and *Byzantium.

BOSPORUS (2) The Cimmerian (or Scythian) B., connecting the Black Sea with the Sea of Azov (modern Straits of Kertch). The Greek cities on its shores were united in what came to be known as the Bosporan kingdom (after 480 BC); this kingdom long served as a centre for the export of grain and slaves from Scythia. Its prosperity continued in the 2nd and 3rd centuries AD, till the gradual penetration of Sarmatians who, together with the Goths, eventually occupied its chief city, Panticapaeum, late in the 3rd century AD.

J. Boardman, *The Greeks Overseas*, 1962.

BOTANY The Greeks never showed much interest in B., nor did their achievements in this field rise to the standards they attained in other sciences, for instance astronomy or anatomy. One incentive to study herbs was their use in magical practices and their usefulness in preparing medical drugs.

It was not before the 4th century BC that a serious approach was made with regard to B. The first botanical work, *On the Nature of the Embryo*, was part of the treatise *On Generation* which was included in the Hippocratic Corpus (*Hippocrates). This work, dating from the first half of the 4th century, discusses the generation of plants from seeds and from cuttings. Though Aristotle's main interest was in zoology, he wrote a work on plants which is not extant. It is thus only with *Theophrastus (*c.*

372–*c.* 286 BC) that any systematical work in B. was undertaken. His two extant treatises, *Inquiry concerning Plants*, and *Causes of Plants*, were modelled on Aristotle's zoological studies. Quite obviously, Theophrastus used information already known in addition to his own observations and studies. He collected and organized data to give detailed accounts of over 400 species, giving their forms, habits, habitats and cultivation, as well as theoretical explanations of the phenomena observed. He showed caution and criticism in his attitude to accepted theories. He pointed out the inadequacy of the theory of spontaneous generation in certain cases, though he did not reject the theory itself. It is evident that he recognized the importance of technical terms to his science, and he took the first steps towards their introduction. His careful research enabled him to distinguish between dicotyledons and monocotyledons – and no further progress was made in the study of the germinating seed until the invention of the microscope. Morphologically, he distinguished between the root, stem, stipule, and flower. He also took notice of the relation of the fruit and the flower, though he had no knowledge of sex in flowers. Another inportant achievement of Theophrastus was his clear view that plant distribution is dependent on climate and soil.

After Theophrastus, no important scientific work was done in B. Such interest as was shown in this field was directed to practical purposes. Among the other botanical writers, Crateuas may be mentioned. He was the physician of Mithridates VI (120–63 BC), and he probably introduced the system of providing illustrations of the plants mentioned in his work, an important innovation at a time when technical terminology hardly existed (this continued to be the case until the 17th century). The botanical information included in the *Natural History* of *Pliny the Elder is mainly based on Greek writings. It deals with the origin, nature, and uses of plants, but is devoid of scientific value. The work was widely read throughout antiquity and the Middle Ages to modern times. The *Materia Medica* of *Dioscorides Pedianus includes short accounts of plants. It was very popular and was translated into many languages, and many of its terms are still used.

R. Cohen – I. E. Drabkin, *A Source Book in Greek Science*[2], 1958.

BOUDICCA Wife of the king of *Iceni in East Anglia. When B.'s husband died in AD 60, he designated the Roman emperor, Nero, as co-heir. The imperial staff subsequently mistreated B. and her daughters. In AD 61, the Iceni rose under B.'s leadership, sacked Camulodunum (Colchester), Verulamium and London, and defeated a Roman army. The Roman governor, *Suetonius Paulinus, hastened back from an expedition in the west and routed the insurgents. Soon after, B. committed suicide.

Frere, *Britannia*, 87ff.

BOULE The main council in Greek states and cities for all forms of government from early times to the Roman period. Its membership and functions varied according to time and place. In monarchies, it was the council of nobles who were summoned by the king to give advice. In oligarchies, it was usually the institution through which the ruling minority governed the state. In democracies, it acted for the *Ekklesia, the popular assembly, and all citizens had the right to become members, after either being elected or, as was more often the case, being chosen by lot.

From Archaic times, Athens had a council which met on the *Areopagus. *Solon introduced a new council of 400 members, 100 to each of the four old tribes. Very little is known about this council, which prepared the agenda for the meeting of the Ekklesia. *Cleisthenes (2) replaced it with a new council of 500 members, 50 to each of his ten new tribes. This council lasted to the later Roman Empire. All citizens over thirty, even *Thetes after the second half of the 5th century, could be appointed by lot after a preliminary selection by the *Demoi. They took office after passing an interrogation by the outgoing B. to confirm their qualifications. Service was for one year and could be repeated only once after an interval. From Pericles' time the members of the B. (bouleutai) received daily payment, which for the poor served only as a partial compensation for their loss of time. The members of each tribe served as a standing committee in turn (*Prytaneis). Only the *strategoi could attend the meetings of the B. and submit proposals. All motions to the Ekklesia (probouleumata) were first discussed and formulated by the B. As a result, all communications with foreign states and their envoys went through the B., which also submitted drafts of treaties to the Ekklesia. The B. had general supervision of the finances (the collection of taxes and rents and disbursements to officials) and the building operations of the state. It had powers of jurisdiction which included cases of *Eisangelia and concerning the illegal actions of state officials, but it could not impose fines of more than 500 drachms. In gerneral terms, the B. took care of the execution of the resolutions of the Ekklesia and coordinated the work of the magistrates. The close cooperation between the B. and the Ekklesia, the sovereign body of the state, was one of the main characteristics of the Athenian democracy.

Aristotle, *Athen. Pol.*; Hignett, *Athen. Const.* (s.v.); Ehrenberg, *The Greek City*, 1960 (s.v.).

BRASIDAS Distinguished Spartan commander in the Peloponnesian War, B. saved the city of Methone from Athenian attack in 431 BC. Next year he became an ephor, and in 425 BC fought bravely against the Athenians at Pylos. B. advocated the continuation of the war against Athens even after the capture of high-ranking Spartans at Sphakteria, which led to the rise of a faction favouring an understanding with Athens. In 424 BC, B. received an independent command and was sent to oppose the Athenians in and around Thrace, leading some 1,700 Helots and Peloponnesian soldiers. On his way, B. thwarted an Athenian attack upon Megara. Exploiting anti-Athenian feelings and claiming he was fighting for the liberation of the Greek cities from Athenian tyranny, B. was soon able to take Acanthus, Stagirus and the important *Amphipolis. His unsuccessful Athenian counterpart in these actions was *Thucydides, the later historian. Although Athens and Sparta concluded a one-year armistice in 423 BC, B. instigated revolts against Athens in several cities. The next year, *Cleon came with strong forces and, in late October, attacked Amphipolis; though B. defeated him, both generals were killed in the battle. B.'s courage, energy and successes in Thrace contributed much to the Spartan recovery in the war. He was honoured by a hero-cult (Thuc. 5.6f.).

BRENNUS (1) King of the Gallic Senones who destroyed the Roman army at Allia on 18 July 390 BC (or 387 BC, according to the chronology of Polybius), and then conquered Rome. B. pronounced the famous dictum

"*Vae victis*", when paid in order to lift the siege of the Capitol. B.'s supposed defeat by *Camillus is a legend.

BRENNUS (2) Leader of a Gallic tribe which attacked the Paeonians in 280 BC. The next year B. invaded Macedonia and penetrated into Greece through Thessaly. As a Greek army was blocking his way at Thermopylae, B. sent a diversionary force to Aetolia; the Greeks retreated from Thermopylae and B. was able to reach Delphi. B.'s forces were constantly harassed and he himself was seriously wounded at Delphi. Retreating northward, the Gauls appointed a successor, and B. committed suicide.

BRIGANTES The most numerous, though primitive and pastoral, of the tribes of Britain, occupying northern England from the line Mersey-Humber to the line Tyne-Solway, excluding east Yorkshire. Their country was conquered by *Cerialis and *Agricola in the AD 70s.
Frere, *Britannia* (s.v.).

BRITANNIA The Celtic name B. superseded the earlier name Albion, recorded as early as the late 6th century BC. The languages of the early inhabitants of B. are unknown; these peoples occupied the "Highland" countries north of the line from the Tyne to the Exe, since Neolithic times. Successive Celtic tribes occupied the "Lowland" countries, apparently from the beginning of the 2nd millenium BC on. The Celts brought Iron Age culture with them, while the earlier inhabitants retained their Bronze Age culture. The latest Celtic arrivals were the *Belgae who, from the early 1st century BC on, occupied southeastern B. The Carthaginians established trade with B., importing tin from Cornwall. In a Demotic papyrus of the 1st century BC, the word *pretan*, i.e. "Britain", is used to denote tin.

Caesar invaded B. twice, in 55 and 54 BC. After Caesar's withdrawal from B. there were no immediate Roman efforts to conquer the island, though Augustus entertained the idea. *Caligula revived the plan but it was left to the Emperor Claudius to invade B. with four legions and auxiliary forces, in AD 43, following the death of Cunobelinus, the Belgic king. Within five years, most of the "Lowland" was subdued and a Roman province was established. The Roman advance was resumed under the Flavian dynasty, several competent generals carrying the border far into the north, culminating in *Agricola's penetration into Scotland. By the end of the 1st century AD, the border was fixed at the Clyde-Forth line. However, after the withdrawal of considerable troops, as well as a revolt in AD 118−9, the Carlisle-Newcastle line was chosen as the frontier, and "Hadrian's Wall" was built along it. As the peoples north of the wall continued to harass the province, *Antoninus Pius decided to push the frontier northward once again, to the Clyde-Forth line, he too building a wall there (the "Antonine Wall"). This frontier stood till the end of the 2nd century AD, when Septimius Severus restored Hadrian's Wall and evacuated the area beyond it. During the 3rd century AD, B. suffered comparatively little from the anarchy afflicting the Roman Empire though there were incursions from the north and sea raids by Saxon pirates. In AD 286−97, B. was separated from central Roman rule, being controlled by *Carausius and *Allectus. *Constantius Chlorus restored imperial rule in B. in AD 297. During the 4th century AD, B. was continuously attacked by Picts, Scots, Saxons and Franks. The Roman garrison was finally withdrawn in AD 407; Rome thus effectively abandoned B.

Roman B. was an imperial province ruled by a consular legate, whose seat was at Camulodunum (Colchester); four legions (later three) were at his disposal which together with auxiliaries, amounted to some 50,000 soldiers. A *legatus Augusti iuridicus* was responsible for judicial matters, and the provincial finances were administered by a procurator. Roman rule fostered urbanization of the country. There were four *coloniae* and more than twenty towns, which began fortifying themselves with walls from the late 2nd century AD on. Under Septimius Severus, B. was divided into two provinces which were increased to four by Diocletian.

Frere, *Britannia*.

BRITANNICUS, Tiberius Claudius Caesar Germanicus Son of Claudius and his third wife *Messalina. Born on 12 February AD 41, he received the surname "Britannicus" after his father's invasion of Britain (AD 43). Claudius was persuaded by his fourth wife, Agrippina, to adopt her son Nero and believed that B. suffered from epilepsy. In AD 54, Claudius showed signs of reversing his cool attitude toward B., but when he died Nero indeed succeeded him. Yet B. remained a menace to Nero's rule. Early in AD 55, B. was poisoned, in the presence of Nero.

BRUNDISIUM (modern Brindisi) The best harbour on the Adriatic coast of Italy. Greek tradition ascribed its foundation to *Diomedes or *Theseus. Actually, B. is a Messapian name, and the settlement there was Messapian. Very little is known of its early history. B. had treaty ties with *Thurii *c.* 440 BC, and in the 3rd century BC it came under Roman hegemony. A Latin colony was settled there in 246 BC, and the Via Appia was extended to B. at about the same time. With the growing interest of Rome in the Hellenistic world in the 2nd century BC, B. became of some importance, it being used by armies and fleets departing to the East. In 89 BC, B. became a *municipium*. Caesar attempted there to block Pompey's retreat from Italy (49 BC), and the next year Caesar himself embarked from B. to Epirus, against Pompey. Mark Antony besieged B. in 40 BC when Octavian tried to prevent his return into Italy. The poet Virgil died at B. in 19 BC.

BRUTTII An Italian tribe that inhabited the southwest part of Italy. The original inhabitants (Oenotri and Chones) came under the influence of Lucanian invaders at the beginning of the 4th century BC. The Oscan language of the new conquerors was adopted by the old inhabitants. The B. (the word means slaves in Oscan) separated themselves from the Lucani in 356 BC. They attacked and took Greek towns on the coast and defended themselves successfully against *Alexander I of Epirus, called in by Tarentum, and *Agathocles. Despite their hostile relations with their Greek neighbours, the B. were influenced by Greek culture. They issued coins at this time. In the years 278–272 B. supported Pyrrhus in his war against Rome and were defeated by Roman armies several times. In consequence part of their land was confiscated. They paid heavily for their support of Hannibal in the Second Punic War; the country was devastated, a large portion of the population was sold into slavery in 213, and more land was confiscated. In fact the Bruttian tribe ceased to exist. Roman colonies were sent to Tempsa and Croton and Latin colonies to Vibo and Copia. Bruttium was a country of shepherds and charcoal-burners and its forest Sila supplied good ships timber, but excessive grazing and the effects of the Hannibalic War caused an economic decline, accompanied by the development of large estates.

A. G. Toynbee, *Hannibal's Legacy*, 1965 (s.v.).

BRUTUS (1), Lucius Iunius According to a somewhat doubtful Roman tradition, B. expelled the tyrant *Tarquinius Superbus from Rome and, by instituting liberty and the consulate, he founded the Republic, in 509 BC. As the Iunii of later times were plebeian, it is argued that B. could not have led the Patricians against the king; but the separation of the orders most probably occurred subsequent to the foundation of the Republic. Certainly many of the stories surrounding B. are legendary. Some constitutional and religious regulations may have been ascribed to him simply because he was said to have inflicted the death penalty on his own sons when they conspired to restore the kingship in Rome. B. was killed during the war in which the Etruscans who supported the exiled king were defeated.

Ogilvie, *Livy*, 916f.

BRUTUS (2), Marcus Iunius Born *c.* 85 BC. B.'s father was put to death in 77 BC by Pompey for participating in the revolt of *Lepidus (2). B.'s mother Servilia, stepsister of *Cato Uticensis, was Caesar's mistress for a time. B. was adopted by his uncle, Q. Servilius Caepio, changing his name to Q. Servilius Caepio Brutus. B.'s uncle *Cato (2) contributed much to his education and character. B. began his political career as *triumvir monetalis* (*c.* 60 BC), and spent 58–56 BC in Cyprus with Cato. B. gained a clientele on the island and made a loan to the people of Salamis (at 48% interest!). B.'s influence and good connections are indicated by the fact that he was able to procure two Senate decrees legalizing the loan. Some time later B. married the daughter of Ap. *Claudius (3) Pulcher. B. rejected *Caesar's proposal to serve with him in Gaul, and went with his father-in-law to Cilicia in 53 BC, as quaestor. Back in Rome in 52 BC, B. appeared against Pompey, and in 51 BC he defended his father-in-law. Despite his hatred for Pompey, B. followed him in the Civil War in 49 BC. B. took part in the Battle of *Pharsalus, but Caesar pardoned him afterward. In 46 BC, Caesar appointed him governor of Cisalpine Gaul, serving there till March 45 BC. B. was on good terms with Cicero, who honoured him with his treatise *De Claribus Oratori-*

Portrait of M. Iunius Brutus on a coin of the 2nd century AD

bus (a survey of Roman orators), naming it "Brutus", as well as with the philosophical treatise *Tusculanae Disputationes*. B. himself wrote philosophical treatises ("On Duties", "On Patience", "On Virtue"), poems and summaries of historical works. As an orator, B. followed the Attic school, but his jejune style was criticized by Cicero.

B. divorced his first wife in 45 BC, subsequently marrying Porcia, Cato's daughter. B. enjoyed Caesar's favour, becoming praetor in 44 BC and consul designate for 41 BC. Perhaps under the influence of his wife, and more probably after Caesar's appointment as dictator for life (early 44 BC), B. joined the conspiracy against Caesar, becoming its leader alongside *Cassius (3). B. no doubt thought that the dictator's elimination would restore liberty, that is, liberty of the aristocracy. The reaction of the populace to the murder compelled B. to leave Rome (April 44 BC). Appointed governor of Crete for 43 BC, B. went to Greece and won the loyalty of Hortensius, governor of Macedonia. Suspecting the intentions of Mark Antony, and more so those of young Octavian, B. levied there an army and seized much of the funds prepared by Caesar for his Parthian expedition; in addition, the quaestors of Asia and Syria backed him financially. The Senate's resolution to declare him a "public enemy", on 28 November 44 BC, was repealed and in February 43 BC the Senate gave him command of Illyricum, Macedonia and Achaea (later adding Asia). During these months B. feverishly collected funds, supplies and ships from the provincials, often by force. Successful against the Bessi in Thrace, B. was hailed *imperator* by his troops. After the establishment of the triumvirate (November 43 BC), B. was outlawed. Meeting with Cassius at Sardes, the two marched to Europe and met Antony and Octavian at Philippi, in October 42 BC. B. won the first battle against Octavian, but was defeated in the second battle (23 October), and ended his own life.

M. Radin, *Marcus Brutus*, 1939;
Syme, *RR* (s.v.).

BRYAXIS Athenian sculptor of the 4th century BC. B. was already sufficiently famous to be commissioned (*c.* 353 BC) to decorate the *Mausoleum at Halicarnassus, along with *Scopas, *Timotheus and *Leochares. According to Pliny the Elder, B. was responsible for the north side of the building (*NH* 36.30), though no particular piece extant can be ascribed to him with certainty. B. made statues of deities for Megara, Patara, Cnidos and Rhodes. B. may have been the sculptor of the statue of Serapis in Alexandria. Copies of B.'s works were later made at Rome.

BRYGUS Athenian potter of *c.* 500 BC. Thirteen pieces signed by B. are extant. B. employed several painters in his workshop, the leading one being known as the "Brygus painter", famous for his vases and red-figure cups.

BUCEPHALUS The beloved horse of *Alexander the Great. B. died at the Hydaspes river in 326 BC, at a spot where Alexander subsequently founded a town, named Bucephala in his memory (modern Jalalpur).

BUREBISTAS Dacian king who built an extensive but short-lived kingdom (60–44 BC). B. carried out a religious reform in his country and prohibited the cultivation

The fall of Troy: Neoptolemus and Priam. Early 5th-century vase-painting by Brygus

of vines. B. defeated his enemies across the Danube and routed Celtic tribes in Pannonia. He harassed various Greek towns on the Black Sea and penetrated as far as Apollonia in Thrace. In 44 BC, Caesar made preparations for an expedition against him, but B. fell victim to a plot at home, and upon his death, his kingdom was divided into several principalities.

BURRUS, Sextus Afranius Born in Vasio Vocontiorum in Gallia Narbonensis, B. began his career as a military tribune and was long a proeurator under Livia, Tiberius and Claudius. *Agrippina (2) induced Claudius to appoint him as sole *praefectus praetorio* in AD 51. After supporting the succession of Nero, whose tutor he had been, in 54 BC, he had effective control of government (in cooperation with Seneca) in the initial years of Nero's reign. After Agrippina's murder (AD 59), B.'s influence declined sharply, mainly because of his opposition to the rejection of Octavia, Nero's wife. B. died in AD 62; the claim that he was poisoned by Nero, repeated by Suetonius and Dio, was not accepted by Tacitus (*Ann.* 14.51).
Syme, *Tacitus* (s.v.).

BUSIRIS An Egyptian word meaning "temple of Osiris"; in Greek mythology B. was an Egyptian king who sacrificed all foreigners who came to Egypt. Finally, *Heracles killed B. with all his priests, on the very altar used for the victims. This popular myth was retold by many Greek and Roman authors, and is depicted on many Greek vases.

BYBLUS (modern Jebeil) Phoenician harbour-city 42 km north of *Berytus, the biblical Gebal. Archaeology has revealed that B. was inhabited already in the 4th millennium BC, and it had commercial ties with Crete and Greece in the 2nd millennium BC. The word *byblos* denotes papyrus in Greek, and is found already in Homer. The hinterland of B. was rich in timber. The city preserved its autonomy within the Persian empire, but soon after its conquest by Alexander the Great (332 BC) it became Hellenized.
Jones, *Cities²* (s.v.).

BYZANTIUM Greek city at southern end of the Thracian *Bosporus (1) on the European shore, founded as a colony of *Megara (*c.* 660 BC). The original settlers included Greeks from central Greece and Peloponnesians. The early constitution was moulded on that of its mother city, that is, an oligarchy. The local dialect and calendar resembled those of Megara; the local cults, Megaran in origin, came under Thracian influence. B. was excellently situated to prosper as a centre of commerce. It became an essential centre for international trade and communications between the lands of the Black Sea and the Mediterranean basin. Custom tolls and fishing were its main sources of income. Its location between Asia and Europe increased its strategical importance, a doubtful advantage which placed the city's independence in jeopardy more than once. *Darius I seized the city in 512 BC, but for a short while B. regaine its independence, during the Ionian Revolt. It was liberated by *Pausanias (1) in 478 BC, but he proved to be a tyrant. *Cimon expelled Pausanias in 476 BC and established a democracy. B. was now part of the Athenian empire, to which it paid a yearly tribute. B. unsuccessfully sought to secede in 440–439 BC, and it revolted again in 411 BC, joining Sparta only to fall under its control after the Battle of *Aegospotami, in 405 BC. The Athenian statesman *Thrasybulus regained B. for Athens (390 BC), and it became a formal member of the Second Athenian Empire, in 378 BC. In 357–356 BC, B. seceded from Athens but when Philip II of Macedonia besieged it, in 340–339 BC, B. sought the assistance of, and was saved by, Athens. The *Galatians wrought havoc to B. in the 3rd century BC, and in 279 BC, the city was compelled to pay them tribute. B. supported *Pescennius Niger against *Septimius Severus, and after a long siege it was captured by the latter, in AD 196, and suffered almost total destruction. *Caracalla, however, restored the city which the Goths sacked *c.* AD 270. *Constantine I founded his "New Rome" on its site in AD 324. The building of the new capital progressed rapidly and it was inaugurated as "Constantinopolis" on 11 May AD 330.

C

CABIRI Gods of foreign origin whose main cult in the Greek world was in *Samothrace (Hdt. 2.51) and *Lemnos. Their Greek name *megaloi theoi* ("great gods") may point to Semitic origin and to their connection with Semitic *Cabirim* ("the great mighty"). Phrigian origin is also supposed – hence their connection with the Great Mother of the gods. The Greek cult of the C. began as early as the 6th century BC, but spread especially during the Hellenistic period. The Greeks connected them with other gods (e.g. Dionysus and Demeter) and composed genealogies for them. Phallic symbols and rites of a chthonian nature marked their cult, but little is known of their mysteries. The C. were considered protectors of seamen, who would invoke them in times of danger. Their number varied, but they were later seen as twins, identical with the *Dioscuri.
Kerényi, *Gods*, 86–8.

CACUS and CACA In Roman mythology Cacus was a monster who was killed by Heracles for stealing his cattle (Verg. *Aen*. 8.190ff.), or by his sister Caca for whom an everlasting fire was kept in a shrine. In origin they were probably fire deities of the *Palatine.

CADMUS In Greek mythology, the son of the king of Tyre. C. left Tyre in search of his sister *Europa, who had disappeared. After wandering amongst various islands and after he consulted the Delphic Oracle, he followed a cow to her resting place, where he founded the Cadmea, which later became the citadel of *Thebes (the Thebans are called "Cadmeioi" in the *Iliad*). In C.'s search for water, he slew a dragon sacred to Ares and sowed its teeth. A host of warriors arose from the ground and slew each other in battle. The five remaining warriors were the ancestors of the Theban nobility. In retribution for killing Ares' dragon, C. worked for him for eight years, and then received his daughter, Harmonia, in marriage. Later on, C. and Harmonia migrated to Illyria and were changed into serpents. C. is said to have brought the alphabet to Greece from Phoenicia, as well as other technical innovations. This myth obviously reflects the cultural ties between Greece and the East; the discovery in 1964 of 36 Babylonian cylinder-seals among Mycenaean objects at the Cadmeia lends historical support. C.'s wedding and the fight with the dragon are depicted on Greek vases.
F. Vian, *Les Origines de Thèbes, Cadmos et les Spartes*, 1963.

CAECILIUS STATIUS Latin playwright, an Insubrian Gaul, probably born in Mediolanum (Milan). During the war against the Insubri (223–222 BC), he was taken prisoner and sold into slavery (the name Statius was generally given to slaves). He took the name Caecilius from his patron on being manumitted. C. spent some time with *Ennius. His first comedies were not successful, but he was encouraged by the actor and director *Ambivius Turpio. Barely 300 verses of his writing survive, but the titles of about 40 of his comedies are known. C. often based his plays on *Menander; an extant fragment shows resemblance to *Plautus' style and metric. Cicero esteemed him highly as a comic poet, though not without reservation. Varro praises his ability to arouse emotions. C. died in 168 BC.
Warmington, *Rem. Ol. Lat*. (Loeb), 1935, 1.

CAECINA (1) ALIENUS, Aulus Native of Vicentia. As quaestor of *Baetica in AD 68, C. supported *Galba (3), who gave him command of a legion. He was then transferred to Upper Germany, where he was very active for the proclamation of *Vitellius as emperor. Given command of the whole army in his province, C. led one column of Vitellius' army to Italy, defeating the *Helvetii on the way. The united army destroyed *Otho's forces at Bedriacum. Vitellius promoted him to the consulate (with *Valens) in September–October AD 68. C. was given overall command of the army against the advancing Flavian army. He was arrested by his own soldiers while trying to come to terms with the enemy. He was saved by the Flavian forces, and later established friendly relations with Vespasian. In AD 79 C. was put to death for taking part in a conspiracy.

CAECINA (2) SEVERUS, Aulus Of an old Etruscan family at *Volaterrae. C. was *consul suffectus* in 1 BC. As legate of Moesia in AD 6, C. fought the Pannonian rebels and repulsed the invasion of Dacians and Sarmatians. The following year he defeated the rebels in a great battle northwest of Sirmium. He was legate of Lower Germany when the army revolted there (AD 14). C. took part in *Germanicus' expedition into Germany (AD 15). While leading his army back to the Rhine through the "Long Bridges", he was attacked by the *Cherusci and it was only with great difficulty that he managed to save his army from destruction.

CAELIUS RUFUS, Marcus   C. was born to an Equestrian family *c.* 84 BC. Though associated with Cicero, C. had a close relationship with *Catiline in 63 BC. In 62 BC, C. served in Africa, looking after his father's interests there. In 59 BC, as a tactic to gain fame, C. successfully prosecuted *Antonius Hybrida for extortion in the governorship of Macedonia. When *Clodia, C.'s mistress for two years, instigated a charge of violence against him in 56 BC, Crassus and Cicero spoke in his defence, and he was acquitted. As tribune in 52 BC, C. supported *Milo and opposed Pompey. As aedile in 50 BC, he spent much money on games, thus adding to his financial difficulties. Expecting Caesar to abolish debts, C. followed him in the Civil War of 49 BC. But Caesar's regulations did not extricate him from his debts and, after the Senate had declared a state of emergency, C. fled to southern Italy. He instigated a revolt with Milo, and was put to death in 48 BC. Seventeen of C.'s letters, preserved in Cicero's *Letters to Friends* (Bk. 8), reveal much about the inner workings of Roman politics and social life.

R. G. Austin (ed.), Cic. *Pro Caelio*[3], 1960; Tyrrell-Purser, 3.

CAEPIO, Quintus Servilius   Roman statesman of a noble family known for three of his actions. As consul in 106 BC, he passed a bill by which senators could again serve in the criminal courts. The same year he captured the sacred treasure of Tolossa (Toulouse) reputedly brought there by the Gauls who had taken Delphi. But the treasure mysteriously disappeared. In 105 BC, he suffered a disastrous defeat at Arausio by the *Cimbri and was removed from his command. Convicted in 103 BC, he was exiled to Smyrna.

CAERE (modern Cerveteri)   Rich Etruscan city on the Tyrrhenian coast, some 50 km north of Rome. *Mezentius was C.'s legendary king. The Etruscan settlement there began quite early, perhaps in the 10th century BC. *Tarquinius Superbus fled to C. after being expelled from Rome. The city had a treasury house at Delphi, and it prospered during the 7th—5th centuries BC, an indication of its trade with the East being the considerable import of Greek pottery. C. is famous today for its cemetery, whose chambered tombs (*tumuli*) are arranged in "streets". There are two versions of the development of C.'s relations with Rome: one, that the Vestal Virgins found shelter here when Rome was captured by the Gauls in 390 BC (for this, C. received the *civitas sine suffragio*); the other, that this status was imposed on C. as punishment after a revolt in the 3rd century BC.

Scullard, *Etruscan Cities*, 97—104.

CAESAR, Gaius Julius   Born 13 July 100 BC; murdered 15 March 44 BC. C. was of a patrician family which claimed royal and divine descent, through Ascanius (Julus), son of *Aeneas. Though some Julii served in important offices in the early Republic, the family of the Caesars was late in acquiring political importance (it had its first consul in 175 BC). The family became prominent towards the end of the 2nd century BC. C.'s father (praetor *c.* 91 BC) died in 85 BC. He had married an Aurelia, of a noble plebeian family which could boast of consuls a hundred years earlier than the Caesars.

More important for C.'s political future was the marriage of his aunt Julia to the famous general *Marius. Whether he willed it or not, C. was considered Marian in the internal political struggles. In 84 BC, he married Cornelia, daughter of *Cinna (1). When *Sulla gained control of the state in 82 BC, he ordered C. to divorce the daughter

Gaius Julius Caesar

of his dead enemy. C. refused and Sulla hunted him, only relinquishing pursuit after the intervention of C.'s relatives. C. felt safer out of Italy, and he served with distinction in the army. Pursuing fame, he successfully prosecuted *Dolabella (consul in 81 BC,) and followed this with an unsuccessful prosecution of Gaius Antonius. This occurred in 77—76 BC. Both men were followers of Sulla. C. left Italy again in 75 BC to study rhetoric in Rhodes. In 73 BC, he was co-opted to the board of the *pontifices*, whose members were mostly Sullan, an indication that until then C. was not considered dangerous to the government.

In 71—70 BC, C. supported the restitution of tribunes' powers and the recalling from exile of the followers of *Lepidus (2). He evidently became popular, gaining support by attacking the Senate and the aristocracy. In 69 BC, he became senator, with his service as quaestor. At this time, C. lost his wife, by whom he had his only daughter. At the funeral of his aunt Julia, C. gave the usual laudatory speech, boasting of his royal ancestors. In 67—66 BC, he supported the bestowal of the extraordinary commands on Pompey against the pirates and *Mithradates VI. In 65 BC, he showed his Marian inclination openly by restoring the trophies of Marius, and he gained much popularity at this time by a generous expenditure on games as aedile.

In 63 BC, C.'s opposition to the Senate was shown in the prosecution of *Rabirius, who was accused of killing Saturinus in 99 BC on the basis of the Senate's decree of emergency (which the *populares* claimed had no legal force). Furthermore, he unsuccessfully opposed the death penalty on the supporters of *Catiline. Nonetheless he was elected Pontifex Maximus in the same year, thanks to his popularity and to large-scale bribery. C. divorced his second wife Pompeia in 61 BC, following her affair with *Clodius.

He was governor of Spain in 61 BC, but was forced to satisfy his creditors -- which he did with the aid of *Crassus (4) -- before he could leave for his province. In Spain, C. carried on a vigorous war, advancing Roman rule to the Atlantic. His administration was good and he acquired much wealth.

Back in Italy, in 60 BC, he sought a triumph and the consulate. As his enemies in the Senate refused to allow him to submit his candidacy *in absentia*, C. entered Rome and gave up the triumph. He made an alliance with Pompey and Crassus, known as the "First Triumvirate", and gained the consulate of 59 BC. He soon clashed with his colleague, *Bibulus, the candidate of Cato's faction (C.'s opponents). C. resorted to force, and Bibulus shut himself in his house, making ineffectual attempts to invalidate C.'s deeds. Pompey's deeds in the East were legalized, and his veterans were alloted land in Campania. The *publicani*, with whom Crassus was probably connected, obtained a reduction of a third of the Asian tax they had contracted in 61 BC. C. published the Senate's transactions and passed a law against magistrates taking money illegally. He got his "share" of the alliance by the law of *Vatinius, which granted him the provinces Cisalpine Gaul and Illyricum for five years. To these, the Senate added Transalpine.

C. left Rome in 58 BC, and over the next nine years, he subjugated and conquered the whole of Gaul to the Rhine. The conquest was not premeditated -- C. was an efficient opportunist. In 58 BC he defeated the invading *Helvetii and the Germans under *Ariovistus, thus winning northeastern Gaul. In 57 BC, he subjugated first the *Belgae and then all the tribes along the Channel. Southeastern Gaul was conquered in 56 BC. One year later, C. made a show of crossing the Rhine, and that same year and again the following year, he invaded Britain. The subjugated Gauls were restless, and revolts frequently occurred. The most serious one, in 52 BC, was under *Vercingetorix. On this occasion, the tribes of central Gaul, including some which had previously cooperated, made a united effort to repulse the Romans. Only after C. had starved Vercingetorix and his army into submission in the fortress of *Alesia did the revolt collapse. The next year, C. completed his subjugation of the country.

From C.'s standpoint, the Gallic wars were a means of gaining political power at Rome. Throughout these years he was involved in Roman politics, employing various agents. He used his enormous war booty to ornament buildings in Italy and the provinces, and to give low interest loans to magistrates and senators, and donatives to kings, provincials and the masses in Rome. He thus gained considerable influence in the Senate, as well as great popularity. In April 56 BC, C. met Crassus and Pompey at Luca and renewed their alliance. In 55 BC, C.'s provincial command was prolonged for five years. Julia, Pompey's wife and C.'s daughter, died in 54 BC, and Crassus was killed at Carrhae (53 BC). Pompey grew jealous of C.'s growing influence, and gradually allied himself with C.'s opponents. C. was able to maintain his command only with the assistance of the magistrates and senators whom he had "bought". After various proposals by C. for a compromise had failed, the Senate decreed a state of emergency (7 January 49 BC). This news reached C. at Ariminum, and he decided to cross the Rubicon on the night of 10 January, thereby initiating civil war.

C.'s rapid advance surprised his unprepared opponents, who had expected his soldiers to desert him. Pompey had already decided on the evacuation of Italy, followed by the consuls and numerous ex-magistrates and senators. Unable to hinder their embarkation from *Brundisium, C. set out for Spain. On 2 August 49 BC, he won a great victory at *Ilerda, securing this part of the empire, as well as the loyalty of seven legions. On his way back to Italy, he brought the siege of Massilia to a successful conclusion. He crossed to Epirus in 48 BC. After the unsuccessful siege of Pompey at Dyrrachium (modern Durazzo) , C. led his army to Thessaly, where he was reinforced by two legions. At Pharsalus, on 9 August 48 BC, Pompey at last agreed to a fight. C.'s veterans, inferior in numbers but of much greater experience, won a total victory. On his arrival in Egypt, C. found that Pompey had already been slain. C.'s attempt to settle the Egyptian royal succession, and his demand for payment of a debt due to him since 59 BC, induced the Egyptians to revolt. C. was placed in a difficult situation, but a force arrived which enabled him to crush the rebellion and install Cleopatra, now his mistress, on the throne. C. proceeded to Asia where he defeated Pharnaces, son of *Mithradates VI, in a short battle at Zela (of *veni, vidi, vici* fame).

After a short pause in Rome, C. crossed to Africa, where he defeated the Pompeians (under *Metellus Scipio) at Thapsus in April 46 BC. C. was now able to return to Rome and on 26 July 46 BC celebrated a quadruple triumph: Gaul, Egypt, Pontus and Africa. But he was again forced to fight Romans when Pompey's sons and *Labienus stirred an insurrection in Spain. After a hard fight, decided by the bravery of his veterans, C. routed his enemies at Munda in 45 BC.

C. sought to redress many of the evils from which the Roman state suffered. The list of those entitled to the corn ration was reduced to 15,000 and C. founded commercial colonies at Carthage and Corinth. His veterans received land in the many colonies founded in Italy and the provinces, and in 49 BC Roman citizenship was conferred upon Cisalpine Gaul. These steps were the starting point for the Romanization of the provinces. In his enlarged Senate, numbering 900, C. included senators from all Italy and the provinces. To secure order, the *collegia* were abolished, magistrates were provided with troops, the penalty for violence was increased, and one third of the shepherds were to be freemen. The current calendar, almost three months ahead of the solar year, was reformed (the Julian calendar remained in use until Pope Gregory XIII replaced it in 1582). Despite his other plans, including comprehensive building operations, he was restless with civil administration and took great interest in his preparations for an expedition against Parthia which were cut short by his murder.

C.'s prime position in the state was intolerable to many of the aristocracy: he was consul several times, appointed dictator for ten years in 46 BC, and for life in 44 BC. Although not deified nor willing to accept kingship, C. was given unusual honours: statues in temples, his visage on coins, a *flamen*, the tribunician sacrosanctity and supervision of morals. Further, C. became impatient and arrogant with senators and the Senate. His famous "clemency" actually put people at his mercy. When made dictator for life in early 44 BC, it became apparent that C. would not freely surrender his absolute power. Under the leadership of Brutus and Cassius, the conspirators decided to eliminate C. and thus restore liberty to the Republic as well as to their own dignity.

C. stated that Sulla showed himself to be ignorant of

the alphabet of politics when he abdicated the dictatorship. C. sought power and knew that he needed money and soldiers to gain it. These were acquired in Gaul, and he used them to gain influence in Rome. In addition to his mastery of political technique, C. was·indeed a leader of men. His troops followed him not only for the generous bounties he gave them but also because C. always displayed his devotion to them. As a general, C. introduced no new tactics — his military success was achieved by an uncanny ability to make the best of a situation, to arrive at quick, courageous decisions, to march at speed, to take advantage of topography and to obtain the maximum from his loyal and experienced soldiers.

C. wrote two books: *Commentaries on the Gallic War*, in seven books, describing wars in Gaul till 52 BC. (An eighth book by *Hirtius completes the description to 50 BC.) *Commentaries on the Civil War*, in three books, describes the progress of the war until the Battle of Pharsalus. This sort of writing was new to Roman literature; C.'s narrative seldom deviates from his subject, it gives the essential, necessary details and, unlike other historical works, is devoid of rhetoric. C.'s ˙style is clear and his accounts of battles are lucid. In an artful way, it also seeks to justify C.'s foreign and civil wars.

Ancient sources include: Caesar's own works, A. J. Peskett, *Civil War* (Loeb), 1921; H. J. Edwards, *Gallic War* (Loeb), 1930. Salust's *Bellum Catilinae*; numerous references in Cicero's works. Caesar's biographies by Plutarch and Suetonius and Appian's *Civil Wars*. Modern literature is vast; note especially, M. Gelzer, *Caesar* (En. tr.), 1968; J. P. V. D. Balsdon, *Julius Caesar*, 1967; T. A. Dorey (ed), *Latin Historians*, 1966.

CAESAREA (1), IOL (modern Cherchel) Harbour on the African coast, some 100 km west of Algiers. C. was a Phoenician trading post, first mentioned in a literary source from the 4th century BC. The early city of Iol was renamed Caesarea by *Juba II, who made it capital of his kingdom. Under Juba, C. was furnished with a good harbour and it became a centre of Hellenistic culture. After *Caligula had the Mauretanian king killed, his kingdom was annexed to the Roman Empire, and C. was made the capital of the new province of Mauretania Caesariensis. A colony of veterans was settled here under the Emperor Claudius. C. prospered and, with an area of c. 370 hectares and a population of about 100,000, it became one of the important cities of Africa. Christianity developed in C. from the 2nd century AD on. The Vandals captured and sacked C., but it recovered and was made capital of the province of Mauretania Secunda in the 6th century AD. Various public and private buildings have been discovered on the site.
S. Gsell, *Cherchell, antique Iol²*, 1952.

CAESAREA (2) MARITIMA On the coast of Palestine, the site of an earlier Phoenician town ("Strato's Tower"). Alexander Jannaeus conquered it at the end of the 2nd century BC, but Pompey separated it from Judaea in 63 BC. The city was granted to *Herod the Great by Augustus in 30 BC. Herod rebuilt it, renaming it C. in honour of Augustus. From AD 6 on, C. was the residence of the Roman governors of Judaea. (An inscription with the name of *Pontius Pilate was found there in 1962.) C. prospered, though the city was disturbed by quarrels between Jewish and Greek elements. Vespasian granted C. the status of a Roman colony. Christianity developed here in the 2nd century AD, and it became the seat of a bishopric.

The Roman theatre at Caesarea Maritime

Origen lived in C. from AD 231 on, and Eusebius was bishop here. C. was destroyed during the Muslim conquest of Palestine.
Jones, *Cities²* (s.v.).

CAESAREA (3) MAZACA Capital of Cappadocia. Ariarathes V, who promoted Greek culture in his country, made it a Greek city. It was renamed C. c. 10 BC. After the Roman annexation of Cappadocia, in AD 17, C. became the residence of the governing procurator.

CAESAREA (4) PHILIPPI (modern Banyas) Hellenized city in Batanea, south of Mount Hermon, earlier known as Panion ("Place of Pan"). The land was given to *Herod the Great by Augustus, and upon Herod's death (4 BC) this part of the kingdom fell to his son Philip, who enlarged the city and renamed it in honour of Augustus (or Tiberius). The appellative, Philippi, distinguished it from other cities of similar name.
Jones, *Cities²* (s.v.).

CAESARION Eldest son of *Cleopatra VII, born in 47 BC. From 44 BC, he was the joint ruler of Egypt with his mother, who claimed that Caesar was his father. *Antonius (4) publicly acknowledged this paternity, and proclaimed C. "King of Kings" in 34 BC, thereby maintaining that C. and his mother ("Queen of Queens") were the rulers of the Asian empire of Alexander the Great. These claims could not be ignored by Octavian, who after his victory over Antony had C. killed (30 BC).

CALAMIS Greek (probably Boeotian) sculptor of the first part of the 5th century BC. Among C.'s famous works was a huge bronze statue of Apollo, commissioned by the city of Apollonia Pontica. A Hermes modelled on a statue of C., made for *Tanagra, appears on Roman coins of that city.

CALCHAS First appears in Homer as a priest of Apollo and a diviner. C. went to Troy with the Greeks and his advice and prophecies rendered them much service. He foretold the helpful role Achilles would play and warned that the bow and arrows of Heracles must be secured to attain the fall of Troy. He is connected with numerous episodes that took ˌplace during the expedition to Troy, and during its siege. In one version, C. died after meeting *Mopsus, who proved to be a better diviner.

CALEDONIA The area of north Scotland beyond the frontiers of the Roman province of Britain. Roman armies first encountered the Caledonii under *Agricola, who won a victory at Mount Graupius (site unknown) in 84 BC. Agricola was recalled, and later Roman emperors did not insist on conquering this part of the British Isles.
S. Frere, *Britannia*, 1967 (s.v.).

CALIGULA (Gaius Julius Caesar Germanicus) Born on 31 August AD 12, to *Germanicus and *Agrippina (2). He was nicknamed "Caligula" ("Little Boot") by soldiers, on account of the military boots he wore as a child. C.'s father would take him on his tours of provincial duty to the Rhine and the East. After his father's death, C. stayed with his mother in Rome. From AD 32 on, he lived with Tiberius on Capri. C. was made Pontifex in AD 31, and quaestor in AD 33. After many other relatives had been killed, C. remained the only serious candidate to succeed Tiberius, who designated him and Tiberius Gemellus as his heirs. With the aid of *Macro, C. became emperor on 16 March AD 37, after the death of Tiberius. C. ruled moderately at first, and was respectful to the Senate. A change occurred in him after a severe illness, in October AD 37 (perhaps because of a brain injury). He squandered the huge treasury left by Tiberius and put numerous people to death. Nothing came of his ambition to conquer Germany or Britain. His rule became more and more despotic, and, in the manner of the Ptolemies, he looked upon his sisters as his wives, and demanded divine honours. It was only due to the intervention of *Petronius, governor of Syria, that C.'s image was not placed in the Jewish temple in Jerusalem. In January AD 41, he fell victim to a conspiracy provoked by his tyrannical rule. His wife and daughter were killed with him.
Suetonius, *Gaius Caligula*; Dio, 59;
J. P. V. D. Balsdon, *The Emperor Caligula*, 1934.

CALLIAS Soldier and statesman of Athens in the 5th century BC. Of a rich family, C. was the brother-in-law of *Cimon and the cousin of *Aristides (1). C. fought bravely in the Battle of Marathon. He is especially known for the "Peace of C.", concluded *c.* 449 BC. There are some doubts as to the authenticity of this peace (perhaps it was an informal agreement) but evidently the war between Athens and Persia, which had begun early in the 5th century BC., did cease after the reported date.

CALLIMACHUS Leading Alexandrian poet and scholar. A native of Cyrene, born *c.* 320–315 BC, C. came to Alexandria *c.* 290–285 BC, where he first earned his living as a teacher in the suburb of Eleusis. He then received a position at the Alexandrian Library and became court poet to *Ptolemy II. Among his many disciples, the most famous were *Apollonius Rhodius, *Eratosthenes and *Aristophanes of Byzantium – all of whom became directors of the Alexandrian Library. C. was still writing poetry in the 40s of the 3rd century BC. The date of his death is unknown.
    A prolific writer, C. is credited with some 800 works on various subjects. His *Pinakes* ("Tablets"), in 120 volumes, was a literary history which included short bibliographies on each writer (the opening words and the number of lines of every work were noted). C.'s writings include treatises on the Athenian dramatic poets, on *Democritus, on the foundation of cities and islands, several encyclopaedias on special topics (such as winds, games and rivers) and collections of Paradoxa. All these important and scholarly works have perished, but C.'s poetry and views on poetry are of much more signifi-

cance. C. opposed the epic genre which, he argued, was merely the repetition of old material or the invention of heroic incidents. He favoured short, refined and carefully written poems (hence the saying "a big book is a big evil" (*mega bibilion mega kakon*)). This brought him into bitter conflict with his own pupil, *Apollonius Rhodius, who, as Director of the Library, was his superior. Apollonius was forced to retire to Rhodes, and C. attacked his rival in the *Ibis*, a work now lost but supposed to have been imitated by Ovid. C. quarrelled with other contemporary poets who were severely critical of him. His *Answer to the Telchines* ("backbiters"), a poem written late in his life, is extant. C. wrote his erudite and polished poetry for an elite. His most famous poem was the *Aetia* ("Causes"), four books of elegiacs of which only some hundred lines have survived from papyri. The poem gave etiological legends on rites, customs and historical episodes, material in which C. could fully display his erudition. Of his *Epigrams*, some sixty are extant and he is represented more fully in this kind of poetry than any other Alexandrian poet. Many of the epigrams were commissioned for inscriptions on tombstones or votive gifts; others were moralistic, dramatic or literary, effectively descriptive in their portrayal of personal traits. C.'s *Hymns* to Zeus, Apollo, Artemis, Demeter, Delos, and the Baths of Pallas are extant; all but the sixth are written in hexameters. These poems were composed for recitation before a literary audience and not for ritual use. In them, C. displays his metrical skill and his antiquarian learning. Occasionally C. alludes to contemporary events (such as the Gallic invasion of 279 BC) with humour, wit and dramatic power. Of C.'s book the *Iambi*, about a thousand lines, mere fragments, are extant, but the contents are sufficiently known from extant summaries. Some are satirically critical of the literary trends of the day, others describe C.'s position and several are etiological stories. C. preferred the epyllion, a narrative poem of several hundred hexameters on some episode in the life of a mythical hero. To demonstrate his point, he composed his famous epyllion *Hecale* (of which some seventy lines — recovered from a wooden tablet — are extant). The epyllion is based on the heroic feat of Theseus, who killed the bull of Marathon. C.'s narrative concentrates on Hecale, an old woman who, without knowing Theseus, entertains him on his way to meet the bull (after his deed, Theseus finds her dead and honours her). C. had a great influence on contemporary and later poets, though many rejected his views on the epic genre. He was often imitated and his popularity was long-lived. Catullus paraphrased C.'s poem "Lock of Berenice" in Latin, and evidently was much influenced by C.'s views on poetry. Ovid to some extent followed the narrative technique of C. The numerous papyri finds with C.'s poetry suggest that he was read more than any other Hellenistic poet. He was often cited by grammarians and scholiasts.
R. Pfeiffer, *Callimachus*, 1949–1953;
A. W. Mair, *Callimachus* (Loeb), 1921;
C. A. Trypanis, *Callimachus' Aetia*, etc. (Loeb), 1958;
T. B. L. Webster, *Hellenistic Poetry and Art*, 1964.

CALLIOPE One of the nine *Muses. In late antiquity, C. was regarded as the Muse of the heroic epic.

CALLISTHENES Greek historian, nephew of Aristotle. C. was Alexander's official historian in his war against the Persian Empire. In his work, he extolled Alexander and supported the notion of his being the son of Zeus. Despite this extravagant flattery, C. opposed and derided Alexander's attempt (in 327 BC) to introduce the custom of *proskynesis*, "prostration", into his court. Soon afterwards, Alexander found the opportunity to implicate C. in a conspiracy, and had him put to death. C.'s history (which has not survived) seems to have been used by many writers on Alexander.

L. Pearson, *His. Al. Gr.*, 1960, 22–49.

CALLISTRATUS Athenian orator and statesman, active in the first half of the 4th century BC. Becoming apprehensive about the ascendancy of Thebes, he brought about a peace with Sparta (371 BC). Because his policy regarding Thebes was not successful, he was prosecuted, and it was only by his excellent oratory that he escaped condemnation (in 366 BC). He was prosecuted again in 361 BC, and condemned to death *in absentia*. An able financier – he had organized the financial arrangements of the Second Athenian League – C. was employed by Macedonia in reorganizing its finances. On his return to Attica, he was executed.

CALLISTUS, Gaius Julius Freedman of *Caligula, who gained much power. C. supported the conspiracy against his former master, and *Claudius (4) appointed him to the important office of *libellis*. He retained his influence as long as Claudius lived.

CALPURNIA *Caesar's third and last wife, whom he married in 59 BC (perhaps out of political considerations). C.'s father, of the noble plebeian Calpurnii Pisones family, duly became consul in 58 BC. Despite Caesar's amorous adventures, C. remained loyal to him. She vainly tried to prevent her husband from attending the Senate on the Ides of March, and after his murder gave his papers and money to Antony.

CALPURNIUS SICULUS, Titus Pastoral poet of the 1st century AD. Seven of his poems have survived, three praising Nero – under whom he seems to have flourished – as the ruler who restored a Golden Age, and one devoted to a description of the amphitheatre built by Nero in Rome. C.'s poems, like other bucolic poems, are composed in dialogue form, and contain, *inter alia*, a love song and some advice on the breeding of goats and sheep. He was evidently influenced by *Theocritus and *Virgil.

J. W. and A. M. Duff, *Min. Lat. Poets* (Loeb), 1934.

CALVINUS, Gnaeus Domitius Roman statesman of a noble plebeian family, elected consul for 53 BC after a complicated bribery agreement (which miscarried) with the consuls of 54 BC. He fought with Caesar in the Civil War and later supported the Second Triumvirate. After his second consulate in 40 BC, he governed Spain and with booty captured there he decorated the *Regia.

CALVUS, Gaius Licinius Roman poet and orator of the 1st century BC, son of the historian *Macer, close friend of *Catullus. His talents were recognized by Cicero and *Quintilian, and his speeches, of which only a few fragments are extant, were models of rhetoric under the Empire. *Or. Rom. Fr.*[3]; Morel, *Fr. Poet. Lat.*

CALYDON Aetolian town, mentioned by Homer (*Il.* 9.530 etc.) which produced several prominent figures of Greek mythology: *Oineus, *Tydeus, *Deianira, and *Meleager (the hero of the Calydonian boar-hunt).

CALYPSO ("The Hidden" or "Hider") In Greek mythology, a nymph. In Homer, Odysseus found shelter on her island after his ship had foundered. C. willingly entertained him and promised him immortality, detaining him on her island for seven years. In the eighth year, she obeyed Zeus and released Odysseus, assisting him to improvise a boat.

CAMARINA Dorian city on the mouth of the river Hipparis in southern Sicily. Though founded by Syracuse (599 BC), for long periods it was its bitter enemy and twice suffered destruction by its mother city (553, 484 BC). Reinforced by *Timoleon (339 BC), C. had its final period of prosperity, but it was seriously damaged in the First Punic War (258 BC) and thereafter declined.

Dunbabin, *Western Greeks* (s.v.).

CAMBYSES Persian king (530–522 BC), son of *Cyrus I. He conquered Cyprus and Egypt in 525 BC, but failed to advance into Ethiopia. He died in Syria on his way to suppress a revolt.

CAMILLUS, Marcus Furius Roman general and statesman, active during the early 4th century BC. C. was the first real personality in Roman history of whose activities and achievements there is reliable evidence, albeit mixed with much legendary material. His first great achievement was the conquest of *Veii, Rome's Etruscan rival, in 396 BC. The siege lasted ten years (a tradition probably modelled on the ten-year siege of Troy), and Rome's influence in southern Etruria was subsequently established. From the booty, a gift was dedicated to the temple of Apollo at Delphi. In legend, C. raised an army and defeated the Gauls who had captured Rome, and even regained the gold paid to them.

C.'s real achievement lay in the work of reconstruction that followed the retreat of the Gauls. He successfully led Roman armies against the neighbouring Volscians, Etruscans and Aequi who tried to take advantage of Rome's defeat. He also promoted military reforms, including the matter of soldiers' pay. At home, he generally supported a policy of reconciliation between the Patricians and the Plebeians, but opposed the attempt of *Manlius Capitolinus to court the poor and crushed his so-called revolution. C. was credited with the building of the temple of Concord. For his military reforms, his victories in the field and his mild policy at home, he was denoted the "father of the country and the second founder of the city of Rome" (Liv. 7.1,10).

Livy, 4–6; Plutarch, *Camillus*.

CAMPANIA The plain stretching from Latium in the north to the promontory of *Surrentum in the south. Famous for its fertility, C. had three to four harvests a year. Grains and vegetables were grown there and, in time, olive groves and vineyards were planted, especially in Venafrum, in the Ager Falernus, and on the slopes of Vesuvius and Massicus. C. had good harbours, notably at *Puteoli. The original population were the Ausones, Greeks settled there from the mid-8th century BC on, founding several colonies: *Cumae, *Neapolis and Puteoli. From the end of the 7th century BC on, Etruscans penetrated into the hinterland of C., founding the city of *Capua, from which C. derives its name. In the ensuing conflict between the Etruscans and the Greeks, the latter were on the defensive until they overcame the Etruscans in 474 BC. Soon after, C. was invaded by the Sabelli, who descended from the Apennines to occupy the entire land, capturing Capua *c.* 425 BC, and Cumae *c.* 421 BC. These new conquerors mingled with the earlier population and imposed their language, which came to be known as Oscan. Roman rule extended over C. from 338 BC on, but only in 90/89 BC were all Campanians given Roman citizenship.

J. Day, *Yale Classical Studies*, 1932, 167–208.

CAMPUS MARTIUS Plain stretching from the Tiber river till the hills of Rome, the Pincius, the Quirinal and the Capitol. In early times, the C. was beyond the city-walls and uninhabited; it was public property and served as a meeting place for the *Comitia centuriata* and for the levying of the army. It derived its name from the altar of Mars which stood there. Eventually, many public buildings were built on it, including markets, temples, the circus of *Flaminius, the Mausoleum of Augustus and the Pantheon of *Agrippa (1). Private owners, too, acquired land there for their villas. Under the Empire, the entire area was densely built-up.

Platner-Ashby, *Top. Dict. Rome* (s.v.).

CAMULODUNUM (modern Colchester) Important Belgic settlement in Britain where a Roman colony was founded in AD 49. It had been the capital city of *Cunobellinus. It was captured and destroyed by *Boudicca in AD 60, but was rebuilt and fortified later.

M. R. Hull, *Roman Colchester*, 1957.

CANABAE Civilian settlements adjacent to Roman army camps, inhabited by various traders, dealers and women, who served the needs of the legionaries. Under the Empire, the C. were augmented by discharged soldiers, artisans and farmers, acquiring some sort of local administration. Some C. gained the status of *municipia* or *coloniae*.

CANNAE Village in Apulia, famous as the site of the crushing victory inflicted by Hannibal on the Roman army in 216 BC. The exact site of the battle, whether north of the river Aufidus (modern Ofanto) or south of it, is disputed. The Roman army, which, according to *Polybius, numbered 86,000, was encircled and routed by 45,000 Carthaginians.

Polyb. 3. 107–118, Livy, 22. 43–9;
Wallbank, *Polybius*, 1, 435ff.

Portrait of Caracalla on a sestertius

CAPITOL, CAPITOLIUM A hill in Rome. The C. was inhabited later than the other hills, probably only in the 6th century BC. It was mainly a public and religious centre, and was famous for the Temple of Jupiter Optimus Maximus, Juno, and Minerva, built by the Etruscan kings of Rome and dedicated, according to Roman tradition, in 509 BC. This temple was burnt and rebuilt several times.

Platner-Ashby, *Top. Dict. Rome* (s.v.);
E. Gjerstad, *Early Rome*, 1960, 3, 168ff.

CAPPADOCIA Country in eastern Asia Minor bounded by Cilicia, the Euphrates, Armenia and the kingdom of Pontus. The population of C. lived in villages and was subject to feudal lords. Large territories were the property of temples and were ruled by their priests. C. was primarily a land of animal breeding: sheep, mules and horses. It was conquered by the Medes and incorporated within the Persian Empire. Ariarathes, the Persian satrap, was killed in 322 BC opposing the Macedonian advance through C. His son, however, regained the country (c. 300 BC), probably with Armenian assistance. Ariarathes III became king c. 225 BC. The dynasty had little success in introducing Hellenization and urbanization into the country. C. was annexed to the Roman Empire in AD 17. See also *Ariarathes, *Ariobarzanes.

Magie, *Asia* (s.v.).

CAPUA Principal city of *Campania. Greek tradition ascribes its foundation to the Trojan Capys, but archaeological discoveries indicate that C. was of Etruscan foundation, probably in the 7th century BC. The fertile Capuan territory constantly attracted enemy invaders. In 338 BC, it lost part of its territory to Rome and was given Roman citizenship without suffrage. The institutions and magistrates of the city continued to function, though from 318 BC on, two Roman prefects were appointed annually for C. and for *Cumae. In the course of the 3rd century BC, C. gained much wealth and, proud of its economic power and resenting the Roman rule, the city joined Hannibal in 216 BC. Rome recaptured it in 211 BC, putting its treacherous aristrocrats to death and confiscating its entire land. The remaining population was later granted political rights but was left without municipal organization, being subject directly to Roman magistrates. A colony was sent there by *Sulla, and under Caesar's agrarian law of 59 BC, the public land, preserved since 211 BC, was distributed to 20,000 colonists, mostly veterans of Pompey. Under the Empire, C. had the status of a *colonia*. It was partially destroyed by the Vandals in AD 456, and ceased to exist after its sacking by the Saracens, in AD 840.

Scullard, *Etruscan Cities*, 190–4.
M. W. Frederiksen, *PBSR*, 1959, 80–130.

CARACALLA, Marcus Aurelius Antoninus Roman emperor, born AD 186 to *Septimius Severus and *Julia Domna; his nickname, C., derived from the Celtic garment he wore. C. accompanied his father on many of his campaigns. After Severus' death (AD 211), he was at first co-ruler with his brother, Geta, whom he later had killed, along with numerous supporters (AD 212). Among his other victims were his wife and the eminent jurist *Papinianus. In July, AD 212, C. issued his famous *Constitutio Antoniniana* granting the entire population of the Empire Roman citizenship — and thereby making it subject to inheritance tax. From AD 213, he conducted wars in Germany, subsequently on the Danubian frontier and later in the East. His plan to conquer Parthia was cut short by his murder, by *Macrinus, in AD 217. C. generally followed his father's anti-senatorial policy. He built huge baths in Rome.

Dio, 77—78, Herodian, 1.

CARATACUS Son of Cunobelinus, king of the Catuvellauni, whose capital was at Camulodunum (Colchester). C. resisted the Roman invasion but was defeated by Aulus Plautius in AD 43. He found shelter among the Silures, whom he led against the Romans in AD 41, and after another defeat, fled to the Brigantes whose queen, Cartimandua, betrayed him. C. was led in a triumph in Rome, but Claudius spared his life.

D. R. Dudley—G. Webster, *The Roman Conquest of Britain*, 1965 (s.v.).

CARAUSIUS, Marcus Aurelius Mausaeus Menapian of low birth, who distinguished himself in military service in Gaul. In AD 286, the Emperor *Maximian appointed him to fight the pirates in the English Channel. C. soon came under suspicion of embezzlement, and crossed over to Britain with his fleet. The attempt to suppress him failed and he was left alone as ruler of Britain. C. managed to add northeastern Gaul to his territory, but was murdered by *Allectus in AD 293.

CARBO Branch of the plebeian clan of the Papirii. The best known member of this line was Gnaeus Papirius Carbo, tribune in 92 BC, who supported *Cinna (1) in 87 BC. He was consul in 85, 84, and 82 BC. He was defeated time and again by Sulla and his lieutenants, and sought refuge in Africa; he was finally captured by Pompey and put to death.

CARDIA Greek city on the western side of the Thracian *Chersonessus (1), founded by colonists from *Miletus and *Clazomenae at the end of 7th century BC. In the middle of the 6th century, Athenian settlers were led there by Miltiades the Elder who governed the city. His nephew *Miltiades left it to the Persians in 493 BC, and after their expulsion from Greece, Athens regained its hegemony. C. opportunely joined *Philip II (351 BC) but was later destroyed by *Lysimachus, who transferred its population to his Lysimacheia. Shortly afterwards it was restored. Its best known natives were *Eumenes (1) and the historian *Hieronymus.

S. Casson, *Macedonia, Thrace and Illyria*, 1926 (s.v.).

CARIA The country of the Carians, mentioned by Homer (e.g. *Il.* 2.867ff.), in southwestern Asia Minor, south of the river Maeander and bordering on Pisidia in the east and Lycia in the southeast. Herodotus says that the Carians considered themselves autochthonous and were formerly called Leleges (1.171), i.e., the pre-Hellenic population of the Aegean world that inhabited the islands and served in the navy of the *Minos (cf. *Il.* 10.428; Athen. 6.272). Greeks settled on the shores of C. as early as the 9th century BC. The most important cities were *Halicarnassus and *Cnidos—but the Carians retained their traditional ways of life up to the 4th century BC. They took part in the Ionian revolt against Parthia in 499—494 BC, and were later under Athenian hegemony. The country was Hellenized by *Mausolus.

CARINUS, Marcus Aurelius Elder son of the Emperor *Carus, Caesar and ruler of the West at the time of his father's campaign against Persia (AD 282); the following year, C. was made Augustus. When *Diocletian became emperor in the East, after the death of C.'s father and brother, Numerian, he clashed with C. at Margus in Moesia. C., however, was killed by his own men.

CARMENTIS Ancient Roman goddess, principally of women in childbirth, whose festival (*Carmentalia*) was on 11 and 15 January. In mythology she was a prophetess, *Evander's mother. Her shrine was at the Capitol.

Latte, *R. Rel.*, 136f.; Platner-Ashby, *Top. Dict. Rome*, 101.

CARNEADES Greek philosopher, born in Cyrene in 214 BC, died in 129 BC. C. studied at the *Academy and became its head. In 155 BC, he was a member of the Athenian embassy to Rome where he made an impression by two persuasive but contradictory speeches on justice. In one speech, he advocated utilitarian behaviour aimed at safeguarding the selfish interests of men or states, while in the other he defended justice on moral grounds. *Cato (1) was alarmed by his argumentation and demanded the dismissal of the embassy.

C. never published any of his writings and it was through the numerous treatises of his pupil, *Clitomachus, that his ideas gained extensive influence in antiquity, though nothing of them has survived. In his philosophical writings, *Cicero reproduced many of the views of C., e.g. concerning gods, fate and the aims of human activity. By preaching Sceptical philosophy, C. continued a tradition held in the Academy since *Arcesilaus. Adopting Stoic terminology, he maintained that reality can be reached only through the medium of "phantasiae", that is, the apparent impressions it makes on the mental faculty or senses; there is no way, however, to judge whether a phantasia is true or not, thus it is preferable that decisions and conclusions be avoided. For practical purposes, decisions and actions should follow the more persuasive (and hence the more likely to be true) phantasiae.

M. M. Patrick, *The Greek Sceptics*, 1929.

CARNUNTUM A Roman military camp on the Danube; from the reign of Tiberius on, belonging to Pannonia. C. was an important crossroads to Italy and the Danube valley. The *Canabae around the camp grew and became the capital of Upper Pannonia (AD 106). Hadrian gave C. municipal status. It flourished in the 2nd century AD, but suffered heavily in the Marcomannic Wars of Marcus *Aurelius, from which it recovered under Septimius Severus, who became emperor there in AD 193, and made it a *colonia*. It was destroyed at the end of the 4th century AD. Most of the legionary camp at C. has been excavated and reconstructed.

E. Swoboda, *Carnuntum*[4], 1964.

CARRHAE (modern Harran, the Haran of the Bible) City in northern Mesopotamia first mentioned in a document from the early 2nd millennium BC. A Macedonian colony was established there by the Seleucids, and it was there that the Parthians defeated *Crassus (4). Marcus Aurelius annexed it to the Roman Empire and Septimius Severus made it a *colonia*. It was conquered by the Arabs in AD 639.

Jones, *Cities*[2] (s.v.).

CARTHAGE A colony of Phoenician Tyre, founded, according to the Greek historian *Timaeus, in 814 BC. Its site on a peninsula in the Gulf of Tunis, with good harbours and a position favourable for commerce, made it the most successful Phoenician colony, although for a long time it remained under the influence of the mother-city. After the downfall of Tyre (in the 7th century BC), C. was able to bring other Phoenician settlements in the western Mediterranean under its hegemony. It managed to subdue the native tribes in North Africa — the Libyans on its eastern boundaries, and the Numidians on the west — thus establishing a continuous rule from the Straits of Gibraltar to Cyrenaica. Seeking to monopolize sea com-

Carthage — a view of the ruins

merce in the western Mediterranean, the Carthaginians inevitably clashed with the Greeks; supported by Etruscans, they defeated a combined fleet of *Phocaea and *Massilia off Corsica, c. 535 BC. Following this victory, C. extended its rule to southern Sardinia and southern Spain, where, some time later, it destroyed the kingdom of *Tartessus. C. also intervened in Sicilian affairs, when the Phoenician settlers were hard-pressed by the Greeks. The Carthaginian general *Malchus established Carthaginian power in the western part of *Sicily before the middle of the 6th century BC; *Lilybaeum, *Panormus and Drepanum were the main strongholds of C. there. The struggle between the Carthaginians and the Greeks continued until the 3rd century BC, neither contestant being able to eliminate the other.

In 509 BC, C. signed a treaty with Rome recognizing Roman hegemony in *Latium, while Rome undertook not to intervene in territories subject to C. (Sicily, Sardinia and Africa) and not to carry commerce into the western Mediterranean. Similar treaties were concluded in 348 and 306 BC. In 279 BC, a treaty was concluded with Rome against *Pyrrhus. These friendly relations terminated in 264 BC, when Rome consented to help free *Messene of Carthaginian domination; the despatch of a Roman army to Sicily began the First Punic War (264–241 BC). After initial Roman successes, *Hieron king of Syracuse signed an alliance with Rome. As C. was determined to continue the fight, Rome realized that the entire island of Sicily must be conquered. Rome won two great naval victories (in 260 and 255 BC), but an expeditionary force sent to Africa, though at first successful, was defeated in 255 BC, and the Roman fleet carrying the survivors was wrecked. As the war dragged on, C. lost ground in Sicily, where only Lilybaeum and Drepanum remained in its hands. Though *Hamilcar's courageous raids greatly harassed the Romans, they maintained their superiority. Only after the Carthaginian fleet was beaten, off the Aegates Islands in 241 BC, did the war come to a close. C. had lost Sicily, and was forced to pay 3,200 talents in indemnity. When C. sought to quell her rebellious mercenaries in Sardinia, Rome again intervened, and C. was compelled to surrender that island and Corsica, and to pay 1,200 talents. These losses were partially made up by Hamilcar's conquest of southern and eastern Spain (237–229 BC); his achievements were consolidated by the diplomacy of *Hasdrubal (1), who was succeeded in command by *Hannibal, son of Hamilcar, in 221 BC. Hannibal's capture of *Saguntum (219 BC) initiated the Second Punic War (218–201 BC). Despite Hannibal's military genius, Rome won the war through its superior manpower, the tactics of *Fabius Cunctator, the boldness of *Scipio Africanus, and the tenacity of the Roman people and its senatorial leaders. After Hannibal himself was defeated at Zama (202 BC), peace was concluded (201 BC). C. had lost all of Spain, surrendered its navy, and was ordered to pay 10,000 talents (in fifty annual installments) and was forbidden to go to war without the authorization of Rome. Despite its crushing defeat, C. soon recovered and its economy flourished. Rome was suspicious of this revival and in all the disputes between

C. and its aggressive neighbour *Masinissa, Rome sided with the latter. In the 150s BC, *Cato Censorius agitated for the destruction of C. The opportunity came when C. attacked Masinissa without Rome's consent. In 149 BC, Rome began the Third Punic War, sending an army to Africa. The Roman general first demanded and received hostages and what arms C. had at its disposal; he then announced that, by the decision of the Roman Senate, C. had to be destroyed and rebuilt 15 miles from the sea. The Carthaginians refused to obey and for three years defended the city. In 146 BC, the Roman commander *Scipio Aemilianus razed C. to the ground.

C. drew its wealth mainly from commerce and its foreign policy was aimed at securing a monopoly for its merchants, who traded with the native tribes of Africa and Spain, supplying cloth, wine, jewellery, agricultural products and Greek pottery in exchange for gold, silver and ivory. Carthaginian seamen explored the Atlantic coast of Africa, reaching as far as Sierra Leone. C. established commercial ties with Britain, trading for copper and tin. Carthaginian agriculture was also well developed, especially in the fertile valley of the Bagradas river (modern Medjerda). It became one of the richest cities on the Mediterranean and its walls are said to have extended 20 miles. *Strabo relates that its population numbered 700,000, which would seem somewhat exaggerated.

The stability of Carthaginian government was admired by Greek political thinkers (notably Aristotle and Polybius) who recognized in C. a mixed constitution. Two annually elected *suffetes* were supreme magistrates who possessed juridical powers. They convened the "council of state" and a weak assembly of the people. The council of state numbered several hundred members, elected for life; it supervised foreign affairs, administered subject territories, dealt with matters of war and peace and decided on army mobilization. Thirty members of the council, including the *suffetes*, formed a permanent board. Maintenance of the constitution and the actions of all officials were supervised by 104 judges from among the members of the council. C. was thus ruled by an oligarchy. From the 6th century BC on, C. relied upon mercenaries, Greeks, Libyans, Numidians and Iberians; the generals, however, were always Carthaginian. The oligarchy often selected only mediocre commanders, out of fear that the mercenaries might be used to establish a tyranny. Unsuccessful generals were often punished by crucifixion.

With the destruction of C. in 146 BC, its territory became a Roman province, *Africa. After the abortive attempt of Gaius *Gracchus to establish a colony in C., Caesar colonized the site, which was reinforced with new settlers by Augustus. C. subsequently enjoyed the status of *colonia*, and grew rapidly, becoming the capital of the province and in the 2nd century AD it was the second largest city in the West after Rome. C. was also a cultural centre, and after the 3rd century AD was a centre of Christianity. The *Vandals made it their capital in Africa, but it was destroyed by the Arabs in AD 697.
G. C. and C. Picard, *The Life and Death of Carthage* (En. tr.), 1968.

CARTHAGO NOVA (modern Cartagena) Town on the eastern coast of Spain, founded by *Hasdrubal (1) in 228 BC on the site of an earlier Iberian settlement (Mastia). C. enjoyed an excellent harbour and there were rich silver mines nearby. It also had a well-developed fishing industry. C. was captured by *Scipio Africanus in a bold and surprising attack in 209 BC. Caesar (or Augustus)

made C. a *colonia*. The town was destroyed by the Vandals in AD 425, but was later rebuilt.

CARUS, Marcus Aurelius Roman emperor, born in Narbo. C. was appointed *praefectus praetorio* by *Probus (AD 276); in AD 282 he rebelled, and Probus was killed by his own soldiers. C. defeated the Sarmatians and the Quadi, and proceeded to the East against Persia, together with *Numerian, leaving *Carinus as Caesar in the West. C. managed to conquer Ctesiphon, but was killed ten months after he had become emperor.

CARYATIDES Columns in the shape of draped females for supporting roofs or cross beams. C. featured in Greek architecture from the Archaic period on; they were also known as *Korai*. Vitruvius says that the name C. is derived from Caryae in Laconia (1.45). Famous C. are those of the *Erechteum in Athens.

A caryatid from the Erechtheum at Athens

Ajax and Cassandra. A vase-painting by the Cleophrades—painter

CASSANDER Son of *Antipater (1), and one of the *Diadochi. C. was born *c.* 358 BC. After the death of his father (319 BC), he contested the rule of the regent *Polyperchon, and within four years managed to bring under his control all Macedonia and the greater part of Greece. During this struggle, C. had Olympias (Alexander's mother) executed; he also executed Alexander's widow, Roxane, as well as his son. Though satisfied with the territories he acquired in Europe, C. fought against *Antigonus (1), who sought to rule Alexander's entire empire. C. took part in the decisive battle of Ipsus in 301 BC, in which Antigonus was defeated and killed. He built two great cities, naming them after himself and his wife: Cassandreia and Thessalonica (modern Salonika). C. died in 297 BC.
Diod. Sicul., 18—20.

CASSANDRA Daughter of *Priam of Troy, also known as Alexandra. In one myth she refused to live with Apollo who had given her prophetic powers; he spat into her mouth and consequently her prophesies were not believed. In another version, she and her brother Helenus acquired their powers when their ears were licked by serpents while they were sleeping in a sanctuary of Apollo. C. thus vainly warned the Trojans of the danger of the Wooden Horse. In the capture of Troy, C. fled to the altar of Athena but was maltreated by *Aias the Lesser. *Agamemnon took her home, where they both were killed by *Clytemnestra. C.'s seizure by Aias was a favourite scene in ancient art.

CASSIODORUS SENATOR, Flavius Magnus Aurelius Roman statesman, scholar and writer (*c.* AD 487—583). He served the Gothic king, Theodoric the Great, and then King Athalaricus. He failed to establish a Christian university at Rome in AD 535, and a few years later left for Constantinople. C. retired from public life and established a monastery of learning at his estate in Bruttium — Vivarium — in AD 555. C. aimed at giving his monks both a Christian education and the best in Classical tradition. For this purpose he established a library, and wrote his encyclopaedic work the *Institutiones* which summarises secular sciences and Christian doctrines, and also gives instructions for the copying of manuscripts. He was thus a very important link in the preservation of Classical literature. His other works include *Chronica* — an outline of world history up to AD 519; *History of the Goths* (only fragments have survived); *Variae Epistulae*, a 12—book collection of letters and edicts composed during his term of public service; and *De Orthographia.*
Th. Mommsen, *Variae; Chronica,* 1934;
R. A. B. Mynors, *Institutions,* 1937.

CASSIUS (1) VECELLINUS, Spurius The only Patrician known to have borne the name Cassius. Consul in 502, 493 and 486 BC, C. was famous for the treaty he signed with the Latins in 493 BC, the *Foedus Cassianum,* which terminated the war between Rome and the Latins, and established a military alliance between them, and an agreement that all war gains would be shared equally. According to a dubious legend, C. was sentenced to death in 485 BC, after planning to win royal power by the agrarian law he proposed in 486 BC.
Sherwin—White, *Rom. Cit.*[2] (s.v.).

CASSIUS (2) LONGINUS, Gaius Known to posterity as the murderer of *Caesar. C. began his career by serving as quaestor under *Crassus (4) (53 BC) and after Crassus' defeat at *Carrhae, C. defended Syria against the Parthians (till 51 BC). He suppressed a Jewish rebellion in 52 BC, enslaving thousands of captives. Plebeian tribune in 49 BC, C. followed *Pompey in the Civil War and was given command of a fleet. After Pompey's defeat at *Pharsalus, C. gave up his command. Caesar pardoned him, and made him praetor (44 BC). C., however, was embittered and it was probably he who initiated the conspiracy against Caesar. Against his better judgment, and due to *Brutus' objections, Mark Antony was spared. Unexpectedly, the populace of Rome was infuriated by the murder and, when the situation became dangerous, C. left Rome (mid-April). He went to the East, where he won over the armies of *Bithynia and Syria. The Senate confirmed his provincial commands after Antony had been defeated at Mutina (April 43 BC). C. was commissioned to wage war against *Dolabella, who was declared a "public enemy". Besieged in Laodicea, Dolabella committed suicide and his army joined C. (July 43 BC). After the establishment of the triumvirate (November 43 BC), C. was outlawed together with the other conspirators. In preparation for the coming war, he ruthlessly levied moneys and supplies from the provincials subject to his rule; he captured and sacked *Rhodes, which had refused to supply the quota imposed on her. C. met Brutus at Sardis (early 42 BC), and in the summer of that year they proceeded to Thrace with their armies. In October, they met their opponents at *Philippi in eastern Macedonia. In the first battle, Antony captured C.'s camp and C., in despair, took his own life. Brutus called him "the last of the Romans". C. was considered an able general, but his military talent was no match for Antony; his judgements were often better than those of Brutus who, however, was more influential. C. was charged with avarice, but this evil, from which the provincials suffered, was common to most members of the aristrocracy, including the "noble" Brutus.
Joseph, *AJ.* 14; Plutarch, *Anton, Brut.;* App. *BC* 2—4; Dio, 40—47; Tyrrell—Purser, 6.

CASSIUS (3) LONGINUS RAVILLA, Lucius Roman statesman of noble plebeian family (consul in 127 BC, and censor in 125 BC). By a law he passed as tribune in 137 BC, the secret ballot was established in trials held before the *Comitia. A severe judge, he introduced the question *cui bono?* ("who benefits?") to judicial inquiry.

CASTOR and POLLUX *See* **DIOSCURI**

CATACOMBS The name used in late antiquity to designate the area along the 3rd mile of the Via Appia where there was an underground Christian cemetery connected with St. Sebastian. These underground cemeteries, with tunnels, tomb-chambers (*cubicula*) and coffin-shaped recesses (*loculi*) for inhumation (not cremation) were used in various places (e.g. Alexandria, Syracuse, Neapolis) and also by Jews. Those of Rome are the largest — the C. of St. Callixtus extends over an area of 61 sq km. This system of burial ceased after the 4th century AD. The paintings found in the C. include both Christian and pagan themes.
L. Hertling — E. Kirschbaum, *Die römischen Katakomben*, 1950.

CATANA (modern Catania) Greek city on the southern side of Mount Aetna in Sicily, founded by *Naxos in 729 BC. Its native Charondas gave it new laws in the 6th century BC. In the 5th century BC, *Hieron I transferred the population to Leontini and named C. Aetna. Subsequently it recovered its old name, but not its independence. From 263 BC it was under Roman rule.
Dunbabin, *Western Greeks* (s.v.).

CATILINE, Lucius Sergius Born in 108 BC to a patrician family long in decline. C. served in the Social War in 89 BC, with Cicero and Pompey. He followed *Sulla in the Civil War of 82—81 BC, in which he slew his brother and two brothers-in-law (thereby gaining their properties). After his praetorship (68 BC), C. governed *Africa (67—66 BC). On his return, he was charged with extortion and thus was unable to present his candidacy for the consulates of 65 and 64 BC. Cicero at one time considered defending him; C. was acquitted thanks to the collaboration of the prosecutor *Clodius. C. cooperated with Gaius *Antonius (3) in the consular elections of 63 BC, and won the support of *Crassus (4). C. was beaten by Cicero and Antonius, and lost again in the elections for 62 BC. A haughty Patrician, C. was very embittered by his failures and conceived the idea of capturing the government by plot, seeking and obtaining wide support with the slogan *tabulae novae*, "abolition of debts"; he himself was heavily indebted. He gathered around himself politically frustrated or impoverished aristocrats, Sullan veterans who had squandered their moneys, persons who had lost their properties under Sulla, and indebted artisans and shopkeepers. C.'s supporters were sent to incite the population in many parts of Italy, especially northern Etruria. Aware of the danger, but lacking good evidence, the consul Cicero initially did not dare attack C. He did, however, succeed in having the Senate proclaim a state of emergency (21 October 63 BC). C.'s plan to murder the consul miscarried, and on 7 November 63 BC, Cicero gave the first of his famous orations in the Senate against C. The following day, C. left Rome to take command of his army in Etruria, leaving detailed instructions with his accomplices. In early December 63 BC, Cicero acquired the evidence he needed, and immediately arrested the ringleaders of the conspiracy. C.'s circle lost support when it was divulged that they intended to free slaves and to set fire to Rome. After a heated debate, the Senate voted the death penalty on the leaders caught in Rome, and five were executed by Cicero's orders. The consul Antonius set out to Etruria with an army, and in a decisive battle at Pistoria, in early January 62 BC, C.'s forces were destroyed and he himself was killed.
Cicero, *In Catilinam*; Sallust, *Bellum Catilinae*;
E. G. Hardy, *The Catilinarian Conspiracy*, 1924.

CATO (1) CENSORIUS, Marcus Porcius Leading Roman statesman, historian, writer and orator, born in *Tusculum in 234 BC. In his youth, C. worked hard on his patrimonial estates, improving his financial circumstances; he became friendly with his neighbour, the noble Lucius Valerius Flaccus, who encouraged and assisted him in entering politics. C. used to go to the Forum and offer his services as a lawyer without payment to those who needed them, thus acquiring wide influence. He did military service in the Second Punic War, taking part in the battle at Metaurus (207 BC), where *Hasdrubal (2) was defeated. C. served as quaestor under *Scipio Africanus in *Africa in 204 BC, and on his return brought *Ennius with him to Rome. As governing praetor of Sardinia in 198 BC, his severity caused the usurers to leave the island. In 195 BC, he was consul with Flaccus. He conducted a successful war in his Spanish province, for which he was awarded a triumph when back in Rome in 194 BC. As military tribune in 191 BC, he distinguished himself in the Battle of Thermopylae, against *Antiochus III. Defeated in the elections for the censorship of 189 BC, C. did become censor with Flaccus in 184 BC, in which capacity he could impose his high moral principles on his fellow senators and on the citizens in general. He levied high taxes on luxurious commodities, expelled offending senators, and severely revised the rolls of the Equites. In leasing public contracts, C. offered difficult conditions, thus gaining money for the Treasury. With Flaccus, he carried out an extensive programme of building; public water-basins were paved with stones, sewers were cleaned and new ones were built. He also undertook the building of the Basilica Porcia.

C. was a conservative who sought to preserve the traditional social order and the old, simple mode of life. He opposed the influx of luxury into Rome. In the course of his life, he made a large fortune, but his standard of living remained simple. He preached his high moral principles in public speeches and sought to impose them by prosecuting corrupt magistrates. C. himself was brought to trial by his enemies 44 times, but was always acquitted. He regarded the predominance of *Scipio Africanus as dangerous to the constitution; C. probably instigated the prosecution of L. *Scipio (3) on a charge of peculation, in which his brother Africanus was implicated. As a result Africanus was forced to retire (184 BC). C.'s concern for the welfare of Roman subjects is shown in his repeated attacks on misbehaving governors. In his last year, aged 85, C. represented the *Lusitani in their prosecution of the atrocious governor Sulpicius Galba.

Having an aversion to Hellenism, C. opposed Roman expansion to the East, but sought well established Roman rule in the West. After visiting *Carthage (153 BC), he strongly demanded its destruction, ending his speeches with *ceterum censeo Carthaginem delendam esse*, "besides, Carthage ought to be destroyed".

C.'s treatise *De Agri Cultura*, "On Agriculture," written *c.* 160 BC, is the oldest Latin prose book extant, though its language was later modernized. It deals with management of estates and is based on personal experience, mainly reflecting conditions in Latium and Campania. No logical arrangement can be discerned in the book, and it includes medical recipes, religious customs and even magic incantations. Of his other works only fragments have survived. C. was the first Roman to write history in Latin; his *Origines* described the history of Rome from its foundation down to his own time, and included the foundation stories of the various Italian cities. He was also the first Roman to publish his speeches (more than 150). C. wrote a didactic encyclopaedia for the education of his son, including in it rules on morals, military tactics, farming and health. He was famous for his witticisms, often crude, and published a collection of sayings.

Cicero, *De Senectute*; Nepos, *Cato*; Plutarch, *Cato Maior*; W. D. Hooper — E. B. Ash, Cato's *De Agri Cultura* (Loeb), 1934; Peter, *His. Rom. Rel.*, 1; Scullard, *Rom. Pol.*², *passim* (esp. 153—176, 232—273); E. Badian in *Latin Historians* (ed. T. A. Dorey), 1966.

CATO (2) UTICENSIS, Marcus Porcius Great-grandson of *Cato Censorius. Born in 95 BC; C.'s father died shortly after his birth, and his mother educated him together with the children of her first husband, Servilius Caepio. C. began public service as military tribune in Macedonia (67—66 BC). As quaestor (64 BC), he closely supervised the work of the Treasury, collected long-standing debts and paid state creditors. As tribune-designate in 63 BC, he persuaded the Senate to vote for the death penalty on *Catiline's accomplices caught in Rome. To weaken *Caesar's popularity amongst the poor, C. induced the Senate to distribute corn cheaply to the people; he strongly opposed Pompey's supporters, and caused friction between the Senate and the Equites by obstructing the revision of Asian tax-contracts. In 58 BC, he was removed from Rome by *Clodius, who sent him to annex Cyprus to the Roman Empire, a delicate task in which large sums were involved. C. executed this successfully but lost his accounts during his return to Rome (56 BC). Pompey and Crassus prevented C. from being elected praetor for 55 BC, through bribery, obstruction and violence. He obtained the praetorship for 54 BC, and, as chairman of the extortion court, was in charge of various important trials. From 52 BC on, he supported Pompey, regarding Caesar as the more dangerous to the Republic. When the Civil War broke out (49 BC), C. followed Pompey and received command of Sicily, which he evacuated to avoid bloodshed. After the Battle of *Pharsalus, C. made his way to Africa, where he reconciled the Pompeian leaders and received special charge of the city of *Utica (hence his epithet). Following the defeat of the Pompeians at *Thapsus (46 BC), he committed suicide.

After his death, Cicero published his *Cato*, a laudatory pamphlet in C.'s honour, to which Caesar replied in a vehement attack (*Anticato*). C. was praised by *Sallust, and in his way of life and the circumstances of his death, he was identified with the cause of the Republic. For Lucan and Seneca he was a freedom fighter and Stoic saint — and this became his traditional image.

Cicero's letters and speeches contain numerous references to C.; other ancient sources: Plutarch, *Cato Minor*, App. *BC* 2.

CATULLUS, Gaius Valerius Born in Verona probably in 84 BC, and died in 54 BC. C.'s father, a man of means with noble connections (notably Caesar), sent his young son to Rome and he stayed there most of his life. He met and fell in love with "Lesbia", devoting 25 poems to her. "Lesbia" was, in reality, *Clodia. *Caelius, C.'s friend, supplanted him as her lover. In 57—56 BC, C. served with C. Memmius, governor of Bithynia, together with his friend Gaius Helvius *Cinna. After the death of his brother in Asia, C. spent some time in Verona. In 55 BC, he attacked Caesar for personal reasons. Nothing is known of C. after 54 BC.

C.'s extant book contains 116 poems. C. himself dedicated a volume of poetry (*nugae*) to *Nepos, but the present collection is evidently larger and was probably made after C.'s death. The book may be divided into three parts: Poems 1—60, polymetric, are short verses on various subjects of amatory or satiric character (mostly written in hendecasyllables); 61—68 are longer poems (the longest, number 64, contains 408 hexameters); 61 and 62 are the earliest surviving Latin *epithalamia*; 63 is based on the myth of *Attis; and 64, an epyllion, tells of the love of Thetis and Peleus; 69—116, elegiac verses, are again short poems (26 lines being the longest); most of them are epigrams on various subjects. Though influenced by *Sappho, C. mainly accepted and practised the literary criteria of Alexandrian poetry, being one of the *neoteri*, "moderns", a sarcastic name coined by Cicero. New genres in Latin poetry (epigram, elegy and epyllion), the introduction of personal sentimental interests into the poems, scholarship, and efforts to perfect language, style and metre are all conspicuous in C.'s poems, and accordingly, he was called *doctus* by later poets such as Ovid and Martial. However, C. combines this technique with elements taken from earlier Latin poetry, using them to express his own personal experience even when following Hellenistic models. The high level of C.'s poetry set a standard for many later poets.

P. Whigham, *The Poems of Catullus* (Penguin Classics) 1966; C. J. Fordyce, *Catullus*, 1961; E. A. Havelock, *The Lyric Genius of Catullus*, 1939; K. Quinn, *The Catullan Revolution*, 1959.

CATULUS (1), Quintus Lutatius Roman statesman of a noble plebeian family. Of C.'s early career nothing is known. He was thrice defeated as candidate for consulship, but with the aid of *Marius, he became consul in 102 BC. As such, he fought against the *Cimbri, who defeated him and forced him to abandon the Po valley. His command was prolonged, however, and he joined Marius in 101 BC, cooperating with him to defeat the Cimbri at the Battle of Vercellae. C. was awarded a triumph for the victory, and used his booty to build a portico on the Palatine. He seems to have quarrelled later with Marius, and when the latter (with Cinna) captured Rome in 87 BC, C. killed himself. C. was a man of letters, writing a history of his war against the Cimbri and some poetry. Cicero considered C. a good orator and made him one of the interlocutors in his rhetorical book *De Oratore*. Malcovati, *Or. Rom. Fr.*³.

CATULUS (2), Quintus Lutatius Son of Catulus (1). C. fled from Rome on its capture by *Marius and *Cinna (87 BC); he fought with Sulla in the Civil War, and became consul in 78 BC. As a supporter of Sulla, he resisted the attempt of his colleague *Lepidus (2) to cancel many of Sulla's reforms and assured Sulla of a public funeral. In 77 BC, C. brought about the defeat of the revolt of Lepidus. Of great influence, he continually sought to defend the Sullan reforms against popular agitators. He opposed the rise of *Pompey, and vainly acted against the passage of the laws of *Gabinius and *Manilius (67 and 66 BC), which conferred extraordinary powers on Pompey. As censor in 65 BC, C. prevented his colleague *Crassus (4) from granting Roman citizenship to the Transpadanes. His influence declined in 63 BC, when Caesar used bribery on a grand scale to defeat him in the elections for the office of Pontifex Maximus; C. died a few years later.

CAUDIUM City of the Caudini *Samnites. In 321 BC a Roman consular army was forced to capitulate in a defile in the territory of the Caudini (Liv. 9.2–6), known as the Caudine Forks (*Furculae Caudinae*). To save the army, Rome concluded a peace treaty with the Samnites. (The defile cannot be identified with certainty.)

CECROPS In Greek mythology, king of Athens; in one version, the first king. C. was the half-human, half-serpent son of Earth, said to have divided Attica into twelve communities, and to have instituted monogamy. He replaced animal sacrifice with offerings of barley-cakes, and was supposedly the first to bury the dead. The invention of writing is also ascribed to him. When C. fled from Athens in fear of his brothers, he was succeeded by his son, Pandion.

CELSUS (1), Aulus Cornelius Flourished in the first half of the 1st century AD; no details of his life are known. C.'s book *Artes* was an encyclopaedia of medicine, agriculture, rhetoric, the art of war and, perhaps, philosophy; the section on medicine is extant, as are fragments of the rest. The brief history of medicine at the beginning of the book is most important. This book was highly esteemed in the Renaissance, and his excellent Latin was considered a model of writing.

W. G. Spencer, *Celsus* (Loeb), 1936–8;
J. Scarborough, *Roman Medicine*, 1969.

CELSUS (2), Publius Juventius Roman senator and jurist. Flourished in the first half of the 2nd century AD. C. was praetor c. AD 106, and consul in AD 129. He governed Thrace and Asia, and was on Hadrian's *Consilium*. C. headed the Proculian School of jurists. Citations from his main work (*Digesta*) are found in the *Digesta* (see *Digesta).

CELSUS (3) Alexandrian philosopher. C.'s work *Alethes Logos*, "True Logos", written c. AD 178, was directed against Christianity in defense of Hellenism, especially the philosophy of Plato. Some arguments against Christianity are represented by Jews, though C. also criticizes Jewish worship. C.'s work is known only through long citations in Origen's *Contra Celsum*, written c. AD 249.

CELTS Large tribal group which ranged from Spain to Galatia in Asia Minor, in various periods. The unity of this large group of peoples was cultural rather than political. Various dialects of one language were spoken, and the art which developed, though diffused over a huge area, displayed common features. Artistic elements were absorbed from both the East and Greece. The origin of the Celtic peoples is obscure and disputed, but it seems to stem from the mixture of the "Urn-field" people with foreign invaders in Central Europe. The Celtic tribes subsequently spread to Western Europe, arriving in Gaul perhaps in the 9th century BC, and in Spain and Britain in the 8th and 7th centuries BC. Other tribes crossed the Alps in the 5th century BC, occupying the Po valley and evicting the Etruscans there. Though the C. captured Rome in 390 BC, their southward advance was eventually blocked by the Romans. Another wave of Celtic tribes invaded Macedonia and Greece in the 3rd century BC. Checked by *Antigonus (2) Gonatas and invited to settle by *Nicomedes I, this Celtic group crossed the *Bosporus (1) and settled in central Asia Minor, in the territory known thereafter as *Galatia. The C. made an overwhelming impression on the Greek and Italian peoples when first encountered. Their warlike spirit and physical superiority could not, however, secure them their initial successes. Lack of unity and inability to persist in long efforts denied them significant political achievements.

T. G. E. Powell, *The Celts*[2], 1960.

CENSOR Roman magistrate whose primary task was to hold the *census*, that is, to prepare a list of Roman citizens and their properties. For this purpose the citizens were required to appear before the C. in the *Campus Martius. Each citizen was registered in one of the tribes of the state and allocated his place in one of the five classes, according to his wealth. The citizens were taxed and called for military service on the basis of this register. The first C.s were elected in 443 BC; earlier, the *census* had been prepared by the consuls. Two C.s were elected every five years for a term of 18 months. With the completion of the *census*, the C.s officiated at a ceremony of purification (*lustrum*). In time the C.s acquired more powers and duties. As controllers of public morals, they checked the list of those fit for cavalry service (the Equites). Contracts for public building, leasing of public land and tax-farming were made by the C.s. Though lacking military power, the C.s enjoyed great prestige, and the office was considered the highest in the political career of a senator. Under the Empire, no C.s were elected, the office having been taken over by the emperor, who often delegated it to his own officials. The last known Italian *census* was made under Vespasian and Titus. The *census* in a province was often made upon its formation, and, subsequently, at irregular intervals.

Jolowicz, *Roman Law*[3], 51–4 (s.v.).
J. Suolahti, *The Roman Censors*, 1963.

CENTAURS In Greek mythology, the C.s were believed to be creatures half-human, half-horse, who lived in the mountains of Thessaly and Arcadia. Homer speaks of them, and various legends connected Greek heroes with them. *Heracles killed the C. Nessus, when the latter tried to rape Deianira. On another occasion, Heracles visited his friend the C. Pholus and was attacked by other C.s who smelled the wine he had brought. Heracles routed them with his arrows and torches. A favourite legend was the war between the C.s and Lapiths. Peirithous, king of the Lapiths, invited the C.s to his marriage. Unused to the wine, which they drank raw, the C.s became drunk and tried to rape the Lapith women. The Lapiths, aided by *Theseus, drove them off after much slaughter. Later, the C.s surprised the Lapiths, who fled to Elis. The C.s would seem to represent the beastly side of human nature. Their myths were favourite themes in Greek art. See also *Chiron.

CEPHISODOTUS Athenian sculptor, son of *Praxiteles, active in the late 4th and early 3rd centuries BC. C. made several statues together with his brother Timarchus. He executed works for Athens, Cos and Pergamum. Fragments and copies of his works have survived.

CERBERUS In Greek mythology, the dog guarding the gates to the netherworld, first alluded to by Homer, and specifically named by Hesiod. C. was the offspring of *Typhon and Echidna. According to Hesiod, he had 50 heads but he is often depicted in art and literature as having three heads and a tail of snakes. C.'s task was to prevent anyone from leaving the netherworld. *Heracles, however, took C. out to show him to Eurystheus and then returned him. *Orpheus overcame him by the charm of his music.

CERCIDAS Native of *Megalopolis, statesman, poet and Cynic philosopher. C. was born c. 290 BC and died c. 220 BC. In politics, he supported *Aratus of Sicyon. C. expressed his philosophical ideas in poems, fragments of which are extant; his works included *Iambi* and *Meliambi*, the latter being his most important work. He was mainly

Heracles, Cerberus, and Eurystheus hiding in a pithos

influenced by *Diogenes of Sinope, but also by *Bion (1), whose "diatribist style" he often employed. C.'s verses reflect the social conditions in the Greece of his time.
A. D. Knox, *Herodes, Cercidas, and the Greek Choliambic Poets* (Loeb), 1929.

CERCOPES In Greek mythology, a ghostly pair of twins who appear in nightmares. The sons of *Oceanus and Theia, the C. disturbed *Heracles' sleep until he caught them. In one version, Heracles released them, but in another, he changed them into apes. Another version has it that Zeus turned them into stone.

CERES Ancient Italian goddess, very early identified with the Greek goddess *Demeter, but also associated with the earth goddess *Tellus. C. was the goddess of crops, and her name reveals her connection with growth. Her antiquity in Rome is evident from her appearance in the Twelve Tables, and from her temple on the Aventine which dates from 493 BC. The institution of C.'s cult was said to have been occasioned by famine on the direction of the Sibylline books, clearly revealing the Greek influence. Her cult was associated with that of *Liber and Libera, and this triad is usually considered parallel to that of the Greek Demeter, Dionysius (or *Iacchus) and Persephone. The Aventine was a centre of plebeian activity, and C.'s Aventine temple was under the control of the plebeian aediles, who were responsible for the corn supply. The foundation day of the Aventine temple was on 19 April, the date of the *Cerialia*, the festival of C. Another festival was held by women in August.
Altheim, *Rom. Rel.* (s.v.).

CERIALIS, Quintus Petillius Roman soldier, relative of *Vespasian. Legate of a legion in Britain, C. was defeated during the revolt of *Boudicca in AD 61. He supported Vespasian's advance to power and was *consul suffectus* in AD 70, the year he subdued the Gallic revolt under *Classicus and *Civilis. As governor of Britain, C. fought the Brigantes and advanced the Roman conquest of northern England. He was *consul suffectus* again in AD 74.

CHALCIS The most important city of *Euboea; its location on the narrowest part of the strait of Euripus gave it a commercial advantage. C. developed commerce with Sicily, Italy and the East, and played an important role in the establishment of the trading settlement at al-Mina in Phoenicia, about 800 BC. C. sent colonies to Italy (*Cumae, *Rhegium), Sicily (*Naxos, Leontini, *Messana) and *Chalcidice, all in the 8th century BC. Its prosperity came from fishing, trade (especially in pottery), and the manufacture of various articles (especially metalwork). C. fought its neighbour Eretria over control of the fertile Lelantine plain. It began issuing coins in the second half of the 6th century BC. Defeated by Athens in 506 BC, it began to decline politically, and its lands were confiscated and settled by Athenians. In 446 BC, C. unsuccessfully revolted against Athens, and had to pay tribute until 411 BC. C. joined the Second Athenian League. *Philip II occupied C. in 338 BC, and used it as a stronghold for controlling Greece; as such it was known as one of the three "fetters" of Greece. C.'s trade continued to prosper in the Hellenistic world.

CHALCIDICE Territory consisting of three promontories (Pallene, Sithonia and Acte) projecting from Macedonia. C. was rich in timber, charcoal and pitch. The earlier population was of Thracian origin and Greek colonization here began in the 8th century BC. Colonists from *Chalcis settled in Sithonia and gave the name C. to the entire region. Other colonists came from *Eretria, Andros (colonizing Acanthus and Stagirus) and Corinth (*Potidaea). The Chalcidic cities were members of the Delian League, but they revolted in 432 BC and made *Olynthus their capital. This league was sufficiently powerful to extend its control westward (at the expense of Macedonia) in the 380s BC. In 379 BC, however, the league was dissolved by Sparta; it was soon reorganized and joined the Second Athenian League. Suspicious of Athens, the C. League made an alliance with *Philip II (356 BC). This unnatural alliance, however, ended in a war, in 349 BC, in which Philip captured and destroyed Olynthus (348 BC). From then on, C. was ruled by Macedonia.
Larsen, *Gr. Fed. St.*, 58—78.

CHALCEDON (modern Kadiköy) Important maritime Greek city on the Asiatic coast of the *Bosporus (1), opposite *Byzantium. Traditionally, C. was founded by *Megara in 685 BC. Herodotus and Pliny report that it was called the city of the blind (*Caecorum oppidum*), because the better site of Byzantium was still unoccupied at the time of its foundation. Still, C. did have a commanding position on the route to the Black Sea, and it took part in the Ionian Revolt against Persia, in 499 BC. A member of the Delian League, it nonetheless tried to preserve its independence against Athens, Sparta and, later, Alexander's successors and the Bithynian kings. C. concluded a treaty with Rome quite early. Generally, its history was connected with that of Byzantium.

CHAERONEA Boeotian town in the Cephissus valley, traditionally the first town settled by Boeotians. C. is first mentioned by *Thucydides (1.113) in 447 BC, at the time under the rule of *Orchomenus. In the 4th century BC, C. was a member of the Boeotian League. Two famous battles were fought at C., situated as it was on the way from northern Greece: *Philip II of Macedonia defeated the Athenians and the Thebans here in 338 BC; and *Sulla routed the army of *Mithridates VI here in 86 BC. *Plutarch was a native of C.

CHABRIAS Athenian mercenary, born *c*. 420 BC and died in 357 BC. C. took his first command in 399 BC with an Athenian force in the Peloponnesus, during which he had little success against Sparta. In 387 BC, he fought for *Evagoras, king of Salamis. C. later helped Egypt against the Persians, and on his return home, was most successful in defending Boeotia against an attack by the Spartan king, *Agesilaus. After defeating the Spartan fleet in a battle of Naxos in 376 BC, C. persuaded many islands and cities to join the Second Athenian League. In internal Athenian politics, he was associated with *Callistratus, with whom he was prosecuted in 366 BC. In the late 360s, C. again went off to fight for Egypt; he returned to Athens in 359 BC, and fell in the naval battle off Chios in 357 BC.
Xenophon, *Hellenica*, 5; Nepos, *Chabrias*;
H. W. Parke, *Greek Mercenary Soldiers*, 1933.

CHARES Athenian general, born *c*. 400 BC. After unsuccessful operations in the Ionian Sea (358 BC), C.'s efforts brought Thracian Chersonesus to join the Second Athenian League. C. was defeated in the naval battle off Chios in 357 BC, and again in 356 BC, but he remained in command. To obtain money for his mercenary soldiers, C. agreed to serve with the Persian satrap Artabazus, for whom he conquered Lampsacus and Sigeum. In 353 BC, he defeated a Macedonian army in Thrace, and soon recaptured Sestos. He was sent as commander of the Athenian army for the defence of *Olynthus, but discovered that *Philip II had already taken the city. C. fought in the Battle of Chaeronea (338 BC). Alexander demanded his surrender in 335 BC, knowing him to have supported *Demosthenes. C. fought with the Persians in 333–332 BC against Alexander. He died *c*. 325 BC.
H. W. Parke, *Greek Mercenary Soldiers*, 1933.

CHARIDEMUS Mercenary commander, native of Oreos in Euboea, who received Athenian citizenship for his services. C. served (*c*. 360 BC) with the Thracian king, Cotys, whose daughter he married, and then with his son Cersobleptes. Though he could not prevent the partition of the kingdom between Cersobleptes and his two brothers, he led the first to cooperate with Athens. Later, C. fought against Macedonia as an Athenian commander. In 335 BC, he escaped to Persia, but *Darius III put him to death (333 BC).
H. W. Parke, *Greek Mercenary Soldiers*, 1933.

CHARISIUS, Flavius Sosipator Latin grammarian of the 4th century AD. Most of his five-book work, *Ars grammatica*, is extant. It is mainly a compilation containing valuable citations of earlier authors, such as *Ennius and *Lucilius, whose works are largely lost.
Keil, *Gr. Lat.*, 1; K. Barwick (ed.), 1925.

CHARITES ("Graces") In Greek mythology, daughters of Zeus, the goddesses of good qualities (Wisdom, Joy, Glory, Beauty, Grace, etc.). The C. originally represented these qualities collectively (like the *Muses of the intellectual powers). As goddesses of beauty and grace, the C. were associated with Aphrodite as early as Homer, who notes two C.s (Pasithea and Cale), though Hesiod's number of three became more accepted. Myrtles, roses and flowers were connected with the C., who sang and danced on various occasions. They were worshipped at various sites, especially in Sparta, Athens and Orchomenus. The C. were often depicted by artists, at first clothed, and from the Hellenistic period on, nude. The Romans called them Gratiae.
Kerényi, *Gods*, 99–101.

The three Charites (Graces). Roman copy of the original probably by Praxiteles

CHARITON Native of Aphrodisias in Caria, lived probably in the 1st or 2nd century AD. C. wrote an eight-book Greek romance, called *Chaereas and Callirhoe*. The romance begins in Syracuse with the marriage of Chaereas and Callirhoe. Chaereas kicks his wife Callirhoe in a quarrel, and thinks he has killed her. Both are then kidnapped and sold into slavery, and, after various ordeals, they meet again and return to Syracuse, where they live happily ever after. C.'s book is the earliest one of its kind to have survived, a novel characterized by a complicated plot with many turning points.
W. E. Blake (ed.), 1938; W. E. Blake (En. tr.), 1939.

CHARON In Greek mythology, the ferryman who carries the spirits of the dead across the river Styx to Tartarus, and who must be paid for his services. In accord with this belief, the Greeks used to put a coin under the tongue of the dead. For not taking this fee from *Heracles when he descended to Tartarus, C. was fettered for a year by *Hades. Virgil's description of him (*Aen.* 6.298–315) as having white hair and burning eyes became the most famous. C. was portrayed by the Greeks in various works of art, the earliest examples dating from the 6th century BC.

CHATTI One of the strongest Germanic tribes, living on the Upper Weser. Though *Drusus (3) invaded their territory in 12 BC, the C. successfully resisted the advance of Roman rule. They took part in the attack against *Varus (AD 9) and thus retained their independence. The C. supported the revolt of *Civilis in AD 69–70. Throughout this period there was hostility between the C. and their neighbours, the *Cherusci. The C. were defeated by Domitian and are not mentioned after the 2nd century AD.
E. A. Thompson, *The Early Germans*, 1965.

CHERSONESUS (1) (modern Gallipoli) Peninsula projecting southwest from Thrace, often called the Thracian C. Fertile soil there produces excellent cereal crops, and its position between Asia and Europe gave C. much importance. Greek colonists from Ionia settled it as early as the 8th century BC. Its most important cities were

Cardia and Sestos. In the 6th century BC, C. came under the control of the Athenian Miltiades, who fortified the Bulair Isthmus against local Thracian attacks. His son *Miltiades the Younger evacuated the peninsula, allowing the Persians to seize it in 493 BC. After the expulsion of the Persians from Greece, Athens took control of C., sending colonists to Sestos and Callipolis (c. 450 BC). Sparta ruled C. in 404–386 BC, but Athens subsequently recovered it. Philip II of Macedonia occupied C. in 338 BC and, after the death of Alexander, various Hellenistic dynasts ruled it. From 189 BC on, C. belonged to *Pergamum, and in 133 BC it became public land of the Roman people. Later on, much of the peninsula belonged to *Agrippa (1).

CHERSONESUS (2) Tauric C. (modern Crimean peninsula). The Greeks were attracted to C. by the fisheries of the nearby *Bosporus (2) and the corn of the hinterland. The first Ionian colonists arrived in C. in the 7th century BC. Its chief city was Panticapaeum.

CHERUSCI Germanic tribe living between the Weser and the Elbe, first mentioned by Caesar. The C. were temporarily subdued by *Drusus (3) and Tiberius, but they revolted in AD 9, under the leadership of *Arminius, who destroyed three legions under Quinctilius *Varus. This defeat brought about the collapse of Augustus' German policy and, despite *Germanicus' efforts to conquer the land, the C. remained free. They successfully beat off the attempt of Maroboduus, king of the *Marcomanni, to extend his rule over them. After the death of Arminius, the C. lost cohesion as a result of internal conflicts and attacks from the *Chatii.

E. A. Thompson, *The Early Germans*, 1965.

CHIMAERA In Greek mythology, a fire-breathing creature composed of a she-goat, a lion and a serpent. This monster was born to *Typhon and Echidna, and was killed by *Bellerophon.

CHIOS Large island off the west coast of Asia Minor (860 sq km). C. was rich in wine, corn, gum-mastic and figs, and its inhabitants were known as the richest of the Greeks. Its population was of Ionian stock. The chief city, C., was situated on the eastern coast and possessed a fine harbour. In politics, it traditionally cooperated with *Miletus. Conquered by *Cyrus (1), C. rebelled (together with Miletus) in the Ionian Revolt of 499 BC. C. was a member of the Delian League, but deserted Athens in 413 BC. It joined the Second Athenian League, leaving it in 357 BC. For a while C. was under Carian control. In Hellenistic times, it was mainly independent. Local tradition claimed that *Homer was born on the island. Many poets, sculptors and writers lived there.

M. M. Cook, *The Greeks in Ionia and the East*, 1962.

CHIRON In Greek mythology, son of *Kronos and the nymph Philyra. In some versions, C. was king of the *Centaurs, though entirely different from them; while they were wild, he was mild and just. Adept in medicine, C. taught this art to *Asclepius. He also educated other heroes, such as *Achilles and *Iason, and it was with his aid that *Peleus married *Thetis. C. was considered immortal, and was worshipped in Thessaly.

CHREMONIDES Athenian statesman in the 3rd century BC. C. was *Zeno's (2) pupil and friend. On C.'s initiative, Athens joined the Peloponnesian League against *Antigonus Gonatas. The ensuing conflict (267–262 BC), known as the Chremonidian War, terminated with the capitulation of Athens. C. fled to Egypt, where he received a naval command.

CHRONOLOGY The present method of dating from the birth of Jesus was introduced by the monk Dionysius Exiguus in the first half of the 6th century AD. He calculated that this was in the year 754 from the foundation date of Rome (actually AD 4). Our chronology of the ancient world is the result of the synchronization of this system with the system and dates used in antiquity, and is based on detailed calculations and a few events dated by astronomical means. The Greeks and the Romans were late to apply satisfactory time-reckoning means. Indeed, no one system was ever followed universally.

The most commonly used system to indicate years was by the name of the principal magistrate, the *archon eponymos* in Athens, the *stephanephoros* in Miletus, the consuls in Rome, etc. Under monarchies, the ordinal number of the year of the reigning ruler was given, a system used also by the Bible. Historians who wanted to indicate events dated by such unsatisfactory systems had to do much work in synchronization, which could have given accurate results only if complete lists of the eponymous magistrates were available. Even the first great historians of the 5th century, *Herodotus and *Thucydides, did not adopt any coherent, systematic method. In reckoning past events they had to resort to traditional genealogies, assuming generations of 30–40 years. Attempts to prepare systematic chronologies were first made in the 4th century BC, mainly by the Atthidographers (*Atthis). At that time, use was made of the Opympiads for time-reckoning. Alexandrian scholars arranged lists of the victors at the Olympian games, with which were associated dated lists of kings. The first Olympian games with names of victors were dated to 776 BC; an Olympiad was a four year cycle. The battle of *Chaeronea (338 BC) would be dated 110.3, i.e. the third year of the 110th Olympiad, which started in 340 (776 is inclusive). The universal historian *Diodorus Siculus used to note the Athenian archon eponymous, the Roman consuls and the Olympian year at the beginning of each year in his narrative. However, it was not only in official documents that local systems were followed; the Seleucids numbered their years from 312 BC, and even historians did not, as a rule, follow the Olympian era. Roman historians sometimes used the foundation date of Rome, A.V.C. (*Ab Vrbe Condita*), but chronologists disagreed on the date; *Varro thought it was 753 BC. The normal method, used by Livy and Tacitus, for example, was simply to note the names of the consuls.

An accurate method of indicating the time of day was not introduced before Hellenistic times. Time was marked as "cock-crow" (dawn), "full market" (mid-morning), mid-day, afternoon, evening etc. Hours, long used in Babylonia, were introduced only in the second half of the 4th century BC, and at first indicated $1/12$ of the actual day or night. Both in Greece and in Rome it was common to reckon hours from the rising of the sun, and only later did the Romans officially reckon hours from mid-night. For measuring time, use was made of the sundial *gnomon* (a pointer that marked the time by its shadow), another Babylonian device first introduced by *Anaximander. Another time-keeper was the water-clock (*clepsydra*), consisting of a vase from which the water passed into a container. Both the above methods were usually inaccurate.

Calendars differed from one state to another, with different names of months and different beginnings. The Athenian months, starting in July, were: Hecatombaion, Metageitnion, Boedromion, Pyanopsion, Maimacterion,

Poseideon, Gamelion, Anthesterion, Elaphebolion, Mounichion, Thargelion, and Scirophorion. Months were named by ordinal numbers, festivals or deities. Months were generally lunar, and attempts were made to adjust the twelve lunar months (properly each of 29½ days but in practice of 29 or 30 days) to the solar year of 364¼ days. The Athenian astronomer Meton (*Astronomy) suggested a system of 7 intercalary months in a 19-year cycle. The one day difference in 4 cycles was corrected by Callipus in the 4th century (*Astronomy). But these methods were not accepted by official calendars. Civil authorities, or the Pontifex Maximus in Rome, were responsible for the intercalation. In Athens, the intercalary month was inserted after Poseideon; in Rome, between the 23rd and 24th of February. Days of the month were normally counted forward by the Greeks, for whom the month was divided into three decades. The Romans indicated days of the month backwards from three main days: the *Kalendae* (new moon) — first day of the month, *idus* (full moon), the 13th day of the month (15th in March, May, July, October), and the *nonae* — the ninth day (counting inclusively) backwards from the *idus* (5th or 7th day of the month). Cicero, for instance, was born *ante diem tertium nonas Ianuarias*, i.e. 3 January.

The Roman calendar originally had only ten months, and the addition of two months was ascribed to *Numa, or, more probably, to *Tarquinius Superbus. Even afterwards the year continued to begin in March and only in 153 BC did January become the first month (on which the consuls entered office). Caesar carried out a reform in 46, when the Roman calendar (of 355 days a year) was 90 days ahead of the solar calendar. He intercalated three months and, for the future, added days to short months so as to make the year total 365 days. This Julian calendar remained in force until the reform of Pope Gregorius XIII (1582), and in Russia it was used until 1917. See *Astronomy, *Annales.

A. K. Michels, *The Calendar of the Roman Republic*, 1967; E. Bickerman, *The Chronology of the Ancient World*, 1968; Samuels, *The Chronological Systems of the Greeks and the Romans*, 1970.

CHRYSIPPUS Stoic philosopher, born in Soli, Cilicia, *c.* 281 BC; died *c.* 207 BC. Arriving in Athens (*c.* 260 BC), C. heard the lectures of *Arcesilaus at the Academy. Very soon he joined the school of the Stoa, where he became a disciple of *Cleanthes and, upon the death of the latter in 232 BC, C. became head of the school. He was a prolific writer, but of his numerous works only fragments have survived. Among his disciples were Zeno of Tarsus and Diogenes the Babylonian; the latter succeeded him. It was C. who systematized and consolidated Stoic philosophy, and he was so successful that the precise doctrines of his predecessors (notably Zeno) were relegated to oblivion, though he differed from them on important issues. C.'s main contribution was in logic and theory of knowledge; he devoted much of his work to fighting the Scepticism of the Academy.

F. H. Sandbach, *The Stoics*, 1975 (s.v.).

CICERO (1), Marcus Tullius Rome's statesman, writer and greatest orator. He was born 3 January 106 BC, at Arpinum (modern Arpino), which had received Roman citizenship in 188 BC. C.'s father, a well-to-do Eques, sent C. and his younger brother Quintus to Rome, to study rhetoric and philosophy; among their teachers were *Scaevola the Augur, Scaevola the Pontifex and Lucius *Crassus (3). C. served in the army under *Pompeius

Head of Cicero, a 1st-century BC statue

Strabo in company with *Pompey and *Catiline, in 90–89 BC. He first appeared at the bar in a civil case in 81 BC, and the following year he defended Roscius Amerinus against a charge of parricide. C. saved his client and, in his speech, passed cautious censure on the regime of *Sulla by attacking the dictator's accomplices who illegally exploited their position. In 79 BC, he and his brother left for Greece; in Athens, he studied philosophy with Antiochus of Ascalon, and at Rhodes, he attended the lectures of *Posidonius.

Back in Rome, C. launched on a political career, being elected quaestor for 75 BC at the very early age of 30. He served in *Lilybaeum in western Sicily and, on his return, realized that his reputation as a good administrator had not reached Rome. To gain a name and influence, he continued to appear in court. In 70 BC, he represented the Sicilians in the prosecution of *Verres who was defended by *Hortensius, acknowledged leading barrister in Rome. The grateful Sicilians assisted C. in the games he gave as aedile in 69 BC. C. was elected praetor for 66 BC.

In an extant speech, C. supported the bill of Gaius Manilius to confer on Pompey the extraordinary command of the war against Mithridates VI. C. already seems to have supported Pompey in 70 BC, and he clearly followed him in politics from 66 BC on. Backed by Equestrian friends and some of the nobility, C. was elected consul for 63 BC against a coalition of Gaius *Antonius (3) and *Catiline, who were supported by *Crassus (4). As consul, C. brought about the withdrawal of the agrarian bill of Rullus, which seems to have originated with Crassus and Caesar. C.'s speeches on this subject are extant. His main achievement was the suppression of the Catiline conspiracy, and he published his anti-Catiline speeches. C. thought that his action established *concordia ordinum*, that is, cooperation of those elements in Roman society interested in preserving the existing form of government, especially the Senate and the Equites.

Backed by a Senate resolution, C. executed five of Catiline's accomplices without trial, an act which made him vulnerable, as the legality of this action was questionable, though he seems not to have realized the danger. In 61 BC, he made *Clodius his inveterate enemy by testifying against him in court. Indeed, as tribune in 58 BC, Clodius passed a law banishing anyone who had executed a Roman citizen without trial. When C. left for Macedonia, three of his estates were plundered by Clodius and his gangs. Alarmed by such attacks, Pompey, supported by *Milo, secured the passing of a bill to recall C. from exile (57 BC). The bill received extensive support from the Equites and the municipal aristocracy. C. returned to Rome on 4 September 57 BC, and for some time was active against the Triumvirate in hope of Pompey's withdrawal; but after the Luca conference (*Caesar), C. lost his independence in politics.

He now turned to busy literary activity, though he also defended the henchmen of the Triumvirate in the courts. Thus, in 54 BC, C. secured the acquittal of *Vatinius, but lost the case of *Gabinius (both of whom he had vehemently attacked in public speeches at an earlier date). In 53 BC, he was elected *augur*. The next year he failed to defend Milo, his staunch supporter, who had been charged with the murder of Clodius. C. did not dare appear before the court, which Pompey had packed with soldiers. His extant speech for Milo was written after his client had been condemned. In 51 BC, C. was sent to govern Cilicia, remaining outside Rome for eighteen months; his administration was just and fair, and he conducted some military operations and entertained hopes of a triumph in Rome.

Soon after C.'s return to Italy, the Civil War between Caesar and Pompey broke out. At first, C. stayed in Italy and did not follow Pompey; then, in April 49 BC, he left for Greece and joined Pompey. Actually, C. contributed nothing to the war effort and, after Pompey's defeat at Pharsalus, gave up opposition. Caesar allowed C. to return to Italy, where he resumed literary activity and refrained from politics. In this period, C. wrote most of his works on philosophy and rhetoric. After the death of his beloved daughter Tullia in 45 BC, he lived in solitude for a time at his villa in Astura. Caesar's murder brought C. back to politics; he believed the chief enemy was *Antonius (4), and that it had been a mistake not to kill him on the Ides of March. C. supported Octavian, blind to his revolutionary actions and to his real aim, the avenging of Caesar. In a series of speeches (*Philippicae*, named after the speeches of *Demosthenes against Philip II), from September 44 BC to April 43 BC, C. constantly attacked and defamed Antony. Under C.'s influence, the Senate conferred military command on Octavian (January 43 BC), but Octavian's true interests led him to cooperate with Antony; late in the year, they formed a triumvirate with *Lepidus (3). Antony could now take revenge on C. and included his name in the proscriptions. C. was caught by Antony's soldiers while trying to escape to Greece, and was murdered on 7 December 43 BC.

As a descendant of a non-senatorial family, C. was indeed successful in his political career. His activities at the bar, the ties he cultivated with influential Equites (including his close friend *Atticus), and senators, and his eloquence enabled him to overcome the handicap of being a "new man" launched on a political career in Rome. He never really felt at ease with the nobility, most of whom disliked him, although he was almost always a supporter of the "establishment". In politics, he consistently defended the existing republican government and social order. C. considered Pompey the man best fitted for this purpose, but he never formed a close friendship with him. In fact, C. never possessed much political power; he was neither a military man, nor a good organizer, nor exceptionally wealthy, and therefore he could not fully utilize the wide influence he had amongst the Equestrian class and the local aristocracy of many Italian towns.

Terentia, C.'s first wife whom he married in 79 BC, bore him a daughter, Tullia, and a son, *Marcus C. C. divorced her (47 BC), partly because of financial disputes, and married Publilia, a young and wealthy woman, whom he soon divorced. C. had a life-long friendship with Atticus, who published his works, gave him financial support and helped administer his affairs. C. acquired considerable property in the course of his life, drawing handsome rewards from his activities in the courts; often his clients named him as heir or legatee. In addition to the patrimony at Arpinum, C. owned several estates in Campania and Latium, and a beautiful house on the Palatine.

C. was a prolific writer. More than 900 of his letters are extant. The 16-book *Ad Atticum* extends over the years 68–44 BC; however, no letters from Atticus to C. survive. C.'s correspondence with various friends (about a hundred correspondents) appears in a 16-book work (*Ad Familiares*). Of C.'s letters to his brother Quintus, 27 are extant. His correspondence with *Brutus (2), 25 letters written in 43 BC, comprise a separate collection. Of his speeches, 58 have survived but not all are complete. The earliest is from 81 BC and the last are the *Philippicae* of 44–43 BC; some are court orations and others are addressed to the people or the Senate. The letters and the speeches are an invaluable source for the study of C.'s times. Several of his books deal with rhetoric; the *De Inventione* is an early work; C.'s more important works were written when he was compelled to retire from politics. *De Oratore* is a dialogue in which famous orators of the previous generation (such as *Lucius Crassus (3) and *Marcus Antonius (1)) take part; it deals mainly with the proper education for an orator. In his *Brutus*, written in 46 BC and dedicated to Brutus, C. gives a concise history of Roman orators. In these works and in the *Orator*, C. discusses the various styles of oratory. His main argument is that all three basic styles (simple, grand and intermediate) are legitimate, and should be used according to the occasion.

C. studied philosophy in his youth and attended the lectures of Academics, Stoics and Epicureans, though he mainly regarded himself as a disciple of the Academy. Late in life, mainly while seeking solitude and consolation after the death of his daughter Tullia, he began writing philosophical works. In a very short time, C. completed several books, mainly following Greek philosophers; he seems, however, to have underestimated his work, saying that he was merely a translator. C., in fact, created Latin philosophical terminology. He deals with matters of ethics, morals, theology and knowledge. In *De Finibus Bonorum et Malorum*, he discusses "supreme good" according to the different schools of philosophy. The dialogue *Tusculanae Disputationes*, containing five books, deals with death, grief and its mitigation, passion and happiness. *De Natura Deorum* and *De Divinatione* expose

Epicurean, Stoic and Academic views on the nature of gods, divine providence and fate. Two books which were read throughout the Middle Ages are *Cato Maior* ("Old Age") and *Laelius* ("Friendship"). In his last philosophical work, *De Officiis*, C. advises his son on practical moral problems; in these, he mainly follows *Panaetius. C. deals with constitutional problems in two books, both in dialogue form: *De Republica*, an analysis of the best constitution, was written as an attempt to solve the social and constitutional problems of the Roman state by means of a mixed constitution with monarchic, aristocratic and democratic elements; it follows the proposals of *Polybius. C. did not publish his second book, *De Legibus*, which dealt with the nature of laws, their divine sanction, and the just and the useful in the administration of public and private affairs; only parts of both these books have survived.

C.'s influence on posterity was far-reaching. It was mainly his philosophical treatises that attracted Christian writers. Others admired his speeches; and his letters, after their discovery in the 14th century, and style always had their admirers (Petrarch, Erasmus, Gibbon). He stood for what was best in Latin thinking and writing.

Loeb. An excellent work is D. R. Shakleton Bailey, *Cicero's Letters to Atticus* (7 volumes), 1965—70. There is a biography of C. by Plutarch. Of modern works note T. A. Dorey (ed.), *Cicero*, 1965;

CICERO (2), Marcus Tullius Son of C. (1), born in 65 BC. In 49 BC, C. followed *Pompey against *Caesar (who spared his life after Pharsalus). After Caesar's murder, C. joined the "liberators", and served with Sextus *Pompeius after *Philippi. C. returned to Italy in 39 BC and co-operated with Octavian, with whom he was consul in 30 BC. He governed Syria and Asia. He evidently lacked the intellectual powers of his father.

CICERO (3), Quintius Tullius. Brother of C. (1), born in 102 BC. C.'s career followed that of his brother, with whom he was educated. C. was aedile in 65 BC, praetor in 62 BC, and governor of Asia (61—59 BC), in which office he had difficulties with Roman tax-farmers. In 57 BC, he went to Sardinia as a legate of *Pompey, and in 54—51 BC, he served with distinction as a legate under Caesar in Gaul. C. was a legate of his brother in Cilicia in 51 BC. In the Civil War, C. followed Pompey but joined Caesar after Pharsalus. C. and his only son were murdered by the Triumvirs in December 43 BC. He had married Pomponia, sister of his brother's best friend *Atticus, with whom he was constantly on bad terms. Four of C.'s letters are extant; one to his brother, and three to *Tiro. The pamphlet *Commentariolum Petitionis* is ascribed to C.; it is addressed to his brother, advising him on the technique of winning the consulate for which he was candidate in 64 BC. Though the work may well have been written later, it is very important for understanding the internal politics in Rome at that time. (It notes, for example, the refraining of candidates for office from submitting "ideological" programmes in their canvassing.)

J. P. V. D. Balsdon, *Cl. Q.*, 1963, 242ff.

CILICIA Southeastern region in Asia Minor, stretching from *Pamphylia in the west to Mount Amanus in the east. The northern boundary between C. and Cappadocia and Lycaonia varied. In the western part of the country (C. Tracheia), the mountains often border on the sea, while in the eastern part there is a fertile plain producing corn, wine, olives and flax. C. Tracheia produced abundant ship-timber. Homer locates the Cilices in the southern Troad, but according to tradition they immigrated to C. after the Trojan War. The early history of C. is obscure. (The *Hilakku* and *Kelekesh* of the Assyrian and Egyptian documents are probably identical with the Cilices.) After the decline of the Assyrian empire, C. was ruled by a local dynasty, under Persian hegemony until 401 BC. Alexander conquered C. in 333 BC, and the region was much disputed by Alexander's successors, though mainly under Seleucid rule. The coast of C. Tracheia, with its many bays and natural ports, was a haven for pirates in the 2nd century BC. Rome sent several commanders to this region to suppress them, from 102 BC on, and they were finally defeated by *Pompey in 67 BC. Cicero was governor of C. in 51—50 BC. Some time later, the province was divided between Syria and Galatia, but Vespasian restored it in AD 72.

Magie, *Asia*, (s.v.).

CILO, Lucius Fabius Native of Baetica. Under *Commodus, C. governed Gallia Narbonensis and *Galatia, and as *consul suffectus* in AD 193 arranged the burial of Commodus. C. served with Septimius *Severus against *Pescennius Niger and later governed Upper *Moesia (AD 195/6) and Upper Pannonia (AD 197/202). After AD 203, C. was *praefectus urbi* (perhaps until AD 211), and consul in AD 203. When *Plautianus was killed (AD 205), he saved *Macrinus. After Septimius Severus' death, C.'s interference in the quarrel between *Caracalla and *Geta endangered his life, but his popularity with the populace and the soldiers saved him.

CIMBRI First Germanic tribe encountered by the Romans. The C. originally came from Jutland. According to Strabo, they began migrating c. 120 BC, after their land had been inundated by the sea. They were joined by the Teutones and Ambrones; checked by the *Boii, the C. deviated and arrived in Noricum in 113 BC, where they defeated a Roman army. They then invaded the land of the *Helvetii and continued into southern Gaul, where they defeated a second Roman army (109 BC) after their request to settle had been rejected. In 105 BC, the C. inflicted two severe defeats on Roman armies, in the Rhone valley and at Arausio (Orange). They then tried to invade Spain, but were repulsed by the Celtiberians. *Marius took over command of the war against the Germanic tribes, defeating the Teutones and Ambrones at Aquae Sextae (102 BC). The C. arrived in northern Italy through Noricum in 102 BC, but they, too, were completely routed by Marius and *Catulus (1), at Vercellae, on 30 July 101 BC.

CIMON Athenian statesman and general. Son of *Miltiades, born c. 510 BC. On his mother's side (Hegesipyle), C. was a grandson of the Thracian king, Olorus. He began his political career as strategos in 478 BC, helping to establish the Delian League with the Ionian cities. He took part in the expedition against the Persians in Cyprus and Byzantium. Until 463 BC, C. usually commanded the Athenian forces; he conquered the Thracian town of Eion, the port of *Amphipolis, from the Persians (c. 476 BC). C. expelled *Pausanias (1) from Byzantium and some time later conquered the island of Scyros, from which he brought the bones of Theseus, who according to legend was killed and buried there. C. won his greatest victory in the battle of Eurymedon (c. 467 BC), where he defeated the Persians on both land and sea. In addition, he annexed the Thracian *Chersonesus to the League, and suppressed the revolt of *Thasos after a two-year siege (465—463

BC). C. thus dominated the foreign policy of Athens for fifteen years and commanded most of the military operations in this period. Though meeting no objections to his military efforts, from which Athens prospered at the expense of Persia, he encountered hostility to his philo-Spartan policy; Themistocles, Ephialtes and Pericles were among those who opposed him. C. also differed with them in internal politics, for he was the leader of the conservative elements in Athens and sought to uphold the *Areopagus council. Wealthy and of noble ancestry, C. was able to pamper the public, thus gaining popularity. His sister Elpinice married the wealthy *Callias, and C.'s own wife was of the aristocratic Alcmaeonid family. The democratic leaders, seeking to ruin C., unsuccessfully accused him of taking bribes during the siege of Thasos. C.'s influence led Athens to agree to send military assistance to Sparta during the siege of the helots in Ithome (462 BC). When C. arrived with the Athenian force, he was sent back to Athens. This disgrace made C. lose influence, and his rivals carried out a democratic coup in Athens. He was ostracized in 461 BC, but after returning to Athens in 450 BC, he was elected strategos to carry on the war against Persia. C. died on that expedition, and Athens soon made peace with Persia, abandoning Cyprus.

Plutarch, *Cimon.*

CINCINNATUS, Lucius Quintius Of a patrician family, most details of his life are legendary, added in the course of time to the few genuine historical facts. In later times, C. was regarded as an example of the simple way of life of Roman statesmen in the early Republic. Probably the only authentic story relates to C.'s dictatorship in 458 BC, when the consul Minucius Esquilinus was trapped with his army on Mount Algidus. C. was called from the plough, appointed dictator and, after winning a brilliant victory over the *Aequi, rescued the consul. Between the call and the triumph, only sixteen days had passed; C., true to his Republican sentiments, then abdicated and returned to his farm.

Ogilvie, *Livy*, 417–8.

CINNA (1), Lucius Cornelius Of a patrician family, C.'s earlier career is unknown. He served with distinction as legate in the Social War of 89–88 BC. Though an opponent of *Sulla, he was elected consul for 87 BC, and as such, he attempted to pass laws contradictory to Sulla's measures, which he had sworn to maintain. Expelled by his colleague Octavius, C. collected an army and, with the support of *Marius, captured Rome late in the year. Many opponents of C. and *Marius were then put to death. C. was consul in succession in 86–84 BC, and his rule was described as tyrannic. He restored order to the state and had several laws passed to regulate debts. During this period, the Italian allies who had received citizenship were first registered. C. made preparations for possible war with Sulla, but his soldiers killed him at Ancona (84 BC), refusing to fight abroad.

C. M. Bulst, *Historia*, 1964, 307ff.

CINNA (2), Gaius Helvius Roman poet of the 1st century BC. A native of northern Italy, C. was a friend of *Catullus and, like him, wrote in the Alexandrian style. He was probably with Catullus in Bithynia in 57 BC. His most famous work was *Smyrna*, on Smyrna's love for her father. C. was probably the tribune of the Plebs in 44 BC, by whose law the two tribunes who opposed *Caesar were deposed. After the murder of Caesar, the mob, mistaking C. for one of the conspirators, lynched him.

CINYRAS In mythology, the Cypriote king who found-ed Paphos and built a temple to Aphrodite. C.'s descendants, the Cinyrades, were responsible for the cult of the goddess there. In one version, C. gave a breastplate to *Agamemnon and promised 50 ships for the Trojan War; but he sent only one ship, along with 49 miniature boats of clay. Apollo then killed C., whose 50 daughters subsequently jumped into the sea, becoming halcyons. In another version, C., being drunk, lay with his daughter Smyrna, who bore him Adonis. When C. discovered the incest, he killed himself.

CIRCE In Greek mythology, a witch living on the island of Aeaea. C. turned all persons who arrived on the island into animals. *Odysseus resisted her magic with the aid of Hermes, compelling her to restore his companions whom she had transformed into pigs. C. had two children by Odysseus, Agrios and Latinus. After a year with C., Odysseus continued his journey according to her directions. In another version, *Jason and *Medea visited the island, where C. purified them from the murder of Absyrtus, Medea's step-brother. The promontory of Circei in southern Latium was identified by the Romans with C.'s home.

CIRCUS Oblong ground for chariot-racing with seating on both long sides, and one of the short sides. At the open end were the stables (*carceres*) for horses and chariots. Down the centre was a divider (*spina*), at either end of which stood pillars, around which the chariots turned. The seven laps of the race were marked by seven marble eggs and dolphins (symbols of the *Dioscuri and Neptune, protectors of horses). In Rome, the Circus Maximus, situated between the Palatine and the Aventine, was the earliest C., with about 60,000 seats at the time of Caesar; it measured 600 by 150 m. In 221 BC, the censor C. Flaminius built a second C. in Rome, in the southern part of *Campus Martius. The C. of *Maxentius, along the *Via Appia, was dedicated in AD 309; it measured 520 by 108 m, and is still well preserved. Four to twelve chariots competed, in four *factiones* (teams), represented by four colours: red, white, green and blue.

Platner-Ashby, *Top. Dict. Rome* 111ff;
Nash, *Pict. Dict. Rome*, 1, 232ff.

CIRTA (modern Constantine) Numidian town, the capital of *Syphax and later of *Masinissa. In the 2nd century BC, C. attracted Italian businessmen, who were subsequently killed there by *Jugurtha in 112 BC. It was colo-

The Circus Maximus — with its surroundings. Detail of a model of the city of Rome

nized under Caesar, and Augustus made it a Roman *colonia*. It enjoyed economic prosperity under the Empire, until partially destroyed in the war against the usurper Domitius Alexander (AD 308–10). After Constantine rebuilt the town, it was renamed Constantina and became the capital of Numidia.

CIVILIS, Gaius Julius Scion of a noble Batavian family, a Roman citizen who had served as prefect in the Roman army in Lower Germany. C. was sent to Rome in chains in AD 68, on suspicion of mutiny, but *Galba released him. Back in his home country in AD 69, he incited the Batavians to revolt. The revolt first appeared to be a war against the government of *Vitellius in support of Vespasian. C. was supported by the Frisii and the *Chatii and, after some success, Gallic tribes and even Roman troops joined him. In AD 70, *Cerialis was sent to quell the insurrection and he subdued the Gauls after his victory at Trier. He then proceeded against the Batavians. C. surrendered in despair; his subsequent fate is unknown.

CLASSICUS, Julius Commander of a Treveri cavalry unit in the army of *Vitellius. In AD 69, C. remained loyal to Rome and fought against *Civilis; the following year, however, he joined the revolt. In AD 70, he was defeated by *Cerialis, but continued service with Civilis. His subsequent movements are unknown.

CLAUDIAN Alexandrian by birth, C. came to Rome as a youth in AD 394, and gained entrée to influential people. In AD 395, he published his panegyric on Probinus and Olybrius, consuls of that year, which immediately won him success and the two brothers of the influential house of Anicii became his patrons. C. soon became a court poet to the Emperor *Honorius, and wrote most of his poetry in honour of *Stilicho, the chief minister. From AD 396 on, C. was, in fact, Stilicho's propagandist, for which he was well rewarded; he was given a statue in Trajan's Forum, an office, a rich wife and the title *vir clarissimus*. He died soon after AD 404.

In addition to the above-mentioned panegyric, C.'s poems include: three panegyrics on the consulships of Honorius (AD 396, 398 and 404); invectives against the opponents of Stilicho at the court of *Arcadius; panegyrics for Theodorus (AD 399) and Stilicho (AD 400); the *Bellum Pollentinum* (or *Bellum Geticum*), in honour of Stilicho's victory over *Alaric at Pollentia in AD 403; a *Gigantomachia* (unlike the others, in Greek; only the beginning has survived); epistles, idylls and epigrams; and *De Raptu Proserpinae*, an unfinished epic in three books. C. was a professional poet and as such was well acquainted with the techniques of the various genres necessary for his profession. His poems contain much historical information, often vitiated by his polemical, tendentious tone. In his panegyrics, he was influenced by rhetorical handbooks; the invectives are more freely composed and are more forceful. C. was especially successful in descriptive and invective passages, and described the high society of his day well. He was thoroughly familiar with the writings of the Latin poets of the Augustan and Silver Ages, and possessed a good knowledge of Greek and Roman writers on history, politics and rhetoric.
M. Platnauer, *Claudian* (Loeb), 1922.

CLAUDIUS (1) (Crassus Inregillensis Sabinus), Appius Consul in 471 BC and *decemvir* in 451 BC. C. supported the demand of the Plebeians for the codification and publication of the laws. He was the leading member of the second decemvirate in 450 BC, in which office he is traditionally regarded as a tyrant. C. was forced to resign

Portrait of Claudius on a coin

after the murder of *Verginia, and is said to have committed suicide or to have been murdered.
Ogilvie, *Livy*, 476–489, 503.

CLAUDIUS (2) CAECUS, Appius Leading Roman statesman in the late 4th and early 3rd centuries BC. C. served as quaestor, aedile (twice), consul (twice), censor and dictator. His most famous office was the censorship of 312 BC, in which he carried out important building projects, the Via Appia from Rome to Capua (by which he secured Rome's communications with, and further expansion into, southern Italy) and the Aqua Appia (the first aqueduct in Rome). C. transferred the cult of *Heracles at the Ara Maxima from private to public administration and he took a controversial step by enrolling low-born citizens in the Senate. It was probably due to his assistance, in 304 BC, that his secretary Gnaeus Flavius was able to publish a book with the legal forms of civil procedure, thus diminishing the patrician control of the courts. C. also took part in the Roman wars of the period, against the Etruscans and the Samnites. In 279 BC, old and blind ("Caecus"), C. gave his famous speech before the Senate against the proposals of *Pyrrhus and under his influence the Senate rejected the proposal, thereby adopting C.'s claim for Roman hegemony in the whole of southern Italy. This speech was still known in the 1st century BC. C., the first Roman to write Latin prose, composed a collection of moral sayings of which the best known is *faber est suae quisque fortunae*.
F. Cassola, *Gr. Pol. Rom.*, 128ff.

CLAUDIUS (3) QUADRIGARIUS, Quintus Roman historian of the early 1st century BC. C.'s *Annales* (at least 23 books) describe the history of Rome from its destruction by the Gauls (387 BC) till his own times. Of C.'s work, often utilized by *Livy, only fragments have survived.
Peter, *His. Rom. Rel., 1*;
E. Badian in *Latin Historians* (ed. T. A. Dorey), 1966.

CLAUDIUS (4) PULCHER, Appius Roman politician. His father, of the same name, was consul in 79 BC, and died in 76 BC, leaving a comparatively small inheritance to Appius, the eldest of his six children. C. started his career in military service in 72–70 BC under *Lucullus, his brother-in-law. After praetorship in 57 BC, he governed Sardinia (56–55 BC). He was consul in 54 BC, and then governor of Cilicia (53–51 BC). Returning to Rome, he was elected censor in 50 BC. In the Civil War, C. was a follower of Pompey (whose son Gnaeus married C.'s daughter). He died in Greece in 48 BC; *Clodius was his brother, and *Brutus (2) married one of his daughters. He was a typical haughty aristrocrat, and plundered the provincials under his governorship.

CLAUDIUS (5) (Tiberius Claudius Nero Germanicus) Roman emperor (AD 41–54). Born in Lugdunum, 1 August 10 BC, to *Drusus the Elder, brother of *Tiberius, and *Antonia (2), younger daughter of Antony. Suffering from chronic illness from childhood, C. was not considered fit for a public career, and thus did not receive a magistracy under Augustus or Tiberius. His early years were devoted to study, including Roman history under *Livy. C. wrote several historical works: in Latin, a history of the reign of Augustus; and in Greek, histories of the Etruscans (20 books) and Carthaginians (4 books). He also wrote an autobiography, a defence of Cicero, a grammatical treatise and a book on dicing. Nothing has survived of his writings.

Until AD 37, C. belonged to the Equestrian order. It was his nephew, *Caligula, who made him a senator, and in July AD 37, C. became *consul suffectus*. After Caligula's illness, C. was often insulted and presumably survived only because he was an easy target for mockery, and seemed unfit to rule. In AD 39, C. married his third wife, *Messalina, who bore him a daughter (Octavia) and a son *Britannicus (c. AD 41). When Caligula was murdered, on 24 January AD 41, the Senate tried to restore the Republic, but the praetorians found C., hiding in fear for his life, and acclaimed him emperor. This intiated the misunderstanding and friction between C. and the Senate. Thankful to the praetorians, C. gave them donatives, which became the normal practice on the accession of every new emperor. That the Roman army was loyal to the new emperor became apparent in AD 42, when *Scribonianus, governor of Dalmatia, revolted with extensive support from senators and Equites; he was murdered, however, by his soldiers. C. sought to make up for his late start in public office, serving four times as consul (AD 42, 43, 47 and 51) and in AD 47 as censor. He also showed interest in the army, and authorized and took part in the invasion of *Britain in AD 43. Under C.'s rule, four provinces were added to the Empire: the two provinces of *Mauretania, and Britannia and Thrace.

C. is criticized and mocked by Seneca, Tacitus and Suetonius, who mainly represented the opinion of the aristocracy. This unpopularity, even hatred, sprang from C.'s excessive interests in jurisdiction, the influence of his freedmen and wives and from his, what seemed to senators, hypocritical demands for their participation in debates and policy decisions in the Senate. After the autocratic reign of Caligula, the Senate could no longer expect to have a genuine share in the administration of the state and the senators well knew who wielded the real power. Another point in dispute was C.'s policy toward provincials, generously extending Roman citizenship. As censor in AD 47–8, he supported the claims of Gallic chiefs to take office and become senators; his oration on this matter in the Senate (AD 48) is extant. When the literary portrait of C. is corrected by other relevant documentary evidence, it becomes apparent that he took his duties as emperor very seriously. The administration of the Empire was under his constant supervision, and to assist him in this, C. promoted his secretaries, all of whom were freedmen. Thus, *Narcissus, his *ab epistulis*

(responsible for the emperor's correspondence), and *Pallas, his *a rationibus* (responsible for the finances), grew quite influential, amassing wealth and thereby causing resentment among the senators. These freedmen also intervened in C.'s private life. It was Narcissus who revealed Messalina's infidelity to C. (AD 48) and then obtained her execution; C.'s fourth wife, his niece *Agrippina (3), was supported by Pallas and, in AD 50, C. adopted Nero, Agrippina's son, who had married C.'s daughter, Octavia. He was now completely under the influence of his wife. When C. seemed to reverse his cool attitude toward his own son Britannicus, in AD 54, Agrippina procured his murder by poison (13 October AD 54). C. was the first emperor after Augustus to be deified.
Tacitus, *Annals*, 11–12; Suetonius, *Claudius*;
A. Momigliano, *Claudius*, 1961 (1934).

CLAUDIUS (6) POMPEIANUS, Tiberius Native of Antioch, of Equestrian origin. After attaining the consulate, C. was governor of Lower Pannonia (AD 167). In AD 169, he married *Marcus Aurelius' daughter, Lucilla, widow of L. *Verus. C. was again consul in AD 173, and from then on was chief commander in the wars against the Germanic tribes. He refrained from public service under *Commodus, who had executed his wife.

CLAUDIUS (7) GOTHICUS, Marcus Aurelius Roman emperor (AD 268–70). Born in AD 219, of Illyrian origin. C. served as military tribune under *Decius and under *Gallienus he became one of the chief commanders. After the murder of Gallienus (AD 268), in which he may have been involved, he was proclaimed emperor by his fellow officers. C. reversed Gallienus' antisenatorial policy and cultivated good relations with the Senate. He was soon called to fight the invading Germanic tribes, first dealing with the Alamanni, on whom he inflicted a defeat near Lake Benacus in the Alps. The Goths, who were devastating the Balkans and were regarded as a major threat, were defeated by C. in two great battles (thus earning him his epithet, "Gothicus"). He also took strong measures against Germanic pirates active in the Aegean Sea. Fully occupied with these tasks, C. did nothing to recover the Gallic Empire established by *Postumus; he had neither the time nor the means to fight *Zenobia, who had taken Egypt, Syria and most of Asia Minor. C. died in Pannonia early in AD 270.

CLAZOMENAE Ionian city on the Gulf of Smyrna, founded by Colophon. In the 6th century BC, C. came under the rule of Croesus, king of Lydia, and subsequently under that of Persia. Probably in connection with the Ionian revolt of 500–494 BC, the population moved to an island opposite the shore, which was later connected to the mainland by a causeway, built by Alexander. In the 5th century BC, C. was a member of the Delian League, paying tribute.
G. E. Bean, *Aegean Turkey*, 1966, 128–36.

CLEANTHES Born in 331 BC (?), at *Assos in the Troad. Of a poor family, C. had to work while studying philosophy in Athens. He was a disciple of *Zeno (2) and became head of the Stoa in 262 BC. He died in 231 BC. Of his extensive writings, only fragments have survived. According to his concept, the sun was the central part of the universe, which he perceived as a living being. C. was interested in cosmogony, and his famous hymn to Zeus glorifies the Logos of the universe. With him Stoicism took on religious aspects.
Diog. Laert. 7.168–176; Arnim, *St. Vet. Fr.*, 1;
F. H. Sandbach, *The Stoics*, 1975 (s.v.).

CLEARCHUS Born c. 450 BC. C. was an able Spartan commander in the latter part of the Peloponnesian War. Appointed governor of Byzantium in 403 BC, he abused his powers and was driven off by Spartan troops. Cyrus II subsequently hired him and C. recruited Greek mercenaries and commanded them in the battle of Cunaxa against *Artaxerxes II, in 401 BC. After the death of Cyrus in the battle, C. and other Greek commanders were deceived and arrested by the Persians, and put to death.

CLEISTHENES (1) Tyrant of the family of Orthagoras, ruler of Sicyon c. 600–570 BC. C.'s rule was marked by an anti-Argive policy; he expelled the cult of the Argive *Adrastus and instituted a festival of Dionysus. C. celebrated the marriage of his daughter Agariste to the Athenian *Megacles with extravagant munificence.
A. Andrews, *The Greek Tyrants*, 1956.

CLEISTHENES (2) Athenian statesman of the noble family of the Alcmaeonidae. C.'s father was *Megacles and his mother Agariste, daughter of *Cleisthenes (1). C. was old enough to serve as archon in 525/524 BC, when Athens was ruled by the tyrant *Hippias. Some time later, however, Hippias exiled the Alcmaeonids. C. is said to have procured the cooperation of the prophetess of Delphi in persuading the Spartans to overthrow Hippias. In 510 BC, Cleomenes, the Spartan king, expelled the Pisistratids from Athens, and all the exiles were able to return. A struggle now began between C. and other aristocrats who had gained power when C.'s opponent Isagoras was elected archon for 508/507 BC. When C. sought to court the people, to counter-balance his rivals, Isagoras invited *Cleomenes I to help him. C. then left Athens, to avoid an unwise clash. When Cleomenes expelled 700 citizens and tried to establish an oligarchy, he faced an uprising and was compelled to leave Athens, followed by Isagoras and his men. C. could then return and carry out his democratic reforms. This, however, may have occurred earlier. The Athenian state was reorganized, and local tribes, each composed of three units from the interior, the city, and the coastal regions, superseded the four old ethnic tribes. The smallest administrative-political units were the *demoi*, that is, villages, townships and urban wards. Everyone who lived in a *demos* at the time of the reform was registered as an Athenian citizen. C. thus enlarged the citizen-body of the Athenian state and broke the power of the aristocracy – which was based on the organization of the old tribes. The new Boule had 500 members, 50 from each tribe; the archontes, strategoi and other boards of the Boule had ten members, one from each tribe. There were ten regiments of infantry and ten of cavalry. The fifty councillors of each tribe served in turn as *prytaneis*, that is, the permanent committee of the Boule. All citizens over the age of 30, excepting the Thetes at first, were entitled to be elected to the Boule. C. is also credited with the creation of *ostracism. He seems to have died soon after his reforms. In any case, nothing is heard of him in later times. The new institutions of C. remained in force for generations, and formed the basis for further democratic development; later on he was commonly believed to have created Athenian democracy.
Hignett, *Ath. Constitution*.

CLEITARCHUS Historian, apparently active in Alexandria. The time of his writing is disputed, but it is likely that his history of Alexander – which has not survived – was written under *Ptolemy II, though some suggest an earlier date. The sensational style of C. made his work very popular, and later historians, such as *Diodorus (book 17), Justinus and *Curtius Rufus used him freely.
L. Pearson, *His. Al. Gr.*

CLEITUS (1) Known as "the Black", he was born c. 380 BC, son of Dropidas. C. served with Alexander in the Persian expedition and was a good cavalry commander. In the battle of the Granicus (334 BC), he saved Alexander from certain death. C. disapproved of Alexander's policy regarding easterners. At a banquet in 327 BC, he was killed by Alexander while both of them were drunk.

CLEITUS (2) Known as "the White". An officer in Alexander's army, C. was sent home in 324 BC. As commander of the Macedonian fleet, he won important naval victories over Athens in 322 BC, during the Lamian War. *Antipater (1) made him satrap of Lydia in 321 BC, which he lost to *Antigonus (1) in 319 BC. After the death of Antipater, C. supported *Polyperchen and, as his admiral, suffered a naval defeat by Nicanor, the admiral of *Cassander. He was killed by *Lysimachus in Thrace in 318 BC.

CLEOBIS and BITON Two brothers, sons of Hera's priestess in Argos. When the oxen which were to draw their mother's chariot for the performance of the rites did not arrive in time, C. and B. harnessed themselves and drew the chariot to the temple, a distance of some eight km. As a reward for their devotion they did not awake from their sleep – according to the belief that death (i.e., everlasting sleep) was the best gift for mortals (Hdt. 1.31). Statues in their honour were erected by Argos in Delphi, which have been found, bearing an inscription.

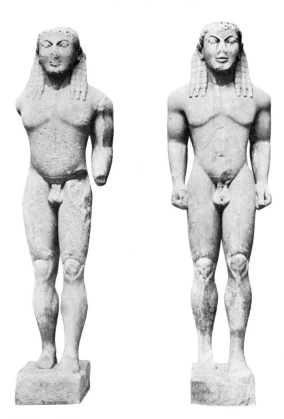

Cleobis and Biton. Two Archaic statues, c. 600 BC, found at Delphi

CLEOMENES (1) I Spartan king of the Agiad dynasty, son of Anaxandridas by his second wife, and half-brother of *Leonidas. C. reigned *c*. 520–488 BC. His general policy attempted to extend Sparta's influence in Greece, to which end he employed unscrupulous methods and brute force if necessary. He opposed interference in overseas affairs. C.'s efforts made Sparta the strongest land power in Greece, though her naval strength was neglected. In 519 – or perhaps 509 – BC, C. urged *Plataeae to ally herself with Athens, in the hope that thereby the latter would come into conflict with Thebes. In the battle of Sepeia (not far from *Tiryns), whose date is not clear (perhaps 494 BC), C. annihilated the Argive army but was unable to capture their city. The chronology of C.'s other actions is more certain. Exploiting the advice of the Delphic Oracle, he brought Athens under siege, driving off *Hippias and his associates (510 BC). He then intervened in the internal conflict between Isagoras and *Cleisthenes (2), but though at first he took control of the city, he later (507 BC) evacuated it. His attempt to restore Isagoras, employing the army of the Peloponnesian League, failed because of the opposition of Demaratus, his fellow king. C. likewise failed in his attempt to restore Hippias to Athens (c. 504 BC). When *Aristagoras came to Sparta seeking aid, for the Ionian revolt against Persia, C. ordered him to leave the city before sunset. Earlier, C. had declined to interfere in *Samos' internal politics. C.'s vigorous policy was again frustrated by Demaratus in 492 BC, when he prevented him from punishing *Aegina for her philo-Persian attitude. C. took vengeance by procuring an oracle from Delphi which said that Demaratus was illegitimate. Demaratus was deposed and left Sparta, but C.'s complicity in the oracle was revealed and he, too, was obliged to flee. He first went to Thessaly and then tried to rouse Arcadia against Sparta. C. soon returned to his country and, according to Herodotus, committed suicide.

G. L. Huxley, *Early Sparta*, 1962.

CLEOMENES (2) III Spartan king of the Agiad dynasty. Born *c*. 260 BC, he ascended the throne in 235 BC, upon the death of his father, Leonidas. C. married Agiatis, widow of *Agis IV, and through her was influenced by the social ideas of her dead husband. A competent general, good organizer and clever politician, C. was able to combine these talents to revive Sparta's power. First, he established his military fame by conquering Tegea, Orchomenus and Mantinea (229 BC). In 227 BC, he won victories against the Achaean League, following which he seized power in Sparta in 227/226 BC, slaying the ephors and expelling his opponents among the great land-owners. C. then implemented the reforms of Agis IV, claiming to restore the Lycurgan constitution. Debts were cancelled and the lands of the rich were confiscated and re-distributed to *perioeci* and metics, who received Spartan citizenship. The number of Spartan citizens, 700 before the revolution, now reached several thousand. C. also revived traditional Spartan education and the simple way of life. He expanded Spartan rule at the expense of the Achaean League, gaining popularity by his social reforms which he introduced into the cities under his control. In 225 BC, he conquered Argos, and the following year, put Corinth to siege. The Achaean leader *Aratus (2) reached an agreement with *Antigonus Doson of Macedonia, and Antigonus advanced to the Peloponnesus and in 224 BC conquered Arcadia. He then organized a Greek alliance against C. C. seized Megalopolis (223 BC), but lost the decisive battle at Sellasia (222 BC). His reforms were

abolished and he fled to Egypt where a new king, *Ptolemy IV, had ascended the throne (221 BC); C. was arrested by him, and after a revolt failed in 219 BC, C. committed suicide.

Polyb. 2; Plut. *Cleomenes*;
B. Shimron, *Historia*, 1964, 147ff.

CLEOMENES (3) Native of *Naucratis. In 332 BC, Alexander the Great put C. in charge of finances in Egypt, the administration of the eastern Delta and the building of Alexandria. C. succeeded in bringing the whole of Egypt under his control. After some resentment, Alexander confirmed C.'s position (323 BC) and made him hyparchos of Egypt, with *Ptolemy I as satrap. C. exploited his financial administration to amass a fortune (8,000 talents), but Ptolemy soon brought serious charges against him and executed him.

CLEON Athenian statesman, active in the first part of the Peloponnesian War. C. was the son of a tanner and thus the first important Athenian leader not of the aristocracy. He first gained fame in 430 BC by attacking *Pericles, after whose death (429 BC) he became the leading personality in Athenian politics. He was responsible for the motion to execute all the citizens of Mytilene (427 BC), which, however, was cancelled the day after it was voted. C. supported an extremist war policy against Sparta, and it was due to him that Sparta's overtures for peace were rejected in 425 BC. Given military command, C. went to Sphacteria where he took the Spartans besieged there as prisoners. He seems to have been responsible for the great increase of the tribute of the Athenian allies. In 422 BC, he campaigned northward and, after initial success, was defeated and killed while trying to recapture *Amphipolis, in which battle the Spartan commander Brasidas also lost his life. C. is described as a demagogue and an unscrupulous politician, but the extant data are derived mainly from sources hostile to him, i.e., Thucydides and Aristophanes.

A. W. Gomme, *More Essays in Greek History and Literature*, 1962, 112ff.

CLEOPATRA The name of several Hellenistic queens.

CLEOPATRA (1) II Daughter of *Ptolemy V and Cleopatra I. C. was married to her brother *Ptolemy VI (175 BC), who became sole ruler of Egypt after the death of his mother in 176 BC. She became co-regent with her husband and his brother, *Ptolemy VIII, from 170 to 164 BC, after which Ptolemy VI became sole ruler. When he died in 145 BC, Ptolemy VIII returned to Egypt and married C. (144 BC). In 142 BC, Ptolemy VIII married C.'s daughter, Cleopatra III, without divorcing C. C. successfully revolted against him in 132 BC, and eight years later, a peace was made. She died in 115 BC.

CLEOPATRA (2) VII Born in 69 BC, daughter of *Ptolemy XII Auletes. After her father's death (51 BC), C. became co-ruler with her brother and husband Ptolemy XIII, who expelled her in 48 BC. Caesar restored C. in 47 BC, and, after defeating her brother who drowned in the Nile, installed another brother, Ptolemy XIV, as her co-ruler and husband. In 47 BC, C. gave birth to a son, Ptolemy XV Caesar, called *Caesarion. In 46–44 BC, C. visited Rome. Probably responsible for the death of her husband, C. made Caesarion joint-ruler in 44 BC. C. first met Antony at Tarsus in 41 BC and she bore him twins, Alexander Helios and Cleopatra Selene. They renewed their close relationship in 37 BC, though Antony did not divorce his wife Octavia until 32 BC. Antony restored to C. the former Ptolemaic territories, Cyrenaica,

Bronze head, presumably of Cleopatra VII

part of Phoenicia and Cilicia. In return, C. supported Antony with money and supplies, after his failure against Parthia (35 BC). The next year Antony named C. "Queen of Queens", and Caesarion "King of Kings", thus officially recognizing them as heirs and rulers of the empire of Alexander the Great. With the final rupture between Antony and Octavian, C. became the main target of Octavian's propaganda, and she was depicted as a national enemy menacing the unity of the Empire. In 32 BC, war was declared against her though not against Antony. C. contributed ships to Antony's fleet, but several of Antony's officers deserted his cause because of her. After the battle of Actium, both fled to Egypt. When Antony committed suicide, C. followed suit, on 10 August 30 BC, rather than submit to the humiliation of a triumph in Rome. C. was evidently an alluring woman; her vices were not exceptional in the Ptolemaic dynasty. She sought to revive the Ptolemaic Empire and to enhance her own power with any means at her disposal. See *Antonius (4), *Augustus, *Caesarion.

H. Volkmann, *Cleopatra*, 1958.

CLEOPHON Athenian democratic statesman, active in the second part of the Peloponnesian War. C. pursued an extreme war policy against Sparta and it was due to his influence that the peace terms of Sparta in 410 BC, and again in 406 BC, were rejected. He also opposed the Spartan peace proposals of 405 BC. C. was responsible for Athenian finances in 410 BC, when he introduced the two obols payment apparently given to the poor. Being the leader of the extreme democrats, it is not surprising that he was condemned to death in 404 BC, after the oligarchs took power.

CLEOPHRADES, Painter The Athenian vase painter and potter active in the late 6th and early 5th centuries BC,

known from a signature on a fragment of a vase. He painted mainly on large vessels, preferring heroic myths for his themes. He is apparently identical with the artist Epictetus.

CLERUCHY Special type of settlement colonized by Athens outside Attica. Unlike the colonists of an *apoikia*, the settlers in a C. retained Athenian citizenship, the new settlement not being an autonomous community. The settlers, *clerouchoi*, incivicually received plots of land (*cleros*). They were registered in the Attic demes and tribes, and were subject to Athenian taxation and military service. They developed local institutions, supervised by Athenian officials. The first certain C. was sent to *Chalcis in 506 BC, and many more were colonized in the course of the 5th century BC. The number of settlers at each C. varied from several hundred to a few thousand In the Hellenistic period, soldiers who received from the king plots of land, actually cultivated by tenants, were *clerouchoi*. The land remained royal domain. The system is known from Egypt.

Graham, *Col. Moth. Cit.* (s.v.).

CLIENS, PATRONUS A social-legal institution in Rome, according to which a free person, the C., was protected by another man, his P. This institution dated from the early history of Rome but its origin is obscure and some of its aspects are disputed. Under conditions of insecurity, poor and weak citizens sought and obtained protection by entrusting themselves to more powerful persons. The P. helped his C. in legal matters and protected him from aggressive neighbours. The C. supported his P. in politics and by escorting him in public appearances, enhanced his social prestige. Through long usage this bond became almost sacred and was recognized by the Twelve Tables as *fides*, that is "duty of fidelity", which existed between the two. Under this special tie, they were not allowed to give evidence against one another in court. The relationship passed on from generation to generation.

A special category of C. was the emancipated slave. The obligations of the freedman to his former master, now his P., were defined by law; the P. was entitled to a share of his freedman's inheritance in certain cases, and wielded some jurisdiction over him. A person representing a C. in court, for instance *Cicero, *Hortensius, and *Crassus (3), was also known as a P. In one way or another he received remuneration for his services, but the ties with the C. were obviously looser. With the extension of Roman power in Italy and the Mediterranean countries, Roman generals and statesmen acquired patronage over communities and individuals who felt that they could benefit from a powerful Roman P. to defend and represent them. Under the Empire, wealthy men used to support numerous clients, who would accompany and salute them in public, as lackeys. See *Amicitia.

J. Carcopino, *Daily Life in Ancient Rome*; E. Badian, *Foreign Clientelae*, 1958.

CLIO One of the nine *Muses. Originally she was a fountain nymph, then a goddess of music, as she appears on vases. In time, C. came to be known mainly as the goddess of history.

CLITHIAS Athenian vase painter, active in the first half of the 6th century BC. His most famous work is the François Vase, discovered at Chiusi in 1884.

CLITOMACHUS Carthaginian philosopher (formerly named Hasdrubal). Born in 187/186 BC, he came to Athens at the age of 24. Four years later, he studied at the Academy under *Carneades, and opened a school of

The famous François vase

his own in 140 BC. After eleven years, C. rejoined the Academy and became its head (127/126 BC). He died in 110/109 BC. None of his more than 400 works has survived, but his lengthy expositions of other philosophers' arguments made him very useful; it was through his writings that the views of *Carneades, who himself never wrote books, were transmitted, to be subsequently reproduced by Cicero.

CLODIA Born *c.* 95 BC, sister of Appius *Claudius (4) and *Clodius Pulcher. C.'s husband was Metellus Celer, consul for 60 BC; he died in 59 BC. Among C.'s lovers were *Catullus (who called her Lesbia in his poems) and *Caelius. For some time she had much influence in Roman society. Cicero's speech *Pro Caelio* is a vivid lampoon against her.

CLODIUS (1) PULCHER, Publius Born *c.* 92 BC, brother of Appius *Claudius (4) and *Clodia. While serving under his brother-in-law *Lucullus, C. incited the soldiers to revolt (68 BC). He was captured by pirates and was subsequently ransomed. C. was in collusion with *Catiline while prosecuting him in 65 BC. He had an affair with Caesar's wife and was caught in Caesar's house disguised as a woman during the annual festival of *Bona Dea in December 62 BC. Cicero testified against his alibi during his trial in 61 BC, though there had been no previous animosity between them; but the jury was well bribed (with *Crassus' (4) money) and C. was acquitted. He was quaestor in Sicily in 60 BC, and the following year became a Plebeian with the assistance of Caesar (then Pontifex Maximus), and tribune of the Plebs for 58 BC. As tribune, C. successfully sponsored several bills, among them: the distribution of free corn to citizens in Rome; the punishment of those who had executed Roman citizens without trial (i.e. Cicero); the restoration of the *collegia*; the annexation of Cyprus; and the granting of new provinces to the consuls of the year. With the support of the restored *collegia*, and audaciously using armed clients, C. dominated the streets of Rome for a while; his men pillaged Cicero's villas and he even attacked Pompey, who subsequently secured Cicero's recall (57 BC). C. was aedile in 56 BC, but although he was popular with the Plebs, his power began to decline. His rivals employed methods similar to his own, and the renewed alliance of

Caesar, Pompey and Crassus in 56 BC enabled them to dominate Roman politics. As candidate for the praetorship, C. was killed by *Milo on 18 January 52 BC. In his striving for power and influence, he was a typical Roman aristocrat. His audacity, unscrupulousness, and the methods he used, increased violence in Roman politics. To a large extent, he was responsible for the anarchy of the 50s BC.
Gruen, *Phoenix*, 1966, 32ff.

CLODIUS (2) ALBINUS, Decimus Probably a native of Hadrumetum (modern Sousse) and scion of a wealthy noble family. C. fought with distinction in Dacia (AD 182–4), and was appointed governor of Britain prior to the death of *Commodus. Septimius *Severus at first recognized C. as Caesar but changed his attitude after his victory over *Pescennius Niger. C. then made himself Augustus and was declared a public enemy, early in AD 196. He advanced into Gaul but was defeated and subsequently killed by Severus at Lugdunum, in February AD 197.
A. Birley, *Septimius Severus,* 1971 (s.v.).

CLUSIUM (modern Chiusi) Etruscan city, one of the oldest in northern Etruria; originally it appears to have been called Camars. *Porsenna, who sought to restore *Tarquinius Superbus to Rome, was from C. The city was also famous for its bronze industry. It was allied with Rome from the 3rd century BC on, and received Roman citizenship in 90 BC.
Scullard, *Etruscan Cities*, 151–6.

CLYTEMNESTRA Daughter of *Tyndareus and *Leda, and sister of the *Dioscuri and *Helen. C.'s first husband, *Tantalus, was killed by *Agamemnon who then married her. When Agamemnon went to Troy, *Aegisthus became her lover. When Agamemnon returned from Troy, the two killed him as well as *Cassandra. C. had three daughters and a son, *Orestes, by Agamemnon. Orestes fled, but when he reached maturity, he returned to kill his mother with the aid of his sister, *Electra. Various motives were ascribed by Greek authors to C.'s infidelity and crime; Homer blames Aegisthus, while according to Aeschylus, C. never forgave Agamemnon for the sacrifice of *Iphigenia. The murders of Agamemnon, Cassandra and Aegisthus were favourite themes among Greek artists.

CNIDOS Greek city on the southwestern coast of Asia Minor. Founded, according to Herodotus, by Sparta, C. is situated on a peninsula, with two good harbours. It took part in the colonization of the Lipari islands (*c.* 575 BC), and became a member of the Delian League from its inception. In 412 BC, however, it followed Sparta. *Mausolus controlled it in the 4th century BC, and in the 3rd century BC it fell under Ptolemaic rule. *Agatharchides, *Ctesias and *Eudoxus were natives of C., and *Praxiteles made a statue of Aphrodite for its temple.
G. E. Bean, *Turkey Beyond the Maeander*, 1971, 135–152.

CODRUS Legendary early king of Athens. His father Melanthus was said to have been driven away from his kingdom by the Dorians. The Spartans waging war against Athens were warned by the Delphic oracle not to kill C. if they wanted victory. When C. was informed of the oracle, he disguised himself as a woodcutter and provoked the Spartans to kill him, thus saving his country. According to another legend, he fell during the very battle in which the Athenians defeated their enemy, and Athenian kingship passed to his descendants. In a later version of the story, C. was the last king of Athens. His grave was shown near the Acropolis in Athens, and he had a hero cult there.

COELIUS ANTIPATER, Lucius Roman jurist, historian and teacher of rhetoric. C. lived in the 2nd century BC (he was still writing after 121 BC). He wrote a history (in seven books) of the Second Punic War, the first historical monograph in Latin. It included speeches, and was apparently fascinating in composition and style, impressing such men as Cicero, Brutus and Hadrian; it was used by Livy, Virgil, Pliny and Plutarch. The famous orator Lucius *Crassus (3) was C.'s pupil.
Peter, *His. Rom. Rel.*, 1.

COHORS Infantry unit in the Roman army. The term was first applied to the troops sent by each of Rome's Italian allies; these allied C.s were of varying size. *Scipio Africanus was the first to use C.s in his war in Spain, combining three maniples and, later, this became the standard tactical unit within a legion, now divided into ten C.s, of six centuries each, numbering 500–600 soldiers. The senior centurion commanded the C. Augustus formed three *C. urbanae*, who policed the city of Rome; they numbered 1,000 men and were commanded by tribunes.
Parker, *The Roman Legions*[2].

COINAGE, GREEK The use of certain objects, cattle, axes, tripods, rings, cauldrons etc., as accepted units for barter, long preceded the invention of coinage in the ancient Orient, Greece and Rome. Use had been also made of metal bars (valued according to weight) as a means of carrying out trade. Iron spits (*oboloi*) were used as a means of exchange; six obols were called a *drachme* (a graspful). The idea of marking ingots, whose weight and alloy had been approved, with special signs, probably originated with traders. Coinage proper was invented by the middle of the 7th century BC in Lydia, whose King *Cyges was probably the first to issue regular, disc-formed pieces of metal, stamped with a design (lion) to guarantee their weight and intrinsic value. They were made of electrum, an alloy of gold and silver found naturally in Lydia. The Ionian cities *Miletus, *Ephesus, *Phocaea, *Chios and *Samos had all adopted the new invention by the end of the 7th century BC.

The Greeks always struck their coins by punching metal blanks of the required weight on an anvil (on which a die was engraved or into which a block with a die was sunk). The anvil-die would produce the required design in relief on the blank. In the second part of the 6th century, the technique was improved by inserting a die in the punch (*character*) with which the metal blank was beaten from above; in this way the coin would have devices in relief on both sides, obverse being the anvil-die side of the coin, reverse the punch-die side. Dies were made of bronze and, from the 4th century, of steel as well. An anvil-die sufficed for twice or thrice as many coins as the punch-die, which was exposed more directly to the blows of the hammer.

King *Pheidon of Argos, who also ruled *Aegina, was said to have been the first to replace iron spits with coins. He probably reigned before the mid-7th century BC and his coins were produced only slightly later than those of Lydia. Other states, such as Corinth, Athens and Megara, adopted the new invention in the late 7th century or early 6th century, and sooner or later all states issued coins. Each state stamped its own distinct images or designs, often with short inscriptions. The owl on the reverse and Athena on the obverse was typical of Athens; the horse Pegasus of Corinth, the nymph Arethusa of Syracuse. Obviously, the images stamped had, in one way or other, some special connection with the state. Metapontum, a grain-growing city, had a wheat-ear on her coins; Cyrene had the silphium plant; Tarentum had its founder, Phalanthus. Often used were symbols of deity or the deities themselves. Kings "published" their images on their coins.

The Greeks usually issued silver coins. The rate of gold to silver fluctuated from $1:13\frac{1}{3}$ in the 6th century to 1:10 in Alexander's time. The rate of silver to gold was about 1:110 in the 5th century BC and dropped to 1:50–70 after the conquest of Alexander. Coins were issued as units of weight, with a few denominations, but there were several weight standards, all based on the Babylonian system of *biltu* (talent), *manah* (mina), and *shekel* (stater), the original relations between them being 1:60:3,600. Though there were considerable variations, the Greeks generally had two main systems, the Aeginetic, associated with Pheidon, and the Euboic which was adopted by Solon for Athens. The first system had a mina (weight unit only) of c. 630 gm, a drachm of c. 6.30 gm, and an obol of c. 1.05 gm. The didrachm (= stater) was a common denomination of c. 12.6 gm. This system was mainly used in Crete, the Peloponnesus and central Greece. The Euboic system had a mina (weight unit only) of c. 430 gm, a drachm of c. 4.3 gm and an obol of c. 0.72 gm. It was used in Ionia, Corinth, Athens, Euboea, Chalcidice, Macedonia and by the western Greeks. Many states issued didrachms, tridrachms and tetradrachms. There were also issues of fractions. Generally, a talent (weight unit) consisted of 6,000 drachms, that is 25.8 kg by the Euboic system, and 37.8 kg by the Aeginetic system. Mention must be made of the Persian coinage which played an important role in Greek politics and economy. When Cyrus defeated Croesus and conquered Lydia in 546 BC, the Persians inherited the Lydian coinage system, which was then bimetallic (gold and silver). They modified it, however, according to the Babylonian weight system and twenty silver pieces were equivalent to one gold piece. Under Darius I, a gold coin with an image of the Great King was introduced, and this famous *dareikos*, as it came to be called, circulated from India to Sicily. Persia's intervention in Greek politics and the close commercial relations between the two countries contributed to its popularity.

For some time after the invention of coins, they were too expensive to play an important role in daily economy. In the long run, coinage proved a most important means for the development of ancient economies, which gradually, or, in some places, rapidly, came to be based on it. The island of Siphnos prospered in the 6th century, thanks to the exploitation of its rich mines for minting, and built an outstanding treasury-house at Delphi (Pausan. 10. 11,2), from which have come some of the finest Greek sculptures. Athens' rise to power was associated with the exploitation of the silver mines of Laurium, and in her heyday she attempted to secure a monopoly of silver coinage. After the acquisition of the mines of Mount Pangaeus, *Philip II was able to finance his way by issuing *Philipeioi*, famous gold staters; hoards of these have been found almost all over Greece, Cyprus, Syria, Egypt, south Russia, Sicily and south Italy. In fact, the right to mint was a corollary of sovereignty, indispensable for a state's economy. Coins are now one of the means for studying ancient history, especially economy. They also provide evidence of art and technical skill.

C. T. Seltman, *Greek Coins*[2], 1955;
G. K. Jenkins, *Ancient Greek Coins*, 1972.

Coin of Demetrius I; on the reverse the goddess of plenty with the horn of plenty (cornucopia)

COINAGE, ROMAN Oxen and sheep were the accepted units of barter in early Rome. The use of crude bronze in weight as a means of exchange began in the second half of the 5th century BC. Following this *aes rude*, came the use of the *aes signatum* (bronze bars produced by casting) in the second half of the 4th century. The next step, established by the early 3rd century, was the *aes grave*, the first truly Roman coins. Also of bronze, they circulated not only in Rome but also in Apulia, Picenum, Umbria, and Etruria. The basic denomination was the *as*, which weighed one pound (*libra*), 327.45 gm, and was hence marked I. Its fractions were based on the duodecimal system and the most important were the *uncia, sextans, quadrans, triens* and *semis* (1/12, 1/6, 1/4, 1/3, 1/2 respectively). The *uncia* was considered to consist of 24 scruples. The nominal value of the coins was always marked.

Rome's involvement with the affairs of Magna Graeca, occasioned by the war against *Pyrrhus, led her to mint silver didrachms, a common type of Greek coin. These so-called "Romano-Campanian" coins of *c.* 7.4 gm had the legend ROMANO with the images of Mars and a horse's head, or Apollo and a horse. Rome continued to issue silver didrachms of lighter weights and with other types, including (as from 269 BC) the Hercules/Wolf and twins. *Quadrigati* first appeared *c.* 235 BC, weighing 6.8 gm. They had the legend ROMA with the images of Young Janus and Victory in *quadriga*. At the same time the *as* dropped to semi-libral (half pound) standard. Rome then had a bimetallist coinage.

Rome faced grave financial problems in the Second Punic War, and had to introduce radical changes in its monetary system. The *as*, once with full value of 1 pound, sank first to triental and then to quadrantal basis *c.* 213 BC. The *victoriatus* replaced the *quadrigatus*, though only half its weight (3.4 gm). Shortly afterwards, *c.* 211–210, appeared the famous silver *denarius*, with the legend ROMA and the devices Roma and Dioscuri. It was equivalent to ten new sextantal *asses* (of 54.6 gm). Other denominations now issued were the *quinarius* (= 5 *asses*) and the *sestertius* (=2.5 *asses*). These three were respectively marked X, V, IIS. In this new bimetallist system the silver coins were the more important. But the *as*, now struck not cast, declined gradually in weight in the 2nd century to one ounce. Shortly after the middle of the century, the *denarius* was retariffed to equal 16 *asses*, and marked XVI or X, the *quinarius* 8 *asses* and the *setertius* 4

asses. By now Rome evidently had token money. Its own coins spread in Italy, while in the provinces use was made of local coinage or special issues modelled on Roman standards, like the *argentum Oscense* in Spain. In Rome the *as* went down to semiuncial standard in the 80s BC and soon the *aes* coinage was discontinued. The issue of gold coins, first known during the Second Punic War, was renewed from *Sulla on.

The Roman mint was under the supervision of special minor magistrates, the *triumviri monetales* (or more fully *tresviri aere argento auro flando feriundo*), traditionally from 289 BC. Occasionally in the 1st century BC other magistrates, usually quaestors and aediles, issued coins. In the course of the 2nd century, the *triumviri monetales* noted their names in abbreviation or, later, more fully; they also came to use symbols with political references. In the 1st century BC, Roman generals made extensive use of this device in their provincial issues; Caesar's portrait appeared on coins and the "Republican" *Brutus (2) soon followed suit.

Under Augustus, Rome had a trimetallist system. The golden *aureus* (7.46 gm) was rated at 1:25 to the *denarius* (3.73 gm). Copper coins included the *as* (16 to the *denarius*) and *quadrans* (¼ *as*); there were also the *sestertius, dupondius* (2 *asses*) and *semis* (½ *as*), of the *orichalcum* alloy. Though the legend *Senatus* (consulto) continued to appear, in the course of time the Senate lost all control of the coinage. Actually, the emperor's slaves and freedmen took control of the Roman mint. Nevertheless, local mints continued to work in the provinces, especially in the Greek East. The portrait of the reigning emperor usually appeared on coins, which were often used as a propaganda means to stress the fidelity of the army, the clemency of the ruler and so on.

From Nero's time on, when the *denarius* was reduced to 3.41 gm, the substantial debasement of Roman coinage began. *Caracalla issued a new coin, the *Antoninianus*, equivalent to two *denarii*, which became the dominant one. But the grave military and economic crisis of the empire forced the government to reduce the amount of silver in the coins. Silver coins became in fact bronze pieces coated with silver. Under these disastrous conditions, when good coins disappeared and bad coins were not trusted, economic relations were more and more based on payment in kind instead of in coins. *Diocletian sought to check this tendency by a thorough reform undertaken in AD 294. This included an *aureus* of 5.45 gm, a silver coin of 3.41 gm, and large and small copper coins. Constantine made some changes, the most important of them being the *solidus*, a gold coin of 4.47 gm, which long remained a trusted coin. However, these and other measures could not in the long run check the rise of natural economy, even though the powers of the officials responsible for the imperial mints (there were fifteen mints under Diocletian) and coinage were more extensive in the later Roman Empire.

C. H. V. Sutherland, *Roman Coins,* 1974; M. H. Crawford, *Roman Republican Coinage,* 1974; H. Mattingly, E. A. Sydenham, C. H. V. Sutherland, R. A. Carson, *Roman Imperial Coinage,* 1923–1967.

COLCHIS   Land on the eastern shore of the Black Sea, bordered by the Caucasus mountains and Armenia. In Greek mythology, *Medea was the daughter of the king of C., and *Jason went there to find the Golden Fleece. It had abundant timber, flax and pitch. There were Greek settlements along its shore, the most important one being Phasis. *Mithridates VI conquered C., but was defeated there by Pompey.

Magie, *Asia* (s.v.).

COLLEGIUM   Term designating private associations and official priestly boards at Rome. Of the latter, the better known are those of *Pontifices, *Augures, Duoviri sacris faciundis* and *septem viri epulonum* (*Epulones). There were private *collegia* of artisans and tradesmen, and for cult and burial purposes. All *collegia* seem to have had a religious character, and they aimed at giving members a framework for social activity. The first *collegia* were allegedly established by the religious Roman king, *Numa. In the 1st century BC, the *collegia* were enlisted for political purposes, and as a result, many were outlawed in 64 BC, though they were used by P. *Clodius (1). Caesar abolished many *collegia,* and Augustus passed a law requiring their legalization. The *collegia* had their own officials and constitutions, and their members paid fees.

J. P. Waltzing, *Etude historique sur les corporations professionelles chez les romains,* 1895;

A. W. Lintott, *Violence in Republican Rome,* 1968 (s.v.).

COLONIA AGRIPPINENSIS (modern Köln)   Roman colony founded in AD 50, by *Claudius (5) on the left bank of the Rhine, and named after his wife, Agrippina. C. was situated in the territory of the friendly Ubii, whom *Agrippa (1) had allowed to settle there in 38 BC. The Ubii and the Roman veterans mixed well and the colony prospered; it had a good port and became a centre of trade. C. was the seat of the governor of Lower Germany. *Vitellius was proclaimed emperor here in AD 69. In the anarchy of the 3rd century AD, it was fortified; it was captured by the Franks in AD 436.

COLONIAE   Roman and Latin settlements outside the territory of the mother-city. The foundation of Roman colonies prior to the mid-4th century BC, related in tradition, is highly dubious. The first C. (*Ostia, *Antium, *Tarracina) were founded to safeguard the coast, up to the 2nd century BC. The number of settlers was quite small (normally 300 families); they remained Roman citizens and had no independent institutions. Citizens in these maritime C. were usually exempt from military service. In the 70s of the 2nd century BC, Roman C. came to encompass several thousand citizens each and the land allotments were larger. They then had their own local institutions, but the colonists still retained Roman citizenship and were subject to Roman magistrates. From the Gracchan period on, colonization was the accepted method "popular" politicians used to obtain land for the poor, and, from the 1st century BC on, for discharged soldiers. When public land in Italy became scarce, C. were founded in the provinces; though the first attempt at this (by Gaius *Gracchus) in *Carthage, failed. From Caesar's time on, provincial colonization became normal until Hadrian. Most of the C. were for veterans, though those at *Corinth and Carthage were commercial. Roman C. under the Empire had extensive rights of local government, and their institutions resembled those of Rome. The chief magistrates were *duoviri,* and there were aediles, pontifices, and a local senate whose members were *decuriones*. The status of C. was highly coveted, and emperors sometimes granted it to provincial municipalities.

Latin C. differed from the Roman in their origin and subsequent history. Originally the Latin C. was a new independent state founded by the Latin League; it had its own political institutions and both Latins and Romans could register in the new foundation (thereby losing their former citizenship). After the dissolution of the Latin League (338 BC), Rome continued to found Latin C., whose constitutions were defined by a law, authorizing their foundation. They had to contribute fixed quotas of troops for the wars of Rome, and their foreign policy was subject to that of Rome. Marriage and commerce with Romans were recognized by Roman law, and colonial citizens also had the right of migration to Rome and permanent residence there, which granted them Roman citizenship. All such C. received Roman citizenship in 90 BC.

E. T. Salmon, *Roman Colonization,* 1969.

COLONUS   Settler in a *colonia.* The term also designated a rent-paying tenant who farmed a plot of land. The *coloni* tended to increase on large domains from the 1st century BC on, with the gradual decrease of slave labour; they were found on private as well as imperial estates. With the increased debasement of coinage, from the times of Nero on, monetary payment was steadily replaced by pay in kind, generally a share of the harvest. Sons usually inherited their parents' holdings. In the 4th century AD, *coloni* were forbidden to leave their farms or to transfer them without the owner's authorization.

R. Clausing, *The Roman Colonate,* 1925.

COLOPHON   Prosperous inland city in Ionia, with a harbour, Notium. It was conquered by Persia in 545 BC, together with other Ionian cities, and in the 5th century it joined the Delian League. In the wars of the *Diadochi, the population was removed to *Ephesus, but the city was later resettled. Claros, the famous oracle of Apollo nearby, belonged to C. The well known philosopher *Xenophanes was a native of C.

COLOSSEUM   The medieval name of the Flavian amphitheatre in Rome. It was built by Vespasian between the Palatine and the Esquiline on part of the former site of the *Domus Aurea of Nero, near the colossal statue of Nero. *Titus dedicated it in AD 80. Its area is approx. 90,000 sq m and it originally rose to a height of 48 m. The three storeys had 80 arched passages, with the usual Doric, Ionic and Corinthian engaged columns, above which rose a podium with Corinthian pilasters. In the intercolumniation stood bronze and marble statues. The C. had seats for about 50,000 spectators, with special boxes for the emperor and the magistrates, and separate rows for Equites. The arena was equipped with elaborate devices for gladiatorial and wild beast shows, but the plan of its substructure is not entirely clear. The C. was several times damaged by fire and earthquakes. The gladiatorial shows were forbidden by *Honorius, and the last games with wild beasts were held in AD 523. In the Middle Ages, the C. was utilized as a quarry.

Platner-Ashby, *Top. Dict. Rome*, 6—11; Nash, *Pict. Dict. Rome*, 1.17ff.

COLUMBARIUM The sepulchral structures used to hold urns with ashes. This kind of burial was used by members of religious clubs, and slaves and freedmen of large households in Rome, from the 1st century BC on; it went out of fashion after the 2nd century AD. Literally, the word means "dove-cote".

COLUMELLA, Lucius Junius Moderatus Native of Gades in the 1st century AD. Of a well-to-do family, C. owned estates in Italy, and his twelve-book *De Re Rustica* is a prime source for agricultural conditions in his day. C.'s work is well organized, and more scientific than those of *Cato and *Varro on the same subject. Book I treats general matters; Book II is devoted to soils; Books III—V deal with vineyards, olive groves and fruit plantations; Books VI—IX, livestock breeding, poultry, fishponds and bees; and Book X, gardens. Books XI—XII were added at the suggestion of a friend and describe the duties of the *villicus* (bailiff) and his wife. C.'s two-book *De Arboribus* seems to belong to an earlier work on the same subject. C. was familiar with earlier Greek and Roman authors on agriculture, but he relied mainly on his own experience in preparing his book. This is C.'s testament to the decline of Italian agriculture, which, he believed, resulted from the great landlords' indifference to their estates.

H. B. Ash — E. S. Forster — E. H. Heffner, *Columella* (Loeb), 1941—1955.

COMEDY, GREEK The performance of comedies was a distinct feature of public life in Athens. The exact origins of the Attic comedy are not very clear. *Komos* was the merry company of men who took part in the festival in honour of Dionysus. Comedy, according to Aristotle (*Poet.* 1449 a 10), originated with the scurrilous songs of those who accompanied the phallus in the Dionysiac cult. These burlesques, full of obscene language, were probably the prototype of the chorus part in the Attic comedy. Another feature of the Attic comedy, the disguise of the participants in masks and grotesque dress, is known from

Comic scene from the New Comedy. A work of c. AD 170

Archaic and not only Attic vase-painting; this shows that the performance of mythological scenes in a burlesque manner was a very old one. But it is not known how, when and where a dramatic performance of a literary comedy developed from these. Beginnings of comedy were to be found in such Dorian states as Megara and Sparta, and one of the first comic playwrights was the Sicilian *Epicharmus who influenced Attic comedy. However, it was only in Athens that comedies became an integral part of public festivals. They were included in the yearly *Dionysia from 486 BC on, and in the *Lenaea from c. 442. In each of these several (usually five) poets each performed one play.

The history of Attic comedy was divided by ancient scholars into: the Old Comedy, to the end of the 5th century; the Middle Comedy, to c. 330–320 BC; and the New Comedy, to the late 4th and 3rd centuries. Of the plays of the Old Comedy, only those of *Aristophanes are extant, all belonging to the last quarter of the 5th century. What is said about Old Comedy consequently depends largely on the works of Aristophanes. Two other important poets of this period were *Cratinus and *Eupolis. The Old Comedy is characterized by its tripartite structure. In the first part, there is a burlesque contest between the chorus and the "hero" of the play. In the undramatic second part, the *parabasis*, the chorus addresses the audience and reveals the poet's intentions. The third part constitutes the sequence to the situation which ended the first part. The play ends with a finale by the chorus. The prominence of the chorus is a major characteristic of the Old Comedy. Many of the plays were named after the choruses, for example the *Acharnians*, the *Knights* and the *Wasps* of Aristophanes. Plots were unreal and fantastic. In the *Birds* of Aristophanes, two Athenians with the help of birds build a new city in the sky. In the *Frogs*, Dionysus descends to Hades to bring back a tragic poet. But the story is only a framework within which the poet deals satirically with political, social and literary themes of his time. The fantastic setting contributed to the festive occasion at which the play was performed. Many of the plays included lampoons of living persons – Socrates was ridiculed in the *Clouds*, Cleon in *Knights*, and Euripides in *Thesmophoriazousae* (by Aristophanes). But the comedies of Crates, who won his first victory c. 450, lacked this element, as Aristotle tells us (*Poet.* 1449 b 7). Sometimes it is not any particular individual who comes under satirical attack but the public in general, or certain tendencies of the public. In the *Wasps*, Aristophanes makes fun of the eagerness of the Athenians to serve in the jury-courts. Thus politicians, artists, intellectuals, the gods, too, are freely parodied and vilified. Exaggeration was used to make an effective impression: with obscene language, grotesque masks, and the huge bellies and phalluses worn by the actors.

The changes in the political and economic conditions after the downfall of the Athenian Empire brought about the transition to the Middle Comedy as revealed in the *Ekklesiazousae* and *Plutus* of Aristophanes, two of his last plays which are extant. In this period, plays of varied form and content were performed. The main tendencies were to limit the role of the chorus, and to do without the *parabasis*; to deal less with politics and more with mythological burlesque, and often with philosophers and intellectuals; to reduce the grotesque appearance of the actors; to present stock characters. Apart from the above-mentioned plays of Aristophanes, not one complete play of the Middle Comedy is extant, and we have to make do with fragments and titles. *Alexis and *Antiphanes were the period's more prominent playwrights.

In the New Comedy, the chorus did not have any part in the plot and only performed interludes of dance and music, between the usual five acts of the play. And the language became more refined. By now, a wide variety of stock characters were treated, including young lovers, soldiers, old men, parasites, and courtesans, all with their typical masks. Plots became quite complicated; love stories, with happy endings and intrigues were common themes, and were often treated pathetically. The leading poets of the New Comedy were *Menander (one of his plays is the only complete one extant), *Diphilus and *Philemon.

Pickard-Cambridge, *Dithyramb*[2]; T. B. L. Webster, *Studies in Later Greek Comedy*, 1953; K. Lever, *The Art of Greek Comedy*, 1956; J. M. Edmonds, *The Fragments of Attic Comedy*, 1957–1959.

COMEDY, ROMAN Roman comedy had its origins in the *Atellana fabula* of Campania and the *Fescenini versus*, improvised dialogues in verse noted for their personal lampoons. The first dramatic performance was given by Etruscan players, in 364 BC, as a ceremonial expiation of a pestilence. Under these influences developed the Roman *Satura, a medley of songs, dances and crude scenes. Such shows consisted of theatrical sketches but lacked any coherent theme and plot. It was only in 240 BC that *Livius Andronicus presented Latin adaptations of a Greek comedy and a Greek tragedy on the occasion of the Ludi Romani. From then on, the *Fabula palliata*, comedies based on Greek models, formed a prominent element in theatrical shows in Rome. Plots and themes were often taken from the Greek New Comedy, the presentation and spirit were largely under the influence of the Old Comedy and the native farce of the Atellana. The native Italian comedy, the *Fabula togata*, in which the actors were dressed in the Roman toga or Italian dress, arose during the 2nd century BC. The most important and prolific poet in the genre was Afranius (born c. 150 BC). He was much influenced by *Terence and he dealt mainly with family themes in a coarse manner. His plays were still performed under the Empire. However, both types of comedy declined at the end of the Republic when there were no playwrights to create new plays. For complete plays of Latin comedies we are limited to those of Plautus and Terence, but there are considerable fragments from other poets. Under the Empire, the *Mime became popular and the *Atellana fabula* was replaced by a kind of farce noted for its low-class themes and coarse characters. All theatrical shows had to compete hard with the entertainments of the circus and the amphitheatre.

For playwrights see: *Livius Andronicus, *Naevius, *Ennius, *Plautus, *Caecilius Statius, *Terence. See also: *Atellana Fabula, *Ludi, *Mimus, *Satura.

G. E. Duckworth, *The Nature of Roman Comedy*, 1952; M. Bieber, *The History of the Greek and Roman Theatre*[2], 1961; W. Beare, *The Roman Stage*[3], 1968.

COMITIA Assembly of the Roman people There were three C. (according to three different units of voting), all governed by the same procedures. The C. could be convened only by magistrates with the appropriate right. The presiding magistrate and those whom he summoned had the right to address the people; there was no right of free speech for all citizens. The magistrate alone could present motions before the assembly, which could pass or reject, but not ammend them. Voting was by unit; the majority in each unit carried that unit's vote. Resolutions had to be ratified by the patrician members of the Senate, a mere formality from the 3rd century BC on. Voting was overt until a series of laws (139–131 BC) introduced the secret ballot. Only citizens who attended the assemblies could vote.

The *C. curiata* was based on the oldest social grouping at Rome, the *Curia. It dates from the monarchic period when it allegedly chose kings and ratified laws. Under the Republic it retained only the formal right to ratify the Imperium of magistrates, adoptions and wills. In the last century of the Republic, thirty lictors represented the thirty *curiae*.

C. centuriata was based on the centuriate organization of the Roman people; citizens were divided into five *classes* by the *censors, according to wealth. Within each *classis*, citizens were grouped into "centuries", which were unequal in numbers, enabling the wealthier citizens to control the *C. centuriata*, though their influence was somewhat reduced by a reform in the 3rd century BC. This assembly elected censors and magistrates with Imperium, was competent to pass laws and ratify proposals of war and peace, and voted on capital cases. Only magistrates with Imperium could convene it. The assembly met outside the *Pomerium in the *Campus Martius. Originally, the centuriate organization (introduced by *Servius Tullius) was for military purposes; it was only later (probably in the 5th century BC) that it was adapted for political use.

C. tributa was based on the division of the Roman citizens into territorial tribes, which increased from the original four to thirty-five by 241 BC. This assembly elected quaestors, curule aediles and military tribunes, passed laws, and voted on minor trials; it was presided over by consuls and praetors.

The C. became corrupt at the end of the Republic and resolutions were quite often passed by force. At this period they certainly did not represent the will of the Roman people, and after 49 BC, they lost their freedom. The C. continued to exist under the Empire, but *Tiberius transferred the election of magistrates to the Senate. The C. ceased to hold trials and to legislate after the 1st century AD.

Jolowicz, *Roman Law*[3] (s.v.).

COMMAGENE Land in northern Syria, extending from Mount Taurus to the Euphrates river. After the disintegration of Alexander's empire, C. was part of the Seleucid empire though its satraps were of the local dynasty which allegedly descended from *Darius. The satrap Ptolemy took C. from Seleucid control in 162 BC and assumed the royal title; his successor, King Samos, is credited with the foundation of Samosata, the capital of the kingdom. Mithridates Callinicus, Samos' son and successor, married a Seleucid princess. His son Antiochus I ruled *c.* 69–38 BC, but submitted to Rome's hegemony in 64 BC, on the approach of Pompey. He built a mausoleum for his father and an imposing tomb for himself on Mount Taurus. Antiochus I was deposed in 38 BC for his support of the Parthians. C. was annexed to the Roman Empire in AD 17. Caligula, and then Claudius, restored the kingdom to Antiochus IV, who reigned from AD 38 to AD 72, when he was deposed for alleged complicity with the Parthians. C. was then annexed to the province of Syria. Hellenism had little influence in C.

COMMODUS, Lucius Aelius Aurelius Roman emperor,

The Emperor Commodus as Hercules

elder son of Marcus *Aurelius, born in AD 161. C. was provided with the best teachers and bestowed with imperial titles as a child. From AD 175 on, C. accompanied his father on provincial journeys, and was made Augustus and co-ruler in AD 177; the same year he married Crispina, daughter of a noble family. Upon his father's death, on 17 March AD 180, C. became sole ruler. He did not continue the policy of war against the Germanic tribes, but evacuated the conquered lands and established peace by paying subsidies. He returned to Rome in October of the same year, and pursued a policy of peace throughout his reign, though there were disturbances in Germany and Dacia, revolts in Gaul and Africa, and an invasion in Britain. In contrast to his father, C. took an anti-senatorial line and was under the influence of favourites. The Empire was, in fact, governed by the praetorian prefects, first Tarrutenius Paternus, then Tigidius Perennis, AD 182–5, and then Marcus Aurelius Cleander, a freedman, AD 185–9. Lucilla, C.'s sister, and her cousin Ummidius Quadratus, conspired against C. in AD 182, and were consequently executed. Paternus fell through the intrigues of Perennis, and Crispina was banished to Capri and put to death *c.* AD 185. C. neglected his duties and gave a great deal of his time to shows and games in which he himself appeared in the arena. Under the influence of his Egyptian chamberlain, Eclectus, he introduced eastern cults, representing himself as Hercules incarnate. Finally, Eclectus, Laetus the praetorian prefect, and Marcia, his concubine, were so exasperated by C.'s excesses that they procured the services of the athlete Narcissus to strangle him on 31 December AD 192.

Dio, 72; Herodian, 1; S. H. A., *Comm.*

CONCILIUM PLEBIS Assembly of the Plebs, dating from the first half of the 5th century BC. Its voting units were the territorial tribes. Patricians, of course, were excluded from it. From 287 BC on, its resolutions (*plebiscita*) were binding on all citizens. The C. elected plebeian tribunes and aediles, passed laws and held trials (mainly with political implications). See *Comitia.

Jolowicz, *Roman Law*[3] (s.v.).

CONON Athenian statesman and general, born *c.* 444 BC. From 414 BC on, C. often served as strategos, mainly as fleet commander. He escaped from the battle of *Aegospotamoi in 405 BC, fleeing to *Euagoras of Cyprus. After the outbreak of war between Sparta and Persia, C. entered service with the Persians, and was commissioned to build and command a fleet in 397 BC; he operated in the southern Aegean, took Rhodes, and in 394 BC, together with the satrap Pharnabazus, won his greatest victory by destroying the Spartan fleet at *Cnidos. As a result, the Spartan maritime empire collapsed. In 393 BC, he returned to Athens where he soon initiated the rebuilding of the *Long Walls with Persian help; he also restored the Athenian *cleruchies in Lemnos, Imbros and Scyros, and was responsible for alliances with several states. In 392 BC, the satrap Tiribazus reversed his policy toward Athens and arrested C., who had come to Sardes. C. made good his escape, once again to Euagoras in Cyprus, where he died shortly after.

CONSILIUM PRINCIPIS A council freely chosen by Roman magistrates under the Republic to discuss public affairs within their administration. Roman emperors continued this practice, with the council of the *amici Caesaris* ("friends of Caesar"), who would also express opinions on current trials. Under *Alexander Severus, a regular council was established, composed of senators, Equites and jurisconsults.

J. A. Crook, *Consilium Principis*, 1955.

CONSISTORIUM Under *Diocletian, the *consilium principis* was reorganized and renamed *sacrum C.;* it consisted of the *magister officiorum* (responsible for the chancellery, court ceremony and security of the emperor), the *quaestor sacri palatii* (minister of justice), *comes sacrarum largitionum* (minister of finance), and *comes rerum privatarum* (who was responsible for the emperor's property). These and other officials were the usual members, and the C. also included jurisconsults. It deliberated on all public questions and served as a supreme court. In the fifth century it lost its real power.

Jolowicz, *Roman Law*[3] (s.v.).

CONSTANS Younger son of *Constantine (1), born *c.* AD 320. When his father died (AD 337), C. ruled Africa, Italy and Illyricum, and from AD 340, when he defeated and killed his brother *Constantine II, he was emperor of all the West. He defeated the Franks in AD 342, and tried to impose unity on the Christian Church, and discipline within the army. He was killed by *Magnentius in AD 350.

CONSTANTINE (1) "the Great", Flavius Valerius Constantinus Born to *Constantius Chlorus at Naïssus (modern Nis) sometime after AD 280. C. stayed with Diocletian when his father became Caesar in the West (AD 293), and his military service began in the East. In AD 306, *Galerius allowed him to join his father in Britain, where he arrived in time to rout the Picts alongside his father

Head of Constantine the Great

who died at York on 25 June. With the support of the army, C. was proclaimed Augustus. He secured Britain and Gaul and, in AD 307, married the daughter of *Maximian. C. did not intervene in the struggle between *Maxentius and Galerius, preferring to secure Gaul against the invading German tribes. In AD 310, after Maximian had committed suicide, C. favoured the worship of the sun-god, *Sol Invictus*, rather than Hercules — Maximian was called Herculius — spreading the story that his father descended from *Claudius Gothicus. He made an alliance with *Licinius in AD 311, and the next year invaded Italy, winning a decisive victory over Maxentius at the Mulvian Bridge (28 October AD 312). To strengthen their alliance, Licinius, who meanwhile had taken control of the entire East, married C.'s sister Constantia (AD 313). The two issued the famous Edict of Milan, legalizing and favouring Christianity throughout the Empire. Soon, however, relations between the two emperors deteriorated, and by AD 316, Licinius was compelled to cede Illyricum to C. After AD 320, Licinius renewed the persecution of Christians and, in AD 323, war broke out between the rivals. After C.'s victories at Adrianople and Chrysopolis (AD 324), Licinius retired to Thessalonica, where he was soon put to death.

Even before this final victory, C. supported Christianity in the West; when he became sole ruler of the entire Empire, Christianity became the official religion, though paganism was tolerated. Christians were assisted in building churches, while in Byzantium (subsequently *Constantinople), no pagan temples were built. C. intervened in Church matters, to assure order and uniformity, but he hardly understood the theological disputes which divided the Church. He also organized the first Church Council at Nicaea which formulated the Nicene Creed, but the schisms continued. He was baptized on his death-bed.

During his administration C. made important reforms though he preserved the administrative arrangements of Diocletian. At the end of his reign, the Empire was divided into four *praefecturae* (Oriens, Illyricum, Italia and Gallia), fourteen dioceses, and 117 provinces. The frontier armies (*limitanei*) were set apart from the field armies (*comitatenses*), who were commanded by a *magister equitum* and a *magister peditum* and received better pay. The praetorians were disbanded in AD 312, and a new unit of bodyguards was created to replace them. The separation of civil and military duties was complete; the praetorian prefects and the *vicarii* (governors of dioceses) no longer had military command, and senators could not take certain offices. In AD 309, C. issued a golden coinage, the *solidus* (72 to the pound), which proved a successful measure. The finances of the Empire, however, were weak; expenditure was high, bureaucracy expanded and grew corrupt, commerce was in decline and, significantly, *coloni* were bound to their farms. The building of Constantinople (begun in AD 324 and dedicated in AD 330) added much to the imperial outlay, though the need for such a capital in the East was obvious. C. secured his frontiers, defeating the Franks, Alamanni, Goths and Sarmatians; but he was forced to make concessions in recruitment, taking more Germans into the Roman army than ever before. He died in AD 337, and was succeeded by his sons, *Constantine II, *Constantius II and *Constans.
A. H. M. Jones, *Constantine and the Conversion of Europe*, 1948.

CONSTANTINE (2) II Second son of Constantine the Great, born in Arles in AD 317. Caesar in AD 317, governor of the prefecture Gallia (Britain, Spain, Gaul), in AD 335, he became Augustus on his father's death in AD 337. He was killed in AD 340, at the battle of Aquileia, attempting to oust his brother *Constans.

CONSTANTINOPLE After *Constantine's (1) victory over *Licinius in AD 324, he decided to build a "New Rome". Byzantium was to become his capital, from which the emperor could effectively supervise the Balkans and his eastern provinces. After six years of construction, both public and private, the new city was dedicated (AD 330) and named Constantinople. The city was conspicuously Christian, with many churches and no pagan temples. As New Rome, it had seven hills, 14 regions, a Senate, praetors, and quaestors. Bread was distributed freely to 80,000 people. The central officials and institutions of the eastern part of the Empire resided in C., and the city grew rapidly, the population soon numbering more than half a million. C. had a university from AD 425 on. The Bishop of C. attained a senior position within the Eastern Church but, overshadowed by the proximity of the emperor, never achieved the power of the Bishop of Rome. Various important public buildings of C. are still extant, including the Hippodrome (famous for the political demonstrations of its mob), the city-walls built by *Theodosius II, and the churches of Hagia Sophia and St. Eirene. C. was captured by the Turks in AD 1453.
N. Baynes, *Byzantium* (1961), 1–33;
M. Maclagan, *The City of Constantinople*, 1968.

CONSTANTIUS CHLORUS, Flavius Valerius Born in Illyria c. AD 250 to a humble family (his supposed descent from *Claudius Gothicus was a later invention). C.'s concubine Helena bore him his eldest son *Constantine (1); he later married Theodora, stepdaughter of *Maximian. C. became *praefectus praetorio*, and in AD 293 was adopted by his father-in-law and made Caesar. In the same year he recovered Boulogne from *Carausius, and three years later took control of Britain after defeating and killing the usurper *Allectus. C. was successful against the Franks, Alamanni and Scots during the following years, and with the abdication of Diocletian and Maximian in AD 305, he became Augustus. In AD 306, Galerius, Augustus in the East, let Constantine join his father. After a victory over the Picts, C. died in York, in AD 306. He was a successful general, and a moderate ruler, lenient in taxation and merciful in the persecution of Christians.

CONSTANTIUS II, Flavius Julius Son of *Constantine (1). Born in AD 317 he was made Caesar in AD 324. After the death of his father (AD 337), C. ruled the East. From AD 338 on, he was fully occupied with the war against Persia. After the murder of his brother *Constans, he defeated the usurper *Magnentius (AD 351). In AD 355, he appointed his cousin *Julian as Caesar in Gaul, and fought in the Balkans. In AD 360, he went to war against Persia once again. Julian revolted in AD 361, but C. died before an open encounter could take place.

CONSUL The two highest magistrates of the Roman Republic. According to tradition, the consulship was instituted after the fall of the monarchy (509 BC); the original title seems to have been *praetor, but this came to be restricted to a third magistrate created in 366 BC. Each of the C.s was invested with *Imperium, giving him full military and civil power to administer the state. The term of office was limited to one year, as were almost all Republican magistracies; by the principle of *par potestas* ("equal powers") one C. could veto measures of the other and, of course, those of lower magistrates. If both C.s remained in Rome, they usually agreed to execute their powers in alternate months. The C.s were elected in the *comitia centuriata. Traditionally, Plebeians gained the right to be elected consuls only in 367 BC; yet thereafter, not many families attained the consulate (which in fact was monopolized by the *nobilitas). The first age-limit for consulship, perhaps 42, was instituted in 180 BC. This was certainly the minimum from 81 BC on. Until 153 BC, the C.s took office on 15 March; thenceforth the date was 1 January. Years were dated by consulships. When C.s died or resigned, substitutes called *suffecti* replaced them. In the post-Sullan period, C.s usually – but not invariably – remained in Italy during their year of office and then proceeded to their provinces. Under the Empire, the elections of C.s were transferred to the Senate but, in fact, were controlled by the emperor. From the 3rd century AD, they hardly had any function.
Jolowicz, *Roman Law*[3] (s.v.).

CONSUS Roman god, probably connected with the storage of corn. C.'s festivals, the *Consualia*, were held on 19 August and 15 December. C. had a subterranean altar in the *Circus Maximus, and a temple on the *Aventine.

CONTIO Roman public assembly held by a magistrate. In a C. only the presiding magistrate and those authorized by him were allowed to speak. A bill had to be read in a C. before the people could vote on it in the *comitia. Magistrates would convene C.s to announce important public information or for political propaganda.

CONUBIUM Marriage recognized by Roman law. The issue of C. was Roman in citizenship, while that of a marriage between a Roman citizen and a foreigner lacking the right of C. did not receive Roman citizenship. Latins had the right of C., and it was later granted to various Italian communities; under the Empire, it was extended to the provinces as well.
Jolowicz, *Roman Law*[3] (s.v.).

CORBULO, Gnaeus Domitius Roman general in the 1st century AD. C.'s father was probably *consul suffectus* under Caligula, who married his stepsister. C. was *consul suffectus* under Claudius and, as commander of the Roman army in Lower Germany, defeated the Chauci and subdued the Frisii (AD 47). He was later sent to Asia, and under Nero, he was appointed governor of Galatia and Cappadocia to conduct the war against Persia for control of *Armenia. C., however, first had to restore discipline in the army, as well as train it. After conquering Armenia (AD 59), and crowning Tigranes, he was made governor of Syria. Tigranes, however, was forced to flee, and Paetus, the Roman commander sent to Armenia in AD 61, had to capitulate to the Parthians. In AD 63, C. reached an agreement with Vologeses, the Parthian king, according to which Tiridates (Vologeses' brother) became king of Armenia, though recognizing Roman hegemony. Nero could not bear the popularity of C. and, late in AD 66, ordered him to commit suicide. Domitian married C.'s daughter, Domitia Longina.
Tacitus, *Annales* 12–15; Syme, *Tacitus*, 1958 (s.v.).

CORCYRA (modern Corfu) Island in the Ionian Sea, approx. 600 sq km in area, with a city of the same name. C. was identified with Scheria of *Nausicaa and *Alcinous, with whom Odysseus found shelter. The first Greek settlers probably came from Eretria, but it was Corinth which founded a colony there. Finds of Late Geometric pottery lend support to the traditional foundation date, 733 BC. C. cooperated with its mother-city in founding *Epidamnus (and perhaps *Anactorium and *Apollonia). It asserted its independence from Corinth, though the tyrant *Periander regained control for a while. C. flourished thanks to its fertility and excellent position on the route between Greece and the West. Defeated in her struggle with Corinth over control of Epidamnus (433 BC), C. sought and received Athenian assistance, one of the secondary causes of the Peloponnesian War. Internal conflict between democrats and oligarchs ensued, in which the latter were massacred. Though repeatedly supported by Athens, C. seceded in 410 BC; it joined the Second Athenian League in 375 BC, but left it in 360 BC. In the Hellenistic period, C. succumbed to foreign rule. The Romans freed it from the Illyrians in 229 BC and it remained under Roman control thereafter.
Hammond, *Epirus* (s.v.).

CORDUBA (modern Cordoba) Probably an Iberian settlement in origin, C. was founded in 152 BC in the rich Baetis (Guadalquivir) valley by M. Claudius *Marcellus (2). Augustus settled veterans there, and at least as early as his time, C. was a *colonia* named Patricia. Under the Empire, C. was one of the four administrative centres of the province of *Baetica. Copper and gold mines, wool and a position well-suited for trade contributed to its prosperity. The *Senecas and *Lucan were natives of C. With the rise of Christianity, C. became the seat of a bishop. It was captured by the Visigoths in AD 572.

CORFINIUM (modern Corfinio) Town of the Paeligni tribe. When Rome's Italian allies revolted in 90 BC, C. was made their capital under the name Italia; when the revolt collapsed C. received Roman citizenship and the status of *municipium*.

CORINNA Poetess, native of *Tanagra in Boeotia. Ancient authors say she was the elder contemporary and rival of Pindar, though on grounds of style and language she may have flourished as late as the second part of the 3rd century BC. Some fragments of her lyric poetry are extant, recovered partly from papyri. These and the titles of her works suggest that C. wrote mainly on Boeotian myths, such as the *Seven Against Thebes, Boeotus,* and *Iolaus.* In one poem C. describes a competition between Mount Cithaeron and Mount Helicon, and in another she tells the story of Asopus and his daughters.
Page, *Poet. Mel. Gr.*; D. L. Page, *Corinna*, 1953.

CORINTH Dorian city on the isthmus between the Peloponnesus and central Greece. C.'s position gave her control of communications between the Aegean and Ionian Seas, especially after the *diolkos* was built to transport ships across the isthmus. The city had two harbours, one on the Saronic Gulf and another on the Corinthian Gulf. In the south rose its magnificent *Acropolis, the Acrocorinth. The Mycenaean settlement at C. seems to have been of little importance and C. rose to significance only after the Dorian migrations. Under the leadership of the Bacchiadae clan, C. developed maritime commerce and a pottery industry. Extensive colonization was initiated in the 8th century BC, with the founding of *Syracuse and *Corcyra. The tyrant *Cypselus took power c. 657 BC, expelling the Bacchiadae, who migrated to Corcyra, Illyria and *Tarquinii. Under Cypselus and his descendants, who ruled for about 70 years, C. reached its zenith and colonized *Epidamnus, *Leucas, *Anactorium, *Ambracia, and *Potidaea. C. possessed a strong fleet, and exported great quantities of pottery to the West. It also issued its own coinage.

With the overthrow of the tyranny (c. 580 BC), C. was ruled by an oligarchy, with eight chief magistrates and a council. It still enjoyed power and prestige, and was on good terms with Sparta, Athens and Thebes. In the war against Persia, C. played a significant role, being the second Greek naval power after Athens. The growth of the Athenian empire, and its interference in the West, led to friction, and the first war broke out in 459 BC. Later, as a member of the Peloponnesian League, C. appealed to Sparta regarding Athens' aggression in Corcyra and Potidaea, which led to the Peloponnesian War in 431 BC. Though Athens lost that war, C. can hardly be considered to have won. Ships and manpower were lost, trade declined and an aggressive and arrogant Sparta had emerged. In the "Corinthian War" (395–386 BC), C. fought alongside Athens, Argos and Thebes against Sparta. Later the newly-established oligarchic regime supported Sparta, though, in fact, C. sought not to interfere in internal political disputes amongst the Greek states. In 338 BC, the Hellenic League of *Philip II of Macedonia was established in C. After the death of Alexander, C.'s strategic position made it the target of many political aspirants. In the 3rd century BC, it was chiefly under Macedonian rule. In 243 BC, the Achaean League controlled it, but it was later taken over by *Cleomenes III though it finally reverted to Macedonia in 222 BC. C. was known as one of the three "fetters" of Greece. In 196 BC, it was declared a free city by *Flamininus and became one of the chief cities of the Achaean League. After the League's defeat by the Romans in 146 BC, C. was destroyed. Caesar sent a

Air view of site of ancient Corinth 1 — columns of the 6th-century temple of Apollo, 2 — remains of a stoa,

colony there in 44 BC which rapidly developed and prospered; the original population of veterans and freedmen having been augmented by elements from the East. C. was now the seat of the governor of the province Achaea. It had a Christian community from the 1st century AD on, and was the seat of a bishop already in the 2nd century AD. The Germanic. Heruli sacked C. in AD 267, as did Alaric in AD 397. C. was destroyed by an earthquake in AD 521, and was rebuilt by Justinian.

J. G. O'Neill, *Ancient Corinth*, 1930;
Rh. Carpenter, *Corinthos. A Guide to the Excavations and Museum*[6], 1960.

CORIOLANUS, Gnaeus Marcius Hero of an old Roman legend which reflected conditions in Rome in the early 5th century BC. The Marcii, a plebeian house which rose in the 4th century BC, considered C. one of its members and cultivated the legend, adding new motifs in succeeding centuries. The name C. is derived from Corioli, a town he supposedly captured in 493 BC. Vehemently opposed to the Plebeians, especially to their demand for corn distribution, C. was subsequently prosecuted and went into exile in 491 BC. He incited the *Volscians to wage war on Rome, and personally led their army. Threatened by this invasion, the Patricians and Plebeians made peace between themselves, though they were no match for C.'s army. The city was saved by the entreaties of C.'s mother and his wife, who revived his love and loyalty for his homeland. The Volscians retreated and — in one version — then killed C. The story was dramatized by *Dionysius of Halicarnassus and by *Plutarch.

Liv. 2; Dion. Hal. 8; Plutarch, *Coriolanus*;
Ogilvie, *Livy*, 314ff.

CORNELIA Younger daughter of Cornelius *Scipio Africanus; *c.* 170 BC, she was married to Tiberius Sempronius *Gracchus (1), one of Rome's leading senators.

Her two surviving sons were the famous tribunes Tiberius and Gaius *Gracchus. C.'s daughter, Sempronia, was married to *Scipio Aemilianus. C.'s husband died in 154 BC, after which she saw to her sons' education, employing the best teachers. She was very cultured. Two fragments of her letters are the only extant prose of a Roman woman. She rejected an offer of marriage from *Ptolemy VIII Physcon. After her sons were killed, she withdrew to her villa at Misenum, where she often received visitors.

J. Carcopino, *Autour des Gracques*[2], 1967.

CORNUTUS, Lucius Annaeus Born *c.* AD 20. Probably a freedman of Seneca, C. taught philosophy and rhetoric at Rome in the days of Claudius and Nero. *Lucan and *Persius were among his disciples, and he was responsible for the publication of Persius' works after his death. He was banished from Rome *c.* AD 64. His only extant work, on Greek mythology, follows usual Stoic doctrine and treats the myths as allegories.

C. Lang (ed.), Teubner, 1881.

CORONIS Greek mythological heroine, daughter of Phlegyas. She took the young Arcadian Ischys as her lover while she was pregnant by Apollo. Artemis, sent by her brother, killed her, and Apollo took the unborn child from the corpse when it was on the funeral pyre; this was *Asclepius. The white crow which brought Apollo the news of C.'s infidelity was turned black, though Pindar (3rd Pythian Ode) says the god being omniscient knew of it already.

CORSICA Island west of Italy, north of and adjacent to Sardinia. The indigenous population was probably of Iberian and Ligurian stock. The Greek Phocaeans established a colony at Alalia *c.* 564 BC, but *c.* 535 BC they were defeated and expelled by the Etruscans, in co-operation with the Carthaginians who later took control of the island. Rome seized C. in 238 BC, but pacification of the native tribes was a lengthy process. C. and Sardinia formed a province under the Republic.

CORTONA Etruscan city near Lake Trasimene. Odysseus was said to have died there, but archaeological evidence points to its having been founded only in the 7th century BC. C. — together with *Arretium — was defeated by Rome, and subsequently made a treaty with her in 310 BC.

Scullard, *Etruscan Cities*, 156—9.

COS Large island of the Sporades group in the Aegean Sea, southwest of the coast of Asia Minor. C. was occupied by Dorian settlers and is mentioned by Homer. It belonged to the Athenian empire in the 5th century BC. The old city was severely damaged by an earthquake in 411 BC. In 366 BC, a new city was built on the northeastern coast. After C. gained independence from Athens in 354 BC, it came first under Persian and then under Macedonian control. During the 3rd century BC, C. was in the Ptolemaic sphere, but it fell to Rome in the following century. *Claudius (5) gave it immunity from taxation. The city was destroyed by an earthquake in AD 139. *Hippocrates was a native of C., and *Theocritus lived here for a while. The famous temple of Asclepius is about 4 km southwest of the city.

A. N. Modona, *L'isola di Coo . . .* , 1933;
J. M. Cook — G. E. Bean, *ABSA*, 1957, 119ff.

COSSUS, Aulus Cornelius Roman hero who, as military tribune in 437 BC or as consul in 428 BC, fought against the Etruscans and killed Lars Tolumnius of *Veii. He consecrated the *spolia opima* (spoils of an enemy leader killed by a Roman commander) in the temple of Jupiter Feretrius. C. and *Marcellus (1) (besides the legendary Romulus) were the only two Romans to accomplish this.

Ogilvie, *Livy*, 563—4.

CRASSUS (1) DIVES, Publius Licinius Born *c*. 240 BC; died 183 BC. A wealthy man, C. was the first of his family to attain high office and political success. As aedile in 212 BC, he held lavish games; he was elected Pontifex Maximus in the same year. C. was censor in 210 BC, and consul in 205 BC. In politics, he cooperated with *Scipio Africanus.

Scullard, *Rom. Pol.*[2] (s.v.).

CRASSUS (2) DIVES MUCIANUS, Publius Licinius A wealthy Roman statesman who was also a good orator and a lawyer. This scion of the Scaevolae family was adopted by Crassus Dives. C. supported Tiberius *Gracchus (2), and replaced him on the agrarian commission after his death. C.'s daughter married Gaius *Gracchus. In 132 BC, he was elected Pontifex Maximus and consul for 131 BC. As proconsul in Asia, he was killed in the war against *Aristonicus in 130 BC.

A. E. Astin, *Scipio Aemilianus*, 1967 (s.v.).

CRASSUS (3), Lucius Licinius Distinguished Roman orator and statesman. Born 140 BC; died 91 BC. C. studied rhetoric under *Coelius Antipater and later under Scaevola the Augur, whose daughter he married. He made his first appearance in public in 119 BC, prosecuting C. Carbo, a renegade Gracchan who subsequently committed suicide. C. supported the foundation of the colony of *Narbo, a "popular" measure, and in 106 BC he favoured the transfer of the courts to the Senate. As consul in 95 BC, he passed a law against aliens who had registered as citizens. In 94 BC, C. was governor of Gaul, and in 92 BC he was censor. C.'s daughter married Marius' son. C. supported the reforms of the younger *Livius Drusus (2) in 91 BC, but they collapsed after he died. Among C.'s

pupils were *Sulpicius Rufus, and Cicero, who regarded him as the best orator. C. is prominent in the rhetorical works of Cicero, advocating a broad education for orators, including history, philosophy and law.

Cicero, *De Oratore; Brutus*; Malcovati, *Or. Rom. Fr.*[3].

CRASSUS (4), Marcus Licinius Born in 115 BC. C.'s father committed suicide after the capture of Rome by *Cinna (1) and *Marius in 87 BC. C. had served with his father in Spain in the 90s BC, and he left Rome to seek refuge there. He followed *Sulla in the Civil War of 83—82 BC, playing a significant role in the decisive battle of the Colline Gate. He made a fortune during the proscriptions of Sulla, and increased it during the 70s BC, apparently becoming the wealthiest man in Rome. In 72 BC, he was appointed commander against *Spartacus, whom he defeated after six months.

C. was consul in 70 BC, alongside his rival Pompey. The two agreed to restore the power of the tribunes and reinstate the Equites in the jury courts. C. sought to secure his position by rendering free legal help, by granting loans without interest, and by supporting various candidates. He assisted Caesar and backed Catiline, until the latter failed in the election for the consulate in 62 BC. As censor in 65/64 BC, he sought to register the Transpadanes, but was foiled by the opposition of his colleague *Catulus (2).

In 60 BC, Caesar persuaded C. to make an alliance with Pompey, the so-called First Triumvirate. Caesar was elected consul for 59 BC and, in deference to C., secured the interests of the tax-farmers. After Caesar had left for Gaul, the hostility between C. and Pompey erupted. C. opposed the restoration of Ptolemy Auletes to the Egyptian throne and gave financial assistance to *Clodius, who openly attacked Pompey. In 56 BC, however, Caesar succeeded in restoring the triple alliance, and the following year, both C. and Pompey were consuls. Having learned from Pompey and Caesar that military power secured political position, C. attained command of Syria for five years, hoping to succeed against *Parthia. In 53 BC, however, he was defeated and killed at *Carrhae. His death left Caesar and Pompey as rivals for power in Rome.

Plutarch, *Crassus*;
F. E. Adcock, *Marcus Crassus, Millionaire*, 1966.

CRASSUS (5), Marcus Licinius Grandson of C. (4), the triumvir. After serving with Sextus *Pompeius and Antony, C. followed Augustus, obtaining the consulship of 30 BC. As governor of Macedonia, he won great victories and killed a king of the Bastarnae. His demand for *spolia opima* was rejected by Augustus. His triumph in 27 BC is the last detail known about his life.

CRATERUS Officer of Alexander the Great, C. participated in the battles of Granicus and Issus as taxiarchos, "commander of a brigade", and at Gaugamella, as commander of the left wing of the phalanx. After the murder of *Parmenion, in 330 BC, C. was Alexander's senior officer, fighting with distinction in independent commands in the wars in Sogdiana and Bactria. He participated in the battle of Hydaspes, and was responsible for the baggage train on the way back to Babylonia. He married a Persian princess at Susa, in 324 BC, and was sent to Macedonia with the discharged veterans to. replace *Antipater as governor of Macedonia and Greece. After Alexander's death, C. cooperated with Antipater (whose daughter he married) against the regent *Perdiccas, but was killed in 321 BC in his first battle against *Eumenes of Cardia.

CRATES (1) Native of Thebes, born *c*. 365 BC, a Cynic philosopher and a pupil of *Diogenes of Sinope. Follow-

ing the example of his master, he lived in poverty (as did his wife and brother-in-law). He wandered about, preaching the Cynic principles of contentment, harmony between people, rejection of earthly possessions and independence. C. won fame and influence for consoling people in trouble — for example, *Demetrius of Phalerum, who had lost power in Athens. C.'s poems were often adaptations of old poetry to which he added Cynic tenets. He also wrote letters and tragedies.
Diog. Laert. 6. 85–93;
Dudley, *Cynicism.*

CRATES (2) Native of Mallos, a philosopher and a scholar who lived in the 2nd century BC. C. was head of the Pergamene Library and was sent by *Attalus II to Rome to represent his interests. His lectures there were successful, and he wrote commentaries on Homer, Hesiod, Euripides, and others. His method of literary ciriticism was different from that of *Aristarchus and other Alexandrian scholars. C. sought to find Stoic doctrines in Homer, and he — and his disciples — applied allegorical interpretations for this purpose. Thus, Achilles' shield (in their interpretation) is a description of the cosmos. The allegorical approach was based on the belief that literature is a representation of truth.
H. J. Mett, *Parateresis,* 1952.

CRATINUS Athenian poet, one of the three great writers of Old Comedy, lived in the 5th century BC. He won the first prize six times at the *Dionysia and three times at the *Lanaca. None of his plays is extant, but 28 titles and more than 450 fragments have survived. As was usual in Old Comedy, C. criticized and ridiculed real persons, such as *Pericles, and one play made fun of his own drunkenness. His *Odysseus,* however, is exceptional in that no real persons appeared in it. Politicians, philosophers, poets and musicians came under his attack. In some of his plays, such as *Dionysalexandros,* the gods were treated irreverently. The structure of C.'s plays probably resembled the works of Aristophanes, on whom he certainly had influence.
Edomonds, *Fr. At. Com.,* 1.

CRATYLUS Greek philosopher, active in the 5th century BC. C.'s land of origin is unknown. He followed *Heraclitus in arguing that things have no constancy, and nothing valid can be ascertained about them. C. is said to have taught Plato philosophy and Plato, in his dialogue *Cratylus,* has him argue that languages are formed naturally and thus the meanings of words are constant by nature.
Diels, *Fr. Vor.,* 2.

CREMERA (modern Fossa di Valca) Rivulet flowing near *Veii, joining the Tiber at Fidaenae. C. was the site of the massacre of 300 members of the Fabian clan by the Etruscans in 477 BC.

CREMONA Latin colony north of the Po river, founded by Rome in 218 BC as a stronghold against the Gauls. In 190 BC, new settlers were sent there to restore the complement after the Second Punic War. In 90 BC, C. received Roman citizenship but its land was confiscated for veterans in 41 BC. Vespasian routed *Vitellius there in AD 69, and then destroyed the colony, which never regained its prosperity.

CREMUTIUS CORDUS, Aulus Roman historian, born in the second half of the 1st century BC; committed suicide in AD 25, when charged with treason. C. covered the Civil Wars of Rome to the reign of Augustus in a book (not extant) with a Republican bias, praising Cicero, Brutus and Cassius, which was considered dangerous. The book

consequently was burned, but C.'s daughter Marcia republished it under Caligula.
Peter, *His. Rom. Rel.,* 2.

CREON ("ruler" or "prince") Name of several kings in Greek mythology, the most famous of which are: (1) Brother of *Iocasta. After the blind *Oedipus departed from Thebes, C. became king there; his son Menoecus killed himself to atone for the slaying of the dragon by *Cadmus, a sacrifice necessary to save Thebes. C.'s refusal to grant burial to the body of Polyneices brought about the suicides of *Antigone, of his own son Haimon and of his wife. In one version, C. was killed by *Theseus. (2) King of Corinth who gave his daughter in marriage to *Jason. In revenge, *Medea killed him and his daughter.

CRESILAS Sculptor, native of Cydonia, Crete, who lived in the 5th century BC. C. worked mainly in Athens; five statue bases bear his signature. According to *Pliny, he made a statue of Pericles (of which Roman copies are extant). He also made a statue of an Amazon, and one of a wounded man.

CRETE Large island (approx. 8,200 sq km), mainly mountainous (its highest and most famous mountain being Ida) with some plains and valleys. Most of the harbours are on the northern coast. Its indigenous civilization was non-Greek. A prosperous Bronze Age civilization, the Minoan culture (named after *Minos), developed in the 3rd and 2nd millennia BC. Its largest cities were Cnossos and Phaestus. The Minoan civilization reached its zenith in the first half of the 2nd millennium BC. C. had a pictorial form of writing, called Linear A, which has not yet been deciphered. C. was largely destroyed (*c.* 1500 BC), probably by an earthquake which seems to have left it open to invasion. The Greeks began to occupy C. *c.* 1400 BC, as can be deduced from a script of this date, the so-called Linear B, which records a group of Archaic Greek dialects. More than 4,000 documents of this script have been found at Cnossos, Pylos, Mycenae and Thebes. The decipherment of the script was first published in 1952. The palace of Cnossos was destroyed in the mid-14th century BC and at about the same time, many coastal settlements were abandoned. The invading Greeks do not seem to have put an abrupt end to the Minoan culture, but in the 11th century BC, invading Dorian tribes overran C., and the Iron Age came to dominate the island.

Homer's *Odyssey* mentions five separate peoples in C. (Achaeans, Cydonians, Eteorcretens, Pelasagians and Dorians) and a hundred towns. The major cities were Cnossos, Lyttus, Gortyn and Cydonia. The structure of Cretan society, an aristocratic citizen-body ruling over a subject population, was an inheritance from the Dorian invasion; it somewhat resembled Sparta, with state controlled education, common meals in groups and military organization. C. prospered in the Archaic period, producing fine pottery in the Geometric and Oriental styles; metallurgy was also well developed. Historically, in both Archaic and Classical periods, C. stood apart from Greece. It declined to fight Persia, but from the 4th century BC on, Cretan mercenaries — famous as archers — were often employed. In Hellenistic times, foreign rulers sought to gain a footing on C. In the 3rd century BC, more than 30 cities formed a Cretan League. There were, however, internal wars, especially between Gortyn and Cnossos. C. was infested with pirates in the 2nd century BC, and in 74 BC, Antonius (3) (father of Antony) was sent to suppress them and was defeated. C. was conquered by Rome in 68–67 BC, and was included together with Cyrene in one province. Under the Empire, peace enabled the economy of C. to revive.

Arist. *Pol.* 10.2; Strabo, 10.474–484;
R. F. Willetts, *Aristocratic Society in Ancient Crete*, 1955; id., *Ancient Crete. A Social History*, 1965.

CREUSA (1) Daughter of *Erechtheus, king of Athens, and wife of Xuthus. Her son Ion, by her husband or by Apollo, was the ancestor of the Ionians. C. is the feminine of *Creon.

CREUSA (2) Daughter of *Priam, king of Troy, and *Hecuba. C. was the first wife of *Aeneas, by whom she bore *Ascanius.

CRINAGORAS Greek poet, native of Mytilene. He was born *c.* 70 BC and was possibly still active at the beginning of the 1st century AD. Several times C. participated in embassies to Rome. His book of epigrams is extant.
M. Rubensohn (ed.), 1888.

CRITIAS Athenian politician and writer, born *c.* 460 BC of aristocratic stock. C. was related to Plato's mother and to *Andocides; he was influenced by Socrates and the Sophists. In politics, he was an extreme oligarch and, in 415 BC, was suspected of participating in the sacrilege of the *Hermae. Surprisingly, he was not active in the oligarchic revolution of 411 BC. He was prosecuted and exiled by *Cleophon (*c.* 406 BC). After the defeat of Athens by Sparta, he returned and became one of the Thirty Tyrants who ruled Athens. He was probably their leader. Xenophon attributes the death sentence on *Theramenes to C. In 403 BC, C. fell in battle against *Thrasybulus. His writing was diversified, including hexameters, elegiacs, tragedies, constitutions (of Thessaly, Sparta) and aphorisms.
Diels, *Fr. Vor.*; Diehl, *An. Lyr. Gr.*, 1³;
A. Fuks, *Eos*, 1956, 47ff.

CRITIUS Athenian sculptor, lived in the first half of the 5th century BC. Six bases bearing his and Nesiotes' signatures have been found on the Acropolis at Athens; the most famous group by them, Harmodius and *Aristogiton (477 BC), was made to replace those of Antenor which had been taken by Xerxes when he captured Athens. These were in bronze (copies are extant) and the group is also reproduced on coins and vases. C. was head of a school. All the known works of C. and Nesiotes were in bronze. A statue of a boy, found on the Athenian Acropolis, dated to *c.* 480 BC, is attributed on stylistic grounds to C. or his school.

CRITO Athenian friend of Socrates. C. tried to rescue Socrates from prison. He appears in several of Plato's dialogues (*Apology, Crito, Phaedo* and *Euthydemus*).

CRITOLAUS Greek philosopher, native of Phaselis in *Lycia. Head of the Peripatetic School in the first half of the 2nd century BC. Together with *Carneades and the Stoic Diogenes of Babylon, C. (at the age of 87) took part in the Athenian embassy to Rome in 156/155 BC. There are some fragments of his works, the titles of which are unknown. In them, C. holds that the world is eternal, that the substance of the soul is the *quinta essentia* ("fifth essence"), and that the best good is composed of three elements of good, with priority given to that of the soul (according to Cicero's exposition). In some fields C. came under Stoic influence; he was an opponent of rhetoric.
F. Wehrli, *Die Schule des Aristoteles*, 1959, 10.

CROESUS King of *Lydia, son of *Alyattes; reigned *c.* 560–546 BC. C. subjected much of Asia Minor up to the Halys river and the coastal cities of Greece, excluding Cilicia and Lycia. He was known as wealthy, was on good

terms with the Greeks, and sent presents to Greek temples. He was not able to stem the advance of Persia. C. was told by the oracle of Delphi that if he crossed the Halys a great kingdom would be destroyed and he wrongly interpreted this to mean Persia. He was defeated by *Cyrus (1); Sardis, his capital, was captured, and Lydia was annexed to the Persian Empire. In one version, C. was killed by Cyrus, but in another he became Cyrus' counsellor.

CROTON (modern Crotone) Achaean colony in *Bruttium, about 8 km from the temple of Hera Lacinia. C. was founded *c.* 710 BC and, in turn, founded several colonies. It ruled over a large territory and was famous for its school of Pythagoreans. Under the command of the famous athlete *Milon, C. destroyed *Sybaris (510 BC). It reached the zenith of its power at this time, even sending a ship to fight the Persians at Salamis. *Petronius called C. *urbs aliquando Italiae prima* ("a city once first in Italy"). Defeated by Rhegium and Locri, and split by internal conflicts (which led to Pythagoras' retirement and afterwards to the expulsion of his society) the city declined. In 388 BC, it was defeated by *Dionysius I; he captured the city in 379 BC and pillaged the temple of Hera. Continual internal and external strife reduced the city's population to a mere 2,000 in 215 BC. C. was ruined during the Hannibalic War. The foundation of a Roman colony there in 194 BC proved unsuccessful.
Dunbabin, *Western Greeks* (s.v.).

CTESIAS Greek physician, native of *Cnidos, of a family of doctors. From 405 BC on, C. lived at the royal court of *Artaxerxes II. He was present at the battle of Cunaxa and, in 398 BC, went on a mission to *Conon. He gained fame through his 23-book *History of Persia*. He also wrote on geography, including a book about India. Only fragments of his work are extant.
Jacoby (ed.), *Fr. Gr. Hist.*, no. 688;
R. Henry (ed.), *Ctesias; L'inde; Les sommaires de Photius*.

CTESIBIUS Engineer who lived in Alexandria in the first half of the 3rd century BC. None of C.'s works has survived, but his practical inventions are significant. He was the first to utilize air pressure for practical purposes; he developed a catapult, an accurate water clock and the pump with valve and plunger. *Philon, *Vitruvius and *Heron describe his inventions.
A. G. Drachman, *The Mechanical Technology of Greek and Roman Antiquity*, 1963.

CTESIPHON City on the banks of the Tigris river. Probably founded by Macedonians, C. became a Parthian settlement and administrative centre opposite *Seleucia. Trajan captured C. in AD 116, and it was recovered in AD 224 by the Sassanid Artaxerxes who made it the capital of his Persian Empire. *Carus captured it in AD 283, but the city later reverted again to the Sassanids. Following the Arab conquest, in AD 637, C. began to decline.
Honigmann, *RE*, Supp. 4, 1102ff.

CUMAE The earliest Greek colony in Italy (though preceded by a trade station at *Ischia). C. was founded by *Chalcis in the mid-8th century BC (though literary tradition ascribed its foundation to 1050 BC). It soon prospered and was able, in turn, to send colonies to *Neapolis, *Puteoli and Zancle. Under *Aristodemus, C. stopped the Etruscan advance in Campania and in 504 BC, it defeated the Etruscans at Aricia. With the aid of *Hiero of Syracuse, C. routed the Campanian Etruscans in 474 BC; but it could not repulse the *Sabelli, who captured it *c.* 421 BC. With the Roman advance into Campania, C. received *civitas sine suffragio* (338 BC), and from 318 BC on was supervised by Roman prefects. C. remained loyal to Rome and obtained full citizenship in 90 BC. It was famous for its *Sibyl and oracle.

Dunbabin, *Western Greeks* (s.v.);

A. Maiuri, *The Phlegraean Fields*, 1957.

CUNOBELLINUS King of the powerful Belgic tribe Catuvellauni (in eastern England) during the first part of the 1st century AD. He extended his rule to the tribe of the Trinovantes and Kent, and moved his capital from *Verulamium to *Camulodunum. Shortly after his death, Britain was invaded by the Emperor Claudius.

S. Frere, *Britannia*, 1967 (s.v.).

CURETES Mythological semi-divine people of Crete who hid the infant Zeus by clattering their weapons and dancing so that *Kronos could not hear his cries. Later they were confused and identified with the Corybantes, the attendants of the Asiatic Mother of Gods *Cybele, and were also associated with the cult of Dionysus.

R. F. Willetts, *Cretan Cults and Festivals*, 1962 (s.v.).

CURIA The house of the Roman Senate, traditionally built by the third king of Rome, *Tullus Hostilius. The C. stood at the end of the Forum, near the Capitol. It was destroyed and rebuilt several times, by Sulla, Caesar, Domitian and Diocletian. Large parts of the building have survived and it has been restored. C. was also the name of local senates in cities under the Roman Empire.

Platner-Ashby, *Top. Dict. Rome*, 142ff..;

Nash, *Pict. Dict. Rome*, 1, 301ff..;

Jolowicz, *Roman Law*[3] (s.v.).

CURIAE Archaic units of the Roman people; the origin and formation of the C. are disputed. The three ancient tribes of Rome, each encompassing ten C., are an arrangement ascribed to *Romulus. All Romans, including the Plebeians, were probably members of the C. The army of Archaic Rome was based on the C., as was the political assembly. With the reforms of *Servius Tullius, and the development of the *comitia under the early Republic, the C. lost their importance.

R. E. A. Palmer, *The Archaic Community of the Romans*, 1970.

CURIALIS Member of a municipal senate (*curia) or any of his male descendants under the Roman Empire. The C. became a hereditary class expected to finance public necessities and, in time, were responsible for various imperial obligations, such as tax-collection. Immunities from such burdens were obtained by Roman senators, imperial officials, shippers and physicians.

Jolowicz, *Roman Law*[3] (s.v.).

CURIO (1), Gaius Scribonius Roman politican, born *c.* 123 BC. A good orator, C. served as tribune in 90 BC, and with Sulla in the east, took part in the capture of Athens in 86 BC. He returned to Italy with his commander to make a fortune in the proscriptions. After his consulate in 76 BC, C. was governor of Macedonia (75—74 BC); for his victories there, he received a triumph (73 BC). He remained active in politics, supported Pompey in 66 BC and Cicero in 63 BC, but strongly opposed Caesar in the 50s BC. He died in 53 BC.

Malcovati, *Or. Rom. Fr*[3].

CURIO (2), Gaius Scribonius Son of C. (1), born *c.* 84 BC. C. married Fulvia, widow of his friend *Clodius. He was friendly with Antony, but followed his father in politics in the 50s BC. C. served as quaestor in 54 BC and tribune in 50 BC; in the latter capacity, he changed sides in politics for various reasons, not the least of which was a huge bribe by Caesar, whose interests he now supported.

The Curia of the Roman Senate. The extant building mainly dates from the rebuilding under Diocletian

C. followed Caesar in the Civil War in 49 BC, took Sicily from *Cato (2), but was defeated and killed by *Juba (1) in Africa.

CURTIUS (1), Marcus Mythological Roman hero who, of his own free will, leapt with his horse into an open chasm in the Forum, and thus sealed it. The myth accounts for the *Lacus Curtius*, a pool which had at one time existed in the Forum.

Ogilvie, *Livy*, 75ff.

CURTIUS (2) RUFUS, Quintus Historian of Alexander the Great; probably lived in the 1st century AD. C. may be identical with Curtius Rufus, a senator of low origin who was *consul suffectus* under *Claudius, governor of Upper Germany, in AD 47, and later, of Africa. C.'s ten-book history of Alexander was in Latin; its first two books are missing, and the extant text begins in 333 BC. He used various sources, good and bad, but was evidently influenced by the hostile tradition of the Peripatetics. C. strove for an attractive history and thus his narrative is marked by speeches, dramatic elaboration and vivid descriptions.

J. C. Rolfe (ed. Loeb), 1946;

H. McQueen in *Latin Biography* (ed. T. A. Dorey), 1967

CYBELE Mother-goddess of Asia Minor. C. had various functions, such as goddess of mountains, fertility, health and prophecy. Her cult probably originated in Phrygia (her chief temple was at Pessinus), but it spread everywhere; thus she became the goddess of the royal dynasty of *Lydia in the 7th century BC. She was associated with *Attis, who always remained a subordinate figure in the native cult. The cult of C., with its ecstasy and rites of

purification, was adopted by the Greeks, who recognized her as a mountain goddess and as the mother of gods, associating her with *Demeter. C., the native name of the goddess, rarely appeared on Greek monuments of Asia Minor. The cult of C. was officially introduced into Rome in 204 BC under the name *Mater Magna*. According to the instruction of the Sibyline books, the black stone of the goddess was brought from Pessinus; a temple was built on the Palatine, and public games, the Megalesia, were instituted for the goddess. The cult, however, was conducted by non-Roman priests (who were self-castrated), since her cult was prohibited to Roman citizens, a restriction removed only by the Emperor *Claudius, from whose reign on, an annual spring festival (15–28 March) of C. and Attis was celebrated in Rome. Under the Empire, this eastern cult spread to the West. The *taurcholium* was part of the cult of C., though perhaps not originally. Under the later Empire, C. acquired a celestial character with cosmic powers, and a belief in after-life was associated with her. See *Adgistis, *Attis.
Cumont, *Oriental Religions*.

CYCLADES Group of islands in the southern Aegean Sea. In a more limited definition, the C. included only those islands concentrated around *Delos. There were Mycenaean settlements on the C., which were later colonized, at the beginning of the 1st millennium BC, by Ionians (though in some cases, by Dorians). Throughout history the C. fell victim to successive rulers, such as *Polycrates of Samos, Lygdamis of Naxos, and Persia (in 490 BC). The C. belonged to the Athenian empire in the 5th century BC, and joined the Second Athenian League in 377 BC. During the Hellenistic period, the islands changed hands several times.

CYCLOPES In Greek mythology, one-eyed giants. Homer's *Odyssey* relates that Odysseus landed in their country and that one of them, Polyphemus, began eating Odysseus' comrades. Odysseus served him wine, and when he was drunk and had fallen asleep, Odysseus blinded him and made good his escape. In *Hesiod, the C. appear as one-eyed creatures, sons of Uranus and Earth, but are described as good artisans rather than savages. They were believed to have built the fortifications of pre-historic Greece, hence the "Cyclopean Walls".

CYCNUS In Greek mythology: (1) Son of *Ares, who robbed pilgrims coming to Delphi; he was killed by *Heracles. (2) Son of *Poseidon, killed by *Achilles and turned into a swan by his father. (3) King of Liguria, who became a swan while lamenting the death of Phaethon, the son of Helios.

CYLON Athenian aristocrat, of the 7th century BC. C. was a winner in the games at Olympia c. 640 BC. He married the daughter of *Theagenes, the Megaran tyrant, and sought to institute tyranny in Athens. Failing to do so, he fled, but his associates were put to death.

CYNICS (Greek kynikoi) A loose philosophical sect of adherents to the doctrines of *Diogenes of Sinope (who was nicknamed Kyon, "Dog", hence their appellation). Famous C. philosophers were *Crates (1), *Bion of Olbia, *Menippus of Gadara, *Meleager of Gadara, *Onesicritus and *Dio (1) Chrysostomos. Diogenes had probably studied under *Antisthenes who, therefore, is often regarded as the founder of this system. C. philosophers taught the blessing of independent life, and voluntary poverty, and opposed social conventions and traditions. They sometimes attacked marriage and religions. Under the Roman Empire, the C. censured bad emperors and outlined their

ideas of the ideal king. Many C. wandered from city to city, living a simple life and teaching their doctrines. They were noted for their wit and shamelessness. There was, however, no comprehensive philosophy of Cynicism, and each C. chose to believe, and taught, what seemed to him to be true.
D. R. Dudley, *Cynicism*, 1937;
F. Sayre, *The Greek Cynics*, 1948.

CYPRUS Third largest island (approx. 9,300 sq km) in the Mediterranean, approx. 70 km south of Asia Minor and 90 km west of the Syrian coast, known for its timber and especially for its copper (whence its name). Its population in Neolithic and Early Bronze times seems to have been from Asia Minor and Syria. In the mid-2nd millennium BC, it was invaded by Mycenaean peoples, who probably encouraged urbanization; writing then appeared there, but the Cypro-Minoan script, related to the Linear A script of *Crete, has not been entirely deciphered. C. also came under Egyptian influence for a short while during this period. The Dorian invasion of Greece resulted in an influx of Greeks into C., apparently all Achaeans. Early in the 1st millennium BC, Phoenician settlers concentrated around Citium. Sargon II of Assyria annexed C. c. 710 BC. At that time, C. was divided amongst cities ruled by local kings. After the collapse of the Assyrian Empire, C. was briefly independent, until its conquest c. 570 BC by the Egyptian king, Amasis. *Cambyses annexed C. to the Persian Empire in 525 BC and, except for short intervals (the intervention of *Cimon, the rise of *Euagoras of Salamis, and the revolt of 350 BC), the island remained under Persian control until Alexander. Though the Persians were, on the whole, lenient rulers, they favoured the expansion of the Phoenicians at the expense of the Greeks, and it is no wonder that the Cypriot Greeks provided Alexander with ships during his siege of Tyre. In the Hellenistic period, C. was part of the Ptolemaic empire; it was annexed to the Roman Empire in 58 BC. In 47 BC, Caesar gave it to *Cleopatra VII, but after *Actium, it again became a Roman province.
S. Casson, *Ancient Cyprus*, 1937;
H. Alastos, *Cyprus in History*, 1955.

CYPSELUS Tyrant of Corinth who seized power c. 657 BC and expelled the ruling aristocracy of the Bacchiadae. According to Herodotus, C. was a typical tyrant; other sources hold that C. brought freedom and was a lenient ruler. It is certain, in any case, that Corinth flourished under him. C. colonized Leucas, Anactorium, and Ambracia, and Corinthian pottery was extensively exported at this time. The first Corinthian coinage was probably issued under C., and he seems to have built the "treasure house" of the Corinthians at Delphi. He died c. 625 BC.
A. Andrewes, *The Greek Tyrants*, 1956.

CYRENE City and country on the Libyan coast. The city was founded by Dorian settlers from *Thera, c. 630 BC. The settlers were led by Battus, whose descendants ruled C. as kings, bearing the names Battus and Arcesilas. C.'s rich territory contributed to its prosperity and other cities were colonized: Barca, Tolmeta, Euesperides and Taucheira. Battus II repulsed an Egyptian attack c. 570 BC, and henceforth encouraged Greek immigration. In 525 BC, Arcesilas III was compelled to submit to *Cambyses, but after *Xerxes' defeat in Greece, C. regained independence. Arcesilas IV won the chariot-race at Delphi in 462 BC, but he was the last of his dynasty (c. 450 BC), and after him, the city received a democratic constitution. In 322 BC, *Ophellas (acting for *Ptolemy I) con-

Air view of Cyrene

quered the country. Under Ptolemaic rule, C. received a new constitution with *strategoi, gerousia* and *ekklesia*. In effect it became an oligarchy, with a large citizen-body of 10,000. Ptolemy was forced to reconquer C. after a revolt, ruling it through his stepson Magas (*c.* 300 BC). Under *Ptolemy II, Magas ceded from Egypt and took the title of king. Toward the end of his reign (*c.* 253 BC), he made peace with Ptolemy II, who married his daughter Berenice. Soon after this time, C. reverted to Ptolemaic control. Ptolemy VIII ruled there in 164–145 BC, and then obtained rule over Egypt as well; in 96 BC, his son Ptolemy Apion left C. as an inheritance to Rome. C. was then organized as a province (74 BC); under the Empire, Crete and C. formed a single province, administered by the Sen-

ate. The large Jewish population of C. revolted in AD 114, and the country witnessed much destruction and bloodshed before they were subdued. Hadrian subsequently settled veterans there as colonists. C. was a corn-growing country, and had extensive olive plantations; it also had a monopoly in growing silphium (a medical plant).

Graham, *Col. Moth. Cit.* (s.v.); Jones, *Cities*[2] (s.v.).

CYRUS (1) Achaemenid ruler who founded the Persian Empire. C. rose to power in 559 BC, and, in 549 BC, defeated Astyages, king of the Medes. He defeated *Croesus of Lydia in 546 BC and annexed all of Asia Minor. After the conquest of the Babylonian empire in 539 BC, he occupied Assyria, Syria, Phoenicia and Palestine. His

rule was mild and he allowed the conquered peoples to retain their traditional ways; he was tolerant in religious matters and assisted the Jews to return to Judaea and rebuild their temple in Jerusalem. C. died in 529 BC.
R. N. Fryre, *The Heritage of Persia*, 1962.

CYRUS (2) II Son of *Darius II, Persian governor of Asia Minor from 408 BC. After the death of his father (405 BC), C. gathered a mercenary force of Greeks to fight his brother, Artaxerxes II. He was slain at the battle of Cunaxa (north of Babylon), in 401 BC.
Xenophon, *Anabasis*.

CYTHERA Island off the southeastern coast of the Peloponnesus. C. is mentioned by Homer, and in the Archaic period, it belonged to *Argos. From the mid-6th century BC on, Sparta controlled it; Athens held it twice (424–421 and 393–386 BC). According to one myth, C. is the birthplace of Aphrodite.

CYZICUS City on the island of Arctonnesus, on the southern shore of the Sea of Marmara. Founded by *Miletus in 756 BC, C. had two good harbours; this, and its position on the route to the Black Sea, led to its prosperity. From the early 6th century BC on, C. issued electrum staters, which soon spread and came to be known as *cyzicenes*. C. was subject to the Persian empire, but after the defeat of *Xerxes it joined the Delian League, contributing nine talents annually. *Alcibiades defeated the Spartan fleet at C. in 410 BC. In the 4th century BC, it was a member of the Second Athenian League, but seceded in 357 BC. During most of the 3rd century BC, C. was under Seleucid control. It regained its independence in 218 BC, and subsequently cultivated good relations with *Pergamum. C. continued to enjoy independence even after the organization of the Roman province of *Asia; disorders led to the curtailment of its freedom in AD 25. In the 2nd century AD, it suffered from earthquakes but continued to enjoy economic prosperity; it was destroyed by an earthquake in AD 534.
C. Roebuck, *Ionian Trade and Colonization*, 1959.

D

DACIA Dacian tribes lived in the land of the Lower Danube stretching east and north. The same area was penetrated by Scythian tribes in the 6th and 5th centuries BC. From the 4th century BC on, the Dacians came under Celtic influence. Commercial relations with the Greeks began in the 3rd century BC. Throughout the centuries the loosely affiliated tribes never formed a strong power, though this changed in the 1st century BC with the rise of *Burebistas, under whose leadership the Dacians united and defeated the *Boii of Pannonia and the *Illyrians. For some two decades the Dacian kingdom spread from the Black Sea to Macedonia. Burebistas was killed *c.* 40 BC and his kingdom subsequently disintegrated. The Dacians were reunited under *Decebalus who fought the Romans in AD 85—9, and gained recognition and a subsidy under *Domitian. *Trajan conquered D. in two campaigns (AD 101—2 and 105), and organized it as a Roman province. This province was at first guarded by three legions; under *Hadrian it was divided into two and then three provinces, but Marcus Aurelius put them under a single governor. There was extensive immigration to D. from other parts of the empire. Indeed, Roman occupation facilitated urbanization throughout D.; the main cities were Sarmizegethusa, Apulum, Dierna, Drobeta and Napoca, all of which were made *coloniae* during the 2nd century AD. The natural resources of D. included gold, silver, lead and iron, all extensively exploited by the Romans. In the 3rd century AD, D. became difficult to hold and, in AD 271, *Aurelian chose the Danube as his new frontier, D. thus becoming the first Roman province to be abandoned. Even later, however, Romanization progressed, the country eventually coming to be called Romania.

DAEDALUS In Greek mythology, a skilful craftsman and inventor. D. was an Athenian who was a descendant of *Erechtheus. Jealous of his nephew Perdix who, though only twelve years old, was the better craftsman, D. killed him and fled to Crete, where he was welcomed by King *Minos. D. built the labyrinth, gave *Ariadne the thread by which *Theseus was able to find his way out of the labyrinth, made wooden toys, and constructed the cow in which disguise Pasiphaë mated with the white bull; for D.'s part in Pasiphaë's infidelity, he was imprisoned in the labyrinth together with his son Icarus.

Father and son escaped with the aid of Pasiphaë, and D. made two pairs of wings for them to fly from Crete. Icarus, however, flew too close to the sun, the heat of which melted the wax of his wings, causing him to fall into the sea, in which he drowned. Arriving in Sicily, D. was sheltered by King Cocalus; Minos pursued him and demanded his surrender, but was killed by Cocalus' daughters while taking a bath.

Many Archaic inventions were ascribed to D.: the potter's wheel, the compass, the saw, the axe and the auger. D. was also said to make figures with movable limbs and, indeed, all Archaic sculpture was related to him. Though reputedly an Athenian (a deme was named for him), Daedalic art was associated mainly with Crete. An actual artist may have stood behind these legends.

W. Miller, *Daedalus and Thespis*, 1931.

DALMATIA The Dalmatae, an Illyrian tribe living in the northwestern Balkans, came to mix with Thracian and Celtic elements; in the 3rd century BC they came under Illyrian control but regained independence in the first half of the 2nd century BC. The Romans fought them several times (156—155, 119—117, 78—77, 51, 48—47, 45—44 BC), but their land was conquered only by *Augustus, in 34/33 BC. Subsequently there was an influx of Roman traders and colonists. The Dalmatae later revolted but were subdued in 11—9 BC and again in AD 6—9, after which two provinces were organized: Upper and Lower Illyricum (later known as Dalmatia and Pannonia, respectively). Pacification of D. was apparently successful and from the Flavian period on there were only auxiliary troops stationed in the province. The province of D. was bordered by *Pannonia on the north, *Moesia on the east and Macedonia on the south, and was governed by a consular *legatus Augusti*. Under Roman rule, urbanization progressed, the main cities being Salona, Jadera, Scardona, Narona and Epidaurum, all of which attained colonial status. The seat of the governor was at Salona. D. was a good recruiting reservoir for the Roman army and, in the 3rd century AD, the Empire was saved by the Dalmatian emperors *Claudius Gothicus, *Aurelian, *Probus, *Carus and *Diocletian.

J. J. Wilkes, *Dalmatia*, 1969.

DAMASCUS An early Syrian city. D. was conquered by Alexander the Great in 332 BC and in Hellenistic times was under Seleucid rule. D. came under Nabataean control in 85 BC, but in 64 BC Pompey made it part of the Roman province of Syria, it remaining so thereafter, except for temporary intervals, under Cleopatra, and under the Nabataeans in the reigns of Caligula, Claudius and Nero until AD 62. Alexander Severus made D. a *colonia*; it was taken by the Arabs in AD 635.

Jones, *Cities*² (s.v.).

DAMNATIO MEMORIAE ("condemnation of a memory") Punishment used in Rome to wipe out the memory of persons condemned of high treason (*maiestas*), or declared public enemies, notably against several emperors after their death. As all mention of such a person should have disappeared, his name was erased from monuments, his images destroyed, and his *praenomen* could not be given to anyone in his family. The D. of an emperor involved the abolition of his *acta*, unless they were specifically ordered to be maintained. Antony, Domitian, Commodus and Elgabalus suffered D. after their death.

DAMOCLES Courtier of *Dionysius I or II. D. so overglorified the happiness of his master that the latter taught him what this happiness was truly like. Serving D. a sumptuous meal, Dionysius had a sword suspended by a mere hair above D.'s head. Thus, D.'s sword has come to symbolize the precarious happiness of the tyrant.

DAMON Athenian of the 5th century BC. D. taught *Pericles music and was his counselor. His political activities led D. to be ostracized soon after 450 BC. D. was one of the first important writers on music; his treatise is not extant though his views are known to have been admired by such persons as Socrates, Plato and Cicero. D. expounded on the influence of music on the soul, its benefits for education and the ethical values of the various rhythms.

DAMOPHON Greek sculptor of the 2nd century BC, native of *Messene. D. made statues of gods for several Peloponnesian cities: Messene, Megalopolis, Aigion and Lycosura. Of the group for Lycosura, several heads are extant. D. was also commissioned to repair *Phidias' statue of Zeus at Olympia. Various other works, including a portrait of the historian Polybius, are ascribed to D. on stylistic grounds.

M. Bieber, *Sculpture of the Hellenistic Age*, 1961, 158.

DANAE Daughter of Argive king Acrisius, great-grandson of *Danaus. Acrisius was told by an oracle that his grandchild would kill him and as D. was his only offspring he incarcerated her. Zeus, however, disguised as golden rain, penetrated into her prison and subsequently D. bore him *Perseus. Acrisius cast the two adrift on the sea in a wooden box, but they arrived safely on the island of Seriphus, whose king, Polydectes, unsuccessfully sought to marry D. After Perseus had petrified the king with the head of the Medusa, mother and son returned to Argos. The myth was often depicted on Greek vases.

DANAÏDS The 50 daughters of *Danaus, compelled to marry their 50 cousins, sons of Aegyptus, whom they killed on the wedding night, except for Hypermestra who helped her husband Lynceus to escape. In one version, all 49 were later killed by Lynceus; other versions have them purified and married off, or condemned in Hades to fill punctured jars with water.

DANAUS In Greek mythology, son of Belus and brother of Aegyptus. D. ruled Libya, while his brother controlled Egypt. Upon their father's death, Aegyptus demanded the marriage of his 50 sons to the 50 *Danaïds.

D. and his daughters fled to the Peloponnesus, where D. became king of Argos. Aegyptus' sons soon arrived, but were slain by the Danaïds. Homer mentions the Danai as an ancient Greek people, and sometimes uses that name for all Greeks; the tradition that the Danai were the descendants of D. was, however, relatively late. One version of D.'s escape from Egypt probably reflects a tradition of the founding of a dynasty at Mycenae by Hyksos elements.

DANUVIUS (modern Danube) The Ister river of the Greeks (first mentioned by *Hesiod, *Theog.* 339), who for long knew only of its lower reaches, below the Iron Gates. The Roman name D. (probably of Celtic origin) was applied to the upper part of the river as well. The entire course of the river became known *c*. the mid-1st century BC. The D. formed the frontier of the Roman Empire in central Europe, and was patrolled by two fleets.

Cary, *Geographic Background*, 273ff.

DAPHNE (1) A nymph, daughter of a river-god, Ladon or Peneus. Apollo fell in love with her, but she fled from him. When he nearly caught her, her mother (Earth) carried her away, leaving behind a laurel tree (Greek *daphne*).

DAPHNE (2) Suburb of Antioch, with a temple of Apollo, dedicated by *Seleucus I. One version of the story of *D. (1) held that she was chased there by Apollo. D. included a stadium and a theatre, and games were held there. Under the Roman Empire, D. was imperial domain.

G. Dawney, *History of Antioch,* 1961.

DAPHNIS In Greek mythology, son of *Hermes and a nymph. He was left in a laurel grove in Sicily by his mother, from which he derived his name. D. was found and raised by shepherds. Pan taught him to play the pipes, and D. came to invent bucolic poetry. D. used to hunt with Artemis, who liked his music. The nymph Echenais became his lover, on condition that he never have another woman. Another nymph seduced him, however, while he was drunk and, in punishment, Echenais blinded him and he died soon after. Another version, related by *Theocritus, is that Aphrodite struck him with a terrible passion, which he resisted, and he subsequently died.

DAPHNIS and CHLOE Pastoral romance by a Greek writer named Longus (of whose life nothing is known). On stylistic grounds, he is variously claimed to have lived in the 2nd to 6th centuries AD. The prose romance, in four books, has a relatively simple, compact plot: D. and C. were found and raised by shepherds in Lesbos. The gradual development of their affection and love is related, until they discover their parents and marry. The charming descriptions of nature, the penetrating psychological treatment, the compact plot, and the elaborate style, distinguish it from other Greek romances and have made it attractive to readers from the 16th century on.

G. M. Edmonds (Loeb), 1955 (1916).

DARDANI Strong Illyrian tribe, with Thracian elements in its eastern fringes. The D. often fought against their southern neighbours, but were defeated by Alexander the Great in 335 BC. Early in the 3rd century BC the D. united and for a time were able to spread as far as the northern Adriatic. The D. were opposed by the Illyrian Ardiaei; *Demetrius II, king of Macedonia, was defeated and slain by them in 229 BC. After the establishment of the Roman province of Macedonia, the D. continued their attacks, and in the first century BC several Roman governors there fought them until they were pacified, by Marcus *Crassus (5). Their territories were incorporated with the province of *Moesia.

J. J. Wilkes, *Dalmatia*, 1969.

DARDANUS Son of Zeus and Electra, whose descendants formed the royal dynasty of Troy. D.'s origin was variously ascribed to Italy, Samothrace, Arcadia and Crete. D. founded Dardania and was considered ancestor of the Dardanians, a tribe on Mount Ida in Phrygia; Homer associated them with the Trojans.

DARIUS (1) I Son of Hystaspes, king of Persia (521–486 BC). D. killed Gaumata who had impersonated Smerdis, Cambyses' dead brother. Until 519 BC, D. was kept busy restoring order to his empire and his efforts in reorganization stood the test well into Hellenistic times. The Persian empire was divided into 20 satrapies; annual taxes were instituted; the army was reformed, and a postal service was introduced, utilizing the extensive road network built at this time. D. continued the policy of religious tolerance instituted by *Cyrus (1), and a flourishing commerce was facilitated by a standardization of currency. D. struck a balance between centralized government and local institutions in the various satrapies. In 513 BC, he made an indecisive expedition against the Scythians, crossing the Bosporus to Europe and advancing into southern Russia. In 499 BC the Ionian cities of Asia Minor revolted, destroying *Sardis; five years were needed to subdue them. D.'s attempts to punish Athens, which had aided the rebels, failed; in 492 BC, the Persian fleet was wrecked off Mount Athos, and in 490 BC D.'s army was defeated at *Marathon. He died in 486 BC.

A. R. Burn, *Persia and the Greeks*, 1962.

DARIUS (2) II Son of *Artaxerxes I. D. had been satrap of Hyrcania and on his father's death became king of Persia (424–404 BC). He married his half-sister Parysatis, who greatly influenced him. D.'s reign initiated a decline of the Persian empire, with revolts in Syria, Lydia and Media. Only in western Asia Minor was Persian power restored, through the Peloponnesian War.

DARIUS (3) III Last of the Achaemenid dynasty. Bagoas, the minister who slew *Artaxerxes III and his son, crowned D. in 336 BC and was then himself put to death.

D. was defeated by *Alexander the Great at Issus and Gaugamella; in both battles, he personally fought poorly and thus lost the allegiance of his subjects. He was murdered by his own satraps in 330 BC.

DASCYLIUM City in Hellespontine *Phrygia, not far from the coast; seat of a Persian satrap.

DECAPOLIS League of ten Hellenistic cities, almost all in Transjordan, organized as a result of Pompey's conquest of Syria and Palestine in 63 BC. The D. included *Damascus, Philadelphia (Amman), Scythopolis (Beth Shean), Gadara, Hippos, Pella, *Gerasa, Raphana, Dion and Kanatha; other cities later joined the D. as well.

DECAPROTOI Colleges of ten members in numerous cities in the eastern provinces of the Roman Empire. The D. were responsible for tax collecting and held office for several years; they disappeared early in the 4th century AD.

Magie, *Asia* (s.v.).

DECARCHIES (Decadarchiai) Ten-member committees of oligarchic inclination, instituted by *Lysander in various cities after the defeat of Athens in the Peloponnesian War. Sparta relied on the D. which also collected taxes for her. With the Peace of *Antalcidas of 386 BC, the last of the D. were abolished.

DECEBALUS King of *Dacia who reunited his people and, from AD 85 on, was at war with Rome. D. defeated Roman armies in AD 85 and 86, but failed at Tapae in AD 88. With the *Marcomannic threat on Pannonia, *Domitian made peace, agreeing to pay D. a subsidy. Trajan, however, renewed the war and in his first campaign (AD 101–2) forced D. to surrender. He allowed him to rule, but with a Roman garrison. War was renewed in AD 105, when D. failed to keep the terms of the peace. Dacia was conquered subsequently and in AD 106 D. committed suicide.

DECELEA Old Attic deme at Mount Parnassus, about 24 km from Athens. The Spartans occupied D. in 413 BC, at *Alcibiades' advice, holding it until 404 BC as a threat against Attica.

DECEMVIRI Board of ten members instituted at Rome in 451 BC, at plebeian demand, to codify Roman law. All

King Darius I and, behind him, Xerxes. A detail from the Treasury building in Persepolis

other magistrates subsequently abdicated and the D. were given full powers; they made ten tables of laws. A second board was supposedly elected for 450 BC, publishing two additional tables; one of the new laws prohibited marriage between Patricians and Plebeians. It is likely that the D. merely codified existing customary law. The second board abdicated after the suicide of *Verginia, and in 449 BC, ordinary magistrates again took office. This Roman tradition may be accepted on the whole as authentic. The Twelve Tables were set up in the Forum, but they perished during the Gallic capture of Rome. The laws were known, however, to later generations, children learning them by heart. They are often cited in extant literary sources, indicating that they included religious, civil, criminal and public law.

Ogilvie, *Livy*, 451ff.

DECIUS, Gaius Messius Quintus Trajanus Roman emperor, AD 249–51; born in Pannonia at the end of the 2nd century AD. In AD 249, the Emperor *Philip appointed him governor of Moesia and Pannonia; his troops forced him to proclaim himself emperor, and Philip was soon killed. D. instituted persecutions of the Christians, whom he considered dangerous to the unity of the Empire. D.'s main efforts, however, were expended in trying to check the Goths in the Balkans. D. lost the battle at Abrittus in June AD 251, where he and his son Herrennius were killed.

DECIUS MUS, Publius (1) Roman hero, consul of 340 BC. He was held to have made a *devotio* at a battle against the Latins; that is, he was killed charging the enemy, after he had devoted them and himself to the infernal gods. This was done to assure a Roman victory.

DECIUS MUS, Publius (2) Son of *D. (1); four time consul and censor. It is more likely that D., rather than his father, made the *devotio* – at Sentinum against the Gauls in 295.

DECUMA ("Tithe") Farmers of the *ager publicus* in Italy were expected to pay a D. of the grain harvest to the state. Contracts for the collection of the D. were leased by the censors to *publicani*. The D. was also collected in the provinces. In Sicily it was based on the law of Hieron II of Syracuse, and encompassed all land except that of the *civitates foederatae* (cities with formal treaties with Rome). The leasing of contracts was made by the Roman governor in Syracuse. The D. was collected in the province of Asia but, by the law of Gaius Gracchus, contracts there were made by the censors in Rome. The same system may have been introduced in various other provinces. By the early Empire, the D. had been replaced by a fixed sum (*tributum*), collected by local magistrates without the service of the publicani.

J. Carcopino, *La loi de Hiéron et les Romains*, 1914.

DECURIONES Under the Roman Empire, members of local councils of Latin and Roman municipalities. The D. and their families formed a privileged class (*ordo splendidissimus*), expected to perform certain municipal duties. Normally, the D. were ex-magistrates appointed for life by the local censors; minimum property requirements and age limits were fixed, with local variations. The D. were personally responsible for the taxes due to the central government, any deficit being at their own expense (see *Curiales*). Local magistrates acted under the directions and decisions of the D. From the 3rd century AD on, the burdens placed upon the D. exceeded the honour involved.

DEDITICII Foreign peoples who had surrendered unconditionally to the Roman state, in anticipation of merciful treatment; the act of surrender was called *deditio in fidem*. The D. were free but had no political rights; their status was usually temporary, until Rome decided how local affairs would be administered.

Jones, *Studies*, 129ff.

DEIANIRA Daughter of the Aetolian King Oeneus (though it was also held that her true father was the god Dionysus). Heracles heard of her in Hades, from her brother *Meleager; he fought *Achelous her suitor, and defeated him. Later, the Centaur Nessus tried to rape D., and Heracles shot him with an arrow; before he died, Nessus gave D. a poisonous garment, promising her it would secure Heracles' love. D. later sent it to Heracles when she heard he was bringing the beautiful *Iole. When the garment led to Heracles' death, D. committed suicide.

DEINARCHUS Orator, active in Athens in the second half of the 4th century BC. D. was associated with *Theophrastus and *Demetrius of Phalerum. Only three of his numerous speeches are extant.

J. O. Burtt, *Minor Attic Orators*[2] (Loeb).

DEINOCRATES Architect and builder, probably a native of Rhodes. D. was employed by Alexander the Great and played an important role in the building of *Alexandria in Egypt.

DEIOTARUS Tetrarch of the Tolistobogii in western *Galatia. *Mithridates VI's aggressive policy led D. to become an ally of Rome. In 63 BC, Pompey expanded D.'s territory, adding parts of Pontus, and he was recognized as king by the Senate. In 51 BC, D. aided Cicero in Cilicia, and in the Civil War supported Pompey until the battle of *Pharsalus. Caesar pardoned him, but limited his rule in Galatia. After Caesar's murder, D. annexed the remaining territories of Galatia and, though he initially followed *Brutus (2), changed sides in time. D. died in 40 BC.

DEIPHOBUS Son of *Priam and Hecuba, and one of the best Trojan warriors. D. married *Helen after the death of *Paris; he was killed by *Menelaus at the capture of Troy.

DELOS Small island (approx. 3.5 sq km) encircled by the *Cyclades. D. is flat, with a mountain, Mount Cynthus, 113 m high. D. was inhabited as early as the 2nd millennium BC, but the indigenous population gave way to Greek settlers *c.* 1000 BC. D. became a religious centre quite early, and *Apollo and *Artemis were said to have been born there. Its sanctuary of Apollo was very famous, and it had early temples of Artemis and Hera. D.'s fame is noted by Homer; by the 8th century BC, an annual festival for Apollo had already been established there, celebrated by the *Ionians with music, games and dances. *Pisistratus purified D., that is, removed graves from the vicinity of the sanctuary. In the 7th and 6th centuries BC, D. had special connections with *Naxos, which built several buildings on D., dedicated various statues and gifts, and its tyrant *Polycrates celebrated the games there.

As a sacred island, D. was the centre of the alliance of the Ionian cities and Athens, established in 478/477 BC to fight the Persians; the treasury of the alliance was kept on the island until its removal to Athens in 454 BC. When peace with Persia was made in 449 BC, Athens converted the alliance into an empire. D. did not pay taxes but the administration of the temples was put under Athenian control. In 426 BC a new purification took place. After the Peloponnesian War, Athens lost control of D., regaining it in 378/377 BC and losing it once again in 314 BC. D. remained free of foreign control until 166 BC and probably was the centre of the League of the Greek Islanders.

Archaic lions of Naxian marble at Delos

Greek population worshipping a chthonic deity. The cult of *Apollo was introduced in a later period, but certainly as early as the 8th century BC; the temple, not necessarily the earliest, was burnt down in 548 BC and subsequently rebuilt with the support of the aristocratic *Alcmaeonid family which had been exiled from Athens. This new temple was destroyed in 373 BC and its replacement was still standing till the 4th century AD.

The exact procedure in consulting the Delphic Oracle is disputed, but can generally be described as follows. A supplicant or supplicants, private or representative of communities, first underwent purification and made a sacrifice; enquiries were then submitted to the priest of Apollo who, in turn, presented them to the *Pythia. The Pythia, inspired by the god while in a state of ecstasy, pronounced her prophecy. This response was rephrased by the priest, usually in verse form, and presented to the supplicant. The oracle was consulted on various matters — economic, political, religious and personal. How the priests could have pronounced prophecies with convincing effect has not been satisfactorily explained. That some of the replies were ambiguously formulated is shown by the case of *Croesus who, wishing to know the outcome of his pending encounter with *Cyrus, was told that a great state would be destroyed if he crossed the Halys. Some replies proved untrue, as when the oracle foretold doom for Athens and Sparta at the time of the invasion of *Xerxes, and counselled submission to Persia. External influence also occurred, as revealed by the cases of *Cleisthenes (2) and *Cleomenes I. Whatever the case, the Delphic Oracle early gained authority, as is shown by its constant consultation prior to the dispatch of new col-

In 166 BC Rome declared D. a free port, giving it to Athens; the old inhabitants were then expelled, to be replaced by Athenian colonists. People from everywhere in the Greek sphere were now attracted to D., including Italian merchants, and it acquired a cosmopolitan character. D. was a centre of banking, of the corn trade and, especially, of the slave trade. The Delian traders were organized in guilds. The prosperity of D. did not, however, last for long, for in 88 BC it was conquered and pillaged by *Mithridates VI, 20,000 of its inhabitants being slaughtered. It also suffered severely from a pirate attack in 69 BC. Thereafter, D. lost its importance, though it was still inhabited under the Roman Empire. The prosperity of D. as a religious and commercial centre has been revealed through archaeological excavations carried out by the French since 1873. The remains of numerous public and private buildings have aided in locating monuments known from literary sources, such as the temple of Apollo, the temple of Artemis and the Sacred Harbour. In addition, numerous inscriptions have been found, facilitating the study of the economic history of the island. Various works of art were discovered, among them mosaics, statues (including parts of that of Apollo), and remains of the impressive Lion Terrace.

W. A. Laidlaw, *A History of Delos,* 1933;
G. A. O. Larsen, *ESAR,* 344ff.

DELPHI City south of Mount Parnassus, celebrated for its sanctuary of Apollo, the most important Greek oracle. There was an *Omphalos ("navel", a sacred stone) in the temple, considered to be the centre of the earth (two such stones were found during excavations there). D. was already settled in the 2nd millennium BC, first by a non-

View of the temple of Apollo at Delphi

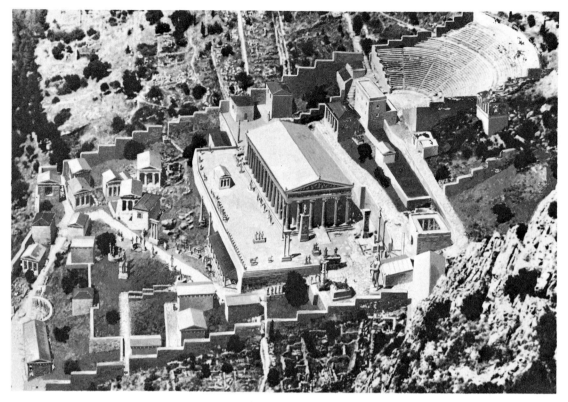

Reconstruction of the buildings of Delphi. Note the temple of Apollo in the centre, the Sacred Way and the treasury-houses along it on the left and the theatre on the top right

onies; that is, from the 8th century BC on. At Sparta, the constitution of Lycurgus (the "Rhetra") was based on a reply of the Delphic Oracle.

By the 7th century BC, D. was regarded as sacred by all Greeks. It became the centre of a league, the Delphic *Amphictiony, which allegedly represented all Greek states. The council of the league took part in the administration of the temple and was responsible for the celebration of the Pythian Games, from 582 BC on. Prior to this the games were held every eight years and included competitions of music, drama, singing and recitation; under Amphictionic control they were held every fourth year, with the addition of athletic competitions and chariot races. The winners were crowned with laurel wreaths, Apollo's tree, gathered in the valley of Temple. The games attracted participants from all Greece as well as from the overseas colonies and states.

The sanctity of D. led to punitive actions against those who violated it. The earliest such war was waged by Athens, Thessaly and Sicyon against the city of Crisa, which controlled the road from the Corinthian Gulf to D. and levied tolls from all who came to consult the oracle. Crisa was destroyed and its land consecrated to Apollo, early in the 6th century BC. The second sacred war was occasioned by the occupation of D. by the *Phocians, in the mid-5th century BC. Sparta intervened to drive them off, but *Pericles restored them in 448 BC; the duration of their control is not known but, by 421 BC, D. was already free. The third sacred war was the most complex,

beginning in 356 BC when the Amphictionic council, influenced by Thebes, imposed fines and threatened war on *Phocis, which had allegedly violated the Crisaean land (consecrated to Apollo) by cultivating it. Phocis then took D., using its treasures to hire mercenaries. The intricacies of Greek politics enabled them to gain the support of Athens and Sparta, and the ensuing war lasted for almost ten years, facilitating *Philip II's intervention in Greek affairs. Philip II finally subdued Phocis and took its place on the Amphictionic council. This was the first time the sanctuary was sacked, for the Persians had only slightly damaged it in 480 BC. In 279 BC it was saved from the attack of the Gauls under *Brennus (2), but later it suffered greatly. *Sulla confiscated its treasures (as he did at other Greek temples), and Germanic tribes pillaged it in the 3rd century AD. It was the decline in the faith of the old gods, however, that truly led to the final neglect of the Delphic Oracle and, with the ban on all pagan cults by *Theodosius I, the temple was closed, in AD 390.

As a revered centre of religion, D. had numerous monuments dedicated by private persons and states. Excavations on the site, from 1880 on, have revealed remarkable remains. The main temple of Apollo stood on a terrace; it was built in the Doric Order, 60m long and 21m wide, with an encircling exterior wall. Within the temple were altars of Poseidon and Hestia, as well as the alleged grave of Dionysus. A sacred serpentine way led from the holy spring of Castalia, whose water purified the worshippers, up to the temple. Along this road the Greek states built treasure-houses, some twenty in number, including those of Sicyon, Siphnos, Potidaea, Syracuse, Athens, Corinth, Cnidos, and Cyrene. Even non-Greek states and rulers — such as *Gyges, *Croesus and Rome — sent dedications to D. The temple of Athena Pronaia, a tholos and a palaestra were discovered lower down the slope. The stadium and theatre have also been excavated. Notable finds include the famous bronze "Charioteer" (part of a group dedicated by Polyzelus of Olla), the tripod of the serpent memorial (dedicated after the victory over Persia, bearing an inscription of the victorious states), a dedication of Lysander (after the battle of Aegospotamoi), sculptures of the pediment of the 6th century BC treasure-house of Siphnos, and the metopes of the Athenian treasure-house. F. Paulsen, *Delphi*, 1920; G. Fontenrose, *Python*, 1959.

DEMADES Athenian orator and statesman in the second half of the 4th century BC. D. began his political career by supporting *Demosthenes, but seems to have changed his views after the battle of *Chaeronea, in which he was captured. D. succeeded in arranging a peace settlement between Athens and *Philip II, and mediated between Alexander and Athens in 335 BC, after the destruction of *Thebes. D. apparently regarded opposition to Macedonia as futile, and he sought good terms with her; he even accepted money to pursue his pro-Macedonian policy. D. passed the resolution for the deification of Alexander in 323 BC. He was convicted of taking a bribe from *Harpalus and was exiled for a short time. He subsequently persuaded *Antipater (1) not to attack Athens for her part in the Lamian War. He also secured the death penalty against Demosthenes and *Hyperides. In 319 BC, D. and his son were executed by *Cassander for their connections with *Antigonus I. Of D.'s speeches, none has survived; he gained much fame through his witty sayings.

DEMARATUS King of Sparta, of the Eurypontid dynasty. On several occasions D. opposed his fellow king, *Cleomenes I; thus, in 506 BC, D. frustrated Cleomenes' invasion of Attica and again, in 491 BC, his attempt to act against Aegina. Cleomenes then procured the support of the Delphic Oracle for his claim that D. was an illegitimate child, and with the aid of the ephors, brought about D.'s abdication. D. left Sparta and went to *Darius I, who appointed him ruler of part of *Mysia. D. accompanied *Xerxes to Greece as an advisor in 480 BC. D.'s descendants succeeded him until the end of the 4th century BC.

DEMETER Greek goddess of agriculture, especially of corn. D.'s name was interpreted as meaning "earthmother" (dubiously deriving the element *de* from *ge*, "earth"). At any rate, D.'s chthonian character is prominent in the Greek myths associated with her. D. bore Zeus a daughter, Core (otherwise known as *Persephone, or, at Rome, Proserpina). *Hades fell in love with Core and seized her; for nine days and nights, D. searched for her daughter without eating or drinking, and on the tenth day she arrived in *Eleusis disguised as an old woman. There D. was hospitably received by King Celeus and his wife Metaneira; she wanted to make his son immortal by putting him in the fire which would burn his mortality away, but Metaneira intervened and broke the magic. Triptolemus, Celeus' other son, revealed to D. that Core had been carried away by Hades. D. then continued to wander, not allowing the trees to give fruit or the herbs to grow. At last Zeus agreed to return Core to D. but, as Core had eaten some pomegranate seeds in the underworld, a compromise was arranged, with Core staying nine months with her mother and three months with Hades

(under the name Persephone). Before returning to Olympus, D. instructed Celeus for the celebration of her mysteries, held ever since at Eleusis; she also sent Triptolemus to teach the art of agriculture, supplied with a plough and seed-corn.

This myth and the rituals associated with it clearly represent the dryness of summer (the period of Core's descent to Hades) and the revival of vegetation in the early autumn. The cult of D. was celebrated in many places under various epithets: D. was called *Kaproforos* ("bringing of friut"), *Thesmoforos* ("bringing of treasures"), *Chloë* ("bringer of seed"), among other appelations. D.'s gloomy character is revealed in other myths: she transformed Celeus' son Abas into a lizard (which lives in dry places); she punished Erysichthon with unsatiated hunger; in Athens the dead were called *demetrioi*; the Titan Iasius, who lay with her in a thrice-ploughed field (the issue was *Plutus) was killed by Zeus with a thunderbolt. Thus, the goddess of abundance was also responsible for dearth, bringing life but also death. It was D.'s benevolent side which found representation in art. D. is usually accompanied by Triptolemus and Persephone. D. was also identified with the Italian corn-goddess *Ceres.
Farnell, *Cults*, 3, 29ff.

DEMETRIAS City built by *Demetrius I on the Gulf of Volos, c. 293 BC. D. was founded by incorporating the adjoining towns of the Magnetes tribe, the entire tribal territory being made over to it. D. possessed strong walls with a circumference of approx. 8 km and good harbours. Until 196 BC, D. served as a Macedonian stronghold, one of the three "fetters of Greece". Rome liberated D. but, after the war against *Antiochus III, it was reoccupied by *Philip V. With the collapse of Macedonia in 167 BC, D. lost its importance.

DEMETRIUS (1) "Poliorcetes" Son of *Antigonus I, born in 336 BC. D. married Phila, daughter of *Antipater (1), and served with his father in the wars of the *Diadochi. D. lost the battle of Gaza to *Ptolemy I in 312 BC. He won Athens (307 BC) and Cyprus (306 BC) after a naval victory over the Ptolemaic fleet off Salamis but he failed to capture Rhodes (305 BC), even though he employed special siege machines, which gave him his surname, *Poliorcetes*, "the Besieger". D. succeeded in extending his power in Greece at the expense of *Cassander and in 302 BC revived the so-called League of Corinth (see *Philip II). D. escaped from the Battle of Ipsus (301 BC), in which his father fell. He was able to preserve his Greek possessions and naval power for several years and, in 294 BC, he became king of Macedonia; eventually, however, he lost his kingdom to *Pyrrhus and *Lysimachus. D. crossed to Asia Minor in 287 BC, but was captured by *Seleucus I, and died in a comfortable prison four years later.
Plut., *Demetrius*.

DEMETRIUS (2) II of Macedonia Son of *Antigonus II Gonatas, born c. 276 BC. D. succeeded to his father's throne in 239 BC; for most of his reign he fought the Achaean and Aetolian Leagues, the so-called Demetrian War. In 229 BC, Macedonia was invaded by the *Dardani. D. suffered defeat at their hands and died.

DEMETRIUS (3) I of Bactria Son of *Euthydemus. D. succeeded his father c. 200 BC, and extended his kingdom by conquering Arachosia and Gedrosia to the south. D. is said to have conquered a large area in India, though this was more probably achieved by a later Demetrius (called

Bronze statue of Hellenistic ruler, presumably Demetrius I Soter

"King of the Indians" by Justin). D. probably died *c.* 185 BC.

DEMETRIUS (4) I Soter of Syria Son of *Seleucus IV, born in 187 BC. D. was held hostage in Rome during his youth, but escaped to Syria in 162 BC and was soon able to recover the Seleucid kingdom. He put down the rebellion of the satrap Timarchus, and quelled the Jewish revolt in Palestine. Fear of D. in Rome led to Roman support for his opponents, *Attalus II of Pergamum and *Ptolemy VI. In 150 BC, D. was defeated and slain by *Alexander Balas.

DEMETRIUS (5) II Nicanor of Syria Son of *Demetrius (4), born *c.* 161 BC. Like his father, D. was held hostage in Rome in his youth, but from 147 BC he fought *Alexander Balas, who died in 145 BC. He was crowned in Antioch with the support of *Ptolemy VI, whose daughter he married. D. failed, however, to suppress the rising power of the Jews and his general, Tryphon, installed the son of Balas as a rival king. D. was captured fighting against Parthia (139 BC) and remained in captivity ten years. After release (129 BC), he sought to recover his kingdom, but was slain in 125 BC.

DEMETRIUS (6) of Phalerum Athenian statesman and philosopher, active in the second half of the 4th century BC. A pupil of Aristotle and friend of *Theophrastus, the pro-Macedonian D. was instituted as *epistates* (governor) of Athens by *Cassander in 317 BC, ruling the city firmly for ten years. Though D. was a philosopher, the spiritual decline of Athens began under him. D.'s legislation made him unpopular and, as a representative of Macedonian rule, he was hated. In 307 BC, when Athens was captured by *Demetrius Poliorcetes, D. fled first to Boeotia and then to Ptolemy I, for whom he became an official. He died in *Ptolemy II's reign. D. wrote an autobiography; the traditional view of him, however, was influenced by his enemies. D. wrote various and numerous works including historical, philosophical, literary, rhetorical, constitutional and fabular ones. Only fragments of his 45 known titles are extant.

DEMETRIUS (7) of Pharus D. cooperated with Rome in the First Illyrian War in 229–228 BC, after which he ruled northern Illyria. In 220 BC, D. renewed Illyrian piratical attacks in the Aegean Sea, leading to the Second Illyrian War, in 219 BC, as a result of which he lost his rule. D. escaped to *Philip V, who resented Roman intervention in Greek affairs, and stayed with him till he was killed in 214 BC.

DEMETRIUS (8) Native of Scepsis in the Troad, born in the late 3rd century BC. D. was an antiquarian scholar, writing a voluminous commentary on sixty lines of Homer (*Iliad*, 2, 816–876), covering various aspects — historical, geographical and mythological.

DEMETRIUS (9) Cynic philosopher, active in Rome in the 1st century AD. D. sharply criticized contemporary Roman rulers, winning the praise of *Seneca (2) for his independence. D. was banished from Rome in AD 66, but returned under Vespasian.

DEMETRIUS (10) of Magnesia Grammarian of the 1st century BC. D. wrote a treatise, *peri homonoia* ("On Concord"), mentioned by Cicero, in 49 BC, and on homonymous writers and cities.

DEMETRIUS (11) IXION Native of Adramyttium in the 2nd century BC. As a grammarian, he first followed *Aristarchus, later going to Pergamum to join *Crates of Mallos, under whom he criticized the method of Aristarchus. D. wrote a commentary on Homer, and perhaps one on Hesiod.

DEMETRIUS (12) LACON Epicurean philosopher of the 2nd century BC, head of the school. He opposed the Sceptic views of *Carneades.

DEMIOURGOI A term having several meanings, but literally meaning public workers. In Homer, D. denotes professional workers such as masons, physicians, heralds, minstrels and seers. In Archaic Athens, the D. formed a class, having two archons in 580 BC. In many Greek states, high officials were called D. (for example *Elis, *Mantinea, *Tegea, *Argos, *Delphi, Larissa and *Naupactus), but their functions were not identical everywhere.

DEMOCEDES Native of *Croton, eminent physician of the 6th century BC. D. was first active at Aegina and Athens, and was subsequently employed by the Samian tyrant *Polycrates. He later served under *Darius I, curing him and his queen. D. later returned to Croton; he was probably a Pythagorean.

DEMOCHARES Son of Laches and nephew of *Demosthenes (2); Athenian statesman and orator, born c. 360 BC. After the expulsion of *Demetrius of Phalerum (307 BC), D. dominated Athenian politics in the war against *Cassander. The walls of Athens were restored, and D. engineered an alliance with *Boeotia. D. soon lost his influence, however, and was banished. Back in Athens c. 287 BC, D. succeeded in adding *Eleusis to Athens and in obtaining financial support from Ptolemy I and Lysimachus. D. died in 275 BC.

DEMOCRITUS Native of *Abdera, philosopher. Details of D.'s life are few and conflicting; he was probably born c. 460 BC, and lived to an old age (in one version, to 104). That he visited Egypt, Ethiopia, Mesopotamia and Persia is doubtful, as is the story that he learned astrology from magi who stayed in Abdera on account of Xerxes' invasion of Greece. D. was a pupil of *Leucippus, perhaps of *Anaxagoras and of a Pythagorean. He wrote numerous works on various aspects of philosophy. *Callimachus prepared a list of his treatises, over 60 of which were later arranged in tetralogies by Thrasyllus (under Tiberius). The main sections consisted of ethical, physical, mathematical, musical and technical works, including cosmology, theory of substance, physiology, astronomy, geography, medicine, mathematics, botany, linguistics, painting, etc.

D. seems to have followed his teacher Leucippus in his theory of atoms, and this theory was ascribed to both of them by Aristotle. Very soon the particular contributions of these two scholars were barely distinguished. Plato considered the theory in his dialogue *Timaeus* (without mentioning D.), but Aristotle apparently thought very highly of him and often cited him. D.'s views on the nature of matter and on the universe found few supporters, though his school in Abdera continued into the Hellenistic period. *Epicurus and *Lucretius took much from him but they were exceptional. Of the voluminous works of D., none has survived. It is mainly thanks to his remarkable sayings that his views have been preserved. D. was called the "laughing philosopher", at least from the 1st century BC on, probably because of his work "On Cheerfulness". A satirical saying about him may have been the origin of the reputation of the Abderites as dull people.

The atomic theory of Leucippus and D. is an answer to the views of *Parmenides and the Eleatic School of philosophy. These maintained that what exists is imperishable, single, motionless and indivisible. Nothing else

is or can be known. Empty space is only a name and there is no place for motion or plurality of units. In the atomist theory, matter consists of indivisible particles which are unchanging, single and imperishable (as the Eleatic maintain); because of their indivisible property they are called atoms. Different atoms have different shapes and sizes but they do not differ in quality nor can they be seen by the human eye. Differing from the "full" and "existent" atoms are the "void", "non-existent" spaces in which the atoms move. Through their movement in the void, atoms combine and create separate formations — the origin of the world. Through movement and collision there are infinite changes and processions. Our world is only one of those created by congregations of atoms. The continual movement and change lead to all sorts of organization, including human society.

On the basis of the theory of atoms, D. explained the nature of sensation and proposed a theory of knowledge. The soul, like everything else, consists of atoms. Sensations result from the impact of atoms from outside on atoms of the soul through the sense organs. But the soul of the sentient cannot receive an exact likeness of the external object; intervening materials, such as air, allow it to receive only distorted images. The conclusion is that sensations are false and poor criteria for knowledge. But D. distinguished between two sorts of knowledge: the "dark knowledge" (*gnome skotie*), that is based on the five senses; and the "trueborn knowledge" (*gnome gnesie*) which depends on an inner sense. The five organ senses can only allude to true knowledge.

In his treatise "On Cheerfulness" (*Peri Euthymias*), D. expounded his views on ethics. For him, pleasure and pain determined happiness (*eudaimonia*); it is best to have as much joy and as little trouble, and in this connection D. is concerned with the soul, not the body — "He who chooses the goods of the soul chooses the more divine." The guiding principle is that of harmony. The pleasure of the soul depends on a state of calm on which also depend its "well-being" and "cheerfulness".
Kirk-Raven, *Presocratic Philosophers.*

DEMOI Smallest political units of Athens, based on natural places of habitation such as villages and town-quarters (but also attested in certain other Greek states, for example *Miletus, *Naxos, *Cos, *Mantinea and *Tegea). *Cleisthenes (2) first gave political function to the Athenian D. Those who had domicile in the D. at the time of his reform were registered as citizens. Each of his ten new tribes consisted of three groups of D. — from those of the coast, of the city and of the interior. The number of D. increased, at one time reaching 174. The D. obviously differed in the number of citizens and the area, and accordingly had different representation in the Cleisthenic Boule of 500. The legal name of each Athenian included his D.'s name. The D. had their own institutions, including an assembly, *demarchos* (chairman), scribe and treasurer; they administered local affairs and had their own cults and festivals. The D. kept registers of members, with assessments of their property on which basis Athenian citizens were taxed and served in the army. Members' sons received membership at the age of 18. Members could change domicile without losing status in the D. Metics were registered in the actual D. of domicile.
Hignett, *Athen. Const.* (s.v.).

DEMOPHON and ACAMAS In Greek mythology, sons of *Theseus and *Phaedra, who went to Troy to save their grandmother *Aethra (Helen's maid). A. had a son by Laodice, *Priam's daughter. D. and A. rescued Aethra during the fall of Troy, and on their way home D. (or variously A.) had a love affair with Phyllis, daughter of the Thracian king. D. (or A.) promised to return from Athens but delayed too long and she died of grief, becoming transformed into an almond-tree. D. or A. opened a casket given to him by Phyllis, became mad from what he saw and died by falling on his own sword.

DEMOSTHENES (1) Athenian general, prominent in the Peloponnesian War. D. was exceptional in his not taking part in the internal Athenian politics. As strategos in 427 BC, D. suffered losses in his invasion of *Aetolia, but shortly afterwards beat off an attack on *Naupactus and then inflicted two defeats on a Peloponnesian and Ambraciot army, winning *Acarnania. D.'s greatest success came in 425 BC when he occupied *Pylos, which led to the capture of a considerable number of Spartans on the nearby island of Sphacteria. ·Next year D. captured Nisaea, the port of *Megara, but the city itself was saved by the intervention of *Brasidas. In the same year he took part in a combined attack on Boeotia; his failure there led to the miscarriage of the entire plan. In 418/417 BC, D. was active in the Argolis and in 413 BC he led the second Athenian expedition to Syracuse, in aid of *Nicias. After the failure to capture Epipolae, D. did not succeed in persuading Nicias to retreat promptly from Syracuse while this was still possible by sea. D. commanded the rearguard of the Athenians trying to escape by land. He surrendered after six days and was put to death.

DEMOSTHENES (2) Athenian statesman and the most famous Greek orator. D. was born in 384 BC; his father was a well-to-do manufacturer of weapons and his mother Cleobule was of Scythian stock. D.'s father died when he was 7 years old and his guardians, his uncles Aphobus and Demophon and a friend, wasted the inheritance through bad administration. At the age of 18, D. set out to recover his patrimony, which proved a tedious task. D. studied rhetoric under *Isaeus. Various stories were later told of his efforts to overcome a stammer and a weak voice. He allegedly would go to the seashore to practice speaking with his mouth full of pebbles trying to overpower the sound of the waves; or he would run while reciting poetry, to perfect his breathing. He also studied law and history and is said to have copied the Histories of *Thucydides eight times to improve his language and historical knowledge. After two years of litigation, when 23 years old, D. obtained what remained of his patrimony. D. now became a *logographos*, that is, a professional writer of speeches for litigants, a profession from which he made handsome profits for many years.

D. entered politics c. 355 BC, with the prosecution of *Androtion, for which he wrote the speech, and of Leptines, in which he himself appeared. His first appearance before the *Ekklesia was in 354 BC, when he delivered a speech *On the Symmories* (the Navy Boards). This was occasioned by the rumour that the Persian king intended to attack Greece. D. argued that Athens was not prepared for war and advocated the strengthening of its naval power. Next year, D. criticized the policy of *Eubulus who was economizing in military preparations. In 352 BC, D. made a speech *For the Megalopolitans*, in which he attacked Sparta. D.'s position within the internal factions of Athenian politics in these years is not clear; on the whole, he seems to have opposed Eubulus, supporting the building of a strong Athenian naval power, to enable Athens to maintain her position in Greece.

The attack of *Philip II of Macedonia on the Thracian king, Cersobleptes (352 BC), marked a turning point in D.'s political career; from then on he became more convinced that Philip was not only the true rival of Athens in the north but also constituted a menace to freedom and the old political order in Greece. In 351 BC, D. delivered his first speech against Philip, the *First Philippic*. That D.'s opinion was indeed correct became apparent in 349 BC, when Philip attacked *Olynthus, which only seven years earlier had seceded from the Second Athenian League and made an alliance with Macedonia. In his three *Olynthiac* speeches (349–348 BC), D. urged the dispatch of a strong Athenian force to Olynthus to fight the enemy. Arguing that the defence of Olynthus was the defence of Athens, and that it was better to fight the enemy while it was still far away, D. proposed supporting the war by cutting off delivery of surplus money to the *Theorika*. When a force was sent, it was insufficient and too late; Olynthus was captured and destroyed. D. now became an even stronger opponent of Eubulus. Meanwhile, Philip consolidated his position in central Greece by defeating *Phocis. In 347 BC, D. served as a member of the *Boule. In 346 BC, he was on the ten-member embassy sent to Philip to negotiate peace (other leading members were *Aeschines, and *Philocrates whose name was given to the peace). In the first debate in Athens, D. supported ratification of the treaty but later, when it became known that Philip was in position to occupy Phocis, he changed his mind. Athens, however, could clearly do nothing to help Phocis, and Aeschines' speech for approval of the peace carried the day.

D. was convinced that Philip was unreliable, and his policy after 346 BC aimed at annulment of the Peace of Philocrates, as well as the destruction of Aeschines. In 345 BC, D. failed in the prosecution of Aeschines, who countercharged Timarchus, D.'s associate. In 344 BC, D. agitated against Philip in the Peloponnesus and when Macedonian ambassadors protested in Athens, D. delivered his *Second Philippic*. Change in the political current in Athens became evident with the condemnation of Philocrates in 343 BC. In that year D. renewed his attack on Aeschines, in his speech *On the False Embassy*, whom he accused as responsible for the disgraceful peace of 346 BC. Aeschines narrowly escaped condemnation. In his effort to renew the war against Philip, he was supported by *Hyperides, but his mission to the Peloponnesus in 342 BC to find allies was a failure. In 341 BC, D. defended Diopeithes' attack on Cardia, which was allied to Philip. D. also delivered his *Third Philippic*, and then his *Fourth Philippic*, in which he advocated war, with the aid of Persia. It was now quite clear that peace could not be maintained for long. In 340 BC, Philip attacked Byzantium and Perinthus, and war was declared. D. was now in control in Athens; his proposal to stop the allocation of surplus money to the *Theorika* was implemented the following year. Thebes joined Athens, but the combined Greek armies were defeated by the Macedonian phalanx at Chaeronea in 338 BC.

D.'s policy had failed and he himself was said to have fled from Chaeronea; but he did not as yet lose his influence. Chosen to read the funeral oration for the fallen at Chaeronea, he served on the committee for the fortification of the city and was elected an administrator of the *Theorika*. In 336 BC, Ctesiphon proposed awarding D. a crown in the *Dionysia, for service to the country, for which Aeschines charged him with *graphe paranomon*.

However, the death of Philip caused an indefinite delay of the trial. Alexander was quick to show that he surpassed his father. Thebes, in whose revolt D. was involved, was destroyed, and the Greek states were forced to submit to Alexander's will. Not much is known of D. in these years. In 330 BC, however, Aeschines renewed his prosecution of Ctesiphon but his speech is directed against D., who replied in a brilliant speech, *peri stephanou* ("On the Crown"), in which he surveyed and defended his policy over the previous twenty years. D. asserted that he had always acted and spoken in the best interests of Greece and Athens; he took full responsibility for the battle of Chaeronea but argued that the outcome was not his fault. His policy had been correct though unsuccessful. D.'s oratory was so impressive that Aeschines secured less than the minimum vote (a fifth of the jury), and he retired to Rhodes. When *Harpalus came to Athens in 324 BC, D. proposed to imprison him and to deposit his wealth on the Acropolis. Next year, D. was charged with taking 20 talents of Harpalus' money, and was fined 50 talents, but he fled to the Peloponnesus. After Alexander's death, D. was active in preparations for war against Macedonia and was recalled from exile. But at the battle of Crannon (322 BC) the Macedonians were again victorious. *Antipater (1) demanded D.'s surrender, and D. was subsequently condemned to death. Again he fled from Athens but, seeing he could not escape his pursuers, committed suicide by taking poison in 322 BC.

Opinion on D.'s policy and significance has changed over the ages; his excellent service to his country was acknowledged already within his lifetime. After D.'s death, his statue was erected, on which was inscribed: "Had his power been equal to his genius, Greece would not have submitted to tyranny". D. has generally been lauded as a champion of freedom and independence in defiance of tyranny, and indeed his orations have served as an inspiration of liberty. The wisdom of his policy, however, has been questioned. On the one hand, his advice to oppose Philip in the north was not fully justified strategically and, on the other hand, his efforts to unite Greece were impracticable in view of the inter-Greek feuds. D.'s senior contemporary and countryman, *Isocrates, was ready to accept Philip as leader of a united Greece against the barbarians. But while opinions vary on D. the statesman, he has been unanimously recognized as the finest Greek orator. Sixty-one speeches, private and public, have come down under D.'s name but, of these, several are spurious. D. took great pains in preparing his speeches, which are not tied by any rigid rules. The style employed was simple or lofty, as the case demanded, and the narrative and arguments are almost always clear and impressive.

A. T. Murray, C. A. and G. H. Vince,
N. W. and N. G. De Witt (Loeb), 1926–1949;
Kennedy, *Persuasion*.

DENTATUS, Manius Curius Roman Plebeian, allegedly of low origin, who rose to the highest offices and won great military successes. As consul in 290 BC, D. defeated the Samnites, bringing the war with them to an end, and subdued the Sabines. For his victories, he was awarded a triumph. As praetor in 283 BC, D. crushed the *Senones, on whose land the colony Sena Gallica was subsequently established. Again consul in 275 BC, he successfully engaged *Pyrrhus in battle, later defeating the *Lucani and gaining a second triumph. D. died in 270 BC, and was regarded as a model of the virtues of the old incorrupt-

ible and frugal Roman generals "whom no one could overcome, by neither sword nor gold" (Ennius, *Ann.* 220).

DERCYLLIDAS Spartan commander. In 411 BC, D. took Abydos and Lampsacus (though Athens soon recovered the latter), and remained *harmost* of Abydos. D. commanded the Spartan army which fought the Persian satraps in western Asia Minor in 399 BC and conquered the Troad. He crossed the Hellespont and defended the Greek cities of *Chersonessus (1) against the Thracians in 398 BC; in 397 BC, he renewed his campaign in Asia Minor but subsequently agreed to an armistice. In the following year, supreme command of the Spartan army in Asia Minor was given to King *Agesilaus and after some time, D. returned to Sparta. D. was again *harmost* of Abydos (394 BC), which he managed to hold for Sparta even after her defeat off *Cnidos; this was the only city left to Sparta in Asia. Nothing more is heard of D. after 390 BC, when he was recalled from Abydos.

DEUCALION (1) Son of *Minos, one of the *Argonauts. According to one tradition, D. was killed by *Theseus.

DEUCALION (2) Son of *Prometheus; the hero of the Greek flood myth. When Zeus decided to send a flood to wipe out mankind, because of the crimes of *Lycaon, D. and his wife Pyrrha built an ark, following the advice of Prometheus. For nine days they floated in the ark while the entire world was flooded. When the waters subsided they landed on Mount Parnassus (or Orthrys in Thessaly, or Mount Athos), where they made a sacrifice to Zeus who told them (in other versions, it was the oracle of Themis) to throw the bones of their mother behind them. They understood this as referring to Mother Earth; throwing the stones over their shoulders, those of D. became men and those of Pyrrha became women. Their son was Hellen, father of the Hellenes. Not all the human race was destroyed in the flood; some escaped to the mountaintops and later revived the crimes of Lycaon.

DEVOTIO Ritual by which a Roman general (or legionary soldier as a proxy) vowed himself and the army of the enemy to *Tellus and the *Manes, deities associated with the netherworld. After reciting the vow according to the instruction of a *pontifex*, the commander would make a suicide attack on the enemy, which would assure victory when the gods accepted the sacrifice. A second D. was not allowed to be made if death did not follow the first vow; indeed, if the general remained alive, a larger than life image was buried in his stead. *Decimus Mus was said to have made a D.

Latte, *R. Rel.* (s.v.).

DIADEM Initially any fillet worn around the head, traditionally invented by Dionysus. A purple D. with white ornamentation was part of the insignia of the Persian kings. Alexander the Great and the Hellenistic kings wore a white D., which for the Romans also signified royal power. Caesar rejected a D. with laurel crown, offered by Antony (44 BC). From Constantine on, the reigning emperor (Augustus) wore the D. (Augusta) with the D.

DIADOCHI The term D. (literally "Successors") refers mainly to the generals of Alexander the Great who fought over his inheritance. These included *Antipater, *Cassander, *Antigonus I, *Lysimachus, *Ptolemy I, *Seleucus I, *Perdiccas and *Craterus. In the last war of the D., Seleucus I defeated and killed Lysimachus at Curupedium (281 BC).

DIALOGUE The literary D. is based on the most familiar form of communication between human beings. It was used by Greek and Roman historians, tragic and

The bathing Diana looked upon by Actaeon

comic writers, poets, prose writers and philosophers. Discourses are found in Herodotus; in his *Melian Dialogue*, Thucydides gives a brilliant sketch of Athenian imperialism. Socrates used the D. as the form most fit to develop his ideas, and his disciples, notably *Plato, *Antisthenes and *Xenophon, adopted this literary form partly to commemorate the conversations they attended and partly to expound their own views. The D. became a literary framework to treat serious themes, literary, philosophical, political, etc. It was more natural and successful when it incidentally gave a characterization of the interlocutors and maintained the conversational setting; it became an artificial means when character portrayals were abandoned and a series of long monologues, whose sole aim was to convey the author's views, replaced the exchange of questions and answers. Plato's D.s offer examples of these two types. To judge by their fragments, Aristotle's D.s were mainly of the second type. Most of the theoretical treatises of *Cicero, on rhetoric, philosophy, theology, and politics, are written in D. form, following the expository type. *Varro chose the D. framework for his agricultural treatise *De Re Rustica*. Tacitus dealt with the decline of oratory in his *Dialogus de Oratoribus*; *Minucius Felix used the D. in his polemical *Octavius*. Of other important writers who used the D., mention may be made of the Greeks *Plutarch and *Lucian and the Latins *Macrobius and *Boethius.
R. Hirzel, *Der Dialogue*, 1895.

DIANA Ancient Italian goddess. Worshipped in many places, D.'s most important temples were on Mount Tifata near Capua and in a grove (*nemus*) on the lake-shore near Aricia. The temple of D. Nemorensis was the centre of an ancient league of Latin cities. The priest of this temple was a runaway slave (*rex nemorensis*) who had killed his predecessor and was liable to be killed by the next runaway slave who would challenge him. According to Roman tradition a temple of D. was established on the Aventine by *Servius Tullius, in an attempt to transfer the religious centre of the Latin League from Aricia to Rome; the text of the treaty between Rome and the Latins was preserved here. Another temple, at the Circus Flaminius, was dedicated in 179 BC. D. was mainly a goddess of women; objects offered to her in the temple of Aricia included figurines of mothers with infants, and votive vulvas. Included in her cult was a procession of women with torches to her Arician temple. She was a goddess of fertility and vegetation and was often associated with woods and hence was also a goddess of hunting. Her lunar nature is uncertain, though she was identified with *Luna, the moon goddess. D. early came to be identified with the Greek goddess *Artemis, no distinction being made between the two.
Latte, *R. Rel.* (s.v.).

DICAEARCHUS Native of *Messana, philosopher, learned and versatile scholar. A pupil of *Aristotle and *Theophrastus, D. lived in the Peloponnesus for a considerable time, and thrived in the last quarter of the 4th century BC. *Varro, *Cicero and *Pliny pay tribute to D.'s erudition. Of D.'s various works only fragments and titles are extant; his treatises dealt with philosophy, politics, history, biography, literature and geography. In his work *peri psyches* ("On the Soul"), D. taught the mortality of the soul, maintaining it to be the mantic organ. D. appears to have been very interested in prophecy and oracles, for he wrote several treatises on the subject. In his "The Descent to the Den of Trophonius", he described the behaviour of the priests of that oracular god; in another treatise, he discussed the self-destruction of man — more men die by war than by natural disaster. D.'s *bios Hellados* was the first of its kind, a cultural history of Greece in three books, based on biographies. D. wrote biographies of various philosophers including Pythagoras and Plato. As a true disciple of Aristotle, D. composed *politeiae* (constitutions) of cities (Sparta and Pallene). In his *tripolitikos*, D. argued against Plato's theory of state and may have suggested a mixed constitution. D. wrote Hypotheses to the tragedies of Sophocles and Euripides, a book on *Alcaeus, treatises on Homer, music and poetry. His geographical works won D. the admiration of Strabo; he prepared a survey of the Greek mountains, and his *periodos ges* described the world.

DICTA CATONIS A handbook of popular morals, probably first composed in the 3rd century AD. The title *Marci Catonis ad filium libri* ("M. Cato's Books to His Son") appears in manuscripts but the work is certainly not by Cato. Popular in the Middle Ages, the D. was translated into many European languages. It is a heterogeneous collection deriving material from various sources, pagan and Christian, Greek and Roman. The influence of Horace, Ovid and Seneca is apparent in various passages. The D. includes: 57 short sayings in prose; four books (each with a preface, often in hexameters) of moral precepts written in hexameters, comprising 288 lines arranged in distichs; and 77 hexameters arranged in monostichs. The distichs are the most important part of the collection. No thematic order can be discerned in the book. Utilitarian and opportunistic tendencies are prominent in many of the proverbs.
Duff, *Min. Lat. Poets.*

DICTATOR Extraordinary Roman magistrate, an office established early under the Republic, though its origins are disputed. In contrast to other magistrates, the D. was nominated by a consul (usually on the proposal of the Senate) and not elected by the *comitia*. The occasion for the nomination was a state of emergency, either external or internal. After nomination, the D.'s *imperium* was voted by the *comitia curiata*. The D.'s original title was *magister populi* (commander of the military citizen-body) and his first act was to appoint a *magister equitum* (commander of cavalry). The D. was superior to all other magistrates, including consuls. His military power was valid within Rome (*domi*) and outside it (*militiae*). Where a consul had twelve lictors, the D. had twenty-four; he was appointed to a specific task and was expected to abdicate with its completion — at most after six months. The *magister equitum*, whose *imperium* resembled that of a *praetor (with six lictors), abdicated along with his D. A D. was sometimes appointed to hold elections (if the consuls were not available), to give games or to perform religious functions. The concentration of powers by the D. was regarded as exceptional and undesirable. With the extension of Roman power beyond Italy in the 3rd century

BC, less D.s were appointed. The dangers of the Hannibalic War occasioned the renewal of the office, the last D. being appointed in 202 BC. *Sulla and *Caesar were D.s but their magistracy differed entirely from the old form. A regular magistrate termed D. existed in several Latin states.
Jolowicz, *Roman Law*[3] (s.v.).

DIDASCALIA A term which originally meant "instruction", especially for the chorus, carried out by the poet himself or a professional teacher. D. also came to denote the official lists which recorded various details connected with theatre performances — titles and authors, actors and flute-players, *choregoi*, year and results of the competition. Such records were used, for example, by *Aristotle in his books *Didascaliai* and *Nicai Dionysiakai astikai kai lenaikai*, both not extant. Subsequent scholars depended on Aristotle's books for this subject. Several inscriptions have survived from the 3rd century BC, giving details of D.; they, too, are based on Aristotle's work.
Pickard-Cambridge, *Dramatic Festivals*, ch. 2.

DIDIUS, Titus Roman politician and general, a *novus homo*. As praetor c. 101 BC, D. received the province of Macedonia, later being awarded a triumph for his victories there. In 98 BC, D. was consul, and with his colleague Q. Metellus Nepos passed a law to regulate legislation, making it illegal to include diverse measures in a single bill and setting a compulsory interval of three *nundinae* (market days) between the promulgation of a bill and the voting on it. In 97–93 BC, D. was governor in Spain and was awarded a second triumph. He was killed in June 89 BC in the war against the Italian allies.

DIDIUS JULIANUS, Marcus Roman senator, associated with Marcus *Aurelius, under whom he served in various provincial posts (Achaea, Africa, Germany and Dalmatia). He also served with *Commodus. When *Pertinax was murdered (March AD 193), D. won praetorian support by promising the highest donatives, and thus became emperor. He was not accepted by the provincial armies, and the Syrian legions acclaimed *Pescennius Niger, and the Pannonian legions, Septimius *Severus. With the advance of Severus upon Rome, D. was deserted by the praetorians and murdered in June AD 193.
Dio, 73.

DIDO Legendary Tyrian princess (called Elissa in Phoenician), first mentioned by the Greek historian *Timaeus and known mainly through *Virgil's account of her love for *Aeneas. D.'s father Mutto (or Belus) was king of Tyre; her brother Pygmalion killed her husband Acerbas (Sychaeus in Virgil). D. escaped to Libya and founded the city of *Carthage. In one version, D. burned herself alive to avoid marriage with the Libyan king, Jarbas. A variant of the legend developed at Rome in the 3rd century BC, in connection with the Punic Wars, introducing *Aeneas to the story (*Naevius and *Ennius probably included it in their narratives). According to Varro's version, it was Anna (D.'s sister) who fell in love with Aeneas and killed herself on the pyre. In Virgil, D. gives shelter to Aeneas after his shipwreck, falling in love with him in spite of herself, as she tried to remain faithful to her dead husband. But "pious" Aeneas obeyed the gods' word, left Carthage and founded a new kingdom in Italy; thereupon D. burned herself on the pyre. The Roman version thus gives a mythological background for the war between Rome and Carthage.

DIDYMA Sanctuary of *Apollo 15 km south of Miletus. As a religious centre, D. was very ancient, perhaps pre-

The remains of the temple of Apollo in Didyma

ceding the Ionian settlement. In the Archaic period, D. was administered by the Branchidae clan. The Archaic temple was built in the 6th century BC and destroyed by the Persians in 494 or 480 BC. The Branchidae were relegated to Sogdiana and their descendants were slain by Alexander the Great for no reasonable cause. Of the Archaic temple, few remains are extant. The statue of Apollo, made by Canachus of Sicyon, was removed by the Persians but restored by *Seleucus I. A new temple was built at the end of the 4th century BC; it was under the control of Miletus, but did not have the same influence as in the Archaic period.

C. E. Bean, *Aegean Turkey*, 1966, 231ff.

DIDYMUS Emminent Greek scholar who lived and taught at Alexandria in the 1st century BC. D. wrote innumerable works on various aspects of Greek philosophy and literature, being credited with 3,500 or even 4,000 books. D.'s vast productivity led him to self-contradictions – for which he was nicknamed "*Bibliolathas*". D.'s works included a reconstruction of the text of Homer according to the recension of *Aristarchus, commentaries on numerous Greek writers (poets, historians, tragedians, comedists and orators), lexicographical treatises on comedies and tragedies, grammatical works and special literary treatises such as "On Lyric Poets". Papyri preserve part of D.'s commentary on the Philippic orations of Demosthenes. D. was evidently a careful compiler of earlier works but his original contribution to Greek philology was meagre. D.'s non-extant books, however, gave easy approach to and summaries of earlier works, and were extensively utilized by later scholiasts. He was thus the direct source of many extant *scholia, such as those of Hesiod, Pindar, Sophocles, Euripides and Aristophanes.

DIGESTA A juristic work treating all fields of Roman law. The first D. was written by Alfenus Varus in the late

1st century BC. Several such works were written by various jurists, the most famous being that prepared on the order of Justinian as part of his codification. A special commission was appointed in AD 530 to excerpt the works of the Classical jurists. The commission of 16 members, under the presidency of Tribonianus, reviewed 2,000 books (with three million lines) and of this vast material 150,000 lines were selected. The final compiled work, titled "D." (called *Pandectae* in Greek), was published in AD 533 and received sanction by the Constitution *tanta* in December of AD 533. It is arranged in 50 books, each with subdivisions and paragraphs. The subdivision titles are based on the praetorian edict, and under each title are passages from the Classical jurists relating to the subject in question. Each passage is headed by a note giving the name of the author and the specific work from which it was taken. Of the many jurists cited, most are from the 2nd and 3rd centuries AD. A third or so of the excerpts are from *Ulpianus and about a sixth from *Paulus. However, as a compilation it could not solve the problems of the day; Justinian's aim had been to provide a valid law, but a judge consulting it often found contradictions amongst the various opinions cited. Though a textbook of law, it contained much irrelevant material, and its awkward arrangement prevented easy consultation. The book is, however, very important for the study of many aspects of the Roman Empire.

DIKASTERION ("lawcourt") Our knowledge of Greek courts is almost wholly limited to those in Athens. It was one of the fundamental characteristics of Athenian democracy that the right of jurisdiction, once exclusively held by aristocratic institutions (*Areopagus, *Archontes), was exercized by the people through a set of courts. The first step had been taken by *Solon who instituted the *Heliaia, a popular assembly which served as a court of appeal against the verdicts of magistrates. In the course of the 5th century, a system of popular juries was established; Athens then became a real democracy because, to cite Aristotle, "the one who rules the courts rules the state".

There were several courts, each presided over by a magistrate or a board of magistrates (e.g. *Hendeca, *Polemarchus, *Thesmotetai). Each court was allocated a certain number of jurors, several hundred or even thousands, to try the cases brought before it. The jurors were appointed by lot from a yearly list. This list consisted of 6,000 men over 30 years old who volunteered to serve as jurors. For each day of hearing a case, they received two obols; by 425 BC, this sum was raised to three obols. The institution of public attorney did not exist in Athens, and any citizen could bring a charge before the appropriate court through the magistrate responsible for it. After a preliminary inquiry by the magistrate to see if there was sufficient reason to start a trial, the case was tried by a jury. At this stage the magistrates neither interrogated the parties and their witnesses nor gave any directions to the jury. The plaintiff delivered his speech and the accused answered him. Both spoke for themselves but could use speeches written by *logographers. Minors, non-citizens and women were represented by relatives or patrons. Documents could be presented and witnesses would appear. Immediately after all the parties had presented their case, the jurors voted by the secret ballot. A simple majority decided the case on which there was no appeal. A tie was considered as an acquittal. Penalties were sometimes fixed by law according to the offence. In other cases, if the accused was found guilty, each party submitted a penalty and the jury voted on which one to accept. Socrates lost his case by proposing far too lenient a penalty, and there were more jurors who condemned him to death than there were who merely pronounced him guilty.

K. J. Bonner—G. Smith, *The Administration of Justice from Homer to Aristotle*, 1930—1938.

DIO (1) COCCEIANUS Surnamed Chrysostomos ("golden-mouthed") for his excellence in oratory, D. was born in Prusa, Bithynia, *c.* AD 40. Of a well-to-do family, D. received rhetorical education and became a pupil of the Stoic philosopher Musonius in Rome. After being banished under *Domitian, D. began a wandering life, during which he preached Stoic and Cynic doctrines. In these years, D. was in Asia Minor and the Balkan provinces. Under *Nerva his punishment was annulled and he was allowed to return to Rome, where he subsequently cultivated relations with Trajan. Several years later, D. settled down in his native town and became involved in local public affairs. The last thing known of him is that he was prosecuted before the governor of the province, Pliny the Younger, in AD 111.

D. attained a vast reputation as an orator, and 80 of his speeches have come down to us (though two are actually of his pupil *Favorinus). D.'s speeches are imbued with Cynic and Stoic ideas, and deal with a wide range of topics, such as literature, mythological questions, the ideal monarch, rhetoric and morals. Some of the speeches are funeral orations and others were delivered before cities (Prusa, Alexandria, Tarsus). D. saw it as his duty to keep alive the inheritance of Classical Greek culture and he did not develop new ideas, but merely followed his predecessors. The philosophical principles that D. taught could not have had much force in his day, well known as they had come to be, and despite the fact that he himself gave a living example. For the historian, D.'s speeches provide a great deal of information on the urban Greek society of his time.

J. W. Cohoon — H. L. Crosby (Loeb), 1932—1951.

DIO (2) CASSIUS (more correctly, Cassius Dio Cocceianus) Native of Nicaea in Bithynia, son of Cassius Apronianus. Like his father, D. rose in the imperial administration to become a senator under *Commodus; he was praetor in AD 194, *consul suffectus* under Septimius *Severus, and later governor of Africa and of Dalmatia. In AD 229, he was again consul, together with *Alexander Severus. D. soon retired to Bithynia. He wrote a book on the dreams and omens of Septimius Severus and a biography of Arrian, but his principal work was his *Roman History*, comprising 80 books and covering the period from earliest Rome to his own second consulate (AD 229). Books 36—54 have survived in full, extending over the years 68—10 BC. Books 55—60, from 9 BC to AD 47, are partly preserved, and there are also parts of Books 79—80. Many of the lost books are known through summaries (*epitome*) made by Xiphilinus (11th century AD) and Zonaras (12th century AD). The first 21 books are represented in Zonaras' *epitome*, which also treats Books 44—68; Xiphilinus abbreviated Books 36—80. D. utilized various authors for his history. D.'s description of the late Republic and early Principate is somewhat misleading and unreliable in many points, for D. interpreted political and constitutional matters from his own experience under autocracy. The narrative is disrupted by the insertion of many tiresome speeches.

E. W. Cary (Loeb), 1924; F. Millar, *Cassius Dio,* 1964.

DIOCLES (1) Syracusan statesman, active in the time of the Peloponnesian War. D. was a leader of the extreme democrats and carried out a constitutional reform in 412 BC, introducing election of magistrates by lot. D.'s opponent was the moderate *Hermocrates, who was exiled in 412 BC. In 409 BC, D. failed to regain Himera from Carthage and was banished. He died after 408 BC.

DIOCLES (2) Mathematician of the 2nd or 1st century BC. D.'s work "On Burning-Mirrors" (*peri pyreion*) is extant.

DIOCLES (3) of Carystus Physician in Athens in the 4th century BC who came to be considered second only to *Hippocrates. He was probably influenced by various personalities (*Empedocles, Hippocrates and Aristotle) and wrote several treatises, of which only fragments survive, including works on anatomy and on dietetics (*hygiena*). Other subjects of interest to D. were botany, physiology, aetiology and prognostics. D. showed concern with methodological questions, emphasizing the importance of individual treatment of patients. On the whole, D.'s theories were a good synthesis of his predecessors' views.

DIOCLES (4) of Magnesia Lived in the 1st century BC. A friend of *Meleager of Gadara, D.'s work on philosophers was used a great deal by *Diogenes Laertius.

DIOCLETIAN, Gaius Aurelius Valerius Born to a low family in Dalmatia after AD 230, D. became a soldier and after long service was appointed commander of the bodyguard of *Carus and, subsequently, of his son Numerian. After the death of Numerian, D. was proclaimed emperor in November 284 AD. D. put Aper, the praetorian prefect, to death as responsible for the murder of Numerian. On his accession to the throne, D. changed his original name, Diocles. D. had to fight *Carinus, Numerian's brother, who had remained as Caesar in the West. At the battle of Margus in Moesia, early in AD 285, Carinus was defeated, and was subsequently killed by his own soldiers. Over the long years of his reign as emperor, D. dealt with all the problems that threatened the welfare and existence of the Roman Empire: external attacks on the frontiers; rival pretenders; loyalty and discipline of the army and its commanders; financial and economic conditions and religious matters.

To cope with the military and administrative problems, D. appointed his old friend *Maximian as Caesar (AD 285) and sent him to the West. After suppressing the revolt of the Bacaudae in Gaul, Maximian was made Augustus (AD 286). In the following years, D. was busy fighting the Alamanni (AD 289), the Sarmatians (AD 289 and 292), and the Saracens supported by Persia (AD 290). In AD 290, D. established Tiridates III as king of Armenia. In AD 292 D. had to deal with a revolt in Egypt; in addition, *Carausius, who since AD 288 had ruled Britain and northern Gaul, came out in open revolt. In view of the simultaneous difficulties in different areas, D. decided in AD 293 to introduce a new system of government, the tetrarchy. D. was to rule the eastern part of the empire (with *Nicomedia as his capital), assisted by a Caesar, for whom he chose his praetorian prefect, *Galerius. Maximian was designated Augustus in the West, assisted by a Caesar, *Constantius Chlorus. (Galerius and Constantius were married to the daughters of D. and Maximian respectively.) D. was still recognized as senior Augustus and, as long as D. remained in power, the new system worked. Constantius recaptured Britain in AD 297, and inflicted a heavy defeat on the Alamanni the following year. Maximian restored order in Africa in AD 297, and in the same year D. himself crushed a serious revolt in Egypt. At this time, Narses, King of Persia, drove Tiridates III out of Armenia, and Galerius, who until then operated in the Balkans, was assigned to right matters there; after an initial setback, he completely defeated the Persians, conquering Nisibis in AD 298. Roman Mesopotamia was extended to the Tigris, and Tiridates III was restored to the Armenian throne as a Roman vassal, compelling Persia to recognize the new arrangement.

The victories of D. and his colleagues established some security on the frontiers and within the empire, and the division of responsibility facilitated defence and administration. A further step was taken in a complete reorganization of the provinces, which now numbered about a hundred. The provincial governors were called *consulares*, or *praesides*, who were of the Equestrian order. Excepting Africa, Asia and Achaea, the provinces were grouped into a dozen dioceses, governed by Equestrian *vicarii* who were responsible to the four praetorian prefects. D. also set about to abolish the military powers of the provincial governors, a reform completed by *Constantine under whom there was a complete separation of military and civil powers. The army was expanded, the legions being increased to about 60. D. also carried out an extensive fortification programme in the provinces. Such building activities (including the huge baths in Rome) and the growing bureaucracy required enormous sums of money, and D. reorganized his taxation system; the units liable to taxation were the *iugum* and the *caput*, and rates were based on the *Indictio*, an assessment made every five years from AD 287 on. Payment was now mostly in kind and the state itself often made payments in kind. To facilitate taxation and secure agricultural production, *coloni* were forbidden to change their places of residence. In AD 294, D. made a comprehensive coinage reform; the new mone-

tary system included gold, silver and copper coins, and mints were established in 15 cities scattered about the empire. The new currency, however, failed to stop the transition to an economy based on kind. Another anti-inflationary measure was taken in AD 301, fixing maximum prices and wages. In general, such attempts to fight economic trends by legislation failed.

D. cultivated court ceremony in order to enhance and secure the imperial status; he was called "Iovius", and Maximian, "Herculius". The elaborate ceremony secluded the semi-divine emperor from mere mortals. D. regarded religion as a unifying factor and sought to enforce the cult of Jupiter throughout the empire. In AD 303, D. began persecuting Christians, whom he regarded as a disruptive element. In the same year, in Rome, he celebrated the twentieth year of his reign. After a severe illness, D. abdicated (AD 305) together with Maximian, and retired to his palace at Salonae. D. lived to see the collapse of the tetrarchy system and the ascendancy of Christianity. D.'s own daughter was executed in the subsequent turbulent years, and he died in AD 316. D.'s provincial reorganization essentially remained in force for many years and, with other measures, contributed to the unity of the empire; and his socio-economic legislation had far-reaching consequences on the ancient world.
Jones, *Lat. Rom. Emp.* (s.v.).

DIODORUS Alexandrian scholar of the 1st century BC, who dealt with mathematics, physics and astronomy. In his *Analemna* (on descriptive geometry), D. was probably the first to give mathematical treatment to the construction of sun-dials. Only part of the treatise has survived, in Latin and Arabic translations.

DIODORUS SICULUS Historian, native of Agyrium in Sicily in the 1st century BC. D.'s literary activity spanned the late Roman Republic and perhaps the early Principate of Augustus. D.'s *Bibliotheke* was a history of the world from the beginning to the conquest of Gaul by Caesar (54 BC); it included 40 books, of which Books 1–5 and 11–20 are extant in full, only fragments of the rest having survived. Book 1 deals with Egypt; Book 2 with Mesopotamia, India, Scythia and Arabia; Book 3 with North Africa; Books 4–6 with Greece and Europe; Books 7–17 with the period from the Trojan War to Alexander the Great; and Books 18–40 with the period from the death of Alexander to Caesar. D.'s system was to follow one particular author for each section, and the value of his work thus varies according to the source used. Among the authors D. relied upon were notably *Hecataeus, *Ctesias, *Ephorus, *Theopompus, *Timaeus, *Duris, *Hieronymus, *Polybius and *Posidonius. The arrangement of the narrative is annalistic but, apart from this, the work is essentially a compilation.
C. H. Oldfather (Loeb), 1933.

DIODOTUS Seleucid satrap of Bactria and Sogdiana, who revolted under Antiochus II, c. 255 BC. D. successfully maintained his independence, thus establishing the Greek Bactrian kingdom. D. was succeeded by his son, D. II, c. 248 BC.

DIOECESIS Under the Roman Principate, the term D. was sometimes used to designate part of a province under the command of a legate. Under the reorganization of the empire by *Diocletian, every few provinces formed a D., governed by a *vicarius*. The *vicarii* were responsible to the four praetorian prefects, and numbered 12 according to their D.s: Oriens, Pontica, Asiana, Thracia, Moesia, Pannonia, Italia, Africa, Hispania, Gallia, Viennensis and Britannia. Certain modifications were made later.

Jones, *Lat. Rom. Emp.* (s.v.).

DIOGENES (1) Greek philosopher, native of Apollonia in the 5th century BC. D. is mentioned by *Aristophanes and *Euripides. Of his "On Nature" (*peri physeos*), only seven fragments are extant. D. followed the Ionian philosophers in dealing with questions of science; he treated physics, cosmology, anatomy and physiology. Like *Anaximenes, D. maintained that air was the basic substance of all existing things, including the soul and mind. In the wake of Ionian tradition, D. held that the earth was flat and round, and, like *Anaxagoras, regarded the stars as stones.

Diels, *Fr. Vor.*, 64;

G. Burnet, *Early Greek Philosophy,* 1930.

DIOGENES (2) of Oenoanda (in Lycia) Epicurean philosopher of the 2nd century AD, known from a fragmentary inscription discovered in 188. D. himself provided the money for the inscription in order to propagate the Epicurean philosophy. The large inscription, in several fragments, covered physics, ethics, advice on old age, sayings of Epicurus, the testament of D., and a letter from a son to his mother. Some scholars ascribe the last to Epicurus, but others to D.

DIOGENES (3) of Seleucia ("of Babylon") Stoic, born *c.* 240 BC and died in 152 BC. D. was a disciple of *Chrysippus and became head of the Stoic school on the death of Zeno of Tarsus. D. came to Rome in 156/155 BC as a member of the Athenian embassy of philosophers. D. dealt with questions of grammar, rhetoric, mantics and the soul, but none of his writings has survived. *Panaetius was his pupil.

DIOGENES (4) of Sinope Greek philosopher, reputedly the first of the *Cynics. Few details of D.'s life are known with certainty, for many legends grew up about him. D. was born *c.* 400 BC and died when about 80 years old. After he and his father were accused of counterfeiting the coinage of Sinope, D. came to Athens, living there and in Corinth for the rest of his life. D. may have been a pupil of *Antisthenes and was surely influenced by his philosophical views. He is said to have expounded his principles in tragedies, but it was through his witty sayings and surprising actions that he and his doctrines gained fame. Anecdotes concerning D. were collected by his pupil Metrocles. Once, when he saw a child drinking from his hands, he threw away his cup, saying that a child had defeated him in simplicity of living. When Alexander the Great asked him what he could do for him, D. supposedly answered "Move away, you are blocking the sun". Again, when people asked him why he was going about with a lamp in broad daylight, D. replied that he was looking for a man. When D. returned from the Olympian games he said that there was a great crowd there but few men; he is also held to have said that the love of money begets all evils, that by their nature gods need nothing, god-like men need little, and that — with regard to his place of origin — he was a citizen of the world. These and other sayings, and D.'s own way of life, reveal his views: Man's happiness does not depend upon external possessions; indeed, they are but a burden; the less man is dependent upon others and material objects, the more happily he lives; the ideal is to attain self-sufficiency (*autarkeia*). Another guiding principle was to live naturally, which can be learned by observing animal behaviour; conversely, human conventions are contrary to nature and should be avoided. In accordance, D. regarded the *polis*, the traditional Greek

state, as unnecessary, as he did all social and religious customs.

D.'s appellation *Kyon* ("dog") is variously explained. Originally it was a nickname given by his enemies, but he and his followers willingly adopted it; it was probably their shamelessness, and their taking animal behaviour as analogies, that earned them the name. In his lifetime, D.'s influence on philosophy was slight, though *Theophrastus was sufficiently interested to describe his way of life. Later, however, the Stoics claimed that he was a link in the chain connecting their doctrine — through *Zeno, *Crates (D.'s pupil) and *Antisthenes — with Socrates.

Dudley, *Cynicism,* 17ff.

DIOGENES (5) LAERTIUS Author of a history of philosophy, the only extant example of its kind. Biographical details on D. are entirely lacking, but the commonly accepted supposition is that he lived in the 3rd century AD. On his own testimony, D. also wrote poetry, which has not survived. D.'s work consists of ten books; he apparently did not consult original works but relied upon earlier histories of philosophy, such as those of *Diocles of Magnesia and *Apollodorus of Athens. D.'s work is thus devoid of intrinsic value but is important in its containing much information otherwise not known. He usually names the works he uses, and the value of his evidence depends on that of his sources. In his biographical sketches, D. gives much anecdotal material which is often worthless, but some parts are of importance, such as those on the Stoics and Epicurus.

D. held that there were two main trends in the development of philosophy: that of the Ionians (the Eastern) and that of the Italians (the Western). Each trend had its succession of philosophers, according to which D. arranged his material, though he accepted that several philosophers had no successors. Following these views, Book 1 treats Archaic figures (including the Seven Wise Men); Book 2, Anaximander, Anaxagoras and Socrates; Book 3, Plato; Book 4, Plato's successors in the *Academy (up to *Clitomachus); Book 5, *Aristotle and the Peripatetic School; Book 6, *Antisthenes, *Diogenes of Sinope and the Cynics; Book 7, the Stoics (*Zeno (2), *Cleanthes and *Chrysippus); Book 8, *Pythagoras and his followers; Book 9, *Empedocles; Book 9, Heraclitus, *Xenophanes, *Zenon of Elea, *Leucippus, *Democritus, *Protagoras and *Pyrrhon; Book 10, *Epicurus.

R. D. Hicks (Loeb), 1925.

DIOMEDES (1) Hero of Greek mythology, son of *Tydeus and Deipyle. D. was connected with several myths, such as the war of the Epigoni against *Thebes, and was one of the leading Greeks in the Trojan War, where he commanded the Argive contingent of 80 ships. He fought *Aeneas, wounded Ares and Aphrodite, and killed Trojan heroes. On several occasions D. cooperated with *Odysseus; they attacked the Trojan camp, murdered *Palamedes, stole the *palladium* from Troy and persuaded *Philoctetes to come to Troy. In the games held in honour of *Patrocles, D. won the race and the javelin competition. Throughout the *Iliad*, D. appears as courageous and prudent. After the fall of Troy, D. returned to Argos, to discover the infidelity of his wife. In one version, D. (rather than his father Tydeus) went to aid his grandfather *Oeneus, king of Aetolian Calydon, who lost the throne to his brother Agrius. D. killed Agrius' sons, crowned Oeneus' son-in-law and took Oeneus with him. Because of his wife's infidelity, D. went to Italy where he helped the king of the Dauni against the

Messapii, and then married his daughter. Various stories were related of the manner of his death or disappearance. D. was worshipped in southern Italy and Umbria, and several places bore his name.

DIOMEDES (2) Latin grammarian of the 4th century AD. D.'s three-book work, *Ars Grammatica*, in which he relied upon several authors, treats prosody and metrical structure in its third book.

Keil, *Grammatici Latini*, 1.

DION Syracusan politician, brother-in-law and son-in-law of the tyrant *Dionysius I; born *c.* 409 BC. D. was much influenced by Plato, who visited Syracuse in 388 BC, and they subsequently had a close friendship. D. served under Dionysius I, acquiring a high position; in 366 BC, he persuaded *Dionysius II to invite Plato to Syracuse and, with his help, Dionysius was to become the Platonic "Philosopher King". D. was soon suspected, however, of conspiracy and was forced into exile in Greece; he returned with a small force in 357 BC, receiving support from Carthage. His following was large and D. won Syracuse from the tyrant with popular support. D. was elected supreme commander (*strategos autokrator*), but lost the support of the masses through his strong opposition to democracy and extreme social and economic reforms. D. quarreled with his assistant, Heracleides, who gained popularity after his naval victory over Philistus, commander of Dionysius II's fleet. For a time, D. went to Leontini but was recalled and brought about Heracleides' murder. D. was now in fact sole ruler of Syracuse. He was suspected of wanting to become tyrant and was murdered in 354 BC, on the initiative of Callippus, himself a pupil of Plato.

DIONE In early Greek religion, D. was probably Zeus's wife (a position later taken by *Hera). In the *Iliad*, D. already appeared as Zeus's mistress. D. was later held to be the daughter of *Uranus and Ge, and mother of Aphrodite. She continued to be venerated as Zeus's wife at *Dodona, and also had a cult at Athens.

DIONYSIA Festival with theatrical performances in honour of *Dionysus. Such festivals were first celebrated at Athens but came to be celebrated in many places. The Attic demes had D.s of their own, but the most famous was held at Athens itself in the month of Elaphebelion (March/April). This festival was instituted by *Pisistratus in the 6th century BC. Dionysus was also called "Eleuthereus" because Pisistratus brought the festival from the village of Eleutherae; at the same time a temple was built for Dionysus on the Acropolis. The theatre was rebuilt in stone, under the supervision of *Lycurgus (2). The festival started with a procession on the road to Eleutherae and then back to the temple, from which the statue of the god was taken to the theatre by the *ephebes*. Ten choruses took part in the dithyrambic contests; and tragedies, satyric plays and comedies were performed in competition, the winning poets in each class receiving prizes.

Pickard-Cambridge, *Dramatic Festivals*.

DIONYSIUS (1) I of Syracuse Born *c.* 430 BC. D. at first supported *Hermocrates, whose daughter he married (she committed suicide in 405 BC). D. rose to power in 406 BC when, at his motion, the Syracusan assembly dismissed the generals who failed to save *Acragas from the Carthaginians, and elected a new board of generals, including D. himself. In 405 BC, D. was elected *strategos autokrator*, and organized a bodyguard. The other generals lost office, and D. in fact became tyrant of Syracuse and was re-elected regularly. D. failed in his

initial operations against the Carthaginians, and had to abandon Gela and Camarina (405 BC). D. then had to suppress an oligarchic rising in Syracuse itself and in order to gain time, he signed a treaty with Carthage, on her terms. He used this respite to secure himself against further internal disturbances, recruiting mercenaries and fortifying the island of Ortygia, from which citadel he could now safely rule the city. He is also said to have enlarged the citizen-body by manumitting slaves, and he distributed the confiscated property of oligarchs to needy citizens, thus gaining popular support. At the same time, D. pursued a vigorous foreign policy, destroying Naxos in 403 BC and sending settlers to *Leontini and Catana; he also extended his rule over the native tribes of Sicily.

D. renewed war against Carthage in 398 BC with an alleged 80,000 troops; he conquered and sacked Motya, a major Carthaginian stronghold, in 397 BC, but then the very able Carthaginian general *Himilco defeated the Syracusan fleet and put the city to siege, encouraging internal dissension. D. was saved by support from Sparta, and, thanks to a plague in the Carthaginian camp, he won a complete victory over the Carthaginian army. Four years later, Carthage unsuccessfully renewed the war and, in 392 BC, signed a peace favourable to D., giving him control over three-quarters of Sicily. D.'s interest in Italy appeared as early as *c.* 398 BC, when he made an alliance with Locri. Supported by Locri and the *Lucanians, he defeated the Greeks of southern Italy (led by *Croton), at the river Elleporus in 388 BC. In 386 BC, D. destroyed *Rhegium and, in the following years, furthered his control along the Adriatic Sea, where he also despatched colonists. In 382 BC, he renewed war against Carthage and, after some initial success, suffered a heavy defeat at Cronium (near *Panormus). As a result, the river Halycus was fixed as the new frontier (*c.* 375 BC). D. again opened war in 368 BC, advancing into western Sicily to besiege Lilybaeum; however, he died during the blockade (367 BC). Under D., Syracuse experienced one of its finest periods; the economy flourished, and the tyrant seems to have enjoyed wide support. D. was a resourceful person, well balanced in time of crisis, internal and external alike, and often used unscrupulous methods. D. also cultivated literary aspirations, writing tragedies, with one of which he won the *Lenaea.

A. G. Woodhead, *The Greeks in the West*, 1962, 89ff.

DIONYSIUS (2) II Elder son of *Dionysius (1) by his wife Doris of Locri; born *c.* 397 BC. D. succeeded his father in 367 BC. Assisted by *Dion, his first act was to end the war with Carthage (366 BC). Unlike his father, D. did not possess a venturing spirit and was content with the empire left to him, seeking merely to enjoy its benefits. As a result, no enterprises were undertaken in foreign policy during most of his reign. D. considered himself a patron of culture, and wrote poetry and studied philosophy. But when Dion tried, with Plato's assistance, to make him the "Philosopher King", D. became suspicious and sent him into exile (365 BC). He re-invited Plato to Syracuse in 361 BC, but did not fulfil his promise to restore Dion, following which further cooperation between the tyrant and the philosopher came to an end. In 357 BC, D. ventured to renew colonization in southern Italy, giving Dion an opportunity to seize Syracuse. The citadel of Ortygia was taken in 355 BC, but D. managed to retain control over Locri in southern Italy and regained Syracuse in 347 BC. In 345 BC, D. again lost Syracuse to Hicetas of Leontini; though he still held Ortygia, he gave himself up to *Timoleon in 344 BC. D. went into exile in Corinth, where he remained to the end of his life, many years later.

DIONYSIUS (3) of Halicarnassus Historian, rhetor and literary critic, active in Rome from 30 BC on. D. taught in Rome until 7 BC. His writings include: "On Imitation" (*peri mimeseos*), fragments of which indicate that he made a stylistic study of the writings of individual authors to determine literary influences; a work on orators, of which the parts on Lysias, Isocrates, Isaeus and Demosthenes are extant; *peri syntheseos onomaton* (*De compositione verborum*, "On the Arrangement of Words"), an extant work which deals with the selection of words and their arrangement in sentences; "On Dinarchus"; "On Thucydides"; "Letters", two to Ammaeus dealing with Demosthenes and Thucydides, and one to Cn. Pompeius on Plato. D. wrote other treatises, not extant, one of which was a defence of rhetoric; he was a severe critic of the Asianic style — that is, the superfluous mannerism which became vogue in the Hellenistic period — preferring the old Attic orators as models. In his *Romaike Archaeologia* ("Roman Antiquities"), D. sought to exemplify his stylistic views; the original work was in 20 books, of which the first ten, part of 11 and fragments of the other books are extant. This history covered the period from the very beginning of Rome to the First Punic War; the extant parts end in 443 BC.

E. Cary, *Roman Antiquities* (Loeb), 1937–1950;
S. F. Bonner, *The Literary Treatises of Dionysius*, 1939.

DIONYSIUS (4) of Heraclea Pontica Stoic philosopher, born *c.* 328 BC. A pupil of Zeno and a prolific writer. Under the influence of severe illness, D. renounced the Stoic doctrine that pain was immaterial to happiness, and instead took on the Epicurean view that pleasure is the criterion of happy life.

DIONYSIUS (5) of Alexandria Greek grammarian, born *c.* 170 BC. Called *Thrax*, D. was the son of Teres, and a pupil of *Aristarchus. He later settled in Rhodes and taught literature and grammar. D.'s fame is due to his extant work "On Grammar", while his other works which dealt with textual interpretation in the Alexandrian manner have been lost. D.'s book is the earliest extant Greek grammar; it had much influence on subsequent grammarians of Greek and Latin and, through them, on other European grammars. Like other grammarians of his time, D. did not treat syntax. Though D. followed Alexandrian scholarship in his book, he also adopted some of the views of the Stoics on grammar. The book treats letters, syllables, accents, parts of speech and inflections.

DIONYSIUS (6) Periegetas ("guide") Probably a native of Alexandria, in Hadrian's time, D. was the author of the treatise *periegesis tes oecumenes* ("Guide of the World"), a geographical description of the earth written in hexameters (1,185 verses). Despite elementary mistakes, the work became quite popular and was probably used as a textbook for schools. D. held that the elliptic earth comprised Libya, Asia and Europe, encircled by the ocean.

DIONYSUS Greek god of vegetation, wine and uncontrolled emotions. The earliest mention of D. is in a Linear B tablet from *Pylos, of the 13th century BC. Various myths are related of D. His father was Zeus and his mother *Semele (otherwise known as Thyone); as she died before D. was born, Zeus put D. in his thigh and delivered him when he was sufficiently mature to be born. *Hera told the Titans to kill D. and, indeed, they tore him to pieces, which they boiled in a cauldron; but he was saved by his grandmother, Rhea, and resurrected. When D. grew up, his adventures carried him to Libya, Egypt, India, Phrygia, Thrace and Greece; wherever he went, people acknowledged his divinity, and those who opposed him became mad and were killed, or they were killed by their kinsmen. D.'s worship spread over the world and finally he was accepted as one of the 12 Olympian gods. D. then descended to *Tartarus and released his dead mother, who had also become an Olympian goddess. Some of the D. myths are late, such as his adventures in India, but others are very early; his encounter with Lycurgus, king of the Edonians in Thrace, is already found in the *Iliad*. Thanks to D.'s popularity, which continued in Hellenistic and Roman times, new myths and motifs grew around him.

The origins of the cult of D. are not clear; his worship seems to have spread from Thrace to Greece, though Phrygia was a second centre from which it came to Greece. Under the overwhelming influence of the ecstatic character of the Dionysiac orgies, D.'s cult expanded rapidly, especially in Boeotia and Attica. The devotees were mainly women, as is reflected in the myths about the *maenads who accompanied D. on his journey from Phrygia to Thrace and Greece; they wandered in the mountains dancing and, at the height of the ecstasy, seized boys (or foals or any other animal in a more refined version), tore them to pieces and ate them raw. In this procession, D. was accompanied by satyrs and *syleni*. It seems that there was some opposition to the introduction of this cult, but in time it came to be a state cult in many cities, as under *Periander at Corinth, under *Cleisthenes (1) at Sicyon and under *Pisistratus at Athens. When the state took control, the disorderly rites were soon limited. Many festivals were celebrated for D., such as the *Anthesteria, the *Dionysia, and the *Lenaea. Many of them were characterized by processions in which phalli were borne, and the god himself appeared in public. The origins of Greek comedy are probably to be traced to the festivities of these processions, in which those who accompanied the phallus uttered verses of mockery. Aristotle at least thought that comedy, as well as tragedy, developed from these phallic songs, and at the Dionysia in Athens there were performances of both tragedy and comedy. Masks, worn by the actors of the Greek theatre, were also characteristic of D.'s cult.

In the course of time, D. came to be known mainly as the god of wine, though this was only one of his aspects. In literature and art, D. is often associated with the wine and the drinking-horn. D. was certainly considered a god of fertility, the phallus being a dominant characteristic of his festivals; also associated with him were the fig, the pomegranate and ivy. That D. was a god of vegetation is reflected in the Phrygian myth that he slept in winter and awoke in summer. D. could significantly take various forms: a lion, serpent, bull, ram or goat. In one myth, D. hired a ship to cross to Naxos, but the sailors were pirates, who sought to sell him into slavery. Thereupon, D. turned the mast into a vine; ivy grew everywhere in the ship; the oars became serpents and he himself became a lion. The pirates leapt into the sea and became dolphins. D.'s vitality and adaptability is shown in his admittance to Delphi and in the fact that he acquired a prominent role in the Orphic cult. In Hellenistic times, new mysteries of D. developed. This new cult (under D.'s other name, Bacchus) had earlier spread to Italy, but became very popular, mainly among the lower classes, at the beginning of the 2nd century BC — so much so that the Senate ordered its suppression (186 BC). In due course, the idea of afterlife was emphasized in the Dionysiac mysteries, D.'s own resurrection in the myth presumably contributing the new concept.

D. was a favourite theme of artists and various scenes from his myths appear in many works of art; these include his birth from Zeus's thigh, the satyrs and maenads; the turning of the pirates into dolphins; and his triumphant procession.
Guthrie, *Gr. Gods*, 145ff.

DIOPHANTUS Greek mathematician at Alexandria, of uncertain date, but not later than the 3rd century AD. Several of D.'s works are known; the *porismata* (propositions on the theory of numbers), "On Polygonal Numbers", and *Arithmetica*. Of the first nothing has remained except several quotations; there is a fragment of the second, and six of the thirteen books of the third are extant, in which D. comes nearer to the conceptions of modern algebra than any other Greek mathematician. The latter book in fact consists of groups of problems, chiefly indeterminate equations; much of this probably stems from Babylonia. For his numbers, D. employs symbols: *Mo* stands for *monades* (units of the determinated number); *S.* stands for *arithmos* (the unknown quantity of *monades*), $\wedge$ denotes *minus*, and he also had symbols for the powers. Solutions to the problems are given in positive numbers.
T. L. Heath, *Diophantus of Alexandria*[2], 1910.

DIOSCORIDES (1) Greek poet from Alexandria, of the second half of the 3rd century BC. D.'s extant epigrams, some 40, reveal that he followed *Callimachus and *Leonidas (2). They deal with various themes, some treat Eastern cults (for example, of Cybele or Adonis), others poets (old, like Sappho, and contemporaneous), and many are love poems.

DIOSCORIDES (2) of Samos Mosaic artist. Two of D.'s works, signed by him, have been found in a villa at *Pompeii, dating from the 1st century BC; they depict scenes from New Comedy.

DIOSCORIDES (3) PEDANIUS Physician of the 1st century AD, under Claudius and Nero. His work in five books, *peri hyles iatrikes* (*Materia medica* in Latin), concerns medicine. Another work, once regarded as spurious, is *haplon pharmakon*, in two books. D.'s drugs and medicines are derived from various sources: animal, vegetable and mineral. With his extensive experience, D. showed interest in precise details and there was no place for magic and superstition in his work. The book became very popular and was translated into many languages, remaining a standard text till the beginning of the modern era. Some of the old manuscripts have excellent illustrations.
M. Wellmann, *Materia Medica* (text), 1907–1914;
R. T. Gunther, *The Greek Herbal of Dioscorides*, 1934..

DIOSCURI ("sons of Zeus") Castor and Polydeucus (Pollux), twin brothers, sons of *Tyndareus. The myths associated with them present different data concerning both their parentage and their adventures. The D. were also known as the Tyndaridae. According to Homer and Hesiod, Tyndareus was their father but later versions say that Polydeucus and *Helen were born to *Leda from Zeus, while Castor and *Clytemnestra were Tyndareus' children. A later version reports that they were born from an egg. When the D. grew up, Polydeucus became the best pugilist and Castor was an excellent fighter and horseman; both were said to have won prizes at the Olympic games. The D. volunteered to accompany *Jason on his search for the Golden Fleece and when King Amycus, the boxer,

challenged the *Argonauts to a match, Polydeucus fought and killed him. Another of the D.'s exploits was to rescue their sister Helen when, a mere child, she was carried away by Theseus. The D. took as wives the daughters of Leucippus, who had been betrothed to their cousins, *Idas and Lynceus (who had also accompanied Jason). In one version, all four participated in a cattle-raid in Arcadia, and quarreled about division of the booty; Castor was killed, but his brother killed the other two. Another version had Idas and Lynceus attacking Sparta and killing Castor; Polydeucus subsequently took vengeance on them. Still another version has Castor killed later. In any event, Polydeucus was carried to heaven after Castor's death, and asked to share his immortality with his brother. From then on the D. lived in heaven and the netherworld on alternate days. For their brotherly loyalty, the D.'s images were set among the stars by Zeus, as the constellation Gemini.

The D. were worshipped in many places: Boeotia, Athens, Argos, Sparta, Messene, Cyrene, Sicily, Rome and Etruria; the cult was especially typical of Dorian states. At Sparta their symbol was the *docana*, two parallel wooden rods connected by two cross-beams; another symbol was made of two amphorae entwined by a serpent. When the Spartan army went to war, its royal commanders took the *docana* with them. The D. were considered the protectors of sailors, whom they would hasten to save, accompanied by sparrows. The D. often appeared to aid contenders in decisive battles. Thus they were believed to have fought with the Spartans several times, with the fleet at Aegospotamoi, with the Locrians at the Sagra river when they defeated the Crotonians who outnumbered them; and with the Romans at the Battle of Lake Regillus, at the Battle of Pydna and at Verona against the Cimbri. The introduction of their cult into Latium occurred quite early, no later then the end of the 6th century BC, as is evident from an inscription found at Lavinium. According to Roman tradition, a temple was dedicated to them in the Forum in 486 BC, for their part in the battle of Lake Regillus. At Rome, the D. were usually called *Castores* and their temple, *aedes Castoris*; they were especially associated with the Equites.

The cult of the twins was known among several ancient peoples – Celts, Germans and Indians – which has led some scholars to suggest a common Archaic origin (the Sanskrit Açvins are connected with horses, like the *Castors*). The D. would appear to have originally been heroes who, owing to their popularity, were deified in the course of time. Another theory has it that they were originally gods who lost their divine character in mythology, like their sister Helen. Artists took themes from the myths of the D., from the 6th century BC on.
Farnell, *Hero-Cults*, 175ff.

DIPHILUS of Sinope One of the three major playwrights of New Comedy (along with *Menander and *Philemon), born no later than 350 BC. D. usually lived at Athens, and died early in the 3rd century BC at Smyrna, but was buried at Athens where his tombstone has been found. None of his 100-odd plays has survived. Sixty of the titles are known, and there are some 130 fragments. D. won competitions at *Lenaea three times. Several of *Plautus' plays were, in fact, Latin adaptations of D.'s works (*Rudens, Casina*, the now-lost *Commorientes* and perhaps *Vidularia*). Some of D.'s plays have mythological characters for their titles (*Theseus, Danaides* and *Lemniae*); one play deals with Sappho, whose suitors are Archilochus and Hipponax, which is an impossible combination on chronological grounds. Other historical characters figure in the titles of his plays, such as Amastris and Tithraustes. The *Hairesiteiches* may have referred to Demetrius Poliorcetes; this play was rewritten and renamed *Stratiotes*. At times, D. seems to refer to actual persons. D. apparently had a sense for theatrical effects and sharp characterization.

T. B. L. Webster, *Studies in Later Greek Comedy*, 1953 (s.v.).

DIPLOMA A duplicate copy, in particular the *diploma militare*. This consisted of two bronze tablets given to soldiers of the **Auxilia*, from the time of the Emperor Claudius, and to officially discharged soldiers of the praetorian and urban cohorts from Vespasian on. The D. was sent by the office *a diplomatibus*, while the original list was kept in Rome. The document confirmed the honourable discharge of a soldier, the legalization of his marriage (*conubium*), and, if he was a non-citizen, as most of the auxiliaries were, the granting of the Roman citizenship to him and his children. From about the time of *Antoninus Pius, children ceased to receive Roman citizenship. Except for a few exceptions, veteran legionaries did not receive the *diploma militare*. More than 200 examples have been found, the latest dating from the early 4th century. Their texts are in CIL XVI 1936.

DITHYRAMB Greek lyrical song performed by a chorus in honour of Dionysus. It is first mentioned by *Archilochus (fr. 77), who says that he knows how to lead others in singing the dithyramb, the song of Dionysus. It appears that the chorus moved in procession while singing it. However, the origins of the word, probably non-Hellenic, and the origins of the D. are far from clear. Herodotus says that at the court of *Periander (*c.* 600 BC), the poet Arion was the first to write, give a name to and sing a D. (1.23); in other words, the D. came to be a literary form dealing with one theme. It was later introduced in Athens, where public competitions of D. were held at the festival of Dionysus from 509 BC. Such famous poets as *Bacchylides, *Pindar and *Simonides took part in these competitions; the latter won 56 prizes. At this stage it apparently had the regular strophe and antistrophe structure and dealt in a narrative manner with mythological themes. From *c.* 470 on, the musical aspect was emphasized, the strophe-antistrophe structure was discontinued, and solo-songs were included. At the same time there began the tendency to use pompous, elaborate language. D. competitions were held in other places apart from Athens where it lasted into the imperial age.

Pickard-Cambridge, *Dithyramb*[2].

DOBUNNI A British tribe. Their chief town Corinum (Cirencester) was originally a military fortress. The native inhabitants were ruled by Belgic conquerors.

Frere, *Britannia* (s.v.).

DODONA Famous oracular centre in Epirus. The sanctuary there dates from remote antiquity and in pre-Hellenic times belonged to *Gaea, who was ousted by *Zeus (under the cult-name Naios) and *Dione. In the *Iliad*, the prophets there are called *selloi*. The place had a sacred oak and a dove, through which the oracles were said to have originally been delivered. Herodotus speaks of Egyptian connections with D. and relates that in his time the replies were reported by three prophetesses; these were called *peleiades* ("doves"). The supplicants would write down their questions on pieces of lead, which

were put in a jar. A considerable number of these leaden pieces have been found in the excavations on the site. D. retained its influence for many centuries, and even its sack by the Aetolians (219 BC) was only a temporary setback. The subjugation of Epirus and the enslavement of its population by Rome (167 BC) led to its decline, though it continued as a religious centre until the 3rd century AD.

H. W. Parke, *The Oracles of Zeus*, 1967.

DOLABELLA, Publius Cornelius The most famous member of his family, of the Cornelii clan, a member of which first rose to the consulate in 283 BC. D. was probably born in 79 BC; he made his first public appearance in 50 BC, unsuccessfully prosecuting Ap. *Claudius (4) Pulcher, then a candidate for the censorship. At that time, D. married Tullia, Cicero's daughter. D. followed Caesar in the Civil War, taking part in the main battles at Pharsalus, Thapsus and Munda. He was heavily indebted and, as plebeian tribune in 47 BC, introduced a bill for the cancellation of debts. His colleagues opposed him as did Antony, but D. was able to retain the goodwill of Caesar and against Antony's opposition, Caesar decided to make him suffect consul before departing on his Parthian expedition. After Caesar's murder, Antony dropped his opposition and D. became consul. At first he showed signs of cooperation with the Republicans, but Antony shared with him the public funds and Caesar's fortune which he had seized and they made common cause. D. was appointed governor of Syria for five years; he left Rome in October 44 BC, without paying his debts (including the dowry he received from Tullia, who had died in 45 BC). D. arrived in Asia in January 43 BC and treacherously killed Trebonius, who had taken part in the conspiracy against Caesar and was governor of the province. After news of this deed reached Rome, D. was declared a "public enemy". *Cassius (3) besieged him in Laodicea and, when D. could no longer resist, he committed suicide.

Syme, *Rom. Rev.* (s.v.).

DOLICHENUS, Jupiter The local Baal of Doliche (Tell Duluk, in Commagene) was identified with Jupiter and became known as *Iuppiter Optimus Maximus*; he was a god of thunder and lightning, as well as of fertility. D.'s consort was identified with Juno. Under the Roman Empire, D. became popular among slaves, traders and especially soldiers. In the 2nd and 3rd centuries AD, D.'s cult spread to Rome and the western provinces; his temple on the Aventine was discovered in 1835. With the extension of his cult, D. was recognized as god of the entire world, who could bring security and military success. On monuments, D. stands on a bull holding a double axe in his right hand and a thunderbolt and lightning in his left; his consort is depicted as standing on a cow or a lioness.

P. Menrat, *Jupiter Dolichenus*, 1960.

DOMITIAN, Titus Flavius Younger son of *Vespasian, born on 24 October AD 54. D. accompanied his father to *Judaea in AD 67, but was in Rome in AD 69 when Vespasian was proclaimed emperor. D. managed to escape the Vitallians and, when Vitellius was murdered, he was hailed by the soldiers as Caesar in Rome. D. was named praetor with consular powers for AD 70 and sought to take control of the administration which, in fact, was under Antonius *Primus and *Mucianus. When Vespasian reached Rome, D. lost all real power and his dream to conduct a campaign in Germany came to nought. As Vespasian adopted a dynastic policy, and *Titus was childless, D. was destined to succeed his brother; yet he had no important share in the government of the empire despite his two ordinary consulships, five suffect consulships and other offices.

D. was named *consors* and *successor imperii* on 23 June AD 79, and became emperor on 13 September AD 81, on the death of Titus. Almost throughout his reign, D. showed concern to secure the frontiers of the empire and at the same time sought to win the military glory he was denied under his father and brother. The main military problems lay in the Danubian and Rhine frontiers. From AD 83 on, D. fought the *Chatii and won a victory which enabled him to occupy Mount Taunus, extending the frontier, which he fortified, from the Main to the Neckar. After this achievement he took the surname Germanicus and celebrated a triumph. This, however, was followed by Dacian victories over Roman armies. Late in AD 85, the governor of Moesia, C. Oppius Sabinus, was defeated and killed, and the situation was sufficiently critical to warrant the presence of the emperor himself. D. found it expedient to divide Moesia into two provinces, Upper and Lower, and to strengthen his troops there; the actual fighting was conducted by the praetorian prefect, Cornelius Fuscus. D. apparently thought the war was over and returned to Rome to celebrate a triumph, but sometime later, probably in AD 87, Fuscus was defeated and killed by *Decebalus. D. was compelled to return and restore order in the Roman army; and in AD 88, the

Romans won a crushing victory over Decebalus at Tapae. Strategical considerations led D. to make peace with Decebalus, who was given formal recognition as king and received a subsidy. (The peace lasted until *Trajan attacked and annexed Dacia.) In the following years, D. had to deal with attacks of the *Marcomanni and *Quadi in Pannonia. In AD 92, he conducted war against the Sarmatians and the Jazygi and, despite several reverses, these wars — in which D. often took part in person — served to strengthen Roman positions along the frontiers in Central Europe from the Black Sea to the Rhine. Significant advances were made for the empire by *Agricola in Britain, in the early years of D.'s reign; Agricola was recalled in AD 84, but this was probably not due to D.'s jealousy, as Tacitus alleges. After six years of service, and in view of his achievements, it was only normal that Agricola should have been replaced.

D. carried out extensive building operations, including a palace on the Palatine, a new temple to Jupiter on the Capitol (after that of Vespasian had burned down, in AD 80), a temple to Jupiter Custos on the Quirinal, a temple to Vespasian, a temple to Isis and Serapis in the *Campus Martius, and his own luxurious villa in the Alban hills. Other heavy expenditure was incurred by the increase of legionary pay, from 300 to 400 denarii per annum, by the prolonged wars and by D.'s generosity to the people. To make up the necessary funds, D. enforced severe and comprehensive tax collection. D.'s concern for economic

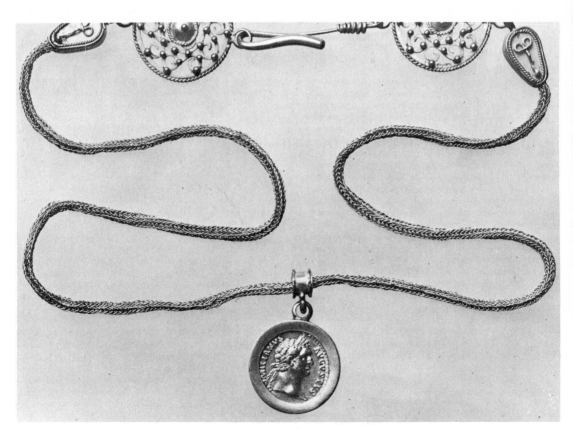

Gold necklace with a Domitian coin pendant

Diomedes in the chariot-race for Patroclus (lower part), and the Calydonian Boar-hunt (upper part). Details from the Francois Vase (c. 510 BC)

Etruscan warrior. Bronze statue from c. 450 BC

problems is seen in the prohibition on the planting of new vineyards, a measure directed to assist Italian agriculture. From his accession on, D. kept strict control of the government of the empire, which brought about efficient and just provincial administration. He also tried to improve the morals of the higher society of Rome, and executed several Vestal Virgins who had been accused of unchastity, but this policy proved unpopular.

Under D., the Principate became an autocracy and, in this respect, he followed Gaius and Nero though in their case the absolutist policy could be ascribed to disturbed, unbalanced personalities. D. held the consulate ten times and, from AD 85 on, was *censor perpetuus*. D. was accompanied by 24 lictors, the traditional number for a dictator; he allowed himself to be called *dominus et deus*, probably unofficially, thus approaching deification. These actions, and the fact that D. would come to the Senate in the dress of *triumphator*, aroused strong senatorial opposition; D., however, showed no respect for the senatorial order, enrolling many new men from the Equestrian class and the provinces into the Senate, which seldom consulted and had little say in imperial matters. The revolt of L. Antonius Saturninus, governor of Upper Germany, in AD 88, though quickly suppressed, was a turning point. D. became suspicious, and the way was open for accusations of *maiestas* (high treason) against innocent persons and real plotters alike. Philosophers, especially Stoics and Cynics, whose teachings of the ideal good ruler were directed against the existing regime, were twice banished from Italy. Many of the leading aristocracy were executed, and a reign of terror began. In AD 95, D. executed his relative Flavius Clemens, whose sons had been D.'s supposed heirs until then. It now seemed that no one was safe from D.'s suspicions, and in AD 96 a conspiracy in cooperation with Domitia, the emperor's wife (and daughter of *Corbulo) and the two praetorian prefects was hatched. D. was murdered on 18 September AD 96. The hatred of the Senate was immediately expressed in the decree of *damnatio memoriae* against D., that is, his official *acta* were annulled, his statues destroyed and his name erased from inscriptions. D. had no children and nominated no heir at the time of his death. Thus, the Senate appointed his successor, *Nerva.

Suet, *Dom.*; Syme, *Tacitus* (s.v.).

DOMITIUS (1) AHENOBARBUS, Gnaeus D.'s homonymous grandfather was the first member of the family to be elected consul (192 BC). He himself was consul in 122 BC and as proconsul in Transalpine Gaul won victories over the Allobroges and Arverni, winning a triumph. The Via Domitia, from the Rhone to Spain, was named in his honour. As censor in 115 BC, D. and his colleague expelled 32 senators from the Senate. He died *c.* 104 BC.

DOMITIUS (2) AHENOBARBUS, Gnaeus Son of *Domitius (1). He took part in the colonization of *Narbo. As plebeian tribune in 104 BC, D. unsuccessfully prosecuted *Scaurus (1), whom he considered responsible for his not succeeding his father as Pontifex. D. passed a law by which election to the four main colleges of priests was by 17 tribes, chosen by lot, instead of the former system of cooption by the colleges themselves. The following year, he was elected Pontifex Maximus, and, in 96 BC, was consul. As censor (with L. Licinius *Crassus) in 92 BC, he issued an edict against Latin rhetors.

DOMITIUS (3) AHENOBARBUS, Gnaeus Son of Lucius *Domitius (4). He was captured by Caesar at Corfinium in 49 BC but, like his father, was pardoned; he may have

been one of the conspirators against Caesar and, after the murder, followed *Brutus (2). He was given command of the Republican fleet in the Adriatic and won a victory; he was able to maintain his force after Philippi and, in 40 BC, was reconciled with Antony. D.'s proscription was annulled, and he was governor of Bithynia in 40–34 BC; in 32 BC, he was consul but, soon after his entering office, fled with his colleague Sosius to Antony. D. could not, however, agree to Cleopatra's presence in Antony's camp, and joined Octavian before the battle of Actium. He died of fever soon after. His son married the daughter of Antony, and their grandson was the future emperor Nero.

DOMITIUS (4) AHENOBARBUS, Lucius Son of Gnaeus *Domitius (2). He made an enormous fortune during the proscriptions of *Sulla, despite his youth. In the following years, D. was active in the courts and in 70 BC supported *Verres. With *Cato (2) (whose sister he married), D. opposed Pompey and later Caesar; his hostility to the "Triumvirate" cost him the consulate of 55 BC, which Pompey and Crassus won. This was a severe blow to him, considered, as he was, to be destined to the consulate from the cradle. D. was consul in 54 BC, but took no province at the end of his office; he was nominated by the Senate to succeed Caesar as governor of Gaul, in 49 BC, and followed Pompey in the Civil War, during which he enlisted his clients and tenants into his army. Caesar captured him at Corfinium, but let him go free. He went to Massilia, to defend it against Caesarian forces, but fled before its fall; he was killed at the Battle of *Pharsalus.

DOMUS AUREA ("Golden House") The magnificent complex of buildings and gardens built by *Nero after the great fire of Rome (AD 64). It extended over the valley between the Palatine, the Caelian and the Oppian. A colossal bronze statue of Nero stood at its entrance. After Nero's death many of the buildings were destroyed. The *Colosseum was built on part of the D. Impressive remains are still extant.

Platner-Ashby, *Top. Dict. Rome* (s.v.).

DONATUS, Aelius Latin grammarian of the 4th century AD. Two of his grammatical works are extant: *Ars minor* treats eight parts of speech, and *Ars maior*, intended for advanced pupils, deals with further material. Commentaries on D.'s works were written and they were used extensively in schools in the Middle Ages. A compilation of D.'s commentary on Terence is extant. Only the preface, *vita* ("Life") and introduction to the *Eclogues* of his commentary to Virgil are extant. (This commentary appears to be identical with what is known as Servius Danielis; see *Servius.) One of his pupils was St. Jerome.

DORIANS Large Greek tribal group, the last to invade Greece. The once accepted view that the D. destroyed the communities of the Mycenean world *c.* 1200 BC is now disputed; it seems more likely that the D. entered Greece during the 11th century BC, in the wake of the so-called "Sea-Peoples" who shattered the Mycenaean world about 1200 BC. Until then, the D. had probably inhabited the northwest of Greece — Epirus and Dalmatia. In Greek mythology, the D.'s migration is reflected in the story of the return of the *Heraclidae, according to which legend they passed Doris, Delphi and Naupactus on their route, and settled mainly in the Peloponnesus. The D. later established themselves in some of the Aegean islands, in southern Asia Minor and in Crete, and later sent colonies to southern Italy and Sicily. The D.'s occupation of the Peloponnesus was a prolonged process.

Communities of D. were characterized by a triple tribal

organization: the Hylleis, Dymanes and Pamphyloi. The more important communities of D. in Greece were Megara, Corinth, Sicyon, Epidaurus, Aegina and Sparta; of the overseas settlements, mention may be made of Rhodes, Melos, Thera, Syracuse, Acragas, Messana and Tarentum. In most places intermixture and equalization of the D., as conquerors, with the former population gradually took place. In Sparta and Crete, the D. developed special institutions to secure their political, economic and social superiority.

DORIS Small country in northern central Greece, around the source of the river Cephissus; it had four small towns: Pindus, Boeum, Cytinun and Erineus. In historic times, it was considered by the *Dorians as their place of origin. From early times, D. was a member of the Delphic Amphictiony. In the 4th century BC, it was controlled by Onomarchus and then by Philip II, and in the 3rd century BC it belonged to the Aetolian League.

DRACO Reputedly the first lawgiver of Athens, who made his reforms c. 624–620 BC. Most of what the Athenians of the 5th and 4th centuries BC knew and wrote about him cannot be authentic. That D. gave Athens a new constitution, or carried out a comprehensive codification, is doubtful, but it seems quite certain that he did introduce new measures, especially in the field of the law concerning murder, aimed at putting an end to the blood-feud. A new element was that the laws were committed to writing and displayed in public on special tablets. The laws came to be regarded as harsh and severe, and hence D.'s law was said to have been written in blood, not ink. Death was the ordinary punishment under D.'s law and no doubt in later times this penalty was considered as unnecessarily extreme. Some of D.'s measures were still in force in the late 5th century BC.
Hignett, *Athen. Const.* (s.v.).

DREPANA (modern Trapani) Coastal town in western Sicily, established by Carthage. It was there that the Romans suffered their only naval defeat in the First Punic War, in 249 BC.

DRUSILLA, Julia Second daughter of *Germanicus and Agrippina, born c. AD 16. D. was present at her father's triumph (AD 17). Her first husband was L. Cassius Longinus, consul in AD 30, and in AD 38 she was married to M. Aemilius Lepidus. D.'s brother, *Caligula, was extremely fond of her, and was said to have committed incest with her. After her death in AD 38, D. was consecrated as Panthea.

DRUSUS (1), Marcus Livius Roman statesman, who first gained fame as a plebeian tribune in 122 BC, when he opposed Gaius *Gracchus by demagogic means. It is disputed whether D.'s proposals to establish 12 large colonies, and to exempt Latins from corporal punishment by Roman magistrates, were carried out. Partly as a result of D.'s activity, Gracchus failed to rewin the tribunate. D. was consul in 112 BC, and won military success as governor of Macedonia, for which he was awarded a triumph. D. died in 109 BC.

DRUSUS (2), Marcus Livius Roman statesman, son of Marcus Livius *Drusus (1). A wealthy man with good oratorial education and talent, D. in association with L. *Crassus (3), created a well-organized clientele in his political career. In 100 BC, D. was active against *Saturninus. His main political activity, however, was as tribune in 91 BC, when he sought solutions to the main political problems of the time. D.'s programme included the following bills: distribution of land and large-scale colonization to provide subsistence for the Roman proletariat; extension of Roman citizenship to the Italian allies of Rome; enrolment of 300 Equites to the Senate and the transfer of the criminal courts to the senators. Whether D. intended to attain a compromise between the Senate and the Equestrian order, or to enhance the Senate's supremacy, is disputed; he met, however, with strong opposition from the Equites who refused to surrender control of the courts, from senators who did not want the influx of Equites into the Senate, and from personal enemies such as his former brother-in-law, Caepio. So long as Crassus could give him his support, D. was successful in passing his bills; after Crassus died, however, the consul Marcius Philippus dominated the Senate, which subsequently invalidated D.'s laws. D. was murdered in his own house, and the failure of his programme led the Italian allies to revolt.

DRUSUS (3), Nero Claudius Born in 38 BC, son of Tiberius Claudius Nero, who was active against Octavian in the late 40s BC. D.'s mother was Livia who, while pregnant with D., was divorced by her husband and married Octavian; his elder brother was the future emperor *Tiberius. D. was quaestor in 18 BC. In 15 BC, D. and his brother Tiberius conquered and organized the province of Raetia; in 13 BC, he was appointed governor of the three provinces of Gaul, and carried out a census there. D.'s claim to fame rests on his military campaigns in Germany in 12–9 BC. In the first season he foiled an attack of the Sugambii and carried the war into the territories of the Frisii, Bructeri and *Chauci; this was made possible by digging a canal to connect the Lower Rhine with the North Sea through the lakes of Holland. In 11 BC, D. was urban praetor in Rome, but returned to continue Roman expansion; he conquered the Usipetes and advanced to the territory of the *Cherusci at the Wesser. For his victories, D. was awarded an *ovatio* (lesser triumph). As proconsul in 10 BC, D. resumed the offensive by attacking the Chatii; in 9 BC, he was consul and fought the Suebii, Chatii, *Marcomanni and Cherusci, advancing as far as the Elbe. This could have been the beginning of the conquest of that country had not D. died after a fall from a horse. His brother Tiberius brought his corpse to Rome, where D. was buried in the mausoleum of Augustus. For his victories, D. and his descendants were granted the appellation of Germanicus. D. married Antonia, second daughter of Antony and Octavia, and had three children: *Germanicus, Livilla and *Claudius (the future emperor). D. was very popular and many writers contrasted him (and his son Germanicus) to his unpopular brother, Tiberius.

DRUSUS (4), Julius Caesar Son of *Tiberius and his first wife Vipsania, born c. 14 BC. When Augustus adopted Tiberius, in AD 4, he forced him to adopt his nephew *Germanicus, who thus was given priority in imperial succession. Yet relations between the cousins remained good, and D. married Livilla, Germanicus' sister. D. was quaestor in AD 11, but his first real commission came in AD 14, when he quelled the revolt of the Pannonian army. In AD 15, D. was consul throughout the year and in AD 17–20 governor of Illyricum. For his achievements there, D. was awarded a triumph and in AD 21 was again consul. The following year D. received the *tribunicia potestas*, which marked him as successor of Tiberius. Sejanus, however, seduced his wife and with her help caused his death by poisoning (AD 23).

DUCETIUS A Sicel of the 5th century BC, who received

Greek education and sought political independence for his people. D. took advantage of Syracuse's weakness after *Hiero I's death in 467 BC to unite the native Sicels and in 464 BC helped Syracuse to rid itself of mercenaries. Some time later, D. made Menaeum his capital, taking the title "King of the Sicels". D. expanded his control in eastern Sicily, winning a success against Syracuse and Acragas. In 450 BC, however, D. was defeated, but was allowed to go to Corinth. He returned *c.* 447 BC to found Cale Acte on the northern coast and died in 440 BC.

A. G. Woodhead, *The Greeks in the West,* 1962, 82f.

DUILIUS, Gaius Roman general and politician, prominent in the First Punic War. D. was consul in 260 BC and was given command of the first large Roman fleet; he routed the experienced Carthaginian fleet off Mylae by employing a new tactic, the essence of which was to board enemy ships after grappling them with the *corvus* ("grapnel"). D. was the first Roman to be given a naval triumph; the *rostra* ("prows") of the captured ships ornamented a column built in the Forum to commemorate the victory. There is extant a copy of the original inscription inscribed on the column. D. used his booty to build a temple to Janus. D. was censor in 258 BC and still alive in 231 BC, when he was appointed dictator, to hold elec-

DURA-EUROPOS Macedonian military settlement with Greek and native populations, established on the Middle Euphrates by *Seleucus I at the end of the 4th century BC. D. maintained its Greek character though in time the Oriental elements became increasingly influential. In the first half of the 2nd century BC, D. was occupied by the Parthians; it was conquered by Trajan when he invaded Mesopotamia, but was evacuated by Hadrian. Under Marcus Aurelius, in AD 165, D. was again conquered, remaining under Roman control until its destruction by the Sassanids, soon after AD 257. D. enjoyed economic prosperity, thanks to agriculture and commerce, lying, as it did, on the caravan route to Syria. Extensive excavations on the site have brought numerous remains to light, including private and public buildings, a Roman camp, papyri and inscriptions. The many works of art found, notably frescoes and reliefs, have proved most important for the study of many aspects of ancient religion as well as ancient art.

M. Rostovtzeff, *Dura-Europus and its Art,* 1938.

DURIS (1) Athenian potter and painter, active in the first half of the 5th century BC. Some 40 of D.'s signed vases are known; in all but two he appears as painter. D. had many followers and some of his vases are outstanding, such as the "Cantharus." (in Brussels) and the "Eos and Memnon" (in Paris).

Fresco from the Synagogue of Dura-Europes

DURIS (2) Tyrant of Samos, born *c.* 340 BC and died in 260 BC. D. studied under the prolific philosopher *Theophrastus and wrote on various subjects: history (Greek, Macedonian and Samian, and on *Agathocles); literature (on Homer, Euripides and Sophocles and on tragedy); music and painting.

DUUMVIRI (DUOVIRI) Many two-member boards existed in Rome and in the Roman Empire. Most notable were: *D. navales*, first elected in 311 BC to maintain and command the fleet defending the Italian coast, and occasionally thereafter elected until the mid-2nd century BC; *D. sacris faciundis*, instituted to supervise the Sibylline books and foreign cults (their number was raised to ten, half Plebeians, in 367 BC, and later, probably under Sulla, to 15); *D. perduellionis*, responsible for cases of high treason; and the two highest magistrates in Roman colonies and *municipia* under the Empire.

Jolowicz, *Roman Law*[3] (s.v.).

E

EBURACUM (modern York) A Roman legionary camp on the east bank of the Ouse. It was established when *Cerialis was governor of Britannia (AD 71–74), and was rebuilt several times. Severus, who died here in AD 211, fortified it in AD 197. The civil settlement that grew on the other bank received the status of *colonia* before AD 237. It suffered some destruction under Allectus but was rebuilt by Constantius Chlorus, who died here in AD 306. E. was the residence of the governor of lower Britain.
Frere, *Brittania* (s.v.).

ECHIDNA In Greek mythology, a monster whose parents were Phorcys and Ceto or Tartarus and Ge (and there were also other versions). She was half-woman and half-serpent. She lived with Typhon and bore him more monsters: Orthus, Cerberus, Hydra, and Chimaera; also the Theban Sphinx and the Nemean lion. She appears on Archaic vases.

ECHO A nymph who entertained Hera with long stories so that Zeus could make love with the other nymphs. As punishment for this, she could no longer use her voice but only repeat what others uttered. She fell in love with *Narcissus, who rejected her. She pined away with sorrow and only her voice remained. In another version, Pan let her be torn to pieces by herdsmen when she did not yield to his courtship. These pieces lie in various spots under the earth where they still resound.

EDESSA (1) The ancient capital city of Macedonia, situated on what was later the *Via Egnatia, at a good spot on the route from the plain to upper Macedonia. It was renamed Aegae. At the end of the 5th century, *Pella became the residence of the king though E. still remained an important centre.
S. Casson, *Macedonia, Thrace,* and *Illyria,* 1926.

EDESSA (2) (modern Urfa) The capital city of *Osroene in northwest Mesopotamia. It was founded by *Seleucus I and was named after E. (1) above. After the disintegration of the Seleucid Empire, Parthia and Rome disputed the control of E. It suffered damage in AD 116 when it was captured by the army of Trajan. Again conquered by Rome in AD 165, it was subsequently made a Roman colony. Later, the Sassanids occasionally captured E. and ruled it. Christianity made progress here quite early and the E. bishopric became the most important one in Syria.
Jones, *Cities*[2].

EDICTUM On taking office, Roman magistrates (holders of *Imperium, aediles, quaestors and censors) made public the rules by which they would carry out their duties.

The right to proclaim was the *ius edicendi*, the method of publication was by exhibiting the E. on a whitened table in a public place, at Rome in the Forum. Every magistrate was free to define for himself these administrative regulations, and was not legally bound by those of his predecessor. In practice, the officials sought legal advice and normally confirmed and perpetuated former measures. The more important edicts were those of the *praetor urbanus* and the provincial governor. As the former was the magistrate responsible for jurisdiction between citizens, the rules he included in his edict determined to a great extent the way justice was administered. It was by these rules that the praetors came to deal with matters not covered by the *ius civile, and to introduce new actions and *formulae*. The praetorian edict created thus a new body of law (*ius honorarium* or *praetorium*) differing from the *ius civile* and characterized by more flexibility. This development came to an end under Hadrian, at whose initiative the jurist Salvius *Julianus published a revised and final edition of the praetorian edict (*c*. AD 130). The provincial edict was of prime importance to the provincials. It included rules concerning the administration of justice (e.g. the maximum legal rate of interest) as well as the execution of their duties to the Roman state (e.g. the collection of the tithe, *Decuma, in Sicily). See *Law (with bibliography), Salvius *Julianus.

EDUCATION, GREEK In the Mycenaean civilization, an intellectual education was apparently given only to the upper class, as may be deduced from the tales about *Chiron, and it probably consisted of some training in speaking and music. Presumably physical and military training were also given; and as writing and poetry existed, there must have been technical education in these arts, but only within a narrow, professional group. Because writing was used only in the administrative centres of the kingdoms, their destruction seems to have ended this practice. However, oral poetry persisted, and its final products were the poems of *Homer and the *Epic cycle.

Organized educational institutions seem to have developed first in Dorian states in Crete and Sparta. The public *gymnasium is said to have existed in Crete in early times, but was for men over 17, while basic education in reading, music and civics was given at home. The aim of the gymnasium was mainly to train the youths to be good soldiers. More is known of the state education of Sparta where children left home at the age of 7, lived in hard conditions, and organized in groups. Each group was under the command of an *eiren*, a youth of 16 to 20 years old, and first priority was given to athletics and physical education, with only elementary instruction in reading, writing and music. Severe discipline was maintained, and the corporal punishment was harsh. The boys ate small quantities of simple food in communal meals. They also received military training. From the age of 16, they became *eirenes* and before completing their training they had to prove themselves in several tests. The whole system aimed at making them good soldiers and citizens, and indeed Sparta came to have the best army in Greece from the 6th to the 4th century. Girls, too, received training in athletics, in addition to dancing, singing and music.

In other Greek states education remained private until the Hellenistic period. It is not clear in what way laws, referred to in Plato *Critias* 50 compelled parents to give their children training in music and gymnastics. Scattered references suggest that schools and elementary education possibly spread from the 7th century and were probably well established in Ionia, Athens and elsewhere by the early 5th century. Elementary education consisted of two main branches, *mousike* and *gymnastike*, which could be completed in the same school. The first was taught by two different teachers, the *grammatistes* and the *kitharistes*. The first instructed their pupils in reading, in writing and, at a later stage, in literature and in arithmetic. According to Plato, writing and reading are to be acquired in three years. The study of poetry was considered as good training in morals; but Homer, the chief poet studied, was severely criticized by Plato in this respect. The teacher would explain the works and the pupils mainly learnt long passages by heart. Teaching was either of individuals or in groups. The *kitharistes* taught music in the narrow sense, mainly how to play the lyre, sometimes the pipe. Music was considered to have good influence on the temper. Gymnastics and sports were taught by the *paidotribes*. There were contradictory views on the possibility of attaining harmony between physical training and intellectual education, the great philosophers Plato and Aristotle giving first priority to the latter. Girls were occasionally taught to read and write but normally were trained to be good housewives. ("Pedagogue" is derived from the Greek word *paidagogos* – a slave who looked after a child and accompanied him to school.)

Higher education was introduced by the *Sophists in the 5th century BC. These were itinerant teachers who claimed that they were qualified to give a better and higher education in general or in particular fields, and for which they asked high fees. Their pupils, they said, were better trained for politics and civic activities. Their teaching included physics, mathematics, philosophy and rhetoric, and they ascribed great value to knowledge. In the 4th century were established the first real institutions of higher education, first the school of rhetoric of *Isocrates, then the *Academy of Plato and later the *Peripatetic school of Aristotle and that of *Epicurus.

The most important development in education that took place in the Hellenistic period was that it came to be provided by the public in most Greek cities, and thus an opportunity was given to all to acquire it. A gymnasium was to be found everywhere and it was there that both intellectual and physical training were given. It was often with the help of private donations that the cities offered these services to their citizens. Public care and supervision of education meant that teachers, appointed anew by the people every year, were paid by the public and were un-

der the control of the yearly officials, the *gymnasiarchos* and the *paidonomos*. The latter was responsible for the education of boys up to the age of 14, both in private and public institutions. The first was responsible for the operation of the gymnasium and for the education of the *epheboi*, aged between 15–17, and of *neoi*, over 17. (The Athenian system of *epheboi* was a case apart.) An account of the teaching of elementary reading and writing is given by *Dionysius of Halicarnassus (late 1st century BC); it was probably the traditional method. The pupils first learnt the letters, their forms and syllables, names, verbs and particles, accentuation, cases, numbers and inflexions, and only then started reading and writing. For exercises they used waxed tablets on which they scratched the letters. There developed a general system of secondary education which consisted of music, physical training, and literature, and mathematics and natural sciences at a more advanced level. For academic studies, one had to go to one of the several centres of learning; the most famous were in Athens, Alexandria and *Pergamum. *Cos and Pergamum had the best medical schools.

H. I. Marrow, *A History of Education in Antiquity*, 1956; F. A. G. Beck, *Greek Education*, 1964.

EDUCATION, ROMAN The old, traditional system of education in Rome was practical and aimed at turning young boys into good citizens. What we know mainly concerns the upper classes of Roman society. Training began under the care of the mother and from the age of 7 the father became the instructor of the son, to a large extent by giving a personal example. By watching his father, the boy would learn to respect the old morals and to know what the proper conduct was for various religious, social, and political occasions. The boys also received basic instruction in reading and writing as well as physical training. After a boy took on the *toga virilis*, at about 15–16, he received political instruction from a senior statesman (this practice was known as the *tirocinium fori*).

From about the middle of the 3rd century BC, Roman education came to be influenced by the Greek system. This brought about the employment of literate slaves as instructors of the younger boys, a practice condemned by *Cato Censorius, who kept to the old system himself giving basic instruction to his son. He regarded law, oratory, agriculture, war and medicine as the proper subjects for instruction. Schools (*ludi*) were introduced in the 3rd century or, if they existed earlier, they became more common then. The *grammaticus*, the Greek teacher, not only taught Greek but also gave a more wide literary education. It was only after the creation of Latin literature, with the translation of the *Odyssey* by *Livius Andronicus and the appearance of the national epic *Annales* by *Ennius, that there was place for a Latin *grammaticus*. The teaching of oratory soon became popular and met with opposition. Philosophers and Latin rhetors were expelled by the Senate in 161 BC, and, in 92 BC, the censors banned the Latin schools of rhetoric – but evidently with no success. In the upper classes, education both in Greek and in Latin became the normal standard. But much as they were influenced by the Greeks, they did not adopt the gymnastic training. According to the 1st century BC scholar *Varro, complete education consisted of grammar, dialectic, rhetoric, geometry, arithmetic, astronomy, music, medicine, and architecture. His work was the first encyclopaedia ever written.

Roman education was very much geared to Greek education in methods and structure, consisting of elementary instruction given by the *litterator*, and secondary education taught by the *grammaticus*; obviously, it included both Latin and Greek teaching. It was only during the late Roman Empire that Greek ceased to be taught in the Latin West. Discipline was severe both in elementary and in secondary schools. Those who wanted higher education would usually go to Athens or, if interested in a special subject, could hire an expert. Oratorical education was important for all who aimed at public careers — as politicians under the Republic, in the courts and in the imperial administration under the Empire. This led to the rise of high schools of rhetoric. But much of the instruction was unrealistic under the new political conditions. The teacher of rhetoric received the highest remuneration. Even Roman emperors found it fit to sponsor rhetorical education. Vespasian appointed professors for Greek and Roman rhetoric with a public salary of 100,000 sesterces. Hadrian founded the Athenaeum in Rome where rhetors and scholars gave lectures and recitations. All this, however, and even the endowments granted by emperors and public-spirited rich persons, did not bring about the establishment of general education. A special Roman development was the rise of schools of law, where acknowledged jurists taught.

A. Gwynn, *Roman Education*, 1926;
I. Marrou, *A History of Education in Antiquity*, 1956.

EGERIA It seems that she was originally a goddess of a brook at *Aricia, where she was worshipped with *Diana. Thence the cult was moved to Rome where E. was worshipped outside the Porta Capena with the Camenae. She also became a goddess of birth, probably through her association with Diana.

EGNATIUS, Gellius A Samnite leader active in the Third Samnitian War. He organized the alliance of the Samnites, Etruscans and Gauls in 296 BC. The following year he commanded the combined armies against Rome, and was defeated and killed. Rome's victory secured her the mastery of central Italy.

EGYPT The land along the lower course of the Nile from the first catract was called *Aegyptos* by the Greeks. The cultivated area was, as it is still now, that part of the land that was watered by the Nile. Thanks to the yearly flood, this strip of land maintained its fertility and could give two crop-yields a year. Here were grown various kinds of wheat, barley, vegetables, and some fruit trees. The country produced little timber and had few minerals, though it had a virtual monopoly or papyrus.

Many centuries of relations of a diverse nature between the Greek world and E. preceded the conquest of the country by Alexander the Great in 332 BC. Many Greek myths took their heroes to E., for instance the myth of Heracles and *Busiris, that of *Io, and that of the *Danaids, but the interpretation and significance of these myths is far from clear. Archaic Greek art shows some Egyptian influence. The commercial relations with E. led to the establishment of *Naucratis as an emporium in the 7th century BC. It was mainly from the islands of the Aegean Sea and Asia Minor that traders came here. In the 6th century, King *Amasis employed Greek mercenaries and sent gifts to Greek temples. *Thales was believed to have founded geometry by studying Egyptian land mensuration. Herodotus visited E., and so perhaps did Democritus and Plato. In the 5th century BC, the war between the Greeks and the Persians led to the Athenian expedition to help the Egyptian revolt (459–454). All

told, these point to Greek interest in E. rather than vice-versa.

After Alexander's conquest, E. was ruled by Ptolemy I, who was appointed satrap of the country in 323 BC. E. became the core of the Ptolemaic Empire, and the Ptolemies were recognized as successors of the pharaohs. The conquest brought about the immigration of Greeks and Macedonians to E. Only a few cities with a Greek constitution and a Greek population were founded, the foremost being *Alexandria and *Ptolemais Hermiou. Under the first Ptolemies, the army consisted almost entirely of Macedonians and Greeks, who also held all the important administrative positions. Many soldiers received plots of land and in this way were scattered all over the country, but mainly in the Fayûm region. Under the Ptolemies, a system of state control and monopoly on all important economic products was the rule. Yearly schedules regulating agricultural production were issued by the royal bureaucracy. The monopoly system included the production and sale of papyrus, oils, textiles, leather, perfumes, the output of the mines, coinage and banking, fishing and hunting, etc. Prices were fixed and protective and fiscal customs duties were imposed on various products. To attain efficient control, registers of land, houses, slaves, livestock, and tax-payers were kept. For administrative purposes the country was divided into *nomoi* (about 36 in the 3rd century); these were sub-divided into toparchies, and villages were the smallest basic units. The *nomoi* were governed by *strategoi*. They were subject to the central officials in Alexandria, the highest of them being the *dioicetes*. The Greeks brought their cultural institutions with them but these were confined to the towns. Alexandria indeed became a main centre of Greek culture in the Hellenistic period, but outside it and a few other towns Hellenism made little progress in E.

The native population kept to its own traditions, and national sentiments were stirred by the success of the native troops in the battle of Raphia in 217 BC. This led to a native uprising ten years later. For about twenty years the district of *Thebes (2) was under the control of native rulers. It was reconquered in 187 BC and the revolt in the Delta was suppressed four years later. However, more revolts occurred. At the beginning of the 2nd century, the Ptolemies lost most of their territories outside E. — in Palestine, Asia Minor and the Aegean. Dynastic feuds contributed to the weakening of the country and only Roman intervention saved it from conquest by *Antiochus IV. Civil wars characterized the history of the country until the end of the Ptolemaic rule. In the first century it was believed in Rome that King Ptolemy XI (who died in 80 BC) bequeathed the country to the Roman people, and *Crassus (4) is said to have planned its annexation. But it was only as a result of the defeat of *Antonius (4), with whom *Cleopatra (2) was inseparably connected, that the Roman conquest occurred in 30 BC.

For the Ptolemies, E. was the mainstay of their empire; for Rome and its emperors it was a rich province from which good revenues could be drawn. The different attitudes led to different policies and consequences. The Ptolemies developed the resources of the country, and while this was done to their own advantage, it also contributed to the welfare of the native population. During the 2nd and 1st centuries, more and more Egyptians received positions in the administration, and there was a mixture of Greeks and Egyptians. Cleopatra, the last Ptolemaic queen, could speak Egyptian; she cared about the living conditions of the Egyptians and showed concern for their religion. Nothing of this was possible under Roman rule. The country was governed by Equestrian prefects who were responsible to Augustus and his successors. Many emperors never visited E. As a portent of future exploitation, much property was confiscated with the conquest and was probably sold cheaply to Augustus' supporters. The Roman absentee landlords were interested in easy profits for themselves and not in the welfare of their tenants. The chief function of E. was to supply corn for Rome. Few changes were made in the administration, which seemed adequate enough to serve the aims of the new rulers. Of course, all the former officials were now subject to the prefect who was assisted by a few Roman officials. He had at his disposal an army which at first numbered three legions but was reduced to two. The development of the system of *Liturgy was typical of the new regime. This meant that state offices were imposed and, while seldom practised under the Ptolemies, liturgics became extensively used in the 1st century AD. In the course of time all state offices were compulsory. In addition, local magistrates became personally responsible for the collection of the imperial taxes. The deteriorating conditions, however, made many tenants flee, and as a result much land went out of cultivation. A more active resistance to Roman rule was centered in Alexandria. Among the Greek-speaking population there developed a kind of national movement in opposition to the foreign rule. The situation was aggravated by the clash between the Greeks and the Jews and riots occasionally broke out. Several of the Alexandrian leaders were executed by the Roman emperors and their deeds and sufferings were recounted in an anti-Roman literature, fragments of which have survived ("Acts of the Pagan Martyrs"). Much devastation and bloodshed was caused by the Jewish revolt of AD 115. After the suppression of the revolt, the Jews no longer caused trouble but the opposition of the "nationalists" continued for many years. Indeed, the Roman emperors never encouraged the Romanization of E. Only small numbers of soldiers settled here and no colonies were founded. After the foundation of Constantinople, E. was obliged to provide food for the new capital. E. remained a part of the Roman Empire until the Arab conquest in AD 638.

E. R. Bevan, *History of Egypt under the Ptolemaic Dynasty*, 1927; Rostovtzeff, *Hellenistic World*; A. C. Johnson in *ESAR*, 2.

EISANGELIA A prosecution in Athens for offences against the state. This procedure existed from the time of *Solon, but underwent changes in the course of time. It was only at the end of the 5th century BC that several specific cases were reserved for E.: treason, attempts to overthrow the democratic constitution, the introduction of motions against the interests of the state which were procured by bribery. But it was possible to use E. for many other offences. In the middle of the 4th century a comprehensive law was passed incorporating former measures relating to E. The charge was brought before the Boule or the *Ekklesia, either of which could try the case; also, it could be handed over to an ordinary court (*dikasterion*). A famous case of E. was that of Alcibiades who was charged in 415 with the mutilation of the Hermae.

R. J. Bonner — G. Smith, *The Administration of Justice from Homer to Aristotle*, 1930.

EISPHORA An extraordinary property tax, chiefly imposed in times of war. It is mainly known from Athens,

but it existed in many other states as well: Aegina, Messene, Miletus, Mytilene, Orchomenus, Sparta, Syracuse, and the Ptolemaic Empire. The kinds of properties assessed and the amounts imposed, as well as the system of collection, varied from place to place, and changed even in the same state during the course of time. The E. existed at Athens at least from 428/427 BC. An important reform was introduced in 378/377: the taxpayers were divided into groups of persons with equal means (*Symmoriai). Each group had to pay a certain percentage of the value of its property when the E. was collected.

R. Thomsen, *Eisphora*, 1964.

EKKLESIA The assembly of citizens in Greek states, also called in some places Halia, *Agora, *Apella. It was considered as representative of the people but its powers and the right to take part in its meetings varied according to the type of constitution each *Polis had. The institution was characteristic of the Greeks from very remote times and is attested to by Homer. In early times it was in fact an assembly of the warriors who were summoned to hear and applaud the announcements of the kings. With the decline of the monarchy and the rise of the aristocracy, and, later, under the oligarchies, important questions, particularly those concerning war, peace and alliances, were brought before the E. for ratification. It also acquired the right to elect magistrates and to try important criminal cases. But the right of attendance under oligarchic constitutions was always restricted according to wealth, birth and age qualifications. It was only under a full democracy that the E. acquired its most extensive powers: all citizens could come to the meetings, speak freely, and initiate motions or amend those proposed; it elected the important magistrates and all officials as well as members of the *Boule; it was responsible for legislation; it decided and gave directions on all work done by the executive organs of the state: the conduct of war, building operations, foreign affairs, expenditure, taxation etc.

There were regular meetings of the E., the number varying in each state, and also extraordinary ones as the necessity arose. The usual meeting-place was in the Agora. The history of the E. in Athens is the only one which is to some extent known in detail. *Solon probably made the first important step by giving the E. judicial powers and the right to pass measures of various sorts. He also extended the right of attendance to all citizens. The next stage was introduced by *Cleisthenes (2) who gave citizenship to all those resident in Athens. He also introduced regular meetings. Further progress was made in the course of the 5th century, in the second part of which the E. attained its widest powers. Each *prytany there were four regular meetings held on the Pnyx, which started early in the morning. The Boule summoned the citizens for the meetings and prepared the agenda, certain matters being required by law, others introduced on the initiative of private citizens who had put forward motions in a previous meeting, and still others recommended by the Boule itself. After the debate, voting was by a show of hands (*cheirotonia*) or by secret ballot. The resolutions (*psephismata*) were put down in writing and were preserved in the public archive and sometimes displayed in public. They were arranged according to a fixed formula. A quorum of 6,000 was required for certain matters, e.g. ostracism, and it seems that attendance of this size was not exceptional. A payment of one obol for attendance was introduced at the end of the 5th century BC and was raised several times;

this helped poorer people but was criticized by the opponents of radical democracy.

In the Hellenistic and Roman periods, E. still existed in Greek cities but they had generally lost their powers.

Hignett, *Athen. Const.* (s.v.).;

V. Ehrenberg, *The Greek State*, 1960 (s.v.).

ELAGABALUS Born in Emessa in AD 204 as Varius Avitus Bassianus to *Julia Sosaemia. He was the priest of the sun-god Ela-Gabal (the god of the mountain), from which he received his name. His mother and his grandmother, *Julia Maesa (the sister-in-law of Septimius *Severus), secured his accession to the throne in AD 218, claiming that his father was Caracalla. *Macrinus, who was responsible for the murder of Caracalla, was defeated and killed. E. took the sacred black stone of his god to Rome and instituted there a cult of the sun-god (*deus invictus Sol Elagabalus*) as the chief god of Rome. E. and his mother soon lost popularity because of their foolishness and religious eccentricities, and Maesa induced him to adopt his cousin Alexianus in AD 221. The following year the praetorians were bribed to kill E. and his mother.

G. H. Hadberghe, *The Cult of Sol Invictus*, 1972.

ELEA (Velia) A coastal colony of *Phocaea in southern Italy, south of *Paestum. It was founded soon after the middle of the 6th century BC. It was famous for its school of philosophy which started with *Parmenides. Many remains and the detailed layout of the town have been revealed in excavations of the site during recent decades.

A. G. Woodhead, *The Greeks in the West*, 1962.

ELECTRA The name of several figures in Greek mythology:

1. Daughter of Oceanus and Tethys, wife of Thaumas, mother of Iris and the Harpyiae.

2. Daughter of *Atlas and mother of *Dardanus and Iasion.

3. Daughter of *Agamemnon and *Clytemnestra, sister of *Orestes. The earliest poet known to have mentioned her is *Stesichorus, and his stories were taken from epic sources. It was, however, with the tragedians that she became a favourite figure, each one elaborating on her character according to his artistic taste and purpose. In all the versions of her story she is responsible, to a lesser or a greater degree, for the retributive murder of her mother and Aegisthus.

ELEGIAC POETRY This comprises a wide variety of poems written on various themes in different moods, but with one common feature, the "elegiac distich". The first verse is a dactylic hexameter, the second a pentameter. In metric terms this can be shown as follows:

$$ \_\ \smile\smile\ \_\ \smile\smile\ \_\ \smile\smile\ \_\ \smile\smile\ \_\ \smile\smile\ \_\ \smile $$
$$ \_\ \smile\smile\ \_\ \smile\smile\ \_ | \_\ \smile\smile\ \_\ \smile\smile\ \_ $$

For Ovid this meant a rhythm of rise and fall (*Amores* 1.1,27). The effect of the pentameter in this combination is to cause some delay, a pause, which can be used for further reflection or to introduce an unexpected element. It seems that *elegos* was associated with the Phrygian flute and that originally the elegiac was a flute-song. Greek EP. first appeared in the late 8th century BC and was a genre used for the expression of personal emotions and views. The marital songs of Callinus of Ephesus (early 7th century) and *Tyrtacas, in which they exhorted their countrymen to fight, were written in elegiac form. *Archilochus wrote wine-songs, and songs on his experiences, in elegiac verses. *Mimnermus used the form to write on

various themes, including erotic poetry, and *Solon used it to express his views on life and politics. *Sappho, *Simonides and *Theognis are among the old poets who wrote EP. Epitaphs, epigrams and lamentations were written in elegiac verses; hence the notion of the elegy as a poem of sorrow.

The elegy long remained a favourite genre of poets. In Hellenistic times, Philetas and *Callimachus were the leading poets to write in this form, which was now employed for narrative and love-poetry. In Rome, poets used it from *Ennius on, and its great period was the late Republic and the Augustan age. The great names are those of *Catullus, *Tibullus, *Propertius and *Ovid. Another important poet who wrote elegies was Cornelius *Gallus. All these poets chose the elegy as the best genre for writing love poetry; and it is interesting to note the love elegies of *Sulpicia, a Roman poetess. Among poets who later used the form were *Petronius and *Martialis, whose epigrams are elegiac verses; much later came *Ausonius and *Claudian.

J. M. Edmonds, *Elegy and Iambus* (Loeb), 1931;
C. M. Bowra, *Early Greek Elegists*, 1938;
G. Luck, *The Latin Love Elegy*, 1959;
J. P. Sullivan (ed.) *Critical Essays on Roman Literature, Elegy*, 1962.

ELEUSIS A very ancient town in Attica on the shore of a bay about 20 km west of Athens. It had a well-defended *Acropolis. Settlement here probably began in the first half of the 2nd millenium BC and developed in the Mycenaean period. E. is one of the very few places where remains of a Mycenaean temple have been found. E. retained its independence for a considerable time after Attica was united and it was perhaps only in the 7th century BC that it was incorporated into the Athenian State, when it became one of the Athenian *Demes. E. was chiefly famed for its mysteries of *Demeter. The temple was built and rebuilt several times, and traces of all periods have been found. *Pisistratus built the *telesterion*, a theatre-like hall in which the performance of the mysteries took place. Its plan was more than once modified and one of the architects who worked on it was *Ictinus. Later additions included the Propylaea begun by Appius *Claudius (4) Pulcher in 50 BC and those of Marcus *Aurelius. The Eleusinean mysteries Athens, bathed in the sea and then went in procession to E., carrying the sacred objects along the sacred way. What precisely happened in the rites at the *telesterion* is unknown. All that can be said for sure is that certain things were said, certain things were shown, and certain things were performed. They were certainly connected with the myths of *Demeter, *Core, and *Persephone, which in turn were connected with agricultural life. The rites apparently went through changes in the course of time, placing emphasis on moral values. They were vital enough to continue even after the triumph of Christianity. It was only in AD 395 that the sanctuary was closed down.

G. E. Mylonas, *Eleusis and the Eleusinian Mysteries*, 1961.

ELIS A country, mainly flat but with some hills, in the northwest Peloponnesus, bordering on *Messenia in the south, on *Arcadia in the southeast, and on *Achaea in the northeast. E. did not have a good harbour anywhere along its coast. The main river was the Peneus. It was an agricultural country and fine horses were bred there. Urbanization made little progress in E. Traces of human occupation in the Stone Age have been found but more important are the numerous finds from the Mycenaean period. It appears that the Greeks came here from the northwest; the local dialect was the one also spoken at Aetolia, Locris, and Phocis. The Eleans extended their territory to the south in about 580 BC, taking control of *Olympia and the Olympian games. They were allies of Sparta but they generally kept out of the main currents of Greek history. In 471, the city of E. was founded on the Peneus. In about the middle of the 5th century, the Eleans conquered the district of Triphylia. In 420, Sparta's support of Lepreum led to E. joining Athens. As a result, Triphylia was taken away from E. after the end of the Peloponnesian War. In the 4th and 3rd centuries, E. fought several times against Arcadia over the control of Olympia. In the 3rd century, E. was an ally of Aetolia. E. joined the Achaean League in 191 BC and, after its dissolution in 146, was subject to Roman control.

EMESA (modern Homs) A town in Syria on the Orontes river. It retained its independence under the rule of the kings, until Domitian annexed it to the Roman Empire. It was the native town of Julia Domna, Julia Mamaea, Elagabalus, and Alexander Severus. The temple of the local sun-god was famous. The Arabs conquered it in AD 636.

EMPEDOCLES A Greek philosopher, native of Acragas, son of Meton. His homonymous grandfather won the horse-race at the Olympian games in 496 BC. He was born at the beginning of the 5th century, some years later than *Anaxagoras, but began his philosophical teaching earlier. He died at the age of 60, but the exact dates of his life are not known. In the course of time many apocryphal tales were told of him and not much that is certain can be said of his life. As *Theophrastus said, he was associated with *Parmenides and the Pythagoreans. Though of an aristocratic family he was probably an active democratic leader in Acragas. He refused to accept the kingship in his home-town; later, things changed and he had to flee from there. He was in *Thurii soon after its foundation. He stayed in the Peloponnesus for some time and probably died there. Aristotle apparently considered him as the inventor of rhetoric. E. was a distinguished orator, famed as a poet and a doctor, and as one able to perform miracles.

The two important works of E. were two poems consisting, we are told, of 5,000 lines. One is "On Nature" (*peri physeos*), of which some 350 lines are known, and the other is "Purifications" (*katharmoi*), of which some 100 lines are known. It is possible that he wrote a book on medicine and it is probable that he did not write the tragedies ascribed to him.

"On Nature" aims at giving a physical explanation of the universe. It is apparent that the theory is a direct answer to the Parmenidean contentions that the real things do not perish and are one, that a void, i.e. empty space, does not exist and as a result motion is impossible. While accepting that real things are imperishable, E. argues that the world, a spherical universe, was never a unity but a plurality. The four original roots, or elements, of all things are Fire, Air, Earth and Water. They indeed fill up the whole space (i.e. there is no place for the void), but they continually mix into one through Love (*philia*) and separate through Strife (*neikos*). What appears to be coming into existence and perishing are only temporary states resulting from the combination in various proportions of the eternal elements and their dissolution. Love and Strife are the forces causing motion in space. In contrast to Parmenides, E. accepts that the senses are a

reliable guide to reality provided that one uses each one for its appropriate function. The never-ending combination and dissolution of the elements goes through a four-stage cycle, two transitional ones and two that are characterized by the rule of one or the other of the motive forces: *a*) Love has complete control of the universe, bringing about a harmonious mixture of the four elements while Strife stays outside; *b*) Love is losing control and Strife is coming into the universe; *c*) Strife has complete control — bringing about a complete separation of the elements while Love stays outside; *d*) Strife is losing control and Love is coming into the universe. The present world was in stage *b*, and in his description of it E. dealt with physiology, botany, and embryology.

There is an apparent contradiction between "On Nature", which excludes the immortality of the soul, and "Purifications", which accepts the belief in the transmigration of the soul. The second poem is concerned with the fall of man from the archaic state of innocence. Again, there are four stages: *a*) Kupris (i.e. Aphrodite, Love) rules the world; *b*) bloodshed and meat-eating cause the fall of man — collectively and individually; *c*) the soul passes through successive incarnations and transmigrations (a period of a "thousand seasons"); *d*) the soul escapes through gradual ascent from re-birth to its original place of abode and state of bliss. It is difficult to accept that E. held two incompatible ideas on the soul at the same time. Either he changed his mind in the course of time, or, as some argue, he made a distinction between the migrating soul and the physical, conscious soul, the second perishing with the body, the first (the life soul) surviving.
Kirk—Raven, *Presocratic Philosophers.*

ENNIUS, Quintus Famous Latin poet, born to a noble local family in Rudiae in Messapia in 239 BC. He later said that he had three hearts, referring to his knowledge of Greek, Oscan, and Latin. In 204 BC he was serving with the Roman army in Sardinia when Cato met him and brought him to Rome. It was here that his literary activity flourished. He established connections with men of influence, but is said to have been poor, living on the Aventine, a plebeian quarter. In 189 BC he accompanied the consul M. Fulvius Nobilior to Greece and the Aetolian War. Nobilior's son gave him Roman citizenship in 184 BC when he established the Roman colonies of Potentia and Pisaurum. He died in 169 BC and his ashes were brought back to his native town.

E. was a poet of remarkable powers and of much creative originality. He wrote tragedies, comedies, various poems, *saturae*, prose works, and an epic. No single work of E. has survived, and the extant fragments only amount to some 1,100 lines. About 24 titles of E.'s plays are known, and some 400 lines. He was apparently more effective as a tragic rather than as a comic playwright. Most of his tragedies were Latin adaptations of Greek originals. Euripides — twelve of whose tragedies (including *Andromeda, Alexander, Iphigenia, Medea*) were translated by E. — was his favourite author. He also adapted some of Aeschylus' tragedies. E.'s tragedies were not mere translations for he added to, modified or omitted from the originals. He also occasionally allowed himself to change the original metre. In *Iphigenia*, there is a soldiers' chorus instead of the original chorus of women. It seems that E.'s plays were more rhetorical and artificial than the originals. E. also wrote two tragedies on Roman themes: *Sabinae* and *Ambracia*.

E. was said to have been the first Roman writer to

write satires in verse. His *saturae* were in four books, written in various metres and dealing with different themes. Of these, some seventy lines have survived. One *satura* was an animal fable in the Aesopic tradition, another a dialogue between Life and Death. It appears that in contrast to *Lucilius and later writers, E.'s *saturae* were not insulting and personal. Their title indicates that they dealt with miscellaneous subjects, with an emphasis on popular moral lessons and humour. The *Epicharmus* was a translation of a poem spuriously ascribed to *Epicharmus. In his poem *Scipio*, E. told the praises of Scipio Africanus. Under the title *Hedyphagetica*, E. translated into Latin the *Hedypatheia*, a gastronomic poem in hexameters by the 4th century poet of Gela, Archestratus. The *Euhemerus* was a work based on the novel of *Euhemerus, *Sacred Scripture*, which claimed that the gods were in fact great men of the past worshipped for their services. In the Latin prose translation this scepticism was applied to Jupiter (=Zeus).

E.'s greatest work was his *Annales*, an epic comprising 18 books of which some 600 verses are extant. It described the history of Rome from Aeneas' arrival to Latium to E.'s time. Following the tradition of the *Annales* of the Pontifex Maximus, the poem was based on the consular years. The content of the books is partially known or can be reasonably surmised. Book 1 ended with Romulus, and Books 2–3 carried the story to the end of the monarchy. Book 6 treated the war against Pyrrhus, Books 7–9 dealt with the Punic Wars, and Books 10–12 were concerned with the war against *Philippus V. The war against Antiochus III came in Book 13, and in Book 16 came the Istrian War. In the opening of the work, E. claimed that it was Homer's soul, formerly incarnated in Pythagoras, that came to dwell in his body. Indeed, E. took the Homeric meter – the dactylic hexameter – for his epic. Though he had to use more spondees than was normal in Homeric usage, the epic was a great success; henceforth, epics in Latin were to be written in hexameter. The epic naturally glorified the achievements of Rome, but it seems that E. was not led to gross exaggerations and distortion of the truth. The extant fragments show him to have been a master of characterization. Some of the lines have gained much fame, for instance the one on Fabius Maximus Cunctator: *unus homo nobis cunctando restituit rem* ("one man for us by lingering saved the state"); or *moribus antiquis res stat Romana virisque* ("the Roman state is supported by old customs and men"). It is no wonder that school-boys were made to learn the epic – from it they came to know of Rome's great heroes and their deeds; and it remained a school textbook and a national epic until it was replaced by Virgil's *Aeneid*.

E.'s poetical power was recognized in his time and his influence was long lasting. *Caecilius and *Pacuvius, his nephew, were his pupils. He also had some influence on *Lucilius and *Accius, and Cicero admired his works. Lucretius and Virgil followed him in writing their great poems in dactylic hexameters. It was only under the Empire that people were no longer attracted to his poetry, and only grammarians showed an interest in his archaic language.

Warmington, *Rem. Od. Lat.*, 2.

EPAMINONDAS Famous Theban statesman and general. His birth date is not known. E. received a good education in rhetoric and music, and was a close friend of *Pelopidas. He first appeared in politics in 371 BC, when he insisted, during a Greek peace congress, that Thebes

should take the oath for all the cities of Boeotia. Sparta would not accept this demand and as a result invaded Boeotia. In the decisive battle at Leuctra, E. employed the new tactics of strengthening his left wing and withdrawing his right wing (*loxe phalanx*). The ten thousand strong Spartan army was destroyed by the Boeotian army of 7,000, and in the winter of 370 BC, E. was free to invade the Peloponnesus. He encouraged the Arcadians to assert their independence against Sparta and to build *Megalopolis. He freed *Messenia, thus putting to an end the centuries-old supremacy of Sparta over the Peloponnesus. After two more invasions in 369 and 367 BC, and naval operations against Athens in 364 BC, E. nearly captured Sparta in 362 BC. He won an inconclusive victory against the Spartans at *Mantinea but his untimely death, from battle wounds, made the victory ineffectual and terminated the supremacy of Thebes.

Xenophon, *Hell.* 6–7; Nepos, *Epaminondas*; Pausan. 9.13.

EPAPHRODITUS Freedman of Nero who discovered the Pisonian conspiracy in AD 65. He helped Nero commit suicide in AD 68 (Dio 63.29). Later, he was the secretary of Domitian, who put him to death in AD 95 (Suet. *Dom.* 14). The philosopher *Epictetus was his slave.

EPHEBOI Greek boys of the 15–20 age group. The special institution of *ephebeia* in Athens is mentioned by Aristotle (*Athen. Pol.* 42) and is first recorded in an inscription of 334/333 BC. Eighteen year old Athenians were given two years of military training. They first had to pass an examination (*dokimasia*) to confirm their age and their lawful descent from a free Athenian family. An elected *kosmetes*, responsible for the training, was helped by ten *sophronistai*, one for each of the ten Athenian tribes. The E. learnt to use swords, spears, bows, javelins etc. and were given physical exercises. After one year of training at Piraeus, they took an oath of allegiance to their country and were given a spear and a shield. They were then assigned to various posts in Attica for guard duties. After two years of service, they enjoyed the full rights of Athenian citizens. In the early 3rd century BC, the service was cut to one year and it was no longer com-

The ephebe of Marathon

pulsory. The daily payment of four obols was also cancelled. As a result, only those who could afford it went through ephebic training, while the *kosmetes* had to spend much of his own money for the maintenance of the institution. By the late 2nd century BC, the character of the training changed from military to literary, rhetorical, musical and philosophical. From 119/118 BC on, foreigners could become E. The Athenian *ephebeia* still existed in the late 3rd century AD, and possibly lasted until the end of the 4th century. Much of the evidence on the E. comes from inscriptions.

C. Pélékidis, *Histoire de l'Éphébie attique*, 1962.

EPHESUS Rich Ionian city on the western coast of Asia Minor, reputedly founded by Argives and Athenians, led by Androcles (son of *Codrus). Originally a Carian settlement, E. owed its prosperity to a good harbour and its location at the end of the long road through the Maeander valley to the East. The Lydian king, *Croesus, took control of E. in the 6th century BC, and helped build the magnificent temple of Artemis, which was burnt (in 356 BC) and rebuilt, and was considered one of the Seven Wonders of the World. E. was subdued by the Persians, and took part in the Ionian revolt; it joined the Delian League but deserted to Sparta at a late stage of the Peloponnesian War. Under Persian rule again in 386 BC, E. fell to Alexander in 334 BC, and passed to his successors. After the death of *Attalus III in 133 BC, it was included in the Roman province of Asia. It was one of the greatest cities of the East, the residence of the Roman governor, and the site of the treasury of the Artemisium, a very successful bank. E. was sacked by the Goths in AD 263. The philosopher *Heraclitus was a native of E. Extensive excavations have revealed considerable remains — streets, temples, a library and other public buildings.

G. E. Bean, *Aegean Turkey*, 1966.

EPHETAI An Athenian court with a jury of fifty-one members which decided on most cases of homicide.

D. M. MacDowell, *Athenian Homicide Law*, 1963.

EPHIALTES Prominent Athenian statesman who adopted an anti-Spartan policy and sought to advance democracy — thus coming into conflict with *Cimon. By a reform he carried out in 462/461 BC, the *Areopagus lost its most important powers. His attacks on Cimon led to the latter's ostracism. E.'s enemies murdered him in 461 BC, and his policy was carried on by his young assistant, Pericles.

Aris. *Athen. Pol.* 25; Plutarch, *Cimon*, 15.

EPHORS Important officials in the Dorian states, especially in Sparta (*epheroi* probably meant "observers"). The institution of the office was ascribed to *Lycurgus (1) or to King Theopompus; lists of E. allegedly date from 754 BC. The powers of the five Spartan E., elected annually by the *Apella, increased with time. By the early 5th century BC, they were responsible for: supervision of the maintenance of the Lycurgan way of life by all Spartan citizens; administration of foreign affairs and mobilization of the army; summoning and presiding over the Apella and the *Gerousia; policing of the *Perioeci and the *Helots; control of the kings, whom they were empowered to prosecute (as they could all other Spartans) and with whom they exchanged monthly oaths for the maintenance of the laws. Two of them went with the king on military expeditions. The year was named after the senior E.

Van den Boer, *Laconian Studies*, 1954, 197 ff;
G. L. Huxley, *Early Sparta*, 1962 (s.v.).

EPHORUS Greek historian, native of Cyme in *Aeolis, born *c*. 405 and died *c*. 330 BC. He studied in Athens under *Isocrates, wrote a history of Cyme, *On Discoveries* (in two books), and a work on world history which comprised thirty books. His general history began with the return of the Heraclids (the Dorian invasion), and ended with the siege of Perinthus by *Philip II in 340 BC. (The last book was written by E.'s son after his death.) Our knowledge of the work is derived from fragments preserved by *Strabo, and the fact that it was the main source for Books 11–16 of *Diodorus Siculus. Though E. read and compared many former works, he shows poor judgement and little understanding of military history. Nonetheless he had a good reputation, and he influenced later historians.

Jacoby, *Fr.Gr.Hist*, ii 70;
G. L. Barber, *The Historian Ephorus*, 1935.

EPIC CYCLE (epikos kyklos) Collection of old epic poems, written by early Greek scholars; artificially arranged in a series to give a historical account of the world from its creation to the end of the Heroic Age. The poems of the collection, apart from those of Homer, were probably written in the 7th–6th centuries BC, and only fragments and summaries have survived. The poems were in the following order: 1) *Theogony*; 2) *Titanomachia*; 3) *Oidipodeia* (the history of the house of Oedipus); 4) *Thebais* (the story of the *Seven against Thebes); 5) *Epigonoi* (conquest of Thebes by the descendants of the Seven); 6) *Cypria* (the origin and first stages of the Trojan War); 7) *Iliad*; 8) *Aethiopis* (the story of the Trojan War up to the death of Achilles); 9) *Little Iliad* (with the story of the Wooden Horse); 10) *Iliou Persis* (the sack of Troy); 11) *Nostoi* (the homecoming of various heroes, including the murder of Agamemnon); 12) *Odyssey*; 13) *Telegonia* (till the death of Odysseus). The poems were read extensively up to the 4th century BC, and their primitive myths were used by later poets and writers, both Greek and Roman.

H. G. Evely-White, *Hesiod, the Homeric Hymns and Homerica* (Loeb), 1936.

EPICHARMUS Greek comic playwright, allegedly born in Cos or Samos, but probably born in Syracuse where he lived at the end of the 6th century and early in the 5th century BC. His were perhaps the oldest Greek comedies; only fragments and titles have survived. The plays were written in the Doric dialect and included mythological burlesques (Hercules, Odysseus and Hephaestus appeared frequently) as well as common characters. The plays of E. were known in Athens; they were esteemed by Plato, and edited and commented on by *Appolodorus of Athens.

Pickard-Cambridge, *Dithyramb*², 230 ff.

EPIC POETRY The epic is the earliest form of Greek literature. It is a long narrative poem about heroic deeds, told in a dignified style, with organic unity and using the hexameter. There are two types of E.P. The first, the original, is the oral epic, a poem recited by bards who thereby commemorated the glorious deeds of the heroes for didactic and entertainment purposes. The bard did not invent his tale but elaborated on traditional material, using such poetical techniques as stock phrases, formulae, and epithets. The *Iliad* and the *Odyssey*, the earliest and the greatest epics ever composed, followed this tradition. The second type is the E.P. written by a poet in his study. He takes as his theme a traditional legend or a national achievement, but revises it freely according to his tastes and purposes by inventing, omitting or modifying details. In this way it becomes an entirely "literary" production lacking the primitive, spontaneous quality of the first type. In Greek literature, epic poems of the first type were not composed after the 6th century, a phenomenon associated with the spread of writing. The second type was used by many poets. In the early 3rd century BC, *Callimachus felt that the genre was already outdated. The *Argonautica* of Apolonius Rhodius largely vindicated his judgement. The genre, however, was still used in antiquity by Greek poets like *Quintus Smyrnaeus in the 4th century AD and *Nonnus in the 5th century.

There was a tradition of oral poems in Archaic Rome whereby young boys at banquets would sing old songs in praise of the achievements of the ancestors. But there is no reason to suppose that these poems, composed in the Latin saturnian verse, were comparable to the Greek oral epics which culminated with Homer. Indeed, this oral poetry was never preserved in writing. Latin EP. developed only under the influence of Greek culture and was wholly confined to the second type. The first epic written in Latin was a translation of the *Odyssey* by Livius Andronicus. The first original Roman epic was the *Bellum Punicum* of Naevius, who still used the saturnian verse. It was Ennius who introduced the Greek hexameter in writing his *Annales*, a versified version of Roman history from remote times to his own. These two treated history with a patriotic attitude, and Virgil followed their line in composing his *Aeneid*. Although Virgil's epic takes as its theme the heroic adventures of Aeneas, the poem from first to last is imbued with an awareness of the greatness of Rome and its role in this world as the realization of divine will. The best Latin epic, it has some structural flaws, especially in the second part, and not everyone would find pious Aeneas to his taste. Of the other Latin poets who wrote epics on historical themes, prominent were Lucan with his *Bellum Civile* (*Pharsalia*), the tale of the civil war between Caesar and Pompey, and *Silius Italicus, whose *Punica* is the longest and the most tedious of the Latin epics. There were others who took Greek myths as subjects for their poems, for instance Valerius Flaccus in his *Argonautica* and Statius in his *Thebais* and *Achilleis*. Claudian, the last great Latin poet, wrote the epic *Rape of Proserpina*.

See *Homer, *Epic Cycle, *Apollonius Rhodius, *Quintus Smyrnaeus, *Nonnus, *Livius Andronicus, *Naevius, *Ennius, *Virgil, *Lucan, *Valerius Flaccus, *Statius, *Sillius Italicus, *Claudian (with bibliographies).
G. Murray, *The Rise of the Greek Epic*[4], 1934;
C. M. Bowra, *Heroic Poetry*, 1964;
J. Higginbotham, *Greek and Latin Literature*, 1969, 162ff.

EPICTETUS Stoic philosopher, native of Hierapolis in Phrygia, born c. AD 55 and died c. 135. E. was the slave of *Epaphroditus who allowed him to study under Musonius Rufus and manumitted him. E. taught philosophy but was expelled from Rome with other philosophers and lived the rest of his life at Nicopolis in Epirus. After his death, his pupil, the historian *Arian, published his *Discourses* (*diatribai*), of which four books are extant, and a *Manual* (*encheiridion*), summarizing his philosophy in 53 extracts. Of deep religious conviction, E. taught that Divine Providence must be trusted in every circumstance. He regarded himself as a doctor able to cure only those who were aware of their infirmity, and he taught people of all social classes. He believed that man can achieve happiness through self-knowledge, and by overcoming external circumstances, for thus he becomes free and gains peace

of mind. E. had a strong influence on later philosophers and rulers.
O. A. Oldfather, *Epictetus* (Loeb), 1938;
F. H. Sandbach, *The Stoics*, 1975 (s.v.).

EPICURUS Greek philosopher, son of Neocles, an Athenian schoolmaster, born in Samos in 341 and died in Athens in 271/270 BC. After completing his ephebic service (*Epheboi) in Athens in 321 BC, he lived with his family at Colophon, and later taught his philosophy at Mitylene (311/310 BC) and at Lampsacus (309–307). In 306 BC he acquired a house and a garden in Athens, and established a school of philosophy that took its name ("the garden") from its surroundings. On his death, E. left the property and the school to his friend and pupil Hermarchus of Mityline.

E. is credited with the writing of some 300 books, of which only some fragments and the following are extant: 1) Letter to Herodotus (an account of E.'s philosophy of Nature); 2) Letter to Pythocles (on meteorological phenomena); 3) Letter to Metrodorus (an account of E.'s philosophy of ethics); 4) *Kyriai Doxai*, "Principal Maxims" — 40 sayings on ethics (these four are all given by *Diogenes Laertius); 5) Vatican Maxims (eighty maxims known from a Vatican manuscript discovered in 1888).

E.'s views are also expounded in the *De Rerum Natura* of *Lucretius. Accepting the atomic philosophy of *Democritus, E. maintained that the world is a natural result of the combination of atoms, and that worlds are produced and destroyed in a never ending coming together and separation of atoms. The gods have no interest in our world, and neither punish wrongdoers nor reward the just. One should therefore not fear death because it is only the disintegration of the atoms of soul and body, with which all senses cease to exist. While man is alive, he should seek the happiness which comes from satisfying his most natural desires. But these moral teachings were not simple hedonism since E. believed that the most important pleasure is the pleasure of the soul which is achieved through meditation, when the soul is undisturbed by material or emotional factors (the ideal state of *atarxia*); abstinence from worldly preoccupations is necessary for this.

Not only men but also women and slaves were attracted by E.'s teachings and joined his school, living a communal life. The Epicurean philosophy spread throughout the Hellenistic world and had many followers in Rome. Additional schools were opened in various places (e.g. Antioch and Naples). The school of E. lasted to the 4th century AD, although Epicureanism encountered much hostility. The Athenian school rivalled the *Academy, where the physical theories of E. were in direct contrast to those of Aristotle. The Stoics, and, later on, the Christians, abhorred Epicurean doctrines about the gods, ethics, the absence of divine providence, and the nature of the world. Epicureanism was abused, and became a byword for hedonism and heresy.

See Diogenes of Oenoanda, Lucretius, Philodemus.
Diog.Laert.10; (ed. R. D. Hicks (Loeb) 1925);
R. M. Geer (Eng. tr.), 1964;
N. W. DeWitt, *Epicurus and his philosophy*, 1954;
B. Farrington, *The Faith of Epicurus*, 1967.

EPIDAMNUS Greek city on the coast of Illyria, founded by Corinth and Corcyra in 625 BC. By the early 3rd century BC, its name changed to Dyrrachium (modern Durazzo). It prospered as the main trading port for Illyria, but, in the 5th century BC, it suffered internal conflicts

The theatre at Epidaurus

between the oligarchy and the lower classes. The dispute between Corcyra and Corinth over E., into which Athens was dragged, was one of the secondary causes of the Peloponnesian War. E. was the main port for Roman armies on their way from *Brundisium to the East. In 48 BC, Caesar failed to besiege Pompey here.

EPIDAURUS Greek city in the eastern Peloponnesus on the Saronic Gulf, with territory extending to the Argive plain. It was conquered by Dorians who came from Argos. Homer knew E. as a member of the *Amphictiony of Calauria (*Il.* 2.561). It took part in the Persian wars, sided with Sparta in the Peloponnesian War, and was later a member of the Achaean League. E. is especially known for its sanctuary of *Asclepius, which was about 8 km inland of the city itself. Originally, the cult of Asclepius (established here by the end of the 7th century BC), was associated with the cult of Apollo, which it later supplanted. E. became a main centre of the cult of Asclepius, which then spread to many other cities. Its buildings included the great temple of Asclepius (built c. 375 BC), temples for Artemis, Aphrodite, and other gods, a gymnasium, palaestra, and accommodations for worshippers. The theatre, perhaps the best extant Greek theatre, and the tholos (round building) attract attention today. Many votive offerings from worshippers who were cured by the god have been found in E.

EPIGRAM Literally "inscription", it came to denote the literary genre that evolved from the writing of verses (usually elegiac couplets) as epitaphs. E.s and epitaphs, the earliest verse inscriptions in Greek, dating from the 8th century BC, tell briefly and quite unemotionally the stories of the dead. The best known early poet who used this genre is *Simonides. Poets continued to write E.s both as genuine epitaphs and as purely poetical works. *Callimachus and other Alexandrian poets, who advo-

cated short poems, preferred the E. on account of its brevity. The E. came to include a wide variety of themes: love and wine, brief accounts of the lives of men and women, works of art, anecdotes, jokes, sayings etc. The first collection of E.s was made in the early 1st century BC by *Meleager (2), and thanks to this and similar collections, many Greek E.s are known.

Like the Greek E.s, Latin E.s had their origin in verse epitaphs; the earliest ones known being those of the *Scipios which date from the 3rd century BC. Under Greek influence, the laudatory short epitaphs developed into a poetical form, and thus we find that *Ennius wrote E.s in honour of Scipio. In the second century BC, E.s were used as erotic poems, and they merged with satire in the works of *Catullus and *Calvus. From then on E.s became a popular form of poetical writing employed by such famous names as Cicero, Caesar, Augustus, Virgil, *Seneca (2) and *Petronius, and culminating with *Martial, who gave the E. its accepted characteristics: conciseness, wit, humour, and a pointed ending. Though E.s were often used after Martial, they were not developed further.

W. R. Paton, *The Greek Anthology* (Loeb), 1916–8;
A. S. F. Gow–D. L. Page, *Hellenistic Epigrams*, 1965;
Morel, *Fr.Poet.Lat.*;
R. Lattimore, *Themes in Greek and Roman Epitaphs*, 1942.

EPIMELETES Officials in Greek cities with administrative or supervisory powers. They were responsible for a wide variety of departments — wells, export and import, dockyards, and festivals. Special officials created for temporary, specific tasks, like the building of public projects, were often given the title E. Officials of private associations were also sometimes called E. Under the Roman Empire, E. were the Greek counterparts of the Latin *curator*.

EPIMENIDES Cretan miracle worker and religious teacher, who allegedly lived 157 or 299 years in the 7th—5th centuries BC. He was also believed to have slept for fifty years and to have purified Athens from the taint of the killing of *Cylon's followers. E. was said to be able to separate his soul from his body at will (cf. *Aristeas). E. R. Dodds, *The Greeks and the Irrational*, 1950, 141f.

EPIRUS "Mainland" northwest of Greece, bordering on the Gulf of Ambracia in the south, separated from Thessaly by the Pindus range in the east, and extending to Acroceraunium in the north. E. is a mountainous country dissected by narrow valleys, with some plains on the Adriatic coast. Its main or better-known rivers are the Aous, Arachthus, *Achelous and *Acheron. Greek *Apoikiai (of which *Ambracia and *Corcyra were the most important) were founded on its borders, and it had a famous oracular sanctuary at *Dodona. The local population, which comprised a considerable Illyrian element, kept to its tribal organization until the 4th century BC; the main tribes were the Thesproti, Molossi and Chaones. E. played no part in Greek politics almost until the 4th century BC. The unification of the tribes of E. was achieved by *Alexander I, the strong Molossian king (brother-in-law of *Philip II), who was the *hegemon* of the Epirote League. After his death in Italy in 330 BC, the Molosian kingdom declined until *Pyrrhus raised the Epirote kingdom to the height of its power in the first quarter of the 3rd century BC. But after the Molossian kingdom was overthrown (in 233 BC), the Epirote League was closely associated with *Macedonia, and, after the downfall of *Perseus (2), it suffered terrible devastation at the hands of the Romans — 150,000 people were allegedly enslaved (167 BC). Later, E. was included in the Roman province of Achaea.
Larsen, *Gr.Fed.St.*, 273—281; Hammond, *Epirus*, 1967.

EPISTATES In many Greek states, *epistatai* were chairmen of various boards and institutions, both private and public. In Hellenistic kingdoms the E. were royal officials, sometimes of high rank, who were responsible for the administration of cities, for local jurisdiction, or for police duties.

EPITAPHIOS Funeral speech given in Athens on behalf of the public in honour of those who had died in battle for the country. The best known E. is that of Pericles, given after the first year of the Peloponnesian War; it was an outstanding exposition of the achievements of Athenian democracy (Thuc. 2.34ff.). No such custom existed in other Greek states (but see the Roman *Laudatio Funebris).

EPRIUS MARCELLUS Roman orator and statesman of the 1st century AD, of humble origin, native of Capua. He made his career under Claudius and Nero (praetor in AD 48 and suffect consul in AD 62), and was one of the main accusers of *Thraea Paetus in AD 66. He survived the anarchy and civil wars of AD 68—9, opportunely collaborated with Vespasian and was governor of Asia in AD 70—3. In his public career and activity at the bar he amassed a fortune (200 million sesterces). Allegedly involved in a conspiracy with *Caecina Alienus, E. was condemned and committed suicide in AD 79.

EPULONES One of the four major priestly *collegia* at Rome, established by a tribunician law in 196 BC. Responsible for the organization and supervision of public banquets at certain festivals, the number of E. was raised to seven, and under Caesar to ten.
Latte, *R Rel.* (s.v.).

EPYLLION ("small epic") Poetical form used by Greek poets in the early 3rd century BC, and fashionable until the 1st century AD. The Greeks Callimachus, Theocritus and Euphorion and the Romans Catullus, Virgil and Ovid are the great names among the poets who wrote *epyllia*. The E. was narrative poetry in several hundred hexameters which usually told the story of a mythological figure.
M. M. Crump, *The Epyllion from Theocritus to Ovid*, 1931.

EQUITES ("horsemen") Traditionally, it was King *Romulus, or *Numa, who enrolled 100 horsemen (*celeres*) for the army out of each of the three old Roman tribes. Later the number was increased to 600, and finally to 1,800 (by *Servius Tullius). Militarily, they were divided into 30-men units (*turmae*), under the command of 3 *decuriones*, and, under the Republic, each legion normally comprised 300 horsemen. They were distinguished by tunics with a narrow purple stripe (*angustus clavus*) and purple embroidered mantles (*trabeae*). Their horses were decorated with silver discs (*phalerae*). The state provided them with horses — hence called *E. equo publico* — which they were required to maintain in good condition. Money for the maintenance came from a special tax on widows and orphans.

The 1,800 E. formed eighteen *centuriae* in the *comitia centuriata*, and were selected and supervised by the *censors. Wealthy men could, if they wished, serve as horsemen with their own horses from c. 400 BC on. A distinct census qualification was required for the E., which was fixed at 400,00 sesterces by the early 1st century (if not earlier). In 225 BC, the number of those who qualified for cavalry service is reported to have been 21,000. While the Roman cavalry was militarily inferior to the infantry and was gradually supplanted by units of the *Auxilia, Roman E. acquired special prestige; and due to the law (129 BC) that excluded senators from the 18 *centuriae*, and to the Gracchan law that gave them the *repetundae* court, this tendency was accelerated. By the law of Roscius (67 BC), *E. Romani*, that is, those who claimed the Equestrian census, were given the first 14 rows in the theatre; by now, they were also distinguished by the wearing of a golden ring. E. were said to form a distinct *ordo*, and their grip on the courts, which brought them into frequent conflict with the Senate, gave this undue emphasis. Socially, they mingled and intermarried with senators, and economically they had much in common with them, the two *ordines* thus forming the upper class in Roman society. Within the heterogenous Ordo Equester, it was mainly the *publicani* who as a more organized and powerful group exerted pressure. In the civil wars of the 80s of the 1st century BC, many lost their lives. Sulla deprived them of the jury courts, and weakened their leadership by adding many of their number to the Senate. The dispute over the courts ended with a compromise which in effect gave them more power (70 BC).

Under the Roman Empire, *E. Romani* were citizens of free birth (with the 400,00 sesterces census), as they had been in the late Republic; but they obviously no longer took part in politics. Augustus revived and reorganized the *E. equo publico*, which had declined with the absence of a regular censorship after 70 BC. They numbered more than 5,000 and had to pass the old inspection (*recognitio*), performed by the emperor. They also had to take part in the 15 July parade (*transvectio*) to the Capitol.

They included young men of senatorial families and were organized into *turmae*, commanded by *seviri equitum Romanorum*. Emperors might also give the title *eques equo publico* to persons who did not have a so-called "public horse" and did not take part in the above-named ceremonies. E. also formed four distinct panels (*decuriae*) of judges (*iudices*), to which Caligula added a fifth. From Augustus on, certain military and administrative positions were reserved for men of Equestrian rank, and in this way the Equestrian career developed as a possible avenue for entering the senatorial rank. These positions included the military tribunates and praefectures, various offices of *procuratores* (including the governorship of minor provinces), and the most important *Praefectus Aegyptu* and *Praefectus Praetorio*. From the time of the Severan emperors, more and more positions were reserved to E. at the expense of senators, and under *Diocletian, almost all the administration and the more important military offices were manned by them.

P. A. Brunt, T. R. S. Broughton, M. I. Henderson, in *The Crisis of the Roman Republic (ed. R. Seager)*, 69–134;
E. Badian, *Publicans and Sinners*, 1972.

ERASISTRATUS An important Greek physician and philosopher, E. lived and had a school in Alexandria in the 3rd century BC. He was influenced by the Peripatetic Straton and especially by the atomic theories of *Democritus and *Epicurus. He held that the body consisted of numerous disconnected atoms in a vacuum. By his anatomical and physiological research work, based largely on pathological surgery, he arrived at advanced views on sensory and motor nerves, though he wrongly speculated on blood circulation and respiration, believing that air flows through the arteries. He used mechanical ideas to explain digestion, and as he believed that diseases were the result of over-nutrition, he advocated dieting as the best medicine. Fragments of his writings are extant.
G. E. R. Lloyd, *Greek Science after Aristotle*, 1973 (s.v.).

ERATOSTHENES Greek scholar, native of Cyrene, born *c.* 274 BC and died *c.* 192 BC. He studied under *Arcesilaus and the Peripatetic Ariston (in Athens) and under *Callimachus (in Alexandria). At the invitation of *Ptolemy III, he became head of the Alexandrian Library and tutor of *Ptolemy IV in 235 BC. On account of his versatility he was nicknamed Pentathlos ("all-rounder"); because he was second in every field, he was also known as Beta. Of his literary works, the most important was the *On Ancient Comedy*, which comprised at least 12 books. His *chronographiai* was the first serious chronological study of history and literature. In mathematics, he gave a solution to the problem of duplicating a cube, and suggested the sieve method for finding prime numbers. He also worked on music, astronomy, and philosophy, and his best achievements were in geography. By an ingenious method, based on observations of the angle of the sun's rays at Alexandria and near Aswan, he made an accurate calculation of the circumference of the earth (252,000 *stades*). His detailed world map, based on meridians of longitude and parallels of latitude, was quite accurate, and superior to all those drawn previously. In his *Geographica*, in three books, he gave a systematic treatment of ethnographical, physical, botanic and zoological geography. His writings are not extant, and his geographical work is mainly known through *Strabo.
J. O. Thomson, *History of Ancient Geography*, 1948 (s.v.).

The Erechtheum, a Ionic temple

ERECHTHEUM The temple of *Erechtheus, one of the most imposing buildings on the Acropolis of Athens, built during the Peloponnesian War (421–407 BC). It consisted of several structures, the central one being divided into four parts. On its southern side was the famous (still extant) porch of the *Caryatids, and on the north side, a monumental porch with six Ionic columns. On its western side, in an open enclosure, was the olive tree given by Athena to the Athenians, and under a vestibule, the salt spring that erupted when Poseidon struck the rock in his dispute with the goddess over the city. The area of the E. had once been occupied by a Mycenaean palace and a temple of Athens dating to the 6th century BC.
I. T. Hill, *The Ancient City of Athens*, 1953, 179 ff.

ERECHTHEUS Mythological king of Athens, sometimes identified with, or said to be the grandson of, the mythological *Erichthonius. He was the son of Earth, but Athena raised him and they had a common cult (Homer, *Il.* 2.257ff.). E. had three daughters, one of whom (Chtonia) was sacrificed for the victory over *Eumolpus, son of Poseidon. In one myth, the Erechtheum was built on the spot where Poseidon killed him.

ERETRIA Prosperous city of Euboea in the Archaic period, mentioned by Homer (*Il.* 2.537), and important in the Greek colonization of southern Italy, Sicily, and the north Aegean. E. was destroyed by the Persians in 490 BC for its participation in the Ionic revolt nine years earlier. It was a member of the Delian League, but seceded from Athens in 411 BC. Despite many vicissitudes E. maintained a leading position in Euboea.

J. Boardman, *ABSA*, 1957, 14 ff.

ERICHTHONIUS Athenian mythological hero, born to Hephaestus and Earth, on whom semen fell while Hephaestus was attempting to make love to Athena. The goddess put E. in a basket, and gave him to the daughters of *Cecrops. Though she had warned them not to, they opened the basket, discovered a serpent with the child (or perhaps E. was half serpent), and killed themselves by leaping off the Acropolis. E. became king of Athens and established the festival of *Panathenaea; he was credited with (among other things) the invention of chariot-driving.

ERINNA Greek poetess, native of the island Telos, probably lived in the second half of the 4th century BC, and died at the age of 19. She wrote a poem of 300 hexameters, *The Distaff*, many lines of which are known

Above: Horseman. Etruscan fresco from c. 510 BC

Battle scene from the Ambrosian Iliad

Above: Fragment of the Ambrosian Iliad: Aphrodite shows Zeus her hand

Below: The Ambrosian Iliad. The Greek drag their boats to sea

Riders on horses — amphora of the 7th century BC

Detail from the pediment of the temple of Apollo at Eretria in Euboea

(primarily from a papyrus). With a delicate touch, she describes her experiences with her friend Baucis, whose death she mourns. Three of her epigrams are extant, two of which are epitaphs for her friend.

Diehl, *An. Lyr. Gr.*, 2.

ERINYES Spirits who pursued the Greeks and punished crimes, especially the murder of kinsmen. They are perhaps the personification of conscience and remorse. Their best known victims were *Orestes and *Alcmaeon. Usually they drove their victims mad. In a euphemistic version, they were placated by Athena with a cult at Athens where they were known as *Eumenides* ("kindly ones"); elsewhere, their cult was uncommon.

ERIS Greek deity, the personification of strife. Homer considered her the sister of Ares (*Il.* 4.440), and Hesiod presented her as the mother of Killing, Discord, War etc. (*Theog.* 224ff.). In her most famous myth, she threw the apple on which was written "for the most beautiful"; Athena, Hera and Aphrodite each claimed it for herself but *Paris awarded the apple to Aphrodite, and won *Hellen. In this way, E. brought about the Trojan War. She appeared in paintings from the 6th century BC on.

EROS Greek god of love (the Roman parallel was Cupid). In one version of his myth, he was the same age as Earth and Tartarus, the oldest of the gods, because without him no one could have been born (Hesiod, *Theog.* 120). But according to the more accepted tale, he was the son of Aphrodite and Hermes (or Ares). E. signifies unmanageable sexual desire. He is violent and cruel, and his victims lose control of their bodies and minds. From Homer on he was always a favourite subject for Greek poets, who ascribed to him all the contradictory feelings of love, best defined by *Sappho as "bitter-sweet". In the Hellenistic period, the theme of Eros tormenting *Psyche (soul) developed. Typically he is beautiful, young and surrounded by flowers. From the 5th century on, the bow and arrow is his weapon for striking victims. The familiar figure of the winged child armed with shafts developed from the 4th century BC on. In works of art, he appeared as an adolescent in the Archaic period, and became the little child in Hellenistic times; often several Erotes, not one E., are depicted in Roman art. E. was worshipped in several places, in Thespiae (in Boeotia) in rough stoneshape, in Athens, where there was a cult of E. and Aphrodite, and at Thebes, by the Sacred Band.

ERYX (modern Monte San Giuliano) High mountain (751 m) in western Sicily, settled in prehistoric times, later by the native Elymians, and then by the Carthaginians. E. was famous for its temple of the Phoenician goddess Astarte, who was identified with the Greek Aphrodite and the Roman Venus. *Hamilcar tried to save *Drepana from the Roman siege in the First Punic War by capturing the old Elymian town, but he failed. In Roman times, the temple *Aeneas was said to have founded for his mother Venus enjoyed various privileges.

ESQUILINE The *regio Esquilina* consisted of the two hills of Rome, Oppius and Cispius. For long periods of time, it served as a cemetery, particularly for the poor, under the late Republic. It was included within the Wall of *Servius. The Gardens of *Maecenas were in the E. and on the Oppius were the main part of Nero's *Domus Aurea* and the *Thermae* of Titus and Trajan.

ETEOCLES Greek mythological hero, elder son of *Oedipus and Iocasta. He and his brother Polynices incurred the wrath of their father who cursed them fatally. Contrary to an agreement, E. refused to give up the throne of Thebes after the first year of his reign. This led to the attack of the *Seven against Thebes, on which occasion the two brothers killed each other.

ETRUSCANS, ETRURIA The people inhabiting the country from the Arno in the north to the Tiber in the south and the east, from the 8th century BC on, called themselves *Rasena*; the Romans called them *Etrusci* or *Tusci*, and the Greeks knew them as *Tyrsenoi* or *Tyrrhenoi*. Their country was E., roughly modern Tuscany. The origins of the E. culture are obscure and their racial and lingual identity is disputed. Herodotus held that half the population of *Lydia was led by Tyrsenos the king's son to settle in Italy (1.94). The ancient historian *Dionysius of Halicarnassus (1.26−30) argued that the language, religion and government of the people of Lydia differed from those of the E., who, in his view, were autochthonous. A modern view is that the E. were Indo-European invaders who came from the north in the late 2nd millenium BC; but the evidence dates from the 4th century BC when the E. were pressed into the valleys of the Alps by Celtic tribes.

The source of the E. language is still a problem; a few lexical entries of E. words and some 10,000 inscriptions, mostly from tombs (where names and stereotyped formulas appeared), do not help much in solving it. There are only five relatively long inscriptions with some 1,800 words − the Zagreb mummy of the 2nd−1st century BC with 1,190 words, and the Capua tile of the 5th century BC are the longest. To these, two inscriptions found at Pyrgi in 1964 were added, but they did not contribute much either, even though they are bilingual (Punic and E.). Thus, despite some knowledge of E. phonetics, morphology and syntax, and although the meaning of many words is known, no significant breakthrough may be reasonably expected with this limited number of texts. That the E. language was not akin to any other language was recognized in antiquity (Dion. Hal. 1.30). It is commonly agreed that it is not an Indo-European language and that it does not resemble any known language, though inscriptions in a similar language were found at *Lemnos. There is therefore no linguistic evidence to show whether E. was a language introduced by invaders from the East, or one spoken by an indigenous population. Archaeological finds have shown that the E. cities developed on *Villanovan sites, while the evidence of objects of Oriental character may have been due to commerce. The E. religion, however, shows significant Oriental elements. It was taught by divine prophets who left books with religious laws. The E. dealt much with celestial phenomena and their significance. They had special priests, the *haruspices*, whose duty it was to interpret signs and omens and to divine the future by inspecting the liver. These religious and astrological practices resemble Oriental customs, notably Babylonian ones. Taken together, the evidence points to an invasion from the East, not in the 13th century as Herodotus says, but during the 8th century BC when groups of warriors conquered the native Villanovan population and mixed with them to some extent. It is important to note that the E. culture developed on Italian soil and reached its dis-

The interior of one of the tombs at Caere

tinctive and familiar characteristics during the 7th century BC, despite Eastern and Greek influence.

The E. culture was an urban one, at a time when the peoples of Italy, with the exception of the Greeks, lived in villages. Religious books and architectural lore gave precise instructions for the foundations of cities, which were marked by straight streets crossed at right angles, with defined locations for temples and altars, and which were defended by walls. The old E. cities were founded on hill tops in places with good natural defences; from *c.* 400 BC on, stronger walls were built on account of the rise of Rome. Some cities were established close to the sea (Caere, Tarquinii, Vetulonia, Rusellae, Populonia), and others inland (Volsinii, Clusium, Perusia, Arretium, Cortona, Veii). The temples of the 6th century BC were almost square shaped, with a colonnade in the front, and comprised three *cellae* for the E. triad of deities. Later temples came under Greek influence. A private house consisted of an entrance room, a central hall and a few rooms at the back. It may have been the precursor of the *Atrium-type house. Cemeteries were outside the city precincts, and, in their later development, resembled the layout of the city itself. Since death was considered as a continuation of life, the dead were equipped with the material apparata they had enjoyed on earth. Most of our knowledge on E. comes, in fact, from these cemeteries.

The E. city was an independent state, like the Greek *polis. In old times it was ruled by kings; the extensive powers of the king (*lauchme*, Latin *Lucumo*) declined in the 6th and 5th centuries BC, with the rise of the aristocracy which eventually established itself. Magistrates were elected annually; the highest ones were called *zilath*. It is not clear what their position was with regard to other magistrates. E. society consisted of the aristocratic class (organized in family groups), who were landowners, and of people who depended on them: tenants, serfs and slaves. The aristocrats (called *principes* in Latin) formed the State council. There is no evidence of the existence of a middle class, but there may have been a class of free farmers prior to the 3rd century BC. Judging by personal ties and dependence, E. society may be termed feudal. The aristocracy, as is known from literature and archaeological evidence, amassed wealth, developed a high level of culture, and enjoyed banquets, music, sports and art.

Agriculture, the basis of the E. economy, prospered thanks to their industry and advanced technology. The E. reclaimed forests, improved soil, and were excellent at drainage and irrigation, constructing canals and underground conduits. Sheep breeding was an old-established activity as was fishing and hunting. The forests provided good timber for building houses and ships, and E. was the only part of Italy with copper and iron mines. This, and the development of trade with central Europe and the East, contributed to the material prosperity of the E.

The E. cities never developed a general political organization, and even when faced with the growing power of Rome which menaced their political independence, they could not achieve unity. A loose league of twelve peoples, or cities, is mentioned in ancient authorities, but it was mainly of a religious character. They had a common sanctuary at Volsinii where an annual fair, festival, and meeting of the representatives of the cities was held. These gatherings had nothing to do with politics, however, and as a result, the E. were not able to retain their supremacy in Italy. The advance of the E. was

achieved through the initiative of the cities or of resourceful individuals, each acting on his own. E. cities appeared first on the coast of E. or close to it, then along the Tiber valley. They later extended to Umbria and the Po valley and to Latium and Campania (but the chronology of this expansion is far from certain). Some places in Latium fell under E. control by the end of the 7th century BC (e.g. *Rome, *Praeneste). At about the same time, Capua became E. In Campania, the E. advanced as far as Salerno (during the 6th century BC), with twelve cities (a stereotyped number). By the end of the 6th century BC, they had advanced to the Alps, where again they founded twelve cities (Liv. 5.33), among which were Felsina (near Bologna) and Mantua. But to judge by archaeological evidence, they settled mainly south of the Po, up to the Adriatic coast. They also challenged the Greeks in the western Mediterranean. With the support of Carthage, and led by *Caere, they won a naval battle off Alalia, thereby establishing control of Corsica. During this period, their trade reached southern France, Spain, Greece, Cyprus, Egypt and the Black Sea.

But is was not long before their power began to decline. They were defeated by *Aristodemus of Cumae in 524 BC, and again in 506 BC (at Aricia); they were expelled from Rome, and lost a naval battle off Cumae in 474 BC. These defeats, together with the occupation of Campania by Samnite tribes during the fifth century BC, deprived the E. of all their southern positions. In the late 5th century BC, the Gauls invaded the Po valley, and by the middle of the 4th century BC, they occupied the whole of this area. But Rome proved to be even more dangerous. Veii was destroyed in 396 BC, and during the next 150 years or so, the E. cities fell to Rome one by one, though they maintained their autonomy (like other Italian cities) until all received Roman citizenship in 90 BC. This brought about the quick Romanization of E., and it is no wonder that within a generation or two, the E. were a puzzle to historians and antiquarians.

E. Richardson, *The Etruscans, their Art and Civilization,* 1964;
Scullard, *Etruscan Cities* (Both works have good bibliographies);
M. Pallotino, *Testimonia Linguae Etruscae,* 1968 (A good collection of inscriptions).

EUBOEA A long island (the second largest in Greece), with an area of *c.* 3,600 sq km stretching from northwest to southeast opposite the eastern mainland coast of Greece. A mountainous island, E. was rich in timber, and cereals, vines and olives were grown on its plains. Its two main cities, *Eretria and *Chalcis, took a leading part in Greek trade and colonization in the Archaic period, but by the end of the 6th century BC, both had lost possessions to Athens. E.'s cities participated in the defence of Greece against the invasion of Xerxes, but the island subsequently belonged to the Athenian empire. Pericles established Athenian *cleruchies on land confiscated after the revolt of 446 BC. Like many other Greek cities, the cities of E. revolted against Athens in 411 BC. They joined the Second Athenian League for several years, starting in 377 BC, and in 371–358 BC came under Theban domination. The cities of E. formed a league in 341 BC, but from then on they were controlled mainly by Philip II and the kings of Macedonia. Rome abolished the league of E. which had been restored by *Flamininus in 196 BC for its support of the Achaean League in 146 BC, and E. became part of the province Macedonia. Under the

Roman Empire, E. was included in the province of *Achaea.

W. Wallace, *The Euboean League and its Coinage,* 1956; J. Boardman, *ABSA* (1957), 1 ff.; Larsen, *Cr. Fed. St.,* 97–103.

EUBULUS (1) Prominent Athenian statesman; born *c.* 405 BC, died *c.* 330 BC; famous for his good financial administration. From 355 BC on, he used his position as administrator of the *Theorica to reduce expenditure and secure sources of income, creating financial reserves with which he built a strong fleet, rebuilt the port of Piraeus, and carried out other public works. In politics, he opposed risky military operations and sought to increase the security of Athens by implementing a defensive policy. He recognized the threat posed by *Philip II, but sought to counteract it by diplomatic means; he was supported by *Aeschines and *Phocion but encountered the hostility of Demosthenes. E. lost his influence after 343 BC.
A. M. Andreades, *History of Greek Public Finance,* 1933 (s.v.).

EUBULUS (2) Prominent comic playwright of the 4th century BC, who won six victories in the *Lenaea. 58 titles of his 104 plays are known. Of these, half are on mythological subjects. Some of the plays were parodies of the tragedies of Euripides, Sophocles and other tragedians, others had contemporary figures or stock characters. Some fragments of his plays are extant.

EUCLEIDES Greek philosopher and native of Megara. A younger contemporary of Socrates, E. lived to *c.* 380 BC. After Socrates' death, his associates, including Plato, stayed for a time with E. who founded the Megarian school. One of E.'s important teachings, preserved by Diogenes Laertius (2.106), concerned the existence of only one good which is called by different names, e.g. wisdom, god, intelligence. Cicero claimed that E. followed the doctrine of monism of the Eleatic school (*Ac.* 2.129).

EUCLID Famed Greek mathematician, lived from the latter part of the 4th century to the early 3rd century BC. E. taught in Alexandria under *Ptolemy I, but very little is known about his life. He became famous with his geometrical textbook *Elements* (*stoicheia*). The book was translated into Latin, Arabic, Hebrew, Syriac and all the important European languages. Commentaries were written on it by *Pappus, *Heron and *Proclus (whose commentary on Book I is still extant). E.'s was the only geometrical system taught before the 19 century AD, and it is still considered useful. In the *Elements,* E. incorporated the achievements of his predecessors, added his considerably original contribution, and with logic and precision provided an excellent exposition of geometry. The work consists of 13 books: 1–4 deal with plane geometry, 5–6 with proportions, 7–10 with arithmetic (10 with irrationals), 11–13 with solid geometry. Books 14–15 were later additions. The clear definitions, the attractive axioms and postulates, the logical sequence of theorems, and the overall treatment secured the book its success. E.'s other works included treatises on music, optics and conics. *Data, On Divisions* (in Arabic), and *Phaenomena,* are extant.
J. L. Heilberg – H. Menge, *Euclidis Opera Omnia,* 1883–1916; T. L. Heath, *Elements*[2], 1956 (1925); G. E. R. Lloyd, *Greek Science after Aristotle,* 1973, (s.v.).

EUDOXUS (1) Prominent Greek scholar, excellent mathematician and astronomer, native of Cnidos, born *c.* 390 BC (or, less probably, in 408 BC) and died *c.* 338 BC.

In his youth, he studied in Athens and went to Egypt to learn astronomy. He taught in Cyzicus, at the court of *Mausolus, and finally in Athens. In his book, *On Proportions,* he laid the foundation for this subject, and his theory was incorporated by *Euclid in the fifth book of the *Elements.* E.'s other important contributions included the so-called "theory of exhaustion" and his work on irrationals. He wrote a work of descriptive geography in seven books. He also wrote on ethics (that pleasure is the highest good) and on the theory of ideas. His most important work was probably in astronomy, and he is considered the founder of scientific astronomy. Accepting Plato's view that astronomy was a mathematical science, E. put forward his theory of "homocentric spheres" which aimed at giving a mathematical explanation for known phenomena. (E. was personally involved in the construction of observatories in Cnidos and Egypt.) Essentially, his theory was based on the assumption that the courses of the sun, the moon and the planets resulted from circular movements of concentric spheres; each of the five planets was surrounded by four spheres, the earth remaining at the centre of all the spheres which circulated at different speeds while their axes were inclined to each other. In this way, E. was able to explain the retrogradations of the planets. The system, however, does not account for the retrogradations of Mars and Venus, nor for other phenomena; these failures were later observed and led to the rise of other theories. Another astronomical work by E. was his *Phaenomena* (on the constellations), on which *Aratus of Soli based his poem. Only fragments of E.'s work are extant.
F. Lasserre, *Die Fragments des Eudoxos von Knidos,* 1966; O. Neugebauer, *Exact Sciences in Antiquity*[2], 1957.

EUDOXUS (2) Greek seaman, native of Cyzicus, active in the 2nd century BC. He was sent twice by Ptolemy II Eurgetes to explore the sea-route to India, and on the second occasion he thought he discovered evidence for remnants of a ship from Gades on the eastern shore of Africa. He therefore sailed from Gades along the western coast of Africa, but had to return by land; he sailed again, and never came back.
Strabo, 2.98–9; E. Hyde, *Ancient Greek Mariners,* 1947 (s.v.).

EUGENIUS, Flavius A teacher of rhetoric in Rome, and friend of *Symmachus, E. was made Augustus in AD 392 by the *magister militum* Arbogast after the murder of Valentian II. His attempt at reconciliation with *Theodosius I failed. E. supported the pagans in Rome. He was defeated and killed by Theodosius in AD 494.

EUHEMERUS Greek writer, native of Messene, served under *Cassander in 311–298 BC, and won fame with his book *Sacred Scripture,* which gave an account of a fantastic voyage to blessed islands somewhere beyond Arabia. It took its name from the Holy Writings which described the achievements of Uranus, Kronos, and Zeus and were inscribed on a golden column on Panchaea, the main one of these imaginary islands. E. wrote that the gods in this utopia had originally been great kings, inventors, heroes and benefactors. This idea suited many traditional accounts of the ancient mythological Greek heroes, and, particularly, the new tendency of Hellenistic kings to develop ruler-cults. Ennius made a Latin adaptation of E.'s novel. Others later accepted this explanation of the nature of the gods. The theory was later used by Christian writers in the polemics against the pagans, and the term

Euhemerism was thus bequeathed to modern times.
Diod. Sicul. 5.41–6; 6.1.

EUMAEUS The swineherd of Odysseus, E. remained faithful to his master during his long years of absence and helped Penelope against the suitors. Although he was the son of a king, he was given to slave-traders (*Od.* 15.402ff.). Not recognizing Odysseus, E. entertained him and later helped him to get rid of the suitors.

EUMENES (1) of Cardia Born in 362/361 BC, served as secretary under *Philip II and Alexander, became chief secretary and was given military command in the last years of Alexander's reign. In the wars of the *Diadochi, he always supported the heirs of Alexander and the regents who stood for the unity of the empire. He was appointed satrap of Cappadocia and Armenia, and defeated *Craterus in 321 BC. Unable to maintain his position against *Antigonus I in Asia Minor, he fled to the eastern part of the empire and raised another army whose loyalty he sought to secure by promoting the cult of Alexander. After a great but indecisive battle against Antigonus in Paraetacene, in 317 BC, his Macedonian soldiers betrayed him at the battle of Gabiene (316 BC) and he was put to death. Being a Greek, his ability to maintain command over Macedonians and in competition with outstanding generals shows his distinct military and diplomatic talents.
Diod. Sic. 18; Plutarch, *Eumenes*.

EUMENES (2) I Ruler of Pergamum 263–241 BC. He defeated *Antiochus I near Sardes in 262/261 BC, and established his independence against the Seleucid kings. *Antiochus II defeated E. and recovered most of the territory lost by his predecessor.
Hansen, *Attalids*[2] (s.v.).

EUMENES (3) II Eldest son of *Attalus I, king of Pergamum 197–160 BC. He followed his father's policy of cooperation with Rome, and supported Rome in the war – which he helped to bring about – against Antiochus III. E. played a decisive role at the battle of Magnesia, and, after the war, was given the Thracian Chersonessus and most of the Seleucid territories in Asia Minor. He retained Roman support until the Third Macedonian War, which he helped to provoke with his accusations against King *Perseus. Due to his political manoeuvres during the war, E. lost the trust of Rome. He was a great philo-Hellenist and helped Rhodes, Delphi and Athens (where he built the Stoa of Attalus). Thanks to E.'s extensive building programme, Pergamum gained magnificent buildings.
Hansen, *Attalids*[2] (s.v.).

EUMOLPUS Greek mythological hero, the eponymous ancestor of the Eumolpidae clan in *Eleusis. Son of Poseidon and Chione, he was said to have founded the Eleusinian Mysteries. He fell in a battle against the Athenian *Erechtheus. According to another myth, he was the son of *Musaeus.

EUNAPIUS Greek Sophist, teacher of rhetoric, and historian, born in Sardes *c.* AD 345 and died *c.* AD 420. He studied in Athens and lived most of his life in Asia Minor. His fourteen-book history, covering the period AD 270–404, had a strong anti-Christian bias. Only fragments are extant – thanks to its use by later historians. His *Lives of the Sophists*, which followed the example of *Philostratus, is extant. A devoted pagan, his hero was Julian. E.'s work was a defence of the old traditions against Christianity.
L. Dindorf, *Historici Graeci Minores*, 1870, 1, 205 ff; *Lives of the Sophists*, ed. C. Giangrande, 1956.

EUPATRIDAI Greek term designating aristrocratic birth; the E. claimed genealogies from mythological heroes. They governed the Greek cities after the decline of the monarchy, and their existence in Athens as the upper class of society was ascribed to *Theseus. The E. were *Archontes, who became members of the *Areopagus, retained the knowledge of religious law, and monopolized certain priesthoods. The reforms of *Solon, which made wealth the criterion for holding office, lost them some of their political dominance; this was finally destroyed by *Cleisthenes (2) and the rise of democracy. The E. managed, however, to maintain their religious duties.
H. T. Wade-Gery, *Essays in Greek History*, 1958, 86ff.

EUPHORION Greek poet of the 3rd century BC, born *c.* 275 (?), native of Chalcis. He studied philosophy in Athens, became rich through his relationship with a wealthy widow, and was installed by Antiochus III as librarian at Antioch in Syria, where he died. Of his works, only titles and a few fragments are extant. His prose included *On the Isthmian Games*, *On the Aleuadae*, a lexicon to Hippocrates in six books, and historical works. A few of his epigrams survive; he generally wrote *epyllia*, and his subjects were mythological. He also seems to have indulged in the writing about obscure myths, aetiological tales, questions of etymology, and difficult phrases. He was evidently influenced by the erudite poets of Alexandria, like *Callimachus and *Apollonius Rhodius, from whom he borrowed material. But poetic erudition was forced and over elaborate, very detailed and repetitious. His *Replies to Theodorides*, a verse epistle, was probably different. For all his shortcomings, E. had influence on subsequent poets like Catullus and Gallus (termed *cantores Euphorionis* by Cicero), and Virgil
J. U. Powell, *Collectanea Alexandrina*, 1925; D. L. Page, *Greek Literary Papyri* (Loeb), 1950.

EUPHRONIUS Greek painter and potter active in the late 6th century and the early 5th century BC. Five red-

Heracles wrestling with Antaeus. A vase by Euphronius, late 6th century BC

figure vases which he painted are extant, the best known of which depicts Heracles and Antaeus. He employed other artists for the painting of his ceramics.

EUPOLIS One of the three great playwrights of Old Comedy. He produced his first play in 430/429 BC — allegedly at the age of seventeen. There is a dubious story that Alcibiades threw E. into the sea in the expedition to Sicily in 415 BC because he had ridiculed him in his *Baptai*. E. died in the Hellespont shortly after 412 BC. He won seven victories, but only fragments and titles of his works are extant. Many of E.'s plays were political, mainly attacking the demagogues: Hyperbolus in the *Maricas*, and Cleon in the *Generation of Gold*. In his *Baptai*, Alcibiades and his associates, in female clothing, worship a Thracian goddess. The Sophists, too, were attacked by him (*Flatterers*). He seems to have been dissatisfied with all the politicians of his day — in his *Demos* (known from papyri), the statesmen of the former generation come from the underworld to help the city. E. was apparently an inventive poet, a master of language (though he may have been more indecent than other comedists), and a successful rival of Aristophanes.

Edomonds, *Fr.At.Gr.* 1.

EURIPIDES Youngest of the three great Athenian tragic playwrights, born in 480 or 485 BC. Many of the known details of his life may be doubted. His family lived at Phlya, on the east side of Mount Hymettus, where it had a local priesthood and was probably well-to-do. E. was a good athlete, was well educated (Anaxagoras was said to have been his teacher), and later moved in philosophical circles with Socrates, among others. He allegedly married twice and had three children. He used to work in a secluded cave in Salamis, and became notorious for his unsociability; his gloomy nature and his addiction to books made him even less popular. All these characteristics were an easy target for Aristophanes' mockery. It was probably E.'s connection with the Sophists that led to his prosecution for impiety by *Cleon. E. left Athens c. 408 BC, accepting the invitation of the Macedonian king, Archelaus, to come to his court. He died and was buried there in 407/406 BC. The Athenians built a cenotaph for him on the road to Piraeus.

E. first participated in dramatic competitions at the Dionysia in 445 BC. But he did not win his first victory until 441 BC, after which he only won three additional prizes during his lifetime. He is reported to have shown no interest in theatrical success. There is more extant writing by E. than by any other Greek playwright: 18 (or 19) plays (out of 92), many fragments, and about 80 known titles. Though underestimated in his own lifetime, his plays were widely read and often performed in later times, more than all the plays of the other tragedians. His popularity has lasted for many centuries.

The following are the plays of E. which have survived:
Alcestis (438) tells the story of Alcestis who volunteered to die instead of her husband Admetus. She is saved by Heracles who fights Thanatos and brings her back to her husband. The play was produced instead of the satyr-play (*Tragedy). Its treatment of Alcestis is serious — but there is also an ironic touch in the description of the gluttonous Heracles and the coarse quarrel between Admetus and his father.

Medea (431) an outstanding tragedy concerning a proud woman who gives everything to her beloved Jason, and is then deserted for a younger woman. In revenge, she inflicts a mortal wound on him by killing their children.

The Children of Heracles (430) tells how Athens (under Demophon, son of Theseus) protects the children of Heracles against Eurystheus who had come to kill them. An insignificant play, produced at the time when Attica was invaded by the Spartans, the ungrateful descendants of the children of Heracles.

Hippolytus (428) in which Phaedra, Theseus' wife, falls in love with her stepson Hippolytus, who resists the temptations of Aphrodite. The fatal encounter of the love-driven woman and the ascetic youth ends in the death of both.

Hecuba (c. 425) is another play that concentrates on the feelings of a woman, one whose children were all killed in the sack of Troy. She takes dreadful revenge on the king of Thrace who has killed her last descendant.

Suppliant Women (c. 420) concerns the Argive women to whom Theseus returns the bodies of the Seven against Thebes; the bodies were refused burial by the Thebans.

Andromache (c. 420) deals with the hostility between Hermione, the wife of Neoptolemus, and his concubine Andromache (the widow of Hector). Hermione does not succeed in killing Andromache. It is considered a second class tragedy.

Heracles (date uncertain) in which Heracles begins by saving his children, his wife and his father from Lycus, who has seized power in Thebes during his mission to bring Cerberus from Hades. Heracles is then driven mad by Hera, and kills his own children and his wife. The accepted myth of Heracles is freely changed by the poet for his purposes, conventional religious behaviour is disregarded, and the hero faces the irrational twists of fate; his feat lies in overcoming his own suffering.

Cyclops (date unknown), a satyr-play which turns the Homeric story about Odysseus and Polyphemus into a burlesque farce. The satyrs, Silenus and his sons, are the slaves of Polyphemus and form the chorus.

The Trojan Women (415), a dramatization of the massacre that occurred in Troy after its capture by the Greeks. Men are killed, women are passed around among the victors, and the city is burnt. The play was produced shortly after Athens had exterminated the men of Melos who refused to join her empire.

Electra (c. 413) presents the myth — concerning the avenging of Agamemnon's murder — which had been used previously by Aeschylus and Sophocles. While living as a peasant's wife, Electra waits for Orestes who finally returns and murders their mother. The matricide is a crime, not a religious expiation, and the avengers are faced with the horror of their deed.

Helen (412), an invention of the poet that turns the old myth into a semi-comedy — Paris takes the phantom of Helen to Troy. Menelaus finds his wife in Egypt, and they both succeed in escaping to their home.

Iphigenia in Tauris (c. 411) in which Iphigenia serves as the priestess of Artemis in Tauris, after the goddess has saved her from being sacrificed by Agamemnon at Aulis. She discovers that the strangers, whom it is her duty to sacrifice, are her brother Orestes and his friend. They all safely escape from the barbarian country.

Ion (c. 411), a tragedy with complications of mistaken identity. Ion, son of Apollo and Creusa, is abandoned by his mother and brought up to serve in the Delphic temple. He is adopted by the childless Xuthus, Creusa's husband. The mother and son try to kill each other, until they discover their true relationship.

Phoenician Women (about 410–408) concentrates on the feud between Eteocles and Polynices, and includes incidentally the story of the house of Oedipus and many other Theban myths.

Orestes (408), the sequence of *Electra*. Orestes, who suffers repeated attacks of madness on account of his deed, is condemned to death with his sister. His hope of being rescued by Menelaus proves false, and he seizes Menelaus' palace and his daughter Hermione. But Menelaus does not give in and only the appearance of Apollo, the *deus ex machina*, prevents the impending catastrophe.

Iphigenia in Aulis, completed and produced after Euripides' death. It concentrates on the internal conflict of Agamemnon, who has to sacrifice his daughter, and on the changing reactions of Clytemnestra and Iphigenia. Artemis probably intervened to save Iphigenia in the play's lost ending.

Bacchae, an outstanding play, written in Macedonia, in which Dionysus comes to Thebes with his Maenads to establish his cult. King Pentheus, though forewarned, tries to suppress the ecstatic worship and is punished by the god. Believing in his power to carry the Cithaeron, he is tempted to watch the Maenads (who are led by his own mother) and is torn to pieces by them. The triumphant god then reveals himself. The play deals with the conflict between traditions and new beliefs, faith and reason, and, above all, with the revelation of the irrational power that governs human nature.

E. was a great poet. There is a story that some of the Athenians captured at Syracuse won their freedom by reciting his lyrics. Aristotle considered him the "most tragic" of tragedians. In many respects, he is the most "modern" of the tragic poets of Athens. He takes his subjects from a variety of myths, sets them in his own world, and uses them for his purposes by free adaptation and even bold invention. His characters are reduced to human proportions, and thus whatever happens to them is of real concern to the spectators. E. provoked his contemporaries with the emotions he excited in his plays, especially with pity. He was interested in and had insights into the workings of the soul and the mind. In his portrayal of people, he deals mainly with depraved characters who suffer from fits of madness or love, from strong, frustrated emotions. His descriptions of the depth of the feelings of embittered women are a great achievement. (His success in portraying degraded women does not mean that he was hostile to them.) Passions for him were not the result of external forces, but rather innate powers causing extreme suffering in their conflicting courses. Hence, he regarded some of the traditional gods as symbols of natural or psychological forces. In several of his plays, Chance predominates, and he seems to deny any divine plan, recognizing the irrationality and cruelty of the forces of nature and hence their inexplicable morality. E.'s contemporaries felt uneasy about these unconventional features, as well as the many allusions to political problems. While his plays contain many anti-Spartan implications, E. also censures specific actions of Athens – its campaign against Melos, its war policy, its demagogues, its extreme democrats, and the deceitfulness of its politics.

While E. could produce perfect plots, this was not his prime concern. The structure of the plays was subordinate to the effects, conflicts and psychological treatment he wanted to produce. Hence, there are many episodic and incoherent plays. A familiar feature of the plays is the special place of the prologues and the epilogues – a role many times given to gods. The prologue supplies the background details necessary for the understanding of the plot. Similarly, the epilogue, pronounced in many plays by the *deus ex machina*, reveals what lies in the future for the heroes. The role of the chorus in E.'s plays declined through the years – this aroused the disapproval of Aristotle. The chorus usually contributes little to the development of the action, and choral passages tend to be lyrical interludes. The elaborately rhetorical passages in E.'s plays are conspicuous, and he was influenced no doubt by the contemporaneous development of the art of rhetoric. Many of his characters' speeches express his own ideas and feelings, and some seem to have been composed mainly for the sake of rhetorical argument. He is more successful in the Messenger's speeches, which often include excellent, vivid descriptions. E.'s language varies from the common – when his style is reduced from the sublime to the ordinary – to the beautiful and lyrical, with ornamental passages and composition. The music of his plays has been lost but in this field, too, he was innovative and encountered much criticism.

With the death of E. and Sophocles, great Attic tragedy came to an end. The next generations were unable to cope with the great problems. E. himself won a posthumous success. His plays were performed repeatedly and they influenced writers of comedy and novelists.

Text: G. Murray (O.C.T.), 1902–1913;
D. L. Page, *Greek Literary Papyri* (Loeb), 1942;
A. S. Way (Loeb) 1912;
D. Grene and L. Lattimore, *The Complete Greek Tragedies*, 1959;
A. Lesky, *Greek Tragedy*[3], 1967;
T. B. L. Webster, *The Tragedies of Euripides,* 1967.

EUROPA Greek mythological heroine, daughter of Agenor or of Phoenix, the king of Tyre or of Sidon. Zeus fell in love with her, and disguised as a beautiful bull, carried her on his back to Crete where she bore him *Minus, *Rhadamanthys and (in a post-Homeric version) *Sarpedon. He gave her three presents (the bronze man Talos who guarded Crete, the hound that did not miss the quarry, and the javelin that did not miss the target) which were all inherited by Minos. Her brother *Cadmus founded Thebes in his search for her. She was identified with a local Cretan goddess and the bull became the constellation Taurus. It is possible that this is an aetiological myth of the Cretan bull-riding rite. But in Boeotia, E. was an earth goddess. The popular theme of E. carried away by the bull is found in an extant *epyllion* by *Moschus, and in Ovid (*Met.* 2.846ff.), and is depicted in a 6th century metope of the Siphnian treasure-house at Delphi, as well as in a temple at Selinus.

EURYBIADES Spartan admiral in 480 BC, commander of the fleet of the Greeks who fought against Xerxes. Accepting the advice of Themistocles, he led the victorious force at the battle of Salamis, but refused to destroy the Persian bridge over the Hellespont.

Herodotus, 8; C. Hignett, *Xerxes' Invasion of Greece*, 1963.

EURYCLES, Gaius Iulius After his father's execution by Antony, E. fought with Octavian at Actium. As a reward, he received Roman citizenship, the island Cythera, and rule over Sparta. With the money he received from *Herod during his visit to Judaea, E. provoked strife in Greece. He was banished by Augustus in 2 BC, and died soon after. His son Laco succeeded him in Sparta. A festival in honour of E. was established at Sparta and Gytheum.

G. W. Bowersock, *JRS,* 1961, 112 ff.

EURYDICE (1) This name ("wide-judging") was given to many mythological figures, especially those of the nether world. The most famous is E. wife of *Orpheus. Bitten by a snake (in her flight from *Aristaeus, according to Virgil's version), she died. Orpheus descended to Tartarus, where he charmed Hades into letting him take back with him E., on condition that he would not look around until she had reached the upper world. But he could not overcome the temptation to look at his beloved, and soon Hermes, the guide of the dead, appeared and took E. back to the underworld. In one version, Orpheus had E. back for only one day. The scene of Hermes returning E. to Hades probably appeared on a relief on the altar of the Olympieum in Athens (late 5th century BC), copies of which are extant. The story was told by many writers; in Plato's *Symposium*, Orpheus receives only a phantom because he is not ready to die for love and he is later killed by the Maenads for his cowardice. Virgil (*Geog.* 4), Ovid, Seneca (*Hercules Furens*), and Statius told the story which later (for *Boethius in *De Consolatione Philosophiae* 3) came to symbolize the impossibility of a return to sensuality once the soul has turned to god.

EURYDICE (2) The name of several Macedonian princesses:
1. Daughter of Amyntas (nephew of Philip II), and wife of Philip Arrhidaeus (son of Philip II) who became joint-king with Alexander's son in 323 BC. She used her husband to intrigue against *Antipater and *Polyperchon. Captured by *Olympias, she committed suicide after the murder of her husband (317 BC).
2. Daughter of *Antipater (1), married *Ptolemy I some time after 322 BC but lost her influence to *Berenice (1) and was divorced by 287 BC. Ptolemy Ceraunus was her son.

EURYMEDON River in Pamphylia, in south Asia Minor, about 170 km long and partially navigable in antiquity. Famous as the site of the double victory (on land and on sea) of *Cimon over the Persians c. 467 BC.

EURYPONTIDAI One of the two royal houses of Sparta. *Archidamus, *Agis II, *Agesilaus and *Agis IV were of this house.

EURYSTHEUS Greek mythological figure, son of Sthenelus and grandson of Perseus, king of Mycenae or Tiryns. By hurrying his birth and delaying the birth of Heracles, Hera made him overlord — and Heracles had to perform the famous twelve labours for him (Hom. *Il.* 19.76ff.). But E. feared him and would not let him enter his palace. After Heracles' death, E. was killed while pursuing his sons.

EUSEBIUS Christian writer and historian, c. AD 262–340, native of Caesarea in Palestine, where he studied under Pamphilius (who sought to preserve the works of Origen). During the persecutions of Diocletian, E. fled but was subsequently imprisoned. His teacher died as a martyr in AD 310. In AD 314, E. was made bishop of Caesarea. Though a supporter of Arius, he tried to arrive at a compromise, and at Nicaea agreed to the condemnation of Arius. He later reversed his position and in AD 335 agreed to the condemnation of Athanasius.

E. was a prolific writer. While in his historical and theological works he criticizes and attacks Greek philosophy, he is ready to recognize its merits as well as the merits of the Old Testament since the two were preparatory stages for the rise of Christianity. His writings include the following: a brief account of world history, with chronological tables from the time of Abraham to

Persian archers from the royal palace at Susa

AD 303 (it is mainly known from an Armenian version and the free translation into Latin by St. Jerome); *Ecclesiastical History*, which gives the story of the Church from its beginnings to AD 324 (in ten books, it maintains that it was God's will that the Church triumphed, and shows the influence of Hellenistic biography and historical writing; it served as an example for all subsequent writers of ecclesiastical history); *Martyrs of Palestine*, a special account of the persecution of Christianity is given; a biography of Constantine; *Praeparatio Evangelica*, in 15 books (demonstrating the superiority of Judaism over pagan philosophy); *Demonstratio Evangelica* (Christianity as the fulfilment of Biblical prophecies); and *Onomasticon* (a lexicon of Biblical places).

Migne, *Patrologiae Cursus, Series Graeca* XIX–XXIV; K. Lake – J. E. L. Oulton, *Ecclestiastical History* (Loeb), 1926–1932; *Chronica* (ed. A. Schoene) 1866–75; (ed. J. Karst) 1911; E. M. Gifford, *Praeparatio Evangelica* (Loeb), 1903; D. S. Wallace-Hadrill, *Eusebius of Caesarea*, 1960.

EUTHYCHIDES Greek sculptor, pupil of *Lysippus, native of Sicyon, where he lived the first part of the 3rd century BC. His best known work is the Tyche of Antioch, of which many copies are extant.

EUTHYDEMUS I Native of Magnesia, he overthrew Diodotus II and became king of Bactria (c. 235 BC). Though defeated by *Antiochus III in 208, he retained his kingdom to c. 200.

EUTHYNA In Greek cities, the procedure for the examination of financial administration and the accounts of

all officials; in Athens it was performed by the *logistai.
If the accounts were not satisfactory, or a charge was
made, the case had to be decided in court presided over
by the logistai. This was supplemented by a second control, the ten eythynoi, who were chosen by lot from the
*Boule and had to investigate any charge brought against
the officials, bringing it to court if necessary.

EUTROPIUS A Roman historian, E. served under Julian
against Persia in AD 363. His Roman history in ten books
is a brief account of the period from the time of Romulus
to AD 364. He used an Epitome of Livy for the Republican
period (1—6) and various sources for the Empire (7—10).

EVAGORAS Born a Teucrid c. 435 BC, of the ruling
family of Cyprian Salamis. E. was exiled in his youth.
With a force he had collected in Cilicia, he took control of
Salamis in 411 BC. He fortified the city and cooperated
politically with Athens. After Aegospotamoi, *Conon escaped to him. While Persia was occupied with Spartan
forces in Asia Minor, E. faced no problems. But after the
collapse of the Spartan Empire with the Battle of Cnidos
in 394 BC, the war with Persia was almost inevitable. It
started in 390 BC. For several years, E. made spectacular
advances, taking control of Phoenicia and part of Cilicia.
But in 381 BC, he was defeated in a naval battle. He
concluded a fair peace treaty by playing off the Persian
commanders against each other. He was murdered in 374
BC.

G. Hill, *A History of Cyprus,* 1940.

EVANDER Greek mythological hero, son of Hermes
and a nymph, or of Echemos of Tegea whose grandfather
was Pallas. Associated with Pan, and worshipped at Pallan-
tion in Arcadia (first mentioned by Hesiod), E. was later
said to have been the first settler at Rome and the son of
*Carmentis. He was associated with *Faunus whose cult
he allegedly established. In Virgil (*Aen.* 8) he meets Priam
and Anchises at Arcadia, migrates to Italy and founds the
settlement Pallanteum, the Palatine. He also established
the *Lupercalia and the cult of Hercules (who killed
*Cacus) at the Ara Maxima. E. helped Aeneas against Tur-
nus, who had killed his son Pallas in battle (*Aen.* 10).

EXECIAS Prominent Athenian potter and vase-painter
active in the second half of the 5th century BC. Eleven
signatures of his are extant. His excellent black-figure
vases include the one with Achilles and Ajax playing dice
(Vatican Museum), Dionysus on the boat (Munich), and
the death of Ajax (Boulogne).

J. D. Beazley, *Attic Black-figure Vase Painters,* 1956,
143 ff.

EXEGETES   An expounder of law. The best known
were the Athenian *exegetai,* attested to from the early 4th
century BC on. One E. was elected by the *demos* from the
*Eupatridai, a second by the Delphic Pythia, and two
more were elected from the Eumolpidae family (from 329
BC) to interpret the sacred law of the Eleusinian Mysteries (*Eumolpus). These E. mainly dealt with sacred
unwritten law as well as secular matters associated with

A vase-painting of Execias showing Dionysius, dolphins and grapes

religion. It is not clear what precise department of law came under each E. They existed in other cities, too; for instance, at the oracle of Telmessos in Lycia (Hdt. 1.78). J. H. Oliver, *The Athenian Expounders of the Sacred and Ancestral Law,* 1950.

EXILIUM ("exile") In Rome, this term originally applied to citizens or *peregrini* who, when prosecuted on a capital crime, left Roman territory before the court issued its verdict. In the late Republic, this customary right was legalized and self-banishment was followed by a formal interdiction (*aquae at ignis interdictio*) by a magistrate. The exiled was liable to the death penalty if caught on Roman territory. E. as an administrative or jurisdictional measure was employed in other cases. One was the *relegatio.* This could be a temporary expulsion from a particular place, ordered as an administrative measure by a magistrate using his coercive powers. It was also used as a penalty, with different degrees of severity, for various crimes. The extreme penalty of E. was the *deportatio,* which meant perpetual expulsion and confinement to a certain place, together with loss of property and citizenship. Under the Roman Empire, E. was a "privileged" penalty, reserved for the high classes.

Jolowicz, *Roman Law*[3] (s.v.).

F

FABIUS (1) One of five leading patrician clans at Republican Rome, prominent from the 5th century BC on. The clan ceased to exist by the early Empire though the name continued to be used. The important branches were the Ambusti, Buteones, Maximi and Vibulani. Traditionally almost the entire clan was destroyed by the Etruscans in the battle of *Cremera. They gave their name to one of the oldest tribes, Fabia.
Scullard, *Rom.Pol.*² (s.v.).

FABIUS (2) MAXIMUS RULLIANUS, Quintus Leading Roman statesman and general in the last quarter of the 4th century and early 3rd century BC. He was five times consul (322, 310, 308, 297, and 295 BC), dictator (315, ? 313 BC), censor (304 BC), proconsul (309, 307, 296 BC) and *princeps senatus*. He won victories over the Etruscans in 325, 310 and 308 BC, the Samnites at Lautulae in 315 BC, and, most notably, over the combined forces of the Samnites, Etruscans and Gauls, in the decisive battle at Sentinun in 295 BC. He was the first to traverse the wooded, and formidable Ciminian mountains in Etruria (310 BC). His achievements were later exaggerated and embellished.

FABIUS (3) MAXIMUS VERRÚCOSUS CUNCTATOR, Quintus Most famous member of the clan, Rome's leading statesman and general in the Second Punic War. He was five times consul (233, 228, 215, 214, 209 BC), twice dictator (*c.* 220, 217 BC), censor (230 BC) and *princeps senatus* from 209 to his death in 203 BC. He was given a triumph for his victory over the Ligurians in 230 BC. It is to F.'s credit that he recognized very early (after the defeat at Trasimene in 217 BC) that in view of Hannibal's new tactics and military genius, Rome was no match for him in a direct battle. He also found the right strategy for fighting him, namely to reduce his forces by a war of attrition and punitive actions against Italian collaborators, while avoiding a direct clash. This strategy, however, seemed shameful to Rome, and won him the nickname Cunctator ("Delayer"). The disaster of *Cannae in 216 BC vindicated his policy, and he was given command several more times. Following F.'s doctrine, Roman generals avoided fighting great battles against Hannibal to the end of the war in Italy. In 209 BC he won back Tarentum from Hannibal. At this period, F. was the most influential statesman of Rome, unscrupulous enough to exploit his

priestly offices (Pontifex and Augur) for political purposes. He exerted his influence to prevent Scipio from carrying the war into Africa (but ultimately failed). F.'s cautious, simple strategy and perseverance saved Rome in its lowest ebb; the derogatory appelation, Cunctator, became an honourable title, and he was the Shield of Rome, *unus homo nobis conctando restituit rem*, as Ennius put it. Plutarch, *Fabius*; Scullard, *Rom.Pol.*² (s.v.).

FABIUS (4) PICTOR, Quintus Roman statesman and historian, active in the Second Punic War. After the disaster of Cannae, he went as senatorial legate to consult the Delphic Oracle on how to change the tide of the war. His *History of Rome*, the first historical work by a Roman, was in Greek, either because he wanted to familiarize the Greeks with Roman traditions, or because Latin prose was perhaps not considered suitable for history. The narrative started with Aeneas and gave a selective, biased account of events down to F.'s own time. The writing of history in Greek was followed by other early Roman historians (L. Cincius, Acilius, A. Postumius). Polybius, though he disapproved of F.'s pro-Roman distortion, used him, as did Livy and Dionysius of Halicarnassus. It was due to his account and authority that members of his clan (Fabian) were portrayed favourably in Roman historiography.
Peter, *His.Rom.Rel.*, 1;
Badian, in *Latin Historians* (ed. T. A. Dorey), 1966.

FABIUS (5) RUSTICUS Roman historian of the 1st century AD, probably from Spain. His *History* dealt with the period of Nero, but its chronological framework is not known. Tacitus seems to have used the work and highly praised F.'s style (*eloquentissimus auctor, Agr.* 10.3). As protégé of Seneca, F. defended his patron and attacked Nero.
Peter, *His. Rom. Rel.* 2; Syme, *Tacitus*, (1958), 289ff.

FABLES Short tales, usually about animal life, with moral teaching, featured in Greek folklore no less than other peoples' folklore. Their use in literature is as old as *Hesiod (the tale of the hawk and the nightingale) and *Archilochus (the fox and the eagle). F. became a distinct literary genre probably by the 6th century BC. The genre was connected with the name of *Aesop and subsequently collections of F. were called Aesopic tales. They were written both in prose and in verse. Babrius (before the 2nd century AD) is the earliest writer whose collection is extant. Roman poets, under the Greek influence (Lucilius and Horace for instance) included F. in their works. *Faedrus is the earliest writer who wrote a collection of F. in Latin. While he drew on the traditional Aesopic tales, he also added many of his own. His aim was to entertain and educate the readers and, possibly, to criticize the contemporary political scene. Also extant is a collection of Latin F. by *Avianus which is inferior.

Editions: B. E. Perry, *Aesopica*, 1952;
Babrius and Phaedrus (Loeb), 1965.
W. R. Halliday, *Greek and Roman Folklore*, 1927.

FABRICIUS LUSCINUS, Gaius Roman statesman and general, of a plebeian family, prominent in the first quarter of the 3rd century BC. As consul in 282 BC, he was awarded a triumph for his victory over the Samnites; again as consul in 278 BC, he won a triumph for defeating the Lucani, Brutii, Tarentines and the Samnites. Thurii erected a statue at Rome in his honour for saving her from the Sabellians. He represented Rome in the negotiations with *Pyrrhus in 280 and 278 BC. F.'s poverty and incorruptibility became legendary, and he was taken as a model of the old Roman virtues.
E. T. Salmon, *Samnum and the Samnites*, 1967 (s.v.).

FABULA Latin term for all kinds of plays, literally meaning "talk" or "story". The different genres of plays were named, and classified, by the costume of actors. F. *palliata* (*pallium*, a Greek cloak) and *crepidata* (*crepida*, a Greek shoe) were Roman adaptations of original Greek comedies; F. *togata* (*toga*, the traditional Roman garment), or *tabernaria*, were comedies about Italian life and characters. But there were no accepted definitions for all kinds of plays, and hence the confused use of terms by ancient authors. The other genres include: F. *praetextata* (*praetexta*, the toga of Roman magistrats), a drama on Roman historical subjects; F. *trabeata* (*trabea*, the typical garment of *Equites) – a comedy about upper-middle class characters, invented in the Augustan period; and F. *riciniata ricinium*, a woman's mantel) – a mimic play. The F. *palliata*, first produced by *Livius Andronicus, flourished more than any other genre and was fully and successfully exploited by *Plautus and *Terence. A native Italian genre of play was the *Atellana Fabula*.
G. E. Duckworth, *The Nature of Roman Comedy*, 1952; W. Beare, *The Roman Stage*[3], 1964.

FACTIONES In Republican Rome, the political groups within the senatorial aristocracy whose henchmen and dependents were from the equestrian and lower classes. In early times, grouping according to family lines had probably been far more important than it was by the late Republic. The role of F. from the 3rd to early 1st centuries BC has probably been exaggerated, and is much disputed. That F. represented different attitudes towards internal and foreign politics is very doubtful; it is equally doubtful that leading personalities restricted their freedom of action to any great extent on account of allegiance to F. It appears that F. were loose combinations, constantly shifting and changing. Influential people based their power on their clients, and cooperated with other members of the nobility, in their own best interests, taking their family and personal relations and obligations as well as state interests, into account. (See also *Races).

L. R. Taylor, *Party Politics in the Age of Caesar*, 1949; Scullard, *Rom.Pol.*[2];
I. Shatzman, *Ancient Society* (1974), 197 ff.

A relief of a mountain town found in Lake Nami

FAESULAE (modern Fiesole) Etruscan town situated on the hills over Florence. It was from here that Hannibal marched to Lake Trasimene to defeat the Romans (217 BC), though F. sided with Rome in the Second Punic War. It suffered much in the Social War, and Sulla confiscated its land to establish a *colonia* for his veterans. *Catiline found many supporters here in 63. *Stilicho destroyed an Ostrogothic army at F. in AD 405. Considerable remains of the 3rd century BC walls as well as a theatre are extant.

FALERII Old town on a commanding site at the confluence of the Treia with the Tiber, traditionally an Argive settlement. It was much contested between Rome and *Veii. After a revolt in 241 BC, the old town, Falerii Veteres (modern Civita Castellana) was destroyed by

Wall and gate of Falerii Novi

Rome, except for its famous temple of Juno (Ovid, *Am.* 3.13), and the population was moved to the plain, Falerii Novi. The inhabitants of F. were the Faliscans, an old population group that once lived in southern Etruria and their language, known from inscriptions, shows close similarity to Latin.

M. W. Frederiksen – J. B. Warde Perkins, *PBSR* (1957), 67 ff.

FASCES Rods (*virgae*) of elm or birch, usually twelve in number, fastened together by a red thong, which were carried by the lictors (attendants) before Roman magistrates holding Imperium. Originally Etruscan, the F. appeared at Rome under the late Etruscan kings of the city. As successors of the kings' powers, holders of Imperium retained the F. Consuls had twelve F., dictators twenty four, praetors six.

FASTI The list of the days of the year on which it was allowed to conduct all public business (*dies fasti*) and those on which it was forbidden for various religious reasons (*dies nefasti*). The aedile Cn. Flavius published this calendar on a marble table in the Forum in 304 BC (Liv. 9.46). Fragments of about twenty calendars are known from inscriptions. The calendars noted supplementary details and hence there came to be lists of the yearly highest magistrates (*fasti consulares*), of triumphs (*fasti triumphales*) and of priests (*fasti sacerdotales*). Such lists were displayed in public in many places and of those extant the most famous are the *fasti Capitolini* (so named because they are preserved in the Capitoline museum), which were compiled and published at the *Regia in 36 BC, but later brought up to AD 13. Also famous are the *fasti triumphales* which were displayed at the same place under Augustus and covered triumphs from the time of Romulus to 19 BC, and of which considerable fragments are extant.

FAUNUS Old Italian deity of shepherds and herds, forests and woods, who was identified with the Greek *Pan. His temple at Rome was dedicated on 13 February 194 BC; 15 February was the celebration day of the *Lupercalia, with which F. is commonly associated. Ovid mentions a local festival for F. on 5 December. Considered as the one who uttered the mysterious voices in nature he was called Fatulcus or Fatuus ("the speaker"). At times he pronounced prophecies. In the plural form, fauns appeared as counterparts to the satyrs and Pans and were depicted as human beings with goat-legs.

F. Altheim, *History of Roman Religion*, 1938 (s.v.).

FAUSTINA (1) ("the Elder"), Anna Galeria Daughter of M. Annius Verus, aunt of the future Emperor Marcus Aurelius, wife (from AD 110) of the future Emperor Antoninus Pius. On her husband's accession to the throne she received the title Augusta. She gave birth to two sons and two daughters and died in AD 141. She was consecrated, and an alimentary fund was instituted in her honour. She had a temple with her husband on the Via Sacra and was buried in the mausoleum of Hadrian.

J. P. V. D. Balsdon, *Roman Women*, 1962 (s.v.).

FAUSTINA (2) ("the Younger"), Anna Galeria Daughter of Antoninus Pius and *Faustina (1), first betrothed to L. *Verus but in 139 to Marcus Aurelius who married her in AD 145. She gave birth to many children; one of them was the future Emperor *Commodus. She was with her husband in the Germanic wars in 170–4 and was given the title *mater castrorum*. When accompanying him to the East, she died in 176. The place where she died was made

The feeding of Romulus and Remus – an altar from Ostia (AD 124)

a *colonia*, she was consecrated and for her, too, an alimentary fund was established.

FAUSTULUS In Roman mythology, the herdsman of Amulius (king of Alba Longa), husband of *Acca Larentia. He found, or received from other herdsmen, the twins Remus and Romulus and brought them up. When he later told Romulus of their true origin, the brothers killed Amulius. Unable to prevent the fatal quarrel between Romulus and his brother, he sought death.

FAVORINUS Greek rhetor and writer, born at Arles *c.* AD 80–90. F. received his education in Massilia and later studied under *Dio Chrysostomus. He visited Greece and taught *Herodes Atticus, *Gellius and *Fronto. He was an enemy of the Sophist Polemon, a friend of Hadrian, and *c.* AD 130 was banished to Chios. Later he returned and lived to the middle of the 2nd century. Two of his speeches are included in those of Dio Chrysostomus and his speech *On Exile* is known from a papyrus. He wrote a Miscellaneous History and a book of memoirs, of which only fragments are known.

FELICITAS Roman goddess who personified success, first attested with the building of a temple for her by L. Licinius Lucullus (consul in 151 BC) for his operations in Spain. The temple, dedicated soon after 146 BC, was on the Velabrum, between the Palatine and the Capitol. In the temple of Pompey for Venus Victrix she had a statue alongside with Honos and Virtus; *Sulla's goddess was Venus Felix. M. Aemilius *Lepidus (3) built a temple in her honour for Caesar's victory in Thapsus. It was mainly under the Empire that she became prominent in official cult in the attempt to secure success for the reigning emperor. She often appears on coins.

Platner-Ashby, *Top.Dic. Rome* (s.v.).

FELIX, Marcus Antonius Freedman of *Antonia (2), brother of *Pallas, procurator of Judaea c. AD 52—60. As judge of St. Paul he kept him two years in prison (*Acts*, 24), and by his cruel and suppressive behaviour provoked the Jews, who unsuccessfully brought him to court.

FENESTELLA Roman historian and competent scholar, 52 BC—AD 19 (or, more probably, 35 BC—AD 36). His historical work, *Annales*, dealt in particular with the last generation of the Roman Republic and perhaps started with the beginning of Rome. The fragments of his work, in at least 22 books, indicate his fields of interest: constitutional, literary, philological, social and economic history. Asconius and Pliny the Elder used him, an epitome (of at least two books) was made of the work and he was rightly compared to Varro (by Lactantius). He also wrote poems.
Peter, *Hist. Rom. Rel.* 2.

FERONIA Italian goddess whose origin (Sabine or Etruscan) and functions are unclear. Livy records her cult at Rome in 217 BC (22.1,18). Her temple there was in the Campus Martius and her festival held on 13 November. Her cult spread in central Italy and the most important sanctuary was the Lucus Feroniae at Mount Soracte in Etruria, where an annual festival was held. It was pillaged by Hannibal (217 BC, Liv. 26.11) but later had a *colonia* (Iulia Felix Lucoferonia). Other sanctuaries were at Trebula Mutuesca in Sabinum, *Tarracina (here slaves were liberated), and elsewhere.
W. W. Fowler, *Roman Festivals*, 252 ff;
Latte, *R Rel.*, 189 f.

FESTIVAL Rites regularly performed at certain times to worship gods. F. consisted — in later times at least — of a procession, sacrifice and feast, and competitions (dramatic, athletic or others). Many of the oldest F.s were associated with the life of agrarian society and held at harvest or sowing times. Those F.s contained both the element of thanksgiving and rejoicing and that of securing the goodwill of the supernatural powers for the future success of the crops. Later every F. was celebrated in association with the cult of a particular god; indeed almost all gods were honoured by F.s In remote times, F.s were celebrated by the family or clan, the village and the local communities, and private F.s still existed in historical times, when the more important F.s were those organized by the city or the state. They were celebrated on fixed day or days, usually at full moon, every year or several years. It was in connection with F.s that athletic competitions developed (foot and chariot races, boxing, wrestling, jumping, etc.) and in fact the great *Agones (Olympic games etc.) were part of F.s for the respective gods. Likewise dramatic performances developed from F.s held for Dionysus (*Dionysia). These F.s were occasions for the gathering of the whole community, and it was quite common that *Apoikiai would send representatives to take part in the F.s of their mother-cities. New F.s were added to old ones, especially in the Hellenistic period (by cities of rulers), to celebrate political achievements.

Roman F.s were called *feriae*. They were not different from those of the Greeks in respect of their origin, regular celebration and essential elements, except for the competitions. Likewise all gods at all important were honoured by F.s The Romans distinguished between F.s held on certain, fixed days of the calendar (*feriae stativae*) and others yearly F.s whose exact date of celebration was determined by the magistrates (*feriae conceptivae*). They,

too, had private or family F.s See *Agones, *Anthesteria, *Apaturia, *Dionysia, *Panathenaea.
Pickard-Cambridge, *Dramatic Festivals*;
W. W. Fowler, *Roman Festivals*;
A. K. Michels, *The Calendar of the Roman Republic,* 1967.

FESTUS (1), Sextus Pompeius Scholar and grammarian of the 2nd century AD. He wrote an epitome in twenty books of the encyclopaedic work *De verborum significatu* of Verrius *Flaccus, of which Books 12—20 are extant. Festus' book was abridged by Paulus Diaconus in the late 8th century.
W. M. Lindsay, *Glossaria Latina,* (1930) .4.

FESTUS (2), Rufius Secretary of the Emperor Valens, author of an extant *Brevarium rerum gestarum populi Romani*, which is a short chronological account of conquests and wars of the Roman people from early times to F.'s own time. He drew the material for his compilation from former epitomes; for the Republic from one dependent on Livy.
J. W. Eadie, *The Breviarium of Festus,* 1967.

FETIALES Roman priestly college responsible for the religious ceremonies associated particularly with signing of treaties and declarations of war as well as other business of the state with other states. The college consisted of twenty members, coopted for life, and included Patricians and Plebeians. In the treaty signing ceremony, one fetial (*verbenarius*) carried herbs (*verbenae*) from the Capitoline Arx and another one (*pater patratus*; the meaning of the term is disputed) read a religious formula: if the Roman people first broke the treaty it would be smitten like the pig that was smitten and killed on that occasion (Liv. 1.24). A two-stages procedure was taken in the declaration of war. First a formula was read by the *pater patratus* in several places of the territory of the would-be enemy calling gods as witnesses to the wrong done to the Roman people. If within thirty three days the offending party did not give satisfaction and the Senate decided to gain satisfaction by *iustum bellum*, the *fetialis* went again to the territory of the wrongdoer, cast a spear in it and declared the war (Liv. 1.32). This procedure has been understood as demonstrating that Rome's early wars were of defensive nature. For wars outside Italy, a fiction was employed for the declaration of the war: a defined area near the temple of the war-goddess Bellona in the Campus Martius represented the territory of the offending party and the spear was thrown at it. This fictitious ceremony was first employed for the declaration of the war against Pyrrhus.
T. Frank, *Roman Imperialism,* 1914 (ch. 1);
Latte, *R. Rel.* 121ff; Ogilvie, Livy, 127ff.

FIDEICOMMISSUM A term meaning "something committed to the faith" of someone. As Roman law debarred, in various degrees, certain persons from receiving inheritances, a way was found to circumvent the legal restrictions by making informal requests to those who benefited from the inheritance. While Augustus made some *fideicommissa* legally enforceable, various enactments gradually took control of this fiction by debarring the same categories of persons who could not legally inherit from benefitting by the *fideicommissa*.
Jolowicz, *Roman Law.*[3] (s.v.).

FIDES Roman goddess who personified good faith; one of the oldest of this type of goddesses. Although the institution of her cult was ascribed to *Numa (Liv. 1.21), F.'s temple was erected on the Capitol only in the middle of the 3rd century BC. The Romans considered good faith as a typically Roman characteristic and this perhaps accounts for their belief in the antiquity of her cult. In the yearly sacrifice held at her temple the hand of the sacrificer was covered with white cloth, and indeed covered hands became her symbol. F. first appeared on coins in the middle of the 1st century BC and later it became part of imperial propaganda to commemorate the loyalty (actual or desired) of legions or the army on coins of F.

Platner-Ashby, *Top. Dict. Rome*, (s.v.);
Latte, *R Rel.*, 237;

FIMBRIA, Gaius Flavius Roman politician and able general whose father was the first of the family (Plebeian) to win the consulate in BC 104. Supporter of *Marius and *Cinna (1), he gained notoriety by killing prominent aristocrats (Caesares and Crassi) after the capture of Rome in 87 BC. As legate in 86 he killed his commander the consul Valerius Flaccus and fought successfully against *Mithridates VI, who escaped thanks to *Sulla. Attacked by the latter in 85, F. committed suicide. He became a model *audax*, that is, an audacious politician who advanced his personal career by unscrupulous methods, behaviour ascribed to the *populares* by their opponents.

FISCUS This term (originally meaning "basket" or "purse") had several meanings from the time of Augustus on. In the first place it denoted the private wealth of the emperor which consisted of the property of Augustus (his patrimony, booty, inheritances and legacies, and estates he acquired) augmented through the years by subsequented emperors who gradually took to themselves sources of income which, under the Republic, went to the *Aerarium. Another aspect of this development was that emperors came more and more to finance what had been definitely public duties. In time this formed a distinct department of finance which was recognized in law and had privileges and a large administrative staff. What categories of public sources of income the emperors took to themselves (and at what time), is a disputed question. F. also denoted the public money held by a provincial governor as well as that held by the emperor by virtue of his proconsular *Imperium* and as governor of provinces. There were also special financial departments for receiving special taxes, though their exact nature is many times unclear (e.g. *fiscus frumentarius, fiscus castrensis, fiscus Alexandrinus*). Jews paid a yearly poll-tax of two denari after the great revolt of AD 66—70, the proceedings of which went to the *fiscus iudaicus*. The *fiscus libertatis et peculiorum* seems to have drawn its revenues from the sums paid by imperial slaves when set free and from the *peculia* of the imperial freedmen and slaves taken after their death.

Jones, *Studies*, 99 ff.;
F. Millar, *JRS*, 1963, 29 ff;
P. A. Brunt, *JRS*, 1966, 75 ff.

FLACCUS Roman *cognomen* whose most important bearers under the Republic were branches of the *Fulvii and the *Valerii; under the Empire many senatorial families used it. Horace too had this *cognomen*.

FLACCUS, Verrius A freedman who was a prominent scholar and antiquarian of the Augustan period. His writings included treatises of various subjects; the most important was *De verborum significatu*, a voluminous encyclopaedic work (several books to each letter). It was epitomized by *Festus (1); none of his works are extant.

FLAMINES Roman priests (*flamen* seems to mean "sacrificer") each of whom served the cult of one particular god. There were fifteen F.; the *flamen dialis* (of Jupiter), *flamen Martialis* (of Mars) and *flamen Quirinalis* (of Quirinus) were *maiores*, the other *minores*. The three *maiores*, who were included in the *collegium* of the *pontifices*, were patrician and the *minores* usually plebeian. The F. performed sacrifices but there is little information available about their other duties. The *flamen dialis* was obliged to abstain from wide variety of actions and events to avoid pollution, and until the end of the third century BC was not allowed to take public offices. Other F. had probably been debarred by similar taboos which were later relaxed. Antony was a *flamen* of Caesar, and later, deified emperors received F.

Latte, *R Rel.* (s.v.).

FLAMININUS, Titus Quinctius Roman statesman and general of a patrician family, prominent in the early 2nd century BC. He was elected consul for 198 without previously holding the aedilship or the praetorship and when only thirty years old, though he had governed Tarentum with extraordinary propraetorian Imperium in 205—204 and had been quaestor. Flamininus, a phil-Hellenist and skilful diplomat, was charged with the conduct of the war against *Philip V of Macedonia. He skilfully attached the Achaean League to the Roman side, negotiated with the Macedonian king, secured the continuation of his command by the Senate to 197 when he defeated the enemy in the decisive battle at Cynoscephalae. F. remained in Greece to work out a settlement after its evacuation by Macedonia. Boeotia was punished and the territorial demands of Aetolia were rejected. Finally in the Isthmian games of 196 (the so-called Corinthian declaration) freedom for the Greeks was proclaimed (Polyb. 18.46). F. remained in Greece to 194, checking *Nabis of Sparta and watching the intentions of *Antiochus III. He received semi-divine honours by the Greeks and returned to Rome to celebrate a three day magnificent triumph. Subsequently he supported the claims of the Greek cities of Asia Minor against Antiochus and in 193/2 helped to suppress Nabis. He was censor in 189 and in 183 was the leading member of the embassy that demanded from Prusias, king of Bithynia, the surrender of Hannibal, who preferred to commit suicide. F.'s position and connection with other leading statesmen, notably Scipio, are disputed; his policy secured a precarious freedom for the Greeks under Roman protectorate. He died in 174.

Polyb. 17—18; Liv. 32—36;
Plut. *Flamininus*;
Scullard, *Rom.Pol.*[2] (s.v.);
Badian, *Titus Quinctius Flamininus*, 1970.

FLAMINIUS, Gaius Roman statesman and general, of a plebeian family, the first of his family to gain the consulship. He sought to solve the social and economic problems of Rome at his time (second part of the 3rd century BC) but his policy and methods encountered the hostility of the senatorial aristocracy. As tribune of the Plebs he passed a law to distribute public land to needy citizens in the *ager Gallicus* (on the Adriatic coast south of the Po valley) which presumably was exploited by the aristocracy. It was described as a dangerous demagogic measure which allegedly provoked the Gauls to attack Rome in 225 and also adversely affected the morals of the people (Polyb. 2.21). He was the first praetor to govern Sicily (227 BC). Consul in 223, he won a victory over the Insubres across the Po despite the attempt of the Senate to call him back; with the people's support he celebrated a triumph, but hostile tradition ascribed his victory to his

soldiers' bravery. As censor in 220 he carried out important building operations: the construction of the Circus Flaminius and the *Via Flaminia. He allegedly was the only senator who supported the *plebiscitum Claudianum* (c. 218), which debarred Roman senators from taking part in maritime commerce, again a measure opposed by the aristocracy. As popular leader, and as opponent of those who conducted the war against Hannibal, he was elected consul for 217. But Hannibal outmanoeuvred him and completely defeated his army at Lake Trasimene, where he died. This defeat, too, was ascribed to his refusal to cooperate with his colleague and his contempt of religious ceremonies and omens.
Z. Yavetz, *Athenaeum*, 1962, 325 ff.

FLAVIUS, Gnaeus Secretary of Appius *Claudius (2) Caecus, son of a freedman. He was aedile in BC 304 and in this office he displayed in the forum a marble table with the calendar of the days on which legal actions could be legally undertaken. It was then or earlier that he published what came to be known as *Ius civile Flavianum*, namely, the *legis actiones*, thereby breaking the monopoly of the *Pontifices* over legal procedure (Pomponius in *Dig.* 1.2.2.6).
A. K. Michels, *The Calendar of the Roman Republic* (1967), 108 ff.

FLORA Italian goddess of flowering said to have been given an altar by the Sabine king, Titus Tatius (Varro, *Lin. Lat.* 5.74). She had a *flamen floralis* and was given a temple in Rome in 238 BC (Plin. *NH* 18.286). The fact that she did not have a festival in the old calendar is probably due to its being *feriae conceptivae* (see *Festival). From BC 173 she was honoured by yearly games held on 28 April (*ludi Florales*, or *Floralia*) which included coarse mimes and were celebrated with much gaiety and lascivious scenes, probably under Greek influence. In mythology she was originally the nymph Chloris but changed by Zephyrus into F. (Ovid *Fasti* 5, 195ff.).
Platner-Ashby, *Top.Dict.Rome*, 209 f.;
Latte, *R Rel.* 73 f.

FLORUS, Lucius Annaeus (or Julius) Author of the extant *Epitome of all the Wars of the Roman People* in two books. The first describes the foreign wars until 50 BC, and the second the civil wars from the Gracchan period to the time of Augustus. Though stated to be an epitome of Livy, it also draws material from other writers (e.g. Sallust and Caesar). It is an encomiastic and rhetorical work and at times inaccurate. The author is identified with the poet P. Annius Florus contemporary and friend of the Emperor Hadrian in the first part of the 2nd century AD. Fragments of F.'s poetry are extant including one of the introduction to the dialogue *Vergilius orator an poeta* (on whether Virgil was an orator or poet).
E. S. Forster, *Epitome* (Loeb). 1929;
Duff, *Min.Lat. Poets.*

FORNACALIA Movable festival (*feriae conceptivae*) held in February on a day announced by the Curio Maximus, but not later than the 17th. Fornax is said by Ovid to have been the goddess who took care that the grain should not be parched (*Fasti* 2.513ff.). The festival was celebrated by the *curiae* and the 17th of February was called "the festival of the stupids" (*stultorum feriae*) because it was on that day that those who did not know their *curiae* celebrated it. (Ovid. *Fasti* 2.531f.).

FORTUNA (or Fors Fortuna) Old Italian goddess whose cult was said to have been instituted at Rome by the King

Servius Tullius and later was identified with the Greek *Tyche. As such she was the goddess of luck, success and chance. Temples for F. were to be found in many places; her most important sanctuary was at *Praeneste, where she had the title Primigenia. In old inscriptions found there she is apparently called "daughter of Jupiter" but attempts have been made to explain away such an affiliation, unique in Italian religion. It was also an oracular sanctuary, and many offerings were found here. "Lots" (*sortes*) were drawn for the consultants; these were pieces of wood inscribed with short lines to be interpreted by the consultants. It appears that whe was worshipped by people of all social classes including slaves. Another important sanctuary with oracular was at *Antium, for *Fortunae* (in plural). At Rome, too, the goddess had a considerable number of shrines: in the Forum Boarium, on the Quirinal, on the Capitol, at the 4th mile on the Via Latina etc. F. was given numerous titles; *felix, muliebris, redux, obsequens, virgo*, etc. Under the Empire she was identified with other deities and hence came *Fortuna Isis* and *Fortuna Panthea*.
Nash, *Top.Dict.Rome* 1, 415 ff;
Latte, *R Rel.* 176 ff.

FORUM (1) Meetingplace of the community for political, administrative, jurisdictional and commercial purpose, hence the market place, the tribunals place and place for the holding of the popular assembly. It consisted of an open area surrounded and encroached upon by various public buildings, temples, and monuments of various sorts. The oldest one at Rome was the *Forum Romanum*, the low area between the Capitol, Palatine, and the Quirinal; it was drained in the 6th century BC and from then on served all the above mentioned purposes. In time numerous buildings were built there during the Republic and under the Empire of which a few may be mentioned here: the *Regia; the temples of Castor, Concordia, Saturn, Divus Augustus, Vespasian, and Diva Faustina; *basilicae*: Porcia, Aemilia, Sempronia, Iulia, Maxentia; the Rostra; the arch of Septimius Severus; and the *Curia (2). The development of the city caused the building of separate markets such as the *forum piscarium* (fishmongers' market) and the *forum holitorium* (greengrocers' market). From Caesar on several emperors built *fora*, each consisting of a temple to a particular deity as well as various buildings for public purposes. The first was that of Caesar: Forum Iulium (Forum Caesaris), dedicated in 46 BC. It was 160 by 75 metres and included a temple of Venus Genetrix. Augustus dedicated his Forum Augustum (Forum Augusti) in BC 2; it was 110 by 83 metres and included a temple for Mars Ultor. Then came the one dedicated by Vespasian in AD 75, the Forum Pacis (Forum Vespasiani) which was 145 by 100 metres and included a temple of Peace (*Pax*). In AD 97 Nerva dedicated the Forum Transitorium (Forum Nervae), which was built by Domitian. It was 120 by 45 metres and included a temple of Minerva. The Forum Traiani, planned and built by *Apollodorus of Damascus, was the largest of the imperial *fora*; the hill of the Quirinal was scraped for its building. A temple of Divus Traianus was built near it by Hadrian.
Platner-Ashby, *Top.Dict.Rome.* (s.v.);
Nash, *Pict.Dict.Rome*, (s.v.).

FORUM (2) Outside Rome, *fora* were market-towns on Roman territory for the country-folk in their vicinity. Roman magistrates came there to administer justice or for other administrative purposes. They were usually named

Right: The Theban king Pentheus is killed by the Maenads. Fresco painting from the House of the Vetii at Pompeii

Fragments from Hadrian's villa near Tivoli

The Roman Forum at the late 19th century

after the Roman magistrate who founded them, on many occasions while constructing a road. Some of them later developed and acquired the status of *colonia* like Forum Iulii (modern Frejus) which was probably founded by Caesar.

FRANKS The name (meaning "free men") applied in the 3rd century AD to a group of German tribes on the middle and lower Rhine; their area was known as Francia. While fighting with other Germans they caused a great deal of trouble by their bold incursions into the western provinces in the second part of the 3rd century. *Maximian fought them and settled part of them within the empire. Later Constantine and Constans signed treaties with them but in 355 they devastated the Rhine area. Julian defeated them and again gave the Salian F. various lands for settlement. They resumed their attacks in the 5th century and after the fall of *Aetius expanded southwards and westwards until in the 6th century they occupied the whole of Gallia.

FRATRES ARVALES Roman priestly college consisting of twelve members known mainly after its restoration by Augustus. In legend the first F. were the sons of *Acca larentia. Their centre was in a sacred grove at the 5th mile of the Via Campana. Their main occupation was with the cult of the old goddess Dea Dia to whom that grove was sacred — there were to be found there a temple, altars and a circus. They celebrated a yearly three-day festival for the goddess in May. The rites performed show the agrarian origin of the cult and, according to one view, the festival was identical with the *Ambravalia. They also worshipped other Roman deities including the *divi imperatores*. Many of their records, the *acta fratrum*

Arvalium, were found in the grove, and supply much information on the organization of the college and the rites and prayer (*carmen Arvale*) it performed. These records spread over the period 21 BC–AD 241.

Latte, *R Rel.* (s.v.).

FREEDMEN Manumission was a common institution in Greek and Roman civilization not less than slavery itself. Manumission secured the ex-slave personal freedom; in the Greek world he joined the free, foreign population of his place of abode (*Metics). Manumitted F. of Roman citizens received Roman citizenship. Skilled slaves who managed to save money could often purchase their freedom from their masters; in other cases it was the nature of the personal relations or the desire of the masters for ostentation that led them to manumit their slaves. In Greece it was common enough to set slaves free by a fictitious sale to a god, as attested by many inscriptions from Delphi and Delos. The juristic evidence on manumission at Rome is much more abundant than on Greek manumission. The three formal methods were by a testament (*manumissio testamento*), by a certain procedure before the praetor known as *manumissio vindicta*, or by a statement of the former master to the censor which led to the registration of the freedman as a citizen (*manumissio censu*). It was far more common to set slaves free in informal ways, by giving a letter or by a statement in the presence of witnesses. For the slave it was important that he should have proof of his manumission. The number of those informally manumitted was apparently so high that Augustus passed a law that gave them a distinct legal status (* Latini Iuniani). He also passed laws to restrict the numbers of slaves manumitted in the formal ways. He seems to have been concerned by the great influx of foreign elements into the Roman citizen-body, but there is not enough information to form any idea of the numbers of F. either in Greece or in Rome.

Many Greek F. had to assume formal obligations to give certain services, including financial obligations, to their former masters. At Rome F. were *clients of their former masters who now became their patrons. They differed from other clients insofar that their duties were defined in law. They owed their patrons *obsequium, reverentia* and *honor*, as well as undefined services (*operae*). The patrons were also given the right to inherit from their childless and intestate F. In the late Empire manumission could be revoked in certain cases. Not many F. rose in society or gained exceptional riches. They often were small traders, artisans, money-changers, shop-keepers, readers etc. However, some did well like Pasion at Athens in the 4th century, Demetrius, Pompey's freedman, whose property amounted to 4,000 talents, or Caecilius Isidorus who owned more than 4,000 slaves and had 60 million sesterces in cash. Others were important writers and thinkers, like *Epictetus. At Rome F. or their descendants acquited political positions (Gnaeus *Flavius), especially under the Emperor Claudius (*Narcissus, *Nymphidus, *Pallas). Roman emperors, who continued in this respect the practice of the great nobles of the Republic, employed their F. in the administration of their private imperial business. The aspirations of F. for social activity and recognition under the Empire were partly fulfilled by such offices as *Augustales and *Vicomagistri.

W. L. Westermann, *The Slave Systems of Greek and Roman Antiquity*, 1955; A. M. Duff, *Freedmen in the Early Roman Empire*[2], 1958; S. Treggiari, *Roman Freedmen during the Late Republic*, 1969; P. R. C. Weaver, *Familia Caesaris*, 1972.

FRONTINUS, Sextus Iulius Senator and writer, lived in the 1st century AD (*c.* 30—101). He was praetor in 70, suffect consul in 73, and as governor of Britain *c.* 74—8 he subdued the Silures. As *curator aquarum* in 97 he was in charge of the water supply of Rome. He was consul in 98 and again in 100. F. wrote books on several technical subjects. Of his two-book treatise of land-surveying only fragments are extant. His book on the art of war, used by *Vegetius, is not extant. The surviving works are a four-book *Strategms* (the fourth possibly by a later writer) and a two-book work on the *Aqueducts of Rome*. The first is a practical guide-book based on military examples arranged according to subjects. The second was written as a guide-book for his own use and that of his successors when he held the office of *curator aquarum*. It gives a description of the whole system of the Roman aqueducts with detailed information on the historical background and technical and administrative matters.
C. E. Bennett — M. B. McElwain, *Stratagems and Aqueducts* (Loeb), 1925; T. Ashby, *Aqueducts of Ancient Rome*, 1935.

FRONTO, Marcus Cornelius Roman senator, writer, and most famous orator of the 2nd century AD (*c.* 100—*c.* 166). Born at Cirta in Numidia, he advanced in the senatorial career to the consulate (143). He was appointed tutor of the young Marcus Aurelius and Lucius Verus, the future emperors, and retained close relationships with them to his death. His high praises by ancient writers as second to none in his oratory cannot be verified since

none of his speeches is extant. The discovery of a manuscript of his correspondence with the Emperor Marcus Aurelius in the early 19th century caused disappointment, since his style here certainly does not vindicate his reputation. The letters show the close ties between the correspondents, touching on trivial matters but also revealing F.'s own view on rhetoric. The style he proposes — what he calls *elocutio novella* — is a mixed Latin consisting of Archaic elements and everyday speech. He preferred writers like Cato Censorius, Plautus, Gaius Gracchus and Sallust, while Cicero's speeches and Seneca's prose came under his criticism; he also raised objections to philosophy. According to Aulus *Gellius F. was the centre of a literary circle (13.29; 19.8 etc.).
C. R. Haines: *Fronto* (Loeb), 1920; M. D. Brock, *Studies in Fronto and his Age*, 1910.

FULVIA Offspring of noble families (*Fulvius and *Sempronius), a woman of strong character, means and ambition. Her husbands, all unscrupulous politicians, were *Clodius, *Curio (2) and *Antonius (4). In Antony's absence from Italy in 41 BC, she helped to instigate the war against Octavian (Perusine War), who spared her; she died in 40, rebuked by Antony.

FULVIUS Roman plebeian clan whose origin was from *Tusculum and whose members were prominent in Roman politics from the late 4th century (first consulate in 322) to the late 2nd century BC. The more successful branches of the clan were the Centumali, Curvi and especially the Flacci and Nobiliores.

FULVIUS (1) FLACCUS, Quintus Prominent Roman statesman in the second part of the 3rd century BC, four times consul (237, 224, 212, 209), censor (231), one of Rome's better generals in the Second Punic War. His greatest achievement was the capture of Capua after siege in 211. In internal politics he was an opponent of Scipio, to whose plan to invade Africa he objected.

FULVIUS (2) FLACCUS, Marcus Roman statesman, supporter of the Gracchi. From 130 BC on, he was member of the agrarian board established by Tiberius to reclaim and distribute public land. He is credited with the first proposal to give Roman citizenship to Rome's Italian allies. Consul in 125, he was sent to fight the Gallic Salluvii and for his achievements won a triumph. He was elected plebeian tribune for 122, unusual for a consular, to help Gaius Gracchus with whom he was killed in 121. Thereafter the Fulvii disappeared from politics.

FULVIUS (3) NOBILIOR, Marcus Roman statesman and general. As praetor in 193 BC he governed Further Spain and gained an ovation in 191. As consul in 191 he defeated the Aetolians and took Ambracia; for his achievements he was awarded a triumph in 187, which he celebrated magnificently. The allegations of his enemies that he used his office for personal profits did not discredit him and he was elected censor for 179, in which office he carried out (with his colleague) extensive building operations. *Ennius, who accompanied F. to Greece, celebrated his achievements in his *Annales*.
Scullard, *Rom.Pol.*[2] (s.v.).

FURIAE The Latin counterparts of *Erinyes.

FUR(R)INA Old Roman goddess who became obsolete in the late Republic. She had a yearly festival on 25 July, *Furrinalia*; and a *flamen Furrinales* (*Flamines). Gaius Gracchus was killed near her shrine on the Janiculum. Her identification with the *Furiae was an old false deduction (Cic. *Nat. Deor.* 3.46). She was also worshipped outside Rome.

G

GABII Old Latin city, situated about 18 km east of Rome on the way to *Praeneste. G. was reputedly founded by *Alba Longa (Dion. Hal. 1.84). Her old treaty with Rome was allegedly found in the time of Augustus, and she is said to have been Rome's ally in the early 5th century (Liv. 3.8). By the end of the Republican period, G. declined and was later known as a desolate place (Hor. *Epist.* 1.11).

GABINIUS, Aulus Roman politician who made his career in cooperation with Pompey. As plebeian tribune in 67 BC, he passed a law to give an extraordinary command to Pompey to fight the pirates. He defeated an attempt by a fellow-tribune to veto the bill when he proposed to abrogate his office, being the only tribune known to have used this tactic since Tiberius Gracchus. Another law of his made it illegal to lend money to provincials in Rome. Subsequently, he served as legate of Pompey (65–63), was praetor (61), and consul (58). By a law of *Clodius, he received Syria as a province (57–55); he checked the publicans, suppressed revolts in Judaea, and restored Ptolemy Auletes to Egypt. Back in Rome he was convicted on a charge of *repetundae* (after aquittal on charge of *maiestas*) and went into exile. He fought on Caesar's side in the Civil War and died in 47. He was the first of his family to gain the consulate.

Syme, *Rom. Rev.* (s.v.).

GADES (modern Gadiz) Old coastal city on an island in southern Spain, founded by Phoenicians from Tyre, supposedly in 1100 BC (this date has not been confirmed by archaeological evidence which does not go back further than the 8th century). G. was erroneously identified with *Tartessus after the destruction of the latter. Its ancient history is obscure. After the First Punic War it was the base for *Hamilcar's conquest of southern Spain. Following the expulsion of the Carthaginians by Scipio, G. entered into a treaty with Rome (206 BC). Caesar gave the city the status of Roman *municipium*. *Balbus and *Columella were natives of G., which was a very prosperous city drawing its wealth mainly from maritime trade and fishery. By the 4th century AD, G. was a desolate place, only to rise again under the Moslems.

GAIA, GAEA, GE The earth goddess; in mythology (Hesiod, *Theog.* 117ff.), she arose after Chaos and bore Uranus (sky) who was her husband and completely covered her; from their union she bore the mountains and the seas, the Titans and the Titanesses, the Cyclopes and the Hecatoncheires (Hundred-handed Ones). After Kronos castrated his father Uranus, she bore from his blood the *Erinyes, *Gigantes and some of the nymphs, but never mated again with Kronos. From her union with Tartarus, she bore *Typhon. The cult of G., the goddess of earth and its powers, was an old one; in many places, she was replaced by other particular gods, as in Delphi where the Chtonian Python was killed by Apollo who took over the oracular function. Occasionally G. was worshipped as Mother Earth, though the theory of an ancient, comprehensive cult of her in this aspect cannot be maintained. She was identified with the Roman *Tellus.

GAISERIC Born in AD 389, he was king of the *Vandals and *Alans (AD 428–77). He led 80,000 of his people on an expedition to Africa in 429, and subsequently occupied the Roman provinces there, defeating the governor Bonifacius in 430. G. captured Hippo in 431, and Carthage (which became his capital) in 439. He was recognized as an independent king by the Emperor Valentian III in 442. Capturing Rome in June 455, G. amassed enormous booty. Subsequently, his naval forces raided and plundered along the shores of the western Mediterranean. In 467, G. defeated a combined attack of the forces of the eastern Roman Empire. On his death, G.'s empire included western Sicily, Sardinia, Corsica, the Balearic Islands, and provinces in Africa.

C. Courtois, *Les Vandales et l'Afrique,* 1955.

GAIUS Roman jurist, lived in the 2nd century AD. There are hardly any biographical details about him. The jurists of the Classical period do not mention him; his authority was acknowledged during a later period, and, thanks to the Law of Citations (AD 426), his writings were given equal force with those of the greatest jurists (Papinianus, Paulus and Ulpianus). Justinian decreed that G.'s book *Institutiones* be given first priority in the compilation of the official new *Institutiones*. G.'s textbook, the *Institutes*, discovered in a palimpsest manuscript in 1816, is the only one of a Classical jurist that has survived. It contains four books, although the subject matter is arranged under three main divisions: *personae, res, actiones*. The exposition is systematic and carefully arranged, the definitions are simple and clear, and the explanations are easy to follow and understand. The book

greatly influenced many generations of students of Roman law. G. also wrote commentaries on several special subjects (the Law of the Twelve Tables, on the edict of the Praetor Urbanus, etc.) and monographs.
F. de Zulueta, *The Institutes of Gaius*, 1946—1953; A. M. Honoré, *Gaius, A Biography*, 1962.

GALATEA Sea nymph, first mentioned by Homer (*Il.* 18.45) and Hesiod (*Theog.* 250). The tale of Polyphemus' love for her was popular with poets and is told by Theocritus (*Id.* 11), Virgil (*Ecl.* 9.39ff.) and in a developed version by Ovid (*Met.* 13.738ff.). Her lover, Acis, son of Faunus, was killed by Polyphemus who caught him listening to his love-song for G. The nymph herself escaped into the sea, turning Acis into a river. The myth was used by painters.

GALATIA, GALATIANS The country of the Celtic tribes (Galatai) who invaded Asia Minor after crossing the Hellespont in 278 BC; also called Gallograecia. It extended from the river Halys in the east to the Sangarius, bordering on Lycaonia, Cappadocia, Pontus, Bithynia and Pergamum, an area of about 60,000 sq km. In the first period after their arrival, the G. caused much trouble with their plundering inroads. For a time, their peace was bought by regular payments, but Pergamum ceased paying after they were defeated by *Attalus I. Hellenistic rulers recruited G. as mercenaries — they fought with *Ptolemy IV at the battle of Raphia and with *Antiochus III at Magnesia. The consul Manlius Vulso subsequently carried out a punitive expedition against the G., but they later stood on good terms with Rome. The G. consisted of three tribes: the Tolistobogii in the western part (main towns — Pessinus and Gordium), the Tectosages in the central part (Ancyra the main town), and the Trocmi in the eastern part (Tavium the main town). Each tribe comprised four subdivisions. After the death of King *Amyntas in 25 BC, G. became a Roman province to which were added adjacent territories. In AD 72, G., Cappadocia and Armenia Minor were organized as one province governed by a legate of consular rank. This was reversed by Trajan who took away some territory and assigned a legate of praetorian rank to govern it.
Magic, *Asia* (s.v.).

GALBA (1) MAXIMUS, Publius Sulpicius Roman politician and general. As consul in 211 BC, he took care of the defence of Rome when Hannibal made his only attempt to attack the city. Subsequently, G. was sent to operate against the Macedonian king, Philip V (210—206). Although he achieved nothing spectacular, G. managed to use a small force to check the king at a time when Rome's main effort lay elsewhere. Again consul in 200, G. initiated the campaign against Philip and won the support of the Aetolians. Later, he was one of the legates who helped *Flamininus to prepare a settlement for Greece (196).
Scullard, *Rom. Pol.*[2], (s.v.).

GALBA (2), Servius Sulpicius Roman politician and general. He became notorious for his treacherous and cruel conduct in governing Further Spain in 151—150 BC, seeking his own glory and enrichment. He was prosecuted on his return to Rome, and though Cato spoke against him, he used emotional tricks to secure his acquittal. His case probably contributed to the establishment of a standing court for cases of *repetundae* (149 BC). G. was consul in 144.
Malcovati, *Or. Rom. Fr.*[3]; Scullard, *Rom. Pol.*[2] (s.v.).

GALBA (3), Servius Sulpicius Roman emperor. Born in 3 BC, he had a long career in the imperial service be-

Battle against the Galatians. A Roman sarcophagus

fore his accession to the throne, winning the confidence and esteem of all the emperors from Augustus to Nero. G. governed Aquitania, Upper Germany, and Africa. From AD 60 on, he was governor of Hispania Tarraconensis. When Vindex, the governor of Gallia Lugdunensis, revolted in 68, G. made his first moves to show his disapproval of Nero. After the latter's death, G. became emperor with the support of the praetorians. But on his arrival in Rome, he very soon lost popularity with unnecessary slaughter and foolish, inopportune parsimony. He made wrong decisions in sending away his Spanish forces and in adopting as his successor L. Calpurnius Piso, a man of noble family but lacking in authority and conspicuous talent. *Vitellius, backed by the armies in Germany, proclaimed himself emperor in January 69; in Rome, *Otho won the support of the praetorians, who were enraged by G.'s refusal to pay the promised donatives. G. was killed by Otho's supporters on 15 January 69. Tacitus marks his reign with a pertinent saying: *omnium consensu capax imperii nisi imperasset* (by consent of all he was capable of ruling — had he not ruled).
Tac. *Hist.*, 1; Plut. *Galba*; Suet, *Galba*; Syme, *Tacitus* (s.v.).

GALEN After Hippocrates, G. (AD 129—99) was the most famous Greek physician, medical writer and anatomist. Native of Pergamum, he studied in Greece and Alexandria and first practised in Pergamum (157) as gladiators-physician. In 162—6, he practised and taught in Rome and won a reputation; the Emperor Marcus Aurelius was his patient. G. returned to Rome in 169 and stayed there for the rest of his life.

G. was a great theoretician and researcher no less than a practitioner and a teacher. He particularly emphasized the importance of practice in the study of anatomy. But his authority was such that anatomy came to be learned from his own books. In his research, he carried out extensive dissections which, together with other experimental work, enabled him to attain his great achievements in anatomy and physiology. G. did excellent work in neurology, and on the muscular system, and his terms are still used. Contradicting previous theories, G. showed that the arteries contain blood and not pneuma. In his numerous writings, he dealt with all aspects of medicine. He also tried to combine medicine with philosophy and the title of his book, *That the Best Doctor is also a Philosopher*, speaks for itself. His somatic views are thus based on many of the traditional theories, including the doctrines of the four elements and the four humours. G. believed in teleology and held monotheistic views. These and his outstanding works secured him a unique influence throughout the Middle Ages.

A. J. Brock, *Galen, On the Natural Faculties* (Loeb), 1916; C. Singer, *Galen, On Anatomical Procedures*, 1956; W. L. H. Duckworth, *Galen, On Anatomical Procedures, The Later Books*, 1962; M. T. May, *Galen, On the Usefulness of the Parts of the Body*, 1968; G. Sarton, *Galen of Pergamon*, 1954; C. E. R. Lloyd, *Greek Science after Aristotle* (1973), 136ff.

GALERIUS (Gaius Galerius Valerius Maximinus) Roman emperor, born *c.* AD 250, an Illyrian of peasant stock. He began his military service under the Emperor Aurelian and rose to power under Diocletian, who made him Caesar of the East in AD 293. G. separated from his wife to marry Diocletian's daughter; his own daughter married *Maxentius. In the following years, he was occupied defending the Danubian provinces against the Sarmatians and Carpi. In 296, he went to the East to check the attack of Persia, and after an initial defeat at Carrhae won complete victory in 298. Diocletian then concluded a peace with the Persian king, Narses and, together with G., he started the great persecution of the Christians. The first edict against them was issued in February 303; G. carried through this policy vigorously in the following years. He became Augustus of the East on 1 May 305, after Diocletian's abdication. He was now the supreme ruler – the new Caesars (Maximian Daia and Severus) were his supporters, and he held *Constantine. But G. had to let him join his father *Constantius, who died in 306. The system of Diocletian soon collapsed as Constantine and Maxentius assumed the imperial titles and defied G.'s authority. He failed to win over Italy from the latter and even the new settlement of Carnuntum in 308 (with Diocletian's approval) miscarried. The persecution of the Christians continued until 30 April 311, when he made Christianity a permitted religion. A few days later, he died of a severe illness.

A. H. M. Jones, *Later Rom. Emp.* (s.v.).

GALLA PLACIDIA Daughter of the Emperor Theodosius I, born *c.* AD 390. After the capture of Rome by *Alaric, she had to marry Athaulf, a Visigoth chieftain. On his death, an agreement was reached for her restoration (416), and the next year, in deference to her brother *Honorius, she married the future emperor, Constantius III (died 421). With the accession of her son Valentian III, a mere child, to the throne in 425, she became the effective ruler in the imperial court of the Western Empire. She sought to strengthen the imperial power by cooperating with the Church, and she was involved in court intrigues. In her later years, she concentrated on building churches in Ravenna, and was responsible for their embelishment. She died in Rome in 450.

GALLIA (GAUL) The land inhabited by the Galli or Celti (cf. Caesar, *Bell. Gal.* 1.1), confined by the Mediterranean, the Alps, the Rhine, the Atlantic Ocean, and the Pyrenees. The Celts, coming in successive invasions of divided tribes, occupied the land from the early 1st millenium on, ousting the former population and mixing with the Ligurians in the south. Greek trade and culture penetrated here mainly through Massalia (modern Marseille), founded *c.* 600 BC. Rome operated here for the first time in 218 BC when Publius Scipio, father of Scipio

Africanus, failed to block Hannibal's march to Italy. The first real campaign was undertaken in 154 on behalf of Massalia, Rome's ally, which was menaced by Gallic tribes. Further operations were taken in southern G. from 125 on, a *colonia* was founded in 118 (Narbo), and in the late 2nd century BC a permanent province, Gallia Narbonensis, was established. Caesar conquered the whole area to the Rhine and the Ocean in a series of wars (58–51), described in his *Commentaries on the Gallic War*. Under the Augustan settlement, the old province was given to senatorial administration and the newly acquired area (Gallia Comata) was organized in three provinces, the *Tres Galliae* (Lugdunensis, Aquitania, Belgica) governed by imperial legates.

The economy of G. flourished under the Roman Empire. The Galli proved themselves good traders and businessmen. They manufactured many previously imported articles, and also exported abroad in competition with local industry in Italy. Wine and pottery, once imported articles, went in mass quantities abroad. Glass and metal manufacture developed, too. The G. provinces were rapidly Romanized, first the old one (Provence) but then the others too. The Latin language was adopted, Roman colonies were established (in Narbonensis), and Latin rights and later Roman citizenship were granted. Gallic chieftains became Roman senators under the Emperor Claudius. Romanization was associated with urbanization, the Gallic tribes becoming *civitates*, and the fostering of the imperial cult. A provincial Assembly (*concilium*) of representatives of the *civitates* of the *Tres Galliae* was established by *Drusus (3) at Lugdunum, which became the main centre of the imperial cult with Narbo as the second centre. The Galli, on the whole, became loyal subjects and citizens of the empire – this was shown in the suppression of the revolt of *Sacrovir under Tiberius and of the national movement of the Treveri (in AD 69–70), who did not succeed in provoking a national uprising. Peace and prosperity were severely interrupted by the anarchy and the devastating invasions of the Germanic tribes, foreshadowed in the civil wars of the time of Septimius Severus. Widespread brigandage also undermined security and hampered normal life. The recovery of the empire in the late 3rd century brought relief but even then the old prosperity was not restored. In the 5th century, G. finally fell to the Germans – first to the Visigoths and later to the Franks.

A. Grenier, in *ESAR*, 3; O. Brogan, *Roman Gaul*, 1953.

GALLIA CISALPINA (CISALPINE GAUL) "Gallia from this side of the Alps" was the name given by the Romans and the Greeks to the part of north Italy from the Alps to the Apennines. The Gauls came here late in the 5th century BC, and by the middle of the 4th century had completely ousted the former population of Etruscans, Umbrians and Ligurians. One group defeated the Roman army and captured Rome itself (traditionally in 390 BC), but later in the 4th century their advance was checked by Rome. The conquest of the whole region had to be resumed after the Hannibalic War and was completed by the middle of the 2nd century. During this period a large part of the Gallic population was exterminated or emigrated, while many Romans and Italians settled here (the first colonies were established before the Second Punic War). In 89 BC, the communities south of the Po received Roman citizenship, while those north of the Po received Latin rights. In 49, Caesar extended citizenship to the Transpadani, and in 42 the region became a part of Italy. From this time on, and for a long period,

Cisalpine Gaul was a main recruiting area for the Roman army. It also became the most prosperous area of Italy, and from here came the poets Catullus and Virgil, and the writers Livy and Pliny. (See *Celts.)

G. E. F. Chilver, *Cisalpine Gaul*, 1941;
C. B. Pascal, *The Cults of Cisalpine Gaul*, 1964.

GALLIENUS, Publius Licinius Egnatius Son of Valerianus, became emperor with his father in AD 253. Almost throughout his reign, he was busy fighting attacks from external powers (German tribes and Persia), and internal usurpers. That he could maintain his rule for fifteen years is an indication of his ability. It was under G. that senators were debarred from taking military positions; this apparently was an attempt to improve the standard of the officers. Soon after his accession, G. saw to the defence of the Danubian and Rhine frontiers while his father unsuccessfully sought to check the Persians in the east. G. gained successes along the Rhine, taking the title *Germanicus* and *restitutor Galliarum*. In 258, he annihilated a force of-the Alamanni at Milan. In 260, his father was defeated and captured by the Persians. At that point, or perhaps it was two years earlier, G. put down the revolts in Pannonia, but he was unable to deal with Postumus who established a separate "regnum Galliarum" in the west. In the east, the defence of the empire was left to *Odaenathus of Palmyra, who suppressed Quietus and took the offensive against Persia. The Goths remained dangerous, repeatedly attacking the Balkan provinces and Asia Minor. In 267, G. seems to have defeated the Heruli who sacked Athens, Sparta, Corinth, and Argos. He could not carry on the war against the Goths as his general Aureolus made himself emperor at Milan. He was the victim of a conspiracy of his own officers in 268.

GALLUS, Gaius Cornelius Roman politician, general, and poet, born in Forum Iulii (*Fréjus*) *c.* 69 BC. Supporter and friend of Augustus, G. played an important part in the occupation of Egypt in 30 BC (after the battle of Actium), and was appointed its first *Praefectus.* He subdued revolts, secured the southern border of the new province, and commemorated his achievements in inscriptions (some on the pyramids). He also erected his own statues. Augustus, provoked by G.'s arrogance and ambition, recalled him, and G. committed suicide in 26. Almost nothing of his poetry has survived. He wrote *epyllia* and four books of erotic elegies (*Amores*), addressed to Lycoris, the pseudonym of his mistress. The tenth *Eclogue* of Virgil, his friend, is about him.

H. Bardon, *La littérature latine inconnue* (1956), 2, 34ff.

GALLUS, Gaius Asinius Roman senator and orator, son of Asinius *Pollio. He was consul in 8 BC and governor of Asia. Tiberius hated him because he married his divorced wife Vipsania, who bore G. five sons. G. severely criticized Cicero's style. He also angered the emperor in his speeches; but it was only in AD 30 that he was arrested, dying in prison after three years.

Syme, *Tacitus* (s.v.).

GANYMEDES (Latin Catamitus) Greek mythological figure, son of the Dardanian king, Tros. His myth, that he was carried off to be the cup-bearer of Zeus, was repeatedly told by poets from Homer (*Il.* 20.231ff.) on. It was his exceptional beauty that attracted the god, who in exchange gave his father marvellous horses or a golden vine. In the early version, G. was carried off by a storm wind, but in the later and more popular version, he was carried away by an eagle (Verg. *Aen.* 5.255), who was Zeus himself (Ovid. *Met.* 10.155ff.). Aristophanes parodied the

A vase-painting showing Ganymedes with a hoop c. 480 BC

myth in his *Peace.* The erotic implications of the myth were often used by poets; in addition the myth was also popular with artists who depicted it in vase-paintings, coins, gems, mosaics etc. A beautiful work of art is the terracotta statue of G. carried by Zeus (Olympia, first half 5th century). The theme of G. loved by Zeus continued to attract thinkers and artists through the Middle Ages to modern times.

GAZA Ancient city of the Philistines on the southern coast of Palestine. It was captured by Alexander in 332 BC and subsequently came under the Ptolemaic rule. With the conquest of south Syria by *Antiochus III, it fell under Seleucid control. Destroyed by the Jewish King Alexander Jannaeus in 96 BC, it was restored by Pompey in 62 BC. Its good commercial location made G. prosper under the Roman Empire.

Jones, *Cities*[2] (s.v.).

GELA Greek city on south coast of Sicily at the mouth of river Gelas, founded *c.* 690 BC by settlers from Rhodes (Lindus) and Crete (modern Gela). G. controlled the nearby fertile plain and extended its power over the native Sicels in the hinterland. In 581, Geloan and Rhodian colonists founded *Acragas. The material prosperity of the city in the 6th century has been revealed in archaeological excavations. The tyrannical brothers Cleander and Hippocrates extended their rule over the whole of eastern Sicily by the early 5th century. But this supremacy ended when their successor *Gelon took Syracuse and made her the centre of his rule. He also removed a large part of G.'s population to his new residence. Despite this, G. was able to revive Camarina in 461. G. also gave important support to Syracuse against the Athenian expedition in 415—413. In 405, the Geloans fled from their city before its capture by the Carthaginian Himilco; the decline of G. continued even after their return. Following a resettlement by *Timoleon, the population was removed to Phintios in 280, and the city was destroyed by the Mamertini. .

Dunbabin, *Western Greeks* (s.v.);
P. Griffo — L. von Matt, *Gela*, 1964.

GELLIUS, Aulus Roman writer of the 2nd century AD, born 130 (or 123). He studied in Rome, perhaps with *Fronto, and was influenced by *Favorinus. He also studied in Athens for a year. In Rome, he tried private cases as a *iudex.* His only work, *Noctes Atticae*, is so called because he began composing it during the long win-

The river-god Gelas on a coin

ter nights of his stay in Attica. Its twenty books comprise a collection of essays, discussions and anecdotes on a wide variety of subjects: philological, literary, philosophical and historical. The importance of the work lies in its numerous extracts and quotations from Greek and Latin writers whose works are otherwise lost. G. also gives a good indication of the literary interests of his contemporaries. The selection and the pleasant presentation of his material won his work a success which continued through the Middle Ages.
J. C. Rolfe, *Attic Nights* (Loeb), 1927–8.

GELON Greek tyrant in Sicily, son of Deinomenes. After the death of the Geloan tyrant Hippocrates (*c.* 491 BC), G. removed the deceased's sons, whose guardian he was, and took power. In 485, G. took advantage of the internal strife in Syracuse and added it to his empire. He made his residence in Syracuse, where he settled many of the Geloans. His brother Hieron governed Gela for him. G. destroyed Camarina and Megara Hyblaea. His reputation led to his being called to assist the Greeks against Xerxes. Instead, he cooperated with *Theron of Acragas to win a decisive battle over a Carthaginian expedition — which may have been coordinated with Xerxes — at Himera in 480. One of the greatest Greek tyrants in Sicily, G. died in 478 and was succeeded by his brother *Hieron.

GENIUS In Roman religion, it was an attendant power in every man. One's birthday anniversary was the feast of one's G. Within the religion of the family, it was the G. of the *paterfamilias* that was worshipped. From this primitive conception developed the belief in G. as the personal spirit guarding a man, comparable to the Greek personal *daimon*. By extension, it was believed that gods, places, the Roman people, and corporations each had their own G. Under the Empire, there was a cult of the G. of the reigning emperor.
F. Altheim, *History of Roman Religion,* 1938 (s.v.);
Latte, *R Rel.* (s.v.).

GENOS Greek social unit whose members claimed a common ancestor in direct male line. In the artificial organization of Athenian society, there were thirty *gene* (of thirty men) to each of the twelve phratries. The G., an

extended family, was mainly an aristocratic organization that survived in Classical Greece from the Archaic period. Where new citizens were taken into the citizen-body, as was done by *Cleisthenes (2) in Athens, they could only artificially be organized in such a supposedly natural framework. Most of the evidence concerns Athens; there, members of the *gene* formed the aristocracy (*Eupatridai), kept their organization, and retained a monopoly on priesthoods, even under the democracy.
Hignett, *Athens Const.* (s.v.).

GENS In Rome, a social unit consisting of a number of families who claimed descent from a common ancestor, in much the same way as a Scottish clan. Members of a clan had the same name (*nomen gentilicum*) and were divided into branches, which again had a distinct name (*cognomen*). The origins of the *gentes* are in dispute; they were already in existence in the archaic society of ancient Rome, and included Patricians and Plebeians. Members of a G. (*gentiles*) had a common cult and a common burial place; they could convene to discuss such matters as testaments, adoption, guardianship of minors and the insane, etc. That during an earlier period property was owned communally by the G. is suggested by the rule that the *gentiles* inherited from a member who died intestate and had no agnates. In the early Republic, *gentes* seem to have played important roles in politics. With the rise of Rome, the gentile organization could no longer cover the largely increased population and the new citizens; it was mainly the aristocracy that retained it. But it is doubtful whether the *gentes* were of much political importance in the middle Republic.
Jolowicz, *Roman Law*[3] (s.v.);
Scullard, *Roman Politics*[2], Ch. I.

GEOGRAPHY Theories and speculations on the nature of the earth together with explorations and mathematical knowledge contributed to the development of the science of G. by the Greeks. The primitive concept of the world as a flat disc surrounded by water on all sides, with the sky above and the underworld below, was a belief that was held by the Semitic peoples of the ancient Orient, and is found in Hesiod (*Theog.* 116ff.) and in Homer (*Il.* 18.483ff.). The first Ionian philosophers were still under the influence of such popular views. *Thales held that the earth floated on water, and though *Anaximander said that it hung freely, it was for him a flat cylinder. The sphericity of the earth, first maintained by Pythagoreans and Parmenides (the latter introduced its division into the five zones), was finally established by Aristotle.

Greek colonization and growth of maritime trade in the Archaic period contributed to greater knowledge of the Mediterranean lands. The first world-maps were drawn by Anaximander and *Hecataeus in the 6th century BC. These showed the world as a circle around the Mediterranean. It always remained a problem whether the continents were islands encompassed by the ocean or not. Descriptions of countries and regions, partly based on journeys and on maritime explorations, were made from the late 6th century on. The first general geographical account was given by Hecataeus, and subsequent accounts often included ethnographical and historical material. Historians from *Herodotus on found it useful to give geographical descriptions in their works. However, until the middle of the 4th century, the geographical knowledge of the Greeks was confined to the Near East, Asia Minor, the Black Sea lands, the Mediterranean countries and part of the western coast of Africa. Following the conquests of

Alexander the Great, better knowledge was acquired of central Asia, Iran, India; the maritime route from Babylonia to India was described by *Nearchus, whose report was used by *Arrian. The rise of Rome attracted interest in Italy and western Europe. *Polybius made research journeys to the Alps and the Atlantic coast and had personal knowledge of Spain and North Africa which he used for the geographical parts of his work. *Posidonius, too, went to study North Africa and the western parts of the Roman Empire. The only comprehensive, descriptive work of G. to have survived is that of *Strabo. In addition to the countries of the Roman Empire he treats Britain, northern and eastern Europe, Ethiopia, Mesopotamia, Persia and India. For him Africa was a triangle north of the equator. A much shorter account is given by *Pliny the Elder in his *Natural History*.

Greek mathematicians achieved good results in their geographical researches. The more important were *Eratosthenes, *Hipparchus (2) and Claudius *Ptolemy. The first calculated quite accurately the circumference of the earth; his result, 252,000 stades, amounts to 39,690 km (if he used a stade of 157.5 m), while the correct figure is 40,009 km. Hipparchus criticized him on descriptive and mathematical points, and carried on Eratosthenes' work in the division of the globe into parallel lines of latitude and longitude which could then be used to mark places on the map. Ptolemy's comprehensive work, in which he used the latitude-longitude parallels to locate places, was marred by serious errors caused by his disregard of astronomical observations. He erred in calculating the earth's circumference as being 180,000 stades. He introduced a land connecting eastern Africa with the Far East, thereby turning the Indian Ocean into a lake. But despite its errors, it was in many ways superior to other accounts and was considered authoritative until the beginning of what can be called modern G. which started at the end of the Middle Ages.

H. E. Burton, *The discovery of the Ancient World,* 1932; J. O. Thomson, *History of Ancient Geography,* 1948.

GERASA (modern Jerash) City in Jordan, founded by *Antiochus IV. It was taken by the Jewish king Alexander Jannaeus. Given autonomy by Pompey, G. was a member of the *Decapolis. A caravan city, it achieved great prosperity in the 2nd century AD. The disruption of trade with the anarchy of the 3rd century caused its decline. It was a bishop's seat. Considerable remains of buildings are extant, including a forum, a theatre, temples, and Christian churches.

C. H. Kraeling, *Gerasa,* 1938; Jones, *Cities*², (s.v.).

GERMANIA, GERMANI The Gauls named all the German peoples after the tribal group G. *cisrhenani* which invaded the west side of the lower Rhine in the 3rd century BC; the Romans continued the usage (Tac. *Germania* 2). The invading group of the G. *cisrhenani* was known to Caesar (*Bell. Gal.* 2.3; 62). The first German tribe with whom either the Greeks or the Romans had direct contact were the Bastarnae, who advanced to the lower Danube at the end of the 3rd century BC. The Macedonian kings, Philip V and his son Perseus, employed them as mercenaries. The first G. tribes to have encountered Rome were the *Cimbri and Teutones, who migrated from central Europe to Gaul after 120 BC and were finally destroyed by *Marius. Caesar, too, fought the G. under *Ariovistus in Gaul. By the 1st century BC, most of the area between the Ukraine and the Rhine was occupied by German peoples.

The confrontation between Rome and the G. at the time of Augustus, who tried to conquer Germany to the Elbe, was finally decided after the annihilation of three legions by *Arminius in AD 9. Despite the efforts of *Germanicus, the frontier line from then on was along the Rhine in western Europe and the Danube in central Europe; a net of fortifications was later added to defend the in-between area (*Limes). As the Rhineland was considered a vulnerable region, eight legions were posted here under the command of two imperial legates — one responsible for Lower (north Rhine region) Germany, and the other for Upper (south) Germany. Under Domitian, these commanders became ordinary provincial commanders. Until then, jurisdiction and civil administration were under the governor of Belgica. While this frontier remained quiet until the 3rd century (and the army was reduced to four legions by Trajan), the Danubian provinces came under pressure from German tribes in the time of Marcus *Aurelius. From *c.* AD 230 on, pressure from the Germans was renewed and the empire was repeatedly invaded and pillaged on all frontiers: the Danubian provinces, north Italy and Gaul. The incessant attacks, though mostly unsuccessful, drained the manpower of the empire; the recruiting of German tribesmen brought disadvantages and disrupted the economy and social life. The settlement of German tribes within the empire and the employment of German chieftains in high positions were only palliative measures which could not save the empire. The destruction of the imperial army under *Valens in 378 and the conquests of Rome by *Alaric and *Gaiseric, were the highlights of the general trend; the deposition of Romulus Augustus in AD 476 was no more than an outward sign of the collapse of the Western Empire and its displacement by the German kingdoms.

See *Cherusci, *Cimeri, *Franks, *Goths, *Marcomanni, *Quadi, *Vandals.

Tacitus, *Germania;*
E. A. Thompson, *The Early Germans,* 1965.

GERMANICUS IULIUS CAESAR Son of *Drusus (3), nephew of *Tiberius, born on 24 May 15 BC. In deference to Augustus, Tiberius adopted him in AD 4 (until then he was Nero Claudius Germanicus), thereby marking him as a likely candidate in the imperial succession. He acquired military experience by serving under Tiberius in Pannonia and Germany. After a consulate in 12, he commanded all the legions of Germania. In 15, he dealt in rather an incompetent and emotional way with the mutiny of the legions of Lower Germany; he ended up by accepting the principal demands of the mutineers. In a series of campaigns in 14–6, G. tried to restore Rome's rule over Germany; he succeeded in burying the corpses of *Varus' army in 15, and defeated Arminius in 16. But Tiberius thought that the conquest of Germany would be too expensive and difficult, and, in 17, he recalled G. After celebrating a triumph in Rome, G. went to the East with *imperium maius* over all the provinces there. Tiberius appointed *Piso (4) as governor of Syria to keep an eye on him. G. organized *Cappadocia and *Commagene as provinces. In 19, he visited Egypt, going against the rule of Augustus which obliged senators to get permission to visit the country. G. quarrelled with Piso and ordered him to return to Rome. Then he became ill and accused Piso of trying to poison him. G. died at Antioch on 10 October AD 19.

Like his father Drusus, G. was popular and is believed to have had "republican" sentiments. The suspicion that he was poisoned was fostered by his wife *Agrippina (2), and there were scenes of grief and popular demonstrations when his body was brought to Rome for burial in the mausoleum of Augustus. The story is artfully told by Tacitus to show that Tiberius and Livia were involved in G.'s death.

G. was also a poet. He wrote epigrams and comedies, and won a reputation with his translation of the *Phaenomena of *Aratus (1) into Latin; none of his works is extant. *Caligula and *Agrippina (3) were two of his nine children.

Tacitus, *Annales*, 1–3; B. Walker, *The Annals of Tacitus* (1952), 110ff.; Shotter, *Historia*, 1968, 194ff.

GEROUSIA Council of Elders (*gerontes*); the name was often applied to the city councils of many Greek cities, mainly in the Hellenistic and Roman periods. It was also the name of the Spartan council. There it dealt with all public matters, and like the Athenian Boule prepared motions to be brought before the popular Assembly (*Apellai). It was also a court for cases dealing with the death penalty and *atimia. It numbered thirty members: two kings and twenty-eight elders, over 60, who were elected for life by the Assembly. Candidates came from the aristocratic families, and thus the G. represented the aristocratic element in the Spartan constitution.

V. Ehrenberg, *The Greek State*, 1960 (s.v.); G. L. Huxley, *Early Sparta*, 1962 (s.v.).

GERYON(ES) In Greek mythology, a monster with three heads and three bodies, the son of Chrysaor and the Oceanid Callirhoë (Hesiod, *Theog.* 287ff.). G. had beautiful red cattle which were guarded by Eurytion and the two-headed dog Orthos, brother of Cerberus. He lived in Erytheia in the farthest west, the place where the sun set. The Tenth Labour of Heracles was to take G.'s cattle. After many adventures, Heracles found the island and killed the herdsman and the dog which tried to stop him. He then fought G., killed him, and drove the cattle away. Painters and sculptors depicted the fight between G. and Heracles.

GIGANTES Mythological giants, sons of *Gaia (earth), who bore them from the blood shed on her when Uranus (sky) was castrated. They were huge and brave warriors (Hesiod, *Theog.* 183ff.); but in Homer they were merely savages dressed in animal pelts (Homer, *Od.* 7.59). Their famous myth concerns their war against the Olympian gods, the *Gigantomachia*. They were provoked by the punishment of their brothers, the Titans, and assisted by their mother. They piled the Thessalian mountains Pelion and Ossa one upon the other and from the top of them hurled rocks against the Olympians. The gods discovered that they could win the war only with the help of a mortal and they used Heracles. While all the gods took part in the battle, it was usually Heracles who finished off the work with his arrows, in addition to killing Alcyoneus. Zeus struck Prophyrion – who tried to rape Hera – with his thunderbolt. Poseidon buried Polybotes under the island of Nisyrus. Apollo shot the left eye of Ephialte and Heracles the right eye. Athena threw the island of Sicily on Encealdes, or he himself became the island when killed. Dionysus killed the giants with his thyrsus. The defeated G. were said to have been buried under mountains and volcanoes.

The myth of the G. developed, and was elaborated on by poets, each repeating and adorning the tale according to his taste. More than 150 names of G. are recorded. They were sometimes confused with the Titans. The G. were accepted as a symbol for the fight against chaos and barbarism by order and civilization, and artists were attracted by the myth. The best known works depicting this myth are the frieze of the archaic treasure-house of the Siphnians in Delphi and the sculptures of the altar of Pergamum.

GLADIATORS *Gladius* means sword, and gladiatorial fights, common in Etruria and Campania, were first held in Rome in 264 BC. They formed part of the funeral rites and were very expensive, costing as much as 720,000 sesterces in the 2nd century BC (Polyb. 31.28,6). Obviously, only the rich nobles could afford them. Nonetheless, the number of combatants grew steadily. Caesar intended to engage 320 pairs for his games in 65 BC. Roman soldiers were trained in the gladiatorial art of fighting in 105 BC as a preparation against the *Cimbri. In the post-Sullan

Battle of the gods and giants (Gigantomachia). Detail from a frieze of the Siphnian treasure-house at Delphi

period, politicians retained G. as bodyguards and occasionally used them for street-fighting (*Milo, for instance); Antony used gladiators in the civil wars.

Under the Empire, the G.'s shows were controlled — only magistrates (praetors and quaestors) could hold them in Rome, and elsewhere official permission had to be obtained. There were several types of G.: the *Retiarius*, who fought with net and trident; the *Dimachaerus*, who fought with a short sword; the *Thracian*, armed with a round shield, who fought with a curved sword, etc. The G. were trained in special schools (*ludi*), and were recruited from slaves, prisoners of war, and (after the late Republic) from free men who volunteered.

Shows were held in amphitheatres and theatres. After a procession (*pompa*), the sign for fighting was given by a trumpet. Fighting was in pairs or in groups. The defeated were usually spared (the raising of the thumb by the giver of the show was the sign), and the winners were awarded prizes. The Emperor Constantine forbade the shows in the East, and Honorius forbade them in the West.

L. Friedlaender, *Roman Life and Manners* (Eng. tr. 1908), 2, 41ff, 4, 166ff.

GLAUCUS The name of several mythological heroes, the more prominent are:

1. G. son of *Sisyphus, king of Corinth and father of *Bellerophon. He used to feed his mares — which he kept at Potniae in Boeotia — on human flesh, so as to make them fiery (Hom. *Il.* 6.154ff.; Apollod. 1.85 etc.). Eventually he himself was eaten by them.

2. G. son of Hippolochos and grandson of Bellerophon, a Lycian chieftain who fought with the Trojans against the Greeks. Finding that his grandfather and Diomedes' grandfather were associated by ties of hospitality, he made a poor bargain by exchanging his golden armour with the bronze armour of Diomedes (Hom. *Il.* 6.234–6). In Homer, Apollo healed him (*Il.* 16.527ff.), but he was killed by *Aias (1) at the battle over Achilles' body.

3. G. of Anthedon in Boeotia, a fisherman who became immortal by eating a magical herb and which changed him into a sea god (Ovid. *Met.* 13.904ff.). G. was thereafter famed for his oracular sayings and had an oracle at Delos. The story was variously told by many writers, Greek and Roman (Athen. 7.296f.).

GNOSTICISM A term used to denote the religious, mystic movement that flourished in the East in the 2nd and 3rd centuries AD. The various Gnostic sects drew their beliefs from various sources: Judaism, Stoicism, Platonism, Zoroastrianism, Christianity. Characteristics of G. included belief in the dualism of the world and in redemption. The world came to being by an accident which caused souls to be locked up in bodies. By revelation (*gnosis*), the souls could be redeemed and returned to their original place of abode in heaven. This could be achieved through the work of a heaven-sent redeemer. Gnostics also believed in life after death for devotees who faithfully performed their rites. Usually it was by allegorical interpretations of old scriptures (Biblical, Platonic, Christian) that these doctrines were expounded. Among the more prominent Gnostic teachers were Basilides of Alexandria (*c.* AD 130), the Alexandrian Valentinus, who taught in Rome (*c.* AD 138– 165), and Marcion of Sinope who also taught in Rome (*c.* 140). For Judaism and Christianity, Gnostics were heretic sects which had to be fought against. Simon Magnus offered a religion with a rival saviour to Jesus. Indeed there were Jews and Christians who followed Gnostic views such as those found in

the writings of Philo, Plutarch, and Porphyry. St. Paul and Plotinus strongly attacked G.

Much concerning the Gnostic movement is still unclear and disputed: its origins, the part of the old religions in it, and even its very nature. Some consider it as the product of the Hellenization of Christianity; others as the result of the Orientalization of early Christianity, and so forth. Further research of Gnostic texts may contribute to the understanding of these and other questions.

J. Doresse, *The Secret Books of the Egyptian Gnostics,* 1960; H. Jonas, *The Gnostic Religion,* 1958; R. M. Wilson, *The Gnostic Problem,* 1958; U. Bianchi, *Origins of Gnosticism,* 1967.

GORDIAN I and GORDIAN II The first, Marcus Antonius Gordianus, a 79-year-old senator who had a long career (consul in AD 223). He was governor of Africa in 238 when proclaimed emperor with the assent of the Senate. Soon thereafter, his son, G. II, fell in a battle against Capellianus, governor of Numidia, and G. I committed suicide — only twenty-two days after his enthronement.

GORDIAN III Grandson of G. I and nephew of G. II, made emperor by the praetorians at the age of 13 in AD 238. From 241 on, the effective power was in the hands of the praetorian prefect Timesitheus, whose daughter G. married. In 242, Timesitheus set out to the East to fight the Persians and occupied Mesopotamia. He died in 243 and his successor, Philip, became emperor after the murder of G. in the following year.

P. W. Townsend, *Yale Classical Studies,* 1934, 59ff.

GORDIUM Ancient city in Asia Minor, west of Ancyra, capital of Phrygia in the 8th century BC (*Midas). A strong city, it was destroyed by the Cimmerians in the early 7th century, but it rose again. By the end of the 3rd century BC, it declined to a village. It is famed for the "Gordian Knot". Gordios, a peasant who became a king, was believed to have founded the city and to have dedicated his chariot to Zeus. The belief was that the man who could untie the complicated knot that fastened the yoke to a pole would master Asia. Alexander the Great visited G. in 333 and solved the difficulty by cutting the knot with his sword (Plut. *Alex.* 18.3 etc.).

GORGIAS Greek Sophist and orator, native of *Leontini (*c.* 485–376 BC). He visited Athens as a member of a Leontine embassy in 427 BC, and won immediate success with his new techniques of rhetoric taught to him by Tisias. G. is said to have amassed riches by his art, and seems to have spent a large part of his life in wandering and teaching rhetoric. Few of his writings are extant: the *Encomium of Helen* (defence of Helen against all possible accusations); *Apologia for Palamedes* (defence of Palamedes against the accusations of Odysseus). There is also a fragment of a funeral oration (*epitaphios*). G. wrote a manual of rhetoric (*techne*) and the speeches he delivered at the Pythian and Olympic games (*Pythicos, Olympicos*) were well known. It was his style, characterized by assonance, antitheses, and balanced and parallel clauses that influenced such writers as Thucydides and Isocrates. G. is also known for the saying that "nothing exists and that if it existed it would be incomprehensible".

Kennedy, *Persuasion,* 61ff.

GORGO or MEDUSA Greek mythological monster, first mentioned by Homer (*Il.* 8.349), with snakes instead of hair and boar's tusks instead of teeth. Her frightful appearance and terrifying eyes petrified those who looked at her. Her two immortal sisters were the Gorgons Sthen-

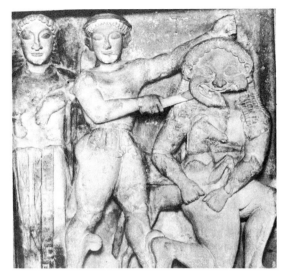

Perseus killing the Gorgo. A metope from temple C at Selinus

no and Euryale (Hesiod, *Theog.* 270ff.). They had wings to fly with and lived in the Far West. Helped by the gods, *Perseus cut G.'s head off but on her death she bore *Pegasus and Chrysaor. The blood of one of her veins was life-bringing, while that of another vein was deadly; both veins were at the disposal of *Asclepius. M. alone, or her killing by Perseus, or the pursuit of Perseus by the two sisters, were popular themes in art from the Archaic period on. In the Hellenistic period, the terrible monster changed into a beautiful maiden.

C. Hulst, *Peseus and the Gorgon,* 1947.

GORTYN Dorian city in south central Crete, about 15 km from the coast, first mentioned by Homer (*Il.* 2.646), probably occupied by Greeks even before the Dorian conquest. It was always one of the important cities in Greek times and became most powerful from the middle of the 3rd century BC. In Roman times, it was the main city of the province Crete – Cyrene, a centre of trade, and it had an imperial mint. As early as the 2nd century AD, it was a bishop's seat. The considerable remains date mainly from Roman times; many inscriptions have been found.

G. is famous for the "Code of Gortyn", a collection of laws known from an inscription dating to the middle of the 5th century BC. These laws, some of which are very ancient, are the most important direct evidence on the early law of any Greek city. The "Code" comprises private and not constitutional laws. It gives regulations on property, slaves, trial procedure, inheritance, adoption, penalties, etc. Criminal law is still largely connected with family law in it.

R. F. Willets (ed.) *The Law Code of Gortyn,* 1967.

GOTHS German people, mentioned by Tacitus (*Germ.* 4), inhabiting the regions north of the Black Sea by the end of the 2nd century AD. Good warriors, they first attacked the Roman Empire in AD 238. From 248 on they made devastating inroads to Asia Minor, the Danubian provinces and Greece. It was the Emperor *Claudius II who checked them by decisive defeats and hence earned the title Gothicus. However, his successor *Aurelian decided to evacuate Dacia, beyond the Danube,

which was then occupied by the Visigoths, one of the two sections of G. (formed about the middle of the 3rd century AD). The other section, the Osthrogoths, remained in the regions north of the Black Sea. The G. kept to these regions for about a century, but under pressure from the Huns the Visigoths crossed the Danube in 376. At Adrianopol, on 9 August 378, they won a great battle over the imperial army under the Emperor Valens and stayed in Moesia until 395. Under *Alaric, they renewed their migration, causing much devastation. In 410, they sacked Rome. They migrated to southwestern Gaul in 418. Under pressure from the Franks, who won a great victory under King Clovis in 507, they moved to Spain. Part of the Osthrogoths joined the Visigoths in their migration in 376, and others made occasional inroads or settled as allies (*foederati*) in Pannonia. Later, they migrated to Italy with King *Theodoric.

GRACCHUS (1), Tiberius Sempronius Important Roman statesman, of a noble plebeian family, active in the first half of the 2nd century BC. He took part in the war against *Antiochus III in 190, and as plebeian tribune (187 or 184) vetoed the imprisonment of L. *Scipio Asiaticus by his colleagues. After curule aedileship in 182, he governed Spain as a praetor (180–179). He won victories and established peace with the Celtiberians by signing moderate treaties, which were the basis of Roman rule for a long period. Consul in 177, he subdued Sardinia and was given a second triumph in 175. He built the Basilica Sempronia and in 169, he carried out his duty as censor with severity. Consul II in 163, he died in 154. He married the daughter of Scipio Africanus. Tiberius Gracchus, Gaius Gracchus and Sempronia, Scipio Aemilianus' wife, were three of their twelve children.

Scullard, *Rom. Pol.*[2] (s.v.).

GRACCHUS (2), Tiberius Sempronius The famous tribune, son of Gracchus (1) and *Cornelia, said to have been influenced by his teachers (the Stoic Blossius of Cumae and the rhetor Diophanes of Mytilene). Quaestor in Spain (137 BC), he used the fame and influence of his father to save a Roman army which fell into an ambush. The personal disgrace involved in the repudiation of the treaty he had concluded was another motive for G.'s policy. Backed by influential nobles, notably his father-in-law Ap. Claudius Pulcher, *Scaevola (1), and *Crassus Mucianus (2), he proposed a sweeping agrarian law. It aimed at distributing small plots of public land to poor citizens, thereby solving the social problems caused by the dispossession of small farmers and the growth of the proletariat and adding to the decreasing manpower by creating propertied citizens who were qualified for military service. The plots were to be distributed by a three-member board from public land (*Ager Publicus) which some people held in excess of the maximum 500 *iugera* (300 acres) allowed; children were possibly entitled to an extra 250 *iugera* each. G. took the unprecedented step of deposing with a second bill his colleague Octavius who vetoed the agrarian law, which was soon passed. The opposition now included not only the possessors of public land and those who feared the acquisition of political power by G. and his supporters but also those who regarded his methods as constitutionally dangerous. His proposal to use the inheritance of *Attalus III to finance the establishment of the new settlers encroached on foreign affairs and finances, which were traditionally administered by the Senate. His intention to be re-elected tribune to complete the reform was interpreted as an attempt to consolidate his personal rule, and he and many of his henchmen were lynched on the Capitol by senators led by the Pontifex Maximus Scipio Serapio. None the less, the agrarian board carried through its work, and much public land was reclaimed and distributed. The tribunate of G. ushered in a new period characterized by the use of violence, the splitting up of the aristocracy, and the adoption of G.'s methods and ideology by the Populares for their own personal careers.

Plutarc, *Tiberius Gracchus*; Appian, *BC,* 1; D. C. Earl, *Tiberius Gracchus,* 1963; E. Badian, "Tiberius Gracchus" in *Aufstieg und Niedergang der römischen Welt* (1972) 1.

GRACCHUS (3), Gaius Sempronius Younger son of Gracchus (1), son-in-law of *Crassus (2) Mucianus, member of the agrarian board of his brother. After serving as quaestor in Sardinia (126–125 BC), he was elected tribune for 123, and re-elected for 122 without encountering violent opposition as his brother did. He carried through a series of laws continuing and extending the programme of his brother. One law reaffirmed the principle — which was not observed by his brother's opponents — that the death penalty should be endorsed by the Assembly. Several laws strengthened the Equites at the expense of the Senate, giving them the right to serve in the jury courts from which senators were barred, and authorizing the selling of the contracts of the Asian taxes in Rome. The *lex frumentaria* gave citizens wheat at a relatively low price. The agrarian and colonial laws established a colony in Carthage (which failed), renewed the distribution of land, and the construction of roads and other operations, and gave work to citizens. Other laws were aimed at checking corruption in trials, easing military service, restricting the Senate's manipulation in the allocation of provinces to the consuls, and so on. G. won popularity with the masses and influence with the Equites, but lost support when he unsuccessfully tried to pass a proposal to give Latin rights to the Italian allies and citizenship to the Latins. The tribune *Drusus (1) weakened G.'s popularity with his own programme of colonization and G. and his most important supporter, Fulvius Flaccus, failed to be re-elected for 121. Prompted by serious disturbances in early 121, the Senate issued the first *Senatus consaltum ultimum.* In the ensuing fighting G. and Fulvius found their death, and G.'s followers were persecuted by the consul Opimius.

A shrewd politician, aware of all the problems of Roman government and society, G.'s failure in the long run was more disastrous than that of his brother. The *lex frumentaria* became a demagogic measure which helped the degeneration of the masses of Rome; the Equites, from whom came the *Publicani*, were more oppressive than the senators in the exploitation of the provincials, and they were probably no better as judges; the military law and the other benefits for poor citizens were not enough to solve the problem of military manpower, and after *Marius the army became more and more an army of professional proletarians rather than one of propertied citizens. G.'s vigorous measures destroyed harmony within the aristocracy and changed the tenor of politics.

Plut. *Gaius Gracchus*; App, *BC,* 1; Malcovati, *Or. Rom. Fr.*[3]; H. H. Scullard, *From the Gracchi to Nero*[2] (1963), ch. 2.

GRAIAE Three mythological sisters of the *Gorgons (Hesiod. *Theog.* 270ff.). They all had only one eye and one tooth. Perseus stole the eye and so forced them to tell him the way to the Gorgo.

GRAMMATEIS These were the annually elected secretaries of the various institutions of the Greek cities. In Athens, the *Boule, the *Ekklesia, and the *Thesmothetai each had their own *grammateus.* They were responsible for writing documents and their preservation, and sometimes for their publication. As non-professionals, they could employ qualified slaves for the technical work, which they often did themselves. This system generally restricted the development of a professional bureaucracy. In Hellenistic kingdoms, notably in Egypt, G. were state officials.

G. Glotz, *The Greek City*, 1927 (s.v.). W. B. Dinsmoor, *The Athenian Archon List,* 1937 (s.v. secretaries, undersecretaries).

GRAPHE PARANOMON In Athens, a proposal submitted before the *Boule or the Ekklesia which contradicted an existing law was liable to legal prosecution, or GP. Any citizen could bring in a GP. against the proposer before a lawcourt administered by the *Thesmothetai. If found guilty, the proposer was fined and the proposal, even if already passed, was annulled. Three convictions led to *Atimia. A year after the passing of a proposal, the proposer was no longer subject to GP. As from the late 5th century BC (the first known case was in 415), this procedure became the most common weapon used by politicians to destroy their rivals. The best known case is that of *Aeschines against Ctesiphon for his motion to give Demosthenes a crown.

Hignett, *Athen. Const.,* 210ff.

GRATIAN, Flavius Roman emperor (AD 367–83), ruler of the Western Empire, son of *Valentian I. Born in AD 359, G.'s tutor was *Ausonius. His effective rule began after the death of his father in 375. After the death of *Valens, he made Theodosius I emperor of the eastern parts of the empire. A devoted Christian, he was the first to give up the title Pontifex Maximus. He supported the claims of the Bishop of Rome for supremacy and fought the pagans. He failed against the usurper Magnus Maximus and was killed at Lyons in 383.

GREECE It has often been said that Greek history was dominated by the geographical features of the land, which is a southeastern extension of the Balkans. Mountains form more than three quarters of G. and the fertile, arable soil is divided among many plains and valleys which were long isolated because of the low level of ancient communications. Hence, numerous independent city-states (*Polis) developed and tribal organization perisisted for long periods. The scarcity of arable land and the proximity of the sea, with good harbours, made the Greeks seafaring men, and led them to overseas trade and colonization (*Apoikia). The main plains, from north to south, are those of lower Macedonia, of Thessaly, of Thebes and the Cephisus valley in Boeotia, of Attica, of Elis, of Messenia, of the Argolid, and of the Eurotas valley in Laconia. The highest mountains are Olympus (over 2,900 m), Parnassus (over 2,400 m), Taÿgetus (less than 2,400 m). The southern part of the Greek mainland, the peninsula of the Peloponnese, is separated from central G. by the Gulf of Corinth and the Saronic Gulf; the Corinthian isthmus is only 6.5 km wide. G. was always poor in mineral resources: the silver mines of Laurium in Attica, the iron mines in Laconia, the gold mines of Mount Pangaeus in Thrace, which attracted Greek settlers, were the notable exceptions. The country does not get much rain. Its few rivers are not suitable for irrigation and are not navigable. Vines and olives were

Mountains and hills at the Gulf of Corinth

grown quite early, but though slope-lands came under cultivation, they could hardly produce enough grain. Hence there was the problem of occasional shortages and a growing dependence on grain import. Livestock consisted mainly of sheep and goats; horses were bred in a few regions, notably Thessaly.

The name G., from the Latin *Graecia*, originated with one small tribe, the *Grai*, or with a place-name *Graia* in Boeotia (Homer, *Il.* 2.498), though it is far from clear why the Italians adopted it. By the end of the 8th century BC, the Greeks called themselves *Hellenes, and their country Hellas, after a small tribe in south Thessaly (for a parallel see *Italy). Other names used by Homer to denote the Greeks in general are Achaeans, Danai, or Argives. They considered themselves the descendants of Hellen, son of *Deucalion, who ruled over Thessaly in ancient times. His sons were Dorus, Aeolus, and Xuthus father of Ion and Achaeus; these were respectively the ancestors of the Dorians, Aeolians, Ionians and Achaeans. The archaeological, literary and philological evidence seems to indicate that the ancestors of the Greek people began to invade G. from the north in the late 3rd millenium BC, and by conquest and some mixing with the earlier population there, developed in the 2nd millenium BC the first great Greek civilization, which was named after *Mycenae (c. 1600–1100 BC). It was these invasions that introduced Greek dialects; the earliest documents written in Greek are those of Linear B, and they may date from the early 14th century. Much of Greek mythology concerns the Mycenaean world, whose society, politics and institutions are reflected to a considerable extent in the *Iliad* and the *Odyssey*. This world suffered destruction in the 12th century, and the Mycenaean civilization came to an end with the invasion of the Dorians who occupied the Peloponnesus and some of the islands, notably Crete, in the 11th century. It was as a result of these destructive invasions that Greeks emigrated to and colonized the Aegean islands and the western coast of Asia Minor. From this period, commonly called the Dark Age (c. 1100–800 BC), emerged the most typical political organization of the Greeks, the polis. During this period, the aristocracy

gradually replaced the kings. But the development of the city-state meant that the Greeks never achieved political unity; indeed, even though certain cultural, religious, institutional and spiritual characteristics were common to all, each state had its own particular gods and heroes, institutions and officials, customs and ways of life. Acting in the framework of the polis, they succeeded settling the shores of the North Aegean, the Hellespont, Sicily and south Italy, the Black Sea, Cyprus, south Gaul, Spain, Cyrene and even Egypt (*Naucratis). Classical G. repulsed the attack of Persia and in the west Carthage was beaten. But the Greeks ruined themselves with internal wars; first Athens, then Sparta and Thebes attempted to win hegemony. The weakness of the Greek states made it possible for Philip II of Macedonia to acquire hegemony over G.; under his successor, Alexander the Great, and the Hellenistic monarchies, Greeks and Greek civilization expanded to the East. In the West, the united Greeks fell victim to several local tribes and finally came under the control of Rome. G. itself came under the control — first indirect later direct — of Rome in the 2nd and 1st centuries BC. By the end of the 2nd century BC, G. had not only lost its political independence but continued to decline economically and no longer produced original cultural achievements.

See *Acarnania, *Achaea, *Aeolis, *Aetolia, *Apoikia, *Arcadia, *Athens, *Attica, *Boeotia, *Dorians, *Elis, *Euboea, *Ionia, *Laconia, *Locris, *Macedonia, *Messenia, *Peloponnesus, *Phocis, *Polis, *Thebes, *Thessaly.

M. Cary, *Geographic Background*;
M. I. Finley, *Early Greece*, 1970;
C. G. Starr, *The Origins of Greek Civilization*, 1961;
N. G. L. Hammond, *History of Greece*[2], 1966;
M. Cary, *A History of the Greek World 323–146 BC*[2], 1951; M. Rostovtzeff, *The Social and Economic History of the Hellenistic World*, 1941; V. Ehrenberg, *The Greek State*, 1961.

GROMATICI Roman land-surveyors, also called *mensores, agrimensores, metatores, divisores*, etc. They took the name from their main tool, the *groma* (derived ultimately from the Greek *gnoma* or *gnomon*), which consisted of two main parts — a pole, and on the top of it, a cross with plumb-lines hung from each of its arms. The technical knowledge and skill of the G. seem to have been originally connected with the divination of the *Augures, who used to divide the space under their observation by a grid system. But it was mainly with the construction of camps, the founding of colonies and the distribution of public land that they came to be associated in the Republic. In such large-scale operations, they were required to define and divide a given area into square blocks (*centuriatio*), leaving spaces for roads, public areas and buildings, etc. The main element in this work was the marking of east-west parallel lines (*decumani*) crossed at right angles by north-south parallel lines (*cardines*); the central of these were called *decumanus maximus* and *cardo maximus*. Air photography has disclosed traces of the centuriation of lands by G. in south Italy and other parts of the Roman Empire. G. were also employed by private owners in land disputes or in divisions of estates. In the course of time, they became skilled professionals. Under the Empire and due mainly to land-taxation needs, *agrimensores* formed a department in the imperial bureaucracy.

Much of the ancient technical literature about the work of G. is extant.

F. Blume, K. Lachmann, A. Rudorff, *Die Schriften der römischen Feldmesser,* 1962 (1848–1852);
J. Bradford, *Ancient Landscapes,* 1957;
O. A. W. Dilke, *The Roman Land Surveyors,* 1971.

GYGES About 685 BC, he became king of Lydia when he murdered the previous king, Candaules. He then married Candaules' beautiful widow. In legend, he was given a magic ring which made him invisible, and it was thus that he took power. In contrast to his predecessor, he attacked the Greek cities in Asia Minor and extended his kingdom to the Hellespont. But soon Greeks and Lydians alike were attacked by the Cimmerians, whom G. first repulsed with the help of Assyria. He was killed (*c.* 652 BC) in another Cimmerian invasion, and was succeeded by his

Fragment of land register showing partition of land by Gromatici

son, Ardys, who finally crushed the invaders. G. issued coins, and was probably the first to do so.
Holt, 1, 8–14; Plato, *Rep.,* 2, 359.

GYLIPPUS Spartan commander who was sent on the advice of *Alcibiades, to help Syracuse against the Athenian expedition in 414 BC. He organized a rescue force from other Greek cities in Sicily, and by his initiative and sound tactics led Syracuse to destroy the Athenian forces. In 412, he returned to Sparta, whence he had fled in 404 after his condemnation on a charge of peculation.

GYMNASIUM A place for sports training and exercise, a typical Greek institution. It consisted of buildings and grounds and was usually outside the city walls at a grove and beside a river. It included a palaestra (a building with the necessary installations for training in wrestling, jumping, boxing, ball games), running courses, bath-rooms, dressing rooms and other facilities; some *gymnasia* had libraries. The more important *gymnasia* in Athens were those of the *Academy, the Lyceum and the Cynosarges. But *gymnasia* were to be found everywhere and in time came to represent the Greek way of life.

H

HADES In Greek mythology, one of the three sons of Kronos (Hesiod, *Theog.* 453ff.), husband of *Persephone. God of the underworld. H.'s name (other older forms were *Aides* or *Ais*) means "the invisible". He received by lot the realm of the dead as his share after the defeat of the Titans (Apollod. 1.6,3). For the Greeks the underworld was "the house of Hades", and only in later times did H. become the place itself. The terrible *Cerberus guarded his realm against intruders. H. himself, the severe, relentless god, punished the sinners. Such a god obviously was not popular. He had no myths except the abduction of Persephone (*Homeric Hymn to Demeter*, 17), but was involved in the tales of heroes that descended to his realm (e.g. Heracles and Orpheus). He was rarely worshipped, except at Elis where he had a temple (Pausan. 25.2). Occasionally he appeared in other places but with different names: Plouton ("the rich one"), Eubouleus ("the good counsellor"), Dis, etc. As god of the lower earth he controlled its treasures and in this respect he was Plouton, from whom prosperity could be asked. From the Archaic period on the grim looking H. occasionally appears in works of art, usually bearded and with sceptre, accompanied by Persephone or his brothers.

HADRIAN (Publius Aelius Hadrianus) Roman emperor (AD 117–38), son of P. Aelius Hadrianus and Domitia Paulina, born at Italica in Baetica in AD 76. A distant relative of Trajan, he was raised in his house after the death of his father in AD 85. He held his first military position under Domitian (AD 95), and advanced to be suffect consul in 108. He was made archon of Athens in 111, accompanied Trajan to the Parthian War and became governor of Syria (114 or 117). After Trajan's death it was made known that he had adopted H., who was proclaimed emperor in Syria on 11 August 117. He sent the news to the Senate, whose privileges he confirmed, and distributed donatives to the soldiers. H.'s adoption and accession to the throne were regarded with suspicion by many senators and senior commanders of Trajan. H. soon abandoned the offensive policy of his predecessor. The new provinces of Armenia, Assyria and Mesopotamia were evacuated and *Lucius Quietus, *Avidius Nigrinus, *Palma and Celsus, four veteran generals associated with the expansive policy, were executed on a charge of conspiracy in 118 (in H.'s absence from Italy). H. himself was

The Emperor Hadrian

busy fighting the Sarmatae and Roxolani on the Balkan frontier, and found it expedient to divide *Dacia into two provinces.

Back in Italy in 118 H. sought to ingratiate himself to the public by popular measures. He cancelled debts to the treasury to the amount of 900 million sesterces, gave gladiatorial shows, donated new funds to the *Alimenta, and helped poor senators financially. He made some important innovations. The jurist Salvius *Julianus published a revised, and final, edition of the *edictum perpetuum* of the urban praetor (*c.* AD 130); this was an important step as until then Roman law had developed to a considerable extent by the inclusion of new measures, suited to new social and economic conditions, in the praetor's edict. Jurisdiction in Italy was given to four circuit consular judges. The imperial administration grew and was manned by *Equites, who also replaced the freedmen as secretaries of the emperor, notably the *ab epistulis* and *a rationibus*. The *Concilium principis* now included jurists and became a more organized institution. He also tried to improve finances and intervened in municipal administration by appointing *curatores*. He carried out considerable building operations which included the *Pantheon, a temple of *Venus et Roma*, and his own mausoleum at Rome, his extensive villa at Tibur and a new quarter, Hadrian's City, as well as public buildings at Athens.

H.'s main concern was for the provinces which he continued to visit almost throughout his reign. After a tour in Gaul, the German frontier, Britain and Spain, and perhaps Mauretania, *c.* 120–2, he sailed directly to the East passing Crete on his way. He travelled through Asia Minor to Syria, and returned to the Balkan provinces (123–4). In 125 he was in Greece and returned to Rome, visiting Sicily on his way, in 126 or 127. In 128 he visited Africa and then from Rome resumed his travels to the East. He went to Athens, Asia Minor, Syria, Judaea, Egypt, and was back in Rome in 131. The Jewish revolt probably occasioned another visit to Syria in 134. These travels were not for pleasure; his aim was to inspect the conditions of the provinces and to introduce, wherever necessary, new measures and arrangements. In Britain he started the building of his wall which was to extend over eighty miles from Wallsend-on-Tyne to Bowness-on-Solway; it was strengthened by a ditch, 6 metres in front of it. When in the Balkans in 124, he made part of Upper Dacia a separate province (Porolissensis). In Asia Minor he occasionally sought to improve the administration of the cities. At Athens he added a new suburb, "the City of Hadrian", and completed the building of the temple of Olympian Zeus which was dedicated in 128. He then received the title Olympius. In Thrace he built a new city Hadrianopolis (modern Edirne). This building activity was unfortunate in Judaea where the plan to found the Colonia Aelia Capitolina in Jerusalem and to erect a temple to Jupiter Capitolinus on the site of the Jewish temple led to the Jewish revolt; a no less important cause was the prohibition of circumcision. The revolt was suppressed only after three years of fighting (132–5) and the devastated country was organized as a separate province (Syria Palaestina). This act was exceptional and was due to Hadrian's enthusiasm for Hellenism. Generally his reign was peaceful, and under him the provinces enjoyed economic prosperity and peace.

In his last years Hadrian stayed at Rome. From his wife Vibia Sabina, whom he married in AD 100, he had

no issue. To secure the succession he first adopted L. Aelius, the father of L. *Verus, and after his death *Antoninus Pius (138). He fell ill in 136 and died in 138. He was deified and buried in his mausoleum (Castel Sant Angelo). H. was a man of letters; he wrote an autobiography, collections of speeches and letters, and a poem addressed to his soul.

B. W. Henderson, *Life and Principate of the Emperor Hadrian*, 1923; R. Syme, *Tacitus*, 1958; H. Bardon, *Les emperereurs et les lettres latins*, 1944.

HADRUMETUM (modern Sousse) Phoenician city on the North African coast, about 100 km south of Carthage, founded late in the 7th century BC. It was the main city of the fertile and well cultivated region of Byzaciun. H. prudently sided with the Romans in the Third Punic War and as a reward became a *civitas libera et immunis* in 146. Caesar punished it in 46. Under the Empire it prospered and was made a *colonia* under Trajan. It was the residence of the imperial procurator of the region and under Diocletian the capital of the new *provincia Byzacena*. A Phoenician *topheth* was discovered there and there are also remains of an amphitheatre, circus, private houses and Christian catacombs.

Z. Foucher, *Hadrumetum*, 1964.

HALICARNASSUS Greek coastal city in Caria said to have been founded by colonists from the Argolid (Troezen or Argos: Hdt. 7.99; Vitruvius 2.8,12) in the 11th century BC but more probably a century or so later. It had a mixed population with Dorian, Ionian and Carian elements. Herodotus says that it was a member of a religious Dorian league. The local rulers came under the control of Croesus and then of Persia in the 6th century BC. H.'s princess *Artemisia (1) fought on Xerxes' side at Salamis, but subsequently H. was a member of the Delian League. In the 4th century BC, H. became the capital city of the Carian satrap *Mausolus, who fortified and adorned it. It suffered considerable damage when sieged and captured by Alexander the Great in 334. It changed masters in the period of the *Diadochi, but for most of the 3rd century was under Ptolemaic control. After 189 BC it was annexed to Rhodes and from 129 BC on was included in the Roman province of Asia. The historians Herodotus and *Dionysius (3) were natives of H. It was famed for the Mausoleum.

Magie, *Asia* (s.v.);

G. E. Bean, *Turkey Beyond the Maeander*, 1971, 101 ff.

HAMILCAR BARCA Prominent Carthaginian general and politician. A daring commander, master of the tactics of "hit and run" (*Baraq* on which his name is based means "lightning"), he attacked and plundered the coast of Bruttium in 247 BC, and later reached as far as Cumae in his sudden inroads. In Sicily he first occupied Mount Heircte (247–244) as a base to operate against the Roman armies in western Sicily, and then (244–241) Mount *Eryx, from which he vainly sought to save Drepana from the Roman siege. After the decisive Roman naval victory at the Aegates Insulae in 241, he concluded the terms of peace with Rome. Subsequently he quelled the revolt of the Carthaginian mercenaries in a bloody and cruel war (241–238). He went to Spain in 237 and in the following years conquered the southern part of the peninsula, first basing his operation on Gades and later on Acra Leuce (near Alicante). The local tribes and cities were required to pay tribute and to surrender hostages. He satisfied the Roman enquiries by claiming that his only aim was to obtain money for the payment of the war indemnity to

Rome. He was drowned in the river Jucar while retreating from a Spanish attack in 229. The army elected his son-in-law *Hasdrubal (1) as his successor in command.

HANNIBAL The greatest Carthaginian general and statesman, the eldest son of Hamilcar Barca, born in 247 BC. According to tradition he swore eternal enmity to Rome before leaving Carthage in 237 to accompany his father to Spain. He showed himself an excellent soldier; he was a junior officer under *Hasdrubal (1), on whose death in 221 he was elected commander-in-chief. He resumed the aggressive policy of his father. He first attacked the Olcades and in 220 the Vaccaei and Carpetani who lived in the north-central part of the peninsula. In 219 he besieged Saguntum which claimed an alliance with Rome. The capture of that city despite Roman protests, the legality of which is doubtful and much disputed, led to the outbreak of the Second Punic War.

H. was confident of his army and his superior tactics, and decided to carry the war to Italy. He reckoned that the Gallic tribes of *Gallia Cisalpina, only recently subdued by Rome, would join him; he also aimed at undermining the loyalty of the Italian allies to Rome. Leaving his brother *Hasdrubal (2) in command of Spain with strong troops, he set out from Carthago Nova in the early spring of 218. He passed the Pyrenees with an army of some 35,000 infantry and 8,000 cavalry, advanced along southern Gaul, and crossed the Rhone despite Gallic hostility, though not intercepted by the Roman army under P. *Scipio (1). With extreme difficulty he crossed the Alps and arrived at the Po valley in October 218 with only some 20,000 infantry and 6,000 cavalry. His first victory was in a cavalry engagement at Ticinus against Scipio who had returned to Italy. At the river Trebia in December he won a great victory over the combined forces of Scipio and the other consul, Sempronius Longus. By these successes he won the support of the Gauls, and was able to allow his army to rest in the winter. In 217 he descended to Etruria and by a classic trap he destroyed the army of the consul *Flamininus at Lake Trasimene. No further actions took place that year due to the strategy of *Fabius Cunctator. H. was also disappointed in that the Italian cities refused to join him and he went through Apulia and Campania devastating the country. He won his greatest victory at *Cannae in 216 where he surrounded and destroyed the numerically superior Roman army. It was now that *Capua and other towns in south Italy joined him, and next year they were followed by *Philip V and *Syracuse.

The brilliant victories and the shrewd strategy, however, failed to defeat Rome. The delaying tactics of Fabius were adopted by Rome, and H. could not gain any more great victories. The vast majority of the Italian tribes and cities remained loyal to Rome and H. was unable to besiege those who refused to join him or effectively protect those who followed him against Roman reprisals. The Roman superiority in manpower, a potential of several hundred thousands, was decisive; in some years as many as 22 legions were recruited, not counting the allies. It was in the years 216–211 that the great first gains were counterbalanced. A Roman expedition to Greece checked Philip V who finally concluded the separate peace of Phoenice (205). The Gauls were blocked in north Italy. At Spain Gnaeus *Scipio (1) and his brother won victories, and conquered Saguntum, thereby depriving Hasdrubal of the opportunity to send reinforcements to his brother, though Scipio and his brother were destroyed in 211. The

same year *Fulvius Flaccus (1) and *Maecellus (1) captured Capua and Syracuse respectively. From now on H. was forced to retreat to the south and in 209 lost Tarentum which he had captured by treachery in 213. The fall of Marcellus in an ambush in 208 was not a great relief. In 207 Hasdrubal arrived in Italy with a strong force but was defeated and killed at the Metaurus before he could join his brother. Next year Scipio Africanus completed the conquest of Spain. Finally in 203, after the spectacular victories of Scipio in Africa, H. left Italy where he had stayed for sixteen years. He lost the final battle of Zama (202) to Scipio who employed H.'s own tactics but had better troops at his disposal.

Carthage's quick recovery after the war was largely due to the reforms H. passed as suffete in 196. By his measures the oligarchic One Hundred Four Court was to be elected annually by the people; he increased the revenues of the state, not the least by making the rich oligarchs pay up for the deficits incurred during their administration. His enemies took revenge by accusing him before Rome that he had contacted *Antiochus III, and so he fled from Carthage in 195 to that king. Antiochus did not follow his advice in his war against Rome, and gave him only a naval command in 190 when he was defeated by the Rhodians. After the king's defeat he found shelter with the Bithynian King Prusias. He committed suicide by poison in 183 (182) when Prusias was about to surrender him to the Romans.

H. was a military genius — one of the greatest of all times — and a great statesman. He showed imagination, inventiveness and superior tactics on many occasions. At Trebia he prepared an ambush and then enticed the Romans to fight on empty stomachs after crossing the cold river. He repeated the ambush tactics at Lake Trasimene taking full advantage of the topography and the avidity of his opponent to fight. He outmanoeuvred Fabius who blocked his retreat way from Campania in 217 by sending oxen with burning fagots at night in one direction while he led his army through the main, now unoccupied, way. His outflanking tactics are best illustrated by the battle of Cannae where he neutralized the superiority of the legionaries by delaying action in the centre while his cavalry routed that of the enemy and then encircled the whole army. He made successful use of reserve forces in battles and was unique in his time in that he knew that a commander should not risk his life by personally fighting. A great leader of men, he retained the loyalty of his soldiers, most of them mercenaries, to the end. His excellent and unusual tactics were matched by his strategic plans. The Romans pursued him in his life and could never forget the awe he inspired; with *Hannibal ad portas* ("H. is at the gates") mothers frightened their children and the people were rallied in times of crisis.

Polybius, 3, 7–15; G. Charles-Picard, *Hannibal*, 1967.

HANNO Carthaginian who explored the western coast of Africa as far as Sierra Leone. His account is extant in Greek. His date is disputed, but he seems to be identical with the H., the Magonid, who ruled Carthage in the 2nd quarter of the 5th century BC.

G. C. and C. Picard, *Carthage*, 1968, 86ff., 115ff.

HARMOST Spartan commander or governor sent abroad. H.'s appeared in the Peloponnesian War and after its conclusion many were sent to govern various cities, such as *Clearchus in Byzantium.

HARPALUS Macedonian high aristocrat, a close friend of Alexander the Great, banished by *Philip II in 337 BC. In

Alexander's expedition he was responsible for the war-chest but for a mysterious reason fled to Greece in 333. He returned in 331, was made the chief treasurer and resided in Babylonia. He used his position to embezzle money and on Alexander's return from India fled to Athens (324). After failing to find shelter there, despite bribes to influential persons including Demosthenes, he went with his money and soldiers to Crete, where he was murdered.
E. Badian, *JHS*, 1961, 16ff.

HARPIES Monstrous birds with women's heads who snatched people and food (Verg. *Aen.* 3.210ff.). Originally they were wind-spirits who carried off the souls. In early mythology they were daughters of Electra, daughter of Oceanus, and Thaumas (Hesiod. *Theog.* 265f.). The *Argonauts delivered the Thracian King *Phineus from their attacks (Apol. Rhod. 2.188ff.), in which they devoured or polluted his food. In art they appeared from the early 6th century BC on, usually described as winged women. In the "Harpy-Tomb" from Xanthos in Lycia there are woman-headed birds.

HARPOCRATION, Valerius Greek scholar of Alexandria, lived after the age of Augustus, perhaps in the 2nd century AD. His collection of florid rhetorical passages, not extant, was used by later lexicographers. His *Lexicon of the Ten Orators*, known from two versions (fuller and abridged), cites many important ancient authors on various subjects, historical, constitutional, religious, etc. The writers he uses include *Hellanicus, *Theopompus, *Aristophanes of Byzantium, *Dionysius of Halicarnasus and *Didymus.

HARUSPICES Etruscan diviners who practised the Etruscan king, Tarquinius Superbus (Liv. 1.56), but it was Rome. Traditionally they came to Rome under the last Etruscan king, Tarquinius Superbus (Liv. 1.56), but it was only from the Second Punic War on that they were extensively consulted by the state. They continued to practise to the end of the 4th century AD. The peculiar art of divination was kept alive within certain families, but by the late Republic the H., who formed a distinct order at Rome, were to be found in other Italian towns and care was taken that young men should be instructed (Cic. *Div.*1.92). The original Etruscan lore was based on the inspection of three kinds of signs: *exta* (the inner organs), *monstra* (abnormal phenomena) and *fulgura* (lightnings). Of these the inspection of the *exta* (especially the liver) was mainly employed at Rome.
Latte, *R Rel.* (s.v.).

HASDRUBAL (1) Carthaginian statesman and general, son-in-law of *Hamilcar Barca. He gained influence by leading the people against the oligarchy. He went to Spain with Hamilcar and returned to suppress a Numidian revolt. He was elected commander-in-chief by the army after the death of Hamilcar in 229 BC. H. founded Carthago Nova and by diplomatic means extended the area under his control. As Rome became suspicious, H. concluded an agreement in which the Ebro was recognized as the limit of the Carthaginian power in Spain (226 BC); yet he established good relations with local tribes even beyond that boundary. He was murdered in 221 by a Celt who thus avenged the execution of his master. In hostile propaganda H. allegedly first attempted to launch a revolution at Carthage and in Spain established his own personal rule.

HASDURBAL (2) BARCA Son of *Hamilcar Barca, younger brother of Hannibal, commander-in-chief of the Car-

thaginian army in Spain from 218 BC. He was defeated in a naval battle by Gnaeus *Scipio at the mouth of the Ebro in 217 and consequently lost northern Spain. His defeat on the Ebro in 215 prevented him from advancing to Italy to help his brother. In the same year he suppressed the revolt of *Syphax in Africa but could not prevent the capture of Saguntum by the Romans. His victory over Gnaeus Scipio in 211 again extended Carthaginian rule to the Ebro. But subsequently P. Scipio captured Carthage Nova (209) and came off better in the battle of Baecula (208). But H. was able to collect his forces and to advance into Italy. He crossed the Alps and with the Gallic reinforcements his troops were 30,000 strong. But the messenger he sent to announce his arrival to his brother was captured by the Romans. Two consular armies came against him, and, at the Metaurus, he lost the decisive battle and his life (207). This was fatal for the Carthaginian cause, for with no reinforcements Hannibal lost hope of restoring his fortunes.

HASDURBAL (3) Son of Gisgo, Carthaginian commander in Spain from 214 BC on. With *Mago (2) he defeated P. Scipio in 211 and then joined Hasdrubal (2) to defeat Gnaeus *Scipio (1). But he and Mago lost the battle of Ilipa to Scipio (206), who thus secured Spain for Rome. He escaped to Africa and by giving his daughter Sophonisbe in marriage to *Syphax, won him for Carthage. He became commander-in-chief and compelled Scipio to give up the siege of Utica (204). But in 203 Scipio set fire to his camp and destroyed his army and then defeated him at Campi Magni. Accused of treason, he took poison before the battle of Zama.

HASDRUBAL (4) Carthaginian commander who was defeated by *Masinissa in 150 BC. He was made commander-in-chief after the outbreak of the Third Punic War and won some successes against the Romans. He surrendered to Scipio in 146 and died in captivity in Italy; his wife and children threw themselves into a fire rather than fall in the victor's hands.

HEBE Greek minor goddess, the personification of youth. Daughter of Hera and Zeus (Hesiod. *Theog.* 922), she is often described as the cup-bearer of the gods (Hom. *Il.* 4.2). She was Heracles' wife after he became a god (Hesiod. *Theog.* 950). She appears in vase-paintings.

HECATAEUS Greek historian and geographer, one of the earliest *logographers. H. was a native of Miletus and lived in the second part of the 6th and early 5th century BC. He failed to dissuade *Aristagoras from the revolt against Persia, and after its collapse sought to obtain mild terms from the Persian satrap in Sardis. In his extensive travels in Asia and Egypt, he collected much geographical information which he used to draw his map of the world. He also wrote a two-book work *Periegesis*, a geographical guide of the world, of which are extant numerous fragments. This work described the peoples and countries, rivers, fauna, flora, cities, history etc. along the coasts of the Mediterranean and the Black Sea, including such remote lands as India and Scythia. He also wrote the *Genealogiai* (or *Historiae*), a history of families with divine or heroic ancestors, of which some fragments have survived. Later writers from Herodotus on used him.
Jacoby, *Fr. Gr. Hist.* 1;
L. Pearson, *Early Ionian Historians*, 1939.

HECATE Ancient Greek goddess of the nether world, probably of Carian origin. She first appears in Hesiod (*Theog.* 411ff., a passage suspected of being an interpolation), where she is the daughter of Asteria, sister of

Leto; i.e., Apollo and Artemis are her cousins. Zeus grants her authority over earth, the sea and the sky; in fact she had enjoyed these powers under the former gods, the Titans. She is so powerful that she can secure all kind of success: material, political, military, etc. She was particularly goddess of women and was considered to bring up children; hence her title *kourotrophos*. She was often identified with *Artemis. Above all she was goddess of the dead and the nether world. She would appear every night with torches accompanied by ghosts, dogs and wolves. She was also associated with magic and sorcery. Euripides made Medea invoke her (*Med.* 394ff.). Her usual cult was at cross-roads where sacrifices were offered her, usually including dogs' flesh. Here her statue would be placed: a three-headed (or bodied) woman. She occasionally appears in art, mostly in the Hellenistic period. Th. Kraus, *Hekate,* 1960.

HECTOR The most courageous and noble Trojan hero, son of King Priam and Hecuba and the husband of Andromache. He is a favourite hero of Homer who makes him lead the Trojans to battle almost throughout the *Iliad.* After he organized the duel between Paris and Menelaus, he drove back the Achaeans and went to retrieve Paris from the city. Here he met his wife and son, Astyanax, for the last time (Book 6). Returning with Paris, he fought an undecisive battle with *Aias (1). Subsequently he beat the Greeks and attacked their camp. He then killed *Patroclus in single combat (Book 16) which caused Achilles to seek revenge. H. refused to seek shelter inside the walls and was killed by Achilles, who dragged the body to the Greek camp (Book 22). After Priam ransoms the body, his funeral is the last scene of the *Iliad.* Hector was worshipped at Troy, Thebes, to which his bones were allegedly transferred, and elsewhere. The name is known from Linear B documents from Cnossos and is probably Greek. Themes from Hector's life appear in vase-paintings, coins and other works of art.

HECUBA Wife of the Trojan king, Priam, mother of Hector, Paris, Cassandra and altogether of nineteen out of the fifty children of the king. A tragic figure, losing her children in the war which she survived, she became a favourite theme of the tragedians, especially Euripides. In his *Hecuba,* she suffered the sacrifice of her daughter Polyxena but she blinded Polymestor who killed her son Polydoros. Because of her terrible sufferings she changed into a bitch before she died.

HEGESIPPUS Athenian statesman of the 4th century BC, prominent in his anti-Macedonian policy. He opposed the peace of *Philocrates in 346 and subsequently sought to undermine it and to renew the war. The extant speech *de Halonneso* was probably written by him.

HEKTEMOROI "Men of the sixth-part", a term mentioned only by Aristotle (*Athen. Pol.* 2.2) and Plutarch (*Solon* 13). They were a separate class at Athens in the early 6th century BC and were probably small farmers who had lost their lands through failure to return loans. They were allowed to cultivate the lands for which they paid one sixth of the produce (or, in another view, only received one sixth). They could be sold into slavery. Solon abolished their debts and restored many who had been sold.

A. French, *The Growth of the Athenian Economy,* 1964, 16ff.

HELEN Greek mythological heroine, daughter of Zeus and *Leda, sister of the *Dioscuri and *Clytemnestra, born from an egg (Zeus coupled with Leda in swan-shape). In a later myth, *Theseus abducted her when she

was 7 years old but she was rescued by her brothers. She was then married to *Menelaus. The most beautiful woman in Greece, Aphrodite promised her to *Paris if he adjudged her the famous apple. He came to Sparta, and abducted her to Troy on her own free will although she was married to Menelaus; she thus became the cause of the Trojan War. In her portrayal by Homer there is no reproach; the Trojan elders considered the war to keep her at Troy worthwhile. She sometimes showed pro-Trojan feelings but was more often loyal to the Greeks. After the capture of Troy, she was reconciled to Menelaus (*Od.* 4.274ff.). Later writers deviated from the Homeric version or added details. Menelaus intended to kill her but was unable to resist her charm, especially as she uncovered her breast. The version of the poet *Stesichorus that it was only a phantom that Paris carried to Troy was taken over by Euripides in his *Helen* and is mentioned by Herodotus and Plato. Achilles was her lover or she lived with him, after her death, in Leuce (the "white island"). Her responsibility for the Trojan War was much discussed by many writers. She occasionally appears in works of art from the 6th century on: with Paris, Menelaus or Theseus.

Originally Helen was probably a pre-Greek goddess of vegetation and fertility. The ancient goddess was transformed by the Dorian conquerors of Laconia to a mythological heroine from whom their rulers descended; only a few vague traces of her original nature remained. In historic times she was worshipped at Sparta, Rhodes and elsewhere.

HELENUS Mythological hero and diviner, son of Priam and brother of *Cassandra. His prophetic power is mentioned by Homer (*Il.* 7.44). In a later version he told Odysseus that Troy would fall if Philoctetes came with his bow. After the fall of Troy he accompanied *Neoptolemus to Epirus where he founded Buthrotum and married *Andromache. Aeneas met him and he foretold his future (Verg. *Aen.* 3.294ff.).

HELIAIA An assembly. At Athens H. denoted the popular assembly by the regulations of *Solon that served as a court of appeal against magistrates' verdicts, and in particular the court of the *Thesmothetai. By the 5th century BC magistrates no longer gave verdicts and H. denoted all the jurors.

Hignett, *Athen. Const.* (s.v.).

HELIODORUS Native of Emessa in Syria, the author of the novel *Aethiopica* or *Theagenes and Chariclea.* He probably lived in the 3rd century AD. The novel tells the story of Chariclea, the daughter of the Aethiopian queen who exposed her. She was brought up at Delphi and became a priestess of Apollo there. Theagenes loved her and, as is usual in such novels, married her at the end after both experienced many adventures. H. succeeds in maintaining tension throughout the novel and, despite the complicated plot, in presenting an orderly and well-constructed narrative. The novel was very popular, praised by critics and translated into many modern languages from the 16th century on.

R. M. Rattenbury, T. W. Lumb, J. Maillon, (Budé) 1935–1943.

HELIOPOLIS (modern Baalbek) Cult-place, town and *colonia* (under Augustus) in Lebanon. The local god *Ba'al Biq'ah* was identified with Jupiter. The town prospered under the Empire. The considerable remains of its temples (of Jupiter and Bacchus) are very spectacular.

HELIOS The Greek sun-god, son of the Titans Hyperion and Theia, brother of *Eos and *Selene. He rises in his

palace in the east every day to drive his chariot drawn by bulls or horses across the sky to the west; thence he floats in a magnificent vessel, made by Hephaestus, along the ocean which encircles the world to his palace in the east (*Athen.* 11. 469f.). Though Helios and his wandering over the sky is mentioned as early as Homer (*Il.* 16.779; 18.239 etc.), he was only rarely worshipped by the Greeks, who considered him a Titan (the only surviving one under the rule of Zeus) and that it took its Olympian god. His mythology was limited to his daily tour, his genealogy and family and the myth of his son *Phaethon. In one of these few tales he punished Odysseus who stole some of his cattle by withholding the day of his return (*Od.* 1.9). It was only in Rhodes that he had an important cult; there it was said that he asked for the island from Zeus even before its emergence from the sea, and that it took its name from his wife, the nymph Rhode (Pind. *Olymp.* 7.54ff.). A special festival was held in his honour, the *Halieia*. It was only natural that as sun he was believed to see and hear everything (Hom. *Od.* 11.109), to witness all good or evil deeds and hence was called upon as a witness of oaths (*Il.* 3.277). In the *Laws* of Plato he is given a joint cult with Apollo, with whom he was identified by the 5th century BC. He became a generally important god with the establishment of the imperial cult of *Sol (Sun) in the 3rd century AD.
Kerényi, *Gods,* 190 ff.

HELLANICUS Greek writer, native of Lesbos, lived in the 5th century BC (*c.* 485–*c.* 400). He was the first to write numerous works on various subjects: mythology, ethnography, chronography, and history. Twenty-four titles of his works are known. In his mythological treatises (*Phoronis, Deucalioneia, Atalantis, Asopis*) he sought to give a comprehensible, coordinated history of the early mythological families. The ethnological works dealt separately with Egypt, Persia, Scythia, Cyprus, Arcadia, Argos, Boeotia, Thessaly, Lesbos, etc. He wrote the first local history of Attica (*Atthis). His chronology of the 5th century is criticized by Thucydides (1.97), but he was the first to compile chronological tables. Nothing of his works is extant but there are a considerable number of fragments.
Jacobly, *Fr. Gr. Hist.* I; IIIB;
L. Pearson, *Early Ionian Historians,* 1939;
The Local Historians of Attica, 1942.

HELLENES, HELLAS Originally a small Greek tribe and its territory in south Thessaly (Hom. *Il.* 684; 9,447 etc.). A close form was *Helloi* or *Selloi* (Hellopia was the area around *Dodona). The form *Panhellenes* to denote all of the Greeks (Hom. *Il.* 2.530) comes earlier than the form Hellenes which is then employed in the general sense by Hesiod (*Erg.* 653). An appropriate genealogy was consequently formed: Hellen, son of Deucalion, had three sons: Dorus, Aeolus and Xuthus father of Ion and Achaeus. These were the eponymous ancestors of the Dorians, Aeolians, Ionians and Achaeans. The process by which the name of the small tribe came to cover the whole people is not known.
V. Ehrenberg, *The Greek State,* 1960.

HELLENOTAMIAI Ten-member board of the Delian League which was responsible for its financial administration. The term means "The Greek Treasurers". Actually they were Athenian officials who were elected annually at Athens, one to each of the ten Attic tribes. Only persons with the highest census qualification (*pentakosiomedimnoi*) were allowed to take the office. They disbursed money as instructed by the Athenian *Ekklesia, mainly for the war operations of the strategoi, but also for purely Athenian purposes. They also delivered 1/60 of the yearly tribute to Athena. The office was abolished after the Peloponnesian War.
B. D. Meritt, H. T. Wade-Gery, F. M. McGregor, *The Athenian Tribute List,* 1939–1953 (s.v.).

HELOTS The subject population of Laconia. This consisted of the old population which had been subjugated by the Dorian invaders after the disintegration of the Mycenaean world as well of the majority of the population of Messenia which was conquered in the 8th and 7th centuries BC. The H. belonged to the state but each was assigned to a particular Spartan whose plot of land (*kleros*) he cultivated and to whom he owed personal services; part of the produce was left to the H. Their status was defined as that "between freemen and slaves" (Pollux 3.83). They were subject to severe supervision and punishment by the secret police (*Krypteia) and by individuals. By the annual declaration of war against them, the Spartans felt they could justly kill any suspect H. In times of emergency H. were occasionally recruited to the army and as a reward for good service might be set free by the state. The H. were numerically superior to the Spartan population. But it was only those of Messenia who sought to gain freedom by revolts, which they accomplished in 369 BC with the help of *Epaminondas. Subject populations resembling the H. existed in other Greek states both in Greece proper (e.g. Argos and Sicyon) and places where Greeks settled (e.g. Crete, Syracuse), but there is only meagre information about them.
R. F. Willetts, *Aristocratic Society in Ancient Crete,* 1955; G. L. Huxley, *Early Sparta,* 1962.

HELVETII Celtic people who under the pressure of German tribes migrated to Switzerland in the 2nd century BC. Part of them joined the *Cimbri and were destroyed with them. According to Caesar, who repelled an Helvetian attempt to migrate to Gaul, they consisted of four *pagi* (*Bell. Gall.* 1.12). Their country was conquered and annexed to Gallia Belgica in 15 BC; later it was part of Upper Germany. The Roman army evacuated the country early in the 5th century AD and subsequently it was occupied by the Alamanni and the Burgundians.

HENDEKA At Athens, a board of 11 officials who were responsible for the prison and presided over one of the jury courts which dealt with cases of theft. They also took charge of executions and the confiscation of the property of condemned persons.

HEPHAESTION Macedonian noble and the best friend of Alexander the Great. He took part in the expedition against Persia and, after the execution of *Philotas in 330 BC, was appointed one of the two commanders of the Cavalry Companions. He advanced in command during the expedition to India and back until he was made "chiliarch" in 324 with powers over the whole empire like those of the Persian vizier. He also married the daughter of Darius III. He supported Alexander with personal devotion in all his new plans, which endeared him more than his not exceptional military talent. His untimely death in 324 was a severe blow for Alexander, who ordered a general mourning and spent 10,000 talents on the funeral pyre.

HEPHAESTUS Greek god of fire and smith god, son of Zeus and Hera. He was born disfigured so that his disgusted mother threw him from the sky. Thetis and Eury-

Hephaestus the smith is about to finish a shield for Thetis

nome rescued him from the sea and reared him. He became a talented smith (Hom. *Il.* 18.395ff.) and was later brought back by Hera to Olympus where he made wonderful works for the gods. His famous works included the armour of Achilles (*Il.* 18.468ff.) and Agamemnon's scepter (*Il.* 2.101ff.). In another version, also in Homer (*Il.* 1.586ff.) Zeus hurled him from heaven when he sought to help Hera. In his fall at Lemnos he broke his legs, and was lame thereafter. He was the butt of the gods' ridicule; when he caught his wife Aphrodite with her lover Ares and called the gods to witness her infidelity, it only amused them (Hom. *Od.* 8.266ff.).

H. probably was a volcanic god of Asia Minor in origin. His association with Lemnos, a volcanic island, was prominent in his myth. In later tales his smithy was under Aetna, the volcanic mountain, but then he was a craftsman's god above all. As such he was associated with the good craftsmen, the *Cyclopes. There was magic in his excellent art. He created *Pandora (Hesiod. *Erg.* 70ff.) and taught mankind various crafts; in this respect he resembled Prometheus. He was worshipped in many places, notably at Athens. At Rome *Volcanus was identified with him. Artists depicted scenes of his mythology from the 6th century BC on. His 5th century temple at Athens (wrongly called Theseum) is extant.
Farnell, *Cults* 5, 374 ff.

HERA Greek goddess, wife and sister of Zeus, daughter of Kronos and Rhea. Her myths are recorded by Homer and Hesiod as well as later writers. She bore Ares, Hephaestus, Hebe and Eileithyai to Zeus, and without him, Typhon. But he enraged her with his numerous amours. Hence she was always on her guard and in her jealousy mercilessly pursued her rivals and their descendants (*Io, *Leto, *Semle) or used tricks against them (*Alcmene). Homer tells how she seduced Zeus on Mount Ida in the Trojan War (*Il.* 14). But once she induced the other gods to revolt against him and as a punishment was hung with a golden bracelet between heaven and earth. On another occasion she was enchained and held in the air on a magic throne by a trick of her son *Hephaestus in revenge for having thrown him from heaven at his birth. Homer made her hostile to the Trojans, as *Paris did not award her the apple, and in this, too, he was followed by Virgil. *Jason and the *Argonauts were helped by her.

Originally H. was a pre-Hellenic goddess: in one view of chthonic character and in another a moon-goddess — both with poor evidence. The invading Greeks took her cult from the former inhabitants, made her the wife of their own god Zeus, but the original name was not preserved (H. probably means "lady"). She was especially a goddess of women and marriage and often connected

Doric temple, probably of Hera, at Metapontum in south Italy

with birth. A very ancient centre of her worship was at *Argos and it is possible that her cult spread from here (Corinth, Sicyon, Tiryns, Olympia, Sparta etc.); *Argeia* was her common title. Another ancient cult was at Samos but she was worshipped everywhere by the Greeks and many of her temples (Heraeum) are known. Cows were usually sacrificed to her, and the peacock was her sacred bird. Her festival, the Heraia, was celebrated in several cities, notably Argos. It included an armed procession, sacrifice, and athletic competitions with a shield as a prize. She appears in many works of art from the Archaic period on, usually depicted as a solemn figure dressed in mantle with sceptre and diadem and pomegranate. She appears in sculpture, vase-paintings and coins, alone or with other gods. The most famous work of *Poly-clitus was the statue of H. he made for the Heraeum of Argos (Pausan. 2.17.4), known only from coins.

Nilsson, *Religion*[2] (s.v.).

HERACLEA The name of several Greek states (near Thermopylae, in Macedonia, Caria, Lucania, Sicily etc.).
HERACLEA PONTICA Greek city on the northern coast of Asia Minor, founded by settlers from Megara and Boeotia before the middle of the 6th century BC. The local population was subjugated. The city had a good harbour and prospered thanks to trade. In the early period it was ruled by an oligarchy. Its great period was in the 4th century BC when it was ruled by tyrants, and then by *Lysimachus. After the latter's death in 280 BC it regained its freedom but subsequently suffered from the Galatians and the kings of Bithynia and Pontus. It became an ally of Rome in 188 BC. After its pillage by the Romans in the Third Mithridatic War it declined. Its native Memnon (lived in the 1st century AD) wrote its history in sixteen books, of which Books 9—16 are known from *Photius.

Magie, *Asia* (s.v.).

HERACLES The most courageous, popular and worshipped of the Greek heroes. His mother was *Alcmene and his father Zeus, who impersonated Alcmene's husband *Amphitryon, king of Thebes, in his absence. By the tricks of the jealous Hera, H.'s birth was delayed and so *Eurystheus was born first and he — not H. — was to rule the house of Perseus. Not content with this, Hera sent two serpents to destroy H. in the cradle, but, though they frightened his twin brother Iphicles, he strangled both of them. He had good teachers for boxing, chariotry, archery etc., but he beat his music teacher Linus and was sent away by his father.

H.'s most famous feats are the Twelve Labours, which he performed for Eurystheus, his overlord. The reason for these exploits is not clear, perhaps to free himself from Eurystheus or as an expiation for the murder of his children, which he did in madness (again a punishment by Hera). The tasks were: 1) to kill the invulnerable Nemean Lion; 2) to kill the Hydra of Lerna; 3) to capture the Hind of Ceryneia; 4) to capture the Boar of Mount Eurymanthus; 5) to clean the stables of *Augeas in one day, which he did by diverting the river *Alpheus; 6) to shoot the Stymphalaian Birds: 7) to kill or capture the Cretan wild bull; 8) to capture the man-eating mares of King *Diomedes; 9) to take the girdle of Hippolyte, the queen of the Amazons; 10) to capture the cattle of the monster *Geryon; 11) to bring *Cerberus from the underworld; 12) to fetch the Apples of the Hesperides. He sailed to those islands in the vessel of Helios; thereafter the mountains on either side of the Strait of Gibraltar were called the Pillars of Heracles.

Many more myths were told about, or associated with, H. In part these originated from attempts to connect or identify him with local legends or heroes. He killed the Libyan giant Antaeus, son of Poseidon and Earth, in a wrestling match. When he returned from the Ninth Labour he came to Troy. There King Laomedon had cheated Apollo and Poseidon and had to give his daughter Hesione as a sacrifice to get rid of a sea-monster. H. killed the monster but Laomedon did not fulfill his promise to give him his famous horses. Thereupon H. killed him and all his sons excepting Podarces, the future King Priam. In another myth which was very popular, and is mainly known from Archaic vase-paintings, he carried off the Delphic sacred tripod and fought Apollo as he was not served by the oracle. He rescued Theseus from Hades in the nether world as well as *Alcestis (again, the motif of the defeat of death). He came to be associated with the legend of the *Argonauts, but left the voyage to search for his boy *Hylas. He served the Lydian Queen Omphale in women's clothes — a theme utilized in satires. He won his second wife *Deianira after a fight with the river god *Achelous. She caused his death by giving him to wear the poisonous garment of the Centaur Nessus. Unable to endure the torments, H. burnt himself on a pyre on Mount Oeta. From there he ascended to heaven and became an immortal god; *Hebe then became his wife.

H. ("the glory of Hera") belonged to the Argolid, though claimed by other Greek cities, notably Thebes. Argos was a centre of a cult of Hera. His relationship to Eurystheus indicates that as a local Argive lord (of Tiryns) he owed service to his overlord the Argive king. Around this, likely, "historical" figure developed extensive mythology enriched by his identification with many other local heroes. This was partly noticed by Herodotus (2.42) and according to Varro there were forty-four heroes named H. There are striking similarities between his myths and those of the Babylonian Gilgamesh. Usually he was worshipped as a hero but in some places as a god. At Rome he was worshipped as *Hercules.

The attitude of the Greeks to H. changed with the changing of their religious ideas and artistic taste and this is reflected in literature and art. He may appear as a young athlete or as a mature, strong man, with beard or shaved, confident and cheerful or thoughtful. In Euripides' *Heracles*, his victory is not physical but spiritual — he overcomes his own sufferings. In art he is distinguished by the lion-pelt, club and bow. His myths are frequently

Three Labours of Heracles on a sarcophagus. The Hydra on the left, the boar in the centre and the Arcadian stag on the right

depicted in vase-paintings, sculpture, and other forms, in all periods. His Twelve Labours appear in the metopes of the temple of Zeus at Olympia (c. 560–550 BC).
Kerényi, *Heroes,* 128 ff.

HERACLIDAE The descendants of Heracles. After the death of their father they fled to Attica and with the help of Theseus killed Eurystheus who pursued them. They were told by the Delphic Oracle that they might return to the Peloponnesus at "the third harvest". They misinterpreted this to refer to the third year and the result was that Hyllus, the eldest son, was killed in single combat. The grandsons, taking the oracle to mean "third generation", renewed the attempt after one hundred years. Led by *Temenus, Cresphontes, and the sons of Aristodemus they conquered the Peloponnesus: the first ruled Argos, the second Messenia, and the last Laconia (hence the dual kingship at Sparta). It was thus that the descendants of Perseus ousted the descendants of Pelops. In fact the Return of the H. was a Dorian attempt to claim Heracles for themselves and to account for their conquest of the Peloponnesus.

HERACLIDES PONTICUS Greek philosopher (c. 390–c. 310 BC), native of *Heraclea Pontica. He became a member of the *Academy from c. 365 and was mainly a pupil of Speusippus but also studied under Plato and Aristotle. He may have been in charge of the Academy during Plato's visit to Sicily (with Speusippus) in 361/360. He left the Academy after *Xenocrates was elected to succeed Speusippus as Head of the school (338) and opened his own school in his native city. H. was a prolific writer; more than 45 titles are given by Diogenes Laertius (5.86–8). His writings included such diverse subjects as ethics, logic, physics, metaphysics, astronomy, history and literature. Only fragments of some of the works are known. His most original work was in astronomy: he held that the earth rotates on its own axis and, possibly, that Venus and Mercury revolve around the sun. This was a step forward towards the heliocentric theory. He used the dialogue form to expound his views and was much admired by Cicero and others for his accomplishment in this genre. His interlocutors were famous persons of the past (e.g. Pythagoras, Empedocles). In his theory of matter H. partly followed *Democritus in that he suggested that matter consisted of numerous loosely tied particles, molecules rather than atoms. He was also extremely interested in Pythagoras. Ostentatious and confident of his importance, he was satirized and criticized for his phantasies or praised for his scientific contribution, and literary achievement.
F. Wehrli, *Heraklides Pontikos,* 1953;
Sarton, *His.Sc.* **1.**

HERACLITUS Important Greek philosopher, native of Ephesus, active toward the end of the 6th century BC. Of a ruling Ephesian family, he is said to have given up the "kingship" to his brother, but there are no trustworthy details of his life. He was, however, hostile to the democratic elements which took power in his native city.

H. was famous for the obscurity of his theories and for his arrogance. Of his work, called *On Nature* but perhaps without title, a considerable number of fragments are extant and enable a reconstruction of his cosmological theory. H. believed that the world is in constant change, either as a whole or each thing is constantly in change; the famous saying *Panta rhei,* "everything flows", is usually attributed to him. Rest and harmony are only apparent; behind them there is the interaction of opposites. These pass through an endless conflict, which is subject to a constant law. Examples for apparent rest are the bow and the lyre which when played on conceal their tension. Among the opposites are day and night, war and peace, love and strife, life and death, etc. In the process of change fire is the most important element: "all things are changed into fire, and fire into things, as goods are an exchange for gold and gold for goods"; "the *Kosmos* (world-order) is an everliving fire". The view that the world is constantly at war betrays a pessimistic attitude, even though this is compensated by the doctrine of the unity of the opposites. Man attains wisdom, that is understands the *logos* of the cosmic order, by self-knowledge.
G. S. Kirk, *Heraclitus, The Cosmic Fragments,* 1954;
Kirk-Raven, *Presocratic Philosophers.*

HERCULANEUM Coastal town on the Bay of Naples about 8 km southeast of Naples, mythologically founded by Heracles. Oscans, Etruscans, Pelasgians are said to have inhabited it in succession (Strabo, 5.4,8). It certainly came under strong Greek influence and was probably settled by Greeks. It became a Roman ally in the late 4th century BC and received Roman citizenship in 89 BC, after its revolt, with other Italian allies, and capture. After a serious earthquake in AD 63, the town was destroyed and it was covered with volcanic ash in the eruption of Mount Vesuvius in AD 79. The search for its treasures began in the late 17th century; more scientific work was done in the 19th century and from 1927 on systematic excavations were carried out. H. prospered in the early Empire, but it was not a commercial town like Pompeii. It was a fashionable place of luxury villas. In a magnificent villa (Casa de Papiri) dozens of statues and papyrus rolls containing the only known prose work of *Philodemus were discovered; it probably belonged to *Piso (2), Caesar's father-in-law.
A. Maiuri, *Ercolano*[5], 1959;
J. D'Arms, *Romans on the Bay of Naple.* 1970.

HERCULES The Greek hero Heracles was worshipped at Rome as H.; his cult at the Ara Maxima, within the ancient *Pomerium, was the first foreign one dating from the pre-Republican period. Here two clans, the Potitii and the Pinarii, were responsible for his worship and only in 312 BC was it taken over by the Roman state. The cult was conducted according to the Greek ritual; women and dogs were forbidden to approach the shrine. In legend he touched at Rome on his return with the cattle of *Geryon and then killed *Cacus. He was particularly worshipped by merchants who considered him a strong protector. Successful businessmen and generals used to dedicate one tenth of their gain to him. He had numerous shrines at Rome besides the Ara Maxima: that of H. Invictus, of H. Custos, of H. Musarum etc. He was also worshipped outside Rome. Emperors later represented themselves as H., notably *Commodus and *Maximinus.
Platner-Ashby, *Top.Dict.Rome,* 251 ff.;
Nash, *Pict.Dict.Rome,* 1,462 ff.;
Latte, *R Rel.* (s.v.).

HERENNIUS MODESTINUS The last of the great Roman jurists of the Classical period, pupil of *Ulpianus. He was Praefectus of the *Vigiles at Rome before AD 244. He is named as one of the five authoritative jurists in the Law of Citations of Theodosius II (*Cod. Theod.* 1.4.3), and is often cited in the *Digesta* of Justinian. He wrote manuals and monographs, one *de excusationibus,* on exemptions from guardianship (in Greek), also *On Manumissions, On Penalties,* etc. There was also a collection of his *Responsa.*

HERMAGORAS Famous Greek rhetor of the 2nd century BC, native of Temnos. His six-book work on rhetoric (*technai rhetoricai*) had extensive influence and was considered essential for a rhetorical education. He gave an elaborate classification of *staseis* ("issues"), namely four aspects by which a case could be approached. His complex differentiation of terms and cases, however, was criticized. The non-extant work is mainly known from *Quintilian and *Hermogenes.

HERMAPHRODITUS Greek mythological being created by the union in one body of the nymph Salmacis with her beloved, the beautiful Aphroditus son of Hermes and Aphrodite (Ovid. *Met.* 4.285ff.). This is an aetiological legend explaining the phenomenon of the hermaphrodite. But at Amathus in Cyprus, Aphrodite was worshipped as Aphroditus, a bearded woman (Macrob. Sat. 3.3.2), and this is possibly a trace of the old maternal religion when the great goddess was attributed virile qualities. In art H. is depicted as a youth with womanish breasts or as an Aphrodite with male organs.

HERMES Greek god, son of Zeus and Maia, the daughter of Atlas. He is first mentioned by Homer and his more important myth is told with humour in the Homeric *Hymn to Hermes*, and by later writers as well. He was born on Mount Cyllene and grew quickly showing his cleverness and deceit on his first day. He stole the cattle of Apollo, who, at first puzzled by his tricks, could not follow the tracks. He invented the lyre by stringing a tortoise-shell with seven strings of cow-gut. He immediately played it and sang the words and music he invented. After Apollo traced him to his cave, he appeased him by giving the lyre. He also invented the pipe. Zeus warned him to refrain from lying and stealing and made him his herald.

Originally H. had been a phallic deity of the pre-Hellenic religion, occupying stones at cross-roads. In the myth are noted his familiar characteristics as he evolved into a Greek god. But probably his most characteristic representation was a herm, that is, a stone or a pillar with a human head or bust on the top and a phallus; such herms were set up at cross-roads and considered as protectors (*Alcibiades was charged with their mutilation at Athens in 415 BC). He was associated with Aphrodite (*Hermaphroditus), a goddess of fertility. His place at the cross-roads made him a protector of all who passed there, but especially merchants, travellers, and thieves. He also had an oracle at Pharae in western Achaea and came to be a patron of music, literature and athletics. As herald, he gave *Calypso Zeus's orders to let Odysseus go. He was the guide to the dead and as such led the suitors of Penelope to the nether world (*Od.* 24.1ff.) and in another myth took *Eurydice back to Hades. As herald he had a broad-brimmed hat, winged sandals and the herald's staff — *kerykeion* (or *caduceus* in Latin). He often appears in works of art from the Archaic period on, usually in his capacity as a herald. There are vase-paintings of his first exploits on his birth day. A famous statue of H. with the infant Dionysius, the work of *Praxiteles, depicts him as young and naked, as he was depicted in later times.
Guthrie, *The Greeks and their Gods,* 87 ff.

HERMIAS Philosopher and tyrant of Atarneus and *Assos, of Bithynian origin. He studied in the *Academy at Athens and took power at Atarneus by murdering the former tyrant Eubulus (*c.* 355 BC). After Plato's death, Aristotle, Xenocrates and other Platonists came to his court. Aristotle, a close friend, married his niece Pythias.

On good terms with Philip II, he was tricked and captured by the Rhodian Mentor, who sent him to Artaxerxes III. He was executed without betraying Philip.
I. Düring, *Aristotle in the Ancient Biographical Tradition,* 1957, 272 ff.

HERMIONE Greek mythological heroine, daughter of Menelaus and Helen. She was betrothed or married to *Neoptolemus, who was killed by *Orestes. She then became the latter's wife, and bore his son Tisamenus, but in another version was *Diomedes' wife. Her name is given as a title to Demeter and Persephone. She is taken as a hostage by Electra and Orestes in Euripides' *Orestes.*

HERMOCRATES Prominent Syracusan statesman and general in the time of the Peloponnesian War. At the congress of Gela (424 BC) he successfully called upon representatives to keep Athens out of the affairs of Sicily (Thucyd. 4.58–64). He later took a prominent part in the defence of Syracuse against the Athenian expedition (415–413 BC) helping *Gylippus. In 412 he commanded a fleet sent to help Sparta and was then sent into exile by the democrat Diocles. He returned to Sicily in 408 and after operations against the Carthaginians found his death in an attack on Syracuse. His daughter was *Dionysius I's wife.

HERMOGENES (1) Important Greek architect of Alabanda, *c.* 200 BC. He built the temples of Dionysus at Teos and of Artemis at Magnesia-on-Maeander; frieze remains of both are extant. They were built in the Ionic Order. He was famous for the harmony of his buildings (Strabo 14.1,40). His principles of proportion (*symmetriae*) were noted by *Vitruvius in his own work, from whose time on H. influenced Roman architecture.
W. B. Dinsmoor, *The Architecture of Ancient Greece³,* 1950, 273 ff.

HERMOGENES (2) Greek rhetor, native of Tarsus, lived in the 2nd century AD. At the age of 15, he declaimed before the Emperor Marcus Aurelius, but later did not practise oratory, only wrote on rhetoric. Two of his works are extant: *Peri Ton Staseon* ("On Issues", cf. *Hermagoras), and *Peri Ideon*, which deals with style. He distinguishes seven main qualities in style (with subdivisions) which, as he tries to show, were perfectly employed by Demosthenes, as well as by other great orators. In this work he depends on *Dionysius of Halicarnassus.

HERMS See **HERMES**

HERNICI Ancient Italian tribe which lived in eastern Latium across the river Trerus. They concluded a defensive treaty with Rome in 486 BC (Liv. 2.40f.) and subsequently fought with her and the Latins against the *Aequi and the *Volscians. After the capture of Rome by the Gauls they joined her enemies for some time but renewed the treaty in 358. Most of them revolted in 306, were defeated and given *civitas sine suffragio* and later full Roman citizenship (Liv. 9.43). Their main town was *Anagnia. Ferentinum (modern Ferentino) remained loyal and kept its independence and received citizenship in 90 BC. Their name means "the Rocky Men".
Alföldi, *Early Rome,* 107 ff.

HERO The main character, together with Leander, of a love story first told in extant literature by Virgil in *Georgics* 3.258ff., though its origin was probably in Alexandrian poetry. Leander used to swim the Hellespont every night from Abydos to visit his beloved H., a priestess of Aphrodite at Sestos. One night he was drowned after a storm put out her guiding light. She then leapt into the sea and died.

HEROD (1), the Great Son of the Idumaean *Antipater

Head of Herod the Great (?) found in Egypt

(2) and the Nabataean Kypros, lived *c.* 73–4 BC. In 47 he was appointed governor of the Galilee where he suppressed Jewish uprisings. After his father's murder he became governor of Judaea but had to flee to Rome in 40 when the Hasmonaean Antigonus was enthroned by the Parthians. A Roman citizen from 47 BC, he was now made king of the Hasmonaean kingdom but could return to Jerusalem only after its capture by the Romans in 37. He kept his position under Augustus who enlarged his territory. Though a resourceful politician and good administrator — he rebuilt Caesarea and the Temple in Jerusalem — he was hated by the Jews and not without reason. He introduced Hellenization to the country, supported Greek cities abroad, appointed High Priests at his will, employed a mercenary army and Greek officials, restricted the powers of the Sanhedrin and was, in native eyes, a foreign Idomaean who had supplanted the native dynasty of the Hasmonaeans. Taxation was heavy and order was maintained by extremely suppressive measures. He was loyal to Rome and promoted the imperial cult in the non-Jewish parts of his kingdom. But his brutality and aggressive policy against Nabataea finally alienated Augustus. He put his beloved wife, the Hasmonaean Mariamne I, to death in 29 BC, her two sons in 7, and his eldest son in 4, besides other numerous victims, and his cruelty became proverbial. After his death his kingdom was divided between his sons Archelaus, Antipas and Philip.
A. H. M. Jones, *The Herods of Judaea*, 1938, 28ff;
M. Grant, *Herod the Great*, 1971.

HEROD (2) ANTIPAS Son of *Herod (1) the Great, confirmed tetrarch of the Galilee by Augustus after the death of his father. He founded the city Tiberias (named after the emperor Tiberius) in AD 17. Jesus the Galilaean was his subject and Pontius Pilate vainly tried to make him responsible for his trial in Jerusalem. He executed John the Baptist who reproached him for marrying his niece Herodias (37). He was defeated by *Aretas IV whose daughter he divorced. After he requested the title of king he and his wife were banished to Lugdunum by Caligula in 39, and his tetrarchy was given to *Agrippa I, his nephew.
H. W. Hoekner, *Herodes Antipas*, 1972.

HERODAS (or Herondas) Greek poet of the 3rd century BC. He wrote *mimiambi*, that is, mimes in iambic scazons (cf. *Hipponax), eight of which were discovered on a papyrus in 1889. In these H. gives sketches of everyday scenes and characters: bawd, pimp, schoolmaster, worshipping women, jealous mistress, shoemaker. The eighth mime alludes to severe criticism of his works. The themes are typical of the genre, which is largely represented by these works in extant literature. H. was good at parody, his characters are vividly described, each with his own peculiar traits, and he produces realistic scenes with monologues and dialogues. In all these there is likeness to the New Comedy. The mimes were probably written for solo performance.
Text and translation: W. Headlam—A. D. Knox, 1922;
A. D. Knox (Loeb), 1929.

HERODES ATTICUS Greek Sophist (AD 101–77), of the Attic deme of Marathon, exceptionally rich, a philanthropist and Roman senator. His father was a governor of Judaea and suffect consul and he himself reached the consulship in AD 143. He was a friend of Hadrian and Antoninus Pius and tutor of Marcus Aurelius and L. Verus. He provided many cities, notably Athens, Delphi, Corinth, and Olympia, with public buildings, of which the most famous is the extant Odeon at Athens. His activities are recorded in inscriptions. But he was unfortunate with his family: his two daughters and younger son died young. The sepulchral inscription of his wife who died in 160 is known. He was considered the best orator of his day, and had much influence. He also wrote a diary and letters, but only one extant speech (*On the State*) is attributed to him.
Philostr. *Vit.Soph.* 2.1; G. W. Bowerseck, *The Sophists in the Roman Empire*, 1969 (s.v.).

HERODIAN Greek historian, younger contemporary of Dio Cassius, perhaps of Syrian origin. His eight-book work (*History of the Period after Marcus Aurelius*) covers the years AD 180–238. He is criticized for his excessive rhetoric, but excepting the speeches, the work is readable and is an important historical source for the period.
C. R. Whittaker, *Herodian* (Loeb), 1961;
E. Echols, *Herodian* (translation), 1961.

HERODOTUS Son of Lyxes, of a well-to-do family in Halicarnassus, lived *c.* 484–*c.* 420 BC, "the Father of History". H.'s family was involved in the political struggle against the tyrant Lygdamis and H. left for Samos, the first station in his extensive travels throughout his life. In his travels he visited Egypt and Cyrene, Palestine, Phoenicia and Babylonia, the north Aegean, the Black Sea, and Scythia, and many other Greek places in the Mediterranean area. He took these travels expressly to get information for his work; some perhaps for commercial purposes as well. He stayed in Athens for a long time, composed and read parts of his work, allegedly taking ten talents for a lecture. He took part in the colonization of Thurii in 443 BC and presumably died there. The last event mentioned in his work is of 430. His work was well enough known in Athens by 425 BC to be parodied by Aristophanes.

H.'s work is the first history ever written. Its subject is the wars between the Greeks and the Persians and their causes. These were the greatest wars fought to his date. The work was later divided into nine books, each named after one of the Muses. Book 1 tells of the attack of Croesus on Persia, the first in the chain of events that led to the invasion of Greece by the Persians. It gives an account of Lydia, of the conquests of Cyrus and of the Persians. A survey of the Persian empire and its peoples to the time of the wars with the Greeks is then taken. Book 2 deals with Egypt, 3 with Cambyses and Darius, 4 with Scythia and Lybia and Darius' attacks on them. Book 5 describes the Ionian revolt, 6 the Marathon campaign, 7 the invasion of Greece by Xerxes to the battles of Thermopylae and Artemisium; the decisive battle of Salamis and its sequel come in Book 8, and the battles of Plataea and Mycale in Book 9. The work often contains digressions inserted by H. to explain the main events or to bring in episodes, customs, events which are of human or historical interest.

Besides being the first historical work ever written, H.'s is also the first large and, on the whole, well-planned prose work in Greek. He obviously collected much material and probably wrote drafts of parts of the work before he designed and wrote it in its present form. It was an *historia*, that is, an inquiry, research. Geography, ethnography and religion were for him part of his historical subject. H. gave what he heard, saw, read and inquired into. His literary sources included poets, travellers, *logographers. His critical methods were poor. He was prepared to recount a good story and let his reader decide on its reliability rather than drop it. Hence some fanciful tales for which he expressly did not claim truth. And yet modern scholarship, based on archaeological finds and documentary evidence not known to him, more often than not corroborate his accounts of Egypt and Babylonia. As a historian his interest was to write the story of what happened; analyses of politics and strategy were beyond him, and even more so economics and social processes. This search for the true story was executed with remarkable success. Though a Greek, he wrote with impartiality on the Persians and showed no sign of racial prejudice. He compared one source of information with another if this was possible. His explanations for what happened took account of fate and chance and divine intervention, but the catastrophe of human *hybris* was not the result of supernatural *nemesis* only. Without giving a formal analysis of the failure of the Persian invasion, he pointed out what he understood the reasons to be in human terms of the Greek victory: their military equipment and tactics, political institutions and social order more than compensated for their numerical inferiority. It was in this connection that he gave an unbiased account of Greek freedom as against the Oriental autocracy and despotism.

Few historians have equalled H. as writers. He did not use elaborate techniques and his sentences were coordinated not subordinated as in the more advanced Greek prose. But he accomplished an attractive history, swiftly told and read, with fascinating character portrayals, dramatic passages and moments of insight into the deep forces of human life.

Text and translations: A. D. Godley (Loeb) 1920–1924; C. Hude (OCT) 1927; A. de Sélincourt (Penguin) 1957. Commentaries and research: W. W. How–J. Wells, 1912; J. L. Meyer, *Herodotus, Father of History,* 1953; H. R. Immerwahr, *Form and Thought in Herodotus,* 1966.

HEROES The H. of the Mycenaean society were simply distinguished nobles and in Homer the word *heros* means no more than "noble" when applied to them. While hero-cult is not attested in Homer, by his time it was already practised by the Greeks. It was probably after the Dorian invasions that the Mycenaean figures, who were later to be recorded by Homer and the epic writers, began to be worshipped as "heroes", that is, semi-divine mortals who performed distinguished feats that put them above normal human beings. The best known were Perseus, Theseus, Achilles, and above all Heracles. They were given divine genealogy, usually with human mothers and divine fathers but also vice versa. H. could include historical personalities, imaginative figures and even such that had been deities in origin. Some were invented for aetiological reasons, others were considered founders of cities, institutions or families. Hero-cult became a typical Greek characteristic and not only figures of the remote past were heroized. Such men as *Aristogeiton and Harmodius, the tyrannicides, and the brilliant Spartan general *Brasidas were given heroic rites after their death for their excellent services to their compatriots. The cult was performed at the tomb of the hero, the *heroon*, and consisted of libations and sacrifices. A few of the H. were worshipped at several places – in each of them they were supposed to have been buried, and Heracles in many, but he became an Olympian god. The cult was performed in order to seek the good will and protection of the H. and in recognition of the supernatural being of the H.

L. R. Farnell, *Greek Hero Cults,* 1921; Kerényi, *Heroes.*

HERON Greek mathematician and engineer of Alexandria, lived after Archimedes and before Pappus, probably in the 1st century AD. He was apparently more interested in practical problems of mensuration and useful devices than in theories, which he nonetheless mastered for his aims. Several works of his are extant either in their original form or in later adaptations. They include *Pneumatica,* on tools operated by compression of air, steam and water. It was here that he severely criticized those (including Aristotle) who denied the existence of vacuum, which he proved by experiments; *On Construction of Automata,* how to construct devices to produce "temple-miracles"; *Mechanica* (extant in Arabic only) which gives the theorems of statics and dynamics, a description of the five main simple machines, and devices for lifting and pressing; *Dioptra,* on the construction of this basic instrument of sighting and measuring used for astronomical observations; *Belopoeca,* on the construction of catapults; and *Catoptrica* (extant in Latin), on the construction of mirrors. These and other extant works are important for the knowledge of the achievements of his predecessors and show his own achievements in constructing siphons, a water-organ, steam machines, mechanical toys etc.

A. G. Drachman, *Ktesibios, Philon and Heron,* 1948; *The Mechanical Technology of Greek and Roman Antiquity,* 1963.

HEROPHILUS Important Greek physician, native of Chalcedon, active in Alexandria in the first part of the 3rd century BC. He emphasized the importance of the study of the human body for medicine and practised vivisection and dissection. His most important work was in anatomy. He carefully studied the brain, which he held as the centre of the nervous system, and the nerves; and he was one of the first to distinguish between sensory and motor nerves. In his study of the eye he distinguished its main membranes. He also studied the heart, the liver and the sexual organs. For clinical purposes his correct assessment and theory of the work of the pulse was most important — and of permanent value. H. also wrote on dietetics and pharmacology, and applied them in practice. He explained diseases by humoral pathology.

L. Edelstein, *Ancient Medicine*, 1967 (s.v.).

HESIOD Greek poet, probably to be dated to the late 8th century BC. The controversy on this point, and on whether he — or Homer — was the first Greek poet started in the 5th century BC and has not been definitely settled. The few certain details of his life come from his own poems. His father, an emigrant from Aeolis in Asia Minor, had a small holding at Ascra near Mount Helicon in Boeotia. After the father's death, his brother Perses disputed the division of the patrimony in court. He addressed a poem to his brother to teach him the virtue of agricultural work and moral conduct, as he won the case by bribery. It was the Muses of Helicon who taught him the art of poetry. To them he dedicated the tripod he won in a funeral contest at Chalcis in Euboea. In later times his tomb was said to be in Orchomenus. Of the poems ascribed to H. the *Theogony* and *The Works and Days* are authentic by common consent. The first gives a comprehensive account of the origins of the world, the genealogy of the gods and the succession of events that resulted in the rule of Zeus. It opens with the hymn to the Muses, who gave him the poetical inspiration for composing fiction and fact. The beginning of the world was with the appearance of Chaos, Earth and Eros. Uranus was the first ruling deity, dethroned by his son Kronus, whose son Zeus finally established his kingdom. Altogether H. gave account of some 300 gods. Similar myths on the succession of gods existed in ancient Mesopotamia. The poem is an essential source for Greek mythology at this early period.

The Works and Days (*Erga kai Hemerai*) is the first didactic poem committed to writing. It is so named after the two main sections that describe the yearly works in peasant life and the list of lucky and unlucky days of the lunar month for various purposes. It also includes myths, notably the tales of Pandora's box and the Five Ages of Man, moral maxims, the fable of the Hawk and the Nightingale, the vivid description of the winter and an account of seafaring. The poem is the only evidence of social conditions at the time. H. takes a rather pessimistic view: the peasant has to work to eke out a poor living. He preaches justice but acknowledges the fact that often injustice is done and might is often right. The poem is written in the Ionic dialect and in hexameter. Its main features — the metre, the inclusion of narrative and descriptive passages, and the loose structure — were to characterize didactic poetry. Wrongly ascribed to H. were the extant *Shield of Heracles* and the *Catalogue of Women* of which fragments have survived.

H. G. Evelyn-White (Loeb), 1936;
T. A. Sinclair, *Hesiod, Works and Days*, 1966 (1932);
M. L. West, *Hesiod, Theogony*, 1966;
F. Solmsen, *Hesiod and Aeschylus*, 1949.

HESPERIDES The mythological daughters of Night and Erebus (Hesiod, *Theog.* 215; 275) or of Atlas and Hesperis. They guarded the tree of golden apples at the far western end of the world, beyond the Atlas mountains. Melanion won his race against *Atalanta by throwing in her way these apples given to him by Aphrodite. The Twelfth Labour of Heracles was to fetch the apples, which he did after killing the dragon Ladon who helped the H. to guard the tree.

HESTIA Greek goddess of the hearth, daughter of Kronos (Hesiod, *Theog.* 493ff.) and the everlasting virgin sister of Zeus. The etymology and functions point to her identification with *Vesta. In primitive times it was essential to continually maintain the hearth fire and hence her place in religion. She also came to symbolize the life of the people, happiness and hospitality. Thus developed both a communal and a private cult. However, she never rose to be a major deity in Greek religion.

HESYCHIUS Native of Alexandria, lived probably in the 5th century AD, wrote a comprehensive lexicon in Greek which is known from an abridged and interpolated manuscript of the 15th century. H. used former lexica for the composition of his work, which even in its present mutilated form is useful, notably for its glosses on Greek dialects.

HETAIRIAI In Crete there were group of citizens who had common meals and a common cult of Zeus Hetaireios. It was in this framework that the military training that they received in youth was maintained; in their youth, they were grouped in *Agelai*. The same term also denoted the political associations or clubs which existed in many Greek cities. The aims of these clubs were sometimes subversive; more often they formed to support the careers of their leading members. They are best known at Athens, where almost all the important statesmen had H. to support them. In later times professional associations or those for worship purposes were called H., like the Roman *Collegia*.

R. F. Willets, *Aristocratic Society in Ancient Crete*, 1955, 22 ff,; G. M. Calhoun, *Athenian Clubs in Politics and Litigation*, 1913.

HETAIROI The Macedonian "companions". These were originally the Macedonian council of nobles who assisted the king and formed his bodyguard. H. was also the name of the Macedonian nobles who served in the cavalry and were given plots of land by the king. They were reorganized by *Philip II. There existed corresponding infantry, probably formed by the king, Alexander II (369 BC). The H. were the select units of the Macedonian army under Philip II and Alexander the Great.

HIERON (1) Greek tyrant in Sicily, brother of Gelon. He ruled Gela after Gelon's departure to Syracuse from 485 BC and succeeded him in Syracuse in 478. He defended Locri against *Anaxilas and his great achievement was the naval victory over the Etruscans off Cumae in 474, which shattered their power in Campania. In 475 he resettled Catania naming it Aetna. H. was a patron of arts and Aeschylus, Simonides, Bacchylides, Pindar and Epicharmus stayed with him. His chariots and horses won victories in the Pythian and Olympian games. He died in 466 BC.

HIERON (2) II Syracusan general and tyrant, *c.* 306—215 BC. He served under Pyrrhus and in 275 took control of Syracuse. After his victory over the Mamertini in 270 he was proclaimed king by his soldiers. With the appearance of the Roman army in Sicily in 264 he made an alliance with Carthage, but after the initial defeats, he made peace with Rome and remained its loyal ally to his death. He helped Rome against Carthage with ships, various equipment and grain. Under him Syracuse enjoyed stability and economic prosperity. He employed Archimedes, who was close to him, in various works. His system of taxation was later adopted by the Romans. His grandson and successor Hieronymus joined Carthage in the Second Punic War and Syracuse was annexed to the Roman province of Sicily.

HIERONYMUS Greek historian, native of Cardia, lived in the second part of the 4th century and the first part of the 3rd century BC and died more than 100 years old. He served under *Eumenes of Cardia, *Antigonus I, *Demetrius I and *Antigonus Gonatas. His work, *History of the Diadochi*, covered the period from the death of Alexander the Great (323 BC) to at least the death of Pyrrhus (272). His description of Pyrrhus' wars in Italy included an account of the origins of Rome, one of the first by Greek historians. His work was used by Diodorus Siculus, Arrian and Plutarch. Only a few fragments are extant.
Jacoby, *Fr.Gr.Hist.* II B.

HIEROPHANTES The priest responsible for the Mysteries of *Eleusis. The office was always reserved for the family of the Eumolpidae (*Eumolpus) and the one chosen served for life. In addition to his main duties he was associated with other festivals in Athens.
G. E. Mylonas, *Eleusis and Eleusinian Mysteries*, 1961, 229 ff.

HIMERA One of the few Greek cities on the north coast of Sicily, founded in 649 BC by settlers from Zancle (*Messana). It was there that the Carthaginians, who came to support the expelled tyrant Terillus, were decisively defeated by *Theron of Acragas and *Gelon of Syracuse in 480 BC. A few years later the city suffered from bloody civil strife. It was destroyed in 409 by Carthage in revenge for the defeat of 480. The remaining population settled in Thermae Himeraeae, the new city founded by Carthage some ten km away in 407. *Stesichorus was a native of H. and Agathocles of the new city.

HIMILCO Carthaginian general who twice almost subdued Syracuse. He conquered Acragas, Gela and Camarina in 406 BC, but the following year could not complete the conquest of Syracuse because of a plague in his army. He concluded peace with *Dionysius I who recognized Carthage's rule over the whole of Sicily except Syracuse, Messana and Leontini. After the outbreak of the war in 397 he was again appointed commander-in-chief and again besieged Syracuse. But, as in 405, his army suffered from a plague and after a severe defeat he managed to rescue the Carthaginian citizen-soldiers. Back in Carthage he committed suicide.

HIPPALUS Greek seaman and merchant who was the first to recognize the regularity of the monsoon-winds and to exploit them for making the voyage to northwest India. Instead of taking the coastal route, he made straight for India from Ras Fartak; this led to the development of busy commerce with India. A part of the Arabian sea and the southwest monsoon were named after him.
R. E. M. Wheeler, *Rome beyond the Imperial Frontiers*, 1955, 154 ff; Thomson, *Ancient Geography* (s.v.).

HIPPARCHUS (1) Younger brother and co-ruler with *Hippias. He invited the poets *Simonides and *Anacreon to his court and introduced the recitation of Homer in the Panathenaic festival. He showed an interest in art and architecture and supported artists. In 514 he was killed by *Aristogeiton and Harmodius.

HIPPARCHUS (2) Prominent Greek astronomer and mathematician, native of Nicaea in Bithynia, lived in the 2nd century BC, and worked in Alexandria and Rhodes. He improved the dioptra, the basic instrument used for sighting and measuring at distance, and carried out a systematic survey of fixed stars (during the years 162—126). He was thus able to note the positions of about 850 stars, and discovered a new star. His famous discovery was that of the precession of the equinoxes. Unlike other Hellenistic astronomers who sought to "save the phenomena" by suggesting theoretical mathematical models, he refrained from developing a theory of the planets and was able to show that all theories to date were not borne out by observation. The first to use trigonometry systematically in his research work, he wrote the first work in this field, *Table of Chords*. He also wrote works on geography (an attack against Eratosthenes) and astrology. Only his *Commentary on the Phaenomena of Eudoxus and Aratus* is extant but much is known from the *Almagest* of Ptolemy.
T. L. Heath, *Greek Astronomy*, 1932 (s.v.); D. R. Dicks, *The Geographical Fragments of Hipparchus*, 1960.

HIPPEIS ("horsemen") Cavalry never played leading roles in Greek armies in the Archaic and Classic periods and was only sparely used before the 5th century. The successes of *Philip II and Alexander the Great were largely due to the extensive use they made of cavalry. In Greek states only the rich could afford to maintain horses and acquire the necessary skill for riding and fighting as horsemen, hence aristocrats and oligarchs were often called by that name. Solon used it as a census qualification for his second class, that is, those whose annual income amounted to 300 to 500 medimnoi of corn.
Hignett, *Athen.Const.* (s.v.);
J. K. Anderson, *Ancient Greek Horsemanship*, 1961.

HIPPIAS (1) Eldest son of *Pisistratus, brother of *Hipparchus (1), with whom he ruled Athens from 527 BC on. He was a liberal ruler and allowed such aristocrats as *Cleisthenes (2) and *Miltiades to serve as eponymous archons. After the murder of his brother in 514 his rule became suppressive. The Alcmaeonids then procured the support of the Delphic Oracle and that of Sparta and in 510 BC *Cleomenes I compelled him to evacuate Athens. He, and his followers, first settled in Sigeum. He then joined Darius and accompanied the Persian expedition that was defeated at Marathon.
Hdt.5.62—5; Thuc. 6.54—9; Arist. *Athen.Pol.* 19.

HIPPIAS (2) Greek Sophist, native of Elis, active in the second part of the 5th century BC. He is mainly known from his portrayal in Plato's dialogues, *Hippias Maior* and *Hippias Minor*. He professed his ability to teach astronomy and mathematics, poetry and music, grammar and heroic history, and claimed that he made his own clothes. He was apparently a successful orator and teacher, but nothing of his extensive writings has survived.

HIPPOCRATES The most famous physician of antiquity, native of Cos, born *c.* 460 BC, lived to old age and died (? 380—370) in Larissa in Thessaly. Very little can be said with certainty about his life. He came from a family with a tradition in the profession of medicine and founded a school of medicine at the famous temple of *Asclepius at Cos. He taught and practised in his many travels throughout Greece, founded scientific medicine and gained eternal fame as the ideal physician. In taking the Hippocratic Oath the physicians of the present swear to maintain the ethics associated with him and his school.

Of the extant collection of medical treatises, known as the *Hippocratic Corpus*, not even one work can be ascertained as definitely H.'s, and probably none is authentic. They cover all fields of medicine: surgery, dietetics, epidemiology, pharmacology, prognostics, therapeutics and ethics. They come from various origins and periods, and do not conform with the views ascribed to H. by writers of the 4th century BC. Presumably they are, in part, remains of the medical literature of the 5th and 4th centuries including that of the Hippocratic school. Among the more important of these are the book on *Epidemics* (with a study of cases) and on epilepsy, which is explained by natural causes. They include *The Oath of Hippocrates*.

E. Littre, *Ouvres complètes d'Hippocrate*, 1939–1861;
W. S. Jones–E. T. Withington (Loeb), 1923–1931;
J. Chadwick–W. N. Mann, *The Medical Works of Hippocrates*, 1950; L. Edelstein, *Ancient Medicine*, 1967.

HIPPODAMUS Greek architect and most famous town-planner, native of Miletus, lived in the early 5th century BC. He is associated with the planning of three towns; Peiraeus (after the Persian wars, Arist. *Pol.* 1267b), Thurii (443 BC) and Rhodes (Strabo 14.2,9), the last one is contested as too late (408 BC). The grid system of town-planning, with parallel streets intersecting at right angles, and divided into regular quarters, was ascribed to and named after him. But the Hippodamian system had been in use before him both in Ionia and the Greek West; he presumably elaborated the system and applied it more skillfully. Apparently he was also a social-political thinker; according to Aristotle he suggested that the ideal city should number 10,000 citizens (*Pol.* 2.5).
R. E. Wycherly, *How the Greeks built Cities*[2], 1962.

HIPPODROMUS Ground for horse and chariot-racing, the Greek counterpart of the Roman *circus. The course of the races was elliptic; that held in honour of Patroclus was in the open plain before Troy (*Il.* 23). Columns marked the turning-points at Olympia (Pausan. 6.20.7). Races were held at many of the public festivals, notably the Olympian, Pythian and Nemean. *Hippodromoi* were to be found in many Greek cities. The victors in the races were much honoured. There is extant a bronze statue of a charioteer, part of a group dedicated by Polyzelus at Delphi to commemorate his victory.

HIPPOLYTUS Greek mythological hero, son of *Theseus and Hippolyte, the queen of the Amazons. Phaedra fell in love with him but he, a devotee of Artemis and averse to sexual desires, rejected her advances. Unable to survive her unfulfilled passion she killed herself, but not without first accusing H. Theseus banished him and called upon his father Poseidon to kill him. A sea-monster terrified H.'s horses as he was driving to Troezen and he fell from his chariot and was dragged to death. H. had a hero-cult at Athens and at Troezen, his supposed place of death. At Troezen he was believed to have been turned into the constellation Auriga. In another version he was restored to life by Asclepius and in the cult of Diana (= Artemis) at Aricia he was identified with a deity by the name Viribus. The myth was used by Euripides in one of his great extant tragedies *Hippolytus* (another is not extant), in which the tormented Phaedra is the more interesting figure. The myth was used by Seneca in his *Phaedra* and by Racine in *Phedra*. It was also told by Ovid (*Met.* 15.506ff.).

HIPPONAX Greek iambic poet, native of Ephesus, lived in the second part of the 6th century BC (Plin. *NH* 36.11). Exiled by the tyrants of his home city he went to Cla-

zomenae. His extant fragments show that he lived in extreme poverty, with low people, which circumstances account for the bitterness in his poetry. A caricatured statue of him made by the sculptors Bupalus and Athenis occasioned his violent attack in verse, said to have caused their suicide. The fragments also refer to his mistress Arete, who is lampooned too.

H. invented the "lame iambic", known as *scazon* or *choliambos*, in which a spondee ends the final foot of the iambic trimeter. He used it to write his satirical verse. Fragments of a mock-heroic poem support the attribution to him of the invention of parody (Athen. 698b). The colloquial vocabulary, with Lydian and Phrygian words, the vivid descriptions, the vigorous style and humour, all make him an interesting poet.

A. D. Know, *The Greek Choliambic Poets*, 1929;
O. Masson, *Les fragments du poete Hipponax*, 1962.

HIPPO REGIUS Ancient Phoenician city in North Africa (at modern Bône in Algeria), allegedly used as a trading centre from the 12th century BC. In the 2nd century it became a residence of the Numidian kings (hence Regius). It was included in the Roman province after *Thapsus, became a *municipium* under Augustus and later a *colonia*. Its bishop *Augustinus died before the Vandals captured and pillaged it (AD 431). The remains include a theatre, baths, and villas.

HIPSALIS (modern Sevilla) Spanish town on the Baetis, first mentioned by Caesar. Colonized by Caesar, it prospered under the Empire thanks to the fertile surroundings and proximity to the mines and to its port (the river is navigable). Throughout history it has maintained its importance. St. Isidore was its bishop in the 7th century.

HIRTIUS, Aulus Roman statesman, soldier and writer, probably native of Ferentinum. He served under Caesar in Gaul from 54 BC on and followed him in the Civil War. After a praetorship in 46 he governed Gaul. Consul in 43, he defeated Antony at Mutina but was killed in the battle (21 April). He completed Caesar's account of the conquest of Gaul by writing Book eight of the *Gallic War* (51–50 BC). He is probably the author of the extant *Bellum Alexandrinum*, the account of Caesar's war at Alexandria in 47 and of the war against Pharnaces which ended with the rapid victory at Zela in Asia Minor (*veni, vidi, vici*). That he wrote the extant *Bellum Africum* (Caesar's war in Africa to the Battle of Thapsus in 47–46 BC) and the *Bellum Hispaniense* (Caesar's war in Spain and victory at Munda in 45), as is reported by Suetonius (*Iul.* 56), is surely unacceptable. His correspondence with Cicero, with whom he had close ties, has not survived.

HISTIAEUS Tyrant of Miletus who accompanied *Darius I with the Ionian fleet in the Scythian expedition. Later the Great King became suspicious and held him at Susa as counsellor. He probably induced his son-in-law *Aristagoras to initiate the Ionian revolt, which he was sent to quell but without success. He was crucified by the satrap Artaphernes in 493 BC.
Hdt. 4–6; A. R. Burn, *Persia and the Greeks*, 1962.

HISTORIA AUGUSTA Collection of biographies of Roman emperors, caesars, and pretenders from Hadrian to Numerianus (AD 117–284), the earliest manuscript of which dates from the 9th century. It was so named by the scholar Casaubon in the early 17th century and is the only extant continuous account of the period but with a lacuna for the years 244–c. 260. The biographies are arranged in the usual pattern of Seutonius' *Twelve Caesars*: date and place of birth of the figure, family and ancestors, life to the accession to the throne, systematic account of the reign according to certain subjects, and death.

The biographies include numerous documents: letters, speeches, *senatus consulta*, acclamations and inscriptions, almost all of which are thought to be forgeries. They appear in minor *Lives* while those of Hadrian, Antoninus Pius, Marcus Aurelius and Septimius Severus, considered more reliable, contain no documents. The biographies are dedicated to Diocletian, Constantine and to private people. Six persons claim to be their authors: Aelius Spartianus, Julius Capitolinus, Vulcacius Gallicanus, Aelius Lampridius, Trebellius Pollio and Flavius Vopiscus. Gibbon extensively used the *Scriptores Historiae Augustae*, the common name for the six, for the writing of his great book but, with other old scholars, had qualms about the number and names of the authors. The "modern problem" of the H. was opened by Dessau who argued in an excellent article (1899) that the *Lives* were forged by a single author at the end of the 4th century AD. The points involved in the "problem" are the number of the authors, the date of the composition, the aim of the writers, and the reliability of the material. Numerous theories have been suggested to date but none seems to have gained common consent. The dates suggested vary from the early 4th century to the late 6th. It has been regarded as pro-senatorial, and anti-Christian, or a propaganda work for the policy of Julian; or simply as aiming to entertain the reader. It has little to recommend it as a literary work and as a historical source it must be used with the utmost care.

Text and translations: E. Hohl (Teubner) 1965 (1927); D. Magie (Loeb) 1922–1932;
A. Birley, in *Latin Historians* (ed. T. A. Dorey), 1966;
R. Syme, *Ammianus and the Historia Augusta*, 1968.

HISTORIOGRAPHY, GREEK Greek H. originally began with the work of the *logographers, the best known of whom was *Hecataeus of Miletus (late 6th century BC), and its best achievements were made in the 5th century: *Herodotus as a narrative historian and *Thucydides as a scientific historian. It was preceded by a long tradition of recording events and preparing lists of kings, priests and magistrates which may have dated from the late 2nd millenium BC. The urge to write history scientifically, that is, to put the accepted accounts of the epics and oral traditions to rational criticism, came in the wake of the rise of science and philosophy in Ionia in the 6th century BC.

The aim of Hecataeus and Herodotus was to preserve the truth and record great deeds. To entertain the readers by interesting stories and good prose was another aim. Thucydides put the search for the accurate truth above all, and stated that to preserve the truth was useful and instructive for future generations. Another Greek historian whose work is extant was *Xenophon and he aimed at recording what happened but his works suffer from partiality. These original aims of H. were later replaced under the influence of literary criticism. Elaborate style and the dramatic story became more important than the truth, which could be distorted on this account. The writing of history was severely damaged by the teachings of Socrates, Plato and *Isocrates. Under the influence of the first two, moral principles came to the fore and the latter, by his pan-Hellenism campaign, introduced national bias and political propaganda. Only few historians perpetuated the tradition of scientific history, notably *Polybius and even he was not above partiality when writing on his Achaea. The worst example of distorting the truth was

*Timaeus according to Polybius; the sensational histories of *Cleitarchus and *Duris were perhaps no better.

Several types of Greek histories can be distinguished: 1) Those which dealt with contemporary or recent events. Under this category come those of Thucydides, Xenophon, *Hieronymus of Cardia, the *Philippica* of *Theopompus, and many others; 2) Monographs, such as those of Herodotus (essentially), Thucydides, the histories of Alexander, etc.; 3) General histories like those of *Ephorus, Timaeus, *Posidonius, *Diodorus Siculus; 4) Local histories which dealt specifically with one city-state only, like the works of the Atthidographers (*Atthis), and the constitutional histories of 158 cities prepared under Aristotle, the Local History of Cyme of *Ephorus and the history of *Heraclea Pontica by Memnon. The writers of local histories usually collected documentary evidence for their works.

Greek H. mainly dealt with political and constitutional history with occasional observations on ethnography, geography and religious institutions. A large part was given to the role of individuals in the making of history. Speeches – genuine or, more often, fictitious – were always included in the narrative.

J. B. Bury, *The Ancient Greek Historians*, 1958 (1908);
M. I. Finley, *The Greek Historians*, 1954.

HISTORIOGRAPHY, ROMAN Roman H. began some three hundred years after the beginning of Greek H. and was under its influence from the first. *Fabius Pictor and his immediate successors wrote in Greek to advertise the Roman achievements to the Greek public and possibly because Latin prose was not developed enough for the purpose at that time. But, as in Greece, the recording of events started earlier, traditionally from the very beginning of Rome and possibly the *Annales included material dating from the 5th century. Family and oral traditions supplemented the documentary evidence and it was thus that Roman historians were able to reconstruct Roman history from the very beginning to their time drawing on Greek mythology as well. *Cato (1) was the first to write history in Latin, and Greek was abandoned for the native tongue shortly after his time.

H., for the Romans, was in the first place a literary genre rather than a search for the truth; a vehicle for national or political propaganda more than an impartial account of what happened. It follows therefore that Roman historians from the start did not write objective, scientific history. The famous maxim of Tacitus *sine ira et studio* ("without prejudice or bias") was presumably professed by many but not followed in practice. Only rarely did the authors try to collect evidence and even when the documents were available they did not usually try to make full use of them. Each one tried to excel his predecessors by elaborate style or better rhetoric. The publication of the *annales maximi* by P. *Scaevola (1) made the work easier and dispensed altogether with the need to find written evidence. Almost all historians were statesmen who took part in the making of history, which led them to pass judgement, take issue and be partial.

The early historians usually wrote general accounts of Roman history and by the end of the 2nd century BC the annalistic framework was established; history was divided and described in yearly instalments. The writing of monographs began with *Coelius Antipater and the first extant of these are those of *Sallust on the *Jugurthine War* and the *Catilinarian Conspiracy*. The *Gallic War* and *Civil War* of Caesar purport to be simple recordings of events; in fact they conceal partisan descriptions. But excepting Sallust and Caesar, the works of other Republican historians are represented at best by fragments. Of the historians who wrote under Augustus and the Empire the great works are those of *Livy and *Tacitus. Both show the merits and defects of Roman historians: the sustained effort to present a stylistically perfect work while neglecting the painstaking search for evidence. The first is devoted to glorify the Roman achievement and the work of Tacitus suffers from his preoccupations with human nature; still it is a masterful description of tyranny. Other extant works — of *Velleius Paterculus, *Florus, *Eutropius, *Festus (2) — are short accounts or abridgements of long periods. They are often superficial and marred by rhetoric, bias or prejudice. The last great Roman historian was *Ammianus Marcellinus and though he sought to attain accuracy he too was not above prejudice. It should be mentioned that much historical work was done by the way of writing biographies, notably *Suetonius (also *Nepos, *Historia Augusta), and that important Roman histories were written by Greeks (*Polybius, *Posidonius, *Appian, *Dionysius of Halicarnassus, and *Dio Cassius).

Roman historians, like the Greek, concentrated on political and military history. Social and economic history were treated only sparely (in fact this is only a modern approach). And they, too, emphasized the importance of individuals in history and were mainly interested in the upper classes.

M. W. L. Laistner, *The Great Roman Historians*, 1947; T. A. Dorey (ed.), *Latin Historians*, 1966.

HOMER The most famous of the Greek poets, believed by the Greeks to have composed the *Iliad* and the *Odyssey*, by far the best epics ever written. Details of his life were disputed even in antiquity. He was variously dated to the Trojan War, to the Ionian migrations, to the middle of the 9th century BC (Hdt. 2.53) and 500 years after the Trojan War. Seven cities claimed to be his birthplace. By extant accounts he was blind and poor, came from Ionia and wandered throughout Greece. The discrepancy among the ancient authorities and the critical analysis of the poems have, in modern times, resulted in the denial of his very existence, but this hypercritical attitude has been proven wrong. Logical considerations, the Ionic dialect of the poems and their internal evidence suggest that he lived in Ionia (as is the tradition), more likely in Chios (the place of the *Homeridae) or in Smyrna (*Pindar's view); that he lived in the 8th century BC; that he was very much like one of the bards described in the *Odyssey* (he never mentions himself in the poems), and that he may very well have been blind.

The subject of the *Iliad* is war, the war of the Greeks against Troy (Ilium), or more precisely, the poet sings about the wrath of Achilles, the most conspicuous hero of the Greeks. Insulted by Agamemnon, who has taken Briseis, his beautiful captive, he shuts himself in his tent and refuses to take part in the war. As a result the Greeks suffer defeats and even the active support of Patroclus, Achilles' friend, does not help, as he is slain by the Trojan hero Hector. Now at last, overcome by grief, Achilles sets out for battle; again he is motivated by anger and the desire for revenge. Almost maddened with fury he pursues Hector, slays him, and for days abuses the corpse. Finally he lets Priam take the body of his son for burial. There are only four days of actual fighting in the poem, and the whole plot takes place in a few weeks at the last stage of

Portrait of Homer on a coin of the second half of the 4th century BC — the earliest known

the war. By way of allusions and flashbacks the whole story of the war, which lasted ten years to this stage, is skillfully told. By relating the exploits of the main heroes on both sides and the part taken by the gods above in the war, as well as by various episodes (such as the funeral competitions for Patroclus) and portrayals, the poet contrives to compose a rich and broad narrative, the essential quality of epic poetry. From first to last, however, the unity of the action is maintained and dominated by the tragic figure of Achilles, the hero who knows he is doomed to die.

The *Odyssey* narrates the ten year adventures of Odysseus on his home voyage from Troy after its sack by the Greeks. In this respect it is a sequel of the *Iliad*. Here again the narrative begins in the last stage, some six weeks in whole, and all other events are told retrospectively. It starts with Odysseus' departure from Calypso; he manages to reach Sicheria, the island of the Phaeacians, after his raft is wrecked by Poseidon. Simultaneously his son Telemachus is induced to go to search for news of his father in Pylos and Sparta; the first four books are devoted to this journey. At Scheria Odysseus narrates his adventures to Nausicaa and her parents at a banquet, a model followed by Virgil in his *Aeneid*. He is then taken to Ithaca where his faithful wife Penelope has been delaying the suitors in the last years. He comes disguised as a beggar, to be recognized only by Eurycleia, his old nurse, and by his old dog. Finally he kills all the suitors. Here, too, there is one central figure, unity of theme with interwoven episodes, a full account of the other characters and many allusions—the Wooden Horse, the Sack of Troy, the murder of Agamemnon etc.

The charm of the Homeric poems is in the simplicity of the narrative, the nobility of the characters and the reality of the action. The unity of the plot is maintained throughout, combined with rich and various episodes. The digressions provide broadness and variety and do not delay the speedy development of the actions in the final climaxes. The language is rich and artfully employed to fit all moments and situations, whatever they may be. A distinct feature are the similes; many more in the *Iliad* than in the *Odyssey*. Short or long, they are made to match the occasion. They are often pieces taken out of the world of nature or the familiar surroundings of the poet's own life and as such add vividness and variety.

The Homeric poems purport to describe the Achaean world at the time of the Trojan War, a world of heroes and heroines, of great warriors, great palaces filled with treasures and spoils of war. They betray, however, that in their final form they were composed several centuries later. While retaining some of the features characteristic of the old civilization, such as chariots and arms, they give evidence of changed conditions, customs and social institutions.

Critical approach to the poems began with some ancient critics who argued that the two poems were written by two different poets. Modern critics collected inconsistencies, emphasized different attitudes, differences in style and vocabulary; the extremists claimed that they were collections made in the 6th century BC out of several earlier layers. All the arguments can be answered; not the least by assuming that the *Odyssey* was the work of the same poet who wrote the *Illiad* at an earlier stage of his life. And much has been done to show that there are similarities in structure and techniques between the two poems. Still it is true that the poems had before them a long tradition of oral epic poetry. The preceding bards told the old tales using conventional phrases and episodes; hence the appearance of formulae and the same lines or passages in the poems. Equally it is true that the poet, or poets, who composed the *Iliad* and the *Odyssey* by the use of the old material achieved remarkable works, consistent in many aspects, with a distinct touch of originality in design, structure, character portrayals, and language — which all show the genius of their author.

The poems, composed in the 8th century BC, were transmitted probably orally for about two centuries. The tradition is that with their introduction to Athens for recitation in the *Panathenaea under Pisistratus a written text was prepared. However, the poems spread in the Greek world in different versions. The Alexandrian scholars, notably *Aristophanes of Byzantium and *Aristarchus, did painstaking research work to establish a correct text, but they were not able to impose it on the public.

The Homeric poems had a unique place in Greek culture. They were learned by cuildren, recited in festivals, cited in political disputes and used as historical sources. Though criticized by Plato on moral grounds, they were admired by Aristotle as masterpieces of epic poetry. This admiration was followed by the Romans and * Virgil modelled his *Aeneid on the Homeric poems. And the influence persisted through all times, to the present: on critics, poets, writers, artists and simple readers.

Text: D. B. Munro, T. A. Allen (OCD) 1912–1920;
A. T. Murray (Loeb) 1919–1924;
C. M. Bowra, *Tradition and Design in the Iliad,* 1960 (1930); G. C. Kirk, *Homer and the Epic,* 1965.

HOMERIC HYMNS A collection of twenty-three poems ascribed to Homer but composed by various anonymous bards from the late 8th century BC on. They were composed as preludes to the recitations of epic poems in public festivals, and were addressed to deities in whose honour the festivals were held. They consist of invocations and praises with myths of the deeds of the gods, written in the epic metre. They include four major hymns: to Demeter, Apollo, Hermes and Aphrodite;

others are short like that for Ares which is of late date.
T. W. Allen–W. R. Halliday–E. E. Sikes (edition and commentary), 1936; H. G. Evelyn-White (Loeb), 1936.

HOMERIDAE "Sons of Homer", a guild of rhapsodes, said to have comprised at first only descendants of Homer, but later others as well. Chios was their main seat. They gave public recitations of the Homeric poems, which thus became known in the Greek world. One of them, Cynaethus, was credited with the writing of the Homeric Hymn to Apollo.

HONESTIORES The social upper classes under the Roman Empire which in course of time acquired some privileges, notably exemption from severe penalties in criminal cases. The inferior classes were called *humiliores*, but there was not any comprehensive legal definition to distinguish between the two groups. The H. included senators, Equites, decurions, and others who managed to join them.
P. Garnsey, *Social Status and Legal Privileges under the Roman Empire,* 1970.

HONORIUS, Flavius Roman emperor in the West (AD 393–423), son of *Theodosius I, born in 384. Until 408 it was *Stilicho who actually governed the empire and then H. had him executed. It was in the reign of H. that Rome was captured and plundered by Alaric, that Britain was evacuated, and Spain lost to the Vandals. He spent most of his time in Ravenna. *Galla Placidia was his sister, and he quarreled with her.)
Jones, *Lat.Rom.Emp.* (s.v.).

HOPLITES The heavily armed infantry soldiers of the Greeks. Citizens with enough resources had to serve as H. with their own equipment. They were armed with short sword, long spear, heavy shield, helmet, breastplate and greaves. They date from the Archaic period, formed the main unit of a Greek army, and were organized in the *Phalanx.
M. N. Snodgrass, *Arms and Armour of the Greeks,* 1967.

HORACE, Quintus Horatius Flaccus Roman poet, son of a freedman, a native of Venusia in Apulia, lived 65–8 BC. His father, a man of considerable means, saw to his education, first at Rome and later at Athens. A republican, he joined *Brutus (2) in the Civil War, was appointed military tribune and fought at *Philippi in 42. Back in Italy, he found himself without means as his father's property was confiscated by the Triumvirs. He says, with humour, that poverty drove him to write poetry (*Epist.* 2.2,41). To make a living he purchased a post of a secretary to the quaestors. His friend Virgil introduced him to *Maecenas in 38 BC and he became a member of the literary circle that was associated with this patron of letters; from him he received his Sabine farm. Through him he became closely associated with Augustus, whose offer, however, to become his secretary he declined. H. enjoyed his close friendship with these great men of the state and retained it throughout his life. He continued to write poetry, which was not always received favourably, for many years and when he died, shortly after his patron Maecenas, he left behind him the finest of Latin lyric poetry

Horace's *Epodes* (called *iambi* by the poet), consisting of seventeen poems mostly in iambic metres, were published about 30 BC and composed in the preceding decade. He expressly modelled them on *Archilochus and claimed that he was the *inventor* of the genre at Rome (*Epist.* 1.9,23ff.). They include furious invectives, more humorous than serious (No. 3 is against Maecenas), love

Greek Hoplite, the "Ariston funerary stele" of the late 6th century BC. Note the helmet, cuirass, the greaves and the spear

themes (again some with a touch of humour), politics, and country scenes. The language is occasionally obscene and the style and techniques show the influence not only of Archilochus but also of Hellenistic poetry.

The *Satires* (*saturae*, also *Sermones*) are two books on a variety of subjects, mainly associated with events in the poet's life, with character portrayals and stories and include views on morality and literary criticism. Book 1, containing ten satires, was published some time after 37 BC, Book 2, containing eight satires, in 30 BC. While the first book presents directly the views of the poet, the second is written in the dialogue form. In this genre H. followed the model of *Lucilius, but without the vehement, personal attacks of his predecessor. He writes with ease and humour on all subjects, even when dealing with serious themes. The epic hexameter is made to fit the changing subjects and moods of the satires, and this highly technical skill is matched by the polished style; however it is the personality of the poet that dominates the *Satires* throughout.

The first three books of the *Odes* (*Carmina*) were published in 23 BC and contain poems written after 30 BC. Their success was limited and it was only in 13 BC that H. published the fourth book of the *Odes*. The first, containing 88 poems, was addressed to Maecenas. The professed models were *Alcaeus and *Sappho, and again H. claimed to have introduced this poetical genre into Rome. But it is evident that he was influenced in points of style and themes by other Greek poets, such as Pindar and especially the Alexandrian poets, such as *Callimachus who put polished verse above all. Again, the poems range over a wide variety of themes and occasions. Friendship, love, wine, countryside scenes, good life, death, politics, religion, are main subjects. But it is not so much the subject matter that draws attention — except perhaps the tendency to treat politics seriously — as the accomplished poetical treatment. A great poet can be judged by his ability to treat old themes in an original manner, which is what H. does in the *Odes*. Original phrases, lovely scenes, charming portraits and tales, combined with humour and passion and that unique art of presenting great truths with ease, all contribute to produce masterly poems. And the great artistry of the poet is amply demonstrated by his complete success in applying the Greek metres to the Latin language. The fifteen poems of the fourth book retain all the traits of the earlier books. The *Carmen Saeculare* was composed on the invitation of Augustus, to be sung in the *Ludi Saeculares* in 17 BC. H. addresses the *Ode* to the Capitoline triad, Apollo, and Diana and celebrates the great services of Augustus. It was performed by a choir of 27 boys and 27 girls.

Book 1 of *Epistles* contains 20 *epistulae* and was published in 20 BC. The second book now consists of two epistles; the second was probably written in 19, the first *c.* 15 BC, the third epistle came to be titled *Ars Poetica*. The verse-letters genre was not H.'s invention; *Catullus and especially *Lucilius used it. The letters are addressed to real persons (Maecenas, Lollius, Tiberius etc.), though not all can be identified and often no serious attempt is made to conceal the fictitious character of the letters. The letter form enables the poet to express his personal views on moral conduct, questions of philosophy and on poetry. H. can thus speak with humour on abandoning poetry for philosophy (1.1; 2.2). In expounding his views, he does not aim at forcing them on his readers. The long epistle of 2.1 deals with the social aspects of the writing of poetry, with special reference to H.'s own time. Throughout an easy mood is preserved, and the treatment of the themes is studded with tales and anecdotes. The same humour and easy treatment is to be seen in the *Ars Poetica*, which can hardly be considered as a serious attempt by H. to produce a guide book for poets. It deals extensively with epic and drama, the two traditionally "respectable" literary genres. The only important advice given to the would-be poet is it be diligent so as to produce accomplished poetry, which H. himself certainly did.

The highly refined poetry of H. in style, language and metre won him followers and imitators from antiquity to modern times; Persius, Juvenal, Petrarch, Ben Johnson, and Pope are only a few of these. His poems were learnt by school children and widely read till the 6th century AD. Subsequently he was known mainly through anthologies. From the Renaissance on, numerous translations were made of his poetry. Wherever and whenever cultured poetry is appreciated he has a place of honour Texts, translations and commentaries: E. C. Wickham (OCD), 1912[2]; A. Kiessling—R. Heinze[9], 1957; C. E. Bennett—H. R. Fairclough (Loeb), 1914—1926; E. Fraenkel, *Horace*, 1957; C. D. Brink, *Horace on Poetry*, 1963; C. D. N. Costa, (ed.) *Horace*, 1973.

HORAE Greek goddesses, daughters of Zeus and Themis: *Eunomia* (*Lawful Government"*), *Dike* (Right), and *Eirene* (Peace; Hesiod, *Theog.* 901). In Attica they personified growth, flowering, and ripeness. In Homer they guarded the gates of heaven, regulated the course of the year, served *Hera and made the corn and grapes ripe. Later they came to symbolize the seasons of the year, Spring, Summer and Autumn, but were also considered four. They often appeared in art and literature with the *Charites and *Muses, and were sometimes confused with them. They were worshipped in several places, notably Athens, Argos and Olympia. They appeared in art as from the Archaic period on, often depicted as dancing.

HORATII (and CURIATII) The three legendary Roman brothers who fought three brothers of *Alba Longa at the time of Tullus Hostilius as representatives of the armies of each side. After the death of his two brothers, the surviving Horatius killed all the C. When his sister mourned one of the C. with whom she was in love he killed her too and was acquitted.

HORATIUS COCLES (the "one eyed") Roman legendary hero who checked the army of *Porsenna from crossing the Sublician bridge until it was destroyed and thus saved Rome. He then crossed the Tiber by swimming. It was probably an aetiological legend occasioned by a statue of a one eyed man which stood near the bridge.

Ogilvie, *Livy*, 258 ff.

HORTENSIUS (1), Quintus Roman statesman, famous for the law he passed as a dictator in 287 BC which made *plebiscita* equal with *leges* — that is, the resolutions of the *Concilium Plebis* became binding on all the Roman people and not only on the Plebs. It was considered as the final victory of the Plebeians in their two centuries of struggle with the Patricians. The bill was occasioned by the only certain historical secession of the Plebs (to the Janiculum). It was prompted by debts and usury and, as it happened, no more secessions were made, and hence the bill resulted in the conclusion of the Struggle of the Orders.

Jolowicz, *Roman Law*[3] (s.v.).

HORTENSIUS (2) HORTAIUS, Quintus Roman statesman and orator, born in 114 BC, of noble plebeian family. He remained at Rome under *Cinna (1), joined *Sulla and became the acknowledged leading lawyer at Rome. Notorious for bribery, he used the ornate ("Asianic") style of orators, but failed to defend his friend *Verres against Cicero in 70. Consul in 69, he was one of the leading Optimates and, with his father-in-law *Catullus (2), an opponent of Pompey. Like his friend *Lucullus (1), he was one of the great *piscinarii*, known for their magnificent villas and luxurious style of life. He died in 50. None of his speeches is extant, and he is mainly known through the writings of Cicero, with whom he appeared for the defence in several cases, notably Sulla (62) and Sestius (56).

Malcovati, *ORF*[3].

HUNS A nomadic people, excellent horsemen, originating perhaps from central Asia, who started the great migrations of the Germans by conquering the Ostrogoth kingdom in the Ukraine *c.* 370 AD. Under their pressure the Visigoths (*Goths) crossed the Danube in 376. From *c.* 400 on they renewed their advance to the west, which caused the migrations of German tribes, notably the *Vandals and the *Alani. By *c.* 430 their empire extended from the Don to the Rhine. At the height of their power under *Attila, they harshly exploited the population under their control and even the Roman rulers of Constantinople and Ravenna bought peace with them by paying enormous sums of money. Their empire collapsed after the defeat of Atilla's sons by a coalition of Germans in Pannonia in 455.

E. A. Thompson, *A History of Attila and the Huns,* 1948.

HYACINTHUS Greek mythological hero, worshipped at Amyclae near Sparta. In the myth he was a beautiful youth loved by Apollo. One day the god was teaching him to hurl the discus and by accident killed him; or it was *Zephyrus who, jealous of Apollo, diverted the discus to strike him on the head. From the youth's blood sprang flowers, the hyacinth, marked *ai ai* — the cries of Apollo on that occasion (Ovid. *Met.* 10.162ff.). Originally, however, H. had been a pre-Hellenic god, supplanted by Apollo. His three-day festival at Amyclae, *Hyacinthia*, was one of the most important for the Spartans. Several other Dorian cities had months and festivals called after H. (Thera, Cos etc.). At Amyclae he was depicted as bearded (Pausan. 3.19,4), but later he appeared as a beautiful boy in vase-paintings.

Nilsson, *Religion*[2], 485 ff.

HYDRA Mythological many-headed monster, offspring of *Typhon and Echidina, living at Lake Lerna in the Argolid. The second Labour of *Heracles was to kill her, but two or three heads grew instead of each one he cut off. It was only when Iolaus helped him to sear the wounds of the monster with burning brands that it stopped sprouting new heads and he could finish his task. The story is first told by Hesiod (*Theog.* 313ff.) and with more details by later writers *Apollod. 2.5,2). It was a favourite theme with artists (vase-paintings, metopes in the temple of Zeus at Olympia, etc.), who represented only several heads while poets attributed her up to 100 (Eur. *Her.* 1190).

HYGIEIA Greek goddess, personification of Health. Mythologically the daughter of *Asclepius, she was commonly worshipped with him. In art she also usually appears with him; in the Hippocratic oath, H. comes next after Asclepius.

HYGINUS (1), Gaius Iulius Roman scholar, probably of Spanish origin, a freedman of Augustus, and librarian of the Palatine Library. He was a teacher and friend of Ovid. H. wrote on various subjects: agriculture, religion, the Trojan families, the origins of the Italian cities, biographies of famous men etc. Only fragments of his work have survived.

HYGINUS (2) Roman land-surveyor (*gromaticus*) in the early 2nd century AD. The extant collection of the writings of the Roman *Gromatici* includes several of his works.

HYGINUS (3) Both a mythological manual in Latin (*genealogiae*) of the 2nd century AD, based on a Greek source, and a Latin astronomical poem have the name of a H. as their author, who cannot be identified with either H. (1) or H. (2). The mythological manual is a poor and inaccurate work.

HYLAS Greek mythological figure, son of the king of the Dryopes. His father was killed by Heracles and H. became a young companion of Heracles who took him on the expedition of the *Argonauts. At Cios he disappeared after nymphs carried him to their springs and Heracles vainly stayed to search for him. It seems to be an aetiological myth to account for the custom of the Cians to wander in the country on a certain day and to call the name H.

HYMENAEUS Greek deity of the wedding ceremony. The idea of such a deity sprang from the custom to call *Hymen O Hymenaeus* at weddings, which is attested as early as the poems of *Alcman and *Sappho. In literature H. first appears in *Pindar as a young man. He is represented as a beautiful youth, with a wreath, pipes, or a torch.

HYPERBOLUS Athenian demagogue, of low origin, active during the Peloponnesian War; "leader of the people" after the death of *Cleon. He was *strategos* in 425/424 BC, pursued an extreme war policy, and in 421 opposed the Peace of *Nicias. He was ostracized in 417 (or 415) after *Alcibiades and Nicias combined against him. He was killed in Samos in 411 by the oligarchs (Thuc. 8.73). He was ridiculed by comic playwrights and vehemently attacked by Thucydides.

HYPERBOREANS Legendary dwellers of the far North, worshippers of Apollo who was said to spend the winter months with them. They are first mentioned by Hesiod. They lived a happy life enjoying everlasting sunshine, immortality, with no grief (Pind. *Pyth.* 10). *Leto came from their country to Delos to give birth to *Apollo and Artemis. Herodotus says that their offering was brought to the Delian temple of Apollo, transmitted from "city to city" (4.33). Their name may mean those "beyond the mountains" or "beyond the North Wind" (*Boreas*). They were neighbours of the *Arimaspoi according to Herodotus, which points to Scythia. In one view their offering were firstfruits sent by an unknown Greek colony in the north of the Black Sea.

HYPERIDES Athenian statesman and orator, son of Glaucippus, of good family, lived 389–322 BC. A pupil of *Isocrates, he started his career as a *logographos* and later was prominent in the courts as a prosecuter. In politics he cooperated with Demosthenes in taking an extreme anti-Macedonian attitude and in 343 succeeded in condemning *Philocrates in court. After *Chaeronea he proposed giving citizenship to metics and manumitting slaves. In 335 Alexander demanded his surrender on account of his hostility, but he was saved and continued his activity at the court. In 324 he joined the prosecution of Demosthenes, on a charge of taking bribes from *Harpalus. He took a leading part in the Lamian War and delivered the funeral oration on the fallen Athenians, one of whom was his friend, the general Leosthenes. After the Macedonian victory *Antipater (1) demanded his surrender and he was put to death.

Considerable fragments of six of H.'s speeches were discovered on papyri in the 19th century, a meagre part of the fifty-two (or 56) speeches known in antiquity. All, excepting the *Epitaphios*, are judicial speeches; *Against Athenagoras* shows him at his best. His restrained tone, humour, inoffensive attitude and tact contributed to his success in the court. In one ancient critic's view he was only surpassed by Demosthenes.
B. O. Burtt, *Minor Attic Orators* (Loeb), 1952.

HYPNOS Greek god, personification of sleep. He was the son of Nyx (Night) and brother of Thanatos (Death; Hesiod, *Theog.* 211f.). In Homer, the brothers carry off the dead *Sarpedon to Lycia for burial (*Il.* 16.666ff.). He lives in Lemnos with his wife Pasithea, one of the *Charites (but Hesiod has him dwelling in the underworld). A winged boy, he brings sleep by touching the foreheads of the weary or by pouring a soporific liquid from his horn. In vase-paintings he and his brother carry the dead to burial.

HYPSIPYLE Greek mythological heroine, daughter of Thoas, king of Lemnos. When the women of the island killed all the males for taking concubines she saved her father. She ruled Lemnos when the *Argonauts touched on the island, entertained them for a year and had two sons by *Jason (1). Later she fell into the hands of pirates and became a nurse of Opheltes son of Lycurgus, king of Nemea. She was saved from punishment by the Seven against Thebes after the child was killed by a serpent. Euripides wrote a tragedy *Hypsipyle*.

A woman taking her child from a nursemaid. A painting on a Lekythos from Eretria

HYRCANUS (1) I, John   Son of Simon, Hasmonaean High Priest and ruler of Judaea (134—104 BC). Early in his rule he had to submit to *Antiochus VII and accompanied him on the expedition against Parthia, in which the Seleucid king died (129). He then regained his independence and extended his rule to Idumaea (whose people he converted to Judaism), Samaria and part of Transjordan. After his rupture with the Pharisees he mainly based his power on the Sadducaeans. He made an alliance with Rome.

HYRCANUS (2) II   Son of Alexander Jannaeus and Salome, Hasmonaean High Priest (76 BC) and king (67). A civil war with his brother Aristobulus, in which he was supported by *Antipater (2) and *Aretas III, ended with the conquest of Jerusalem by Pompey. H. was now High Priest and ruled Judaea, Samaria, Galilee and Peraea as ethnarch. But in 57 Gabinius deprived him of his secular powers. The effective ruler was Antipater, though in 48 H. was again made ethnarch by Caesar. In 40 the Parthians carried H. off to Babylonia.

I

IAMBLICHUS Neo-Platonist philosopher, native of Chalcis in Syria, active in the early 4th century AD. He was a pupil of Porphyry in Rome, and later had a school of his own in Syria, probably the school of Apamea. Mysticism, theosophy, mathematics and astrology were his main interests. His extant works are: 1) *On the Life of Pythagoras;* 2) *Protrepticus*; 3) three works on mathematics. All these works are concerned with Pythagoreanism, on which they give some valuable information, while revealing the limited knowledge and understanding of the author. Another extant work *De Mysteriis* ("On Mysteries") is probably by I. It is a valuable source of information for contemporary beliefs. I. wrote other works, dealing with Gods, souls, Chaldaean mythology, and commentaries on Plato and Aristotle, whose teachings he misrepresented. But his extraordinary ideas had a fascination of their own and he had admirers for many of whom he was the "divine Iamblichus".
J. M. Dillon, *Iamblichi Chalcidiensis . . . Fragmenta*, 1973.

IAMBULUS Greek writer, perhaps of the 3rd century BC. He wrote a work on an imaginary voyage he made to the happy Island of the Sun, somewhere in the Indian Ocean. After seven years he returned home. The people of the island lived a blessed life: they were organized in groups of 400, ruled by the elders, had women and children in common, and at old age or when ill sought death voluntarily. The story partly followed old tales on the life of bliss in remote islands or places, and partly the utopian views of *Euhemerus. An account of the tales (not extant) is given by Diodorus Siculus (2.55–60).

IBYCUS Greek lyric poet, a native of Rhegium who lived in the 6th century BC. He left his home city for the court of *Polycrates of Samos after refusing to accept the tyranny. According to a late story, he was killed by robbers who were identified by the birds who witnessed the crime. He was buried in Rhegium. Of his poems, edited in seven books by Alexandrian scholars, only fragments are extant. In his early poems he was influenced by *Stesichorus, who used epic themes for his lyrical poems. In the extant fragments there are indications that I. treated such themes as the birth of Athens and the fall of Troy. His poetry probably included mainly choral poems as well as love-songs. I. is credited with part of an encomium of Polycrates, probably the tyrant's son, known from a papyrus. It is a choral song which sings the praises of Polycrates' beauty. The fragments show that I. used various metres, was sensitive to nature scenes and expressed his emotions with power and imagination.
Page, *Poet. Mel. Gr.*; Bowra, *Gr. Lyr. Poet.*

ICARIUS Eponym of the deme Icaria in Attica to whom Dionysius presented the vine for his hospitality. The neighbouring peasants killed I. after they drank his wine and thought that they had been poisoned. His dog led his daughter Erigone to the corpse and thereupon she hanged herself. Zeus made I. the constellation Boötes, his daughter Virgo and the dog, Canicula. A pestilence sent by Dionysius ended only after the institution of the festival of the Aiora in memory of Erigone. The myth probably reflects opposition to the introduction of the cult of Dionysius.

ICARUS Son of *Daedalus who flew away with his father from Crete to escape from King *Minos. I. came near to the sun so that the wax of which his wings were made melted and he fell into the Aegean. The part of the sea between Samos and Icaros and Cos was named the Icarian Sea after him. This aetiological myth was recorded by many poets and writers; the version of Ovid is best known (*Met.* 8.183ff.). The flight to the sun has been taken to symbolize illusory schemes.

ICENI Celtic tribe in East Anglia (Norfolk and Suffolk) who were on good terms with Rome at the time of the Roman conquest under the Emperor Claudius. They retained their autonomy until the revolt of *Boudicca, the widow of their last king, in AD 60. Their main city was at modern Caistor (near Norwich).
Frere, *Britannia* (s.v.).

ICTINUS Prominent Greek architect of the 5th century BC. His greatest work was the *Parthenon on which he worked from 448 to 437 BC; he worked in collaboration with another architect, Callicrates, and under the supervision of *Phidias. In view of the complicated problems — topographical and aesthetic — involved in the task, it is not surprising that he wrote an account of his work. He was probably the architect of the famous temple of Apollo at *Bassae. The Telesterion (Hall of the Mysteries) of Eleusis was rebuilt by him. In his buildings he succeeded to combine the decorative elements of the Ionic Order with those of the severe Doric Order.

W. B. Dinsmoor, *The Architecture of Ancient Greece,* 1950 (s.v.).

IDAS and LYNCEUS Greek mythological heroes, sons of Aphareus, the Messenian rivals of the *Dioscuri. I. was the "strongest of men" and L. had the sharpest eyes. When *Apollo tried to carry off his bride Marpessa, I. fought him and retained her after she chose him over the god. I. and L. took part in the voyage of the *Argonauts and in the Clydonian boar-hunt (*Meleager). They both died in their final encounter with the Dioscuri after one of them killed Castor.

IDUMENEUS The valorous, if rather old, king of Crete who fought with the Greeks in the Trojan War. On his homeward voyage he·made a vow to sacrifice to Poseidon the first thing he would meet if he survived the storm. It turned out to be his son, and he was later compelled to go into exile as an expiation. This common mythological motif is known only from the commentary of *Servius (2) to Virgil (*Aen.* 3.121).

ILERDA (modern Lerida) Old Iberian city in northeast Spain, the site of one of Caesar's important battles in the Civil War. By defeating the legates of Pompey (*Afranius and Petreius) in 49 BC he took over Spain. It became a *municipium* under Augustus.

ILLYRICUM, ILLYRII The country of the large tribal group of the I. extended along the Adriatic Sea and into the hinterland of the Balkans from the eastern Alps to the Gulf of Valona, roughly corresponding to modern Yugoslavia and Albania. The I. proper were only a small tribe but the Greeks applied the name to all those tribes who bordered on Macedonia and Epirus and later the Romans extended the use of the name. Both hostility and trade marked the relations between the I. and the Greeks and the Macedonians for many centuries. The tribal spirit was too strong for the I. to unite into a powerful state. It was only in the 3rd century BC that some tribes became strong enough to harass the Greeks and the Macedonians by land and sea. The *Dardani inflicted a heavy defeat on Macedonia in 229 BC. Meanwhile the powerful kingdom of the Ardiaei clashed with Rome by their attack on Italian traders (*Teuta). As a result of the First and Second Illyrian Wars (229/228; 219 BC), Rome established a protectorate there. Always prone to piracy, the I. brought upon themselves another Roman attack in 168 BC, following which the kingdom of Gentius was divided into three parts, a treatment similar to that administered to Macedonia in 167 BC. I. was Caesar's second province during his Gallic Wars. In the 30s BC Octavian operated against several Illyrian tribes but it was only by the campaigns of Tiberius from 13 BC on that Roman control reached the Danube. An imperial province of I. was established, but after the great revolt of AD 6 it was divided into two provinces later known as *Pannonia and *Dalmatia. See *Dalmatia, *Pannonia, *Dardani.

Hammond, *Epirus*; J. J. Wilkes, *Dalmatia,* 1969.

IMAGINES Masks made of wax representing those who held curule offices at Rome. They were kept by their families in the *Atrium with short inscriptions describing their careers and deeds. These descriptions were often falsified and led to distortion of Roman history. I. were worshipped, and were carried in funeral processions of members of families who held curule offices.

IMPERATOR Originally the term designated a Roman magistrate, holder of *Imperium. It came to denote par-

ticularly a general who was acclaimed I. by his soldiers after a victory, an act which was sometimes confirmed by the Senate. This was a honorific title added to the name and its use is not known before the 2nd century BC. Later, generals tended to emphasize the number of times they were acclaimed with the title. Caesar always added the title to his name and this usage was followed by the Roman emperors. Under the Empire it was the emperor who received the credit for the victories of his legates; hence he held the triumph and in writing down his name the number of the acclamations to date was affixed to the title. In addition, emperors from Augustus on used I. as a praenomen and thus the formula ran: Imp. Caesar . . . Vespasianus . . . Imp. III. Since senatorial governors ceased to command armies they practically had no occasions to be acclaimed I. The last case was that of Junius Blaesus governor of Africa (AD 22), as is noted by Tacitus (*Ann.* 3.74).

D. McFayden, *The History of the Title Imperator under the Roman Empire,* 1920;
R. Combes, *Imperator,* 1966.

IMPERIUM The supreme and unlimited power of the Roman kings, which was given to the highest magistrates of the Roman Republic after the expulsion of the kings. It gave the right to command in war, to administer justice (including the death penalty), to initiate legislation and pass motions in the *Comitia and the Senate, and to do everything which the holder of I. deemed good for the state. The I. was held by the consuls, dictators, consular tribunes (445—367 BC), praetors, *magistri equitum* (masters of the horse), pro-magistrates (first case in 327 BC) and rarely (only from the Second Punic War) by *privati.* The principle of *par potestas et ad tempus* ("equal power limited in time") was applied to reduce the dangers of such extensive power, that is, the two consuls that held it could each veto the actions of the other and served for one year. Holders of I. had *fasces, twelve in the case of consuls, whose powers were higher than those of praetors. The adoption of the principle of *provocatio* by the *leges Valeriae* (at the latest by 300 BC) abolished the right to inflict the death penalty without a trial in the *Comitia.* Even citizens serving in the army were later granted the *ius provocationis.* A special type of I. was the *I. maius* which is known from the late Republic; holders of such I. were given the right to interfere in the *provinciae* of other magistrates with I. and to override their actions. Augustus was given *I. maius* against senatorial governors in 23 BC. *Agrippa and Tiberius were also given such an I., each when he was considered as a likely successor. The bestowal of the I. was confirmed by the *Comitia curiata,* a mere formality.

Jolowicz, *Roman Law*[3] (s.v.).

INDICTIO Purchase of supplies irregularly requisitioned under the Roman Empire as from the early 2nd century AD. *Diocletian made it a regular tax in AD 287. A certain amount of supplies was levied from each of the new fiscal units (*caput,* human, *iugum,* unit of hand) and that amount was assessed every five years; from 312 every 15 years.

Jones, *Lat.Rom.Emp.* (s.v.).

INSTITUTIONES Elementary, systematical handbooks such as the book of rhetoric of *Quintilian (*institutio oratoria*) but mainly of Roman law. Many jurists wrote such works but the only extant ones are those of *Gaius and that prepared by Tribonianus and his collaborators at the direction of *Justinian.

INSUBRES Powerful Gallic tribe that came to inhabit the northwestern part of the Po valley in the late 5th century BC. Their main city was Mediolanum (modern Milan). In the 220s BC, Rome sought to advance her control over their territory and in 222 *Marcellus (1) defeated them at Clastidium, winning the *spolia opima* by killing their king. They supported Hannibal in the Second Punic War and were defeated and pacified in the years following the war. See *Gallia Cisalpina.

INTERCESSIO The right of a Roman magistrate to veto proceedings of a colleague with the same power or of a lower magistrate. Tribunes of the Plebs, however, came to have the right not only among themselves but against all other magistrates. It was a gradual process and by the end of the 4th century BC they could use it even against dictators who otherwise were immune from the I. as having no equal colleagues.
Jolowicz, *Roman Law*[3] (s.v.).

INTERREX Traditionally the man chosen by the Senate after the death of a king to hold authority and conduct the proceedings for the election, or acclamation, of a new king. Under the Republic it was an official appointed to conduct the election of new consuls when the serving consuls died or abdicated. Only patrician senators were appointed, each for five days, and only the second appointed was allowed to hold the election. In 53 BC *interreges* were appointed in succession for several months as they could not perform their task because of obstructions.
Jolowicz, *Roman Law*[3] (s.v.).

IO Greek mythological heroine, priestess of Hera at Argos, daughter of the river god Inachus. Zeus loved her and changed her into a heifer, which did not escape the suspicious Hera who sent *Argos (2) to watch her. After Argos was killed by Hermes, I. was pursued by a gadfly sent by Hera and wandered from Greece to Egypt where Zeus restored her human shape. Epaphus, her son by Zeus, was the ancestor of *Danaus. After her death she became a constellation. In Aeschylus' *Prometheus* she meets Prometheus in her wanderings and tells him her story. Later she was identified with the Egyptian goddess Isis. Originally she may have been a moon-goddess represented with cow-horns.

IOLAUS Greek mythological hero, nephew, companion and charioteer of Heracles. He helped him to kill the *Hydra. In one version he killed or captured *Eurystheus after Heracles' death. He was mainly worshipped at Thebes, where he was honoured by a festival, but also at Athens and elsewhere. In many places his cult was associated with that of Heracles.

IOLE Daughter of Eurytus, king of Oechalia. Eurytus was defeated in an archery competition by Heracles and killed with his sons after his refusal to surrender I. as had been agreed. I. tried to commit suicide by leaping from the city wall but was saved. In trying to regain Heracles' love, *Deianira caused his death and at his wish his son Hyllus married I. The myth was variously told by many poets, among them Sophocles (*Trachiniae*), and details of it appear in vase-paintings.

ION (1) Greek poet of the 5th century BC, native of Chios, mainly active at Athens, where he had close ties with *Cimon. He wrote tragedies, dithyrambs, epigrams, elegiac poems, the history of the foundation of Chios, among other works. He once won the first prize in the *Dionysia. Though he was extolled by the Alexandrian critics and commentaries were written on his plays, only meagre fragments are

extant. His meeting with Sophocles at Chios is recorded by Athenaeus (13.605 c).
F. Jacoby, *ClQ*, 1947, 1ff.

ION (2), IONIA, IONIANS Ion son of Xuthus (or Apollo) and *Creusa (1), the eponymous ancestor of the Ionians, is first mentioned by Hesiod. He served Apollo at *Delphi and, after the death of his grandfather *Erechtheus, he became the king of Athens. The four Ionian tribes were named after his sons: Aigikoreis, Argadeis, Hopletes, and Geleontes. Pressed hard by the invading *Dorians, the Ionians of the Greek mainland emigrated to the Aegean islands and to the western coast of Asia Minor, where the region colonized by them was called Ionia, bordering on *Aeolis in the north and *Caria in the south. Their main cities and islands were *Miletus, *Ephesus, *Smyrna, *Phocaea, *Chios, and *Samos. Later Athens claimed to be the mother-city of all these foundations, a claim only partly justified as was recognized long ago by Herodotus (1.46–7). The Ionians came to use a distinct dialect of Greek, attested at Ionia, the *Cyclades, *Euboea and Attica. They had a common festival at *Delos. Ethnically they consisted of mixed elements as the immigrants intermarried with the local population especially in Caria. The rise of Greek civilization was mainly due to them. It was in Ionia that science and philosophy began; Greek colonization (*Apoikia) in the Archaic period was largely their work; the early great poets were Ionians (*Homer, *Archilochus, etc.) and it was in Athens that the early achievements in art, literature and philosophy were realized. For the peoples of the East, Ionians was the generic term of the Greeks (*Yawani*). Politically however, Ionia was dominated successively by *Croesus, Persia, and by Athens in the 5th century. Their preoccupation with arts and literature led to exaggerated contrast between the womanly Ionians and the virile Dorians.
J. M. Cook, *The Greeks in Ionia and the East*, 1962.

IPHICRATES Prominent Athenian general and mercenary soldier in the first half of the 4th century BC. In 393 he was given command in the Corinthian War against Sparta and made inroads into the Peloponnesus. In 390 he cut a Spartan unit to pieces at Corinth. After the conclusion of the Peace of *Antalcides in 386 he became a mercenary captain. He entered service with the Thracian King Cotys and married his daughter. Employed by the Persians he defeated the rebellious Egyptian kings in the 370s and was back at Athens in 373. He failed to help the Spartans against *Epaminondas in 369 or to regain *Amphipolis, and returned to the service of Cotys in 360. He was again Athenian commander from 357 on in the war against the allies and successfully defended himself against a charge of treason by *Chares. He died in 353. I. showed great skill in ambushes and hit-and-run tactics, in which his *peltasts won for the first time victories over the fully armoured *hoplites.
H. W. Parke, *Greek Mercenary Soldiers*, 1933.

IPHIGENIA Greek mythological heroine, daughter of *Agamemnon and *Clytemnestra. To appease Artemis who prevented the Greek fleet from sailing from *Aulis to Troy, the soothsayer *Calchas said she should be sacrificed to the goddess. Agamemnon sent for his daughter under the pretext that he wanted her to be married to Achilles. In one version, followed by *Aeschylus in his *Agamemnon*, she was sacrificed, but in a version used apparently by Euripides, she was substituted at the last moment by a hind and taken by Artemis to be her priestess at Tauris in the Crimea. As such she had to con-

Relief of Isis and her child Horus (= Harpocrates)

duct the sacrifice of all strangers to the goddess. Her brother *Orestes with his friend Pylades arrived there to fetch the image of the goddess and she recognized him; they all made good their escape with the image. She then became Artemis' priestess at Brauron in Attica, where later the goddess was worshipped with the title Tauropolos. Here I.'s grave was shown and the myth was recalled in the custom to feign a sacrifice by slightly cutting a man's throat. She was worshipped elsewhere too, and there were variants to the myth in one of which she became immortal and married Achilles. She does not appear in Homer whose Iphianassa (*Il.* 9.144f.) was said to be identical with I. Originally I. probably had been a by-form of the pre-Hellenic Great Goddess identified with Artemis.

Kerényi, *Heroes*, 331 ff.

IPSUS Location in Phrygia, known for the defeat and death of *Antigonus I by *Lysimachus and *Seleucus I in a great battle in 301 BC; this sealed the division of the empire of Alexander the Great. The exact location of the place is not known.

IRIS Greek goddess of the rainbow, messenger of the gods, daughter of the Titan Thaumas and the Oceanid Electra (Hesiod, *Theog.* 266ff.). In Homer she usually serves Zeus, but later poets assign her especially to Hera. The rainbow as connecting sky and earth perhaps looked like a messenger. There is little mythology about her and she had no cult. She appears in art from the 6th century BC, in vase-paintings and sculpture (the Parthenon frieze), winged or wearing winged boots.

ISAEUS Attic orator and rhetorician (*c.* 420–350 BC), native of Chalcis in Euboea, pupil of *Isocrates and teacher of *Demosthenes. Little is known or certain about his life. He was a professional speech-writer (*logographos*) and never delivered his speeches himself. Twelve of his speeches are extant, all pleas in cases of inheritance. They date from 390 BC (or 377) to 353. In antiquity fifty genuine speeches of his were known. It is apparent that he was expert on the Athenian law of inheritance, and the extant speeches are the main source for this subject. He expounds his cases with lucidity and apparent objectivity, with simple and factual language.

E. S. Forster, (Loeb) 1957 (1927); W. Wyse (commentary) 1904; Kennedy, *Persuasion*.

ISCHIA Island in the Bay of Naples otherwise known as Pithecusae or Aenaria. Settlers from *Chalcis and Eretria established there the first Greek settlement in Italy in the first part of the 8th century BC. It was a centre of trade between the East, Greece and various parts of Italy, especially Etruria. It fell under Roman control in 326 BC.

Dunbabin, *Western Greeks* (s.v.).

ISIDORUS Bishop of Seville (AD 601–36). Of his various

works the most important for the preservation of the classical tradition was the *Etymologiae* or *Origines*, which he did not complete. In this encyclopaedic work, which was divided into twenty books after his death, he tried to present information for educational purposes on a wide variety of subjects. By explaining words he treats the liberal arts, medicine, geography, law, philosophy, theology, natural history, war, minerals, food, etc.

Text: W.L. Lindsay, (*Etymologiae*), 1911.

ISIS The cult of this Egyptian goddess, wife of Osiris and mother of Horus, began to spread in the Hellenistic world from the 4th century BC. Ruler of heaven, the world, and nether world (with Osiris), I. came to be worshipped all over the Mediterranean in later times. Capable of doing miracles, she would give protection against illnesses, especially bites of scorpions and snakes. Originally a private cult performed by Egyptian priests, it soon became public in many Greek cities with official priests. Her cult, like that of other Egyptian deities, was Hellenized. The language used was Greek and the temples and statues were usually not different from the Greek. The main characteristics of the cult included initiatory ceremonies, processions, the use of the sacred water of the Nile, and music. These elaborate mysteries would arouse deep religious emotions in the participants. She has been identified with *Demeter by Herodotus but later with Aphrodite, and in Egypt with Ptolemaic queens. Other Egyptian gods — notably *Sarapis — were worshipped in her numerous temples. Her best preserved temple is at Pompeii. *Apuleius gives a detailed account of the mysteries of her cult, the popularity of which is attested by the appearance of symbols in numerous finds of jewellery objects and the tomb reliefs.

F. Cymont, *Oriental Religions* (s.v.);
R. E. Witt, *Isis in the Graeco-Roman World*, 1971.

ISMENE Local mythological heroine of Thebes where her name was preserved in many places, including an oracle of Apollo Ismeneios. She was later said to be the daughter of *Oedipus and Jocasta, and sister of *Antigone, and her timid character as described by Sophocles in his *Antigone* became the conventional one. Her killing by *Tydeus is depicted in a vase-painting of the 6th century BC.

ISOCRATES Athenian orator, rhetorician and publicist, born in 436 BC to a wealthy family which was ruined in the Peloponnesian War. He studied under *Gorgias and *Theramenes, and *Protagoras, too, is said to have been his teacher. To earn a living he became a professional speech-writer in the years following the Peloponnesian War. Handicapped by a weak voice, he could not make an effective appearance in public, and in *c.* 393 BC established a school of rhetoric. He won much success and fame all over the Greek world. Among his pupils were politicians, orators and scholars such as *Hyperides, *Timotheus, *Lycurgus (2), *Isaeus, *Androtion, *Ephorus, and *Theophrastus. He communicated with the leading rulers of his age including *Agesilaus and *Archidamus III of Sparta, *Evagoras of Cyprus, *Jason (2) of Pherae and *Philip II. In his writings he reacted to contemporary political events. He ended his life in 338 BC by starvation at the age of ninety eight.

In a series of public addresses and letters that spanned more than forty years, I. dealt with the political, economic and social problems of Greece. The Greeks were ruining themselves by civil wars — within and between cities. There was an ever increasing number of impover-

ished Greeks living the lives of exiles who always constituted a menace to peace and security. The solution he suggested was a kind of national Hellenic crusade against Persia, the traditional enemy, which would remove the vagabonds, unite the Greeks and provide new territory for settlement. The earliest speech in which he expounded his view on the subject, *Panegyricus* (at Olympia in 380), presents Athens as the Greek state most fit to lead the crusade. Subsequently he turned his eyes to other rulers and finally to Philip II. His programme, with an important account of conditions in Greece, is explained in the *Philippus*, addressed to the Macedonian king. His last great treatise, the *Panathenaicus* was completed in 339. It is hard to say to what extent his ideas influenced his contemporaries.

Twenty-one of L.'s speeches are extant as well as nine letters. Of these, six speeches belonged to the period he worked as a professional speech-writer. The *Helen* (390) and the *Busiris* (391) are exercises in which he praises two mythological figures who were traditionally censured. Other rhetorical exercises include *To Nicocles*, *Nicocles* and *Evagoras*, which deal with the question of the ideal ruler. In the *Plataicus* (373), *Archidamus* (366), *Areopagiticus* (355), and *De Pace* (355), he expresses his views on comtemporary politics in Athens and Greece. The *Antidosis* (353) was composed after his failure to defend himself in court from service as trierarch (*Trierarchy). In this autobiographical treatise he expounds his educational theory and practice.

I. was a master of prose writing. Without distorting the usual order of words, he manages to avoid hiatus or clash of dissonant consonants. There is rhythm and music in this balanced prose, though occasionally the longer speeches are too complicated.

G. B. Norlin – L. Van Hook (Loeb), 1928–1945;
Kennedy, *Persuasion*, 174 ff.

Ismene killed by Tydeus. An amphora-painting of the mid-6th century BC

Mountainous landscape in Italy (Sabinum)

ISOPOLITEIA This term, which means "equal citizenship", denoted the grant of the citizenship of one state to citizens of another state, usually made on reciprocal basis. I. appears from the 4th century BC on, occasionally attested by inscriptional evidence. The two states kept their independence, and the grant became effective only when a citizen of a city with the right came to live in the city that gave it.
Larsen, *Gr.Fed.St.*, 262 ff.

ISTHMIAN GAMES Athletic games held at the Isthmus of Corinth for Poseidon. Traditionally founded by the Corinthian king, Sisyphus, in honour of the sea-god Melicertes Palaemon, they became pan-Hellenic in 581 BC (or 570). The games were held every two years; the winners were given a crown of wild celery. They attracted many spectators, especially from Athens, where it was told that they were founded by *Theseus after the killing of the robber Sinis. It was at the games of 196 BC that * Flamininus proclaimed the "freedom" of Greece.

ITALICA (modern Santiponce, near Seville) Spanish town founded in 206 BC by *Scipio Africanus who set-

tled veterans of his army there. By the end of the Republic it was a *municipium* and under Hadrian received the status of *colonia*. A prosperous town, it was a centre for oil export. It was the native town of the emperors Trajan, Hadrian and Theodosius I.

ITALY *Italia* as a geographical term was first used by Greek writers; it was derived from *Vitelia* which meant "calf-land". By the middle of the 5th century BC it denoted the most southern part of the peninsula, close to the Straits of Messina (modern Calabria); gradually it extended to the north. By the late 4th century it included south I. up to Campania; in the 3rd century all the peninsula south of the Po and by the middle of the 2nd century the whole country south of the Alps. I. extends over some 214,000 sq km; its greatest length is 1,100 km and its breadth 220 km. Hills and mountains cover about 70% of the country. Plains are to be found in the Po valley, which was politically incorporated only in 43 BC, and along the coasts, the larger on the western side, Etruria, Latium, and Campania, and only Apulia on the eastern coast. The Apennine mountains are dissected by rivers that usually flow eastward or westward. As a result the Po valley forms a close unit, encircled as it is by mountains on three sides. It is well watered and fertile. In other parts of the country it rains only in winter, and the summer is dry. The mouths of the rivers tend to be silted by the torrential rains. Ancient authors exaggerated the good soil and climate of I. (Varr. *RR.* 1.2; Verg. *Gerog.* 2.136ff.). It was mainly the Po valley and Campania that were exceptionally fertile. Excepting some parts of Etruria, Latium, and a few valleys in the mountains, the country was poor. Besides, there was need of extensive drainage, dykes, canalization and afforestation before the country could be cultivated. Some poor regions suffered from overgrazing in later times and became desolate (wars were another factor). The only minerals that I. had were copper in north Etruria, iron in Elbe and gold in Piedmont.

Traces of human settlement in palaeolithic times were found in several places in the Apennines, Liguria and even near Rome. Copper began to be used in the second half of the 3rd millenium BC and the Bronze Age dates from about the 18th century BC. After the *Terramara settlements, limited to the Po valley (probably from the 16th century), came the *Villanovans. Ceramic finds of what is called Apennine Culture were found all over the Apennines south of the Po valley. The historical peoples of I. spoke Indo-European languages, but there are also traces of a different, and earlier language family. It is commonly agreed that the Indo-European speaking peoples came to I. in the 2nd millenium BC; how they came, from central Europe across the Alps or from the Adriatic, is disputed. Nor is it clear whether the above mentioned cultures were the results of mass migrations only or of the infiltration of Indo-European elements and their mixture with the former local population.

At the dawn of historical times, I. was inhabited by various peoples who spoke different dialects and languages. The old tribes of south I. are called in literary sources Itali, Oenotri, *Brutii, or Ausones. The eastern coast was inhabited by Illyrian tribes — Dauni and Messapii (who came quite early under Greek influence), Picentes and possibly the Veneti. The Umbro-Sabelli occupied the central parts of the country. The Latini and the Falisci (*Falerii) lived in Latium, the area north of which was controlled by the Etruscans. The Ligurians lived in the northwestern part of the peninsula from the Arno to the Alps. Greeks settled on the coasts of south I. and Campania. The Gauls came in the late 5th century. It was left to *Rome to bring about the political unification of all these peoples, which was accomplished by the 2nd century BC.

Cary, *Geographic Background,* 103 ff;
J. Whatmough, *The Foundations of Roman Italy,* 1937; J. Heurgon, *Rome et la mediteranée occidentale,* 1969 (Eng.tr.1974).

ITHACA Small, mountainous island in the Ionian Sea, the famous kingdom of Odysseus. Archaeological finds, mainly vases, attest to its occupation from Mycenacan times on as well as to its importance for the trade with the West in the early Archaic period.

ITHOME Salient mountain in *Messenia (802 m) famous as the stronghold of the resistance of the Messenians against the Spartans. Twice they withdrew here: in the First Messenian War (*c.* 735–715 BC) and in the Third Messenian War (464–456 BC) and each time they had to capitulate after a long siege. The city of *Messena was founded by *Epaminondas on the western

slopes (369 BC). At the summit there was a temple of Zeus for which *Agelades made a statue.
G. L. Huxley, *Early Sparta* (1962), 34 ff.

IUDEX Judge, especially in Roman civil law procedure. Civil cases were held in the first stage (called *in iure*) before a Roman magistrate (normally praetor) and in the second stage (*apud iudicem*) the case was handed over to a private person, the I. He had to give a verdict according to the evidence and the formula of the case as was directed by the magistrate. There was a list of judges (*album iudicum*), senators and, later, *Equites as well. The defendant had the right to reject the names suggested by the plaintiff. The I. could consult advisors, but he alone gave the verdict. He might pronounce the case as undecided if he could not arrive at a decision. His verdict was final but it was not his duty to enforce its execution.
Jolowicz, *Roman Law*[3] (s.v.).

IUDICIA POPULI Trials held by the Roman people, that is, before the *Comitia. All capital cases had to be tried before the *Comitia centuriata* by the right of the Roman citizen to *Provocatio. For political and other reasons ex-magistrates could be brought to trial before the people not only on capital charges; and there is a view that only political cases, not ordinary crimes, were brought before the people. Such cases were often brought by plebeian tribunes. In fact the trial was conducted as a *Contio in which the prosecuting magistrate conducted the investigation (*anquisitio*) and then the assembly voted on his motion according to what everyone concluded from the evidence.
Jolowicz, *Roman Law*[3] (s.v.); A. H. M. Jones, *The Criminal Courts of the Roman Republic,* 1972.

IURIDICUS Circuit judge appointed by Roman emperors from the time of Marcus Aurelius to Diocletian. Of praetorian rank, the I. tried civil cases, each one in his region.

IUS CIVILE The term was used in two main senses: that section of Roman law that concerned Roman citizens only (likewise the particular law of any state); and that part of the Roman law which was based on legislation and its interpretation in contrast to what magistrates introduced by their right of issuing edicts, the *Ius Honorarium* (*Edictum).
Jolowicz, *Roman Law*[3] (s.v.).

IUS GENTIUM The term was used in two main senses: 1) That section of Roman law which concerned citizens and non-citizens alike. It was largely associated with the activity of the *praetor peregrinus* who tried cases between foreigners or between foreigners and citizens. The term also came to be used in cases involving Roman citizens only and included institutions of the *ius civile.* 2) That part of the law which was common to all states alike by natural reason. Otherwise it was called *ius naturale.*
Jolowicz, *Roman Law*[3] (s.v.).

IUS ITALICUM Under the Roman Empire this was the right to enjoy the legal and fiscal privileges of Italy in the provinces, i.e., exemption from *tributum capitis* and *tributum soli* and the right to own land according to Roman law. For fiscal and other reasons, it was not given to all colonies or to provincial cities that received the status of *colonia.*
A. N. Sherwin-White, *The Roman Citizenship*[2], 1974 (s.v.).

IUS LATII The Latin rights which originated from the special relations of the *Latins with Rome in the early Republic. They included the right of *Conubium and

Commercium as well as the right to migrate to Rome and become a Roman citizen by settling there permanently. The right of migration was limited in the 2nd century BC because of the complaints of the Latin allies that they were losing their citizens. By the end of the century, magistrates in Latin cities automatically became Roman citizens. The I. was conferred on the communities of Transpadene Gaul in 89 BC, on Sicily by Caesar, and on many other provincial communities under the Empire.

Individuals and communities who received it, later obtained the full Roman citizenship.

A. N. Sherwin-White, *The Roman Citizenship*[2], 1974 (s.v.).

IXION Greek mythological figure, the first to kill a kinsman. Though purified by Zeus, he tried to rape Hera, but the goddess substituted another form for herself on which he fathered the *Centaurs. As a punishment he was tied to a revolving wheel (Pindar, *Pyth.* 2).

J

JANICULUM Long hill stretching from north to south on the right bank of the Tiber at Rome. The name indicates an association with *Janus. The cult of the old Roman deities here (*Furrina) was ousted by that of Oriental gods under the Empire. Here was shown the grave of *Numa, and it was on the J. that Gaius Gracchus found his death. *Augustus included the J. in his reorganization of Rome into 14 regions, and later it was within the wall of *Aurelianus.

JANUS A gate or barbicon was *ianus*, and J. was the deity of such a public monument. Especially known is his temple on the north side of the Forum Romanum; it had double gates and was called *Ianus geminus*. It was thought important that the army should pass through such a monument in the right way when going out to war. From his association with gates, through the passing of which every action must start, he became a god of beginnings. But it was only in 153 BC that Januarius, J.'s month, became the first month of the year. The closing of his temple at the Forum symbolized the restoration of peace and its opening signified the beginning of war. It was closed once by King *Numa, the second time in 235 BC, and the third time by Augustus. Nero and Vespasian also closed it. A second temple of J., built by *Duilius at the Forum Holitorium, was restored by Augustus. A festival for J, the Agonium, was held on 9 January. By the late Republic he was considered a great god; finally, he was considered a sky-god. He was represented by a gate or a double-faced head which appeared on the first bronze coins of Rome.
L. A. Holland, *Janus and the Bridge,* 1961.

JASON (1) Greek mythological hero, son of Aeson, king of Thessalian Iolcus (excavations have shown that this city, on the Bay of Volo, was a Mycenaean centre). He was educated by *Chiron after his uncle Pelias usurped the throne. When he grew up, he returned to claim the kingship. As he wore only only one sandal, having lost the other when crossing a torrent, Pelias knew by an oracle that he must beware of him and provoked him to fetch the Golden Fleece. This was the origin of the voyage of the *Argonauts. He succeeded in accomplishing his task with the help of *Medea, who fled with him from Colchis. She tricked Pelias' daughter into killing her father. But later J. deserted her and married the daughter of *Creon (2). Medea took revenge by killing her rival as well as her

children from J. He found his death when part of his ship, the Argo, fell on him.

JASON (2) Tyrant of the important Thessalian city Pherae (*c.* 385–370 BC), son or son-in-law of Lycophron, the first tyrant there. Able and vigorous, he organized a strong army, removed his rivals, notably Polydamus of Pharsalus, and united the whole of Thessaly under his leadership as Tagos (374 BC). He maintained good relations with Macedonia, Thebes and Athens, and became the dominating power in northern Greece at the time. He intervened to conclude an armistice between the Thebans and the Spartans after the battle of *Leuctra (371). The following year he mobilized the Thessalian army but was murdered before making clear his intentions. Thessaly was then again torn apart by internal feuds.
H. D. Westlake, *Thessaly in the Fourth Century,* 1935.

JAVOLENUS PRISCUS, Gaius Octavius Roman senator and prominent jurist. After service in Dalmatia, Africa and Britannia, he was *consul suffectus* in AD 86, and subsequently governed Upper Germany, Syria and Africa. He was a member of the *Consilium Principis of Trajan and died after AD 120. His important juristic work was the 14 books of *Epistulae,* occasionally cited in the *Digesta* of Justinian. Intelligent and critical in his epitomes of former jurists and in expressing his own views, he carefully avoided dogmatism.

JEROME, Sophronius Eusebius Hieronymus Prominent Christian Latin scholar (*c.* AD 348–420). He was born in Strido in Dalmatia and studied under the famous scholar *Donatus in Rome. After studies at Trèves, he became interested in an ascetic life, and went on a pilgrimage to Jerusalem in 373. He spent three years in the desert where he learnt Greek and Hebrew. He became a priest in Antioch in 379, and from 382 to 385 was in Rome. Here he revised the Latin text of the Bible at the invitation of Pope Damasus. Back in the East in 386, he spent the rest of his life in a monastery founded at Bethlehem by a rich follower, Paula. An excellent Latinist, he produced good translations of the Bible and the Gospels. His Latin Bible became the accepted version and was known as the Vulgata in the Middle Ages. Important also is his *Chronica,* a free Latin adaptation of the chronological account of world history by *Eusebius, expanded to AD 378. His *Of Illustrious Men* included brief accounts of Christian writers who wrote on the Scriptures. He translated several other works and engaged in polemical writing. His letters give evidence of his attractive personality and his scholarly work.

R. Helm (ed.), *Chronica*, 1913.

JERUSALEM Old city in Palestine, first settled in the early 3rd millenium BC, and first mentioned in contemporary documents in the middle of the 2nd millenium. It became the capital of the kingdom of David and the main religious centre of the Jews. Destroyed by Nebuchadnezzar (586 BC), it was resettled by the Jews under *Cyrus I (538). The Second Temple was dedicated in 516 BC, and the walls were repaired in the mid-5th century. Alexander the Great allegedly visited it. As a result of the wars of the *Diadochi, it came under Ptolemaic rule and subsequently (198 BC) it came under Seleucid rule. With the support of Hellenized Jews, *Antiochus IV attempted to establish a Greek city here ("Antioch in Jerusalem"). A gymnasium was set up near the Temple, which was soon dedicated to the Olympian Zeus (167). A fortress, the Acra, was built to secure Seleucid domination. Soon, persecutions led to the Maccabean revolt and in 164 the Temple was rededicated to Jahweh. Although the Acra was only captured by Simon in 142 BC, J. had already become the capital of the Hasmonaean High Priest in 152. The Hasmonaeans fortified the city which grew in size with the growth of their power. Pompey captured J. in 63, and it was again taken by the Romans in 37 BC. Herod the Great carried out extensive building operations which included a new building of the Temple. The still standing "Wailing Wall" was one of the external walls of the Temple, other parts of which have recently been excavated. Other remains of Herodian buildings include the lower course of the tower of Phasael, popularly known as the Tower of David, and parts of the fortress of Antonia. J. was captured and destroyed by *Titus in AD 70. On its ruins was built the camp of a Roman legion (X Fretensis). After the suppression of the revolt of *Bar-Cochba, Hadrian's plan to establish the *colonia Aelia Capitolina* was carried out. Some features of the Roman city can still be recognized in the present Old City. Numerous Christian churches, the first of which was the Church of the Holy Sepulchre (AD 335), were built from the time of Constantine the Great on. The city was captured by the Persians in 614, recaptured in 627 and taken by the Moslems in 638.

JEWS The J. were dispersed in many parts of the Greek-Roman world. Their main centres were in Judaea, Mesopotamia and Egypt. The first settlement of J. in Egypt dates from the 6th century BC (excepting of course that of old Biblical times). Here the J. well served the Persians and subsequently the Ptolemaic kings, under whom a large Jewish population grew, especially in Alexandria. They engaged in all kinds of economic activity and even in military service. From the above-mentioned centres, J. migrated to Cyrenaica, Cyprus, and Asia Minor in the Hellenistic period, and later were to be found in Italy and the western provinces of the Roman Empire.

The attitude of the J. to Greek civilization was ambivalent. Greek became the spoken language wherever J. lived with Greeks and even in Italy. The translation of the books of the Bible and other scriptures allegedly dates from the 3rd century BC (Septuagint). There were J. who became aware of the cultural achievements of the Greeks, and tried to show that those of the J. were not inferior. There developed a Jewish-Greek literature which was not only written in Greek but also used Greek literary

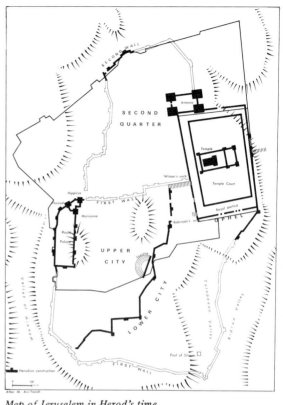

Map of Jerusalem in Herod's time

forms, notably the epic and drama, to deal with Jewish themes. The historical writings of *Josephus show the influence of Greek historiography and the philosophy of *Philon owes much to Greek philosophers. In Judaea, it was no less the Hellenized J. than *Antiochus IV who sought to turn Jerusalem into a Greek city. However, despite the Hellenistic tendencies of their upper classes, and the influence resulting from the communications of daily life, the J. kept to their religious beliefs and practices and maintained their autonomous institutions wherever they went. Indeed, within rabbinic circles there was always strong opposition to Greek learning.

Some Greeks were ready to recognize the cultural achievements of the J. But the first anti-Semitism developed from the encounter between the Greeks and the J. Matters became complicated under the Roman Empire. In Palestine, there was frequent friction between the Roman governors and the J. which culminated in the Great Revolt of AD 66. In the same year, the J. of Caesarea were massacred by the Greeks there. Generally, the J. enjoyed religious liberty under the Roman Empire, but proselytizing was forbidden and led to severe punishments. However, under *Trajan and *Hadrian the J. suffered greatly. When long-standing enmity flared up in 115, a devastating war spread between the J. and the Greeks in Cyrenaica, Egypt and Cyprus. Enormous atrocities were perpetrated and it was only with difficulty that Rome restored order after three years of fighting.

The plan of Hadrian to establish a colony in Jerusalem and the ban on circumcision led to the revolt of *Bar-Cochba. The ban was revoked a few years later by Antoninus Pius and Jews did not suffer any further discrimination until the triumph of Christianity. See *Judaea.

S. W. Baron, *A Social and Religious History of the Jews*, 1952; M. Stern, *Greek and Latin Authors on Jews and Judaism*, Vol. 1. 1974; V. A. Tcherikover, *Hellenistic Civilization and the Jews*, 1959.

JORDANES Gothic historian of the 6th century AD. His history of the Goths, *Getica*, is an abridged version of *Cassiodorus' work on the same subject. He also wrote a chronological outline of Roman history, *Romana*. Both works were completed by AD 551.

Th. Mommsen (ed.), *Monumenta Germaniae Historica*, VI, 1. 1882; Ch. Mierow, *Getica* (Eng. tr.) 1915.

JOSEPHUS, Flavius Jewish historian, born AD 37/8. Of a priestly family, he became one of the leaders in the Jewish revolt in 66, though he opposed the extreme zealots. Appointed to the command of the Galilee, he was besieged in Jotapata and captured by Vespasian in 67. He gained Vespasian's confidence, and saved himself by predicting that Vespasian would rule Rome. After the destruction of Jerusalem, J. settled in Rome and received Roman citizenship. He translated his seven books of the *Jewish War* into Greek from the original Aramaic. As a background, he gives an account of Jewish history from the Maccabaean revolt to the outbreak of the Great Revolt. His second work, *Jewish Antiquities*, appeared in AD 93/4. Its 20 books tell the history of the Jews from the very beginning to AD 66. In his autobiography, he defended his behaviour as commander of the Galilee. His *Contra Apionem* is a polemical work against Greek anti-Semites.

Text and translation: H. Thackeray, R. Marcus, L. H. Feldman (Loeb) 1926–1965.

JOVIAN Roman emperor (AD 363–4). Born in 331, he succeeded *Julian with whom he went on the expedition against Persia. He made a 30-year peace with the Persian king, Sapor II, giving up much territory. J. restored the privileges of the Christians and for a while adopted an anti-pagan policy. He died on his way back to Constantinople.

JUBA (1) King of Numidia who was hostile to Caesar and sided with Pompey in the Civil War. He defeated *Curio (2) in 49 BC and helped the Pompeians after *Pharsalus. After Caesar's victory at *Thapsus (46), J. fled but then died in a suicide pact.

JUBA (2) Son of *Juba (1), J. was educated in Italy and received Roman citizenship. On good terms with Augustus, he was made king of Mauretania in 25 BC. His first wife was Cleopatra Selene, daughter of Antony and Cleopatra. He made *Caesarea (1) Iol his capital and developed it. J. was a cultured man with scholarly inclinations and did much to Hellenize and Romanize his kingdom. None of his many historical and literary works is extant. He died c. AD 23.

JUDAEA The country of the tribe of Judah, later the southern part of the kingdom of David, from which the kingdom of Israel separated under the successors of King Solomon. It was destroyed by King Nebuchadnezzar of Babylonia in 586 BC, but *Cyrus I allowed the Jews to return to their homeland (539 BC), after which time *Yahud* became a sub-province (*medinta*) of the Persian empire, with Jerusalem as its main city. It was conquered by Alexander the Great and changed hands in the wars of the *Diadochi, but after *Ipsus (301) it was ruled by the Ptolemaic kings. The Seleucid Antiochus III conquered it

Reconstruction of the Herodian Temple

in the Fifth Syrian War (202–198 BC) and granted privileges to the Jews. The clash between the Hellenizers and the orthodox Jews under his son *Antiochus IV, who eventually forbade the practice of Judaism, led to the revolt of Mathatias the Hasmonaean and his sons. Under Judas Maccabaeus, the Jews regained Jerusalem and their religious liberty. After Judas' death, his brother Jonathan was acknowledged as governor of J. and High Priest by *Alexander Balas. He was succeeded by his brother Simon in 143, who shortly afterwards captured the Seleucid fortress (Acra) in Jerusalem.

The first expansionist steps were taken by Jonathan and Simon. John *Hyrcanus I (134–104) conquered Samaria and Idumaea; his sons Aristobulus (104–103), who took the royal title, and particularly Alexander Jannaeus (103–76), extended their rule to the whole Palestinian coast, the Galilee, Peraea and a large part of Transjordan. Wherever they went the Hasmonaeans enforced Judaism on the local population; this policy was especially successful with the Idumaeans and the Ituraeans. Alexander Jannaeus was succeeded by his wife Salome (76–69), who made peace with the Pharisees; they had been opposing the Hasmonaeans since John Hyrcanus. The quarrel between her sons led to Pompey's intervention and a Roman protectorate (63 BC). Hyrcanus II was made High Priest and was left with J., Samaria, Galilee and Peraea to rule as ethnarch; the royal title was abolished. Under him there rose to power the Idumaean *Antipater (2), whose son *Herod the Great eventually became king of J. After the deposition of his son Archelaus in AD 6, J., Samaria and Idumaea were ruled by Roman procurators, with a short interval in AD 41–4 when the province was given to *Agrippa I. Economic and social distress and maladministration by the procurators caused constant unrest and sporadic uprisings which culminated in the Great Revolt (AD 66–70). This was suppressed by Vespasian and Titus. Jerusalem was destroyed in 70 and *Masada, the last fortress, was captured in 72.

J. was now ruled by imperial legates who had under their command a legion (X Fretensis) in Jerusalem. Peaceful conditions fostered a quick recovery and Jabneh (Jamnia) became the new centre of Palestinian Jewry. The great revolt of the Jewish Diaspora (115–7) had but minor repercussions here but fifteen years later the revolt of *Bar-Cochba (132–5) began. This time J. was ruined and consequently the Galilee became the centre of Jewish life.

See *Jerusalem, *Jews (with bibliographies).

F. M. Abel, *Histoire de la Palestine*, 1952;
M. Avi-Yonah (ed.), *A History of the Holy Land*, 1969.

JUGURTHA The illegitimate grandson of *Masinissa, J. was adopted by the Numidian king, Micipsa, and succeeded to the throne with his two step-brothers in 118 BC. He procured the murder of one of them and the second escaped to Rome. After Roman intervention, J. received the western part of Numidia and Adherbal, his surviving brother, received the eastern part. J. renewed his aggression in 112, captured Cirta after a siege, and killed his brother – despite the appearance of Roman embassies. Because he killed Italian businessmen, a war was declared on him. But it was conducted inefficiently and several Roman commanders were convicted on charges of corruption in 109 by a special court. The consul of that year, *Metellus (2) Numidicus, won successes over J., but was not able to end the war. He was replaced by *Marius who was elected consul in 107 thanks to popular agitation and a promise to terminate the war quickly. But J., although defeated on the battlefield, continued to evade the Romans. And it was only in 105 that the Mauretanian King Bocchus betrayed him to Sulla. He was put to death a few days after Marius' triumph (1 January 104). The war is the subject of the *Bellum Iugurthinum* of *Sallust, who chose it as his subject because it revealed the internal evils from which Rome was suffering. Famous is J.'s saying on Rome: *o urbem venalem et mature perituram, si emptorem invenerit* – "that corrupt city, soon to perish when a purchaser will be found" (Sall. *B. J.* 35.10).

R. Syme, *Sallust*, 1964 (chs. 10–11).

JULIA The only daughter of Augustus (and Scribonia). Born in 39 BC, she married first *Marcellus (4) (25 BC) and after his death (21) *Agrippa (1) from whom she had several children, including *Agrippina (2) and *Agrippa (2) Postumus. After Agrippa's death, Augustus compelled Tiberius to marry her (11), an unhappy marriage for both of them. On revealing her amorous affairs, J. was banished by Augustus in 2 BC. She lived a miserable life until her death in AD 14.

JULIA DOMNA Daughter of Bassianus of Emessa in Syria, she married Septimus *Severus, the future emperor, in AD 185. She bore him his sons Caracalla and Geta. She accompanied her husband on his campaigns, and hence was called *mater castrorum*. After some estrangement from her husband due to the influence of the praetorian prefect Plautianus, she regained her dominant position after the prefect's downfall (205). She vainly tried to make peace between her sons after the death of her husband and was present at the murder of Geta. She committed suicide after the assassination of Caracalla (217). An intellectual woman, she gathered around her a literary circle which included Philostratus, whom she urged to write the life of *Apollonius of Tyana and who called her "the philosopher".

A. Birley, *Septimius Severus*, 1971 (s.v.).

JULIA MAESA Sister of *Julia Domna and mother of *Julia Sosaemias and *Julia Mamaea. She lived at the im-perial court in Rome and in AD 217 returned to Syria. Here she procured the support of the army to proclaim her grandson *Elagabalus as emperor (218). She then went back to Rome and had much influence on the government of the empire. She helped the accession to the throne of her other grandson, *Alexander Severus (222) and died in 226.

JULIA MAMAEA Younger daughter of *Julia Maesa and mother of *Alexander Severus. With her mother she secured the succession to the throne of her son in AD 222 and subsequently had much influence on the government of the empire. She was murdered with her son in 235.

JULIA SOSAEMIAS Daughter of *Julia Maesa and mother of *Elagabalus. With her mother, she secured the accesion to the throne of her son in AD 218. She was involved in the extravagance of her son, and was killed with him by the praetorians in 222.

JULIAN ("the Apostate"), Flavius Claudius Julianus Nephew of Constantine the Great, born in AD 331. He survived the massacre of his father and most of his kinsmen, engineered by *Constantius II, in 337. He was brought up in a secluded place in Cappadocia and became an admirer of Greek culture. Influenced by the pagan scholar *Libanius, J. secretly converted to paganism. Constantius II made him Caesar and governor of Gaul and Britain in 355. He defeated the Alamanni and the Franks, secured the Rhine frontier and improved financial conditions in his provinces. He thus became popular with the army and the civil population. In 360, he was acclaimed emperor by his soldiers, and a war with Constantius II was avoided by the latter's death in 361.

As sole emperor, J. revoked the privileges of the Christians and sought to revive paganism. He built temples, appointed priests and gave financial aid to foster the pagan cults. The Jews were allowed to rebuild their Temple in Jerusalem. He gave preference to pagans in the administration. His administrative measures aimed at cutting expenditure by abolishing offices. He chose Antioch as a base for his campaign against Persia and started the expedition on 5 March 363. Though he defeated a Persian army at Ctesiphon, he was later wounded and died on 27 June. His successor *Jovian soon restored the Christian privileges.

A good soldier, and an intelligent and industrious emperor, with a clear understanding of administrative and financial problems, J. was also a mystic and believed in the practices of the old religion. He took seriously the revival of paganism and would himself attend the performance of the rites. But the old religions were dying and his policy failed. His memory was denigrated by the Christian tradition. He was a prolific writer and some of his writings are extant – though not his *Against the Christians* – and include eighty letters, eight orations, hymns for gods and speeches. The *Misopogon* is a satiric work against the people of Antioch who insulted him, and the *Caesares* is a humorous description of Roman emperors who go into contest.

W. C. Wright (edition and tr. in Loeb) 1913–1923;
J. Bidez, *La Vie de l'empereur Julien*, 1930.

JULIANUS SALVIUS Roman senator and administrator, one of the greatest Roman jurists. He was born (*c.* AD 100) near *Hadrumetum and studied under *Javolenus. He began his public career under Hadrian, was a member of the *Consilium Principis, consul in 148 and subsequently governor of South Germany, Nearer Spain and Africa. His *cursus honorum* (course of offices) is

Julia Mamaea and Alexander Severus on sarcophagus

known from an inscription. He was prominent enough at the age of 30 to be appointed by Hadrian to revise the praetorian edict. Commentaries were written to his edition and many parts of it were included in the *Digesta* of Justinian. But his most important work was the *Digesta* in 90 books which treated the civil and praetorian law in a masterly way. This work, too, was excerpted by the editors of the *Digesta* of Justinian. J. was an erudite scholar, but it was thanks to his independent thinking, sharp insight and originality that he influenced the development of Roman law and was often cited. He died *c.* 170.

JUNO Ancient Italian goddess, mainly associated with the life of women and childbirth. Many of her titles, representing earlier minor deities which she had supplanted, refer to her functions in various stages in the life of women. With the rise of the state, she became the main goddess in many places (e.g. J. Curitis in *Falerii, J. Sospita in *Lanuvium, J. Regina in *Veii). In Rome she was one of the Capitoline triad (with Jupiter and Minerva), whose cult was established by the Etruscan kings. Her name was given to a month in the calendars of several Latin cities including Rome (hence June). As J. Caprotina she had a festival on 7 July, and on 1 March the festival of Matronalia was held in her honour. Her functions and position facilitated the identification with *Hera.
Platner-Ashby, *Top. Dict. Rome,* 288 ff.;
Latte, *R. Rel.* (s.v.).

JUPITER (Iuppiter) The old Italian sky-god, with whom various heavenly phenomena were associated. As J. Luce-

tius he was the god of the light of the sky, As J. Fulgur he was the god of lightning, as J. Tonans he was the god of thunder, and as J. Elicius he was the god of rain; there were other titles that represented his association with the weather (Caelestinus, Pluvialis, Serenus). Various sacred stones were used to take oaths in the name of J. Lapis. J.'s oldest state cult in Rome was as J. Feretrius, at whose shrine (on the Capitol) *spolia opima* were consecrated (*Cossus). The god of the Latin League was J. Latiaris, whose cult and festival were held on the Alban mountain. But the most famous was *Iuppiter Optimus Maximus,* the best and greatest J. whose cult was instituted on the *Capitol by the Etruscan kings of Rome. At his cult here he was worshipped with *Juno and *Minerva. As such he became the main Roman god and temples for J. in future Roman towns all over the empire were modelled on that of the Capitoline temple. Roman generals would climb on their knees to the Capitoline temple at the final stage of the triumphal procession (as Caesar did in 46 BC). J. was associated with the *Idus* of the month (*Chronology). The *Ludi Romani* and the *Ludi Plebeii* were celebrated in honour of J. The special priest of J. was the *Flamen Dialis. As sky-god and supreme god, J. was identified with various foreign gods, foremost of all Zeus.
Platner-Ashby, *Top. Dict. Rome,* 281 ff.;
Nash, *Pict. Dict. Rome,* 1, 518 ff.; Latte, *R. Rel.* (s.v.).

JURISPRUDENCE *Iurisprudentes* were experts on Roman law, also called *iurisconsulti* or *iurisperiti.* Knowledge of law was confined to the *Patricians and especially the

*Pontifices in early Rome. One of the demands of the Plebeians was the publication of the laws, which occurred when the *Decemvirs published the laws of the Twelve Tables. But the Roman legal system, like many other legal systems, made it always necessary to consult jurists for their advice. The jurists helped not only private citizens but also magistrates, mainly the praetors, and the *Iudex, before whom civil cases came. Until the last years of the Republic, most jurists (e.g. *Scaevola) were senators who were also lawyers. It is highly unlikely that the opinions of the jurists, which were expressed in their answers, *responsa*, were ever binding on the judges. But it was by this activity and especially by their literary work that the jurists contributed greatly to the development of Roman law. Indeed, Roman legal literature is the product of the jurists. See *Scaevola (3), *Labeo, *Sabinus, *Javolenus, *Julianus Salvius, *Gaius, *Papinianus, *Paulus, *Pomponius, *Ulpianus, *Herennius Modestinus.

F. Schulz, *History of Roman Legal Science,* 1946.

JUSTINIAN (Flavius Petrus Sabbatius Iustinianus) Emperor of the Eastern Roman Empire (AD 527–65), born *c*. 482. In 522, he married the actress Theodora, who much influenced and helped him. He ascended to the throne in 527 on the death of his uncle, Justin, and reformed the provincial administration of the empire, making financial improvements to cut expenditure, and carrying out extensive building operations, the most famous of which is S. Sophia. He had to conduct long, defensive wars against Persia in the East and against various peoples in the Balkans. In the West, his general Belisarius defeated the Vandals and recovered North Africa (533) and then conquered Italy from the Ostrogoths (535–40). After the successful uprising of the Ostrogoths, Belisarius renewed the campaign (546–9), and the final conquest was completed by the general Narses (550–4). A very religious man, J. intervened in the internal conflicts of the Christians and vigorously enforced the laws against heretics, Jews and pagans. He also closed the last Greek schools of philosophy, including the *Academy. Very important was the codification of Roman law carried out under his instructions by *Tribonianus. It consists of the *Codex Iustinianus* (a collection of imperial constitutions from Hadrian on in 12 books), *Digesta*, *Istitutiones*, and *Novellae* (new imperial constitutions). These works ended and summed up the development of Roman law, and were to influence the development of law in Europe. For this legal work some date the "end" of the ancient world at J.'s period.

Jones, *Lat. Rom. Emp.*

JUVENAL (Decimus Iunius Iuvenalis) One of the greatest Roman satirists. Details of his life in ancient biographies are contradictory and untrustworthy. A native of Aquinum, in central Italy, he was middle-aged *c*. AD 100; therefore he must have been born *c*. AD 60–5. He may have practised rhetoric. He was exiled from Rome by Domitian for writing a lampoon. This probably ruined him and caused his poverty, to which he refers in his poetry. *Martial is the only contemporary who mentions him (7.91,1). His circumstances were later improved, probably thanks to Hadrian. He died after AD 127, a year in which he was still writing.

The sixteen satires of J. are written in hexameter and arranged in five books (I 1–5, II 6, III 7–9, IV 10–12, V 13–16). The books appeared in this order, in the course of some 25 years (from after AD 100 to after 127). He states his case for writing satires in satire 1: the immortality and corruption of Roman society. But he declares that his attacks will be directed only on the dead for reasons of safety. Satires 2 and 9 are attacks against homosexuality; 3 – Rome, Megalopolis, full of vice and poverty, where honest men cannot make a living; 4 – a satiric account of the meeting of Domitian's council; 5 – a client is abused at a dinner given by his patron; 6 – a vivid invective against women and marriage; 7 – the miserable conditions of intellectuals and literary people; 8 – nobility without virtue is to be reproved; 9 – a male prostitute complains; 10 – men do not know the real things to be wished for (hence this satire was called by Johnson *The Vanity of Human Wishes*); 11 – the simple dinner is compared with the fashionable extravagance; 12 – friendship is discussed on the occasion of the survival of a friend at sea; 13 – consolation to a friend, some of whose money was embezzled; 14 – the evil of avarice if this is the example shown by parents to their children; 15 – inhuman behaviour, exemplified by a scene of cannibalism in Egypt; 16 – soldiers' life.

J. is usually too indignant to be humorous, but his descriptions are vivid and vigorous. He uses irony and sarcasm with great force. Granted poetical exaggeration, his satires told the truth, though not the whole truth. It was only from the 4th century that his fame rose. Lactantius, Ausonius and Sidonius refer to him and commentaries were written to his poetry. He was very popular in the Middle Ages and has influenced many a satirist to modern times.

Texts and translations: W. V. Clausen, 1959 (Oct.); G. G. Ramsay, 1925 (Loeb), G. Highet, *Juvenal the Satirist,* 1954.

K

KOLAKRETAI Officials in Athens who were responsible for the treasury of the state by the time of Solon (Aris. *Athen. Pol.* 7.3). They disbursed money for various purposes and had to submit accounts to the *Boule. They are not heard of after 411 BC, and their functions were probably given to the *Hellenotamiai.

KRONOS Greek mythological god, one of the Titans, son of Uranus (Heaven) and Ge (Earth). He castrated his father and married his sister Rhea, who bore him Zeus, Poseidon, Hades, Hera and Demeter. He swallowed all of them except Zeus, the younger son, whom Rhea concealed in Crete while giving him a stone to swallow instead. With the help of Rhea, Zeus made K. vomit up the children he swallowed. The gods then conducted a war against K. and the Titans who were defeated and banished after a long struggle. The story is first told by Hesiod (*Theog.* 453ff.). K. was worshipped in several places and had a festival, the Kronoia. He was identified with the Roman god *Saturnus.

Farnell, *Cults*, 1,23ff.

KRYPTEIA The secret police of Sparta, its main duty being to supervise the *helots. The young Spartans who served in the K. would go out at night and kill the helots they met (Plut. *Lyc.* 28).

The Fair-haired Ephebe (c. 480 BC)

Laocoön and his sons killed by the serpents. **This famous Hellenistic marble group, made by three Rhodian sculptors in the second half of the 1st century BC, has been much praised but also considered theatrical.**

L

LABEO, Marcus Antistius A Roman senator and an important jurist, he died about AD 10/11. L. was an erudite and prolific writer who showed much originality in his writings. Among the known titles of his works are *Epistulae, De Iure Pontificio, Responsa* and *Pithana.* He was highly esteemed in his time and by later jurists. The jurist Gaius Ateius Capito, a conservative in his legal views, was his rival. But L.'s fame persisted, whereas Capito was rarely mentioned after his time. Their disputes gave rise to two schools of jurists (*Sabinus).

LABERIUS, Decimus A Roman writer of mimes (*Mimus), born *c.* 110 BC. Of his works, 43 titles and over 150 lines are known. He wrote on various subjects and in his plays women acted for the first time. Though a knight, he himself appeared on the stage at Caesar's insistence in 46. He died in 43 BC.

LABIENUS, Titus Roman senator and general, native of Cingulum in Picenum (*c.* 100–45 BC). He presumably advanced in his career by cooperating with *Pompey. Tribune of the Plebs in 63, he helped Caesar to be elected Pontifex Maximus. He was legate and chief officer of Caesar in the conquest of Gaul (58–50), but followed Pompey in the Civil War. He took part in all the important battles and was finally killed at the battle of Munda in Spain (45 BC).
Syme, *Rom. Rev.* (s.v.).

LABRANDA A religious centre in Caria, first mentioned by Herodotus (5.119). The local deity came to be known as Zeus Labraundos or Zeus Stratios, and his cult gained much fame.

LABYRINTH The famous complicated building, a sort of maze from which no one could escape, built by *Daedalus for *Minos, king of Crete. It was here that the Athenian youths and maidens were killed by the Minotaur, until Theseus killed it. All buildings with a complicated structure came to be called by that name. Etymologically it is connected with *labrys*, the Cretan double axe which was a religious symbol, and the story may have reflected an old rite associated with a maze. The L. often appeared on Cretan coins, Greek vase-paintings and Roman mosaics. It was depicted as a square and sometimes as a round structure.

LACHARES Popular leader in Athens, friend of *Cassander, who took control of the city with his mercenary soldiers in 300 BC. He remained in power until 295 when he could not defend the city against his enemies who were helped by *Demetrius Poliorcetes. L. then escaped to Boeotia.

LACONIA Region in the southeastern Peloponnesus, bordered by the Argolid in the north, Arcadia in the northwest, and Messenia in the west. Its main features are the valley of the river Eurotas stretching from northwest to southeast, on the west of it the range of Taÿgetus and on the east Mount Parnon. The plain of the Eurotas, the Homeric "hollow Lacedaemon", is the fertile part of the region and it widens towards the south. In the south, there are two promontories ending with Cape Malea and Cape Taenarum and between them the Laconian Gulf. The only important port was that of Gytheum on the northwestern shore of the Gulf. The Mycenaean kingdom of L., whose centre was near Sparta where ruins of a palace-fortress were traced, broke up in the Late Bronze Age and the whole of L. was subsequently occupied by invading *Dorians. L. was ruled by *Sparta, from the end

*The eagle eating **Prometheus' liver**. A Laconian vase-painting of the 6th century*

of the 8th century BC until well into the 2nd century BC. Under the Roman Empire there existed an independent league of Laconian cities, which first consisted of twenty-four members.

See *Sparta (with bibliography).

LACTANTIUS, L. Caecilius Firmianus Christian Latin writer, native of North Africa, born in the mid-3rd century AD and died c. 320. He taught rhetoric at Nicomedia at the invitation of Diocletian but had to resign when the persecution of the Christians began in 303. Subsequently, he went to the West and later (c. 317) he was tutor to Constantine's elder son at Trèves.

Only the Christian works of L. are extant, but even these show his thorough knowledge of Latin literature. Besides Cicero, his favourite author, he quotes Varro and Sallust, Ennius, Plautus, Terence, Horace, Lucretius, Virgil and many others. Style was very important for him and in this respect he followed Cicero. He was highly appreciated during the Renaissance and Pico della Mirandula called him "the Christian Cicero". His works include *De Opificio Dei* (304), a study of human physiology to prove providence; *Divinae Institutiones* (303–13) in 7 books, an exposition of the Christian doctrines with refutations of the arguments of its critics; *De Mortibus Persecutorum* (written late in life), on the failure of all who persecuted the Christians. It deals mainly with the persecutions of his own time. His *Phoenix* is a poem which tells the legend of this bird, whose resurrection he takes as a symbol of Christ.

R. Pichon, *Lactance*, 1901.

LAELIUS (1), Gaius Roman general and statesman, a *Novus Homo*. Friend of Scipio Africanus and his chief officer in all the campaigns in Spain and Africa in the Second Punic War (210–202 BC). After the war, he launched on a political career, was helped by Scipio, and advanced to the consulate of 190 as the colleague of L. *Scipio (3). Subsequently, he took part in several diplomatic missions. He lived to an old age and in 160 gave information to Polybius about Scipio.

Scullard, *Rom. Pol.*[2] (s.v.).

LAELIUS (2), Gaius Son of the above; a soldier, statesman and orator, he was born c. 190 BC. He served with *Scipio Aemilianus in the Third Punic War, was governor in Spain in 145, and consul in 140. At one time, he proposed a bill for agrarian reform, but withdrew it in the face of oppostition. It is unlikely that it was his prudence on this occasion that gained him the nickname *Sapiens*. His friendship with Scipio Aemilianus is commemorated in Cicero's treatise *De Amicitia* ("On Friendship"). As an interlocutor he also appears in the *De Republica.*

A. E. Astin, *Scipio Aemilianus*, 1967 (s.v.).

LAESTRYGONES Legendary race of cannibal giants whom Odysseus met on his voyage. Their king, Antiphates, killed one of Odysseus' companions for his dinner, and then the L. sunk all but one of Odysseus' ships (*Od.* 10.81ff.) Their nights were so short that herdsmen taking out the flocks for pasture met those returning, a detail probably based on tales of travellers to the north. Later they were believed to have dwelt in Sicily or in southern Italy.

LAEVIUS Latin poet of the early 1st century BC, author of the *Erotopaegnia*, amatory poems noted for their great variety of metres and fantastic language. L. was thus a pioneer of Latin poetry in the Alexandrian style (*Catullus). Only a few fragments are extant.

Morel, *Fr. Poet. Lat.*

LAMACHUS Athenian general whose first command was c. 436/435 BC when he went on an expedition with Pericles to the Black Sea (Plut. *Per.* 20). Along with *Alcibiades and *Nicias he was elected to command the expedition against Syracuse, where he was killed in 414. Though Aristophanes ridiculed him in the *Acharanians*, he praised him after his death.

LAMBAESIS Legionary camp and town in Numidia (modern Lambèse), dating from at least AD 81. Hadrian's speech to the soldiers on his visit to the place (AD 128) is recorded in an extant inscription. It became the main city of the province under Septimius Severus and it was later made a *colonia*. Besides the excellently preserved camp, there are many other remains.

LAMIA (modern Lamia) City in the northern part of the Sperchus plain which belonged to the Malians by the 5th century BC. Thanks to its position it commanded the main route from Thessaly to central Greece. It is mainly known for the failure of the Greeks to capture it in 323/2 when they besieged *Antipater (1) here during the "Lamian War".

LAMPSACUS (modern Lapseki) Prosperous Greek city in the northern Troad, an early Phocaean foundation. It owed its prosperity to its position on the route to the Black Sea, though for most of its history it was controlled by foreign states: Lydia, Persia, Athens, Sparta. It was one of the cities given to *Themistocles by Artaxerxes I after the former's escape from Athens. L. was one of the cities that suffered from *Verres.

J. M. Cook, *The Troad*, 1973.

LANUVIUM (modern Lanuvio) Ancient Latin city on the southern slopes of the *Alban hills. It received Roman citizenship in 338 BC. It was one of the few old cities of Latium that was still prosperous under the Roman Empire. L. was the home town of *Milo and *Antoninus Pius. It was especially famous for the cult of Juno Sospes.

A. E. Gordon, *Cults of Lanuvium*, 1938.

LAOCOÖN Legendary Trojan prince, son of Capys, brother of *Anchises and priest of Apollo (or of Poseidon). His story is mainly known from later tales, especially one by Virgil (*Aen.* 2.45ff., 199ff.). He tried to dissuade the Trojans from drawing the Wooden Horse left by the Greeks into the city. Two serpents then appeared and killed him and his two sons, a punishment either by Poseidon for his marriage or by Athena, the patroness of the Greeks. The scene is the subject of one of the most famous Greek sculptures, a marble group made by three Rhodian sculptors (Agesander, Athenodorus, Polydorus) in the 1st century BC. It was brought to Rome by Titus, and was much praised by Pliny (*NH* 36.37). The sculpture was discovered in 1506 and is now in the Vatican Museum. Highly esteemed by such artists as Michelangelo and Bernini, it was used by Lessing in his essay on the difference between poetry and the fine arts.

LAODICE The name of several Hellenistic princesses. One was the wife, and cousin, of *Antiochus II. She bore him two sons and three daughters, but he then married Berenice, daughter of *Ptolemy II. After his death, L. had Berenice and her son murdered, and a war ensued with *Ptolemy III (the "Third Syrian War", 246–241 BC). It was L.'s son — *Seleucus II — who ruled the Seleucid Empire.

Will, *His. Pol.* (s.v.).

LAODICEA The name of several Hellenistic cities, almost all in the Seleucid Empire.

1. L. (modern Latakia) in Syria ("at the sea"), was

Centaur carrying a Lapith woman; west pediment of the temple of Zeus at Olympia

founded by *Seleucus I at the mouth of the Orontes and thus named in honour of his mother. A prosperous city, thanks to trade and industry, it became a "free city" under Augustus. It was still an important city in the late Roman Empire.

2. L. of Asia was founded by *Antiochus II and named in honour of his wife *Laodice. It was situated on a hill above the valley of the Lycus in southwest Phrygia. The city flourished, and although it was hit by earthquakes in the 1st century AD, it was again prosperous in the 2nd century. It was here that *Dolabella died in 43 BC.
Jones, *Cities*[2] (s.v.).

LAPITHS Primitive tribe that lived in Thessaly after driving away the Pelasgi (Hom. *Il.* 2.738ff.). They are mainly known in Greek mythology for their war against the *Centaurs. Helped by Theseus, the L. defeated the Centaurs when the latter tried to carry away their women at the wedding of the daughter of Perithous, their king. Later, however, the L. were defeated by them and fled to the Peloponnesus. The war was a favourite theme in Greek art, the L. representing civilization, the Centaurs beastly nature. It appeared in the sculptures of the temples of Zeus at Olympia, of Apollo at *Bassae and the *Parthenon.

LARES Minor Roman deities, guardians of roads, of travellers by land and by sea, and of the state. They were worshipped at cross-roads and in the houses. Their cult was mainly attended by slaves, servants, freedmen and other humble people. A temple for the *Lares Permarini*

was dedicated in Rome in 187 BC. It is unlikely that they were originally the ghosts of the dead.
Platner-Ashby, *Top. Dict. Rome*, 314ff.;
Latte, *R. Rel.* (s.v.).

LARISSA The most important city of Thessaly, situated in a fertile plain (Pelasgiotis), and inhabited by the time of the Mycenaean civilization. The city was dominated by the local aristocratic family of the *Aleuadae. It is first mentioned in literature by Herodotus (7.6,2), and by *Pindar who was invited to stay here by the Aleuadae. L. supported Xerxes and consequently had to defend itself against a Greek expedition. It was the centre of the opposition against the tyrants of *Pherae and it offered *Philip II the chance to take control of Thessaly. The Romans made it a free city in 196 BC (*Flamininus), and it became the leading city of the Thessalian League.
Larsen, *Gr. Fed. St.*, 12ff.; 281ff.

LATIFUNDIA (sing. latifundium) Large estates. Though no ancient author defines their size, the term seems to indicate estates of more than 300 acres. Pliny the Elder says that the L. destroyed Italy, and his saying probably refers to contemporary conditions rather than to the 2nd century BC, when large estates began to form. The development of the L. was due to the rapid enrichment of the upper class of Roman society and the impoverishment of the small farmer — both processes occasioned by the overseas wars of Rome. The exploitation of the *Ager Publicus also contributed to this development. It was only during the late 1st century BC and the early Empire that large estates became dominant. A change in the system of cultivation came about under the Empire. Earlier, the estate was cultivated by slaves, and it was in the L. that vineyards, olive groves and other new crops were fostered. When slave labour ceased to be cheap, the land was given to *coloni* (*Colonus) for cultivation, and the absentee landowners showed little interest in their estates. Nonetheless the large estates became common throughout the Roman provinces, and prominent among them were the imperial ones.
M. I. Rostovtzeff, *Social and Economy History of the Roman Empire*, 1952 (s.v.).

LATINI The inhabitants of *Latium, a mixed race according to ancient authors and modern scholars. They included *Aborigines, Pelasgi, Arcades, Siculi, Aurunci, Rululi*, and *Osci*, according to Pliny the Elder (*NH* 3.56; cf. Dion. Hal. 1.9; 60). *Latinus, their eponymous king, is first recorded in Hesiod (*Theog.* 1011–16), and the *Latinoi* are mentioned in the first treaty between Rome and Carthage dating from 509 BC (Polyb. 3.22,11). It seems that "Southern *Villanovans" appeared here in the Iron Age, and to them some would ascribe the introduction of Latin.

The old L. lived in small settlements, and at one time there were numerous Latin *populi*. It was under the impact of the Etruscans that they were amalgamated into larger states from the 6th century BC on. Though not united politically, the archaic *populi* had a sense of social and religious unity and consequently had among themselves rights of *Conubium and *Commercium. They had several religious leagues, the more important of which were connected with the cult of Jupiter Latiaris on the Alban Mount, and the shrine of Diana at *Aricia.

According to Roman tradition, supremacy over the L. passed to Rome after the destruction of *Alba, the mother-city of the Latin cities. The supremacy of Rome was in fact attained by its Etruscan kings in the course of the 6th century BC. It is reflected by the transference of the cult of Diana to the *Aventine by *Servius Tullius. Soon after the downfall of the monarchy, a powerful Latin League (comprising Tusculum, Aricia, Lanuvium, Lavinium, Cora, Tibur, Pometia, Ardea) successfully contested Roman hegemony at the Battle of Lake Regilius (496). A defensive alliance was signed between the L. and Rome in 493 (Foedus Cassianum) which was joined by the *Hernici in 486. Together, they now fought the *Aequi and *Volsci, shared the booty and founded Latin *coloniae*. The ascendancy of Rome in the late 5th century caused apprehension and brought about a renewal of hostilities, especially by Tibur and Praeneste, after the Gallic catastrophe. The Latins and the Volscians finally attempted to assert their independence in the Great Latin War (340–338), but were defeated. The Latin League was now dissolved by Rome, several cities were annexed and their citizens received Roman citizenship. The rest had to subject their foreign policy to Rome, and for some time lost their mutual rights of Conubium and Commercium; they also had to supply troops to Rome. The type of rights they were granted by Rome came to be known as the *Ius Latii; this was conferred on subsequently established Latin colonies and, later on, on many cities in the Roman Empire; and this helped the process of Romanization. The original L. and Latin colonies in Italy received Roman citizenship in 90 BC during the *Bellum Sociale.

A. N. Sherwin-White, *Rom. Cit.*[2];
A. Alföldi, *Early Romans and the Latins,* 1965.

LATINI IUNIANI Legal status introduced by a *lex Iunia*, probably in 17 BC, but possibly in AD 19, and applied to slaves informally manumitted by Roman citizens. The freedom of the freedman was thus recognized by Roman law — he did not receive Roman citizenship, as did slaves formally manumitted, but had the Latin rights with some restrictions (the most important of which being that on his death his property reverted to his former master). The LI. could acquire citizenship in several ways and their children became Roman citizens. The institution was abolished by Justinian in AD 531.

Jolowicz, *Roman Law*[3] (s.v.).

LATINUS The eponymous king of the Latins first mentioned by Hesiod, according to whom he was the son of Odysseus and Circe and the king of the Tyrrhenians (*Theog.* 1011ff.). A later version has him marrying Rhome, daughter of Aeneas, who bore him Rhomus (Remus) and Romulus. This was chronologically impossible and was corrected in another version by *Cato Censorius, essentially followed by Virgil and Livy; here Aeneas married Lavinia, L.'s daughter, and subsequently killed Turnus, her former fiancé.

LATIUM Old L. (*Latium Vetus*) was the area stretching from the Tiber to Circeii, bordered by the *Volsci in the southeast, the *Hernici in the east, and the *Aequi in the northeast. The expansion of Rome led to the extension of L. over the territories of these peoples, and over the Aurunci, and this part was known as *Latium Adiectum*. L. was a populous country in early times, well cultivated, and successive invaders found it an attractive area. But it seems that extensive colonization (*Colonia) and numerous wars drained its manpower. By the late Roman Republic, many of its old towns were in decay, and malaria was endemic in some parts. In imperial times, its once great towns (e.g. *Tibur, *Praeneste) became locations for fashionable villas. Under Augustus' organization, L. and Campania formed the first region of Italy and

as from the late Roman Empire the name Campania was applied to both regions (hence the modern Campagna for L.). See *Latini, *Ius Latii (with bibliography).

T. Ashby, *The Roman Campagna in Classical Times,* 1927.

LAUDATIO FUNEBRIS Laudatory, funeral oration publicly given in Rome in honour of deceased persons. The personal merits and public achievements of the dead and of his ancestors were excessively praised as the Roman aristocratic families vied with one another for glory. The use of the L. as a historical source caused much distortion in Roman historiography. The tradition of L. had some part in the development of Roman *biography.

D. R. Stuart, *Epochs of Greek and Roman Biography,* 1928, 209ff.

LAURIUM Southern district of Attica, on the eastern coast near Cape Sunium. L. owed its importance and fame to its seams of silver which were exploited from early times. It was, however, only *c.* 484–483 BC that rich layers were discovered which helped the Athenians, with the initiative of *Themistocles, to build a navy which proved decisive in the war against *Xerxes. The mines were state property and were operated by slaves; they were the only places where these workers were ruthlessly exploited. By the end of the 2nd century BC the mines were exhausted and practically abandoned.

LAUS PISONIS Poem of 261 hexameters by an unknown writer on one Calpurnius Piso, probably the one involved in the conspiracy against Nero (*Piso (5)).

Duff, *Min. Lat. Poet.*

LAVINIUM (modern Pratica di Mare) A town in Latium, known as the place of landing of *Aeneas. It had several important cults — of Venus, Jupiter Indiges, Vesta and the Penates. It declined by the end of the Republic. Remains of thirteen archaic altars were found here.

A. Alfoldi, *Early Rome and the Latins,* 1965, 246ff.

LAW, GREEK Our knowledge of the legal systems of the Greek states is at best meagre, or non-existent, the only exception being Athenian law. The Homeric poems and Hesiod do not give sufficient information to form a clear picture of the machinery of justice and the legal institutions of their time when law was based on custom and related to religious conceptions. Under the monarchy, the king was the judge (cf. Homer, *Il.* 9.99), but with the decline of the kings the administration of justice passed to the aristocracy.

It was only in the 7th century BC, under the impact of new social and economic conditions, that laws were first committed to writing. This was the work of special legislators, *nomothetai*, who were given complete authority to publish codes. The earliest of them was *Zaleucus, whose laws were adopted in many Greek cities in Sicily and Italy. Another was Charondas of *Catana (6th century), whose laws were received not only in his native city but in other Chalcidic cities, notably Rhegium. In Athens, laws were first laid down by *Draco, and more names of legislators are known. It would seem that at this stage the legislators, themselves aristocrats, simply published the customary law. Their work included such departments as penal law, homicide law, adoptions and inheritance. The only direct evidence available on the early law of any Greek city comes from the "Law Code" of *Gortyn. An exception to the above development occurred in Sparta where customary, unwritten law prevailed, and a *rhetra* ("order") was ascribed to *Lycurgus (1) forbidding the introduction of written laws.

In Athens, the social conflicts led to the appointment

of *Solon as a lawgiver after Draco. He adopted many of the laws of his predecessors, abolished some, introduced innovations (e.g. in the fields of personal law and the law of property) and was later regarded as responsible for the Athenian legal system. The work of the *nomothetai* and the machinery of legislation in Athens show that, for the Greeks, legislation required exceptional procedure. Though the popular assembly (*Ekklesia) was the sovereign body, it could only pass decrees (*psephismata*), which had to conform with existing laws (*Graphe Paranomon). Every year, in the first meeting of the Assembly, a motion could be put forward to revise any of the laws. If the Assembly voted for acceptance of the motion, drafts for new laws were introduced by the interested parties to the *nomothetai*, who were chosen by lot from the year's jurors. The Assembly appointed five men to defend the old laws and both they and the proposers of the new laws delivered speeches before the *nomothetai*, who then voted on the bill. (Special *nomothetai* were appointed in 411 and 403, a measure occasioned by the oligarchic revolutions.)

It is commonly said of the Athenians and the Greeks that they were fond of legal disputes. Trials for them were *agones*, that is, competitions. But this interest in the courts and in the operation of justice did not produce for them a legal literature as was produced in Rome. Witnesses and legal documents could be introduced but more important were the speeches of the plaintiff and the defendant. They were allowed to use speeches written by *logographers, but could not be represented by lawyers. See *Dikasterion, *Thesmothetai.

R. J. Bonner — G. Smith, *The Administration of Justice from Homer to Aristotle,* 1930–1938;
J. W. Jones, *The Law and the Legal Theory of the Greeks,* 1956.

LAW, ROMAN Early Roman law was based on custom and related to religion. It was as a result of the struggle between the Patricians and the Plebeians that laws were first committed to writing and published by the *Decemvirs in the mid-5th century BC. The laws of the Twelve Tables published by them was the first code of Roman law and remained the only one to the late Roman Empire. After the Twelve Tables the development of Roman law involved passing new laws and interpreting the existing law. Until 287 BC laws (*leges*) could be passed only by motions voted for by the *Comitia, through which the people of Rome (*Populus Romanus*) expressed its wish. No special procedure was needed for passing laws. From 287 decisions of the Plebs in its assembly (*Concilium Plebis) were binding on the whole people, that is, *plebiscita* had the same force as *leges*. But in practice the legislation of the Assembly was mainly concerned with public law and only rarely with private law. Thus it came about that changes were slow and mainly connected with the activities of the urban praetors through the publication of their edicts. The transition from the Republic to Empire led to the decline of the work of the Comitia and by the end of the 1st century AD they no longer passed bills. At the same time the decisions of the Senate (*senatus consulta*) gradually acquired the force of law but normally they did not deal with private law. In fact, legislation became the prerogative of the emperors; for *Gaius in the 2nd century AD, the imperial *constitutiones* are laws. They consisted of *edicta* which usually were ordinances of a general character, *decreta*, decisions taken by the emperors in trials, and *rescripta* (or *epistulae*), which were decisions on legal points given in answer to private petitions or addresses of magistrates.

Three stages are distinguished in the development of the procedure of civil law at Rome. The old system, that of the *legis actiones*, was characterised by extreme formalism. The litigants had to use solemn oral forms, any deviation from which caused the loss of the case. This system was replaced by the formulary system. The essence of this was the formula, that is, not an inflexible oral form but in each case a formula defining the case had to be concluded between the litigants before the praetor. The formula consisted of two parts, the *intentio* in which was defined the claim of the plaintiff and the *condemnatio*, which gave authorization to condemn the defendant or to discharge him according to the evidence and arguments. This flexible system was first used in cases not covered by the *Ius Civile, and was first applied to some cases of the Ius Civile by the *lex Aebutia* (c. 150 BC), and finally two *leges Iuliae* (17/16 BC) terminated the use of the *legis actiones*. In both these systems there were two stages in the trial. The first, called *in iure*, was held before a magistrate, normally the praetor. The magistrate checked if the law was applicable to the case, which was then defined. Finally a *Iudex was appointed. In the second stage, called *apud iudicem*, the Iudex heard the case as formulated and pronounced judgement against which there was no appeal. A third system, *cognitio extra ordinem*, began to develop from Augustus' period on. The case was heard from first to last by special officials appointed by the emperors or a magistrate. In the late Roman Empire it remained the only system in use. Under this system appeals were possible and this was applied to cases tried in the formulary system.

Criminal cases were dealt with originally by magistrates with *Imperium. The right of *Provocatio led to the rise of the *Iudicia Populi which were used in cases involving capital punishment and high fines. The system of *Quaestiones was introduced by the establishment of a permanent court for cases of *Repetundae in 149 BC. It was largely extended by *Sulla. A new procedure, also called *cognitio extra ordinem*, began in the 1st century BC, at first in the provinces. It gradually replaced the Quaestiones which disappeared in the 3rd century AD. Trials in this procedure were held by the emperor or other imperial officials appointed by him. Certain criminal offences, such as damage to property, assault and fraud, came under the rules of the civil procedure. See *Digesta, *Edictum, *Iudex, *Iudicia Populi, *Iuridicus, *Ius Civile, *Ius Gentium, *Justinian, *Jurisprudence, *Lex, *Quaestio, *Repetundae.

J. Crook, *Law and Life of Rome,* 1967;
Jolowicz, *Roman Law*[3].

LECTISTERNIUM Roman religious rite in which the gods took part in a feast. The feast was held at a private house or a temple and statues of the gods were placed on couches.
Latte, *R. Rel.* (s.v.).

LEDA Greek mythological figure, wife of the Spartan King *Tyndareus, mother of the *Dioscuri, *Helen and *Clytemnestra. Zeus made love to her in the shape of a swan and Helen and Polydeucus were born of the union; Clytemnestra and Castor, however, were Tyndareus' children. The myth was told in many versions. The important detail was that some of the children were hatched from an egg, which is said to have still existed in Sparta in the 2nd century AD (Pausan. 3.16,1). In one version of the myth

Helen was the daughter of Nemesis and Leda brought her up as her daughter after she was hatched from the egg. In Homer Leda appears as mother of the Dioscuri, but he does not mention the egg motif. The epiphany of the gods in bird-shape, however, goes back to the Minoan religion, and the poet may simply have ignored it. Indeed in later times the Greeks regarded the story with scepticism. In art the motif of the swan approaching Leda has been very popular not only with the Greeks and the Romans but with many later artists such as Leonardo da Vinci and Michelangelo. It has also attracted philosophers and poets many of whom regarded it as a symbol or gave it psychological interpretations (e.g. *Leda and the Swan* by W. B. Yeats).

LEGATUS (pl. legati) L. was originally an official envoy sent to represent the Roman people in its dealings with foreign states, in particular one sent by the Senate. Senatorial commissions (*legationes*), consisting of 2–10 members, were usually sent on diplomatic missions. They normally assisted Roman generals at the conclusion of wars in negotiating the peace treaty or in organizing the provinces of conquered territories (though not always in the post-Sullan period).

L. were also the chief assistants of Roman governors and generals and were delegated powers by their superior commanders. At first they were appointed by the Senate but in the 1st century BC a few generals were allowed to nominate their own L. As such they were often given command over part of the army. Under the Empire the governors of imperial provinces had the title *Legati Augusti pro praetore*, that is, they governed the provinces as delegates of the emperor "acting as praetor" (whether they had served as praetors or consuls or not). The title of the commander of a legion was *legatus legionis*. Such commanders were normally senators of praetorian rank; in Egypt they were Equites and had the title *praefectus legionis*.

T. R. S. Broughton, *The Magistrates of the Roman Republic*, 1951–2; H. M. D. Parker, *The Roman Legions*[2], 1958.

LEGION The most important unit of the Roman army, originally consisting of the whole army, which then numbered 3,000 soldiers. The number was doubled in the late regal period, but after the foundation of the Republic, each of the consuls received command of a L., now half the army. Subsequently a consular army normally numbered two L.s, and to each L. were given six Tribuni Militares. By the 3rd century BC L. was organized in the manipular system. It consisted of 1,200 *hastati* (soldiers of the first line), 1,200 *principes* (second line) and 600 *triarii* (third line), and 1,200 *vetites* (light-armed soldiers). Each L. was assigned 300 horsemen organized in ten *turmae* 30 apiece, and each *turma* consisted of three *decuriae*. The three lines consisted of 30 maniples (*manipuli*), each numbering 120 in those of the *hastati* and *principes* and 60 in those of the *triarii*. A maniple consisted of two centuries (*centuriae*) and had two centurions; the senior of them was its commander. Each maniple had its *signum*. After the experience of the Second Punic War the manipular system gradually gave way to an organization based on the *Cohors as a tactical unit and this system was finally established by the reforms of *Marius. The L. now consisted of ten cohorts, each numbering 500–600 men, and sixty centuries. This organization gave the L. a great deal of flexibility.

The organization of the L. remained unchanged under

Attack of Roman legionaries, covered by shields (testudo), on a Dacian camp; column of Trajan

the Empire and normally only citizens served in it. The original annual pay, 120 *denarii* (or 112½), was raised to 225 by Caesar and to 300 by Domitian. The term of service was raised by Augustus from 16 years to 20 (with the addition of 4–5 years *sub vexilio*). Under the Flavians normal service was raised to 25. The number of L.s was at first 28 and 25 from AD 9 after 3 were destroyed in the disaster of *Varus. The commander of a L. was a *legatus legionis*. In the 4th century AD the number of the L.s increased but their strength was reduced. The L.s of the field army (*comitatenses*), commanded by tribuni, were 1,000 each, those of the frontier army (*limitanei*), commanded by praefecti, were stronger. See *Armies, Roman, *Primipilus, *Signa Militaria, *Tribuni Militum.

H. M. D. Parker, *The Roman Legions*[2], 1958; G. Webster, *The Roman Imperial Army*, 1969.

LEMNOS A fertile, once volcanic, island in the north Aegean sea, of about 480 sq km. It had been settled by a pre-Hellenic population and its early inhabitants were described by ancient authors as Pelasgians and Tyrsenoi (Etruscans). A grave inscription found there is supposed to be written in a language very close to Etruscan. The island, which is mentioned by Homer, came under Greek influence in the Archaic period and was conquered by *Miltiades at the 6th century BC. It received an Athenian cleruchy in the mid-5th century, and, except for some intervals (notably the second half of the 4th century), it remained under Athenian control for many centuries. L. was devastated by the Goths in AD 267.

LENAEA Festival in honour of Dionysus at Athens, held on 12th of Gamelion (January–February). Its chief features were a procession and dramatic competitions. The performances originally took place in the Lenaion precinct, between the west slope of the *Acropolis and the *Areopagus. The L. began about 442 BC and included comedies and tragedies. Two playwrights gave each two tragedies, though at first comedies were given preference. Pickard-Cambridge, *Dramatic Festivals*[2], 68ff

LENTULUS Branch of the Cornelian clan the first member of which to become consul was L. Cornelius L. (327 BC; the attribution of the name L. to C. Cornelius, the consul of 478 BC, is obviously a later addition). The branch was prolific and had subdivisions (e.g. Caudinus, Lupus, Spinther). Numerous Lentuli attained the highest offices as from the late 4th century BC to the 1st century AD but none rose to dominant position comparable, for instance, to that of the Fabii or Scipiones.

LENTULUS GAETULICUS, Gnaeus Cornelius Relative of *Sejanus, praetor in AD 23, consul in 26 and commander of the army in Upper Germany in 30—9. He survived the downfall of Sejanus but in AD 39 was put to death by Caligula for his involvement in conspiracy. He wrote erotic epigrams which were followed by Martial.

LEOCHARES Prominent Greek sculptor of the 4th century BC. He was commissioned to make works for many places, and he worked for Philip II and Alexander the Great, among others. He mainly worked in bronze but also in marble and gold and ivory. His statues of gods were famous and in one of them Ganymedes was shown carried by Zeus's eagle (Plin. *NH* 34.79). An extant marble group (in the Vatican) of this theme is supposed to be a copy of L.'s original. His other famous works include the frieze and sculptures of the *Mausoleum, where *Bryaxis and *Scopas also worked, and a gold and ivory group of Philip, Olympias, Alexander, Amyntas and Eurydice at Olympia. The famous statue of Apollo Belvedere may be a copy of an original bronze work by L.
M. Bieber, *The Sculpture of the Hellenistic Age*[2], 1961.

LEONIDAS (1) King of Sparta who succeeded to the throne after the death of *Cleomenes I, whose daughter he married. He commanded the Spartan troops that marched to central Greece to face the invasion of Xerxes in 480 BC. After two days of fighting at Thermopylae, the Persians outflanked the Greek army with the help of a traitor. Leonidas remained with his 300 Spartans and a Boeotian detachment to cover the retreat and he and all his men died fighting. A famous warrior-bust of the 5th century, found at Sparta, may likely be his portrait.
Hdt. 7.204—39;
C. Hignett, *Xerxes' Invasion of Greece*, 1963.

LEONIDAS (2), of Tarentum Prominent Greek elegist. L. was poor and lived a wandering life in the first half of the 3rd century BC. Of his poetry some 100 epigrams are extant in the Greek *Anthology. He differs from his contemporaries in taking as his main subject the life of humble people (artisans, fishermen, sailors, etc.), with whom he identifies himself. His mood is usually pessimistic. Most of the epigrams are dedications and epitaphs. His fine poetry, with accomplished technique, won him the admiration both of later Greek and Roman poets (notably *Propertius).
A. S. F. Gow—D. L. Page, *The Greek Anthology*, 1965;
T. B. L. Webster, *Hellenistic Poetry and Art*, 1964.

LEONTINI (modern Lentini) Greek city in eastern Sicily, founded in 729 BC by *Naxos (Thuc. 6.3) at the south corner of the plain of Catana. Its tyrant Panaetius was the first one in Sicily. It was taken by the tyrant Hippocrates of Gela in the early 5th century and subsequently was subject to Syracuse. It made an alliance with Athens in 433 BC and supported its intervention in Sicilian affairs. The famous orator *Gorgias was a native of L. The city was

Torso of Greek soldier, known as "Leonidas", c. 480 BC

captured and plundered by the Romans in 214 BC.
Dunbabin, *Western Greeks* (s.v.).

LEOSTHENES Athenian general who recruited and maintained mercenaries discharged by Alexander (324/3 BC). After the death of Alexander he used this force in the attempt to liberate Greece from Macedonian rule. Supported by Phocaeans, Aetolians and Thessalians he succeeded in blockading *Antipater (1) in *Lamia, but was killed in the siege (322). His friend *Hyperides honoured him in his funeral oration on the Athenians who fell in the war.

LEOTYCHIDES Spartan king, born c. 545 and succeeded to the throne c. 491 BC. He commanded the Greek force that defeated the Persians in a naval and land battle at Mycale (479 BC), the last great battle associated with Xerxes' invasion of Greece. Shortly afterwards he led a Greek army in a punitive campaign against the pro-Persian *Aleuadae of *Larissa. As he failed to accomplish his mission he was accused of taking bribes and went into exile to Tegea (c. 476).

LEPCIS (LEPTIS) MAGNA The eastern of the three Phoenician cities, at first trading posts, on the coast of Tripolitania. A prosperous city, thanks to agriculture and trade, the city was subject to *Masinissa after the Second Punic War. It belonged to the province Africa Proconsularis under the Empire and it was made a *colonia* under Trajan. The Emperor Septimius *Severus was a native of L. and granted it the *Ius Italicum. He built a new harbour and lavishly decorated the city with many public buildings. It had bishops by the mid-3rd century AD. L. declined from the late 4th century and disappeared as a town after the Arab conquest. The remains of L. are among the finest of Roman provincial cities and include the Augustan forum, hunting baths, Severan collonades, etc.
D. E. L. Haynes, *The Antiquities of Tripolitania*, 1956;
G. Caputo—E. V. Caffarelli, *Buried City*, 1966.

LEPIDUS (1), Marcus Aemilius Leading Roman states-man of the first half of the 2nd century BC. After govern-ing Sicily as praetor in 193, he was consul in 187 when he built the Via Aemilia from Ariminum to Placentia. He became Pontifex Maximus in 180, and in 179, as censor, built the Basilica Aemilia and carried out other building operations with his colleague. He was again consul in 175 and *Princeps Senatus from 179 to his death in 152.
Scullard, *Roman Politics*[2] (s.v.).

LEPIDUS (2), Marcus Aemilius Roman statesman; he opportunely followed *Sulla in the Civil War and largely profited in the proscriptions. Elected consul of 78 BC, despite Sulla's attempt to prevent it, he soon sought to abolish the latter's reforms. In the following year he open-ly started a war but was defeated by *Catullus (2), helped by *Pompey, and escaped to Sardinia where he died from a broken heart at his divorce. His followers fled to Spain to join *Sertorius.

LEPIDUS (3), Marcus Aemilius The younger son of Lepidus (2), he followed Caesar in the Civil War and after governing Nearer Spain in 48—47 BC was given a triumph. Consul in 46, and *Magister Equitum of Caesar (46—44), after Caesar's murder he became Pontifex Maximus with the support of Antony. He then went to govern Gallia and Nearer Spain and in 43 formed the Triumvirate with An-tony and Octavian. He was again consul in 42 and re-mained in Italy to be deprived of his provinces after *Philippi. In 40 he received Africa but lost all power in 36 when his army went over to Octavian. However he re-mained Pontifex Maximus to his death in 12 BC.
Syme, *Rom. Rev.* (s.v.).

LEPIDUS (4), Marcus Aemilius Consul in AD 6, he fought in Pannonia under Tiberius, and subsequently governed Nearer Spain (14) and Asia (c. 26—8). Able and clever, Augustus said he was capable of reigning but de-spised it (Tac. *Ann.* 1.13).
Syme, *Tacitus*, 1958 (s.v.).

LESBOS Fertile island, the largest of those off the coast of Asia Minor, about 1,615 sq km. Of the five cities of the island Mytilene was the strongest, and its name was sometimes given to the whole island. The island was oc-cupied in the Bronze Age, and, in Homer, Achilles con-quered it as being under Trojan influence. Subsequently the population, mainly of Aeolian origin, had trade and agriculture as its main occupations. Lesbos owes its fame to its great poets, *Alcaeus and *Sappho. It was also the birth place of *Theophrastus.

LETO Titaness, mother by Zeus of *Apollo and *Ar-temis. This is told as early as Homer (*Il.* 26.605ff.), and Hesiod (*Theog.* 918ff.). Delos was commonly believed to be the place where she bore them. The myth of the birth is told in the Homeric *Hymn* to the Delian Apollo, and also by *Callimachus in his fourth hymn (with a different ver-sion of how Hera sought to prevent the birth). Another important myth, beside the birth, tells of her punishment of *Niobe. She was worshipped in several places, partic-ularly in Lycia, and was probably of Asian origin. L. with her children appears in art from the 7th century BC on.

LETTERS L. were used by the Greeks and Romans for various purposes and there are still extant collections of L. of various types. Generally a distinction can be made between L. which were used as a means of communica-tion, in private or official correspondence, and L. which were used as a literary form. Of the former the most important are those of Cicero. They are a mine of infor-mation on political, social, economic and personal matters

and form the best extant documentary evidence for un-derstanding the mind and character of the ancients. They are mainly news L., but by their nature many mat-ters are mentioned in passing. A special category are the L. of recommendation, mainly to be found in Book 13 of the *To His Friends.* In this collection there are also L. by many contemporaries including Caesar, Pompey, Cato, Antony, Brutus, Cassius and Pollio.

Greek private L. are known from papyri. Many of the official L. of Hellenistic rulers are known because they contained administrative rulings and grants of privileges and so were inscribed on durable material and other-wise committed to writing. The L. of *Pliny the Younger in-clude one book of his official correspondence with Tra-jan, and private L. The latter are much more literary in tone than those of Cicero, though they generally cover the same topics. The L. of *Fronto are purely personal. L. as a literary genre were used by philosophers, poets and other writers. Of this type are extant the philosophical L. of *Plato only some of which are genuine, *Seneca the Younger, and *Epicurus; the political L. of *Isocrates; the verse L. of *Horace and *Ovid; the fiction L. of Alciph-ron (Greek writer of *c.* 3rd century AD who composed L. allegedly written by Athenians of the 4th century BC); and many others. Many L. of writers, both pagan and Christian, of the late Roman Empire are extant including *Libanius and *Julian, *Jerome and *Augustine. Extant also are spurious L. of various authors. See also the authors mentioned above with bibliographies.
R. Hercher, *Epistolographi Graeci*, 1973; D. Brooke, *Private Letters,* 1929; C. B. Welles, *Royal Correspondence in the Hellenistic World,* 1934.

LEUCAS Mountainous island in the Ionian Sea, very close to the coast of *Acarnania. It was inhabited in My-cenaean times and some identify it with Ithaca, but this is unlikely. The island was colonized by settlers from Corinth in the second half of the 7th century BC, who maintained close connection with their mother-city. It took part in the Persian Wars. Capital of the Acarnanian League in the 3rd century, L. was made a free city by Rome in 167. According to legend *Sappho, desperate with love, ended her life by leaping from its precipitous promontory.

LEUCIPPUS (1) Greek philosopher of the 5th century BC, said to have been born in Elea, Abdera or Miletus; the last is the most probable. Of the two works ascribed to him, *The Great World System* and *On Mind*, almost nothing is known. L. was the first to develop the atomic theory, but it is impossible to define his own contribution to the theory which is known from his disciple *Demo-critus. See *Democritus (with bibliography).

LEUCIPPUS (2) In Greek mythology, a king of Messenia whose daughters Hilaeira and Phoebe (Leucippidae) were carried away by the *Dioscuri. *Idas and Lynceus were his sons.

LEUCOTHEA The "white goddess", a sea-goddess who was said to have been originally Ino, daughter of Cadmus and wife of *Athamas. She helped Odysseus to reach the island of Phaeacia (Hom. *Od.* 5.333f.).

LEUCTRA Location in Boeotia famed for the defeat of the Spartan army in 371 BC. With this battle Sparta's hegemony in Greece ended and that of Thebes began. See *Epaminondas.

LEX (pl. leges) In Roman public life L. normally was a law passed in one of the *Comitia (*centuriata* or *tributa*).

There was a view which associated the term with *legere*; that is, it was a "selection" out of the whole body of statutes (Cic. *Leg.* 1.19). But more probably it was connected with *ligare* (to bind), that is, it was a binding agreement between two contracting parties; hence one could also speak of *lex privata*. A bill passed by the Comitia was a *lex rogata* (the magistrate asks, *rogat*, the Assembly to accept his motion). It went through three stages: *legislatio*, the public advertisment (*promulgatio*) of the bill in a *Contio or an edict; *rogatio* (at least three *nundinae*; market days, after the *legislatio*), the voting on the bill; and *publicatio*, the formal publication of the law (if approved), copies of which were kept in the *Aerarium. Not every *lex rogata* had a sanction, hence the jurists distinguished the following: *lex imperfecta*, a law which did not invalidate the act it prohibited nor fix a penalty for it; *lex minus quam perfecta*, a law which fixed a penalty but did not invalidate the act prohibited; *lex perfecta*, a law which invalidated the act prohibited; *lex plus quam perfecta*, a law which both penalized the offender and invalidated the act. The abolition of a L. was carried out by passing a new L. called *abrogatio*. As from 287 BC, decisions of the Plebs (*plebiscita*) were binding on the Roman people; they, too, passed the same procedure. A L. was normally called by the name of the magistrate who passed it (the clan name was used) hence, e.g., *lex Iulia* is a law passed by one of the Julian *Gens.

The administrative regulation of a province, a unilateral act performed by a Roman magistrate holding *Imperium and normally on the advice of a senatorial board, was called a *lex data*. The municipal constitutions of cities, which were occasionally given by Roman magistrates in Italy and the provinces, were also *leges datae*. The term L. was also applied to a contract between the state and a private individual (or a *societas*). Such L. normally concerned the collection of taxes, the operation of mines and the construction of roads or public buildings. For this purpose the state was represented by the censors or other magistrates with Imperium. *Leges agrariae* dealt with the distribution of the *Ager Publicus; *Leges annales* regulated the minimum age limits for offices and the intervals between them; *leges frumentariae* introduced the distribution of cheap — and from 58 BC free of charge — corn to the masses of Rome; *leges iudiciariae* concerned the institution, composition and procedure of the jury courts (*Quaestiones); *leges sacratae* outlawed their offenders (the offender became *sacer*); the *leges tabellariae* introduced the secret ballot to all kinds of Roman assemblies (legislative, electoral and judicial). The *leges regiae* were a collection of laws ascribed to the regal period and dealt with homicide law, family law, and obligations; *lex curiata* was a law passed by the *comitia curiata*. A special law was passed by that body for the sake of magistrates holding Imperium. Until recently the common view was that it confirmed the Imperium of the magistrate. An alternative theory is that it confirmed the right of the magistrate to take the auspices (*Auspicium). See *Comitia, *Law, Roman.

G. Rotondi, *Leges Publicae Populi Romani*, 1912; A. Berger, *Encyclopaedic Dictionary of Roman Law*, 1953, 544ff.; D. Daube, *Forms of Roman Legislation*, 1956; Jolowicz, *Roman Law*[3] (s.v.).

LIBANIUS The leading Greek rhetorician and Sophist of the 4th century AD (314–93). Born at Antioch to a wealthy and socially prominent family, he first studied there and later in Athens (336–40). He taught rhetoric at Constantinople, Nicaea and Nicomedia and then again at Constantinople. From 354 to his death he held a chair of rhetoric at Antioch. His reputation ran high and among his pupils, pagan and Christian alike, were John Chrysostom, Basil and Gregory of Nazianus and *Ammianus Marcellinus. He showed much interest in the revival of paganism by *Julian, his former student, and deplored his death. Although a convinced pagan, he managed to cultivate good relations with the Christian emperors.

L.'s literary output was enormous and thanks to his popularity much of it has survived. His extant writings include 64 speeches, numerous declamations and rhetorical works and about 1,600 letters. The more famous speeches are his funeral eulogy of Julian, his autobiography (AD 374), and the encomiastic description of Antioch. His letters, of which many are addressed to emperors and high officials, deal with personal matters, public affairs and literary questions and are a mine of information on the 4th century. His model was Demosthenes, of whom he wrote a biography, but he was also influenced by Isocrates and other writers.

R. Foerster — E. Richsteig, *Libanii Opera*, 1963 (1903–1927); *Selected Works* (Loeb), 1969; L. Petit, *Libanius*, 1956.

LIBER Old Italian god of fertility particularly associated with wine and usually having the epithet *pater*. It was only natural that he became identified with the Greek god of wine *Dionysus; at Latium he was so identified by the early 5th century BC at the latest. His merry festival, the Liberalia, was celebrated on 17 March and was the usual occasion for boys to take on the *toga virilis*. At Rome he was worshipped with Libera and *Ceres on the Aventine. In some way he became associated with Jupiter, who occasionally has the epithet L.

A. Bruhl, *Liber Pater*, 1953.

LIBERTAS "The state of being free", established — so the Romans believed — by the expulsion of the kings and foundation of the Republic. Hence, for them, L. meant the Republican constitution. As a political idea, the notion went through changes in the late Republic and early Empire. L. was also the goddess that personified personal liberty; a temple was dedicated to her in 238 BC.

Ch. Wirszubski, *Libertas as a Political Idea at Rome*, 1950; Platner-Ashby, *Top. Dict. Rome*, 296f.

LIBRARIES Books in Greece and Rome were rolls of papyrus or parchment. Their use was very limited in Archaic Greece and it was only in the 4th century BC that they became more widespread there. Yet the first private L. are ascribed to the tyrants *Polycrates of Samos and *Pisistratus of Athens who indeed were patrons of the letters. Small collections of books may have been at Athens in the 5th century. The *Academy of Plato presumably had a L. but the first large and systematically organized L. was established by *Aristotle for his school. The first public L. were founded in the Hellenistic period and the largest and the most famous of antiquity was that of Alexandria. It dates from the time of *Ptolemy I and was founded in association with the *Museum. *Ptolemy II supported it lavishly and it is said to have included 700,000 volumes. The chief librarians, appointed by the Ptolemaic kings, were prominent scholars such as *Zenodotus, *Eratosthenes, *Aristophanes of Byzantium, and *Aristarchus. These and others who worked in the L., like *Callimachus, founded literary and textual criticism and were responsible for the editing of the writings of many Greek authors. Their work was thus decisive for the preservation of Greek literature. A catalogue (*pinakes*) was prepared by Callimachus. The L. was badly damaged in the Alexandrian war of Caesar. The second great L. was established by the kings of Pergamum, and there were many others, both private and public.

The Romans were very late in establishing L. The first were spoils captured in the Eastern wars: Aemilius *Paullus brought the library of King *Perseus and *Sulla brought the manuscripts of Aristotle. But in the 1st century BC many of the Roman aristocrats had private L. and indeed trade in books flourished. *Cicero had L. in several of his villas. Caesar's plan to open up a public L. was abortive and it was Asinius *Pollio who first founded one. Augustus soon founded two public L., connected with temples, and was followed by many emperors. The most magnificent was the Bibliotheca Ulpia of Trajan. This had separate divisions for Greek and Latin books. It had reading-rooms. The rolls lay on shelves or stood vertically in boxes. Public L. also became common in many cities in Italy and the provinces.

J. W. Clark, *The Care of Books,* 1909; F. G. Kenyon, *Books and Readers in Ancient Greece and Rome*[2], 1951.

LIBYA In early times L. meant for the Greeks the coastal land west of Egypt. When more geographical information became known, L. denoted the continent of Africa and by the 5th century BC was regarded as being separated from Asia at Suez. See *Africa.

LICINIUS The name of a Roman plebeian clan, members of which are recorded as tribunes of the Plebs in the 5th century BC. *Stolo was a member of the clan. *Crassus and *Lucullus were the most prominent branches of the clan.

LICINIUS, Valerius Licinianus Roman emperor (AD 308–23), of peasant origin, native of Dacia south of the Danube, born *c.* 250. He was a close friend of *Galerius under whom he served against Persia in 297. Though declared Augustus of the West in 308, he could not assert his authority over *Maxentius and *Constantine. After the defeat of *Maximinus Daia in 313, he annexed the eastern provinces to his rule, but by 316 lost part of his Balkan provinces to Constantine. He renewed the persecution of the Christians in 320 with the growing differences between him and Constantine. In 324 he was defeated by Constantine and he was put to death in 325.

Jones, *Lat. Rom. Emp.* (s.v.).

LICTORES Low rank officials, of Etruscan origin, belonging to the administrative staff of Roman magistrates and priests. They carried the *Fasces before holders of *Imperium, each holding one, and arrested, summoned, flogged or, before the establishment of *Provocatio, executed people on their orders. In the late Republic 30 L. represented the *curiae* in the *Comitia curiata (*l. curiatii*). L. also attended senators on official business.

LIGURIANS (Ligystinoi, Ligyes, Ligures) The large, old tribal population that once extended from northwest Italy (north of the Arno) to the Iberian peninsula. Some authorities connect them with the neolithic population of these regions. They are first mentioned by *Hecataeus but though known through Greek colonies in southern Gaul, very little is told about them by Greek writers. They were pressed by, and in part intermixed with, the *Celts. Roman magistrates subjugated the disunited Ligurian tribes in the course of the 2nd century BC, partly to ensure communications with Spain and to establish security and partly to gratify their own ambition for glory and booty.

J. Whatmough, *Foundations of Roman Italy,* 1937.

LILYBAEUM (modern Marsala) Major Carthaginian city in western Sicily, founded in 396 BC, after the destruction of Motya (old Phoenician town on an islet near the Sicilian western coast) by *Dionysius I. A strong and flourishing city, it became the main Punic base in Sicily and the Romans failed to capture it in the First Punic War, despite a long siege (250–241 BC). It was the residence of one of the two quaestors of the Roman province of Sicily. Augustus made it a *municipium* and *Pertinax (or Septimius Severus) a *colonia*.

LIMES Originally a boundary way, this term came to signify the frontier fortifications of the Roman Empire. Although the Romans had been always good at fortification, the idea to construct a line of defence along the frontiers developed late and is associated with the decision not to embark on further expansion. In Europe the defence of the empire was based on the rivers Rhine and Danube, after the collapse of the German policy of Augustus. Along the rivers it was sufficient to establish legionary forts, at intervals, but in Upper *Germany and *Raetia the whole frontier line was fortified. To the system of signal-towers constructed under Domitian along the Taunus was added a palisade under Hadrian. In the 3rd century the *L. Germanicus* consisted of an earthen rampart and a ditch and the *L. Raeticus* of a stone wall. Thus there existed a continuous defensive line from the Black Sea to the Northern Sea. Hadrian's Wall in Britain, constructed AD 122–6, extended from Wallsend-on-Tyne to Bowness-on-Solway. Its eastern part was made of stone, the western of turf, and it was strengthened by turrets and towered gates. In front of the wall and behind it there ran ditches; there were some outposts in front of the wall and the military way behind it connected its large garrison forts. When *Antoninus Pius advanced the frontier he built an earthen wall from the Forth to the Clyde (AD 142). It had a wide fosse in front of it, out-post forts and garrison forts, smaller than those of Hadrian's Wall. A similar stone wall with a fosse was constructed on the southern frontier of Numidia. In other parts of the empire, small or larger garrisons along a frontier road were established at intervals to secure the borders. The whole system was good for supplying information and preventing small inroads, while the major war operations were reserved for the legions to take in the open fields. The system worked quite well until the 3rd century but it was ineffective against the persistent invasions of the German tribes and the Persian attacks.

LINDUM (modern Lincoln) Originally a legionary fortress, established about the mid-1st century AD; a *colonia* was founded here, probably after the campaigns of *Agricola. It belonged to Lower Britain by the time of Septimius *Severus and was an important town to the 4th century AD when it had a bishop.

Frere, *Britannia* (s.v.).

LINEAR B The modern name given to the script discovered in the course of archaeological excavations on several sites in Greece and Crete. Clay tablets and some jars painted in this writing were found mainly in Cnossos, *Pylos and *Mycenae but also at *Tiryns, *Thebes, *Eleusis and few other places. In all some 4,000–5,000 tablets were discovered. Those of Cnossos, discovered first, date from the 14th century BC and were preserved because they were hardened by fire at the destruction of the palace. Those from the mainland date from the 13th century. Linear B evidently was the script used by the peoples of the Mycenaean civilization. The script was deciphered by Michael

A fort (Qasr al-Hêr) on the Syrian frontier

Ventris, helped by J. Chadwick, who used a "grid" system to arrange the pictographical signs and on the assumption that its language was Greek. The results were first published in 1952, and after much debate it is now commonly agreed that the script represents an Archaic Greek dialect. It also indicates that the Mycenaean civilization, with its palaces and monarchs, was the first developed by the Greeks, a conclusion long contested by those who identified Greeks with the *Polis only. The tablets themselves are mainly accounts and lists of articles prepared by the administration of the palaces. They use some 87 syllabic signs.

M. Ventris – J. Chadwick, *Documents in Mycenaean Greek*[2], 1973; J. Chadwick, *The Decipherment of Linear B*, 1960.

LITURGY (Leiturgia) Originally, the duty of the citizen to do service for the state. At Athens in the 5th and 4th centuries BC, it signified several duties, regular and irregular, imposed on rich citizens and metics by the state to be performed at their own expense. The *trierarchy was an irregular L. A regular one was the *choregia*; the person appointed to this duty (*choregos*) had to pay the expenses of a chorus, whose members he selected for the dramatic performances (including comedy, dithyramb and tragedy), and to each *choregos* was assigned one of the poets who took part in the competitions. A *choregos* whose chorus won the prize received a crown. Appointments were made in some cases by the *Archontes or *Strategoi and in others by the tribes. A person appointed to a L. might demand that another citizen, considered by himself wealthier, perform the duty, or that they exchange properties (*antidosis*). If the other refused, a court decided who was the wealthier, and he had to perform the

L. The L. was a duty and an honour, and public minded persons, or those seeking popularity, would occasionally volunteer. In Greek cities of the Hellenistic period the L. was assimilated to other regular offices, and those elected were expected to spend lavishly for the public needs. The system persisted under the Roman Empire when the Greek L. of the eastern provinces was similar to the *Munus in the West.

Pickard-Cambridge, *Dithyramb*[2]; *Dramatic Festivals*; Rostovtzeff, *Hellenistic World* (s.v.); *Roman Empire* (s.v.).

LIVIA Of a noble family, born 58 BC, she first married Tiberius Claudius Nero, *c*. 43 BC. Her husband, himself of a noble family, though a follower of Caesar in the Civil War, showed Republican inclinations after the latter's murder. L. followed him in his escape to Sicily in 41, but in 39 they divorced and Octavian married her. She bore two sons to Nero: Tiberius, the future emperor, and *Drusus (3) who was born about the time of her second marriage. To Octavian (Augustus) she bore no children. A woman of intelligence and charm, she was much respected by Augustus, who adopted her in his will; thus she became Julia Augusta after his death. Though Tiberius respected her, he did not like her intervention in government and relations between them became somewhat strained. After her death in AD 29, Tiberius refused to allow her to be deified and did not execute her will. Under the Emperor Claudius, her grandson, she was deified. The insinuations of Tacitus as to her sinister character and intrigues derive from gossip and rumour.

H. Syme, *Tacitus*, 1958 (s.v.).

LIVIUS ANDRONICUS, Lucius Important Latin poet. A Greek born in Tarentum, L. was captured in the war

against *Pyrrhus (or in 272 BC when his home town was conquered) and manumitted by his master, a Livius. He thus acquired the name Livius and Roman citizenship. With L. Latin literature began. At Rome he taught Latin, and was induced to translate the *Odyssey* which was the usual work Greek children learnt. In his free translation he used the native Saturnian verse instead of the hexameter, and his *Odyssia* was very influential and used as a schoolbook down to the 1st century BC. Of this, his most famous work, only 46 verses are known. He was the first Latin playwright, and produced his first play, probably a tragedy, in 240 BC. Of his tragedies and comedies, which were Latin adaptations of Greek plays, only few titles and some lines are extant. L. himself acted in his plays. He won public recognition and in 207 was commissioned to write a hymn for the gods (*Partheneion*). He was also allowed to found a guild of actors and writers at the temple of Minerva on the Aventine (207 BC).
Warmington, *Rem. Ol. Lat.*, vol. 2; Morel, *Fr. Poet. Lat.*; Beare, *Rom. St.*

LIVY (Titus Livius) Roman historian, native of Patavium (Padua), 59 BC–AD 17 or 64 BC–AD 12. He began his studies in his home town but came to Rome quite young and stayed there for a considerable part of his life, of which very little is known. He composed philosophical dialogues and wrote a treatise on rhetoric. He began his major work, a history of Rome (from the foundation of the city – *Ab Urbe Condita*) early in his life and used to read parts of it as the work progressed. Augustus showed interest in it, and L. himself encouraged Claudius, the future emperor, to produce his own Roman history. L. died in his home town.

L. devoted his whole life to the writing of his great work. He published Book 1.19,3 before 25 BC. His original plan was to arrange his work in pentads and decades. Books 1–5 cover the story of Rome from its foundation to its sack by the Gauls (390 BC), 6–10 carry the story to 293 BC; 11–15 bring it down to the beginning of the First Punic War, and 16–20 relate the story of that war and the period just before the start of the Second Punic War, which is given in Books 21–30. Books 31–45 carry the story to 167, with the Macedonian and Syrian Wars as its main themes; (Book 40 ends with the death of Philip V and 45 with the triumph of Paullus over Perseus). With the progress of the work and the growth of the material at his disposal, L.'s description became more detailed; for the period after the death of Sulla (which ended Book 90) he could no longer retain the pentad arrangement. The final work comprised 142 books and ended with the death of *Drusus (3) in 9 BC. Of these are extant Books 1–10 and 21–45, 35 books in total, which cover the years 753–293 and 218–167 BC. Of the abridgements made of the work, one is mentioned by Martial (14.190). One abridgement, commonly called *Periochae*, is extant; it includes all the books except 136–137, but it is more of a detailed table of contents than an abridgement and suffers from many errors and inaccuracies. In addition there are epitomes of Books 37–40, and 48–55, known from the Oxyrhynchus papyri, as well as a few short fragments.

L. came in the wake of a long tradition of Roman historiography. The idea of writing the whole history of Rome from the beginning down to the author's own time was not new; indeed the first Roman historian *Fabius Pictor did it, though probably, in some parts, in a discursive manner. The early Roman historians wrote short works; *Piso (1) covered the whole history of Rome to

the mid-2nd century BC, probably in seven books. L.'s immediate predecessors wrote at greater length; *Valerius Antias expounded Roman history to his own time in 75 books. L. wrote on a grand scale, but while in the early parts he treated several years in one book, in the later parts, he treated one year in several books. This was a direct result of the sources he used which were former historians — only seldom did he consult original documents — and as far as these were short or long, so was his narrative.

As a historian L. followed the conventions of his literary genre. In the preface to his work he states his aim as to present to the reader conspicuous models of exemplary conduct taken from real examples, and in contrast, examples of bad undertakings ending in disaster. It is obvious that, for L., historiography is in the first place a didactic and ethical exercise. The search for truth and accuracy is at best a secondary matter. This approach, which was quite conventional, dictated his manner of work and the main problem was to choose the right historian for each period or subject. Yet at times he consulted several authors, compared their narratives and either reproduced the one he preferred (usually later historians rather than earlier) or noted divergent versions. Occasionally he follows different authors in the same section for different subjects, without realizing the differences between them. This system accounts for some discrepancies, repetitions and chronological confusion. It also occasioned some omissions. He hardly mentions his authorities, except when they differ or when he changes the authors he follows. His authorities include *Polybius, *Coelius Antipater, *Claudius Quadrigarius, Licinius *Macer and *Valerius Antias. Some of L.'s defects can be ascribed to the use of an author like Valerius, notorious for his exaggerations and some of his merits to the use of an author like Polybius, famous for his search after truth and accuracy. L.'s geography is often poor — indeed he never took the trouble to visit the places about which he wrote — and his understanding of military affairs is limited. He was one of the few Roman historians who only wrote history and took no part in the making of it. This may explain the shallowness of his political accounts and his incorrect interpretations as well as his neglect of important themes. Obviously he hardly touches upon social and economic history; it would have been exceptional had he done so.

L.'s defects as an historian were rather those of Roman historiography in general than his own. But by contemporary standards he was successful. He gives a full, broad description of the rise of Rome, treating inner politics and foreign expansion. The processes he describes are explained by the character of his people and by the very course of events; occasionally he adds his explanations of the causes. The speeches he inserts help to illuminate the given situations and characters, besides being great rhetorical and psychological pieces. He is aware of the importance of individuals in history but does not give them undue place in his narrative. He deals with details but does not lose sight of the whole. He cares for the truth and never deliberately distorts it. But he is proud of the achievement of Rome, and the work is permeated with a basic conviction of its historical mission — to rule the world in an orderly manner. How Rome accomplished the task is told in an artistic fashion to please the readers.

L. is a master of his subject and he has the necessary breadth to expound it. His vocabulary is rich and he varies his style according to the various situations he deals with. He can be brief and factual in relating simple narrative; otherwise his language can be vivid and poetical, notably in his first books. On occasions he shows rhetorical power and dramatic skill. Generally his style was considered "milky" (Quintil. 10.1,32), that is, smooth and rich. Thus his style, language and achievement in creating a great picture of a great past won him immediate success as well as admirers from his time down to nowadays. Pliny the Younger relates that a Spaniard went to Rome simply to see him and then returned to Spain (*Ep.* 2.38). His eloquence and trustworthiness were recognized by Tacitus (*Ann.* 4.34) and Quintilian praised his charming narrative and diction (10.1,101). What *Pollio meant by criticizing his Patavinitas is not clear; perhaps he was referring to some nuances or peculiarities of vocabulary or pronunciation, or the naive, moral character of his work. Dante spoke of him as "Livy who does not err", and a major work of Machiavelli is his discourse on the first decade of L. No doubt he is one of the most important Latin prose-writers, and for the periods they treat, his books are indispensable to modern historians.

Text and commentary: G. Weissenborn – M. Müller (Teubner), 1858–1914; Text and translation: B. O. Foster, F. G. Moore, E. T. Sage, A. C. Schlesinger (Loeb), 1919–59. Ogilvie, *Livy*; P. G. Walsh, *Livy*, 1965; T. A. Dorey (ed.), *Latin Historians*, 1966; T. A. Dorey (ed.), *Livy*, 1971.

LOCRI EPIZEPHYRI (Locroi) Important Greek city, on the eastern coast of the toe of Italy, founded by settlers from *Locris in the early 7th century BC. It prospered and founded other colonies. Politically L. was associated with Syracuse and in rivalry with its Italian neighbours *Rhegium and Croton. Zaleucus, the first Greek law-giver, was a native of L.
A. G. Woodhead, *The Greeks in the West,* 1962 (s.v.).

LOCRIS Country in central Greece divided into the Opuntian Locrians in the east on the coast of the Euboean straits and Ozolian Locrians in the west, north of the Corinthian Gulf, without direct land communication between the two parts. It is supposed that the once united state was divided by the occupation of its centre by Phocians. For a long period the two parts retained their political association. The Locrians always remained insignificant communities in Greece and suffered from encroachments by their neighbours. *Amphissa was the main town of the western Locrians.
L. Lerat, *Les Locriens de l'ouest,* 1952.

LOGISTAI Board of auditors at Athens responsible for the examination of the financial reports that all magistrates were required to submit. They numbered 30 in the heyday of the Athenian Empire in the 5th century BC but only ten in the 4th century. If they found fault in the accounts, or if any citizen brought a charge, they had to take the case to the *Dikasterion and presided in the trial. See *Euthyna.

LOGOGRAPHERS (logographoi) The term was first used to signify the predecessors of *Herodotus who wrote prose works with some historical content. By criteria of later times they were poor writers in respect of style and language and their works were marred by errors and fictitious details. The most famous of them is *Hecataeus of Miletus. They wrote various kinds of works, on mythology, geography, and chronology, and also on the founding of cities. The other main meaning of L. is a speech writer. Lawyers were unknown at Athens and citizens had

to represent themselves in court and to deliver their speeches. It was common to apply to the service of a L., who would write the speech. The citizen would learn it by heart and then deliver it in court. *Isocrates began his rhetorical career as a L.
L. Pearson, *Early Ionian Historians,* 1939.

LOLLIUS This Roman senator, a *Novus Homo, was a follower of *Augustus. He governed Galatia (25 BC), Macedonia (*c.* 18 BC) and Gaul. He acted as an adviser to Gaius Caesar (Augustus' grandson, and son after his adoption), and incited him against Tiberius. He died in AD 2.
Syme, *Rom. Rev.* (s.v.).

LONDINUM (London) Originally a trading-station on the Thames, L. grew to be the capital city of Upper Britain under Septimius Severus. The Roman settlement began as early as AD 43, but L. was sacked in the revolt of *Boudicca (61 BC). The mint established here under *Carausius was closed in AD 326. A flourishing city, it probably became the capital of the *Dioecesis of Britain. In the 4th century, it had a bishop.
Frere, *Britannia* (s.v.).

LONGINUS The anonymous Greek writer of the treatise *On the Sublime (peri hypsous)*, who was once identified with Cassius Longinus, a Greek rhetorician of the 3rd century AD. It is now agreed that the treatise was written in the 1st century AD. The author professes to have been induced to write it by the unsatisfactory account of the subject made by one Caecilius of Calacte. He sets out to describe the five elements that constitute an impressive literary style. These are grandeur of conception, intensity of feeling, appropriate thoughts and figures of speech, nobility of diction, and ordered composition. It is an important work on literary criticism, and the author cites examples of what he considers to be good literary works. The author also shows originality and independent judgement. The work was often translated and had considerable influence until relatively recent times.
Text and translation: W. Rhys Roberts, 1907[2].

LONGUS The author of *Daphnis and Chloe.

LONG WALLS The name given to the walls – almost 6.5 km long – that connected Athens with *Piraeus and Phalerum. The first two walls were completed by 456 BC, and a third was added in 445. Destroyed by Sparta after the Peleponnesian War they were rebuilt by *Conon. They protected the supplies imported from abroad and brought to Athens through the port of Piraeus. In the Peleponnesian War, the population of Attica was evacuated and found shelter here.

LOTOPHAGOI (Lotus-eaters) A legendary people met by Odysseus during his voyage (Hom. *Od.* 9.82ff.). They lived on lotus fruit and were peaceful. Those of Odysseus' men who ate the lotus did not wish to return home. Various sites on the North African coast have been suggested as their place of abode, one of them the island of Djerba where Odysseus was said to have dedicated an altar. A few authorities locate the L. in Sicily.

LUCANUS (Marcus Annaeus Lucanus) Latin poet (AD 39–65), native of Cordoba, nephew of the philosopher *Seneca (2). His father (M. Annaeus Mela), a rich Roman knight, settled in Rome when L. was an infant. He received a good education and studied rhetoric, and probably philosophy under the Stoic *Cornutus; he went to Athens to complete his studies. Famous for his rhetorical powers and literary pursuits, he was recalled by Nero to join his circle of intimate friends. In AD 60, his poem in praise of Nero won a prize; soon thereafter, he embarked on his great work, an epic on the Civil War between Caesar and Pompey. The first three books appeared by AD 63. His relations with Nero became strained and the emperor forbade him to recite his poems in public. L. took part in the conspiracy of Piso and was ordered to commit suicide (3 April 65).

Of L.'s extensive writings, only titles and some fragments are known, the exception being the *Bellum Civile*, which is often called *Pharsalia*. This work consists of ten books and was left uncompleted on his death. L. begins it with an introduction and only in the second half of Book 2 does the description of the war itself begin (with Pompey's escape from Italy). Book 3 describes Caesar's operations in Italy and the siege of Massilia, and Book 4 concerns his operations in Spain and the victory at Ilerda. The events leading to Pharsalus occupy Books 5 and 6, and the battle at Pharsalus takes the whole of Book 7. The last three books carry the story to Caesar's occupation of Pharos at Alexandria. It seems that L. intended to end his epic with the death of Caesar.

L. showed much technical skill in the composition of his epic. Nevertheless, it is marred by serious faults. There are admirable epigrams, eloquent speeches, and occasionally colourful passages, and the metre is technically faultless. But L. had no sense of the right proportion, though he was wise enough to abandon the divine machinery. He indulged in minute and boring accounts; the numerous digressions are tedious, the exaggerations are often ridiculous, and the metre is monotonous. But most seriously, the epic lacks heroic dimension. Caesar might have been the hero, but L. came to hate the man and all that he stood for. For all his efforts, L. could not arouse sympathy for the tragic Pompey and the pedantic Cato. However, the spirit of liberty, the high emotions and the imaginative passages in the work, and the circumstances of L.'s death (it could be said in the cause of freedom), earned him much admiration through the ages, including that of Dante, Marlow, Shelley, Southey and Macauley.

Editions: A. E. Housman, 1926; J. D. Duff (Loeb) 1928. M. P. O. Morford, *The Poet Lucan*, 1967.

LUCANIA The mountainous region of southwestern Italy, bordered by Campania in the northwest, Bruttium in the south, the Gulf of Tarentum in the east, and separated from Apulia in the north by the river Bradanus. It took its name from the Sabellic tribe, Lucani, which had occupied the land by the early 4th century BC. The Oenotri and Chones were the earlier populations, and Greeks founded colonies on several coastal sites (e.g. Metapontum, *Paestum, *Elea). The Lucanian aggression against *Thurii led to Rome's intervention, and finally to the arrival of *Pyrrhus (who was invited by *Tarentum). The Lucanians supported *Hannibal and suffered much from the Romans — a large part of their territory was confiscated and became *Ager Publicus. They took part in the *Bellum Sociale and were subsequently annihilated by Sulla in the Civil War.

E. Magaldi, *Lucania Romana*, 1947.

LUCIAN Famous Greek writer, Sophist and satirist, native of Samosata in *Commagene, born *c.* AD 120. Of non-Greek origin, L. received a Greek education in Ionia. He studied rhetoric, travelled extensively, and gave public lectures in Asia Minor, Greece, Macedonia, Italy and Gaul. At the age of 40, he settled in Athens where he devoted himself to philosophy for about twenty years until, under *Commodus, he accepted a post in Egypt.

Some eighty works of L. are extant. They are written in good Attic, mainly in dialogue form. They include orations, essays, letters and short novels (none of his works is long). He was mainly influenced by *Menippus of Gadara, Greek comic playwrights (notably *Aristophanes and *Menander) and writers of mimes (*Mimus). L. also modelled some of his dialogues on those of Plato. He was not a profound thinker but a satirist, sensitive to human follies and with the literary talent to present his subject-matter with humour. Sceptical and ironic, L. showed no reverence for philosophers, gods, and writers. He despised superstition (and hence did not spare Christian fanatics); he commented on art, and criticized contemporary manners, religious beliefs, and ideas. Of his dialogues, the better known are *The Dialogues of the Dead, Dialogues of the Courtesans, Sailor's Dialogues*. Indeed, the satiric dialogue was his very own contribution to Greek literature. His *The True History* is an excellent parody of travellers' stories — all of which are lies. In the epistolary genres were written *How to Write History, Peregrinus and Alexander* (the Christian fanatic and religious impostor). That he wrote *Lucius or The Ass* is disputed (*Apuleius). He has always been popular with people sensitive to human follies (e.g. Erasmus).

A. M. Harmon, K. Kilburn, M. D. Macleod (Loeb), 1911–1967; G. W. Bowersock, *The Sophists in the Roman World*, 1969.

LUCILIUS (1), Gaius Latin poet (*c.* 180–102/101 BC), native of Suessa Aurunca, of a wealthy family. He settled in Rome, established connections with members of the upper classes, and was on especially good terms with *Scipio (5) Aemilianus, with whom he was in *Numantia (134–133 BC). His brother was a senator (and some conjectured that he, too, was a senator), and his niece was the wife of *Pompeius Strabo and the mother of Pompey. He had estates in southern Italy, Sicily and Sardinia. Independent and with powerful friends, he could freely attack men of the highest rank in the Roman aristocracy. He died in Naples where he spent his last years.

L. was the first Latin satirist, but of his thirty books of poetry only some 1,300 verses have survived in fragments. From first to last his satires bear the stamp of his personality, being presented as a sort of autobiography (Hor. *Sat.* 2.1) — Book 3, for instance, describes a journey to Sicily. According to Horace, L. was much influenced by Aristophanes and the Old Comedy (*Sat.* 1.4). The satires were characterized by criticism of and personal attacks on living persons (such as Cornelius Lentulus Lupus). Though he later became especially known for his invective and wit, L. dealt not only with people but also with philosophical, literary and grammatical questions. Books 26–30 were the first to be published (*c.* 125 BC); here he used various verse forms, including the hexameter which he employed in all his other books (Books 1–21 appeared 123–106 BC and the rest appeared thereafter). His verse was not polished and was even carelessly written. Horace later said that people, influenced by L., thought that careless composition was a prerequisite of free criticism. Otherwise it is his fierce spirit and vigorous descriptive powers that characterize L.'s writing. He was widely read and had much influence on satirists, notably Horace, who adopted the hexameter for this genre and also indulged in personal invective.

Warmington, *Rem. Ol. Lat.*, 3; J. Wight Duff, *Roman Satire*, 1937.

LUCILIUS (2) IUNIOR, Gaius Known as the friend of

*Seneca (2) the Younger who was his senior by some years. L. was born in Campania to a family with little means. Apparently talented, he made a fortune, became a Roman knight, and made an equestrian career. Under Claudius and Nero he served as procurator in Alpes Graiae, Macedonia, Africa and Sicily. Seneca's *Epistulae Morales*, *De Providentia* and *Quaestiones Naturales* are addressed to him. Intellectual and with literary interests, he wrote poems and a philosophical treatise (not extant). It has been suggested, but not very convincingly, that he is the author of the *Aetna*.

LUCRETIA In Roman tradition, a beautiful Roman lady who was raped by Sextus, son of the King *Tarquinius Superbus. Unable to endure life, she informed her husband Tarquinius Collatinus of what had happened and committed suicide. Under the leadership of *Brutus (1) the enraged people rose and expelled the king and his supporters. Her husband joined the revolt and was allegedly one of the first consuls, but later, being a Tarquin, he went into voluntary exile. The Rape of Lucretia was a favourite theme with poets (e.g. Shakespeare) and painters (e.g. Botticelli, Titian).
Ogilvie, *Livy*, 218ff.

LUCRETIUS (Titus Lucretius Carus) Roman poet and Epicurean philosopher of whose life only a few details are known. Jerome says that he was born in 95 BC and lived 44 years; but it would appear from Cicero that he was dead by 54 BC; perhaps, then, he was born in 99 BC. He dedicated his great poetry to Memmius, a mediocre contemporary statesman (with whom *Catullus, too, was associated). His name is that of the old aristocratic family of Lucretii, but if Memmius was socially his superior, then L. could hardly have belonged to the distinguished Lucretii. Jerome says that L. was driven mad by a love-potion, wrote during intervals of sanity, and finally committed suicide. But his major poem is certainly not the work of a lunatic, and Jerome's testimony is probably a Christian slander on the author of such poetry.

The *De Rerum Natura* ("Concerning Nature"), his only work, is a didactic poem in 6 books and comprises some 7,400 verses. L. did not complete it and, again according to Jerome, Cicero "emended" it; this seems to indicate that he edited it. L. had one overriding purpose: to give a lucid exposition of the physical theory of *Epicurus and thereby to liberate men from superstitions and fears of gods and death. The physical theory is based on the atomic theory of *Democritus and Leucippus. Book 1 starts with a justifiably famous invocation of Venus; he then demonstrates the existence of matter in the form of small particles, and of void as empty space. The particles are the "atoms" — solid, indivisible and indestructible. Earlier physical theories of *Heraclitus and *Empedocles are then refuted, and the final conclusion is that the universe is infinite. In Book 2 the view is introduced that atoms, which are in state of motion, are characterized by their size and shape, and not by other qualities such as heat, colour and smell. The book ends with the theory of the formation and disintegration of the many worlds. Book 3 shows the material, atomic nature of the soul which is therefore mortal and does not last after death. Death, then, is not to be feared. The final section is a hymn on the mortality of the soul. Book 4 deals with sensation, vision, thought, dreams and sleep. All are given a physical explanation. It also includes an attack on the passion of love. Book 5 deals with the beginning and the development (and the end) of the world, of vegetable and of animal life, of man and of civilization. Book 6 deals with various meteorological and terrestial phenomena, including thunder and lightning, earthquakes and volcanoes, and ends with the famous description of the plague at Athens.

For L., his poem was in the first place a philosophical work. In this respect he was an admirer of Epicurus, the teacher who showed the way to be freed from superstition and to overcome hardships on earth. But L. was too much of a true poet to simply expound in verse the philosophy he was devoted to. He had the eye and the ear and the intelligence to observe the peculiarities and the phenomena of the world around him. His imagination and vivid language transform even passages on abstruse themes into interesting and attractive pieces. He had an innate vigour and, though he found Latin a poor vehicle for his subject, he mastered the language and produced eloquent passages and vivid descriptions of nature. His use of the hexameter, however, included blemishes and could not be compared to that of Virgil — but for L.'s time it was a great success. He also used archaism, alliteration and assonance. Technical considerations aside, it is the majestic treatment of a lofty subject that makes *De Rerum Natura* a great poem.
Edition, translation and commentary: C. Bailey, 1947; D. R. Dudley (ed.), *Lucretius*, 1965.

LUCULLUS, Lucius Licinius Roman general and statesman. His grandfather was the first in his family to attain the consulate, in 151 BC, and he elevated the rest of the family to the nobility. After service in the *Bellum Sociale under *Sulla, L. followed him in the capture of Rome (88 BC), and in the Mithridatic War, in which he showed diplomatic skill and military capacity. After his praetorship in 78, he governed Africa. As consul in 74, he curbed agitation against the Sullan reforms and received the command against *Mithridates VI. He achieved a spectacular success in the war, occupied Pontus and defeated the Armenian King Tigranes, whose capital he captured (69 BC). However, Mithridates escaped and recruited new troops, L.'s army mutinied and, in Rome, his personal enemies intrigued against him. Many who had invested their money in loans in Asia suffered from his financial reorganization in the province and now took revenge. His provinces were taken from him and in 66 Pompey was given the command against Mithridates. It was only in 63 BC that L. was allowed to celebrate a triumph. In so far as he took part in politics he acted against Pompey, but after 59 BC he found his sole pleasure in living luxuriously. He died in 55. L. was a great military commander, and a good administrator, with a sense of justice in his dealings with provincials. But in his time, he was too much of a disciplinarian to win the devotion of his soldiers, and too conservative and high minded to seek popularity in Rome.
Plut. *Lucullus*; J. Van Ooteghem, *Lucullus*, 1959.

LUDI The term *Ludus* (pl. *Ludi*) refers in particular to the games, contests and spectacles which were associated with the religious festivals in Rome (*Feriae). They were originally thought of as rites. The following types of L. can be distinguished according to their list of events: races (horse and chariot), athletics, theatrical performances (*Ludi Scaenici); gladiatorial shows (which properly speaking were *munera*), religious dances (*Salii); wild-beast shows (*venationes*), competitions in the Greek style (*Agones). These last were first introduced in 186 BC but became common later with contests in music and Greek and Latin poetry as their special characteristics. There were also exceptional shows such as mimic sea-fights (*naumachiae*). Shows that were given in the *Circus were *L. Circenses*, shown on the stage — *L. Scaenici*. The games were given either by the public (the state or any city outside Rome) or by private men. There were regular games and irregular games (the latter were given on certain occasions — voted in battle (*L. votivi*), or in honour of the deceased (*L. funebres*)).

In early times, the L. were limited to one day, but eventually they were extended over several days. Of the public games held during the late Republic, the following may be noted: 1) *L. Romani* (or *Magni*) — 4—18 September (they were *scaenici* and *circenses* and held in honour of Jupiter); 2) *L. Plebeii* — 4—17 November (originally only *circenses* but very soon also *scaenici*); 3) *L. Cereales* — 12—19 April (*scaenici*, with one day of *circenses*, in honour of *Ceres); 4) *L. Apollinares* — 6—13 July (in honour of Apollo, mainly scenic shows with only one day for the circus); 5) *L. Megalenses* — 4—10 April (in honour of the Magna Mater (*Cybele), only one day for the circus and the rest for the scenic shows); 6) *L. Florales* — 28 April—3 May (in honour of the goddess Flora).

Evidently, the L. occupied a large part of the year and under the Empire their duration was extended and their number was added to. Some L. were only only later celebrated on fixed dates. The L. usually started with a solemn procession, and some included a public banquet. The Senate allocated a sum of money (that of the *Plebeii* was 600,000 sesterces in the 1st century BC), but the magistrates responsible — mainly aediles — were expected to add to it from their own pockets. The passion for L. was strong and they were held all over the Empire; every city had its own theatre and amphitheatre, and often had more than one.

The term *Ludus* also signified a school building — for ordinary education and teaching as well as for the training of gladiators. And L. meant any game — with a ball, with toys etc.

LUDI SCAENICI Theatrical performance was first given in Rome in 364 BC as a propitiatory rite to get rid of the pestilence. The players (*ludiones*) were from Etruria; they performed a dance in mime, with musical accompaniment from a double pipe and without words (Liv. 7.2). LS. subsequently became irregular shows consisting of the Etruscan mimetic dances with Roman Fescennine verses and with music. The first performance of a Greek play in a Latin adaptation was given by *Livius Andronicus in 240 BC, and he was followed by *Naevius (*c.* 225 BC, Gell. 17.21,44). Most of the regular Ludi were devoted to theatrical performances, which now consisted of *Ludi Graeci* (that is, Latin adaptations of Greek plays), and *Ludi Latini* (that is, original Latin plays in terms of content, language and spirit). Under the Empire, mime and pantomime were the main performances and for a long time the shows were given on temporary wooden platforms around which the spectators arranged themselves as best as they could. It was felt that a permanent building devoted to these shows would lead to the corruption of morals. The first permanent theatre in Rome was built by Pompey in 55 BC — but others had been built earlier in various Italian cities.

See *Atellana Fabula, *Comedy, Roman, *Fabula, *Ludi, *Mimus.

Bear, *Rom. St.*

LUGDUNUM (modern Lyon) This city, near the confluence of the Rhône and Saône, was founded by L.

Munatius *Plancus as a *colonia* (later Colonia Copia Claudia Augusta. With good communications, it prospered and was the capital of the province Gallia Lugdunensis, with an imperial mint. In the wars of Septimius *Severus, it was seriously damaged and thereafter it declined somewhat. An altar of Rome and Augustus was founded by *Drusus (3) in 12 BC near the city, and it became the centre of the imperial cult of the Gallic provinces. In the 5th century, L. became the centre of the *Burgundi. The Emperor Claudius was born here and an inscription with his famous speech on the acceptance of provincials into the Senate was found here. The four Roman aqueducts at Lyon are the best examples of inverted siphons; there is also a theatre and odeon.
P. Wuilleumier, *Lyon*, 1953.

LUNA The Italian moon-goddess, said to have been introduced to Rome by the Sabine King Titus Tatius. She was worshipped on the Aventine, with a temple that was burnt in the fire during Nero's time. Another temple was on the Palatine. The moon-goddess was identified with goddesses of birth (*Iuno, *Diana).
Platner-Ashby, *Top. Dict. Rome*, 320; Latte, *R. Rel.*, 232f.

LUPERCALIA Old Roman festival celebrated on 15 February in honour of *Faunus. The rite took place at the Lupercal, a cave at the foot of the Palatine where the she-wolf fed Romulus and Remus; *Evander was thought to have built a shrine to Faunus (identified with *Pan) here. The rite was performed by the Luperci. It started with the sacrifice of a goat and a dog and then the young Luperci, wearing only girdles, ran around the bounds of the Palatine — whipping by-standers with strips of goatskin. The whipped were thought to be assured fertility. The purification of the bounds and their securing against wolves were the ideas associated with the ceremony.
F. Altheim, *A History of Roman Religion*, 1938, 206ff.

LUSITANIA The country of the Lusitani, a great tribal group of Ibero-Celtic origin, in the west of the Iberian peninsula. The Romans fought them, at intervals, from the early 2nd century BC. A long war was conducted against their great leader *Viriathus from *c.* 150 BC until his treacherous murder in 139 BC. They supported *Sertorius and it was only with great difficulty that Pompey conquered them. Augustus completed the conquest and pacification of their country; the southeastern part of it was included in the province *Baetica. He organized the province L. which was bounded by the rivers Anas (Guadiana) in the southeast and Durius (Douro) in the north. From then the peaceful province gradually developed its economic resources.
C. H. V. Sutherland, *The Romans in Spain*, 1939;
Van Nostrand, *ESAR*, 3.

LUSIUS QUIETUS Roman general, a Moor by origin, first employed by Domitian. He served with his native cavalry under Trajan in the conquest of Dacia and for his achievements was made a senator with praetorian rank (and later was *consul suffectus*). He took part in Trajan's Parthian expedition, suppressed the revolt of the Jews in Mesopotamia and then, as a legate, quickly stopped the disturbances in Judaea. He lost the command of his troops after the accession of *Hadrian, and in AD 118 was executed on a charge of conspiracy.
Syme, *Tacitus*, 1958 (s.v.).

LUSTRATION Various rites of purification were used by the Romans; they dated from remote times, and at an early stage they were mainly associated with primitive agricultural societies. The essential element in such a rite (*lustratio*) was to form a procession around the object – a person, a piece of land, or a city – that had to be purified with materials that were considered to have magical power. Sacrifices were also made. Such a purificatory rite was carried out for the Roman people every five years by the *censors, on completing their duties (*lustrum*). Rites correctly performed were thought to banish evil and secure the good.

See *Ambarvalia, *Lupercalia.

LUTETIA (or LUTECIA) PARISORUM The capital of the Parisii (modern Paris), first settled in the 3rd century BC and originally confined to an island on the Seine. It is first recorded by Caesar (*Bell. Gall.* 6.3). Under the Empire, it was called by the name of the tribe only (*Parisia Civitas*), and was an important ship station on the Seine but not a great city. Julian was proclaimed emperor here (360 BC).
P. M. Duval, *Paris antique*, 1961.

LYCAON See *ARCAS.

LYCAONIA The country of the Lycaonians in central Asia Minor, north of Mount Taurus, bounded by Cilicia, Cappadocia, Phrygia (later Galatia) and Pisidia. The boundaries shifted in the course of time with the various political changes that took place thereabouts. It was subject to Persia, the Seleucids and Pergamum, and, after 133 BC, to Rome. Under the Roman Empire, the country was organized in several ways, with attachments to the adjacent provinces. The main cities were Iconium and Laranda.
Magie, *Asia* (s.v.).

LYCIA Mountainous country in southwest Asia Minor, bounded by Pamphylia, Pisidia and Caria. The Lycians, first mentioned by Homer (*Il.* 2.876f.), were the allies of King Priam in the Trojan War, led by *Glaucus and *Sarpedon. Herodotus writes that they originated in Crete and had been called Termilae by their neighbours, a name known from inscriptions. The country was subdued by *Cyrus I, but it was included in the Athenian Empire for a short period in the mid-5th century BC. After the conquest of Alexander the Great and the wars of the *Diadochi, it belonged to the Ptolemaic kings until 197 BC. Rome assigned it to Rhodes after the defeat of *Antiochus III (188 BC), but made it free from 169 BC. It was organized as a Roman province, with Pamphylia, in AD 43. However, even under foreign rule, the Lycians retained some autonomy and the local rulers tended to cooperate with each other. The main cities were Telmessus, Xanthus, Patara, Myra and Phaselis (the most eastern). A Lycian League, *Koinon*, was established in the Hellenistic period, with a central council in which the constituent cities had representatives according to their relative size. The League struck coins with the lyre as the main device, but the individual cities continued to have their own coins. The Lycians were Hellenized and from the 3rd century on used only Greek in their inscriptions.
Magie, *Asia* (s.v.); Larsen, *Gr. Fed. St.*, 240ff.

LYCO Pupil of *Strato and his successor as head of the *Peripatetic School (*c.* 268–*c.* 224 BC). He was interested more in worldly affairs than in philosophical research and of his few writings very few fragments are extant. Though a good speaker, he was ranked a low thinker by Cicero (*Fin.* 5.13). He died *c.* 228/224 BC.

LYCOPHRON (1) Tyrant of *Pherae (*c.* 405–390 BC). He rose to power by courting the low classes against the Thessalian aristocracy, and won a victory over the aristocrats of the Thessalian cities, notably Larissa, on 3 September 404. His alliance with Sparta did not win him the hegemony of Thessaly which continued to be torn by internal feuds. The tyrant *Jason (2) was probably his son.

LYCOPHRON (2) Greek poet and scholar, born at Chalcis in Euboea *c.* 320 BC. He came to Alexandria under Ptolemy II and received a post in the Library, where he worked on the preparation of a catalogue of comedies. It was probably in connection with this work that he wrote the treatise *On Comedy* (in at least nine books), which has not survived. But he was mainly renowned as a tragedian and was one of the seven poets of the tragic Pleiad. Twenty titles of his 46 (or 64) tragedies are known, but only one fragment of four lines from the *Pelopidae* is extant. The extant poem *Alexandra* is attributed to L. It consists of 1,474 iambic trimeters in which a slave reports the prophecies of his charge, *Cassandra (= Alexandra), to her father King Priam. Cassandra predicts the destruction of Troy and the sufferings of the Greeks on their homeward voyage, and also the rise of Rome to power. As the lines 1,446–50 allude to *Flaminius' victory (197 BC), the poem must have been written by a later poet; but they possibly refer to the war against *Pyrrhus. The poem is very obscure and the poet indulges in recondite erudition, bizzare idioms and metaphors, and tantalizing allusions.
W. A. Mair, *Callimachus, Lycophron, Aratus* (Loeb), 1921.

LYCORTAS Achaean statesman, native of Megalopolis and father of the historian *Polybius. He supported the policy of his friend *Philopoemen against Sparta and sought cooperation with Egypt. He quelled the insurgent Messenians after the death of his friend, but lost his influence in the late 170s BC.

LYCURGUS (1) The Spartan legislator to whom were ascribed all the institutions of Sparta: constitutional, social and military. He is first recorded by Herodotus (1.15) who relates that he was a guardian of King Leobotes (*c.* 900 BC), but other authors dated him between the 11th and the 8th century BC. By the 5th century, he was worshipped as a semi-god in Sparta. The doubts expressed by modern scholars as to his very existence, occasioned by chronological and other difficulties in the stories about him, are not justified, although some reforms were erroneously ascribed to him. It seems that the social customs associated with him had their roots in tribal times and that the economic measures and peculiar austerity of the Spartans were a later development (*c.* early 6th century BC). His main work was the political organization of Sparta which was introduced by the Great Rhetra (Plut. *Lyc.* 5–6) he brought from Delphi, probably in the 8th century BC.
Plut. *Lyc.*; G. L. Huxley, *Early Sparta*, 1962;
A. J. Toynbee, *Some Problems of Greek History*, 1969.

LYCURGUS (2) Athenian statesman and orator (*c.* 390–*c.* 325 BC). He was of the priestly family of the Eteobutadae and the son of Lycophron. He supported Demosthenes in his anti-Macedonian policy and rose to power after the battle of *Chaeronea. For twelve years, he administered the finances and the public works of Athens, though it is not known what his exact title and powers were. He largely increased the revenues of the state (to perhaps 1,200 talents a year), enlarged the navy, improved the harbours and rebuilt the theatre of Dionysus (now made of stone). He also commissioned the erection of statues of Aeschylus, Sophocles and Euripides and the preparation of official copies of their plays. Of his speeches only one is extant, *Against Leocrates*. It was delivered in his prosecution of Leocrates in 331 BC. The speech shows L. as a man devoted to the service of his state, severe and intransigent, and this was his reputation in antiquity. In style he was influenced by Isocrates, but he cared more for content than for elegance.

Kennedy, *Persuasion*; Burtt, *Min. At. Or.*

LYCURGUS (3) Mythological king of Thrace. He drove away Dionysus (Hom. *Il.* 6.130ff.) and as punishment was blinded and driven mad.

LYDIA Country in western Asia Minor, bounded by Caria in the south, Phrygia in the east, and Mysia in the north; another old name for it was Maionia. The *Ionians settled on its western coast (e.g. *Smyrna, *Ephesus) and thus it was profoundly influenced by Greek civilization. A powerful kingdom was established by the local dynasty of the Mermnads (*c.* 700–546 BC) whose kings sent many rich offerings to Delphi. The first king was *Gyges and he was succeeded by Ardys, Sadyattes, Alyattes and *Croesus. The first coins ever struck appeared under Gyges. The Greeks soon followed his invention – and this was not the only thing they received from the Lydians. (Tyrant was probably a word of Lydian origin.) Ardys, Gyges' son, destroyed the Cimmerians who had wreaked havoc in the country. The last king, *Croesus, consulted the Delphic Oracle before he went to war against *Cyrus. The conquered country became a Persian satrapy, with Sardes as its capital, and it remained such until conquered by Alexander the Great. After the wars of the *Diadochi, L. mainly belonged to the Seleucids; from 189 BC it belonged to the Attalids of Pergamum. It became part of the Roman province of Asia in 133 BC.

G. E. Bean, *Aegean Turkey*, 1966.

LYDUS, Joannes Laurentius Greek author, native of Lydia (hence his name), born AD 490. He studied in Constantinople and received a post under the praetorian prefect. His rich wife died shortly after their wedding. After 40 years of service he retired, *c.* AD 552 and wrote his works, the most important of which is *De Magistratibus Populi Romani* (*peri archon tes romaion politeia*) in two books. This treats the magistracies of Rome from the regal period to the Empire. His other two works are *De Mensis* (only partly extant) and *De Ostentis*.

Carny, *John the Lydian* (tran.), 1965;
A. H. M. Jones, *JRS*, 1949, 38ff.

LYGDAMUS Latin poet, the author of six poems included in Book 3 of Tibullus' works. He aims at regaining the affection of Neaera with his tedious love-elegies. The names of the poet and his beloved are probably pseudonyms and their true identity is not known.

LYRIC POETRY, GREEK The term *lyricos* is very late (first attested in the 2nd century BC), and was probably first used by the Alexandrian scholars who distinguished between different genres of poetry. By their criteria, LP. was that composed to be sung to the lyre, while epic poetry was for recitation, accompanied by the flute. Earlier lyric was properly called *melos*, and a lyric poet, *melopoios*. The Alexandrian scholars also listed nine poets in their canon of LP.: *Alcman, *Sappho, *Alcaeus, *Stesichorus, *Anacreon, *Ibycus, *Simonides, *Pindar, *Bacchylides. There were two types of lyric – the monody, a poem composed for a solo performance, and the choral. Sometimes, choral poems consisted of a solo by a leader and an answer by the chorus. The choral (*molpe*) was performed normally with a dance in religious festivals. The monody was usually performed on private oc-

casions and essentially expressed the feelings of the individual. It was simpler in structure and wording and included personal experiences (e.g. love) in its themes. But these were not hard and fast rules and monody could be performed in public and choral on private occasions.

The Homeric poems give evidence of ballads performed by solo singers and of choral songs: the dirge (a song sung for the dead), hymn (any poem addressed to the gods), *hyporchema* (a song with mimetic dancing), maiden-songs, marriage-songs. The processional song (*Prosodion*) was performed by the 8th century, though it is not mentioned by Homer. It is clear that these types of LP. go back to prehistory. The songs were composed to be performed on particular occasions and for centuries they retained this character. The dinner party or symposium came to be the commonest occasion for the performance of the monody. An important type of the choral came to be the *dithyramb, associated with the cult of Dionysus. The *Encomium* was a song composed to celebrate the achievements of prominent persons, and in this respect the *Epinician*, a song composed for a victor in one of the pan-Hellenic games, was an *Encomium*. The decline of LP. from the late 5th century on was partly associated with the rise of democratic life, when the customs and ideas associated with the aristocracy lost their vitality. The dithyramb persisted through its association with the tragedy, and the *Nomos*, an astrophic poem with emphasis on music, was the main form of monody. The old distinctions were not retained in the Hellenistic period when poetry was recited, not sung. Poets then composed poems which had no real association with the social background of the old genres.

See the poets mentioned (with bibliographies).

Page, *Poet. Mel. Gr.*; Bowra, *Gr. Lyr. Poet.*;
A. D. Campbell, *Greek Lyric Poetry*, 1967;
D. L. Page, *Lyrica Graeca Selecta*, 1968.

LYRIC POETRY, LATIN The essential element of the LP. of the Greeks – that the poems were to be sung – was never applied to the Latin lyric. Latin literature came under Greek influence, and indeed developed only by this influence, at a time when the Greek lyric had already lost this essential characteristic. Except for the *Partheneion* of *Livius Andronicus and the *Carmen Saeculare* of *Horace, lyric poems were written to be read and not sung. And nor can the Latin lyric be termed "lyric" according to the modern criterion, as it was not poetry designed to give expression to personal feelings in short poems. The only two great Latin poets to write LP. were *Catullus and Horace. It was mainly the use of the metres of the Greek lyric that made them lyric poets, although some of the lyric poems – by modern standards – of Catullus were not composed in these metres. The accomplished poems of these two can be ranked with the best of the ancient LP. Generally, however, LP. was not much to the taste of the Romans. Seneca the Younger includes choral odes in his tragedies, and Statius has two lyric poems (*Silvae* 4.5 and 7), but these are not comparable to the former's work. The next lyric poet of importance is *Prudentius in the late 4th century AD.

J. P. Sullivan (ed.), *Critical Essays on Roman Literature, Elegy and Lyric*, 1962;
G. Gordon, *Tradition and Originality in Roman Poetry*, 1968.

LYSANDER Spartan statesman and general who rose to prominence in the last stage of the Peloponnesian War. He was given command of the Spartan fleet in 408/407 BC

Man playing a lyre, mid-5th century BC

and defeated an officer of *Alcibiades at Notium (406 BC), after winning the confidence and support of *Cyrus (2). By his victory over the Athenain fleet at *Aegospotamoi (405) he left no hope for Athens, which he took in 404 BC. At his initiative, the Athenian democracy was abolished and the power to rule was given to the *Thirty Tyrants. He established oligarchies in most of the cities formerly allied to Athens (*Decarchies). But his policy was opposed by the Spartan government which allowed Athens to restore the democracy. L. tried to regain his influence by supporting *Agesilaus II, but the latter was far from grateful to him. L. was killed when he invaded Boeotia at the beginning of the Corinthian War (395 BC). One of the best generals Sparta had, he made himself unpopular by his arrogance and personal ambition.
Plut. *Lysander*.

LYSIAS Attic orator, born before 450 BC, died *c.* 380–375 BC. His father Cephalus, a prosperous Syracusan, settled at Athens at the request of Pericles. Plato's *Republic* opens with a discussion in the house of Polemarchus, the

eldest brother of L. These two, with their third brother, Euthydemus, went to live in *Thurii. In 412 BC, they returned to Athens and had success as manufacturers of shields. In 404, Polemarchus was put to death by the *Thirty Tyrants but L. escaped to Megara and returned with the restoration of the democracy. In recognition of his services, he was given Athenian citizenship, but this was cancelled on a technical point. L. thereafter worked as a *logographer; as a *metoikos* he was not allowed to appear in court. He also probably taught rhetoric. He is said to have died at the age of 80.

Of L.'s more than 200 speeches, 35 are extant, but some of them are spurious. The cases vary: homicide, embezzlement, bribery, negligence of public duties, high treason, etc. They cover various aspects of contemporary life: political, social and economic. Few of the speeches were delivered by him; one of these is an outstanding oration, perhaps the best of L., *Against Eratosthenes*. Eratosthenes was one of the Thirty Tyrants, responsible for the execution of Polemarchus. The speech gives excellent evidence of L.'s personal experience in that period of terror, and has eloquence and elegance with irony. He also delivered the *Epitaphios*, on those who fell in the Corinthian War, and the *Olympiacus*, of which only part of the oxordium survives. Other notable speeches are *For the Cripple* and *Against Simon*. L. was famous for his simple, clear style. He was careful not to use unfamiliar words and exaggerated figures of speech. His speeches have logical sequence and are noted for their smoothness. What perhaps made L. a successful logographer was his ability to make his clients speak naturally and express their personality.

Edition: W. R. M. Lamb (Loeb), 1930;
Kennedy, *Persuasion*; K. J. Dover, *Lysias*, 1968.

LYSIMACHUS Son of Agathocles, one of Alexander's companions, L. was born *c.* 360 BC and rose to power in the wars of the *Diadochi. He was given command of Thrace and of northwest Asia Minor and married the daughter of *Antipater (1). He joined *Seleucus I, *Cassander and *Ptolemy I against *Antigonus I in 315 BC and established his power from the Aegean to the mouth of the Danube. In 309 BC, he founded Lysimachia as his capital at the isthmus of the Thracian Chersonese. He helped Rhodes during her siege by *Demetrius (1), and, in 302 BC, conducted a defensive campaign against Antigonus I in Asia Minor, until the arrival of Seleucus I. They both defeated their enemy at the battle of Ipsus, and L. received most of Asia Minor to Mount Taurus. He was captured across the Danube in 292 BC, but regained his freedom by giving up territory. He won Macedonia and Thessaly from *Demetrius I and *Pyrrhus in 285 BC. At the height of his power, his house suffered from a feud between his wife *Arsinoe (2) and Lysandra, his daughter-in-law, as a result of which he executed his son Agathocles. His rule was oppressive and he became hated. In 281 BC, L. was defeated and killed by Seleucus I at Curupedium; his kingdom disintegrated after his death.

Will, *His. Pol.* (s.v.).

LYSIPPUS Important Greek sculptor, native of Sicyon, active in the 4th century BC. He mainly worked in bronze but also in marble. According to Pliny the Elder (*NH* 34.65), L. introduced new proportions in his sculptures: the head became smaller and the body more slender. This had the effect of making his figures appear taller. He also introduced movement in his statues, with the different parts (head, trunk, limbs) facing different directions; the total impression is one of potential dynamism. L. said that the Doryphorus of *Polyclitus was the major influence on his work, but he differed from his predecessor whose statues were characterized mainly by strength and stability. But L. perpetuated the athletic ideal, and his masterpiece is the Apoxyomenos, a young athlete scraping himself with a strigil. It was made in the late 4th century and is known from a Roman copy, in the Vatican Museum. Many other works are attributed to L. The Heracles Farnese, signed by Glycon, is a copy of Heracles made by L. for Sicyon, of which there are other copies. The Heracles Epitrapezios (of which there is a Roman copy in the British Museum) was the statuette Alexander used to carry with him (Alexander allowed only L. to sculpt him). This statuette is described by Martial (9.44) and Statius (*Silvae* 46) and copies of it are extant. L. also made a relief of Seleucus I. He was known for his colossal statues and animal figures. Because of his new proportions, large scale compositions and realism, he had much influence on Hellenistic art.

LYSISTRATUS Greek sculptor, brother of *Lysippus, whose main interest was in portraits. Pliny the Elder says that he invented the art of taking casts from statues (*NH* 35.153). That such an important innovation, which was later extensively used to supply copies to Romans interested in Greek art, was made in the 4th century BC has been doubted. Pliny also says that he made plaster casts of his models and poured wax on them so that he could make exact likenesses. Apparently he was interested in realistic portraits — but no examples are extant.

M

MACEDONIA Country bounded by Mount Olympus and the Pindus range in the south, Epirus and Illyria in the west, and Thrace in the northeast; the peninsula of *Chalcidice in the southeast was colonized by Greeks. Its frontiers shifted in the course of time: once the Strymon was its boundary with Thrace but later it was extended to the Nestus. The main features of Upper M. are its mountains, with valleys and elevated plains between them. Lower M. is the plain on the Theramic Gulf into which flow the rivers Axius (Vardar), Lydias, and Halicamon. The country was thus divided into several regions which for a long time retained their separate dynasts and opposed a strong central government, especially in Upper M. Its communications with the outer world were not easy — those with the south were via the sea (but no important port developed on the Theramaic coast until later times), or by land to Thessaly through the vale of Tempe. The Axius valley provided a route to the north and an eastward route could be taken via Mygdonia to the Strymon valley. Agriculture and stock-breeding were the main means of subsistence and the country was rich in timber and silver.

M. was inhabited since Neolithic times and by the 7th century BC its population was of mixed origin: Illyrian, Greek and Thracian. In Classical Greece the Macedonians were considered barbarians, though the royal house claimed descent from Argos — a claim which was recognized in the case of *Alexander I, under whom Hellenization and closer political relations with the Greeks began. As long as the dynasts of Upper M. successfully maintained their independence, M. could not rise to power. But when *Philip II put an end to these separationist tendencies, recruited the available manpower and exploited the natural resources of the country, M. became the strongest power in Greece. The conquests of Alexander took the Macedonian army as far as India, but under him and the *Diadochi, M. was drained of its population — hence the decline in the 3rd century. *Antigonus Gonatas and his successors managed to maintain some control in Greece, but M. was not a match for Rome. After the defeat of *Perseus (2) in Pydna (168 BC), M. was divided into four republics and in 146 it was organized as a Roman province.
S. Casson, *Macedonia, Thrace and Illyria*, 1926.

MACER, Gaius Licinius Roman senator and historian. As tribune in 73 BC he attacked the reforms of *Sulla. He was praetor in 68 BC and in 66 was convicted of extortion and committed suicide. He wrote a history of Rome from early times in the annalistic manner. He used the *libri lintei* ("Linen Books"), a list of magistrates, which was not a great improvement, to supplement his sources. His work extended to at least 16 books and reflected M.'s "popular" tendencies. *Livy and *Dionysius of Halicarnassus occasionally used his work.
Ogilvie, *Livy*, 7ff.

MACHON Greek comic playwright of the 3rd century BC. Born in Corinth or Sicyon, he lived in Alexandria. Of his plays nothing has survived except two fragments. His collection of anecdotes, in iambic trimeters, is preserved in Book 13 of *Athenaeus. It consists of some 460 verses — anecdotes concerning Athenian parasites, *hetairai* (courtesans) etc.
A. S. F. Gow, *Machon*, 1965 (text and commentary).

MACRINUS Native of Caesarea in Mauretania, born in AD 164. He advanced in his equestrian career and was appointed praetorian prefect in AD 212. He took part in the Parthian expedition of *Caracalla whose assassination he engineered in AD 217. He then became the first non-senator to be proclaimed emperor. He did not pursue the Parthian War and soon lost the loyalty of his soldiers who resented his strict discipline and his parsimony. *Julia Maesa gained the support of a legion to promote her grandson *Elagabalus, allegedly Caracalla's son, to the throne. M. was defeated in AD 218 and executed.

MACRO, Q. Naevius Cordus Sutorius Native of Alba Fucens. As prefect of the Vigiles he arranged the arrest and execution of *Sejanus, in AD 31, whom he replaced as praetorian prefect. He helped *Caligula to succeed to the throne in AD 37, but soon thereafter was compelled to commit suicide with his wife.

MACROBIUS, Ambrosius Theodosius Latin writer of the early 5th century AD. Of his life nothing certain is known; he was probably a pagan, possibly from Africa. His extant works are: 1) *Commentarii in Somnium Scipionis* — a commentary on the dream of Scipio contained in the last book of Cicero's *De Republica*. This neo-Platonist treatise was widely read and influential in the Middle Ages; at that time, Cicero's treatise was not known. 2) *Sa-*

turnalia — the conversation recorded at a symposium on the occasion of the festival. Among the interlocutors are *Symmachus, *Avienus and *Servius (2). This work in seven books is modelled on the *Noctes Atticae* of *Gellius and the symposium of *Athenaeus. Many and various themes are discussed (e.g. dancing, drunkenness), but the main interest is in literature and philology. The main poet discussed is Virgil, but many others are cited by way of comparison and illustration. These citations often provide fragments from poets whose writings are not otherwise preserved, notably *Ennius and *Lucilius.

Text: J. Willis (Teubner), 1963;
T. Whittaker, *Macrobius*, 1963;
A. Cameron, *JRS*, 1966, 25ff.;
H. de Ley, *Macrobius and Numenius*, 1972.

MAECENAS, Gaius Roman politician, patron of letters, and friend of Augustus. Born to an Etruscan family in *Arretium, M. supported Octavian (Augustus) from the beginning of his career and carried out many diplomatic missions for him. He preferred to remain a Roman knight and did not try for a senatorial career. M. was the trusted councellor of Augustus who left him in charge of his affairs when he went abroad. Wealthy and with luxurious habits, he was interested in literature and helped many poets, among them Virgil, Horace, and Propertius. Of his own writings, which came under criticism, only a few fragments are extant. On his death in 8 BC he made Augustus the sole heir to his enormous property. His name has become synonymous with patronage of the arts.

MAENADS (BACCHAE) The frenzied women who accompanied *Dionysus on his triumphal procession from Phrygia to Thrace and Greece. Other women who joined them also became M. In the myth, they went about the mountains wearing skins and garlands of ivy and carrying the thyrsus (a stick with bunches of grapes). They danced and sang in honour of Dionysus, and were free from all social conventions. They had unnatural strength and in their ecstasy would kill animals and eat the raw flesh. While in this state they were incapable of recognizing their close kinsmen — and so *Pentheus was killed by his own mother. The myths of the M. were favourite themes in literature and art. The plays of Aeschylus associated with them (e.g. *Pentheus*) are not extant., but *Euripides' *Bacchae* is preserved. M. appear in vase-paintings from the 6th century on. One extant statue of a dancing Maenad is ascribed to *Scopas.

MAENIUS, Gaius Of a plebeian family, he was elected consul of 338 BC. He then defeated the *Latins and the fleet of *Antium. The beaks (*rostra*) of the captured ships decorated the speaker's platform in the forum, and the platform was henceforth called *rostra*.

MAGISTER EQUITUM ("master of the horse") The first action of a Roman *dictator on his appointment was to appoint a ME., an official who assisted him to carry out his task either as commander of the cavalry or in other matters. The *Imperium of the ME. was ranked with that of the praetors. The ME. held his office as long as the dictator did.

Jolowicz, *Roman Law*³ (s.v.).

MAGISTRI MILITUM Generals instituted by Constantine to command the army after he left the praetorian prefects with only civil duties. There were the *magister peditum* and *magister equitum*. The title was also given to the commanders of the army assigned to the residence of the emperor (*magistri praesentales*).

Jones, *Lat. Rom. Emp.*, 608ff.

A maenad on a red-figured painting by the Cleophrades painter, c. 500 BC

MAGNA GRAECIA The name which designated the part of southern Italy that was colonized by the Greeks. It was in use by the end of the 6th century BC. The Greeks of MG. were called *Italiotes*. Among the Greek cities here were *Cumae, *Neapolis, *Paestum, *Elea, *Rhegium, *Locri Epizephyrii, and *Thurii. The cities here suffered from the same evils as those in Greece: internal upheavals and inter-city feuds. They came under pressure from local tribes and it was only with difficulty and with Roman help that they managed to survive. They lost their independence and suffered much in the Hannibalic War.

Dunbabin, *Western Greeks*;
A. G. Woodhead, *The Greeks in the West*, 1962.

MAGNENTIUS, Flavius Magnus He murdered the Emperor *Constans in Autun (AD 350) and proclaimed himself emperor. He was recognized in the West, but was defeated by *Constantius II at Mursa in Pannonia (AD 351). He was defeated again in AD 353 and committed suicide.

MAGNESIA (at the Maeander) City in Ionia on a tributary of the river Maeander, colonized by the Magnetes, the old inhabitants of Thessaly. It is first mentioned by Herodotus (1.161). M. was subject to foreign powers from the 6th century BC on. It was given to *Themistocles by Artaxerxes I. The ruins of the temple of Artemis were excavated; a frieze of this temple is extant. Another M. (ad Sipylum) was situated north of *Smyrna at the foot of Mount Sipylus.

G. E. Bean, *Aegean Turkey*, 1966, 246ff.

MAGO (1) The ancestor of the powerful Magonid dynasty which ruled Carthage from the mid-6th century BC to *c.* 375 BC. He restored Carthaginian power in Sardinia, shattered after the defeat of *Malchus (*c.* 550 BC). M.

reorganized the Carthaginian army into a mainly mercenary force, with Carthaginians serving only as officers. The following is a list of the Magonid "kings": M. (c. 550–c. 530 BC), Hasdrubal, son of M. (c. 530–c. 510 BC); Hamilcar, grandson of M. (c. 510–490); Hanno the Navigator (c. 480–c. 440); Hannibal (440–406), Himilco (406–396); Mago (396–375).

G. C. and C. Picard, *The Life and Death of Carthage*, 1968.

MAGO (2) The youngest brother of *Hannibal under whom he served in Italy (218–216 BC) and in Spain (from 215). He annihilated the Roman army under P. *Scipio (1) but was defeated by *Scipio (2) at Ilipa (206 BC). He escaped and recruited more troops but was forced to leave Spain. After landing at Minorca (where the port of Mahon perpetuates his name) he went to Liguria and from there operated against the Romans. But he was defeated (203), and died of wounds on his homeward voyage.

MAIA One of the Pleiades (daughters of Atlas) and mother of Hermes by Zeus (Hom. *Od.* 14.435; Hesiod, *Theog.* 938). She was confused with the Roman goddess Maia who was associated with growth and after whom a calendar month was named. A sacrifice was consequently made for her on 1 May. She also became associated with the Roman *Mercurius, who was identified with Hermes.

MAIESTAS This term literally means "greatness", "eminence", in particular of the Roman people and its representatives (*M. populi Romani*). Actions that decreased the greatness or dignity of the Roman people (*M. minuta or laesa*) were considered as treason (Cic. *Invent. Rhet.* 2.53). It was first defined as a crime by a law of L. Appuleius *Saturninus (103 BC), which supplemented the law of *Perduellio that was confined to cases of actual hostility against the state. The law of Saturninus applied also to negligence of duty by magistrates, and was occasioned by the Roman defeats in the war against the *Cimbri. Its scope was enlarged by a law of *Sulla who made it a crime for a Roman magistrate to lead an army outside his province without authorization by the Senate. He also established a permanent jury court (*quaestio*) to deal with these cases. Another law was passed by Caesar or Augustus. With the establishment of the Principate, hostile acts, libel and slander against the emperor and his family (e.g. adultery with his daughter) came under the scope of the law. Informers (*delatores*) were often welcomed and would receive a quarter of the property of the accused if condemned. Confiscated property, death and *Damnatio Memoriae* came to be the penalty of the law, though if the man concerned committed suicide before the trial he was spared the extreme application of the law. Under the Empire these cases were tried by the old jury court, the Senate, or the emperor himself.

Bowman, *The Crimen Maiestatis in Roman Republic and Augustan Principate*, 1967; *Impietas in Principem*, 1974.

MAJORIAN, Julian Roman emperor of the West (AD 457–61). With Ricimer he contrived the abdication of Avitus, and was then made emperor. After the failure of his expedition against *Gaiseric, Ricimer had him murdered.

MALALAS, Johanes The Greek author of a world chronicle (*Chronographia*) in 18 books, from the creation of the world to the end of Justinian's reign. He lived in Antioch from the late 5th century to AD 578, perhaps in Constantinople in his last years. His is the earliest extant Byzantine chronicle, though in the present form it has passed through some abridgement. It is also known from excerpts of a Slavonic translation. The author concentrates his narrative around his home city, though in Book 18 emphasis is given to Constantinople. It is an unclear work with many errors, but it contains material not known from other sources.

Text: L. Dindorf, 1831. Translation: M. Spinka and G. Downey, 1940 (part of the Slavonic text).

MALCHUS (perhaps a title, Semitic *melek* is "king") Carthaginian general recorded by Justin (18.7) and Orosius (*Hist. Ad. Pag.* 4.6,7ff.). He won success in western Sicily but was defeated in Sardinia. He is also credited with success over the Libyans. M. was exiled with his army to Sardinia, returned and took control of Carthage but was soon put to death. Some doubts have been raised about his exploits.

MAMERTINI ("sons of Mamers", i.e. Mars) Campanian troops, once the mercenaries of *Agathocles. They captured *Messana some time after 288 BC, and ravaged eastern Sicily until they were defeated by *Hieron (2) of Syracuse (c. 270–265). To protect themselves against him they received a Carthaginian garrison, but simultaneously asked for the support of Rome. The arrival of the Roman army started the First Punic War. Messana became an allied city (*civitas foederata*) of Rome.

MANES The spirits of the dead who originally were not individualised but thought of collectively; hence they were called *Di Manes*. Their name is probably derived from *Manus*, an old Latin adjective meaning "good" (Varro *Lin. Lat.* 6.4). The common formula that was inscribed on graves was *Dis Manibus Sacrum* (or abbreviated D.M.). Under the Empire, the name of a dead person was given in the genitive or dative case in inscriptions. The M. were associated with three festivals (Feralia, Parentalia and Lemuria), but it is doubtful whether these involved worshipping the dead. Each ceremony was a kind of magical rite to get rid of the souls (in the Parentalia it was perhaps a repetition of the burial ceremony). The name M. was used by poets to denote the realm of the dead. Only in the late Republic do we hear of the use of M. to denote the soul of an individual dead person.

MANETHO Egyptian high-priest in Heliopolis in the second half of the 3rd century BC. He wrote a history of Egypt (*Aigyptiaca*) up to the 31st dynasty. Only parts of the work are extant, partly through Josephus and Eusebius.

W. G. Waddell, *Manethon* (Loeb), 1940.

MANICHAEISM Religious movement, associated with Gnosticism, founded by Mani (AD 216–76). Mani was born in Ctesiphon and came under Gnostic influence, but he had two visions that made him believe that he was the Paraclete. He wandered to India, then returned and preached his mission with the protection of *Sapor I. He died in prison under Bahram I (274–7). The theological doctrine of M. had various sources: Gnostic, Christian, Persian, Babylonian and Indian. Originally there had been two separate realms, one of light and one of darkness. The present world is a contamination of the realm of light by that of darkness, so that good and evil are mixed. The five hypostases of the light are reason, mind, intelligence, thought, and reflection; those of the other realm are darkness, smoke, fire, wind and water. The Father is identical with light. The Son of God appeared as Jesus to save his own soul. Only the Elect will be redeemed from transmigration. Mani, the "Seal of the prophets", founded the holy community. By asceticism the gospel is taught and the light is preserved from dispersion. The non-Elect in the community, the Hearers, could hope for rebirth as the Elect, provided that they behaved morally. This mystic religion of redemption had much success and many followers in the West as well as in the East. In one way or another it survived for many centuries in Europe and spread as far as China.

H. Ch. Puech, *Le Manicheisme*, 1949.

MANILIUS, Marcus Latin writer of the first half of the 1st century AD. He is the author of *Astronomica*, a didactic poem in five books on astronomy and astrology. Book 1 recounts the creation, the organization of the heavenly bodies with their different zones and circles; Book 2 deals with the signs of the zodiac — their characteristics and relations to the gods and the parts of the human body; Book 3 is concerned with the division of the signs into twelve *sortes* with instructions for the horoscope; Book 4 describes the influence of the signs on the characters of men born under each of them, with a discussion of the influence of the signs on the parts of the earth governed by them; Book 5 discusses the influence of the signs that are outside the zodiac on those born during the rising of these signs. The work was written at a time when astrology was very popular. But it was not successful, perhaps because it could not be used as a practical manual by a believer. That M. could have written quite good verses on such a technical subject shows that he was a poet of some talent. One of the greatest works of textual criticism is the edition of the *Astronomica* by A. E. Housman (in 5 volumes, 1903—1930); and two other great scholars, Scaliger and Bentley, have commented on the text.

MANLIUS CAPITOLINUS, Marcus Of a patrician family, consul in 392 BC, hero of a Roman legend. Awakened by the cackling of the sacred geese, he saved the Capitol from a night attack by the Gauls. But this seems to be an aetiological myth to explain the name Capitolinus, borne by a branch of the Manlian clan which lived on the Capitol. In 385 he allegedly attempted to make a revolution, but failed and was executed; thereafter no Patrician was allowed to live on the Capitol. The later historians told the story in the light of the Gracchan reforms.

Ogilvie, *Livy*, 734f.

MANTINEA City in east Arcadia, founded by the *Synoecismus of five demes in the late 6th century BC. It was situated on the northern part of an elevated plain, over 600 m above sea level; the control of this area was often disputed between M. and *Tegea, another Arcadian city (in the southern part of the plain). The Mantineans fought with the Spartans at Thermopylae (Hdt. 7.202). The constitutional reform of Nicodorus introduced a democratic government in the mid-5th century. At about the same time, M. expanded its control over the plain. It joined a coalition against Sparta (420 BC), with whom it had maintained good relations since the Persian Wars (Thuc. 5.29). But Sparta won a complete victory at M. (418 BC) over the Mantineans and their allies (Elis, Argos, and Athens). As relations remained hostile Sparta compelled the Mantineans to destroy their walls and to settle in villages (387), with an aristocratic instead of a democratic government. The city was re-established with a democratic constitution after the battle of *Leuctra (371). In 362, Epaminondas defeated the Spartan army at M. Thereafter the decline of the Arcadian League led M. to cultivate good relations with Sparta. Though a member of the Achaean League by 230 BC, M. supported the Spartan king *Cleomenes III and massacred an Achaean garrison (226). Three years later, it was destroyed and its

population was either sold into slavery or deported to Macedonia. The Achaeans refounded it as Antigonea.

MANUBIAE Technically this term signified that part of the booty which a Roman general assigned for himself. He was entitled to use it for his personal needs, though many a general devoted a part of his share for public purposes (temples, theatres, roads etc.). In common language it came to be confused with *praeda*, that is, booty or spoils in general.

I. Shatzman, *Historia*, 1972, 177ff.

MARATHON Large deme on the northeast coast of Attica, the centre of an old religious league (Tetrapolis). It was probably situated near modern Vrana (not at modern Marathona). One of the most renowned battles in Greek history took place in the plain of M. in 490 BC. Here, the Athenians with a Plataean contingent defeated a Persian force which was guided by the ex-tyrant *Hippias. The leading Athenian commander was *Miltiades; *Aeschylus and *Aristides also fought in the battle. It was the first time that Greeks won a victory over Persians in a pitched battle. The story concerning the runner who was sent to tell the news and who died from exhaustion after his arrival in Athens comes from a late source. Herodotus states that Pleidippides, the Athenian runner sent to ask Sparta's help before the battle, covered more than 200 km in two days (6.1056). M. was also the scene of the battle in which *Pisistratus secured his power for the third time (c. 545 BC).

W. K. Pritchett, *Marathon*, 1960.

MARCELLUS (1), Marcus Claudius Prominent Roman statesman and general, five times consul, of the plebeian branch of the Claudian clan. He fought in the First Punic War and thereafter advanced his senatorial career. As consul in 222 BC, he defeated the *Insubres and killed their king, thus winning the *Spolia opima* (*Cossus) and a triumph at Rome. He served in the Second Punic War in various areas in Italy and won some success against Hannibal. In late 214, he was sent to Sicily; he conquered *Leontini and, after a long siege, captured Syracuse in 211 (Archimedes was killed on this occasion). M. returned to Rome, was elected consul IV (210), continued in command as proconsul in 209, and was again consul in 208. He was then killed while reconnoitring near Venusia. Vigorous and able, M. was, with Fabius Cunctator and Scipio Africanus, one of the best generals Rome had in the war against Hannibal. M. was called the Sword of Rome, and was one of the first phil-Hellenists in Rome.

Plut. *Marcellus*; Scullard, *Rom. Pol.*[2] (s.v.).

MARCELLUS (2), Marcus Claudius Grandson of M. (1), prominent Roman statesman. He was praetor in 169 BC and governor in Spain (169—8). As consul in 166 he fought in Liguria, where he operated again as consul in 155. He attained the consulate for the third time in 152. He was governor of Nearer Spain and concluded a peace with the Celtiberians. M. was drowned in 148. He was the only one to be thrice elected consul during this period.

Scullard, *Rom. Pol.*[2] (s.v.).

MARCELLUS (3), Marcus Claudius Descendant of M. (1), bitter enemy of Caesar. As consul in 51 BC he opened a campaign to terminate Caesar's command of Gaul. He joined Pompey in the Civil War, but after Pharsalus he desisted from further fighting. Caesar permitted him to return to Rome, but he was murdered in Piraeus (45).

MARCELLUS (4), Marcus Claudius Son of Gaius Marcellus (consul in 50 BC) and nephew of Augustus, born in 42 BC. He married *Julia, Augustus' daughter, in 25 BC and

thereafter was considered as the likely heir to his uncle. But he never advanced beyond the office of aedile and he died in that office (23 BC). He was the first to be buried in the mausoleum of Augustus. The Theatre of M. in Rome, largely preserved, was named after him. The grief over his loss is manifest in Virgil's *Aeneid* (6.860–86). Propertius wrote a poem on his death (3.18).
Syme, *Rom. Rev.* (s.v.).

MARCIANA, Ulpia Trajan's older sister. Trajan gave her name to two new cities: Marcianopolis, in Lower Moesia (in Bulgaria), and Colonia Ulpia Marciana Traiana (Thamugadi). He also gave her the title Augusta.

MARCIANUS Born *c.* AD 400; the son of a soldier, he became emperor of the Eastern Roman Empire in AD 450, when he married Pulcheria, the sister of *Theodosius II. After the death of *Attila, he settled within the empire peoples formerly subject to the Huns. His reign was generally a peaceful one, and he was able to improve the imperial finances. Under him the Council of Chalcedon was convened. He died in 457.
Jones, *Lat. Rom. Emp.* (s.v.).

MARCOMANNI ("inhabitants of the marshes") German tribe, of the Suebic group, first recorded by Caesar. They left their original country around the middle Elbe during the early 1st century BC and later joined *Ariovistus in the invasion of Gaul. They retreated from their settlement around the Main to Bohemia after their defeat by *Drusus (3) in 9 BC. Their King Marobodius extended his power over the neighbouring Germans in Silesia and Saxony. He was considered too dangerous and Augustus prepared an expedition against him, but it was never carried out because of the revolt in Illyricum. *Arminius fought against him and in AD 19 Marobodius lost his throne and was allowed by Tiberius to live in Ravenna. The M. gave help to Vespasian in 69, but *Domitian had to resume war against them and in 97 they invaded Pannonia. Thereafter, they became dependent on Rome. They renewed their pressure on the empire in 166, and Marcus *Aurelius had to conduct long wars against them. In the 3rd century they invaded the Balkan provinces several times. Diocletian defeated them in AD 297. The M. migrated to Bavaria in the early 6th century.

MARDONIUS Son of Gobryas, nephew and son-in-law of *Darius I. He let the Ionians establish democracies after the suppression of the great revolt, and restored Persian power in Thrace in 492 BC. He took a leading part in Xerxes' invasion of Greece and received general command when the Great King left after the battle of Salamis. M. lost the battle of Plataea and was himself killed in it (479).

MARIUS, Gaius Roman general and statesman, native of *Arpinum, born to an equestrian family *c.* 157 BC. He served under *Scipio Aemilianus at Numantia and thereafter probably engaged in business. After a few years he launched on a political career, presumably assisted by the Metellan family. He was quaestor *c.* 123 and as tribune in 119 he passed a law to curb dishonest interference with voting. This caused friction between him and one Metellus and it was only with difficulty that he won the praetorship of 115. He afterwards governed Spain and in 112 married Julia, Caesar's aunt. He was a legate of *Metellus (2) Numidicus in the Jugurthine War and was elected consul of 107 by popular agitation. A special law gave him — instead of Metellus — the command against Jugurtha. As a general, M. introduced military reforms. He was the first to recruit *proletarii*, that is, citizens without means,

Barbarians surrendering to the emperor Marcus Aurelius

into the army. This was the first important step towards changing the citizen-army of Rome into a professional army; and the proletarian soldiers of the 1st century were more attached to their command than to the state.

The war against Jugurtha was more protracted than M. expected and it was only through the diplomacy of *Sulla that it was brought to end. From 105 to 101 M. was continuously elected consul and given command against the *Cimbri. He reorganized the legion, which was now based on the *Cohors as its main sub-division, thus consolidating a long development. He defeated the Teutones at Aquae Sextae (102) and the Cimbri at Vercellae (101). As consul in 100 he first cooperated with *Saturninus, who proposed to colonize the veterans of M. But when riots broke out, M. suppressed Saturninus and his supporters and so lost his popularity; earlier on he had incurred the hatred of many of the aristocracy by driving Metellus into exile. M. now went to Asia for a while and returned after he was made an augur. In 92, he helped to condemn his enemy *Rutilius. He was given command in the *Bellum Sociale but his success was limited. In 88, the tribune Sulpicius Rufus passed a law to give the command against *Mithridates VI to M. instead of Sulla, who thereupon led his army to occupy Rome. M. fled to Africa but returned in the following year. He organized an army and, with *Cinna (1), captured Rome. He now took revenge on his enemies; among his victims were *Atonius (1) and *Catulus (1). He was consul for the seventh time in 86 BC (the only one to achieve this under the Republic). He was given the command against Mithridates, but he died before he could take up the command.

A good soldier, an able commander, and ambitious, M. was the first Roman general to establish his dominance by popular means. His own experience and his novel method of recruiting for the army introduced new elements into Roman politics. His intrigues and his clash with aristocratic adversaries embroiled Rome in seditions and civil wars. It was his nephew Caesar, more than anyone else, who learnt from the experience, and had the talent and the daring to exploit it.

T. F. Carney, *A Biography of Gaius Marius*, 1961; J. Van Ooteghem, *Marius*, 1964.

MARMOR PARIUM A marble stele with an inscription which was found in Paros, one of the Cycladic islands. One fragment is preserved in Oxford, the other in the local museum of the island. The inscription is a chronological list of events dated by Athenian kings and archons and by their relations to the year 264/263, which was the last year of the list. The list covered the years 1581/1580 BC to 264/263 BC; in the present form, years 354/353 to 337/336 and those after 299/298 are missing.

Jacoby, *Fr. Gr. Hist.* no. 239.

MARS Important Italian god. In historical times, he was clearly a war-god but there were agricultural elements in his cult. It has been suggested that originally he had a different character (a chtonian god, a supreme god, etc.), but as to that opinions vary. His name was given to the first month of the year in the old Roman calendar, and many other Italian cities named a month after him. Several festivals were dedicated to him in Rome. The ritual in these festivals seems to have been a sort of preparation for war or purification of weapons. A Roman general would go to the *Regia and shake the sacred spears of M. before departing for war. The *Flamen Martialis was M.'s priest, and the wolf and the woodpecker were his sacred animals. In old times the Roman army was assembled in the *Campus Martius.

As a war-god it was quite natural that he should be identified with *Ares. As a result he inherited the myths attaching to his Greek counterpart. He thus came to be a lover of Venus, the Roman counterpart of Aphrodite. This was a theme often depicted by artists. A temple to M. was dedicated in 388 BC (Liv. 6.5,8), and he had other temples. A temple of M. Ultor ("Avenger") was built on the Capitol under Augustus (who took revenge on those who had murdered Caesar).

Latte, *R. Rel.* (s.v.).

MARSI A tribe in central Italy which was Latinized very early in its history and maintained good relations with Rome from early times. The M. were one of the leading peoples in the *Bellum Sociale, and for this reason it was occasionally named *Bellum Marsicum. After the war, the M. became Roman citizens.

MARSYAS In mythology, the satyr or silenus who learnt to play the flute, or oboe, which Athena invented but discarded because it distorted her face when playing. He was so confident of his talent that he challenged Apollo to a musical contest, the winner of which would do whatever he liked with the loser. Apollo won with his lyre and had him bound to a tree and flayed alive. From his blood the stream Marsyas sprang, or, in Ovid's version (*Met.* 6.391ff.) from the tears of the satyrs and the nymphs. M. is mentioned as early as Herodotus (7.26). Originally, he was probably a Phrygian river-god, and, at Celaenae, a guardian god (Pausan.16.39.9). The legend has been the theme of many famous works of art. The sculptor Myron made a bronze group for the Acropolis in the 5th century, which is known from Roman copies. It also appeared on vase-paintings. Another famous sculpture is the tied, bearded M. from Pergamum. Renaissance painters, too, were attracted by the subject (e.g. Titian's "Flaying of Marsyas").

MARTIAL, Marcus Valerius (c. AD 40–c. 104) Latin poet, famous for his epigrams, native of Bilbilis in Spain. Born on 1 March (hence his name), he was educated there and moved to Rome in 64. Presumably helped at first by Seneca the Younger and Lucan, Spaniards like himself,

Mars approaching Rhea Silvia. A relief on a 3rd century AD sarcophagus

The Flaying of Marsyas, an early 2nd century BC statue by an unknown sculptor

after their death he had to depend on the generosity of patrons. His means remained always modest. M. was on good terms with such contemporary writers as Juvenal, Quintilian, Frontinus and Pliny the Younger. After the death of Domitian, the new regime was less favourable for his literary activity and, helped by Pliny, he returned to Spain where a patroness, Marcella, gave him a small estate where he completed his last book before dying.

Liber Spectaculorum is the earliest extant book (AD 80). It commemorates the gladiatorial games given by Titus at the inauguration of the *Colosseum. The *Xenia* (now book 13) and *Apophoreta* (now book 14) contain mottoes for gifts given at the Saturnalia, almost all in elegiac couplets. The 12 books of epigrams (*Libri Epigrammaton*) appeared at intervals of a year or more from AD 86 on. But it took M. three years to complete the last book. He prepared a special selection from books 11 and 12, and added prose prefaces to several books.

M.'s essential talent was for conciseness, and it was in the epigram that he found the best form in which to express himself. His theme was the social life he knew and this included all classes from the emperor down to humble people. With a keen eye for the essential, characteristic or humorous aspect of a figure or a situation, he achieved his descriptions in a brief, economic way. The elegiac couplet was precisely the genre for such a purpose and talent, and he is the greatest Latin epigramatist. Indeed, he provides the model for the epigram with a contrast, a pun, and a pungent and surprising ending. A witty satirist, he avoided personal attacks and used invented names. He could indulge in obscenity and abusive language but also wrote lyrical pieces. Himself a bachelor, he loved children (a few of his poems are about Erotion, whose death M. lamented). His books contain some 1,560 poems, the vast majority of which are short poems. Besides elegiacs, he also wrote hendecasyllabic and choliambic poems and a few iambics and hexameters. His longest poem is of 51 verses. Not a great thinker, narrator or lyricist, his artistry has won him fame and readers down to our times.
W. C. A. Ker, *Martial* (Loeb), 1919–1920.

MARTIANUS CAPELLA Latin writer, native of Carthage, lived in the first half of the 5th century AD. In his old age, he wrote his only known work *De Nuptiis Mercurii et Philologiae* (or *Disciplinae*), which he dedicated to his son. It describes, in nine books of prose and verse, the wedding of Philologia to Mercury — the hand-maids of the bride are the Seven Liberal Arts (grammar, dialectic, rhetoric (the *Trivium*), and geometry, arithmetic, astronomy and music (the *Quadrium*)). Two books are devoted to the married couple and one to each of the Arts. Thanks to its allegorical setting and educational material, the book was widely read from the Carolingian period on. But it is a tedious work, essentially compilatory, with no original contribution from M.
Edition: A. Dick (Teubner), 1925.

MASADA Natural fortress on the western mountains of the Dead Sea. First fortified by Jonathan (Joseph. *BJ*, 7.285), it was extensively built as a palatial residence and citadel by Herod the Great. He built a wall with towers, a garrison-barracks and storage rooms. The water supply was secured by skillfully planned aqueducts. A detailed description of M. is given by Josephus (*BJ*, 7.280–300). The fortress was occupied by the Zealots at the beginning of the Great Revolt in AD 66, and it was the last fortification to be captured by the Romans. The siege was commanded by Flavius Silva who surrounded the rock with eight camps and a circumvallation. After the wall was breached on the western side, the 900-odd defenders destroyed the buildings by fire and committed mass suicide (May 72). Two women and five children survived the destruction. The site was completely excavated in 1963–1965.

Y. Yadin, *Massada*, 1967.

MASINISSA Numidian prince, son of Gaia the king of the Massyles in eastern Numidia. He fought with the Carthaginians against Rome in Spain, but in 206 BC he changed sides. After his father's death, M. escaped from his kingdom which was partly occupied by *Syphax. He fought with Scipio against Carthage and did important service with his cavalry at Zama (202). King of all Numidia, he was an ally of Rome and Rome persistently supported his encroaching on the territory of Carthage in the decades after the Second Punic War. He finally provoked the Carthaginians into open warfare and defeated them (150). This was a breach of the treaty terms with Rome, who used it as a formal excuse to open the Third Punic War. M. appointed *Scipio Aemilianus to execute his testament and after his death (148) his kingdom was ruled by his sons (Micipsa, Gulussa and Mastanabal). M. was the greatest king the Numidians had. He developed agriculture and town life and introduced the Punic culture. Strong and brave, he was a great fighter and cavalry commander. He kept his vitality to old age and on his death had a four-year-old son. Energetic and crafty, he rose to such power that Rome finally became apprehensive of his aims; but apparently he also knew his limits, unlike his grandson *Jugurtha.

P. G. Walsh, *JRS*, 1965, 149ff.

MASSALIA (Latin Massilia, Modern Marseille) Greek city founded by settlers from *Phocaea, *c.* 600 BC. The name is probably Ligurian in origin. The city flourished and won control of the whole coast of southern Gaul to Spain, along which she founded several colonies, including Nicaea (Nice), Antipolis (Antibes) and Emporium (Ampurias). The Phocaeans brought with them the cult of Artemis and Apollo.

M.'s trade expanded to Gaul, Liguria and Spain, and with it Greek culture penetrated into these regions. Her only rival in the western Mediterranean was Carthage, and though she had to yield some posts, she successfully maintained her prosperity. Her good relations with Rome and interests in Spain seem to have contributed to Roman involvement on the Iberian peninsula, and a formal treaty of friendship was established. Rome helped her against the neighbouring Gallic tribes and the series of wars Rome conducted from 125 ended with the establishment of the first Gallic province of Rome late in the 2nd century BC. Her decision to support Pompey cost her much as Caesar captured her (49), confiscated her treasury, and reduced her territory. Many remains have been found in excavations.

MASTARNA An Etruscan hero said by the Emperor Claudius to be identical with *Servius Tullius. Etruscan wall paintings, from the François Tomb at Vulci, show M. (*macstarna*) releasing Caeles Vibenna (*caile vipinas*) from chains and Gnaeus Tarquinius Romanus (*cneve tarxu rumax*) killed. It is likely then that M. was a Roman king of Etruscan origin.

A. Momigliano, *Claudius*[2], 1961, 12ff., 85ff.

MATHEMATICS The earliest mathematical works of Greeks, by *Autolycus (1) and *Euclid, date from the late 4th century BC but it is clear enough that since the 6th century Greeks had been showing interest in mathematical theories and problems. What is difficult to assess is to what extent, and at what time, they received mathematical knowledge from the Babylonians. The latter had achieved considerable advances in arithmetical calculations as well as in algebra. Their number-system was based on the place-value principle, with sixty as their base (not ten), and they could handle quadratic equatations. Curiously enough, a tradition dating from Eudemus, a pupil of Aristotle, and preserved in essence by *Proclus, ascribed the invention of geometry to the Egyptians, whose mathematical knowledge was far inferior to that of the Babylonians. Among the main geometers were *Thales, who allegedly received the science from Egypt, *Pythagoras, *Anaxagoras, Hippocrates of Chios (*c.* 470–400 BC), Plato and his pupil Theaetetus, and *Eudoxus of Cnidus. But it is doubtful whether any authentic knowledge was preserved of the mathematical activities of the Ionian philosophers who tended to deal with speculations; and theorems ascribed to Thales are probably apocryphal. On the other hand the Pythagoreans were certainly interested in the theory of numbers. They classified numbers according to their properties, discovered arithmetical analogues for geometrical facts, and knew simple geometrical theorems including the one called after Pythagoras — the square on the hypotenuse of a right-angled triangle is equal to the sum of the squares on the two adjacent sides. But this had been known to the Babylonians, too. The Greeks classified numbers as even or odd, square (e.g. 4, 9) or oblong (e.g. 6, 12). The root of a square number was its "side", and the root of any other number was "inexpressible". As they were geometrically minded, they used points to express number patterns. Hippocrates of Chios investigated the problem of doubling the cube and discovered that this was equivalent to finding the two mean proportionals. It was left to the Pythagorean Archytas (first half of the 4th century BC) to solve it by geometrical means, using two half-cylinders. Menaechmus (4th century BC) solved the problem with the help of two conic sections. To the Pythagoreans was also ascribed the discovery of the irrationality of $\sqrt{2}$. This was known before Plato and is described by the mathematician Theodorus of Cyrene (*Theaetetus* 147 d), who also used geometrical terms, showing that the diagonal of a square is incommensurable with its side.

The notable feature of the work of the Greek mathematicians is not so much that they proposed correct theorems as that they based them on rational proof. As this was all important they came to develop methods of proof. The *reductio ad absurdum*, a particular form of their analytic method, was used in the case of the diagonal and the side of a square: if we assume that the diagonal of a square is commensurable with its side, this leads to the impossible consequence that the same number is both even and odd; hence the assumption is wrong and the diagonal is not commensurable with the side. The analytic method, as defined by Euclid, is to assume as true the thing to be proved and to show it involves an admitted truth; the synthesis method is to show that a certain admitted truth involves the new proposal.

Geometry attracted the Greeks more than any other department of M. It was characteristic of them, as we noted above, that they applied geometrical proofs to arithmetical and algebraic problems. Euclid, for instance, gives geometrical solutions to quadratic equations (6.28

and 29). It is well known that no one could enter the *Academy without knowing geometry. Much work was done in the fourth century BC, notably by *Eudoxus, but, as was said before, not much is known of it. And then we have the work of Euclid, which includes plane and solid geometry, ratios and proportions, and theory of numbers. He evidently took much from his predecessors, added original contributions and reorganized the whole body of theorems to give them an axiomatic exposition. The two greatest mathematicians of antiquity — Archimedes and *Apollonius of Perge — worked in the 3rd century BC. With his new theorems on conoids and spheroids, Archimedes anticipated modern integral calculus, and he also invented or established the sciences of statics and hydrostatics. Apollonius' achievement in his *Conics* was of equal magnitude. After them no great work was done in geometry. Spherical trigonometry was probably founded by *Menelaus (2) of Alexandria. Plane trigonometry was also known and used by *Hipparchus (2). The Greeks never developed algebra and the work of *Diophantus (? 3rd century AD), which absorbed old Babylonian tradition, is an exception.

M. contributed to the development of *astronomy; *Eratosthenes, *Hipparchus (2) and Claudius *Ptolemy are the great names in this field. Even when no new original work was produced, the interest in M. persisted and was shown in commentaries written to the works of the great masters, notably by *Pappus, *Theon and *Proclus. See the names referred to above (with bibliographies).

T. L. Heath, *A History of Greek Mathematics*, 1921; M. Thomas, *Greek Mathematical Works*, 1939—41.

MATIDIA Daughter of *Marciana and niece of Trajan. Her daughter Sabina married Hadrian (AD 100). Trajan gave her the title Augusta after the death of her mother. Hadrian deified her after her death (119) and gave her and Marciana's name to a temple he built in Rome.

Nash, *Pict. Dict. Rome*, 1, 36.

MATUTA, MATER A minor Roman goddess of growth, with a festival (Matralia) on 11 June. That she was a goddess of dawn, as Lucretius says (5.656), is disputed. Her temple is in the Forum Boarium.

Platner-Ashby, *Top. Dict. Rome*, 330f.; Nash, *Pict. Dict. Rome*, 1, 411.

MAURETANIA The country of the Moors, stretching west of *Numidia to the Atlantic. The locals were called *Maurysioi* (Pol. 3.33.15) or *Mauri*. According to one view, they were a Lybian people, but there was also a belief that the Medians, Persians and Armenians came to Africa and were called *Mauri* (Sall. *BJ*, 17ff.). The Phoenicians established trading posts along the coasts (hence Lixos, Cartenae, Icosium etc.), and Moors often served in the Carthaginian army. Tribal organization persisted throughout antiquity, even though strong rulers rose in the 2nd century BC. M. became involved with Roman affairs during the Jugurthine War. King *Bochus of M. received western Numidia for the betrayal of *Jugurtha, his son-in-law. *Sertorius recruited Mauretanian cavalry with which he returned to Spain. Rome annexed the country after the murder of King Ptolemy (AD 40), the successor of *Juba II. M. was organized into two provinces with procurators as governors: M. Caesariensis (with *Caesarea Iol as its capital) and M. Tingitana (with Tingi as its capital). Though some *coloniae* were established and the use of Latin spread, a large part of the country retained its old traditional life.

J. Carcopino, *Le Maroc Antique*[2], 1947.

MAUSOLEUM One of the Seven Wonders of the World (Strabo 14.656), the tomb of *Mausolus was built of white marble by his widow *Artemisia (2) at *Halicarnassus. In the excavations held here in 1857, large parts of the frieze were found and they are now in the British Museum. The architect, Pythius, designed it in the Ionic Order. He described his work in a book which is not extant but is mentioned by Pliny the Elder (*NH*, 36.30—1) and Vitruvius. The tomb was probably built on a base of about 100 by 121 feet, though there are other calculations. The battle between the Greeks and the Amazons was depicted on its low frieze. Colossal statues of Mausolus and his family were placed inside the building. A chariot stood on top of the structure. The sculptures were made by four prominent masters of the time: *Scopas, *Bryaxis, *Leochares and Timotheus.

MAUSOLUS The local ruler of Caria (377—353 BC), formally a satrap within the Persian Empire. He joined a revolt against Persia in 362, but prudently deserted it at the right time. Vigorous, and with diplomatic skill, M. expanded his realm to Lycia and Ionia and made *Halicarnassus his capital (instead of *Mylasa). He ousted Athens and established hegemony over Rhodes and Cos. M. introduced Hellenism to his country.

MAXENTIUS, Marcus Aurelius Valerius Son of *Maximian, born c. AD 279. He married the daughter of *Galerius, but despite his connections was not included in the imperial succession after the abdication of Diocletian and his father in 305. Next year he was proclaimed emperor by the praetorians at Rome. He overcame the attacks of Severus (the new Augustus after the death of Constantius Chlorus) and of Galerius, and his own father's attempt to depose him. His authority was recognized in Italy and for some time in Spain and Africa. He followed a policy of tolerance towards the Christians. It was his support of the privileges of Rome that enabled him to maintain his rule, but he was not a match for Constantine who destroyed him at the battle of the Mulvian Bridge at Rome (312). Constantine passed a *Damnatio Memoriae* against him after his death.

MAXIMIAN (Marcus Aurelius Valerius Maximianus) Of peasant origin, he was born near Sirmium in Pannonia c. AD 240. He served in the army under Aurelius and Probus in the main campaigns of the period: in the East, the Balkan peninsula, Germany and Britain. He was made Caesar by his old friend *Diocletian in 285 and was sent to restore order in Gaul. In 286 he was elevated to Augustus and given the title Herculius (Diocletian was Iovius). During the following years, M. operated against the German peoples — Burgundians, Alamanni, Heruli — who invaded Gaul. Under the arrangement that Diocletian made in 293, he was to take control of the West with *Constantius Chlorus as his Caesar. Constantius, who married M.'s daughter Theodora, conquered Britain from *Allectus. M. was first engaged on the Rhein frontier and, in 296, in the suppression of a revolt in Africa where he fortified the *Limes. He rigorously persecuted the Christians in Africa. In Rome he built the Baths of Diocletian. A year after his abdication with Diocletian (1 May 305), he came to support his son *Maxentius. He resumed his title and arranged the surrender of Severus in Ravenna (307) and an alliance with Constantine; the latter married his daughter Fausta. As the result of a conference at Carnuntum in 308, M. had to resign. In 310, he committed suicide after the failure of his revolt against Constantine.

W. Seston, *Diocletian et la Tetrarchie*, 1949.

MAXIMINUS THRAX (Gaius Iulius Verus) Roman emperor (AD 235–8), of peasant stock from Thrace, born in 173. He had a military career under Septimius *Severus and his successors, but never rose to high command. He was proclaimed emperor by the army at Mainz after the murder of *Alexander Severus. He engaged in successful wars in Germany and on the Danube but the revolt of *Gordianus I in Africa led to his downfall. When he could not take Aquileia, his own soldiers murdered him (May–July 238).

MAXIMINUS DAIA (Gaius Galerius Valerius) Nephew of *Galerius, who adopted him and helped his advance in the army. On the abdication of Diocletian, M. was made Caesar in the East. He proclaimed himself Augustus in 310 and, after the death of Galerius, took control of Asia Minor. He tried to revive paganism and encouraged anti-Christian measures and propaganda. M. was defeated by *Licinius in Thrace (30 April 313), succeeded in escaping and died in Tarsus.

MEASURES AND WEIGHTS, GREEK The basic linear measure was the foot (*pous*). Subdivisions were the finger (*daktylos*), palm (*palaste*), span of all fingers (*spithame*). For longer distances the basic units were the *bema*, *orgyia*, *plethron*, and *stadion*. The three main standards were the Attic foot of *c.* 295 mm, the Olympic of 320 mm, and the Aeginetic of 333 mm.

2 *daktyloi* (fingers) =		1 *kondylos*
4 *daktyloi*	=	1 *palaste*
8 *daktyloi*	=	1 *hemipodion*
12 *daktyloi*	=	1 *spithame*
16 *daktyloi*	=	1 *pous*
20 *daktyloi*	=	1 *pygon*
24 *daktyloi*	=	1 *pechys*
2.5 feet	=	1 *bema*
6 feet	=	1 *orgyia*
100 feet	=	*plethron*
600 feet	=	*stadion.*

Areas were measured by square feet and square *plethra*. The *plethron*, considered to be the area ploughed by a yoke of oxen in a day, was then 10,000 feet. There were different measures of capacity for liquids and solids. The basic unit was the *kotyle*, with standards varying from 0.21 of a litre to over 0.33 of a litre. The dry measures were: 4 *kotylai* = 1 *choinix*; 8 *choinikes* = 1 *hekteus*; 6 *hekteis* = 1 *medimnos*. The liquid measures were 12 *kotylai* = 1 *chous*; 12 *choes* = 1 *metretes*.

There were several weight standards (see *Coinage). The barley corn was considered as the natural unit. Hence 12 barley corns = 1 obol; 6 obols = 1 *drachma*; 100 *drachmae* = 1 *mina*; 60 *minae* = 1 talent.

MEASURES and WEIGHTS, ROMAN The foot (*pes*) (of 296 mm) was the basic linear measure, and a unit (*as*) was divided into twelve *unciae*; hence *as* = 12 *unciae*; *deunx* = 11 *unciae*; *dextans* = 10 *unciae*; *dodrans* = 9 *unciae*; *bes* = 8 *unciae*; *septunx* = 7 *unciae*; *semis* = 6 *unciae*; *quincus* = 5 *unciae*; *triens* = 4 *unciae*; *quadrans* = 3 *unciae*; *sextans* = 2 *unciae*; there were also fractions of the *uncia*. In another system, the *pes* was divided into sixteen fingers (*digiti*). For longer distances the Romans had: 5 *pedes* = 1 *passus*; 125 *passus* = 1 *stadium*; 1,000 *passus* = 1 mile (95 yards shorter than the English mile).

The *actus quadratus* was the area that could be ploughed by a yoke of oxen in a day, but the basic measure of area was the *iugerum*. It had the following subdivisions: 2½ *pedes* = 1 *gradus*; 2 *gradus* = 1 *passus*; 2 *passus* = 1 *decempeda*; 12 *decempeda* = 1 *actus*; 2

actus = 1 *iugerum* (= 28,800 square Roman feet); 100 *iugera* = 1 *centuria.*

For measuring capacity, the *sextarius* was the basic unit and equalled 0.546 of a litre. The smallest subdivision was the *cochlear*: 4 *cochlearia* = 1 *cyathus*; 6 *cochlearia* = 1 *acetabulum*; 12 *cochlearia* = 1 *quartarius*; 24 *cochlearia* = 1 *hemina*; 48 *cochlearia* = 1 *sextarius*.

For dry measures: 8 *sextarii* = 1 *semodius*; 16 *sextarii* = 1 *modius.*

For liquid measures: 12 *heminae* = 1 *congius*; 8 *congii* = 1 *amphora*; 20 *amphora* = 1 *culleus.*

The basic weight unit was the *libra* of 327.45 gr, with the same subdivisions as the *pes* (above).

MEDDIX Oscan magistrate. The *M. tuticus* was the senior magistrate in Oscan states. He was a yearly magistrate and had administrative, judicial and religious authority.

MEDEA The mythological daughter of Aeetes, king of Colchis, niece of *Circe and granddaughter of *Helios. She was considered a priestess of *Hecate and a sorceress. When *Jason (1) came with the *Argonauts, she fell in love with him and helped him to fetch the Golden Fleece. She delayed her father, who pursued them, by scattering the limbs of her brother. Back home at Iolcos, she restored Jason's father to youth by boiling him with magic herbs. She then tricked the daughters of Pelias into killing their father by giving them useless herbs for the old man's rejuvenation. M. and Jason then fled to Corinth where Jason deserted her for Creusa, the daughter of *Creon. She took revenge by sending the bride a poisoned garment. Not satisfied with the death of Creusa and Creon, M. killed her two own children by Jason and fled to Athens. She married *Aegeus, and had a son, Medius. Failing to kill *Theseus, she fled with her son who gave his name to the country Media.

M. is not mentioned by Homer and first appears in Hesiod (*Theog.* 958). The story was told, in many variations, by numerous Greek and Latin writers. The tragedies of Aeschylus and Sophocles that dealt with her are lost, but the *Medea* of *Euripides, one of his greatest plays, is extant. The most interesting part of the *Argonautica* of *Apollonius Rhodius is the description of her love to Jason. Seneca's *Medea* is modelled on that of Euripides, a tragic woman overcome by her strong passions, but he exaggerates his description of her. Various themes of the myth appear on vase-paintings from the 6th century on.

MEDICINE The art of healing in Greece in early times was partly based on experience and partly on religious beliefs, superstition and magic formulae. Homer mentions two physicians: Machaon and Podalirius, sons of *Asclepius, who himself was believed to have been taught the art by *Chiron; Achilles, too, was a disciple of Chiron. In those remote times, and for a considerable period, the physicians were craftsmen, and the popular practices of these physicians persisted throughout antiquity.

The foundation of scientific M. is generally ascribed to *Hippocrates (1) of Cos, but it seems now that not even one of the works ascribed to him was in fact written by him. As it is difficult to date the various views and theories in the *Corpus Hippocraticum*, it is hardly possible to trace the development of Greek M. until fairly late. It is clear, however, that the various schools developed in addition to the medical tradition which was a matter of inheritance in certain families. Such a school existed at Cos, associated with the temple of Asclepius and Hippocrates himself. Another important one was at Cnidos. Greek cities had their own public physicians. In

Athens, there were several, chosen by the Assembly. Many physicians travelled from city to city and were followed by pupils.

The rise of a scientific attitude to disease is reflected in the famous account given by Thucydides of the plague in Athens. The basic idea is that illness is associated with a rational and not a divine cause. The first important thing to do about disease generally is to get to know the phenomena, and hence Thucydides gives a precise account of the symptoms and progress of this particular illness. The anatomical and physiological studies carried out by Greek scholars were most important and it was the great physicians who did the best work in these fields. The first attested anatomist was Alcmaeon of Croton, a younger contemporary and disciple of Pythagoras. He dissected animals and made note of the passages between the nose and the ear cavities as well as of the optic nerves. He held that the brain was the centre of thought and feeling. Blood was a subject for much research and speculation. For a long time it was believed that the blood vessels contained *pneuma* (air and breath). In accordance with the doctrine of four elements of *Empedocles, there developed the doctrine that the body consists of four humours (Blood, Phlegm, Black Bile and Yellow Bile). This belief was maintained until relatively modern times. Aristotle contributed a little to anatomy, including his erroneous belief in the heart as the seat of thought. Important work was done by *Herophilius of Chalcedon. He carried out dissections as well as vivisections on human subjects, using condemned criminals for his research. He studied the brain, the nerves, the sexual organs, the liver, the eye and the vascular system. His achievements were noteworthy: he concluded that the brain was the seat of intelligence and the centre of the nervous system, he distinguished between sensory and motor nerves and between arteries and veins, and recognized the work of the pulse etc. *Erasistratus of Chios, too, carried out vivisections and dissections and proposed the best theory concerning the circulation of blood until Harvey. He also studied the nervous system and achieved better results than Herophilus. The next greatest and the last physician of antiquity to conduct anatomical and physiological research was *Galenus, although he used animals and not humans as his subjects. He worked on the blood-system, the muscles, the bones, the spinal cord etc.

But the advance of knowledge of the human body had no direct influence on the practitioners. As noted above, the better physicians recognized the importance of observation. The work *Epidemics* contains several detailed case-histories, which includes precise observations extending in some cases to the 120th day of the disease. It is thanks to the accumulation of knowledge of this kind that the physicians who came later could understand the symptoms they were confronted with. The work *Prognostics* instructs the physician as to what questions he should ask when he visits a patient. As the means of the ancient physicians to help their patients were limited, they suggested preventive treatment (including diets, gymnastics, hygiene and right modes of life). The therapeutic repertoir included purgatives, dietetics, baths, bleeding, cupping, inunctions and clysters. Drugs were also used and it was essential for a doctor to know how to select the right herbs. Surgery was also practised. Homer gives descriptions of wound-treatment, but great advances were made after his time. Physicians treated fractures, dislocations, wounds. There were doctors who did skull operations, treated cataracts surgically, removed nasal polyps and extirpated goitres. The operating theatre was well equipped and the importance of hygiene was known. Numerous surgical tools have been found in excavations, notably at Pompey.

The Romans, according to Pliny the Elder (*NH*, 29.11), had no physicians for centuries. They, too, based healing on religious beliefs and on experience; hence rites, magical means and drugs were used. The earliest extant work that contains medical instructions is *On Agriculture* by *Cato (1). He mentions the use of herbs, and simple surgical approaches for wounds and dislocations which include magic incantations. Greek medical science came to Rome gradually from the 3rd century BC. The physician Archagathus practised in Rome from 219 (Pliny *NH*, 29.12), and even received Roman citizenship. *Asclepiades (2) of Prusa gained fame in Rome in the 1st century BC. The most important Latin medical writer *Celsus (1), who is immensely indebted to the Greeks. In a preface he gives an account of the four different Greek Schools of M.: the Dogmatic, the Empiric, the Methodic, and the Pneumatic. It was the philosophical views adopted by the physicians that determined the division, and they were the followers, respectively, of the Stoics, the Epicureans, the Sceptics, and the Eclectics. Galen, who lived in Rome, did not commit himself to any of the schools and took ideas from all of them, but mainly from the Dogmatists and Stoics.

M. was transformed into a science, then, when a natural cause and not a supernatural power was considered to be behind a disease. This realization was arrived at by the Greeks in the 5th century BC. The study of the human body and its diseases proceeded thereafter on scientific lines − even though it was somewhat confused by philosophical doctrines. But popular beliefs and practices persisted even after the best achievements were attained. In the long run, research work came to an end, so that Galen's writings were accepted as the last word until the end of the Middle Ages. Greek and Latin terminology is still used in medical practice.

J. Scarborough, *Roman Medicine*, 1969;
E. O. Philips, *Greek Medicine*, 1973.

MEDIOLANUM (modern Milan) A town founded by the *Insubres at the early 4th century BC; by the 3rd century it had become important. Rome conquered it in 194 BC. Like other Transpadane communities it received the Latin rights in 89 and Roman citizenship in 49 BC. It became a *colonia* under Hadrian. Its importance grew owing to its central position in northern Italy and it was often the imperial residence from the 3rd century AD. In the 4th century AD it became the capital of Liguria and the seat of the praetorian prefect.

MEGACLES A member of the aristocratic family of the *Alcemaeonidae in Athens; he married (c. 575 BC) Agariste, the daughter of *Cleisthenes (1). Leader of the Paraloi (in south Attica), he successfully opposed *Pisistratus, leader of the Diakrioi (in northeast Attica), in his first attempt to establish tyranny. Soon he reversed his policy and helped Pisistratus, who married his daughter, to gain the tyranny. But they quarreled and M. with Lycurgus, leader of the Pedieis, expelled the tyrant (c. 556). He was father of *Cleisthenes (2).

MEGALOPOLIS ("the great City") A city founded by *Epaminondas after 370 BC by the incorporation of the population of forty Arcadian villages; it became the centre of the Arcadian League. Situated in a plain, it was strongly fortified. The area of the city was larger than the population needed. Its theatre was the largest in Greece. The general Assembly of the Arcadian League met in the Thersilion. Many of the buildings have been excavated. Sparta opposed its foundation and subsequently sought to destroy it. M. cooperated with *Philip II. The Spartan king *Agis III was defeated at M. by *Antipater (1) in 331 BC. Aristodemus became tyrant of M. *c.* 270 and pursued pro-Macedonian policy. After him Lydiadas became tyrant and repulsed a Spartan attack. Lydiadas brought M. into the Achaean League (235/234 BC), and was its general several times until his death in a battle against *Cleomenes III. M. was sacked by the latter in 223, but recovered. Its native *Philopoemen became the leading Achaean general until his death. The historian *Polybius was a native of M. By Strabo's time it had declined, but it was still able to issue coins in the early 3rd century AD.

MEGARA One of the oldest towns of Greece, situated on two low hills in a plain on the isthmus of Corinth. It still bears the same name. In Attic tradition it had been part of Attica, and the geographers Strabo and Pausanias still regarded its region (Megarid) as part of Attica. The early population came under Dorian influence.

From the mid-8th to the mid-6th century BC, M. played an important role in the Greek colonization. Among the colonies it founded were: *Megara Hyblaea, *Heraclea Pontica, *Chalcedon and *Byzantium. In the late 7th century a tyranny was established in M. by *Theagenes. After him M. lost its leading position, in consequence of internal conflicts between the aristocracy and democracy. It lost Salamis to Athens and the western territory to Corinth. In the second half of the 6th century it joined the Peloponnesian League. In the 5th century it fought in the Persian Wars and was involved in the struggle between Athens and Corinth and Sparta. The ban against trade with M. proclaimed by Athens (the "Megarian Decree") contributed to the outbreak of the Peloponnesian War. It revived in the 4th century BC when it managed to maintain neutrality. The Megarian School of philosophy, founded by *Eucleides, mainly followed the theories of *Parmenides. Its members had a reputation as skillful dialecticians.

E. L. Highbarger, *The History . . . of Ancient Megara*, 1927.

MEGARA HYBLAEA Greek city on the eastern coast of Sicily, about 20 km north of Syracuse. It was founded by settlers from *Megara *c.* 729 BC. It prospered and was able to found *Selinus in the next century. *Gelon destroyed it in 483 BC (Thuc. 6.4). *Timoleon re-established it (*c.* 340 BC) but it was destroyed again by *Marcellus (1) in 214 BC.

Dunbabin, *Western Greeks* (s.v.).

MEGARON In Homer the M. is the main hall of the royal palace, and by extension the whole palace. The main hall was preceded by a columned court (*aule*), and all the other rooms of the palace were built around it. The single hall-house was the dominant type of building in the Aegean world from the late 3rd millenium BC. It has been found in archaeological excavations in numerous sites in Greece, the islands and Troy. It was a rectangular building with a hearth in the middle which was for domestic use and worship. The M., preceded by a covered or opened vestibule, was the basic unit of the house in Greece It was also the main element of the Greek temple.

MEGASTHENES The Greek author (*c.* 350–290 BC) of *Indika*, a four book work on India. It dealt with the geography, ethnography, society, religion, mythology and history of India. M. went on several diplomatic missions, in the service of *Seleucus I, to the court of the Indian ruler Chandragupta. He thus had first-hand knowledge of the land. His work is not extant but it was used by many subsequent writers including *Strabo, and is the main source of the extant *Indika* of Arrian. What was known in the West on India was thus mainly due to M.'s work.

MEIDIAS PAINTER The artist who worked for the Athenian potter Meidias. He was active in the late 5th century BC and is known for his refined, graceful style. The rape of the Leucippidai and Heracles with the Hesperides are the themes on an extant Hydria (British Museum).

MELA, Pomponius The author of a geographical work in Latin, *De Chorographia*, in three books. He was native of Tingentera in south Spain and wrote under the Emperor Claudius. Book 1 opens with a general description of the earth: the hemispheres, the five zones, the continents and the seas, and then describes the countries from Mauretania to Egypt, and the coastal lands from Egypt to the Bosporus. Books 2 and 3 continue the description of countries. The work is a mixture of fables and scientific material. M. gives an account of northern Europe (but curiously not of central), of India and of eastern Asia (but not of central Asia).

MELAMPUS Greek mythological figure, son of Amythaon and Eidomene, brother of Bias. While a child, snakes licked his ears and from then on he understood the languages of all creatures. By listening to the voices of birds he was endowed with prophetic powers. In one case he consulted a vulture to discover why Iphiclus had no children; he discovered the cause and cured him. He cured the daughters of *Proetus, though one died. He and his brother married the remaining two and each received a third of the kingdom of Argos. M. is first mentioned by Homer (*Od.* 285ff. *et al.*). According to Herodotus he was the founder of the cult of Dionysus in Greece (2.48f.). A detailed account is given by Apollodorus (1.96ff.). He was considered the ancestor of the prophetic family of the Melampodidae who told his myth.

MELEAGER (1) Greek mythological hero, son of Oeneus, king of *Calydon, and Alathea; his wife was Cleopatra, daughter of *Idas. His story is first told by Homer (*Il.* 9.529ff.). He quarreled with his mother and refrained from helping his city when attacked by the *Curetes; he participated in the defence only after they forced their way into his own house. In particular he is related to the Calydonian boar hunt. After his father forgot to sacrifice to Artemis, the goddess sent a monstrous boar to ravage the Calydonian country. He invited heroes from all over Greece to hunt the boar (the list came to include, among others, the *Dioscuri, *Idas and Lynceus, *Theseus, *Jason, *Admetus, *Peleus, *Nestor, and *Amphiaraus). In a later version of the myth, dating at least from the early 5th century BC (it was told by Phrynichus and appears in Bacchylides), *Atalanta took part in the hunt. M. fell in love with her and though he killed the boar, he awarded her the prize (the boar's head), as she was the first to wound the beast. A quarrel with his uncles ensued and he killed them. His mother then ended his life in the following manner. At his birth she was visited by the *Moirai who said he would live as long as a firebrand, then on the fire, was not burnt. Alathea always kept it but when M. killed his uncles she burnt it and M. died. The Calydonian boar hunt was a favourite theme in sculpture and vase-paintings in the Archaic and Classical periods.

MELEAGER (2) Greek poet and philosopher (c. 100 BC), native of Gadara. He lived in Tyre and in his last years in Cos. He excelled in the epigram form and was the first to compile an *anthologia* (garland) of poetic epigrams. About a hundred of his epigrams are in Greek *Anthology. They are mostly love poems. He also wrote Menippean Satires, but these are not extant.
T. B. L. Webster, *Hellenistic Poetry and Art*, 1964.

MELOS The great southwestern island of the Cyclades. Rich with obsidian, it was inhabited from Neolithic times. Archaeological excavations have shown its close connections with the Minoan and Mycenaean civilizations. The island was occupied by the Dorians and later was considered as a Spartan foundation (Hdt. 8.48). The Melians fought at *Salamis and *Plataea and pursued a neutral policy thereafter. This did not save them from Athens in the Peloponnesian War. They were first attacked in 426 BC by Nicias and in 416 were conquered; the men were killed and the women and children were sold to slavery. This was one of the more brutal manifestations of Athenian imperialism, the nature of which is discussed by Thucydides in the famous *Melian Dialogue* (5.85—113). Athens founded a cleruchy on the island.

MEMNON (1) In mythology, the son of *Eos ("Dawn") and Tithonius, king of Ethiopa. He came to help his uncle Priam after the death of Penthesilea. He killed Antiochus, son of Nestor, but was killed by Achilles. His myth was told in the lost epic *Aethiopis* and is mentioned by Hesiod (*Theog.* 894f.), Alcman and Pindar. Some associated him with Susa. Seti I built a temple for Osiris at *Abydos which was known as Memnoneion. The same name was given to a temple of Seti in the Egyptian Thebes. The colossal statues of Amenhotep III were associated with him. They "sang" at sunrise after they were slightly damaged by an earthquake (27 BC) and thus attracted tourists. After Septimius *Severus restored them they ceased making the peculiar sounds. His myth was a favourite theme in vase-painting. There is a famous cup by *Duris (1) showing Eos carrying the body of her son.

MEMNON (2) Rhodian mercenary captain, younger brother of *Mentor (2). He married Barsine, his sister-in-law, after the death of his brother. He also succeeded to the command his brother had had in the service of Persia and won victories against the generals of *Philip II. He survived the battle of Granicus and was appointed commander-in-chief in Asia Minor. M. then conducted a successful maritime war but suddenly died (333 BC).

MEMPHIS The old capital of Lower Egypt, the White Wall (Thuc. 1.104). In old times the main god was Ptah. In Ptolemaic time it was a centre of the cult of *Sarapis, supported by the Ptolemies, who had here a famous temple, the Sarapeum. It was the second largest city in Egypt but under the Roman Empire it declined. A legionary camp was built opposite it.

MENANDER (1) Greek comic playwright (342—292 BC), the leading writer of the New Comedy. Of good Athenian family, he attended the lectures of *Theophrastus, was influenced by *Epicurus and associated with *Demetrius (6) of Phalerum. He wrote his first play in 321 and until his death composed more than 100 plays, of which almost 100 titles are known; however, he won only eight prizes. Until 1957 his works were known only by numerous fragments from papyri (over 1,000) which showed his wide popularity. A complete play was then discovered, the *Dyscolus* ("Bad-Tempered Man"). There are more than 1,000 fragments of his work, some of them quite substan-

tial. Besides the *Dyscolus*, the other better known plays include *Arbitration*, the *Hero*, the *Woman of Samos*, the *Shorn Girl*, the *Man of Sicyon*. In *Arbitration* the husband discovers that his newly-wed wife exposed her baby, which later is shown to be his own child. Another recognition scene occurs in the *Shorn Girl*: a jealous soldier cuts his mistress' hair; discovering that she is the daughter of his rich neighbour he marries her. In the *Dyscolus*, a peevish father is rescued by the suitor of his daughter whom he had rejected; he now consents to the wedding.

M. became famous after his death; in his lifetime his rival *Philemon was far more successful. His outstanding talent was his ability to reflect life in his plays, that is, his characters appeared lifelike. His plays used figures already common in the comedy, but he was able to endow them with individual traits. His language fits his characters, and so the contrast between the characters is more conspicuous. His figures are taken from all social circles. They are often not ordinary types (e.g. kidnapped daughters) but by his treatment they are convincing and credible. His plots are well constructed and full of surprises. In his themes he prefers the love-motif, but he treats it in many different ways, and in fact the true theme is often not love itself. He is fond of using the false identity of a character to create situations and develop the plot until the final recognition. With humour and irony he touches on various amusing sides of human nature. And he often has moralizing sayings to add for dramatical purposes. His plays were produced at Athens after his death and were known at Rome through their free Latin adaptations by Plautus and Terence, and through them greatly influenced the comedy of manners in European literature.
P. Vellacott, *Menander, Plays and Fragments* (tr.), 1960;
E. W. Handley, *The Dyskolos of Menander*, 1965;
T. B. L. Webster, *An Introduction to Menander*, 1974.

MENANDER (2) The most famous of the Indo-Greek kings, he ascended to the throne quite young (c. 155 BC) and died in 130. Reputedly a great conqueror (Strabo 11.516), his precise achievements are not sufficiently clear. His coins have Pallas Athena on the reverse and some the Buddhist Wheel of the Law. He adopted Buddhism and is known as Milinda in the Buddhist tradition.
A. K. Narain, *Indo-Greeks*, 1957;
G. Woodcock, *The Greeks in India*, 1966.

MENELAUS (1) Son of *Atreus, younger brother of *Agamemnon, king of Sparta, and the renowned husband of *Helen. His wife's escape with *Paris and his will to take revenge was the cause of the Trojan War. He is thus one of the prominent figures in the *Iliad*, but not its main hero. Why the Greeks agreed to go into war on his behalf is explained by the way he won Helen. Her father *Tyndareus obliged her suitors to help the man whom he would choose as his son-in-law. His main exploits at Troy are his duel with Paris, who is saved only by the intervention of Aphrodite (*Il.* 3), and the prominent part he plays in the battle for *Patroclus' body (*Il.* 17.1ff.). But otherwise his role is subordinate. He is one of the few Greek heroes who returns safely home, and he tells his adventures on that voyage in Book 4 of the *Odyssey*. Many details and versions were developed for his life before and after the Trojan War by later writers. At the fall of Troy he is determined to kill Helen, but is overpowered by her charm. He then returns with her to Sparta where they live happily (*Od.* 4). In Euripides' *Helen*, it is a phantom of his wife that is taken by Paris, and Menelaus finds his real wife in Egypt. Theocritus has a wedding-song for Menelaus and Helen (*Idyll.* 18). In historical time he had a hero-cult in the Menalaion at Sparta (Pausan. 3.15,3) a site of Mycenaean origin. He appears in many works of art.

MENELAUS (2) Greek mathematician and astronomer, native of Alexandria. The astronomical observations he made, recorded by Claudius *Ptolemy, help to date him to AD 98. His only extant work, in Arabic translation, is the *Sphaerica* which is a three book work on spherical geometry. M. is the first known mathematician to give theorems on spherical trigonometry.

T. L. Heath, *History of Greek Mathematics*, 1921, Vol 2.

MENENIUS LANATUS, Agrippa Roman consul of 503 BC. He is famous for his success in reconciling the Plebs in the first secession (494 BC) which he achieved by telling them the parable of the Belly and Limbs (Liv. 2.32; Dion. Hal. 6.83ff.), probably an old popular tale. He died so poor that the costs of his funeral were paid by the state.

MENIPPUS of Gadara Author of the first half of 3rd century BC. M. was a slave at Sinope who bought his freedom and studied philosophy under the Cynic, Metrocles, at Thebes; he became a citizen of that city. His writings were a mixture of prose and verse and he treated serious philosophical subjects in comic manner. Hence rose a distinct genre called after him, the *Menippeae Saturae* (Quint. *Inst.* 10.1, 95). Thirteen titles of his works are known including, *Descent to the Underworld, The Sale of Diogenes, The Wills of the Philosophers, Epistles from the Gods*, and *Symposium*. The Menippean Satire was used by *Varro (2) and *Seneca the Younger. *Meleager (2) of Gadara, *Lucian and *Petronius were also influenced by him. None of his works are extant.

Diog. Laert. 6.95, 99–101.

MENTOR (1) The friend of Odysseus who, too old to go to the Trojan War, stayed at Ithaca to take care of his affairs. Athena took his form to give *Telemachus advice in his search for Odysseus. His name became proverbial for a loyal adviser.

MENTOR (2) Rhodian mercenary captain, elder brother of Memnon (2). He served with *Artabazus, the Persian satrap of Daskylium, from 366 BC, and was his brother-in-law. He and his brother fought in the Satraps' Revolt (362–360) and he was given Ilium and other territory by Artabazus. He supported the revolt of Artabazus (356), and after its collapse he fled to Egypt and Artabazus to Macedonia. M. later helped the Persians to take Sidon and arranged the return of Artabazus and his own brother. He was given command and served in the reconquest of Egypt (343). M. then had great influence and was given general command in Asia Minor to restore the Great King's authority over the local dynasts who had pro-Macedonian sympathies. One of them was *Hermias whom he captured and put to death (342). M. died soon after.

MERCURIUS (Mercury) The Roman god of traders, who was probably the Greek *Hermes introduced into Rome, under a name implying his character (*merx; mercator* = trader). He lacks the features of the old Roman gods, neither a *Flamen not a festival in the old calendar. According to another view he was originally an old Graeco-Etruscan god, but the difference is only relevant to the question of how the Greek god came to Rome. He received a temple at Rome on the Aventine in 495 BC (Liv. 2.21 and 27) and its foundation date (15 May) was the festival of the traders. Almost all his mythology was modelled on that of Hermes, and he also had the same

attributes: the herald's staff; winged cap and shoes. Under the Roman Empire his cult was widespread especially in the West. This was the result of his association with local deities, whose names were preserved in the titles given to him. His popularity is attested by hundreds of dedications to him. His image in mediaeval Europe was influenced by the astrological powers ascribed to his planet.

Latte, *R. Rel.*, 162ff.

MESOPOTAMIA "The country between the rivers", i.e. the area between the Tigris and the Euphrates. Properly applied, the name refers to the northern part of modern Iraq, north of Bagdad, and so it was used by classical writers; Babylonia was the southern part of the area. The Aramaic name of the country (*beyn nahrin*) has the same meaning. But by convention it includes the whole country from the mountains of Iran to the Syrian and Arabian deserts and from the mountains of Kurdistan to the Persian Gulf. *Seleucus I took control of M. in the wars of the *Diadochi (312 BC) and it remained under Seleucid rule until the death of *Antiochus VII Sidetes (129 BC). The Seleucids built many new cities (e.g. *Edessa (2), *Dura-Europos, *Seleuceia (1)). After the Parthian occupation a gradual decline of the Greek cities began. The Euphrates came to be the border line between Parthia and Rome, who, from the mid-1st century BC on, occasionally were at war. *Trajan was the first Roman to conquer M. (AD 114–7), but his successor *Hadrian evacuated it. It was again conquered by L. *Verus (162–5) and by Septimius *Severus (197–9), but only part of it became a permanent Roman territory. The main city under the Parthians was *Ctesiphon.

F. Stark, *Rome on the Euphrates*, 1966;
Jones, *Cities*[2], ch. 9.

MESSALA CORVINUS, Marcus Valerius Roman statesman and general, 64 BC–AD 8. Of old patrician family, he studied at Athens (45 BC), and was known as orator. After the assassination of Caesar, he followed the tyranicides and fought with distinction at *Philippi. He thereafter followed *Antonius (4), but soon left him for Octavian. He took part in the war against Sextus Pompeius (36 BC), the Illyrian War (35–34) and conquered the Gallic Salassi (34–33). Consul in 31 BC, he fought at *Actium. He continued his military exploits by subduing the Aquitani as governor of Gaul and was awarded a triumph in 27 BC. He was the first to be appointed *Praefectus Urbi (25 BC), but presently resigned presumably because he regarded his appointment as unconstitutional. With the spoils of his campaigns he reconstructed public buildings. Himself a renowned historian and orator, he was a patron of poets (*Tibullus, *Sulpicia). There is extant a rather inferior poem (212 hexameters) that tells his praises, *Panegyricus Messalae* (the 4th book in the poems of Tibullus).

J. Hammer, *The Military and Political Career of M. Valerius Messala Corvinus*, 1925; Syme, *RR*. (s.v.).

MESSALINA (1), Valeria Granddaughter of *Octavia (1). At the age of 14 she married *Claudius, the future emperor (AD 39/40). She bore him *Britannicus and Octavia (2). M. was notorious for her shameless love-affairs, but her cuckold husband, 34 years older than her, was the only one unaware of her conduct. She went as far as to marry her lover C. Silius, but then *Narcissus, Claudius' freedman, secured her execution (AD 48).

MESSALINA (2), Statilia A descendant of *Statilius Taurus, who became the third wife of *Nero after he put her fourth husband to death. Beautiful, intellectual and of personal charm she retained her high position even after Nero's death.

MESSANA (modern Messina) A city on the commercially favourable position between Sicily and Italy which was founded by settlers from *Cumae (c. 730–725 BC); it was originally named Zancle. It prospered and was able to found its own colonies. After the collapse of the Ionian Revolt it received refugees from *Samos and *Miletus. It was captured by *Anaxilas (490/489 BC), the tyrant of Rhegium, and changed its name to Messene after receiving settlers from Messenia (but later its coins show the form Messana). It allied itself with Syracuse against the Athenian intervention in Sicily, and was involved in the feuds between Ionian and Dorian cities. Destroyed by the Carthaginians in 396 it was soon resettled by *Dionysius I. In the mid-4th century BC it had its own tyrant who was defeated by *Timoleon. After him M. was under *Agathocles. In 288 it was captured by the *Mamertini who 24 years later sought Roman protection and unwittingly led to the conquest of Sicily by Rome. M. remained a free "allied city" (*civitas foederata*) and was an important trade centre.

Dunbabin, *Western Greeks* (s.v.).

MESSAPIA The region of the Messapii in extreme southeastern Italy. The Mesapii were part of the Japyges who included other ethnical groups in this area: Peucetii, Calabri, Salentini (Pol. 3.88). They were probably of Illyrian origin but came under Greek influence. Their relations with the main Greek city in the area, *Tarentum, varied. For their support to Tarentum in the Pyrrhic War, they were conquered by Rome.

J. Whatmaugh, *The Foundations of Roman Italy*, 1937.

Walls and towers of Messene

MESSENE After the defeat of Sparta at *Leuctra (371 BC), Epaminondas helped the Messenians build this city (369). It was situated on the western side of Mount Ithome and was fortified by strong walls (9 km long). These are the best preserved walls in Greece. It was the capital of Messenia. Many buildings have been excavated including a theatre and a temple of Artemis. The main cult of M. was of Zeus Ithomas on Mount Ithome. See *Messenia.

MESSENIA The southwest country of the Peloponnesus, bounded by *Elis in the north, *Arcadia in the northeast and *Laconia in the east. The most fertile part of M. was its lower plain and the worst part was in the west. Curiously, it was in the west bare part of the country that civilization developed in the 2nd millenium BC. The legends about the great kingdom of *Nestor at *Pylos, with implications of material prosperity, have been proved true by archaeological excavations at several places. These give evidence of the existence of palaces and a considerable population. It is clear that M. belonged to the Mycenaean world and had close connections with Crete. The country was conquered by the Dorians and this is reflected in legend by the story of the return of the *Heraclidae; then the fugitives from M. found shelter in Athens.

M. was evidently fertile enough to attract the expansionist Spartans in the 8th century BC. The First and Second Messenian Wars (8th–7th century BC) ended with the Spartan conquest of M. The remaining Messenians became *helots and had to cultivate the land of the Spartan lords. They tried to regain freedom by taking advantage of the great earthquake from which Sparta suffered in 464 BC, but the Third Messenian War ended in the capitulation of the rebels on Mount Ithome. They were allowed to leave and settled at Naupactus. It was only in 369 that the Messenians regained their freedom with the help of *Epaminondas. Sparta naturally sought to reconquer M., which consequently tended to ally itself with other powers: Athens and Philip II. After the death of Alexander M. fell under the control of various rulers. From the mid-3rd century it allied itself to Aetolia, Achaea and *Philip V in succession. It suffered from the same social and economic problems that disturbed the Greek world at that time. M. was saved from the Spartan tyrant *Nabis by the intervention of *Philopoemen. But the relations with the Achaean League were strained and on one occasion Philopoemen was captured and put to death. In revenge *Lycortas conquered Messene. The city was still prosperous under the Roman Empire.

C. A. Roeubuck, *A History of Messenia*, 1941.

METELLUS (1) MACEDONICUS, Quintus Caecilius Of a noble plebeian family, he was praetor in 148 BC and quelled the revolt of *Andriscus in Macedonica (hence Macedonicus). He was awarded a triumph in 146. As consul (143) he was in charge of Nearer Spain and pursued a successful war against the Celtiberians. He was censor in 131 with Q. Pompeius — the first plebeian pair of censors. On that occasion he delivered a famous oration to encourage an increase in the birth rate. M. was an opponent of *Scipio Aemilianus and opposed the Gracchi. He was one of the leading senators of his day and established the pre-eminence of his family. He had four sons and three daughters; three of his sons had attained the consulate at his death in 115 BC.

A. E. Astin, *Scipio Aemilianus*, 1967 (s.v.).

METELLUS (2) NUMIDICUS, Quintus Caecilius As consul in 109 BC, he was given the command against Jugurtha, at a time of great popular agitation against the nobility. In open war his success was complete: he twice defeated the enemy in pitched battles. But Jugurtha escaped and resorted to guerilla tactics. When his legate *Marius announced his intention to stand for the consulate, M. told him to wait for his son (who was very young and had to wait many years for the consulate) and thus incurred his violent enmity. By intrigue and popular agitation, Marius was elected consul of 107 and superseded M. in the command against Jugurtha. M. was awarded a triumph and was censor in 102. In 100 he refused to swear to uphold the agrarian law of *Saturninus (1) and was compelled to go into exile. After a year or so his son M. (3) succeeded in securing his recall.

METELLUS (3) PIUS, Quintus Caecilius Son of M. (2), under whom he served in Africa. In 99 BC received the name Pius for his devotion to his father whose recall from exile he secured. Praetor in 89, he fought in the *Bellum Sociale. After *Cinna (1) took control of Rome in 87, he left for Africa. He fought for Sulla in the Civil War and was his colleague in the consulate of 80. From 79 on he fought against *Sertorius in Spain. But it was only with the help of Pompey that the war was concluded. He returned to Rome in 71 and received a triumph. He was Pontifex Maximus until his death in 63; Caesar was elected the next Pontifex Maximus.

METELLUS (4) PIUS SCIPIO, Quintus Caecilius By birth and adoption he was successor of many noble families. His father was a Scipio Nasica and *M. (3) Pius adopted him at his death. He was praetor by 55 BC and celebrated a triumph after governing an unknown province. Pompey married his daughter and helped him to become his colleague in the consulate of 52 BC. M. was a sworn enemy of Caesar and proposed the motion to declare him a public enemy in 49. He governed Syria and commanded the centre in *Pharsalus. He succeeded to escape to Africa, became the supreme commander and died after *Thapsus.

Syme, *Rom. Rev.* (s.v.).

METICS (Metoikoi) This term which means "those who lived with" designated resident aliens in Greek states. It was a formal status and not all foreigners who lived in a Greek city attained it. At Athens, the M. had to have an Athenian citizen as a sponsor (*prostates*), who probably represented him in court, was registered in the deme where he had a domicile and paid a special tax (*metoikion*) of 12 drachms a year. In addition he was subject to the other taxes and paid the *eisphora* at a higher rate. Ordinarily a metic was not allowed to own houses or land nor could he enter into a legal marriage with a citizen; some M., however received special privileges. The M. were called for military service. They were protected by law (their case came before the court of the *Polemarchos) and were free to practise their professions. *Lysias, *Aristotle and *Anaxagoras are only few of the many famous M. that lived in Athens. The M. played an important role in the economic life of the communities where they lived. V. Ehrenberg, *The Greek State*[2], 1969 (s.v.).

METIS The Greek goddess that personified council. She first appears in Hesiod (*Theog.* 886ff.) as "the wisest of gods and men". Zeus took her as his wife but swallowed her to prevent her giving birth to a son who would supplant him. But then *Athena sprang from his head.

METTIUS FUFETIUS Dictator or king of Alba Longa. The duel between the *Horatii and Curiatii was held at his suggestion. For his treachery, the Roman King *Tullus Hostilius executed him by binding each of his limbs to horses who were set free. This was not the Roman way of execution and Livy states that this was the first and last time it was applied (1.28,11).

MEZENTIUS The Etruscan king of *Caere who came to help *Turnus against Aeneas. In the early version, *Ascanius defeated M. In Virgil's *Aeneid* M. is a blood-thirsty warrior, brutal and godless (*contemptor divium*). After killing Lausus, Aeneas' son, he is slain by Aeneas. In another version he demanded the first-fruits of the vintage from his allies (Ovid *Fasti* 4. 884ff.) or from Aeneas (Dion. Hal. 1.55).

MICON Painter and sculptor in Athens in the 5th century BC. He executed paintings in the Theseum and the Stoa Poikile. The themes were probably the War of the Amazons and the War of the Centaurs. He also made statues of athletes.

MIDAS (1) Mythical king of Phrygia who is involved in several myths. He once judged a musical contest between Apollo and *Marsyas (or Pan) and gave the prize to the second. Apollo in revenge turned his ears into ass's ears, which only his hairdresser knew, as he hid them with a special bonnet. But the barber could not keep the secret to himself and whispered it to a hole he dug in the earth. The reeds there grew and repeated what he said. In another story he once found the satyr Silenus drunk in his marvelous garden and he told him wonderful stories. He thus entertained Silenus who was too drunk to follow his leader, Dionysus. The latter, who had been concerned about Silenus, then promised to give M. anything he wanted. He asked that everything he touch become gold and then discovered that he could neither drink nor eat. He was told to wash in the river Pactolus and after he did so, the river sand became golden.

MIDAS (2) King of Phrygia (738–696 BC). He opposed Assyrian expansion but in 707 became subject to Sargon. He killed himself by drinking bull's blood after the Cimmerian invasion. M. is said by Herodotus to have been the first Barbarian king to present a gift to Delphi.

MILETUS The most renowned Ionian city in southwestern Asia Minor. It was occupied from the early 2nd millenium BC. The city probably appears in a Hittitie text as *Milatawa* belonging to the king of *Achiyyawa*. According to Homer, the Carians of M. fought the Achaeans in the Trojan War (*Il.* 2.868). There was another tradition that Miletus of Crete fled with his followers from Minos and founded the city. The Ionians, led by Neleus, came from Athens and took the city from the Carians, and had their wives for themselves. The Ionians, the last to come, became the dominant element of the city, which prospered in the Archaic period and sent many colonies northward including *Abydos, *Cyzicus and *Sinope. According to Strabo, the Milesians founded *Naucratis ("Milesian" Fort) in the reign of Psammetichus. Pliny the Elder says that M. founded 90 cities (*NH* 5.112). M. also developed trade relations with the West, mainly with *Sybaris. Its exports included the famous Milesian wool and furniture (in particular beds). M. was one of the first cities to mint coins. In the late 7th century it was ruled by Thrasybulus, notorious for his cool cruelty. It was a centre of intellectual activity in the 6th century; *Thales, *Anaximander, *Anaximenes and *Hecataeus were from M.

M. came under the Persian rule in 546 BC. The Milesian tyrant *Aristagoras was responsible for the start of the Ionian Revolt in 499, which ended with its destruction.

The *Taking of Miletus* was a play by *Phrynichus, which so grieved the Athenians for the misfortunes of the Milesians that the author was fined and performances of the play were forbidden. M. was resettled after the Greek victory over Persia and became a member of the Delian League. For some reason Athens sent a garrison there. It deserted Athens in 412 but thereafter came under the Persian control. It gained its freedom after the victory of Alexander at Granicus (334), and in the Hellenistic period managed to retain its autonomy. Included in the province of Asia, M. prospered under the Roman Empire.

A. G. Dunham, *History of Miletus* 1915; Magie, *Asia* (s.v.).

MILO, Titus Annius Prominent Roman politician in the 50s BC. M. was one of those Roman senators who used gangs to intimidate and drive away their political rivals, and so they replaced constitutional rule with anarchy. He began using this method to counterbalance the dominance of *Clodius (1) who preceded him in the use of violence. As tribune in 57, he bought a gang of gladiators and also armed his clients. He was thus able to help Cicero return from exile. He was praetor in 55, but when a candidate for the consulate he killed Clodius (18 July 52 BC). He was prosecuted and convicted (Cicero failed to deliver his speech as he was alarmed by the troops Pompey posted). M. went to Massilia in exile. He returned in 48 and tried to raise a revolt with *Caelius Rufus but was put to death.

MILON The famous wrestler of Croton who won six times at the Olympian games and six at the Pythian games (second half of the 6th century BC). Many anecdotes were told about his extraordinary strength, and he was compared to Achilles and Heracles. He carried a heifer to the stadium, killed it with one blow and then completely ate it in a day. He led his compatriots against Sybaris and defeated it. He was also considered a disciple of Pythagoras and his daughter married the famous doctor Democedes. He once tried to split a tree apart and was eaten by wolves when he was caught in the cleft.

MILTIADES Son of Cimon, of the aristocratic family of Philaïdae in Athens; born *c.* 550, died *c.* 489 BC. M. went to the *Chersonesus (1) and made a personal rule there. He married Hegesipyle, the daughter of the rich Thracian King Olorus, who bore him *Cimon. He took part in the Scythian campaign of *Darius I. M. supported the Ionian Revolt and after its collapse escaped to Athens. Here he was charged with having created a "tyranny" in the Chersonesus but was acquitted. As general in 490 M. was the commander that took the decisive resolution to fight at *Marathon. In the following year he failed to capture Paros, was wounded, fined, and soon died.

A. R. Burn, *Persia and the Greeks*, 1962 (s.v.).

MIMNERMUS Greek elegist and musician, of Smyrna and Colophon, lived in the second half of the 7th century BC. Two books of his elegies are known. *Nanno*, named after his beloved flute-girl, consisted of poems on various themes of mythology and history and probably erotic verses as well. The *Smyrneis* was a historical poem on Smyrna. He also wrote iambic verses. Only fourteen fragments are extant, five from the *Hanno*. One is a description of the night journey of Helios (sun) in his magic bowl to the east. Another tells of the pleasures of youth – only the young can enjoy love, and old age is worse than death. This fleeting nature of life recurs in his love-poems. Indeed the love of pleasure is conspicuous in his work. The little that has remained shows a sense for rythm and music in this genre.

Diehl, *An. Lyr. Gr.* 1; Bowra, *E. Gr. El.*, 17ff.

MIMUS This term denotes both the actor and the performance of simple, dramatic sketches which were common in Greece and Italy from early times. It was essentially mimetic and improvised, with stock characters and themes taken from daily life or mythology. The mimes were performed on private occasions or in religious and rustic festivals, by solo performers or troupes which were often wandering. The characters were of middle and low social classes. The mimes consisted of monologues and dialogues. Sophron of Syracuse (5th century BC) was probably the first to compose literary mimes, in rhythmical prose. They were divided into male and female. There is one considerable fragment and many citations of his mimes. *The Tunny-fisher*, and *Women at Breakfast* were among his subjects. Plato, who admired his mimes, is said to have imitated them in some of his dialogues. Xenophon (*Symposium*) gives an account of a mime *Dionysus and Ariadne* which was played by a wandering company (a boy, a girl and a flute player) from Syracuse at the house of Callias. Dance, acrobatics, music and the dialogue are the elements in this mime. In the Hellenistic period *Theocritus and *Herodas, influenced by Sophron, composed mimes. Mimes were very popular in Sicily and Magna Graecia. The performers of the informal farce here were called *phlyakes*, gossips, and were compared to the *autokabdaloi*, improvisers, of Greece. The popular performance of mimes on the stage started at Rome from the 3rd century; here it was called the *Fabula riciniata*. The actors, male and female, appeared without masks (at the festival of the Floralia *mimae* appeared naked). The mimes were given as an after piece to the programme. In the 1st century BC *Laberius and *Publilius Syrus composed literary mimes. Under the Empire a new genre came to the fore, the pantomime. The pantomime was performed by a single masked actor with a chorus and players of flutes, pipes, cymbals and other instruments. The actor played all the roles and hence changed the mask several times. The actor used gestures, postures and dances with conventional meanings. Librettii were written by such poets as Lucan and Statius. Both the mime and the pantomime enjoyed tremendous popularity in all social classes. The licentiousness of the actors was notorious and there were those who deplored the degradation of morals. Yet the coarse, indecent scenes were liked by the emperors as well and it was quite fitting that Theodora (Justinian's wife), a former *mima*, became an empress.

L. Friedlaender, *Roman Life and Manners under the Early Empire*, 1908–13, 2, 100ff.;
M. Bieber, *The History of the Greek and Roman Theatre*[2], 1961.

MINERVA The Italian goddess of arts and crafts who was identified with the Greek *Athena. Her cult was widespread in Italy, notably in Sabinum, but was introduced to Rome, as far as is known, only with the foundation of the Capitoline temple. There she was one of the Triad Capitoline and worshipped with *Jupiter and *Juno. Through her identification with Athena she also acquired the military character of the Greek goddess, and in course of time her worship supplanted that of Mars. An important centre of the worship of Minerva was at her temple on the Aventine, first attested in 207 BC. The flute-players celebrated their festival there on 13 June, and the guild of actors (*histriones*) and writers (*scribae*) was placed there. The cult of M. also spread to the Gauls under the Roman Empire.

Latte, *R. Rel.*, 163ff.

MINOAN CIVILIZATION The modern, convenient name, so called after the fabulous King *Minos, for the Bronze civilization of Crete in the 3rd and 2nd millenium BC. It was first used by Sir Arthur Evans who excavated Cnossos from 1900 on. This long period is conventionally divided into three main periods: Early, Middle, and Late Minoan and each of these is subdivided into I, II, III. This is a schematic system, based not on historical information but on archaeological finds and it has been proved unsatisfactory with the growth of archaeological evidence since the first excavations of the early 20th century. To fit the new evidence, more subdivisions have been suggested, but it is well to bear in mind that the periodization is based on changes in the techniques and decorations of ceramics, and the study of layers in the ruins. These give relative chronology and even when there are absolutely datable objects they do not help to evaluate the pace of change. The following is the common division: Early Minoan: *c.* 3000–2300 BC, Middle Minoan: 2200–1600 BC, Late Minoan: 1600–1200 BC.

The people of the MC. were not Greek. It is thought that at the beginning of the Early Minoan period they came from Asia Minor or Syria and occupied the island that had already been inhabited in the Neolithic period. The language was not Indo-European and they had trade and cultural relations with Egypt and the East. The most important centre was Cnossos, near modern Iraklion, about 5 km from the north coast. Another important centre was at Phaestus in the centre of the south side of the island. The small centre of Hagyia Triada is known only from archaeological excavations and so are many other sites (notably Mallia). Great palaces are characteristic of the MC. The palaces were not only the residences of the rulers but administrative and storage centres. They were two storeys or more and had central courts, halls, throne rooms, secondary courts with staircases, passages, and colonnades; and such an enormous complex of building (that of Cnossos covered an area of five acres) was probably at the base of the legend of the *Labyrinth. The palaces were also religious centres, though worship was also performed in caves and on high hills. A Mother Goddess was at the centre of the Minoan religion with the double axe as her cult-attribute. The palaces arose at the late 3rd millenium BC at Cnossos and Phaestus, but whether this was the result of an invasion or due to local development is disputed. This was the beginning of the great prosperity of the island which lasted to the 15th century BC. The population grew, new sites were occupied, and large cities developed around the palaces. The art of pottery was perfected at the early 2nd millenium BC. The palaces of Cnossos and Phaestus were destroyed for some reason or other but were rebuilt (18th century BC) and rose to high prosperity evidenced by the fine jewellery, frescoe paintings, metal work and gem engraving. The MC. reached its zenith all over the island probably in the 16th century. At that time Crete was a great power governed by a centralized administration from Cnossos. Then the island was destroyed in the early 15th century BC, after which only Cnossos still flourished. The island suffered further reverses in the early 14th century after which MC. declined sharply.

Writing was known at Crete by the early 2nd millenium BC. The first type of script was pictorial and is mainly known from seal-stones. It developed into a syllabic script about 1800 BC; this so-called Linear A script was used until the 15th century BC when it was replaced by *Linear B. Unlike Linear B, Linear A has not been deciphered. The use of Linear B is restricted to Cnossos where some 9,000 clay tablets have been found. It indicates that by that time the place was occupied by Greek-speaking people, apparently the Achaeans of the Greek epic. The memory of the MC. was preserved in Greek mythology, notably by the legends about *Minos and *Daedalus.

H. Kantor, *The Aegean and the Orient*, 1947;
S. Marinatos–M. Hirmer, *Crete and Mycenae*, 1960;
R. W. Hutchinson, *Prehistoric Crete*, 1962;
J. W. Graham, *The Palaces of Crete*, 1962;
J. D. S. Pendlebury, *The Archeology of Crete*, 1963 (1939).

MINOS The mythological king of Crete who probably preserves the memory of the great ruler of the island during the *Minoan civilization. He first appears in Homer where he is said to be son of Zeus (*Il.* 11.449) and a Phoenician mother (*Il.* 14.321) who is *Europe in all accounts. He had special relations with Zeus, who brought him up, raised him to the throne and through him, gave the first laws to mankind. According to Plato, M. went every ninth year to a cave to renew his friendship with Zeus. M.'s brothers were Rhadamanthys and *Sarpedon, and he married Pasiphaë, daughter of *Helios, perhaps a moongoddess. In other words, the king and queen of Minoan Crete were probably considered divine. M. secured his kingship by praying to Poseidon to send a bull as a divine sign for his right, promising to sacrifice it to the god. But he could not make himself kill the beautiful animal and as a punishment Poseidon made Pasiphaë fall in love with it. Disguised as a cow with the help of *Daedalus she mated with the bull and bore the Minotaur, a monster half man, half bull, which M. kept in the *Labyrinth. To M. she bore *Ariadne, Phaedra and Androgenus. When the Athenians killed Androgenus, M. made war on him and ended it after they consented to send him every year seven youths and seven maidens whom he gave to the Minotaur, until *Theseus killed it. This myth may represent a genuine conflict between Athens and Crete in the past. Indeed to M. was ascribed the first Thalassocracy, that is sea-empire (Thuc. 1.4).

M. himself died in Sicily when he came there to seize Daedalus. After his death he became one of the three judges of the underworld, with Rhadamanthys and Aeacus. This is how he appears in the Roman poets, and also in the *Inferno* of Dante.

MINTURNAE Town of the Aurunci, south of ancient *Latium, close to the coast, on the *Via Appia. Rome subdued it in the second half of the 4th century BC and established a Roman *colonia* there in 295 BC. The local goddess Marica was identified with *Circe (or Venus or Diana). Remains of many public buildings with inscriptions have been excavated there.

J. Johnson, *Excavations at Minturnae*, 1933.

MINUCIUS (1) RUFUS, Marcus Roman statesman, consul in 221 BC, but mainly known from his exploits in 217. Appointed *Magister Equitum of the dictator Fabius Cunctator by the Assembly, an exceptional procedure, he won some success over Hannibal. He was then promoted as co-dictator and is said to have been rescued by Fabius, perhaps an invention. He died in *Cannae.

Scullard, *Rom.Pol.*[2] (s.v.).

MINUCIUS (2) FELIX, Marcus Christian author of a dialogue in Latin, *Octavius*, in the first half of the 3rd century AD. The dialogue is a conversation between Octavius, a Christian convert, and Caecilius Nata, who uses Scepticism to criticize Christianity.

Text and translation: G. H. Rendall (Loeb), 1931.

MINYANS A prehistoric people who lived at *Orchomenus in Boeotia and at Iolcus in Thessaly. Their eponymous ancestor was Minyas who founded Orchomenus. In Pausanias' time, 2nd century AD, Minyas, "treasury" was known at Orchomenus. Schliemann has shown that it was a Mycenaean beehive-tomb. He called the fine pottery he found at Orchomenus "Grey Minyan", but it is not connected with the M. The M. were associated with the legend of the *Argonauts.

MISENUM Town at the northern promontory of the Bay of Naples. In legend it was so named after Misenus, the trumpeteer of Aeneas who was drowned here after incurring the wrath of a *Triton (Verg. *Aen.* 6.162ff.). Under Augustus, M. and Ravenna became the two main stations of the Roman fleet (Pliny the Elder was the commander of the fleet when Vesuvius erupted in AD 79). The town was a favourite sea resort.

J. D'Arms, *Romans on the Bay of Naples*, 1970.

MITHRAS The Indo-Iranian god of light and truth, the ally of Ahuramazda and enemy of Ahriman. With some important changes his cult spread to the Roman Empire from the 1st century AD. Evidence of Mithraic cult have been found almost all over the empire particularly in the great centres of trade and commerce and army sites, which implies that the worshippers were mainly soldiers and traders. Plutarch tells that the pirates of Cilicia already practised the mysteries of M. in the 1st century BC. Only men could take part in the ritual ceremonies of the cult. The evidence on the cult is partly literary and mainly archaeological and epigraphical. The first evidence in Latin literature for the cult is in Statius (*Theb.* Book 1).

Those who took part in the cult had to go through seven grades of initiation: Raven (*Corax*), Bride (*Nymphus*), Soldier (*Miles*), Lion (*Leo*), Persian (*Perses*), Sun's courier (*Heliodromus*), and Father (*Pater*). The rites were secret and took place in caves or artificial underground structures. The scene of M. slaying the bull (tauruoctony) was depicted in these temples of the god (*Mithraea*). In the scene the god plunges a knife into the bull's shoulder while a dog and a snake drink the blood. The god is accompanied by two torch bearers and wears the Persian cap and trousers. Other themes depicted in the Mithraic monuments include his birth (from a rock) and his association with the Sun-God. The slaying of the bull was a symbol, a kind of promise of life (the bull-blood) after death. M. is victorious over evil and death alike. The initiators go through a baptism and take a sacred meal. Mithraism was also associated with astrological beliefs — as is amply shown in Mithraic art. The tremendous popularity of Mithraism was in that as a saviour and a foe of death (evil) it promised rebirth to immortals. In this respect, the promise of salvation, Mithraism proved to be serious competition to Christianity.

While there is no doubt that the origin of M. is Oriental, including the qualities ascribed to him (truth, light, the victory over death and evil), it is equally clear that Mithraism as a mystery-religion with the tauroctony (with all that it symbolizes) as its most important element belongs to the Roman cult. In the course of time, Graeco-Roman gods were associated with him (e.g. Minerva and Mercury), and Mithraic art is mainly Roman and not Oriental.

M. J. Vermasseren, *Corpus Inscriptionum et*

The port of Misenum

Monumentorum Religionis Mithraicae, 1956–1960; *Mithras, the Secret God*, 1963; A. L. Campbell, *Mithraic Iconography and Ideology*, 1968; J. R. Hinnells (ed.) *Mithraic Studies*, 1975.

MITHRIDATES (1) KTISTES ("Founder") The founder of the Pontic kingdom, of a noble Persian family, allegedly descending from *Darius I. Born *c.* 338 BC, he served with distinction under *Eumenes (3), and then served under *Antigonus I. When Antigonus I put his relative Mithridates II of Cius to death (302), he fled, and after the downfall of Antigonus established himself at Pontus. He made *Amaseia the capital of his kingdom and took the royal title in 281. He died in 266 BC.

MITHRIDATES (2) V EUERGETES King of Pontus (*c.* 150–120 BC), descendant of M. (1). He astutely followed a philo-Roman policy, and as an ally sent ships and troops to the Third Punic War. In 133–129 he also helped in the war against *Aristonicus. Pylaemenes, king of Paphlagonia, made him his heir and on the Asian settlement after the suppression of the revolt of Aristonicus he received Phrygia. He married his daughter Laodice to *Ariarathes VI of Cappadocia, which he came to control. He was murdered in *Sinope, which had become the capital of the Pontic kingdom under his rule. He introduced Hellenism into his kingdom and his phil-Hellenism is evidenced in his dedications to Delos.

MITHRIDATES (3) VI EUPATOR DIONYSUS Son of *Mithridates (2) V, born *c.* 132 BC. He fled after the death of his father and in 112 returned and captured Sinope. He killed his brother and married his sister Laodice. Embarking on an expansionist policy, he organized a strong army trained in Greek fashion. His first conquests included the northern country of the Black Sea (the Bosporan kingdom), eastern Pontus and Colchis. He thus gained large revenues, the control of a corn supply and extensive military manpower. He also extended his rule to Armenia Minor and, but for the Roman intervention, he would have safely controlled Asia Minor. As it was, his incursions on Cappadocia and Paphlagonia after 105 (the chronology is complicated) were opposed by Rome; in 96 *Sulla compelled him to evacuate Cappadocia. In 88 BC started the First Mithridatic War, after *Nicomedes IV of Bithynia, incited by Roman businessmen and senators to whom he was indebted, invaded Pontus. M. quickly overran Asia Minor generally without opposition because of the population's hatred of the Romans and Italians who had been exploiting them. It is reported that on his orders, 80,000 Italians were killed in one day. He also conquered most of the Aegean islands and Greece. But in 87−86 *Sulla defeated his armies (*Chaeronea) and drove him from Greece. He was almost captured by Fimbria, another Roman general, but Sulla (an enemy of Fimbria) let him escape and concluded a peace treaty at Dardanus (85/4 BC) in which M. only surrendered the territories he had conquered. The Second Mithridatic War, which started when Murena, the governor whom Sulla had left in Asia, invaded Pontus, was short as M. successfully defended himself and peace was restored (81 BC). But in 74 M. started the Third Mithridatic War after Rome decided to accept Bithynia which *Nicomedes IV left to it in inheritance. Again M. won victories at first; Bithynia was occupied and he advanced to the Aegean. But *Lucullus destroyed his army at Cyzicus and conquered Pontus (72−71). M. escaped and sought help from *Tigranes I of Armenia, his son-in-law, who too was defeated by Lucullus. But then M. was able to regain control of large part of his kingdom after a mutiny in Lucullus' army. In 66 Pompey was invested with the command against him. M. was defeated and fled to the Crimea. Here he planned to raise an army and to proceed to Italy, but met opposition, including that of his son Pharnaces, and he committed suicide (63 BC). His corpse was sent to Pompey. M. was the greatest opponent met by Roman generals in the East. Energetic, of great physical strength, ambitious and brave, he lacked, however, the political wisdom of a *Masinissa. Overpowered by his ambitions and impulses he overestimated his power and misunderstood Rome's policy and determination.

Magie, *Asia* (s.v.).

MOESIA Roman province in the Balkan that took its name from the tribal group of the Moesi, which was probably distinct from the Thracian tribes. They lived in part of Serbia and northwest Bulgaria. *Crassus (5) conquered them in 29 BC. At first they were subject to the Roman governor of Macedonia who was represented by a prefect. A separate province of Moesia existed by AD 6. The province extended from the Drina in the west to the Black Sea, bounded by Dalmatia and Pannonia in the west, Macedonia and Thrace in the south and the Danube in the north, that is, Serbia, north Bulgaria and Dobrudja. The province occasionally suffered from inroads by peoples from across the Danube. Its garrison numbered three, or sometimes two legions. After AD 57 the governor, Plautius Silvanus Aelianus, secured the border, defeated the Sarmatians and other tribes and settled more than 100.000 of those tribes south of the Danube. Domitian divided M. into two provinces, Upper (the western part) and Lower (the eastern part). M. was the base for the Dacian wars of Trajan after which part of the land north of Danube and

east of the Abita was added to Lower M. Under Diocletian M. was divided into five provinces. M. was a corn and livestock-breeding country. The Roman peace helped to develop the agricultural resources of the province. The legionary camps were centres for Romanization and urbanization. Indeed many of the towns arose around such camps (e.g., Singidunum, modern Belgrade).

V. Parvan, *Dacia*, 1928; A. Mócsy, *Pannonia and Upper Moesia*, 1974.

MOGONTIACUM (modern Mainz) A legionary fortress, with two legions, was established between 18 and 13 BC at the mouth of the river Main, on the left bank of the Rhine, as a base for the Roman advance to Germany. A large town developed near the fortress and the place was the residence of the governor of Upper Germany. The civil settlement (*Cannabae) received the status of *municipium* under Diocletian. The Roman garrison was evacuated in the 4th century AD.

MOIRA (pl. moirai; literally "share", "portion") The three M. first mentioned by Hesiod (*Theog.* 904−6), were the daughters of Zeus and *Themis: Clotho ("spinner"), Lachesis ("getting-by lot"), and Atropos ("the one who cannot be turned"). But they were also said to have been born to Night and according to Plato to Necessity (Ananke). Clotho spins the thread of man's life, Lachesis measures man's lot with her rod, and Atropos cuts the thread when man dies. The basic idea behind this myth is that a man gets a "share of life". In Homer the idea of one's "share" is mainly abstract, and M. as goddesses who are responsible for the personal fate is a later development. M. is both what is due to happen in life and the final destination of all − death. The original idea was that the gods measured the M. of individuals. At Delphi two M. were worshipped: that of Birth and that of Death. The M. were Parcae in Latin.

MOLOSSI Tribal group in Epirus which extended from the Pindus range to the Gulf of Ambracia in the first half of the 4th century BC. The official name of their state was "The Molossians and their Allies". The Molossian kings considered themselves descendants of *Neoptolemus, son of Achilles, and Heracles, too, was included in their genealogy. The earliest king known is Tharypas in the 5th century BC. With the help of Philip II, *Alexander (3) united all Epirus as *hegemon*. The Molossian kingdom reached its height under *Pyrrhus, but in *c.* 233 BC the royal house of the Aeacidae was overthrown, and the Mollossians became members of the Epirote League.

Hammond, *Epirus*.

MONETA This is found only as a title of *Juno, and probably means "the one who warns" (from *monere*). According to Cicero, a voice from the temple of Juno gave warning to make the appropriate sacrifice after an earthquake (*Div.* 1.101), or by the warning of Juno the Capitol was saved. A temple to Juno Moneta was dedicated on the Arx of the Capitol in 344 BC (Liv. 7.28; Ovid, *Fasti* 6.183ff.; the sacred geese of Juno had saved the Capitol from the Gauls by their cackling). Near that temple the Roman mint which was named by the title of the goddess was located and thus *moneta* eventually came to signify mint. Juno Moneta received another temple in 168 BC (Liv. 42.7).

Platner-Ashby, *Top. Dict. Rom.*, 289f., 345f.

MONS SACER ("The Sacred Mountain") A hill near Rome beyond the Anio so called because when the Plebeians seceded to it they returned only after their rights were sanctioned by a *lex sacrata*.

MONUMENTUM ANCYRANUM The inscription found at Ancyra in 1555 on the walls of a mosque, originally a temple of Rome and Augustus. It is a copy, in Greek and Latin, of the original document which Augustus left with the Vestal Virgins and which was read in the Senate after his death. It is, as he phrased it, *index rerum a se gestarum* that is, a record of his deeds. According to his wish the record was inscribed on two bronze tablets which were placed at his Mausoleum (Suet. *Aug.* 101). (Augustus left three other documents with the Vestals.) Copies of the original documents were published in the same manner in the provinces, and another, fragmentary, inscription, only in Greek, was found at Apollonia in Pisidia (first in 1821 and then in 1930). A fragmentary Latin copy was found at Antioch in Pisidia in 1914 (*Monumentum Antiochenum*); there was a Roman colony there and hence there was no need of Greek translation. With the three inscriptions, the original text of the *Res Gestae Divi Augusti*, as the document of Augustus is otherwise known, can be fairly reconstructed.

Augustus tells of his achievements in first person. In the first part he describes his rise in 44 BC and the offices he received (1–14); in the second his personal expenditure on the public (15–24), and in the third the wars and conquests (25–33). The final part (34) is a definition of his position which is of much interest. Augustus claims that he has restored the Republic and that after 27 BC he had no more power (*potestas*) than his colleagues, and was superior to them only in his *Auctoritas*. The document was composed by AD 13, and was somewhat revised after that. There is also an appendix which gives a summary of the sums of money spent by him. Though the style is that of triumphal inscriptions and eulogies, it is a unique document and gives Augustus' version of what he had done — a version that may be, and has been, contested.

Editions, translations and texts: E. G. Hardy, 1923; J. Gage, 1935; P. A. Brunt – J. M. Moore, 1967.

MOPSUS Two mythological diviners bear this name. The one is son of Ampyx (or Apollo) and Chloris. He took part in the Calydonian boar hunt, fought the *Centaurs and was the diviner of the *Argonauts. He died on the way back in Libya bitten by a snake. The second was son of the Cretan Rhacius and of Mantho, daughter of *Tiresias. *Calchas met him at Claros and was beaten by him in a competition of divination and then died. He founded the oracular temple at Mallos in Cilica.

MORPHEUS Son of Hypnus (Sleep), brother of Icelus and Phantasus. He is the personification of dreams and visions and is best known from the description of the Caves of Sleep by Ovid, who says that he is an expert in simulating the human figure (*Met.* 11.633ff.).

MOSAICS The earliest Greek M., dating from the 5th century BC on, have been found in several places, notably in *Olynthus (excavated 1928–38). It seems that from the 4th century this form of decorative art spread to many parts of the Greek world and archaeological excavations have revealed remains in Pella, Athens, Sicyon, Corinth, Olympia, Delos, Asia Minor, Alexandria and Sicily. The earliest mosaicists worked in natural pebbles, mainly black or white but also coloured, and composed geometric designs with animals or mythological scenes. The improved cube technique came to the fore in the 3rd century BC, either from the Orient or from Sicily. In this *opus tesselatum* technique, the stones (marble and tile) were cut into cubes, polished and smoothed on the surface, and pressed one beside the other into a mortar lay. The *opus vermiculatum*, a more refined technique, was used by the 2nd century BC. In this material, not only stone but also glass and even wood, was cut irregularly, then curved and smoothed and arranged so as to fit the patterns desired by the artist. The squared pieces of the *opus tesselatum* imposed restrictions on the artist while the new technique was subtler and could produce paintings of three dimensions; the art of M. then was capable of reproducing original paintings. Indeed some Roman paintings are copies of famous Greek M. One of the best known M., the *Alexander Mosaic* from Pompeii, is probably after a work of Philoxenus of Eretria (late 4th century BC).

Alexander and Darius III in battle. A mosaic from Pompeii

It is evident that M. were very popular all over the Graeco-Roman world. They were generally used as decorations for the floor, like a carpet. This was the dominant use in Italy, Africa and the western provinces. In villas of the wealthier classes, both in town and the country, the owners could enjoy a carpet-like design from wall to wall. In the Hellenistic world the *emblema*, a panel, was quite common to the 4th century AD. It consisted of a central figured scene, surrounded by decorative motifs and was regarded as a picture. In addition there were to be found, mainly in the West, mural M., made of glass-paste tesserae, in various buildings. There were variations in taste, and so the known M. show black-and-white, or multi-coloured painting, geometric and floral designs or figure scenes or composed ones, mythological, historical or everyday scenes, country and town life etc. The art of M. was introduced into Christian churches, but there the pagan motifs disappeared by the late 4th century and were replaced by Biblical and Christian themes.

D. M. Robinson, *Excavation at Olynthus*, V, 1933;
D. Levi, *Antioch Mosaic Pavements*, 1947;
B. R. Brown, *Ptolemaic Paintings and Mosaics,* 1957.

MOSCHUS Greek pastoral poet of Syracuse, also called a grammarian, lived in the 2nd century BC. Three fragments of his *Bucolica*, all together 30 verses, are known from the anthology of *Stobaeus. Two short poems of his — *The Runaway Eros* and an epigram — also in hexameter, are in the *Anthologia Palatina (9.440; 16.200). The *epyllion Europa* (166 hexameters) is attributed to him — it is a description of the Rape of Europa, but in true Alexandrian fashion 25 hexameters are devoted to the flower-basket of Europa. The finest poem attributed to him, *The Lament for Bion*, was not written by him, as M. was older by a generation than Bion.

Ph. Legrand, *Bucoliques grecs*, 2, 1927;
A. Long, *Theocritus, Bion, Moschus*, 1928 (translation).

MUCIANUS, Gaius Licinius Roman senator, mainly known for his support of *Vespasian. He served under *Corbulo, was governor of Lycia-Pamphylia and then *consul suffectus* in AD 65. Governor of Syria from 66, he played an important role in the proclamation of Vespasian as emperor in 69 and set out with the army to Italy. But by the time he arrived there the war was over as Antonius Primus had defeated the army of *Vitellius. M. took control of the government until the arrival of Vespasian and thereafter was his main adviser. He was *consul suffectus* in 70 and 73. His geographical book was an important source for Pliny the Elder.

Syme, *Tacitus* (s.v.).

MUMMIUS ACHAICUS, Lucius Roman statesman and general. Praetor in 153 BC, he governed Further Spain and for his achievements against the Lusitanians was awarded a triumph in 152. As consul in 146 he received the command against the Achaean League, in which he replaced *Metellus (1) Macedonicus who already won initial success. M. defeated the main Achaean force under Diaeus and captured Corinth. The city was plundered and destroyed and the population sold into slavery. Further, the Achaean League was dissolved. M. took part in the reorganization of Greece with senatorial envoys (*Legati), and statues were erected in his honour. He sent the works of art of Corinth to Italy and celebrated a triumph. In 142 BC he was censor with *Scipio Aemilianus.

MUNICHIA (or MUNYCHIA) The steep hill (87 m.) on the east part of Piraeus; on its eastern side there was a small harbour with the same name and on its south-eastern side the larger harbour of Zea. The old theatre of Dionysus was on its northwestern side. M. was a key-position for the control of Piraeus and hence, of Athens, and therefore was fortified and garrisoned. The Macedonians held it almost continuously from 322 to 219 BC.

MUNICIPIUM (pl. municipia) The origin of the Italian M. is not clear enough in the sources and is disputed by modern scholars. The name signifies that such a community was liable to a duty (*munus*) with regard to Rome, and if this was a unilateral duty, it would follow that it was of an inferior status. But there is evidence suggesting that originally the rights and duties were reciprocal. In this view the M. was an Italian community with *civitas sine suffragio* (citizenship without political rights). This involved at first an exchange of certain rights (*Commercium and *Conubium) between Rome and the Italian community. Citizens of such communities could become Roman citizens by settling in Rome. In other words they were like those who had the *Ius Latii. The Italian M. continued to enjoy full autonomy in local affairs but their foreign policy was subject to Rome, and eventually they had no foreign policy. They also had to supply troops to Rome. Some of them, called *praefecturae*, were reduced in course of time to an inferior status; in these, Roman officials, *praefecti*, had jurisdiction, It seems, then, that the first M. originally came to possess the *civitas sine suffragio* status on equal terms. But later, as Rome rose, it was considered a limited franchise and Rome gave it to conquered people, like the Sabines. Some M. received the full Roman citizenship and were called *municipia civium Romanorum*. After the Roman citizenship was given to all the Italians in 89 BC, all communities, whether the Italian M. or the Latins, were called *municipia civium Romanorum*. As a result of this change, a M. came to be regarded as a community which runs its local affairs with its own institutions and is not administered from outside. This was important for the future, as the status was conferred on provincial communities which became Romanized. When the Ius Latii was given, it was a *M. Latini iuris*, but there came into existence M. with the full Roman rights. When a provincial city was made a M. its territory was defined and all within it enjoyed the rights. The M. had a local council (*Decuriones) and magistrates.

A. J. Toynbee, *Hannibal's Legacy*, 1965, Vol. 1;
Sherwin-White, *Rom. Cities*[2] (s.v.).

MUNUS (pl. munera) Duty or service that is performed for the state, the city or any individual; for instance, guardianship of a relative was a *M. privatum*. Service in the army was a public M. Under the Roman Empire citizens were liable to duties, to the state but particularly to the local community. Some received immunity (*immunitas*). With the deterioration of economy from the second half of the 2nd century AD the duties became more demanding; the most burdensome were the local magistracies as their holders were personally held responsible for the collection of the imperial taxes. See *Curiales, *Decuriones, *Liturgy.

MUSA, Antonius The physician who saved Augustus when he was suffering a serious illness in 23 BC; a statue was erected in his honour (Suet. *Aug.* 59 and 81). His speciality was drugs and hydropathy. The extant works that are attributed to him were written by a later writer.

MUSAEUS Mythical poet, associated with *Orpheus (in one version, he was Orpheus' son). According to one account he officiated at the mysteries in *Eleusis. Poems and oracles were attributed to him.

MUSES Daughters of Zeus and Mnemosyne ("memory"), (Hesiod, *Theog.* 54ff., 76ff.), Greek goddesses of all intellectual and artistic sciences and professions. They were born at the foot of Mount Olympus and their sacred mountain was Mount Helicon in Boeotia. That they were nine and gave knowledge of song is first found in extant literature in Hesiod and was generally followed in antiquity. The Greeks regarded them as patronesses of the arts collectively and only in Roman times were they each assigned a distinct department; but there were variations in their names. The more accepted are the following: Calliope — heroic epic, Clio — history, Terpsichore — lyric poetry, Euterpe — flutes and music, Erato — hymns, Melpomene—tragedy, Thalia — comedy, Polyhymnia — mime, pantomime (and geometry), Urania — astronomy (the names are already in Hesiod *Theog.* 76ff.).

The M. danced and sang for the gods and heroes on appropriate occasions, and naturally *Apollo was their leader. They were chosen to judge the competition between Apollo and *Marsyas. They themselves defeated the *Sirens, who then leapt into the sea. Another who suffered for venturing to contest them was the Thracian singer Thamyris who was blinded and could not sing any more. They had cults in many places (Pieria, Athens, Chaeronea, Delphi, Olympia, Tegea, Sparta, etc). A special type of cult were the schools founded by Plato and Aristotle: these were association for the worship of the M.; and Museum was "the place of the Muses".

MUSEUM A place where the Muses were worshipped — normally with an altar, rarely with a temple — was a M. Because of this association, M. came to be a place serving educational purposes, and institutions for study and research were dedicated to the Muses (in this respect the *Academy was a M.). The greatest M. in antiquity was that founded in Alexandria by Ptolemy I. *Demetrius (6) of Phalerum, who had helped the foundation of the *Peripatetic School, was probably the adviser of the king in that matter. It was an association for the cult of the Muses presided over by a priest who was nominated by the king (the king also appointed the members). But in fact it was an institution of research. The members were given accomodation and the kings provided the money needed to upkeep them and the institution. The M. included a central dining room where symposiums were held, and an exedra for lectures and discussions, in which the kings took part (Strabo 17.793). The number of the members is not known. The list of the famous scholars who were members is very long (*Aristarchus, *Eratosthenes, *Apollonius (3) of Perge, *Herophilus, etc). The Roman emperors supported the M. after the conquest of Egypt. The M. continued to work, despite the destruction it suffered *c.* AD 270, to the late 4th century. *Theon is named as its last member.

M.s in the modern sense of the term did not exist in antiquity, though there were collections of works of art, in particular among the Romans.

Frazer, *Alexandria* (s.v.).

MUSIC M. played a dominant part in Greek life for private and public occasions. This is amply known from Greek literature, works of art (notably vase-paintings), education, religion and theatre. Greek poetry, especially *lyric poetry, was composed to be sung, not to be read. M. was conspicuous in many religious ceremonies, in banquets and marriages. Musical competitions were introduced at the great games (Pythian, *Isthmian, and Nemean games) as well as at city festivals. Soldiers marched to battle accompanied by song and M., and choral songs (*Dithyramb) were important to dramatic performances. M. was regarded as essential to education. Plato considered M. to be instrumental in the formation of character and gave regulations for musical education in his ideal state. Of the various musical modes he endorsed only the Dorian and Phrygian. Aristotle, too, thought that M. had moral influence. And it was widely believed that the different musical modes had each distinct ethical and emotional effect. In ordinary education the *kitharistes* taught M. and lyric poetry. Heracles was a bad pupil and killed his music-teacher, Linus, by a blow of the cithara. But he apparently was an exception. To sing and to play the lyre was normal with laymen, and of course there were professionals.

Greek M. was in the first place vocal; the instruments were there to accompany the singing or dancing. Choral performance was more common than solo pieces, and in certain forms, chorus and solo were combined. Of the numerous instruments known to the Greeks only a few were of importance: the lyre and cithara of the strings, the aulos (double flute, really resembling the clarinet or oboe) of the wind-instruments, and the tambourine of the percussion-instruments. The lyre had strings of equal length and was normally played with a plectrum, seldom with the fingers. The cithara and the lyre accompanied lyric poetry. The aulos, made of reed, wood or bone, had several lateral holes (3—6). It was a very popular instrument and apparently there were artists with reputation, not unlike modern soloists. The tambourine as well as the cymbals predominated in ecstatic cults and popular shows. Brass instruments were used for military purposes.

There are extant several theoretical musical works, the earliest and most important is the *Harmonics* of *Aristoxenus (4th century BC). Most works are of much later periods, dating from the 2nd century AD (Claudius *Ptolemy, *Nicomachus of Gerasa, *Aristides Quintilianus, *Boethius). The Pythagoreans were the first to study M. For them numbers represented principles of all things and this they discovered in M., that is, the numerical ratios of musical harmonies (the octave by the ratio of 2:1, the fifth by 3:2, and fourth by 4:3). But it is doubtful whether this research had anything to do with the musical practice. The theoretical treatises and other evidence provide a fair knowledge of Greek M., though there are important matters that are not sufficiently known and are in dispute. There are several characteristics that make Greek M. different from Western M. In the first place they had a large number of modes, each one of them had its own sequence of intervals, and tonality. Secondly the Greeks had a variety of intervals not comparable with the tones and semitones of modern M. Whether this would be to our taste is questionable. The modes were regarded as having ethical effect and they were called by ethnic names: Dorian, Phrygian, Ionian, Lydian, Mixolydian, Locrian, etc. The Dorian was considered of austere mood, the Mixolydian as plaintive, and the Ionian and Lydian as effeminate, even lascivious. The musical sounds were noted alphabetically. The symbols in poetic works were written above the syllables. It is believed that there was one system for vocal and one for instrumental M. It seems that the symbols indicated durations and pitch, but the evidence is fragmentary and controversial. Only a few musical texts with notations are extant, the most famous is the Delphic Hymn to Apollo. Others are known from papyri and stone inscriptions.

Street musicians. An excellent mosaic painting by Dioscorides of Samos from the so-called villa of Cicero at Pompeii

The attitude of the Romans to M. was completely different from that of the Greeks. To play musical instruments was a socially inferior profession. Musical training was not included in the regular curriculum. This is not, of course, to say that there Romans had no M., only that M. did not have the social esteem it had among the Greeks. In religious rituals and dramatic performance M. did have a role. Needless to say, the Romans did not show the same interest as the Greeks in the study of the theoretical aspect of M.

R. P. Winnington – Ingram, *Mode in Ancient Greek Music*, 1936; *New Oxford History of Music*, 1957 (s.v. "Ancient Greek Music", "Roman Music"); W. D. Anderson, *Ethos and Education in Greek Music*, 1966; G. Wille, *Musica Romana*, 1967.

MUSONIUS RUFUS, Gaius Stoic philosopher, *c.* AD 3– *c.* 100, native of Volsinii in Etruria. He was a Roman knight. His views caused him to go into exile several times, the first about AD 60 when he voluntarily followed Rubellius Plautus to Asia Minor. He returned and was exiled in 66 after the conspiracy of *Piso (5). Again in Rome after the downfall of Nero, he was exiled by Vespasian, but recalled by Titus. M.'s reputation ran very high and he had many pupils. He did not write any books, but his pupils recorded his conversations and sayings many of which are extant (in *Stobaeus). Ethics were his main concern and he advocated ascetic conduct to philosophers. His most famous pupils were *Epictetus and *Dio (1) Cocceianus Chrysostomus.

Edition: O. Hense (Teubner), 1905; M. P. Charlesworth, *Five Men*, 1936, 33ff.

MUTINA (modern Modena) Originally a Boian town, M. was an important base for the Roman advance in Cisalpine Gaul by 218 BC. It was made a Roman colony in 183, captured by the Ligurians in 177 but soon recovered. *Brutus Albinus was besieged there in 43 BC by M. Antonius (4), who failed to take the city and suffered defeat by *Hirtius and *Pansa. Favourably located, it was a flourishing town.

MYCENAE This, the most famous city of pre-historic Greece, was situated on the foothills northeast to the Argive plain. The position there gave it access to – and control of – the routes to the Corinthian isthmus, to the inner part of the Peloponnesus and to the sea, a distance of approximately 13 km. But it is questionable whether this is enough to explain its greatness and prosperity in the 2nd millenium BC, thanks to which the whole Late Bronze Age civilization in Greece and the islands is named after it by modern convention.

Until a century ago M. was known as the capital of the mythological great king *Agamemnon, the overlord of the Greeks, the commander of the Greeks who fought against Troy. It belonged to the world of poetry and legends rather than to history and reality. Then in 1876, Heinrich Schliemann, who had already discovered Troy, found a circle grave on the site of M., known as Circle A. The contents of the 6 graves within the circle ("shaft-graves") were splendid: ornamented swords, gold masks, breast plates etc. The objects were luxurious and it was evident that they belonged to a powerful authority. Further archaeological excavations (including another circle grave, Circle B, discovered only in 1951) brought the M. of the past to life. The archaeological finds help to trace in outline the development of the city. In mythology it was founded by *Perseus (1). Its human occupation began in the second half of the 3rd millenium BC, apparently by pre-Hellenic people. The Greeks took the site *c.* 1900 BC and under them the place grew in importance, which is re-

Above: *Various scenes in a mosaic-painting from a Roman villa in Piazza Armerina, Sicily*

Overleaf left: *Detail of the wall mosaic from the church of San Vitale, Ravenna. It shows the head of the Emperor Justinian, with a golden diadem and a halo.*

vealed at the end of the so-called Middle Helladic period (1900–1600 BC) by the finds in Circle B (*c.* 1600), and those of Circle A which is about a century later. The circles were outside the settlement which was concentrated on the hill itself. The negative archaeological evidence indicates that at this period the structures of the citadel were not of stone. The rulers were surely wealthy warriors, and they wanted to commemorate their power in their deaths. M. was at its height in the early 14th to the mid-13th century BC. The hill was surrounded with Cyclopean walls, first constructed in the mid-14th century and later extended so that Circle A was included within the precincts. A palace was built and from *c.* 1300 extensive building operations were carried out. The area within the citadel was densely covered with various rooms and structures, the famous Lion Gate appeared, and outside the walls tholos tombs, the renowned Treasury of Atreus and Treasury of Clytemnestra were constructed. The citadel served the king, the high officials, the bureaucracy of the kingdom; on the slopes around it lived the other population that was increasing. Evidently the king of M. wielded great power but the evidence from other sites of the Mycenaean civilization indicate that there existed other kingdoms at the same time, who seem to have been more independent than what is suggested by a superficial reading of Homer.

M. was destroyed in the early 12th century; one of the many places in Greece and elsewhere that were sacked by a widespread migration of peoples from the north. It continued to be inhabited thereafter but the great palace was not restored, the material prosperity disappeared and the population declined. It was further destroyed by the Dorians in the late 12th century BC and sank to oblivion in the Dark Age of Greek history. By the late 7th century BC a *polis of some importance grew at M. It took part in the Persian War (Hdt. 7.202; 9.28 and 31) but was destroyed some years later by Argos (Diod. Sic. 11.65).

C. E. Mylonas, *Ancient Mycenae*, 1957; *Mycenae and the Mycenaean Age*. 1966.

MYCENAEAN CIVILIZATION The so-called MC. is a modern term used to denote the Late Bronze Age civilization (*c.* 1600–*c.* 1200 BC) that developed in Greece and the Aegean islands and whose influence spread to the coastal parts of Asia Minor and Syria and to Sicily and southern Italy. Archaeological finds have revealed uniformity of material culture but politically the Mycenaean world was divided, and even in Greece proper, the authority of the most powerful king, that of Mycenae, was rather regional than "continental".

Numerous Mycenaean sites have been identified, more than 400 in Greece proper. The main centres were at *Mycenae, *Tiryns and *Pylos in the Peloponnesus, *Athens, *Thebes and *Orchomenus in Boeotia and Iolcos in Thrace. In Crete, Cnossos was occupied in the late 15th century BC by Mycenaean people. After the decipherment of *Linear B it is now commonly agreed that the people associated with the MC. were Greek-speaking and that they should be identified with the Achaeans of the Homeric poems. The notable characteristic of the MC. is the great centralized power of the kings. This is evidenced, more than anything else, by the great palaces and citadels, the royal tombs and the imposing Cyclopean walls. The treasuries found in the graves of the early period of the MC. show that even at that time the rulers amassed great wealth and that art and craft techniques were at an advanced stage. The objects found include

jewellery, vases with fine geometrical and floral decorations, good metal work (including swords) and precious stones. And all this the kings took to their graves. That power and prosperity grew is shown by the appearance of the tholos (or bee-hive) tombs. These were circular, vaulted structures, dug into a hillside with a long approach, all covered with earth. They appeared in the 15th century BC. The Treasury of Atreus has a diameter of 15 m, a height of 13 m and some of its blocks weigh over 100 tons. It is indicative of the outlook of those who constructed the tholos-tombs that they only later (two, three or more generations) built the great palaces and citadels. These fortress-like palaces, the kernel of which was the *Megron-house, were centres of government and administration as well as storage and arsenal. Storage-rooms, halls, corridors, and courtyards surrounded the main part of the palace. It is evident that the Mycenaean world was that of warriors and traders. The heavy fortifications, the armour finds, the battle scenes in art (admittedly not numerous) and, not the least, the myths of the Greeks, reflect a warrior society. The spread of Mycenaean objects, in particular vases, to the East (Cyprus, Syria) and to the West (Mycenaean objects even arrived in southern England) show the trade society.

Inscriptions in Linear B, mainly on clay-tablets and some on jars, were found in several places. Most of them come from Pylos and Cnossos, others from Mycenae, Thebes, Tiryns and Orchomenus. The language is Archaic Greek. The content is prosaic. For the most part they are bureaucratic documents, lists and inventories associated with taxation, land-tenure and offerings to the gods. But they are important for the knowledge of the social and political order. Mycenaean society was hierarchic, with centralized bureaucratic government. The king, *wanax*, was all powerful. Under him were the *lawagetas*, Leader of the Host, and then various officials, the aristocratic group. These were the main land-holders. There were various, clearly distinct, classes of artisans, masons, goldsmiths, potters, weavers, spinners, etc. At the bottom were the slaves, and there were many of them. The Linear B inscriptions also shed some light on the Mycenaean religion. They list names of gods and so we know that Zeus, Hera, Poseidon, Athena, Hermes, and Artemis (and surprisingly, the name of Dionysus appears in a Pylos tablet) were worshipped and were served by a special personnel of priests and priestesses.

The Mycenaean centres declined in the second half of the 13th century BC. This may have resulted from internal wars and need not be taken as evidence for the incredibility of the tradition of the Trojan War (conducted by the Mycenaean Greeks), even though there are chronological difficulties. But in the early 12th century a general destruction put an end to the citadels and palaces, never to be reconstructed. Those responsible for the catastrophe presumably came from the north, and the cataclysm was associated with widespread migrations of peoples. Later in the 12th century the Dorians came and wiped out the remnants of the MC. It took the Greeks several centuries to develop another great civilization, which was very much different from the MC.

E. Vermeule, *Greece in the Bronze Age*, 1964;
W. Taylor, *The Mycenaeans*, 1964;
E. E. Mylonas, *Mycenae and the Mycenaean Age*, 1966;
Desborough, *The Last Mycenaeans and their Successors*, 1964; M. Ventris — J. Chadwick, *Documents in Mycenaean Greeks*[2], 1973; F. Matz, *Crete and Early Greece*, 1962.

MYLASSA (modern Milâs) Important, ancient city in Caria with a temple to a local god which the Greeks identified with Zeus (Zeus Carius). It was a member of the Delian League in the mid-5th century and after some years seceded. Subsequently it came under Persian control and in the early 4th century was the residence of Hecatomnos, the satrap of Caria. His successor *Mausolus probably moved it from its earlier site (Peçin Kale) to Milas, but later made Halicarnassus his capital. In addition to the above mentioned temple, there were two other important temples, of Zeus Osogos and of Zeus Stratius. It suffered damage in 40 BC at the hands of Q. Labienus (son of T. *Labienus), who conquered Caria for a while with the Parthian army, but remained an important city under the Roman Empire. There are remains of beautiful buildings near M., notably a Roman mausoleum.

MYRMIDONS Ancient Greek tribe in south Thessaly the eponymous ancestor of which was Myrmidon. In the *Iliad* they are commanded by *Achilles in the Trojan War and after his death by *Neoptolemus.

MYRON Prominent Greek sculptor, native of Eleutherae in Attica, pupil of *Agelades, active *c.* 475–445 BC. He executed many works for Athens, Delphi, Olympia, Argos etc. and had an interest in symmetry. His most famous work is the Discobolus, "Discus-thrower". There is a detailed account of it by Lucian which has helped to identify several Roman copies of it in marble. It is also known from engraved gems. The best copy is in the Therme Museum in Rome. It shows a young athlete taken at a point in the throwing of a discus, with body leaning forward, and head turned back, one arm stretched out and the other almost touching the knee and yet the whole is a harmonious composition. Another work of M., a group of Athena and Marsyas (Plin. *NH* 34.57), is known from

representations on coins of Athens as well as from Roman copies of an Athena and a Marsyas. The original group was on the Acropolis. A few other works are attributed to him, but with insufficient evidence. The Ladas, an athlete about to run, is attributed to M. M. was not alone at this period in his interest in motion and new poses, but his are surely of the best statues.

MYSIA The country of the Mysi, a pre-Hellenic people, in northwest Asia Minor, whose border with Phrygia the Greek geographers found difficult to mark (Strabo 12.564). It extended from the Hellespont southward to *Lydia. *Telephus, king of M., is associated with the Trojan War in Greek mythology. Greek colonization on the shores of the Hellespont and in the Troad must have brought them in direct contact with the local population. Magie, *Asia* (s.v.).

MYSTERIES Certain ancient deities were worshipped by secret cults. Only those who passed through initiatory rites were admitted to the cult of the deity and the initiates, *mystai*, were forbidden to divulge the M. of the cult. Generally, the actions performed at the rites had symbolic and mystic significance. The initiation rites were normally gradated and the initiates had to advance from one stage to the next. The chief deities who were worshipped in this way were *Demeter and *Dionysus. The most famous were the M. of Demeter at Eleusis, but there were several others of this goddess: at Phlya in Attica, at Pheneus in Arcadia etc. The M. of the *Cabiri at Samothrace were very popular. The orgia of Dionysus assumed mystery aspects, which in the Hellenistic period became prominent. The Orphic M., too, attracted many people. Oriental gods such as Cybele and Attis, Isis and Osiris became popular in the Graeco-Roman world precisely because of the M. associated with them: and elements of the mystery cults were to be found in the Gnostic sects. The origins of the M. were in remote times, and were probably part of the agrarian cult of the religion of the family. What precisely was performed is in many cases unknown because of the prohibition against making the knowledge public; indeed to tell it was to profane the M. and in Athens, for instance, the wrongdoers were liable to punishment by the State. There were, of course, differences between the M. but all had an appeal to the individual as such. They gave purification, hopes, protection, and direct contact with the divinity. Some were associated with moral values and under the Roman Empire they offered salvation and after-life. See *Bacchus, *Cabiri, *Demeter, *Dionysus, *Eleusis, *Gnostics, *Isis, *Mithras, *Orpheus (with bibliographies).

MYTILENE This, the most important city of *Lesbos, was situated on the southeast coast of the island. It stood on a hill and had two harbours, the northern, the bigger, was commercial, and the southern was military. M. was an Aeolian city, as the rest of Lesbos. The city fell under tyrants and suffered from civil strife from the late 6th century BC. It also lost Sigeum (in the Troad) to the Athenians. It came under Persian rule and took part in the Ionian Revolt. But when M. decided to leave the Delian League it was severely punished (428 BC). The Athenians at first voted to exterminate the grown up men but reversed their decision. It remained allied to Athens in the 4th century. It changed rulers in the 3rd century but thereafter became practically independent. Though sacked in 80 BC by the Romans it regained its free status and remained an important city under the Roman Empire. *Alcaeus and *Sappho were natives of M.

The Discobolus of Myron. A Roman copy

N

NABATAEANS Arabic people, called *nabatu* in their inscriptions, who inhabited Transjordan from the late 4th century BC, and later spread northward and to southern Palestine (Negev), Sinai and the coast of the Red Sea. The attempt of *Demetrius (1) Poliorcetes to subdue them in 312 BC failed. They prospered thanks to the control of much of the caravan trade with the Far East (via southern Arabia). They transported such precious Oriental commodities as spices, incense, pearls and perfume to the Mediterranean coast. But they were also skilful farmers and made great achievements in agriculture in dry areas. The first Nabataean king known of is Aretas I (169 BC) and under him the N. expanded to Moabitis. Their first encounter with the Romans was in 66 BC, when *Aretas

Relief of Atargatis, the goddess of fertility, from the Nabataean temple at Khirbet et-Tannur (Trans Jordan)

III was compelled by *Scaurus (2) to evacuate *Judaea. They lost the territory they held in northern Transjordan to *Herod the Great. Trajan conquered their country (AD 106) and made it the Roman province of Arabia. Their capital was Petra, but after the organization of the Roman province, Bostra was the residence of the Roman governor; it became a colony under Septimius Severus. There is an excellent Roman theatre at Bostra.

N. Glueck, *Deities and Dolphins, the Story of the Nabataeans,* 1966; M. I. Miller, *The Spice Trade of the Roman Empire,* 1969 (s.v.).

NABIS Son of Demaratus, last king of Sparta (207–192 BC). N. took the throne by force after the death of the young king, Pelops. Maintaining power through mercenary troops, he set many helots free, exterminated rich Spartans and distributed lands, thus restoring the programme of *Cleomenes III. He made an alliance with the Cretan pirates, and sought to extend his power at the expense of Achaea and Messenia but was defeated by *Philopoemen in 201 BC. N. cooperated with *Philip V in the Second Macedonian War and received Argos, where he introduced his revolutionary programme. But soon he joined the Roman side. The Achaeans accused him of tyranny and in 194 he was compelled to evacuate Argos and the towns of the *Perioiki. His attempt to recover the ground lost was defeated by Philopoemen and in 192 BC he was murdered. N. is regarded by some as a social reformer, a "Champion of the have-nots"; others, however, deny this view and consider him a tyrant, pure and simple.

F. W. Wallbank, *Philip of Macedon,* 1940 (s.v.).

NAEVIUS, Gnaeus Latin poet and playwright, native of Campania, born *c.* 270–265 BC. He fought in the First Punic War, so he said (Gellius 17.21,45), and in *c.* 235 made his *début* on the Roman stage. For the next thirty years he wrote tragedies, comedies and poetry. Haughty and outspoken, he abused even important senators, and his quarrel with the Metelli was famous. Of them he said *fato Metelli Romae fiunt consuls* ("The Metelli become consuls by fate"; i.e., not by their ability). He was even imprisoned. He left Rome *c.* 204 and some time later died in Utica.

N.'s talent lay in comedy rather than tragedy. But the remains of his work are few and fragmentary. Over thirty titles are known as well as 140 lines. The *Tarentilla* is the only one that can be somewhat reconstructed. The style is lively and it appears that N. was influenced by the Greek New Comedy. Only few fragments and titles of the tragedies are extant. But N.'s importance in this field is that he was the first to write on Roman subjects, *Fabula Praetexta (Clastidium,* on M. *Marcellus (1), and *Romulus).* N. was also the first poet to write a Roman epic. This was the *Bellum Punicum,* composed in the Italian saturnian verse. Some regarded it as his most important work. He wrote it in his old age, and later it was divided into seven books; only fragments are extant. Either in the opening or in digressions N. dealt with the mythological background of Rome, including the wanderings of *Aeneas from Troy. N.'s influence was wide; *Plautus was indebted to his comedies and *Ennius and *Virgil to his epic.

Warmington, *Rem. Ol. Lat.;* Beare, *Rome. St.*[2].

NAMATIANUS, Rutilius Claudius Roman official and Latin poet, active in the first quarter of the 5th century AD. Of a Gallo-Roman family (at Toulouse?) and a pagan, he was *Praefectus Urbi in 414, and two years later went to Gaul to inspect his Gallic property, which suffered damage by the barbarian invasions. He gave a description of his voyage in an extant poem, *De Reditu Suo.* The two-book work, written in elegiacs, is incomplete taking the description of the voyage to Luna but no further. He reveals his adherence to paganism and detestation of Judaism and Christian monks. There is also an invective against the dead *Stilicho. The most famous passage of the poem is a passionate eulogy of Rome. N. was the last Latin pagan poet of any note.

Duff, *Min. Lat. Poet.*

NAMES The normal Greek usage was to give a man only a personal name and for further qualification to note his father, which might be given as patronymic. N. could denote physical or mental characteristics, place of origin, have honorific meaning or be derived from the N. of deities. Nicknames and surnames were also sometimes used. The full name of a citizen in official language consisted of the personal name, the patronymic, the name of the *Genos, and the deme. Numerous personal Greek N. are known.

The Romans in the Early Republic had two N.: the *praenomen,* personal name, and the *nomen,* the name of the *Gens. By the late 4th century BC many of the upper class had a third name, *cognomen,* which denoted a distinct branch in the Gens; for instance Gaius Iulius Caesar. The addition of a *cognomen,* and even more N., had later on nothing to do with the Gens, as Roman citizenship was extended to foreign peoples. Not many *praenomina* were used and only a few dozen are known. Approximately 20 N. were used by the senatorial class. *Praenomina* denoted physical characteristics, external circumstances, or were of honorific nature. *Cognomina* were mainly derived from physical and mental characteristics. Women came to be denoted by the feminine adjective of their Gens without the *praenomen.* In official language, the father's and grandfather's name as well as the tribe's name were added. An adopted man took the N. of his new family and, from the 2nd century BC, could have an additional name formed from his original *nomen.* Under the Empire people of the upper classes tended to have many N., associated with various circumstances. Freedmen received the *praenomen* and *nomen* of their patron.

I. Kajanto, *Latin Cognomina,* 1965.

NARBO (modern Narbonne) Old Gallic settlement (the name appears in *Hecataeus), at which Rome founded a colony in 118 BC, the second outside Italy (the first was Iunonia of Gaius *Gracchus (3), but it failed). It became the capital of the Roman province, which was called Gallia Narbonensis. The city prospered, was made the centre of the imperial cult under Augustus, and, thanks to its position on road and river communications, was a centre of trade. Many artisan and trade *collegia are known from N. The city declined in the 3rd century AD and was encircled with walls.

C. H. Benedict, *A History of Narbo,* 1941.

NARCISSUS (1) Greek mythological figure, son of the nymph Liriope and the river-god Cephisus (in Boeotia). He was a beautiful youth, and once he looked at his reflection in the water and fell in love with it. He pined away and died turning into a flower (Pausan. 9.31, 7–8). In another version, told by Ovid (*Met.* 339ff.), the nymph, *Echo, died of grief after he rejected her love. The myth has been variously interpreted as indicating the magical danger of looking at one's own reflection; as a punishment for opposing god or for vanity in physical beauty which can be fatal. There is, of course, also a psychological interpretation. The myth was the subject for works of arts, mosaics, reliefs etc.

NARCISSUS (2) The powerful freedman and secretary (*ab epistulis*) of the Emperor Claudius. He intrigued in court politics, raised and brought down senators and amassed immense riches (400 million sesterces). Vespasian was helped by him to receive command of a legion. It was N. who disclosed to Claudius the marriage of *Messalina (1) to Silius and arranged her execution. After Claudius' marriage to Agrippina, N.'s influence declined and in AD 54, following the murder of Claudius, he was compelled to commit suicide.

NAUCRATIS Greek trading centre in Egypt, on the Canopic canal of the Nile. The settlement began in mid-7th century BC when *Miletus was allowed to use the place and *c.* 560 King *Amasis gave concessions to Phocaea, Clazomenae, Rhodes, Halicarnassus, Aegina and Samos. Originally N. was the only port where the Greeks were allowed to trade in Egypt (Hdt. 2.178). It retained some commercial importance even after the foundation of Alexandria, and still had a Greek constitution (i.e. autonomy) under the Roman Empire.
C. Roebuck, *Ionian Trade and Colonization,* 1959.

NAUKRARIAI Old local districts of Attica which had each to supply and man one ship. The exact nature of the N. is, however, disputed. As there were 48 N. (twelve in each of the four old tribes), the Athenian fleet numbered the same number of ships. But the duty may have been based on social units, not territorial. The N. were also used for some administrative purposes. Each ship was commanded by a *naukraros*. The reforms of *Cleisthenes (2) dispensed with this system of organization.
Hignett, *Athen. Const.* (s.v.).

NAUMACHIA A mock naval battle, first given at Rome by Caesar in 46 BC. Sometimes *naumachiae* were modelled on famous naval battles. In the N. that the Emperor Claudius gave in AD 52, 19,000 men took part.

NAUPACTUS (Lepanto) Town of western Locris, on the northern side of the entrance to the Corinthian Gulf. It had a good harbour, but was isolated from the hinterland by mountains. A natural stronghold, the Athenians settled the Messenian rebels who survived the Third Messenian War (*c.* 459 BC; see *Messenia) there, and used it as a base for their operations in the west. The Messenians were expelled by Sparta in 399 BC, and in 338 *Philip II gave N. to the Aetolians.
L. Lerat, *Les Locrens de l'Ouest,* 1953 (s.v.).

NAUPLIUS A hero in several Greek myths. In one version he was one of the *Argonauts. In another myth, he was father of *Palamedes and, to avenge the death of his son, wrecked the Greek fleet returning from Troy by setting false a light in Euboea.

NAUSICAA Daughter of *Alcinous, king of the Phaeacians, who, while playing ball with her maids, met Odysseus, all naked after his shipwreck. She gave him food and clothing and led him to her father. This is told by Homer (*Od.* 6.15ff.), and was the subject of several works, including a lost play by Sophocles.

NAVIES With the growth of Greek maritime commerce and colonial expansion from the 8th century BC on, the need arose of some Greek states to have N. to protect these activities. Obviously inland states were not touched by this development. The importance of N. grew when Greek states, and there were many such, came to depend on foreign supply of vital commodities such as grain. But the maintenance of ships was expensive, and so even rich states found it difficult to maintain large permanent N. The result was that N. were often potential, rather than an active force. In other words, it was important to have a nucleus of a navy, the necessary equipment and suitable manpower, and sources of supply for the construction of ships. When the need came, all this was mobilized to form a fleet ready for battle. The absence of permanent fleets guarding the sea facilitated the spread of piracy.

The earliest known battle between Greek N. was that between Corinth and *Corcyra in 664 BC (Thuc. 1.13). The great naval battles of the 5th century are well known (*Salamis, *Eurymedon, *Aegospotamoi), and there were many others. In battle, the method was to ram the enemy ships, to disengage and let them sink. With the appearance of the *trireme a new tactic developed, the *diekplus*. A single line of ships swept between the ships of the opposing line, causing damage to their oars, and then charged from the rear. This manoeuvre became the usual tactic from the early 5th century BC. The strongest naval power was Athens, and the way Athens built its first great fleet is indicative of the economic difficulties of raising a navy. After the discovery of new silver lay, in Laurium, *Themistocles persuaded his compatriots to build 200 triremes instead of distributing the profits among themselves. Earlier fleets were much smaller. Athens retained its naval supremacy to 322, when its fleet was destroyed by the Macedonians. It is noteworthy that it maintained a large navy even after the downfall of its empire in the Peloponnesian War; this it was able to do by the system of the *trierarchy. Fleets of 100–200 ships were the normal in the Hellenistic period, when the quinquereme replaced the trireme as the main war ship, and only the great powers could afford to raise such fleets.

Rome maintained only a small fleet until the First Punic War and it had little experience in naval war. The dominant maritime power in the western Mediterranean had been *Carthage. But in the course of that war the inexperienced Romans defeated the Carthaginian fleets time and again, and only once themselves suffered a defeat. Their success was due to their tactics: they turned the naval battle into a land battle by landing soldiers on the enemy ship to which they attached their own ships with grapnels. Their success was so complete that in the Second Punic War, Carthage did not really challenge them

Roman legionaries on board of a warship

on the sea. But under the Republic, even Rome did not maintain a permanent navy, especially after the downfall of Macedonia (168 BC). This fact, and the decline of Rhodes, gave rise to piracy, which was firmly checked by *Pompey only in 67 BC. In the civil wars of the last two decades of the Republic enormous fleets were raised, and in the battle of *Actium, between 800 and 900 ships were engaged. It was only Augustus who established a permanent navy. The main bases were at *Misenum and *Ravenna and other units were stationed in various parts of the Mediterranean, the Black Sea, the English Channel and the Rhine and Danube.

W. L. Rodgers, *Greek and Roman Naval Warfare*, 1937; J. H. Thiel, *Studies on the History of Roman Sea-Power*, 1946; C. G. Starr, *The Roman Imperial Navy*, 1960; M. Amit, *Athens and the Sea*, 1965.

NAXOS (1) The largest (440 sq km) and most fertile island of the *Cyclades. It had been inhabited in the Bronze Age — small lead models of ships, perhaps from the mid-3rd millenium BC, were found here. The early population was said to have consisted of Cretans, Carians and Thessalians. Later, it was an Ionian island. In legend, Theseus left *Ariadne here — and then Dionysus married her. Naxos' great period was in the 6th century BC and its artists played an important role in the development of Archaic Greek sculpture and architecture. The best building and sculpture in Delos were Naxian offerings. Her tyrant Lygdamis expanded his control over the adjacent islands. The Persians failed to take it in 500 BC, but after the suppression of the Ionian Revolt they sacked it (490 BC). N. joined the Delian League and was subdued by Athens when it tried to secede.

NAXOS (2) The first Greek *apoikia* in Sicily, on the eastern coast of the island. It was founded by Naxians and Chalcidians in 735 BC. N. colonized *Leontini and *Catana. It was subject to *Gelon and *Hieron in the 5th century. *Dionysius I destroyed it in 403 BC.

Dunbabin, *Western Greeks* (s.v.).

NEAPOLIS (modern Naples) Greek town on the coast of Campania founded by *Cumae. Her first name was allegedly Parthenope, after one of the *Sirens, who were worshipped in N. (Plin. *NH*, 3.62). When Cumae was captured by the Sabelli (*c.* 421 BC), N. became the most important Greek city in Campania, and gave shelter to the Cumaean refugees. It was captured by Rome in 327 BC, but it retained its autonomy until 89 BC, when it was accorded Roman citizenship and became a *municipium*. Under the Empire it was made a colony.

NEARCHUS Native of Crete, close friend of Alexander the Great, who took part in the expedition against Persia. He was entrusted with several duties, but his most famous achievement was his voyage from the mouth of the Indus to the Persian Gulf. He wrote an account of this voyage which included a description of India. The work, not extant, was used by Strabo and Arrian.

Pearson, *His. Al. Gr.*, ch 5.

NELEUS Greek mythological hero, son of Tyro and Poseidon. He and his brother Pelias were abandoned by their mother; when they grew up, Pelias killed Tyro's stepmother who had maltreated her. N. was king of *Pylos and father of *Nestor by Chloris. When he refused to purify Heracles, the latter killed all his sons except Nestor.

NEMAUSUS (modern Nîmes) Originally a Gallic town, it probably became a *colonia* under Augustus. It was encircled with walls in 16 BC. Its prosperous period was in the 2nd century AD when it became the capital of Gallia Narbonensis. The Pont-du-Gard at N., part of a 49 km aqueduct, is 275 m long and 49 m high. Other remains of note are a temple, built by Agrippa in 16 BC ("Maison Carée") and an amphitheatre.

NEMEAN GAMES The pan-Hellenic games that were held every two years in Nemea, a valley in the north Peloponnesus. One of the feats of Heracles was the killing of the Nemean lion, after which he established the games. In another version, the N. were established by *Adrastus. The games became pan-Hellenic in 573 BC, and in the 5th century were conducted by Argos. The victors received crowns of wild celery. The competitions included horse races, foot-races, jumping, wrestling, *pankration*; during the Hellenistic period, musical and other contests were added. The games were held in honour of Zeus. Remains of the great temple (4th century BC), palaestra and gymnasium have been excavated.

NEMESIANUS, Marcus Aurelius Olympus Latin poet, native of Carthage, lived in the second half of the 3rd century AD. Two works of his are known: *Eclogae*, four short pastorals (319 lines), which show the influence of Calpurnius Siculus and Virgil; *Cynegetica* ("hunting with dogs"), a didactic poem on hunting with dogs (incomplete, the poem ends before an account is given of the hunting itself).

Duff, *Min. Lat. Poet.*

NEMESIS In Greek mythology, daughter of Night, with whom, in one version, Zeus mated in the shape of a swan. She laid the egg from which, under the care of *Leda, *Helen was born. Zeus made love to her at Rhamnus in Attica, and it was there that she had her best known cult. The myth of N. tells nothing of her distinct characteristics as a goddess. In Boeotia she was worshipped as N. Adrasteia, that is, the "unescapable" N., because it was thought that no one could escape from her retribution (though, in the myth, her worship in this form was established by Adrastus). N. was the goddess who punished pride and presumption. She was the personification of divine indignation provoked by human presumption, *Hybris*. This sequence then of pride and punishment was considered unescapable, but some attempts to avert N. were made. Apprehensive about his excessive fortune, *Polycrates threw his ring into the sea, but it was brought back to him and, eventually, he was punished. Spitting was considered an effective defence against her.

NEOPLATONISM The modern term used to denote the philosophy of the pagan Graeco-Roman world from the 3rd century AD to the closing of the philosophical schools by *Justinian in AD 529. The Neoplatonists based their philosophy not only on Platonic doctrines but also on Aristotelian, Stoic and other elements of early Greek philosophy. In studying the old masters, the Neoplatonists were influenced by Christianity and Gnosticism, movements to which they were at the same time hostile. Their most prominent philosopher was *Plotinus, whose teacher Ammonius Saccas (first half of the 3rd century AD) surely played a very important part in the development of this syncretic philosophy, although he wrote nothing. Other important philosophers were *Porphyry (3rd century), *Iamblichus and *Proclus (5th century). In the 4th century, N. expressed the pagan opposition to Christianity. Christian thinkers were influenced by N. until the late Middle Ages.

E. R. Dodds, *Select Passages Illustrating Neoplatonism*, 1924; C. J. de Vogel, *Greek Philosophy*, 3, 1959.

NEOPTOLEMUS Greek mythological hero, also known as Pyrrhus, son of *Achilles and Deidameia. After the death of his father, he came to Troy, proved to be an excellent warrior and was one of those who entered Troy by the stratagem of the Wooden Horse (Homer, *Od.* 11.508f.). N. killed *Priam during the sacking of Troy. He was one of the few who returned home safely, and he married *Hermione (*Od.* 3.188f. and 4.5ff.). Later writers gave other versions, in which he never came home but was killed at Delphi; also, that he had a son (by *Andromache), Molossus. The Molossian kings in Epirus claimed descent from him (as Pyrrhus). N. had a hero-cult at Delphi. He appears in vase-paintings; his killing of Priam and Astyanax is the best known scene.

NEPOS, Cornelius Roman writer (*c.* 100–*c.* 24 BC), native of Cisalpine Gaul, came to Rome *c.* 80 BC and lived there thereafter. He kept out of politics, and was a friend of *Catullus (who dedicated his poems to him), of *Cicero and of Atticus.

N. wrote a large number of books, but most of these are not extant: a *Chronica* (world history) in three books, *Exempla*, a collection of anecdotes in five books, *Lives* of *Cato* and *Cicero*, a geographical work and love poems. Of his *De Viris Illustribus* ("Lives of Famous Men"), 25 short biographies are extant. Its subjects included Romans, Greeks and others, kings, generals, historians and poets. Pieces on Hannibal, Themistocles, and Alcibiades are among those extant. Also extant is the biography of Atticus. N.'s style is jejune and the historical value of his biographies is slight. His aim was eulogistic, but he was hardly successful. His biographies are the earliest extant in Latin.

Edition and translation: J. C. Rolfe (Loeb), 1929.

NEPTUNUS Italian god of water, streams and fountains. He came to be a sea-god only after his identification with *Poseidon, and this was by *c.* 400 BC. N. had a temple at Rome in the Circus Flaminius. His festival, Neptunalia, was held on 23 July.

Platner – Ashby, *Top. Dict. Rome*, 366f.

NEREUS Old sea-god, son of Pontus (Sea) and Gaea (Earth). The Oceanid Doris bore him the Nereids, of whom there were fifty or a hundred and with whom he lived in the deep sea. N., "the old man of the sea", was regarded as wise, righteous and benign. He is first mentioned by Homer, and many later authors refer to him (e.g. Pindar, Bacchylides, Horace). His beautiful daughters spent their time dancing or spinning. Amphitrite married Poseidon; *Peleus won Thetis after a wrestling bout and bore him *Achilles. N. took many forms in his fight with Heracles. He and his daughters appear in works of art as from the 6th century. In the François Vase he presents gifts at the wedding of Thetis and Peleus.

NERO (1), Gaius Claudius Roman statesman and general in the Second Punic War. As praetor in 212 BC, he served in Campania and took part in the siege of Capua. He continued as propraetor (211 BC) and went to Spain where he restored Roman power north of the Ebro. As consul in 207 BC he won his most important achievement, the defeat of *Hasdrubal (2) at the Metaurus; he was helped in thsi by the other consul, M. Livius Salinator. He was censor in 204 BC.

NERO (2) (Nero Claudius Caesar) Roman emperor (AD 54–68), born on 15 December AD 37 in Antium. His father was Cn. Domitius Ahenobarbus, and his mother *Agrippina (3). He ascended to the throne after his adopted father, the Emperor *Claudius, was poisoned by Agrippina. In his first years as emperor, N. was modest and let his former tutors (*Seneca the Younger and *Burrus) control the government of the empire. But the roots of his later extravagance were already there. He was very enthusiastic about art, music and the theatre and he was an easy prey to flatterers. He was also good at intrigues. He began to resent the control and influence of his mother and killed his step-brother *Britannicus by poison. His relations with his mother gradually deteriorated and in AD 59 he arranged her murder. After the death of Burrus and the prudent retirement of Seneca, which in the long run did not save him, no one was left to control N. He killed his wife *Octavia (2) and married his mistress Poppaea Sabina, a good match for his passions.

N. was totally committed to the arts — not only did he establish festivals and encourage artists, but he himself

Neptune in a relief showing the busy port of Ostia, 3rd century AD

and regarded himself as an artist (*artifex*). Among his favourites, for some time, were *Lucan and *Petronius. But he rapidly lost the popularity he enjoyed in the first years of his reign. Many were scandalized by his appearance on the stage, and his activities, together with the wars in Britain and against Parthia, emptied the treasury. N. was also intoxicated by his absolute power and, being suspicious of members of the old aristocracy, executed many rich senators, whose property was confiscated. He was accused of having set the fire to Rome in AD 64 and his persecution of the Christians did not help him to regain the confidence of the public. The building of the sumptuous *Domus Aurea further increased his outlays. In AD 65, a conspiracy to kill the tyrannical N. and replace him with a figure-head like *Piso (5) failed and many executions followed; among the victims were Seneca, Petronius, Lucan and *Thrasea Paetus. The same year Poppaea died (after N. kicked her when she was pregnant). Anyone who showed exceptional ability was immediately suspect. In AD 66, N. went on an artistic tour to Greece and there compelled Corbulo to end his life. The reign of terror continued and disaffection spread to the army. In March 68, Vindex, the governor of Gallia Lugdunensis, revolted. He was suppressed, but *Galba, too, revolted, and at Rome the praetorians transferred their loyalty to him. N. fled and on 9 June AD 68 committed suicide; his last words were *Qualis artifex pereo* (What an artist dies!).

N. was the last emperor of the Julio-Claudian dynasty. Allegiance to the emperor was deep rooted and it took a long time before the army was alienated – but N. did everything that could have been done to be hated by everyone, or almost everyone. The Greeks long remembered him and expected his return, and more than one false N. did in fact appear.

Tac. *Ann.* 13–16; Suet. *Nero;*
B. H. Warmington, *Nero*, 1969.

The Emperor Nero

NERVA, Marcus Cocceius Roman emperor, born in AD 30. He was a friend of Nero, rose to the consulate under Vespasian (AD 71), and was again consul under Domitian (90). After the murder of Domitian, in which he may have been involved, he was elevated to the throne by the praetorian prefects. The Senate gave him support as he was of a noble family and had a good reputation. A decision of *Damnatio Memoriae* was passed against Domitian, and N. did much to announce his policy of freedom, which is reflected in Tacitus' work (*Agricola* 3.1). But the praetorians were furious over the assassination of Domitian; the persecution of the supporters of the dead emperor prevented the restoration of normal life; and the loyalty of the armies in the provinces could not be counted on as N. was not a military man. Worst of all, he was old, childless, and the succession to the throne was not clear. The situation was similar to that under *Galba in AD 68. N. found the solution in adopting a son, and his choice proved excellent. In September AD 97 he adopted *Trajan, governor of Upper Germany. And N. died on 25 January AD 98, without even seeing his adopted son. He was soon deified.

Even in his short reign, and under complex political conditions, N. was able to attend to social and administrative problems personally. He instituted the system of the *Alimenta (by imperial subsidies), improved the corn and water supply of Rome, reduced extravagance in public spending and accepted financial responsibility for the postal services in Italy, thus marking the beginning of a new era.

Syme, *Tacitus* (s.v.);
M. Hammond, *The Antonine Monarchy*, 1959.

NESTOR The mythical king of Pylos, he was the son of *Neleus and lived to be a very old man; he took part in the Trojan War with his son, Antilochus. In the *Iliad*, he is a man of experience, capable of giving advice – but apparently it was not always helpful. As is the habit with old men, he tended to dwell on his past exploits. In the *Odyssey*, he is back at Pylos and is visited by *Telemachus. Post-Homeric writers were not greatly interested in him.

NEXUM Old legal institution at Rome, associated with the contracting of a loan. It is not clear whether the debtor was immediately in bondage to the creditor, that is, if he pledged his body to guarantee payment, or whether N. gave the creditor the right to enslave the debtor – without the authority of a court – when the latter failed to repay a loan on time. The problem of *nexi* (bondsmen) was a serious one in the 5th–4th centuries BC and was the cause of much social unrest. The Lex Poetilia Papiria (*c.* 326 BC) banned loans involving bondage.
Jolowicz, *Roman Law*[2] (s.v.).

NICAEA (modern Iznik) Important Greek city in Bithynia, founded by *Antigonus I as Antigoneia and renamed Nicaea by *Lysimachus – in honour of his first wife. It profited from its location on a main road into central Asia Minor, but it was always contending with the rivals of Nicomedia. It was known for its perfect square layout. Pliny the Younger and Dio Cocceianus give much information on social conditions prevailing in the city. It suffered damage from the Goths and from earthquakes. N. is famous as the seat of the first Church Council (AD 325), during which the Nicene Creed was defined.
Jones, *Cities*[2] (s.v.).

NICANDER Greek poet, native of Colophon, probably lived in the 3rd century BC (or in the 2nd century). He

wrote didactic poems of which the following are extant: *Theriaca* — an account of poisonous reptiles, giving remedies for their bites; *Alexipharmaca* — an account of various poisons and their antidotes. His *Georgica*, on farming, influenced Virgil. His *Heterioioumena* ("metamorphoses") was used by Ovid. He wrote almost all his works in hexameters though he is also known to have written in prose. The obscurity of his style interested grammarians. However, the mere use of poetical forms was not enough to turn his work into real poetry.
A. S. F. Gow—A. F. Scholfield, *Nicander*, 1953.

NICIAS (1) Athenian statesman and general (c. 470–413 BC); a leading figure in Athenian politics during the Peloponnesian War. He was exceptionally rich (Plutarch couples him with *Crassus (4) in his *Parallel Lives*). In politics, he is said to have followed Pericles, after whose death he became the main rival of *Cleon, opposing the extreme, uncompromising imperialists. As strategos, in 427 BC, he conquered the island of Minoa near *Megara and won a victory over Tanagra in 426, but these were not major achievements. His aim was to conclude the war against Sparta and he succeeded in bringing about the armistice of 423 BC, which was followed by a peace treaty in 421 (the Peace of Nicias). He continued to oppose imperialistic plans but was not able to prevent *Alcibiades' intrigues in the Peloponnesus and the expedition to Sicily (N. even found himself appointed to command it with Alcibiades and *Lamachus in 415 BC). But Alcibiades deserted, Lamachus died, and N. was hesitant about making bold decisions. The siege of Syracuse, which was progressing well in 414 BC, failed, and not even the arrival of *Demosthenes (1) with more forces could improve matters. Finally the Athenians themselves tried to escape but were defeated and N. was put to death. N. was to a large extent responsible for the disastrous loss of the Athenian army.
Plut. *Nicias*;
H. D. Westlake, *Individuals in Thucydides*, 1968.

NICIAS (2) Athenian painter who lived during the second half of the 4th century BC. He painted statues for *Praxiteles, and was known for his treatment of light and shade which made his figures stand out. His themes were probably mainly mythological; none of his works is extant. Andromeda and Perseus, a wall painting from Pompeii (now in the Museo Nazionale in Naples), is perhaps modelled on his Andromeda (Plin. *NH* 35.132).

NICOLAUS OF DAMASCUS Greek writer who lived during the second half of the 1st century BC. He became a friend and adviser of *Herod (1) the Great and visited Rome with him twice. After the death of Herod, he represented his son Archelaus in Rome but was not his courtier. N. wrote tragedies and comedies and philosophical and scientific works — none of which is extant. He also wrote a biography of Augustus — a tendentious, eulogistic work, of which there are excerpts (only to mid-44 BC). His great work was a Universal History in 144 books — from early times to the death of Herod the Great (4 BC). It was a great work of its type, second only to that of *Ephorus. There are excerpts from Books 1–7 which dealt with the ancient Orient (including the Persian Empire). Other excerpts are known from the works of *Josephus.
Jacoby, *Fr. Gr. Hist.* ii (A, 324 and C, 229).

NICOMACHUS OF GERASA Neo-Pythagorean mathematician, lived *c.* AD 100. His works are *Introduction to Arithmetic*, which treats the Pythagorean theory of numbers in two books (it was translated into Latin by *Apuleius and freely adapted by *Boethius); *Handbook of Harmony; Theologoumena Arithmeticae*, a mystic treatment of numbers of which excerpts are extant.
T. Heath, *History of Greek Mathematics* 1, 1921, 97ff.

NICOMEDES Several kings of Bithynia had this name:
I. Ruled from *c.* 280 BC until his death in 255 BC. His main adversary was *Antiochus I. In his struggle against him, N. made use of the cooperation of *Heraclea Pontica and of *Antigonus (2) Gonatas, and finally brought the Gauls into Asia Minor (*Galatia). He sought to Hellenize his country and founded *Nicomedia.

II. Ruled from 149–c. 127 BC. Supported by *Attalus II, he revolted and put his father, Prusias II, to death. He pursued a pro-Roman policy and lent his support in the war against *Aristonicus — but he was not given Phrygia, which was assigned instead to *Mithridates V.

III. Ruled from *c.* 127–94 BC. He was called "Euergetes" for his donations to Greek cities. He apparently suffered from the activities of Roman businessmen who enslaved his subjects. He failed to extend his country at the expense of Paphlagonia and to gain control of Cappadocia.

IV. Ruled from 94–75/74 BC. Son of III, he was expelled from his kingdom by *Mithridates VI. He regained it with the help of Rome. But he became heavily indebted to Roman businessmen and was driven to invade Pontus, thereby provoking Mithridates VI to start the First Mithridatic War. Sulla restored him at the conclusion of the war. Caesar went to him to get ships for the blockade of Mytilene (80 BC), and their relations became the subject of obscene lampoons (Seut. *Iul.* 2.49; Plut. *Caes.* 1). On his death, he bequeathed his kingdom to Rome.
Magie, *Asia* (s.v.).

NICOMEDIA The capital of Bithynia, founded by *Nicomedes I (*c.* 265 BC), but little is known of it under the Bithynian kings. The Romans retained it as capital of the province organized after the death of *Nicomedes IV. N. recovered from the damage it had suffered in the Mithridatic Wars and its leading position in the province was recognized when the temple of Augustus and Roma, built in 29 BC, became the meeting-place of the provincial assembly of Bithynia. Its prosperity under the Roman Empire was due to its good harbour and its position on the main road from the Balkan peninsula to the East. It was hit by many earthquakes and *c.* 257 it was sacked by the Goths, but it rose again to become the residence of Diocletian.
Magie, *Asia* (s.v.); Jones, *Cities*[2] (s.v.).

NIGIDIUS FIGULUS, Publius Roman senator and scholar with wide interests. He helped *Cicero in 63 BC against *Catilina, was praetor in 58, followed Pompey in the Civil War and died in exile in 45 BC. In his works, he dealt with divination, astrology, theology, natural science and grammar. He was immensely interested in occult teachings and was said to have practised magic. Only fragments of his works are extant.

NIKE Greek goddess of Victory, in fact a personification of it. In mythology, she is the daughter of Pallas and Styx, and the sister of Rivalry, Strength, and Force. She came to symbolize victory not only in war but in every contest, particularly the athletic competitions of the *Agones. She thus appears in Epinician poems (*Lyric Poetry, Greek). The cult of N. was widespread in Greece; it was promoted by Hellenistic rulers and passed to Rome

Nike with wine cup. A vase-painting (c. 480 BC)

as the cult of Victoria. N. was a favourite theme with Greek artists − painters, and particularly, sculptors. In many works, N. appeared as a young woman with wings, accompanying the victors. Her attributes are a crown, a fillet, and a helm or a shield. None of the famous N.s of Phidias has survived, but several equally famous N.s are extant: for instance, N. by *Paeonius (Olympia Museum) and N. of Samothrace (Louvre Museum). On the pediment of the Parthenon, she is shown crowning Athena; and the temple of Athena N. can still be seen on the Acropolis.

NIOBE Daughter of *Tantalus and wife of *Amphion of Thebes in Greek mythology, first referred to by Achilles to Priam (*Il.* 24. 602). She had six (or seven or nine etc.) sons and six daughters and was so proud of this that she had the daring to say that she was superior to *Leto (who indeed had only two children, Apollo and Artemis). The result was that Leto's children killed all her children (and her husband, too, in some accounts). N. wept for nine days and nights and was turned into stone on Mount Sipylum. The stone was seen by Pausanias, who considered it a natural formation (1.21,3). The story gives a good example of pride and punishment, *hybris* and *Nemesis. The dead children, Niobids, and the weeping of N. were a favourite theme of Greek artists.

NISIBIS Old city in northeastern Mesopotamia, resettled with Macedonians by *Seleucus I and renamed Antioch of Mygdonia. But the old name persisted. The city became important under the Parthians, though it was for some time under the control of *Tigranes I and it was captured by *Lucullus (68 BC). Temporarily occupied by *Trajan (AD 114), it was regained by L. *Verus and made a *colonia* by Septimius Severus. It also received the honourary title Septimia. Subsequently, it sustained many attacks by the Parthians and the Sassanids, but in AD 363 the Emperor *Jovian gave it to Persia. At this time, a large

part of the population preferred to leave the city. Christianity spread to N. by the 3rd century, and it had a bishop.
Jones, *Cities*[2] (s.v.).

NISUS Fabulous king of Megara, brother of *Aegus and father of Scylla. He had a lock of red hair on which his life and the independence of his city depended. Out of love for, or because of a bribe from, King *Minos, who was besieging Megara, Scylla cut the lock. N. then became a sea-eagle, and Scylla a bird called Ciris. The legend is told by Ovid (*Met.* 8.1ff.) and in the poem *Ciris* included in the *Appendix Vergiliana.

NOBILITAS The Patricians were the Roman aristocracy in the early Republic. After the Plebeians became legally equal to the Patricians and all offices were open to them, a new aristocracy rose, termed N. *Nobiles* were those "known" to the public by their exploits and particularly for holding magistracies. In the course of time only the position of consul was considered high enough to confer the social prestige of N. and hence those belonging to this small circle sought to monopolize the consulate. But occasionally, non-nobles were elected (e.g. *Marius, *Cicero). N. then was a social and not a legal concept. Under the Empire, the term was used in a non-technical way, but it was also used to denote the descendants of consular families of the Republic.
A. Afzelius, *Classica et Mediaevalia*, 1938, 40f.; 1945, 150ff.;
M. Gelzer, *The Roman Nobility*, 1969.

NOLA (modern **Nola**) Campanian town, allegedly founded by Chalcidians, it was for some time under Etruscan control; later, it was occupied by a Sabellian population. It was subdued by Rome *c*. 313 BC but remained loyal to Rome in the Second Punic War. It took part in the *Bellum Sociale but thereafter it became Romanized. In 73 BC, it was plundered by *Spartacus. Augustus died in N. in AD 14.

NOMOPHYLAKES ("protectors of the law") Greek officials known in several cities. In Athens, there were seven of them in the late 4th century. They attended meetings of the *Boule and the *Ekklesia and had the power to veto motions which they considered illegal.

NOMOTHETAI ("legislators") This term was used to denote the Greek law-givers of the Archaic period (like *Zaleucus), as well as the special Athenian committee, appointed to revise laws. See *Law, Greek; *Thesmothetai.

NONIUS MARCELLUS Latin grammarian and lexicographer, native of Thubursicum Numidarum, lived probably in the 4th century AD. His work *De Compendiosa Doctrina*, in twenty books, is extant (with the exception of Book 16). The first twelve books treat grammatical matters and other sundry themes like drinks, food, ships etc. Each item is explained and illustrated by quotations. The main importance of the work is in the many citations of works no longer extant.
Edition: W. M. Lindsay, 1903.

NONNUS Greek poet of the 5th century AD. His epic *Dionysiaca* in 48 books is a detailed account of the myths associated with Dionysus. The work shows much learning and has much on the love affairs of the god. Dionysus' conquest of India forms the main bulk of the book. It was written in an age which was again attracted by epic poetry.
Text and translation: H. W. D. Rouse (Loeb), 1940; R. Keydell, 1959.

NORBANUS, Gaius Roman politician, a *Novus Homo*, who as tribune of the Plebs in 103 BC succeeded in condemning *Caepio. Later he was accused of his actions but was successfully defended by M. *Antonius (1). After his praetorship, he governed Sicily efficiently (c. 90–87 BC). He became consul in 83 BC and was defeated time and again in the Civil War by *Sulla and *Metellus (3) Pius. He succeeded in escaping from Italy but committed suicide in Rhodes.

NORICUM Roman province bounded in the west by *Raetia, in the north by the Danube and in the east by *Pannonia, corresponding to a large extent to Austria. The original Illyrian population of the country was Celticized by the 2nd century BC and the various Celtic tribes united to form a state, called N. after the Norici. Under Augustus, the Regnum Norici was organized as a Roman province c. 16–10 BC. The annexation was peaceful and only a small army was stationed in N. which had an equestrian governor. The capital of the province was Virunum. In the Marcomannic wars at the time of Marcus *Aurelius, N. suffered from German invasions and a legion was stationed here. It was now governed by the legate of the legion. *Diocletian divided N. into two provinces. N. was lost to the Empire in the 5th century AD.

G. Alföldi, *Noricum*, 1974.

NOTITIA DIGNITATUM This document gives an account of the high offices, civilian and military, in the late Roman Empire, one part for the West and one part for the East. Each entry gives the title, rank and functions of the office, as well as of the subordinate officers; it also lists the army units of military commanders. The extant copy gives illustrations of the insignia of the offices, the shields of the army units, weapons etc. It is thus an important source for the organization of the empire, the distribution of the army and so on. The extant copy was made in 1551 from an original manuscript now lost. There is evidence to show that the N., a sort of aid manual, was first compiled in about AD 395, but that the extant copy is from a revision made some 30 years later.

Jones, *Lat. Rom. Emp.* 3, 347ff.

NOVEL This literary genre was late to develop, in one view as late as the 2nd century AD, but, to conclude from papyrus fragments, more probably in the Hellenistic period. The genre did not even have a distinct name: *Photius called it *drama*, and, because of the themes they chose, the authors were called *erotikoi*. The origins of the N. are variously ascribed to the love-elegy, to sentimical-mythical historiography and to religious sources. The Greek N. is invariably a love-story in prose, in which the hero and heroine are separated and go through many adventures before coming together again to live happily. The plots are full of surprises — but these always have the same pattern. The characterization of the heroes and other figures is superficial. The descriptions are sentimental and rhetorical. Within the main story come digressions with secondary stories. There are extant five complete N.s by *Achilles Tatius, *Chariton, *Heliodorus, Longus (*Daphnis and Chloe*), and *Xenophon Ephesius. But the considerable number of papyrus fragments indicate that the genre was popular with a large part of society under the Roman Empire. The Latin N. was a rare phenomenon. Only the *Satyricon* of *Petronius and the *Metamorphoses* of *Apuleius can with justification be classed as such.

S. Trenkner, *The Greek Novella in the Classical Period*, B. E. Perry, *The Ancient Romances*, 1967.

NOVUS HOMO A "new man"; this designation was applied to two different types of individual in the late Republic: to those who were the first of their family to be elected consuls or to those who were the first of their family to become senators. Those of the first category ennobled their descendants (*Nobilitas), those of the second category joined the senatorial aristocracy, and they usually came from equestrian families (see *Equites). It was characteristic of the senatorial aristocracy that it always absorbed new men; and although the consulate was jealously guarded by the nobility, it was occasionally won by a "new man".

See *Nobilitas (with bibliography).

NUMA POMPILIUS The second king of Rome who, according to tradition, was the founder of the religious institutions of Rome and reigned from 715–673 BC. He may have been a real figure, but the religious institutions associated with him were a natural development and not the invention of one man. The following are ascribed to him: the introduction of the priestly colleges (*Flamines, *Salii, *Vestales, *Pontifices), the reform of the calendar (12 months instead of 10), the foundation of *collegia of artisans, the distribution of land etc. He was said to have been a pupil of *Pythagoras, who lived two centuries after him.

NUMANTIA Very old settlement in Spain, on the confluence of the Douro and the Merdancho. It was a Celtiberian town by the 3rd century BC. The Celtiberian wars of Rome in the 2nd century were often conducted against the Numantians. After a period of a relative peace, they successfully defended themselves against the attacks of C. Fulvius Nobilior (consul 153 BC) and of *Marcellus (2). From 144 BC, Roman governors in Spain conducted a war against N. but suffered reverses; in 137 BC, a whole Roman army capitulated and was only saved by Tiberius *Gracchus (2). After a siege of eight months, *Scipio (5) Aemilianus conquered N. and destroyed it. The place has been thoroughly excavated.

A. Schulten, *Numantia*, 1913–31;
A. E. Astin, *Scipio Aemilianus*, 1967.

NUMIDIA The country of the Numidae, which extended westwards and southwards from Carthaginian territory, the eastern part of modern Algeria. The Numidae, nomad herdsmen of Berber stock, were excellent horsemen. Until the late 3rd century BC they lacked political unity and split into small tribal units; they were subject to Carthage, paying it tribute and serving in its army. But *Syphax succeeded in forming a strong kingdom of the Masaesylii. And he was outdone by *Masinissa, who united the whole country and whose descendants ruled N. until the Civil War of Caesar and Pompey. As *Juba I supported Pompey, N. was annexed and organized as the province of Nova Africa. It was again a client kingdom under *Juba II and then it was annexed to the old Roman province of Africa. Only under Septimius *Severus was it made a separate province.

N. was mainly an agricultural country. Cereals, olives and grapes were cultivated in the valleys and plains, while the uplands were used for livestock breeding. The main cities during the time of Roman rule were *Lambaesis, *Theveste and *Thamugadi. N. also profited from trade from the Sahara. Under the Roman Empire, the southern frontier suffered from sporadic attacks and the *limes was fortified under Hadrian.

R. M. Haywood, *ESAR*, 4; T. R. S. Broughton, *The Romanization of Africa Proconsularis*, 1929.

NYMPHIDIUS SABINUS, Gaius Son of a freedwoman and a gladiator (but he claimed that Caligula was his father). He advanced under Nero and was appointed prefect of the praetorians. In AD 68 he instigated the praetorians to revolt against Nero. He sought to become emperor but was killed by his own soldiers.

NYMPHS In Greek mythology, female nature spirits, residing in mountains, woods (Dryades, Naphaeae), trees (Hamadryades), waters (Naiads etc.) and many other places. They were beautiful young women, daughters of Zeus. N. were endowed with special powers but were mortal (see *Echo, *Daphne). There were numerous N. — in addition to those associated with various types of places, there were those connected to particular places. On occasion, they favoured men, but they were often wild and pernicious. They were associated with Pan and Satyrs and followed Dionysus. *Daphnis was blinded by N. and Hylas drowned. The N. were worshipped everywhere, often in caves and groves, but also in towns. N. in works of art are usually unimpressively portrayed.

NYX Greek personification of night, one of the primaeval divinities. She was born of Chaos, was the mother of Aether, and lived with Hemera in the west (Hesiod *Theog.* 744ff.). All the gods were her descendants, and she gave them advice. Her garment was black, spotted with stars. Her descendants represented evils: *Eris, *Nemesis, etc.

OBSEQUENS, Iulius Latin author of a list of prodigies from 249 to 12 BC (only the section from 190–12 BC is extant). The author used an abridged version of Livy; he probably lived during the 4th century AD.

OCEANUS Greek god, son of Uranus (Sky) and Gaea (Earth), father of the Oceanids and the River-gods. He first appears in Homer where he is the river that encircles the world, the place where the sun and the stars rise and set; in other words, he is more an element of nature than a personification. And Hesiod states that he is the source of all other rivers (*Theog.* 786). He was considered to belong to the old generation of gods, and he never assumed a distinct personal character. Poseidon – and not O. – became the Greek god of sea. But O. appears in the tragedy *Prometheus Bound* by Aeschylus. In art, he is depicted from the 6th century BC on. In Roman times, it was common to depict him on sarcophagi.

OCTAVIA (1) Augustus' sister, born *c.* 70 BC. She bore *Marcellus (4) and two daughters to her first husband, and, after his death in 40 BC, she married M. *Antonius (4). She lived with him for short periods and after his departure for the East, in 37 BC, they were practically separated, though Antonius only divorced her formally in 32 BC. From Antonius she had two daughters: *Antonia Maior (1) and *Antonia Minor (2). O. took under her care Antonius' children by *Fulvia and *Cleopatra and brought them up with her own children. She died in 11 BC.

OCTAVIA (2), Claudia The elder daughter of the Emperor *Claudius and Messalina was born *c.* AD 40 and married to *Nero in AD 53. Nero, however, preferred his mistresses *Claudia Acte and *Poppaea Sabina and divorced her in AD 62 (allegedly because of her sterility). She was practically imprisoned in Campania, and, soon afterwards, accused of adultery; exiled to Pandateria, she was put to death on 9 June AD 62.

OCTAVIA (3) This Roman tragedy, the only extant one on an historical subject (*Fabula Praetexta), takes *Octavia (2) as its subject. Since Nero's downfall is accurately predicted by the ghost of his mother *Agrippina (3) the Younger, the tragedy was surely written after AD 68 and so could not have been written by *Seneca (2), though it is included in his tragedies.

OCTAVIUS Roman plebeian clan of which the first member to attain the consulate was Gnaeus O. (163 BC). For his exploits in the war against *Perseus in 168 BC, when he was praetor, he was awarded a triumph. He was apparently a rich man and had a beautiful house on the Palatine. A famous member of the clan is Marcus O. who as tribune in 133 BC vetoed the agrarian bill of Tiberius *Gracchus (2) and was removed from office by the *Concilium Plebis, an exceptional procedure. Gaius O., *Augustus' father, did not belong to this clan, although he had the same name.

ODAENATHUS, Septimius The local ruler of *Palmyra who became prominent after Emperor *Valerian was captured by the *Persians (AD 260). For his success against *Sapor I, he was made *dux* by *Gallienus and commander of the Roman army in the East. He subdued the usurper Quietus, defeated the Persians and recovered Mesopotamia (AD 262–7). For his achievements, he was honoured with the title *imperator*, but he himself took the royal title. He and his eldest son were assasinated in AD 267, perhaps with the connivance of his wife *Zenobia who succeeded him.

ODOACER Born *c.* AD 430, served in the army, and with the support of German soldiers deposed the last Roman emperor of the West, *Romulus Augustulus. He then became the first German king of Italy, but acknowledged the formal authority of the Roman emperor of the East. His good administration won him the support of the Senate. In AD 489, however, he was attacked by *Theodoric. The war dragged on until AD 493 when O. was killed by Theodoric after having concluded an agreement with him.

ODYSSEUS One of the leading Greek heroes in the *Iliad* and the hero of the *Odyssey*. His Latin name Ulixes is also known from vase inscriptions (*Olyxeus, Olysseus* etc.). He was the son and successor of *Laertes (king of Ithaca), the husband of *Penelope and the father of *Telemachus. His versatility is fully described in the *Iliad*: clever and prudent, his advice is good and esteemed; brave and enterprising, he fights with distinction. With *Diomedes, he attacks the Trojan camp at night (10.242f.). Together with Ajax and *Phoenix, he brings Agamemnon's offers of reconciliation to Achilles (9.168ff.). He wins the foot race and draws a wrestling-match with Ajax in the funeral games held in honour of *Patroclus.

The *Odyssey* is the epic of his adventures on his homeward voyage after the fall of Troy for which he, more than anyone else, was responsible. These adventures take ten years and during all the time that he is away his wife continues to wait for him. In his adventures, O. meets various peoples and exceptional figures. He visits the *Lotophagoi and has a fateful encounter with the *Cyclops Polyphemus. Thereafter, he is pursued by Poseidon who wants to avenge the blinding of his son Polyphemus. This is a major cause for the delay of O.'s homecoming. He meets *Aeolus (2), barely escapes the *Laestrygones and lives for a year with *Circe. She advises him about his return home and his visit to the nether world. The story of his descent and meeting with the ghosts (*nequia*) is told in Book 11. Here *Teresias prophesies that after his coming home he will have to take an oar to a people whose food is unsalted and who, not knowing anything about boats, use the oar as a winnowing-fan. There he will offer a sacrifice and appease Poseidon for the blinding of Polyphemus. He will then return home and in old age will find an easy death "from the sea".

O. then continues his voyage, survives the *Sirens and the *Scylla and Charybdis, but incurs the anger of Helios, whose cattle O.'s crew ate. The ship is sunk and O. alone succeeds in reaching the island of *Calypso. She entertains him for seven years and when she lets him go, after being instructed to do so by Zeus, his ship is destroyed by Poseidon. Exhausted and naked, he arrives in Scheria, the island of the Phaeacians. Here he is received with generous hospitality by *Nausicaa and *Alcinous. From Scheria, O. finally makes his way home, but disguised as a beggar. He kills Penelope's suitors, reunites with her, and a quarrel with the relatives of the suitors is prevented through the intervention of Athena.

In Homer, O. is the "good hero". That he is cunning and tells lies is due to the circumstances and is to his credit. He is the resourceful hero who excels in a desperate situation. For some reason, this version did not appeal to later writers, who represented him as a scoundrel rather than one who lied out of necessity; as a coward and not a courageous hero; as cunning rather than honest; as one without any moral scruples. Thus he did not want to go to Troy, he contrived the murder of *Palamedes, he tricked *Philoctetes to come to Troy, and he stole the *Palladium (all with *Diomedes). This change began with the epics, now lost, was taken up by Sophocles (*Philoctetes*) and Euripides (*Hecuba*), and followed by Virgil in his *Aeneid*. For the Sophists and philosophers who criticized the immoral character of the Homeric poems, he was an easy target. A different line was taken in the lost epic *Telegonia* — which told of the further wanderings of O., taken to fulfil the prophecy of *Teresias. He finally found his death at the hands of Telegonus, his own son by Circe, who raided Ithaca while wandering in search of his father. Later philosophers gave allegorical interpretations to the traditional stories of O. The interest in O. was not confined to Greek and Roman writers. O. as a cunning, deceitful hero, even a magician, or a restless man wandering in the world to find new things, knowledge and experience, has been portrayed by numerous writers in the Middle Ages and modern times. He of course appears in the *Inferno* of Dante and in this century was the subject of two great novels, one by James Joyce (*Ulysses*) and one by Nikos Kazantzakis (*Odyssey*).

In historical times, O. had a hero-cult in several places. His deeds and adventures were apparently a great inspiration to artists and they appear in works of art from the Archaic period on: O. with Polyphemus, with the Sirens, with Nausicaa, with Circe etc.
M. I. Finley, *The World of Odysseus*, 1956;
W. B. Stanford, *The Ulysses Theme*[2], 1962.

OEDIPUS Greek mythological figure, son of Laius, king of Thebes, and Iocasta. His myth is first told by Homer who says that O. unknowing married his mother and committed incest; after she discovered the truth, she hanged herself. O. continued as king of Thebes (*Od.* 11.271ff.), and later died in battle (*Il.* 679f.). O. is also referred to by Hesiod (*Erg.* 162f.). It is clear that O. belonged to the Theban cycles of legends, which were developed and fully treated in the lost epics *Thebais* and *Oidipodia* (*Epic Cycle). It was from this source that the tragedians drew their versions of the story. Of the trilogy of Aeschylus which dealt with the subject (*Laius, Oedipus, Septem Contra Thebas*), only the third is extant. Of Sophocles' plays, *Oedipus Tyrannus* and *Oedipus Coloneus* deal with O., and *Antigone* with the subsequent story of his house. Also extant is the tragedy *Oedipus* by Seneca the Younger.

O. had a curse on him even before he was born. His father Laius (son of Labdacus, grandson of Polydorus and great-grandson of *Cadmus) kidnapped Chrysippus, the favourite son of his host *Pelops. Pelops cursed the kidnapper and Laius was warned by the oracle of Apollo that his son would kill him. He ignored the warning and had a son by his wife Iocasta (or Epicaste in Homer). Laius exposed the child whose feet he pierced with a spike or a pin; hence he was "swell-foot" — *Oedipus*. He was saved by chance and was brought up by the childless Polybus, king of Corinth, as his son. O. too, was warned by the Delphic Oracle that he would kill his father and marry his mother — and he accordingly decided not to return to Corinth, mistaking Polybus as his true father. On his wanderings, he met Laius and killed him during a quarrel; he next came to Thebes and solved the riddle of the monstrous Sphinx, who thereupon killed herself; Iocasta was then married to him and he became king of Thebes. They had four children: *Eteocles, Polynices, *Antigone and *Ismene. As punishment for the pollution, Thebes was later afflicted by a plague and the truth was discovered. Iocasta hung herself and O. blinded himself (or was blinded) and went into exile. After prolonged wanderings with Antigone, he was received with hospitality by Theseus and disappeared in a sacred grove at Colonus. The curse passed to his descendants: Eteocles and Polynices killed each other and Antigone ended her life by suicide. Some of the episodes in O.'s story are depicted in vase-paintings, notably his encounter with the Sphinx. The story was used by modern writers and the "Oedipus complex" is Freud's well-known psychoanalytic interpretation of a male child's mother-fixation.
Kerényi, *Heroes*, 88ff.

OENEUS ("wine-man") The mythological king of *Calydon, son of Portheus, father of *Deianira and *Meleager (1) by Alathea, and of *Tydeus by his second wife, Periboea. He may have been originally a wine-god who was supplanted by Dionysus; the latter was considered as the true father of Deianira. When O. was old, his brother, or his nephews, deprived him of his kingdom, but his son Tydeus, or his grandson *Diomedes, restored it to him.

OENOMAUS "O. of Gadara" was a Cynic philosopher of the 2nd century AD of whose life nothing is known. The titles of several of his works are known as well as considerable excerpts preserved by *Eusebius. He is also known from the polemic of Emperor *Julian against the immorality of the Cynics. O. attacked all accepted beliefs and had no reverence either for gods or for men. In his work on oracles, he denied the influence of the gods on dreams and rejected the truths of the oracles.

OENONE This nymph of Mt. Ida in the Troad was once the beloved of *Paris, but when the opportunity presented itself he left her for *Helen. Out of jealousy, she refused to help him when he was fatally wounded by *Philoctetes. She changed her mind when it was too late and then killed herself. Later they had a common grave (Strabo 13.596; Apollod. 3.154f.).

OGULNIUS GALLUS, Quintus Roman plebeian statesman, the most famous of his clan. As tribune in 300 BC, he gave five places to Plebeians in the college of the *Augurs and four in the college of the *Pontifices. In 296 BC he erected a figure of the she-wolf with the twin brothers Romulus and Remus, and, in 292 BC, he was the leading member of the mission that brought *Asclepius from Epidaurus. He was consul in 269 BC.

OLBIA Greek city at the mouth of the Hypanis (modern Bug), founded by *Miletus in the second half of the 7th century BC. Its subsequent prosperity was due to the dependence of the cities of Greece on the importation of various products from southern Russia, notably grain and slaves. It was also the centre from which the Scythians acquired Greek commodities. By the 3rd century BC, its decline started, as did its dependence on the neighbouring Scythian tribes. It was half destroyed by *Burebistas in the mid-1st century BC but it survived and in the 2nd century AD it received a Roman garrison.
H. Minns, *Scythians and Greeks*, 1913.

OLYMPIA The most famous and important temple of Zeus in Greece, situated in *Elis, about 20 km from the sea, in a beautiful, serene vicinity, at the foot of hills. The site had been occupied in the Bronze Age and traces of Mycenaean civilization were found here. The original cult at the site was devoted to a goddess, while that of Zeus was introduced by the Greeks who brought it with them when they occupied the place. In tradition, it was *Pelops and *Hippodameia who founded it. Zeus was worshipped in the grove of Altis at the foot of the hill of his father Kronos (Kronos Hill). In the Altis, Pelops and Hippodameia were also worshipped in two enclosures. For long periods, the cult of Zeus was held at an altar in the open air and not in a temple. The first temple, made of wood, was built for Hera in the 7th century BC. It was probably reconstructed and extended in the 6th century (and there were subsequent supplements), and parts of the columns are still extant. Various Greek states built treasury-houses in a row on a terrace north of the temple; the number of these went up to eleven. The building of the great temple of Zeus took place in the second quarter of the 5th century BC. It was built of local stone covered with stucco, and with Parian marble for the tiles and the sculpture of the metopes and the pediments. The west pediment depicted the battle between the Lapiths and Centaurs which was decided by the majestic intervention of Apollo in favour of the former. The Labours of Heracles were depicted on the frieze. The famous cult-statue of Zeus was made later by *Phidias. Only the foundations and the bases of the columns of this temple are

Remains of the temple of Hera at Olympia

extant. Numerous other buildings and monuments of every sort were built in the course of time. The old stadium, east of the sanctuary, was replaced by a very large one in the early 5th century. There were administrative buildings: a Prytaneum and a Bouleuterium. Of the palaestra, only a part of the portico is extant. Kings and Roman emperors added more buildings. The place must have been very cluttered with all these constructions.

O. was traditionally under the control of *Elis (though *Pheidon once presided over the Games). It remained a cult centre until late antiquity. In addition to the cults mentioned, numerous other deities and heroes were worshipped here: Athena, Apollo, Artemis, Pan and Aphrodite, Alpheus, etc. It was damaged during the German invasion c. AD 265—70. The cult was closed down by Theodosius I (AD 391) and in AD 426 the sanctuary was set on fire. The workshop of Phidias was turned into a church. The place was first excavated in 1881 and numerous objects, offerings of devotees, have been found, as well as remains of the magnificent sculptures of the temple of Zeus.

E. Gardiner, *Olympia, Its History and Remains*, 1915; B. Ashmole — W. Yalouris, *Olympia*, 1967.

OLYMPIAN GAMES The Greek tradition that the festival at Olympia was founded by Heracles probably reflects its origin from Mycenaean times, though Olympia is not mentioned by Homer. The offerings found at Olympia suggest that some competitions were held very early in the 1st millenium BC. But the regular games, held every four years, began in 776 BC. They attained pan-Hellenic recognition and when they were celebrated everyone was required to refrain from hostilities. A list of the victors in the OG. is preserved by Eusebius. Well established, they became a standard basis for time-reckoning (*Chronology). They were abolished by Theodosius I (AD 393). The games formed part of a festival in honour of Zeus. The competitors had to be free Greeks and had to swear to keep to the rules. The judges (*Hellanodikai*) supervised the competitors, fined those who broke the rules, and presented chaplets of wild olive to the winners. By the early 5th century BC, the festival lasted for five days. After performing sacrifices and rites on the first day, the competitions started on the second day with chariot- and horse-races and the pentathlon (men). The third day was devoted to boys' competitions. The other contests for men were held on the fourth day and the fifth day was again devoted to sacrifices; a banquet for the winners closed the event.

E. N. Gardiner, *Olympia*, 1925; H. A. Harris, *Greek Athletes and Athletics*, 1964.

OLYMPIAS Daughter of the Molossian King Neoptolemus, wife of *Philip II (357 BC), to whom she bore *Alexander the Great (356) and Cleopatra. She is said to have been a devotee of the cult of Dionysus, and certainly had a passionate, domineering nature. Unable to get on with the other wives of Philip, she left him, and, after her husband's death was cruel to her past rivals. Alexander was devoted to her, but did not let her have influence on the government of Macedonia. She hated *Antipater (1) who, however, was left in control of the kingdom during all the years that Alexander was in the East. After Alexander's death she renewed her campaign against Antipater and, after his death, against his son *Cassander. She succeeded in getting control of Macedonia with the help of *Polyperchon, but she abused her power (among the others she killed was Philip III, the feeble-minded son of Philip II). This enabled Cassander to regain Macedonia and to arrest O. After a trial by the army, she was put to death.

G. H. Macurdy, *Hellenistic Queens*, 1932.

OLIMPIEUM Various temples of Zeus were called O. The building of the temple of Zeus at Athens began under *Pisistratus, who left it incomplete at his death. Work on the building was only resumed by *Antiochus IV Epiphanes and completed by *Hadrian.

OLYMPUS The highest mountain in Greece, part of a vast range on the borders between Macedonia and Thessaly, whose peak rises to 2,900 m. O. was thought to reach the sky and to be the domicile of the gods. When the *Gigantes tried to attack the Olympian gods they piled Mount Ossa on Mount Pelion to reach it. It formed a natural barrier in north Greece. There were other mountains called by the same name.

OLYNTHUS This city in *Chalcidice, about 4 km from the Gulf of Torone, was inhabited by people called Bottiaean (by Herodotus) and destroyed by the Persians in 479 BC. It was resettled by Greeks from Chalcidice and for some time it was under Athenian control. O. grew in size and population and became the main city of the Chalcidian League. Sparta captured it in 379 BC after a prolonged siege and dissolved the League. It was restored after the defeat of Sparta by Thebes. At first, O. cooperated with Philip II against Athens (357—356 BC), but in the late 350s BC tried to enlist Athens' support against him. Despite the eloquence of Demosthenes, the Athenian help was ineffective and Philip captured and destroyed O. in 348 BC. The site was thoroughly excavated from 1928 on and it revealed the layout of the city and many works of art, including the earliest Greek mosaics, were discovered.

M. Gude, *A History of Olynthus*, 1933; *Gr. Fed. St.*, 55ff.

OMPHALE Mythical queen of Lydia, to whom Heracles was sold into slavery as a purification for his killing Iphitus. The price of the transaction was paid to Eurytus, father of Iphitus. While in her service, Heracles caught the *Cercopes and took part in the voyage of the *Argonauts. In one account, she also assigned him to do women's work. She had a son from him, Lamus.

OMPHALOS It means "navel" and it was the name given to navel-shaped objects which were associated with various cults. The best known is the O. of Delphi; two *omphaloi* have been found on the site. The function of the O. is not clear. It might have been used as an altar or as a tombstone. The O. of Delphi was considered to mark the centre of the earth.

J. Fontenrose, *Python*, 1959, 374ff.

ONESICRITUS of Astypalaea Pupil of the Cynic *Diogenes, took part in Alexander's expedition to India and in the voyage of *Nearchus to the Persian Gulf. After Alexander's death, O. wrote a work on him on account of which he was considered a liar. The work was seldom used by subsequent writers on Alexander. O.'s account of Alexander describes him as a Cynic who introduced culture.

T. S. Brown, *Onesicritus*, 1949.

ONOMARCHUS Phocaean statesman and commander in the Third Sacred War, brother of Philomelus, after whose defeat and death in 354 BC, O. became the supreme commander of Phocis. He organized a mercenary army with the treasuries he confiscated from Delphi. With this army at his disposal he attained control of central Greece and even defeated *Philip II (353). O. also de-

Above; Apollo intervenes in the battle between the Lapiths and the Centaurs. Scene from the west pediment of the temple of Zeus at Olympia (c. 460 BC)

Overleaf left: Statue of Nike (Victory) of Samothrace, colossal sculpture of early 2nd century BC

Overleaf right: Departing from the dead. Attic grave-relief, c. 400 BC

"The Orator", a bronze statue of an Etruscan magistrate, c. 100 BC

Omphalos found at Delphi

selves. Politically they stood for the existing constitutional order, that is, they defended the government of the state through the *Senate with its traditional control over the legislative activity of the magistrates, especially the *tribunes of the Plebs, and administration of the finances, foreign affairs and of the provinces. Socially they defended the superiority of the upper class in general and particularly of the *Nobilitas. In the struggle against the P., the oligarchy succeeded in rallying the supporters of the "establishment" within the equestrian class (*Equites) and to maintain to a large extent its influence on the low classes through the personal ties of *clients to patrons. It is noteworthy that the O. were far more successful in the elections for magistracies than in controlling the legislation. This may be explained by the peculiar system of voting at Rome. The citizen had to come to the voting-place in Rome to cast his vote. This gave an advantage to those who lived in Rome, a large proportion of whom in the late Republic were a proletariat easily gained by popular agitation. For the yearly elections far more people came from outside Rome, but not for the legislative assemblies throughout the year. Secondly, legislation was normally carried out by the *Concilium Plebis; the praetors and consuls were elected in the timocratic *Comitia Centuriata.

P. was a derogatory term used by the O. to denote their opponents, who invoked the rights of the People (*populus*) but were regarded as demagogues. There were several points at issue. The P. sought to establish the sovereignty of the people in practice by making the Assembly the body that administered the state, and hence they opposed the traditional powers of the Senate. They also sought to liberate the people from the control of the nobility, and hence defended the secret ballot. In their attacks against the nobility they insisted on merit rather than right of birth. They showed their concern for the people by introducing laws for the foundation of colonies, distribution of land and sale of cheap (eventually free) grain. By such legislation and by agitation against the dominance of the nobility they won popularity. Tiberius and Gaius *Gracchus (2, 3) were P. in their programmes as well as in their methods. The same methods were exploited by those who simply sought to advance their political career. Significantly many of the P. came from the nobility. As they were not able to maintain their political position (and to attain magistracies) within the oligarchic class, they resorted to the new methods: such people were *Saturninus (1), Licinius *Macer and *Clodius. And there were those who, at one stage of their career, used "popular" methods and later were supporters of the "establishment".

L. R. Taylor, *Party Politics at Rome in the Age of Caesar*, 1949; Ch. Wirszubski, *Libertas as a Political Idea at Rome*, 1950, Ch. 2.

feated the Locrians and Boeotians and resettled *Orchomenus. Before he could successfully conclude his campaign against Thebes, the persistent enemy of Phocis, he was called to Thessaly against Philip II by his ally Lycophron of Pherae. He then fell in battle (352 BC).

OPHELLAS "Companion" of Alexander who was commissioned by *Ptolemy I to conquer *Cyrene (322 BC). He accomplished his task and remained governor of the territory, but was practically independent of the king. Allied with *Agathocles, he collected a large force to assist his ally against Carthage. He suffered losses on his march to Carthage to join Agathocles but the latter had him killed (c. 309). Agathocles took over his troops, but the settlers who came with his army scattered or died. Cyrene was regained by Ptolemy.

OPIMIUS, L. Roman senator who, as praetor in 125 BC, destroyed Fregellae for its rebellion. He was an opponent of Gaius *Gracchus (3) and as consul in 121 used the Senate's decree of emergency (*Senatus Consultum Ultimum*) to crush the Gracchans. Gaius Gracchus, *Fulvius (2) Flaccus and numerous others were killed and more were convicted by a special court. To commemorate the achievement he built a temple of Concord. He led a senatorial mission to Africa which divided the kingdom of *Jugurtha from that of *Adherbal and was later accused of bribery. He was convicted in 109 BC and went into exile.

OPTIMATES, POPULARES These two terms came to the fore in Roman politics after the political experience of the Gracchi. The O., "the best men", was the self-styled term by which the Roman oligarchic class denoted them-

ORACLES There were many places where gods were consulted and gave *Oracula* (*manteia, chrestereia*), i.e. responses, to questions put to them regarding private as well as public matters. The O., then, were a distinct category of divination. The consultation started only after the consultant performed sacrificial and purificatory rites. There were several methods of receiving the answer of the god. In many oracular sanctuaries, the god gave his answer through an intermediary, a man or a woman, who was inspired by him. The most famous oracle of this kind was that of Apollo at *Delphi. There, after paying a fee, offering a sacrifice, which should show good omens, the consultant was led to ask his question. The answer was given through the Pythia who was in a state of ecstasy (*mania*). She sat on a tripod and was thought to be inspired under the influence of exhalation from the earth or of laurel leaves which she chewed. What she said was rephrased by the priests of the shrine, and many oracular answers are known, but many of them are fictitious. Another common way to receive an oracle was by incubation. This was a very common practice in the Graeco-Roman world. The consultant went to sleep in the sanctuary of the god who would appear in his dreams and give him the right prescription for his illness or any trouble. Often the questions and the answers were given in writing. In some oracular shrines the method of getting the answers was by observation of signs or by the casting of lots.

Apollo was the foremost oracular god and had many other shrines in addition to Delphi, notably *Didyma and Claros (*Colophon). The most famous oracle of Zeus was at *Dodona. *Asclepius was the most prominent god consulted for healing by the incubation method — at *Epidaurus, *Cos, *Smyrna, *Pergamum, Rome and many other places. *Amphiaraus, too, was consulted by incubation, notably in Oropus. Of foreign O. the best known was that of the Egyptian Ammon at Siwah in the Sahara, identified with Zeus by the Greeks. In Italy the prophecies of the Cumaean Sibyl were famous and at Rome the Sibylline Books were kept under the control of the state. The only important oracular sanctuary in Italy was that of *Fortuna Primigenia at Praeneste.

H. W. Parke, *The Greek Oracles*, 1967;
The Oracles of Zeus, 1967.

ORCHOMENUS Important Boeotian city, once the most powerful in the country, situated in the northwestern part of the Copaïc plane. It is mentioned in the Ship Catalogue in the *Iliad* where it is associated with the Minyans (2.511f.). In old times its wealth was proverbial. In those times Lake Copaïs was probably drained. Its wider interests are indicated by its membership in the *Amphictiony of Calauria. It probably became a member of the Boeotian League only in the 5th century BC, but was not able to resist Thebes whose power grew at its expense. Even its adherence to Sparta was not of much help in the 4th century and in 364 BC it was destroyed by the Boeotians at the initiative of Thebes. Some years later O. was resettled but never regained its power. At O. Sulla won one of his two great battles against *Mithridates (3) VI (86 BC). Of its remains, the walls and the fortifications of the Acropolis are the most conspicuous.

O. was the name of two more cities: in *Achaea Phtiotis and Arcadia.

Larsen, *Gr. Fed. St.* (s.v.).

ORESTES Son of *Agamemnon and *Clytemnestra who killed his mother and her lover *Aegisthus. The myth is first told by Homer according to whom O., a mere child at his father's death, avenged the death of his father after spending seven years in exile in Athens. He only implies that O. killed his mother. This simple tale of crime and revenge was developed and elaborated by later Greek writers, especially the three great tragedians. In the post-Homeric version, based apparently on the non-extant *Oresteia* of *Stesichorus, the infant O. was rescued at the murder of his father and was brought up by Strophius, king of Phocis. He was fated to kill his mother and Aegisthus and returned with his companion Pylades, son of Strophius. His sister *Electra took part in the act of ven-

geance. After the murder he was pursued by the *Erinyes (Aeschylus), really phantasies of remorse (Euripides). He finally came to Delphi and was told by the oracle to go to Athens. Here the court of the *Areopagus pronounced him not guilty and in gratitude he set up an altar (Pausan. 2.31,4). However, other places claimed the honour of purification (Troezen; Pausan. 2.31,4). The myth was told by many writers and there were many variations in details. In one of them, O. went to fetch the statue of Artemis from Tauris to be cured from his madness. He there met *Iphigenia, as told in Euripides' *Ipigenia in Tauris*. The fact that there were more variants than those known from extant literature is clear from works of art which treat the myth.

M. Delcourt, *Oreste et Alcméon*, 1959.

ORIBASIUS Greek physician and medical writer of the 4th century AD. Native of Pergamum, he studied in Alexandria and later became closely associated with Julian whose personal physician he was. O. was not an original writer; his aim was to compose medical anthologies. The anthology he prepared from the writings of *Galen is not extant, but of his huge anthology from medical writers from 5th century BC to his own time (*Collectiones Medicae*) 25 books are preserved (out of about 70). He himself made abridgements of this anthology (*Synopsis ad Eustathium* and *Ad Eunapium*) which were used by later writers and translated into Latin; parts of his work were translated into Arabic. He preserves material from writers whose works have not survived.

ORIGEN (Origenes Adamantius) Important Greek Christian writer (*c.* AD 185–*c.* 255). A native of Alexandria, O. studied under his father and in the Catechetical school of Clement; he succeeded the latter in 202 after his departure on account of the persecution. O. also studied under Ammonias Saccas (*Neoplatonism). He remained in Alexandria until 231 when he was expelled by the bishop, Demetrius, who was exasperated after O. had been ordained by other bishops. The self-castration of O. was also used as a reason for the expulsion. He settled in Caesarea and died after his torture in the persecution of *Decius. O. was a prolific writer, but only few of his works have survived. He wrote commentaries on the Scriptures, and on theology. A famous work of his was the *Hexapla* which gave a synoptic text of the Bible — six versions of the Old Testament including the Hebrew texts with various Greek translations. Only fragments are extant of this work in which he sought to establish a critical text. He engaged himself in the polemics between Christians and pagans and wrote an answer to the attack of *Celsus (3). His *Against Celsus* is preserved and in fact the work of Celsus is known through its detailed exposition by O. His important work on Christian dogma, *First Principles*, is known from its Latin adaptation and from fragments. His views were influential but controversial.

G. L. Prestige, *Fathers and Heretics*, 1948; D. Daniléo, *Origen* (En. tr.), 1956; H. Chadwick, *Early Christian Thought and the Classical Tradition*, 1966.

ORION The mythological lover of Eos who was killed by Artemis. The myth of this huge and handsome hunter, son of Poseidon and Euryale according to one version, is known as early as Homer (*Od.* 5.121ff.). In one version O. fell in love with Merope, whose father Oenopion rejected him. Once, when drunk O. raped Merope and Oenopion blinded him when he fell asleep from the wine. He wandered to the furthest east where Eos fell in love with him and her brother Helios restored his sight. There are various versions of his death. Artemis killed him by mistake or because in some way he offended her; or he boasted that he would destroy all wild animals from Earth who then sent a scorpion to kill him. After his death he continued to hunt wild animals in Hades or was transformed into the constellation O. which is still pursued by Scorpion.

ORODES II King of Parthia c. 56—c. 38 BC. It was under his command that the Parthians defeated *Crassus (4) at Carrhae in 53 BC (the commander was Surenas), but the invasion of Syria under his son Pacorus failed. In 40 his armies again attacked the Roman Empire led by Pacorus and Q. Labienus (son of T. *Labienus). Despite the initial success (Syria, Palestine and large part of Asia Minor were occupied), by 38 BC the Parthians were repelled and Pacorus was killed. O. was killed by his own son, Phrates IV.

OROPUS The coastal part of extreme southeastern Boeotia, with a town at modern Skala Oropou, famous for the oracular sanctuary of *Amphiaraus. Athens controlled O. in the 5th century until 412 BC; it had various rulers thereafter. It was in Boeotian control 312—171 BC and was then set free. The temple of Amphiaraus was famous for giving health remedies by incubation (see *Oracles). Excavations at the site have yielded remains of a temple, a hall, a small theatre and other buildings.

OROSIUS, Paulus Christian writer of the first half of the 5th century AD, a native of Spain and a pupil of St. Augustine. At the suggestion of Augustine he wrote *Historiae adversus Paganos*, a world and Roman history to AD 417. He used the works of Eusebius and Hieronymus as well as Roman historians such as Justin, and an epitome of Livy. The book was an answer to the pagan accusation that Christianity was responsible for the calamities of the empire which culminated in the capture of Rome by *Alaric.
Edition: K. Zangemeister (Teubner), 1889.

ORPHEUS The mythical son of the muse Calliope (or Polyhymnia) and of a Thracian king (or Apollo), the greatest singer and musician who ever lived. The music he played was so charming that he could make wild animals, trees and even stones do what he desired. He took part in the expedition of the *Argonauts and helped his fellows to stand the hardships by playing his lyre. In particular he helped them pass through the Symplegades (Clashing Rocks) and overcome the temptations of the *Sirens. He married *Eurydice (1) on their return and after she died, he descended to the underworld and charmed its master to give him his wife back. But he looked back before they reached the upper world and so lost her forever. He later arrived in Thrace where he was torn to pieces by the *Maenads or by Thracian women. But his head, still singing, and his lyre floated by the river Hebrus and the sea to Lesbos.

The myth of O. developed from the late 7th century BC. Many oracles and poems were ascribed to him and he is mentioned in the Homeric Hymns and by *Ibycus. Aeschylus took the myth of O. and Eurydice as the theme for his lost tragedy *Bassarae*. Numerous writers told the myth of O. in brief or longer forms. The popularity of the myth is also evidenced in many works of art where his departure from Eurydice, the charming of the wild animals and the manner of his death appear. According to one view he was a historical person.
W. K. C. Guthrie, *Orpheus and Greek Religion*, 1953.

ORPHISM Greek mystery religion which was said to have been founded by *Orpheus. This religious movement

started as early as the 6th century BC and lasted till late antiquity. There existed a whole Orphic literature, which was associated with Orpheus himself, and a list of Orphic poems is extant as well as some of the later poems. The Orphic mythology had a distinct version of the creation: the never aging Chronos (Time) fashioned an egg in the Aether from which Phanes was hatched. This was the creator of all, himself double-sexed, golden-winged and with the heads of a lion, a serpent, a bull and a ram. Phanes was also called Eros and he bore Night and with Night created Gaea (Earth), Uranus (Sky), Sun and Moon. Then came *Kronos and after him Zeus. Persephone bore to Zeus Dionysus otherwise called Zagreus. The evil Titans, enemies of the new child, killed and ate him. His heart was saved by Athena, then Zeus created a new Dionysus and destroyed the Titans. There were variants to this myth.

But the evil of the Titans did not disappear as men descended from them. As a result man had a double nature: the wicked element inherited from the Titans themselves and the divine element inherited from Zagreus whose flesh the Titans devoured. His soul then was imprisoned in the body which some called tomb (*soma; sema* = sign). Death does not relieve the soul from the punishment of the body as it is condemned to reincarnation. The believers (in contrast to the followers of Dionysus) abstained from killing animals and eating meat. The Orphics went through initiation and purification rites and were promised that with their complete purification they would be delivered from the corporeal bonds and live happily in the nether world In tombs in Crete and southern Italy have been found gold leaves with inscriptions from the Hellenistic period. They give evidence to the kind of belief, shared by Orphics with other mysteries movements (it is not certain that the leaves are Orphic). They instruct the dead to drink from the Lake of Memory after presenting himself in the underworld as son of Earth and Heaven. After drinking he will join the other heroes.
W. K. C. Guthrie, *Orpheus and Greek Religion*[2], 1953.

OSCANS (Greek: Opicoi; Latin: Osci) The ancient population of south Italy to Campania. From the 5th century BC on the O. lost ground to the Sabelli who expanded from central Italy. But the language of the new tribes in these areas, notably *Samnites, *Lucani, *Bruttii, was called Oscan. Oscan was still spoken in Campania in the 1st century BC and many Oscan inscriptions are extant.
J. Whatmough, *The Foundations of Roman Italy*, 1937.

OSTIA Reputedly the oldest Roman colony, founded by King *Ancus Marcius at the mouth of the Tiber. The earliest archaeological finds on the site are not earlier than the mid-4th century BC. The tradition, however, is at least correct in that it reflects the interest of the early Romans to exploit the salt-beds in the area and there may have been some settlements whose traces have not been discovered. The territory of O. (*ager Ostiensis*) is mentioned by Livy in connection with the year 340 BC (8.12,2) and traces of a well-planned grid-like settlement, with strong walls, belong to about the same time.

Situated about 26 km from Rome, O. was the important harbour for the great city and with Rome's growth O. also grew in size and population. In the first two Punic wars O. was the main naval base of Rome. From the 2nd century BC on, it was through it that Rome imported much of its grain and other commodities from abroad, though *Puteoli was always a hard competitor. O.

Entrance gate to a big warehouse in Ostia, one of the best preserved Roman cities

suffered damage in the civil wars of the 80s BC and also from the activity of the pirates but with restoration of peace and security under Augustus it expanded rapidly and prospered. Many new buildings were built and a new harbour was constructed under Claudius to which Trajan added a more protected basin. The greatest prosperity of O. was in the 2nd century AD, but it sharply declined in the 3rd century as a result of the military anarchy that disrupted trade and normal life all over the Roman Empire. Thereafter it still had rich citizens but was less and less a trading city. The new harbour of Claudius and Trajan, some 3½ km to the north, answered the needs of the trade and around it developed a new town Portus which was made independent of O. by Constantine. O. is one of the few Roman cities of which there are considerable remains, though its buildings were used for building materials by subsequent generations. Modern excavations, begun in the 19th century, have revealed the material development of the city with numerous inscriptions. These give ample evidence on the social, economic and religious history of the city. It had the traditional Roman deities (there are considerable remains of the Capitolium built by Hadrian), but it was only natural for a trading city like O. that the cult of Oriental gods spread there in the Empire.

R. Magie, *Ostia*[2], 1970.

OSTRACISM The establishment of the procedure of O. is ascribed by Aristotle (*Athen. Pol.* 22) to *Cleisthenes (2).

Every year in the 6th prytany, the Athenian *Ekklesia took a vote whether to proceed with an O., and if it so decided, another meeting was held for this purpose. Each citizen wrote on an *ostrakon* (a potsherd, thus the name of the procedure) the name of a citizen whom he wanted to be expelled from Athens. The citizen against whom the majority of the votes were cast, provided there was a quorum of 6,000 — or in another version, that at least 6,000 votes were cast against — was expelled from Athens for a period of ten years. The ostracized person did not lose his citizenship or property, but he had to leave Attica within ten days and at the end of the period of exile could return without any restrictions. The explanation given for the institution was that it protected the Athenians against would-be tyrants. But it was only in 487 BC that the first O. took place — twenty years after the reforms of Cleisthenes; hence some argue that it was instituted later than Cleisthenes. Some prominent Athenian statesmen were ostracized including *Aristides (1), *Themistocles, *Cimon and Xanthippus, father of Pericles. The last case was that of *Hyperbolus in 417 BC. Thereafter the *graphe paranomon* was found to be a better method of attacking political rivals. Almost 1,000 *ostraka* were found at the excavations in the Athenian *Agora. A similar system was used in Megara, Argos, Miletus and Syracuse.

Hignett, *Athen. Const.*, 159ff.; R. Thomsen, *The Origins of the Ostracism*, 1972.

Sea donkey, a mosaic from Ostia

OTHO, Marcius Salvius Born AD 32, he was a dissolute youth who for a while was a close friend of *Nero. But the emperor fell in love with his wife *Poppaea Sabina and O. was removed from Rome to govern Lusitania (AD 58). There he proved a competent governor for the next ten years. Poppaea married Nero in 62. In 68 O. declared for *Galba, but when the latter did not appoint him as his heir, he won the allegiance of the *Praetorians, murdered Galba and became emperor (15 January AD 69). His authority was widely recognized but the legions of Germany had already proclaimed their allegiance to *Vitellius. The Vitellian legions invaded Italy under *Caecina Allienus and Fabius Valens, and O. suffered a crushing defeat at Bedriacum and committed suicide (16 April AD 69).

Plutarch, *Otho*; Suetonius, *Otho*.

OVID (Publius Ovidius Naso) Prominent Roman poet, 43 BC–AD 17. Native of Sulmo (a Paelignian town in central Italy). Of an equestrian family, O. studied at Rome and began an official career. He was helped by *Messala Corvinus and naturally was acquainted with other poets of his time; with *Propertius and *Tibullus he had close ties. He married three times and had one daughter, probably by his second wife. In the midst of his literary and social success, Augustus banished him to Tomis (Constanza) on the Black Sea (AD 8). O. only alludes to the reasons for his banishment: a poem he wrote and an error. What this error was has been variously explained but not convincingly. The poem was his *Ars Amatoria*. Apparently this *Art of Love* so offended Augustus that public libraries at Rome were not allowed to keep his works. Tomis was a bad place for O. to live in: with a population only partially Hellenized, bad climate and frequent inroads of Scythian tribes. In his *Tristia* and *Epistulae ex Ponto* he often expresses his hardships. Time and again he asked to be pardoned but was rejected both by Augustus and Tiberius. He died in exile.

The extant poems of O. are extensive: 1) *Amores*. These love poems, originally in five books (*c.* 20 BC), were edited in three books *c.* 2 BC. There are 49 short poems mainly addressed to one Corinna, an imaginary beloved; 2) *Heroides*. Verse love-letters by mythical women (Penelope, Deianira, Helen, Ariadne etc.) to their husbands or lovers. To the original 15 letters (that of Sappho is suspected of not being genuine) O. later added another five poems (letters and replies). The letters are more like monologues and O.'s rhetorical training is clear in them; 3) *Medicamina faciei Femineae*. A poem on cosmetics, only 100 verses are extant; 4) *Ars Amatoria*. A three book didactic poem which gives instructions how to win and retain a lover. The first two books are for men; O. added the third for women, in response to a request ("to provide amazons with arms"). Original and accomplished, it is written with witticism, and parodies didactic literature; 5) *Remedium Amoris*. A sequel of the former work, this poem teaches how to end a love affair; 6) *Metamorphoses*. While all other poems of O. are written in elegiac couplets, this is an epic written in hexameters. Here O. drew on the vast mythological material in Greek and Roman literature relating to changes from one form into another and presented them within one poem. Thus all legends deal with one theme: the change of shape. But he succeeded in giving unity to the different stories by providing ingenious ties between them (including a story within a story) and by the chronological sequence. The last change is that of the transformation of Caesar into a god. The poem is in the tradition of Alexandrian poetry, with resemblance to the *Aetia* of Callimachus. The erudition is not elaborate, and yet the material was so vast that the poem extends over 15 books. It was incomplete when he was banished and he reacted by burning it; but his friends had copies of it. The epic remained extremely popular till modern times and has had extensive influence on writers and artists; 7) *Fasti*. A verse account of the calendar of Roman religion. Each month was assigned one book but O. was banished after completing only 6 books. For such an erudite poem, there was no appropriate library available in Tomis and so he was never able to finish it; 8) *Tristia*. Five books of elegies written in exile and describing his journey to Tomis and his new experiences and conditions; 9) *Epistulae ex Ponto*. Four books of elegies with the same mood and motifs as the *Tristia*; 10) *Ibis*. A curse in verse on an unknown enemy. The other works which O. wrote, including a tragedy, *Medea*, are not extant.

Erudite poet, master of language and metre, witty and inventive, O. wrote accomplished poems. If his main theme is the passionate emotions of the heart, he is too much of a cynic to treat it in complete seriousness; irony,

reason and ease govern his erotic poetry. He wrote poems for enjoyment, both his own and his readers'. The external circumstances of his last years obviously influenced his poetry, but even in them he shows his usual technical accomplishment. And his gay, graceful and artistic poetry has always been enjoyed by readers.

Text and translation: Loeb; *Fasti* : J. G. Frazer (text, trans. and comm.), 1929; *Amores* etc.: E. J. Kenney, 1961. L. P. Wilkinson, *Ovid Recalled,* 1955; B. Otis, *Ovid as an Epic Poet,* 1966.

OXYRHYNCHUS HISTORIAN The author of a historical work known from a papyrus fragment found in 1926 at Oxyrhynchus in Egypt. Only 900 lines are extant and these give a detailed description of Greek history in 396–395 BC. The author was apparently a competent historian and well-informed. It is thought that, given the large space devoted to such a short time, the work dealt with a limited period, probably starting in 411 BC (end of Thucydides) and ending in 394 BC (Battle of Cnidos). *Theopompus and *Ephorus are among those who have been suggested as the author, but no one has offered conclusive arguments for the identification.

Text: Jacoby, *Fr. Gr. Hist.* ii A 66; I. A. F. Bruce, *An Historical Commentary on the Hellenica Oxyrhynchia,* 1967.

Tragic masks on a sarcophagus

P

PACUVIUS, Marcus Roman tragedian, 220–*c*. 130 BC, native of Brundisium, nephew of *Ennius. P. was the first Roman poet to compose tragedies only. He was also a painter. Twelve titles and over 400 fragmentary lines are all that have survived from his writings. The titles show that he reproduced Greek tragedies in Latin. Only one title is on *Fabula Praetexta, that is, on a Roman subject. This is *Paullus*, probably the one who defeated the Macedonian king, Perseus. From what is said about him by ancient authors and from the known verses it appears that he was an artificial poet, characterized by a copious style with neologisms and uncouth compound words. But he had a good reputation and Cicero regarded him as the greatest Roman tragedian.

Warmington, *Rom. Ol. Lat.* 2, 158ff.

PAEONIUS Greek sculptor of the 5th century BC, native of Mende in Thrace. His original work, a flying *Nike, was discovered in 1875 in Olympia and is known as Nike of Olympia. The statue was a dedication of the Messenians, presumably after the defeat of Sparta at Sphacteria (424 BC). That P. is the sculptor and that he also made the acroterial figures of Zeus' temple at Olympia is stated in the inscription on the base of the statue. The novelty is in the treatment of the drapery – blown but transparent and clinging to the body.

PAESTUM Greek city on the coast of *Lucania at the southern side of the Gulf of Salerno, originally called Poseidonia, founded by settlers from *Sybaris in the late 7th century BC. The city prospered but was conquered by the Lucanians in the early 4th century. Still the Greeks tried to maintain their ways of life and in 332 were helped by *Alexander I, but the Lucanians retained their supremacy in the city. Rome established a Latin colony at P. in 273 BC, which was loyal to her in the war against Hannibal. P. remained a rather prosperous *municipium* under the Empire. It is renowned for its excellently preserved temples, the walls, and pottery. The walls, about five km long, date from the 6th century BC. The temples include the so-called Basilica of the mid-6th century, in truth a Doric temple of Hera, and the temple of Ceres, which was really a temple of Athena (late 6th century BC). In both temples there are some influences of the Ionic style. A third extant temple is commonly called the temple of Poseidon, but it really was another temple of Hera built *c*. 460 BC. It is unique in that part of its second tier of columns inside the *cella* (the interior chamber) is preserved. Another great temple of Hera at the mouth of the river Silaris (Sele), about 8 km from P., was built in the late 6th century; some excellent metopes are extant. The sculptures of the P. temples, however, have not been preserved. Excavations have revealed remains of many other temples, a forum, a theatre, an amphitheatre, paintings from tombs, etc.

Dunbabin, *Western Greeks,* 25ff.;

P. C. Sestieri, *Paestum*[4], 1956.

Aerial view of the temples of Paestum

PAGASSAE Important harbour city of Thessaly on the northwestern shore of the modern Gulf of Volos (once the Gulf of P.). In one version the *Argonauts started their expedition from P. and not from Iolchus, but it was only after the decline of the latter that P. rose to importance. In historical times it was under the control of *Pherae and served as its main port for exports. P. became free of Pherae after its capture by *Philip II, but with the foundation of the nearby *Demetrias (c. 393 BC) it became subject to the latter. Its strong walls date from the 4th century BC and were built either by the tyrants of Pherae or, more probably, by Philip.

PAGUS (pl. pagi) A term which denoted the country districts in ancient Italy, the smallest unit of a state in the rural areas. It is not clear to what extent Rome contributed to the extension of the administrative system of *pagi*, but these were the basic administrative units within the Roman territory in such areas. With the growth of urbanization, *pagi* were incorporated in the territories of cities and this became normal in the 1st century BC. The Romans introduced the system to the provinces. The *pagi* had their own magistrates (*aediles, magistri*) but their number and powers varied.

F. F. Abbott – A. C. Johnson, *Municipal Administration in the Roman Empire,* 1926.

PAINTING The earliest extant paintings from Greek countries are works from the Minoan civilization which date from the late 3rd millenium on. Minoan P. is known from vase- and wall-paintings. At its height, 17th–15th century BC, Minoan P. was colourful, figurative, decorative and gay. There was a great deal of convention in this art. Figures were depicted in profile and often at a point in movement – violent like that of acrobats or gentle like that of the women on a social occasion. The extant Minoan murals are excellent evidence of the refined tastes and luxury of that society. The people of the Mycenaean civilization continued the techniques of the Minoans but concentrated on other subjects which indicate their different attitudes and outlook: battle, hunting and sport scenes. The destruction of the Mycenaean world terminated this art, both in the medium of frescoes as well as vase-paintings, as it did to other departments of Mycenaean civilization.

The major part of Greek P. has not been preserved. It is only the painted decorations of Greek pottery that can be closely followed from the end of the Mycenaean world. But pottery painting was only one field of Greek P. and in its techniques it differed from the wall paintings, mosaic paintings, wooden plaque paintings, terra-cotta paintings etc. That the painting of statues are not preserved is considered an advantage in some views. And yet there are many paintings extant from certain periods and areas as well as literary sources that make possible the reconstruction of the development of the art. The first attempts at figuration, after the Mycenaean period, were made in the 8th century BC. The figures are in silhouette, schematized, composed of front and profile views and in two dimension. The colours were flat and mainly red, yellow, blue, black and white. A head was on a circle with a dot for a frontal eye. It was only gradually that the bodies and limbs became fully drawn, but even in the 7th century the two dimensional representation remained. Fine examples of 7th century P. are the painted terracotta metopes from Thermum. They were painted in the same technique as the pottery. The colours are black, red, white and yellow, and the theme is mythological. A well

preserved painting depicts Perseus running with the head of the Gorgo. In this period the painters were influenced by Oriental art as evidenced by decorative motifs from vase-paintings: monsters and wild animals, birds and fish. Of interest are remains of mural paintings from Gordium in Phrygia which include a scene from the gymnasium as well as birds, flowers and griffin heads. According to Pliny the Elder, early Greek P. was invented in Corinth (*NH* 35.15), and indeed the archaeological evidence shows the leading role of Corinth in this field. Etruscan wall paintings and terra-cotta plaques of the same period (7th to early 5th century BC) have been discovered in tombs. There is no doubt that they were influenced to a large extent by Greek paintings. They consist of daily life scenes, religious ceremonies and banquets.

The loss of Greek P. can be fully appreciated when one considers that no paintings of the 5th to mid-4th century BC have survived; and this is the period when the great advance was made in this art and in which the great artists worked. This great development can only be partially followed in the contemporary vase-paintings. According to Pliny, Cimon of Cleonae invented faces with varied expressions and discovered the folds of drapery. Indeed the painting of the *Cleophrades painter and other artists of his time reveal these same inventions. *Polygnotus was considered as the great inventor. He gave expression to motions and grouped his figures on different levels. He did large mural paintings at Delphi and at Athens. Agatharchus of Athens (c. 430 BC) made great advances in perspective (he made scenery for a tragedy of Aeschylus) and Apollodorus (c. 430) in shadowing. The latter is said to have been the first to have represented "real appearance". *Zeuxis, who "entered the door opened by Apollodorus", is credited with discovering the principle of light and shade and his pictures were noted for the realistic expression of motions). *Parrhasius of Ephesus (second half of 5th century) developed the art of outline and of facial portrayal. All these inventions and discoveries gave the third dimension to P. and paved the way for realistic P. of the succeeding artists. Of the realistic artists the most famous was *Apelles and as evidence of his great artistry it was said that live horses neighed at his picture of a horse; the same idea is behind the anecdote that birds flew at grapes painted by Zeuxis. Aristides of Thebes is said to have been the first to represent the soul, affections and emotions. *Nicias (2) excelled in that his figures stand out from the background. The technique of encaustic painting was developed by Pausias of Sicyon who was able to paint flowers in a very realistic style. In the 4th century panel paintings came to the fore. It was also in this period that the art of mosaic paintings developed, and, when better techniques were found, it rose to high achievements both in the Hellenistic and the Roman world. Landscape, still-life, and common people-paintings came to the fore in the Hellenistic period.

Roman P. is known from mosaic, panel and mural paintings and there is no doubt that it developed under the influence of Greek P. Indeed, Greek works of art were brought to Italy in great quantities from the late 3rd century BC on, either as booty or purchases. But the demand exceeded the supply of originals and so reproductions were made. Copying from Greek works was very common, and the models taken ranged over different periods and styles (5th–2nd centuries BC). It is interesting to note, however, that a member of the patrician family of the Fabii was a painter (hence called Pictor), and he

The "Feeding of Telephus". A prominent wall painting from the basilica of Herculaneum. Heracles, Telephus' father, stands at the right; on the left — Arcadia

Cock fight — a mosaic from Pompeii

Feston, a mask, flowers and fruits — a mosaic from Pompeii

made decorations for the temple of Salus in 304 BC.
*Pacuvius was a painter, not only a poet. Pliny the Elder
says that Roman generals commissioned artists to paint
pictures illustrating their victories. In such themes, as well
as in those of gladiatorial shows, the Romans had nothing
to copy from the Greeks. Landscapes were also favourite
themes especially in wall-paintings. But the subjects also
included mythological, genre and still-life paintings. There
were large-scale panoramic pictures as well as small, and
the art of portraiture rose to a high level. Unlike the
Greek paintings there are extant considerable Roman
paintings, notably from Pompeii but also from many
other sites.

M. Robertson, *Greek Painting*, 1959;
M. Pallotino, *Etruscan Painting*, 1958;
A. Maiuri, *Roman Painting*, 1957.

PALAMEDES Greek mythological hero, son of *Nauplius and Clymene (or Hesione), reputedly clever and an
inventor like *Prometheus, *Cadmus and *Daedalus. He
was credited with the invention of letters, weights, measures, dies etc. When Odysseus feigned madness to avoid
going to the Trojan War, P. proved him false by throwing
the infant *Telemachus before his plough at which Odysseus stopped ploughing. But Odysseus took his revenge by
forging a letter from *Priam that purported to show that
P. had betrayed the Greeks; he provided further proof by
hiding a sack of gold in P.'s tent. P. was sentenced to
death and stoned by the army; there are other versions of
his death. All this was post-Homeric; his encounter with
Odysseus first appeared in the lost *Cypria.*

PALATINE (Palatium) One of the seven hills of Rome,
traditionally the first to have been occupied. The earliest
archaeological traces at Rome come from the P. They
consist of archaic cisterns and post-holes for archaic huts;
these latter are known from models. By the 2nd century
BC, the P. had become the aristocratic quarter of Rome.
One of the earliest magnificent houses at Rome was that
of Gnaeus *Octavius on the P. Other famous figures that
had houses here include *Catullus (1), *Crassus (3) the

orator, *Drusus (2), *Hortensius and *Cicero. The enormous complex of buildings of the Roman emperors on
the P. began under Augustus, who acquired the houses of
*Hortensius and Catullus and other property as well. Al-
most each of the following emperors added buildings including a large palace by Tiberius and monumental buildings and gardens by Domitian. As the residential palace of
the emperors, the P. became proverbial and hence became
synonymous for such buildings in many languages.

Platner-Ashby, *Top. Dict. Rome* (s.v.);
Nash, *Pict. Dict. Rome*, 2. 163ff.

PALINURUS The story of P., Aeneas' helmsman, is told
by Virgil in *Aeneid* (5.814ff.; 6.337ff.). On the voyage from
Africa to Sicily he was not able to resist the temptation of
the god of Sleep, fell to sea and when cast ashore was
killed by the Lucanians. Later his ghost begged Aeneas to
help him find rest, but he was rejected as his body was
not properly buried. But he was honoured by a shrine,
and Cape Palinurus (modern Capo Palinuro) in Lucania
bore his name (cf. Dion. Hal. 1.53). The place is known
for the disasters that Roman fleets suffered there from
storms (253 BC, 36 BC).

PALLADAS Greek poet of the 4th century AD, lived in
Alexandria and found it hard to make a living at his profession as schoolmaster. More than 150 of his epigrams
are preserved in the Greek *Anthology, noted for their
bitterness, pessimism and satirical tone.

PALLADIUM In mythology, the sacred statuette of Pallas Athena given by Zeus to his son *Dardanus, the
founder of Troy. This image of the goddess was a guarantee for the security of the city. One of the exploits of
*Odysseus and *Diomedes — in a post-Homeric version —
was the stealing of the P. and by so doing the city became
vulnerable. This version was taken by Virgil in his *Aeneid*
(2.161ff.). In another version, Aeneas rescued the P. at
the fall of Troy and ultimately it arrived in Rome and was
preserved in the temple of Vesta as a guarantee for the
safety of the city (Dion. Hal. 1.69). The P. was in fact a
sacred object believed to protect the city, and there were

View of the Palatine, an aristocratic quarter under the Republic, hill of the imperial palaces under the Empire

other cities which possessed talismans called P. after that of Troy.

PALLADIUS, Rutilius Taurus Aemilianus Latin writer of the 4th century AD, the author of an extant work on agriculture, *Opus Agriculturae*. It consists of an introduction, twelve books, one for each month, and a last book in verse. A work on veterinary medicine is considered to be the 14th book of this work. P. used former writers on farming, such as *Columella, but as the owner of estates himself could also rely on his own experience.

PALLAS, M. Antonius Freedman of *Antonia (2) and powerful financial secretary (*a rationibus*) of the Emperor Claudius. He was involved in court intrigues, amassed great wealth and was hated. After the death of *Messalina (1) he helped *Agrippina (3) to become Claudius' wife and engineered the adoption of Nero by his step-father. With the decline of Agrippina's influence under Nero, he was relieved from his office (AD 55) and, in AD 62, was put to death on account of his wealth.

PALMA FRONTONIANUS, Aulus Cornelius Native of Volsinii; after his consulate in AD 99 he governed Nearer Spain (Tarraconensis) (*c.* 101) and Syria (*c.* 104). He occupied the Nabataean kingdom and organized it as a province (AD 105/6) and received "triumphal ornaments" and another consulate (109). With other veteran generals of Trajan he was executed under Hadrian (AD 118).
Syme, *Tacitus* (s.v.).

PALMYRA (Aramaic: Tadmor) Very ancient oasis city in the Syrian desert about 230 km northwest of Damascus. It grew to importance in the 1st century BC when it came to control the caravan trade between Syria and Mesopotamia. M. *Antonius (4) failed to capture it but it was annexed to the Roman Empire, with special privileges, by *Germanicus (*c.* AD 17/8). Its special status was secured under Hadrian and Septimius *Severus made it a *colonia*. It rose to the height of its power under *Odaenathus and *Zenobia, but never revived after its capture by *Aurelian (AD 273), though it had a Roman garrison. The rich city, with Aramaic-Arabic population, was Hellenized to some extent. Many Aramaic inscriptions have been found which give evidence about the social, economic and religious life of the city. The remains are impressive and include a theatre, a monumental arch, several temples (notably that of Bel) and colonnade streets. These and the sculptures from the necropolis show a fusion of Oriental and Hellenistic elements.
M. Rostovtzeff, *Caravan Cities*, 1932;
I. A. Richmond, *JRS*, 1963, 43ff.

The gods of Palmyra on a relief

PAMPHYLIA The coastal country in the central part of south Asia Minor, bounded by *Cilcia in the east, *Pisidia in the north and *Lycia in the west; the boundaries, however, were not constant. The main cities were Aspendus, Side, Magydus, and Perge. P. had been colonized by Greeks from various origins — the name means "the land of all tribes" — and the mythical *Amphilochus, *Mopsus and *Calchas were considered to be its founders. Subject to the Persians until the conquest of Alexander the Great, the Pamphylian cities were alternatively under Ptolemaic and Seleucid control until 189 BC. After the defeat of *Antiochus III at Magnesia they were allied to Rome. P. was probably part of the province Cilicia in the 1st century BC, was given to *Amyntas (2) of Galatia in 36 BC and was organized with Lycia as a separate province in AD 43.
Magie, *Asia*; Jones, *Cities*[2], 124ff.;
G. E. Bean, *Turkey's Southern Shore*, 1968.

PAN Originally the Arcadian god of shepherds and herdsmen, son of Hermes (the name of his mother varies in different versions) with a human body and the horns, ears and legs of a goat. He is first mentioned in literature in the Homeric *Hymn to Pan*, which describes him as a hunter of the wilds, and tells of his birth to Hermes. A god of fertility, he was amorous and would make love to young men and women. Once he pursued the nymph Syrinx who became a reed-bed, from which he made his pipes; the shepherds played Pan-pipes. With *Selene he was more successful giving her a sheep fleece. He used to sleep in the afternoon and it was well not to disturb him, otherwise he would cause "panic" terror, frighten flocks and cause nightmares. But he could be also benevolent. For his help to the Athenians in the Battle of Marathon he was given a cave-shrine on the Acropolis (Hdt. 6.105). It seems that from that time on his cult began to spread in Greece. In literature he became patron of pastoral poets. As from the 5th century BC on P. (or several Panes) appear on vase-paintings. In a fine group statue from Delos (2nd century BC) he is shown trying to seduce Aphrodite.

PANAENUS Athenian painter, brother or nephew of *Phidias, whose statue of Zeus in Olympia he painted. He is credited by some sources with the painting of the "Battle of Marathon" in the Stoa Poikile in Athens (460—450 BC), otherwise ascribed to *Polygnotus or *Micon (Plin. *NH* 35.57).

PANAETIUS Stoic philosopher, *c.* 185—109 BC, native of Lindus in Rhodes, pupil of *Crates of Mallos at Pergamum and of Diogenes the Babylonian and Antipater of Tarsus (heads of the Stoa in succession) at Athens. He went to Rome *c.* 145 and became close to *Scipio Aemilianus and his literary circle. When Scipio went on a tour to Greece and the East (*c.* 140—138) P. accompanied him. After Scipio's death (129), P. returned to Athens and became Head of the Stoa. P.'s works are not preserved, but his views are discussed by Cicero in his *De Officiis* ("On Duties"). It appears that P., though a Stoic, also followed the doctrines of Plato and Aristotle. His ties with Roman statesmen induced him to present Stoicism in a way appropriate to the Roman aristocracy. He thus tried to combine the traditional moral and political concepts of the Romans with Stoic ethics. In his system, the more active virtues of Stoicism, such as liberality and benevolence, were given emphasis. He also insisted on the supremacy of the state's interests over personal interests and regarded the Roman constitution as the best.
J. M. Rist, *Stoic Philosophy*, 1969, 173ff.

PANATHENAEA The yearly festival held at Athens on 28th Hecatombaeon (July/August), the anniversary of Athena, traditionally instituted by *Erichtonius or *Theseus. The festival was celebrated with greater magnificence every four years. It was a four day festival and it consisted mainly of sacrifices, games and a procession. The main event was the procession which made its way through the city to the Acropolis to present the goddess the new *peplos*, an embroidered robe which was hoisted on the mast of a ship; this was carried on a wagon at the head of the procession. After the wagon, came the *ergastinai*, the women who wove the *peplos*, the *canephoroi*, the maidens who carried baskets with sacred implements, the youths who led sacrificial animals, citizens, metics and at the end young horsemen. Scenes of the P. were depicted in the frieze of the *Parthenon.

PANDORA The myth of P. is first told by Hesiod (*Theog*. 501ff.; *Erg*. 60ff.). She was the first woman fashioned by Zeus to punish mankind. He sent her with a box to Epimetheus ("After thinker"), whose brother *Prometheus had helped men. She opened the box and all evils and diseases which were in it escaped, save Hope which remained. This is an anti-feminist myth, but P. ("all gifts") was probably an old earth-goddess, the "giving all" goddess.

PANEGYRIC In Greece P. was a speech held before a general public, like the one that assembled at the pan-Hellenic festival from all parts of the Greek world. The best extant Greek P.s are the *Panegyricus* and *Panathenaicus* of *Isocrates. At Rome the P. was an eulogistic speech in honour of a person. Under the Empire, by a decision made by the Senate in Augustus' time, the consuls had to enter their office with a speech of thanks to the emperor and the gods. Twelve such speeches are extant; the earliest is of Pliny the Younger but most belong to the later Roman Empire.
R. A. B. Mynors, *XII Panegyrici Latini* (OCT), 1964;
T. A. Dorey (ed.), *Empire and Aftermath*, 1975, 143ff.

PANGAEUS A massif (group of mountain peaks), about 25 km long with peaks almost 2,000 m high on the borders of Macedonia and Thrace. P. was rich in gold and silver which were exploited from the 6th century BC, first by *Thasos, then by Athens and, in the mid-4th century, by *Philip II.
S. Casson, *Macedonia, Thrace and Illyria*, 1926.

PANNONIA The country of the Pannonii, a mixed Illyrian-Celtic people, south of the Danube extending to the Save valley; corresponding to west Hungary and part of Yugoslavia. After some operations in 35 BC the systematic conquest of P. was undertaken in 13 BC under *Agrippa (1) and completed by Tiberius after the latter's death. At first, the conquered area was annexed to *Illyricum. However, a great revolt broke out in AD 6, and after its suppression Illyricum was divided into P. and *Dalmatia. Under Trajan, P. was divided into Upper P., the western part with *Carnuntum as its capital, and Lower P. with *Aquincum as its capital. The provinces of P. were always imperial, governed by *Legati Augusti pro praetore of consular rank (except Lower P. until Caracalla's time); as from *Gallienus they were governed by equestrian *praesides*. Further division of the provinces were made under *Diocletian. As from the late 1st century AD there were four legions in P. The first colonies and *municipia* appeared under Tiberius and the colonization and municipalization of P. reached its height in Hadrian's time. To protect the province from the barbarian tribes from across the Danube the fortification of the Danube's *Limes began under Domitian and was advanced under Hadrian. But P. suffered much in the Marcomannic Wars under Marcus *Aurelius, though it recovered under *Commodus and Septimius *Severus. The prosperity was interrupted by the new invasions of the mid-3rd century. Thereafter there were sporadic inroads but it was only after the defeat of *Valens in Adrianopol (AD 378) that numerous *Alani, *Goths and Huns settled in P. The Pannonian provinces were lost in the early 5th century.
P. Oliva, *Pannonia and the Onset of Crisis in the Roman Empire*, 1962; A. Mócsy, *Pannonia and Upper Moesia*, 1974.

PANORMUS (modern Palermo) An important Phoenician city on the northern coast of Sicily. Founded in the 7th century BC, P. became the main Carthaginian stronghold against the Greeks. *Dionysius I devastated its area in 397 BC but only *Pyrrhus was able to capture it for a while before the Roman conquest. The Romans captured P. in 254 BC in an attack by land and sea. A colony was established there under Augustus. After the Arab conquest P. became the capital of Sicily.

PANTHEON It was normal usage in Greek and Roman religions to add an appeal to "all gods" when addressing the deities. The temple which *Agrippa (1) built in the *Campus Martius (27–25 BC) was called P. because it contained many gods and its circular plan resembled the sky (Dio 53.27). The building was destroyed by fire in AD 80, restored by Domitian, burnt again in AD 110 and completedy rebuilt under Hadrian. Later it was repaired by Septimius Severus and Caracalla. In the P. there is still preserved the inscription that says that M. Agrippa built it. The P. had a rectangular forecourt and gardens around it. Its peculiar feature is the huge rotunda, with an internal diameter of 43.3 m, approached through a pedimented portico, with columns of granite Corinthian. The cylindrical wall of the rotunda is sunk with four rectangular and three semicircular recesses, fronted by pairs of columns. The ancient bronze doors are still extant.
Nash, *Pict. Dict. Rome*, 2, 171ff.

PANTICAPAEUM Important Greek city on the eastern side of the Crimea, founded by *Miletus in the early 6th century BC. Its prosperity was due to fishery, viticulture and trade, especially the export of grain. It founded other cities and retained its prosperity for centuries. P. came under the control of *Mithridates (3) VI whose descendants continued to rule under Roman protectorate. Its decline started with the occupation by the Goths and the Sarmatians in the 3rd century AD.

PAPHLAGONIA The territory of the central coast of northern Asia Minor with its hinterland, separated by river Halys on the east from Pontus and bordering on Bithynia in the west. In Greek mythology P. is mentioned in connection with the Trojan War and the voyage of the Argonauts. It was mainly an agricultural country with a few Greek cities on the coast from *Heraclea Pontica to *Sinope. The conquest of the country under Alexander the Great was nominal. In the period of the *Diadochi a local dynasty established itself in the inland part, and this came to be known as Inner P. This local dynasty suffered from the expansionist tendencies of Bithynia and Pontus. Augustus annexed P. to the province of Galatia. The rest of P. had been included in the province of Pontus – Bithynia, organized by Pompey (63/2 BC).
Magie, *Asia* (s.v.).

PAPHOS City in west Cyprus, about 1 km from the

coast, near the modern village of Kouklia. The city was in the sphere of the *Mycenaean civilization in the 14th–13th centuries BC, when it was already of importance. It was famous for its temple of *Aphrodite, which is mentioned as early as Homer (*Od.* 8.363). P. was ruled by the dynasty of the Cinyrads, whose supposed ancestor was *Cinyras. The kings were also the priests of Aphrodite. A new P. was built by Nicocles on the coast about 15 km to the north. This became the capital of the island in the Ptolemaic and Roman times.

G. Hill, *A History of Cyprus*, 1940 (s.v.).

PAPINIANUS, Aemilius Roman official and prominent jurist. He advanced under Septimius *Severus and became praetorian prefect in AD 203. As he refused to justify the murder of Geta, Caracalla's brother, he was put to death by the emperor (AD 212). His main works were *Quaestiones* in thirty seven books and *Responsa* in nineteen books. *Ulpian wrote *Notes* to the latter and *Paulus to both; these two were P.'s assessors. P. had an excellent reputation as jurist. Other jurists as well as imperial constitution cited him as an authority, and in the Law of Citations of Theodosius II (426) his view was given preference in cases when other jurists were divided equally. He was original and practical, with consideration for equity and ethics. His language is brief and precise.

PAPIRIUS CURSOR, Lucius The most prominent patrician statesman and general of Rome in the last quarter of the 4th century BC. He was consul five times (326, 320, 319, 315, 313) and dictator twice (325, 309). Severe disciplinarian, he played a leading role in the Roman recovery after the reverse in the Caudine Forks (*Caudium), but family tradition and the rhetorical exaggeration of Roman historians prevent an accurate assessment of his achievements.

PAPPUS of Alexandria Prominent mathematician, contemporary of Constantine the Great. The most important work of P. is the *Synagoge* ("Collection"), a manual of Greek mathematics of which Books 3–8 are extant. It is particularly important as it gives information on works now lost including those of *Euclid and *Apollonius of Perge on higher geometry and those of *Archimedes on semiregular solids and mechanics. However, he also offers contributions of his own. Of his other works there is extant, in Arabic, Book 10 of the commentary on the *Elements* of Euclid, part of the commentary on the *Almagest* of Claudius *Ptolemy. An extant Armenian geographic treatise is based on a geographic work of P.

T. Heath, *History of Greek Mathematics*, 1921, 2, 335ff.

PARIS Son of *Priam and *Hecuba, also named Alexander; his abduction of *Helen from Sparta, which was the cause of the Trojan War, is told as early as Homer (*Il.* 3.443ff.). P. is not prominent in the *Iliad* and when he goes to a duel with *Menelaus it is Aphrodite who saves him. In post-Homeric literature important details and myths were added. Exposed as an infant, he grew up with shepherds, distinguished himself in games and returned home. Asked to judge who was the most beautiful of Athena, Hera, and Aphrodite, after *Eris threw her Apple of Discord, he gave the prize to Aphrodite who promised him Helen. Thus the Judgement of Paris, in fact a folktale, became the cause of the war. A distinguished archer already in the *Iliad*, he was said to have killed Achilles by an arrow. He himself was killed by *Philoctetes. The main events of the myth associated with him were favourite themes for artists.

PARMENIDES One of the most influential pre-Socratic philosophers, a native of *Elea. Biographical details are few and unsatisfactory. He lived in the 5th century BC, is said to have visited Athens and met Socrates, and to have given laws to his home city. He wrote a philosophical poem in hexameters, considerable excerpts of which are preserved by Simplicius (6th century AD). The first part is a description of his journey from night to day and meeting a goddess who is purported to give the philosophical doctrines of P. There are two ways, that of Truth (*aletheia*) and that of Illusion (*doxa*) or Opinion. The first is related to "to be"; this is eternal, indivisible, motionless and definite. It comes out that what we perceive with our senses (coming to being, perishing, movements) is illusory, and that the way of Opinion does not give us reality. P. was the founder of the theory of knowledge, he introduced method into philosophical thinking and all subsequent philosophers had to cope with the view that reality was one, motionless and definite.

Kirk-Raven, *Presocratic Philosophers*.

PARMENION Son of Philotas, the leading general of *Philip II. He was responsible with *Antipater (1) for the conclusion of the Peace of *Philocrates (346 BC) and in 337 commanded the advance guard in Asia in preparation for the great expedition against Persia. In the expedition of Alexander he was given independent commands and in the great battles was second-in-command of Alexander, commanding the left wing, while Alexander carried the attack on the right wing (Issus, Gaugamela). He was the main representative of the "old guard", the Macedonians who opposed the new ideas of Alexander on the government of the empire and the relations with the conquered. With the advance to eastern Iran, he was made responsible for the communications with Europe, with his base at Ecbatana; in fact Alexander had deposed him from his senior position. After the execution of Parmenion's son *Philotas, Alexander sent men to murder him (330 BC).

E. Badian, *Transactions of the American Philological Association*, 1960, 325ff.

PARNASSUS Huge mountain in central Greece with a peak of 2,450 m. *Delphi is situated in an upper valley on its southern side. It was considered a sacred mountain. Apollo, through his Delphic temple, was associated with P. and Dionysus had special connection with it and its followers held their orgies on its slopes. It was also considered as the place where *Deucalion landed after the flood. In Roman times it came to be the Mountain of the Muses and was hence associated with poetry.

PAROS Large island in the *Cyclades, 22 km long and 15 km wide, renowned for its marble. It was settled already in Neolithic times and in historic times had an Ionian population. In the Archaic period it was a centre of trade and was considered the richest of the Cycladic islands. *Thasos was colonized by settlers from P. in the early 7th century BC. The poet *Archilochus, a native of P., tried his luck in Thasos. In the same period P. had a prosperous pottery industry. In the 5th century P. was a member of the Delian League and, in the 4th century, of the Second Athenian Empire. The marmor quarries of P. were still exploited under the Roman Empire. The inscription known as *Marmor Parium came from P.

PARRHASIUS Greek painter, son of Evenor, native of Ephesus, active in Athens probably in the second half of the 5th century BC. Extravagant and proud, he won a reputation, and is introduced as Socrates' partner in the discussion of painting in the *Memorabilia* of Xenophon. He painted mythological themes and was known for the grace of his

Southeast front of the Parthenon

figures. According to Quintilian, P. discovered the subtlety of outline.

PARTHENIUS Greek poet, native of Nicaea, who was captured in the Third Mithridatic War (*c.* 73 BC), and manumitted in Italy. His elegiac poems have not survived. Extant are the *Erotic Tales*, in prose, a collection of love-story plots, intended to be composed as elegies for Cornelius *Gallus.
Text and translation: S. Gaselee (Loeb), 1916.

PARTHENON The temple of Athena Parthenos ("Virgin") on the *Acropolis, the main part of the building operations of *Pericles. The work was begun in 447/446 BC, completed in 438, but the sculptures were finished in 332 BC. *Phidias apparently was in charge, and also made the cult statue of Athena, a standing armed figure with a helmet, a shield and a lance, made of gold and ivory. The architect was *Ictinus with whom Callicrates worked. The temple, which was built on the foundations of an earlier temple, is of Pentelic marble and is the finest temple of the Doric Order, both in its perfect proportions and refined structure. It had seventeen columns on the sides and eight at the ends. Its dimensions are 228 by 101 feet. It had two inner porches of 6 columns each, a *cella* with inner colonnades on the sides and rear, within which was the statue. There was also a small room with an entrance from the back. The sculptures of the metopes, frieze, and pediments included the battle of the Lapiths and Centaurs, that of the gods and Gigantes, Greeks and Amazons, the birth of Athena, and the pan-Athenaen procession. It was a superb work, the symbol of the grandeur of Athens. The temple was made a church under Justinian and a mosque under the Turks. Well preserved until 1687, it was then severely damaged when the Turkish gun-powder stored in it was hit by a Venetian shell and exploded. Much of the sculpture was acquired by Lord Elgin and is still in the British Museum. The outer colonnades have been restored.
W. B. Dinsmoor, *Architecture of Ancient Greece*, 1950.

PARTHIA Territory in the southeast of the Caspian Sea (corresponding to Chorasan), a Seleucid satrapy which was occupied in 247 BC by the Parni, a nomad people who came from east of the Caspian. The new masters were called thereafter Parthians and were ruled by the Arsacid dynasty who took the name of their first king, Arsaces, as an official title. The Arsacid era began in March/April 247 BC. At the time of *Antiochus III they had to recognize the overlordship of the Seleucid king. After the death of *Antiochus IV, King Mithridates I (*c.* 171–138 BC) extended his rule over Media, Babylonia and Elymais, and as a heir to the Achaemenids took the title of Great King. His empire extended to the Indus and his successors retained, with various degrees of success, the claim to this vast area. With the extention of the Roman Empire of the east, the Euphrates became the frontier line between the two great powers. Occasionally wars broke out, in particular in connection with the overlordship over Armenia. Trajan conquered Mesopotamia for a while, and part of it became a Roman province in the late 2nd century AD. Throughout this long period the Parthians remained foreign rulers for the Persians. The latter, under the dynasty of the Sassanids, terminated the Parthian kingdom in the first half of the 3rd century AD (*c.* 227, the death of the last Arsacid).

The Parthians were a feudal aristocracy who adopted the Persian religion and continued the Persian-Seleucid organization of their empire. Their capital was Ecbatana in Media with *Ctesiphon as an occasional residence. They were tolerant of the Greeks under their rule and took advantage of their administrative experience and scientific achievements. They were excellent horsemen and based their army on cavalry, as cataphracts or arch-men. However, they suffered from the weaknesses of a feudal state until they succumbed to the rising power of their Persian vassals.
N. C. Debevoise, *A Political History of Parthia*, 1938;
M. A. R. Colledge, *The Parthians*, 1967.

PASITELES Important Greek sculptor in the first century BC, native of Magna Graecia. He received Roman citizenship in 89 BC. At his time there was a great demand in Rome for copies of Greek sculptures. P. was probably one of those who introduced accurate copies by making casts of originals and applying the pointing process. None of his works is extant.

PATAVIUM (modern Padua) The capital of the *Veneti in northern Italy. Subject to Rome since at least 174 BC, it was made a *municipium* in the 1st century BC. With good communications, both by land and sea, it was a prosperous city and had a successful wool industry. *Livy, *Asconius and *Thrasea Paetus were natives of P.

PATER FAMILIAS The head of the Roman family under whose authority (*patria potestas*) were his wife (if married under certain conditions), his natural children and their descendants through the male line; not affected by this authority were married daughters, who came under the authority of their husbands (again if married under certain conditions), and children adopted by others or emancipated from a father's authority. A man's adopted children came under his authority. In early times, PF. could sell his children in the same way that he could sell his property. He had the authority of life and death over them, though actual cases of the exploitation of this right are rarely mentioned. According to Roman law, the PF. was the only one of the family who owned property, and any property in the possession of his children was considered as his own (see *Peculium). At the death of a PF., each and every male person directly under his authority became a PF.

PATER (PARENS) PATRIA ("Father of the Country") Traditionally, Romulus and *Camillus were called by this title. *Cicero was called PP. for his handling the Catilinarian conspiracy in 63 BC, and a Senate resolution honoured Caesar with the title after *Munda. Augustus agreed to receive it from the Senate, the equestrian order, and the Roman people, in 2 BC (*Mon. An.* 35.1). Except for Tiberius, all subsequent emperors received it during their reigns.

PATRICIANS (patricius, pl. patricii) The aristocratic class in early Rome. They had special privileges which included the exclusive right to hold magistracies, especially the consulate, membership in the priestly colleges, and the power (exercised by patrician senators) to confirm the resolutions of the popular assemblies (*Patrum Auctoritas). P. were appointed *Interrex and *Princeps Senatus. Marriages between P. and Plebeians were not legitimate until 445 BC. The P. also had what amounted to exclusive knowledge of the law until the publication of the Laws of the Twelve Tables by the *Decemvirs, and even afterwards they were the experts (see *Flavius). Various theories have been suggested, by ancient and modern scholars, to explain the privileged status of the P.: that they were the heads of the families (*patres*) appointed to the Senate by Romulus; that they were a conquering class; that they were the cavalry of the kings etc. Apparently, they were especially connected with the Senate as their name is derived from *pater*, that is, a member of the Senate. But it is doubtful whether they were ever the only members of this body. It seems that the class, formed during the late regal period and the beginning of the Republic, included those families which were economically, socially and politically successful and were able to give legal status to their superiority. But their number continuously decreased and by the early 3rd century BC they had conceded almost all their privileges to the *Plebeians. Augustus and subsequent emperors bestowed the rank of P. to new families. About fifty patrician clans are known.
Jolowicz, *Roman Law*[3], (s.v.).

PATROCLUS Son of Menoetius, the slightly older companion of *Achilles. He accompanied his friend to the Trojan War. When the Trojans attacked the Greek camp, Achilles let him have his armour and P. led the *Myrmidons to battle, but he was killed by Hector (Homer, *Il.* 16.786ff.). Achilles then avenged his death and gave splendid funeral games in his honour (*Il.* 23).

PATRUM AUCTORITAS The confirmation of the decision of the *Comitia* by the *paters*, i.e. (most probably), the patrician members of the Senate. By a *lex Publilia* (339 BC), this had to be given in advance in cases of legislation, and, by a later law, *lex Maenia*, in elections. It thus became a mere formality. The decisions of the *Concilium Plebis were probably not subject to this procedure. Jolowicz, *Roman Law*.[3] (s.v.).

PAULLUS, Lucius Aemilius An influential patrician statesman. His homonym father was consul when he defeated *Demetrius (7) of Pharus in 219 BC; he died in Cannae (when he was again consul). P.'s sister, Aemilia Tertia, was married to Scipio Africanus. As praetor in 191, P. governed Farther Spain where, after an initial reverse, he defeated the Lusitanians. As consul in 182 BC, P. was successful against the Ligurians. His greatest achievement was in 168 BC when, again consul, he defeated *Perseus (2) at Pydna and thereby not only terminated the Third Macedonian War but also the Macedonian monarchy. He subjugated and ruthlessly enslaved the population of Epirus according to the Senate's resolution. He had five children, two of whom were adopted. His two younger sons died at the time of his triumph in 167 BC. His elder sons were Q. Fabius and P. Scipio Aemilianus. His daughter married Cato's son. P. was censor in 164 BC and he died in 160. Said to have been a phil-Hellenist, he was rather conservative in politics, way of life and outlook.
Plut., *Aemilius*; Scullard, *Rom. Pol.*[2] (s.v.).

PAULUS, Julius Leading Roman jurist, active in the first quarter of the 3rd century BC. He was an assessor of *Papinian and a member of the *Consilium principis* under Septimius Severus and Caracalla. He became praetorian prefect under Alexander Severus. P. was a prolific writer (over 300 books). Among his writings were commentaries on the praetorian Edict and the earlier jurists, monographs on various subjects (constitutional, private and criminal law), and *Responsa*. Numerous passages from his works are cited in the *Digesta of Justinian, in which

A relief from the monument of Paullus at Delphi showing Romans fighting Macedonians

A fresco detail from Cnossos, known as "The Parisian"

A Greek fighting an Amazon. Marmar copy of the shield of Athena Parthenos by Phidias

he is the most quoted author after *Ulpian. The extant *Pauli Sententiae* is based on a selection made of his work. Despite his fame, he was basically a compiler, competent at expounding his topics and not an original thinker.

PAUSANIAS (1) Of the Agiad royal family at Sparta, nephew of *Leonidas (1). He was the commander-in-chief of the Greeks at the battle of Plataea (479 BC) and played a decisive role in attaining the victory. He made a dedication to Delphi with his name which the Spartans replaced with the names of the cities that took part in the battle. During the next year he captured Byzantium, but by his haughty manners he alienated the allied Greeks and thus he unwittingly helped Athens to form the Delian League. He was also suspected of establishing secret ties with Xerxes, but was twice acquitted on this charge. Finally, he was suspected of having intrigued to get the helots to revolt — he fled to the temple of Athena Chalkioikos and was starved to death.

PAUSANIAS (2) Spartan king of the Agiad family, succeeded to the throne in 408 BC (as a minor after the deposition of his father, he was the nominal king in 445—426 BC). He took part in the blockade of Athens in 405 BC, and in 403 reversed the policy of *Lysander with regard to Athens: the democrats were allowed to take control and the Thirty Tyrants left Athens. For his conduct in the war against Boeotia in 395 BC, in which Lysander fell, P. was sentenced to death, but he escaped.

PAUSANIAS (3) Greek traveller and writer. He lived during the 2nd century AD and his important work, *Description of Greece*, is extant. It includes ten books: Book 1, Athens, Attica and Megara; Book 2, Argolis and Corinth; Book 3, Laconia; Book 4, Messenia; Books 5—6, Elis and Olympia; Book 7, Achaea; Book 8, Arcadia; Book 9, Boeotia; Book 10, Phocis and Delphi. P. is mainly interested in artistic monuments: buildings, tombs, statues, writing about them as if for tourists. He gives a historical outline of the places he describes, describing the topography of, and the mythological and religious customs and beliefs associated with, the various sites. His work is a very important source for all these subjects and he has been proved to be an accurate writer.

J.C. Frazer, *Pausanias' Description of Greece*, 1898 (text, tran. and commentary); W. H. S. Jones — R. Wycherly (Loeb), 1918.

PECULIUM Persons under the power of a *Pater Familias* did not have the right of ownership in Roman law. For practical reasons, however, such persons, sons or slaves, were given property for their use which they administered freely, but which in law remained the property of the giver (father or master). This was the P., and slaves who did well with it used their profits to buy their freedom.

PEDIUS, Quintus Of an equestrian family on his father's side, he was the son or grandson of Caesar's sister Julia. He served with Caesar in Gaul, followed him in the Civil War and was praetor in 48 BC. For his achievement in Spain he was given a triumph in 45 BC. After Caesar's death, P. gave his share in the inheritance (one eighth) to Octavian with whom he became consul on 19 August 43 BC. He passed a law against the tyranicides and died in November 43 BC.

Syme, *Rom. Rev.* (s.v.).

PEGASUS The fabulous winged horse which was born to *Gorgo when *Perseus (1) killed her (Hesiod, *Theog.* 280). *Bellerophon, aided by Athena or Poseidon, caught him at the spring of Pirene at Corinth. With such a horse,

Pegasus on the reverse of a Corinthian coin

Bellerophon fought successfully against the *Chimaera and the *Amazons. But rather than allow Bellerophon to fly to heaven, P. threw him. P. created the spring Hippocrene on Mount Helicon by stamping his hoof; he created many other fountains in the same way. His birth and the fights against the Chimaera and the Amazons were frequently depicted in vase-paintings. In later times he became a symbol of immortality.

PELASGIANS One of the people mentioned by Greek writers as the former occupiers of Greece before the arrival of the Greeks. They are said by Homer to have dwelt in Thessaly. And in later times the region around Larissa was called Pelasgiotis. Their name, originally that of a distinct people in northern Greece, was applied by the Greeks to many other peoples.

PELEUS Greek mythological hero, son of Aeacus of Aegina, who was banished after killing his half-brother. He was purified by Eurytion of Phthia, whose daughter, Antigone, he married. He took part in the Calydonian boar hunt, and had the misfortune to kill Eurytion. He fought the Centaurs and took part in the voyage of the *Argonauts. His most famous myth connected him with the Nereid *Thetis. He had to wrestle with her and in the contest she changed into water, fire, wind, a lion, a snake etc., but he persisted and at last won. All the gods took part in the wedding and brought presents. The Muses and the Moirai sang, and the Nereids danced, but *Eris, who was not invited, threw the Apple of Discord which required the judgement of *Paris and thus brought about the Trojan War. Thetis bore P. *Achilles and made him immortal except for his heel. Various episodes of P.'s myth were used by artists: his wrestling with Thetis, his wedding and his wrestling with *Atalanta in the funeral games for Pelias (the uncle of *Jason (1)).

PELLA (modern Agii Apostoloi) The capital of Macedonia from the late 5th century BC until 167 BC. Situated at the river Lydias, it had good communications to the sea. After the organization of the Roman province of Macedonia (146 BC) Thessalonica replaced P. in importance.

Hunting scene. A mosaic painting from Pella

PELOPIDAS Theban statesman and general. He escaped from Thebes in 382 BC when the Spartans captured the Cadmea, but he recaptured it in 379. Thereafter, P. and his friend *Epaminondas became the leaders of Thebes. The Boeotian League was revived and P. distinguished himself on several occasions, notably at *Leuctra. He died in action in 364 in the battle which he won against *Alexander (2) of Pherae.
Plut., *Pelopidas.*

PELOPONNESIAN LEAGUE The modern term used to denote what the Greeks called "the Lacedaemonians (i.e. Sparta) and their allies", which lasted from the 6th to the 4th century BC. This organization grew as Sparta acquired a dominant position in the Peloponnesus. It had one main concern: the conducting of common war. The dominance of Sparta is seen in its commanding of the wars and in the fact that the assemblies were held and presided over at Sparta. In the assemblies, each member city had one vote; after the acceptance of a decision, the Spartan assembly had to ratify the resolution. When no common war was conducted, each member was allowed to wage wars as she pleased. By signing new treaties of alliance, Sparta enlarged the scope of the League (for instance with Athens after the Peloponnesian War).

PELOPONNESIAN WAR (431—404 BC) The war between Sparta and her allies against Athens; it was caused, according to Thucydides, by the fear of Athens. Not only Corinth, which directly suffered from the growing power of Athens, but even Sparta was apprehensive of her. There were also contributory causes, like the war between Corinth and *Corcyra, the revolt of *Potidaea and the embargo upon Megara by Athens. The strategy of Pericles was to avoid contesting Spartan supremacy on land while evacuating the population of Athens, which could find shelter within the walls of Athens; he also took advantage of the naval superiority of Athens to devastate the coasts of the enemy and to cause damage to its trade. But in the second year of the war a large part of the Athenian population died as a result of a plague, described by Thucy-

dides. Pericles himself died in 429. In the following years Athens won important successes despite the initial devastation of Attica by the Spartan army which in the first years was led by *Archidamus II (hence the Archidamean War). In 425 BC the Athenians won Pylos, a good base in the enemy's country, and in addition captured important Spartans. Sparta now wanted peace but the extreme imperialists, notably *Cleon, rejected the offer. In 424, however the extremely able Spartan general *Brasidas undermined the Athenian position in Thrace and conquered Amphipolis. He and Cleon died in 423 and in 421 a peace based on status quo — the Peace of Nicias — was concluded.

But not all were satisfied, and Alcibiades intrigued against Sparta in the Peloponnesus, and won Argos, Elis and Mantinea. Sparta however won a decisive battle in 418. The imperialists were influential enough in 415 BC to pass a decision to send an expedition to Sicily. But the whole force, with an additional one under *Demosthenes (1), was lost (413). Sparta now occupied Decelea in Attica from which it could easily operate. It was at this time that the subject states seceded from Athens, which managed to recover to some extent from the Sicilian disaster. She rebuilt her fleet and Alcibiades won some victories. But *Lysander organized a Spartan fleet with Persian money and, after his victory at *Aegospotamoi, Athens had to surrender (April 404 BC).
Thucydides; Xenophon, *Hellenica* 1.; Plut., *Pericles; Nicias, Alcibiades, Lysander;* G. B. Grundy, *Thucydides and the History of His Age,*[2] 1948; C. E. M. de Ste. Croix, *The Origins of the Peloponnesian War,* 1972.

PELOPONNESUS ("Isle of Pelops") The great southern peninsula of Greece, named after the mythological *Pelops, with an area of approximately 21,400 sq km. It consisted of *Elis, *Messenia, *Laconia, *Argolis, *Arcadia and *Achaea and was connected with central Greece by the isthmus of Corinth.

PELOPS Greek mythological figure after whom the Peloponnesus peninsula was named. His father *Tantalus cut him up into little pieces and offered his flesh to the gods, but practically all of them refrained from eating it. The exception was Demeter, who ate a part of the shoulder, being absent-minded with grief over the loss of Persephone. The gods then restored P. to life and gave him an ivory shoulder. He became the favourite of Poseidon, who gave him a golden chariot and wonderful horses. When he grew up, P. wanted to marry Hippodamia, the daughter of King Oenomaus of Elis. But Oenomaus had been forewarned that he would be killed by his daughter's husband. As he had divine horses, Oenomaus announced that any one could carry Hippodamia off in his chariot, but he would be pursued and, if beaten in the chariot race, he would be killed. Thirteen competitors had been killed before P. came along. He bribed Myrtilus, the charioteer of Oenomaus, to remove the pins from his master's chariot, and the latter was killed. P. did not keep his promise to Myrtilus, but drowned him in the sea, thereafter named Myrtoan. Myrtilus, or Oenomaus, cursed P. before he died, and thus was responsible for all the calamities that befell P.'s sons *Atreus and Thyestes and their descendants. P. himself was wealthy and had many children. In memory of his victory he instituted the *Olympian games. This story is told as early as Pindar (*Olym.* 1). P. was worshipped at *Olympia and his chariot-race was the scene depicted on the east pediment of the temple of Zeus at Olympia.

PELTASTS The *pelte* was a small, light, round shield used by lightly armed soldiers who were named after it. Originally, P. were Thracian soldiers and were considered as auxiliary troops. They rose to importance in the 4th century BC, and, under *Iphicrates, the P. won victories as independent troops. At the same time, their armour changed and they used much longer spears and swords.
A. N. Snodgrass, *Arms and Armours of the Greeks,* 1967.

PENATES DI The deities of the store room who were worshipped in every Roman household with Vesta; a characteristic cult of the religion of the family. But there was also a public cult to them.
Alföldi, *Early Rome*, 258ff.

PENELOPE The loyal wife of *Odysseus, and mother of *Telemachus, her tale is recounted by Homer in the *Odyssey*. In her husband's absence, suitors, the nobles of Ithaca, come to live in her house and ask her to remarry. She puts them off by saying that she will marry after finishing a shroud for Laertes, her father-in-law. But at night she unravels the work that she does in the day. After three years, her ruse is revealed and she is compelled to finish the work. Following the advice of Athena, she promises to marry the one who can bend Odysseus' bow and shoot an arrow through a series of axes. No one is able to do this except Odysseus, who arrives disguised as a beggar, joins the competition, and then kills the suitors. Thereafter P. reunites with her husband whom at first she did not recognize. From Homer on P. has been a symbol of faithfulness. But in the lost epic *Telegonia* she remarried Telegonus, Odysseus's son by Circe. She appears in a few works of art.

PENTAKOSIOMEDIMNOI One of the four classes established by *Solon at Athens, which included those people who had a yearly income of at least five hundred *medimnoi* of grain (*medimnos* ≅ 48 litres) or the equivalent income in oil. It appears that this criterion was introduced when barter was still the normal method of conducting economic transactions. When the use of coinage was established a drachm came to be considered as equal to a *medimnos*, and thus not only landowners were included

in the class (Plut. *Sol.* 23.3). By the 4th century BC, as a result of inflation, the P. were no longer exceptionally rich. Only P. were allowed to become *Tamiai and probably *archontes (Aris. *Athen. Pol.* 7.4; 8.11).

PENTHEUS King of Thebes, son of Echion and Agave, whose maternal grandfather was *Cadmus. He opposed the introduction of the cult of *Dionysus into his country, but the god, in disguise, enticed him to go to the mountains to watch the women at worship. In their ecstasy the women mistook him for an animal and, led by his own mother Agave, tore him to pieces. The myth is the theme of the *Bacchae*, one of the best tragedies of Euripides. The death of P. appears in vase-paintings.

PERDICCAS (1) King of Macedonia (*c.* 450/445–413 BC). His reign is marked by changing alliances and hostilities with Athens whose control on the Macedonian coast he tried to curb. He was also beset by the separatist tendencies of the local dynasts of the Macedonian cantons. Skillfully manoeuvering and changing sides (he supported the revolt of *Potidaea and allied himself with *Brasidas), P. was able to impose his authority in Macedonia, to repel the invasion of the Thracian King Sitalces (429 BC) and to survive the Athenian attacks. Before his death he was again allied with Athens.

PERDICCAS (2) Son of Orontes, rose in command during the Persian expedition of Alexander the Great to become "Bodyguard" in 330 BC and successor of *Hephaestion in 324. He was thus second-in-command to Alexander, became regent after his death and tried to preserve the unity of the empire. His authority and policy, however, were contested by *Antipater (1) and *Craterus (and the latter found his death in the battle against *Eumenes (1), P.'s man), and when he tried to invade Egypt he was killed by his own soldiers, influenced as they were by his opponent *Ptolemy I.

PERDUELLIO Act of hostility against the Roman state, noted as a crime as early as the Twelve Tables; originally probably with reference to treason and co-operation with the enemy. But the law was found insufficient to deal with misdeeds by magistrates and in the late Republic was supplemented by the laws of *Maiestas.

PEREGRINI From the Roman point of view, these were the free citizens of foreign communities. Some of the P. received rights of *Conubium and *Commercium. Lawsuits in which P. were involved were under the jurisdiction of the *praetor peregrinus*. Roman citizenship was sometimes conferred on P. on an individual basis; these then ceased to be citizens of their communities as double citizenship was not allowed in Roman law. All the Italian allies of Rome ceased to be P. with the bestowal of Roman citizenship in the *Bellum Sociale (89), and all provincial P. became Roman citizens by the Constitutio Antoniniana (AD 212) of *Caracalla.

PERGAMUM (Pergamon, modern Bergama) Ancient city in the Caïcus valley in *Mysia, situated on a high hill about 25 km from the sea. It is first recorded in extant literature in 400 BC, but its importance dates only from the Hellenistic period. *Lysimachus chose it as a secure place for his treasure but the commander of the place *Philetaerus became independent and established the Pergamene kingdom of the Attalids. The fortification and development of the city continued gradually under the successors of Philetaerus. The buildings were built in terraces on the slopes of the hill, the top of which was occupied by the palace and citadel. The peculiar conditions of the site were taken into account by the architects and P. presented an excellent example of town-planning. It had arsenals, barracks, a splendid theatre and, with the enthusiastic support of the kings, an outstanding library (the second after that of Alexandria), a museum, and a great temple of Asclepius. It became a centre of learning, had a flourishing school of sculpture; the fragments of the sculptures of the great altar of Zeus (dedicated by Eumenes II) are very famous. *Pergamene* ("parchment"), the fine writing material made of sheepskin, was invented in P. from which it received the name.

P. was the centre of the kingdom of the Attalids, but they let her have a Greek constitution. From this centre they were able to expand their rule and became dangerous competitors to the other great Hellenistic kingdoms, notably the Seleucids. Its greatest power was under *Eumenes II (197–159 BC). P. was a flourishing city and drew its wealth from the textile and parchment industries, agriculture and livestock breeding and silver mines. After the death of *Attalus III the kingdom became the Roman province of Asia, but the city retained its constitution.

Hansen, *Attalids*²; Magie, *Asia*; Jones, *Cities*?

PERIANDER Son of *Cypselus and tyrant of Corinth (*c.* 625–585 BC), under whom the city rose to the height of its prosperity. He probably founded Apollonia, regained control over *Corcyra, and established relations with Egypt, the Lydian King *Alyattes and the tyrant Thrasybulus of Miletus. He had a strong navy and constructed the *diolkos*, a system of rails on which ships were pulled over the Isthmus; he is even credited with planning to dig a "Corinthian canal". Under him Corinthian crafts and industry flourished and Corinthian pottery was extensively exported, especially to the West. When his father-in-law Procles of Epidaurus incited his son against him, P. conquered Epidaurus. P. probably dedicated the Chest of Cypselus at Olympia, which *Pausanias (3) was able to see even in his time. P. was a patron of arts and letters and had at his court the poet Arion (see *Dithyramb). Plutarch set the *Symposium of the Seven Sages* at his court. His nephew Psammetichus succeeded him but was soon murdered and the oligarchic government was restored at Corinth.

A. Andrews, *The Greek Tyrants,* 1956.

PERICLES Born *c.* 495 BC, he was the leading Athenian statesman during the mid-5th century; under him the Athenian democracy became in fact the rule of one man. He was the son of Xanthippus, a prominent statesman in the Persian wars, and the Alcmaeonid Agariste. His first public appearance was in 472 BC when he was Choregos for the *Persae* of Aeschylus. He prosecuted *Cimon in 463 and supported *Ephialtes in his attack on the *Areopagus. Democratization of the Athenian constitution and imperialistic policy were his main pursuits thereafter. According to Plutarch, he became the leader of the people after Ephialtes' death. His measures probably included the extension to the *Zeugitae of the right to serve as *archons; the introduction of payment to the jurors; the institution of the *Theorika, and the law that made Athenian citizens only of those whose mother and father were citizens. In 446 BC he quelled Euboea, saw to the withdrawal of the Spartans from Attica (by bribery?) and concluded the Thirty-Year Peace with Sparta. His only rival at this time was *Thucydides (1) son of Melesias, who opposed the imperialistic policy of P.; but he was ostracized *c.* 443 BC.

P. was responsible for the transformation of the Delian League into an Athenian Empire. Those allies who

tried to secede after the Peace of *Callias were apparently forced to stay and P. established *cleruchies on the territory confiscated. He founded *Thurii in southern Italy (443 BC) and in 440/439 subdued the revolt of the important island of Samos. P. was responsible for the extensive building operations of the period, in particular those on the *Acropolis (*Parthenon, *Propylaea), in which he was helped by *Phidias. For this he used the contributions of the allies, and when he was criticized, he answered that as long as Athens defended the allies she could dispose of the money as she wished. His prestige was high and from 443 BC he was continuously elected strategos. His policy finally led to the outbreak of the *Peloponnesian War in which he was responsible for the plan to evacuate Attica and to base Athens' operations on her naval superiority.

At the height of his power, P.'s enemies attacked his favourites: *Anaxagoras, *Phidias and his mistress (or wife) *Aspasia. After the plague of 430 BC he was prosecuted, fined and had to abdicate from his office (430). He was again elected strategos (429 BC), but he died shortly afterwards. The funeral speech he delivered in honour of the Athenians who died in the first year of the war is a monument to the achievements of Athens under his leadership (Thuc. 2.35ff.).

A. R. Burn, *Pericles and Athens,* 1948; V. Ehrenberg, *Sophocles and Pericles,* 1954.

PERINTHUS Greek city on the Thracian shore of the Propontis, founded by settlers from *Samos *c.* 600 BC. Due to the nature of the site, on the slope of a hill, the city resembled an amphitheatre (Diod. Sic. 16.76). P. came under the control of Persia, was a member of the Delian League in the 5th century and of the Second Athenian Empire in the 4th century. It successfully repelled a famous siege by *Philip II in 341/340 BC. *Philip V succeeded in taking control of P. in 202 BC and after 189 BC it was subject to the Attalids of Pergamum. Later it was under the control of the Roman governor of Macedonia. The modern name Erekli preserves its later name Heraclia.

PERIOIKI ("those who live round about") This Greek term denoted those groups of the population that were subject to Greek states, and had personal freedom and their own governing institutions. The groups frequently comprised only half-citizens, but they had to tender services to the states on which they each depended. They are known from various places including Crete, Elis, Argolis, Boeotia, Thessaly, and especially Sparta where the P. inhabited the Laconian cities on the coastal and mountain districts "around Sparta", and numbered around 100. They differed from the Spartiates in that they were not subject to the economic and social regulations of the Licurgan constitution; nor did they have the political rights of the Spartiates; but none the less they served in the army. They had their own constitution for self-government. Originally, they had been independent of Sparta and under Augustus the Laconian towns were not dependent on Sparta.

E. Michell, *Sparta,* 1952 (s.v.);
V. Ehrenberg, *The Greek State,* 1960 (s.v.).

PERIPATETIC SCHOOL The school Aristotle founded in Athens in 335/334 BC at a sacred grove of Apollo Lyceus and the Muses was called Lyceum, after the epithet of the god. Later, it was called Peripatetic after the covered walk (*peripatos*) which was included in the buildings which Theophrastus, Aristotle's successor, gave to the school.

Theophrastus bequeathed the property to certain scholars and was succeeded as Head by Strabo. The School passed in succession to later Heads. In Aristotle's time and under Theophrastus the scholarly activities of the members of the School were very extensive and their writings were numerous. The subjects studied included mathematics, music, botany, medicine, politics, history, metaphysics, and ethics. But later no great scholars worked here and even the works of Aristotle were neglected. The only scholar of importance in the 2nd century BC was *Critolaus. With the decline of scholarship, the School could not claim to offer its own distinct doctrines; none the less, it lasted until the 4th century AD.

I. Düring, *Aristotle in the Ancient Biographical Tradition*, 1957.

PERIPLUS Term applied to the circumnavigation of an island, or a coast; also the account given of such a voyage, as well as practical guide books for such a purpose. The earliest extant P. is that of *Hanno the Navigator (translated into Greek). The P. of *Nearchus is known through its use by *Arrian. *The Periplus of the Erythraean Sea* is an extant account by an anonymous author of the route from Egypt to India. Another extant P. is *Stadiasmus Maris Magni* (see also *Scylax).

A. Diller, *The Tradition of the Minor Greek Geographers*, 1952.

PERSEPHONE (Latin: Proserpina) Greek goddess of the underworld, wife of Hades and daughter of Zeus and *Demeter, originally a pre-Hellenic deity who was identified with Core ("maiden"). In the myth she was abducted by Hades and her mother finally reached an agreement whereby she would spend half a year with Hades and half a year with her mother on earth. While she was with Hades the earth was barren, and when she rejoined her mother everything grew — a myth that shows P. as a goddess of vegetation. In the Orphic religion (see *Orphism) she was the mother of Zagreus-Dionysus by Zeus. P. Core was usually worshipped with her mother Demeter and in works of art she was also depicted with her. She usually carries a sceptre or torches. The *Rape of Proserpina* is a poem of *Claudian, and he is only one of many poets and artists who were attracted by her myth.

PERSEUS (1) Greek mythological hero, son of Zeus and Danaë. In the myth his mother was shut in a bronze building by her father Acrisius who had been warned by an oracle that his daughter's son would kill him. But Zeus came to her as a shower of gold, and after P.'s birth, Acrisius put him and his mother in a chest and set it afloat on the sea. They were rescued and found shelter in Seriphus. When P. grew up, Polydectes, the king of the island, sent him to fetch the head of the *Gorgo (Medusa). Hermes gave him winged sandals and Athena gave him a magic helmet that made him invisible, and so he succeeded in decapitating the monster and in rescuing *Andromeda on his homeward voyage. When he came back, he turned Polydectes and his companions into stone for molesting his mother. Later he took part in a discus competition and accidentally killed his grandfather Acrisius who was one of the spectators. He then gave up Argos, his legitimate inheritance, and became king of Tiryns. The main events in the myth of P. were very popular with artists from the 7th century on: the decapitation of Gorgo (a metope from Selinus, vase-paintings), the *Graiae, the rescue of Andromeda (depicted in wall paintings in Pompeii), and the turning of Polydectes into stone.

J. M. Woodward, *Perseus*, 1937.

PERSEUS (2) Son of *Philip V, born 212 BC, the last king of Macedonia (179—168 BC). In his youth, he took part in the Second Macedonian War against Rome. He also opposed the pro-Roman tendencies of his brother, Demetrius, and brought about his execution by Philip in 181 BC. P. had a strong army and was at first success ous policy and succeeded in advancing his influence: he defeated the Bastarnae in Thrace, married the daughter of *Seleucus IV, and skillfully interfered in the affairs of Greece. But he was mainly interested in the Balkan hinterland of Macedonia. The growth of his power provoked Rome and led to the Third Macedonian War (171—168 BC). P. had a strong army and was at first successful against the Romans, but he was defeated in the decisive battle of Pydna (168 BC) by L. Aemilius *Paullus. Here the superiority of the Roman legion over the Macedonian phalanx was amply proved. He had to take part in the triumph of Paullus (167 BC) and died two years later.

PERSIAN WARS It was Herodotus who first wrote the story of the wars of the Greeks and the Persians. After the defeat of *Croesus, king of Lydia, by *Cyrus I (546 BC), the Greeks of Asia Minor were ruled for the next sixty-five years or so by Persia. The first war was that of the Ionians of Asia Minor. Known as the Ionian revolt it was instigated by *Aristagoras, the tyrant of Miletus, who exploited the widespread discontent with the Greek tyrants who represented the Persians. A contributory motive may have been the commercial competition of the Phoenicians, favoured by Persia. The revolt started in 499 BC, the tyrants were overthrown, a league of the Ionian cities was established, but the rebels received only little support from the Greeks of Greece: twenty ships from Athens and five ships from Eretria. In 498 BC they burnt down Sardes, the seat of the Persian satrap, and in 497 BC defeated a Phoenician fleet off Cyprus. But, thereafter, disunion and insubordination spread among the Greeks and in 494 BC they were defeated in a naval battle at Lade; Miletus as well as other cities were captured and destroyed, and Persian rule was restored, but not the tyrants.

Persia now took the offensive. *Mardonius secured control of Thrace and Macedonia (492 BC) and in 490 a strong force was sent against Eretria and Athens as a punitive measure for their support of the Ionians. Eretria was taken and burnt but at the Battle of *Marathon the Athenians, supported only by a small force of Plataeans, won an overwhelming victory. It took Persia almost ten years to launch another attack, but when it came it was on a grand scale. The size of the Persian army — hundreds of thousands — reported by Herodotus is difficult to believe, but it must have been huge. In addition *Xerxes secured the cooperation of Thessaly, Delphi, Boeotia and Argos, and it is said that the Persian attack was coordinated with a Carthaginian attack on the Greeks of Sicily. But the Greeks had prepared themselves. Athens had built a strong fleet and a Hellenic League was founded in 481 BC at the Isthmus. The Persians overpowered the defence of *Thermopylae by *Leonidas (1) and compelled the Greek navy to abandon its position at Artemisium. They now occupied central Greece, and sacked Athens whose population had been evacuated before the Persian advance. But the Persians lost the decisive naval Battle of *Salamis (480 BC) and Xerxes returned to Asia. *Mardonius was left in command, but he lost the great land battle and his life at Plataea (479 BC). Those Persians who survived the battle now left Greece. At the same

Greek hoplit attacking a Persian warrior. A red-figured amphora

of the damaging effects of vice on the soul; Satire 4 calls on a young statesman to study his own self; Satire 5 eulogizes Cornutus and Stoicism; Satire 6 gives advice on how to make good use of wealth. P.'s style is contorted and mixed; he uses obscure allusions and digressions, indulges in slang and rare words and his verses are rough. His aim was to condemn immorality, notably that of Nero and his court, and he did it in earnestness but without humour. He had his readers in his time and in the Middle Ages, but he is the least readable of the Roman satirists. Text and translation: G. G. Ramsey (Loeb), 1918; J. Wight Duff, *Roman Satire,* 1937.

PERTINAX, Publius Helvius Born AD 126, of humble origin, he embarked on a military career and was made a senator under Marcus Aurelius. He fought in Raetia (AD 171), was *consul suffectus* (c. 174), and governed Moesia, Dacia, Syria, and Britain. At the time of the murder of Commodus (AD 192) he was consul and prefect of the city and was hailed emperor by the praetorians. After a short reign, he alienated the praetorians who were incited by their prefect Laetus to kill him (28 March AD 193). Dio 73.

PERUSIA (modern Perugia) Etruscan city which was under Roman control since 295 BC (Liv. 30.31 and 37). In 41 BC, L. Antonius, brother of M. *Antonius (4), was besieged here by Octavian. This, the so-called Perusine War, was ended with the sacking of P. But P. recovered and was a prosperous city under the Empire. C. Shaw, *Etruscan Perusia,* 1939; Scullard, *Etruscan Cities,* 159ff.

PERVIGILIUM VENERIS A poem of 93 trochaic verses of unknown authorship and date (not earlier than the 2nd century AD). It is a hymn to love and passion on the eve of the spring festival of Venus in Sicily. A lively, passionate poem, it captivates the reader with its bright descriptions of nature and its powerful refrain — but in the end a sad note appears to the effect that the springtime of the author has not come yet.

PESCENNIUS NIGER JUSTUS, Gaius Born c. AD 135, of an equestrian family, he served in the army and was made a senator by Commodus. He governed Syria from AD 191 and was proclaimed emperor (April AD 193) after the murder of Pertinax. But he was not a match for Septimius *Severus who defeated him at Cyzicus and Nicaea. He retreated to Syria, lost another battle at Issus, and was later put to death (AD 194).

PETRA ("Rock") The capital city of the Nabataean kingdom. Its flourishing period began in the late 1st century BC. After the annexation of the Nabataean kingdom to the Roman Empire, Bostra became the capital. Hadrian visited P. in AD 131, when it received the title Hadriana Petra Metropolis. It remained a religious centre until the late Roman Empire. There are numerous ruins around the site but it is the splendid temples and the tombs cut in the rock around the city that are its main attraction.

PETREIUS, M. Roman soldier and senator, a henchman of Pompey. He defeated *Catiline in 62 BC and from 55 BC governed Farther Spain as legate of Pompey. He fought in the Civil War and after *Thapsus he killed King *Juba (1) in single combat and then he killed himself.

PETRONIUS ARBITER, Gaius Roman senator, governor of Bithynia and consul (the dates are not known). Tacitus gives a fascinating account of P. (*Ann.* 16. 18–19). He was an able administrator but he excelled in the art of pleasure and thus became a favourite of Nero. As *arbiter elegantiae* ("Arbiter of Taste") he helped the em-

time, the Greek fleet, commanded by King *Leotychides of Sparta, routed the Persian fleet off Cape Mycale. The Ionians now revolted and the Greek fleet under *Pausanias (1) captured Byzantium. The Athenians under Xanthippus, father of Pericles, captured Sestos (478 BC) and at this point Herodotus ended his story. But *Athens organized the Delian League and carried the war into Cyprus and Egypt, and it was only in 449 BC that an agreement was reached, known as the Peace of *Callias. Herodotus; A. R. Burns, *Persia and the Greeks,* 1962; C. Hignett, *Xerxes' Invasion of Greece,* 1963.

PERSIUS FLACCUS, Aulus Latin poet (AD 34–62), of an equestrian family from Volaterrae in Etruria, was a pupil of the Stoic *Cornutus who published his poems after his death. These are in a book of six satires written in hexameter with a preface in scazons; in these P. followed *Lucilius and *Horace. Satire 1 is an attack on the unrealistic, fashionable poetry of his day; Satire 2 is a derisory attack on prayers; Satire 3 is a clinical diagnosis

The imposing rock-cut façade of a Nabataean tomb on the approach to Petra

peror to choose the right pleasures. But he fell victim to the intrigues of the praetorian prefect Tigellinus and was compelled to commit suicide. Unlike others, he did not lose his spirit — he sent a letter to Nero with a full account of his debauches and he destroyed a vase that the Emperor coveted.

P. the courtier is probably identical with the author of the *Satyricon*, a unique novel based on the adventures of the disreputable Encolpius, Ascyltus, and the boy Giton. The adventures, narrated by Encolpius, took place in Campania and in southern Italy. Of the 16 books only fragments of Books 15 and 16 have survived. The narrator takes us to the world of the low classes, to the taverns frequented by rich freedmen. The work is in prose interspersed with occasional verses and colloquial language and slang is used — it is one of the rare works of this kind in extant Latin literature. Of the extant books the main section is the *Cena Trimalchionis* (Trimalchio's Feast). It gives a splendid description of the type of character that Trimalchio was: a vulgar, extravagant, pretentious, multimillionaire freedman. The fragments also include poems on the Fall of Troy and the Civil War. It has been suggested that the novel is a parody of the romantic Greek novels or (according to another view) of the wanderings of Odysseus. Also extant is a collection of poems of P.
M. Heseltine (Loeb), 1913; J. Sullivan (tran. Penguin), J. P. Sullivan, *The 'Satyricun' of Petronius,* 1968.

PHAEDRA Greek mythological heroine, daughter of *Minos and Pasiphaë, and sister of *Adriadne. She married Theseus and became the step-mother of his grown-up son *Hippolytus, with whom she fell in love. But Hippolytus rejected her and in revenge she accused him before Theseus of attempting to seduce her. This led to his death and she hanged herself. The myth is the subject of Euripides' *Hippolytus* and of Seneca's *Phaedra.*

PHAEDRUS Latin fabulist, born in Macedonia *c.* 10 BC, came as a slave to Rome and was set free by Augustus. Of his fables, five books of verse fables and probably thirty more fables in prose are extant. P.'s tales follow the model of *Aesop. He was the first to use this genre in Latin. In his animal tales, P. sought to amuse his readers. He was also a moralizer, didactic, and he occasionally included satyrical pieces on the politics and society of his time. In this way he enraged Sejanus and was punished in some way. Little known in his day, his reputation rose later. *Romulus,* the prose version of his fables that was written during the later Roman Empire, was very popular in the Middle Ages.
Text and translation: B. E. Perry (Loeb), 1965.

PHAETON The legendary son of *Helios and Clymene who asked his father if he could drive the chariot of the sun for a day. But he was too weak to restrain the immortal horses and Zeus killed him with a thunderbolt to prevent the world from being set on fire by the horses. P. fell in the river Eridamus and his sisters turned into amber-dropping trees from excessive mourning. The myth was told by Euripides in his *Phaeton* and it is recounted with details by Ovid (*Met.* 1.750ff.).

PHALANX The infantry section of the Greek army which was arranged to do battle in a solid body. The soldiers were drawn in lines usually eight deep. It was difficult but of vital importance to keep the lines unbroken during a charge. Gaps in the lines were dangerous. The strength of the P. was in its compactness and shocking power; but it was inflexible, not suited to uneven terrain and, if outflanked, it could be easily routed. The

Macedonian P. under *Philip II and Alexander was far superior to the Greek P. The soldiers were equipped with a longer pike (*sarissa*), were given thorough training and were organized in subdivisions. It was somewhat flexible, and with the support of lightly armed soldiers and the excellent Macedonian cavalry, it was not easily outflanked and could thus fight freely. The armies of the Hellenistic kingdoms did not reach this standard and proved inferior to the Roman *legion.
F. E. Adcock, *The Greek and Macedonian Art of War,* 1957.

PHALARIS Tyrant of *Acragas (*c.* 570–554 BC), renowned for his cruelty. He had a hollow bull made of bronze in which he roasted his victims alive. He succeeded in securing his city against the local Sicans but was finally overthrown. The *Letters of Phalaris* were in fact written in the 2nd century AD, as was shown by R. Bentley.

PHARSALUS Important city in southern Thessaly near *Achaea Phtiotis which it controlled for long periods. Parts of the city walls are still in existence. In the early 4th century BC the city came under the control of the tyrants of *Pherae, and thereafter it was not able to retain its control of Achaea Phtiotis. P. supported *Philip II of Macedonia and its cavalry served with Alexander the Great in Asia. In this period it recovered its prosperity but it suffered much as a result of its participation in the Lamian War. In the 3rd century it belonged to the *Aetolian League. P. is especially famous for the great battle fought near it between Caesar and Pompey (9 August 48 BC) and *Lucan's poem on the Civil War is commonly called *Pharsalia.*

PHASELIS Greek coastal city in east Lycia; founded by Rhodes in 690 BC, probably on a Phoenician site. Thanks to its good harbour, the city prospered and took part in the foundation of the Greek emporium at *Naucratis. It became subject to Persia with the conquests of *Cyrus I, and after the victory of *Cimon at Eurymedon (468 BC) joined the Delian League (it was the easternmost city of the League). It was still independent in the 4th century BC, but it became subject to foreign rulers in the Hellenistic period.
G. E. Bean, *Turkey's Southern Shore,* 1968.

PHEIDON Son of Aristodamidas, king of Argos, who probably lived in the first half of the 7th century BC though the evidence for this date is unsatisfactory. Herodotus knew him as a tyrant (6.127). P. was probably the first to strike coins in Greece, and is said to have dedicated to Hera the spits which were formerly used as means of exchange. He presided over the Olympian games and seems to have extended his rule in the Peloponnesus.
A. Andrews, *The Greek Tyrants,* 1956.

PHERAE Important Thessalian city situated in the southern plain with fertile land. P. benefited from its control of *Pagassae, the only port city of importance in Thessaly through which Thessaly exported its products, notably corn. In the first half of the 4th century the tyrants of P. (*Lycophron, *Jason (2), *Alexander (1)) dominated Thessaly. But *Philip II occupied P. and made Pagassae independent of her, and thereafter it lost its importance.

PHERECRATES Athenian comic playwright, active in the second half of the 5th century BC. He won victories in the *Dionysia and the *Lenaea and of his plays 19 titles and numerous fragments are known. The fragments show his inventive powers and adaptation of old material; thus in his *Miners* the world of Hades appears as a world of plenty.

PHIDIAS Leading Athenian sculptor, son of Charmides, born in the early 5th century BC. P.'s first works were paintings, but sculpture became his main occupation. He worked mainly in bronze, ivory and gold and all his great works were statues of deities. He made a colossal statue of Athena Areia for Plataea and a group for Delphi. His two great works were the colossal cult statues of Zeus· in *Olympia and of Athena Parthenos for the *Parthenon, both made of gold and ivory. The first depicted Zeus seated and was very famous all over the Graeco-Roman world, but there are no copies or representations of it. Of the second there are Roman copies. Another famous statue was the Athena Promachos, a colossal statue, approximately 30 feet high, which stood on the Acropolis. It could be seen, we are told, from as far as Sunium. A smaller statue was the Athena Lemnia. P. was appointed by Pericles to plan and supervise the public building on the Acropolis. He was thus responsible for the construction of such buildings as the *Parthenon and the *Propylaea. The extant remains of the sculptures of the Parthenon, for the designs of which he was certainly responsible, are a testimony to his grand and yet simple style.

P. was accused of embezzling gold in 432, an indirect attack against Pericles, and he died soon afterwards.

PHILEMON Greek comic playwright, native of Syracuse or Soli in Cilicia, born c. 363 BC, died c. 262 BC, aged about 100 years old. He became a citizen of Athens where he lived for a long time. He was highly esteemed during his lifetime and later he was considered second only to *Menander. Of the almost one hundred comedies which he wrote, and he was active to the end of his life, about 64 titles are known. His first victory at the Dionysia was in 327 BC, and he often came first, ahead of Menander. In addition to the large number of fragments, several of P.'s plays are also known from their Latin adaptation by *Plautus: *Mercator* (from *Emporos*), *Trinummus* (from *Thesauros*) and *Mostellaria* (probably from *Phasma*). Except for the *Myrmidones* and *Palamedes*, which seem to have been mythological, comic plays, the setting of the plays was contemporary with the usual themes and characters of the New *Comedy. Though P. was less esteemed later than during his lifetime, he was still noted for his wit, realistic characters, apt maxims and carefully planned plays (Apul. *Florida* 16).

Edmonds, *Fr. At. Com.*; Webster, *Lat. Gr. Com.*, 125ff.

PHILEMON and BAUCIS The tale of this mythological couple from Phrygia is told by Ovid (*Met.* 620ff.). P. and his wife B. were the only ones who gave hospitality to the wandering Zeus and Hermes. The gods punished their neighbours by sending a flood but P. and B. were forewarned to leave the place, became priest and priestess in a magnificent temple and were then transformed into trees.

PHILETAERUS Son of the Macedonian Attalus and a Phaphlagonian mother, the founder of the Attalid kingdom of Pergamum. He was appointed commander of Pergamum by *Lysimachus; his special business there was to guard the huge treasure of 9,000 talents. P. transferred his allegiance to *Seleucus I just in time (282 BC) before the downfall of his master, and remained nominally under Seleucid rule until his death (263 BC). He succeeded in defending his territory against the Galatians, and helped Greek cities. Himself an eunuch, he was succeeded by his nephew *Eumenes I whom he had adopted. His portrait on the coins of his successors is one of the best of the Hellenistic coin portraits.

Hansen, *Attalids²*; C. M. Kraay, *Greek Coins,* 1966 (737—9).

PHILETAS Greek scholar and poet, active in Cos in the early 3rd century BC. Among his pupils were the future King *Ptolemy II Philadelphus and the scholar *Zenodotus. A bronze statue was erected in his honour by the Coans, and he had considerable influence on the Alexandrian poets and Latin poets who followed them; for Theocritus he was the master (7.40). But only fragments of his writings survive. His *Miscellanea*, a sort of a lexicon of unusual words, won great success, and his reputation as an elegist and epigrammatist ran high. It was the combination of mythological learning and finished poetry that made him a forerunner of the Alexandrian poets.

PHILIP (1) (Philippus) II Son of *Amyntas (1) III, king of Macedonia (359—336 BC). Born c. 382 BC, he was held hostage during his youth in Thebes (368—365 BC), where he was able to learn the new tactics of *Epaminondas. As regent after the death of his brother Perdiccas (359 BC), he skilfully eliminated pretenders, defeated the Illyrians and the Paeonians and subsequently took the royal title. He captured *Amphipolis in 357 BC and, in the following year, Pydna and Potidaea, in each case forming an alliance, respectively, with Athens and the Chalcidian League so as to have war only on "one front". In 356 BC he also defeated an Illyrian—Thracian coalition which was supported by Athens. This gave him control of Mount *Pangaeus, and a yearly income of 1,000 talents from its mines. He now extended his power to Greece, took control of Thessaly, defeated the Phocian *Onomarchus (in 352 BC, after initial reverses) and made *Pagassae a Macedonian base. He was able to further his influence in Illyria and Thrace at the same time, and by 348 BC also concluded the conquest of *Chalcidice with the sack of *Olynthus (348 BC) — the Athenians, as was usual in their dealings with P., arrived too late to save this city. He now consolidated his power in central Greece by subduing *Phocis and making the Peace of *Philocrates with Athens (346 BC). He became archon of Thessaly for life, and busied himself extending his power in Thrace, but he failed to take *Perinthus. And in the meantime *Demosthenes' (2) activities led to a final test of power. P. then won a crushing victory over Athens and Thebes at *Chaeronea (338 BC). He now organized a Hellenic League, the so-called League of Corinth, whose Hegemon he was elected, and he began preparations for the expedition against Persia — a mission *Isocrates called him to take to relieve Greece from its social, economic and political problems. But while still engaged in these preparations he was murdered at the wedding of his daughter (336 BC).

A cunning diplomat, a great organizer, and an able general, P. made Macedonia the strongest power of his time. He put down the separatist tendencies of the dynasts of the Macedonian cantons. By training, new tactics and new organization he made the Macedonian *phalanx the most efficient army. He fostered agriculture, trade, and urbanization. It was this new Macedonia which he left that was capable of providing the means by which his son and successor Alexander conquered Persia.

P. Green, *Alexander of Macedon,* 1970, Chs. 1—3;·
S. Perlman, *Philip and Athens,* 1974.

PHILIP (2).V Son of *Demetrius (2) II, born in 239 BC, was adopted by *Antigonus (3) III Doson and became king of Macedonia on the latter's death in 221. As Hegemon of the Hellenic League, he successfully waged war against Aetolia, Sparta and Elis (Social War, 220—217 BC). He received Messenia into the League, conquered Elis and defeated the Dardanians. In 218 BC he put his powerful minister Apelles to death and in 217 concluded the Peace of Naupactus with the Aetolians. Disturbed by the Roman intervention in Illyria, he concluded a treaty with *Hannibal in 215 BC, but in the First Macedonian War, the Romans, allied with *Aetolia, were able to check him (215–205 BC). After the withdrawal of the Roman army he concluded a peace with Aetolia and in 205 BC one with Rome (Peace of Phoenice). After the death of *Ptolemy IV, he made an agreement with *Antiochus III to divide the Ptolemaic territories so that Thrace, the Aegean islands and west Asia Minor were to be his share. When he applied brutal force to take possession of his share, he encountered the opposition of Rhodes and Pergamum, and suffered a naval defeat (201 BC). The Roman Senate, instigated by Attalus I and Rhodes, initiated a new war against him, the Second Macedonian War (200–197 BC). After long diplomatic and military manoeuvres, P. lost the decisive Battle of Cynoscephalae in Thessaly (197 BC), in which the Roman legion proved superior to the Macedonian phalanx. In the settlement which followed, and which was partly announced at the Isthmian games in 196 BC, the Greek cities became free, and P. had to evacuate Greece and Asia Minor, pay a war indemnity of 1,000 talents, and give hostages (including his son, Demetrius). In the following years, P. loyally supported Rome against *Nabis, the Aetolians and Antiochus III. For this support he got his son back and was given some compensation in Thrace as well as a remittance of part of the indemnity. He now concentrated on the development of Macedonian resources, improved the country's finances, fostered the growth of the population and amassed supplies. He also carried out military campaigns against the Thracians (184, 183, 181 BC) to consolidate his power in the Balkan peninsula. Induced by his elder son *Perseus (2), he put the pro-Roman Demetrius to death (180). The following year he died in Amphipolis.

P. began his reign with spectacular military achievements, and he was always a good commander. But by his senseless brutality and occasional political blunders he lost his position in Greece and made it possible for Rome to interfere in Greek affairs. His administration of Macedonia in the last period of his reign showed that much could be achieved by concentrating on the natural resources of the country – however, a too strong Macedonia provoked a Roman reaction, and the last phase of the conflict came under P.'s son *Perseus (2).
F. W. Wallbank, *Philip V of Macedonia*, 1940.

PHILIP (3) the ARAB (M. Julius Verus Philippus) Roman emperor, native of Arabia, born c. AD 204. He was appointed praetorian prefect in AD 243 by *Gordian III, and ascended to the throne after inducing the soldiers to kill Gordian (244). P. ended the war against Persia (conducted since 242) with a peace treaty and returned to Rome to celebrate a triumph. In AD 247 he celebrated the Secular Games for the thousandth anniversary of Rome, but he faced serious troubles. There were pretenders to the throne in Mesopotamia and Syria and the Goths invaded Moesia. *Decius, the general P. sent to fight the Goths, became dangerous, and in a battle against him at Verona (September AD 249) P. was killed.

PHILIPPI Originally a Thracian settlement, this city on the plain northeast of Mount Pangaeus was established and renamed by *Philip II in 356 BC. It served as a centre for the exploitation of the rich mines in the district. P. is famous for the great battle that took place near it between *Brutus (2) and Cassius (3) against Octavian and M. *Antonius (4). The latter were victorious in two battles (October 42 BC), first against Cassius and then against Brutus. M. Antonius (4) founded a colony of veterans there, which was augmented with more veterans by Augustus after Actium; and still more veterans were settled there in the Flavian period. P. is also known as the first town in Europe with a Christian community founded by Paul.
P. Collart, *Philippes*, 1937.

PHILIPPUS (1), Q. Marcius Roman statesman in the first half of the 2nd century BC. He is known for two of his deeds: the suppression of the Bacchanalian worshippers in 186 BC when he was consul (see *Bacchus) and the diplomatic negotiations with *Perseus (2) before the Third Macedonian War. During the negotiations he gained time by unscrupulous diplomatic manoeuvres, the *nova sapientia* which was said to be contrary to the traditional, honest Roman diplomacy. He was censor in 164 BC.
Scullard, *Rom. Pol.*[2] (s.v.); J. Briscoe, *JRS*, 1964, 66ff.

PHILIPPUS (2), L. Marcius An astute Roman statesman of the first quarter of the 1st century BC. As consul in 91, he opposed the programme of Livius *Drusus (2) and succeeded in invalidating his laws. He was censor (86 BC) under *Cinna (1), but when *Sulla returned to Italy he followed him and became the leading figure in the Senate in the early 70s BC. It was because of him that Pompey received the command against Sertorius.
J. Van Ooteghem, *Lucius Marcius Philippus*, 1961.

PHILISTION Of Locri, a physician, apparently during the 4th century BC, famous in his time. He adopted the theory of *Empedocles concerning the four elements and regarded hot, cold, moist, and dry as corresponding to fire, air, water, and earth. He laid emphasis on the importance of breathing which, he believed, cooled the innate heat. He presumably influenced Plato in the *Timaeus*.

PHILISTUS Historian and statesman in Syracuse (c. 430–356 BC). He helped *Dionysius I to establish his tyranny, and became his chief minister and the governor of the city. But on some occasion (? /386 BC) he enraged the tyrant and was expelled, to return only under *Dionysius II. He served his new master well and played an important part in the banishment of *Dion. As commander of the fleet he failed against Dion (357 BC) and died in battle or committed suicide. P.'s *History of Sicily* (*Sikelika*) probably consisted of 13 books. The first seven books covered the period from early times to the sacking of Acragas in 406 BC, the last ones concentrated on the reign of Dionysius I. P.'s work was extensively used by later historians (notably Ephorus, Timaeus) and he was compared to Thucydides; he is only known from citations in later works.
Jacoby, *Fr. Gr. Hist.*, 3 B 556.

PHILOCHORUS Son of Cycnus, of Athens, lived c. 340–260 BC. He held religious offices ("prophet and victim inspector" – *mantis kai hieroskopos*), wrote extensively and is the most prominent of the atthidographers (*Atthis). His most important work was the *Atthis* in seventeen books. It covered the whole history of Athens but concentrated on the history of P.'s own time, ending in 261 BC. The work is known only from citations (altogether some 230 fragments) by later writers who were mainly interested in the earlier parts of it. Its subjects included constitutional, religious and cultural matters.
Jacoby, *Fr. Gr. Hist.*, iiiB 328.

PHILOCRATES Athenian statesman, mainly known for the peace he arranged with *Philip II in 346 BC, the Peace of P. He was a member of the ten member embassy (including Demosthenes and Aeschines) which went to negotiate the peace with Philip and succeeded in passing the motion for the acceptance of the treaty, helped by Demosthenes. After a second mission, he was also responsible for the proposal to proceed with the implementation of the alliance. In 343 BC he prudently left Athens when prosecuted for accepting bribes in the peace negotiations, and was condemned to death *in absentia*.

PHILOCTETES Greek mythological hero, companion of Heracles who left his bow and arrows to P. before he died. This is known from post-Homeric writers. In Homer, he leads seven ships to the Trojan War, but is left behind on the island of Lemnos after a snake bites him (*Il.* 718ff.), and later returns home (*Od.* 3.190). In the full story he remained on the island for ten years and then *Odysseus, *Diomedes and *Neoptolemus came to take him to Troy as the Greeks discovered that only with his help could the city be captured. On his arrival at the Greek camp he was cured by Machaon and he killed *Paris with his arrows. Aeschylus, Euripides and Sophocles wrote tragedies on the subject but only the *Philoctetes* of Sophocles survives.

PHILODEMUS Of Gadara, Epicurean philosopher and epigrammatist (*c.* 110–*c.* 40/35 BC). He came to Rome in the 70s BC and won the support and friendship of *Piso (2). Many papyri rolls with fragments of his writings were discovered in a magnificent villa (probably of Piso) which was excavated at Herculaneum in the mid-18th century (with numerous statues). P. gained influence in Roman upper society to which he expounded Greek philosophy in his writings. For this purpose he composed an outline of the theories of the Greek philosophers. He also wrote epigrams of which some thirty (not all of them genuine) are preserved in the Greek *Anthology. In these fine epigrams, erotic themes are dominant, which is quite appropriate for one known as *lascivus*.

PHILOMELA The mythological daughter of Pandion, king of Athens, whose sister Procne was married to the Thracian King Tereus. Tereus invited P. on some pretext and then raped her and cut her tongue out. She told the horrible story to her sister by weaving a piece of embroidery. The two sisters then killed Itys, son of Tereus and Procne, and gave his flesh to his father to eat. When he discovered what he had eaten Tereus pursued the women but by divine intervention he was transformed into a hoopoe, Procne a nightingale and P. a swallow (Ovid, *Met.* 6.424ff.) – but there were other versions in which the sisters reversed roles.

PHILON (1) Of Byzantium, follower of *Ctesibius, author of a book on mechanical works (*mechanike synataxis*). Of this, Book 4 and parts of Books 7 and 8 are extant in Greek as is an Arabic translation of Book 5. They deal with war catapults (and some have been reconstructed and could be operated), pneumatic works and works employed in sieges.
A. G. Drachmann, *Ktesibios, Philon and Heron,* 1948.

PHILON (2) Of Larissa. Pupil and successor (109 BC) of *Clitomachus as Head of the *Academy. He escaped to Rome in 88 BC on account of the First Mithridatic War. He does not seem to have returned and by 80 BC he was probably dead. P. won much success in Rome and his most loyal pupil was Cicero who expounds P.'s views in his own philosophical writings (*Acad. Pr.; Lucullus*). P. followed the sceptical doctrines of *Arcesilaus as modified by *Carneades, that is, the impossibility of attaining knowledge about which one can be certain. P. was the last Head of the Academy to take this position. His successor as Head, *Antiochus of Ascalon, revolted against it.

PHILON (3) Of Alexandria (Philo Judaeus) *c.* 30/15 BC–*c.* AD 45. Greek-Jewish philosopher and writer, of a wealthy and influential Jewish family; his nephew *Tiberius Julius Alexander was later prefect of Egypt. Biographical details of P. are scanty and various dates have been suggested for his birth. He evidently received a good Greek education (Greek was his mother language and he does not seem to have known Hebrew). In AD 39 he went to Rome on a mission to ask *Caligula to exempt the Jews from the obligation to join the emperor cult. He failed, but the request was later granted by the Emperor Claudius. P. described his experiences in the *Embassy to Gaius.* But this is almost the only episode known from P.'s life.

P. wrote many works, large parts of which are extant. He dealt with ethics, metaphysics, theology, commentaries to the Bible, and apologetic works. In the *Embassy to Gaius* and *Against Flaccus* (who was a prefect of Egypt) he argues that God eventually punished the persecutors who, by their own deeds, bring about the reaction. Another apologetic work is the *Life of Moses* in which Moses is described as an ideal ruler and legislator. In his *On the Contemplative Life* he gives an account of the Therapeutae, a Jewish sect which was associated with the Essenes. Generally, what P. tried to do was to present the Jewish traditional teachings in terms and conceptions taken from Greek philosophy. In this he was influenced by various Greek philosophers and systems, including Plato, the Stoics, and *Posidonius. In his theology he introduced intermediaries between the world of God and the world of man, the most important of which is the *Logos* (Word, *Dabar* in Hebrew). By this separation of the two worlds, P. was able to account for disturbing phenomena on earth. His doctrines had great influence both on the neo-Platonists and Christian writers, and this influence lasted until the Middle Ages.
F. H. Colson – G. H. Whitaker (Loeb), 1932–62;
E. R. Goodenough, *An Introduction to Philo Judaeus,* 1962; H. A. Wolfson, *Philo* ², 1948.

PHILOPAPPUS (C. Julius Antiochus Epiphanes Philopappus) Grandson of King Antiochus IV of Commagene; he was an Athenian archon, and Roman consul (AD 109). P. is mainly known for his sepulchral monument in Athens, on the Museum Hill, which is now called after him. This monument, built in AD 114/6, contains the statues of P. and his ancestors.
C. C. Vermeule, *Roman Imperial Art in Greece,* 1968, 80ff.

PHILOPOEMEN Son of Kraugis, native of Megalopolis, Achaean general and statesman (253–182 BC). P. fought with distinction against *Cleomenes III when he attacked Megalopolis (223 BC) and again at the battle of Selassia. He spent ten years as a mercenary soldier in Crete but returned and became general of the Achaean League in 208/207 BC. He trained the army in the Macedonian fashion and won a victory at Mantinea over the Spartan army whose commander he himself killed. He was general of the League on several occasions but he left for Crete during the Second Macedonian War when his line to keep neutrality was not followed. He returned, became general several more times, annexed Sparta to the League and then Messene and Elis. In 182 BC he was captured by the Messenians and was forced to take poison.

P. sought to expand the power of the Achaean League all over the Peloponnesus and to make it independent of all foreign powers. To some extent he achieved this aim, but soon it became dangerous to create too strong a power, which would only provoke Roman suspicion. P. was "the last of the Greeks" according to Plutarch (*Philop.* 17).

Plut., *Philop.*; R. M. Errington, *Philopoemen*, 1968.

PHILOSTRATUS The name of a family of Sophists and writers from Lemnos during the 2nd and 3rd centuries AD. To distinguish between the members of the family and to assign the extant writings to each of them correctly was a vexed question and difficulties still exist. But the following four members are known quite well:

(1) P. Verus, a Sophist who wrote in the 2nd century AD.
(2) Flavius P., born *c.* AD 175, died under Philip the Arab (AD 244–9). He was a member of the philosophical circle of *Julia Domna, wife of Septimius *Severus. At the initiative of the empress, P. wrote the *Life of Apollonius of Tyana* in eight books and *The Lives of the Sophists* in two books. He probably wrote other works.
(3) P. of Lemnos, born *c.* AD 190, son-in-law of the former, wrote the *Eikones*, a description of pictures kept in a collection at Naples.
(4) P. IV, grandson of the former, who wrote further *Eikones*.

F. C. Conybeare, *Life of Apollonius* (Loeb), 1912;
C. C. Wright, *Life of the Sophists* (Loeb), 1922;
A. Fairbanks, *Eikones* (Loeb), 1931.

PHILOTAS Son of *Parmenion, *c.* 360–330 BC. He was commander of the Guards Corps in the expedition of Alexander against Persia and distinguished himself as cavalry commander, but the king came to distrust him. The causes of the estrangement are not sufficiently clear; presumably, P. opposed the policy of Alexander towards the subject peoples. When Alexander discovered that P. did not warn him of a conspiracy, he accused him in front of the army (after torture). P. was found guilty and executed. Alexander then sent men to execute his father Parmenion, without trial.

PHINEUS Mythological king of Thrace who suffered from the *Harpies. This was a punishment for letting his second wife blind his children by his first wife who was the daughter of *Boreas (but there were other versions to explain his punishment). When the *Argonauts got to him they saved him from the monsters and he told them how to reach *Colchis.

PHOCAEA Important Ionian city in the 7th–6th centuries BC, situated north of Smyrna. P. founded *Lampsacus and *Massalia and had a large share of the trade in the western Mediterranean, with many trading sites along the coasts. The Persian conquest of Asia Minor brought an abrupt end to the Phocaean prosperity. Most of the population preferred to leave the place and were received at Elea in southern Italy. The Phocaeans also suffered a naval defeat from the combined Carthaginian-Etruscan fleets off Alalia in Corsica (*c.* 535 BC). Thereafter, they did not play a major part in trade or politics.

J. M. Cook, *The Greeks in Ionia and the East*, 1962;
G. E. Bean, *Aegean Turkey*, 1966.

PHOCION Athenian statesman and general of the 4th century BC. P. was the most popular general in Athens; he was elected Strategos forty-five times (even more than Pericles). He began his military career under *Chabrias in 376 BC and by 365 was elected general for the first time. He deposed the tyrant of Eretria in 348 BC but was not able to save *Olynthus. He was successful against *Philip

II and his supporters on several occasions: he defended Megara (343 BC), drove out the tyrant of Eretria in 341 BC and in 339 helped Byzantium to repel Philip's attack. He also did mercenary service for Persia. But despite his reputation as a general, P. recognized the military superiority of Macedonia and in politics joined those who advocated a policy of cooperation with Philip, thus acting with *Aeschines and *Eubulus. After the battle of Chaeronea, P. helped in the negotiations with Philip and in the following years helped *Demades to maintain the peace. He opposed the Lamian War, but when the need came he succeeded in defending Attica. After the war he collaborated in establishing a limited democracy in Athens but failed to defend Piraeus which was captured by *Cassander. After the restoration of the democracy (318 BC) he was condemned to death for high treason. But by the next year he was honoured with a public funeral and a statue.

Plut., *Phocion.*

PHOCYLIDES Greek poet of the 6th century BC, native of Miletus. He used hexameters and occasionally elegiacs in his poems. His poems are noted for their maxims, and begin with "Also this is by Phocylides" . . . For him virtue is righteousness and nobility by itself has no value.

Diehl, *Ant. Lyr. Gr.*, 1.

PHOEBE ("Bright") In Greek mythology, the Titaness daughter of Uranus and Gaea (Sky and Earth), mother of Leto (Hesiod *Theog.* 136 and 404ff.). Apollo/Phoebus and Artemis were therefore her grandchildren. Her name signifies the Moon and it was also used for her granddaughter.

PHOENIX (1) In mythology, son of *Agenor, who, like his brother *Cadmus, went to find their sister *Europa but never came back. He was the eponymous ancestor of the Phoenicians.

PHOENIX (2) The mythological son of King Amyntor who seduced the concubine of his father at the instigation of his mother. P. escaped but his father cursed him to be childless. He was received hospitably by *Peleus, became the tutor and counsellor of Achilles and went with him to Troy (Homer, *Il.* 9.447ff.).

PHOENIX (3) The legendary bird which was worshipped at Heliopolis in Egypt, as is told by Herodotus (2.73). Every 500 years, the P. died on a funeral pile and then it came alive. Herodotus says that he saw a figure of the bird with red golden feathers. Tacitus tells that the P. appeared in Egypt in AD 34 (*Ann.* 6.28), but this was not 500 hundred years after its former appearance. In poetry, the cycle was increased to 1,000 years. The myth of the P. is the theme of an elegiac poem by *Lactantius (*Phoenix*) in which it is treated as a symbol for the resurrection of Christ. The P. appears in many works of art.

R. Van den Broeck, *The Myth of the Phoenix*, 1972.

PHORMION Athenian general, contemporary of Pericles. He took part in the war against Samos (440/439 BC) and in 432 BC fought in Acarnania and did good service in Chalcidice. His greatest achievements were the two naval victories over two superior fleets of Sparta and her allies, which enabled him to secure Acarnania for Athens (Tuc. 2.81 and 83). He is not mentioned again after 428 BC.

V. Ehrenberg, *AJP*, 1945, 113ff.

PHOTIUS The most learned Byzantine scholar and patriarch of Constantinople (AD 858–67, 877–86). It is his *Bibliotheca* that makes him so important for the Classical student. It gives an account of some 280 works that P.

read, and it deals with a wide variety of subjects, such as medicine, lexicography and oratory, but mainly with history and theology. P. also gives extracts from the works he read and thus he is the sole, or the important, source of historians and other writers whose works have not survived, notably *Ctesias, Memnon (see *Heraclea Pontica), *Agatharchides, *Diodorus Siculus and *Arrian. Extant also is his *Lexicon*.

Text and French translation of the *Bibliotheca* by R. Henry, 1959–

PHRAATES IV King of Parthia who ascended to the throne after killing his father *Orodes II (c. 38 BC). He successfully repelled the attack of M. *Antonius (4) in 36 BC but in 20 BC reached an agreement with Augustus and returned the standards and the prisoners who were captured from *Crassus (4) and Antonius. His murder was contrived by the intrigues of his wife and his son (2 BC).

PHRATRIA (pl. phratriai) Old social groups, based on kinship, of Greeks and other Indo-European peoples. The P. ("brotherhood") consisted of several families (*Genos) and was a subdivision of the tribe (*phyle*). In Athens there were three P. to each of the four tribes (before the reforms of *Cliesthenes (2)). Theoretically, the members of a P. were the descendants of a common ancestor and only the sons of a member could themselves become members. This was probably true in remote times, but with the growth of free society, outside members could enter the P. In old times, the membership of a P. was the only criterion for being a citizen, and hence the *phrateres* formed the citizen-body of the state. In Athens, *Cleisthenes (2) made citizenshp dependent on deme-membership (see *Demoi), but he did not abolish the organization of the P. In old times, the members of a P. lived in the same vicinity and this locality remained its centre even when, owing to changing conditions, the members scattered over the country. The P. had its own institutions and regulations, with annual meetings and common property. Each P. had a cult of its divine protectors, normally including Zeus Phratrios. Although the P. survived in one form or other in some places until Roman times, they declined in the Hellenistic period.

A. Andrewes, *Hermes*, 1961, 129ff.;
Hignett, *Athen. Const.* (s.v.).

PHRYGIA In northwest Asia Minor, the country of the Phryges, who — according to Herodotus (7.43) — came from Macedonia and Thrace. They are probably referred to in Assyrian records as Mushki; Mita is probably identical with the Greek *Midas (2). The original territory was very great, but, with the coming of the Mysians (*Mysia), and the Bithynians, and the rise of the kings of *Lydia in the 7th century BC, it was reduced. In the 8th century BC, P. was the greatest power in Asia Minor under the reign of Midas who made Gordium his capital. It was also the prosperous period of the material culture of P., from which date monumental buildings and ivory and bronze works. It was in this period that writing began. But the Phrygian kingdom collapsed under the attacks of the Cimmerians in the early 7th century BC and the growth of the Lydian kingdom prevented any chances of recovery. For the Greeks, P. was known as a barbaric country with a slave population. The Phrygian musical mode was a violent one; Phrygian was a synonym for slave, and from P. came ecstatic cults.

W. M. Ramsay, *Cities and Bishoprics of Phrygia*, 1895–7;
T. J. Dunbabin, *The Greeks and their Eastern Neighbours*, 1957.

PHRYNICHUS Athenian tragic poet, predecessor of Aeschylus, said to have been a pupil of *Thespis. He won his first victory at the dramatic competitions c. 511 BC. In c. 492 he produced the *Capture of Miletus*. This dealt with the destruction of *Miletus by the Persians two years earlier. The performance provoked such profound emotions that the Athenian spectators burst into lamentation. We are told by Herodotus that P. was fined 1,000 drachms for his too vivid reminder of the disaster that befell Athens's ally, and that the play was forbidden to be staged again (6.21). P. produced another historical tragedy in 476 BC, the *Phoenician Women* (on the then recent Persian defeat), with Themistocles as *Choregos*. His other tragedies dealt with mythological subjects, including the *Aegyptii, Antaeus, Alcestis*, and *Danaids*. P. was known as the first to introduce female characters and to use the tetrameter. His fame rested on the sweetness of his lyrics and the wide variety of the dances he invented, and he was considered one of the founders of the Attic tragedy. Only fragments of his works are known. He died c.470 BC.
Pickard-Cambridge, *Dithyramb²*, 63ff.

PHRYNICHUS ARABIUS Lexicographer and rhetorician of the 2nd century AD, native of Bithynia, rival of *Pollux. He dedicated his *Sophistike Paraskeue*, a collection of terms with examples, to Commodus. This work in 37 books is known only through *Photius and from fragments. In his *Atticestes*, a selection of Attic words and terms, he took an extreme attitude as to which words were correct Attic words. He based it on such prose writers as Thucydides, Plato, the Ten Orators and the poetry of Aeschylus, Euripides, Sophocles and Aristophanes; Menander's usage, for instance, he rejected. There is an abridgement of this work (*Ecloge*).

G. W. Bowersock, *Greek Sophists in the Roman Empire*, 1969, 571f.

PHYLARCHUS Athenian historian of the 3rd century BC whose work, *Historiae*, covered the period 272–220/219 BC, that is, from the death of Pyrrhus to the death of *Cleomenes III. Only fragments of the work are known, mainly preserved by Athenaeus. P. used *Duris (2) of Samos and like him he wrote sensational-emotional history. It appears that he dealt with the entire Hellenistic world. As an historian, he was criticized by Polybius, and Dionysius of Halicarnassus criticized him for his style. He was the main source for Plutarch's *Lives of Agis and Cleomenes* — and he was also used for the *Lives of Pyrrhus and Aratus*.

T. W. Africa, *Phylarchus and the Spartan Revolution*, 1961.

PHYLE (pl. phylai) This term ("tribe") was used by the Greeks to denote both the older, large ethnic groups, subdivisions of the Ionians and Dorians, which were based on supposed ties of kinship, and the later main divisions of the citizen-body of a state, often artificial units. The four Ionian (Geleontes, Hopletes, Aegadeis, and Aigikoreis) and the three Dorian P. (Hylleis, Pamphyloi, and Dymanes) were to be found respectively in many Ionian and Dorian cities in historic times. But where the Greek invaders did not eliminate the former population, the latter tended to organize themselves into tribes of their own (for instance at *Sicyon). And when Greeks founded a new city (*Apoikia), the tribal organization of the mother-city was introduced there; since, however, the population sometimes came from different cities, a new organization had to be established. Normally, P. consisted of several *phratriai*. The P. and the *phratriai* were the basis of the aristocracy and as long as the aristocratic form of government persisted, the P. formed the military and administrative division of the state. At Sparta in the 6th century BC five territorial tribes became the main divisions of the state, each contributing a regiment (lochos); and there were five *ephors. At Athens, ten territorial tribes replaced the ethnical ones after the reforms of *Cleisthenes (2). Hence the *Boule was composed of 500 members, fifty (*prytaneis) to each tribe, and there were many boards of ten members, probably one to each tribe (notably *Archontes, *Strategoi); and the army consisted of ten infantry and ten cavalry units – one of each to each tribe. Even in the dramatic contests of the choruses, each P. contributed one chorus.

Hignett, *Athen. Const.* (s.v.);
C. Roebuck, *TAPA*, 1961, 497ff.

PIAZZA ARMERINA This small town in east-central Sicily is known for the extensive remains of a Roman villa of the 4th century AD which were discovered a few km from it. They present some of the best examples of Roman mosaics. Whoever owned this villa must have been very rich, and according to one view it was the residence of *Maximian.

M. Guido, *Sicily, An Archaeological Guide*, 1967.

PICENUM The eastern region of central Italy stretching from the river Aternus in the south to the Aesis in the north. The Picentes (*Pikentinoi* in Greek) became allied to Rome in 299 BC, and were subdued in 268 BC. Rome founded here the Latin colonies Hadria and Firmum and the Roman colonies Castrum Novum, Potentia and Auximum. Other important cities were *Ancona and *Asculum. As a result of the *Bellum Sociale – which began at Asculum – P. received Roman citizenship. It was known for its wine, oil and fruits. Large estates apparently developed here by the 1st century BC and one of the great landlords was Pompey.

J. Whatmough, *The Foundations of Roman Italy*, 1937.

PINDAR Reputedly the greatest Greek lyric poet (518–438 BC), native of Cynoscepalae in Boeotia. He came from an aristocratic family, the Aegeidae (according to him), and moved in aristocratic society, cultivating relations with tyrants and kings. He first learnt the art of poetry and music at home and later was sent to Athens where he apparently had accomplished teachers. His first extant poem dates from 498 BC and it was written for a member of the aristocratic *Aleudae of Larissa in Thessaly. At about the same time he won a dithyramb competition. To tell the story of his life is to recount his relations with the various patrons he had. In 490 BC he wrote an ode (*Pyth.* 6) in honour of Xenocrates, the brother of the tyrant *Theron of Acragas. In the next few years he wrote poems for a member of the *Alcmaeonid family (*Ol.* 14 and *Pyth.* 7). Some time later he established his life-long connections with the Aeacidiae from Aegina, again a powerful and cultured family. He went to Sicily in 476–474 BC and celebrated the victory of *Hieron I of Syracuse in the Olympian horse-race (*Ol.* 1) as well as that of Theron in another chariot-race (*Ol.* 2). *Bacchylides and *Simonides too were at the court of Hieron at about the same time. Later, P. sent Hieron odes from Greece – thus *Pyth.* 1 was written in honour of Hieron's victory in the chariot-race of 470. P.'s reputation spread all over the Greek world and his poems were written for persons from various places, from citizens of Abdera to King Arcesilas of Cyrene (whom he perhaps visited). His last extant poem (*Pyth.* 8) was written in 446, and it

The warrior from Capestrano in Picenum. A unique statue of the 6th century BC

celebrates a victory won by a young Aeacid from Aegina.

The poems of P. were edited in 17 books by the ancient editors. They included various kinds of *lyric poetry: Hymns, Paeans (each one book), Dithyrambs, Processional-songs, Maiden-songs, Hyporchemata (each two books), one more Maiden-song book, Encomia, Dirges (each one book) and four books of Epinician poems. Of these the Epinician poems survive complete and in addition there is a considerable number of fragments of the Dithyrambs and Paeans. The fragments, partly known from papyri, show the same sublime style that characterizes the Epinicians.

The Epinicians contain 44 poems written in honour of victories in the four great pan-Hellenic games: Olympian, Pythian, Nemean and Isthmian. P. is very brief in his reference to the victory itself. He occasionally refers to former victories, the god in whose honour the games are celebrated, the charioteers etc. He obviously includes a laudatory piece on the victor, and his achievements, his family and his country. He almost always inserts a myth, briefly told, meditations on the victory, praises himself as a poet, praises poetry, and includes general religious and moral observations. Though the Epinician is occasioned by the victory of a man, for P. it is an occasion for celebrating and praising the gods. In victory, which is the achievement of a human being, a man for once excels and shows his virtue — which is a sign of some divine element in him. A religious man himself with a deep sense of morality, P. finds it fit to insert moralizing maxims in the poem; these are profound and skilfully interlaced with the poem. He often tells the myths for their moral lesson and hence he occasionally gives the versions of myths appropriate for his purpose. The poems vary in length; some are short and others quite long, some were written for recitation at the games, others at celebrations in the hometown of the victor. The poems are composed of strophes or triads with a strophe, an antistrophe and an epode. P. uses a great variety of metres; and each poem differs metrically from the others. P. is proud of his noble birth, and believes that he writes under divine inspiration; he considers himself the prophet of the Muses. For him a song gives light, which is divine. And P.'s poetry is bright, full of metaphors and similes and obliges the reader to use his imagination.

C. M. Bowra, *Pindari Carmina*[2], 1947;
R. Lattimore, *Pindar* (tran.), 1947;
C. M. Bowra, *Pindar*, 1964.

PIRAEUS Peninsula on the Attic coast 6 km south of Athens. Until the early 5th century BC, Athens used Phalerum, an open, ill protected area close to it as its harbour. It was Themistocles who understood the importance of P. as a naval base and started to fortify it when he was archon in 493/492 BC. The circumference of his walls was over 10 km (Thuc. 2.13). With the growth of Athenian sea power, for which Themistocles, too, was responsible, P. became a first-rate base for Athens' power. There were three natural harbours at P.: *Munichia, Zea and Kantharos. The last, on the west, was the largest — it became mainly a trade harbour and had quays, storage-houses and docks and other buildings. The first two were used by the Athenian navy, with arsenals and ship-houses for some 200 ships. The city of P. was planned by the famous architect *Hippodamus of Miletus (mid-5th century BC). It was connected to Athens by the *Long Walls. The growth of the Athenian Empire made P. a thriving centre, and its residents, finding their sub-

sistence from the maritime Athenian Empire, were the main supporters of the imperialistic policy of democratic Athens. The walls were destroyed by Sparta at the end of the *Peloponnesian War, but they were rebuilt by *Conon in 393 BC.
M. Amit, *Athens and the Sea*, 1965.

PIRITHOUS The mythological king of the *Lapiths, who is mentioned as early as Homer. He was the son of *Ixion, or more accurately of Zeus and Ixion's wife (*Il* 2.741; 14. 317f.). He was a close friend of *Theseus, and in fact most of the tales about him present him in the company of the latter. At his wedding with Hippodamia, the *Centaurs got drunk and tried to rape the bride and the Lapith women and a great battle ensued in which Theseus helped the Lapiths to win the day. P. took part in the war against the Amazons and helped Theseus to abduct *Hellen. Then they decided to descend to Hades to carry off Persephone for P., so that both of them would have daughters of Zeus as wives. But Hades caught them. Theseus escaped, or was set free by *Heracles, and P. remained to suffer.

PISIDIA Mountainous inland country in south-central Asia Minor, bounded by Phrygia in the north, Caria in the west and Pamphylia in the south. It was too backward and unimportant for the rulers of Asia Minor to subdue it. After the conquest of Alexander the Great it belonged to the Seleucids, and from 189 BC it belonged to Pergamum; in the early 1st century BC it was annexed to the Roman province of Cilicia. It was only under Augustus that P. was pacified and then it was included in the province of *Galatia. The main cities were Termessus, Sagalassus and Selge. Augustus established colonies for veterans here.
Magie, *Asia;* Jones, *Cities*[2];
B. Levick, *Roman Colonies in S. Asia Minor*, 1967.

PISISTRATUS The Athenian tyrant, of an aristocratic family, son of Hippocrates. Through his mother he was related to Solon. He was born in the early 6th century BC and distinguished himself in the war against Megara by conquering Nisaia (*c*. 565 BC). In politics, he became the leader of the Diakrioi, apparently the small landholders from northern Attica, and in 561 BC took control of the state after he was given a bodyguard by the Athenians themselves (Hdt. 1.59; Arist. *Athen. Pol.* 14). But after five years, the Paralioi (of the coast) and Pedieis (of the plain), with *Megacles and Lycurgus as leaders, regained power and P. went into exile. He returned after coming to an agreement with Megacles but was again forced to leave. He now amassed wealth at the mines of Mount Pangaeus, established ties with powerful men in Naxos, Thebes, Thessaly and Argos, and in 546 BC returned with mercenary troops. He was victorious against his enemies and retained his tyranny until his death in 527 BC.

P. was a benevolent ruler. He helped the small peasants and encouraged the extension of the areas under cultivation. Artisans were supported and under him the products from the Attic potteries dominated the markets of the Greek world. He also carried out building operations, notably the *Olympieum, Propylaea to the Acropolis and other temples. These must have given employment to many. P. introduced a tithe, and other taxes, issued coins, and thus was able to finance his public programmes. His foreign policy was not less successful. He retained his base in Macedonia at the Gulf of Thermus, won Sigeum in the Troad (important for the trade with the Black Sea) and kept his good ties with other rulers. He also succeeded in effecting the reconciliation of the aristocrats and did not change the constitutional reforms of Solon. In addition to all this, he helped the arts and literature. It was probably under him that a definitive edition of Homer was compiled; poets were invited to his court and the festivals of the *Panathenaea and *Dionysia were magnificently celebrated. He thus consolidated the foundation for the cultural superiority of Athens.

A. Andrewes, *The Greek Tyrants*, 1956.

PISO (1) FRUGI, Lucius Calpurnius Roman statesman and historian. As tribune in 149 BC he passed a law which established the first permanent jury court at Rome, used for cases of *Repetundae*, He was consul in 133 BC, the year Tiberius *Gracchus (2) was tribune, and censor in 120 BC. In his *Annales*, he dealt with the whole history of Rome from the very beginning to his own time. Unlike later annalists, he gave short accounts and so seven books were sufficient for him to reach the year 158 BC. He interpreted legends rationally and was much appreciated by later writers; but only fragments of his work have survived.

Peter, *Hist. Rom. Rel.* 1; Ogilvie, *Livy*, 14ff.

PISO (2) CAESONINUS, Lucius Calpurnius Roman statesman. Caesar married his daughter *Calpurnia, and P. became consul in 58 BC following Caesar's consulate. By cooperating with *Clodius Pulcher he received Macedonia as province, and, according to Cicero, he abused his authority to make profits (57–55 BC). He was censor in 50 BC and in the Civil War he refused to side with any of the contestants, not even with his son-in-law. P. was probably the owner of the magnificent villa at Herculaneum which was discovered in the mid-18th century, and contained a rich library. The fragments discovered there included prose writings by the Epicurean *Philodemus, who was P.'s friend.

Syme, *Rom. Rev.* (s.v.).

PISO (3), Lucius Roman senator, son of P. (2), born in 48 BC. P. was consul in 14 BC. Two years later he was sent to quell a revolt in Thrace and after three years he received the "triumphal ornaments". He later became the prefect of the city and retained this office until his death in AD 32. He was apparently a patron of artists and was known for his easy ways. But he was a good administrator and he was able to survive almost twenty years under Tiberius, which was quite a feat.

PISO (4), Gnaeus Calpurnius P. is known for his quarrel with *Germanicus. Tiberius gave P. the province of Syria shortly before the arrival of Germanicus in the East, probably so that P. should watch him. Relations between the two men deteriorated and Germanicus ordered P. to leave the province. When Germanicus died shortly afterwards (AD 19), his wife and friends accused P. of poisoning him, and many believed the story. P. was tried before the Senate but committed suicide before the end of the trial. Tacitus' account of this episode reflects the attempts to implicate Tiberius and Livia in the death of Germanicus, as if P. was responsible for it (which he was not) and carried out their instructions.

Syme, *Tacitus* (s.v.).

PISO (5), Gaius Calpurnius The head of the "Pisonian conspiracy" under Nero. He was of the highest nobility, but never showed much interest in a political career. P. was banished by Caligula but restored by the Emperor Claudius and was *consul suffectus*. He won a reputation for his oratory, and because of his popularity he was suspected of conspiracy as early as AD 62 (Tac. *Ann.* 14.65). When the conspiracy was revealed he committed suicide.

PITTACUS Statesman of Mytilene, born *c.* 650 BC. With the brothers of the poet *Alcaeus he removed the tyrant Melanchrus (612 BC) and distinguished himself in the war against Athens for Sigeum. After the death of the tyrant Mysilus, P. was elected Aesymnetes, that is arbitrator and sole ruler, for ten years. In this role he opposed the aristocrats, passed laws and succeeded in putting an end to civil strife. Ten years after resigning his powers, he died (*c.* 570 BC). P. was considered one of the Seven Sages of Greece.

PLANCUS, Lucius Munatius Roman statesman and soldier of the 1st century BC. He served under Caesar in Gaul and followed him in the Civil War. He was governor of Gaul in 44–43 BC, and founded the colonies *Lugdunum (Lion) and Raurica (August). In 43 BC he joined M. Antonius (4), deserting the cause of the Republic, contrary to his promises to Cicero. He was awarded a triumph and became consul of 42 BC. He lost his army to Octavian in the Perusine War (41 BC) and went to Greece to join Antonius in whose service he remained until 32 BC. He transferred his allegiance to Octavian before the war of Actium and returned to Italy. It was P. who proposed the title Augustus to Octavian in 27 BC. He was censor in 22 BC.

Syme, *Rom. Rev.* (s.v.).

PLATAEA Boeotian city close to Attica, mentioned in the Ship Catalogue of Homer (*Il.* 2.504). From the late 6th century BC, it was closely associated with Athens and opposed Thebes. It was the only Greek city whose soldiers fought with Athens at the battle of Marathon. P. was sacked by the Persians in 480 BC, and during the next year the land army of Xerxes, commanded by *Mardonius, was defeated near P. by the Greek army under *Pausanias (1). In the Peloponnesian War, the Thebans failed to capture P. (431 BC), which however was blockaded by Sparta. After a long siege (429–427 BC), it was captured and the defenders were put to death (but most of the population had been evacuated). The Plataeans were restored to their city in 386 BC.

PLATO The great Greek philosopher, son of Ariston and Periktione, both from prominent Athenian families, *c.* 428–347 BC. After the early death of his father, his mother married Pyrilampes, a rich man and a close friend of Pericles. Through his mother P. was related to the oligarchic *Critias. Despite these family relations, P. did not take part in Athenian politics and he himself gives the explanation in his *Seventh Letter* (probably genuine). He could not stand the politics of his time, and this was why he came to the famous view that the ideal government would exist when philosophers became kings and kings became philosophers. P. was a pupil of Socrates for some eight years until the latter's execution in 399 BC. This association was a descisive influence on his whole philosophy and life. Socrates appears in all his dialogues (excepting the *Laws*) and P. is indebted to him for a large part of his philosophical doctrines. The execution of Socrates deterred P. from ever taking part in the politics of his home city. He left Athens and for some time stayed in Megara with *Eucleides and other pupils of Socrates. In the following years he travelled much and visited Italy and Sicily and perhaps Egypt and Cyrene. In Italy he came to know closely the Pythagorean Archytas of Tarentum and in Sicily began his close friendship with *Dion of Syracuse. P. returned to Athens, *c.* 387 BC, and founded the *Academy, the first institution of high education. And he stayed there for practically the rest of his life, except for two more visits to Sicily. After the death of *Dionysius I (367 BC), he was invited by Dion to "make" the tyrant *Dionysius II into the philosopher-king. But things went wrong, Dion was banished by the tyrant, and Plato returned to Athens. He was induced to go back to Sicily in 360 BC on Dionysius' promise to cooperate, but the attempt again ended in failure, and P. returned to Athens where he remained until his death.

It seems that all the published writings of P. are extant. There are 25 dialogues, the *Apology*, thirteen letters (not all genuine) and some of the poems under his name that are in the Greek *Anthology. P.'s first writings probably date to before the death of Socrates and in his last years he worked on the *Laws*, but the chronological order of the writings is not known. It is usual to divide the treatises into three groups: the early period which includes *Apology, Crito, Laches, Euthyphro, Hippias Minor*; the middle period, to which belong *Phaedo, Symposium, Republic, Gorgias, Phaedrus*, and the late period of *Theaetetus, Sophist, Politicus, Philebus, Timaeus* and *Laws*.

The earlier dialogues concentrate on Socrates and his methods. Their aim is to discover what is Good; and this depends on knowledge. The method employed is the conversation and each dialogue tests the accepted definitions of a certain "good" ("courage" in *Laches*, "piety" in *Euthyphro*). If one knows what is "good", one surely will not do wrong. But people only think they know, and Socrates, by his questioning proves their definitions and conceptions to be wrong. It is important that the false notions should be exposed, as this will lead to the search for true knowledge. Four of P.'s works deal with the prosecution of Socrates. Of these the *Apology* comprises not only the defence of Socrates in court, but is also an explanation and defence of Socrates' method, which irritated many who pretended to or supposed that they had knowledge, and were proved wrong. The dialogues deal with a wide range of subjects: *Cratylus* with linguistics, *Phaedo* (dealing with Socrates' imprisonment before his execution) with the immortality of the soul, *Symposium* with love, *Gorgias* (the famous orator) with rhetoric and right and wrong in politics, *Meno* with the question whether "goodness" is teachable. In his search for knowledge, P. shows that people do not know what things truly are; nor do they know that their definitions are at best limited to examples. Neither he himself (nor Socrates) in the early dialogues offers an answer to the question posed. But this search leads to the theory of Ideas or Forms. This is fully developed in the *Republic* which belongs to the middle period. This dialogue in ten books starts with a conversation about Justice. Socrates disproves the theory of Thrasymachus that Right is Might and as the dialogue develops other subjects are discussed. It concentrates on what is the best state and includes a discussion of education and a severe criticism of poetry. There is an underlying assumption that goodness is the aim of the state and hence the state should be governed by philosophers. But in discussing the ideal state, P. expounds his theory of Ideas. This is where we find the famous parable of the men in the cave. They cannot look at the light, and they see only its shadows on the wall. In other words, P. distinguished between the Forms, which are absolute, perfect and invisible, and hence above the world of the senses, and their representations. The things we see are only reflections of the Forms. The latter, invisible, are reached by thought. Concerning things, we

have opinions and not knowledge, which is confined to the absolute, unchangeable Forms. The world of Forms is that of reality, and the visible world is unreal. It is by teaching and recollection that knowledge of the Forms can be acquired. In the *Phaedrus*, P. describes the world of the Forms as that beyond the vault of heaven where the gods drive in chariots. Souls, which are immortal, can look at this world and later on, while on earth, can reminisce about it. An earthly beauty will remind them of the Form of Beauty. The Form of Good is supreme among the Forms.

In a later dialogue, *Parmenides*, severe criticism is raised against the theory of Forms. Some would like to explain it away, but without success. Indeed, some of the later dialogues have in common this element of rigorous, damaging examination of cardinal problems. In the *Theaetetus*, the theory of Knowledge (*episteme*) is criticized. The common answers are rejected since perception is false and even true opinion is not reliable. In the *Sophist*, which concerns metaphysics (Being and not-Being), P. attacks Eleatic doctrines. The *Philebus* deals again with the Good, and since this cannot be grasped, knowledge of it can be approached through "beauty, proportion and truth". Cosmology, or natural science, is the subject of the *Timaeus*. Here again he makes the distinction between the world of Forms and the world of Becoming. The Creator (*Demiurgos*) modelled the latter on the former. P. gives a detailed account of man, his soul and his body. He firmly adheres to his doctrines that no certainty is possible concerning the world of things. But P. stresses that the universe is governed by a rational, intelligent principle. The importance of this doctrine for natural science is that it provides the incentive to discover the rational rules that operate in nature. What the *Demiurgos* does is not the creation of the matter — rather, he takes an existing matter and by putting it in order creates the world. P.'s belief in the rationality of the world was the basis for all the mathematical studies in astronomy and physics. The *Timaeus*, however, is unique among the dialogues of P., which all deal with moral questions. Problems of politics and the state occupied P. to the end. In *Crito* we find the story of the lost kingdom of Atlantis. In the *Politicus* he argues, as elsewhere, that as government is a profession it should be entrusted to professionals, not amateurs. Hence a state which is ruled by experts has the best constitution. Of the existing constitutions, the scale is from constitutional monarchy, aristocracy, and democracy to their depraved forms of tyranny, oligarchy and lawless democracy (these six forms were later followed by many political thinkers). In his last work, *Laws*, P. describes an imaginary city, not the ideal one as in the *Republic*, but the best that can be achieved in view of the Greek experience and conditions. It gives precise details: the number of citizens (5,040), the governing institutions (Assembly and Council), magistrates, means for subsistence, laws, etc.

The writings of P. do not present the whole of his philosophical thinking and he himself considered his teaching in the Academy as more important. Indeed, Aristotle, in the last book of the *Metaphysics*, mentions doctrines that are not included in the dialogues. Even so, his teachings during his lifetime and his writings have always served as a challenge to the mind and have been a source of inspiration to students of philosophy, politics, and other disciplines. The profundity of his thought and his ingenious methods are matched by a remarkable style. His

A comic scene on a mosaic from Pompeii

language varies from simple prose to passages of great pathos, from rational, though delightful narratives to poetic myths. He is liberal in his use of metaphors and similes, has a sense of humour, and can use a pun. By common consent his is the best Greek prose. As for his philosophy — he has had his critics, and not only admirers, since antiquity; these have increased in number in modern times. While some have welcomed the communist element in his political doctrines, others have emphasized the danger his views present to an open, free society.

Text: J. Burnet (OCT), 1903—1915;
Translation: B. Jowett (4th revised ed.), 1953;
M. E. Taylor, *Plato* (5th ed.), 1948;
K. Popper, *The Open Society*, 1, 1957;
J. M. Crombie, *An Examination of Plato's Doctrines*, 1962—3.

PLAUTIANUS, C. Fulvius Native of Lepcis Magna, the hometown of Septimius *Severus to whom he was related and under whom he rose to importance. He served with Septimius from AD 193, was appointed prefect of the Vigiles in 195 and praetorian prefect in 197. In the following years he acquired unlimited influence over the emperor and became all-powerful. His daughter was married to *Caracalla and he was consul with Geta in AD 203. He treated *Julia Domna, Severus' wife, contemptuously, but was finally executed on suspicion of conspiracy, engineered by Caracalla (AD 205).
A. Birley, *Septimius Severus*, 1971 (s.v.).

PLAUTUS, Titus Maccius Roman comic playwright. There is very little reliable information concerning his origin, the details of his life, and even his name. According to Cicero, P. died in 184 BC and his birthday may be placed in the mid-3rd century BC. He is said to have been born at Sarsina in Umbria, to have worked in a theatre and, after acquiring some money, to have turned to comedy writing. He became very popular and many plays passed under his name. Of the 130 plays ascribed to him, Varro listed 21 which were commonly accepted as genuine. It seems certain that these are the extant 21 plays of P.

His plays are of the *Fabula Palliata sort, that is, adaptations of Greek comedies. The plots of a few of them may be briefly given here. In the *Amphitruo*, a tragicomedy according to P., Jupiter (Zeus) seduces Alcumena (Alcmene) by taking the form of her husband Amphitruo (Amphitryon). The return of the jealous husband causes comic complications, but Alcmene remains a dignified figure until she gives birth to twins and everything is explained by Jupiter. In the *Asinaria* (a comedy about asses), a father, Demaenethus, helps his son to rescue his mistress with money which the wife kept for buying asses. When she discovers what happened, it is too late. The *Aulularia* ("The Pot of Gold") tells the story of the miser Euclio who has discovered a hoard of gold. He is now terrified lest someone should find it. His daughter is about to marry but before the wedding takes place she bears a child and his gold disappears. But it all ends happily: the father of the infant explains everything, and it was his slave who took the gold. He will marry Euclio's daughter and Euclio gets his gold back. The comedy is according to the conventions of the Greek stage. In P.'s plays, singing played a much more important role than in the original; the *Cantica*, that is, the passages to be sung, featured largely in his plays. There were scenes with arias or duets which were probably accompanied by dancing; other scenes were recited to musical accompaniment; there were also scenes with no music at all. P.'s vocabulary was rich and ranged all over the Latin language; and he made effortless use of metaphors from all fields of human life. He also used all the ornaments of artistic Latin: rhyme, alliteration, assonance, and word-play. Thanks to his inventive powers, his witticisms and humour, and his comic, lively plots, P. won great popularity, which lasted to the early Empire.

Text: W. M. Lidsay (OCT), 1904—5;
Text and translation: P. Nixon (Loeb), 1928—38;
G. E. Duckworth, *The Nature of Roman Comedy*, 1952.

PLEBS, PLEBEIANS All non-patrician Roman citizens were Plebeians. In early Rome, the *Patricians monopolized the magistracies and the priestly colleges. They were the only ones who had knowledge of law, and intermarriage between the Orders was not allowed. How the differentiation between the Orders came about is a vexed question. That the Plebeians were a conquered race, that they were the clients of the Patricians, or that the latter were selected by Romulus, are untenable explanations. It seems that the politically and economically more successful families in Rome separated themselves from the rest of the people in the late regal period or at the beginning of the Republic. The internal history of Rome until the early 3rd century is largely the struggle of the P. to acquire equal rights with the Patricians. In the course of this struggle they developed their own Assembly (*Concilium Plebis), and elected their own officials (*Tribuni Plebis, *Aediles Plebis), and had their centre on the Aventine (at the temples of Diana and Ceres). Their demand that the laws be published was achieved in mid-5th century (*Decemviri); the consulate was open to P. in 367 BC and the priestly colleges in 300; the laws of debt were relaxed, and by a law passed in 287 a resolution of the Concilium Plebis (*plebiscitum*) became binding on all the people, that is, it had the force of *lex. Even before the conclusion of the struggle, wealthy and successful P. became members of a new aristocracy (*Nobilitas) and by the late Republic P. were simply the lower classes of Roman society.

Jolowicz, *Roman Law*³ (s.v.);
Z. Yavetz, *Plebs and Princeps*, 1969.

PLINY THE ELDER (Gaius Plinius Secundus) Roman soldier, administrator and writer (AD 23–79). Native of Comum in northern Italy, of a well-to-do family, he held equestrian posts mainly in the armies of the German provinces (c. AD 47–58). In the next ten years he was occupied with grammatical and rhetorical studies – he apparently could not make himself serve under Nero, the "enemy of the human race", as he denoted him (*NH* 7.46). He again entered the imperial service under Vespasian, with whose son Titus he had served in Germany. He was procurator in several provinces: Gallia Narbonensis, Africa, Hispania Tarraconensis and Belgica. He returned to Italy c. AD 77 and got a position in Vespasian's court. As commander of the fleet of Misenum in AD 79, he tried to help those who suffered from the eruption of Vesuvius, and was killed while trying to watch the phenomenon. An account of this is given in a letter (*Ep.* 6.16) by his nephew, Pliny the Younger.

P. wrote several works: on the use of the javelin by horsemen; a life of Pomponius Secundus; a history of the Germanic Wars of Rome (in twenty books), used by Tacitus; an introduction to the study of rhetoric; a Roman history in 31 books, beginning where the work of the historian Aufidius Bassus ended (the date is not known; c. AD 50). All these are lost.

The *Naturalis Historia* ("Natural History") in 37 books is extant. In the preface to the work, P. says that there are 20,000 notable "facts", excerpted mainly from 100 authors. This vast encyclopaedia is unique; it is based on the reading of 20,000 volumes, and is a result of the work of an indefatigable, curious man. The work is dedicated to Titus. Book 1 contains an introduction with indexes of the other books; Book 2 deals with the universe; Books 3 to 6 with geography, Book 7 with man, Books 8 to 11 with animals, Books 12 to 19 with botany, Books 20 to 27 with the medical use of plants and herbs, Books 28 to 32 with the medical use of drugs derived from animals, and Books 33 to 37 with stones. The work is a mine of information and though P. is an indiscriminate writer and not a scientist, his work is invaluable for the study of several aspects of Greek and Roman antiquity.

Text and translation: H. Rackham, W.H.S. Jones, D. E. Eichholz (Loeb), 1938; T. A. Dorey (ed.), *Empire and Aftermath*, 1975, 57ff.

PLINY THE YOUNGER (Gaius Plinius Caecilius Secundus) Roman senator and writer. Born at Comum, in AD 61/2 and died c. 112/3. He lost his father in his childhood and was educated by his uncle, Pliny the Elder. The latter adopted him and made him his heir in his will. He studied rhetoric under Quintilian. In AD 79, he observed the eruption of the Vesuvius at which his uncle died. By that time he had begun his career at the bar. P. served as military tribune in Syria c. AD 82. He continued his activity in the courts on his return, entered the Senate (c. AD 89), and became praetor in AD 93. He was prefect of the military *aerarium* (c. AD 94–6) then of the *aerarium* (c. AD 96–8), and in the year 100 became consul. He was then a member of the board responsible for the Tiber and the drainage system of Rome. He was sent to govern Bithynia–Pontus (c. AD 110) where he probably died.

One speech and ten books of letters are extant. The speech is a revised version of the *Panegyric* he delivered as consul in the Senate (AD 100) in honour of Trajan. As usual, it praises the emperor and P. finds it easy to contrast the benevolent rule of the living Trajan with the tyrannical rule of the dead Domitian. But despite the assertion that this depends on the will of the emperor. The first nine books of letters appeared during P.'s lifetime. They contain 247 literary letters which give a lively account of various events and matters: politics, trials, society, personal business and so on. Among P.'s friends and acquaintances were Tacitus, Martial and Suetonius. The letters are a good corrective and complement of the social criticism of the satirist. They give a picture of civilized society and of the senatorial way of life. Carefully written, they are elegant and readable. The tenth book contains the correspondence of P. with Trajan when the former was in Bithynia. As such they are unique and very important for the study of the provincial administration at the time. They also contain an account of the Christian community in the province, which sheds much light on the official attitude towards it.

Text and translation: Melmoth-W. M. L. Hutchinson (Loeb), 1921–7; A. N. Sherwin-White, *Pliny's Letters, A Social and Historical Commentary*, 1960; Syme, *Tacitus* (s.v.); T. A. Dorey (ed.), *Empire and Aftermath*, 1975, 119ff.

PLOTINUS Neo-Platonist philosopher (AD 205–70), native of Egypt, pupil of Ammonius Saccas (see *Neoplatonism) in Alexandria. He took part in the Persian expedition of Gordian III (AD 242–3) in the hope of learning from the Eastern sages. The expedition was a failure and after staying in Antioch for some time P. went to Rome where he taught until the end of his life. In Rome he won a reputation and had various pupils, including members of the senatorial aristocracy. His published works were teaching aids for his courses. These writings were later edited by his pupil *Porphyry and were arranged in *Enneads*, groups of nine, of which there were six altogether. The extant writings are from the carefully edited work.

P. is regarded as the founder of neo-Platonism. His system combines elements from early Greek philosophy, Plato, Aristotle, and Oriental ideas (how much he owes to the Eastern doctrines is disputable). In his writings he deals with all the familiar subjects: ethics, physics, cosmology, metaphysics, logic, and knowledge, but in all these he has one central philosophical doctrine. All realities emanate or expand from the First Principle, the One, which P. identifies with the Good in the *Republic* of *Plato. This expansion from the One takes the form of concentric circles and there are several intermediaries between Matter (the sensible world) and the One: Nature, World-Soul, World-Mind (*Nous*). There is a depreciation of value in this emanation, and the more distant the circle is from the One, the more it loses its unity. Through the intellect and especially through ecstasy, it is possible to penetrate from the outer circle to the inside. P. himself attained unification with the One on three occasions.

Text and French Trans.: E. Brehier (Budé), 1924—38; Eng. Trans.: S. Mackenna and B. S. Page, 1962; W. R. Inge, *The Philosophy of Plotinus*, 1929; J. M. Rist, *Plotinus*, 1967.

PLUTARCH Of Chaeronea, Greek philosopher and biographer, born *c.* AD 45/50 and died *c.* 125. He came from a distinguished family in his home city. P. went to Athens to complete his education and learnt rhetoric and philosophy. His teacher was a Platonist but he was also influenced by the Stoa. He travelled through the whole of Greece, Egypt, and Asia Minor, and visited Italy on several occasions to represent the interests of Chaeronea. He established close relations with influential people in Rome and is said to have become procurator of Achaea under Hadrian. At the age of 50 he became a priest of Apollo at Delphi, but he always remained a patriotic citizen of his hometown where he had official duties and ran a school.

P. was a prolific writer and a substantial part of his writings is extant. The number of works ascribed to him in an ancient list is 227. The extant works include the famous biographies (50) and all the other miscellaneous works (78) which are commonly called *Moralia*. The *Parallel Lives* (*Vitae Parallelae*) include 50 biographies of leading Greeks and Romans, arranged in pairs (one Roman and one Greek), who are then compared to each other. There are 23 such pairs but only 19 are now provided with the comparisons. In addition there are biographies of Galba and Otho. The pairs are sometimes artificially arranged. P. writes as a moralist rather than as an historian. In the construction of the biography he follows a standard pattern: the family background, the up-

bringing, the course of the life, with digressions and emphasis on those points which seem to him instructive on the character of the man. But there is no clear chronology, and there are omissions and inaccuracies. Anecdotes largely feature in the biographies whose value for the historian varies according to the sources used by him. The schematic pattern is convenient for the writer but not always suitable for the man. But the *Lives* are lively, with diverse details and moralizing lessons. For many generations, the biographies have presented a picture of what Greeks and the Romans were really like. They also influenced European literature. Shakespeare took the subject matter for his *Coriolanus, Julius Caesar* and *Antony and Cleopatra* from the translation by Sir Thomas North.

The *Moralia* include writings on philosophical, religious, literary, historical and scientific subjects. They are presented in the form of dialogues and essays. His *Roman Questions* and *Greek Questions* supply much information on the ancient religion of the Romans and the Greeks. The famous *The Malignity of Herodotus* is a curious attack on the Father of History. Many short treatises deal with questions of popular philosophy. In his religious treatises he deals with oracles, divination, and mysticism. These writings were apparently popular and had, like the *Lives*, a great influence on many thinkers and writers.

Text and translation: F. C. Babbit etc. *Moralia* (Loeb), 1927; B. Perrin, *Lives* (Loeb) 1914—26; D. M. Russel, *Plutarch*, 1973.

POLEMARCHOS It seems that the original P. was the Athenian archon who commanded the army after the disappearance of the monarchy. The importance of the P. declined in the early 5th century BC. The last Athenian P. mentioned as commanding an army is Callimachus who was, at least nominally, the commander-in-chief of the Athenian army at *Marathon (490 BC). But after the reforms of *Cleisthenes (2) and the establishment of the *strategoi, the latter seem to have encroached on the P.'s duties. As *archontes began to be elected by lot after 487/486 BC, the military duties of the P. were transferred

Walls of the small Polis Aegosthena

to the strategoi. Thereafter, the P. was responsible for the funeral ceremonies of those fallen in war and for some sacrifices and judicial cases (Aris. *Ath. Pol.* 58). The office of P. as commander of the army also existed in other Greek states.

Hignett, *Athen. Const.* (s.v.).

POLEMON I King of Pontus. A native of Laodicea, he defended his home city against the Parthians in 40–39 BC. As a reward M. Antonius (4) gave him part of Cilicia to rule, and, from 37 BC, the kingdom of Pontus. He was taken prisoner by the Parthians in the Parthian expedition of Antonius (36 BC). But he was ransomed and in 34 BC received Armenia Minor, which he held until Augustus deprived him of it after Actium. He annexed the Bosporan kingdom with the help of *Agrippa (1) in 15 BC. P. was killed by rebels in 8 BC and was succeeded by his wife Pythodoris.

Magie, *Asia* (s.v.).

POLETAI ("sellers") Athenian officials, mentioned as early as Solon, responsible for the selling of public property. They also leased public property, issued rights to exploit public mines, to collect taxes and so on. There were ten P. in the 4th century BC, elected by lot, one for each of the the *Rhylai.

POLIS The Greek city-state, their most remarkable political institution. Originally, it denoted the "citadel", which was later called the *Acropolis. The origins of the P. go back to the Dark Age of Greek history when, following the destruction of the *Mycenaean civilization, the powers of the kings declined. By the 8th century BC the idea of the P. had occurred, and wherever the Greeks settled outside Greece they established new *Poleis* (see *Apoikia).

There were several characteristics of the P. In the first place it was small, both in the number of its citizens and its territory. In his *Laws* *Plato gives a population of 5,040 as the appropriate number for his ideal, workable constitution, and here he certainly took into account actual conditions. From this follows another important characteristic: the participation of the citizen in the affairs of his P. The P. was a tangible reality for the citizen and not an abstract idea. The citizen, *polites*, was a member of the P. and took part in its affairs (*Ta politika*), not once a year, or once every several years, in elections, but on frequent occasions, political, social and religious. Aristotle regarded it as a natural, social organization which was ultimately based on the family, and a Greek citizen for him was a "political animal". Thirdly, the P. was regarded as the sum of its citizens, and therefore, e.g., the Athenian P. was not Athens but "The Athenians". Further, the embodiment of the P. was a town with its Acropolis, Bouleuterium (council building) and *Agora (centre of civic life). Citizens might reside in the country, and every P. had a territory beyond its walls, but the P. was governed from the city. Another characteristic of the P. was its particularism. Though the Greeks had much in common, each P. had its own magistrates, traditions, cults, festivals, laws, in short, a distinct way of life. From this followed the desire to maintain autonomy, autarky and liberty. Understandably, there were numerous city-states, many of them very tiny indeed. (Athens with its more than 40,000 citizens in the 5th century BC was an anomaly.) This fact was due to the way in which the P. rose as well as the geographical features of Greece. In each of the numerous natural divisions of the Greek territory the population sought shelter in a place that was naturally

fortified. In these, once isolated, centres, the spirit of particularism developed.

There was never a uniform kind of government in the Greek P. states. In the course of Greek history, the P. were ruled by aristocracies, tyrants, oligarchies or democracies. The political rights of the citizens depended on the type of constitution the P. had, but in all cases the citizens were a privileged body as against *metics and inferior inhabitants (see *Perioiki, *Helots). In democracies all citizens participated in the government, in oligarchies this right was restricted to some minority. But whatever constitution the P. had, government was by Assembly (*Ekklesia), Council (*Boule) and magistrates. The internal struggles often caused changes of government and one of the problems Greek political thinkers dealt with was how to create a constitution that would be stable and terminate the "Change of Constitutions" (*metabole politeion*). The continued internal strife (*staseis*) and the inter-state wars, largely connected with the attempts of first Athens and then Sparta to maintain hegemony over Greece, as well as the deterioration of economic conditions in the 4th century BC, led to the decline of the P. Among the signs of decline were the rise of mercenary armies in place of the citizen-army and the corruption of democracy. With the rise of Macedonia under *Philip II and Alexander the Great, the Greek P. states lost much of their political power. Although they continued to exist, and many more were founded in the East, the leading political powers were the great Hellenistic kingdoms and the leagues in Greece. The P. was still a political body and it tried to administer its affairs without outside control, yet under the new conditions they were mainly noted for their Greek way of life with the *gymnasium and other cultural institutions as characteristics.

V. Ehrenberg, *The Greek State,* 1960;
A. H. M. Jones, *The Greek City from Alexander to Justinian,* 1940;
W. G. Forrest, *The Emergence of Greek Democracy,* 1966.

POLLIO, Gaius Asinius Roman statesman and writer. Despite his republican tendencies, he followed Caesar in the Civil War, and fought in Sicily, Africa and Spain. He was praetor in 45 BC, and at the death of Caesar was governor of Farther Spain. He joined M. *Antonius (4) in 43 BC and in 41 BC helped Virgil. Consul in 40 BC, he was governor of Macedonia in 39 BC and celebrated a triumph for his victory over the Illyrian Parthini. Thereafter, he left politics and declined to take part in the struggle between Octavian and Antonius.

P. was a man of letters. Among his friends were the poets *Catullus, *Cinna (2), and Horace, and he supported Virgil. He was a distinguished orator and a poet (he wrote erotic poetry and tragedies), a grammarian and an historian. His *Historiae* began in 60 BC and described the Civil Wars of Rome up to 42 BC. He founded the first public library in Rome, for which he used his booty. P. had an art collection and was the first to give public recitations of new works. A severe literary critic, he attacked Cicero and Caesar, criticized Sallust for his use of archaisms and Livy for his Patavinitas, probably "provincialism". His style was simple. None of his works is extant.

Peter, *Hist. Rom. Rel. 2*; Syme, *Tacitus* (s.v.).

POLLUX Of Naucratis, scholar of the 2nd century AD. He was appointed to the chair of rhetoric at Athens, beating his rival *Phrynichus Arabius, and was attacked by the latter as well as by *Lucian. P. wrote an *Onomastikon*; to each of its ten books he added a letter addressed to the Emperor Commodus. It is known from incomplete copies (with considerable variants) of an early epitome. It is arranged by subjects and not in alphabetical order. A large variety of subjects is dealt with (science, religion, music, arts, cookery, etc.); important are the citations from earlier literature and a few sections like the one on the theatre (Book 4) and that on Athenian law (Book 8). The work mainly lists terms and P. owes a great deal to former lexicographers.

POLYAENUS The author of *Strategica*, a work in eight books consisting of a collection of stratagems. P. wrote the work after the outbreak of the war against the Parthians under Marcus *Aurelius (AD 162). It gives examples from all peoples (Greek, Macedonian, Roman, Scythian, Persian, Egyptian, Celt) and from all periods. He used earlier collections of this sort, and in some cases the examples are informative.

POLYBIUS The most important Hellenistic historian (*c.* 200–after 120 BC), son of *Lycortas, native of Megalopolis. His father was a leading Achaean statesman, and P. became active in politics soon after completing his education. He served as the Hipparch (cavalry commander) of the Achaean League in 170/169 BC, and after Pydna (168) was sent to Italy with 1,000 other Achaeans who were known as anti-Roman or as too independent. He had the good luck to become the friend and adviser of *Scipio (5) Aemilianus, and was allowed to move more freely than the other detainees. But for the next 16 years he could not return to his home country. P. travelled much, largely with Aemilianus, and probably visited Spain, Africa, and Gaul. He was with Scipio at the destruction of Carthage, helped the Achaean cities after the destruction of Corinth, continued his travelling and was perhaps in *Numantia in 133 BC. He died in old age after falling from a horse.

In addition to his major work, P. wrote a biography of *Philopoemen, for whose ashes he arranged a funeral in 182 BC; *Tactics*; a history of the Numanitine War – but all are lost. His *Histories* comprised 40 books of which Books 1–5 are extant, in addition to excerpts of varying length from the other books, known from later writers. The subject of the work was the rise of Rome to dominance of the Mediterranean world from the Second Punic War to 146 BC; in the original plan, the work was to terminate after the battle of Pydna. The first two books surveyed the period from the First Punic War (264 BC) to 220 BC. The last book summarized the work.

P. wrote to provide statesmen with historical accounts that could be useful for their profession. He wrote pragmatic history, that is, political and military history with analyses of causes, processes and effects. Time and again he criticized other historians who wrote rhetorical and sensational histories to please their readers. The great historical event that he had to explain was the Roman expansion. As this ultimately concerned the whole Mediterranean world, an account of the developments in the various areas, particularly Greece and the Hellenistic kingdoms, had to be included. And the narrative was divided between accounts of the events in the different areas. As to the Roman achievement, this was explained by the type of its constitution, and the army. For that reason, Book 6 was devoted to an analysis of the development of the Roman constitution and a detailed account of the military system of the Romans. In this analysis, P. was influenced by the Greek experience, that is, the frequent changes of constitutions (*metabole politeion*; see *Polis). The solution of Greek thinkers to that endless cycle was a mixed constitution, one composed of monarchic, oligarchic and democratic elements. According to P., this kind of constitution developed in Rome. His theory of the check and balances between the constituent elements of the Roman constitution was very famous and has been erroneously taken as a theory of "separation of powers".

P. was a scientific historian, not an accomplished writer. His style is dull and periphrastic. But his method of writing history can only be admired. His aim was to write accurate history. For this purpose he checked documents, where these were available, travelled to acquaint himself with the geography and peoples of his history, talked with people, and studied early works. And he had political experience and a critical mind, so he used the material he collected to present a comprehensive, intelligible account of the historical phenomena. But he also had his shortcomings. There was some prejudice against the enemies of his country (notably *Aetolia and *Cleomenes III of Sparta) and bias towards the Scipionic family. He neglected some subjects, for instance the inner politics of Rome and, as did all the ancient historians, he ignored the economic aspects. But these defects are negligible when compared to the positive aspects of his work, which is one of the very few good ancient histories.

Text and translation: W. R. Paton (Loeb), 1922–7; F. W. Walbank, *A Historical Commentary on Polybius* (two volumes, the third in preparation), 1957–   ; F. W. Walbank, *Polybius*, 1974.

POLYCLITUS Prominent sculptor, native of Argos. He lived during the second half of the 5th century BC. Possibly a pupil of *Agelades, P. established a school of his own. He worked with almost all kinds of material but particularly in bronze. He made statues of the gods, notably a chryselephantine statue of Hera for Argos, but athletes were his speciality. His most famous works were the "Doryphorus" ("spear bearer") and "Diadumenus" (a youth fastening a band around his head). The first is described by Pliny (*NH* 34.55) as a youth with a spear, a work which was used as a model for artists. Roman copies of this statue have been identified. P. was interested in rhythm and proportions and, as Pliny says, he wrote a book on the subject. In the "Doryphorus" he illustrated his view, and indeed even the copies, notably the one in the Naples Museum, show his high achievemenet in harmony and proportion. Copies of the "Diadumenus" reveal the same qualities. These statues are a magnificent achievement in presenting the human body. Two other famous works of P. are also known from copies, the "Cyniscus", and the "Amazon" which he made for Ephesus in competition with Phidias. His most famous work was the colossal seated Hera, described by Pausanias (2.17,4) and considered by some as superior to the Olympian Zeus of Phidias (Strabo 8.372). It is known from representations on coins.

POLYCRATES Tyrant of Samos. Son of Aeaces, he took control of the island with his brothers *c.* 540 BC and after a few years became the sole ruler. P. reduced the power of the aristocracy, encouraged craftsmen to settle in Samos, extended the harbour and built ship-houses. Under him, Samian products were exported to remote parts of the Mediterranean. He also developed agriculture on the island, and the period of his rule was a prosperous one. P. was a patron of poets and artists; *Anacreon and *Ibycus were among those who came to his court. He cooperated with Lygdamis, the tyrant of Naxos, helped Arcesilas III, the deposed king of Cyrene, and had ties with *Amasis of Egypt. He had a strong navy and for several years established a maritime empire. Rich and fond of luxury, he sought to escape from the revenge of *Nemesis by throwing his precious ring into the sea, but a fisherman brought back a fish with the ring, an ill omen. P. was tricked by the Persian satrap of Ionia, captured and crucified (c. 522 BC).

P. N. Ure, *The Origin of Tyranny*, 1922;
A. Andrewes, *The Greek Tyrants*, 1956.

POLYGNOTUS Of Thasos, prominent Greek painter, active c. 480–c. 440 BC. His father Aglaophon, a painter, was his teacher. He came to Athens, became an Athenian citizen and was the friend of *Cimon (and some said that Cimon's sister Elpinike was his mistress). His most famous works were the "Sack of Troy" and the "Nekyia" (descent to the Underworld) in the Cnidian Lesche (assembly-hall) in Delphi. In Athens he painted other famous murals ("Capture of Troy") for the Stoa Poikile. Other works of his were the "Rape of the Leucippidae", and the "Battle of the Greeks and Amazons" for the Theseum. Pausanias (10.25–31) and Pliny (*NH* 35.59) give accounts of his works and he is mentioned by many other writers, but his works are lost. His special achievement was in giving expression to emotions and thoughts and placing the figures on different levels to produce spatial effects.

POLYPERCHON Macedonian officer of Alexander the Great, appointed commander of an infantry brigade after Issus (333 BC) for his distinction. He was sent home with *Craterus (1) in 324 BC, and, on the recommendation of *Antipater (1), became the Macedonian regent after the

latter's death (319 BC). But he was a failure, lost control of Macedonia and gradually of other positions and, after several years, disappeared from the historical scene.

POLYXENE The daughter of *Priam and Hecuba. According to a post-Homeric version of her myth, she was sacrificed to the ghost of Achilles after the fall of Troy. In another version, known from many works of art, she and her brother Troilus were attacked by Achilles. The brother was slain but she escaped.

POMERIUM The sacred line which encircled a city founded according to the augural rites. When first established, the buildings of such a city were obviously within that line, but the city usually extended beyond the P. as it developed. The P. was often considered to closely border on the city-walls. The intra-P. area was considered as a non-military zone. Hence the lictors did not carry axes in the *Fasces before magistrates, except the *dictator, holding *Imperium within the P. The *Comitia Centuriata, once the assembly of the citizen-soldiers, was convened in the *Campus Martius which was outside the P. The area within the P. was called *domi*, that beyond it, *militiae*. The P. was extended several times in the course of Roman history, but there is much uncertainty about this.

POMPEII Port city on a volcanic hill in southern Campania, about 8 km from Vesuvius, at the mouth of the river Carnus. The original population (Ausones) came under Greek influence in the 8th century BC and Etruscan influence in the late 7th century BC. The Greeks resumed their dominance in the second third of the 5th century BC but during the late 5th century the city was occupied by *Samnites. It was then enlarged and fortified. The city

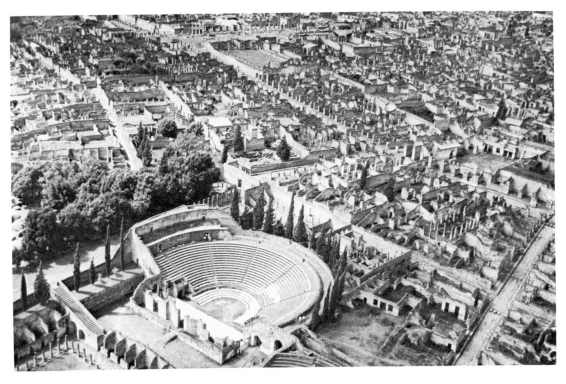

Aerial view of Pompeii

retained its political autonomy until the early 1st century BC. P. had its magistrates (*Meddix, aediles, quaestors) and assembly, but it became dependent on Rome. It joined the Italian allies of Rome in the *Bellum Sociale and under Sulla a colony of veterans was founded here (*colonia Veneria Cornelia*). Until then P. retained its Oscan language, attested to by inscriptions, and its native culture. Romanization now spread rapidly: in language, institutions, titles of magistrates, and architecture. Romans of the upper classes like Cicero acquired villas near P. which was a prosperous city deriving its wealth from trade and agriculture. It was severely damaged in an earthquake in AD 62 and it was destroyed by the eruption of Vesuvius in AD 79, which is described by Pliny the Younger (*Ep.* 6.16 and 20) who was in Naples at the time. P. was discovered in 1748 and since then excavations have been held, first by art-hunters but as from the mid-19th century by more scientific investigators. Most of the city has been unearthed and it is today one of the rare sites where an ancient city may be examined. The finds have revealed the material development of the city and its social and economic history. Numerous inscriptions give evidence of the lively municipal life. And, of course, it provides very important examples of Graeco-Roman architecture and art. The rich material, including statues, wall paintings and mosaics, can be seen on the site or in the Naples Museum.
R. C. Carrington, *Pompeii*, 1936;
A. Maiuri, *Pompeian Wall Paintings*, 1960.

POMPEIUS MAGNUS, Sextus Younger son of *Pompey and his first wife Mucia, born *c.* 66 BC. After the murder of his father, which he witnessed, he escaped to Africa, and, after *Thapsus (46 BC), to Spain. He remained in Spain after the defeat of his elder brother Gnaeus in *Munda and was successful against the Roman governors. In the summer of 44 BC the Senate agreed to give him compensation for the confiscated property of his late father and to his return to Italy. But he was careful and he delayed his return. In 43 BC he was outlawed and proscribed by the triumvirs. PM. now captured Sicily and with his strong fleet devastated the Italian coast, giving shelter to the fugitives. In the treaty of Misenum in 39 BC Antonius and Octavian recognized his control over Sicily, Sardinia, Corsica and Achaea and he agreed to stop the blockade of Italy. But Octavian renewed the war and despite initial defeats he destroyed PM.'s power in 36 BC (in the battles of Mylae and Naulochus). PM. escaped to Asia and was put to death by Antonius's officer, M. Titius.
M. Hadas, *Sextus Pompeius*, 1930; Syme, *Rom. Rev.* (s.v.).

POMPEIUS STRABO, Gnaeus Roman statesman and general, the father of Pompey. A rich man, he had estates in Picenum; as legate (90 BC) and consul (89 BC) he was sent to that area in the *Bellum Sociale. He took *Asculum and was awarded a triumph. In the same year he gave the Latin rights to Transpadane Gaul. When the consul of 88 BC was sent to take command of PS.'s army, he was killed by the latter's soldiers. PS. maintained an independent position in 87 BC in the Civil War when *Cinna (1) attacked Rome. But he died in an epidemic "hated by men and gods".

POMPEY (POMPEIUS), Gnaeus Born in 106 BC, the son of Pompeius Strabo, under whom he served in the *Bellum Sociale, P. died in 48 BC. His rise to power began in 83 BC when he raised an army of three legions from his clients and his father's veterans in Picenum and fought for Sulla. He won Sicily from *Carbo, whom he killed, and

Head of Pompey

Africa, and when he returned he was given an unprecedented triumph for an Eques. He married Mucia, a relative of the powerful family of the Metelli, and in 77 BC was given a command to suppress the rebellion of *Lepidus (2). During the same year he was given a special command to fight *Sertorius in Spain. The war dragged on for several years and only after the assasination of Sertorius was it brought to an end. He returned in 71 BC, routed the remnants of the army of *Spartacus and became consul in 70 BC with *Crassus (4). The tribunes were given full powers, and the Equites and the Tribuni Aerarii (close to the Equites in wealth and social position) got two thirds of the seats in the jury courts; thus were abolished two important laws of *Sulla. In 67 BC, P. was appointed to fight the pirates, and he completed his mission in three months. The next year he was given command against *Mithridates VI. In the following years he not only completed the conquest of Pontus (Mithridates escaped to the Crimea and committed suicide), but he also conquered Syria, intervened in *Judaea and reorganized the Roman provinces in the East.

Back in Italy in 62 BC, he sent his soldiers home, and triumphed. He divorced his unfaithful wife and vainly tried to connect himself to *Cato by marriage. He was induced to ally himself with Crassus and Caesar in 60 BC ("First Triumvirate"). P. married Caesar's daughter Julia, and in 59 BC Caesar satisfied his demands concerning the confirmation of his administrative actions in the East and the distribution of land to his soldiers. In 57 BC P. was given a command to secure the corn-supply of Rome. He helped *Cicero (1) return from exile and suffered from the attacks of *Clodius Pulcher. He renewed his alliance with Caesar and Crassus in 56 BC, and became consul with the latter in 55 BC. Spain was given to him for the next five years but he governed it by proxy. Julia died in 54 BC and Crassus was killed in 53 BC; thereafter, the rivalry between P. and Caesar increased. P. became sole consul in 52 BC and married the daughter of *Metellus (4) Scipio. During this year he passed a law that enforced an interval, of at least five years, between service as praetor or consul in Rome and provincial governorship. He came to support the enemies of Caesar and in 49 BC took command of the army against Caesar. But he was not sufficiently prepared and he left Italy for Macedonia after successfullly defending Brundisium, his port of embarkation, from a siege by Caesar. In the East, P. mobilized a strong army and in the first encounter, at Dyrrachium, caused losses to Caesar. The decisive battle took place at *Pharsalus and P.'s defeat was complete. He escaped to Egypt and was murdered on landing ashore — while his wife was watching from the ship.

For his early achievements, P. was called Magnus ("Great"). For thirty years he dominated Roman politics. His beginnings were unconstitutional: the raising of a private army and the command given to a young man who was not even a senator (he became a member of the Senate only during his first consulship). He met strong opposition in the oligarchy but knew how to establish his power beyond the military commands. In Italy and the eastern and western provinces he had numerous *clients, including dynasts and kings, and many senators and Equites were attached to him. Cicero considered him capable of carrying out the reforms necessary to heal the Roman state. But it seems that P. lost something of his political mastery in the 50s BC, and, in the final test of power, failed before one better than he.

Syme, *Rom. Rev.*; Badian, *Foreign Clientelae,* 1958; J. Van Oeteghem, *Pompée le Grand,* 1954.

POMPONIUS, Sextus Roman jurist of the 2nd century AD. He was a prolific writer and in his numerous works he covered various fields of Roman law. His most bulky work was a commentary on the *Edictum of the urban praetor. His Enchiridium (*liber singularis enchiridi*) was an historical outline of Roman law and it dealt with jurists, magistrates and legal sources. A considerable excerpt from it is included in the *Digesta of Justinian (1.2.2), and it gives unique information on the subject. He is often cited in the *Digest*.

PONTIFEX (pl. pontifices) The main priestly college in Rome comprised an advisory board of P. who were responsible for the correct performance of the religious cults at Rome. Their number at first was three and by the end of the Republic it increased to 16. By the Lex Ogulnia of 300 BC the Plebeians were first admitted to the college. They gave advice to the magistrates and the Senate in all cases concerning the public — for instance, dedications, vows and sacrifices. They were also consulted on the correct performance of rites by private citizens, for instance in funerals. They were considered to be experts in religious law. The P. Maximus was the head of the college of the P., and as such was responsible for the State religion and had control over all other priests. He was also responsible for the arrangement of the calendar, including intercalation. The P. Maximus was appointed by the members of the college, but in the late republic he was elected by 17 tribes selected by lot. After the death of M. *Lepidus (3), the reigning emperor was always the P. Maximus. Latte, *R. Rel.* (s.v.).

PONTIUS PILATUS Roman governor of Judaea (AD 26—36). According to Philo, he was inflexible, cruel and corrupt (*Legatio ad Gaium* 38). He enraged the Jews by carrying the images of the emperor into Jerusalem and also by appropriating money from the Temple treasury for the construction of an aqueduct. He condemned Jesus, handed to him by the Jewish Sanhedrin, to death, and the sentence was executed in the manner reserved by the Romans for non-Romans, that is, crucifixion. In AD 36 he was deposed from office by the governor of Syria after the Samaritans complained about him. According to Eusebius, P. committed suicide. He became the subject of various tales and was said to have sent a report on the trial of Jesus to the Emperor Tiberius. He is mentioned in an inscription discovered at *Caesarea Palaestinae in 1961. A. N. Sherwin-White, *Roman Society and Roman Law in the New Testament,* 1963.

PONTUS Country in eastern Asia Minor, bordered by the river Halys in the west, *Cappadocia in the south and *Armenia Minor in the east. The Greeks established cities on the coasts, among them Amisus, Sinope and Trapezus. The non-urban population lived in villages, ruled by a feudal aristocracy or by the priests of the great temples. A mountainous country, with fertile valleys and plenty of water, P. had been part of the Persian Empire, and it became the kingdom of *Mithridates I and his descendants from *c.* 300 BC. After the downfall of *Mithridates VI, Pompey organized it as one province with Bithynia, though he gave some parts of it to neighbouring dynasts. Part of it was ruled by *Polemon I and his successors until this, too, was annexed under Nero (AD 64). Magie, *Asia* (s.v.).

POPILIUS LAENAS, Gaius Roman statesman, of a plebeian family that became powerful in the 170s BC. He was consul in 172 BC, and is famous for the way he dealt with *Antiochus V in 168 BC. The latter occupied Egypt and PL. came to him on an official embassy to demand the evacuation of the country. When Antiochus hesitated, PL. drew a line around him and insisted on receiving an answer before the king left the circle. Antiochus decided to leave Egypt. Scullard, *Rom. Pol.* [2] (s.v.).

POPPAEA SABINA Of an aristocratic family, born *c.* AD 30, she first married a praetorian prefect under the Emperor Claudius, and later married Otho, the future emperor. A beautiful woman, she is said by Pliny to have bathed in ass's-milk (*NH* 28.183). She became Nero's mistress and Otho was sent to Spain (AD 58). According to Tacitus, she was responsible for the murder of Nero's mother and the downfall of *Octavia (2). After the murder of the latter (AD 62), PS. married Nero and gave birth to a daughter, who soon died. She died in AD 65 after Nero kicked her while she was pregnant. There was a story that she was interested in Judaism (Josephus *AJ,* 20.195). Syme, *Tacitus* (s.v.).

PORCIA Daughter of *Cato (2). Her first husband was *Bibulus and in 45 BC she married *Brutus (2). She was involved in the conspiracy against Caesar but did not go with her husband to the East. She committed suicide in 43 BC.

PORPHYRY Greek scholar and philosopher (*c.* AD 233 —*c.* 305), native of Tyre, whose original name was Malchus. He studied philosophy and other subjects at Athens under the rhetorician Longinus, and came to Rome in AD 263 where he became a pupil and an admirer of *Plotinus.

An ascetic and a mystic, he suffered from depression. On the advice of Plotinus, he left Rome (AD 268) and travelled, going to Lilybaeum in Sicily. After Plotinus' death, he returned to Rome and became Head of his school. He collected the writings of Plotinus and published them, *c.* 301—5, and shortly afterwards died.

P. was a prolific writer and his writings covered a wide variety of subjects, mainly associated with religion and philosophy. He wrote a history of philosophy until Plato, and commentaries on Plato, Aristotle, Theophrastus and Plotinus. He also wrote a biography of Plotinus. His *introduction to the Categories of Aristotle, Isagoge*, was translated into Latin by *Boethius (who also wrote two commentaries on it), and the Latin version was the accepted textbook of logic in the Middle Ages. P. was also a philologist and in his early Homeric studies interpreted allegorically the cave in the *Odyssey* (see 13.102ff.). In his work *Against the Christians*, in 15 books, he applied philological criticism. It was a vehement attack on both the Old Testament and the New Testament, and in particular on the Christian dogmas. Christian writers tried to refute his arguments and finally the book was publicly burnt (AD 448), but fragments of it are extant.

J. Bidez, *Vie de Porphyre*, 1913.

PORSENNA , Lars P. was an Etruscan, who came from *Clusium and conquered Rome sometime at the end of the 6th century BC (Tac. *Ann.* 3.72; Pliny, *NH* 34.139). In the patriotic Roman tradition, he tried to help *Tarquinius Superbus after the latter's expulsion but failed to seize Rome. With him were connected legendary figures such as *Horatius Cocles and Scaevola ("left handed"). The latter allegedly tried to kill P. in his camp and when caught put his right hand in a fire to convince the Etruscan of his bravery.

Alföldi, *Early Rome*, 51ff., 72ff.

PORTICUS ("Portico") The Roman P.s were sometimes independent hall-like structures with colonnaded P.s, or more often rectangular open areas enclosed by colonnaded P.s, or simply colonnaded passages. The colonnaded P. was also used in private buildings and not only in public ones.

PORTORIUM (pl. portoria) Duties levied by the Roman government for merchandise passing through harbours or certain points on inland routes. The aim was fiscal, not protective. The letting out of P. to *Publicani in Italy in 199 BC is mentioned by Livy (32.7). The Italian P. were abolished in 60 BC but Caesar reintroduced them. The rate varied, but normally it was 2.5% or 5%. Only on the frontier of the Roman Empire in the East were rates of 25% attested to and they were probably protective in aim. From the late 2nd century AD the collection was taken by the imperial procurators.

S. J. de Laet, *Portorium*, 1949.

POSEIDON Greek god of water, including fresh water, river water, spring water and sea water. His antiquity is indicated by the fact that he is mentioned in documents of Linear B (*Po-se-da o*). He was considered responsible for earthquakes and his titles referred to his special association with earth, *enosichthon, ennosigaios* ("shaker of earth"). His name probably means "Husband of Earth", and as god of water he indeed fertilized the earth. He was also especially associated with horses, and one of his titles was *hippios*. In mythology, he mated with *Demeter in horse-shape and fathered the marvellous horse *Pegasus on the *Gorgo.

P. was one of the great gods and this is reflected in mythology. He was a son of *Kronos and Rhea and was generally thought to be the elder brother of Zeus, except in Homer. With their third brother, *Hades, P. and Zeus overthrew their father. In the allotment of the rule of the universe, Zeus won the sky, P. the sea and Hades the underworld. P. married the Nereid Amphitrite (a minor figure compared to Hera of Zeus and Persephone of Hades) who bore him *Triton. But his indifelity was notorious. In one version his beloved *Scylla was turned into a sea-monster by the jealous Amphitrite. The *Cyclops Polyphemus was P.'s son by the nymph Thoosa, and *Orion by Euryale (daughter of *Minos). Among his many other sons may be mentioned *Eumolpus, *Neleus, Agenor (father of *Europa) and the giant Antaeus, who was killed by *Heracles. He was also the father of the Athenian Theseus, otherwise known as the son of *Aegeus. In one myth, he contested the rule over Attica with Athena and to support his claim thrust his trident into the Acropolis. On the salt spring that sprang forth there was built a shrine (see *Erechteum). But it was Athena who won Athens. In the *Iliad*, P. appears as an enemy of Troy — seeking revenge against Laomedon, father of *Priam, who cheated P. of his pay for building the walls of the city (21. 441ff.). In the *Odyssey* he pursues Odysseus for his treatment of Polyphemus. In art, P.'s attributes are the trident, a fish and a dolphin. The famous bronze statue that was found near Artemisium (now in the National Museum in Athens) is either of P. or of Zeus. His struggle with Athena over the rule of Athens was depicted in the west pediment of the Parthenon.

POSIDONIUS Stoic philosopher and scholar (*c.* 135—51/50 BC), native of Apamea on the Orontes, pupil of *Panaetius in Athens. His scientific travels to Spain, Gaul and North Africa were probably completed before he settled down in Rhodes where he had a famous school. In 87 BC he represented Rhodes at Rome. In 78 BC Cicero attended his lectures in Rhodes. Pompey, too, visited him during his wars in the East and P. came to be his supporter and friend.

Despite his fame and numerous writings only a few fragments are extant. P. wrote on history, philosophy, and geography. His *Histories* was a work in 52 books which covered the period from the end of the *Histories* of Polybius. An admirer of Pompey, P. added an appendix in which he dealt with the wars of the latter in the East. The work was not merely an account of events with an analysis of causes, processes and effects. P. tried to find a purpose in history and regarded the Roman Empire, which included all the peoples of the world, as the human brotherhood. He thus justified the growth of the Roman Empire, even though his accounts of the wild tribes (Celts, Iberians) show that he appreciated the good customs that they had. In writing his history he took sides. As a believer in aristocratic regimes he criticized the activities of Tiberius and Gaius Gracchus and others who attacked senatorial control. He also held the view that the course of history shows a progression of moral decadence. P.'s travels gave him material for his ethnographic and geographic works. He noted the connexion between tides and the cycles of the moon (but his explanation was inadequate), calculated the circumference of the earth and his result, 240,000 stades, was quite accurate (but it was based on incorrect figures); he also constructed a sphere and prepared a map. His interests also included mathematics, meteorology and astronomy. The study of the passions was important for P. Here he took the view that the *psyche* consisted of rational and irrational elements.

Bronze statue of Poseidon or Zeus, found in the sea off Cape Artemisum

The irrational, inborn emotions can be satisfied or exhausted, and their existence explains the passionate behaviour of men and the roots of evil. P. then suggested ways of treating the irrational elements, probably stressing diet.

As has been noted, P. had a wide range of interests. This was in keeping with the Stoic theory, which P. modified and developed, of *Sympatheia*, that is, the sympathetic connexions between the parts of the whole. He believed that all the constituents parts of this world work together, including man. To understand the whole one has to know its parts. The world is the product of a divine power — it is an ordered world, intelligible to the human mind. Hence everything was of interest to him.

P. has been compared to Aristotle in the scope of his subject-matter, and in his interest in details as a basis for building a system. But not much has been preserved of his writings and there is much controversy over what views in later writers can be ascribed to him. That he was a mystic, once a popular view, has been strongly contested; and his influence on subsequent philosophers and writers is not as certain as once was thought.

H. Strasburger, *JRS*, 1965, 40ff.
L. Edelstein and I. G. Kidd, *Posidonius*, 1, 1972;
F. H. Sandback, *The Stoics*, 1975, 129ff.

POSTUMUS, Marcus Cassianus Latinus Governor of Gaul and commander of the Rhine frontier under *Gallienus, he captured Cologne and killed Gallienus' son and his guardian, the praetorian prefect (AD 360). P. made himself emperor and won control of Spain and Britain as well. He established a separate empire, with his own Senate and magistrates. By his defence of the Rhine frontier he gave some security to the West, and Gallienus was unable to overcome him. But in AD 268, after putting down the revolt of Laelianus in Mogontiacum, P. was killed by his own soldiers.

POTIDAEA Greek city on the isthmus of Pallene (the western promontory of *Chalcidice), founded *c.* 600 BC by Corinth (under *Periander). It was still under the influence of its mother-city in the 5th century, when Corinth sent her the supreme magistrate every year (Thuc. 1.56). But at that time P. was a member of the Delian League after it had fought the Persians in 480—479 BC. The revolt of P. against Athens in 432 BC was one of the contributing causes of the Peloponnesian War. Athens, however, captured the city after a siege (430 BC), and sent cleruchs to settle there. P. was set free after the Peloponnesian War and joined the Chalcidian League. In 364 BC it again came under Athenian control but in 356 BC *Philip II captured P. and later destroyed it. *Cassander founded his new city Cassandreia on the site (316 BC), which received the whole of Pallene as its territory.
J. A. Alexander, *Potidaea*, 1963.

POTTERY The importance of P. in ancient times was immense. It supplied the basic implements for domestic life. Pots were used for cooking. Liquids were stored, served and transported in vessels made of P. Even dry foods, especially grains, were stored and transported in jars. The importance of P. to trade cannot then be overrated. Terracotta lamps were a part of the P. industry and in certain places and periods large jars were used for burial.

The use of clay for manufacturing P. dates from Neolithic times in Greece and elsewhere. At first, P. was only hand and home-made. In all the stages of production — the preparation of the clay, the forming of the vessel and its firing improvements were introduced with time. An important invention was that of the potter's wheel. Henceforth P. production became an occupation for professionals. From early times, craftsmen used to decorate the vessels, and although this was a non-essential addition for practical purposes, it came to be one of the flourishing forms of art.

Clay is a plastic material. In preparing it the craftsman had to clean it and to remove pebbles and other coarse particles. This was done by sifting, immersing in water, and kneading. A few pots, mainly small bowls, were directly shaped by hand. Before the invention of the wheel, larger vessels were shaped by the technique of coiling. P. was also formed by using moulds. With the introduction of the potter's wheel (dating from the 4th millenium BC in Sumer, from the early 2nd millenium BC in the Minoan civilization), the craftsman would throw a lump of clay on a turning wheel. Large vessels were produced in sections and then fastened together with a thin clay which covered the joining points. After the vessels dried they were fired in a kiln (the use of a kiln dates from Neolithic times). Temperatures of $700°-800°$ C were needed to fire the vessels; tests conducted on P. finds have shown that Mycenaean kilns produced temperatures of over $1,000°$ C. Vessels were decorated prior to the firing stage. This was done by covering the surface with a protective layer of diluted clay on which the decoration was applied. The diluted clay (slip) was a kind of varnish, but not strictly speaking a glaze. The best achievements in this technique, which show a remarkable knowledge of the firing process, were made by the Attic potters of the 6th and 5th centuries BC who produced the black figure and red figure vases. They used clay which contained iron and the colours, black, red or brown, were obtained by firing the same slip in three stages. In the first, when the kiln was open to air, the entire vessel turned red by the oxidizing fire. In the second, air was not admitted to the kiln and the vessel and the slip turned black. In the third stage only the diluted parts of the slip reoxidized then turned red while those areas with a thicker slip remained black (or grey).

By its nature clay can take on any shape that the craftsman wants to produce. However, certain types of vessels were repeatedly used for a special purpose. The amphora with two handles was the main vessel for carrying liquids and other materials. It was so commonly used that it came to be a unit of capacity measure (see *Measures). The stamnos and the pelike, also with two handles, served the same purpose. There were several shapes of drinking cups: the two-handled kylix, skyphos, and headed-shaped vessels, like the rhython. Wine and water (only the wild *Centaurs drank wine neat) were mixed in the krater, a large vessel with a wide mouth. Wine was cooled in the psykter. The large jar for carrying water from a fountain was the hydria with three handles. The single-handled oinochoe was the wine-jug, the single-handled lekythos was the oil-jug. The aryballos was an oil and perfume vessel. Jewellery and toilet articles were kept in the pyxis. These are only the main shapes, and though the essential features lasted for centuries, there were changes and variations.

P. is an excellent medium for decoration. In addition to the shape which can be artistically produced, the craftsman can incise, stamp, work in relief, glaze or paint. The most important art was that of painting. The surface of the vessels was used to apply ornamental motifs, geometric patterns, plants, and scenes with realistic or imaginary figures. Mythological themes as well as subjects from

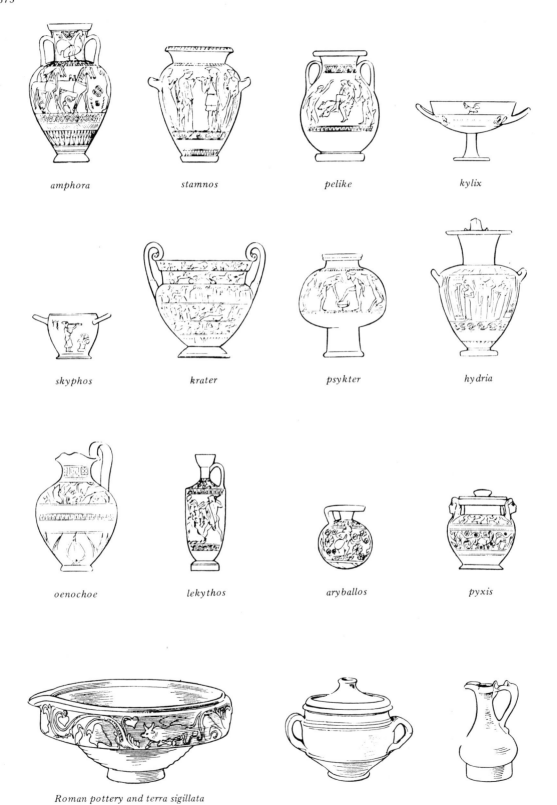

amphora

stamnos

pelike

kylix

skyphos

krater

psykter

hydria

oenochoe

lekythos

aryballos

pyxis

Roman pottery and terra sigillata

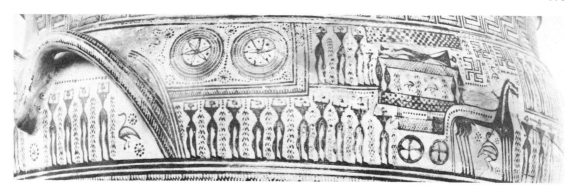

funeral procession, geometric style, 8th century BC

Attic red-figured amphora, c. 440–430 BC   *Attic black-figured amphora, c. 525 BC*

daily life were painted. In the history of Greek vase-painting, several periods are noted, but obviously there were local variations. Minoan vase-painting had mainly ornamental motifs with floral and marine subjects. During the height of the Mycenaean civilization, vase-painting was mainly abstract and stylized and lost some of the Minoan brightness. The 11th–10th centuries BC are known as the proto-geometrical period, characterized by curvilinear ornaments which occupied only parts of the surface. They developed into the geometric style of the 9th–8th centuries BC with more complicated designs which covered the whole surface of the vases. In addition to the geometric patterns (zigzags, network, meander, swastika, etc.), the artists now included animal and human figures either singly or in groups. The figures were painted in silhouette (later in outline) and the usual scenes were battles, funerals or dances. In the late 8th century BC, under the impact of the connexions with the East, the Orientalizing period began. Eastern floral patterns, notably the lotus and the palmette, eastern animals and monsters, like panthers and sphinxes, were painted in addition to or instead of the geometric patterns which also changed. Outline drawing was introduced alongside the silhouette and use was also made of polychromy, and the patterns became less orderly. Corinth and Attica were the main P. centres in Greece but it was also the great period of the east Greek P. There were several other important centres. In the course of the 6th century BC Athens came to dominate the international P. market while Corinth's influence declined: Attic ceramics were exported to all the Mediterranian countries and to the Black Sea region as well. The Attic artists first developed the black-figured style and later (c. 530 BC) the red-figured style. The scenes painted included myths of gods (Zeus, Apollo, Athena, Dionysus etc.) and heroes, notably Heracles, Theseus and Perseus. Other myths, such as the battles of the Amazons and the Greeks, of the Centaurs and the Lapiths, were also favourites. But the artists also painted everyday scenes. With the new style, the two dimensional drawing was gradually replaced by the three-quarter view which became dominant in the 5th century BC. Some painters achieved great works of art and are known by name or from the works they produced (e.g. *Execias, *Cleophrades, *Brygus, *Duris (1), *Meidias).

The developed painting and bronze craftsmanship proved a successful competitor to painted P. in the 4th century BC. Though the rich, vigorous style of the Attic artists continued, a new element was introduced: the relief decoration. This clearly came as an imitation of bronze works. Fine works were produced but this did not save Greek vase-painting which ended in the 3rd century BC.

Greek P. was exported to southern Italy and Etruria from early times. But a local industry always existed in Italy. In so far as vase-painting developed it was in imitation of the Greek models. The Etruscan contribution in the Archaic period is the "buchero" style, that is, dark-clay P. with a burnished black surface. This was decorated by incision or relief. The other main contribution from Italy was the *terra sigillata* under the Roman Empire. This was often produced in moulds, incorporated reliefs and was noted for its red outer layer. The most famous centre was *Arretium.

A. Furumark, *The Mycenaean Pottery*, 1941;
J. N. Coldstream, *Greek Geometric Pottery*, 1968;
J. V. Noble, *Techniques of Painted Attic Pottery*, 1965;
R. J. Charleston, *Roman Pottery*, 1965;
J. D. Beazley, *Etruscan Vase-Paintings*, 1967.

PRAEFECTURA The administrative unit within Roman territory which was subject to the authority of a *praefectus* delegated by the *praetor urbanus*. Such prefects were sent to administer justice in the local centres of rural areas and also occasionally to *Municipia with *civitas sine suffragio*. Two special *praefecti* were sent to *Capua and *Cumae from 318 BC on; from 211 BC they were elected and not appointed by the praetor. After the extension of Roman citizenship to all of Italy, as a result of the *Bellum Sociale, the Italian municipalities were given wider powers of jurisdiction, and these *praefecti* disappeared.

A. J. Toynbee, *Hannibal's Legacy*, 1964–5 (s.v.).

PRAEFECTUS (pl. praefecti) The title of many military officers and civil officials at Rome. The commanders of the *alae* were P. The *Cohors of the *Auxilia was commanded by a P. In Egypt the commanders of the legions were P. The *P. castrorum* was the commander of a legionary camp. The *Annona, *Alimenta and *Aerarium were administered by P. under the Empire. The commanders of the *Vigiles and the Roman *navy (in Ravenna and Misenum) were also P. The highest officials who bore the title P. were the *P. Aegypti* (governor of *Egypt), the *P. Urbi, and the *P. Praetorio.

PRAEFECTUS PRAETORIO Commander of the *praetorians. The office was instituted by Augustus in 2 BC, who at that time appointed two men of the Equestrian order to command the praetorians. His example was normally followed by subsequent emperors and except for a few occasions these units were commanded by two equestrian PP. The position gave great powers to the PP. — they commanded the most important troops in the capital, since, from AD 23, the praetorians were concentrated in Rome. In cases of anarchy, some PP. played the role of emperor-makers; *Macrinus and *Philip the Arab used the office to make themselves emperors. In the course of time they also acquired civil powers. They were members of the *Consilium Principis and from the 2nd century AD their jurisdiction extended to include cases in Italy beyond the 100 mile area from Rome. They also heard appeals from both senatorial and imperial provinces, and acquired financial duties. Some PP. had a large share in the administration of the empire — for instance, *Sejanus under Tiberius, *Burrus under Nero and *Plautianus under Septimius *Severus. Others were prominent jurists, like *Papinianus, *Ulpianus and *Paulus. With the administrative reforms of *Constantine the nature of the office changed; the PP. lost their military functions and became the supreme civil officials of the dioceses. By the late 4th century AD the empire had four territorial prefectures: East, Illyricum, Italy and the Gauls. The prefects were now senators, not Equites, and were often given the consulate and the honorary title of *patricius*.

Jolowicz, *Roman Law*[3] (s.v.);
L. L. Howe, *The Praetorian Prefect from Commodus to Diocletian*, 1942; Jones, *Lat. Rom. Emp.* (s.v.).

PRAEFECTUS URBI At Rome, according to tradition, a delegate of the king on his absence from the city and of the consuls under the Republic. Only on rare occasions were such delegates appointed under the Republic. Augustus revived the office but his first choice, *Messala Corvinus, resigned and only late in his reign did he appoint another man. The PU. was always a senator and normally of consular rank. He was invested with *Imperium, had the *cohortes urbanae* (see *Cohors) under his command

and was responsible for the maintenance of order in Rome. In connection with his duties he had jurisdiction which in the course of time extended to 100 miles from Rome and replaced that of other magistrates. *Constantine II instituted a PU. for Constantinopole (AD 359).
W. Sinnigen, *The Officium of the Urban Prefecture during the Later Roman Empire*, 1957;
Jolowicz, *Roman Law*[3] (s.v.).

PRAENESTE (modern Palestrina) City in Latium, situated on a high site 23 km east-southeast of Rome. In mythology, it was founded by a son of *Latinus, or by Telegonus son of *Odysseus. It was under Etruscan influence in the 7th century BC and after the decline of Etruscan power south of the Tiber it became one of the important Latin cities (5th century BC). It was one of the leading Latin cities which fought Rome in the 4th century. After the defeat of the Latini in 340–338 BC, it lost territory (Liv. 8.14) but retained its autonomy until the *Bellum Sociale. The homonymous son of *Marius was besieged here by Sulla, who plundered P. and settled a colony of veterans on land confiscated here. For his victory in P., Sulla instituted annual games here. Many fashionable villas were built in P. under the Empire and it was famous for its great oracular temple of Fortuna Primigenia. The earliest Latin inscription comes from P., the Fibula Praenestina (6th century BC).

PRAETOR Regular Roman magistrate, holder of *Imperium instituted in 367 BC and first elected for the year 366 BC. P. had originally been the name of the two supreme Roman magistrates who were instituted with the foundation of the Republic and who were later called *consuls. The P. had all the power inherent in the Imperium but his was inferior to that of the consul and hence he was accompanied by only six lictors, and not twelve. A second P. was instituted in 242 BC to deal with judicial cases in which one of the parties was a foreigner. The original P. was known as *P. urbanus*, and the new one came to be known as *P. peregrinus*. In 227 BC two new P.'s were instituted to be governors of the Roman provinces of Sicily and Sardinia, and two more were added a

The famous marine mosaic from Praeneste (cf. Plin NH 36.25)

few years after the Second Punic War for Spain (196 BC). The P. actually had unlimited power in his province. Sulla added two more to the office (81 BC) to be chairmen of the *Quaestiones. Sulla also established a minimum age of 39 years for the office. Caesar increased the number of P.'s to 16 and under Augustus the number varied from 10 to 16. Their judicial functions made the edicts (*Edictum) of the *P. urbanus* most important for the development of Roman *law. Under the Empire the P.s lost effective powers and only minor cases were left to them. However, the office remained an essential one for advance in the imperial service. The only function left to the P. was the celebration of games which the P. himself financed. Constantine made the office of P. a *munus*. Jolowicz, *Roman Law*[3] (s.v.).

PRAETORIANS The soldiers of the *cohors praetoria*, the personal bodyguard of the Roman general from the 2nd century BC. *Augustus followed this usage to organize a special force of nine cohorts to serve as his bodyguard in 27 BC. Each cohort numbered 1,000 soldiers (but in one view only 500, and 1,000 only from the time of Septimius *Severus). From the time of *Domitian there were ten cohorts. Three of them were stationed near Rome and the rest in Italy. In 2 BC he instituted the office of the *praefectus praetorio*, when two such officials were given command of the P. Each cohort was commanded by a tribune who was an experienced soldier. The P. were moved to Rome by *Sejanus (AD 23) and their camp, *castra praetoria*, is still in existence and used by the Italian army. Their proximity to the centre of government made the P. politically important. This was first divulged in AD 41 when Claudius was made emperor by the P. after the murder of Caligula, while the Senate held a discussion about whether or not to restore the Republic. The P. again showed their hand in the downfall of *Nero, the murder of *Galba and the elevation of *Otho. In fact, these were exceptional cases, which were again repeated with the murder of *Pertinax and the elevation of *Didius Iulianus. The Guard was finally abolished by Constantine (AD 313).

The P. were an elite corps and were given better conditions than the legionaries (see *Armies, Roman). Septimius Severus replaced the old P., who were mainly recruited in Italy, with provincial soldiers, mainly from Illyria. See *Armies, Roman (with bibliography).

PRAXITELES Son of Cephisodotus, leading Athenian sculptor of the 4th century BC. Several of his works achieved wide renown. His most famous statue was the "Aphrodite of Cnidos", which is known from many Roman copies. The goddess was totally nude, an unusual representation, holding her drapery in her hand. A model of beauty, it was considered by Pliny the Elder as the finest statue ever produced (*NH* 36.20), and Lucian noted the gentle smile on her lips (*Eikones* 20). Another famous work of P. is that of Hermes with the infant Dionysus. It was described by Pausanias (5.17,3) and was found in Olympia in 1877. The opinion that this is a Roman copy or that Pausanias referred to another P. is untenable. Other works of P. include the "Apollo Sauroktonos" (Lizard-Slayer) known from copies of an original bronze, the "Aphrodite of Aries", "Artemis of Gabii", the "Eros of Thespiae", the base statue from Mantinea (original) with Apollo, Artemis, Muses and Marsyas, the Eros of Parium, and satyrs.

P. was enormously successful and his works were imitated and copied in the Graeco-Roman world. He worked mainly in marble and his statues were noted for their

Head of the statue of Hermes by Praxiteles found in Olympia, probably the original

grace and their elegant expression of motion.

PRIAM Son of Laomedon, king of Troy at the time of the Trojan War. His wife was *Hecuba and by her and his concubines he had numerous sons and daughters, among them *Hector, *Paris, *Deiphobus, *Helenus, and *Cassandra. In the *Iliad* he is a great and rich king with a large kingdom at the beginning of the war. In his youth he had fought the *Amazons but now he is a wise old man. He dislikes the war but is gentle to *Helen who caused it. He goes to the Greek camp to redeem the body of Hector and makes a strong impression on Achilles. He loses his sons in the war and at the fall of his city he is killed by *Neoptolemus (Verg. *Aen.* 506ff.) at the altar of Zeus. He became known as the one who lived through contrasting extremes of fortune. Two themes of his story were often painted: the ransoming of Hector's corpse and the manner of his death at the sack of Troy.

PRIAPUS Phallic god of fertility who originated from *Lampsacus in the Hellespont region. In the wake of Alexander's conquest his cult spread to the Greek world and was to be found in many places, notably Attica, Alexandria, and other great cities; it also reached Italy. In the Greek myth about him, Dionysus was his father and his mother was a nymph or Aphrodite herself. P. was represented as a figure with an enormous phallus (cf. *Hermes). Donkeys, considered to be the embodiment of lust, were sacrificed to him in Lampsacus. P. was capable of giving or withholding sexual potency. However, in the Graeco-Roman world he lost some of his primitive vitality, and his red-painted, grotesque figure with a large phallus was often presented as a sort of scarecrow and protector of gardens. Greek and Latin poets wrote poems about him and there is one extant collection, *Priapea*. It includes 85 short Latin poems addressed to P., written under Augustus by unknown poets. Some of the poems are allegedly by Virgil, Tibullus, and Ovid. The poems describe in obscene language the phallus of the god and the punishment to be suffered by those who sinned against him.

E. Baehrens, *Poetae Latini Minores* (Teubner), 1, 1879.

PRIENE Old Ionian city in Caria, whose original site is not known (Pausan. 7.2,10). The city was resettled north of Miletus in the mid-4th century BC. During the German excavations (1895–8), the plan of the city was revealed in detail. The walls encircled the city itself and the high citadel (*Acropolis) adjacent to it. It was planned according to the Hippodromic grid system with the *Agora in its center. The other public buildings, well-planned according to the grid pattern, were also excavated. The Agora was an open courtyard with colonnaded halls. Among the other public buildings of interest are the Bouleuterium (council hall), the theatre, the old gymnasium and the temple of Athena Polias. Many inscriptions were also discovered and one of them records a dedication of Alexander.

G. E. Bean, *Aegean Turkey*, 1966, 197ff.

PRIMIPILUS The senior centurion in the Roman army. In the manipular system of the *Legion the two centurions of the first maniple of the *triarii* were of this rank. After the development of the *Cohors, and under the Empire, the P. was the senior centurion of the first cohort of the legion. One who reached this rank was able to advance in his equestrian career.

PRINCEPS ("the first") The term P. (pl. *principes*) was used by Latin writers under the Republic and under the Empire to denote leading men of the Roman state as well as chieftains or senoir statesmen of foreign states. Those Romans to whom the term was applied were normally of the *Nobilitas and all had attained the consulate. The *P. civitatis* ("leaders of the state") were those who had control of the Senate and the government of the state. The term denoted a social-political reality and not legal status.

P. Senatus was the title given to the senator placed first in the list of the senators which was prepared by the censors. The custom was to appoint to this position the oldest patrician *censorius* (one who served as censor).

Above all P. was the unofficial title which *Augustus chose for himself; *principatus* (Principate) was his kind of regime. His constitutional powers were accumulated over the years and there was not an official title to designate the sum of them. This was in line with his policy to keep as far as possible to the Republican institutions. The obvious Republican precedent for the use of the term was *Pompey who had been preeminent in the Roman state during the years 80–50 BC. P. was not one of the *principes civitatis*, but the P. referred to in singular by Cicero.

But whatever Cicero meant by his *P. civitatis*, the constitutional and extra-constitutional powers of Augustus were wider. Augustus himself applied the term to his rule in his *Res Gestae* (see *Monumentum Ancyranum) and Roman historians, notably Tacitus (*Ann.* 1.1 and 9) emphasized his choice of this term. Augustus' aim was to avoid the bad connotations associated with titles like Rex or Dictator and to stress his conformity with the Republican tradition. His successor Tiberius revealed the different aspects of his position in his saying that he was *dominus* (master) of his slaves, Imperator of his soldiers and P. of all the rest (Dio 57.8,2). All Augustus' successors assumed the title but it never appeared in their official titles as they are known from inscriptions and other documents. However, the name could not disguise the facts and in common usage, even by historians and jurists, it was another name to designate the emperor. Hence there is the saying "*princeps supra leges*" (the P. is above laws) and that which the P. wished had the force of law.

M. Gelzer, *The Roman Nobility*, 1969;
M. Hammond, *The Augustan Principate*[2] , 1968.

PRISCIANUS Important grammarian, native of *Caesarea Iol in Mauretania, lived in the early 6th century AD. He taught in Constantinopole and is mainly known for his *Institutiones Grammaticae*. This work in 18 books deals mainly with the parts of speech (Books 1–16) as well as syntax. P. made extensive use of former grammarians, both Greek and Roman, and gives many citations to illustrate his points. He is noted for his use of the comparative method in the treatment of the grammar and syntax of the two languages. The work became a standard school book in the Middle Ages and various commentaries were written on it. Several other works of P. are extant including a treatise on Roman numerals and coins, a metrical treatise, a panegyric on the Emperor Anastasius and a poem based on the geographical work of *Dionysius (6) Periegetes.

Keil, *Gr. Lat.*, 3, 306ff.;
E. Baehrens, *Poetae Latini Minores*, 5, 1883, 264ff.

PRISCUS Greek rhetorician and historian of the 5th century AD, native of Panium in Thrace. He was an official in the imperial service of the Eastern Empire and travelled abroad, visiting – among other places – Atila (AD 449), Egypt and Rome. He wrote a history of his time which covered at least the years AD 433–72. This is known only from considerable excerpts included by later writers; it was used by *Cassiodorus for his description of the Huns.

E. A. Thompson, *A History of Attila*, 1948 (s.v.).

PROBUS, Marcus Aurelius Roman emperor (AD 276–82). Of low origin, he advanced in the military service and in AD 276 revolted against Florian, the successor of the Emperor *Tacitus (2). Florian was killed by his own soldiers at Tarsus after they were made restless by the delaying tactics of P. In the six years of his reign, P. continued the vigorous policy of *Aurelianus. He defeated and expelled the *Alamanni, *Burgundians and *Franks from Gaul (AD 276–9), and then defeated the Vandals in the Balkan peninsula. He suppressed several revolts and in AD 281 was able to celebrate a spectacular triumph. The army however was provoked by his rigorous discipline and when the praetorian prefect *Carus revolted in 282 P. was killed by his own men.

PROCLUS Important neo-Platonist philosopher (AD 410 or 412–85), native of Lycia. He came to Athens as a young student to complete his studies and stayed there for almost the rest of his life. He succeeded his teacher Syrianus as Head of t   *Academy. Immensely learned, P. was a prolific writer and much of his writings are preserved. These include the short *Elements of Theology* and the work *Platonic Theology* in six books; commentaries on the *Timaeus, Republic, Parmenides, Alcibiades* and *Cratylus* of Plato; short essays on Fate, Providence and Evil. In his philosophical work, P. presented a synthesis of Greek philosophy blended with mythological and religious ideas, and this had wide influence in medieval times. He also wrote *Outline of Astronomical Hypotheses, Elements of Physics,* commentaries on Euclid and Claudius Ptolemy and literary works. In his works he elaborated on the geometrical doctrines of Plato.

L. J. Rosan, *The Philosophy of Proclus*, 1949.

PROCONSUL and PROPRAETOR Roman magistrates were elected and given powers for one year only. But experience showed that it was better sometimes to prolong the powers of the magistrates. The first case was in 326 BC when the Assembly passed a motion to extend the Imperium of *Publilius Philo "in place of consul" (*proconsul*) after the termination of his consulate. He was thus able to complete the siege of Naples and to capture it. Thereafter the "prorogation of Imperium" (*prorogatio imperii*) of consuls and praetors became a usual method and normally this was done by the Senate. Occasionally, private men were given Imperium "instead of praetor". The prorogation of the Imperium of praetors and consuls after their year of office, with the assigning of provinces, became frequent in the course of the 2nd century BC. Some praetors received Imperium *proconsule*, when they had a larger army and important duties (as such they had twelve *lictors, not their usual six). Proconsuls and propraetors then were those who were invested with the Imperium of consul or praetor respectively. From 23 BC on Augustus governed his province with *imperium proconsulare*.

W. F. Jashemski, *Origin and History of Proconsular and Propraetorian Imperium*, 1950.

PROCOPIUS Greek historian and Byzantine official, native of Caesarea in Palestine, born *c.* AD 500 and died after AD 560. He studied rhetoric and law and became a counsellor to Justinian's leading general, Belisarius, in AD 527. He was with Belisarius in his wars against Persia, the Vandals (Africa) and the Ostrogoths (Italy). After AD 540 he returned to Constantinople and wrote his works while still in the imperial service. He later became prefect of Constantinopole (AD 562).

P.'s main work is the eight-book *History of the Wars of Justinian* (there are other titles). It mainly covers the wars of the period: against Persia (Books 1–2), in Africa (Books 3–4), and in Italy (Books 5–7). The eighth book contains more material on these areas with accounts of the wars up to AD 553. The work also includes accounts of the inner politics of Constantinople and events in other parts of the empire. P. wrote in a clear style, used documents and aimed at establishing what really happened. At the same time, he wrote his second historical work, the *Secret History* (*Anecdota*), which was completed *c.* AD 550. The work certainly appeared after Justinian's time and probably after P.'s death. It is an abusive attack on Justinian and his policy. The emperor is depicted as an oppressor and a murderer responsible for every mishap of the period. Several scurrilous chapters are also devoted to Justinian's wife Theodora. Even Belisarius is criticized. Sometime around AD 553 P. was commissioned by Justinian to write an account of the latter's building operations. The resultant work *On the Buildings* is arranged geographically and is an excellent account of contemporary monuments and art (Constantimople, Asia, Armenia, Balkan peninsula and Africa).

Edition: J. Haury (Teubner), 1962–4.

PROCURATOR P. was the term applied to one who took care of the affairs of another person, whom he represented. Under the Empire it was the title of many and various imperial officials. Most of them were *Equites, others were freedmen. The following were the main types of P.: first, those who were responsible for the management of the emperor's properties in senatorial provinces. They sometimes performed other duties for the emperor and in the course of time were given jurisdiction in cases associated with the *Fiscus: second, P.s who were responsible for the finances in imperial provinces, their main duties being to collect the taxes and other imperial revenues and to pay the army; third, P.s who were governors of several lesser provinces including *Thrace, *Noricum, *Judaea, and *Mauretania. In the early Principate they bore the title Praefectus. In addition to the above, officials responsible to the imperial estates, in the administration of the *Annona and the imperial mint, for the collection of indirect taxes, etc. bore the title P. In the course of time a hierarchy of office was established and the different grades were marked by different payments: *sexagenarii* whose annual salary was 60,000 sesterces, *centenarii* (100,000), *ducenarii* (200,000), and *trecenarii* (300,000).

Jones, *Studies,* 19ff.; F. Millar, *Historia,* 1964, 180ff.; P.A. Brunt, *Latomus,* 1966, 460ff.

PROCUSTES Mythological robber, son of Poseidon, the last one whom *Theseus encountered on his way to Attica. P. lived in Attica or at Eleusis and used to torture to death those who happened to pass by him. He had two beds, one short and one long. He would hammer out his short victims to the length of the long bed or fit the longer victims to the short bed by cutting off their limbs. Theseus used the same method to kill him. P. is sometimes called by other names which describe his deeds (Procaptas, Damastes, Plypemon).

PRODICUS Greek Sophist of the 5th century BC, native of Ceos. He occasionally represented his city in diplomatic embassies and visited Athens several times. He had a high reputation as a teacher of rhetoric and paid special attention to differentiating between terms with similar meanings. That Socrates appreciated his moral teaching can be seen from the *Protagoras* of Plato. P. is famous for his myth about Heracles standing at the crossroads and preferring the hard way of Virtue to that of Vice.

PROEDROI The chairmen of the Athenian *Ekklesia and *Boule from the early 4th century BC (earlier, this duty fell to the chairman of the *Prytaneis). The chairman of each meeting was drawn by double lot from the members of the Boule.

Arist., *Athen. Pol.*, 44.

PROETUS Son of Abas, mythological king of Argos. After the death of his father he fought with his brother Acrisius over the succession and was later helped by Jobates, his father-in-law. Finally, he left Argos to his brother and took Tiryns for himself. He sent *Bellerophon to Jobates to be killed after his wife pretended that he tried to seduce her. His daughters were driven mad by Hera or Dionysus and were cured by *Melampus who received a part of P.'s kingdom.

PROLETARII Roman citizens who had no property to declare before the *censors except their children (*proles*). The censors assigned them all to one "century" in the *Comitia Centuriata. As they had no property, they were normally not recruited into the army. This changed after the reforms of Marius who recruited P. into his army.

Jolowicz, *Roman Law*[3] (s.v.).

PROMETHEUS ("forethought" or "foreseeing") One of the Titans in Greek legend, son of Iapetus and Gaea (or Clymene), brother of Atlas and Epimetheus ("afterthought"). His myth is told by Hesiod (*Theog.* 507ff., 565ff.) and many other writers. P. was wiser than the other Titans and did not take part in their war against the Olympian gods. He also helped Zeus give birth to *Athena from his head. But he cheated and enraged Zeus. In the first place he made man from clay (Pausan. 10.4,4) and taught him his arts. Later, when Zeus took fire away from man, P. stole a spark of fire from the fire of Hephaestus, or from the chariot of Sun. With this he lit the pith of the stem of a giant fennel and so was able to give fire back to man. On another occasion he tricked Zeus to choose the bones of a sacrifice which P. wrapped in fat, and in this way man won the better parts of the flesh. Zeus took revenge first by creating woman. This was *Pandora whom Zeus sent to Epimetheus. But Zeus also chained P. to a rock in the Caucasian mountains and sent an eagle to tear out his liver, which grew again every night. P. was finally released by Heracles who killed the eagle with his arrow.

Of Aeschylus' plays that took the myth of P. as their subject, only *Prometheus Bound* is extant. In this P. is the benefactor of man who fights against the tyranny of the Olympian god Zeus. P. knows a secret which endangers the reign of Zeus — that *Thetis will give birth to a son mightier than his father — but he refuses to reveal it. For this he suffers further punishment. But P. the freedom-fighter, creator of man and his protector is a later development. Originally he had an amoral character and was the embodiment of deceit and trickery. He was worshipped by potters, smiths and craftsmen generally, especially in Attica. To some extent then he competed against Hephaestus.

Themes from the myth of P. appear in art from the 7th century BC on. It was only natural that his suffering, his fight against Zeus and his services for mankind attracted Christian thinkers, modern writers, painters and poets — each one picking out that motif of the myth that suited him.

PROPERTIUS, Sextus Roman elegiac poet, native of Assisi in Umbria, born to a well-to-do family *c.* 48 BC. His father died when he was still a child and part of the family property was confiscated by the triumvirs in 42—41 BC. He was sent to Rome to study law but turned to poetry instead. In Rome he met, and became one of the lovers of, the courtesan he calls Cynthia; her real name was Hostia. His relations with her had a great effect on his poetry and in his first book of twenty-two elegies he mainly writes of her and himself. The publication of the book (by 28 BC) won P. fame and he was admitted to the literary circle of *Maecenas. The next book was published *c.* 26 BC. Much of this is also about Cynthia. Book 3 appeared *c.* 22 BC and by that time P.'s affair with Cynthia had ended after lasting for some six years. Book 4 followed after a longer interval, appearing in 16 BC. No more is heard of P. and the date of his death is not known.

P.'s first book was written under the impact of his fresh experience with his mistress. With grace and power P. tells of his passion for Cynthia, and his attempts to liberate himself from her. From the first poem of Book 2 it appears that the poet was asked to help spread official propaganda. But, as he says, to write on great achievements is not his field. His are erotic themes and the book is indeed of this kind. Book 3 contains various types of poems. P. adopts the Alexandrian style and uses Callimachus as his model. There are love poems, but in these P. treats the subject in a mainly general fashion, examining the psychology of love as he already did in Book 2. In one of the poems (9) he seeks to excuse himself for not writing court poetry. And yet one elegy is about Actium. Book 4 also deals with various subjects. In one poem P. imagines himself as a guide for the religious calendar of Rome. But the astrologer he guides shows him that his genre is love poetry. And yet there are a few more learned antiquarian elegies as well as several remarkable poems like those on Cynthia (7,8) and Cornelia (11).

To sum up, P.'s poetry presents a variety of themes but he is above all a poet of love. The poems extend from those in which his passion takes possession of him to those in which he is the mouthpiece of all lovers. In the Alexandrian tradition he can be very learned and obscure, making allusions that are difficult to follow. He shifts mood and thought in the same poem and this, too, makes him difficult to follow. He is noted for his wit and remarkable visual imagination. On Quintilian's evidence some considered him the most elegant of the Roman elegists (10.1,93).

H. G. Butler (Loeb), 1912;
H. E. Butler and E. A. Barber (Ed. and commentary), 1933;
Ezra Pound, *Hommage to Sextus Propertius*, 1934;
N. Hubbard, *Propertius*, 1974.

PROPYLAEA In Greek architecture, a monumental gateway. The most famous one was that at the western entrance of the Athenian Acropolis. It was built by Mnesicles under Pericles in 437—432 BC, and it consisted of a central wall with two Doric porticoes, one to the west from which the Acropolis was approached by a steep slope, and one to the east. The wall was broken by five doorways, the central large one being for the sacrificial animals. There was a projection to the north and one of the rooms so formed was the Pinakotheke, a picture gallery in which there were, among other things, paintings by *Polygnotus. The structure was roofed and the ceilings were known for their decoration. The P. was built of white Pentelic marble with some additions of black Eleusinian stone. Mnescicles planned to attach other new buildings but the Peloponnesian War interrupted and brought an end to the building activity, and the P. was never finished.

W. B. Dinsmoor, *Architecture of Ancient Greece*, 1950, 198ff.; J. Bundgaard, *Mnesicles*, 1957.

PROTAGORAS Greek *Sophist, (*c.* 485—*c.* 415 BC), native of Abdera, P. won a reputation and charged high sums for his teaching. He taught in several places, particularly in Athens. In 444 BC he was selected to give the code of laws for the new city of *Thurii. He is said to have been convicted of impiety in Athens in 416 BC. As a Sophist, he claimed to teach virtue (*arete*), that is, efficiency in winning success. His famous saying was: "Man is the measure of all things", which summed up his scepticism about the possibility of gaining absolute knowledge. He also took an agnostic attitude to the question of the existence of gods. In Plato's dialogue *Protagoras*, P. is attacked by Socrates for making the teaching of virtue his profession.

K. Freeman, *The Pre-Socratic Philosophers*, 1946.

PROTEUS Sea god, shepherd of the herds of the sea, servant or son of Poseidon. He has the power of prophecy and of changing his shape. But if grasped hard, he takes his true shape and gives answer to questions. In the *Odyssey* (4.349ff.) he lives on the island of Pharos in Egypt and yields to Menelaus and answers his questions. *Aristaeus, too, succeeds in consulting him (Verg. *Georg.* 4.387ff.). Herodotus (2.112f.) says that he was the king of Egypt who preserved Helen for Menelaus.

PROVINCIA The original meaning of this term was any sphere of action of a magistrate holding Imperium. In the course of time the Senate acquired the right to define and assign the *provinciae* to magistrates who would draw lots or divide them by agreement. In later times *provinciae* were also assigned to quaestors and promagistrates. The term at first, then, did not have the territorial meaning which it had after the expansion of Roman power in overseas countries. The *praetor urbanus* (see *Praetor), for instance, had the *provincia urbana*, consisting mainly of the administration of justice. The normal province of the *praetor peregrinus* (see *Praetor) was the administration of justice in cases where one of the parties was a *peregrinus* (foreigner). This concept began to change after Rome conquered lands outside Italy. The first territorial provinces to be constituted were Sicily and Sardinia (227 BC), only 14 and 11 years respectively after Rome took possession of them from Carthage. Two new praetors were then instituted and they would draw lots for these provinces. The area conquered in Spain in the Second Punic War was probably organized in 197 BC and then two more praetors were instituted. The number of praetors was not added to until Sulla (81 BC), though a few more provinces were constituted: Africa and Macedonia (146 BC), Asia (133 BC), and Gaul (late 2nd century BC). To administer the increasing number of *provinciae*, the system of *proconsuls or propraetors was applied. But the rise of the *Quaestiones, which were reorganized by *Sulla, who added two praetors, occasioned adjustment in the administration of the provinces. Normally, the magistrates, consuls and praetors, remained in Italy during their year of office, the praetors serving as presidents of the jury courts (*quaestiones*). But even before their election, the Senate, by the law of Gaius *Gracchus (3), determined which provinces the consuls would hold, and the rest naturally would go to the praetors. At the end of their annual term in office the magistrates would proceed to their respective provinces. But if the need arose, the Senate would direct them to go to the province earlier. Even in the 1st century BC the term P. retained its old meaning and in not a few cases it was a task to be executed in Italy or in the overseas areas, without definite geographical limits.

The frontiers of the territorial provinces, notably Spain, were not clearly defined for long periods, and the province was more an amalgamation of different political units than a territory under uniform administration. Some cities had treaties with Rome (*civitates foederatae*) and theoretically were free and outside the authority of the Roman governor. Others had informal rights of autonomy given to them at the organization of the P. but not confirmed by the Senate and the Roman Assembly (*civitates immunes et liberae*). The rest were formally subject to the governor and paid tribute (*civitates stipendiariae*). In some areas the population consisted of tribes, not settled in cities, which retained their forms of organization. However, in course of time the Roman governors asserted their authority in practice, even on the *civitates foederatae*, although the current administration was largely left to the provincials because of the aversion of the Roman government to develop a costly civil service. The basis of the organization of the province was the "law" (*lex provinciae*) issued by the Roman general, helped by a senatorial commission and backed by a Senate's resolution. This was done when the P. was first constituted or later after a major war. The law dealt with administration, taxation and jurisdiction. But every governor issued his *Edictum in which he defined the regulations according to which he would administer the P. In fact, the governor had absolute power, and the only redress the provincials had was to prosecute him under the law of *Repetundae after the end of his office. The governor was assisted by a quaestor and legates to whom he could delegate his authority. He had some administrative staff and would use friends in his entourage (*comites*) and residential Romans for his council. He was responsible for internal security, the administration of justice and the defence of the P. and supervised the municipal and tribal affairs. The collection of indirect taxes was left to the *publicani* and even those provincials who paid fixed sums of money employed taxfarmers for their collection.

The establishment of the Principate of Augustus brought about major changes. Those provinces which he and subsequent emperors had were "imperial". These were governed by the *Legati Augusti pro praetore*, delegates of the emperor, and their finances were assigned to *Procurators. Almost all the provinces with armies were included in this category. The remaining provinces were "senatorial", that is, subject to the authority of the Senate, theoretically as it had been under the Republic but in practice and by his *imperium maius* the emperor could always intervene. Of the senatorial provinces only Africa retained an army for some time, and not after the 1st century AD. Some provinces changed their status from senatorial to imperial and vice versa, and generally the large provinces were divided (notably Gaul and Illyrium). There was some improvement in the behaviour of the governors due to somewhat efficient control by the emperors. One source of oppression was removed by the removal of the *publicani* and the gradual abolition of taxfarming. In the course of time more and more posts were reserved to Equites and under *Gallienus senators could no longer hold military positions. But the system established by Augustus lasted essentially until the 3rd century AD when it was totally reformed by Diocletian.

For individual provinces see: *Achaea, *Africa, *Arabia, *Armenia, *Asia, *Assyria, *Bithynia, *Britannia, *Cappadocia, *Cilicia, *Corsica, *Crete, *Cyprus, *Cyrene, *Dacia, *Dalmatia, *Egypt, *Epirus, *Galatia, *Gallia, *Germania, *Illyricum, *Judaea, *Lycia, *Macedonia, *Mauretania, *Mesopotamia, *Moesia, *Noricum, *Numidia, *Pamphylia, *Pannonia, *Pontus, *Raetia, *Sardinia, *Sicily, *Spain, *Syria, *Thrace.

G. H. Stevenson, *Roman Provincial Administration*, 1939; F. F. Abbot and A. C. Johnson, *Municipal Administration in the Roman Empire*, 1926.

PROVOCATIO The right of P. was that of appeal for a hearing before the *Comitia Centuriata* in cases involving capital punishment. The legal right against summary execution within the *Pomerium by a magistrate with *Imperium was given to Roman citizens by a *lex Valeria*, traditionally in 509 BC, but probably only by the *lex Valeria* of 300 BC. Traditionally, also, the *Decemviri and the *Dictators, until the 3rd century, were exempt from this limitation on their power. Some guarantee of the right of the citizen to a trial before the *Comitia Cen-

turiata in capital cases was given by a law of the Twelve Tables, but it is far from clear to what extent the magistrate's jurisdiction was limited before 300 BC. No doubt in practice the Plebeians under the tribunes exercised a restrictive influence on the magistrates. However, though the principle of appeal was legalized in 300 BC, it proved to be insufficient. It was extended to the military sphere by a *lex Porcia* in the 2nd century BC. After what happened to his brother, Gaius *Gracchus (3) once again enacted the principle that in capital cases the citizen had the right to a hearing before the Roman people (i.e. the Assembly). But in cases of emergency the *Optimates claimed, and applied, the right of the consul to summary execution on the authority of the Senate.

There is much controversy about the P. The orthodox theory, associated with Mommsen, is that the P. was an appeal against a magistrate's sentence and that all capital cases had to be tried by a *Iudicium Populi. A recent view is that only important and political cases came before the Assembly and ordinary crimes were always dealt with by the magistrates.

A. H. M. Jones, *The Roman Criminal Courts*, 1970; Jolowicz, *Roman Law*³ (s.v.).

PRUDENTIUS (Aurelius Prudentius Clemens) Christian Latin poet, born in Spain in AD 348. After a successful public career, he retired and devoted himself to the writing of Christian poems. In these he sought to fight heresy and defend the Church, to attack paganism and to praise the Christian martyrs. His *Cathemerinon*, a collection of hymns for everyday use, and the *Psychomachia* ("Battle for the Soul"), an allegorical poem, are his best known works. In the latter, Pride and Humility (and other pairs) fight over man's soul. Some of his hymns are still used. He also wrote *Peristephanon* ("On the Crown of Martyrs"), *Apotheosis* ("On the Nature of Christ"), *Hamartigenia* ("Origin of Sin"), and *Contra Symmachum*, a polemic against paganism. P. used a wide variety of Latin meters, hexameters, iambics and trochees; he wrote lyric verses and had talent and originality, but he could be tediously long. His works were known in the Middle Ages and had an influence on poetry and art.

H. J. Thomson (Loeb), 1949.

PRUSIAS I, Cholus ("Lame") Son of Ziaëlas, king of Bithynia (*c.* 230—*c.* 182 BC). A warrior and a diplomat, and ambitious, P. attempted throughout his reign to extend his kingdom. Allied with Rhodes he fought Byzantium but could not retain his gains (220 BC). In 218 BC he repelled an invasion by Gauls. In alliance with *Philip V he fought *Attalus I of Pergamum and annexed parts of Phrygia and Mysia. He refounded Cius and Myrleia, given to him by Philip, as Prusias and Apameia (202 BC). Neutral in the Roman war against *Antiochus III, he refused to give back the territory he had taken from Attalus and was defeated in the war that followed (188—183 BC). He then evacuated the area and was about to extradite Hannibal when the latter committed suicide.

PRUSIAS II, Cynegus ("Hunter") Son of Prusias I, king of Bithynia (*c.* 182—149 BC). He cooperated with *Eumenes II against Pharnaces I of Pontus (181—179 BC). His loyalty to Rome amounted to servility (Pol. 30.18). He failed in his war against Attalus II (156—154 BC) and in 149 BC was executed by his own son *Nicomedes II.

Magie, *Asia* (s.v.).

PRYTANEIS ("presidents") The highest magistrates in many Greek cities, especially in western Asia Minor and the adjacent islands. In Athens they were the standing committee of the *Boule. As each of the ten tribes (*Phyle) after the reforms of *Cleisthenes (2) had 50 members of the Boule, there were 50 of the 500 members serving in rotation as P. for one tenth of the year (or for one twelfth of the year after the addition of two tribes in 307 BC). The P. had an office building, the Tholos, situated at the southwest side of the *Agora near that of the Boule (Bouleuterium). A third of the P. under their chairman (*epistates*), who was chosen by lot every day, had to stay in the Tholos day and night. The *epistates* of the P. was also the chairman of any meeting of the Boule or *Ekklesia but this duty was transferred to the *Proedroi in the early 4th century BC. The P. were responsible for the current business of the Boule. As a citizen could serve only twice in the Boule and only once as an *epistates*, many citizens must have had a share in the actual government of the state.

Arist., *Athen. Pol.* 43—4; P. J. Rhodes, *The Athenian Boule*, 1972.

PSYCHE ("soul") The myth of P. and Eros (= Cupid) is a late invention and is best known from *Apuleius' *Metamorphoses*. P. was a young girl whose lover Eros would come to her at night, and she was not allowed to look at him. One night when he fell asleep she looked at him and recognized him, but a drop of oil from her lamp awakened him and he vanished. She went wandering all over the world in search of him and finally found him and lived happily with him.

In Homer the souls of the dead, who resemble their living selves but do not have a memory, inhabit the Underworld. In the *Nequia* (descent to Hades), Odysseus offers them blood to drink which gives them vitality. In art the souls of the dead are often represented as human figures; and according to the myth the battle of *Achilles and *Memnon was decided by the weighing of their souls by Zeus. In another conception, also revealed in art, the souls were like butterflies or birds which left the body at the moment of death. This conception of the soul as a different essence from the body was developed by philosophers. In the Orphic religion (*Orphism), the body is the tomb of the soul. In the *Phaedrus* of Plato, the chariots of the souls are driven by Eros. This connection between Love and Soul became well known and was represented in art and poetry from the 4th century BC. A Hellenistic marble sculpture known as Invention of the Kiss showed P. and Eros together and is known from Roman copies. A psychological version showed Eros tormenting P.

PTOLEMY I SOTER Son of the Macedonian Lagus and Arsinoe, friend of Alexander the Great, the founder of the Ptolemaic (or Lagid) dynasty of Egypt. He was born *c.* 367/366 BC and died in 283/282 BC. Suspected by *Philip II, he was exiled but restored by Alexander after the latter's accession to the throne. He became Alexander's companion and bodyguard and took part in the Persian expedition. He captured Bessus, the Persian satrap who killed *Darius III. In 323 BC he became satrap of Egypt, put *Cleomenes (3) to death and took possession of the body of Alexander which he buried in Memphis. He skilfully repelled the attack of *Perdiccas and defended himself against *Antigonus I. P. gave shelter to *Seleucus I and helped him to regain Babylonia. In 312 BC he won an important battle over *Demetrius I at Gaza. In 306 BC he lost against Demetrius in a naval battle off Salamis in Cyprus. The following year he took the royal title after Antigonus had set the example. He did not participate in the final battle of *Ipsus (301 BC)

Portrait of Ptolemy I Soter on a coin

but was able to occupy Palestine and Phoenicia, which for the next century became the bone of contention with the Seleucids. He also took control of Cyprus, and many Aegean islands and territories in Asia Minor, as well as *Cyrene. P. laid the foundation for all the institutions of the Ptolemaic Empire. He established the cult of *Sarapis, organized the army and the Egyptian economy (with royal monopolies and state control), and developed Alexandria. Under him the *Museum and the *Library were established and this was the beginning of flourishing literary and scientific activities. Under Alexander he had married a Persian noble woman but he divorced her and married Euridice, and then *Berenice (1). His daughters married *Lysimachus and *Pyrrhus. In 285 BC he made his son *Ptolemy Philadelphus co-ruler. In his last years he wrote a history of Alexander, which was the main source of *Arrian.

For P. as historian: L. Pearson, *His. Al. Gr.*;
For all the Ptolemaic kings see: E. Bevan, *A History of Egypt under the Ptolemaic Kings*, 1927;
T. C. Skeat, *The Reigns of the Ptolemies*[2], 1969.

PTOLEMY II PHILADELPHUS Son of Ptolemy I and Berenice I, born in 306 BC, co-ruler from 285 and king (282–246 BC). It seems that many of the economic, military and administrative systems of Egypt were due to P. His military campaigns and coastal garrisons in Aethiopia and Arabia aimed at securing trade relations with India. He also contributed much to the development of Alexandria, encouraged scholarship and literary activities. He adopted an expansive policy and acquired territories in Asia Minor and the Aegean Sea and in the First Syrian War (c. 274–271 BC) against *Antiochus I. Thus Cilicia, Pamphylia, the Cyclades and other islands, including Samothrace, came under his dominion. He supported Athens in the Chremonidean War (266–261 BC) against Antigonus II Gonatas but without success, and suffered a naval defeat off Cos (? 255 BC) which gave Antigonus control of the Aegean. The Second Syrian War (c. 260–253 BC) was concluded by the marriage of *Antiochus II

and P.'s daughter Berenice. P. married his sister *Arsinoe II (c. 277), who exercised great influence on his reign. He established the cult of his parents, and of his dead wife and himself as Theoi Adelphoi.

PTOLEMY III EUERGETES Son of Ptolemy II, born c. 285 BC, succeeded his father in 246 BC. By his marriage to *Berenice (2) he got control of Cyrene. In the Third Syrian War (246–241 BC) against *Seleucus II, P. took control for a while of much of the Seleucid territory in Asia Minor and Syria. He supported *Cleomenes III of Sparta and the Aetolians against Macedonia. In Alexandria he followed his predecessors in supporting scholarship. But his military operations imposed a heavy financial burden and he had to contend with discontent. He died in 221 BC.

PTOLEMY IV PHILOPATOR Son of Ptolemy III, and Berenice (2), born c. 240 BC, succeeded his father in 221 BC. In the Fourth Syrian War (221–217 BC), he won the battle of Raphia (217 BC) after suffering initial reverses and thus secured Ptolemaic dominion in Palestine and Phoenicia until the end of his reign. But the victory was won with the help of Egyptian troops who now became conscious of their power. This led to a revolt and whole districts were for considerable periods under the control of native rulers. P. himself did not show any further interest in government and foreign affairs and lived a life of profligacy according to Polybius (5.34). He died in 205 BC.

PTOLEMY V EPIPHANES Son of Ptolemy IV, he was born in 210 BC and succeeded to the throne in 205 BC when he was only a child. The country was governed by his ministers (Sosibius, Agathocles etc.), and for most of his reign native rulers maintained their power in the Thebaid. Antiochus III conquered Palestine and other territories in Asia Minor in the Fifth Syrian War (202–198 BC). Indeed almost all the Ptolemaic possessions in the Aegean and in Asia were lost — only Cyprus and Cyrene were retained. The native rulers were only suppressed in 184 BC. He died in 180 BC.

PTOLEMY VI PHILOMETOR Son of Ptolemy V, a mere child of about five years on the death of his father, he was under his mother's guardianship until her death in 176 BC. He married his sister Cleopatra II in 175 BC. But for Roman intervention, *Antiochus IV would have conquered Egypt in 168 BC. From 170 BC he ruled jointly with his wife and brother Ptolemy VIII. He escaped from his brother in 164 BC, and on his return he had sole rule from 163 BC. He died after a victory over *Alexander (6) Balas in 145 BC.

PTOLEMY VIII EUERGETES II Brother of Ptolemy VI with whom he was co-ruler from 170 to 164 BC. He was king of Cyrene in 163–145 BC, and bequeathed his kingdom to Rome in his testament, the first Hellenistic king to do so (but nothing came of it). After his brother died, he became king of Egypt (145 BC), married his sister *Cleopatra II and in 144 BC killed Ptolemy VII who was her son from his brother. In 142 BC he married Cleopatra III, the daughter of his wife. He lost control of Egypt to Cleopatra II who revolted in 132 BC. He only regained Alexandria in 127 BC. From 124 BC peace was restored and he had a joint rule with the two Cleopatras. He died in 116 BC.

PTOLEMY IX SOTER II LATHYRUS Son of Ptolemy VIII and Cleopatra III, born in 142 BC; he was made joint ruler with his mother after the death of his father (116 BC). He divorced his sister Cleopatra IV to marry his sister Cleopatra Selene. He escaped from Egypt to Cyprus c. 108 after his mother established a joint rule with his brother Ptolemy X. P. returned in 82 BC and ruled the country until his death in 81 BC.

PTOLEMY XII THEOS PHILOPATOR PHILADELPHUS NEOD DIONYSUS (Auletes) Illegitimate son of Ptolemy IX, born c. 110 BC, ascended to the throne in 80 BC. For a long time Rome did not recognize his title as it was believed that Egypt was bequeathed to Rome by Ptolemy X (brother of Ptolemy IX), who died in 88 BC. He secured this recognition in 59 BC by promising a huge sum of money to Caesar, and he had to flee from Alexandria in 58 BC. After his restoration by *Gabinius in 55 BC, *Rabirius Postumus was made finance minister to collect money for the repayment of debts to the Romans. P. married his sister Cleopatra V Tryphaena who bore him *Cleopatra VII. He died in 51 BC.

PTOLEMY, Claudius Greek mathematician, geographer and astronomer. He lived in the 2nd century AD and was active in Alexandria from AD 127 to AD 151. His most important work was the *Mathematike Syntaxis* in 13 books, known from its Arabic name *Almagest*. This is a comprehensive treatment of astronomy in which P. uses spherical trigonometry to establish the eccentric-epicyclic explanation for the courses of the planets (see *Astronomy). The system is based on the achievements of *Apollonius (3) of Perge and of *Hipparchus (2), but P. adds important original contributions and corrections, partly based on his own observations. He modifies the theory of the moon and presents an elaborated system for the five planets. The precise, comprehensive and clear account became the accepted astronomical system until the end of the Middle Ages. Other astronomical works of P. include the *Hypotheses of Planets* in two books, which gives a summary of P.'s astronomical system; the *Phases of Fixed Stars*, a list of the rising and setting of fixed stars; *Catalogue of Stars* (with calculations of ecliptic coordinates). In music, P.'s work *Harmonica* gives the mathematical basis for the theory of harmony. Extant also (in Latin translation) is his work *Optics*. The *Tetrabiblos* is a scientific exposition of astrology.

P.'s most famous work was his *Geography* in eight books. When he wrote it, P. had far more geographical data than his predecessors had at their disposal. He systematically located places by altitude and longitude which, however, were calculated from travellers's observations. The book also contained a world map. The basic defect in the system was that P. did not try to verify the geographical positions of the places by astronomical observations. Further major defects resulted from his assumption that the circumference of the earth was 180,000 stades, 70,000 stades less than the more accurate calculation of *Eratosthenes. Obviously, this led to incorrect gradations. Among the many other misconceptions there was a land mass connecting eastern Africa with the Far East; Scandinavia was presented as an island and India as a rectangle. Despite its errors the work improved on all that had been done previously and became the authoritative textbook of geography until the end of the Middle Ages.

R. Catesby Taliaferro, *Ptolemy, The Almagest* (tran.), 1952; F. E. Robbins, *Ptolemy, Tetrabiblus* (Loeb), 1940; C. L. Stevenson, *Geography*, 1932.

PUBLICANI The contractors who under the Roman system of government collected taxes and various public revenues and executed various kinds of services for the government, notably providing supplies for the army and constructing public buildings (roads, temples, basilicas etc.). The contracts were awarded in a public auction, normally by the censors (for the major operations), but also by other magistrates. As the sums of money needed for such work were vast, the P. were organized in companies (*societates publicanorum*). Those who invested money in the business were *socii* and they had a *magister*, director, who was the legal representative of the company. They were mentioned in the Second Punic War when 19 P., organized in three *societates*, undertook to supply the Roman army in Spain (Liv. 23.48–9). The extension of Rome's military operations in the 2nd century BC, the increases in public building, and the leasing of the silver mines in Spain led to the enrichment of the P. The law of Gaius *Gracchus (3), by which they collected taxes in the rich Roman province of Asia, further increased their wealth and importance. They were well organized, formed the active element in the equestrian class (see *Equites) and sought to secure their interest by political pressure. Their grip on the jury courts, made possible by the law of Gaius which transferred the courts to the Equites, involved them in a bitter struggle against the Senate. Only the compromise of 70 in the consulate of *Pompey established better relations with the Senate. Yet several senators – as individuals – acquired shares in the businesses of the P. In the provinces, the P. oppressed the provincials, usually with the cooperation of the senatorial governors. Under the Empire they lost most of their opportunities for gain as most taxes were directly collected by quaestors in the senatorial provinces and by procurators in the imperial provinces.

E. Badian, *Publicans and Sinners*, 1972.

PUBLILIUS PHILO, Quintus Prominent Roman general and statesman in the second half of the 4th century BC, of a plebeian family. He was the first plebeian dictator (339 BC), four times consul (339, 327, 320, 315 BC), and censor. In 339 BC he passed three laws which allowed Plebeians to be elected censors, made *plebiscita* binding on the whole people (but see *Hortensius (1)) and turned the *auctoritas patrum* into a mere formality (see *Patricians). P. was the first *proconsul and as such captured Naples (326 BC).

PUBLILIUS SYRUS Latin comic playwright of the 1st century BC. He came to Rome as a slave and was set free. In the competition arranged by Caeasr he won against *Laberius. P. wrote mimes (*Mimus), but these have not survived. Extant is a collection of the sayings of P.

Duff, *Min. Lat. Poet.*

PUNIC WARS The wars between the Romans and the Carthaginians (Puni). There were three such wars: the First Punic War (264–241 BC), the Second Punic War (218–201 BC), the Third Punic War (149–146 BC). The First War ended with the Roman conquest of Sicily; Sardinia and Corsica were conquered in 238 BC. In the Second, also known as the Hannibalic War, Carthage lost Spain and Rome remained the only dominant power in the western Mediterranean. The Third ended with the destruction of Carthage and the establishment of the Roman province *Africa. For details see *Carthage and *Hannibal.

Sources: Polybius, Livy (21–30), Appian, *Libyca*;
H. H. Scullard, *Scipio Africanus*, 1930;
A. Toynbee, *Hannibal's Legacy*, 1965;
A. E. Astin, *Scipio Aemilianus*, 1967;
G. C. and C. Picard, *Carthage*, 1968.

PUTEOLI (modern Pozzuoli) Greek city on the Bay of

Campanian harbour, a wall painting from Stabiae

Naples, founded by Cumae in 531 BC as Dicaearchia. It is not known when it acquired its name P. It became a Roman *Praefectura, and was an important naval base in the Second Punic War. A Roman colony was founded here in 194 BC. In the course of the 2nd century BC, with the commercial expansion of Italians to the East, P. became a major port and a flourishing trade centre. As the harbour of Ostia was not developed yet, Rome received most of its supplies through P. It was connected to the Via Appia by the Via Domitiana, and thus it had good connections with Rome. The city retained its prosperity and commercial importance until the 5th century AD. From the 1st century BC, Romans of the upper class (e.g. *Hortensius (1), *Sulla) acquired luxury villas in its vicinity.

A. Maiuri, *The Phlegraean Fields*, 1957;
J. D'Arms, *Romans on the Bay of Naples*, 1970.

PYDNA City in southern Macedonia, first annexed by King *Archelaus I. It is known for the defeat of *Perseus (2) by *Paullus that took place near it in 168 BC.

PYGMALION Mythological king of Cyprus who fell in love with an ivory statue which he made of a woman. The statue was changed into a living woman by Aphrodite. This woman, Galatea, bore P. Paphos through whom P. was the grandfather of *Cinyras. The myth is best known from Ovid (*Met.* 10.243ff.), as well as from modern adaptations.

PYLOS The kingdom of *Neleus (in the western Peloponnesus) whose son *Nestor took part in the Trojan War. It was identified by Strabo (8.3,14ff. and 26ff.) with P. in Triphylia (south of the river Alpheus); this is accepted by some modern scholars. In another view (Pausan. 4.36,1f.), the Mycenaean kingdom is identified with P. in Messenia, north of the Bay of Navarino. In the whole region many Mycenaean traces were found, including a palace northeast of the Bay. However, Mycenaean traces were also found at P. in Triphylia, including beehive-tombs. At any rate, the archaeological evidence, which include Linear B tablets, vindicates the Homeric tale.

E. L. Bennett, *The Pylos Tablets*, 1955;
C. W. Blegen and M. Rawson, *A Guide to the Palace of Nestor*, 1962.

PYRAMUS and THISBE The love story of this pair of lovers from Babylon is mainly known from Ovid (*Met.* 4.55ff.). Their parents refused to let them marry but they managed to talk through a crack in a wall and agreed to meet at the mulberry tree near the tomb of Ninus. On getting there, T. encountered a lion and, in her flight from it, lost her veil. P. found it stained with blood, thought that she had died, and killed himself. Finding his body, T. killed herself, too. And since that time the fruit of the mulberry (which was white and was stained by their blood) has been red.

PYRGI (modern Santa Severa) Coastal Etruscan city which served as the port of nearby *Caere. Its rich and well known temple of Leucothea was plundered by *Dionysius I of Syracuse (Diod. Sic. 15.1,4). The Roman colony established here is first mentioned in 191 BC (Liv. 36.3,6). In the course of the excavations that were held on the site since 1956, two temples of the early 5th century BC (one earlier than the other) were found. The most interesting discovery came in 1964 when three inscribed sheets of gold leaf were found. One was written in Punic and apparently had the same text as one of the other two that were in Etruscan. The bilingual texts, however, have not helped much in solving the riddle of the Etruscan language. They record a dedication of the king of Caere to the Etruscan goddess Uni, identified with the Phoenician Astarte. But they do show the strong Carthaginian influence in Etruria at the time, only briefly referred to in literary sources.

J. Heurgon, *JRS*, 1966, 1ff.

PYRRHON Of Elis, son of Pleistarchus, Greek philosopher (c. 360–c. 270 BC), the founder of Scepticism. In his early life he was a painter and took to the theories of *Democritus. With Anaxarchus of Abdera he arrived in India with the expedition of Alexander the Great and was influenced by the native sages. P. did not elaborate on his views in writing and what is known of them comes from later writers. He drew logical conclusions from the impossibility of reaching true knowledge as a result of the shortcomings of sense perceptions. No positive or absolute views can be maintained with regard to all things. Hence one's way of life should be based on probabilities. This means being indifferent and imperturbably calm at all times. And P. indeed was a living example of this philosophy, adapting his way of life to it on his return to Elis.

Diog. Laert. 9.61ff.;
M. M. Patrick, *The Greek Sceptics*, 1929;
L. Robin, *Pyrrhon et le scepticisme Grec*, 1944.

PYRRHUS The greatest Molossian king of Epirus, born in 319 BC, ascended to the throne as a minor in 307 BC. In 302 BC he escaped from *Cassander to *Demetrius (1)

War elephant on a south Italian bowl. The Romans first encountered elephants in the wars against Pyrrhus

Poliorketes with whom he fought at *Ipsus before becoming his governor in Greece. In 297 BC he married Antigone the step-daughter of *Ptolemy I, and the king helped him to regain Epirus. P. soon got rid of Neoptolemus, his co-ruler, and after the death of Antigone married *Agathocles' daughter, thus obtaining *Corcyra and Leucas. By conquest and additional marriages he also acquired parts of Illyria and Macedonia, Ambracia and Acarnania. In 294 BC he made Ambracia his capital and beautified it. Fighting a war against Demetrius from 291 BC, he conquered half of Macedonia with *Lysimachus as an ally (288 BC); he also obtained Thessaly, and liberated Athens from its siege by Demetrius. But in 283 BC he lost his part of Macedonia to Lysimachus. In 280 BC, P. went to Italy to help Tarentum against Rome and won the first battle at Heraclea at a high cost; hence his famous dictum "one more victory like this and we are lost" (Diod. Sic. 22.6,2). He had only 25,000 troops and twenty elephants when he came to Italy and quickly became aware of the manpower superiority of Rome. He tried to conclude a peace settlement. But his diplomat Cineas failed to persuade the Senate and Appius *Claudius (2) Caecus carried the day with his famous oration on the right of Rome to the whole of southern Italy. A second costly battle at Asculum (279 BC) did not help P. and he was happy to receive an invitation to come to the help of the Greeks against the Carthaginians in Sicily. He almost won the entire island through his spectacular victories but failed to take Lilybaeum and quarrelled with the Greeks. P. returned to Italy and fought an unsuccessful battle against the Romans at Beneventum (275 BC). He lost hope of gaining anything in Italy, left a garrison in Tarentum and returned to Epirus. He now attacked *Antigonus (2) Gonatas, invaded the Peloponnesus and, while trying to force his way to Argos, he was killed in a street fight (272 BC).

A great general and leader, P. wrote on tactics and diplomacy and deemed himself a new Alexander. His spectacular achievements impressed his contemporaries and in antiquity he was put on the same level as Alexander and Hannibal. But he lacked the patience to consolidate his achievements and was constantly enticed to new adventures. In the end, all his external conquests were ephemeral and only the consolidation of the Epirot kingdom, which for him was a modest achievement, proved viable.

Plut., *Pyrrhus*; Hammond, *Epirus*.

PYTHAGORAS (1) Greek philosopher, son of Mnesarchus, native of Samos, lived in the 6th century BC. He left his home country (c. 532 BC) because of the tyrant *Polycrates and settled in *Croton in southern Italy. Here he formed a religious society which consisted of men and women, maintained an ascetic way of life, including vegetarianism, purification rites, silence, the examination of conscience and taboos. P. was a devotee of Apollo and at Croton was identified with Apollo the *Hypoborean. In his time, Croton rose to the height of its power and destroyed the luxurious *Sybaris. Because of internal conflicts, P. left the city and settled in Metapontum where he died c. 496 BC.

P. became a legend after his lifetime and it is difficult to separate facts from the myths that are associated with

him, and to define to what extent his followers supplemented his theories. He believed in the transmigration of souls, that is, that souls continuously reincarnated as men, animals and plants. His memory was so good that he could remember his former lives. The special way of life of his sect aimed at releasing the soul from the cycle of reincarnation. This doctrine had a profound influence on *Empedocles and *Plato. In his studies, P. discovered the simple numerical proportions (2 : 1, 3 : 2, 4 : 3) between intervals of the musical scale: the octave, the fifth, and the fourth. This led him to believe that "all things are numbers", regulated by harmonic ratios. Hence P. and the Pythagoreans aimed in their scientific studies to discover the laws of harmony in nature. For them the heavenly bodies were arranged by ratios, and they believed in the musical harmony of the spheres. P. may well have discovered the "Pythagoras" theorem, though this had been known to the Babylonians.

P.'s followers continued their studies of "numbers" after the death of their master but the society was expelled from Croton in the second half of the 5th century. Some of them settled in Tarentum, and Plato on his visit there learnt the Pythagorean theories from Archytas. The Pythagoreans were the first to suggest the sphericity of the earth, which was scientifically established by Aristotle.

K. Von Fritz, *Pythagorean Politics in Southern Italy*, 1940;
J. E. Raven, *Pythagoreans and Eleatics*, 1948.

PYTHAGORAS (2) of Rhegium. Greek sculptor, native of Samos, considered by ancient writers as one of the leading figures in sculpture in the first half of the 6th century BC. He excelled in rhythm and symmetry (Diog. Laert. 8.46) and in shaping muscles and hair (Plin. *NH* 34.59). None of his statues has been identified. He mainly made statues of athletes, victors in the Panhellenic games.

PYTHIA, PYTHON Pythia was the priestess of *Apollo Pythius in Delphi (Hdt. 1.13). Apollo took possession of Delphi after killing the formidable dragon Python which was the guardian of the place. The myth is told in the Homeric *Hymn to Apollo*. Pythia was the medium through which the god gave his *oracle to those who came to consult him, and was subordinate to the priests of the sanctuary. She was also called *prophetis* or *promantis*. When consulted she would sit on a tripod and, in a state of ecstasy, caused by an exhalation from the earth or by chewing laurel leaves, she would utter the replies. The names of some of the Pythian priestesses are known. A few of them were corrupted to give answers politically advantageous to the consultors (see *Cleisthenes (2)).

H. W. Parke and D. E. W. Wormell, *The Delphic Oracle*[2], 1956.

PYTHIAN GAMES The Panhellenic games held at Delphi in honour of Apollo Pythius. In early times, the festival was held every eight years and included musical contests. As from 582 BC it was held every four years, on the third year of each Olympiad. Dramatic competitions, music, singing, recitations, athletics, and chariot races were included in the reorganized games. The famous bronze statue of a charioteer was dedicated by Polyzelus (brother of *Hieron (1)) after his victory. The prize for victors was a crown of bay-leaves.

Four-horse chariot on the reverse of a tetradrachm from Syracuse

Runner on a 6th century BC amphora

QUADI German tribe, first mentioned by Caesar in 58 BC as the most strong and warlike of the Suebi (*Bell. Gal.* 4.1,3). At that time they lived in the Main region, but *c.* 8 BC, following the German Wars of *Drusus (3), they migrated to the east with the Marcomanni and settled in Moravia. During the 1st century AD they became dependent on Rome, but under *Domitian they fought against Rome. Former relations were reestablished under Nerva and lasted until the reign of Marcus *Aurelius. The Q. now joined the Marcomanni in the attacks on the Roman Empire, but in AD 172–3 they were routed. *Commodus did not carry out his father's plan to annex them to the empire and concluded a peace with them. After AD 260 they resumed, with the Sarmatians, their inroads on the Roman provinces. In AD 283 *Carinus won a victory over them. After the mid-4th century AD they are heard of again, and in AD 375 the Emperor Valentian died while conducting peace negotiations with them. Part of the tribe migrated with the Vandals to Spain in the 5th century AD.

QUAESTIONES Roman criminal courts consisting of a magistrate with a jury. Originally, criminal cases were dealt by the magistrates or by the Assembly, according to the right of *Provocatio. Occasionally the Senate or the Assembly would appoint a commission to try a case or a series of cases, under a magistrate with *Imperium. This was a *quaestio* and such a procedure was taken to deal with serious public crimes. There was no appeal against the sentence of the *quaestio*. The first permanent *quaestio* was established by a law of *Piso (1) in 149 BC to deal with cases of *Repetundae, and the jurors were senators. Gaius *Gracchus (3) made it a criminal court, excluded senators from the jury and reserved the right for *Equites. Several more Q. were established, including one for *Ambitus. With few exceptions (see *Caepio), only Equites were jurors until *Sulla transferred the courts to the senators. He also revised the laws of the Q. and increased their number to at least seven, each under the presidency of a praetor or a *iudex quaetionis* (one specially appointed to preside over the court, usually a former Aedile). In 70 BC, a law was passed which gave a third of the places to senators, a third to Equites and a third to Tribuni Aerarii (a class close to the Equites but less wealthy). The parties chose a jury for each case by a special procedure from three jury panels (*decuriae*). Normally, any citizen could bring a charge before the magistrate as there was no public attorney. The jurors voted by secret ballot and the magistrate pronounced the sentence.

The system established in 70 BC persisted to the Empire. Augustus added a fourth panel and Caligula a fifth. Under the Empire, new courts gradually supplanted the Q. The important cases were tried by the Emperor and his delegates or by the Senate, and ordinary crimes in Rome and Italy by the *Praefectus Praetorio and *Praefectus Urbi. But the Q. were still functioning under Septimius *Severus and his successors.
A. H. M. Jones, *The Roman Criminal Courts*, 1970; Jolowicz, *Roman Law*³ (s.v.).

QUAESTOR The original Q.s were officials who assisted the consuls in prosecuting capital cases before the *Comitia Centuriata. These *quaestores parricidi* existed only under the early Republic. The regular Q.s of the Republic were magistrates whose main function was with finances. They were first appointed by the consuls to help them in financial matters but from 447 BC were elected by the *Comitia Tributa. Their number was raised from two to four in 421 BC when the office was opened to Plebeians. Two remained in the city (*quaestores urbani*) and were responsible for the *Aerarium under the Senate's control and each of the others was attached to one of the consuls. In 267 BC four more were added, called *quaestores classici*, and they were associated with the administration of the navy and various matters in Italy. Sulla raised the number to twenty, Caesar to 40, but Augustus fixed it at twenty. Each Q. was assigned a *Provincia, so-called, and thus one was attached to Ostia (Q. Ostiensis), another dealt with the water-supply, but most were attached to the governors of the provinces. These latter were responsible for the finances of their superiors and performed other duties including military command. They normally remained as proquaestors when the *Imperium of their superior was extended.

The quaestorship became the first compulsory stage in a senatorial career and censors normally listed ex-Q.s as senators in the 2nd century BC. Sulla fixed the age-limit for holding the office at 30 and enacted that ex-Q.s should become senators automatically.

The administration of the Aerarium was finally taken

from the Q.s by Nero after this was done by Augustus but reversed by Claudius. Like other Republican magistrates, the Q.s lost their real duties in Italy but in the senatorial provinces they continued to be responsible for finances.

The *Quaestor sacri palatii* was a high office in the late Empire (at least from the early 4th century AD). His functions were like those of a minister of justice, and he was a member of the *Consistorium.
Jolowicz, *Roman Law*³ (s.v.).

QUINDECEMVIRI SACRIS FACIUNDIS One of the four major priestly colleges of Rome. Originally their number was two; it was raised to ten in 367 BC and by the first century BC it was fifteen. Their special duties were to supervise the foreign cults allowed to be worshipped at Rome and to consult the Sibylline books (which they kept). They were requested to do so when unnatural phenomena occurred, for instance public calamities and pestilences.

QUINQUEREME (Greek Penteres, "five rowed") Type of warship which appeared in the 4th century. In Athens, it was first attested to in 325 BC. The nature of the "five rowed" system is obscure. It is certain that it had more rowers than the *trireme. It was the common type of warship until the 1st century BC.

QUINTILIANUS, Marcus Fabius Roman rhetorician and famous teacher, born in Calagurris (modern Calahorra) in Spain *c.* AD 35. After studying in Rome in his youth, he returned to Spain but came back to the capital with Galba in AD 68. He now won a reputation, and was given a salary by Vespasian (as professor of rhetoric). Pliny the Younger was one of his pupils. He was also a successful advocate and became very wealthy. After twenty years, he retired, but was made tutor to Domitian's grandnephews. His wife died young and so did his two children. Q. died *c.* AD 100.

Of Q.'s speeches, lectures and treatise *On the Causes for the Corruption of Oratory*, nothing survives. But his great work *Institutio Oratoria* ("The Education of an Orator") in twelve books is extant. For Q., as for Cato three centuries before him, the orator was "a good man skilled in eloquence" (*vir bonus dicendi peritus*), and hence the work is an educational treatise and not only a manual of rhetoric. The first book deals with education in childhood and is noted for its advanced ideas and humane attitudes. Some would prefer it to most of the modern educational treatises. Book 2 is on oratorical education and is noted for its discussion of the good teacher. Books 3–11 give a detailed account of the art of rhetoric, its characteristics, functions, speech structure, style, figures of speech etc. In Book 10, Q. advises on the literature to be read for the education of the orator, and he gives a critical comparison between Greek and Roman literature, obviously from the standpoint of oratory. The last book depicts the orator produced by the educational system of Q. The large part of the work is technical but where, as noted above, Q. deals with questions of education and literature, he is interesting and worthwhile reading.
H. E. Butler (Loeb), 1921;
G. Kennedy, *The Art of Rhetoric in the Roman World*, 1972;
T. A. Dorey (ed.), *Empire and Aftermath*, 1975, 98ff.

QUINTUS SMYRNAEUS Greek epic poet of the 4th century AD. He is the author of *Posthomerica*, a poem which describes the Trojan War from the point where the *Iliad* ends and until the beginning of the *Odyssey*. These events were told in the poems of the *Epic Cycle, but the poet aims at retelling them in the Homeric manner, and shows some poetical talent.
A. S. Way (Loeb), 1913.

QUIRINIUS, Publius Sulpicius Roman senator and general under Augustus, native of Lanuvium, a *Novus Homo. He was consul in 12 BC and some time later pacified the Homanadenses, a predatory tribe in central Asia Minor. When the young C. Caesar (Augustus' grandson and adopted son) was in the East, Q. assisted him. As governor of Syria in AD 6 he carried out the census of Judaea on its annexation to the Empire and quelled disturbances. He died in AD 21.

QUIRINUS Old Italian god whose cult in Rome was on the hill of Quirinal, which was probably called after him. The settlers on the hill, one of the earliest inhabited in Rome, were Sabines, and Q. is said to have been a Sabine god. A temple to Q. was dedicated on the Quirinal in 293 BC and after its destruction was lavishly rebuilt by Augustus. Q. had a *Flamen and his festival was on 17 February. Q. probably had been the war god of the Quirinal population but lost his position to *Mars after the unification with the *Palatium.

R

RABIRIUS (1), Gaius Wealthy Roman knight (Eques), who took a leading part in the suppression of the sedition of *Saturninus. For this he was prosecuted on a charge of *Perduellio* (high treason) by *Labienus in 63 BC. The prosecutor, and Caesar (who probably stood behind the prosecution) wanted to contest the legality of the execution of Roman citizens without trial, with reference to *Senatus Consultum Ultimatum. When they made their point, the instigators of the trial ended it before sentence was passed. R. was defended by Cicero.

RABIRIUS (2) POSTUMUS, Gaius Roman knight, banker and proprietor whose business spread to many parts of the Empire. He received an inheritance from his uncle *Rabirius (1) who adopted him in his will. RP. was one of a group of Roman bankers who gave loans to *Ptolemy XII Auletes in 59 BC and thereafter, and in 55 BC was appointed minister of finanace (*dioiketes*) of Egypt to collect the debts. He enraged the Alexandrians and had to flee for his life. He was charged with receiving illegal money from *Gabinius and was acquited, with Cicero as his lawyer (54 BC). He followed Caesar in the Civil War and was praetor in 45 BC. After Caesar's death he helped his heir Octavian.

RACES (horse and chariot) It was a very old Greek custom to hold races on certain occasions. The funeral games given by Achilles in honour of *Patroclus in the *Iliad* included chariot-races. *Pelops won his wife Hippodameia in a chariot-race against her father. Horse- and chariot-races formed part of the programme of the Panhellenic games. In very early times the races were held in an open plain but later in the *Hippodrome. The number of chariots varied and could rise to some tens. Only wealthy men could spare the money for participation in chariot-racing, and some of the tyrants (for instance *Hieron (1)) made a name by this means.

In Rome, the chariot-races were part of the *Ludi Circenses. They were held in a *Circus and there were several such, the earliest being the Circus Maximus. The races were preceded by a procession (*pompa*) to the circus and a parade in it. The usual chariots were drawn by two, three, or four horses (*bigae, trigae, quadrigae*), but under the Empire there were sometimes competitors with a larger number of horses to a chariot. Races normally consisted of seven laps. Originally, only four chariots took

Four-horse chariot. An amphora painting of the 6th century BC

part in a race and only a few races were held. But the number of the chariots and the number of the races were increased until they lasted all day. Five days of the *Ludi Romani were devoted to racing. The charioteers represented the four *factiones*, companies, of the circus, each with its distinct colour: blue, green, white and red. Domitian added a purple one and a gold one, but later there were only two: the blue and the green. The drivers were slaves, freedmen or low class people. But victorious drivers won a reputation and became rich. The rivalry between the *factiones* was fierce and was accompanied by betting and sometimes by riots, in the most famous of which (the Nika rebellion) *Justinian almost lost his power.

L. Friedlaender, *Roman Life and Manners* (Eng. tran.), 1908–1913.

RAETIA The country of the Raeti, an Illyrian-Celtic people, was conquered by Rome under Augustus about 15 BC. The Roman province of R. consisted of eastern Switzerland, Tyrol and parts of Bavaria bounded by *Noricum in the east, Upper Germany in the west and the Danube in the north. It thus included (in the north) the Vindelici as well. It was an imperial province governed by a procurator (at first a prefect) whose residence was in Augusta Vindelicorum (modern Augsburg). Under Marcus *Aurelius, when the Danubian provinces were invaded by the Germanic tribes, the province was given to a senatorial legate who had a legion under his command. The frontier was fortified even earlier but this did not save the province from Alamannic inroads in the 3rd century AD. From the late 4th century the Alamanni expanded to the province and in the 5th century they conquered it.

RAVENNA The origins of this city in eastern Cisalpine Gaul are obscure, but it came to be inhabited by Umbrians. It had a treaty with Rome and only in 49 BC did it receive Roman citizenship. It was Caesar's starting point for his invasion of Italy in the Civil War. Augustus chose it as a base for the imperial navy (38 BC) and for that purpose the city was connected by a canal with the harbour that was built on the coast. The prefect of the imperial fleet was in charge of the administration of the city. Under the Empire the city prospered through trade and industry. The Emperor *Honorius made it his residence and so it remained under his successors, including *Odoacer, and *Theodoric the Great. The latter adorned the city, improved the water supply and built many buildings, including his palace and his mausoleum. Justinian's general, Belisarius, conquered it in AD 540 and until its conquest by the Lombards (mid-8th century AD) it was the centre of the Byzantine power in Italy.

There are extant various buildings dating from the 5th century AD and later, including the tomb of *Galla Placidia, the mausoleum of Theodoric and several churches with remarkable mosaics (S. Apollinare Nuovo, S. Vitale).

G. E. F. Chilver, *Cisalpine Gaul*, 1941 (s.v.).

REGIA The official building of the *Pontifex Maximus, situated on the east side of the Forum (but he did not dwell there). Traditionally the home of *Numa, it now appears from archaeological excavations that the first R. was only built at the end of the regal period *c.* 500 BC. The building was restored several times, and in 36 BC Gnaeus Domitius Calvinus rebuilt it of marble, using his booty. The college of the Pontifices held its meetings here, and the Pontifex Maximus presented in front of the R. the annual table on which he noted the main events (see *Annales). Those were preserved in the R.

REGULUS, Marcus Atilius Roman statesman and general of a plebeian family in the first half of the 3rd century BC. As consul in 267 BC he conquered Brundisium. In 256 BC he was again consul and won an important naval victory against the Carthaginians. After landing in Africa, his colleague returned with the navy and R. won a victory over the Carthaginians on his own. Carthage refused to accept his terms for peace and the following year R. was defeated and captured. According to Roman tradition, he was sent on parole to Rome on a peace-mission or to negotiate an exchange of prisoners but he dissuaded the Senate from accepting the Carthaginian proposals. He then returned to Carthage where he died. His wife tortured Carthaginian prisoners in Rome and the story went that she did it in revenge for the torture of her husband. R.'s heroic devotion to his country and his honourable return to Carthage made him a national hero.

REPETUNDAE Cases of taking money by Roman senators by whatever means or pretexts from Roman allies and provincials. Such cases were first dealt with by special commissions until in 149 BC a permanent *Quaestio was instituted by *Piso (1). It was presided over by a praetor and its members were senators. The prosecution aimed at restoring the money taken to the one from whom it was taken. Gaius *Gracchus (3) transferred the court to the *Equites (for later charges see *Quaestiones) and introduced a double repayment. It allowed the magistrates and senators (and fathers or sons of senators) to receive a certain amount of money. The law gave certain prizes to successful prosecutors. Later laws covered also those who received the money from the senators, made expulsion from the Senate obligatory in case of condemnation and introduced exile as well. In 59 BC Caesar passed his comprehensive law which dealt with all the various aspects of such cases, and his law lasted to the Empire. By a special Senate resolution (4 BC), Augustus made it possible to bring such cases before five senatorial judges who would simply secure repayment. In practice, both under the Republic and the Empire, it was difficult to convict offenders as the jurors (even Equites) declined to convict members of their own class.

J. P. V. D. Balsdon in *The Crisis of the Roman Republic* (ed. R. Seager), 1969.

REX ("king") According to Roman tradition Rome was founded by *Romulus, who was the first R., and after him there were six kings until the Republic was established in 509 BC. Kingship was also ascribed to other Latin or Etruscan cities as is revealed in the myths of such figures as *Latinus and *Mezentius. The kingship at Rome did not pass in inheritance but after the death of a R. the new R. was nominated by an *Interrex. The king traditionally had *Imperium which was free from the limitations which were imposed under the Republic. He thus commanded the army, was the high priest, administered justice, and controlled foreign affairs, but legislated through the *Comitia Curiata. It is clear that Roman historians who wrote on the regal period reconstructed the form of the Roman archaic kingship and had little, if any, reliable information. But there is no doubt that in early times Rome was ruled by kings. The *Rex Sacrorum, Interrex and possibly the *Regia and the oldest inscription found at Rome (Lapis Niger) in which the word R. is mentioned, are all evidence for the old kingship. The last kings of Rome were Etruscans and, recently, new evidence on Etruscan kings at Caere was found in the inscriptions from *Pyrgi. The kingship came to an end in a revolution against the tyrannical regime of *Tarquinius Superbus (509 BC). Since then the term R. acquired bad connotations and in the late Republic it could be used in slanderous political propaganda. Even when Rome was again ruled by a monarch he was called by other names (Princeps, Caesar, Augustus) and not by the old one.

REX SACRORUM Roman priest, second in seniority after the Pontifex Maximus in the college of the *Pontifices, also called *rex sacrificulus* or *rex*. He was the priest who took over the sacral functions of the *Rex after the abolition of the kingship at Rome in 509 BC. He regularly performed certain rites and sacrifices. Only Patricians could be chosen for this priesthood which was for life. The wife of the RS. was *regina sacrorum* and was responsible for certain rites. This priesthood also existed in several other Latin cities.

RHADAMANTHYS The mythological son of Zeus and *Europa and brother of *Minos and *Sarpedon. His name indicates a pre-Hellenic origin and he is mentioned as early as Homer who says that R. did not die but went to Elysium, the abode of the blessed. He was considered as a law-giver of Crete and a just person, and as such is one of the judges in the nether world, with Minos and Aeacus.

RHEGIUM (modern Reggio) Greek coastal city on the southwest side of the "toe" of Italy, founded by *Chalcis some years after the foundation of *Messana, that is, c. 720 BC. Messenians in the 7th century BC and Phocaeans in the 6th century BC found refuge here. The early government of the aristocracy, with laws by the famous law-giver Charondas of Catana (6th century), was replaced by the tyranny of *Anaxilas (494–476 BC), whose children were expelled several years after his death. R. was always an enemy of Locri and in 387 BC it was destroyed by *Dionysus I of Syracuse. It was refounded and joined *Timoleon. The Campanian mercenaries who took control of the city in 280 BC were executed by Rome after the capture of the city in 270 BC. Since then R. had a treaty with Rome, was loyal to her and received Roman citizenship after the *Bellum Sociale.

G. Vallet, *Rhegiom et Zancle*, 1958;
A. G. Woodhead, *The Greeks in the West*, 1962.

RHESUS In Homer, R. is a Thracian king who comes to Troy with excellent horses to help Priam (*Il.* 10.435ff.). *Diomedes and *Odysseus attack his camp at night, kill him and take his horses. Later scholars said that Troy would have been impregnable had the horses not been captured before grazing in the Trojan fields and drinking from the Scamander. Various notices indicate that R. had originally been a Thracian daemon or deity. In the extant play *Rhesus*, which is attributed to Euripides, R. is the son of the river-god Strymon and a Muse.

RHETORIC and ORATORY O. was obviously practised by the Greeks long before R., the art of persuasion, was invented. The development of a democratic way of life, both in politics and in the courts, made persuasive O. an indispensable means for success. This also gave rise to the *logographers. The importance of speeches in Greek life is shown by the custom of historians to include orations, fictitious or genuine, in their works. This began as early as the great masters *Herodotus and *Thucydides. The first to write a manual of R. was Corax of Syracuse in the 5th century BC. Corax is said to have taught the division of a speech into proem, arguments and peroration and the use of probability, exaggeration and understatement. His manual also dealt with O. in the law-courts. His pupil Tisias, who lived a wandering life and taught in several

places, is also credited with writing a manual. The *Sophists at Athens also taught R. and when *Gorgias of Leontini came to Athens in 427 BC he won immense success with his public speeches. *Antiphon composed model speeches. The aim of these new techiques was to ensure success in the courts or in the Ekklesia — a necessity for all Athenian citizens. The right of free speech (*parhesia*) was one of the essential characteristics of Athenian democracy. A good speaker was able to make a weak argument into a strong one in a debate. Teachers of R. laid rules on how to accomplish this. The speech was divided into proem, narrative, argumentation (in which the possible arguments of the rival were also taken into account and refuted), and peroration, in which the case was summarized. Later, speeches were divided into three types: judicial, political and epideictic or panegyric. The pupil was taught the art of invention, how to compose the material, elocution and gesticulation. Much importance was ascribed to style which led to the use of figures of speech, prose rhythm, assonance and parallelism.

R. as an amoral, superficial art of persuasion was criticized by Socrates and Plato. A new direction in R. was given by *Isocrates. He began his rhetorical career as a logographer but in the school of R. he opened c. 393 BC he aimed at giving a moral education to the would-be statesmen through R. His speeches were polished with much artistry. Among his pupils were scholars and politicians such as *Hyperides, *Timotheus (1), *Lycurgus (2) and *Theophrastus. After Isocrates, R. was masterfully dealt with by *Aristotle in his *Rhetoric* — both as a technical means of persuasion and as an art.

Political O. lost its importance with the decline of the *polis and the rise of the great Hellenistic kingdoms. In this new world, R. was considered as an indispensable element in the education of a Greek. The Alexandrian scholars prepared a "canon" of the great Ten Attic Orators. These were: *Antiphon, *Andocides, *Lysias, *Isocrates, *Isaeus, *Lycurgus (2), *Aeschines, *Demosthenes, *Hyperides and *Dinarchus. Schools of R. developed in many places, but the leading ones were in Athens, Rhodes and Pergamum. The new centres of R. in Asia gave their name to the Asianic style, maneristic, bombastic and rich in contrast to the Attic style, which was simple and clear. The rivalry between Asianism and Atticism passed later to Rome.

In Rome, as in Greece, O. preceded R., and was occasioned by the same causes: the need to speak before an audience in courts or for political purposes in the Senate or the Assembly. The earliest speech to be recorded was that of *Claudius (2) delivered in the Senate against the peace proposals of *Pyrrhus and still known in the 1st century BC. R. developed only under Greek influence. *Cato (1) Censorius was against the Greek influence, although he himself was a veteran orator (more than 150 of his speeches were known to Cicero). For him the orator was "a good man skilled in speaking" (*vir bonus dicendi peritus*), and this was still the ideal of *Quintilian under the Empire. His maxim was "get the matter and the words will follow" (*rem tene, verba sequuntur*). In the 2nd century Rome became a profitable place for Greek teachers to give courses in R.

R. also contributed to the development of Latin style. The two leading orators of the late 2nd century were Lucius *Crassus (3) and M. *Antonius (1). The first, according to Cicero, insisted on a broad education, including philosophy, for the training of the orator; the second was known for his vigorous style and did not have much esteem for learning. He was the second (after Cato) to write a rhetorical treatise. The earliest extant manual of R. is the *Rhetorica ad Herrenium* of the 80s BC. *Cicero wrote several treatises on R.; the earliest *De Inventione* is a short handbook. In his other works he emphasized the importance of a comprehensive education for the good orator and in his *Brutus* he gave an historical outline of Roman orators and O. The apogée of Roman O. was in the last generation of the Republic when accomplished R. was of prime importance for political success in the Senate, the Assembly and the courts. But of the many known leading orators, including Caesar and *Crassus (4), only the speeches of Cicero are extant in a complete form.

With the establishment of the Principate under Augustus, O. lost its vitality. Policy was not decided by the Assembly nor even by the Senate. In his *Dialogue on the Orators*, Tacitus traces the decline of O. to the loss of political freedom. Paradoxically, the early Empire was a flourishing period for schools of R. The study of O. was regarded as essential for education, even though the courses taken were of an academic nature, as the themes of the *Declamations* practised reveal. Professors of R. could earn much money. The outstanding work on the education of the orator was the *Istitutio Oratoria* of Quintilian, a work which was still influential in the Middle Ages, the Renaissance and even in modern times. Thus, although for practical purpose O. was confined to the courts, it became a part of cultural life under the Empire, and the public interest is manifest in the success of orators like *Dio (1) Cocceianus Chrysostom and Aelius *Aristides (2).

D. L. Clark, *Rhetoric in Greco-Roman Education*, 1957;
G. Kennedy, *The Art of Persuasion in Greece*, 1963;
Id., *The Art of Rhetoric in the Roman World*, 1972.

RHETORICA AD HERRENIUM The earliest extant handbook of rhetoric in Latin, written by an unknown author in the 80s. BC. The work in four books is addressed to one Gaius Herrenius (hence the name). It deals with invention, composition, elocution and style. It is evident that the author is an experienced rhetorician and well-versed in the Greek traditions.

H. Caplan (Loeb), 1954.

RHIANUS Greek poet of the 3rd century BC, native of Crete, a slave and gymnasium keeper in his early life. He is mainly known for his epics which included *Achaeica, Thessalica, Eliaca* and *Messeniaca*. His writing epics indicates that he did not follow the literary view of *Callimachus. The titles and the fragments show that these were ethnographic poems with emphasis on geographic and mythical themes. The *Messeniaca* is the better known as it was one of the sources of Pausanias (4.17ff.) for his account of the Second Messenian War and the adventures of its hero Aristomenus. R. also wrote epigrams and prepared an edition of the *Iliad* and *Odyssey* which is known from scholia to Homer.

J. U. Powell, *Collectanea Alexandrina*, 1925;
D. L. Page, *Hellenistic Epigrams*, 1965.

RHODES The great island southwest of Asia Minor, approximately 1400 sq km. Objects from the Mycenaean civilization have been found on the island, which was later occupied by the Dorians who formed three city-states, Ialysus, Lindus and Camirus. In legend, Helios (Sun) had three children by the nymph Rhodes: Ialysus, Lindus and Camirus, the eponymous ancestors of the three cities. Lin-

dus took an important part in the Greek colonization, notably in *Gela. The Rhodian cities were members of the Delian League but seceded from Athens in 411 BC. They now united to form one state with a new capital, Rhodes, which was founded at the northern end of the island (407 BC). With the help of *Conon, Rhodes liberated itself from Sparta in 396 BC, was a member of the Second Athenian League and in 356 BC became dependent on *Mausolus and Persia. It was liberated by Alexander the Great in 332 BC and in 305 BC withstood the famous siege by *Demetrius (1) Poliorcetes ("Besieger"). As a memorial to this event the famous Colossus of Helios was erected, one of the Seven Wonders of the ancient world. It fell in an earthquake in 227 BC.

Rhodes had a democratic form of government. It became a prosperous trading city and with its strong navy policed the seas against pirates. The aggressive policy of *Philip V caused her to ask, with Pergamum, for Roman help. It remained loyal to Rome and in the war against *Antiochus III won a naval battle against Hannibal. In the settlement of Apamea (188 BC) it was given large parts of Caria and Lycia, but after the Thrid Macedonian War, it lost this territory. Its trade prosperity suffered from the rise of *Delos which Rome made a free port (167 BC), and it could no longer secure the seas against pirates. In 88 BC *Mithridates VI failed to capture R., but in 42 BC *Cassius (3) conquered it, and plundered it. With the restoration of peace under Augustus, R. recovered and under the Empire it flourished.

In the Hellenistic period, R. became a centre of culture. The famous sculpture group of *Laocoon was made by three Rhodian sculptors. The poet and scholar *Apollonius of Rhodius left Alexandria for R., from which he acquired his name. *Panaetius and *Posidonius lived in R. Caesar went to R. to complete his studies and Tiberius retired to the island in 6 BC.

Rostovtzeff, *Hellenistic World* (s.v.);
P. M. Frazer and G. E. Bean, *The Rhodian Peraea and Islands*, 1954.

RHOECUS Of Samos, Greek architect and bronze-sculptor of the 6th century BC. He often worked with his compatriot Theodorus, notably in the building of the great temple of Hera at Samos. The art of modelling in clay and the bronze-casting of images was attributed to R. and Theodorus.

ROME The history of R. may be divided to the regal period (until 509 BC), the period of the Republic (509–31 BC) and the Empire. The Republican period is divided into early (509–264 BC), middle (264–133 BC) and late Republic (133–31 BC). The subdivisions of the Empire period are the early Principate (Augustus, the Julio-Claudian emperors and the Flavians, 31 BC–AD 96), the Antonines (AD 96–192), the Severan emperors and the military anarchy (AD 193–283), and the late Roman Empire. Obviously this is a schematic plan and other systems of periodization or titles for periods may be used.

According to Roman tradition, R. was founded by Romulus in 753 BC (or 814, 751, 748, 721 by other calculations) who was the first king (*Rex). For a time he shared the kingship with the Sabine Titus Tatius and after him R. was ruled in succession by six more kings: *Numa Pompilius, *Tullus Hostilius, *Ancus Marcius, *Tarquinius Priscus, *Servius Tullius, and *Tarquinius Superbus. Much of what the Romans told about the history of the regal period and the 5th and 4th centuries BC was legendary or unreliable material (see *Annales and *His-

Air view of Lindus, the most important city of the island of Rhodes before Rhodes itself was founded. It is situated on a naturally fortified Acropolis

toriography, Roman). They ascribed to the kings the establishment of their various institutions, political, social and religious. They connected R. with Troy in the legend of *Aeneas who left his home city after its sack and settled in Latium. Most of the details are surely fictitious but the Roman traditions contained a kernel of truth. The study of the archaeological, religious and linguistic evidence contributes largely to the literary tradition.

The earliest traces of human habitation on Roman soil date from the 2nd millenium BC. Continual settlement probably started on the Palatine and the Quirinal in the 10th–9th centuries, and these two communities, representing the *Latins and *Sabines of the literary tradition, may have united in the 8th century. Burial was both by cremation and inhumation which might indicate the double ethnical elements of R. Other hills were also occupied. But it was probably only under the Etruscan kings in the 6th century that R. became a strong united state out of her constituent communities. The Forum as the centre of civic life was drained *c.* 575 BC. The old three ethnic tribes were replaced by four territorial tribes (*tribus*) by *Servius Tullius who also instituted the system of the *census* with the division of the people into *classes* and *centuriae* according to census-qualifications. The *Comitia Centuriata he founded lasted until the Republic, when, with modifications in its organization, it became a main electoral, legislative and judicial institution. Trade and industry developed and the Etruscan kings extended Roman power in *Latium. The area of the Roman territory (Ager Romanus) has been estimated as approximately 800 sq km. Roman hegemony in Latium is seen in the first treaty between R. and Carthage (Pol. 2.23) and the modern attempts to play down her position under the Etruscan kings are not convincing.

The monarchy came to an end in a revolution against the tyrannical rule of *Tarquinius (2) Superbus. The tradition has been contested both in respect of the nature of the fall of the monarchy and its date. Again, the later date (*c.* 450 BC) and the gradual decline suggested for the end of monarchy bring up such difficulties that it is better to accept the Roman tradition. The expulsion of the king did not wipe out the Etruscan influence. The great temple on the Capitolium for Jupiter, Juno and Minerva was an Etruscan work; the *Triumph, *Lictors and the magisterial insignia were an Etruscan inheritance various religious practices and institutions were of Etruscan origin and for some time Etruscan families remained in R. and retained their political position.

For the Romans, the expulsion of the kings and the establishment of the Republic meant the institution of *Libertas. There were three elements in the new constitution: the People (*Populus*), Senate, and Magistrates (with the consuls as supreme). The inner history of the early Republic is that of struggle between the Patricians and the Plebeians which led to the development of that form of government which *Polybius later called "mixed constitution". In the course of this struggle new magistracies were instituted and the Plebeians were gradually admitted to all of them including the priestly colleges (*Consul, *Praetor, *Dictator, *Quaestor, *Censor, *Pontifex, *Augur, *Aediles). The laws were published by the *Decemviri in the mid-5th century BC and the rules of legal procedure in 304 (*Flavius); the Plebeians won recognition of their own institutions (*Tribunes and *Concilium Plebis); the laws of debt were made less harsh and the poor citizens received land. By the early 3rd century the struggle was over and a new aristocracy rose, the patrician-plebeian *Nobilitas.

The internal struggle was accompanied by the expansion of Roman power all over Italy, though not without some reverses. After the fall of the monarchy, R. lost her hegemony in Latium and under the threat of external foes (*Volsci, *Aequi, *Etruscans) found it useful to form an alliance with the *Latins (493 BC) and with the *Hernici (486 BC). Only in the last third of the 5th century was R. able to resume the offensive, which culminated in the capture of *Veii by *Camillus (396 BC). About ten years later (387 BC) the Gauls routed the Roman army at Allia and captured R. (387 BC). The next half-century passed in wars to recover the lost positions in Latium, during which R. improved her military system and the city was strongly fortified. After the last war against the Latins (340–338 BC), the Latin League was dissolved, a few Latin cities were incorporated into the Roman state and the rest, including Volscian cities, were attached to her separately. Roman rule was secured in Latium and she also established a foothold in Campania. In the next half-century, R. defeated the *Samnites, Gauls and Etruscans and by alliances and military power established her hegemony in central Italy from the Adriatic to the Tyrhenian. No sooner had R. finally defeated the Boii (283 and 282 BC), than her attention was drawn to southern Italy with the request of *Thurii for help against the Lucanians. This led Tarentum to ask *Pyrrhus for help. But the Hellenistic king did not save the Greeks and, after the third battle (275 BC), he evacuated Italy and Tarentum was reduced in 272 BC. Italy from the Straits of Messina to the Po valley was practically under Roman rule.

The expansion of Roman power in Italy was due partly to defensive wars and partly to the search for land for the increasing population, and in part to aggressive Roman statesmen. R. succeeded because she constantly improved her military system and skilfully manoeuvred against her enemies. The Latin and Italian communities were allowed to administer their own affairs, and did not pay taxes to R. — they only supplied troops, according to treaties, to serve with the Roman army. This was important; by 225 BC R. had at her disposal a huge potential in military manpower: 700,000 infantry and 70,000 cavalry. In many cases R. conferred its citizenship to her allies or former enemies. R. also secured her control of Italy by founding colonies in various strategical places. She thus achieved the political unification of Italy.

R. had signed a friendship treaty with Carthage in the first year after the foundation of the Republic and since then kept good relations with her. But in 264 BC she was requested by *Messana to send military help, which Carthage regarded as a hostile action, and so began the struggle between the two great powers. In the course of the first two *Punic Wars (264–241 BC, 218–201 BC), R. established her rule over the western Mediterranean and organized her first provinces: *Sicily, *Sardinia and *Corsica, and *Spain. She also began the conquest of Cisalpine Gaul which was completed only in the first decades of the 2nd century BC. At the same time, R. became involved in the affairs of the Hellenistic world by the Illyrian Wars (229–228 BC, 219 BC) and the wars against *Philip V (214–205 BC, 200–196 BC). Thereafter followed the war against *Antiochus III (191–189 BC) and after that Roman hegemony was well established over

Greece and the Hellenistic kingdoms. The wars against *Perseus (2) (172–168 BC), *Andriscus, the Achaean League and the Third Punic War resulted in two new provinces, Macedonia and *Africa. Roman power, directly or indirectly, extended by that time all over the Mediterranean. The conquest of Spain was a long process completed only under Augustus. These external wars of the middle Republic profoundly changed Roman society and economy. The class of *Equites rose while many of the small farmers lost their lands. The senatorial and equestrian upper classes acquired the lands of the impoverished and occupied public lands. The dispossessed farmers were largely replaced by slave labourers and became an embittered proletariat. Meanwhile, R. was opened to the cultural influence of Greece which led to the development of Roman literature and theatre and to the rise of luxury and a more sophisticated way of life. The great influx of wealth was used to build many public buildings and to decorate the city.

In the late Republic the empire was further extended. The province of *Asia was organized in 129 BC after *Attalus III bequeathed his kingdom to R. and the revolt of *Aristonicus was suppressed. The province of *Gallia Narbonensis was established in the late 2nd century BC and thereafter *Cilicia was added. More provinces were acquired in the post-Sullan age: *Cyrene, *Bithynia, *Crete, *Cyprus, *Pontus and *Syria by Pompey and *Gallia and *Numidia by Caesar.

The last hundred years of the Republic are characterized by such violent inner political struggles that some would call the period "the Roman Revolution". The tribunate of Tiberius *Gracchus (2) ushered in the conflict between Populares and *Optimates. The legislation of his brother Gaius *Gracchus (3) consolidated the equestrian class and led to the struggle over the courts (*Quaestiones). The reform of *Marius regarding military recruitment transformed the former citizen-militia into a proletarian army whose soldiers looked to their commander for pay and bounty. When the legislation of *Drusus (2) failed in 91 BC, R. was faced with a serious revolt by her Italian allies and was able to suppress it only after conferring her citizenship to all Italy. Thereafter followed the civil wars of the 80s in which *Cinna (1) and *Sulla were the main figures. The latter tried to re-establish the authority of the Senate by a series of laws, but they all collapsed because on the one hand the senatorial aristocracy was corrupt or incompetent and on the other hand the personal ambitions of political leaders outgrew the constitutional framework of the Republic. As Sallust saw it, each politician fought for his own power. The most successful of all after Sulla was *Pompey who, in the course of his wars against *Sertorius in Spain, the pirates and *Mithridates VI, established his dominance in the state. But he faced strong opposition from aristocrats, prominent among whom was *Cato (2). In 60 BC *Caesar succeeded in forming a coalition with Pompey and *Crassus (4), the famous First Triumvirate. His prize was the governorship of Gaul which he exploited to extend Roman power to the Rhine and at the same time increased his personal influence at R. After Crassus was killed by the Parthians (53 BC) the two remaining partners of the Triumvirate were not able to arrive at a compromise and Pompey drifted to the enemies of Caesar. This finally led to the Civil War of 49–45 BC which ended with the total victory of Caesar. But the old aristocracy was not ready to acquiesce to his personal rule and he fell victim to a conspiracy with *Brutus (2) and *Cassius (3) as its leaders. Fresh civil wars ensued (44–42 BC) at the end of which *Antonius (4) and Octavian (*Augustus) emerged as the new masters of the empire. The relations between them were never cordial and after removing *Lepidus (3) and Sextus *Pompeius (36 BC), Octavian overcame Antonius in the final test of power to remain the sole ruler of the whole Roman Empire (31 BC).

In 27 BC Octavian "restored" the Republic; in truth, he founded the Principate (*Princeps). While retaining the Republican forms of government, he had all the power; he commanded the armies, governed directly several provinces and indirectly (by his *Imperium maius*) all the others, had a huge clientele and enjoyed immense prestige.

In the next 41 years until his death he carried out extensive reforms. The army was organized, the security and food- and water-supply of the city of R. were dealt with adequately; the administration of the provinces was improved; the foundations of the civil service were laid; various laws were passed to raise the birth-rate and to secure the integrity of the family among the upper classes; measures were taken to revive the Roman religion and extensive building operations adorned R. and many other cities in Italy and the empire. While peace was restored within the empire, Augustus carried out a vigorous foreign policy; he pacified Spain and created several new provinces in areas newly or recently occupied: *Raetia, *Noricum, *Pannonia, *Moesia, *Galatia, and *Egypt. After the disaster of *Varus (AD 9), no further advance was made in central Europe and the line Danube-Rhine became the frontier, and essentially remained as such until the later Roman Empire.

Augustus was succeeded by *Tiberius (AD 14) who had been made almost an equal partner in the reign since AD 4. The contention between the emperors and the Senate is the main issue of the inner politics of R. in the early Principate. Few people seriously believed that the Republic could have been restored and only once, after the death of *Caligula, did the Senate discuss the question. The conflict arose from the attempt to reserve some share in the government of the empire for the Senate, from the opposition to the autocratic rule of the emperors and the suppressive means which the emperors took against the Senate. The suspicious Tiberius, with and without his praetorian prefect *Sejanus, executed many senators in the *Maiestas trials. He was followed by Caligula and *Nero, both of whom ruled in an autocratic manner. Even *Claudius who, like Tiberius, sought to cooperate with the Senate, could not find an adequate solution for the strained relations between emperor and Senate. The advance of freedmen in the imperial civil service and in high positions in the central administration exasperated the senators who also begrudged the admittance to the Senate of Gallic chieftains. The struggle continued under the Flavian dynasty and ended only with the accession to the throne of *Nerva. In the course of this struggle most of the old Roman aristocracy was eliminated. But relations between the emperors and the Senate had little effect on the empire. The administration was generally efficient and peace ushered in a period of prosperity. There were some wars on the frontiers but they were not serious, except for the major campaign of *Claudius (AD 43) for the conquest of *Britannia. *Thrace and *Mauretania were two other provinces which were annexed. The Julio-Claudian dynasty came to an end with the death of *Nero (AD 68)

which was followed by the Year of the Four Emperors; *Galba, *Otho, *Vitellius, *Vespasian (AD 69). It demonstrated the possibility of making an emperor elsewhere than in Rome, by the wishes of the armies in the provinces. The administration of Vespasian was efficient, the civil service was developed and the finances of the state were improved. The frontier of Britannia was advanced under *Domitian who began to fortify the frontiers on the Danube and the Rhine. But his reign was marked by terror and he finally succumbed to a conspiracy (AD 96).

*Nerva, *Trajan, *Hadrian, *Antoninus Pius, and Marcus *Aurelius (AD 96–180) are known as the Good Emperors. Their reputation rests on their establishing good relations with the Senate, which Tacitus and Pliny the Younger magnified as the restoration of liberty, and the great prosperity of the empire. In contrast to the Julio-Claudian and Flavian emperors under whom the imperial succession was confined to the imperial family, it seems that these emperors adopted the Cynic-Stoic doctrine of the good ruler by adopting suitable successors and bequeathing the throne to experienced administrators and generals. The truth is that none of them had sons and the one who had, the Stoic Emperor Marcus Aurelius, bequeathed the reign to his son *Commodus. On the frontiers there were some major wars and a few annexations. Trajan conquered *Dacia and *Mesopotamia and annexed the kingdom of Nabataea. Marcus Aurelius had to conduct a series of wars both against Parthia and in the Danube provinces — a foreshadowing of what was to devastate the empire in the next century. That the empire had reached its extreme expansion became evident with the fortification of the frontier lines (*Limes). The 2nd century was the zenith of the Roman Empire. The cities flourished, more and more provincials received Roman citizenship and became Roman senators and Equites. The imperial administration was manned to a large extent by provincials. Trade, industry, and agriculture expanded — but by now Italy lingered behind the provinces in these fields. In the mid-2nd century AD the orator Aelius *Aristides (2) delivered his speech "*To Rome*" in which he depicted the empire as an aggregate of happy, flourishing city-states living under the benign, paternal rule of the emperors, with equal opportunities for all the good and cultured citizens to take part in the government. For Gibbon, writing 16 centuries later, there has never been a similarly blissful period in the whole history of mankind. But under Marcus *Aurelius the first signs of decline appeared. The centralized government and increased bureaucracy became cumbersome and, as a result, municipal initiative declined. Inefficient government and wars drained the financial resources of the empire, and there was a shortage of coins. The system of recruiting and army organization created a gap between the army and the civilian population.

When Marcus Aurelius died (AD 180) he was succeeded by his son Commodus, who abused his power and was killed (after twelve years). His successor *Pertinax was also murdered (AD 193), and, in the struggle that followed, Septimius *Severus emerged victorious. Except for a few cases, from this time on the emperors were military men who mainly relied on the army, promoted the Equites in the imperial service, and did not cooperate with the Senate. *Caracalla completed a long process by conferring Roman citizenship on all the provincials. Of Severus' successors only *Alexander Severus maintained good relations with the Senate and he fell victim to a military revolt (AD 235). In the next 50 years the empire was continually under attack from abroad, from German tribes in Europe and from the new Persian kingdom in the East. Numerous pretenders to the throne killed and were killed in turn. Social life and the economy were disrupted, never to recover the same prosperity. The building of the walls of R. by *Aurelian (AD 270—5) was a symptom of the general insecurity. Several military emperors, mainly *Claudius Gothicus, Aurelian and *Probus (AD 268—82) saved the empire from foreign foes and paved the way for Diocletian.

The administrative, social and economic reforms of *Diocletian, which were later supplemented by those of Constantine the Great, reshaped the empire. The Principate became dominant and elaborate court ceremonial emphasized the distinction between simple mortals and the semi-divine emperor with his diadem and purple robe; and even prostration was introduced. The old Republican institutions lost their functions and the Roman Senate became a council of the city of R. There was a complete reorganization of the provinces whose number increased to almost 120. The military and civilian services were separated; the taxation system was reorganized (see *Indictio). Economic activity was subjected to state control and numerous laws fixed the duties of citizens to the state. Municipal and state obligations became hereditary (*Munus, *Curiales). The *coloni* were attached to the soil, and prices and salaries were fixed. All these factors, with the growth of the hierarchic bureaucracy, contributed to the decline of the economy and social activity. Many aristocrats preferred to develop and live in their country estates which later became fortress-like. And yet the empire was thriving enough to maintain its huge army and administration and to supply the means for vast building operations, including the building of the new capital, Constantinople.

The political system Diocletian envisaged for secure and peaceful succession collapsed after his abdication (AD 305) because of the personal ambitions of the Caesars. The wars between his successors and other pretenders (*Galerius, *Licinius, *Maximian, *Maxentius, *Maximinus Daia) ended with the complete victory of Constantine and the unification of the empire (AD 324). With him Christianity also triumphed, though the conflict with the revived paganism continued until the 5th century. The empire was again divided between his sons after his death (AD 337) but it was the renewed attacks of the German tribes that shattered it. In AD 378 the *Goths routed the Roman army under the Emperor *Valens at Adrianopole. In the 5th century they sacked Rome (AD 410) and subsequently established themselves in southwestern Gaul and Spain. The *Vandals, *Alani and some of the *Quadi crossed the Rhine frontier in AD 406, advanced to Spain and finally occupied North Africa under *Alaric. In AD 455 he captured and plundered Rome. The *Burgundians crossed the Rhone c. AD 406 and occupied a large part of Upper Germany and eastern Gaul, with Worms as their capital. When they tried to advance to *Belgica they were heavily defeated by *Aetius. The *Franks crossed to Gaul in c. AD 425. They were checked by Aetius, but later (under Clovis) they occupied northern and western Gaul (AD 487); and by the defeat of the Visigoths (AD 507) extended their power to central and southwest Gaul. Most of the Roman garrison of Britain was evacuated in the early 5th century.

The last sole emperor of the whole empire was *Theo-

dosius I, who bequeathed the Eastern Empire to his son *Arcadius and the Western Empire to *Honorius (AD 395). Most of the emperors of the West were puppet-rulers while the real power was in the hands of their generals and ministers, notably *Stilicho and Aetius. In AD 476, the last Western Emperor *Romulus Augustulus was deposed by *Odoacer, who ruled as king of the Germans in Italy. The Eastern Empire fared better. It survived and repelled the barbarian invasions and the Persian attacks and under Justinian a successful attempt was made to recover part of the Western Empire. This Byzantine Empire lasted until AD 1453 when Constantinople was captured by the Turks.

The question why the Roman Empire declined and fell has been differently defined and variously answered. Surely there is no simple, single explanation. Perhaps stress must be placed on the long survival which indicates the vitality and the strength of the Roman Empire as well as the grandeur of the Roman achievement. The Roman government, administration, military and legal systems were far superior to any of the others of the ancient world. It took several hundred years to exhaust this powerful edifice. The continual attacks of the barbarian peoples from abroad in Europe and of Persia in Asia drained the military manpower and financial and economic resources of the Roman Empire. The barbarian elements in the Roman armies became more and more dominant after Constantine. Economic and social life were disrupted by these as by the accompanied growth of bureaucracy. Separatist movements and the political ambitions of army commanders caused internal wars. And each factor aggravated the others. The diffusion of the Oriental religions and especially the rise of Christianity gradually changed the cultural outlook of the Graeco-Roman world. It was a weakened and altogether different empire from that of the Antonines that disintegrated in the 5th century under the onset of the renewed barbarian invasions.

Bibliography: See the Select Bibliography.

ROME (city) The ancient city of R. was built on the seven famous hills rising over the Tiber valley, the *Palatine, *Capitol, *Aventine, Caelian, Quirinal, Esquiline and Viminal. The earliest settlements were on the Palatine, Quirinal and Esquiline, dating from the 10th and 9th centuries BC. For a long time the valleys between the hills remained uninhabited and served as cemeteries. The security that the hills provided and the ford over the Tiber, with the Tiber island, were probably what attracted people to occupy the place. The original buildings were urn-shaped huts, and post-holes for these were discovered on the Palatine. The growth of the city is marked by the drainage of the *Forum by the Cloaca Maxima and the end of its usage as a cemetery in the early 6th century. The last kings of R. built the temple of Diana on the Aventine, fortified the city and erected the Capitoline temple of Jupiter, Juno and Minerva. Other archaic buildings, from the regal period or early Republic were the *Regia, the temple of Vesta and that of the Senate (*Curia). In the 5th century the Aventine became a centre of plebeian activity while the Forum became the centre of civic life. In the latter were built the temples of Saturn (497 BC), Castor (484 BC), and Concordia (336 BC). In early times it was also a market place but later some of the traders and shopkeepers were removed elsewhere, especially on the Tiber bank. From the 2nd century BC several basilicas were built. After the sack of the city by the Gauls (387

Aerial view of Rome

BC), the city was surrounded by the "Servian Wall", remains of which are still extant. During the censorship of *Claudius (2) Caecus (312 BC) the first aqueduct of R. was constructed and the Via Appia, which connected R. with Capua and Campania, was built. Other aqueducts followed, notably the Aqua Marcia built in 144 BC. The influx of wealth and booty in the 2nd century was used by the victorious generals to build many public buildings. As censor in 184 BC, *Cato (1) improved the sewerage system. By now the city had become crowded and a fashionable aristocratic quarter developed on the Palatine. The selling of parts of the Campus Martius, a public land, by Sulla gives evidence of the need for new areas for the increased population in the early 1st century BC. It was a period of luxury building by the upper classes, with houses costing 10–20 million sesterces each. The refined taste also led to the building of gardens, and Caesar left his gardens over the Tiber to the public. He also built his Forum Iulium and began the building of the Basilica Iulia. The Capitoline temple which was destroyed in the Civil War of Sulla was rebuilt by *Catullus (2). The first permanent theatre was built by Pompey. By now the population of the capital may have reached 1 million.

Augustus received R. built in bricks and left it in marble. He rebuilt many temples, added new ones, established the imperial palace on the Palatine, and among his other buildings were the Forum Augustum and the mausoleum. His chief assistant, Agrippa, repaired the old aqueducts, built new ones and erected many new public buildings in the Campus Martius, notably the *Pantheon. For administrative purposes, the city was divided into 14 regions and 265 subdivisions (*vici*), and measures were taken to defend the city from floods by the Tiber. Many new buildings were added by Augustus' successors in the 1st century AD, including a circus by Caligula, aqueducts by *Claudius, the *Domus Aurea by Nero, the *Colosseum by Vespasian, and the Forum of Nerva. Trajan (Forum, aqueduct) and Hadrian (mausoleum and the Pantheon) followed this tradition. In addition, various arches and mon-

uments were built. R. presented a mixed appearance: squalid quarters and magnificent public buildings, and luxurious private houses. Of the later buildings the notable ones are the great baths of Caracalla, and of Diocletian, and the basilica of Maxentius. But significantly for the new conditions of the empire, Aurelian (AD 270–5) encircled R. with a new wall. The emperors were too busy defending the empire after the 2nd century to spend much time in R.

Constantine built Constantinople and Honorius made the secured Ravenna an imperial residence. R. ceased to attract the building initiative of the emperors. Worse than that she was sacked in AD 410 and AD 455 by Alaric and Gaiseric.

Platner-Ashby, *Top. Dict. Rome*; Nash, *Pict. Dict. Rome*;

ROMULUS and REMUS The legendary twin brothers, founders of Rome. Their grandfather Numitor king of Alba Longa was deposed by his brother Amulius. To safeguard himself, the latter made his niece, Rhea Silvia, a *Vestal Virgin, but she bore twins and said Mars was the father. Amulius put her in prison and cast the twins into the Tiber. Carried ashore by the current, they were suckled by a she-wolf and later found by the shepherd *Faustulus. He and his wife *Acca Larentia reared them as their own children. When grown up, they excelled in courageous deeds and Remus was once caught by the king. Romulus saved him, they killed Amulius and reestablished their grandfather as king of Alba Longa. They now set out to found a city of their own. In a quarrel, Romulus killed his brother because he leaped over the sacred furrow that Romulus had made. After the foundation of Rome, Romulus attracted people to settle in it and provided them with wives by carrying off the Sabine women, who were invited to take part in a festival. The mothers of the Sabine girls made peace between their husbands and the Romans and the Sabine Titus Tatius became joint-king with Romulus. After Titus' death, Romulus remained sole king. He instituted the Senate, the three old tribes (Ramnes, Tities, Luceres), the *curiae* and the old calendar. After reigning for almost forty years (753–715 BC) he disappeared in a whirlwind. But there was another version: the senators killed him in the Senate-house and each took a part of his body and so nothing remained of him. At any rate he was identified with the Sabine god *Quirinus whose cult was on the Quirinal. The grave of Romulus was said to have been beneath the Lapis Niger, a black marble pavement in the Forum which has been found with an inscription.

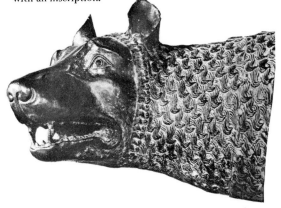

The Capitoline she-wolf, probably an Etruscan work

In old legends Romulus was the son of *Aeneas but when it was realized that this was chronologically impossible a lineage was composed to cover the gap. The myth contains typical motifs: a divine father, the casting into the water, the rescue by an animal etc. The name Romulus is obviously derived from that of the city. The famous bronze statue of the she-wolf dates from the 6th century BC and is an Etruscan work. From Livy we know that a statue of the she-wolf was dedicated in 296 BC.
Ogilvie, Livy (s.v.).

ROMULUS AUGUSTULUS The last Roman emperor of the West. His father Orestes had been a secretary and an officer of Attila. Orestes overthrew the Emperor Nepos and made his little son (Augustulus = little Augustus) emperor (August 475 AD). But the following year *Odoacer killed Orestes and sent RA. to live in Campania. Thus the last Roman emperor ironically had the name of both the first and second founders of Rome.

ROSCIUS, Sextus In 80 BC he was accused of killing his wealthy father and was defended by Cicero. The prosecutors were his relatives who added the name of R.'s father to the proscription list with the help of Chrysogonus, *Sulla's favourite freedman. For Cicero it was his first important appearance in court and the case attracted general attention because many nobles were provoked by the position of Chrysogonus. Cicero handled the case tactfully and presumably won it.
Cicero, Pro S. Roscio Amerino.

ROSCIUS GALLUS, Quintus One of the most famous Roman actors, free-born, noted for his appearance both in comedy and tragedy, though he excelled in the former. Rich and popular, he was made a Roman knight (Eques) by Sulla for his artistry. In one year he played 125 times. Because he squinted, he played with a mask, except when he took the role of a parasite. He was admired by Cicero, who was his advocate in a civil suit, and who mentions him in his writings. RG. had a dramatic school and wrote a treatise on acting and oratory.

ROXANE R. was the daughter of a Bactrian chieftain named Oxyartes who sent her and his wife to an impregnable mountain stronghold, known as the "Soghdian Rock". Alexander's soldiers captured the place by Alpine climbing, and the king, so some sources say, fell in love with her, the loveliest woman in Asia after Darius III's wife. Alexander married her (327 BC) to win over the local population. She gave birth to a posthumous son, Alexander IV, the only son of Alexander. After Alexander's death, R. contrived the murder of his other wife,

Statira. After *Antipater (1) died she fled to Epirus but returned with *Polyperchon and *Olympias. She was betrayed to *Cassander who after several years killed her and her son (310 BC).

RUBICO (RUBICON) The little river flowing from the Apennines into the Adriatic north of Ariminum (Rimini). By the early 1st century BC it was the boundary between Italy and Cisalpine Gaul. Which of the rivers in this area is the ancient R. it is not known for sure. R. is famous for Caesar's crossing of it in 49 BC by which he opened the Civil War against Pompey. On the night of 10 January 49 BC Caesar was still hesitant and when he arrived at his final decision to cross it he pronounced the famous saying: alea iacta est ("the die is cast") and hence "to cross the Rubicon" is to commit oneself to an action.

RUFUS, Cluvius Roman senator and historian of the 1st century AD. He was consul (at an unknown date), rich and eloquent, but, as Tacitus says, avoided prosecutions. During Nero's tour of Greece he was his herald in the theatre. In AD 69 he was governor in Spain and after Galba's death made his allegiance to Vitellius. In December of that year he was witness to the negotiations between Vitellius and Vespasian's brother Flavius Sabinus. His Histories probably dealt with the period of Caligula, Claudius, Nero and the year AD 69.
Peter, Hist. Rom. Rel.²; Syme, Tacitus (s.v.).

RUTILIUS RUFUS, Publius Roman statesman and writer, born c. 160–155 BC. He served as a military tribune under Scipio Aemilianus in *Numantia (134–133 BC) and was praetor by 118 BC. He failed to win the consulate of 115 BC and prosecuted the successful candidate *Scaurus (1), and was prosecuted by him. RR. became a Stoic after studying philosophy under *Panaetius; he also studied law under *Scaevola (1). He served successfully as legate of *Metellus (2) Numidicus against Jugurtha (109) and as consul in 105 BC introduced new methods of training soldiers in which he was followed by *Marius. RR. was legate of *Scaevola (3) in Asia (94 BC) and while helping the provincials he clashed with Roman businessmen. In 92 BC he was prosecuted on a charge of *Repetundae and was condemned by the equestrian jurors, a famous case of distortion of justice. *Drusus (2) was prompted to introduce his reforms as the result of this trial. RR. settled in Smyrna where he wrote his historical work which is not extant. RR. wrote on events and persons with whom he was involved, and his work was a vent for his embittered feelings.
Malcovati, ORF², 168ff.

S

SABELLI The peoples of central Italy, prominent among them were the Samnites, who migrated and conquered Campania and Lucania in the second half of the 5th century BC. The growth of population and the scarcity of land induced them to spread by the custom of *Ver Sacrum (Sacred Spring). Their language became *Oscan; ancient authors identified them with the Sabini.
J. Whatmough, *The Foundations of Roman Italy*, 1937;
E. T. Salmon, *Samnium*, 1967.

SABINI (The country is Sabinum) The Rape of the Sabines − the abduction of the Sabine girls by *Romulus and his men − is probably the best known episode about the S., but this belongs to the sphere of legend. The S. were an old Italian people who inhabited the Apennine mountains east of the Tiber with Reate (modern Rieti) and Amiternum as their main towns, though they mainly lived in villages. They were variously said to be the original inhabitants of the region or − in the view of ancient writers impressed by their bravery and morality − Lacedaemonians, or Cimbrians; it was also thought that various peoples originated from them, notably the Samnites. Legends and linguistic and religious evidence indicate that the S. formed one of the ethnic elements of ancient Rome, living on the Quirinal. The prominent clan of the Claudii came from Sabinum to settle in Rome in the late 6th century BC. Occasionally, however, there were wars between Rome and the S. who used to make inroads on Roman territories until the mid-5th century BC. The Sabines were subdued by the Roman general Marius Curius *Dentatus in 299 BC and received Roman citizenship. They were Romanized soon thereafter.
E. C. Evans, *Cults of the Sabine Territory*, 1939;
E. T. Salmon, *Samnium*, 1967.

SABINUS, Masurius Roman jurist of the first half of the 1st century AD. His main work was a textbook in three volumes on the *Ius Civile*, in which he gave a systematic description of Roman private law without committing himself to any doctrine. Later writers followed his arrangement in their treatment of the subject. One of the two schools of jurists, the *Sabiniani* was named after S.; the other, *Proculiani*, was named after Proculus, a jurist who was S.'s contemporary. But the nature of these schools is obscure. Among S.'s successors were *Javolenus and Salvius *Julianus.

SABRATHA The western of the three Phoenician trading posts (hence Tripolis) on the coast of the Lesser Syrtis. It was founded in the 5th or 4th century BC and depended on Carthage, and it later came under the control of *Masinissa. From Augustus on it was included in the province of Africa Proconsularis and in the 2nd century AD it was made a Roman colony. S. derived its prosperity from trade. The site has been largely excavated. The more important buildings are a basilica, a theatre, temples (Hercules, Isis etc.) and an ampitheatre. The city had a bishop in the 3rd century AD.
D. E. L. Haynes, *The Antiquities of Tripolitania*, 1956.

SACRED WARS Wars conducted by the *Amphictiony of Delphi against those members who committed sacrilege against the Delphic sanctuary of Apollo. For details see *Delphi.

SACROVIR, Julius Chieftain of the Gallic *Aedui who revolted against Rome in AD 21, in which revolt the Treveri participated. He occupied *Augustodonum but after his defeat by the Roman commander of Upper Germany, he committed suicide.

SAGUNTIUM (modern Sagunto) This Iberian city is mainly known for the part it played in the outbreak of the Second Punic War. When *Hannibal attacked it in 219 BC, Rome demanded that he stop the siege on the claim that S. was her ally. But he persisted and after eight months conquered it; Rome thereupon declared war against Carthage.

Because of the resemblance in name, the city was said to have been founded by Greek settlers from the island of Zacynthus. The site was situated close to the coast some 25 km north of Valencia. Its territory was fertile and its figs, cereals and pottery were well known. *Scipio (1) and his brother conquered it in 212 BC. Under Augustus it became a *Municipium.

SALAMIS (1) This island (approximately 90 sq km) in the Saronic Gulf opposite Piraeus is best known for the decisive victory that the Greeks won here over the Persians in September 480 BC. The battle was fought in the narrow straits between the island and the Attic coast. The numerically inferior Greeks were inside, and the Persians, hampering each other, were routed as they advanced inward. *Xerxes, with the Persian land army, watched the battle from the shore and thereafter hurried to leave

Greece. The battle is described by Aeschylus in the *Persae*.

Athens won S. from *Megara in the time of *Solon (*c.* 600 BC) and made it a cleruchy in the late 6th century. Euripides used to compose his tragedies in a cave in S. *Cassander occupied S. in 318 BC and, with some interval, it remained under Macedonian control until *c.* 230 BC when *Aratus (2) handed it to Athens.

C. Hignett, *Xerxes' Invasion of Greece*, 1963, 193ff. and 468ff.

SALAMIS (2) The most important Greek city in Cyprus, situated on the east coast, some 6 km north of modern Famagusta. Its legendary founder was Teucer, brother of the greater Ajax (*Aias (1)). In the nearby Enkomi there had been a Mycenaean settlement. The names of S.'s kings are known from coins dating from 520 BC. The most famous king was *Evagoras who established his rule almost all over the island (*c.* 411–373 BC). At S. the Persians defeated the Cypriot Greeks in a naval battle (498 BC), and the Athenians won a victory over the Persians (*c.* 450 BC). *Demetrius (1) defeated the navy of Ptolemy I here in 306 BC but was not able to conquer the city, which was the residence of the Ptolemaic governors in the Hellenistic period. After the annexation of Cyprus by Rome (58 BC), the Salaminians suffered from *Brutus (2) who charged 48% on the loans he gave to the city. In the Roman period *Paphus replaced S. as the capital of the island. The prosperous Jewish community of S. ceased to exist after the revolt of AD 116. Refounded by Constantine II, it was called Constanta. The remains include a gymnasium, a theatre and a basilica.

V. Karageorghis, *Salamis in Cyprus*, 1969.

SALII College of minor priests at Rome whose name derived from *Salire*, "to dance". The Roman S. were priests of Mars consisting of two associations (Palatini and Collini) each of twelve members. They were Patricians and their chief function was to perform ritual dances at the opening and closing of the war season, March and October. They were armed with a sword, an 8-shape shield (*ancilia*) and a spear, and wore a red *tunica*, a *trabea* (a short cloak) and an *apex* (a high conical hat). Many Italian and Latin cities each had their own S. who were normally, as in Rome, associated with the god of war.

SALINATOR, Marcus Livius Roman politician and general born in 254 BC. For his victory as consul in the Second Illyrian War (219 BC) he was awarded a triumph. But the following year he was accused of embezzlement of public money and left Rome. He was later allowed to return and as consul in 207 BC won, with C. Claudius *Nero (1), the important battle against *Hasdrubal (2) at the Metaurus. He was given a second triumph and was proconsul for the next three years. He attained the censorship in 204 BC.

Scullard, *Rom. Pol.*[2] (s.v.).

SALLUST (Gaius Sallustius Crispus) Roman politician and important historian (86 BC–34 BC), native of the Sabine town Amiternum, of a well-to-do, non-senatorial family. He lived a profligate life in his youth, to which he alludes in his own works. He was quaestor *c.* 55 BC and as tribune in 52 BC was prominent in the public demonstrations after the murder of *Clodius (1) by *Milo, which led to the burning down of the *Curia, the Senate house. Expelled from the Senate by the censor Appius *Claudius (4) Pulcher in 50 BC, he followed Caesar in the Civil War. He was praetor in 46 BC and fought with Caesar. He

became the first governor of the new province Nova Africa (the former kingdom of Numidia) and amassed riches at the expense of the provincials. Barely escaping condemnation on a charge of *Repetundae on his return, which cost him a bribe of more than one million sesterces to Caesar, he quit politics to enjoy the amenities of his famous gardens in Rome and to write history.

S. wrote three historical works. The first is the *Bellum Catilinae* which gives an account of *Catiline's conspiracy in 63 BC. S. aims at sketching and explaining the moral and political decadence of Rome in his time, and he takes the Catilinarian conspiracy as an example. The main corrupting factors are avarice (*avaritia*), ambition (*ambitio*) and luxury (*luxuria*). Rome had once been a frugal, patriotic and well-ordered society. But the expansion of the empire led to an influx of wealth and the elimination of Carthage removed all fear of external foes. From then on, every one sought to indulge in luxury and in political power, whether he belonged to the oligarchy in power or to the Populares. But even in such a state of society great talents must be noted by the historian, and at the time of the conspiracy there were two who excelled: Cato and Caesar. There is a vast literature on what S.'s aim is in this monograph, but the once popular interpretation that it is a piece of Caesarian propaganda cannot be maintained. It is probably no more than what it claims to be: an artistic analysis of the state of Roman society by which the author seeks to gain a name; and he did.

The *Bellum Jugurthinum* is a monograph on the war against *Jugurtha. The main theme is essentially the same as that of Catiline's conspiracy: the vices of the *Nobilitas which selfishly exploited its power, and its corruption and incompetence which endangered the interest of Rome. S. takes the Jugurthine war as his subject because, he says, it was then that the supremacy of the nobility was challenged for the first time. In the mouth of the *Novus Homo *Marius, S. puts the view that true nobility is not an inheritance one receives from one's ancestors but one's own excellence. Yet Marius is hardly S.'s hero and while the venality of the Roman aristocrats is fully exposed the historian also gives full credit to the achievements of *Metellus (2) Numidicus.

S. also wrote a full scale historical work, but of his *Histories*, in five books, covering the years 78–66 BC, only fragments, including some important speeches and letters, are extant. Three other small works are ascribed to S.: an invective against Cicero and two letters to Caesar. Opinions vary about their authenticity and they were probably written by later writers.

S.'s defects as an historian are considerable. Accuracy is not his aim and as a result he is often vague or wrong on chronology and geography. This is largely because he regarded his works as expositions of his historical conceptions and interpretations. He thus antedates the conspiracy of Catiline by one year or more. He also writes for dramatic effect and for this purpose he presents Sulla as alive at a time when he was dead. His philosophical and political views are regarded as commonplace or unoriginal. However, though he has been refuted in some points of detail, and though credit must be given to former thinkers for his general views (which are not so important for the historical works as such), his verdict on the state of Roman society, the causes of its decline and of the change in political behaviour, is essentially true. As a writer, he is noted for brevity, dramatic construction, use of archaisms, sayings, and unusual words. The terse style, contrasted with the verbosity of many other writers, won success and was to influence Tacitus.

J. C. Rolfe (Loeb), 1921;
D. C. Earl, *The Political Thought of Sallust*, 1961;
R. Syme, *Sallust*, 1964.

SALMONEUS In mythology, king of Elis, son of Aeolus and brother of *Sisyphus. Hated by his people he claimed to be Zeus, hurling torches into the air for the god's lightning bolts and dragging cauldrons of bronze behind his chariot so as to make a noise for the thunderbolts. Zeus struck him with a real thunderbolt. S.'s actions were probably part of a mimic charm to bring rain.

SALONAE or SALONA (near modern Split) Coastal city in Dalmatia, once inhabited by Thracians, it was occupied by Dalmatians and was conquered by the Romans in 78 BC. Thereafter it attracted Roman settlers and was made a *colonia* by 44 BC. After the organization of the province of Dalmatia by Augustus, it became its capital. *Gabinius died here in 47 BC and Diocletian built his palace near the city where he lived after his abdication from the throne in AD 305.

J. J. Wilkes, *Dalmatia*, 1969, 22ff.

SALUS Old Roman goddess who stood for the welfare and security of the state. A temple was built to her on the Quirinal in 302 BC. By the early 2nd century BC she was identified with the Greek goddess *Hygeia. Augustus built an altar to S. *Populi Romani* (S. of the Roman People),

Pax (peace) and *Concordia*. Her attributes on coins are the sacred snakes and a sceptre.

SALVIDIENUS RUFUS, Quintus Roman general, probably of low origin, rose as a supporter of Octavian after Caesar's murder. After an initial success against Sextus *Pompeius in 42 BC, he soon suffered a defeat near Rhegium (42 BC). He fought with Octavian in the Perusine War (41 BC) and was made governor of Gaul in 40 BC. But Octavian discovered that he secretly negotiated with Antony and the Senate declared him a public enemy; he thereupon killed himself.

SAMNIUM The country of the Samnites (*Saunitae* in Greek) in south-central Italy. The Samnites, a Sabellic people, consisted of four tribes: Caudini, Caraceni, Hirpini and Pentri, which had some federal institutions. The growth of the population led them to expand to Campania in the 5th century BC and those who remained at home renewed the expansion in the 4th century. They made a treaty with Rome in 354 BC but the latter's intervention in the affairs of Campania led to the First Samnite War (343–341 BC). This is sometimes considered as an invention, but at any rate Rome soon established her hegemony in Campania, following which the Second Samnite War began in 327 BC; and with an interval of several years after 321 BC, it lasted until 304 BC. The Samnites proved dangerous enemies and in 321 BC trapped a Roman army near *Caudium. But Rome improved her tac-

Samnite soldiers. A tomb-painting from Paestum. Early 4th century BC

tics and armour and with tenacity continued the war (and meanwhile expanded her control to Apulia and south Campania) until she won it. In the Third Samnite War (298–290 BC) the Samnites were again defeated and their territory was reduced. But whenever they had the opportunity the Samnites fought Rome: with *Pyrrhus, *Hannibal and in the *Bellum Sociale. Latin colonies (Beneventum, Aesernia) were founded to secure Roman control and after the Second Punic War large parts of S. were confiscated. In the Civil War in 83–81 BC the Samnites fought with Sulla's enemies and he annihilated them.
E. T. Salmon, *Samnium and the Samnites*, 1967.

SAMOS Large island off the west coast of Asia Minor, stretching east–west with a length of 45 km and an area of approximately 490 sq km. It is separated from the mainland by 1.8 km wide straits. Occupied as early as Neolithic times, it was settled by Ionians in the early 1st millenium BC. S. sent settlers to various places including *Perinthus, *Naucratis, and *Samothrace. The seafaring Samian Colaeus reached the kingdom of *Tartessus in the mid-7th century BC (Hdt. 4.152). By trade and industry the island prospered from the 7th century on.

The early kingship was replaced by a landed aristocracy and in the 6th century BC *Polycrates established a tyranny (c. 540 BC). Under him, S. became mistress of the seas and a centre of arts, crafts and letters. After the execution of the tyrant, S. became dependent on the Persians and took part in the Ionian Revolt. Following its suppression, many Samians immigrated to *Messana. The Samians fought on the Persian side at *Salamis but joined the Delian League. After the suppression of its revolt (441–439 BC) by *Pericles, it had a democratic government. For their loyalty to the democratic cause during the oligarchic revolution in Athens (411 BC), the Samians received Athenian citizenship but were conquered by *Lysander. S. opposed the Second Athenian League and was conquered by *Timotheus (1) in 365 BC. The former population was expelled and a cleruchy was established. In the Hellenistic period its masters varied (Ptolemies and Seleucids) and for its support of Rome in the war against *Antiochus III it was made free (188 BC).

S.'s great period was in the 6th century, though the great philosopher *Pythagoras, a Samian by birth, migrated to Italy. It had famous architects and sculptors (*Rhoecus and *Theodorus) and at the court of Polycrates poets such as *Anacreon and *Ibycus were active. It had a famous aqueduct which was tunneled into the city and the even more famous great temple of Hera. The Samian engineer Mandrocles constructed the bridge over the Bosphorus for Darius I. Other known Samians are the historian *Duris (2) and the astronomer Conon, a close friend of Archimedes, who discovered the constellation Lock of Berenice.

SAMOSATA (modern Samsat) The capital city of *Commagene, situated at a crossing point on the right bank of the Euphrates. It was an important caravan city. After the annexation of Commagene by Vespasian (AD 72), S. was the centre of one of the four territorial divisions of the country. *Lucian was a native of S.

SAMOTHRACE Island with a 1,600 m plateau and an area of 180 sq km in the northeast Aegean. It was settled by colonists from *Samos. In most periods S. was under foreign control: Athens in the 5th and part of the 4th centuries BC, later Macedonia and various rulers in the Hellenistic period – Rome made it a "free city". It was famous for the mysteries of the *Cabiri whose sanctuary

there was very old (8th century BC). It was supported by the Ptolemies in the Hellenistic period; later the cult attracted Romans. The famous statue Nike of S. that was found there is in the Louvre.
K. Lehman, *Guide to Samothrace*, 1966.

SAPOR (1) I Son and successor of *Artaxerxes (2) I, the founder of the New Persian Empire. A short time before he died, his father made him co-ruler in AD 241. S. commemorated his achievements in a trilingual inscription where he calls himself "King of Kings of Iran and non-Iran" instead of the usual "King of Kings". His armies pillaged the eastern provinces of the Roman Empire time and again and he even captured the Roman Emperor *Valerian in AD 260. Occupied by other problems, *Gallienus was not able to set out against him and it was *Odaenathus of Palmyra who saved the East for the Empire. Under S., Mani the founder of *Manichaeism was allowed to work, though S. himself adhered to Mazdaism.

SAPOR (2) II Sassanid king of Persia, "brother of Sun and Moon" (Amm. Marc. 17.5.3), AD 309–79. After Christianity became the state religion in the Roman Empire, he persecuted the Christians, and fought continually against *Constantinus II. He thrice failed to capture *Nisibis (338, 346, 350). *Julian's attack against him miscarried, and thereafter *Jovian gave him Nisibis.

SAPPHO The famous poetess of Lesbos, born to an aristocratic family at Eresus in the late 7th century BC. Probably owing to civil strife, she had to leave her country in her youth and spent some time in Sicily. However, she returned and lived in Mitylene. She was married and called her daughter Cleis after her mother. S. had around her a group of young girls who were organized in an association for the worship of the Muses and Aphrodite. With these she had close ties of passionate relationship and wrote her lyrical poems about them and her feelings for them. It is from this that the term Lesbian originated. In legend, because of unrequited love for Phaon, she ended her life by leaping into the sea from a cliff on the island of *Leucas.

S.'s poetry was edited by the Alexandrian scholars but only fragments, which are mainly known from papyri, are extant. Love and her personal feelings were her subject matter, and it is no wonder that Aphrodite is the goddess to whom she turns. The only complete extant poem of hers is an address to Aphrodite from Book 1. She was highly emotional and in her poems describes the physical effects of her passions. Provoked by the sight of a girl speaking and laughing with a man, apparently her bridegroom, she becomes pale, is speechless and her ears buzz. She aptly says of Eros that he is "sweet-bitter" – a state from which there is no escape. But she also wrote marriage songs for her girls in which she followed the traditional themes. The setting of love for S. is the surrounding world of nature. In expressing her feelings she tells of flowers, the sun, the moon and the stars. In her poems S. also reveals her other affections. She is furious with her brother Charaxus who fell in love with a slave courtesan and she recounts the faults of rivals for the love of her girls.

Writing in the vernacular dialect of Lesbos, S. composes her poems in varied metres, uses melodious words and is most successful through her directness, intensity and simplicity of expression. Lyric poetry for the Greeks was poetry to be sung accompanied by the lyre. S.'s poetry is the personal lyric and in this she and *Alcaeus were the first in a long tradition.
Page, *Sappho and Alcaeus*, 1955; Bowra, *Gr. Lyr. Poet.*, 176ff.

SARAPIS (SERAPIS) Graeco-Egyptian god. His cult originated from the belief that the Apis bull of Memphis was turned into Osiris after its death, and was addressed as Osorapis. The cult was originally associated with the temple of Memphis beneath which the Apis bulls were buried. *Ptolemy I promoted the cult as a state god of the Greeks and the Egyptians and associated with it a cult statue which he brought from Sinope in accordance with a dream. A temple, Sarapeum, was built in Alexandria and there the god was represented in a seated, bearded figure (traits characteristic of Zeus), with a fertility symbol on his head and a Cerberus figure at the right knee. S. had mixed elements — he was an underground god like Osiris, a supreme god like Zeus and a god of healing like Asclepius. His cult soon spread to the Hellenistic world and was found in many centres like Athens, Corinth, Delos and Rhodes. He was also identified with many other gods including Dionysus, Helios and in Roman times, Jupiter. Wherever the cult of the Egyptian deities was introduced he occupied a prominent place. In Rome he had a temple dating from the 1st century BC, but under the Empire the mysteries of Isis attracted more worshippers.

T. A. Brady, *The Reception of the Egyptian Cults of the Greeks*, 1935; F. Cymunt, *Oriental Religions in Roman Paganism*.

SARDES (or SARDIS) The capital city of Lydia, situated at a foothill in the fertile valley of the Hermus with good communications to inner Asia Minor as well as to the coastal districts, S. developed from the Late Bronze Age. The nearby Mount Tmolus was rich in gold, silver and electrum (cf. Hdt. 1.93), and it was in S. that the first ever mint was established by *Gyges, king of Lydia. After the victory of Cyrus I over Croesus, S. became the residence of the Persian satraps. In the Ionian Revolt it was burnt down (498 BC), but it was soon restored and remained the centre of the Persian rule in west Asia Minor to the conquest of Alexander the Great. In the period of the *Diadochi it belonged to *Antigonus I, and, after Ipsus (301) fell, to the Seleucids. After the defeat of Antiochus III, Rome gave S. to *Eumenes II (188). In 133 BC it came under Roman rule with all the Attalid kingdom of Pergamum.

H. C. Buller (ed.), *Sardis*, 1922ff.; Magie, *Asia* (s.v.); G. M. A. Hanfmann, *A Short Guide to the Excavation at Sardes*, 1962.

SARDINIA The large island of the Sardi was in legend settled by Sardus son of Heracles and was associated with other Greek mythological heroes including Daedalus and Aristaeus; the Trojans were also said to have come there after the fall of their city. It was settled in prehistoric times. It attracted the commercial expansion of Carthage in the 6th century BC. *Malchus failed to conquer it but by the end of that century Punic rule was established in its coastal districts. Rome used the mercenaries' revolt against Carthage, after the First Punic War, to annex it (238 BC) and made it one province with Corsica (227 BC). But the island was pacified only in the course of the 2nd century thus giving several Roman generals opportunity to win triumphs. Under the Empire a few of its cities received colonial status. The grain supply was its main asset for Rome.

SARPEDON Mythological hero of Lycia who was also associated with Crete. In Homer he came to Troy to help his ally Priam and to gain distinction in the attack on the Greek camp (Book 12). But *Patroclus killed him. His father Zeus mourned him, and Sleep and Death returned the body for burial to Lycia (Book 16). In a later version he was the son of *Europa and Zeus and became king of Lycia after quarreling with his brother *Minos. To account for the chronological gap between the later version and the Homeric tale he was credited with a three-generation life. In historical times he had a hero-cult in Lycia.

SASSANIDS The royal dynasty of the New Persian Empire, founded by *Artaxerxes (2) I, grandson of Sasan. Throughout their existence the S. were formidable enemies of the Roman Empire and several times they overran Asia Minor. With the Arab conquest of Mesopotamia they ceased to be a menace. See *Artaxerxes (2) I, *Sapor (1) I, *Sapor (2) II.

R. Ghirshman, *Iran, Parthians and Sassanians*, 1962.

SATURA Satire, the word *satur* meaning "full" or "stuffed". Though there were Greek works with satirical elements, the S. was predominantly a genre developed by the Romans. According to Livy there had been in the 4th century BC a kind of dramatic performance, called S., which was a medley of music, song and mimetic dancing (7.2). This disappeared but the term S. was applied to a literary form noted for its mixed character. *Ennius was the first to write such verse satires noted for their humour and variety. But the creator of the true satire was *Lucilius. He mainly used the hexameter, wrote in conversational style with disregard to stylistic niceties and gave prominence to personal, mocking attacks. Subsequent satirists admired him, but only fragments of his thirty books are preserved. *Varro (2) introduced the Menippean satire, a medley of verse and prose, and also wrote verse satires. Only fragments of the first are known. Next came Horace and though he was a follower of Lucilius in this genre, his satires are more refined and lack the intensity of the personal lampoon. The Lucilian satire was also followed by *Persius and, under Nero, *Seneca the Younger wrote his *Apocolocyntosis* and *Petronius his *Satyricon*, both Menippean satires. The last great satirist was *Juvenal who in his 16 satires attacked not only individuals but the whole Roman society. See the poets mentioned (with bibliographies).

C. Hignett, *The Anatomy of Satire*, 1962.

SATURNINUS (1), Lucius Appuleius Roman statesman, good orator and agitator, of a praetorian family, prominent at the end of the 2nd century BC. As quaestor, some time before 103 BC, responsibility for the corn supply was taken from him and given to *Scaurus (1). Henceforth, he became a fierce enemy of the senatorial oligarchy, one of the extreme Populares and a supporter of *Marius. In his first tribunate (103 BC), he passed a law to establish a court of *Maiestas cases and an agrarian law to distribute lands to Marius' veterans in Africa. He was again tribune in 100 when he cooperated with the praetor Glaucia and for some time with the consul Marius. The former passed, then or earlier, a law to restore the court of *Repetundae to the Equites. S. passed a law to distribute lands outside Italy to Marius' soldiers in the recent wars against the *Cimbri. As *Metellus (2) Numidicus refused to swear obedience to the law he was expelled from Italy. S. sought to be tribune again in 99 with Glaucia as consul. But the elections were accompanied by riots. Marius then changed sides and, acting on the basis of a *Senatus Consultum Ultimum, took steps to suppress S. and his followers. S. and Glaucia were lynched and the colonization programme was not implemented.

The Sassanid king, Chosroes, shown hunting. A silver plate relief

SATURNINUS (2), Lucius Antonius Roman senator and general under the Flavians, consul *c.* AD 83, he was thereafter made governor of Upper Germany. In 89 he started a revolt in his province against Domitian, but he was promptly defeated and killed by the governor of Lower Germany. From then on Domitian became hypersuspicious and introduced a regime of terror.

SATURNUS Old Roman god whose origins are not clear. According to some modern views he was Phrygian, Illyrian or Cretan in origin. There is, however, better evidence to associate him with Etruria. According to the more common view he was god of the sowing (*satus* means "sown"), his festival was held in December, after the sowing season of the autumn. The ancients believed him to have been Greek in origin and identified him with *Kronos. As such he was father of Zeus/Jupiter. In poetry he was the first ruler in the Golden Age.

In early times the Capitolium had been S.'s hill and his temple, consecrated in 497 BC, stood on the slope of the hill. It served as the Treasury of the state (*Aerarium Saturni) and there are extant impressive remains. The festival of S. (17 December) was the Saturnalia, the greatest festival of the agricultural year. It was celebrated with much festivity, and slaves were given permission to take part in the day and night carnival. Gifts were exchanged (*Martial wrote mottoes for such gifts) and there were a *Lectisternium, a public banquet and a Mock King. Under the Empire the merry festival spread to the provinces and in the 4th century BC the festivities became an element of the New-Year's Day.

Platner-Ashby, *Top. Dict. Rome,* 463ff.; W. W. Fowler *The Roman Festivals of the Republic,* 1899.

SATYRS Daemons of woods and hills, creatures half-man, half-animal, notorious for their mischievous and lustful character, sometimes associated with *Dionysus. In a passage of Hesiod, the earliest author who mentions them, they are called "good-for nothing" and "play-mates of the nymphs" (Strabo 471). In literature they were often confused with *Sileni. In vase-paintings they were represented as human beings with horse tails and pointed ears. Later in Hellenistic and Roman times they had goat legs and horns and appeared in association with Pan and Faunus. But they lost something of their wild nature and acquired an idyllic, pensive character in Hellenistic poetry and art. The Satyr pouring wine is the best known of the copies of the Satyr-statues of *Praxiteles.

The poet Arion (*c.* 600 BC) may have introduced the singers of the *Dithyramb in costumes of S. (Hdt. 1.23), and according to Aristotle the early plays were of a satyric character. The poet Pratinas from the Peloponnesus was known as the inventor of the satyr-play and to have introduced it into the dramatic competitions at Athens in the late 6th century. This type of play was so-called because it had a Chorus of S. It became a regular feature of the dramatic competitions in the early 5th century BC. Each of the poets who took part in the competitions produced a satyr-play after his trilogy. The most accomplished in this genre was Aeschylus, but only fragments of one of his plays are preserved. A large part of the *Ichneutae* of Sophocles is extant as well as the complete *Cyclops* of *Euripides. These were rather burlesque-type plays but in subjects and form were like those of the tragedy. In the above plays the precise bestial character of the S. is not stated and it seems that they could appear in more than one shape.

Pickard-Cambridge, *Dithyramb,* 60ff.

SCAEVOLA (1), Publius Mucius Roman statesman and renowned lawyer, of a plebeian family. Tiberius *Gracchus (2) consulted him on his agrarian reform, and as a consul in 133, S. refused to use illegal force against him, though he did not approve of the way he carried out his bill. After the death of his brother *Crassus (2) Mucianus, S. became Pontifex Maximus and published the *annales maximi* (*Annals).

T. P. Wiseman, *Athenaeum,* 1970, 152f.

SCAEVOLA (2), Quintus Mucius ("Augur") Roman statesman and prominent lawyer, son-in-law of *Laelius (2). Praetor by 120 BC, he was accused by *Albucius of *Repetundae for his governorship of Asia. He was acquitted and became consul of 117 BC. In 100 he was one of the opponents of *Saturninus and in 88 of *Sulla when the latter occupied Rome. S. was influenced by the Stoic philosophy. He had many pupils including his son-in-law *Crassus (3), Cicero, *Sulpicius Rufus and *Atticus. He appears as an interlocuter in several dialogues of Cicero (*De Amicitia, De Re Publica, De Oratore*). S. died in 87 BC.

SCAEVOLA (3), Quintus Mucius ("Pontifex") Son of Scaevola (2) the Augur, Roman statesman and distinguished jurist, *c.* 140–82 BC. Tribune in 106 and praetor by 98, he was consul in 95 BC with *Crassus (3) as his colleague. They expelled non-citizens from Rome and instituted an investigation against those who had acquired citizenship illegally. In 94 he governed Asia with P. *Rutilius Rufus as legate and his provincial *edict became a model of equity for subsequent governors. But his arrangements reduced the free exploitation of the provincials by the *Publicani, who later took revenge by prosecuting Rutilius. S. became Pontifex Maximus in 89 and remained in Rome under the regime of *Cinna (1), but was killed in 82 on the order of Marius the Younger. In his reputation as jurist, S. excelled all his contemporaries including his father. In a famous case he appeared against his brother-in-law the famous orator *Crassus (3). He wrote a comprehensive work on the *Ius Civile, the first of its kind.

SCAMANDER River of the Troad (modern Menderes Su), mentioned by Homer. Later it was said that had the horses of *Rhesus drunk its water, Troy could not have been captured.

SCAURUS (1), Marcus Aemilius Influential Roman statesman and the leading figure in the Senate in the late 2nd century BC and the 90s BC. Born *c.* 162 BC of an impoverished patrician family, he started his political career after first improving his financial circumstances. He was aedile in 122, praetor by 119, and consul in 115. After his rival for the consulate P. *Rutilius Rufus failed to convict him on a charge of *Ambitus, Scaurus counter-prosecuted him but also failed. As consul, he was sensitive to his dignity and punished a praetor who did not show him due respect. He won a triumph for his war against the Ligurians and used the booty for building the temples for Mens and Fides. The censors appointed him *Princeps Senatus, a position endorsed by all further censors to his death. Despite his suspicious links with *Jugurtha, he was one of the chairmen of the commission which investigated the misbehaviour of Roman senators in their dealings with him (109 BC). He was censor in 109 but had to abdicate after the death of his colleague. He clashed with *Saturninus (1) when he took over his supervision of the corn supply (before 103). After his son from his first marriage died, he married a Metella, a daughter of the influential Metellan family who bore him three children including

*Scaurus (2). In 100 S. took a leading part in the suppression of the sedition of Saturninus in cooperation with *Marius, with whom he had some business relations. S. gave his support to the reforms of *Drusus (2). He died in 89.

S. was an astute politician and shrewd businessman. His authority was immense. Prosecuted at old age he won the case by simply asking the jurors whether they believed him or the prosecutor. He wrote an apologetic biography. For Sallust he was the typical corrupt senator, but Cicero admired him.

I. Shatzman, *Ancient Society*, 1974, 197ff.

SCAURUS (2) The notorius spendthrift son of *Scaurus (1). He served under Pompey in the East and took bribes from Aristobulus, brother of *Hyrcanus (2), and from *Aretas III. The games he gave as aedile in 58 BC were the most extravagant ever given at Rome. In the same year his villa at Tusculum was burnt down with a damage of 30 million sesterces. He was prosecuted for *Repetundae in 54 BC for his governorship of Sardinia but was acquitted. In 53 he was convicted on a charge of *Ambitus and went into exile.

SCEPTICS The main doctrine of the Sceptic philosophers was that there is no way to attain certain knowledge, mainly because of the unreliability of the senses. Hence they maintained agnostic views, and opposed the dogmatic teachings of other philosophers. The founder of Scepticism was *Pyrrhon. Scepticism was dominant in the *Academy from *Arcesilaus to *Antiochus of Ascalon, but there was no school of Scepticism. See *Arcesilaus, *Pyrrhon, *Sextus Empiricus (with bibliographies).

SCHOLIA (sing. scholion) Notes in the margins of manuscripts which comment on the subject matter and language of the text. Those who wrote or copied them may have used various ancient commentaries and the S. in manuscripts of an author need not be identical. Normally S. originate from commentaries of ancient scholars, though the manuscripts are of late dates. There are S. on many Greek and Latin authors, mainly poets, but their value varies.

SCIPIO (1) CALVUS, Gnaeus Cornelius Of the patrician Scipionic family which was dominant in Roman politics from the 4th to the 2nd century BC. The family burial place was discovered near Rome on the Via Appia with a sarcophagus of Lucius Cornelius Scipio Barbatus, the grandfather of S. Barbatus, who was consul in 298 BC and the inscription on the sarcophagus, the earliest of its kind, briefly enumerates his career and exploits.

As consul in 222 BC, S. fought the *Insubres and captured their capital *Mediolanum. After the outbreak of the Second Punic War, he was sent to Spain (218) to carry the war into the Carthaginian area. Next year he won a naval victory over *Hasdrubal (2) off the Ebro and was joined by his brother Publius. The latter, who had been consul in 218, failed to intercept Hannibal on his way to Italy and was defeated by him in a cavalry engagement at the Ticinus and at the battle of Trebia. In the following years the two brothers prevented Hasdrubal from joining his brother Hannibal in Italy and won an important victory in 215. They captured Saguntum in 212, but the following year were defeated and killed.

SCIPIO (2) AFRICANUS, Publius Cornelius Roman statesman, and Rome's brilliant commander in the Second Punic War. Born in 236 BC, he fought under his father, the consul of 218. After his father and his uncle, *Scipio (1), were killed in battle in Spain (211) he was appointed

by the People to command the Roman army in Spain in 210; this was an unusual procedure especially as he was a private man and not a magistrate. He retained this popularity almost to the end of his life. By training and new organization he made the legion more flexible, and by daring decisions and surprise outflanking tactics he won spectacular achievements. He captured *Carthago Nova in 209, defeated *Hasdrubal (2) at Baecula (208), and in 206 won the decisive victory at Ilipa over *Mago (2) and *Hasdrubal (3), the son of Gisco. He thus expelled the Carthaginians from Spain and laid the foundation of Roman rule in the Iberian peninsula.

Back in Rome S. was elected consul for 205. The Senate, influenced by *Fabius (3) Cunctator, gave him limited permission to invade Africa and he first went to Sicily. He landed in Africa in 204 but failed to take Utica. In 203 in a night attack he destroyed the camps of *Syphax and *Hasdrubal (3) by fire and won a great victory over the latter at the Campi Magni. At Zama in 202 he won his crowning victory by defeating Hannibal. Both tried to develop outflanking tactics and thus cancelled out each other's movements; the battle was decided by the superiority of the Numidian cavalry of *Masinissa and the skill of the legionaries. This ended the Second Punic War and S. was given the surname Africanus.

On his return, S.'s prestige and influence in the state were supreme. He was censor in 199 and, from then to his death, *Princeps Senatus. He was elected consul again for 194 and in 190 was a legate of his brother Lucius in the war against *Antiochus III. Due to his illness, he did not take part in the decisive battle at Magnesia. His exceptional eminence and popularity always seemed dangerous to *Cato (1) who instigated a prosecution against his brother for embezzlement of public money in the war against Antiochus. S. at first repelled this attack by his prestige but he could not save his brother and after 184 he retired from politics to his estate in Liternum where he soon died. His wife, sister of *Paullus, bore him two sons and two daughters. Of the latter, one was married to *Scipio (4) Corculum and the other, *Cornelia, to Tiberius *Gracchus (1). S. was one of the greatest generals of antiquity, in one view the best of all. In his tactics he learnt from Hannibal, and the Romans compared him to Alexander the Great. He was a great leader of soldiers and legends grew round him and the divine providence behind his success. His military achievements and vigorous policy were decisive for the growth of the Roman Empire. The great clientele he had and the personal attachment of the army to him foreshadowed the great political figures of the 1st century BC; he had no intention, however, to use them to secure himself against the attacks of his rivals.

H. H. Scullard, *Scipio Africanus, Soldier and Statesman*, 1970; *Roman Politics*[2] (s.v.).

SCIPIO (3) ASIATICUS, Lucius Cornelius Roman statesman and general, brother of *Scipio (2) Africanus. He served under his brother in Spain and Africa in the Second Punic War. As praetor he governed Sicily, and as consul in 190 received the command against *Antiochus III whom he defeated at Magnesia in the winter of 190/189. He was given a triumph in 188 but, to undermine the position of his brother, he was charged with embezzlement of public money received from Antiochus (probably in 187). He was saved from imprisonment by the veto of Tiberius *Gracchus (1), but the accusation was enough to shatter the predominance of the Scipions.
Scullard, *Roman Politics*[2] (s.v.).

SCIPIO (4) NASICA CORCULUM, Publius Cornelius
Prominent Roman statesman in the mid-2nd century BC,
grandson of *Scipio (1) Calvus. He fought at *Pydna
(168), was consul in 162 and censor in 159. As consul for
the second time in 155, he fought in Dalmatia. After the
death of *Lepidus (1) he became Pontifex Maximus, and
Princeps Senatus. He is mainly famous for his opposition
to the destruction of Carthage, a policy pursued by *Cato
(1) in the 150s BC. The removal of the external foe, he
argued, would be detrimental to the preservation of the
morals of Roman society; *Sallust claimed that the decadence of Roman morals began after the Third Punic War.
Scullard, *Roman Politics*² (s.v.).

**SCIPIO (5) AEMILIANUS AFRICANUS NUMANTINUS,
Publius Cornelius** Roman statesman and general,
184–129 BC, prominent in the third quarter of the 2nd
century BC. Son of *Paulus under whom he fought at
*Pydna, he was adopted by the son of *Scipio (2) Africa-
nus. He established a life-long friendship with *Polybius,
who was deported to Italy after Pydna. In 151 he served
in Spain and in 149–148 distinguished himself in the Third
Punic War. His popularity was such that he was elected
consul for 147, despite strong opposition in the Senate
and against the legal requirements which were circum-
vented by special legislation. He received the command
against Carthage, imposed severe discipline and captured
the city in 146. Back in Rome he held a spectacular
triumph and won the admiration of the Greeks after he
restored various works of art which had been captured
through the years by the Carthaginians in Sicily. Thereafter he was censor in 142 and went abroad on a diplomatic mission to the East (140–139). He was largely responsible for the repudiation of the treaty by which his
brother-in-law Tiberius *Gracchus (2) saved the Roman
army from the Numantines in 137. He was granted dis-
pensation from the law that forbade a person to hold
more than one consulate and was elected consul of 134.
He then received the command against *Numantia, and
set out for Spain with many volunteers from among his
friends and clients. He captured and destroyed Numantia
in 133, and sold the population into slavery. He again
celebrated a triumph (132). S. soon lost his popularity by
leading the opposition to the work of the agrarian commission set up by Tiberius *Gracchus (2), and died suddenly in 129. The suspicion that he was murdered is
probably wrong. He was childless and thus the line of
Scipio Africanus was extinguished.

S. had round him a group of close friends who were
interested in Greek literature and philosophy, the so-
called Scipionic Circle. Among these were *Laelius (2),
*Lucilius, *Terence, *Pacuvius and P. *Rutilius Rufus.
This group is referred to by Cicero (*De Amicitia* 69), but
it is very doubtful whether it was associated with politics.
With them were also associated the historian Polybius and
the Stoic philosopher *Panaetius. But it seems that the
cultivation of Greek culture was, so to speak, an academic
pursuit. As a statesman, S. followed traditional ruthless
Roman methods in dealing with foreigners. He was largely
responsible for the uncompromising policy against *Viriathus and Numantia, and was not satisfied with less than
the complete suppression and destruction of the latter. He
apparently opposed the reform of Tiberius Gracchus but
had no alternative solution for the social and economic
problems of the day. A good soldier and organizer with
wide popularity, he was, however, not above the selfish
motives and personal interests of ordinary Roman statesmen. It is only Cicero's admiration of him as defender of
the once good constitution of Rome that made him an
exceptional figure.
H. H. Scullard, *JRS*, 1960, 59f.;
A. E. Astin, *Scipio Aemilianus*, 1967.

SCOPAS Native of Paros, leading Greek sculptor and architect of the 4th century. He was the architect of the temple of Athena Alea at Tegea; he executed the statues of
Asclepius and Hygeia for it and probably designed the
sculptures of the pediments. The subjects were the Calydonian boar-hunt and Achilles and Telephus. Of these
there are some remains, including several spoiled heads
with sunken eyes and furrowed brows which are very impressive in their strong expression. However it is not certain whether S. made these. S. also worked in the temple
of Artemis in Ephesus and made sculptures for the *Mausoleum of Halicarnassus. Again there is no certainty in the
attribution of the extant remains to him. One of these is a
fight between Greeks and Amazons (British Museum). A
Maenad in the Dresden Museum is probably a Roman
copy of the famous Maenad of S. noted for its violent
movement and expression. In contrast, the Pothos
("Longing") known from many Roman copies, is a youth,
quite delicately fashioned, with a tender gaze. This testi-
fies to the versatility of S. who gave expression both to
violence and tenderness in his works.

SCRIBONIA After she was married twice, to men of
consular rank, S. was married to Octavian as a political
means to secure better relations with her relative Sextus
*Pompeius. She gave birth to his only child *Julia. But in
39 BC he divorced her and married Livia. S. lived to an
old age and survived Augustus.

SCULPTURE, GREEK The origins of S., or more correctly of the making of statues, is associated in Greek
traditions with the legendary *Daedalus. This is correct in
so far as it reflects the fact that the artists of the Minoan
civilization and of the Mycenaean civilization made figurines of terra-cotta or bronze and ivory or pottery statuettes. The monumental relief of the famous Lion Gate in
Mycenae is exceptional among these works. At any rate
Greek S. as it developed from the mid-7th century BC was
not a continuation of this tradition, nor even of the figurines and statuettes of the geometric period (c. 1000–700
BC).

Greek S. consisted of S. in relief and S. in the round.
It was essentially religious in the sense that statues of
deities were made to be placed inside the temples which
were also decorated by architectural sculptures, notably
in the friezes and the pediments. Both types of work were
also employed in grave monuments. The materials used
included marble, limestone, bronze, wood, terra-cotta and
chryselphantine. Stone and terra-cotta sculptures were
painted. The notably characteristic of Greek S. is that
even when it was closely associated with religion (and in
later times this was frequently not the case) the artists
were not limited by religious beliefs. They sought to give
realistic presentation to the human – or animal – body in
idealized or natural forms. In some way this was obviously connected with the anthropomorphic conception
of the gods.

The Archaic period of Greek S. begins in the mid-7th
century BC with the appearance of statues of full or col-
losal size and continues to the early 5th century BC. The
life size sculpture in stone was first developed under influence from Egypt. There are two major types of it in
the extant statues of this period: The "Kouros" (youth),

The charioteer. Bronze statue found at Delphi. Dedication of Polyzelus of Gela

a male figure, and the "Kore" (maiden), a female figure. The "Kouroi" are standing, nude statues. They are erect, stiff, with the head straight, the left leg advanced, and the arms hanging down or clenched; the shoulders are broad and the waist narrow. It is a solid block in which the human body is symmetrically fashioned with stress on the essential parts — not a correct anatomical representation. *"Cleobis" and "Biton" belong to this type of statue. The "Korai" are standing, clothed statues of women and it was in the shaping of the drapery that the artists gradually showed their skill. In a few cases Korai were seated. In architectural S. and funerary monuments the sphinx or the lion were sometimes fashioned. Figures reclining or in movement were sometimes made for works in relief, the pediments of temples or in some minor S. The frieze of the Treasury House of Syphnos in Delphi is a good example. The stele of Ariston, which belongs to the late Archaic period (*c.* 500 BC), is a fine example of the funerary monuments.

The influence of the Egyptian S. at the beginning of the Archaic period is manifest in the frontal pose, the rendering of the faces and the anatomical description. The changes in the fashion of the human body from the 7th to the early 5th century BC offer an instructive evidence as to the difference in the outlook of life between the Greek and Oriental artists. The latter continued to follow the stylised, traditional forms for hundreds of years. The Greeks sculptors constantly improved the fashioning of the human body: relaxation replaced stiffness; the body became more and more articulated; the figures were animated by turning and reclining; the anatomy of the body became more accurate. Thus at the end of the Archaic period Greek sculptors all over the Greek world reached the stage of naturalistic representation of human figures. This progress was the result both of increased knowledge of the human body and of better techniques; for instance the modelling in clay and the casting of bronze and iron images.

The Classical period of Greek S. lasts from *c.* 480–320 BC. Several great masters worked in this period, and it is one of the great losses that, except for the Hermes of Praxiteles, none of their original works have survived. Many of their works were of bronze but these were later melted for re-use. A few have survived. One is the famous charioteer of Delphi (474 BC) which is notable for the fine fashioning of the folded cloth, the confident and upright position, and the austere expression of the face. Equally impressive is the bronze statue of *Poseidon from Cape Artemisium noted for the coordination of the parts and the majestic position (475–470 BC). Almost all other S. in the round is represented in copies of the Hellenistic or Roman times. Thus the "Dyscobolus" of *Myron, a masterpiece in arresting movement (as were his other works), is known from Roman copies. *Polyclitus studied the harmonious proportion of the body and his statues became model-works. The copies of his "Doryphorus" and of the "Diadumenus" reveal his great art. Other important sculptors of the 5th century were *Cresilas, *Agoracritus, *Calamis, and *Paeonius. But *Phidias was considered the great master for his cult-statues of Athena Parthenon (known from copies) and of Zeus of Olympia. To the rendition of naturalistic forms, a stage reached by the late Archaic period, were now added serenity, majesty and harmony. The Greek classical sculptors mastered their material to produce complicated positions and to express, in a severe way, emotions.

Original extant works are the decorative sculptures of the *Parthenon of Athens and those of the temple of Zeus in Olympia. In these, as in other architectural sculptures by this time, relief developed to carving in the round. The subjects of these are mainly mythological and large spaces allowed the artists to depict consequential scenes. They used them to produce symmetry or contrasts with various stances: sitting, standing, running, fighting, crouching, falling etc. For those of the Parthenon, Phidias was responsible. In the west pediment of the temple of Zeus in Olympia we have the majestic *"Apollo" who, in an unemotional gesture, restores order, by his appearance and stretching out his arm. The artists of the 5th century are economic in the expression of emotions and succeeded in revealing the inward feelings and spirit without exaggeration rather by way of allusion. The grave steles provide some of the finest examples of such rendering. In the 5th century portraiture also began in Greek S. and so we have some copies of the original statues of Themistocles and Pericles. But though the making of portraits continued, Greek sculpture was not subjected to "realistic" style; the aim was to give an artistic expression to nature at her best.

Gods, goddesses, athletes and myths remained the favourite themes in the 4th century BC, but a change in style came about. Austerity, majesty and serenity were replaced by grace, anxiety, intensity and delicacy. Style became more polished and the whole range of poses were fashioned with repose and violent action in the extremes. Essentially the tendency was to give a human quality to the figures, with stress on individualistic traits instead of the impersonal, idealized figures of the 5th century.

The great masters of the 4th century were *Praxiteles, *Scopas and *Lysippus. The latter introduced new proportions and movements to his statues thus giving them the impression of potential dynamism. He was also noted for large scale compositions and realism. His masterpiece was the "Apoxyomenus". Scopas was noted for the passionate expression of his statues. He was one of the sculptors who decorated the Mausoleum. The famous work of Praxiteles was the "Aphrodite of Cnidos", a model of the nude female beauty fashioned in a standing, graceful position. It was also noted for its gentle smile. His "Hermes and infant Dionysus" is extant in the original, a work remarkable for its delicacy. Other sculptors of note in the 4th century were *Cephisodotus, *Bryaxis, *Timotheus

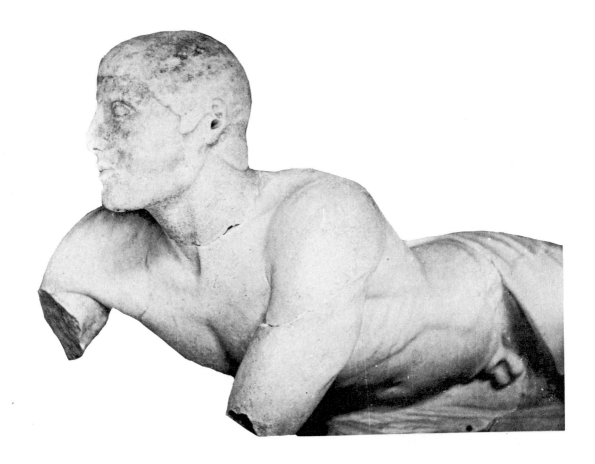

The river-god Cladeus. A statue from the temple of Zeus at Olympia

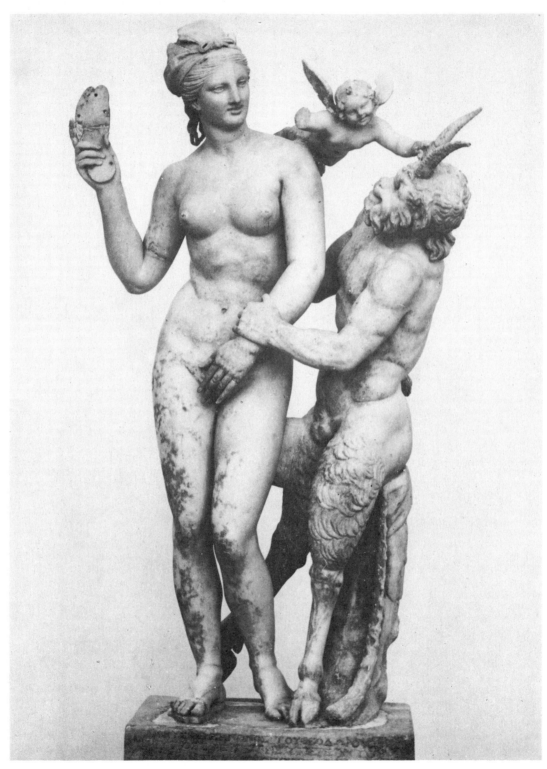

*Pan tries to seduce Aphrodite but is pushed away by Eros, while the goddess is about to hit him with her sandal.
Roman copy (the original dates from c. 100 BC)*

Marble statue of a man in a toga, (late 4th century AD)

(2) and *Leochares. Relief sculptures in grave steles and votive offerings remained restrained in the expression of the emotions, but the figures are often heroized. In contrast, scenes of the most violent action are depicted in the Alexander Sarcophagus. There is no doubt that the changes in style came about with the new social and political conditions, that followed the long wars for hegemony in Greece (notably the *Peloponnesian War). Suffering and misery were now quite familiar and occupied much of the public life of the Greeks as is evidenced in the writings of *Isocrates. It is also characteristic that with the rise of the individual, the art of portraiture was further developed and there are extant Roman copies of portraits of Sophocles, Euripides, Socrates and *Plato, made in the 4th century.

The new conditions of the Hellenistic World that followed the conquest of Alexander the Great resulted in great changes in the art of S. (late 4th–1st century BC). Sometimes this is called a period of decadence. But it was hardly so, and some of the characteristics of the new age had originated in the former period. The new centres of art were outside Greece: Rhodes, Pergamum, Alexandria, Antioch, etc. Human or divine beings at extreme situations were favourite themes. These gave the artist the stimulus to render strong emotions and expressions. The "Tyche of *Antioch" (c. 300 BC) is a forerunner of the new style in that the contrasting directions of its constituent parts render animation to apparent repose. More expressive is the *Marsyas tied before his flaying by an unknown artist. The dying Gaul is another example. Aged and deformed men, men in agony or despair are in line with this tendency. the *"Laocoon Group" made by Rhodian sculptors in the 1st century BC is a masterpiece of this style and has often been considered the best piece of Greek S. Other great works noted for the ostentatious rendering of emotions are the frieze of the altar of Zeus at Pergamum and the "Nike of Samothrace". In all these the essential quality was that of realism — this had begun in the 4th century and steadily increased to become predominant in the early 2nd century BC. No wonder the Hellenistic

period was also the age of portraiture. Thus we have copies of original portraits of Demosthenes and Epicurus. Alongside these monumental works appeared sensuous Satyrs and Fauns, frenzied Maenads, and lively boys. At the same time, there were artists who perpetuated the Classical tradition.

The increased demand of Romans for copies of statues of the Classical period from the mid-2nd century BC on arrested the development of the Greek S. The realistic, vigorous style gradually declined (though the "Laocoon" was made in the 1st century BC). The admiration of the past drained the creative power of the artists. Still it is thanks to this tendency that we have the "Venus of Milo" and many other representations and imitations of Classical statues.

G. M. A. Richter, *The Sculpture and Sculptors of the Greeks*, 1950; *Three Critical Periods in Greek Sculpture*, 1951; R. Lullies and M. Hirmer, *Greek Sculpture*, 1957.

SCULPTURE, ROMAN In a famous passage Virgil says that ruling was the part assigned to Rome in this world; to draw "breathing images from bronze and carve alive faces out of marble" was the art given to others, that is, Greeks (*Aen.* 6.683). And yet S. was introduced to Rome by the Etruscans as early as the regal period. The cult-statue of Jupiter in the Capitoline temple was commissioned from the artist Vulca of Veii according to Pliny the Elder (*NH* 35.157). The earliest statues were made of wood or terracotta, and only later were of bronze or marble. With the growth of Rome, many Greek statues were brought to Rome and, as from the 2nd century BC, Greek artists found employment in Italy.

Strong as was the tendency to acquire the admired original works or even copies of the great Greek masters, Roman S. had native characteristics of its own. The first was the preference of realistic portraiture. While the anthropomorphic concept and rendering of deities were imported from abroad, it was an old Roman custom to make *Imagines, that is, waxed masks of the faces of men of the nobility after their death. The marble bust came in

A hunting scene from the "Alexander" sarcophagus found in the royal tombs at Sidon

the wake of this tradition and included the head, the neck and the upper part of the chest. The idea was that the descendants of the deceased would be able to see their ancestors alive — hence came the utmost care for realism. This tendency to emphasize the role of the individual is also reflected in the concentration of Roman historians on personal achievements. The Forum became crowded with honorary statues and according to Pliny all unauthorized statues were removed in 158 BC (NH 34—30). There are many examples of portraits of historical figures: Pompey, Cicero, Antony, Caesar, Brutus, Vespasian, etc.

Characteristically Roman are also the historical reliefs, also noted for their realism. It was an old Roman tradition that the victorious generals carried in their triumphs plastic descriptions of their military achievements. Later they came to commemorate their victories in arches and monuments with relief sculptures which depicted the fighting and success of their campaigns. The Arch of *Titus and the Column of Trajan (with a hundred and fifty scenes and some two thousand five hundred figures) and that of Marcus *Aurelius belong to this tradition. The realistic, narrative style of the two latter has enabled historians to reconstruct the stories of the wars of these two emperors. And there were many other arches with realistic descriptions. The impression conveyed by the scenes of Trajan's column is that of a conquering, irresistible army led by an indefatigable emperor. The sense of realism is also noted in the numerous relief sculptures all over the Empire which take as their themes everyday scenes including traders and artisans at work. In the *Ara Pacis Augustae, on the other hand, allegorical figures represent the blessing of the Augustan period. This tendency for abstract, allegorical or idealized representations are known from sarcophagi, arches and also from some statues of emperors.

D. E. Strong, *Roman Imperial Sculpture*, 1961;
J. M. C. Toynbee, *The Art of the Romans*, 1965.

SCYLAX Explorer, a native of Caryanda in Caria. S. was sent by *Darius I to explore the Indus and after reaching its mouth sailed to the Red Sea (Hdt. 4.44). The extant account of Mediterranean countries and those on the coasts of the Black Sea (Periplus) that bears his name was composed in the second part of the 4th century BC.
V. Müller, *Geographici Graeci Minores*, 1855.

SCYLLA and CHARYBDIS S. was a sea-monster that lived in the straits of Messina opposite the whirlpool C. The latter sucked and emitted the water thrice a day destroying any ship that happened to be there. S. had six heads with six ferocious dogs around her belly. She ate fish and passing sailors. In one version she was turned into a monster by *Circe (Ovid. *Met.* 14.1ff.), in another by Amphitrite wife of *Poseidon who was her lover. In a rationalized version she was said to be a rock. The *Argonauts and Odysseus survived their encounter with the S. and C. The S. appears in coins of Acragas and in vase-painting. To go between the S. and C. has become a proverb for facing two dangers, the one worse than the other.

SECESSIO The secession of the Roman *Plebs to the Aventine or the Sacred Mount as a pressure on the *Patricians to yield to their demands. Five such secessions are recorded: 494, 449, 445, 342, and 287 BC. Whether they are all historical is contested, though each was associated with a specific matter, for instance, with the organization of the Plebs, the downfall of the *Decemviri and the law of *Hortensius (1) which gave *plebicita* the force of *leges*.
Ogilvie, *Livy*, 309ff.

SECOND ATHENIAN LEAGUE The League founded by Athens in 378 BC to oppose Sparta. In view of the experience of the Delian League, Athens undertook not to impose tribute or garrisons; not to interfere in the internal politics of the members of the League or to send cleruchies. After *Leuctra, *Thebes left the League. After 365, when Samos was captured and the foundation of cleruchies was renewed, Athens resumed its imperialistic methods and aims as in the 5th century BC. But in 357 Rhodes, Chios and Byzantium left the League and Athens suffered defeat at the naval battle off Chios. The League declined and was abolished after the battle of *Chaeronea.

SECULAR GAMES (Ludi Saeculares) Dramatic games and rites held at Rome every one *saeculum*, that is, every hundred years. There were such games in 348, 249, and 148 — but not in 49 BC. Augustus manipulated the dates so that he could celebrate the Games in 17 BC, and they are known from the *Carmen Saeculare* of Horace and a long inscription. They lasted three consecutive days and nights. But the Emperor Claudius celebrated them again in AD 47; and in 248, the 1,000th anniversary of Rome, they were celebrated by the Emperor Philip.

SEGESTA The capital city of the native Elymians in the mountains of northwest Sicily. The Elymians were in continual enmity with *Selinus until the latter was plundered by Carthage in 409. Thereafter S. came under the control of the Carthaginians. It was captured by Agathocles in 307 BC and it sided with Rome in the First Punic War. Under Rome S. had the status of "free city", but it declined under the Empire. The Segestans were Hellenized very early as can be seen from their coins, the Greek characters of their writing and their architecture. Of the impressive remains, the most notable is the great Doric temple which was never completed.

SEJANUS, Lucius Aelius The famous assistant of *Tiberius, native of Volsinii, of an equestrian family. Tiberius made him praetorian prefect in AD 14 and he later became sole prefect of the praetorians. He concentrated all the praetorian cohorts in a camp at Rome thus making them a political factor. He was said to have caused the death of Tiberius' son *Drusus (4), whose wife he seduced. He was responsible for a large number of *Maiestas condemnations thus getting rid of his personal enemies. After Tiberius' retirement to Capri (26), he in fact ruled Rome. In 29 he was responsible for the deportation of *Agrippina (2). But in 31, when S. was consul and possibly aimed at seizing power, Tiberius struck back. With the help of *Macro, S. was arrested and put to death.
Syme, *Tacitus* (s.v.).

SELENE ("Moon") The moon-goddess of the Greeks, sister of *Helios and *Eos (Hesiod, *Theog.* 371). Like her brother and sister she had a chariot to drive in the sky. She fell in love with the beautiful Endymion and had fifty daughters by him. At her request Zeus gave him eternal sleep. (In another version this was a punishment for his love of Hera.) In another myth S. was seduced by *Pan who gave her a sheep fleece. In some versions she was the mother of Dew or Hours or the Nemean Lion. As goddess of the moon she was identified with the Roman Luna. The Greeks identified her with Artemis and both with Hecate.

SELEUCIA (1) The greatest city of the Seleucids founded by *Seleucus I on the Tigris after he regained Babylonia in 312 BC. Connected by a canal with the Euphrates, it became the greatest trade centre in Mesopotamia and grew in size and population. In the 1st century AD the population amounted to 600,000. It was a Greek city though it also had a local and a Jewish population. It is remarkable that the Greek elements maintained their way of life for so long a period after the conquest of Mesopotamia by the Parthians in the 2nd century BC; this was due to the phil-Hellenism of the Parthian kings. But the liberal policy changed in the 1st century AD and S. revolted for seven years (AD 35–42). Thereafter *Ctesiphon became the capital and Vologasia was built as a rival centre. Trajan set S. on fire; it was restored only to be finally destroyed by *Avidius Cassius in AD 164.

SELEUCIA (2) in PIERIA This city, founded by *Seleucus I c. 300 BC, served as the harbour of *Antioch. Except for one interval (c. 245–219 BC), it remained under Seleucid rule until the disintegration of the kingdom. When *Pomepy conquered Syria, he made S. a free city.

SELEUCUS (1) I Macedonian noble, c. 358–281 BC, the founder of the Seleucid kingdom. S. took part in the expedition of Alexander the Great against Persia and after the death of the king gained Babylonia. But in 316 *Antigonos I took control of this country and S. found refuge with *Ptolemy I. He returned in 312 and won Babylonia as well as Iran. But when he sought to extend his power to India he encountered the Indian ruler Chandragupta (Sandracottus in Greek sources). S. handed over the eastern provinces (Gedrosia, Arachosia and Aria) to him and received 500 elephants (304). These later played an important part in the final battle against Antigonus I whom S. defeated with Lysimachus at *Ipsus. His new kingdom then extended to Asia Minor. In 281 S. defeated *Lysimachus but when he landed in Europe to gain Macedonia he was murdered (280) by Ptolemy Ceraunus (son of *Ptolemy I and Eurydice). S. was a great Hellenizer and founded many Greek cities including *Seleucia (1), *Seleucia (2) and *Antioch. After his treaty with Chandragupta and the battle of Ipsus he made Syria the centre of his empire and so it remained under his successors.
Will, *His. Pol.* (s.v.);
Rostovtzeff, *Hellenistic World* (s.v.).

SELEUCUS (2) II Callinicus Son of *Antiochus II and Laodice, c. 265–225 BC, succeeded to the throne in 246. Early in his reign Bactria was lost to *Demetrius (1) I and the *Parthians established themselves in north Iran. His brother Antiochus Hierax took control of Asia Minor and S. failed to regain it (c. 239–236). Also, he at first lost Syria to *Ptolemy III Euergetes in the Third Syrian War (246–241). However, he recovered much of the lost territory from Ptolemy, except Phoenicia and *Seleucia (2). It was left to his son *Antiochus III to regain all the lost parts of the Seleucid Empire.

SELEUCUS (3) IV Philopator Son of *Antiochus III, c. 218–175 BC. His father shared the throne with him after his defeat by the Romans at Magnesia (190/189). S. became sole ruler in 187 after Antiochus was killed in an attempt to plunder a temple. In his twelve year reign he maintained peace and good relations with Rome, Macedonia and Egypt. S. was murdered by his minister Heliodrus and was succeeded by his brother *Antiochus IV.

SELINUS (modern Selinunte) Greek coastal city in southwest Sicily founded by *Megara Hyblaea (on the eastern coast of Sicily) in 628 BC or 651 BC. Situated round a low Acropolis with fertile territory, S. flourished particularly by trade. The city faced the hostility of the nearby local population of Elymians and preferred to ally itself to the Carthaginians. S. fought against the Elymian

Tetradrachm of Seleucus I

city *Segesta in the mid-5th century and when hostilities broke out again the latter asked for Athenian help. This was the occasion for the expedition Athens sent to Sicily in 415 under *Alcibiades, *Nicias and *Lamachus. But Segesta allied itself to Carthage in 410 and in 409 the latter destroyed S. Resettled shortly afterwards, it remained under Carthage's control until destroyed by it in 250 BC, never to be refounded.

S. was very wealthy and built a series of temples in the 6th and 5th centuries BC. The remains of these are very impressive. They are marked by letters as the names of their gods are not known. The remains of the architectural sculptures are now in the museum of Palermo.
Dunbabin, *Western Greeks* (s.v.).

SEMELE The mythological daughter of *Cadmus and Harmonia with whom Zeus fell in love. As usual this provoked Hera who came disguised and enticed S. to ask Zeus to appear in his true form to prove his divinity (Ov. *Met.* 3.259ff.). As the god first promised S. to do whatever she asked, he could not refuse her request. The result was that S. was caught in the fire of his lightning and thunderbolt but Zeus took the child of her womb, the immortal *Dionysus. Later Dionysus went to the underworld and brought back his mother who then became a goddess. S. might be another form of *Selene. She was also called Thyone. S. is a non-Greek name and in one view she was originally the Phrygian earth-goddess Zemelo.

SEMO SANCUS DIUS FIDIUS Roman god, perhaps an amalgamation of two separate gods. The component Fidius shows his connection with *Fides, and the god is indeed associated with actions in which the latter was involved, notably treaties and oaths. His temple on the Quirinal dates from 466 BC.
Latte, *R. Rel.* (s.v.);
Platner-Ashby, *Top. Dict. Rome*, 469ff.

SENATE (Senatus) The S. was originally the council of the Roman kings and in theory it remained a council of the supreme magistrates until the late Republic. As late as 91 BC, the consul *Philippus (2) said that as he could not govern the state with the S. at his disposal, he would choose another council. It seems likely that in the regal period the kings were largely free to select the members of the council. Yet Romulus was believed to have established a S. of 100 members which was enlarged to 300. The 300-member S. allegedly consisted of the heads of the *gentes*: ten to each of the ten *curiae* of each of the original three ethnical tribes of Rome. Until the early 1st century this was the number of the senators. It seems that Plebeians were chosen senators even under the kings. The formal address to the S. was *patres (et) conscripti*, the first were the patrician members, who had certain privileges (*Patricians), and the second the plebeian members. Under the Republic, the consuls chose the members of the S. At some time in the 4th century this function was given to the censors who were required to give preference to worthy ex-magistrates. By 216 BC curule aediles, praetors and consuls were assured of a place, but at that time these could have numbered, at most, half of the S. and the censors were able to select members according to personal interests. But in the 2nd century plebeian aediles and then tribunes were assured of a place in the S. after completing their office. Sulla (81 BC) ruled that the quaestors, now twenty, should automatically become senators. As a result the number of senators rose to 600. Of course, the censors could always expel those senators of whose conduct they did not approve. Thus on one occasion a senator was disqualified because he divorced his wife without holding a family council. The censors of 70 BC expelled 64 senators — the largest number under the Republic.

The classic description of the powers of the S. is in Book 6 of Polybius. By that time the S. had acquired extensive functions which were not based on written laws but on custom. In contrast the *Patrum Auctoritas of the patrician members had become mere formality. The S. in practice supervised the finances, foreign policy, religion and legislation of the state. It became customary to discuss all motions in the S. before bringing them to the Assembly. The S. assigned the provinces to the consuls, prolonged the Imperium of magistrates (*Proconsuls) and allocated them moneys for their administrations; it fixed the rate of the *Tributum; sent embassies on diplomatic missions and to help governors in the organization of the provinces; received foreign embassies and representatives of Rome's allies in Italy; directed the military operations of the state, took a decisive part in declaration of war and conclusion of peace and treaties — subject of course to the confirmation by the Assembly which usually did what the S. advised; controlled the *Aerarium and allocated moneys to the censors for their major building operations and at times ordered them to revise the contracts with the *Publicani; consulted the priests on religious matters and directed the magistrates on the means to be taken accordingly (for instance, the case of the *Bacchanalia). In brief, almost everything the magistrates did was on the advice of the S. A decision of the S. (*senatus consultum*) was not a law under the Republic, but the S. might invalidate laws on technical points as it did in the case of *Drusus (2) or grant dispensations from certain laws. The validity of the *Senate consultum Ultimum*, however, was in dispute.

The S. was convened by magistrates with *Imperium, normally the consuls, or tribunes in the late Republic. The meetings took place in the *Curia or in any temple in Rome or within one mile of it and lasted from dawn to sunset. The presiding magistrate introduced the subject to be discussed and asked the opinions of senators starting with the *Princeps Senatus (or designated consuls in the post-Sullan period) and then ex-censors, ex-consuls, ex-praetors and so on. But he was not obliged to maintain this order or to ask every one and normally only the senior members had the chance to express their opinions. Once a senator was asked to state his view he could speak without limitation in time. After the discussion, the voting on the motions was taken by a division, and hence those senators who could express their opinions only by walking in the voting were called *pedarii* ("pedestrian"). The decision of the S. was a *senatus consultum*, and if vetoed by a tribune, a *senatus auctoritas*. The decisions were recorded in writing and kept in the Aerarium.

The senators formed the aristocratic class of Roman society and the existence of such a class was indirectly recognized by Roman law, though no privileges were given them in private law. Senators wore a tunica with the *clavus latus* — a broad purple stripe (Equites had a narrow stripe — *clavus angustus*). Praetors usually appointed senators as judges (*Iudex), and the panels of the *Quaestiones, except for the period between Gaius *Gracchus (3) and *Sulla, were manned exclusively or partly by senators. Senators often received official standing when going abroad to administer their private business (*legatio libera*). They were not allowed to take part in maritime commerce and state contracts, though some found ways to circumvent the law. Large expenses were incurred in the course of a senatorial career but there were also opportunities for enrichment, mainly in wars or at the expense of provincials. But the senatorial class was never closed and members from non-senatorial families were always added, though the *Nobilitas jealously tried to retain the consulate (see *Novus Homo). From Sulla on the number of new members extensively increased.

In the late Republic the S. lost much of its authority and prestige and with the establishment of the Principate, Augustus became the real master of the Roman Empire. Still, he sought to retain the appearance of a Republican constitution and under the Empire the S. represented the Republican tradition. It controlled the Aerarium and certain provinces ("senatorial provinces") and from AD 14 elected the magistrates. It became a court for its own members and in the course of time the S.'s decision acquired the force of law. Though the S. retained its prestige and by its decision a new emperor was recognized as legitimate, even under good emperors it obediently did what it was told to. From the late 2nd century AD the emperors generally pursued an anti-senatorial policy. The provinces were more and more ruled directly by the emperors. Constantine instituted a new S. in Constantinopole. The formula *Senatus Populusque Romanus* ("the Senate and Roman People") was still used (as even now at Rome) and the S. passed decisions, but it was more the council of the city of Rome than an imperial institution.

The S. in the post-Sullan age included many Italian senators and Caesar even introduced provincial members. This policy was cautiously followed by Augustus and with more liberality by Claudius. In the 1st century AD the new senators mainly came from the Western provinces later from the Eastern and from Africa. In the early Empire many imperial positions were reserved for senators, but gradually they were replaced by *Equites. In the 3rd century *Gallienus excluded senators from military posts. But while the S. lost its powers, the senatorial class retained its economic and social supremacy until the late Roman Empire.

Jolowicz, *Roman Law*[3] (s.v.);
R. Syme, *Rom. Rev.*;
M. Hammond, *The Augustan Principate*[2], 1968;
The Antonine Monarchy, 1959;
I. Shatzman, *Senatorial Wealth and Roman Politics*, 1975.

SENATUS CONSULTUM ULTIMUM The modern name for a special decision of the Senate which called upon the consuls to take great care in defending the state. It was interpreted by the *Optimates as authorizing the consuls to execute citizens who, by their actions, could be presumed to be enemies. Sometimes these citizens were called by name in the decision. But such a procedure was hotly opposed by the Populares who were the obvious victims. Several such declarations of emergency were passed in the late Republic: against Gaius *Gracchus (3) in 121 BC, *Saturninus (1) in 100 BC, *Lepidus (2) in 77 BC, *Catiline in 63 BC, 62 BC, and 52 BC, Caesar in 49 BC, *Caelius Rufus 48 BC and 47 BC, and in 43 BC first against Antonius, and then Octavian.

Ch. Wirszubski, *Libertas as a Political Idea at Rome*, 1950; A. W. Lintott, *Violence in Republican Rome*, 1968.

SENECA (1), Lucius Annaeus, "the Elder" or "Rhetor" Latin writer, native of Corduba, of an equestrian family, *c.* 55 BC–*c.* AD 40. He studied rhetoric at Rome in his youth and in one way or another became wealthy. He had three sons, one of them was *Seneca (2) the philosopher and the other father of the poet *Lucan. Unlike his son he did not take to philosophy and was old fashioned in his style of life.

Of S.'s history of Rome nothing is preserved. He retained his interest in rhetoric and to amuse his sons he composed a collection of extracts from rhetoricians he had heard with prefaces, anecdotes and digressions of his own. The work consisted of 10 books of *Controversiae* (speeches on legal points) and at least 2 of *Suasoriae* (speeches addressed to a historical personality). Of these are extant 1, 2, 7, 9, and 10 with an abridgement of all the former and one book of the latter. These constitute the best extant evidence on the art of rhetoric at Rome in the age of Augustus and Tiberius. With an exceptional memory S. cites passages of more than one hundred declaimers which show each with his own distinct style. He records their epigrammatic sayings (*sententiae*), headlines (*divisiones*) and aspects of presentation (*colores*). In general the trend was towards an ostentatious exciting style in an attempt to win the applause and favour of the public. S. shows good sense in his criticism of over enthusiasm for such a style and himself prefers the elegant style of Cicero.

Edition: A. Kiessling (Teubner), 1872; W. A. Edward, *Suasoriae* (with Eng. tran.), 1928; S. F. Bonner, *Roman Declamation in the Late Republic and Early Empire*, 1949; G. Kennedy, *The Art of Rhetoric in the Roman World*, 1972.

SENECA (2), Lucius Annaeus Roman statesman, philosopher and writer (4/1 BC–AD 65). son of *Seneca (1) and Helvia, native of Corduba, he came to Rome in his youth and studied rhetoric, grammar and then philosophy. He went to Egypt to visit his aunt who was married to the prefect of the country. On his return, she helped him to become quaestor. His fragile constitution helped him to survive the jealous Caligula who was persuaded that S. was going to die soon anyway. But Claudius ban-

ished him to Corsica (AD 41) for alleged adultery with Caligula's sister. Under the influence of *Agrippina (3), he was allowed to return (AD 49), and became a tutor of Nero. After the accession of the latter to the throne (AD 54), S., as the adviser of the emperor, became, with *Burrus, responsible for the government of Rome. He was *amicus principis* (see *Concilium Principis) and *consul suffectus* in AD 56. The first good years of the reign of Nero are attributed to his and Burrus' influence. But he also knew how to use his position to amass enormous wealth and became the subject of slanderous rumours. Gradually Nero drifted away from his influence and S. became associated with his crimes, notably the murder of Agrippina; he allegedly composed Nero's speech of justification on that occasion. After the death of Burrus (AD 62) he was allowed to retire. During his life he was cowardly and assented to his master's crimes, but when he was ordered to commit suicide in AD 65 for his alleged involvement in the conspiracy of *Piso (5), he ended his life with Stoic courage.

S. was a master of rhetoric, but none of his speeches is extant. His writings include the following:
Ten treatises, known as "Dialogues" (though they are not dialogues), in 12 books. They treat Stoic morality and except for *De Ira* (On Anger) in three books, they are short: *De Providentia* (On Providence), *De Constantia Sapientis* (On the Constancy of the Sage), *Ad Marciam De Consolatione* (Consolation to Marcia; she lost her son); *De Vita Beata* (On the Happy Life); *De Otio* (On Leisure – a justification of retirement from public life); *De Tranquilitate Animi* (On Calmness of the Soul); *De Brevitate Vitae* (On the Brevity of Life); *Consolatio Ad Polybium* (Consolation to Polybius; written to gain the favour of Claudius' freedman whose brother died); *Ad Helviam De Consolatione* (Consolation to his mother on his exile).
Two long treatises: *De Clementia* (On Clemency), addressed to Nero, and *De Beneficiis* (On Beneficence), addressed to a friend – it deals in seven books with what constitute acts of beneficence.
Naturales Quaestiones, deals in seven books with various natural phenomena (earthquakes, comets, lightning etc.).
Epistulae Morales, 124 letters in twenty books addressed to Lucilius; in truth fictitious letters, essays on the right conduct in life.
Apocolocyntosis, a Menippean satire on the Pampinification of the Emperor Claudius; it is a parody of the deification of Claudius and provides interesting evidence of the hostility of the upper class to him.
Nine tragedies: *Hercules Furens, Troades, Phoenissae, Medea, Phaedra, Agamemnon, Thyestes,* and *Hercules Oetaeus* (of doubtful authenticity). The tragedies are mainly modelled on those of Euripides, Sophocles, and Aeschylus; several are the result of a "contamination" of sources. They were composed for recitation and not for performance on a stage. They suffer from exaggeration – in rhetoric, emotional treatment, and occasional passages of horror. Yet there are also good, dramatic passages with real poetry.

Of S.'s other poems only a few epigrams are known.

There is no originality in S.'s philosophy and instead he treats commonplace themes in a popular manner. His reputation as a moralist has suffered perennial damage by his own way of life which was more like that of an Epicurean than that of a severe Stoic. As a prose writer he is noted for his short sentences, elaborate rhythm and the use of metaphor, paradox and epigram with a rich vocabulary. His prose won immediate success and was to influence subsequent prose writers from antiquity to early modern times. He also had a special appeal for Christians who were apparently not aware of the gulf between his writing and his conduct. A correspondence between him and St. Paul was invented and St. Jerome made him a Christian saint.

Text and translation in the Loeb series: *Naturales Quaestiones* (1910), *Apocolocyntosis* (1913), tragedies (1916–17), (1917–1925), and philosophical writings (1932–5); C. W. Mendell, *Our Seneca*, 1941; D. N. Costa, *Seneca*, 1974.

SENONES Gallic tribe which invaded Italy from the early 4th century and according to one tradition was the one which sacked Rome in 390 BC. The S. settled on the Adriatic coast from the Rubico to Ancona. In 283 BC Rome routed the S. and they are not heard of thereafter. Their territory became public land, which was used for colonization and in 232 BC for individual distribution of plots of land to needy citizens by *Flaminius.

SERTORIUS, Quintus Roman politician and general who had an extraordinary career. He served in the war against the Cimbri under *Caepio and *Marius and then in the 90s BC in Spain. He was quaestor in 90 BC and legate in the *Bellum Sociale. In the Civil War in 87 BC he followed *Cinna (1). After his praetorship (c. 83 BC) he became governor of Spain but in 81 BC lost his position to the governor of the Sullan regime. He escaped to Mauretania and returned at the request of the Lusitanians. His bravery and leadership and the superstition of the Spanish tribes (the white fawn that accompanied him was considered as a sign of the divine protection of Diana) helped him to win a widespread following, and he controlled a large part of the peninsula. Those who survived the massacres of Sulla fled to him and he posed as the lawful Roman governor and organized a Senate of his own. He also sought to promote Romanization and set up schools for this purpose. Metellus (3) Pius was sent against him but made no progress. In 77 BC the survivors of the revolt of *Lepidus (2) found refuge with S., and in the same year Pompey was sent to help Metellus. Despite the unfavourable odds, S. succeeded in maintaining his power for several more years. He also tried to cooperate with the pirates and *Mithridates VI. But as his opponents steadily became more successful, his popularity declined, and in 72 BC he was murdered by one of his lieutenants. After that, the revolt collapsed.
Plut. *Sertorius*.

SERVIANUS, L. Iulius Ursus Roman senator and administrator, born in the mid-1st century AD. He was *consul suffectus* under Domitian and governor of Upper Germany after Trajan was adopted by *Nerva. In AD 102 he was again consul. S.'s wife was the sister of Hadrian but the latter did not show him any favour after he became emperor. S. was again consul in AD 134. To ensure the succession, Hadrian caused the death of the aged S. who was suspected of opposition to the heirs.
Syme, *Tacitus* (s.v.).

SERVILIA Of a noble family, granddaughter of *Caepio and step-sister of *Cato (2). She was the mistress of Caesar and hence there arose the rumour that he was the real father of her son *Brutus (2). With all her connections she had much political influence but this is only partially revealed in Cicero's letters from 44 BC.
Syme, *Rom. Rev.* (s.v.).

SERVILIUS (1) VATIA, Publius Roman statesman and general, of a noble family, on his mother's side the grandson of *Metellus (1) Macedonicus. He was awarded a triumph in 88 BC but failed to attain the consulate of 87 BC. He followed Sulla in the Civil War (83–81 BC) and became consul of 79 BC. In the next four years or so he pacified Cilicia and reorganized it as a Roman province. Back in Rome he was given a second triumph (74 BC), and was surnamed Isauricus for his war against the Isaurians. He was a leading senator even as a very old man and in 55 BC was censor.

SERVILIUS (2) ISAURICUS, Publius Roman statesman, son of *Servilius (1) Vatia. Praetor in 54 BC, he followed Caesar in the Civil War and became consul of 48 BC. Next he was governor of Asia. In 43 BC he opportunely followed Antony, and his daughter was betrothed to Octavian (though the latter eventually did not marry her). He was again consul in 41 BC. A cautious politician, he was always careful to follow the winning side.

SERVIUS (1) TULLIUS The sixth king of Rome (578–535 BC) who is credited, in Roman tradition, with several important reforms. These include the reorganization of the Roman people into four local tribes instead of the three old ethnical ones and the institution of the *Comitia Centuriata. He is also said to have built the walls of Rome and a temple for Diana on the Aventine to serve as a religious centre of the Latin League. S. was surely a historical figure. His constitutional reforms are probably genuine in essence and though he surely did not build the walls of which there are remains (they date from the 4th century BC), he may have constructed some fortifications. And despite attempts to refute the tradition there is no compelling argument to doubt the institution of the Latin federal cult of Diana on the Aventine.
H. Last, *JRS*, 1945, 30ff.; A. Momigliano, *JRS*, 1963, 106ff.; Ogilvie, *Livy*, 156ff.

SERVIUS (2) Latin scholar and grammarian of the late 4th century AD. He is mainly known for his commentary on the poems of Virgil. The extant manuscripts give two versions of the commentary, a shorter and a longer one. The latter is called *S. Auctus* or *S. Danielis* after the name of Pierre Daniel who first published it. This includes material from another commentary, probably by Aelius *Donatus.

SESTIUS, Publius Roman politician. As quaestor in 63 BC he helped Cicero against *Catiline and as tribune in 57 BC he was active against *Clodius (1), employing gangs of his own. He supported the passing of the law to allow Cicero to return from exile and in 56 BC was defended in court by him (the speech *Pro-Sestio* is extant). Cicero won his acquittal in another case when S. was accused of *Ambitus in the election for the praetorship. In the Civil War he first followed Pompey but, after Pharsalus, he served under Caesar.

SESTOS Greek city on the coast of the Thracian *Chersonesus, with a good harbour and in a favourable position to benefit from the maritime traffic between the Aegean and the Black Sea. It came under Persian rule with *Darius I and was liberated by the Greeks in 478 BC (Herodotus ends his history with this event). Thereafter it came under the dominance of Athens until the end of the Peloponnesian War, when Sparta took control of it (404 BC). It joined the Second Athenian Empire in 365 BC and after the failure of its revolt, Athens sent a cleruchy to S. (312 BC).
S. Casson, *Macedonia, Thrace and Illyria*, 1926.

SEVEN AGAINST THEBES Heroes of a Theban legend

associated with the legend concerning the house of Oedipus. For some reason Oedipus cursed his sons *Eteocles and Polynices who agreed to reign alternately in Thebes. But Eteocles refused to quit the throne when the time arrived, and his brother sought the help of *Adrastus whose daughter he married. Adrastus arranged an expedition to take Thebes for his son-in-law in which the following also took part: *Amphiaraus, *Tydeus, Capaneus, Hippomedon of Argos and Parthenopaeus, son of *Atalanta. Polynices and his brother died fighting each other and of the Seven all except Adrastus were also killed. Ten years later, Adrastus returned with the sons of the Seven, the Epigoni, and captured Thebes.

SEVEN WISE MEN (SEVEN SAGES) There are various versions of the fabulous Seven Sages: seven men famous for their wisdom in philosophy or politics, all belonging to the late 7th and early 6th centuries BC. Plato (*Protagoras* 343) is the earliest to give a list. The usual names included in the list are *Thales of Miletus, Cleobulus of Rhodes, Bias of Priene, *Pittacus of Mitylene, *Solon of Athens, *Periander of Corinth, and the ephor Chilon of Sparta. Of these, Thales, Bias, Pittacus and Solon appear in almost all the versions. Others who are sometimes included are *Anacharsis, *Epicharmus of Cos, and *Orpheus. They were credited with popular maxims such as "know yourself", "nothing too much", "seize the opportunity". Plutarch wrote the *Banquet of the Seven Wise Men*.

SEVEN WONDERS OF THE WORLD The concept of seven outstanding achievements in building and sculpture was known by the time of *Strabo (17.1,33). There is extant a treatise on the Seven Wonders of the World attributed to Philo of Byzantium, who may have lived as late as the 5th century AD. The usual list consists of: the Pyramids of Egypt, the Hanging Gardens of Babylon, the statue of Zeus at Olympia by *Phidias, the temple of Artemis at *Ephesus, the *Mausoleum at Halicarnassus, the Colossos of *Rhodes, and the lighthouse of the Alexandrian Pharos. The last was a 300 foot tower, comprising three storeys with a statue of Poseidon on top. It was built by Sostratus of Cnidos and dedicated in 279 BC. Other buildings sometimes mentioned in the list include the Walls of Babylon, the Capitoline temple of Jupiter and the Temple of Jerusalem.

SEVERUS, Lucius Septimius Roman emperor, AD 193—211, native of *Lepcis Magna, of an equestrian family. He launched on a senatorial career, was quaestor, tribune and praetor, and served in various provinces, including Sicily and Gallia Lugdunensis where he was governor. In AD 190 he was consul and then governor of Upper Pannonia. After the murder of *Pertinax, with whom S. was closely associated, he was proclaimed emperor and easily took control of Rome. He discharged the praetorians, who killed Pertinax, and from then on recruited legionaries from the provinces for this service. S. had two rivals for the throne: *Clodius (2) Albinus in Britain and *Pescennius Niger in Syria. He first went to the East to deal with the latter. Pescennius was defeated at Issus, was later captured and put to death. After taking measures against those who supported his rival and dividing Syria into two provinces, S. returned to Italy. He promoted his son Caracalla to Caesar and made himself an adopted son of the Antonines. In AD 197 he routed Clodius at Lugdunum and the latter committed suicide. Thereafter, all those who supported, or were suspected of giving support to, Clodius and Pescennius Niger were severely punished. In the following years he

again operated in the East. He conquered Mesopotamia and organized it as a province. His other military campaign was in Britain in AD 208, but his invasion of Scotland was a failure.

S. carried out extensive reforms in addition to the reorganization of the praetorians. Generally, he distrusted the Senate and preferred to rely on Equites in the imperial administration. His main interest was in the strengthening of the army and of the empire. He raised the annual pay of the soldiers from 375 to 500 denarii, and soldiers were permitted to contract legal marriages. He founded new colonies, mainly in his home country, Africa, and in Syria, the home-country of his wife *Julia Domna. It is noteworthy that great jurists worked under him, including *Papinian, who was praetorian prefect from AD 205 and *Paulus and *Ulpian. The ruthless persecution of his enemies gave him the opportunity to amass enormous properties for which a special department was instituted, *Res Privata*. Though he spent much money on the army, on extensive building operations, on the *Alimenta and other donations to the people, the revenues far exceeded the expenditure. This was achieved by severe exactions and taxation. Vigorous and on the whole successful in his public administration, he was gravely disappointed by the conduct of his son Caracalla and the hostile relations between him and his other son Geta. He died in York in AD 211.
A. Birley, *Septimius Severus*, 1971.

SEXTUS EMPIRICUS Greek philosopher and physician probably of the second part of the 2nd century AD. He was a Sceptical philosopher and thanks to his extant writings the views of the Greek Sceptics are known. Three works are preserved:
Outline of Pyrrhonism. In three books it gives an account of the Sceptic philosophy and a refutation of the dogmatic schools of philosophy.
Against the Dogmatists. In five books, it gives a detailed criticism of the major philosophical systems.
Against the Professors. In 6 books, a critical treatment of teaching in education.

As a philosopher, S. emphasises the lack of valid criteria for judging the truth, but he is mainly important for his information on previous philosophers.
R. G. Bury, *Sextus Empiricus* (Loeb), 1933—49;
M. M. Patrick, *The Greek Sceptics*, 1929.

SHIPS There were two main types of S. in the Mediterranean in ancient times: merchant S. and warships. The first were broad, heavy and slow with a large space for cargo. They had a mast and depended on a sail for propulsion. The warships were slim and speedy with little space for the crew and the soldiers. They were mainly operated by rowers. Warships were made of lighter wood and to prevent rotting they had to be hauled out of the water whenever not in use. Merchant S. were made of durable timber and were left in the water. The S. were steered by two rudder-oars.

The earliest Greek warships were the *pentekonteres*, which were rowed by fifty oarsmen, twenty-five to a side, and had only one bank. This type was replaced by the *trireme in the 6th century BC. Its crew numbered 170 oarsmen, in addition to soldiers and other sailors: altogether not more than 200. In the late 4th century BC the *quinquereme was introduced and became the main type of warship in the Hellenistic period. Warships had rams with which they fought the enemy and were decorated with eyes on the prow. Their success depended on speed

Sailing ships with a tower on the left Fragment of a sarcophagus

and ability to manoeuvre. The speed of a trireme on a long voyage was 8 knots. The quinquereme had a larger crew. The Romans, who used land war tactics in their naval engagements, built larger S. to make room for a large number of soldiers (over one hundred).

Merchant vessels were decked from the late 5th century BC on. They advanced at a speed of 4–5 knots per hour. Those of the common type were called *holkades*. Remains of one of this type indicate a length of about 82 feet. The Roman common type was called *navis oneraria*. Some S. were exceptionally large, like the one built by Archimedes for Hieron II or that of *Ptolemy II Philadelphus. The latter allegedly had over 4,000 rowers and 2,850 soldiers. The ship of Hieron could carry over 1,000 tons. However, ordinary merchant vessels had a capacity of several tens of tons.

L. Casson, *The Ancient Mariners*, 1959; S. Morison R. J. Williams, *Greek Oared Ships*, 1969.

SIBYLLA (SIBYL) The legendary prophetess whose place of abode was variously located in early times. From the 4th century BC on the belief grew that there were several S.s who dwelt in different places. S. then became a generic name. According to Varro there were ten S.s, but there were more places with an alleged S. than were mentioned in his list. A famous description of the Cumaean S. is given by Virgil in the *Aeneid* (6.67ff.). The Cumaean S. also prophesies in the 4th Eclogue of Virgil, the Messianic Eclogue. The old S. appears in the *Metamorphoses* of Ovid. The prophecies of the S. were given in verse form. According to legend, a S. sold a collection of three books of prophecies to King *Tarquinius Priscus. These were preserved by the priestly college of the *Quindecemviri Sacris Faciundis. They consulted the books on the order of the Senate whenever there were unusual phenomena and gave advice as to what actions to take. After the destruction of the books in 83 BC, a new collection was made which was destroyed only on the instructions of *Stilicho.

The oracular prophecies of the S. were freely forged and were current in Jewish and later in Christian circles

(14 books of these forgeries are preserved). As a result, the S. acquired a position in Christian literature similar to that of the old prophets.

SICILY Greek colonization in S. began in the 8th century BC with the establishment of *Naxos (2) in 735 BC, *Syracuse (c. 733 BC), *Messana (c. 730 BC), *Catana (729 BC), *Leontini (729 BC), *Megara Hyblaea (728 BC; but on archaeological evidence perhaps earlier, c. 750 BC) and Mylae (modern Milazzo, c. 717 BC). Many other colonies were founded in the 7th and 6th centuries BC: *Gela (688 BC), *Selinus (651 or 628 BC), *Himera (c. 648 BC), *Camarina (c. 599 BC), *Acragas (580 BC), and Morgantina (in east-central S., c. 560 BC). The original population of the island consisted of the Sicili in the eastern part of the island; the Sicani in west-central part and the Elymi in western S. The Sicili probably came from Italy, as is said in literary sources (Thuc. 6.25; Dion. Hal. 1.22) and corroborated by archaeological evidence. The Greeks replaced the indigenous population wherever they established themselves: generally along the coasts, in particular the eastern and southern sides of the island. Few cities were established inland, but even those on the coast expanded their territories as far as they could into the hinterland. Most of the cities prospered and even colonized other cities and there was Hellenization of the locals.

Two or three main issues characterize the political history of the island until the third century BC. The first is the long struggle between the Greeks and the Phoenicians. The latter had settled in S. even before the Greeks, according to Thucydides (6.2). They established themselves in the western part of the island with *Panormus and Motya (see *Lilybaeum) as their main centres. From the 6th century BC it was the Carthaginians who fought the Greeks replaced the indigenous population wherever conducted wars among themselves: inter-city wars or internal wars between tyrants or between the aristocrats and the democrats. The great tyrants were *Gelon and *Hieron I in the 5th century BC and *Dionysus I and

*Agathocles in the 4th century. Though at times it seemed as if one side was about to eliminate the other, neither Carthage nor the Greeks ever succeeded in ousting their enemies. Even Athens was attracted to S. but her expedition against Syracuse in the *Peloponnesian War ended in complete disaster. In the continual wars many cities suffered and some were completely destroyed and even when refounded remained in decline.

Rome conquered S. in the First Punic War (264—241 BC) and in the Second Punic War her rule was expanded over *Syracuse who joined Carthage and was captured in 211 BC. Under Roman rule there were several categories of cities. Messana and *Tauromenium were *civitates foederatae* that is, formally independent cities with treaties with Rome. Five cities had the status of *civitates liberae et immunes*, that is, "free cities", and the rest were under direct Roman control and paid a tithe or, in cases where the land became *Ager Publicus, a tithe and rent. The system of taxation was based on that of *Hieron II. Roman governors (praetors or propraetors) let even the subject communities administer their own affairs, but whenever they wished they could intervene even in the affairs of the "independent" cities. The seat of the Roman governor was in Syracuse and he was assisted by one quaestor there and another at Lilybaeum. Under the Republic, S. was the main granary of Rome and at times large quantities of corn were purchased in addition to the tithe. In these cases the sale was compulsory. By the second half of the 2nd century BC many Italian businessmen established themselves on the island and apparently not a few Romans acquired estates there. Great estates grew and S. suffered twice from slave revolts (135—132 BC and 104—100 BC). The provincials also suffered from exploitation by Roman governors though not all were as rapacious as the notorious *Verres. In the civil wars, after the death of Caesar, Sextus *Pompeius took control of the island and for several years Rome suffered from a food-shortage until Octavian conquered it (36 BC). Caesar had given Latin rights to the Sicilians and Augustus gave Roman citizenship to a few cities, notably Messana. He also founded several colonies for discharged soldiers. Under the Roman Empire the *coloniae* and most of the *municipia* did not pay the old taxes, and the tithe was replaced by a fixed tax. Thanks to peaceful conditions the island flourished, in both the large and small estates.

Dunbabin, *Western Greeks*;
L. Bernabò Brea, *Sicily Before the Greeks*, 1957;
A. G. Woodhead, *The Greeks in the West*, 1962;
M. I. Finley, *History of Sicily*, 1968.

SICYON Greek city in the northern Peloponnesus, about 15 km west of Corinth and 3 km from the Corinthian Gulf. It was subdued by the Dorians when they invaded the Peloponnesus and for a long time there existed there a subdued population (*Helots). The Dorian supremacy was shattered when Orthagoras — one of the earliest tyrants in Greece — established a tyranny in S. (c. 670/660 BC). Under his grandson *Cleisthenes (1), S. reached the height of its power (c. 600—570 BC). At this time the Argive hegemony over S. came to an end and the non-Dorian section of the population, organized in the tribe of the Archelaoi, rose to power. Cleisthenes took a leading part in the First Sacred War of the *Amphictiony of Delphi against Crisa and destroyed the latter (c. 580 BC). He gained fame by the sumptuousness with which he celebrated the wedding of his daughter Agariste to the Alcmaeonid *Megacles. But a few years after his death the

tyranny of his house was terminated by Sparta. Since then S. became a member of the *Peloponnesian League but it never played an important part in politics. Led by its chief citizen *Aratus (2) it joined the Achaean League in the mid-3rd century BC. In AD 25 it suffered extensive damage in an earthquake.

S. was known for its schools of art, its painters and sculptors. Its most famous artist was the sculptor *Lysippus.

C. H. Skalet, *Ancient Sicyon*, 1928.

SIDE Important harbour city of Pamphylia, said to have been founded in 1405 BC. The Greeks here were influenced by the local population. S. issued coins by the 5th century BC. It was always under foreign rule but with the disintegration of the Seleucid Empire in the 2nd century BC, it became a base for pirates. It came under direct Roman control with the organization of the province of *Cilicia. There are considerable remains including the walls and a theatre.

Jones, *Cities*[2] (s.v.).

SIDON Ancient and important coastal city of Phoenicia. Unlike Tyre, it did not show opposition to Alexander and the native dynasty was allowed to remain in power. It came under the rule of *Ptolemy I in the wars of the *Diadochi and some time later a sort of republican government replaced the monarchy. With the rest of Phoenicia it was taken over by *Antiochus III in the Fifth Syrian War, but it became a free city in 111 BC. It received the status of a Roman colony under *Elagabalus. The prosperity of S. was due to trade and industry, notably purple dyeing and glass-blowing.

Jones, *Cities*[2] (s.v.).

SIDONIUS APOLLINARIS Latin writer (c. AD 430—c. 480), of a Gallo-Roman aristocratic family, native of Lugdunum. His father-in-law Avitus became Roman emperor in AD 455 and SA. addressed him with a panegyric. He composed another panegyric for the Emperor *Majorian whom he first opposed after the dethronement of Avitus. In AD 468 he composed his third panegyric for the Emperor Anthemus and was made Praefectus Urbi. Next year he became bishop of Clermont and led the resistance of Auvergne against the Visigoths. But in AD 475 the region was given up by Rome to the Visigoth king. After a short imprisonment SA. returned to his ecclesiastical position. His extant writings consist of poems, in which are included the panegyrics, and nine books of *Letters*. The letters were partly written for publication and were partly revised before publication. As such they are in the tradition of those of *Pliny the Younger. They are an important source for the study of the political, social and cultural conditions at the time.

W. D. Anderson (Loeb), 1936;
C. E. Stevens, *Sidonius Apollinaris*, 1933.

SIGNA MILITARIA The standards of the Roman army. The *vexillum* (pl. *vexilla*), a small scarlet flag, was the ensign of the general and was hoisted as a signal for battle. It was also the standard of the cavalry of the legion, of the *alae and of special detachments (*vexillationes*). From Augustus to Flavian, veteran legionaries were required to serve five more years *sub vexillo* after completing their twenty year service (*Legion). Such a veteran corps was also called *vexillatio* and had a *vexillum*. The *aquila* (eagle), made of silver, was the standard of the legion from *Marius' time. In the manipular system of the Roman *legion each maniple had a *signum*, a pole with a hand figure over it. Later this was a spearhead adorned with metal discs (*phalerae*), crowns (*coronae*) and images of animals. With the introduction of the *cohors*, its *signum* was that of the first maniple in it. Under the Empire, almost all units had *imagines*, standards with images of the reigning emperor. The century had no *signum*.

SILANION Athenian sculptor of the 4th century BC who also wrote on art, particularly on proportion. He made statues of famous figures (e.g. Sappho) and portraits. One of these was a portrait of Plato for the Academy which is probably the original of the extant Roman copies.

SILENI Like the *Satyrs, with whom they were confused, the S. were the spirits of woods and hills. They were thought of as men with horse-ears, with flattened noses and sometimes with horse-tails and horse-legs. In art and literature, it is often Silenus (in singular) that is the subject of the tales. He is depicted as a bearded man with horse-ears on the François-vase (*c.* 570 BC). One famous tale was that King *Midas (1) caught him drunk in his gardens, whereupon he told the king wonderful stories. After entertaining him for several days, the king helped Silenus to return to Dionysus. This motif of the captured Silenus appears in various tales, including the 6th Eclogue of Virgil. Unlike the other S. he was wise and at one time was the tutor of Dionysus. With the rise of the satyr-play the S. appeared as comic, drunken figures in the chorus. Socrates was compared to Silenus on account of his ugliness and wisdom. In art there were representations of both the wise, sober Silenus and the drunken one.

SILIUS ITALICUS, Tiberius Catius Acconius Roman senator and poet (*c.* AD 26–*c.* 101). He was consul in AD 68, supported *Vitellius but was able to become governor of Asia under Vespasian (AD 77). Thereafter, he retired from public affairs and devoted the rest of his life to art and literature. An admirer of Virgil, he restored his tomb in Naples. In a letter which supplies most of the information about him, Pliny the Younger says that he starved himself to death because of an incurable disease (3.7). SI. is known for his *Punica*, the longest epic in Latin (consisting of 12,000 lines in 17 books). It treats the Second Punic War with much learning, and it shows knowledge of the epic techniques, but it is done in a boring way and with little talent for such a task. It justifies Pliny's verdict that he wrote with "more diligence than talent" ("*maiore cura quam ingenio*").

J. D. Duff (Loeb), 1933.

SILVANUS Roman god of the wild land, a spirit of the woodland and hence identified with *Satyrs and *Sileni. He guarded the boundaries of his territory and it was well to appease him before encroaching upon it.

SIMONIDES Greek lyricist and elegist (*c.* 556–*c.* 468 BC), native of Iulis in Ceos. He was a court poet and charged high fees for his poems. For some time he stayed in Athens at the court of *Hipparchus (1) son of Pisistratus. Thereafter, he went to Thessaly and mainly stayed with the Scopads. By 490 BC he was again in Athens and wrote an epitaph on the Athenians fallen at Marathon. He commemorated the other great battles against the Persians in 480–479 BC and had close ties with Themistocles. S. moved to Syracuse in 476 BC and stayed with his nephew the poet *Bacchylides at the court of *Hieron I. He reconciled his patron with his brother *Theron. He stayed in Sicily until his death, and was buried in Acragas.

Of all S.'s poetry only fragments (with some 100 lines) are extant. He wrote various sorts of *lyric poetry including paeans, hymns, hypochremes and in particular Epinicians, which he wrote for many patrons and developed into long, choral poems. He was known for his dirges (one for his patrons the Scopads who were killed in

Head of Plato, Roman copy of an original probably by Silanion

the collapse of their house) and he excelled in the restrained tone of his epitaphs. For Leonidas and the Spartans who fell with him at Thermophylae he composed the deservedly well-known couplet "the stranger, go and tell the Lacedaemonians that we lie here in obedience to their laws". In another famous poem S. describes in a tone of subdued pathos the agony of *Danaë when cast to the sea in a chest with her little son Perseus. He took part in the *Dithyramb competitions and was credited with numerous victories. Poetry for him was "speaking painting". His melodious words, simplicity, conciseness, harmonious style and careful thought can be appreciated even in the remaining fragments.

Page, *Poet. Mel. Gr.;* Bowra, *Gr. Lyr. Poet.*[2], 1961.

SINON Pretending to be a deserter from the Greeks, S. tricked the Trojans into taking the Wooden Horse into their city. At night he helped the hidden Greeks inside it to get out and sack Troy. He is not mentioned by Homer, but appeared in lost epics and his story is best known from Virgil (*Aen.* 2.57ff.).

SINOPE Greek city on the central Euxine shore of Asia Minor, founded by *Miletus in the 8th century BC and resettled in the second part of the 7th century BC after its destruction by the Cimmerians. For centuries it was a flourishing commercial city and took a substantial part of the trade of the Black Sea. As a result of the expedition of Pericles to the Black Sea, a number of Athenians settled in S. It managed to retain its independence for long periods but in the 2nd century BC Pharnaces I, king of *Pontus, took control of it and thereafter it became the capital of the kingdom. *Lucullus made it a free city again and Caesar sent a Roman colony here. Its most famous citizen was the Cynic philosopher *Diogenes (4).

Magie, *Asia* (s.v.).

SIRENS These mythological singers of the sea are first mentioned by Homer. They lured sailors to their island and all died there. Odysseus took precautions by filling the ears of his crew with wax and arranged to be tied to the mast of his ship so that he could listen to their music without endangering himself. The *Argonauts were saved from the temptation of their singing by *Orpheus who excelled them with his singing. In the post-Homeric literature they appeared as the daughters of Earth, and accompanied the dead, whom they mourned and consoled, to the underworld. In early works of art they were shown as half-women and half-birds (with wings), and often as bearded men. Later they became beautiful women and sometimes they also appeared in the famous shape of women with fish-tails. Their association with music, without the original sinister aspects, was emphasized, and they were even said to have been the daughters of a Muse.

SIRMIUM Important city on the Savus in Pannonia, a military centre of the Romans since the conquest of the province. A Roman colony was founded here under Vespasian. Situated at a centre of good communications (both by land and by river), its importance increased in the troubled times of the late Roman Empire. It had an imperial mint, and the emperors frequently made it their residence.

A. Mócsy, *Pannonia and Upper Moesia*, 1974 (s.v.).

SISCIA Important city in Upper Pannonia, occupied by Octavian in the Dalmatian War (35 BC). It was a military centre, with a legion and a fleet. A colony was founded here by Vespasian. In the later Roman Empire it had an imperial mint.

M. Mócsy, *Pannonia and Upper Moesia*, 1974 (s.v.).

SISENNA, Lucius Cornelius Roman statesman and historian. He was praetor in 78 BC, probably governed a province, appeared for *Veres in 70 BC and died as legate of Pompey in 67 BC. His *Historiae* was a work on contemporary history with the *Bellum Sociale and the Civil War of *Sulla at its centre. It is mentioned and praised by Cicero. S. was also known as an orator. Only a few fragments of his history are known.

Peter, *Hist. Rom. Rel.* 1.

SISYPHUS Greek mythological figure, son of *Aeolus (1), and grandfather of *Bellerophon (Hom. *Il.* 6.154f.). He is famous for the punishment (recounted as early as Homer (*Od.* 11.593ff.)) that he suffered in Hades. He had to roll a boulder up a hill but whenever it reached the top, it rolled down again; hence a "Sisyphean work" is a futile, endless one. Why he was condemned to such a labour was later variously explained, always with reference to his ingenuity. In one version Zeus sent Thanatos (Death) to punish him because he told Asopus where Zeus had taken his daughter Aegina. But S. tricked Thanatos and bound him so that no one could die until Ares released him. Before he was taken to Hades he told his wife Merope not to perform the funeral rites for him. He was therefore permitted to return to arrange the right burial. But contrary to his promise he remained on earth and lived to an old age. Only then was he given the famous punishment so that he could not run away. Known for his cunning, he out-tricked *Autolycus (1) who used to steal his cattle by inscribing the words "stolen by Autolycus" on their hooves. And in this version he seduced his daughter Anticlea (wife of *Laertes) who bore him Odysseus. It was also fitting that *Sinon was said to be his son. His cunning thus became proverbial.

SLAVERY For Aristotle, S. was a natural condition because some people were so inferior that by their very nature they were the slaves of others. Hence he could speak of the slave as a property with a soul. In this respect he expressed the usual Greek attitude to the institution of S. The term used by the Greeks for a slave, *doulos*, was also applied to a state of serfdom and there were various kinds of bondsmen like the *Helots. These were mainly the local population subdued by Greek conquerors and were to be found in various areas in the Peloponnesus, Thessaly and Crete. But in Archaic Greece a state of serfdom also resulted from the inability to pay debts; such were the *Hektemoroi in Athens, where debt-serfdom was ended by the reform of *Solon.

S. and enslavement existed in the Mycenaean civilization and are attested to in the Homeric poems. War and piracy, the two main means for enslavement known throughout the Graeco-Roman world, were also then the common practice for acquiring slaves. In addition, there were some home-bred slaves. However, it seems that in those remote times the number of slaves was low and they were mainly employed in service duties in the households of the nobles. In Classical Greece and the Hellenistic World, slaves became numerous. In one view, the brilliant achievements of Athens in the 5th and 4th centuries BC were made possible because the slaves did all the work and the Athenian citizens thus had all their time free for politics and cultural pursuits. This is surely wrong. According to a reasonable estimate of the population of Athens on the eve of the Peloponnesian War, there were about 172,000 citizens, 28,500 metics and 110,000 slaves at the time; that is, the free population was almost twice as large as the slave population. Due to the wars, the free population declined and the relative number of slaves increased. It seems, however, that to own slaves was a very common practice and every one who had a bare minimum of means acquired one or two slaves.

Slaves were employed in every kind of work, productive and unproductive, particularly in domestic service and in mines. Small farmers had a few slaves to assist them with their agricultural work and slaves also worked in industry. *Lysias and his brother employed some 120 slaves in their workshops; *Nicias had 1,000 slaves in his mines, but he was exceptional. The largest number of slaves were employed in the silver mines of Attica and they may have numbered as many as 30,000 when these were intensively exploited. Only mine-slaves were treated badly while others were given much freedom. The oligarchic author of the Athenian constitution ascribed to Xenophon complains that one cannot distinguish a slave from a free man in the streets of Athens. Many were allowed to work in separate workshops and their masters were only interested in collecting their earnings. Such slaves could save money to buy their freedom.

The situation in Athens is obviously better known than in other Greek states. There were local and regional changes in the numbers of slaves and their occupations. From Thucydides one learns that in the 5th century BC S. was rare in agriculture in the Peloponnesus (1.141). This was probably also true in Boeotia, Locris and Phocis. In other regions slaves were more numerous, notably where large estates tended to develop. Corcyra and Chios had a large number of slaves, about half of their population. In the great industrial centres of the Hellenistic world, there was a large population of slaves.

Slaves were generally barbarians bought and transported from abroad. But both in Classical Greece and during the Hellenistic period it was the common practice to sell the populations of conquered Greek cities into S., often after killing the men. Athens enslaved the population of *Melos in 416 BC, *Philip II that of *Olynthus in 348 BC. The Athenians who capitulated to Syracuse in the Peloponnesian War (413 BC) were sent to the quarries. In addition, Greeks sometimes exposed their children who became the slaves of any one who brought them up. However, most of the slaves were either barbarians from Asia Minor and the East (Phrygian was synonym for slave) or from the tribes of the Black Sea countries. The public slaves of Athens were Scythians. Certain places became centres of the slave-trade, like Ephesus, Byzantium, and Delos in the 2nd century BC. It is noteworthy that both through the lack of common interest between the slaves, and the generally good treatment they received, revolts were rare. The great revolt of *Aristonicus in Pergamum (133–129 BC) was exceptional in that it had national and utopian aspects.

In early Rome, slaves were few. Creditors had the right to sell into S. those who failed to pay their debts, but this procedure was practically abolished by the end of the 4th century BC. In those times the small farmers did not need slaves and they were the bulk of the population. The law of 367 BC that required landlords to employ a certain number of free labourers instead of slaves is probably a projection from the 2nd century BC.

Conditions changed in the 3rd century BC. In the course of the First Punic War Rome sold a large number of people into S. and at the same time the general increase in wealth enabled landlords to acquire slaves. There is some evidence to show that at the end of the 3rd century

BC slave labour existed even in small farms. The overseas wars of Rome in the 2nd century BC resulted in a tremendous increase in the number of slaves in Italian agriculture. In 167 BC, the Senate ordered *Paullus to enslave the entire population of Epirus, some 150,000 men. Wars and piracy were the main suppliers; the slaves reached Italy indirectly after being purchased from the slave-traders, and the great international centre was at Delos. A medium-sized estate of 50–100 acres had a staff of some 15 slaves (not counting those employed in domestic service). For seasonal work, free labourers were hired. The number of slaves on large estates was very considerable. The elder son of Pompey recruited 800 of his agricultural slaves in the Civil War against Caesar. The rich freedman C. Caecilius Isidorus (died 8 BC) had 4,116 slaves, most of them surely employed on his estates. In Sicily the concentration of slaves and their harsh treatment led to two serious revolts (135–132 BC, 104–100 BC), in which the slaves were led by competent leaders. And it took the Roman government several years to suppress them. In Italy, *Spartacus was able to lead tens of thousands of slaves in his revolt which lasted some three years and was quelled only by six legions. Slaves were also employed in industry and in building. The Roman *Publicani employed 40,000 slaves in the silver mines in Spain. *Crassus (4) had a staff of 500 architects and masons. In the households of the great rich there were probably tens or even hundreds of slaves. Under the Empire there was a decrease in the sources of supply. The owners of large estates tended to cultivate them with the help of tenants instead of slaves (see *Colonus). Large numbers of slaves were employed in the imperial household and administration. The regular staff of the aqueducts of Rome numbered 700 slaves. For the social standing of the high nobility it was important to maintain a great number of slaves.

Roman law gave complete authority to the master over the slave. The lot of those who worked in the mines was a very hard one and mortality was high. For *Cato (1), slaves were in the first place property to be exploited for profit. He was more liberal with his skilled slaves, but also for reasons of profit. On the large estates, and not only in the mines, slaves often worked in fetters. Marriages between slaves were not legal and their offspring became slaves. Domestic slaves were better treated, but even they could be ill-treated by cruel masters. On the other hand, slaves were allowed to celebrate certain festivals, notably the Saturnalia. The educated among them and those who held a profession were allowed to save mony (*Peculium) and, with their savings, acquire their freedom. Masters used to manumit slaves, and this practice became so widespread that *Augustus passed laws to limit the numbers. But even he allowed a master to set free up to 100 of his slaves in his will. It is noteworthy that under Roman law manumitted slaves became Roman citizens, though with some restrictions (see *Freedmen). Their descendants could rise high in society in one generation or two. *Horace was of servile origin and so were the aedile *Flavius (who first published the procedural rules of the civil law) and the Emperor *Pertinax.

R. H. Barrow, *Slavery in the Roman Empire*, 1928; W. L. Westermann, *The Slave Systems of Greek and Roman Antiquity*, 1955; M. I. Finley (ed.), *Slavery in Classical Antiquity*, 1968; P. R. C. Weaver, *Familia Caesaris*, 1972.

SMYRNA Ancient Greek city on the western coast of Asia Minor, founded in the early 1st millenium BC. It was one of the cities of Ionia, though there were Aeolic elements in the population. It was one of the seven cities that claimed Homer as their native – probably with more justification than the others, except Chios. It was favourably situated to benefit from trade with inner Asia Minor through the valleys of the Hermus and the Maeander. However, it was insignificant until the Hellenistic period. It was refounded on a new site about 5 km from the old site by the end of the 4th century BC, and after that time it grew in size and population. Its prosperity lasted until the Roman period. The poets *Mimnermus and *Quintus Smyrnaeus were natives of S.

C. J. Cadoux, *Ancient Smyrna*, 1938;
G. E. Bean, *Aegean Turky*, 1966, 41ff.

SOCRATES The famous Athenian philosopher (469–399 BC), son of the sculptor Sophroniscus and the midwife Phaenarete, of the Attic deme Alopece. His wife was Xanthippe, notorious for her bad temper. He was a good Athenian citizen and fought in the campaigns at Potidaea (432 BC), Amphipolis (422 BC), and Delium (424 BC) where he distinguished himself. In 406 BC he was one of the Chairmen of the Ekklesia and he showed his courage and independence by his refusal to let the Assembly vote on an illegal motion concerning the strategoi who did not save the Athenians in the naval battle of Arginusae (but they were nevertheless condemned to death). In 404 BC he courageously refused to obey the orders of the *Thirty Tyrants. In 399 BC he was accused of having introduced new gods and corrupted the young. There has been much debate on the true aims of the prosecutors who may have been concerned about the negative influence of S.'s views for the restored democracy. By his uncompromising behaviour S. pushed the judges to condemn him to death. And though he could have escaped from prison, he refused to break the law and ended his life by drinking hemlock. S.'s defence in his trial and his last days in prison are told in the *Apology*, *Crito*, and *Phaedo* by Plato.

In his early life, S. pursued the study of natural science. In his play, *Clouds*, Aristophanes gives a ridiculous description of S. as a natural philosopher and Sophist. In fact he opposed the Sophists and by the time Aristophanes wrote his play he had devoted himself to the investigation of the right conduct in life. This began with the Delphic Oracle who told his friend Chaerephon that there was no wiser man alive than S. He regarded it as his mission to check the truth of the oracle's statement. He would go to public and private places in Athens and ask questions and discuss various subjects with people who claimed to have knowledge while he pretended ignorance (the famous "Socratic irony"). By his questions he showed that they only thought they had knowledge whereas in fact they were ignorant. And so he contested the claim of the Sophists that they could teach knowledge. He was wiser because he knew that he knew nothing. He also believed that he had been given a divine sign which directed his actions on exceptional occasions. S. discussed ethical and moral problems. Only the possession of true knowledge of values could enable one to choose the right conduct. In his investigations he developed the dialectical method and built a body of ethical doctrines.

S. had a profound influence on a large number of followers. He was ugly and was compared with the ugly and wise *Silenus. Alcibiades praises him in the *Symposium* of Plato. His circle of followers included *Plato, *Euclides, *Xenophon, *Critias and *Antisthenes. He wrote nothing and it is difficult to determine how much of Plato's philoso-

Statue of Sophocles, Roman copy

phy is derived from him. The early dialogues of Plato probably owe much to him. In a way he was a forerunner of the Sceptics in that he showed that he knew nothing, and the Stoics claimed him for themselves through Antisthenes.
A. E. Taylor, *Socrates*, 1932; A. Chroust, *Socrates, Man or Myth*, 1957.

SOL ("Sun") The old Roman sun-god was Sol Indiges. He was the god of the agricultural year and was not in any way important. With the diffusion of Oriental religions under the Empire, the cult of the gods of the sun spread to the West. *Elagabalus made the sun-god of his native city *Emesa, El Gabal, the principal god of the state, and he himself was its priest. *Aurelian established a state-cult of Sol Invictus and this cult became the chief one in the official religion of the state under Diocletian and his associates.
G. H. Halsberghe, *The Cult of Sol Invictus*, 1972.

SOLON Athenian statesman, legislator and poet. Of an aristocratic family, he is said to have been a merchant. He took a leading part in the war against Megara for the possession of *Salamis (*c.* 600 BC). In his poems he exhorts his compatriots not to give up but to go and fight for the island. He was archon in 594/3 BC and after carrying out his reforms he travelled abroad for ten years in Greece, Egypt, Cyprus and Asia Minor. On his return he found Athens suffering from the factional-regional rivalries which gave *Pisistratus the opportunity to seize power. S. failed to organize resistance to the tyrant but before he died (*c.* 560 BC) he saw the first expulsion of

Pisistratus. He was thought to be one of the Seven Sages of Greece and his answer to *Croesus, that only when one died could it be said whether one had lived a happy life, became famous.

When S. became archon Athens suffered from an economic-social crisis. Small farmers fell into debt, some were about to lose their properties, others lost their properties and became *Hektemoroi; and there were Athenians who were sold abroad as slaves because of their insolvency. He was accepted both by these people and by the aristocracy as a mediator and he seems to have been given special authority to legislate. His most important measures were called *Seisachtheia*, the throwing-off of the burdens. Borrowing on the security of the person was forbidden, debts for which the security was personal freedom or land were cancelled, land was restored to the owners and those sold into slavery were set free. He is also credited with a series of economic measures, including new Attic coinage, support to trade and industry and the conferring of citizenship on foreign artisans. The third part of his reforms was constitutional. He established the division of the people into four classes according to certain degrees of income (in terms of corn, oil, and wine): *Pentekosiomedimnoi, *Hippeis, *Zeugitai, and *Thetes. Only the first two classes were allowed to become archontes and hence members of the Areopagus. A new council (Boule) of 400 members was instituted — 100 members to each of the four tribes, of which, Zeugitai could become members. He also instituted the *Heliaea to which Thetes were admitted, as they were to the Ekklesia. And he also replaced all the laws of *Draco (with the exception of those on homicide) with more liberal laws.

S. is sometimes regarded as the founder of Athenian democracy. He certainly took the first important steps in the rise of the democracy in Athens in that he gave jurisdiction to the people (Heliaea), rejected aristocratic ancestry as a right for governing the state, gave some political rights to the low classes, and secured personal freedom. But none of the parties was satisfied. The poor wanted more and the rich aristocracy grieved over what it had lost. Hence arose the tyranny of *Pisistratus. But S. was venerated and in Athenian politics of the 5th and 4th centuries BC politicians sought to strengthen their case by applying to his authority. He was the first Athenian poet, and in his elegiac and iambic poems he described the political issues of the period. These were later used as sources for accounts of his reforms, and fragments are extant.

Diehl, *An. Lyr. Gr.*; Arist. *Athen. Pol.*; Plut. *Solon*; W. J. Woodhouse, *Solon the Liberator*, 1938.

SOPHISTS Wise men, experts in any kind of profession; in particular those scholars-philosophers of the 5th century BC who professed to have knowledge of a subject. They would go from place to place, teach their special subjects and receive high fees. The aim of the teaching was to give the pupils some knowledge which would assure them of success in life. Many S. taught the art of persuasion, as this was important both in politics and in the courts. Some taught Virtue. But though they all used the same methods, each of the S. had his own special doctrine and they differed from one another. *Protagoras and *Lysias were S., and some even considered Socrates to be one. The Sophist Thrasymachus appears in the *Republic* of Plato and expounds a theory of selfishness with the claim that what the strong man does in his interests is just. He is an expert in teaching how to win success — regardless of

morality. Because of the S.'s emphasis on being successful regardless of truth and moral conduct, their reputation was a bad one in the 4th century BC when the term S. acquired a pejorative connotation.

In the 2nd century AD the term S. was applied to orators and professors of rhetoric (e.g. Aelius Aristides (2), Dio (1) Cocceianus Chrysostomos).

W. Jaeger, *Paidea* (Eng. tr.), 1939—1945; G. W. Bowersock, *Greek Sophists in the Roman Empire*, 1969.

SOPHOCLES One of the three great Athenian tragic playwrights (496—406 BC), son of a wealthy arms manufacturer, native of Colonus, a village at Athens. Handsome, skilled in music and dancing, he played the lyre and led the chorus of the paean for the victory at Salamis (480 BC). S. was a good citizen and an amiable man. He was one of the *Hellenotamiai in 443/2 BC and a Strategos in 440 BC in the Samian War (with *Pericles as a colleague) and another time with *Nicias (1) as a colleague. In 413 BC he was a member of the special ten-member committee that was appointed to take the necessary measures after the disaster of the Athenian expedition against Syracuse. He was a priest of a healing god and Asclepius was worshipped at his house until the completion of his temple (420 BC); for this he was honoured as a hero after his death. He lived in Athens all his life and rejected the invitations of kings to come to their courts. He saw the rise and fall of the Athenian Empire but, dying in 406 BC, was spared the final collapse.

S. was interested in the theory of poetry, wrote a prose treatise *On the Chorus* and was the leading member of a literary association. He appeared in two of his plays but as his voice was weak he was the first tragedian to give up acting on the stage. Amid much public excitement he won his first victory in the dramatic competitions in 468 BC, defeating the veteran Aeschylus. More prolific and successful than Aeschylus, he was credited with the composition of 123 plays, and 24 victories, which means that he was successful with 96 of his plays. With the remainder he came second, never third (or in the last place). Of these there are extant seven plays; the *Ajax* was probably earlier than *Antigone* (produced in 441 BC). *Philoctetes* was produced in 409 BC and the last play *Oedipus Coloneus*, in which he wrote a charming ode in praise of Colonus, his place of birth, was produced after his death in 401 BC. There are also many fragments and titles of his other plays including a part of a satyr-play (*The Trackers*). Of these many dealt with Theban legends and the Trojan War and the others with a wide variety of subjects. According to Plutarch, S. noted three stages in the development of his style: the pompous style in the manner of Aeschylus, the severe and artificial style, and the best and most expressive one of moral disposition. All the surviving plays belong to the third stage.

S.'s earliest extant play *Ajax* is about *hybris* and its punishment. Ajax was one of the leading Greek heroes in the Trojan War. He was always proud and arrogant and when the armour of Achilles was allotted to Odysseus he regarded it as an unbearable insult to his honour and decided to kill the Achaean leaders responsible for the decision. But Athena intervened to drive him mad and in his madness he slaughtered sheep and oxen, believing them to be the hateful Greeks. When he regained his senses and realized what he had done he could not survive the humiliation and killed himself. His brother Teucer contested the decision of the Greek leaders to dishonour him by leaving him unburied. And it was no one less than Odysseus, his would-be victim, who intervened to allow the burial: he did not enjoy the humiliation of his enemy, being aware that his lot was the same. Though the play is traditional in taking the sequence of pride and punishment, the hero is not conscious of his guilt and this is the beginning of a new treatment of the theme.

The legend of the fate of Oedipus' children is the subject of the *Antigone*. After Polynices and Eteocles killed each other in the war of the Seven Against Thebes, the new King Creon forbade the burial of the first because he was a traitor to his country. Polynices' sister Antigone would not obey his order; acting in the name of a divine law, she discharged the obligation to the dead by performing funeral rites and covering his body. Creon condemned her to death and persisted in his decision despite the appeal of his son Haemon who was betrothed to Antigone. She killed herself and Haemon and his mother Euridice also committed suicide. In the third part of the play Creon gives in to the threats of the seer Tiresias — but it is too late and in the last scene the resolute tyrant finishes as a desolate man. The central problem of the play is the clash between human laws and divine laws, and in this S. was reacting to Sophistic rationalism and criticism of traditional beliefs. But the greatness of the play is in the portrayal and handling of the main characters.

The Women of Trachis takes the myth of Deianira and Heracles as its subject. The loving and faithful Deianira tries to regain her husband's love when she hears he is bringing a new concubine, the young and beautiful Jole. She then sends him a garment with the blood of the Centaur Nessus who told her before he died that it was a love charm. But it contained a harmful poison. Soon her son Hyllus arrives and curses her for murdering his father. Thereupon Deianira kills herself without saying a word. At last Heracles arrives, exhausted by his pains, and orders his son to arrange a funeral pyre for him and to marry Jole. He leaves the stage with a procession to the pyre. His son bursts with accusations against the gods, but in his last words admits that everything in this world, including what befell his father, is attributable to Zeus. What happened to Heracles was in fact foretold in an old prophecy, and the play turns on human blindness and the work of divine destiny.

The *Oedipus Tyrannus* has been considered the best of S.'s plays. The story is familiar. Laius, king of Thebes, had a son Oedipus by his wife Jocasta despite the warning of the oracle. To undo what he did, he abandoned the infant who was saved and brought up as the son of the king of Corinth. Oedipus later killed his father Laius, without knowing who he was, married his mother Jocasta and became king of Thebes. When the play opens Thebes is suffering from a plague and to end it the king is told by the Delphic Oracle to purify it from the pollution caused by the murder of Laius. Oedipus gradually discovers the truth and there is much irony in his searching after the murderer — himself. He is renowned for his cleverness but in truth he is blind. When the truth is finally revealed Jocasta ends her life by suicide, Oedipus blinds himself and leaves Thebes, led by his daughters. From first to last Oedipus proceeds to the final catastrophe through no fault of his. His fate was predestined by divine power even before he was born. S. notes the sequence of events but does not call into question the divine working.

The *Electra* tells of the avenging of the murder of Agamemnon by his daughter Electra and son Orestes against the murderers Clytemnestra and Aegisthus. It is the same subject as the *Libation Bearers* (*Choephoroe*) of Aeschylus. But in S.'s play the dominant figure is Electra. S. concentrates on her thoughts, feelings, reactions and plans. For years she has kept waiting for the return of her brother Orestes in the hope of being able to take revenge. When the false news comes that he was killed in a chariot-race at Delphi, she at first despairs but then decides to act on her own. The climax of the play is in the recognition scene between Electra and her brother; the murder of Clytemnestra and Aegisthus comes as a secondary element. By concentrating on the figure of Electra, S. pays little attention to the legend, and the sequence of crime and punishment and of the working of divine destiny is of little importance.

In the *Philoctetes*, Odysseus and Neoptolemus are sent to the uninhabited island of Lemnos to bring Philoctetes to Troy as only with the help of his bow can that city be conquered. But Philoctetes hates the Greeks who abandoned him on the island when he was bitten by a snake ten years earlier. Much to his dislike, Neoptolemus cooperates with the cunning Odysseus to deceive Philoctetes. But at the decisive moment, he tells Philoctetes the truth and returns the bow. The latter refuses to go to Troy, even though by doing so he can find a cure for his pains, and Neoptolemus is ready to take him home. Heracles, the original owner of the bow, saves the situation by his appearance, and Philoctetes obeys his order to go to Troy.

One of the greatest plays of S. is *Oedipus at Colonus*, and it is remarkable that he wrote it when he was over ninety. At the end of his life, a blind beggar, Oedipus comes to Colonus near Athens where he knows from the oracle that his wanderings will end. The citizens of Colonus, the chorus of the play, want to expel him from the grove of the Eumenides but are persuaded to await the decision of Theseus. Meanwhile an oracle has predicted that whichever of the two brothers, Eteocles and Polynices, gets the help of their father Oedipus, that one will be victorious in the struggle for the rule over Thebes. Oedipus, however, refuses to help either of them, and does not relent in his hatred for them despite Theseus' intervention. The latter recognizes that Oedipus is innocent despite his crimes and shows him hospitality in Athens. When Creon, sent by Eteocles, and Polynices come to ask his help he remains obdurate in his vindictiveness against his sons who did not prevent his expulsion from Thebes. At the end, when Oedipus is called to his grave by a voice and thunder from heaven, he is led there by Theseus and disappears.

In the *Ichneutae* ("Trackers"), the only remaining part of the satyr-plays of S., the chorus of satyrs, led by Silenus, track the thief who stole Apollo's herd. They are attracted by the tones of the lyre, newly invented by the young Hermes, and they will tell Apollo that Hermes the inventor is surely the clever thief.

Aristotle tells us that S. introduced the third actor. This innovation helped him to include more characters in his plays, to compose complex plots and to develop the dialogues. Almost all his known plots are noted for their unity and careful structure. Unlike Aeschylus, his trilogies did not treat a single subject and this enabled him to build his plots freely. He was especially noted for the dramatic irony of his plays, particularly in the dialogues. His characters were often ignorant of the true meaning or significance of what they said (as is best known from *Oedipus Tyrannus*). The chorus in his plays played a lesser part than in the plays of Aeschylus, but it still had a significant and often a dramatic character. His style was marked by its flexibility; it was dignified but also adjusted to the emotions of the character. He is reported to have said that he portrayed men as they ought to be, whereas Euripides portrayed them as they are. His characters indeed belonged to the heroic world, but even though he lacked the psychological insight of Euripides, he treated them as human beings, only nobler. They were motivated by strong wills and passions. What befell them was due to the gods, but their heroic and tragic nature was seen in their human and yet exalted reactions and behaviour. S. was a religious man and found the subjects for his dramas in the traditional Greek myths. There was more than enough in their heroic world to create sublime tragedies, which he exploited so successfully.

A. C. Person (O.C.T.), 1928; F. Storr (Loeb), 1913;
E. F. Walting (Penguin Classics), 1947, 1953;
C. M. Bowra, *Sophoclean Tragedy*, 1965;
B. M. W. Knox, *The Heroic Temper*, 1965.

SORANUS Of Ephesus, Greek physician of the first part of the 2nd century AD. He was the leading figure of the Methodist physicians (followers of the *Sceptics). Of his works, which are preserved in Greek or in Latin translations, the more important are on gynaecology and pathology.

I. E. Drabkin, *Caelius Aurelianus, On Acute Diseases and Chronic Disorders* (tr.) 1950; O. Temkin, *Soranus' Gynecology* (tr.), 1956.

SOSIUS (1), **Gaius** Roman politician and general, of a praetorian family. He was a follower of Antony and after holding the quaestorship became governor of Syria and Cilicia in 38 BC. The Parthians had already been expelled by *Ventidius and S. proceeded to subdue Judaea and Jerusalem where they had installed the Hasmonaean Antigonus. He captured Jerusalem and was awarded a triumph (37 BC). As consul in 32 BC he attacked Octavian but soon fled with his colleague and many senators to the East. He took part in the battle of *Actium and his life was spared after it thanks to *Arruntius.

Syme, *Rom. Rev.* (s.v.).

SOSIUS (2) **SENECIO**, **Quintus** Son-in-law of *Frontinus, leading figure in the administration of Trajan. Details of his career are only partially known from chance references. He was consul in AD 99 with *Palma, another important genreal of Trajan, as his colleague. He seems to have taken part in the Dacian War and was again consul in AD 107. Pliny the Younger was his friend and Plutarch, also a friend, dedicated his *Parallel Lives* and other works to him.

SPAIN (Hispania) The oldest inhabitants of S. were the Ligurians, but in historic times the population of the Iberian peninsula consisted mainly of Iberian and Celtic elements. The Iberians were the old inhabitants and the Celts arrived in S. in the early 1st millenium BC. They were divided into many tribes which lacked unity. In the mountainous regions, which form most of the country, the population of each small locality was attached to the nearby local hill-fortress. The Phoenicians were attracted to S. from early times and the traditional date of the foundation of *Gades is c. 1110 BC. Although some date it to the 8th century BC, from which time Sexi on the south coast also dates, it is clear that the Greeks came later. *Phocaea established trading posts, but after its de-

cline it was its colony *Massalia that became the most important Greek factor in S. It founded colonies on the Mediterranean coast, including *Emporium (modern Ampurias), Rhodae (Rosas) and Artemisium (Denia). But from the late 6th century BC Carthage tried to oust the Greeks. It destroyed the native kingdom of *Tarteseus c. 500 BC and established its hegemony over the old Phoenician cities: Gades, Abdera and Malaca. It concluded treaties with the native tribes of southern S. and was able to recruit mercenaries and to exploit the silver mines. Later the Carthaginians sought to monopolize the trade of the peninsula. But it was only in the 3rd century that the Greeks were ousted. A large Carthaginian empire was established by *Hamilcar and his successors *Hasdrubal (1) and *Hannibal. All this ended with the spectacular victories of *Scipio (2) Africanus in the Second Punic War, who expelled the Carthaginians from S.

The Romans organized the area conquered from Carthage into two provinces (197 BC): Nearer S., in the coastal regions of east S. from Emporiae in the north to north of Baria in south; Farther S., in the southern part of the peninsula. The conquest of the whole of S. spanned over the 2nd and 1st centuries BC. At the end of the first series of wars (197–179 BC), Tiberius *Gracchus (1) secured Rome's position in the central plateau by concluding mild treaties with the Celtiberians. The second series of wars (154–133 BC), of which the hero was the native leader *Viriathus, ended with the destruction of *Numantia, and by this time Rome had established direct rule over the central part of S. In subsequent wars, Roman rule gradually extended to the western parts but it was only under Augustus that S. was pacified. Augustus reorganized the peninsula: Baetica in the southern part was a senatorial province; Lusitania in the west from the Durius in the north to the Anas (Guadiana) in the southeast (mostly modern Portugal), and Tarraconensis (in the northern, central and eastern parts) were imperial provinces.

The Roman conquest was accompanied by exploitation on the one hand and Romanization on the other hand. Many of the wars under the Republic were due to the ambition of Roman generals to win glory and booty in war. Enormous quantities of silver and gold were brought to Rome by victorious generals in the 2nd century BC; in addition they distributed donatives to their soldiers and officers and enriched themselves. The rapacity of the governors and the complaints of the provincials contributed to the establishment of the court of *Repetundae (149 BC). The mines were let out to *Publicani. The Spaniards were required to pay fixed sums in money and to deliver corn on demand. The first Roman settlement dates from 206 BC when *Scipio (2) Africanus settled some of his veterans in *Italica. There was some immigration of Italians to S. in the 2nd century BC and it increased in the 1st century BC. Caesar and Augustus founded many colonies and many other cities became *Municipia. In some regions, notably Baetica, the native population adapted itself to the Latin culture. By the time of the Augustan period, the tribe of the Turdetani had forgotten its own language and spoke Latin.

After the wars of Augustus, S. became a peaceful area and the garrison of three legions was reduced to one by Vespasian. Agriculture, industry and trade prospered in the 1st and 2nd centuries AD, and Spanish products, including oil, wool and fish, were exported. The unique Monte Testacio at Rome consists of numerous potsherds of Spanish amphorae. Vespasian gave the Latin rights to all the Spanish towns. The first Roman senator from S. dates from the early 1st century BC. In the 1st and 2nd centuries AD, very many Roman senators were from S. Trajan and Hadrian were natives of Italica. Many writers were also from S., including the two Senecas, Columella, Lucan, Quintilian and Martial. Compared to other provinces, S. suffered less in the 3rd century AD from the inroads made by German tribes, though the Franks got as far as there. But in the 5th century AD the Vandals, the Suebi and the Alani first plundered and then settled in S. However, the Vandals and the Alani were severely defeated by the Visigoths and crossed to Africa in AD 428. Thereafter the Visigoths ruled S. until the Moslem conquest in the early 8th century AD.

J. J. Van Nostrand, in *ESAR*, 3; C. H. V. Sutherland, *The Romans in Spain*, 1939; Dunbabin, *Western Greeks*; A. Arribas, *The Iberians*, 1964.

SPARTA The archaeological finds from the site of S., situated on the western bank of river Eurotas in the southern Peleponnesus, indicate that it was insignificant in Mycenaean times, despite its description as the centre of the kingdom of *Menelaus by Homer. It seems that at that time Amyclae, south of S., was much more important. In the early 1st millenium BC, the area was conquered by the Dorians who settled in villages. When five of these villages united to form a new city (*Synoecismus), the history of S. began, and this may have been in the 9th century BC.

In later times, the Spartans attributed all their institutions to the legislation of *Lycurgus (1). It is not unlikely that he was a historical figure and that he was responsible for the political organization of S. He brought the Rhetra, an ordinance, from Delphi, which is quoted by Plutarch (*Lyc*. 6). This briefly authorized the main institutions of S.: the two kings (called *archagetai*), the *Gerousia and the *Apellai. It regulated the meetings of the Assembly, fixed its meeting-place, and established its sovereignty. A later rider empowered the kings and the council to set aside "crooked" decisions of the Assembly, and subsequently the *ephors were added as the supreme regular magistrates. Lycurgus was also said to have forbidden the writing down of laws. And the Spartans indeed did not have written laws. As for social institutions it seems that in part they go back to the early tribal organization and way of life. The economic measures came later, by the early 6th century.

In later times, Greek thinkers regarded the constitution of S. as superior to the other constitutions of Greek states — consisting, as it did, of democratic, aristocratic and monarchic elements. The origins of the dual kingship at S. are obscure; it may have been associated with the union of different communities. There were two royal families, the Agiadae and Eurypontidae, and both claimed descent from Heracles. In early times they surely held extensive powers, military, judicial and religious. Of these they retained the command of the army, some judicial power (for instance, in cases of adoption) and they enjoyed some privileges and honours. They were members of the Gerousia. Their influence on foreign affairs and internal politics was largely reduced from the early 5th century BC. This was associated with the rise of the ephors, with whom they had to exchange an oath to observe the laws. The latter exploited the discord between the kings to weaken their position, and thus they replaced them as chairmen of the Assembly. In fact, S. was ruled by an aristocracy. The Assembly could not discuss motions, only vote.

"The Lacedaemonioi" was the official name of the Spartan state; Spartiatai were the Spartan citizens as compared to the other sections of the population. It seems that after the five villages of S. united, the expansion of the city began. It subdued the population of *Laconia in the course of the 8th century BC. The subject population, the old inhabitants as well as the Dorians, became *perioikoi or *helots. In the second part of the 8th century, S. also subdued *Messenia (the First Messenian War) and the population was reduced to the status of helots. The Messenians revolted in the first half of the 7th century BC (the Second Messenian War) and it was with much difficulty and great effort that S. quelled the rebels. In the 7th century BC, S. was still like other Greek cities. It had its poets (*Tyrtaeus and *Alcman), it colonized Tarentum (c. 700 BC), and it was successful in industry and commerce. But to secure itself against the subject helots and perhaps the *perioikoi*, the whole way of life changed. Children were taken from their parents from a very early age (5 years) and were given military training and a severe *education. Arts and literature disappeared. Life became simple and austere. The use of silver and gold coins was forbidden, and the equality of property was maintained. The manufacture of fine objects was discontinued. The citizens were organized into groups, and they lived a communal life, eating their meals together. The whole life of the citizen was supervised by the state in an attempt to make him an efficient soldier devoted to his country.

The political hegemony of S. in the Peloponnesus began before the mid-6th century BC. S. overthrew the tyranny in *Sicyon, defeated *Argos and organized the *Peloponnesian League. King *Cleomenes I pursued a vigorous foreign policy and extended the interests of S. to central Greece. S. was universally acknowledged as the most powerful state in Greece and, in the war against Persia, it was given the leadership, not only on land but also on the sea. However, S. declined to commit herself to overseas operations and it was Athens who became the leader of the Ionian Greeks. The earthquake of 465 BC caused much damage and it took several years to subdue the revolt of Messenia. Thereafter, S. became involved in a war against Athens which ended in a thirty-year truce (446 BC). S. defeated Athens in the *Peloponnesian War; it tried to maintain hegemony over Greece and became involved in war in Asia Minor. This embroiled S. in wars against Persia as well as Athens, Thebes, Corinth and other Greek cities. It succeeded in asserting its supremacy by the Peace of *Antalcidas (386 BC). But in 371 BC its power was broken for ever in the Battle of *Leuctra. As a result, Messenia regained its freedom, *Arcadia became an independent league and *Megalopolis was founded. S. was defeated again in the Battle of *Mantinea (362 BC). The decline was associated with the change in the way of life at S. after the Peloponnesian Wars. Equality had not been completely maintained even earlier on, but now there was luxury and, with the passing of a law (397 BC), the alienation of land by bequest or gift had been legalized. Soon, inequality became obvious and many Spartans lost their full rights as citizens because they no longer kept their plots of land. By the mid-3rd century there were only 700 full citizens. *Agis IV and *Cleomenes III sought to restore the Lycurgean constitution. The latter increased the citizen-body by granting plots of land and citizenship to some 4,000 people. But he was defeated at the Battle of

Aerial view of the Eurotas valley, with the modern city of Sparta at the centre, the site of ancient Sparta to the right, and the Taygetus mountains in the background

Selasia by Antigonus Doson. After the fall of the tyrant *Nabis, S. became a member of the Achaean League. Under the Roman Empire it prospered, though the cities of the *perioikoi* were independent. With other cities of the Peloponnesus it was destroyed in AD 267 by the German Heruli and in AD 395 it was sacked by *Alaric.

Thucydides aptly remarks that later generations will hardly believe in the greatness of S. if they will have to form an opinion on the basis of its temples and public buildings. No wonder that the extant remains of buildings which were poor even when standing cannot impress the visitor. But S.'s power was in its men. For centuries it had no walls, an exception in the Greek world. It was properly walled only in the 2nd century BC. *Pausanias (3) gives a description of the city. Its most famous buildings were the temple (Bronze House) of Athena Chalkioikos, where *Pausanias (1) was starved to death, the temple of Artemis Orthia (where Spartan boys underwent the ordeal of whips), and the Scias, the Assembly hall.

H. Michel, *Sparta,* 1952; G. L. Huxley, *Early Sparta,* 1962; B. Shimron, *Late Sparta,* 1972.

SPARTACUS The Thracian gladiator who escaped with 70 other gladiators from the gladiatorial schools in Capua in 73 BC. Numerous slaves followed him and at the height of his power he had an army of 90,000 men. With such a force, mainly of Thracians, Celts and Germans, he won extraordinary victories over Roman armies, including those of the consuls of 72 BC. But his fellow-leader, Crixus, separated with a considerable following and was annihilated with all his force in 72 BC. And when S. and his army came to Cisalpine Gaul, his followers refused to return to their home countries. He led them again to southern Italy and tried to cross to Sicily but could not acquire the necessary ships. In 71 BC his whole army was finally destroyed by *Crassus (4), who had six legions; S. himself fell during the fighting. Those who were captured alive were crucified, and Pompey, returning from Spain, finished off some remnants. S. was a great leader and a courageous warrior. His exploits soon became legendary. His revolt, however, was an exceptional ocurrence and did not bring about any change in the institution of slavery at Rome.

Plut. *Crassus*; Appian, *BC.* 1.116f.

SPEUSIPPUS Greek philosopher (*c.* 407–339 BC), nephew and pupil of Plato whom he succeeded as Head of the *Academy in 347 BC. Of his numerous works only fragments are preserved. He is credited with having abandoned his master's theory of ideas. He concentrated on mathematical research, mainly on the elements of numbers; but in contrast to the Pythagoreans he rejected the view that everything could be explained in terms of numbers. His other major occupation was biology, in which he attempted through classification of plants and animals to implement his views on the definition of species. On his death he was succeeded by *Xenocrates.

SPHINX Legendary monster with a lion's body, a human head, and often with wings. It originated in Egypt and it spread to the East and to Greece in Mycenaean times. In Greek mythology, it is associated with the Theban legends about Oedipus. To punish Thebes, Hera (or Apollo in a later version) sent the S. which sat before the city and asked all those entering it a riddle: who walks on four legs in the morning, on two at noon and on three in the evening? Those who did not answer correctly (and for a time no one solved the riddle) were killed and devoured by the monster. Finally, Oedipus came and correctly answered that it was man: as an infant, as a grown-up person and in old age. Thereupon, the S. killed itself or was killed by Oedipus. Figures of the S. were placed on tombstones and appeared frequently in Greek art. They were popular in vase-paintings of the orientalizing period, notably at Corinth and Rhodes. In Archaic art they were usually represented as females, but sometimes as bearded males. They also appeared in frieze sculptures. As from the 5th century the image of the S. changed and instead of a sinister figure it was represented as a beautiful, mysterious being.

SPOLETIUM (modern Spoleto) Ancient city in Umbria, dominated by Rome by the early 3rd century BC. It received a Latin colony in 241 BC and Roman citizenship in the *Bellum Sociale (90 BC). Under the Empire it was a prosperous city. There are impressive remains.

STADIUM The Greek ground for foot-races, a rectangular structure about 600 feet long and 90 feet wide. The starting and finishing points were marked by pillars. Short races were of one, two or four times the length of the S. There were also longer races up to 24 times the length of the S. as well as the race in hoplite armour. In races of more than the single length of the S., the runners would run up and down, turning round the pillars. Rows of seats were built along the ground for the spectators. Several stadia have been preserved in quite good condition, for instance those in Delphi, Athens and Epidaurus.

E. N. Gardiner, *Athletics of the Ancient World*, 1930.

STATILIUS TAURUS, Titus Roman politician and general, one of the best commanders of Augustus. He pre-

sumably followed Augustus quite early and was *consul suffectus* in 37 BC. The following year he took an important part in the war against Sextus *Pompeius and after the removal of *Lepidus (3) proceeded to his province, Africa, to establish Octavian's authority there. For his achievement he was awarded a triumph in 34 BC. He fought in Illyricum, Actium and Spain and was again consul in 26 BC. In 16 BC he was appointed Praefectus Urbi. ST. amassed riches during his career and inscriptions show that he had numerous slaves at Rome, as well as property in Istria. He was a *Novus Homo and his descendants in the next two generations held high positions. *Messalina (2), Nero's third wife, was his descendant.

Syme, *Rom. Rev.* (s.v.).

STATIUS, Publius Papinius Latin poet, native of Naples (AD 45–96). His father, a poet and a school-master, was his tutor. S. moved to Rome where he won success with recitals of his poetry. His libretti for pantomimes (see *Mimus) were profitable though he did not depend on these for his living as he seems to have been well-off. He moved in the circles of high society, and Domitian, whom he flatters in his poetry, was one of his patrons. His marriage was childless and his adopted child died in youth. He came first in a poetry competition *c.* AD 89 but failed in a competition in 94. His last years were spent in Naples where he also died.

S.'s *Silvae*, in five books, consists of 32 poems on various subjects. They are addressed to several people, including S.'s wife and Domitian. The occasions for the poems are festivals, weddings, dedications of a statue, births, funerals etc. One of them eulogizes S.'s father. S. has an elaborate technique of flattery when he deals with Domitian. The best known of the collection is the poem addressed to Sleep (5.4). Most of the poems are written in hexameters and only a few are in lyric metres. S. shows ingenuity and learning in recounting the praises of his subject. The poems were not known in the Middle Ages

The Delphic stadium, 182 by 28 metres

until the discovery of a manuscript by Poggio in Constance in 1417.

S. was mainly an epic poet. As he himself says, it took him twelve years to compose his main epic, the *Thebaid*. Its twelve books give a narrative of the quarrels of Eteocles and Polynices and the war of the Seven Against Thebes. It is a highly artificial epic comprising erudite allusions, melodramatic passions, sentimental scenes, and apalling slaughters. S. did not live to complete his second epic, the *Achilleid*. In the two books of it which he managed to write he told the story of young Achilles: his education by the Centaur Chiron, the attempt of his mother Thetis to prevent his participation in the Trojan War by hiding him among the maidens of Lycomedes in Scyros and the way Ulysses and Diomedes detected him.

The epics of S. were very popular in the Middle Ages. He is alluded to by Chaucer; Dante thought him a Christian and made him his guide in the last part of the *Purgatorio*.

J. H. Mozley (Loeb), 1928.

STEPHANUS of BYZANTIUM Greek grammarian of the 6th century AD. He wrote *Ethnica*, a work in sixty books, which dealt with place-names, arranged in alphabetical order, and various matters associated with them. The work is known from an abridgement. The work is important because the author used various sources, some of which are not extant.

STESICHORUS Greek lyric poet (*c*. 630–*c*. 553 BC), native of Mataurus in southern Italy, lived in Himera, spent some time in Greece, and died in Catana. His lyrical poems were edited in 26 books, but only fragments are extant. He used mythical themes from the epics to compose choral poems on a grand scale. His *Oresteia*, comprising several hundred verses, was arranged into two books. His themes included the Sack of Troy, the Calydonian Boar-hunt, the Labours of Heracles (the cattle of Geryon, Cerberus), and the Argonauts. In his handling of the traditional myths he introduced innovations to adjust them to his aims; for instance, he was the first to describe Heracles with a lion-skin and a club, and not with a bow and arrows. It was said that he was punished with blindness for making Helen responsible for the Trojan War. He then recounted the myth in a palinode in which he said that it was only a phantom of Helen that arrived at Troy; Homer was to be blamed for the impiety against her. The narrative style of S. was not followed by choral lyricists, but the other innovations ascribed to him, the strophe, antistrophe, and epode structure, became common.

C. M. Bowra, *Greek Lyric Poetry*[2], 1961.

STILICHO, Flavius A German who did military service in the Roman army under the Emperor *Theodosius I and advanced to high positions. After the death of Theodosius (AD 395), he was the chief minister and general of *Honorius and practically ruled the Western Empire. In AD 395 he engineered the murder of Rufinus, the main minister of the Eastern Emperor *Arcadius. Despite some success, he failed to defeat the Visigoths in Greece. Subsequently, he won two victories over *Alaric at Pollentia and at Verona (AD 402 and 403), but did not follow up his success and instead bought the Germans off with money. He routed a mixed force of Germans in AD 405, but subsequently lost his influence and was executed with his family by Honorius in AD 408.

STILPON Greek philosopher (*c*. 380–300 BC). Head of the Megarian school of philosophy which was founded by *Eucleides, under whom S. studied. He was also perhaps a pupil of *Diogenes (4) of Sinope. Among his own pupils was *Zeno (2) who founded Stoicism. To maintain the imperturbability of the soul was a guiding principle for him: the wise man is free from external happenings and above earthly possessions and needs no friends. He was also interested in logical paradoxes and through Zeno influenced the logic of the Stoa.

STOA (1) (STOICISM) The school of philosophy which was established at Athens by *Zeno (2) of Citium *c*. 300 BC. Zeno taught in a hall of the Stoa Poikile ("Painted Porch") from which the school acquired its name. His successors as heads of the school were *Cleanthes, *Chrysippus, Zeno of Tarsus (early 2nd century BC), *Diogenes (3) of Babylon, Antipater of Tarsus (defended Stoicism against the criticism of *Carneades and *Panaetius). The school lasted until the time of the Roman Empire, though little is known of it in later times.

Three periods are usually distinguished in the history of S.: the Early Stoa (to the middle of the 2nd century BC); the Middle Stoa which began with Panaetius; and the Late Stoa, that of the Roman Empire. The revision of S. by Panaetius made it more acceptable to people of the Roman nobility and he had a large following at Rome, notably *Scipio (5) Aemilianus, C. *Laelius (2), P. *Rutilius Rufus, and *Scaevola (2) the Pontifex. *Posidonius carried further the revision of S. and he too was associated with Roman statesman, notably Pompey. The leading Stoic philosophers under the Empire were not associated with the Athenian school: *Cornutus, *Seneca (2), *Musonius, and *Epictetus; the last great figure was the Emperor Marcus *Aurelius.

None of the writings of the founder and early Stoics survives. For their views one depends on quotations and information provided by later writers, notably *Diogenes Laertius, *Didymus, *Cicero; also by opponents of S., like Plutarch and *Sextus Empiricus. On the other hand, there are extant the complete writings of later Stoics: Seneca, Epictetus and Marcus Aurelius.

Zeno laid down the foundation for all the doctrines of the Stoic philosophy, but his system was elaborated and completely reshaped by Chrysippus so that it was through the latter that S. was mainly known. Ethics stand at the centre of the Stoic philosophy, that is, the doctrine of the right conduct man should pursue. This also includes the relation of man to the world in which he lives, and hence doctrines were introduced concerning the natural world and the knowledge of the universe by man. The Stoics maintained that virtue causes happiness and depends on knowledge. A virtuous man is a happy man and as he is wise he always knows what constitutes right conduct. The ordinary good or bad things are immaterial to the virtuous man, because morally they are neutral, neither good nor bad. In other words, such things as wealth and poverty, ugliness and beauty, health and sickness are immaterial for the state of happiness. What counts is man's attitude towards them. A man who relies solely on himself can face with equanimity the vicissitudes of external conditions. And yet one may have preferences if in so doing one acts virtuously. Certain things are preferable – by the criterion of natural life, not moral life. To maintain natural faculties and powers, then, is preferable to losing them: to be blind is against nature. The aim of life is "to live consistently" or, as was differently defined by some Stoics, "to live consistently with nature". The true Stoic aims at controlling or abolishing passions. He is perfect in that he is not moved by his material conditions.

It was essential to the Stoic doctrine of virtue as dependent on knowledge that the Stoics developed a positive theory of perception and knowledge. They argued that man has the mental faculties which make him capable of grasping and acquiring knowledge of external things (this was contested by the Academy under *Arcesilaus and *Carneades). According to the Stoic doctrine, God, which is Logos, gives shape to matter and so forms the world. God is also Fate and Providence. The universe is guided by divine reason and is subject to dynamic process. Hence there is a cycle in which the world turns to fire and then a new world, identical with the one consumed, emerges.

Not all Stoics adhered to the doctrine of the conflagaration of the world. *Panaetius abandoned it. He also modified the Stoic doctrine of ethics, which concerned itself only with the absolutely wise, virtuous man. He maintained that there were four main virtues: wisdom (= the knowledge of the truth), justice, bravery, and sense of propriety (*sophrosyne*). Of these, the first is theoretical but the others are practical. They can be achieved not only by the absolutely wise man but by others, each one according to his capacity. To live consistently is to live according to one's natural capacity and conditions.

The figure of the passionless Stoic, the wise man, and yet one who fulfills his duties as a citizen (as defined by Panaetius), made S. successful at Rome. *Cato (2) became a symbol of Stoic fortitude. In the 1st century AD Roman adherents of S. defied the autocratic emperors and were ready to, and did in fact, die for their cause. At that time S. spread not only among the upper classes but to the intellectual middle class. After Seneca the Stoics neglected all other questions except those of conduct, and it was mainly this aspect of S. that had a lasting influence. It had its influence on *Neo-Platonism and was absorbed by Christian thinkers, including Augustine.

J. Rist, *Stoic Philosophy*, 1969;
F. H. Sandbach, *The Stoics*, 1975.

STOA (2) A typical Greek building characterized by colonnades. Colonnades were attached to various buildings, but the name S. was mainly applied to the oblong hall opening to a colonnade. Such buildings were used for various purposes, notably commercial and judicial, and as council-halls. The S. Poikile in Athens was decorated with pictures by many painters, notably *Polygnotus. In the 2nd century BC, *Attalus II built an enormous S. at the Agora of Athens. See *Porticus.

STOBAEUS Greek anthologist of the 5th century AD. His work consisted of four books in two parts, entitled *Eclogae* and *Anthologion*. It includes extracts from prose and verse writers arranged according to subject matter. S. cites hundreds of writers and in many cases the citations he gives are not otherwise known.

STOLO, Gaius Licinius Roman plebeian statesman who, with L. Sextius Lateranus, was responsible for epoch-making legislation in 367 BC. According to Roman tradition, they were tribunes for several consecutive years (five or ten) and stopped the regular working of the constitution until the Patricians yielded to their demands. The Licinio-Sextian laws opened the consulate to the Plebeians, introduced them to the college of *Quindecemviri Sacris Faciendis (then only of ten members), restricted the amount of public land allowed to be occupied by individuals, and arranged a payment of debts (the interest to be deducted from the principal and the remainder to be paid in three years). The details of their agrarian law

are disputed and may have been confused in the tradition with a later law, but there is no reason to doubt that their legislation included economic measures.

K. V. Fritz, *Historia*, 1951, 1ff.

STRABO Greek historian and geographer (64/63 BC– AD 21 or after), native of Amaseia in Pontus, apparently of a well-to-do family. He studied at home and abroad, adopted the Stoic philosophy and was an enthusiastic admirer of the Roman Empire. He visited Rome several times and travelled in Egypt and Asia Minor. The aim of his writing was didactic and he believed that his works were of practical value for people engaged in public affairs.

Nothing is preserved of the *Historical Sketches* of S., a work in forty-seven books. His *Geography* in 17 books is almost completely extant; only the last part of Book 7, on Thrace and Macedonia, is missing. In the first two books he expounds his views on geography, including cartography, and criticizes the views of his predecessors, notably Eratosthenes, Polybius and Posidonius. In the following books he gives a systematic description of countries: Books 3–10 give an account of the European countries from west to east: Spain, Gaul, Britain, Italy, Sicily, central, northern and eastern Europe including the Balkan peninsula and Greece. The next six books (11–16) deal with the countries of Asia, including the Black Sea regions, Asia Minor, India, Persia, Mesopotamia, Palestine and Arabia. The last book deals with Africa. S. accepts the sphericity of the earth which for him consists of three continents encircled by an ocean. His interest is in historical and ethnographical geography, less in physical and mathematical geography. Though he is selective in giving details, his work is a mine of information.

H. L. Jones, *The Geography of Strabo* (Loeb), 1917–1933.

STRATEGOI (sing. strategos) The Greek term to denote army commanders. In various states the S. were the chief magistrates, notably in the Achaean League and the Aetolian League. In the Hellenistic kingdoms, the S. were governors of cities or regions and had various powers. The term was used as the Greek translation for the Roman *praetor; *strategos hypatos* was used for *consul.

Ten annual S. were instituted as regular magistrates at Athens in 501/500 BC. At first one was elected for each of the ten new tribes of *Cleisthenes (2) and each one commanded the troops of his own tribe. From 487 BC on, the S. replaced the *polemarchos as the supreme commanders of the army, as the latter was thenceforth elected by lot (like the other *archontes) and it was felt that such a system could not guarantee the election of the right men. With this change, the S. became the most important Athenian magistrates. They were responsible both for the land army and the naval forces of Athens and presided over trials of all matters associated with military service and the duties of the Athenians. In the 5th century BC, there was no division of duties, and often several S. together commanded the forces abroad; three commanders were appointed for the expedition against Syracuse in 415 BC: Alcibiades, Nicias and Lamachus. By Aristotle's time, several of the S. were given specific duties: one commanded the infantry, one was responsible for the system of the *Trierarchy, one for the defence of Attica and two more for the defence of Piraeus. The S. had the exclusive right to attend the meetings of the *Boule and to submit proposals to it. The office thus became a key position in Athenian politics in the 5th century BC. Most of the leaders then were from aristocratic families; they actively sought the office which combined military command with political activity. All the dominant figures in Athens until the 5th century BC were S.: *Themistocles, *Aristides (1), *Cimon, *Pericles, *Cleon, *Nicias (1) and *Alcibiades. However, some S. were merely military men, like *Demosthenes (1) and *Lamachos. In the 4th century BC, this became the rule, and men like *Eubulus, *Aeschines and *Demosthenes (2) did not regard the office as important for their poli

The original rule that each tribe elected one S. was modified in the 5th century BC when Pericles was continuously elected (from 443 on), so that other members of his tribe could be elected. In the 4th century BC the S. were no longer elected according to tribes. The S. were under constant supervision. In every prytany (*Prytaneis) a vote of confidence was taken on each S. and one who failed to win it was brought to trial; when the S. ended their term of office they had to submit reports which were examined by the *Logistai and were subject to the process of *Euthyna.

Hignett, *Athen. Const.* (s.v.).

STRATO Of Lampsacus, Greek philosopher, head of the *Peripatetic School (c. 286–268 BC). S. was the last important original scholar of the school and he was interested in various subjects, including logic, politics, ethics, zoology, and psychology. But his main work was in physics and he came to be called *Ho Physicos*. In contrast to Aristotle, S. maintained the existence of vacuum in nature, to which conclusion he arrived through observation and experimentation. In his use of experiments as a means to test physical theories he was quite exceptional among the Greek philosophers, and such men as *Philon (1) and *Hero were indebted to him. By observation and experimentation he also contradicted the theory of Aristotle on the difference between heavy bodies which tend to the earth and light bodies (air, fire) which tend upwards. He simply regarded this as a result of the falling of the heavier bodies. He generally rejected the explanation of the phenomena as the action of a deity, and argued that they were to be explained by natural causes.

STRATONICEIA (modern Eskihisar) Macedonian city in Caria, probably founded by *Antiochus I who named it after his wife, Stratonice. He have it to Rhodes under whose control it remained, save for the interval under *Philip V, until 167 BC. It was a free city under the Roman Empire. Near S. were two renowned temples, that of Hecate and that of Zeus Chrysaoreus.

P. M. Fraser–G. E. Bean, *The Rhodian Peraea*, 1954.

STYX River in Arcadia flowing from the northeastern slopes of Mount Chelmos and falling down a deep, steep rock. There was a story that water from the S., considered to be poisonous, was sent to Alexander the Great and caused his death. The river S. was regarded as one of those of the underworld; the dead were carried over it by the ferryman *Charon. In one version *Thetis immersed her son Achilles in its water – every part of him except the heel by which she held him – to make him invulnerable. In Homer, the gods swear by it and so did the Arcadians, according to Herodotus (6.74).

SUDA (SUIDAS) The title of an encyclopaedic dictionary which was compiled in the late 10th century AD. It is mainly based on former lexica, scholia, and anthological works. It includes unreliable material and many absurdities in addition to important and unique information. It is especially valuable for its literary articles.

SUETONIUS (1) PAULINUS, Gaius Roman senator and general in the 1st century AD. After the execution of Ptolemy, the king of Mauretania, by Caligula, he was sent to pacify and organize his kingdom as a province (AD 41–2). He wrote an account of his expedition, in which he was the first Roman to traverse the Atlas mountains. He was made governor of Britannia in AD 58 and expanded Roman rule to the West. In AD 61 he quelled the rebellion of *Boudicca but was replaced in his command. Despite his active support of *Otho in AD 69, he made peace with *Vitellius.

Syme, *Tacitus* (s.v.).

SUETONIUS (2) TRANQUILLIUS, Gaius Roman writer, of an equestrian family, born c. AD 70. His father was tribune in the army of *Otho at the battle of Bedriacum. S. was a friend of Pliny the Younger who recommended him to Trajan. He received a position in the imperial court and advanced to become a secretary of Hadrian. In this post he was able to consult the imperial archive and thus used various original documents, including the private letters of Augustus, in his writings. But in AD 121 he was dismissed from office because he did not show due respect to the emperor's wife. Thereafter he devoted himself to literary activity and was still writing after AD 130.

S. was a scholar with antiquarian interests and wrote on various subjects, including notorious courtesans, critical signs used in books, Greek terms of abuse, Roman festivals, the Roman year, and the names of clothes. All these writings are lost, and he is mainly known as a biographer. His *Lives of Famous Men* included short biographies of poets, rhetoricians, orators, philosophers, and historians. Part of this work is extant, including the Lives of Terence, Virgil, Horace and Lucan. The section on grammarians survives almost completely. It appears that he used to cite from documents and the original writings to illustrate or demonstrate points at issue. St. Jerome used his biographies for his *Chronicles*.

The most famous work of S. is the *Lives of the Caesars*, which is completely extant. It consists of the biographies of twelve Caesars from Julius Caesar to Domitian. He presents his material according to a fixed pattern: birth, family background, early life, public career, personal qualities – physical and mental, good and bad – and death. In so doing he gives up any attempt to give a chronological account which is a serious shortcoming from the standpoint of a historian; but he was not a historian. Nor does he try to arrive at a general appreciation of the personality. In fact, the biographies are a collection of material, arranged under rubrics and presented in a plain style. The reader is left to form his own view of the Caesars. S. is often attracted by the gossip and anecdotes concerning the personal lives of the Caesars but he aims at writing the truth, and this for him was mainly a matter of reproducing his sources – which are not always reliable. His success was great. He became a model for various biographers, including Einhard in his *Life of Charlemagne*, and has been popular with readers until modern times.

J. C. Rolfe (Loeb), 1924; G. B. Townsend in *Latin Biography* (ed. T. A. Dorey), 1967.

SULLA, Lucius Cornelius Roman statesman and general (138–78 BC), prominent in the 80s BC. Of an impoverished patrician family, he managed to live in a profligate way in his youth and to improve his circumstances by inheritances, one of which was from his mistress. He was quaestor under *Marius in Numidia and by his diplomatic skill persuaded Bocchus of Mauretania to surrender

Portrait of Sulla on the reverse of a denarius

*Jugurtha. This was the source of the later enmity of Marius who became exasperated when S. claimed that he had concluded the war. He served in the war against the *Cimbri, was praetor in 97 BC, and thereafter enthroned Ariobarzanes I in Cilicia to thwart the ambitions of *Mithridates VI. He was prosecuted on his return by a friend of Marius but nothing came of it. He distinguished himself in the *Bellum Sociale and became consul of 88 BC with the support of Metelli, after he married Metella the widow of *Scaurus (1).

In 88 BC, S. was given the command of the war against Mithridates VI, but the tribune *Sulpicius Rufus passed a law to transfer it to Marius. S. did not give in and led his army, which was stationed in Campania, and took Rome by force. Sulpicius was killed and his laws abolished, but Marius escaped to Africa. S. passed several laws to strengthen the authority of the Senate but was not able to prevent the election of *Cinna (1) to the consulate of 87 BC though the latter swore to respect S.'s laws. After S.'s departure for Greece, Cinna took control of Rome and outlawed S. His wife succeeded in escaping and went to Greece. S. twice routed the armies of Mithridates in Greece, sacked Piraeus and Athens and plundered the treasuries of the Greek temples. He concluded a treaty with Mithridates at Dardanus by which the king was free to govern his kingdom, Pontus, but had to evacuate the territories he still occupied and to pay war indemnity. He took control of the army of *Fimbria who committed suicide. S. returned to Italy and a civil war ensued in 83–82 BC. He was followed by *Metellus (3) Pius, *Pompey and *Crassus (4). After repeated victories over *Carbo and his associates, and a final victory over the Samnites and the Lucanians at the Collina Gate of Rome, he became the master of the state.

S. was elected dictator with special powers to make new laws and to restore the Republic. He published "proscription" lists of his enemies who were thereby outlawed and had their properties confiscated; about 100 senators and 1,000 Equites were killed and the total number of the victims was well over 4,000. S. used his powers to carry out a thorough reform of the Roman constitution. According to his laws, tribunes were not allowed to advance to higher offices, could not submit bills before the Assembly without obtaining the endorsement of the Senate beforehand, and their right of veto was reduced. The Equites lost their right to serve as jurors in the *Quaestiones but many Equites were included in the 300 new members whom he now added to the depleted Senate. He fixed minimum ages for holding magistracies: quaestor – 30, praetor – 39, consul – 42. He raised the number of praetors to eight and the number of quaestors to twenty and these latter automatically became senators on ending their year of office. He passed new laws to expand the system of the Quaestiones which were now to be manned by senators. He extended the scope of the law of *Maiestas to curb the ambition of governors to initiate wars. He used the vast confiscated lands of his enemies to establish colonies for his veterans and to help his supporters to enrich themselves. He was consul in 80 BC and after resigning his powers as dictator became a private citizen in 79 BC. He died the following year.

S.'s aim was to make the Senate the governing body of the state and to eliminate those who endangered his position: the Populares (see *Optimates) who acted through the tribunate and the army commanders. Caesar said that by abdicating from the dictatorship S. showed that he did not know the alphabet of politics, but this is more revealing about Caesar's aims than about S.'s. Once he thought that he had done what he could to strengthen the Senate, he resigned. However, the constitutional reforms were weaker than the political and social forces at work. The aristocracy was sharply divided, personal ambitions had no limits, and no radical solution was found for the growth of the Roman proletariat. The system of S. was brought down by his own men, Pompey and Crassus, in 70 BC.

Plut. *Sulla*; E. Badian, *L. Cornelius Sulla*, 1971.

SULPICIA Roman poetess, of aristocratic family, probably the niece of *Messalla Corvinus. She is the author of six short elegies preserved in the Tibullus collection. In these she freely tells of her love for a young aristocrat she calls Cerinthus. The poems are remarkable for the frank and unaffected expression of her warm passion.

SULPICIUS RUFUS, Publius Roman politician, of an old aristocratic family, albeit one for long in decline. He was a pupil of L. *Crassus (3) and made his first appearance in public by prosecuting Norbanus, an associate of *Marius. As tribune in 88 BC, he proposed a law to register the new Italian citizens in all the 35 Roman tribes so as to give their votes equal force with those of the old Roman citizens. He met strong opposition from the *Optimates who sought to neutralize the law that gave the Italians citizenship by registering them in only a few tribes. S. had some equestrian supporters and he now passed a law to transfer the command in the war against Mithridates VI from *Sulla to Marius. With his new supporters he passed the law by force, but this led to the capture of Rome by Sulla, and he was executed and his laws were repealed.

SUNIUM The southern promontory of Attica, the site of a temple of Poseidon built in the Doric Order c. 440 BC. There are only a few but nonetheless impressive remains of the temple. The place was fortified in the Peloponnesian War to secure the maritime corn-supply of Athens.

SUSA The capital city of Elam, mentioned as early as the 3rd millenium BC in Babylonian documents. The city became a residence of the Achaemenides, and *Darius I built his famous palace, the Apadana, here. The famous mass-marriages of Alexander the Great and his officers to Iranian wives took place at S. A military cleruchy was established under the Seleucids and the city seems to have received the status of a polis under Antiochus III. It retained its autonomy under the Parthian kings and had a mixed population. In the excavations on the site, remains of various temples and public buildings have been found and it seems that the city extended over a huge area, perhaps 2,000 acres.

W. W. Tarn, *The Greeks in Bactria and India*, 1938 (s.v.).

SYBARIS Greek city in southern Italy on the west coast of the Gulf of Tarentum, founded by settlers from Achaea and Troezen *c.* 720 BC. The city prospered by trade and agriculture and one of its colonies was *Paestum. Its wealth and the luxurious way of life of its population became legendary. The city aroused the jealousy of other Greeks and in 510 BC it was captured and wiped out by *Croton. Athens established a new city *Thurii near the old site (443 BC), but the old Sybarites who joined the new foundation were soon expelled.

J. S. Calaway, *Sybaris*, 1950; A. G. Woodhead, *The Greeks in the West*, 1962.

SYKOPHANTES (pl. sykophantai) It is not clear why professional accusers at Athens were called by this name, which refers to some gesture with a fig (*sykon*). Under the Athenian legal system the office of public attorney did not exist and it was left to the initiative of private citizens to start a case. The S. were attracted by the rewards that the Athenian law gave to successful accusers in some cases. They could also start a prosecution in order to blackmail the accused or to represent a third party who paid them. Laws were passed to reduce abuses of this kind.

SYMMACHUS, Quintus Aurelius Roman statesman, *c.* AD 340–*c.* 402. Of a noble family, S. was the leading orator of his time and a firm defender of paganism. He was governor of Africa (373), Praefectus Urbi (384, 385) and consul (391). In 382 the altar of Victory was removed from the Senate-house following the anti-pagan legislation of the Emperor *Gratian. S. led the pagan aristocracy in an attempt to alter the decision but his eloquent appeal was unsuccessful, largely because of the opposition of St. Ambrose. Of his speeches some fragments are extant as are his letters, arranged in ten books. Following the model of Pliny the Younger, the latter consist of nine books of private letters and one of official Bonner–Smith, *The Administration of Justice* 2, 1938, 39ff.

Aerial view of the mound of Susa

letters. The language is artificial and the content of little interest.

H. Bloch in *The Conflict between Paganism and Christianity in the Fourth Century* (ed. A. Momigliano), 1963; R. H. Barrow, *Prefect and Emperor*, 1973.

SYMMORIA (pl. symmoriai) Under the reform of the *Eisphora at Athens in 378/7 BC the Athenian taxpayers were organized in groups with more or less equal means. Each such group, the S., had a president, a treasurer and a registrar. The collection of the tax was carried out by the S. The new system was used for the upkeep of the ships in a reform of the *trierarchy which was made in 357/6 BC. The wealthiest citizens of Athens were grouped into twenty S. and each S. was given a number of ships to maintain. Within the S. a sub-group of a few members was responsible for the maintenance of one ship.

H. Michell, *The Economics of Ancient Greece*, 1957 (s.v.).

SYMPOSIUM The Greek drinking-party which followed the evening dinner. It opened with a libation and a hymn to the gods and heroes and was accompanied by flute girls and often by performances of dancing and miming. The wine was mixed with water in different proportions in separate mixing-bowls. Conversation, wine-songs, games and riddles were part of the occasion. The participants wore garlands of flowers. The party would last late into the night even to the morning. An account of the discourse in a S. came to be a literary genre; the most famous work of this kind is the *Symposium* of Plato. In that the discussion was on one theme, love. The S. of Xenophon is an account of a party at which Socrates was a guest and deals with several themes. Several more *Symposia* are extant, including those of Plutarch, *Athenaeus, and *Macrobius.

SYNOECISMUS The unification of two or more communities to form one city-state. This could be accompanied by the concentration of all the constituent member communities in one centre (a new city or one of the old), but often the population continued to live in its old place. Athens became the city-state of Attica by the S. traditionally ascribed to *Theseus. *Sparta became a city-state by the S. of five villages. *Demetrias and *Megalopolis were founded by the S. of a large number of villages from a whole region.

V. Ehrenberg, *The Greek State*, 1960 (s.v.).

SYPHAX King of the Numidian Masaesyli whose capital was Cirta. In his war to free himself from the Carthaginian control, he established connections with P. and Gn. *Scipio (1) in Spain (213 BC). *Hasdrubal (3), son of Gisco, won him for the Carthaginian cause by giving him his daughter Sophonisba, renowned for her beauty and intelligence. S. occupied the land of the Massyli whose chieftain *Masinissa escaped and shortly afterwards joined *Scipio (2) Africanus. He was twice defeated by the latter; captured later, he died in captivity in Italy.

SYRACUSE (modern Siracusa) The greatest Greek city in Sicily, founded on its eastern coast by settlers from Corinth in 733 BC. The first settlers, led by Archias, occupied the island of Ortygia but as the population grew the city expanded to the mainland, Achradina, and a causeway connected the two parts. On one side of the causeway was the lesser harbour of the city and the great harbour was on the inner side. The Greeks subjected the native population which was compelled to cultivate the lands of the aristocracy, the *gamoroi*. S. prospered and sent several colonies including *Camarina.

S. suffered from internal conflicts in which the aristocrats were banished and which enabled *Gelon of Gela to seize it (485 BC). He transferred the population of Camarina and Megara Hyblaea to S. and defeated the Carthaginians at Himera (480 BC). He was succeeded by his brother *Hieron I who was a great ruler and patron of arts and letters. Pindar, Bacchylides, Simonides and Aeschylus stayed at his court. He won victories in the pan-Hellenic games at Olympia and Delphi and with Cumae defeated the Etruscans of Campania (474). After his death a democracy was established in S. (466). As in Athens the chief institutions were an Assembly, a Boule and strategoi. S. lost some of its influence in Sicily under the democracy but its prosperity continued. It defeated the Athenian attacks in the Peloponnesian War (427–424, 415–413), but was not able to save *Acragas from Carthage (406). This gave *Dionysus I the opportunity to seize power. After some difficulties, Dionysius controlled most of Sicily and extended his rule to south Italy. He built strong walls, over 25 km long, which included the plateau of Epipolae with the fortress of Euryalus. His son *Dionysus II lost his rulership to *Dion (356) and thereafter the city suffered from internal conflicts. The reforms of *Timoleon led to some recovery, but it was only under *Agathocles that S. rose again to supremacy in Sicily. After the latter's death (289) the Greeks in Sicily were so hard pressed by Carthage that they invited Pyrrhus to help them. *Hieron II took power in S. in 265 and after first opposing Rome in the First Punic War concluded a treaty with it to which he remained loyal till his death (215). His successor made the mistake of following Carthage in the Second Punic War and the city was captured and sacked after a prolonged siege (213–211). From then it became the residence of the Roman governor of Sicily.

There are only a few remains of the ancient city; they include the walls of Dionysus I, the theatre, the temples of Apollo and Athena and traces of the Olympieum.

A. G. Woodhead, *The Greeks in the West*, 1962.

SYRIA S. was a satrapy in the Persian Empire until the conquest of Alexander the Great. After the battle of *Ipsus (301 BC), *Ptolemy I occupied its southern part, Coele S., and the northern part became the centre of the Seleucid Empire with *Antioch as its capital. The Seleucids founded many cities and military colonies and sought to Hellenize the country, and were ready to give special rights to Hellenized cities. *Antiochus III conquered Coele S. from Ptolemy V in the Fifth Syrian War (202–198 BC), but after the death of his son *Antiochus IV, the Seleucid Empire declined and various cities and dynasts acquired independence, notably Judaea, Commagene and the Nabataean kingdom. In the 1st century BC *Tigranes, king of Armenia, annexed S. to his kingdom (83) but was ejected by *Pompey who made it a Roman province. All the local dynasts and cities which were given autonomy were in fact subject to the Roman governor of S.

With the establishment of the Principate, Augustus made S. an imperial province and so it remained under the Empire. From the 1st century BC on it was a key position for the advance against, or defence from, Parthia. It was governed by a legate of a consular rank who had at his disposal four legions. The Great Revolt of the Jews resulted in the organization of Judaea as a separate province with one legion; after the revolt of *Bar Cochba this province was called S. Palaestina. There were other reorganizations of the province such as the annexation of

Athenian red-figured drinking cup (Rhyton) in the shape of a bull's head (c. 460 BC)

*Commagene (AD 72) and the division into S. Coele (north S.) and S. Phoenice under Septimius Severus. The Romans did not follow the policy of urbanization of the Seleucids and no new cities developed under the Roman Empire. In the 3rd century S. suffered much from the invasions of the New Persian Empire, but it remained a Roman province until the Arab conquest in the 7th century.

F. M. Heichelheim in *ESAR*, 4;
Jones, *Cities*², 227ff.

SYRINX An arcadian nymph who was turned into a reed-bed to escape from Pan. From the reeds Pan made his pipe — *syrinx.*

SYSSITIA A group of citizens at Sparta whose members ate communal meals. Each member had to provide a share of the food. A new member was received only by the general consent of the members, and the voting was secret. All the citizens of Sparta were organized in such groups and one who was not a member of a S. was not a full citizen. A similar system existed in Crete.

Bronze statue of Poseidon (or Zeus) of c. 460 BC. It was found at Antemisium in 1953

Romulus, Remus and the she-wolf. A marble group from Hadrian's villa at Tivoli

T

TACFARINAS Numidian chieftain who served in the Roman army and started a revolt in AD 17. He ravaged the Roman province for several years and as long as he personally survived the Romans were not able to quell the revolt despite repeated victories. It was only in AD 24 that he was killed.

TACITUS (1), Cornelius Roman senator, orator and outstanding historian, born *c.* AD 55. His family was probably from Gallia Narbonensis or North Italy. He began his career under Vespasian, continued under Titus and advanced higher under Domitian – as he himself tells (*Hist.* 1.1). His experience under the Flavian dynasty, especially his connections with the tyrant Domitian, was decisive for the whole of his historical outlook and coloured his historical writings. In 78 he married the daughter of *Agricola, then became senator, and praetor and *Quindecemvir Sacris Faciundis in 88. He apparently held a provincial position in 93 when his father-in-law died. He was in Rome in the last years of Domitian's reign. As *consul suffectus* in 97, he delivered the funeral oration for *Verginius Rufus and in 100 prosecuted, together with his friend Pliny the Younger, the ex-governor of Africa, Marius Priscus. He was governor of Asia about 112 and was probably still alive in AD 117.

T. was greatly admired as an orator and one of his first works is the *Dialogus De Oratoribus*, probably composed *c.* AD 98–100. It purports to reproduce conversations he attended in his youth (AD 74) on the decline of Roman oratory. Two reasons are given: that contemporary rhetorical education is inadequate, in comparison with the thorough education of the ancients; and that the high eloquence of the late Republic was an integral part of the turbulent politics of that time, while under the Principate judicial cases and politics were of relatively minor importance. T.'s talent of portrayal of characters is manifest even in this early work. About the same time he published a biography of his father-in-law, the *Agricola*, and an ethnographic monograph, *Germania*. The large part of the biography is devoted to Agricola's campaigns and achievements in Britain. Despite T.'s shortcomings in geography and military matters, the work is important for the information about Britain. The few chapters on the relations between Agricola and Domitian herald the Tacitean treatment of another tyrant, Tiberius. The *Germania* is the only extant Latin treatise of its kind and the only relatively comprehensive account of the Germans and other tribes beyond the imperial frontiers on the Rhine and Danube. It is a literary rather than a scientific work, and it seems that one of T.'s aims was to criticize the corruption of Roman society by giving an idealized picture of the Germans, who were something akin to the Noble Savage.

T.'s two major historical works are the *Histories*, probably written between 104 and 109, and the *Annals* written in the 110s AD. The first begin in AD 69, the year of the Four Emperors and probably ended with the downfall of Domitian in 96. The first four books and part of the 5th book are extant and carry the story to the siege of Jerusalem and the revolt of Julius Civilis in Gaul in 70. The complete work probably consisted of twelve books. The *Annals* begins in AD 14 with the death of Augustus (T.'s title was "From the Death of Augustus") and ended with the death of Nero in AD 68. Extant are Books 1–4 complete, parts of 5 and 6 and 11, 12–15 complete and part of 16, ending in AD 66. Books 7–10 and, probably, 17–18 are missing and covered the years 37–47 and 66–68. T. planned to write a history of Nerva and Trajan but did not live to accomplish it. His historical works thus covered the years AD 17–96, i.e., the early Principate.

The central theme of the historical works of T. is the rule of the Roman Empire by the Roman emperors, and their relations to the senatorial aristocracy. He would have preferred to have a Republican government at Rome, and he makes clear his view that Rome had been better under the Republic. But he had no illusions and knew all too well that the restoration of the Republic was impractical because of the new conditions. The question was whether a settlement could be reached which would give the Romans a constitutional liberty under a rule of an emperor. From this point of view he sketches the history of the Principate. But he was pessimistic about human nature, and for him, as for other Roman historians, history is in the first place the work of the people in power. T. fully endorses the view that power corrupts and absolute power corrupts absolutely. Of all the emperors, Vespasian was exceptional in that he changed for the better on his accession to the throne. Some began well and ended as the worst tyrants. T. indeed started with

Tiberius but there are indications that he had come to the conclusion that the roots of the evil went back to Augustus' time. The first chapters of the first book of the *Annals* sum up the new conditions as well as the means by which Augustus made himself sole ruler. What is worse, as much as the rulers incline to tyranny, society inclines to servility. Hence, the other theme which occupied him constantly: how should one behave under the rule of a tyrant? Certainly this is connected with his association with the Flavians; in a sense he was a collaborator. T. condemns both servility and open defiance of the emperor. The behaviour of *Thrasea Paetus and his like may be admired but is not to be recommended. One has to retain his dignity as a human being and senator (and T. writes for the senatorial class), to remain active in the public service but to be prudent. T. claims that the reigns of Nerva and Trajan restored *libertas*; the panegyric of his friend Pliny the Younger makes it clear that the emperors still remained absolute rulers. It was not constitutional guarantees but the character of the new rulers that brought the change.

The emperor, the court, the senatorial aristocracy and the wars in the provinces are the subjects treated by T. He is not interested in ordinary, every-day occurrences and only rarely gives information on the administration of the empire. His history is like a gallery of portraits, and T. is a highly skilled painter. Great and secondary figures appear, directly and indirectly portrayed: Tiberius, Claudius, Nero, Sejanus and Seneca, Livia, Messalina and Agrippina, and a host of others. It is the weak and evil side of human nature that attracts T. He also gives masterly accounts of situations, social groups, the Senate, the army and so on.

T. claims to write *sine ira et studio* ("without prejudice or bias") and no one can say that he directly presents incorrect details as facts. But he has his views and as a superb writer he forces them on the reader even when he does not have solid facts to substantiate them. By innuendo, implication, repetitions, rumours and carefully selected words and phrases he produces the impression he wants to convey to the reader of certain figures. The sinister figure of Tiberius and his reign of terror emerge not by direct accusations but by an ingenious method which employs the above indirect means. As a student of human nature, T. presents his views in unforgettable brief phrases. His damaging verdict of Galba is a good instance: *omnium consensu capax imperii nisi imperasset* ("by common consent he was capable of reigning had he not reigned"). Sarcasm and irony characterize his short sayings on men and human behaviour and accompany his narrative throughout. He is not a great thinker and his psychological treatment of the historical phenomena is not particularly profound, but his comments are apt and instructive and show his insight. T.'s language is varied with rare verbs, archaisms, poetical words, and idiosyncratic phrases. The style is terse, complex, full of intensity, and the occasional long sentences only serve to emphasize his usual rapidity. All these make the reading of his works an unusual intellectual experience.

M. Hutton, *Agricola, Germania* (Loeb), 1914;
W. Peterson, *Dialogus* (Loeb), 1914;
C. H. Moore, *Histories* (Loeb), 1925–31;
J. Jackson, *Annals* (Loeb), 1931;
Syme, *Tacitus*, 1958;
D. R. Dudley, *The World of Tacitus*, 1968.

TACITUS (2), Marcus Claudius Roman emperor, ascended to the throne in November AD 275 on the rare occasion when the army, after the murder of Aurelian, asked the Senate to name an emperor. Himself a senator, his reign was too short for making considerable changes in the position of the Senate. After winning a victory over the Goths, he was murdered in 276.

TAGOS The supreme Thessalian magistrate, chosen only from time to time and holding his powers for indefinite period. As Thessaly suffered from rivalries between cities the office was often dormant. Several of the family of *Aleuadae held the office. The tyrant *Jason (2) of Pherae ruled Thessaly with the title T.

TALOS The bronze man who was given as a present by Zeus to *Europa to guard Crete. He walked three times a day around the island and frightened away or burned those who dared to land. On their way back from Colchis the *Argonauts encountered T. when they tried to approach Crete. *Medea bewitched him, opened his vital vein and so he died bleeding. He may have been originally a god.

TAMIAS (pl. tamiai) T. was a treasurer, and the most important T. at Athens were the ten treasurers of Athena. They were officials elected annually by lot, one to each tribe and until the 4th century BC only *Pentekosiomedimnoi were allowed to take the office. They were in charge of the property of Athena Polias and Athena Nike which was stored in the Opisthodomos on the Acropolis. The revenues included the first fruit of the tribute of the Athenian allies, i.e. 1/60 of the sums paid, various rents, a tithe of booty and confiscated property, and certain fines. The T. disbursed money for various purposes, notably religious, according to the resolutions of the *Ekklesia. A separate board of T. existed for the "the other gods" from 434 to 406 and from 385 to 341. Two T. and seven *epistatai* were in charge of the sancturies of Eleusis. The Ekklesia, Boule etc. had each a T. of its own. T. was the Greek equivalent for the Roman quaestor.
W. S. Ferguson, *The Treasurers of Athens*, 1937.

TANAGRA Town of Boeotia, important until the rise of Thebes in the 4th century BC. Thousands of Hellenistic terra-cotta figurines have been found in the graves of its district, and T. became the common name for such little figures. T. is also known as the place of the defeat of the Athenian army by Sparta in 457 BC. The poetess *Corinna was native of T.

TANTALUS Greek mythological figure, son of Zeus and Pluto, king of Sipylos in Lydia (a region rich in precious metals) and father of *Pelops and *Niobe. He is famous for the punishment inflicted on him by Zeus in the Tartarus. The usual version is that he stood in water up to his waist or chin and whenever he tried to drink, the water receded; and when he tried to grasp the delicious fruit that hung above him from a tree the wind carried it away. In another version, he was also in constant fear lest a huge overhanging stone should fall upon him. Various reasons were given for the punishment. In one he killed his son Pelops and served his flesh to the gods to test their omniscience. But they were not deceived and brought Pelops back to life. In another version he was invited to a banquet of the gods and stole their Ambrosia and Nectar to give them to his fellow mortals. The myth is told by many authors and is as early as Homer.

TARENTUM (Greek: Taras, modern Taranto) Greek city on the Gulf of Tarentum, founded in 706 BC by Spartans led by Phalantus, who later appeared on Tarentine coins. The settlers were said to be the offspring of the Spartan women and helots born when the Spartan

A woman draped in himation. A terracotta from Tanagra

men were away in war in Messenia. The city prospered from agriculture, trade and industry but was always faced with the hostility of the neighbouring Italian tribes. After the decline of the Greek cities in south Italy in the 5th century BC it remained the most important city in that region. In 433 it founded the colony Heraclea (modern Policoro), on the western coast of the Gulf of Tarentum, and T. became the leading power in the league which made the new foundation its centre. T. rose to the height of its power under the leadership of the Pythagorean philosopher, Archytas, in the first half of the 4th century.

The growing power of the Italian tribes after the mid-4th century induced T. to ask help of generals from abroad. King *Archidamus II of Sparta, King *Alexander I of Epirus and Cleonymus of Sparta fought for her, but either failed or were unable to crush the Italians. In the meantime T. signed a treaty with Rome by which the latter agreed not to send her navy to the Gulf of Tarentum. Rome's intervention on behalf of *Thurii led T. to invite *Pyrrhus to Italy. But he did not save her and after his return to Epirus (275), T. was unable to oppose Rome any longer and it fell in 272. It retained some autonomy and was still flourishing until the Second Punic War. Hannibal captured it in 213 and it was sacked when the Romans took it in 209. Thereafter it declined.

TARPEIA The legendary daughter of the Roman commander of the Capitolium who was so greedy that she was ready to help the Sabines capture the citadel if they would give her their golden armlets. They, however, killed her with their shields. This was an aetiological story for the Tarpeian Rock — the cliff on the southwest side of the Capitolium from which traitors and conspirators were thrown off.

Ogilvie, *Livy*, 74f.

TARQUINII (modern Tarquinia) Etruscan city, situated some 7 km from the sea, considered to be the leading member in the league of the twelve cities of the *Etruscans. In legend it was founded by Tarchon (brother of Tyrrhenus) who led the Etruscans from Lydia and was an ally of Aeneas. The city is especially renowned for the rich paintings which have been found in its chamber tombs. These and the other finds in the tombs supply much of the evidence about the Etruscan culture. Two of the Etruscan kings of Rome were said to have been from T., *Tarquinius (1) Priscus and *Tarquinius (2) Superbus. The latter tried to recapture Rome after his expulsion with the help of T.

H. Hencken, *Tarquinia and Etruscan Origins*, 1968.

TARQUINIUS (1) PRISCUS The fifth king of Rome (616—579 BC), whose father, the Greek Demaratus of Corinth, settled down in *Tarquinii. He is credited with various exploits, some of which are otherwise attributed to *Tarquinius (2) Superbus. There is no doubt that Rome was ruled by Etruscan kings but some of the details associated with T. may be doubted. He introduced Etruscan cults and craftsmen to Rome, drained the Forum and constructed the Cloaca Maxima (great drain), brought the Sibylline Books, enlarged the Senate and founded the Capitoline temple. In his wars he extended Roman rule in Latium. He was murdered and his wife Tanaquil helped *Servius Tullius to ascend to the throne.

Ogilvie, *Livy*, 145ff.

TARQUINIUS (2) SUPERBUS The last king of Rome (534—510 BC). In Roman tradition he killed his father-in-law, *Servius Tullius, to win the throne. He established his rule over the Latins and dedicated the Capitoline tem-

A dancing youth from the "Tomb of the Leopards" in Tarquinii, 6th century BC

ple. He is depicted as a Greek tyrant and his tyrannical rule led to his expulsion from Rome. This was achieved after his son raped Lucretia wife of *Tarquinius Collatinus. He found refuge in *Caere and was given help by *Veii, *Tarquinii, *Porsenna and the Latins (Battle of Lake Regillus) but failed to regain power and died in exile. T. was certainly a historical figure and the Roman hatred against *Regnum* indicates that the traditional picture of the character of his reign is genuine. The view that Rome did not control Latium under the last Etruscan kings (in contrast to the literary evidence) is not convincing.

Ogilvie, *Livy*, 194ff.

TARQUINIUS (3) COLLATINUS, Lucius Nephew of *Tarquinius (2) Superbus in Roman legend. After his wife *Lucretia was raped by the king's son, he led the revolt with *Brutus (1) with whom he was consul in the first year of the Roman Republic. But he later went into a voluntary exile because of his family relationship to the king.

Ogilvie, *Livy* (s.v.).

TARRACINA (modern Terracina) Coastal town in southwest Latium, called Anxur when occupied by the Volscians in the early 5th century BC. Rome subdued it in the 4th century and founded a colony there in 329 BC. There are impressive remains of the temple of Jupiter on the Acropolis above the city.

TARRACO (modern Tarragona) Spanish town on the northeast coast of Spain. It came under Roman rule when P. *Scipio (1) and his brother Gnaeus Scipio operated in Spain in the Second Punic War. Caesar made it a colony and it was resettled by Augustus. Henceforth the north-central province of Spain was called Hispania Tarraconensis, and T. was the residence of the Roman governor. After T. was ruined by the Franks in AD 264, Barcino (modern Barcelona) became the leading city in the province.

TARTESSUS Kingdom in the region of the Baetis (Guadalquivir) in south Spain probably with a city by that name as its capital. It was famous for its wealth which was in part due to its extensive trade. The connections it had with the East are reflected in the biblical story of Jonah who tried to escape to Tarshish. The kingdom was destroyed by Carthage *c.* 500 BC.

TAUROBOLIUM This rite of purification had its origin in Asia Minor, became part of the cult of *Cybele and spread to the West under the Roman Empire. Prudentius gives a detailed description of it (*Peristephanon* 10.1011ff). The worshipper stood in a pit to receive, touch, drink, and wash himself with the blood of a bull, or a ram, which was slain above him.

R. Duthoy, *The Taurobolium*, 1969

TAUROMENIUM (modern Taoromina) Greek city on the east coast of Sicily slightly north of *Naxos (2), founded by *Dionysius I in 392 BC on the site of a settlement which was established four years earlier by *Himilco. It came under the control of Syracuse under *Agathocles and under *Hieron II. In the Second Punic War it became an ally of Rome when Syracuse revolted and thus it was the second city in Sicily with a treaty with Rome (*civitas foederata*) — the other being *Messana. Augustus made it a *colonia* and under the Empire it prospered. The historian *Timaeus was native of T. and his father was a tyrant of T. in the mid-4th century BC. Octavian was defeated off T. by Sextus Pompeius in 36. There are fine remains, including those of a theatre.

TEGEA Important city of *Arcadia, situated on the southeastern part of an elevated plain, about 600 m high. It was always a rival of *Mantinea and except for few intervals pursued a pro-Spartan policy until the mid-4th century BC. Its temple of Athena Alea was famous; the architect was *Scopas and he probably was also responsible for the sculptures of the temple. A rare beautiful marble head of a woman, usually called Hygieia from T., was found there. It is now in the National Museum at Athens.

TELEMACHUS Son of *Odysseus and *Penelope who left Ithaca to search for his father. This is told by Homer in the *Odyssey*. He came to Pylos to ask information from *Nestor and proceeded to Sparta where he met *Menelaus. Athens then instructed him to return home. He met his father and helped him to get rid of the suitors. In the lost epic *Telegonia* he married *Circe.

TELEPHUS The mythological son of Heracles and Auge the daughter of King Aleos of Arcadia. As his mother bore him in the sacred shrine of Athena Alea, the goddess sent signs of her displeasure and Aleos discovered what his daughter had done. He ordered the child to be exposed and his daughter to be sold. T. was suckled by a hind and brought up by a shepherd. He later came to Mysia and found his mother who was with King Teuthras. T. became king of the country and when the Greeks were on their way to Troy he was wounded by Achilles. Later Achilles cured him, and he took them to Troy. The suckling of T. by the hind appears in wall-paintings from Pompeii.

TELLUS The old Roman goddess of earth whose temple was on the Esquiline. Her festival was the *Fordicidia* when

Hygeia of Tegea, mid-4th century BC

a cow in calf was sacrificed to her. It was celebrated on 15 April. Her Greek counterpart was *Gaea.

TEMENUS When the *Heraclidae reconquered the Peloponnesus, T. received Argos and probably Corinth. He was killed by his own sons for the favour he showed to his son-in-law. His reign, however, passed to his son-in-law.

TEMPLE The T., according to ancient religious concepts, was a building to house the image of the god and votive offerings for it. It seems that in the Mycenaean world the notion to build a house for the god with his cult-statue was not developed. Traces of what may have been T.s were found only in very few places: Ceos, Delos, Eleusis, none of them great Mycenaean centres. Apparently an altar in an open space was normally considered sufficient for the cult of the gods. The altar usually remained in the open air even when the god was housed in a T. The altar and later the T. stood in a sacred precinct (*temenos*) which was often walled. In Delphi and Olympia this was very large area and included all the treasure-houses, sacred groves and other structures connected with the cult.

The first T.s were built of wood and originally were mere huts. But in time the architectural concept of the T. became quite definite. The kernel of the T. then consisted of a central rectangular hall (*naos* or *cella* in Latin), in front of which came a columned porch (*pronaos*), usually with another at the back (*opisthodomos*) which had no opening to the *naos*. A colonnade (*peristylion*) was added, usually all around. This peristyle was for decoration and became common by the early 6th century BC. Sometimes columns were set up in the interior of the *naos* to hold the roof and for decoration. This was the basic plan. A colonnade of one row of columns is peripteral, with two rows — dipteral. The number of the columns at the ends varied: 6, 8, 10, 12; and so did that of the sides: 12—18 and even 21 in very large T.s, for instance that of Artemis at Ephesus which was dipteral. A T. can be hexastyle, octostyle (and so on) if it has six or eight columns at the front. Many T.s were built from east to west, and in early times the far end could be apsidal. Obviously there were variations and architects sought to find out the best proportions between the constituent elements of the T., and the interrelation between height, width and length.

The T. was usually built above a three stepped platform. Sometimes a second hall was added between the *naos* and the *opisthodomos* — the *adyton* or sacred inner holy room. The cult-statue of the god stood in the *naos*. T.s were built in the style of one of the Orders: Doric, Ionic or Corinthic (see *Architecture), but sometimes architects preferred to use elements of two orders. The decoration of the T.s was achieved both by the columns and by the sculptures of the friezes and the pediments. The roofs were decorated by antefixes and acroteria. The walls of the *cella* were not decorated on the outside; sometimes they had paintings on the inside.

In the great sanctuaries, notably Delphi and Olympia, Greek cities used to build "treasuries" to house their votive-offerings to the gods. These normally consisted of one room with a portico in the front, usually of two columns (distyle), and were decorated by sculptured friezes and pediments, akroteria and caryatids.

The earliest Roman T.s seem to have been introduced from Ertruria. The Etruscan T. consisted of three rectangular *cellae* side by side, with the central broader, and with a deep porch in front of them. This plan sometimes persisted even after Roman architecture came under the influence of Greek concepts and practice. A characteristic of the T. was that it always stood on a high platform (*podium*) to which steps led only on one side. The portico in front of the T. was very deep, but often there was only one *cella*. The Capitoline T. and those modelled on it retained the three *cellae* — to Jupiter, Juno and Minerva. The T.s were decorated by engaged columns and sometimes were non-peripteral altogether. The *cella* at the inner end sometimes had an apse. Finally, many Roman T.s were circular; they could be a circular *cella* surrounded by a row of columns or simply a row of columns supporting the roof.

See *Architecture (with bibliography).

TERENCE (Publius Terentius Afer) Roman comic playwright, of African stock, born in Carthage *c.* 190 BC. He arrived in Rome as a slave and attracted his master the senator Terentius Lucanus by his beauty and talents. He was given an education and, after his manumission, took the name of his former master, as was usual. He won the friendship of certain aristocrats including the young *Scipio (5) Aemilianus and *Laelius (2). These connections and his perfect Latin gave rise to the allegations that they wrote some or parts of his plays. He died on a voyage to Greece in 159 BC.

T. composed six plays, all modelled on Greek originals (*Fabula Palliata), and all are extant. The earliest is *Andria*

The temple of Hephaestus in Athens, Doric temple of c. 450–440 BC

("The Girl from Andros") which was staged in 166. It was based on two plays by *Menander. Pamphilius has a mistress, Glycerium, who is the girl from Andros. But his father wants to marry him to a daughter of his friend. After various intrigues, it is discovered that the mistress is in fact the lost child of the friend. Pamphilius marries his beloved mistress, and her sister is betrothed to Pampilius' friend. *Hecyra* ("The Mother-in-Law") was twice a failure and only on the third performance (160 BC) did it attract an audience. It is based on a play by *Apollodorus (1). In the play Philumena bears a son too soon after her marriage. Her husband Pamphilius refuses to live with her and his father is angry with his wife (the mother-in-law) because he thinks she has expelled Philumena from the house. The happy ending is reached when it is discovered, with the help of Bacchis (Pampilius' former mistress), that Pamphilius is the father — as he ravished his wife in a nocturnal festival before he married her. *Heauton Timorumenos* ("The Self-Punisher"), based on Menander, was performed in 163. It is about the love-affairs of two young men; the father of one of them is permissive, the other very strict. After many intrigues, in which a slave takes part, it is discovered that the beloved of one of the young men is the exposed sister of the other. He is now betrothed to her and his friend is given a wife too. *Eunuchus* ("The Eunuch"), again modelled on a play of Menander, came in 161. It consists of the love-intrigues of two brothers with the courtesan Thais and her slave-girl. One of them succeeds in entering Thais' house disguised as a eunuch. The slave-girl turns out to be a free-born

woman and is betrothed to her lover while his brother at the end can easily get Thais because she becomes a client of his father. *Phormio*, produced in 161, is based on a play by *Apollodorus (1). It takes its name from the parasite Phormio who is hired by Antipho to help him marry a girl against his father's will. In the intrigues is included Antipho's cousin who falls in love with a flute-girl. It turns out that Antipho's beloved is the daughter of his uncle from a woman the latter once had at Lemnos — without the knowledge of his wife at Athens. *Adelphoi* ("The Brothers"), produced in 161 and based on a play by Menander and one by Diphilus, turns on the education of two brothers, one by his father and the other by his uncle. The father is strict and the uncle is indulgent, and the first reproaches his brother for the way he spoils his son. But it turns out that the spoilt young brother has carried off a harp-girl for his respectable brother. The strict father then becomes amiable.

Though T. allowed himself — and was accused for it — to use elements from more than one original Greek play (*Andria, Eunuchus, Adelphoi*), in spirit, costume and setting his plays are pure Greek. Only the language is Latin. He explained and defended his method of writing in the prologues to his plays, which was a novel procedure, as usually the prologue gave the background of the plot to the audience. He used simple metres and avoided the lyric *cantica*. He was very careful to construct a consistent plot and had a skillful power of invention. He preferred to represent ordinary human characters unlike the exaggerated, caricatured types of *Plautus. He wrote with

The north porch of the Erechtheum, with Ionian columns

The Olympieum in Athens, a Corinthian temple, begun before 527 BC, later completed by Hadrian

moderation and restraint and his language was refined and pure. This was not to the coarse taste of the Roman public and could appeal only to the well educated. None of his plays was a great success though the famous actor *Ambivius Turpio produced them. But his elegant Latin and simple style secured almost perennial success to his plays. They were used as textbooks and were extensively read to modern times. He was admired by critics and the Church Fathers; his plays were performed in the Renaissance and greatly influenced the commedy of manners. Only in modern times, because of anxiety for the morals of the young pupils, have his plays been excluded from school-books.

J. Sergeaunt (Loeb), 1914;
G. Norwood, *The Art of Terence*, 1923.

TERMINUS The boundary mark which, in Roman religion, was considered to have a divine power (*numen*). Hence offerings and sacrifice were made to these marks which were erected with a special ceremony. In addition an annual feast, the *Terminalia*, was held for them. The god Terminus had been the original deity of the Capitolium and his image remained there after the building of the Capitoline temple for Jupiter, with the roof left open to give him a clear sky above.

TERPANDER Greek poet and musician of the 7th century BC, native of Antissa in Lesbos, worked in Greece, mainly in Sparta. He is credited with musical innovations, notably the introduction (or reintroduction) of 7-string lyre. He wrote nomes (melodies to epic lines — his or of others), preludes (probably hymns), and drinking songs. The extant fragments attributed to him are hardly authentic.

TERRAMARA The name given to a Bronze Age culture in north Italy, so named because of the black soil (*terra marna*) which is dominant in the places where the settlements were found. The settlements were discovered in the 19th century in a limited region in the Po valley around Parma, Modena and Piacenza. They do not seem to antedate the 16th century BC. The T.'s people lived in villages in huts, often built on poles with ditches for protection. They lived on hunting and agriculture and raised livestock. They were good potters and bronze-smiths. They cremated their dead and kept the ashes in urns. It is supposed that they were invaders from central Europe. The view that the Romans were their descendants has been discarded.

TETRICUS, Gaius Pius Esuvius The last of the emperors of the separate ."Gallic Empire" which began with the usurpation of *Postumius in AD 260. He ascended to the throne in 270 and gave himself up to *Aurelian in 274 who spared his life.

TEUCER (1) The mythological ancestor of the royal family in Troy.

TEUCER (2) Son of Telamon and half-brother of *Ajax. He appears as a prominent archer in the *Iliad* and is renowned for his loyalty to his brother. By his persistence, and with the help of Odysseus, he succeeds to bring his brother to burial.

TEUTA Wife of the Illyrian king, Agron, and the effective ruler after his death (231 BC). Her aggression and attacks of Illyrian pirates on Italian merchants and Roman envoys led to the First Illyrian War of Rome (229–228 BC). She was defeated and Rome established a protectorate in Illyrium.

The front of the Pantheon

THALES Greek philosopher and scientist, by common consent in antiquity one of the Seven Sages. A native of Miletus, he had wide interests including politics, geography, astronomy, and mathematics. There was a belief that he predicted the solar eclipse of 28 May 585 BC — now discredited. He seems to have visited Egypt, tried to explain the Nile floods and to measure the height of the pyramids. He was regarded as the founder of geometry. According to Herodotus, T. advised the Ionians to establish a common council and a federation with a centre at Teos (1.170). He was the founder of science in that he sought to explain nature without any reference to deities or supernatural powers. He held that the world originated from, and was made of, water; also that the earth floated on water whose waves were the causes of earthquakes. It seems that he did not write anything.
Kirk — Raven, *Presocratic Philosophers*, 74ff.

THAMUGADI (modern Timgad) Colony of veterans in Numidia founded under Trajan in AD 100. It had all the usual public buildings and was well planned in the traditional grid system of a Roman camp. The colony flourished and extended beyond the original settlement. In the 7th century it was captured by the Arabs. T. is famous for its well-preserved buildings, including streets, a theatre and the huge Capitoline temple, second only to *Lepcis in Africa.
C. Courtois, *Timgad, Antique Thamugadi*, 1951.

THANATOS Death personified as a god, son of Night, never a great figure in Greek mythology or literature. With his brother, Sleep, he carried off the body of *Sarpedon to Lycia in Homer; he also appears in Hesiod. He was beaten by Heracles when he came to take *Alcestis and was duped by *Sisyphus.

THAPSUS Phoenician coastal city in Numidia known for the battle in which Caesar defeated the Pompeian forces under *Metellus (4) Scipio in 46 BC. Though Caesar still had to fight Pompey's son in Spain in Munda (45), T. was the last great battle of the Civil War. *Cato (2) committed suicide after the battle and Caesar was able to return to Rome to celebrate his triumphs.

THASOS Island in the north Aegean, a few km from the Thracian coast, settled by Greek colonists from Paros in the early 7th century BC. The first colonists had to fight the Thracians and one of those who tried to improve his fortunes in T. but found conditions hard was the poet *Archilochus. However, the rich gold mines of T. and those at Mount Pangaeus on the mainland were exploited by T. which became one of the richest Greek cities. The wealth accumulated enabled the Thasians to commission great works of sculpture in the 7th and 6th centuries. T. also developed vineyards and its wine in later times was a major source of revenue exported as it was to the Balkan, Syria and Egypt. T. joined the Delian League in 477 and when it tried to secede in 465 it was besieged and subdued by Athens (463 BC). Thereafter there was some decline and the "liberation" of the island from Athens after the Peloponnesian War was accompanied by civil strife. In the 4th century T. became an ally of the Second Athenian League but was conquered by Philip II (340). Rome made it a free city in 196 BC after the defeat of *Philip V. Subsequently T. regained some of its prosperity and there was public building.
The painter *Polygnotus was a native of T., but he mainly worked abroad and became an Athenian citizen.
S. Casson, *Macedonia, Thrace and Illyria*, 1926.

THEAGENES Tyrant of *Megara. He seized power from the aristocracy some time after the mid-7th century BC and depended on troops to maintain his rule. He supported his son-in-law *Cylon in his attempt to establish tyranny in Athens, but the latter failed. T. was finally expelled from Megara.

THEATRE In its developed form the Greek and Roman T. had three main elements: the orchestra, the *theatron* (*cavea* in Latin), that is, the auditorium, and the *skene*, that is the stage. Dramatic performances began in Greece with choral dances which took place in the orchestra, a large circular surface with hard earth and an altar at its centre. The spectators originally sat on wooden stands which in Athens collapsed *c.* 496 BC. Hence the normal Greek auditorium was a semi-circular open structure on a slope of a hill with lines of seats supported by walls on its outer sides. It was intersected by passages radiating up from the orchestra. Constructed on a hillside, the auditorium had no outside façade. The originally wooden seats were replaced by stone benches from the 4th century BC on. Where it was possible the seats were cut in the rock as in Syracuse. Special seats of honour were made in the front tiers for priests and officials; otherwise seats were of equal quality for all spectators. The stage, *skene*, was a simple structure constructed behind the orchestra to enable the actors to change costumes and to make their entrances and exits. The originally wooden and low stage was replaced by the 4th century by a stone elevated building. In addition, a *proskenion* — a stone platform supported by columns in front of the *skene*, which was used as a stage — developed. This became a common feature in T.s built in the Hellenistic world. The spectators entered the T.s through open passages (*parodoi*) that separated the *skene* from the *theatron* and led to the orchestra and then to the *theatron*.
The T. of Dionysus on the south slope of the Acropolis at Athens is the earliest extant Greek T. It dates

Stage rehearsal. A mosaic from Pompeii

from the 5th century though it was re-built in stone *c.* 330 BC. The orchestra is a circle of about 27 m. The T. of Epidaurus, built in the mid-4th century BC, is the best preserved Greek T. Its acoustics are extraordinary. T.s were built all over the Greek world and everywhere in sanctuaries.

The Roman T. differed from the Greek in several essential aspects both in structure and concept. In the first place it was a complete building with roofed stage and partly roofed auditorium. It had a semicircular orchestra, with a low, deep stage and behind it a high wall (*scaenae frons*) decorated with niches and pillars. There were special rows of seats in the orchestra for senators and by a law of 67 BC the first 14 rows were reserved for Equites. The auditorium was a substructure with vaulted entrances, staircases and decorated gallery. Unlike Greek T.s, Roman T.s were not associated with sanctuaries. The first permanent T. in Rome was built by Pompey in 55 BC; until then T.s were temporary constructions made of wood. Remains of numerous Roman T.s have been found both in Italy and in the provinces. The T. of Marcellus at Rome is partly preserved and was partly restored under

Mussolini. Fine remainings of T.s are at Pompeii, Orange, Taoromina and Aspendus.

M. Bieber, *History of the Greek and Roman Theatre*[2], 1961.

THEBES (1)   Important city of Boeotia known in Greek mythology for the legends of *Cadmus and those of *Oedipus and his house. The rich legends indicate a prominent position in the 2nd millenium BC and close ties with the East. This has been supported by various archaeological discoveries. These date from Mycenaean times and include Linear B tablets. Of special interest are Mesopotamian cylinder seals, found in 1964, which give special colour to the story that Cadmus introduced writing to Greece. In legend T. was sacked by the descendants (Epigoni) of the Seven Against Thebes.

When the Boeotians occupied Boeotia, before and after the Trojan War, T. recovered but very little is known about it. In the late 6th century *Cleomenes I of Sparta embroiled Athens with T. by advising the latter to support *Plataea. T. sided with the Persians in the invasion of Xerxes and as a result lost its leading position in the Boeotian League. Athens controlled Boeotia in the 450s

BC until its defeat in 447 BC. Thereafter began the rise of T. which sided with Sparta in the *Peloponnesian War. In the 4th century it reversed its policy and fought against Sparta in the Corinthian War but was compelled to accept the Peace of *Antalcidas (386 BC) which curtailed its power over the Boeotian towns. The Spartans captured its citadel in 382 but lost it in 378. T. rose to a leading position in Greece as a result of the Battle of *Leuctra (371) and under the leadership of *Epaminondas. But after his death it could not retain its supremacy, and was routed by *Phocis in the Sacred War. With Athens, T. was defeated by *Philip II in the Battle of Chaeronea (338) and it was destroyed by Alexander for its revolt (335 BC). It was later refounded.

THEBES (2) Ancient city of Egypt and at times capital of the Pharaohs. It was the centre of the revolt of the Egyptians against the Ptolemies in the late 3rd and early 2nd centuries BC when the whole region (Thebaid) was under the control of native rulers. Cornelius *Gallus plundered it in 30 BC. T. was famous for its ancient temples and the colossus of *Memnon (1).

THEMIS Old Greek goddess, in mythology a Titaness, daughter of Gaea and Uranus, mother of the *Moirae and *Horae by Zeus (Hesiod, *Theog.* 901ff.). She was associated with oracles, considered to have possessed Delphi, established rites and instituted laws. In an Attic vase-painting of the 5th century she is seen on the Delphic tripod and in Aeschylus she appears as prophetess, mother of Prometheus. She came to personify justice and divine law.

THEMISTOCLES Athenian statesman (c. 528–462 BC), of a good family, prominent in the first third of the 5th century BC. Archon in 493, he began the building of Piraeus. He was a tribal commander in 490 and in the following years was involved in fierce inner political struggle in which he defeated his opponents. Megacles the *Alcmaeonid, Xanthippus father of Pericles and *Aristides (1) were all ostracized in the course of his struggle. His involvement is attested to by the large number of ostraca from these years with his name (*Ostracismus). In these years (487) the law introducing the election of the *Archons by lot was passed. This was a democratic measure which was to diminish the influence of the *Areopagus and to increase the power of the *strategoi; T. was probably associated with the innovation. His influence and prudence is clear from his success in passing a motion to use the revenues of the new silver mines of Laurium for the construction of 200 triremes (483). The new fleet was decisive in the war against Xerxes.

T. was strategos in 480 and though the general command of the Greek forces was given to the Spartans, his strategy was followed. His aim was to fight the Persians in the north and when the Persian army penetrated to central Greece, Athens was evacuated according to his motion. A great naval battle took place at Salamis on his initiative and his choice of these straits was decisive for the Greek victory and the complete Persian failure. He soon exhorted the Athenians to build the walls of the city while he outtricked the Spartans who opposed this undertaking. Thereafter his enemies, mostly of the aristocratic families, won the confidence of the Athenians and he lost his influence. He was ostracized and in his exile agitated against Sparta in the Peloponnesus. Sparta then accused him of treacherous negotiations with Persia and he barely escaped and was condemned to death (early 470s BC). He had the daring to seek refuge at the Persian court and

*Artaxerxes I gave him three cities to rule in Asia Minor, including Magnesia and Lampsacus. And so the Greek who defeated the Persians ended his life in their service.

Thucydides composed an excellent obituary to T. and noted his unique ability to foresee the future and to choose the right course (1.135f.). Indeed T. was a brilliant statesman both in his judgement and his operation. His foresight, strategy and tact saved Greece in its hour of peril. He was also the founder of the Athenian maritime empire and his activities led to the rise of the low classes and Athenian democracy.

Plut. *Themistocles*; A. R. Burn, *Persia and the Greeks,* 1962.

THEOCRITUS Greek pastoral poet, native of Syracuse, c. 300–c. 250 BC. Profoundly influenced by the landscape and rural life of his native Sicily, he was unable to attract a patron in Sicily (*Hieron II apparently was not interested) and he went abroad after 275 and secured the protection of *Ptolemy II Philadelphus. He was first in Cos and then in Alexandria. Other details of his life are obscure.

T.'s poems are called *eidyllia*, that is, "little pictures". He is especially renowned for his pastoral poems. They are the oldest extant poems of this genre and have influenced all bucolic poets not only in Greek and Latin (notably Virgil) but in European languages as well. Unlike later pastoral poetry which was noted for its artificiality, T.'s poems are alive and have the touch of the real life of the shepherds and goatherds. Love is a prominent theme: that of the Cyclops Polyphemus for Galatea (Nos. 6, 11) or that of the young girl, tormented by strong passion, who uses incantations and a love potion to win back her lover (No. 2), or Heracles' love for the boy Hylas (No. 13). There are several short poems on myth of heroes like Heracles, Pentheus, and the Dioscuri. Some poems are epigrams. A famous poem is the *Adoniazusae*: a mime about two women of Syracuse, now settled at Alexandria, who take part in the festival of Adonis. In one poem T. addresses himself to Hiero and in another to Ptolemy II (Nos. 16, 17).

Like his contemporaries T. wrote short, polished poems. Unlike the Alexandrian poets he refrained from composing erudite, allusive poetry. In his poetry he excels through his vivid descriptions, genuine feelings, acute observations, wit and dramatic talent.

A. S. F. Gow, *Theocritus²*, 1952 (Text, tr. comm.); J. M. Edmonds, *The Greek Bucolic Poets* (Loeb), 1912.

THEODORIC ("the Great") Son of Theodemer, king of the Ostrogoths. T. spent his youth as a hostage in Constantinople and succeeded his father in AD 471. He led his people to Italy in 489 with the consent of the Emperor Zeno. After four years of fighting, he murdered *Odoacer in Ravenna (493) and became king of Italy. Yet he acknowledged the Eastern emperors as his superiors. Under him was built the church of Sant' Apollinare Nuovo renowned for its excellent mosaics with a representation of T.'s palace. His rule brought peace to Italy and he cultivated good relations with the barbaric kings of the West. In his last years he became suspicious and executed *Boethius for alleged treason. He died in 426 and was buried in Ravenna where his tomb is still extant.

THEODORUS Versatile Greek artist, architect and inventor, native of Samos, lived in the 6th century BC. In many of his works he cooperated with *Rhoecus with whom he visited Egypt. He was the architect of the great dipteral temple of Hera in Samos which was known as the

"Labyrinth". It was an enormous building and T. built special towers to enable its construction. The inventions of bronze casting and modelling in clay are attributed to him. He also built the Scias in Sparta, the Assembly hall of the Spartan *Apellai.

THEODOSIUS (1) I ("The Great") Son of Theodosius, who was a successful general of *Valentian I, born c. AD 346 and began his military career early in life. Though his father was put to death in 376, *Gratian gave T. the command against the Goths after the death of the Emperor Valens at the battle of Adrianopole (378). The following year he was made Augustus of the eastern part of the empire. He ended the wars against the Visigoths by letting them settle in Thrace (382). In 387 he defeated and executed Magnus Maximus who had murdered Gratian (383) and placed Valentian II over Gaul. In 394 he defeated the usurper Eugenus.

T. took an active part in the ecclesiastical disputes of his time. He took strong measures against the heretics and enabled the Christians to occupy pagan temples. He finally suppressed all pagan worship and closed down pagan temples (AD 391) and in accordance abolished all the pan-Hellenic games (393). He was the last emperor to rule the whole Roman Empire and on his death the empire was divided between his son *Honorius who received the West and *Arcadius who received the East.

Jones, *Lat. Rom. Emp.* (s.v.).

THEODOSIUS (2) II Emperor of the East, son of *Arcadius, ascended to the throne on his father's death in 408 AD. He was much influenced by his sister and wife, and the empire in fact was ruled by his chief ministers. While the Persians were checked at the Eastern frontiers, the only successful means against the Huns was paying them regular sums of money, and the attempt to recover Africa from the Vandals failed completely. Under T. the second codification of Roman Law since the publication of the Twelve Tables by the *Decemviri in the mid-5th century BC was executed. The Theodosian code was published in AD 438 and contained sixteen books with laws enacted from the time of Constantine the Great.

Jones, *Lat. Rom. Emp.* (s.v.).

THEOGNIS Greek elegiac poet, native of Megara, active in the second part of the 6th century BC. In the extant 1,300 lines that are ascribed to him there are short passages of *Tyrataeus, *Solon and *Mimnermus and it is supposed that the original poems of T. were included in a wider collection. Hence there is uncertainty as to the authenticity of parts of the extant lines. T. is an aristocrat who has no illusions about the decline of his class and the old Greek morals but insists on maintaining their standards. He writes about his love for the young Cyrnos in many poems. The poems were probably composed for singing at *symposia* (drinking-parties). T. included moral maxims in his poems and it was these that made his poetry famous.

D. Young, *Theognis* (text), 1961;
C. M. Bowra, *Early Greek Elegists*, 1938.

THEON OF ALEXANDRIA Greek mathematician and astronomer, lived in the 4th century AD. Several of his works are extant including commentaries on the *Almagest* and astronomical tablets of Ptolemy. He also edited the work of Euclid. His daughter Hypatia had a good knowledge of mathematics and astronomy. She herself wrote commentaries (not extant) on the works of *Diophanthus and Apollonius. An active neo-Platonist, she was lynched by the fanatical Christian mob of Alexandria (c. AD 4).

Coin of Theodosius I

THEOPHRASTUS Greek philosopher, native of Eresus in Lesbos, c. 371–c. 288 BC, pupil and friend of Aristotle, and head of the *Peripatetic School after his master's death (322 BC). His researches and writings embraced almost all branches of human knowledge including politics, ethics, rhetoric, logic, religion, education, physics, methaphysics, astronomy, meteorology and botany. He reputedly lectured to 2,000 students and the extant catalogues of his works, going back to the Library of Alexandria, include about 270 titles; many of his treatises consisted of several books. But out of this enormous output only a small portion is extant.

T. was in the first place a scientist with a critical attitude to his predecessors including Aristotle, and a research worker, intent on empirical work rather than on speculations. Like Aristotle he worked on a grand scale with a view to correct methodology and appreciation of the importance of classification. Of the extant complete works the most important are *Enquiries Into Plants* in nine books and *Aetiology of Plants* in six books. In these T. did for *botany what Aristotle did for zoology. Having collected and organized enormous amounts of data, T. carefully described and classified the species and their physiology and added theoretical discussions of various questions, notably generation. Even more famous is his *Characters* in which he treats thirty human types, all of bad character. Here, too, T.'s sense for order, accurate observation and classification is noted, but he writes with humour and it has been suggested that the work was intended for entertainment at dinner parties in the School. In another view they were useful for the orators and comic poets who dealt with stock characters. Also extant are several short treatises which reveal T.'s critical and research method, for instance *On Fire* and *On Stones*. The latter was the best systematic treatment of minerals until modern times. In his *Metaphysics*, T. showed the inadequacy of Aristotle's theory of final causes but only fragments survive. His work *Opinions of Natural Philosophers* in 18 books was a comprehensive history and criticism of the theories of natural science and philosophy. This and other works of T. had much influence in antiquity, but in mediaeval Europe and particularly in France in early modern times it was his *Characters* that was popular and influential.

A. F. Hort, *Enquiry into Plants* (Loeb), 1926;
R. E. Dengler, *Theophrastus De Causis Plantarum Book One*, 1927; J. M. Edmonds, *Characters* (Loeb), 1929;
E. R. Caley and J. F. C. Richards, *Theophrastus on Stones*, 1956; P. Vellacott, *Characters* (Penguin Classics), 1967.

THEOPOMPUS Greek historian, native of Chios, born *c.* 378 BC. Expelled with his father for his pro-Spartan attitude, he was restored by Alexander the Great and after the latter's death escaped to Egypt. T. was a prolific writer but only fragments of his works have survived. The best known were his *Hellenica* and *Philippica*. The former, a 12-book work, continued the history of Thucydides from 411 BC to 394 BC — the Battle of *Cnidos. The view that it is preserved in the work of the *Oxyrhynchus historian is not convincing. The *Philippica* was a 58-book work which covered the period of *Philip II (359–336 BC) on a grand scale. T. devoted himself to historical work under the influence of his teacher *Isocrates. He was diligent researcher and an erudite man but in his work he gave vent to his personal judgement of politics and politicians.

THEORIKA ("spectacle moneys") This was a characteristic institution of the Athenian democracy. It was a fund instituted by Pericles, from which money was paid to citizens of Athens to enable them to attend the dramatic performances. In the 5th century BC each Athenian who was properly registered as citizen received two obols to this end. A board of officers elected for four years to deal with the fund was instituted. By a law passed in the 4th century all surpluses in the various public departments were to go to the T. Only in wartime could money be taken from it by a regulation of Demosthenes, otherwise a death penalty was inflicted on anyone who proposed using the T. for military purposes in peace time.
H. Michell, *The Economic of Ancient Greece*[2], 1957.

THERA (modern Santorini) The southern island of the Cyclades, occupied from the 3rd millenium BC. Minoan objects have been found on the island including Linear A signs. The island suffered a volcanic eruption *c.* 1500–1450 BC but though the destruction was terrible, it was not abandoned. The volcanic deposits added to the fertility of the soil and T. was renowned for its wine. It was colonized by Dorians from Laconia in the early 1st millenium BC and prospered in the Archaic period. In the 7th century BC it was overpopulated and it was decided to send out a colony; this led to the foundation of Cyrene (Hdt. 4.153). In the 5th century BC T. was an ally of Athens. In the Hellenistic period it was controlled by the Ptolemies.

THERAMENES Athenian statesman, prominent in the second part of the *Peloponnesian War. After the failure of the Athenian expedition to Syracuse, he took a leading part in the activities that led to the establishment of the oligarchic council of the Four Hundred (411 BC). But he did not agree with the extremists and helped to overthrow this council and to institute a limited democracy with 5,000 full citizens (the wealthier). In the following year full democracy was restored but T., who was abroad, managed to retain his influence. He fought at the Battle of Arginusae (406) and was largely responsible for the trial and execution of the *strategoi who did not save the Athenians whose ships were wrecked; this was done in an illegal procedure which was vainly opposed by *Socrates. T. was responsible for the peace negotiations with Sparta at the end of the war (404) and became one of the *Thirty Tyrants. But his moderate policy was not to the liking of *Critias and his associates and he was condemned and executed. Aware of the weaknesses of Athenian democracy, T. sought to work out a moderate democratic constitution as a compromise but this was unacceptable to both the oligarchs and the democrats.

THERMOPYLAE ("Hot Gates") The defile between the mountains and the sea southeast of the Malian Gulf, a natural defensive position against armies intending to invade central Greece from the north. It was there that King

Greek hoplits before battle. A painting on a red-figured vase (kylix) of the 5th century BC

*Leonidas (1) of Sparta attempted to block the advance of the Persian army under Xerxes in 480 BC. The Greek army was outflanked by the Persians who were guided by a traitor along the Anopaea Path in the mountains above. Thereupon Leonidas sent away the main body of his army and kept on fighting with his royal guard of 300 Spartans, helots and 1,100 Boeotians. They all died in battle and in their honour *Simonides composed his famous epitaph. This weak side of the passage, which today is much wider, was exploited on several more occasions: by the Thessalians in the 6th century BC, *Brennus (1) and the Gauls in 279 BC, and by *Cato (1) in the war against Antiochus III (191 BC).

A. R. Burn, *Persia and the Greeks,* 1962, 407ff.

THERON Tyrant of *Acragas in 488 BC and a close associate of the tyrant *Gelon who married his daughter. Together they routed the Carthaginians in a great naval battle off Himera; the latter was captured by T. in 483 BC. T. was a great ruler and under him Acragas prospered but after his death his son was expelled.

Dunbabin, *Western Greeks* (s.v.).

THERSITES An exceptional figure in the heroic gallery of the *Iliad*; ugly, mean and of a low birth, he impudently reproaches Agamemnon but is beaten and stopped by Odysseus. In later versions he was of a better disposition and was killed by Achilles for insulting him in reference to the latter's relation to the Amazon Penthesilea.

THESEUS The national Athenian hero, son of King *Aegeus (or Poseidon) and Aethra of Troezen. Aegeus married Aethra with the encouragement of her father, King Pitheus, and left Troezen without waiting to see what she would bear him. But he hid his sandals and sword beneath a heavy rock. When T. grew up he was told by Aethra to lift the rock which he did with no difficulty. He then set out to see his father but chose the dangerous way by land and not the safe route by sea. On his way he encountered various brigands and notorious ruffians. By his exploits he showed that he was the equal of Heracles. He first killed Periphetes, who lived at Epidaurus and used to club his victims to death; from then on T. carried the iron club of the brigand. He dispatched Sinis, who lived on the Isthmus of Corinth, in the same manner that the latter killed those he overpowered, namely by tying them to two bent trees which tore them apart after he released

them. After killing *Sciron, *Procrustes, Cercyron the wrestler, Phaea the monstrous sow of Crommyon in Attica, and many others, he arrived at Athens. Here he met *Medea who had become his father's wife and knew who he was, while his father was still ignorant of his existence. She tried to poison him but Aegeus recognized the sword T. wore and saved him. He annihilated all the fifty sons of his uncle Pallas who attacked his father and saved the Athenians from the bull of Marathon. On his way to capture the beast, he met an old woman Hecale who offered him hospitality without knowing him. When he came back she was dead; this episode was the theme of the famous epyllion *Hecale* of *Callimachus.

The next adventures brought T. to Crete. He volunteered to go with the seven boys and seven girls Athens had to send annually to *Minos. But he was able to kill the monstrous Minotaur in the *Labyrinth and to escape with the aid of *Ariadne. On their way back he landed at Naxos where he conveniently forgot to take Ariadne. He and his companions visited Delos where they danced at the "altar of the horns", what later was known at Delos as the "crane dance", which imitated the twists of the Labyrinth. On his return, as he forgot to hoist a white sail, the agreed sign for his safety, his father committed suicide and he succeeded him.

As king, T. brought about the *synoecismus of Attica and in one version established the *Panathenaea. He annexed Megara, fought the *Amazons but married Hippolyte who bore him *Hippolytus. Another woman he married was *Phaedra. He abducted *Helen but later lost her. He became a friend of *Pirithous, king of the Lapiths, and helped him to defeat the Centaurs at his wedding. They both descended to the underworld to abduct Persephone and were imprisoned by Hades. *Heracles released him when he went down to fetch the Cerberus. T. took part in the Calydonian Boar-hunt with *Meleager (1) and in the voyage of the *Argonauts. He gave hospitality to Oedipus in the latter's old age, as is told by *Sophocles in *Oedipus at Colonus.* He was finally driven from Athens and sought refuge in Scyros, but King Lycomedes caused his death by throwing him from a cliff. When *Cimon conquered Scyros in the 5th century he found bones which were believed to be those of T. He brought them to Athens where they were buried and a hero-shrine was erected there for T.

Theseus landing at Delos, a detail from the François vase, c. 570 BC

The legends of T. were largely modelled on those of Heracles. But in addition they referred to various Athenian institutions and political claims, and to historical events. It is possible that some historical figure was at the root of the legends. The story is best known by the *Life of Theseus* by Plutarch. Themes of the legends are known from works of art from the 7th century on, in sculpture and in vase-paintings.

THESMOPHORIA Greek festival in honour of Demeter which was held for three days in the autumn. Men were excluded from the T. which aimed at securing the growth of the seed-corn about to be sown at that season of the year. One of *Aristophanes' plays is about the women who celebrate the festival and plan to take revenge on Euripides.

THESMOTHETAI The six minor *archontes at Athens, instituted by the 7th century BC. Like all archontes they became members of the *Areopagus on completing their year of office and from 487 BC were elected annually by lot. The T. acted collectively. They were responsible for the drawing of lots for the appointment of officials elected by this method. Their functions were judicial and legal. They presided over various sorts of cases, private and public, and they were responsible for the examination of laws and the appointment of *Nomothetai. They had the authority to put to death persons condemned to exile for murder if they were caught in Attica. They also distributed the courts to the various magistrates who were to try the cases.

THESPIAE One of the main cities of Boeotia and the leading one in the southern section of the country. Unlike other Boeotian cities, notably *Thebes (1), T. fought the Persians in the invasion of Xerxes. A detachment from T. fought and fell with *Leonidas (1) in the Battle of *Thermopylae.

THESPIS Of Icaria in Attica, the oldest tragic writer, the first to introduce the speaking actor. By adding the prologue and the dialogue between the actor and the chorus leader to the choral song, he became the founder of tragedy. T. apparently produced one-actor tragedies for some time before the first official performance of tragedies took place at the *Dionysia in Athens in 534 BC — and on that occasion T. won the first prize. Horace says that he took his plays about on a wagon in Attica before he came to produce them in Athens, but this is disbelieved. He is also credited with the invention of the mask, but its use surely antedated him. Of his works nothing survives; forgeries were produced after his time and attributed to him.
Pickard-Cambridge, *Dithyramb*[2] 69ff.

THESSALONICA (modern Salonika) Macedonian city, situated on the northeast of the Theramic Gulf, founded by *Cassander who synoecized the villages of the region. With a good harbour and communications it became the main Macedonian harbour and eclipsed Pella. After Macedonia became a Roman province (146 BC), T. was made the residence of the Roman governor. Under the Empire, it enjoyed prosperity, but it was made a Roman colony only in the mid-3rd century AD.

THESSALY Country in north Greece separated from Macedonia in the north by the Cambunian range and Mount Olympus, and from Epirus in the west by the Pindus range, and with Mount Othrys in the south as a border. The Thessalian plain, believed by the Greeks to have once been a lake, is enclosed by all these mountains and is the largest in Greece. The ranges of Mount Ossa and Mount Pelion in the east blocked T. from the sea, and the narrow vale of Tempe provided the only access through the mountains to the northeast. Through this vale flows the river Peneus. This river drained the whole of T. The vale of Tempe could be easily blocked against invaders from the north, but there was another pass west of Mount Olympus through which Xerxes invaded. *Pagassae was T.'s only port with good communications to the interior.

T. consisted of four regions: Hestiaeotis in the northwest, with the city of Tricca; Pelasgiotis in the east, with the cities of Crannon, *Pherae, and *Larissa; Thessaliotis in the southwest; and Pthiotis in the southeast. Thanks to its fertile plain, it was one of the few regions in Greece which had abundant supplies of grain. It was a good region for rearing livestock. It was also famous for its horses. Indeed, the Thessalians had the only good cavalry in Greece. There is evidence, archaeological and other, that T. was inhabited from Neolithic times on. The Thessali invaded T. during the general migrations that occurred in the 12th century BC. They occupied the more fertile parts of the country and subjected the local population. Though T. always suffered from separatist movements and rivalries between its cities, a loose federacy was developed and T. turned into a strong state in the 6th century BC. It lost its predominant position in the 5th century because of the inter-cities rivalries which weakened it for a long period. For a short time *Jason (2) of Pherae succeeded in uniting it but after his death it was again torn apart by feuds and rivalries. *Philip II came to control T. and ruled it as a Thessalian archon for life. T. was practically always under Macedonian rule until the Romans made it free in 196 BC. The Thessalian League was then restored. In 146 BC T. became part of the Roman province of Macedonia.
Larsen, *Gr. Fed. St.*, 12ff., 281ff.

THETES The lowest class in Greek society, consisting of the poor free labourers who worked for hire. They formed the lowest class in Athens after the reform of *Solon, but perhaps even earlier. All citizens whose income was below 200 medimni of corn (or a corresponding amount in other forms of wealth) belonged to this class. According to the law of Solon they could attend the *Ekklesia and *Heliaea. In the course of the 5th century BC they were admitted to magistracies.

THETIS A Nereid whom Zeus and Poseidon dared not seduce because they were told that her son would be stronger than his father. She was given to *Peleus but he had to fight hard to win her especially as she took on various shapes (fire, wind, a lion etc.). All the gods came and brought presents to the wedding which took place on Mount Pelion. She bore *Achilles to Peleus and made her son invulnerable except for his heel. In one version she bore seven children and tried to make them immortal by throwing them into fire, but they died and this was the reason why she left Peleus. Later, she hid Achilles with the daughters of Lycomedes of Scyrus to prevent him from going to the Trojan War because she knew he would die there. After *Hector captured Achilles' armour from the corpse of *Patroclus, she presented her son with new armour made by Hephaestus. Her wrestling, wedding and the presentation of the armour — all these were favourite themes with Greek artists from the 6th century BC.

THEVESTE (modern Tebessa) Old town in Numidia, captured by the Carthaginian general Hanno the Great in the mid-3rd century BC. The city prospered under the Roman Empire and became a *colonia* in the early 2nd century AD. There are considerable remains, among the best in Africa, notably the fortifications from Byzantine times, an arch of Caracalla and the temple of Jupiter.

THIRTY TYRANTS Group of thirty oligarchs who, due to *Lysander's intervention, were appointed by the Athenian *Ekklesia in 404 BC to introduce a new constitution for Athens. They introduced a reign of terror and were known as the Thirty Tyrants. The leading members were the moderate *Theramenes and the extremist *Critias. They set up a new *Boule and dismissed the popular courts (*Dikasterion). They put to death some 1,500 citizens and metics who were known or believed to be devoted democrats, but this aroused the dissension of Theramenes who was then put to death by Critias. The exiled democrats led by *Thrasybulus captured Piraeus and Critias lost his life in his attack on them. Thereafter, the moderates regained power and established a constitution of 3,000 citizens. The Spartan King *Pausanias (2) organized an agreement between the democrats in Piraeus and the oligarchs and the democratic constitution was re-established. The survivors of the Thirty and the extreme oligarchs left for Eleusis.
Hignett, *Athen. Const.*

THOLOS (pl. tholoi) A circular building with concentric colonnades. Such buildings were to be found mainly in the precincts of sanctuaries, and are known from Delphi, Olympia and Epidaurus. But it is not known what they were used for. The T. in the *Agora of Athens served as the hall for the *Boule. (For T.-tombs see *Mycenaean Civilization).

THRACE The country of the Thracian tribes which extended from the Danube in the north to Macedonia in the south, with changes in its frontiers during the course of several centuries. The Greeks came into direct contact with them when they established colonies on the coastal fringe of T. on the Black Sea, the Propontis and the Hellespont, notably *Byzantium, *Perinthus and *Abdera. The Thracian tribes were never united. *Darius I extended his rule over them but the failure of his son against the Greeks in 480–479 BC enabled T. to regain its independence. The king of the Odrysae, Teres, was the first to organize a large kingdom of T. in the 5th century BC; it lasted to the mid-4th century BC and was involved in Greek politics. The kingdom disintegrated after the death of King Cotys and King *Philip II annexed parts of T. to Macedonia and extended his rule of the Thracian tribes. *Lysimachus and the Macedonian kings until 168 BC checked or sometimes effectively controlled T.

The establishment of the Roman province of Macedonia brought the Romans into direct contact with the Thracians. Until the end of the Roman Republic, governors in Macedonia almost always had the opportunity to conduct wars against the Thracians. Augustus did not conquer T. but established a protectorate over the native kings. It was annexed by the Emperor Claudius in AD 46. The Roman province of T. was bounded by Lower Moesia in the north, with Mount Haemus as the border line, the Black Sea in the east, the Propontis and the Aegean in the south, and in the west the river Nestus which formed the border with Macedonia. The Thracian *Chersonessus (1) was imperial property from the time of Augustus. T. was governed by procurators and from Trajan's time by legates of praetorian rank.
S. Casson, *Macedonia, Thrace and Illyria*, 1926;

THRASEA PAETUS, Publius Clodius Roman senator and Stoic, *consul suffectus* in AD 56. He admired *Cato (2) Uticensis and wrote his biography which was used by Plutarch (*Cato Minor* 25). He is mainly known from Tacitus who did not approve TP.'s defiant behaviour in the Senate and regarded it as a theatrical gesture and an unnecessary provocation of the emperor. His republicanism and the free way in which he expressed his opinions finally led to his condemnation. He ended his life in the same dignified manner in which he lived it.
Syme, *Tacitus* (s.v.).

THRASYBULUS Athenian democratic statesman and general, prominent in the late 5th and early 4th centuries BC. When the oligarchs took control of Athens in 411 BC, he organized the democratic opposition in Samos which eventually caused the fall of the oligarchic council of the Four Hundred, and he took a leading part in the naval recovery of Athens. When the *Thirty Tyrants took power in Athens in 404 BC he escaped and after a few months captured Piraeus. He repelled the attack of the oligarchs whose leader *Critias fell in the battle. There followed the intervention of the Spartan King *Pausanias (2) and as a result T. was able to return to Athens and to restore the democratic constitution (403 BC). He continued to play an important role in Athenian politics and sought to recover the leading position of Athens. He was killed in 388 BC while commanding an Athenian army in Pamphylia.

THUCYDIDES (1) Son of Melesias, Athenian statesman, mainly known as the opponent of *Pericles. After the death of *Cimon, to whom he was related, he became the leader of the conservative elements in Athens. He criticized Pericles for his building operations, arguing that Athens did not have the right to use the tribute of the allies for this purpose. In an ostracism held *c.* 443 BC, T. lost his case and had to leave Athens for ten years. Thereafter, he was not active in politics. Thucydides the historian was probably his descendant.

THUCYDIDES (2) Son of Olorus, the greatest ancient historian (*c.* 455–400 BC). His father was probably a descendant of Olorus, the Thracian king who was the maternal grandfather of *Cimon. T. himself owned property in the region of Strymon in *Thrace and was buried in the family vault of Cimon; obviously, he was his relative. He was probably related to *Thucydides (1) son of Melesias, the opponent of Pericles. However, he came to follow and admire Pericles. As strategos in 424 BC, T. was sent to the Thracian region but was not able to secure Amphipolis which fell to *Brasidas, the brilliant Spartan commander. In his absence, he was condemned to exile and he returned to Athens only after the war ended (404 BC). A few years later, he died.

T. wrote the history of the war between Athens and Sparta known as the Peloponnesian War. The *History* in eight books is extant and ends in 411 BC. His aim was to carry it to 404 BC but apparently he did not live to finish it. Three historians started their works where he finished and of these only the *Hellenica* of *Xenophon is extant (see *Theopompus and *Oxyrhynchus, historian). The *History* of T. consists of the following parts: an introduction in which T. explains the importance of the Peloponnesian War, expounds his historical methods and views and analyses the causes of the war (Book 1); the first phase of the war, that is, the years 431–421 BC to the Peace of Nicias, the so-called Archidamian War (2–5.24); the peace interlude with the campaign of Mantinea and the Melian dialogue as the main events in the years 421–416 BC (5.24–116); the Athenian expedition to Sicily,

Above: *Koure, marble head found on the Athenian Acropolis, c. 510 BC*

Overleaf: *Remains of a Doric temple (c. 650 BC) on the Acropolis of Selinus*

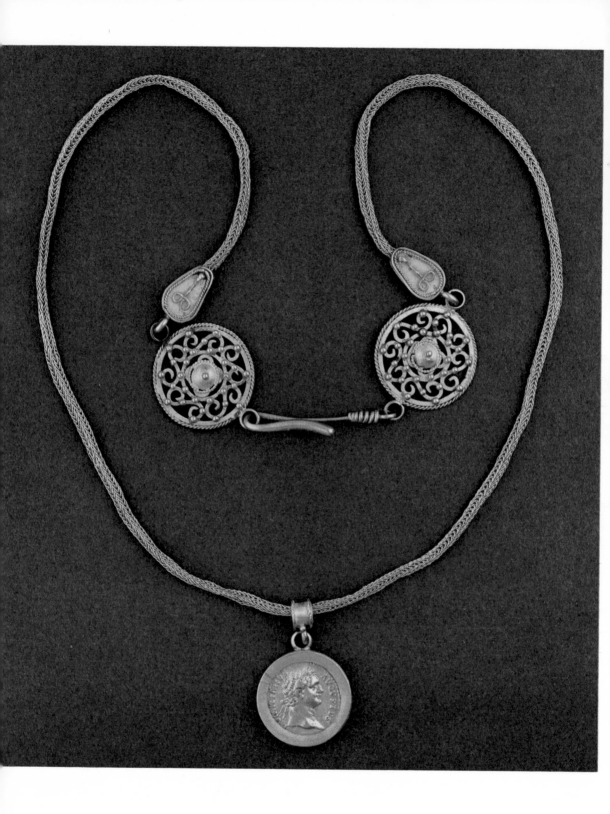

Gold necklace with Emperor Domitian coin pendant

415—413 BC (Books 6—7); the war in Greece, known as the Decelean War, 413—411 BC (Book 8) — which T. left incomplete.

T. claims that he realized the magnitude of the war and started collecting material from the first. The order in which he composed his work and extent to which he revised it are disputed questions. It is certain that T. devoted his time to getting as much accurate information as could be obtained from both sides. For the first years of the war he had personal knowledge of Athenian politics. Thereafter, he questioned people involved in the events and took the trouble to check documents. The texts of nine treaties are given in his work. He also included speeches in his work; these take up more than a fifth of the *History*. He claims that he introduced speeches only on those occasions when they were actually delivered, but he expressly says that his are not the exact reproductions of the real speeches. His principle was to give in the speeches the arguments appropriate for the occasion and at the same time to remain as faithful as possible to what the speaker actually said. It is evident that in the speeches his aim was not accuracy; he used them as a dramatic means to illustrate views, to present situations, and to reveal inner motives and forces. They certainly were not his free invention, as it is sometimes maintained, but adaptations of real speeches to his purposes, and it can be assumed that some are more accurate than others. The theme of T.'s work is war, but in his account of it the military operations are only one — and not the more important — part of the story. The main subject is Athenian imperialism and the causes of the war are given in reference to it. The growth of Athenian power accompanied by the abolition of the autonomy of Greek states spread fear for their independence in other states. It seemed that Athens was about to subjugate the Greek states. The other great Greek state, Sparta, felt insecure of her own power — and so the Athenian aggression and the Spartan fear were the basic causes of the war. But T.'s analysis of Athenian imperialism is not confined to this case only. In a direct account and in several speeches (that of the Athenians at Sparta before the war, the Funeral Speech of Pericles, the speech of the Syracusan Hermocrates, and the Melian Dialogue) he expounds an outstanding theory of imperialism. In their actions men are motivated by fear, honour and the quest for gain. From these simple foundations, T. shows the operation of general laws of human behaviour. His account of the civil strife in Corcyra is a brilliant analysis of the degeneration of man under the stress of war and hatred, of the distortion of truth, and the loss of human values in such situations. T. has been critized for neglecting the economic causes of the Peloponnesian War. The truth is that he did not neglect them; he examined them and concluded that economic resources were important for the conduct of the war but economic motives were at most secondary for the outbreak of the war.

T. is a model of the scientific historian. He aimed at giving an accurate description of what really happened as well as an explanation of the causes and processes and their effects. For this purpose he collected vast amounts of information and selected the relevant evidence. An Athenian and an admirer of Pericles, he wrote without prejudice on Sparta and Athens's enemies. In contrast to Herodotus and many other ancient, and modern, historians, he explained the course of history in human terms, not in reference to supernatural causes. His ac-

count of the plague in Athens, which affected him, too, is read as a pure medical report; and the success or failure of statesmen and states are explained by their deeds and misdeeds, by their resources and policies. He gave individuals their share and did not neglect classes and society. He did not write to entertain but to give a reasonable account from which an intelligent reader could take advantage in the future. He wrote his history in a unique style, noted for its conciseness, speed, antithetical construction, and use of abstract phrases. Above all, he wanted to express his thoughts rather than achieve elegant effects; hence some of his sentences are loosely constructed. And yet there is a difference between the simple narrative, which is lucid, and the speeches and theoretical discussions which are complicated and not clearly expressed. This has made him difficult to read; but his work has always been what he said of it: an eternal acquisition.

C. F. Smith (Loeb), 1919—23;
R. Warner (Penguin Classics), 1954;
G. B. Grundy, *Thucydides and the History of his Age*[2], 1948;
A. G. Woodhead, *Thucydides on the Nature of Power*, 1970.

THURII Greek city in southern Italy near the former site of *Sybaris, founded by Pericles as a pan-Hellenic enterprise in 443 BC. *Herodotus and *Lysias were among the colonists, the former died there and the latter returned to Athens. The city suffered from civil strife and the Sybarites were expelled. To protect herself against the Lucanians, T. applied for Roman help and this was the background for the summoning of Pyrrhus by *Tarentum against Rome. A Latin colony was founded here after the Second Punic War (193 BC), but it was a failure and the place became desolate.

A. G. Woodhead, *The Greeks in the West*, 1962.

TIBERIUS (Tiberius Julius Caesar Augustus) Roman emperor (AD 14—37). Born in 42 BC, his mother *Livia was divorced from his father, Tiberius Claudius Nero, in 38 BC to marry Octavian — the future Augustus. The circumstances of his childhood and the way he was brought up may have contributed much to his gloomy character. Under Augustus he attained outstanding achievements. In 20 BC he brought back the Roman standards lost to the Parthians by *Crassus (4). In 16 BC he conquered *Raetia with his brother *Drusus (3). He was responsible for the conquest of Pannonia (12—9 BC) and, after his brother died he took command of the Roman army in Germany (9 BC). His career was interrupted in 6 BC by his retirement to Rhodes. The reasons were partly his bad relations with his second wife *Julia, Augustus' daughter. He had been compelled to divorce his first wife in 12 BC to marry her; but she was a licentious woman and he was an austere man and the marriage was an unhappy one. He was probably also embittered by the preference Augustus showed for his grandchildren Gaius and Lucius, the two sons of *Julia from her former husband *Agrippa (1). T. returned from Rhodes early in AD 2. The death of Lucius and Gaius left T. as the only possible heir and Augustus adopted him (AD 4). He gave T. the two powers indicative of his position as the likely heir: the *Imperium Proconsulare and the tribunician power. T. was now the chief general of Augustus. He conducted the war operations in Germany and in AD 6—9 was responsible for the suppression of the rebellion in Pannonia and Illyricum. In AD 13 his powers were renewed for ten years and in AD 14 he succeeded Augustus.

T. came to the throne at the age of 56. He was an

Portrait of Tiberius on a gold coin

experienced soldier, a diplomat and an administrator, but also an embittered man. Even when Augustus appointed T. as his heir he compelled him to adopt *Germanicus as his own heir. The administration of the empire was efficient and no major wars were embarked on to extend the frontiers. T. checked Germanicus who tried to renew the expansionist policy in Germany. In contrast to Augustus, T. spent little money on public building and entertainment and reduced all expenditure. On his death, he left 2,700 million sesterces.

T.'s reign, however, is known as one of terror. This applied only to his relations with the Senate and the aristocracy. From the start there was no understanding between them. T. was basically a republican; he tried to avoid innovations and to retain republican forms of government. He was considered a hypocrite. There followed the *Maiestas trials, the death of Germanicus and the trial of *Piso (4). The rise of *Sejanus and his sinister influence added to the unpopularity of T. and in AD 26 he retired to Capri and tried to rule from there. His own son died in AD 23 by the machinations of Sejanus who also caused the death of two sons of Germanicus. Their mother *Agrippina was starved to death (AD 33). Sejanus and many of his associates were executed in AD 31.

According to Tacitus, T. was wicked from the start but, being a master in the art of simulation, he only gradually revealed his character. This evaluation may be doubted. The stories of his debauchery in Capri, well known from the *Life* of Suetonius, are hardly credible. But he was hated and therefore everything was believed about him. His positive achievements were forgotten and the rumours and executions were stressed by the historians.

G. Marañon, *Tiberius, A Study in Resentment*, 1956;
R. Seager, *Tiberius*, 1972.

TIBERIUS JULIUS ALEXANDER A Jew by origin, a nephew of *Philon Judaeus, he became a Roman. He governed Judaea (AD 46–8), served under *Corbulo and then became prefect of Egypt. As such he was the first to declare allegiance to Vespasian (1 July AD 69). His provincial edict is known from an inscription.

TIBULLUS, Albius Roman elegiac poet, born in the mid-1st century BC and died in 19 BC. He was of equestrian rank, and despite some loss of property remained well-off and had a villa at Pedum (beyond Tibur). Horace and Ovid were his friends and he was closely associated with *Messala Corvinus.

Two books of poems by T. are extant and a third, not by him, and divided into two, is attached to them in the manuscripts — these are known as the *Corpus Tibullianum*.

Most of the poems are love poems. Book 1 consists of five poems for the courtesan Delia and three for the boy Marathus. There is also a poem in honour of Messala in addition to one against war. Book 2 contains three poems for the courtesan Nemesis, a charming poem on the festival of *Ambarvalia, a poem for the birthday of Cornutus and one for the admission of Messala's son to the college of the *Quindecemviri Sacris Faciundis. The third book consists of poems written by poets of the circle of Messala. There are six poems by Lygdamus, a panegyric of Messala by an anonymous poet, and the poems of *Sulpicia.

T. writes refined poetry, smooth and melodious. He is noted for his simplicity and his avoidance of erudite allusions and myths. Instead, he finds attraction in life in the countryside and describes it.
J. P. Postgate (Loeb), 1913.

TIBUR (modern Tivoli) Ancient Latin city, about 25 km from Rome, on the Anio. It took control of several nearby towns and was one of the main Latin cities that contested Roman hegemony in Latium. But it was defeated in the war of 340–338 BC, and lost a part of its territory. It received Roman citizenship only in 90 BC but even before that time it had become a fashionable place for the Roman aristocracy. Horace had a little villa here; that of Hadrian was a magnificent complex. The building-stone of T. was famous.
E. Bourne, *A Study of Tibur*, 1916;
S. Aurigemma, *The Villa Adriana near Tivoli*, 1955.

TIGELLINUS, Gaius A Sicilian by origin, exiled allegedly on a charge of adultery with Calligula's sister, he rose to power under Nero who made him praetorian prefect. By flattery and intrigues he caused many deaths. He survived Nero but was compelled to commit suicide under *Otho.

TIGRANES I ("The Great") King of Armenia. He ascended to the throne with the support of Parthia in the early 1st century BC. He married the daughter of *Mithridates VI of Pontus. He advanced his power at the expense of Parthia, established control over north Mesopotamia and conquered Syria, Phoenicia and Cilicia (80s BC). But he became involved in the war of his father-in-law against Rome and was defeated by *Lucullus. Subsequently, he gave himself up to Pompey. In the new provincial organization of Pompey, T. retained only his original kingdom of Armenia (63–62 BC).

TIMAEUS Greek historian (c. 356–260 BC), native of Tauromenium, son of Andromachus. His father became tyrant of his home city, but T. escaped from Sicily through fear of Agathocles, tyrant of Syracuse (c. 312 BC). For fifty years he lived in Athens, studied rhetoric and composed his historical works. His *Histories* was a thirty-eight book work which concentrated on the history of Sicily and south Italy, but included digressions on events in other countries, and thus also dealt with Rome. T. used the Olympiads as a basis for his chronology and achieved a high degree of accuracy in this respect. He was erudite, according to Cicero, but he was accused of lacking knowledge, distorting facts, and innacuracy, notably by Polybius. It is difficult to ascertain the validity of the accusations against him. He certainly took the trouble to collect evidence and it is difficult to prove that he wrote with prejudice.

T. S. Brown, *Timaeus of Tauromenium*, 1958.

TIMOLEON The Corinthian statesman and general who had spectacular achievements to his credit in Sicily. He managed to take control of Syracuse in 344 BC and sent the tyrant *Dionysus II away to Corinth. He used the extraordinary powers which were given to him to introduce a moderate oligarchic constitution. Thereafter, he sought to abolish, and succeeded in abolishing, the tyrannies in other cities. He also won a great victory over the Carthaginians (341 BC). In addition, T. took measures to revive various cities, including Camarina, Gela and Acragas. He died c. 334 BC. T. evidently was an extraordinary leader and statesman. His opposition to tyranny was a driving force. What is no less remarkable is his success in bringing about a new period of prosperity to the old Greek cities in Sicily.

W. D. Westlake, *Timoleon*, 1952.

TIMON Citizen of Athens, lived in the 5th century BC, mainly known from Plutarch (*Anton.* 70). He became proverbial as a misanthrope and Aristophanes referred to him in his plays. He also appeared in a dialogue by *Lucian.

TIMOTHEUS (1) Athenian statesman and general, son of *Conon and pupil of *Isocrates. In the first year of the *Second Athenian Empire, he carried out successful measures to annex more members. He then entered the service of Persia and fought against the Egyptian rebels. When he returned (366 BC), he resumed a vigorous expansionist policy, but with little result. In 356 BC he failed in his military operation, was brought to trial and condemned. He died in 354 BC.

TIMOTHEUS (2) Greek sculptor of the 4th century BC. An inscription in the temple of Asclepius in Epidaurus records that he worked for the decoration of that temple. Pliny the Elder says that he was one of the sculptors who worked on the *Mausoleum in Halicarnassus. However, it is impossible to attribute with certainty any of the parts to T.

TIRESIAS The legendary seer in the Theban myths, first described in Homer. Though blind he was very wise and could see the future. When *Odysseus descends to the underworld, T. tells him of his future adventures. Two explanations were offered for his blindness. In a version told by Callimachus, this was a punishment for seeing Athena taking a bath; but he was given the power to prophesy in recompense. In another version he saw snakes mating and beat them with his stick and thereupon turned into a woman. Years later he struck them again and became a man again. Some time later he was chosen to arbitrate in the argument between Zeus and Hera about who gets more enjoyment from sex, and from his experience answered that it was the woman. The enraged Hera blinded him but Zeus granted him prophetic power and longevity. But he is mainly known from his role in the myths about Oedipus and Antigone as described by Sophocles in *Oedipus Tyrannus*. He also appears in the *Bacchae* of Euripides.

TIRYNS Ancient city in the southern part of the plain of Argos, only one mile from the sea. In Greek legends it was ruled by *Proeteus, *Perseus, and *Eurystheus. *Heracles had special connections with it and the legends about him may have been based on a real ruler of T. The site, a rock which rises above the plain around it, was first excavated by Schliemann almost 100 years ago, after his excavations in Troy and Mycenae. The site had been occupied from the 3rd millenium BC on. Traces of destruction are thought to have been caused by the arrival of the Greeks about 2200–2100 BC. Several phases of the settlement can be distinguished. In the 3rd millenium there was a circular house at the top of the hill; other buildings must have existed on the plain. In the 16th century a large building was built with frescoes. The city extended to its maximum size in the 14th–13th centuries BC. A wall was built and was later twice enlarged – apparently there was a need for a large, fortified space. Significantly, concerning its economic resources, large store rooms were built. There developed a complex palace on the southern part, with courts, propylaea, a great hall, a bathroom, an altar and other chambers. It was destroyed by fire in the late 13th century BC, though the site remained inhabited. A polis later developed and T. was one of the Greek cities which fought the Persians at *Plataea (479 BC). But about ten years later, T. was destroyed by Argos.

There are impressive remains in T. These include the Cyclopean Walls made of huge blocks, vaulted galleries, and subterranean passages.

TISSAPHERNES Persian satrap in western Asia Minor who played an important role in the Peloponnesian War from 412 BC. He then received *Alcibiades who fled from Sparta. Though he supported Sparta on the whole and acted against Athens, his aim was to weaken all parties so as to make possible the restoration of Persian authority. After the arrival of *Cyrus (2) II (408 BC) he was sent to Caria and failed in his policy with regard to the Greeks. His relations with Cyrus were bad and his accusations of treason almost cost the latter his life when *Artaxerxes II ascended to the throne. When Cyrus began preparations for the expedition against his brother, T. personally went to Artaxerxes to warn him. He played a decisive role in the final battle at *Cunaxa (401 BC) and in the capture of the Greek commanders who were with Cyrus. Thereafter he received his former satrapy in western Asia Minor and fought the Spartans. After his defeat by *Agesilaus II (395 BC), he was executed.

TITANS The pre-Olympian gods, children of *Gaea (Earth) and *Uranus (Heaven). The Titan *Kronos took control of the world and married his sister Rhea after castrating his father. But his sons *Zeus, *Hades and *Poseidon defeated him and after that the Olympian gods ruled the universe (Hesiod, *Theog.* 154ff.; 453ff.). *Hyperion, *Oceanus, *Mnemosyne and *Themis were Titans and so was *Prometheus.

TITUS (Titus Flavius Vespasianus) Roman emperor (AD 79–81), son of *Vespasian, born 30 September AD 39. He served in the army in Germany and Britain and after his quaestorship he served under his father as legate in the war in *Judaea. After his father became emperor he was left to end the war and in AD 70 captured Jerusalem and burned the Temple. He commemorated his achievement in the Arch of T. at the Forum in Rome, which is still extant.

Vespasian made T. almost his equal partner in the rule of the empire. He received the tribunician power (AD 71) and was continuously consul with his father. Even the title Augustus seems to have been given to him in his father's lifetime. He was also a praetorian prefect and was responsible for the execution of *Caecina (1) Alienus and *Eprius Marcellus. He ascended to the throne on 23 June AD 79, on his father's death. During his short reign he became very popular because of his liberality. His rule was mild and he curbed the hated *Maiestas trials. He gave help to those who suffered from the eruption of Vesuvius in AD 79 and from the fire and plague in Rome in AD 80. T. completed the building of the *Colosseum and the Baths of T. He died on 13 September AD 81 and was deified; his good reputation is reflected in Suetonius who calls him "the pleasure of the human race" (*Titus* 1).

T. was twice married and his only child died before he did. His affair with the Jewish princess *Berenice (3) was notorious at Rome. Their relationship started during the war in Judaea. Though it was very unpopular, he lived with her for some years (*c.* AD 75). In deference to public opinion, he did not marry her, and, when she came to Rome again in AD 79, he sent her back.

TORQUATUS, Titus Manlius Roman statesman and general, a popular hero in Roman tradition. To account for the cognomen Torquatus borne by a branch of the patrician clan of the Manlii, it was told that T. won a collar (*torques*) in single combat against a Celtic chieftain (361 BC). A severe disciplinarian, as consul he ordered the execution of his son who successfully, but contrary to orders, fought the enemy in a duel (341 BC). Apart from all this, his main exploit was the decisive victory over the *Latins in 340 BC in a war which left Rome the unquestionable master of Latium.

TRAGEDY The evidence on the origin of Greek T. is scanty and disputed. According to Aristotle, T. originated from the leader (*exarchon*) of the *dithyramb — that is, the actor developed from the man who used to lead the dithyramb; also, in origin it was a satyr play (*Poetics*, 3ff.). The members of the chorus appeared as *satyrs and as such displayed the features of goats (*tragoi*); *Tragodoi*, then, were "goat singers" and *tragodia* a "goat song". But the dithyramb was associated with the cult of Dionysus and the dramatic element of T. may have been developed from mimetic rites performed in the cult of this god. But there is also evidence that a "tragic chorus" performed in the cult of the Dorian hero *Adrastus, and that in Sicyon this was replaced by a cult of Dionysus by *Cleisthenes (1).

Two names are associated with the origins of T. The first is *Arion (2) who is credited with the invention of the "tragic manner" and "the first performance of tragedy", and with introducing "satyrs speaking in verse". This shows that the word "tragedy" existed by Arion's time (*c.* 600 BC), but in his time it certainly did not refer to the same type of dramatic performances known later from Athens. Arion probably made the dithyramb a static performance with a literary form — which eventually helped to develop T. The second name is that of *Thespis who was responsible for the introduction of an actor and the inclusion of prologues and dialogues between the actor and the leader of the chorus. His plays included a narrative and elements of action, that is, the beginnings of drama, but even in the plays of *Phrynichus there was little action.

As T. developed the chorus no longer appeared as a group of satyrs and it was disassociated from the primitive, crude aspects of the performance. The part of the chorus diminished and that of the actors increased. To the first actor (*protagonistes*) *Aeschylus added a second

(*deuteragonistes*) and *Sophocles a third (*tritagonistes*). T. then consisted of a prologue and several scenes with a set of speeches or dialogues between the actors, with choral odes and dances at intervals. Plots became complex and later the chorals were mere interludes. Speeches and dialogues were in the Attic dialect, usually in the iambic metre; the choral odes in the Doric dialect and in various lyric metres.

T. was an Athenian achievement. The performance of T. was a religious ceremony and a public occasion. Tragic competitions were included in the festival of the Great *Dionysia by *Pisistratus in 534 BC. In the 5th century BC each of three poets produced four plays each (tetralogy): three tragedies (trilogy) and one satyr-play. In the *Lenaea two poets produced two tragedies each. Poets who wanted to take part in the competitions recited their plays to the *Archon Eponymous (or the Archon Basileus in the Lenaea) who was responsible for the selection of those who would produce the plays in the festivals. He gave each poet a *choregos* and a chorus. The poets themselves appeared as actors until Sophocles, whose voice was too weak for him to appear on the stage. At some time the state also undertook to supply the protagonist for the poet. The victorious poets received an ivy crown and probably money prizes as well. There were ten judges, each appointed by lot from one of the ten Athenian tribes. T.s were also performed in the rural festivals of Dionysus. While the chorus of the satyr-play consisted of satyrs, that of the T. was of human or other beings. Actors and chorus wore masks. Only men played and each actor played the several parts. Use was made of some technical equipment, notably the *mechane*, a sort of a crane which enabled the actors to fly (hence *deus ex machina*), and the *enkyklyma*, a rolling platform. T. was performed in the *Theatre.

Of all the tragedies, a thousand and more, which were composed by the Athenian tragedians, only 34 complete plays are extant: of *Aeschylus, *Sophocles and *Euripides. Almost all tragedies took their subjects from Greek mythology. The *Capture of Miletus* of Phrynichus and *Persae* of Aeschylus, and a few other plays are exceptional in taking historical themes. The myths, however, were reproduced with free inventions by the poets; indeed the myth was a setting for the performance of a human drama, in which the poets used to express religious, moral or political beliefs, or to insert references to contemporary events. Obviously each tragedian had his own characteristics. According to Aristotle, T. is an imitation of a serious, complete action of a certain magnitude which by pity and fear causes the purgation (*catharsis*) of these emotions. The characters of a T. are like us but nobler. It is in the nature of T. that the prosperous hero, who is neither perfect nor debased, brings about his own downfall through error; logical, causal events lead to the unexpected catastrophe. Not all tragedians and plays conformed to this view and only Sophocles achieved perfection according to these criteria. But tragic conflicts or tragic situations were dominant and the concepts of Greek T. became part of the Classical inheritance.

Tragedies were composed and produced after the 5th century BC and everywhere in the Greek world. But they never reached the level of the great tragic playwrights of the 5th century. T. appeared in Rome in the second part of the 3rd century BC under Greek influence and continued to be produced to the end of the Republic. But it was not as popular as in Greece and later it became a literary genre: to be read or recited and not for performance.

For Roman T. see: *Livius Andronicus, *Naevius, *Ennius, *Pacuvius, *Accius, *Seneca (2), *Fabula Praetexta, *Ludi Scaenici.

P. Pickard-Cambridge, *Dithyramb*²;
M. Bieber, *The History of the Greek and Roman Theatre*²,
1961;
H. D. F. Kitto, *Greek Tragedy*, 1965.
A. Lesky, *Greek Tragedy*, 1965.

TRAJAN (Marcus Ulpius Traianus) Roman emperor (AD 98–117). Native of Italica in Spain, born in AD 53, T. served in the army from his youth and advanced in his senatorial career. He saw service in Syria, Spain and Germany, and was consul in 91. He was governor of Upper Germany in AD 97 when *Nerva adopted him and made him his successor. On the latter's death (27 January AD 98), T. ascended to the throne, and was consul, but he only came to Rome in AD 99 after a tour of organization on the Rhine and Danube frontiers. As consul in AD 100, Pliny the Younger delivered the usual panegyric in his honour (T. was the other consul) in which he stressed the constitutional manner of his rule. Tacitus, writing about the same time, emphasized that under Nerva and T. *libertas* was restored. This line of policy, the cooperation with the Senate, remained in force throughout T.'s reign and became traditional under the Antonine emperors. It did not make the rule of T. and his successors less absolute in practice, only in appearance and theory.

T. was a warrior emperor. His first campaigns were conducted on the Danube frontier against *Decebalus and the Dacians. He invaded Dacia, defeated the enemy and captured the capital, Sarmizegethusa, and was content with imposing peace terms (101–2). But Decebalus renewed the hostilities in AD 105 and this time T. conquered Dacia and annexed it as a province of the Roman Empire (AD 105–6); Decebalus committed suicide. The second area of his campaigns was in the East. The Parthian aggression in *Armenia gave him his opportunity. He left Rome in AD 113, conquered Armenia in AD 114 and proceeded to occupy north Mesopotamia. The following year he conquered the whole of Mesopotamia with *Ctesiphon; he advanced as far as the mouth of the Tigris. But revolts broke out in Mesopotamia and among the Jews in Cyprus, Cyrene and Egypt. Though the Jews were suppressed and

T. restored his control in Mesopotamia, the costs were huge. In AD 117 he began his journey back to Rome but died in Cilicia.

T. was a hard-working emperor and devoted much of his time to supervising the administration of the provinces, Italy and Rome. He constantly corresponded with the governors and decided on various matters, as can be learnt from Pliny's correspondence with him (Book 10 of the *Letters*). He annexed the kingdom of the *Nabataeans (Arabia Petraea) and founded *Lambaesis and *Thamugadi in Numidia. Himself a Spaniard on his mother's side, he introduced many provincials to the Senate. He enlarged the civil service and manned it with Equites instead of freedmen. He distributed money to the populace in Rome on several occasions but generally he was economical and strict. He used the booty of the Dacian wars to carry out extensive building operations, including his *Forum, arches (those in Benevento and Ancona are still extant), and his famous column. On top of this column there was a statue of T. but it was replaced by one of St. Peter in 1587. T. built baths and a new aqueduct to Rome. He continued or introduced the system of the *Alimenta. His military achievements, cordial relations with the Senate, liberality and amiable character made him dear to all. First unofficially and from AD 114 officially he was styled Optimus Princeps – and so he was remembered to succeeding generations. His deification after his death was decreed by a grateful Senate.

B. W. Henderson, *Five Roman Emperors*, 1927;
F. A. Lepper, *Trajan's Parthian War*, 1948;
L. Rossi, *Trajan's Column and the Dacian Wars*, 1970.

TRALLES (modern Audin) City in *Caria situated in a fertile plain in the valley of the Maeander, first mentioned by Xenophon. It flourished in the Hellenistic period when its name was Seleucia. After the death of Attalus III (133 BC), it became part of the Roman province of Asia.

Magie, *Asia* (s.v.).

TRAPEZUS (modern Trebizond) Greek coastal colony in the southeast region of the Black Sea, founded by *Sinope or *Miletus, according to tradition in 756 BC. For centuries it was an insignificant city but it developed from the 1st century BC on. Under the Empire it prospered and was made a free city under Nero (AD 64). It was plundered by the Goths in AD 259.

Magie, *Asia* (s.v.).

TRASIMENE, LAKE The largest lake in Etruria, mainly known as the locality of the crushing defeat *Hannibal inflicted on the consul C. *Flaminius in 217 BC. The Roman army was advancing along the lake when it was attacked by the Punic army from ambush positions on three sides. Some of the Roman soldiers died in the lake.

TRIBONIANUS A learned jurist and an advocate, a high official and Justinian's right-hand man in legal matters. He was a member of the commission that prepared the first *Codex Justinianus*, and was then appointed (AD 530) to set up a commission and prepare the *Digesta. Later, he was responsible for the preparation of the *Institutiones* and the second edition of the Codex. It is evident that, in addition to his legal expertise, T. was a good administrator. Alterations in classical texts in the Digesta ("interpolations") are called *emblemata Triboniani*.

TRIBUNI MILITUM The senior officers of the legion, six to each legion, attached to the commander. The T. of the four regular legions (two to each consul) were elected by the *Comitia Tributa* and called *tribuni militum*

Head of Trajan

a populo; tribunes of other legions were appointed by the commander of the army and called *Rufuli*. Normally, they were young men at the beginning of their careers, of senatorial or equestrian origin, but there were exceptions. *Cato (1) Censorius served as a military tribune in the war against Antiochus III, after he had been consul. Under the Empire, a distinction was made between T. of senatorial families with the *clavus latus* (broad purple strip) and those with the *clavus angustus* (narrow purple strip) of equestrian origin. Later, a man advancing in an equestrian career served as a prefect of a cohort, T., and a prefect of an *ala*. Under the Empire, and especially from the 4th century, T. were commanders of various units.

J. Suolahti, *The Junior Officers of the Roman Army*, 1955; Jones, *Lat. Rom. Emp.*, 640ff.

TRIBUNI PLEBIS   The officials of the Plebs, traditionally instituted in the first *Secessio. Whatever their original number was, it was increased to ten by the mid-5th century BC and so it remained. The office was in a sense revolutionary because it was in defiance of the regular institutions of the Roman state that the *Plebeians organized their own institutions. The T. derived their powers from the fact that the Plebeians were ready to support them by force and took an oath to defend their *sacrosanctitas*, which meant that anyone who harmed them was regarded as "sacred", that is, to be slain. The original purpose of the office was that the T. would defend the Plebeians against arbitrary actions of the patrician magistrates; hence came the *ius auxilii ferendii*, that is, the right to veto any coercive procedure by magistrates (later including dictators) against Roman citizens. The citizen could appeal to one of the T., who would intervene or reject the appeal at his discretion. From this evolved their general right of *intercessio*, that is, the right to veto all acts of magistrates — electoral, legislative, consultative (with the Senate or the Comitia), even in the recruitment of the army. They could also veto the acts of their colleagues. The T. presided over the meetings of the *Concilium Plebis* and passed motions; hence, when by the law of *Hortensius (1) in 287 BC *Plebiscita* became laws, the T. had power to legislate and many of the laws under the Republic were tribunician laws. The T. also acquired coercive powers. By bringing motions against ex-magistrates in the Assembly, over which they presided and at which they conducted the interrogation, they also played the role of public prosecutors and had some jurisdictional power. In the 2nd century the T. became members of the Senate after completing their office and at some time they acquired the right to summon the Senate for meeting.

The T. lost their revolutionary character in the 3rd century BC after the Plebeians achieved all their aims and the formation of a patrician-plebeian aristocracy, the *Nobilitas. Usually they would discuss their bills in the Senate before submitting them to the Assembly, but not always. Tiberius and Gaius *Gracchus (2)(3) opened a new revolutionary activity and in the late Republic many of the Populares who opposed the senatorial aristocracy and the *Optimates acted as T.s. *Sulla curtailed their powers but by 70 BC all his limitations were removed. The fall of the Republic and the establishment of the Principate ended their free activity. But *Augustus received the tribunician power (*tribunicia potestas*) and under the Empire the conferment of this power marked the successor to the emperor.

Jolowicz, *Roman Law*[3] (s.v.).

TRIBUS ("tribe")   The original T.s of the Roman people were ethnical: Tities, Ramnes, Luceres. *Servius Tullius replaced them by local T.s, that is, administrative divisions of the people based on territorial divisions. At his time there were four T.s of the city of Rome — *tribus urbanae*. As the Roman state expanded, new territorial acquisitions were organized into new T.s but no new T.s were added after their number reached 35 (241 BC); instead all new additions were annexed to the existing T.s and it so happened that a tribe did not form a continuous territory but consisted of several units distributed over several regions of Italy.

Every citizen was registered in a T. and this system persisted to the Empire when more and more citizens were provincials. The censors were responsible for the registration and the T.s were the constituent units of the *Concilium Plebis* and the *Comitia Tributa* (tribal assembly) and were related to the *Comitia Centuriata*.

L. R. Taylor, *The Voting Districts of the Roman Republic*, 1960.

TRIBUTUM   Originally the direct tax levied from the Roman citizens by the decision of the Senate. It was levied only when the state did not have sufficient money to cover its expenditure, and it could be returned as was done in 187 BC. The normal tax (*tributum simplex*) amounted to 1/1000 of the property of the citizen as evaluated by the censors. After the Third Macedonian War, when Rome captured the treasury of *Perseus (2), the tax ceased to be levied — but it was not abolished. In the turbulent times after the murder of Caesar, the Triumvirs renewed the levy but this was not continued.

T. was also used to denote the direct taxes imposed in the provinces. This was either a land-tax (*tributum soli*) or a poll-tax (*tributum capitis*). Roman citizens in *coloniae* with the *Ius Italicum, citizens of "free cities" and those specifically exempted did not pay it. Under the Republic the tax was levied either by the provincials themselves or by the *Publicani, but under the Empire a direct collection was introduced.

TRIERARCHY   The Athenian institution for the maintenance of the navy by way of a *liturgy. Each year the strategoi appointed wealthy citizens as trierarchs. Each paid from his own pocket for the upkeep of one trireme whose captain he was. The expenditure was quite considerable but it enabled Athens to maintain the largest and best Greek navy. As costs grew the expenditure was shared by more than one man for a ship; first the burden was divided between two and from 357 BC several citizens contributed the expenses with the introduction of the system of the *Symmoria.

TRIPOLIS   Three Phoenician cities on the coast of north Africa: *Sabratha, Oea, and *Lepcis. They passed from the Carthaginian control to *Masinissa's in the 2nd century BC. Part of the province Africa Proconsularis since Augustus, the cities and their territory were made a separate province — Tripolitana — by Diocletian with Lepcis as the residence of the governor. Only Oea (Tripoli) remained after the Arab conquest in the 7th century.

D. E. L. Haynes, *The Antiquities of Tripolitania*, 1956.

TRIREME   The dominant type of ship in the Greek world, introduced in the 6th century BC and lasting throughout antiquity in the east Mediterranean; it was replaced by the *quinquereme in the Hellenistic period. A T. had 170 oarsmen and soldiers, marines and special crew members raised the total to some 200. How the oarsmen were arranged is disputed but it is now commonly accepted that each rower had an oar; perhaps there were three rowers to each bench. The ship was armed with a ram in the prow on either side of which there was an eye, originally painted but later often made of marble. Originally undecked, later the T. was sometimes fully or partially decked. It had a mast which was dismantled before battle. It could reach a speed of 7 or 8 knots per hour.

J. S. Morrison and R. T. Williams, *Greek Oared Ships*, 1968.

TRITONS In Greek mythology, half-man half-fish creatures, mer-men. Their origin may have been pre-Hellenic, and they never played a major role in mythology. In the *Aenid*, *Misenus was drowned by Triton for challenging him to a musical contest. In art the T. were usually depicted as blowing a conch-shell.

TRIUMPH A Roman general, the holder of Imperium and fighting under his own *Auspicium who defeated an enemy with 5,000 dead was entitled to a T. which had to be confirmed by the Senate. The Senate also allocated money to the general for the costs of the T., but he was also free to use the booty he captured in the war for this purpose. The T. was introduced to Rome from Etruria, and it is not clear to what extent it was influenced by Hellenistic ideas and practice. The T. was held in Rome and consisted of a procession to the temple of Jupiter on the Capitolium. The army, spoils, captives, magistrates and senators took part in the procession in addition to the general. He wore a gold and purple toga and had his face painted red; he stood on a four-horse chariot and a slave stood beside him holding a crown over his head. The procession started in the *Campus Martius and after a long circuit approached the Capitol from the Via Sacra past the Forum. When the general climbed the Capitol and offered the booty and sacrificed to the god, enemy prisoners were led aside and put to death. This was not always done but in this way *Vercingetorix ended his life. Under the Empire only the emperor could celebrate a T.

H. S. Versnel, *Triumphus*, 1970.

TRIUMVIRI Various three-member boards at Rome, like the *triumviri* (*tresviri*) *monetales* (*Coinage, Roman). The so-called First Triumvirate was a private pact between *Caesar, Crassus, and Pompey and had no constitutional basis. The Second Triumvirate of M. *Antonius (4), Octavian and *Lepidus (3) originated from a private pact between the three but then a law gave them special powers to rule the state in order to reorganize it.

Jolowicz, *Roman Law*[3] (s.v.).

TROAS (TROAD) The northwest region of Asia Minor, south of the Hellespont so called because it was believed to have been subject to Troy. Few Greek colonies (e.g. *Assos, Sigeum) were founded along the coasts which are separated from the interior by chains of mountains.

J. M. Cook, *The Troad*, 1973.

TROGUS, Pompeius Roman historian, of Gallic origin who lived in the period of Augustus. His main work was a forty-four book history called *Historiae Philippicae*. It covered the period from the Ancient Orient to the Roman conquests in Greece and the East as well as in Gaul and Spain. It did not deal with Rome and Italy. The work is only known from an abridgement made by Justinus, a later writer probably of the 3rd century AD.

TROILUS Son of the Trojan King Priam who in post-Homeric versions was ambushed and killed by Achilles; his sister *Polyxena succeeded in escaping. T.'s love for Cressida (i.e., Chryseis, the daughter of the priest of Apollo who was captured by Agamemnon) is a Medieval inven-

tion. His death was a favourite motif of Greek artists.

TROPHONIUS Greek oracular god whose sanctuary was at Lebadeia (modern Livadia) in Boeotia; the site has been identified. The oracle was very famous and many came to consult the god. The manner of the consultation was uncommon. After elaborate initiation rites, the worshipper was thrown down, in an ingenious way, into an underground construction. There he underwent a unique experience with voices and revelations after which it took him some time to return to his normal behaviour. Pausanias devoted a long account to its description (Book 9).

TROY (modern Hissarlik) Until 1870 Troy was a city which belonged to the world of Greek mythology, famous for the war the Greeks made against it, as was related by *Homer in the *Iliad*. But Heinrich Schliemann, a successful merchant, amateur archaeologist and great believer in Homer, decided to find and unearth it. An examination of the topographical details in Homer convinced him that the hill of the Hissarlik, a few km from the straits of the Dardanelles was the site of Troy (or Ilium as the city was also called). He began his excavations in 1870 and continued them during the following twenty years (with intervals to excavate in *Mycenae and *Tiryns). Schliemann indeed found what he was looking for.

The excavations of Schliemann and subsequent archaeologists have shown that the mound consisted of the ruins of several cities which were piled up in the course of many centuries. Ten main layers with subdivisions have been recognized, the earliest dating from the early 3rd millenium BC. T. was a strong, fortified site with imposing walls, citadels and towers. The second layer from the bottom was very prosperous and yielded rich jewellery made of gold and bronze. The rich treasures induced Schliemann to identify that layer with the Homeric T., but in fact it dates from about 2300–2200 BC and it was destroyed by fire. Usually it is T. VIIa that is identified with the Homeric T. which was destroyed by Agamemnon and the Greeks. However, there are chronological difficulties. According to the chronology of Greek tradition, T. was destroyed in 1184 BC, which date is improbable in view of the destruction of the *Mycenaean civilization by that time. But T. VIIa dates from the mid-13th century BC and at that time the Mycenaean Greeks had the resources and organization to conduct the great war.

In historic times T. was occupied by Greeks and was called Ilium. When Alexander the Great landed in Asia Minor he went to Ilium and made a sacrifice at the tombs of Achilles and Ajax.

H. Schliemann, *Troy and its Remains*, 1876; C. W. Blegen, *Troy and Trojans*, 1963.

TULLUS HOSTILIUS The third king of Rome (673–642 BC), traditionally a warlike figure. His main exploit was the destruction of *Alba Longa whose population he transferred to Rome. He is also credited with the building of the Senate-house (the Curia Hostilia), and is famous for the barbaric punishment he inflicted on *Mettius Fufetius. There is reason to regard him as a historical figure, though his military achievements are generally mythological inventions.

Ogilvie, *Livy*, 105ff.

TURBO, Quintus Marcus General and high official under Trajan and Hadrian. Native of Dalmatia, he advanced in military service from the lower ranks. After commanding the navy in Misenum, he was appointed by Trajan to sup-

press the furious revolt of the *Jews who had been rav-
aging Cyrene and Egypt from AD 115. After much bloodshed he completed his mission and was given similar task
in Mauretania. Under Hadrian he was given first command
in Pannonia and Dacia and by 126 BC was appointed
praetorian prefect. This was his last office and it is not
known that Hadrian dismissed him.

TUSCULUM Old city of Latium, situated about 25 km
southeast of Rome on a high hill above modern Frascati.
T. was one of the more important Latin cities that opposed Rome after the fall of the monarchy and led the
Latin League in the Battle of Lake Regillus (496 BC). But
with other Latin cities it became allied with Rome in the
Foedus Cassianum (*Cassius (1)), and took part in the
wars against the Aequi and the Volsci. According to Roman tradition, T. received Roman citizenship in 381 BC,
and by the next generation T. won the consulate in
Rome; notably the family of the *Fulvii. Another Tusculan who came to be a leading Roman statesman was
*Cato (1) Censorius. By the early 1st century BC, T. be-
came an attractive place for Roman aristocrats to own
villas. The estate of *Lucullus extended over several
square km, that of *Scaurus (2) was worth 30 million
sesterces. Cicero was fond of his Tusculan villa and one of
the works he composed here he called *Tusculan Talks*.

Alfödi, *Early Rome* (s.v.).
G. McCracken, *A Short History of Ancient Tusculum*,
1939.

TWELVE TABLES *See* **DECEMVIRI**

TYCHE The term, T., was used by Greek writers, painters,
historians, philosophers and others with various meanings:
chance, luck, success, fortune, lot, either as a separate
force governing each individual and city or a general
power. Essentially, and ethymologically, it was what happened to man. It was used either as an idea or came to be
personified as goddess. Sometimes it was independent or
even above gods, occasionally it was subordinate to gods.
A cult for T. was established in Thebes and Athens in the
4th century and *Praxiteles made a statue of T. A statue
of the personal T. of *Antioch was made by Eutychides in
the 3rd century BC, and later many cities had cults, each
of its own T. The usual attribute of T. was the rudder.
Decrees of city-states from the 4th century BC on opened
with the phrase *agathe tyche* ("with good luck").

TYDEUS Greek mythological hero, son of *Oeneus, husband of Deiphyle and son-in-law of *Adrastus. His son was
*Diomedes. He is mentioned as early as Homer. Adrastus
undertook to restore Polynices and T. each to his respective kingdom but began with the latter, hence T. took
part in the war of the *Seven against Thebes. A terrible
warrior, he killed forty-nine of the fifty Thebans who
ambushed him when he came to submit Polynices' demands (Homer, *Il.* 4.38ff.). In the attack on Thebes he
was fatally wounded by the Theban hero, Melanippus, but
succeeded in killing his opponent. At his request, the head
of the Theban was brought to him and he split it open
and ate the brains, an act which deterred Athena from
giving him an elixir which would have given him immortality. This scene and his killing of *Ismene are shown
in Attic vase-paintings.

TYNDAREUS Greek mythological hero, king of Lacedaemon, husband of *Leda who bore to him – or to Zeus
– the *Dioscuri, *Helen and *Clytemnestra. In one version of the myth it was *Heracles who gave him Lacedaemon after killing the former king. Many suitors came
to ask for his daughter *Helen and on *Odysseus' advice

he pledged them all to take an oath to support the man he
would choose for her. He chose *Menelaus who succeeded
him; because of the oath the Greek leaders were obliged
to follow Menelaus in the Trojan War to win back Helen.

TYPHON Mythological monster, offspring of *Gaea and
Tartarus (Hesiod, *Theog.* 820f.), with a hundred heads, a
hundred feet and a hundred hands, sometimes said to be
one of the *Gigantes. In some versions, T. was the father of
the *Hydra, the *Chimera and *Cerberus by Echidna. He
fought Zeus and seriously wounded him. But the latter was
helped by Hermes, and overcame T. with his thunderbolts.
Zeus had T. buried under Mount Aetna from which he tried
occasionally to get out and caused the volcanic eruptions.

TYRE Old Phoenician city, first mentioned in Egyptian
documents from the 2nd millenium BC; originally situated
on the coast, it then expanded to an island 700 m opposite
it. T. founded colonies along the Mediterranean coasts, the
most important of them was Carthage. The old commercial
and cultural relations of Greece with T. are reflected in the
legends about *Cadmus. Under the Persian empire it often
supplied the Persians with the main navy for the wars
against the Greeks and was often in conflict with the Greeks
of *Cyprus. Alexander the Great destroyed it after a long
siege in 332 BC (it had once withstood a 13-year siege by
Nebuchadnezzar). However, it was refounded and prospered. It was under Ptolemaic control in the 3rd century
BC, passed to *Antiochus III in 200 BC, and gained its
independence in 126 BC. Later it was subject to the Roman
governor of Syria and was given the status of *colonia* with
the *Ius Italicum by Septimius Severus.

Jones, *Cities*[2] (s.v.).

TYRTAEUS Greek elegist of the 7th century BC who
seems to have been a Spartan though there is no direct
evidence. He was a commander in the Second Messenian
War and in his poems wrote about it. Only fragments of
several poems survive and include exhortations to the
Spartans in the war and part of a poem on the Spartan
constitution. T.'s poems are those of a devoted patriot
who sings the praises of those who are courageous enough
to fight and die for their country. His poems were used as
marching songs by the Spartans. They are valuable evidence on Archaic Sparta.

Diehl, *An. Lyr. Gr.* 1;
C. M. Bowra, *E. Gr. El.,* 1938, 397ff.

The goddess Tyche with signs of the Zodiac

U

ULPIANUS, Domitius Prominent Roman jurist and high official, active in the first quarter of the 3rd century AD. He was assistant of the praetorian prefect and the great jurist, *Papinian, and rose to power under Alexander Severus. He was praetorian prefect but in 223 was killed by the praetorians. U. was a prolific writer. He wrote a comprehensive commentary (81 books) on the Edict of the praetor and a short one on the Edict of the curule aediles. He dealt with various magistracies, laws and institutions of the private law in separate monographs. He wrote a systematical account of the private law in his *Ad Sabinum*. U. was especially skilful in summing up and expounding the works and views of former jurists, and the compilers of the *Digesta of Justinian found him very useful; almost a third of that work consists of excerpts of his work, far more than any other jurist. The extant *Epitome Ulpiani* is a later abridgement of a compilation based on the works of several jurists including U.
F. Schulz, *Roman Legal Science*, 1946.

UMBRIANS Ancient people of Italy who lived east of the middle- and upper-Tiber and extended to the Adriatic coast; at one time they also occupied part of Etruria. The relation of the archaeological evidence in this area to the ancient literary evidence is confused and disputed. The Umbrian language, a dialect related to the Oscan, is known mainly from the Iguvine Tables. These are nine bronze tablets (two have been lost) which were found in 1444 at Gubbio and contain ritual records and directions.

Umbria was subdued by Rome in the course of the 4th and 3rd centuries BC and received Roman citizenship in 90 BC.
J. W. Poultney, *The Bronze Tables of Iguvium*, 1959;
W. V. Harris, *Rome in Etruria and Umbria*, 1971.

URANUS ("Sky") In tales about the creation of the world, literary and philosophical rather than the mythological, U. was the son and husband of *Gaea (Earth). He was father of the *Cyclopes whom he cast to Tartarus and of the *Titans. The latter rebelled against him and their leader *Kronos castrated him.

UTICA (modern Utique) The oldest Phoenician city in North Africa according to tradition (1101 BC), though the earliest archaeological finds are from the late 8th century BC. In ancient times it was situated on the coast, at the mouth of river Bagradas. It came under the control of Carthage but was always a flourishing city. *Scipio (2) Africanus failed to capture it in 204 BC. In the Third Punic War U. cooperated with Rome and as a reward received part of the territory of Carthage. It then became the residence of the Roman governor of the province, Africa. In the Civil War in 49 BC it was a centre of resistance to Caesar and he imposed a heavy fine on it after its capitulation. *Cato (2) was its governor and committed suicide there after *Thapsus (46); hence his surname Uticensis. It became a *municipium* under Augustus and a colony under Hadrian.
A. Lézine, *Carthage, Utique*, 1968.

The seven-branched candlestick of the Jerusalem Temple. A relief from the Arch of Titus. The treasures of the Temple were carried off by the Vandals when they captured Rome in AD 455

V

VALENS (1), Fabius A native of Anagnia, of Equestrian origin, V. commanded a legion in Lower Germany in AD 69 and took a leading role in making *Vitellius emperor. He led one column of the Vitellian army to Italy and with *Caecina (2) won the decisive battle of Bedriacum against Otho. He was made consul but later, after the defeat of the Vitellian army at Cremona by Antonius Primus, fled to Gaul where he was executed.

VALENS (2) Emperor of the Eastern Roman Empire (AD 364–78), so appointed by his brother Valentian I. V. is mainly known for the crushing defeat which the Visigoths inflicted on him at the Battle of Adrianopole (9 August 378). He himself was killed in the battle and henceforth the Visigoths remained within the frontiers of the Empire.

VALENTIAN (1) I Roman emperor, ascended to the throne after the death of *Jovian (AD 364). V. devoted himself to the defence of the empire in western Europe and therefore appointed his brother *Valens (2) as emperor of the East. He appointed *Ausonius as tutor for his son Gratian and made the latter emperor in 367. He was successful in his wars against the Germans and was about to sign a peace treaty with the *Quadi when he died (AD 375).

VALENTIAN (2) II Son of *Valentian I, ascended to the throne after the death of his father (AD 375). He was given Italy and Africa by his brother Gratian but lost Italy to the usurper Magnus Maximus (383). After the victory of Theodosius I over the latter (387) he regained his rule but died in 392.

VALENTIAN (3) III Born in AD 419, Roman emperor of the West (AD 425–55), son of *Galla Placidia. The empire was in fact ruled by his mother and later by *Aetius. He is mainly known for the enactment which made the bishop of Rome supreme over other Christian priests. For his killing of Aetius he was killed by the latter's men in 455.

VALERIANUS, Publius Licinius Roman emperor with his son *Gallienus in AD 253. Attacked on all sides, the empire was in a desperate situation. V. left his son to organize the defence of the West and went to the East to fight the Persians. But he was defeated and captured by *Sapor I and never came back. It was only thanks to *Odaenathus of Palmyra that the Persians were repelled.

VALERIUS (1) POPLICOLA, Publius Consul in the first year of the Republic who is credited with several measures and achievements all highly suspect as later inventions. They included the first law of *Provocatio*; the introduction of the quaestorship, addition of senators, as well as military achievements.
Ogilvie, *Livy*, 250ff.

VALERIUS (2) POTITUS, Lucius Consul in 449 BC with M. Horatius Barbatus. The first consuls after the *Decemvirs, they traditionally introduced several laws: to give the force of law to the decisions of the Plebs (*plebiscita*); to confirm the right of *Provocatio*; to confirm the sacrosanctity of the tribunes. All are suspect as unhistorical.
Ogilvie, *Livy*, 497ff.

VALERIUS (3) CORVUS, Marcus Leading Roman statesman and general in the 4th century BC; six times consul (348, 346, 343, 335, 300, 299 — only *Marius surpassed this record) and twice dictator (342, 301). He acquired his surname because a raven (*corvus*) helped him to overcome a Gallic warrior in a duel. He won victories over almost all enemies of Rome. He was also responsible for the law (300 BC) that instituted the right of *Provocatio*.

VALERIUS (4) ANTIAS Roman historian of the 1st century BC whose *History* covered the whole history of Rome from early times to his own. V.'s work was largely fictional; he invented speeches, accounts of battles, debates and achievements. Himself of the Valerian clan, he attributed to members of that clan victories and gains and ascribed exaggerated losses to Rome's enemies. Despite his criticism of V., Livy often used him.
Ogilvie, *Livy*, 12ff.

VALERIUS (5) MAXIMUS Roman writer of the first half of the 1st century AD. The senator, Sextus Pompeius, was his patron and V. went with him to Asia in AD 27. His main work is the nine-book *Memorabilia*, a collection of various episodes, anecdotes and sayings intended to illustrate bad or good conduct. The books are divided into chapters with headings and under each are given the appropriate examples, first of Romans, then of other people, notably Greeks. The work is moralistic in tone and aim, the style is pompous and the presentation of the tales is marred by excessive rhetoric. V. uses various sources, but only occasionally gives information of real importance for the historian. And yet its anecdotal nature made it quite popular and there are even two abridgements of it.
Edition: E. Kempf (Teubner), 1888;
T. A. Dory (ed.), *Empire and Aftermath*, 1975, 1ff.

VALERIUS (6) FLACCUS, Gaius Roman poet, apparently of the upper class as he was a *Quindecemvir Sacris Faciundis*. He died shortly before his mention by Quintilian, about AD 90. He did not live to finish his epic the *Argonautica*. The work, in eight books, has survived and takes the story of the *Argonauts and Jason to the acquisition of the Golden Fleece and the flight of the Argonauts pursued by Absyrtus, Medea's brother. The poem is basically modelled on that of *Apollonius Rhodius, although there is some influence by Virgil and some original episodes. Thus Jason helps Aeëtes in his war against his brother, but Aeëtes breaks his promise to give him the Fleece and only then does Medea fall in love with Jason. In this treatment, Jason comes better than in that of Apollonius. V. apparently intended the complete work to consist of twelve books; he probably planned to take the Argonauts *via* the Danube, Rhine and Britain and in that case would have ample opportunity to exploit his descriptive power.

J. H. Mozley (Loeb), 1934.

VANDALS A German people who originally lived in south Scandinavia but migrated to eastern Europe and, in the 3rd century AD, launched attacks from across the Danube on the Roman provinces in the Balkan. In the 4th century they advanced westward and in 406 invaded Gaul together with the Alani and Suebi and caused havock wherever they passed. Thereafter they occupied Spain. But the expansion to Spain of the Visigoths, who exterminated part of the V., induced them to cross to Africa with the Alani under *Gaiseric in 429. They established a strong kingdom in North Africa with Carthage as capital. In 455 they sacked Rome for two weeks. Their mastery of the sea enabled them to carry out plundering inroads. Their kingdom was destroyed by Justinian's general, Belisarius, in AD 533—4. Vandalism became proverbial for destruction of works of art.

C. Courtois, *Les Vandales et L'Afrique*, 1955.

VARRO (1), Gaius Terentius Roman statesman and general, probably of a non-senatorial but rich family, active in the Second Punic War. As consul in 216 BC, he commanded, with his colleague, the Roman army at the Battle of *Cannae which he survived. His *Imperium was prolonged by the Senate in 215—213 when he operated in Picenum, and he was again given command in 208—207 when *Hasdrubal (2) arrived in Italy. V. evidently retained his influence after Cannae which was fought against the strategy of *Fabius (3) Cunctator. This probably caused his denigration by *Fabius (4) Pictor, on whom extant accounts seem to have been based.

Scullard, *Roman Politics*[2] (s.v.).

VARRO (2), Marcus Terentius Roman statesman and scholar, 116—27 BC. A native of Reate, he studied under the philologist, C. Aelius Stilo, at Rome and under the philosopher, *Antiochus of Ascalon, in the *Academy. He served as praetor at an unknown date and in politics he followed Pompey, under whom he served in several campaigns. He fought against Caesar in the Civil War in Spain but was pardoned; Caesar intended him to be Librarian of the first public library at Rome. V. was proscribed by the Second Triumvirate, escaped but lost some of his extensive property and his libraries were plundered. Thereafter he was able to resume his studies in which he engaged for the rest of his life.

V. was a prolific writer and the most prominent Roman scholar. At the age of 78 he had already written 490 books and the titles of over fifty of his works are known. Of this vast material only his *De Re Rustica*, "On Agriculture", in three books is extant complete. This work, written when V. was eighty years old, deals in a dialogue form with agriculture proper, livestock breeding on a grand scale and livestock breeding in a small estate. It is based on V.'s own experience as well on literary works, and is the only work of its kind of the time. Of his *De Lingua Latina*, "On the Latin Language", Books 5—10 are substantially preserved. The work dealt with etymology, declension and conjugation, and syntax. It contains many citations of older authors. Of V.'s other works only fragments are preserved and that not of all. That V.'s work have not survived is a great loss in several cases. His *Antiquitates Rerum Humanarum Divinarum*, "Antiquities", dealt in twenty five books with human affairs and in sixteen books with the religious institutions and gods of Roman religion. It was an encyclopaedic work on various aspects of Roman life and much that is in later authors was derived from it. The *Saturae Menippeae*, "Menippean Satires", were humoutous satires in prose mixed with verse and the extant fragments show a great variety of tones with a talent to compose vivid descriptions. His *Disciplinae* in nine books was an encyclopaedia of the liberal arts and the subjects treated in the first seven books were known in the Middle Ages as the *trivium* and *quadrium*. The *Imagines* contained 700 biographies of Greeks and Romans with their pictures. V. also wrote on rhetoric, philosophy, chronology (his date for the foundation of Rome was 753 BC), geography, music, medicine, etc. His erudite works had much influence on many subsequent generations.

W. D. Hooper and H. B. Ash, *On Agriculture* (Loeb), 1934; R. G. Kent, *On The Latin Language* (Loeb), 1938; J. Wight Duff, *Roman Satire*, 1937; B. Tilby, *Varro the Farmer*, 1973.

VARUS, Publius Quinctilius Roman administrator and general under Augustus. A scion of old patrician family, V. was favoured by the Augustus, governed Africa, Syria (when he suppressed Judaea) and is mainly known for his disaster in Germany in AD 9. His three-legion army was ambushed and annihilated, and he committed suicide. This induced Augustus, who thereafter used to lament the loss of the army, to abandon the expansion to the Elbe. Thereafter, no new legions were raised to replace those lost.

VATINIUS, Publius Roman politician. As tribune in 59 BC, he passed the laws that gave Caesar the governorship of Illyricum and Cisalpine Gaul for which he was handsomely recompensed. He also passed the bill to endorse the administrative arrangements of Pompey in the East. Thereafter he followed Caesar and served under him in Gaul. He was praetor in 55 and fought with Caesar in the Civil War winning a victory in 47; in that year he became consul. Later (42) the Triumvirs let him have a triumph. In 56 Cicero delivered a slanderous speech against him but by 45 BC they had become reconciled.

L. G. Pocock, *A Commentary on Cicero In Vatinium*, 1926; Syme, *Rom. Rev.* (s.v.).

VECTIGAL (pl. vectigalia) A term used to denote the revenues of the state both from its property and by indirect taxes. After the levying of the *Tributum was discontinued in Italy, the Italians paid only V. which, under the Republic, consisted of *Portorium and a tax of 5% of the value of slaves set free. Under the Empire several more indirect taxes were introduced including those for the maintenance of the *Aerarium Militare and a tax of 4%

on sales of slaves. Under the Republic and early Empire V. were collected by the *Publicani; later they were gradually replaced by *Procuratores.

VEGETIUS RENATUS, Flavius The author of a military handbook, written after AD 383 and before 450. Book 1, addressed to the reigning emperor, is on recruiting and training; Book 2 is on the organization of the legion; Book 3 is on tactics and logistics; and Book 4 is on siege operations and naval warfare. V. is not a soldier and his work is mainly based on reading of former works. It is the only Latin work of its kind to have survived.

Text: C. Lang (Teubner), 1885.

VEII Etruscan city, developed on a Villanovan site, about 15 km north of Rome. Under the rule of the Etruscan kings of Rome, good relations were maintained with V. and King Tarquinius commissioned the artist, Vulca of V., to make the statues for the Capitoline temple. Only Roman aggression in the course of the 5th century brought V. in conflict with it. After a long siege, traditionally of ten years, V. was destroyed by *Camillus in 396 BC. Its territory became *Ager Publicus and was later distributed to Roman citizens. The archaeological excavations on the site lend support to the Roman tradition that tunneling was used to capture the city.

Scullard, *Etruscan Cities*, 104ff.

VELLEIUS PATERCULUS Roman historian, soldier and senator, *c.* 19 BC–after AD 30. Of a well-to-do family from Campania, he served under Tiberius (as did his father and grandfather under Tiberius and his father) in Germany and Illyricum, was quaestor in AD 7 and praetor in 15. V. is the author of two-book *Roman History*, addressed to his friend M. Vinicius, the consul of AD 30. The first book covered the history of Greece and Rome to 146 BC. But the larger part of it is not extant including the period from the foundation of Rome to 168 BC. The second book takes the story to AD 30 and is more fully told. It is mainly of value for the period of Augustus and Tiberius for which in some cases V. is the only author, though he is clearly biased in favour of Tiberius. This, however, has to be taken into account against other prejudiced works, notably Tacitus'. V. included accounts of Roman colonization (1.14–15), Roman provinces, and literature, but in the main his work concentrates on individuals and in his character portrayal he is rather successful.

F. W. Shipley (Loeb), 1924;
T. A. Dorey (ed.), *Empire and Aftermath*, 1975, 267ff.

VENETI The inhabitants of the northeast part of the Po valley who occupied that region in the early 1st millenium BC. In Roman legend they were the Eneti of Paphlagonia who, led by the Trojan Antenor, settled in Venetia. This perhaps was invented to account for the good relations between the Romans and the V. Their main cities were *Patavium and Ateste. They succeeded in repelling the advance of the Etruscans and subsequently of the Gauls to their region, but later came under Roman control. The V. received the Roman citizenship in 49 BC.

J. Whatmough, *The Foundations of Roman Italy*, 1937.

VENTIDIUS, Publius Roman politician and general, with an extraordinary career. In his youth he was one of the Italian allies who marched in the triumph of *Pompeius Strabo (89 BC), and afterwards became wealthy as an army contractor. He followed Caesar and became a senator when the latter took control of the state in the Civil War. After Caesar's murder he became a supporter of Antony, brought him three legions after the battle of Mutina

and became *consul suffectus* of 43 BC. He gave lukewarm support to Antony's wife, *Fulvia, and brother in the Perusine War. He won his best achievements against the Parthians who invaded Asia Minor and Syria in 40. His victories were crushing and he drove them off from the occupied territory and received a triumph in 38 BC. In fact he was the first Roman to achieve such a success against Parthia.

VENUS Old Italian goddess, who was worshipped in many places and whose name meant "charm" or "beauty". Originally she was the deity (*numen*) associated with vegetables and ensured their fertility. How she has become identified with the Greek goddess Aphrodite is obscure; probably the meaning of her name was the cause of this identification and it was the Aphrodite of Mount *Eryx in Sicily, whose cult there came to be considered as a foundation of Aeneas, that was first called V. A temple for V. Erycina was erected on the Capitol in 217 BC and from then on the Latin V. acquired all the functions, legends, and attributes of Aphrodite. As a goddess who brings luck V. Aphrodite was the protective divinity of

Venus of Cyrene, supported by a dolphin. A statue from c. 50 BC

*Sulla who, though an excellent general, believed in luck as the power behind his achievements. Pompey built a temple to V. Victrix in his theatre in 55 BC. As the Julian clan claimed descent from Aeneas son of Aphrodite, the cult of V. Genetrix, "the one who begets", spread under the Julio-Claudian dynasty. This had begun under Caesar who built a temple to and instituted games for her in 46 BC. And V. Genetrix, the creator of all things, appears in the invocation at the beginning of *On the Nature* of *Lucretius.

VER SACRUM ("consecrated spring") This custom was mainly of the peoples of central Italy. Whenever the population outgrew the means of subsistence they consecrated to the gods all the children who would be born in the subsequent spring. When those children became twenty years of age they were sent to find out a place of living outside their territory and in this way the *Sabelli expanded to Campania and south Italy.

VERCINGETORIX King of the Gallic tribe of the Arverni and leader of the great Gallic revolt against Caesar in 52 BC. He realised that he could not face Caesar in a pitched battle and resorted mainly to guerrilla tactics attacking Caesar's lines of communications and taking positions in strong fortresses. But Caesar surrounded him at *Alesia and, after a long siege, V. surrendered. Caesar led him in his triumph in 46 BC and executed him afterwards. V. was the only leader who succeeded in uniting the Gauls for a national effort.

VERGINIA Heroine of a Roman legend associated with Appius *Claudius (1) the Decemvir. The latter came to be described in Roman tradition as a Greek tyrant and as such wanted to violate V. But her father Verginius, rather than let him satisfy his lust, killed her and exposed her body in public. This led to a rising of the people and ended the regime of the *Decemvirs.
Ogilvie, *Livy*, 576ff.

VERGINIUS RUFUS, Lucius Roman senator and general with a unique reputation for his behaviour in AD 68–9. He was consul (AD 63) and governor of Upper Germany (AD 67) under Nero and in 68 suppressed the revolt of *Vindex. His soldiers wanted to make him emperor but he declared his allegiance to *Galba (3). He became consul under Otho and again declined to become emperor after the latter's death. Many years later *Nerva made him serve with him as consul but he died (97). Tacitus delivered the panegyric for him. V. became proverbial for his lack of ambition and for his loyalty to the country.

VERONA Old city of Cisalpine Gaul occupied by the Gallic Cenomani in *c.* 400 BC. V. prospered under the Empire and became a *colonia*. There are impressive remains notably the well preserved ampitheatre. The poet *Catullus was a native of V.

VERRES, Gaius Roman senator, notorious for his avarice and his exploitation of whoever came under his power. His family was new in the Senate. As quaestor he used the circumstances of the Civil War of *Carbo and *Sulla to embezzle the public money at his disposal and joined Sulla at the right time to profit in the proscriptions. Thereafter he served under Dolabella, the governor of Cilicia, and robbed the provincials both in the province and on his way there and back. Responsible for civil cases as *praetor urbanus* in 74, he accepted bribes. He governed Sicily in 73–71 and plundered the provincials and even Roman businessmen. On his return in 70, the Sicilians brought a prosecution against him and Cicero took upon himself to represent them. V. had powerful patrons,

notably *Hortensius (2) and several of the Metellan family. He also tried to use a great deal of bribery and Hortensius sought to postpone the trial to 69 when he would be consul. But Cicero outtricked him by shortening the process and caused much agitation in his first speech. On the advice of Hortensius, V. went into exile to Massilia. The total sum, the prosecution stated, he had illegally acquired in Sicily was 40 million sesterces, and he succeeded in retaining much of it. In 43 he was proscribed and killed by the Triumvirs for his wealth.
T. P. Wiseman, *New Men in the Roman Senate*, 1971 (s.v.).

VERULAMIUM Capital of the powerful British Belgic tribe of the Catuvellauni, near St. Albans (Herts.). After the conquest of Britain by the Emperor Claudius, it probably received a status of a *municipium. V. was sacked in the rebellion of Boudicca in AD 60, and at that time had a population of about 15,000; after some time it was rebuilt and was strongly fortified under Hadrian. The city survived to the late 5th century AD. Remains of private and public buildings have been excavated including a theatre, a forum and temples. St. Albans was martyred here probably in the early 3rd century AD.
R. E. M. and T. V. Wheeler, *Verulamium*, 1936; Frere, *Britannia* (s.v.).

VERUS, Lucius V.'s father L. Aelius was Hadrian's first choice as his heir, but when he died Hadrian induced *Antoninus Pius to adopt Marcus *Aurelius and V. as his heirs. V. was born in AD 130 and first became consul in 154. On M. Aurelius' accession to the throne he made V. co-emperor with the title Augustus – probably the first time that this title was shared by two emperors. V. operated in the East against the Parthians (163–6) and was with Aurelius in the campaign against the Germans in 168. He had married his colleague's daughter in 164 and died in 169.

VESPASIAN (Titus Flavius Vespasianus) Roman emperor (AD 69–79). Native of Reate in Sabinum, of an equestrian family, born in AD 9. He served in the army, became a senator and, after his praetorship (40), was a legion's commander under Claudius in the invasion of Britain. He was *consul suffectus* in 51 and later was governor of Africa. It is said that he offended Nero by falling asleep while the emperor was singing in the tour in Greece (66). However, he was regarded as trustworthy enough to be given a large army to fight against the revolt of the Jews in *Judaea. He was in Judaea when Nero fell, and transferred his allegiance to Galba and then to Otho, but not to Vitellius. He was supported by *Mucianus, the governor of Syria, and *Tiberius (2) Julius Alexander, the prefect of Egypt. The latter was the first to swear allegiance, with his two legions, to V. on 1 July 69, which date became the official beginning of V.'s reign. The war against Vitellius was decided by Antonius Primus who dashed to Italy with the Danubian army and won the battle at Bedriacum. Primus occupied Rome and killed Vitellius (20 December 69) but could not come in time to save V.'s brother.

V. entered Rome only late in 70. The Senate had recognized him as emperor – the first not to belong to an aristocratic family. A law was passed which specifically and at one time gave him all powers which former emperors had accumulated; it is known only partly from an inscription. A "new man", to stress his position V. served often as consul and so did his sons. He carried out a thorough financial reorganization which included increased taxation, the sale of imperial properties and rigid economy where this could be imposed with profit. He was thus able to make up the deficit and to accumulate a surplus. He then undertook extensive public building including his Forum, the Temple of Peace, the restoration of the Capitoline temple, burnt down in 69, and the *Colosseum (completed by Titus). V. reorganized the army. The rebellions in Judaea and Gaul were subdued, the frontier was extended to north England in Britain but there was no increase in the number of legions. In the provinces V. extended the Roman citizenship and the Latin rights; all the Spanish communities received the latter. He also took the censorship to introduce many new members from new Italian and provincial families to the Senate.

V. was a man of simple manners and had a coarse humour. When his son, Titus, protested against a certain tax he gave him a coin to show that it had no smell. When he felt he was dying he said, "I am going to become a god". Tacitus, who believes that power corrupts, says that of all emperors he was the only one to change for the better on his accession to the throne. Though there was some senatorial opposition to his dynastic policy, on the whole he was on good terms with the aristocracy and there were few executions. He died on 23 June 79, was deified and succeeded by *Titus.

Suetonius, *Vespasian*.

VESTA, VESTAL VIRGINS V., as a goddess of the hearth (like the Greek *Hestia), belonged to the religion of the family, an older substratum in Roman religion that preceded the state cult. But, with the rise of the king and the state, the royal hearth acquired importance for the whole of the community. A circular building was built for her in the Forum near the Regia where an eternal fire was kept. This was said to have been taken from Troy and the temple was ascribed to *Numa. The priestesses of V. were the *Vestales*, the Vestal Virgins. Except for old times, their number was six, they were chosen by the *Pontifex Maximus and served for thirty years. Thereafter they were

allowed to marry. The Vestals were highly honoured, were free from the tutelage of their parents, but subject to strict discipline under the control of the Pontifex Maximus. They were scourged if the sacred fire died (and had to light it by friction of wood), and buried alive if they broke their obligation to remain virgins. In 113 BC two *Vestales* were so punished and this occurred again under Domitian. The Vestals lived in the Atrium Vestae near the Forum. They were not allowed to use water from mains and had near their building the fountain of the nymph Juturna, for their water. There are some remains of the temple, of their building and of statues of Vestals.

VIA AEMILIA Important road which was constructed by M. Aemilius *Lepidus (1) and connected *Ariminum with Placentia (modern Piacenzza). Various other roads branched out from it and it was an important means for the establishment of Roman rule in Cisalpine Gaul. It gave its name to the region known as the Emilia.

VIA APPIA The road built by Appius *Claudius (2) Caecus, as censor in 312 BC, from Rome to Capua, a distance of 132 miles. In the 3rd century BC it was extended to Brundisium on the Adriatic coast *via* Beneventum (Benevento) and Tarentum. It thus became the main line of communication between Rome and south Italy and the East. Major improvements were made on several occasions, and thus Trajan cut the coastal rock at *Tarracina, a work which was commemorated by an inscription.

VIA EGNATIA Roman road from the Adriatic coast which started at Dyrrhachium (with a branch from Apollonia) and led across Macedonia to *Thessalonica and thence along the Thracian coast to Byzantium. With the *Via Appia from Rome to Brundisium it formed the main line of land communications with the East.

VIA FLAMINIA The main road from Rome to north Italy, constructed by C. *Flaminius as censor in 220 BC. It extended over 300 km from Rome to Ariminum on the Adriatic coast. Much care was taken to maintain the road in good condition. The road had several branches.

VIA LATINA Ancient road which connected Rome with Campania in an inland route passing on the northern outskirts of the Alban Hills, through the Trerus valley, near Fregellae, to Venafrum and thence turning south to join the *Via Appia.

VIA SACRA ("Sacred Road") Famous street of Rome which connected the Forum with the Velia, starting near the temple of Vesta and the *Regia and passing the house of the Vestals. It was through this road that the Roman imperator approached the Forum in the triumphal procession.

VICOMAGISTRI The *vici* were the smallest administrative subdivisions of the city and the V. were their chairmen and responsible for the maintenance of the local cults in them. Augustus reorganized the system. There were 265 *vici* in Rome organized in 14 regions. There were then four *magistri* to each *vicus* and the local cult included that of the *Genius of the emperor.

VICTORIA The Roman goddess of victory, counterpart of *Nike, mainly worshipped in the army. She had a temple on the slope of the Palatine dating from 294 BC. Augustus dedicated an altar to V. in the Senate in 29 BC. This became the centre of the last struggle of the pagans against the Christians when *Gratian ordered its removal. *Symmachus appealed for its restoration, but, except for a short restoration, it disappeared from the Senate.

VIGILES These were both policemen and firemen, 7,000 in number and organized in seven cohorts, each one to

The temple of Vesta at the Forum Boarium

Nike of Samothrace, early 2nd century BC

pottery. There is a great deal of controversy as to their origins, chronology, and their relation to the historical peoples of Italy. In one view they had immigrated to Italy from central Europe across the Alps. Others regard their culture as Italian in origin, with elements from the *Terramara and Appenine cultures. The V. appeared probably in the tenth century BC. Later they came under Greek and Oriental influence. A most remarkable aspect is that Etruscan cities developed on Villanovan sites. This is relevant to the problem of whether the *Etruscans were indigenous or came from abroad. But this is still a moot point.

Scullard, *Etruscan Cities*;
H. Hencken, *Tarquinia, Villanovans and Early Etruscans*, 1968.

Fourth-century mosaic pavement of Roman villa at Beth-gubrin in Judaea

two of the 14 regions of Rome. They were all freedmen. The force was instituted by Augustus in AD 6 and he appointed a prefect of the V. (*Praefectus Vigilum*) to command it. He was of the equestrian class and only the prefect of the Annona and the praetorian prefect were superior to him in rank. Until the establishment of the V. Rome had no police force and fire-fighting was left to the initiative of private citizens.

P. K. Baillie Reynolds, *The Vigiles of Imperial Rome*, 1927.

VILLA The V. was the building, or group of buildings, of an estate. It consisted of the *villa urbana*, the dwelling-building, and the *villa rustica*, the workshops, stables and other buildings associated with the productive part of the farm. The term V. was also used to denote the entire estate, especially a small farm where poultry, fishes, bees etc. were raised. V. was also used to denote a luxurious house in the city or in the country.

VILLANOVANS An Iron Age people whose cemeteries have been excavated in two main areas: Bologna-Ravenna ("northern Villanovans") and Etruria ("southern Villanovans"). The modern name is after a town near Bologna where the first cemetery, with the typical material finds of the Villanovan culture, was found in 1853. A main characteristic of the V. is the conical urns. They lived on hunting, agriculture and bred livestock, and developed fine

Remains of the Attrium Vestae at the Forum Romanum

Head of Constantine the Great

VINDEX, Gaius Iulius Governor of Gallia Lugdunensis, V. revolted against Nero in AD 68. He was of Aquitanian origin and secured widespread support from the Gauls. However, he was routed and killed by *Verginius Rufus.

VINDOBONA (modern Vienna) City on the Danube in Upper Pannonia with a Roman garrison. Under Trajan it became a legionary camp, and it only acquired the status of a *municipium* in the 3rd century AD. It was lost to the Barbarians in the early 5th century AD. The Emperor Marcus Aurelius died at V.

A. Mócsy, *Pannonia and Upper Moesia*, 1974 (s.v.).

VIRGIL (Publius Vergilius Maro) The greatest Roman poet, 70–19 BC, born near Mantua in Cisalpine Gaul, probably of a family of means. He was given a good education; he first studied in Cremona, then went to Mediolanum and later to Rome to study rhetoric. But though he even appeared in an actual case, he realized that oratory was not his field and he abandoned it for philosophy and poetry. He does not seem to have taken active part in the Civil War of Caesar and Pompey but when Octavian confiscated estates to distribute land to soldiers in Italy V.'s paternal property was seized too. It seems that it was later returned to him. Be that as it may, V. won powerful friends including *Pollio and Cornelius *Gallus. He also became friendly with Horace and then established ties with *Maecenas and Octavian. His situation improved and he received estates from his patrons. His poetry, in which he celebrated the blessings of Octavian's regime, won him fame. In 19 BC he went on a tour to Greece and fell ill. He was taken to Brundisium where he died on 20 September. His body was buried near Naples and the epitaph, allegedly composed by V. on his deathbed, says: "Mantua begot me, Calabria took my life, and now Naples holds me; I sang of flocks, farms and heroes".

V.'s earliest poems are the *Bucolics* ("Pastoral Poems") also called *Eclogues* ("Select Poems"). With these poems V. made his name and won the support and friendship of Maecenas. They were published by 39 BC. They are composed after the model of Theocritus. Poems 1 and 9 refer to the events of the periods and the appropriation of lands. Tityrus, apparently V. himself, is thankful for the land that has been secured for him by *deus*, which refers to Octavian. But, despite the feelings of gratitude, the hard times of the period are manifest. Poem 4, known as the "Messianic Eclogue", is the most famous of the collection. Here V. tells of the future birth of a miraculous child who will introduce a period of peace and the return of the Golden Age. To the Christians in the Middle Ages this seemed to be a prophecy concerning the birth of Christ. What V. had in mind was probably the future birth of the son of Antony and Octavia, Octavian's sister. Poem 6 tells of two shepherds who catch a silenus asleep. When he awakes, he sings to them about the creation of the world and then they let him go free. Poem 10 is written to V.'s friend and poet Cornelius Gallus. In Poem 5, there is a reference to the death and deification of Caesar. Most of the poems are a mixture of Arcadian and Sicilian scenery, with Italian elements. Shepherds' life is depicted, with their loves and hates. Generally, there is an air of idealization but there is some Roman realism. The poems are noted for their elegance, charm and sweetness.

The next poems were the four books of the *Georgica*. V. was invited to write them by Maecenas and they can be regarded as part of the official propaganda of Octavian who sought to revive old Italian virtues. The poems were published in 29 BC, and in fact they are didactic poetry on farming, the oldest work of this genre being the *Works and Days* of Hesiod; V., however, was also influenced by *Nicander. Book 1 of the collection treats crops with a description of signs of good and bad weather; Book 2 treats vines and olives; Book 3, livestock breeding; Book 4, bee-keeping. In writing this poetry, V. was influenced by Hesiod, Lucretius and *Aratus (1). The books have the air of an agricultural manual. They give a detailed account of the work of the farmer. It is hard work; but it is the work that produces men. V. inserts several digressions, mostly short, such as those in praise of country life. But there is one exception, the story of Aristaeus and Orpheus and Eurydice. This takes a substantial part of Book 4. Deep religious belief is revealed in the poems, with influence from Lucretius in the attitude to the great powers of Nature. But V. is not Epicurean and stresses divine providence. His interest in living creatures makes it a true poem about nature. He is pathetic, not sentimental in the description of a dying ox. Sensitive to the various appearances of life, he did not give a manual of farming but a pure poetical monument.

The most famous work of V. is the *Aeneid*, but he did not finish it. In 19 BC he intended to devote three years to completing it, after having worked on it the last ten years; and he asked that it should be burnt should he die before. However, Augustus intervened and instructed V.'s friends, the poets Varius and Tucca, to publish it.

The *Aeneid* is the story of the wanderings of Aeneas from Troy, after its sack by the Greeks, to Italy. It is also the epic of the Roman people with its future grandeur. The epic is in twelve books. Book 1, after the introduction in which it is related that the destiny of Aeneas is in Italy but he is pursued by Juno, describes the storm sent against Aeneas by the goddess. His ships are scattered and he is driven to the African coast. Here he is brought to Dido of Carthage who receives him with hospitality. She arranges a banquet for him in which she asks him to tell his story. In Book 2 Aeneas tells of the fall of Troy and his escape with his family but without his wife; her ghost had told him that his destiny would be to settle in Italy. He continues his story in Book 3 with his wanderings to Thrace, Delos, the Strophades, Epirus to Sicily. Book 4 describes the love of Dido and Aeneas; but Aeneas is instructed by Mercury, Jupiter's messenger, to continue his voyage to the destined land. As he sails away, Dido commits suicide. This part of the poem is perhaps the best, a tragedy within the epic. In Book 5 Aeneas arrives in Sicily and celebrates funeral games for his father on the anniversary of his death. Aeneas has been told by the seer Helenus and by the shade of his father that he should descend to the underworld. In Book 6 he consults the Sibyl of Cumae who forewarns him on his wars in Italy and instructs him to get the golden bough for the descent. This he succeeds in finding and the Sibyl leads him across the Styx to meet the spirit of his father. Anchises foretells the future of the Roman people, and that he is to lay the foundation for such a glorious future, including the achievements of Augustus.

The theme of the next six books is that of wars but V. contrives to reduce their description. In Book 7 Aeneas arrives at Latium and a war is stirred up between him and Turnus, who demands Lavinia, the daughter of King Latinus, for himself as wife; she, however, prefers Aeneas. In Book 8 he arrives in Rome where he is received by King Evander and his son Pallas. While he spends the night there, Vulcan, Venus' husband, prepares him a magnificent shield (clearly a counterpart of Achilles'), with scenes of the future history of Rome including Actium. Book 9 describes the attacks of Turnus on the Trojan camp in the absence of Aeneas. In Book 10 Aeneas arrives with Pallas at the camp and a fierce battle ensues. Pallas is killed by Turnus but Aeneas kills the mighty Etruscan tyrant, Mezentius. With a few intervals for burial of the dead and negotiations, the war continues in Book 11 with the Trojans victorious over Turnus and the Latins. In Book 12 an agreement is reached to decide the war by a duel between Aeneas and Turnus, but the latter's sister, the nymph Juturna, induces his people, the Rutuli, to resume fighting in truce time to save him from the duel. Aeneas is wounded but is healed with the help of Venus and kills Turnus in the duel.

V. exploited a vast literature for the composition of his *Aeneid*. He absorbed in his work numerous ideas, episodes, names, adventures and motifs from Greek and Roman literature. He made extensive use of the Homeric epics and of Apollonius Rhodius. To take only few notable examples: the descent of Aeneas to the underworld can be compared to that of Odysseus; the shield Aeneas is given is like that of Achilles; the funeral games for Pallas parallel those for Patroclus; not to mention the many phrases and especially the adaptation of similes. Dido, though a woman with her own characteristics, is largely based on the Medea of Apollonius Rhodios; V.'s Dido is, however, coloured by the contemporary figure of Cleopatra. The basic legend of his epic was Greek. But in addition he included — with great mastery — purely Roman traditions and institutions in his work and — what is more important — his epic is far more than the mere sum of its ingredients. The concept of the poem as a national epic, treating the role of Rome in the world as predestined by divine providence with Aeneas as a forerunner of Augustus, is entirely Virgilian. V. also has given an artful portrayal of human beings and their struggles in this world. Though incomplete, the *Aeneid* is noted for its masterly structure. This is not simply the division into the two parts: the six books considered as an *Odyssey* and the last as an *Iliad*; and not only the periodical climaxes in the even-numbered books and recessions in the odd-numbered books. The plot is so constructed and the various chapters of the story are so entwined that, though we know at the very start what the end will be, the dramatic development is maintained throughout the whole epic. The hero of the epic has been often criticized. By some standards he seems to be a weak personality, without strong feelings or character — particularly as revealed in his love for Dido. But Aeneas is above all a Roman hero. He is Pius; his sense of duty to his father, people and god, overrides all other considerations including his personal happiness. He is human in that he has doubts, sufferings and struggles, but as a true Roman he masters them in order to fulfil his destiny. He was never criticized on this score by ancient critics.

The *Aeneid* soon replaced the *Annales* of Ennius as the national Roman epic. V. was recognized as the greatest Latin poet and he became to the Romans what Homer was to the Greeks. His epic became the accepted textbook for schools. In the 1st century AD several poets were induced to compose epics under his influence but none approached his standards. And yet scholars found faults in his works; in particular his imitations of other poets were collected and considered as plagiarisms. "Vergiliomastix" ("the scorge of V.") became the name of such critics. But the critics disappeared and a cult of V., the greatest poet ever, grew under the Empire. Copies of his books were kept in temples and were consulted for fortune-telling (*sortes Vergilianae*) and this was bequeathed to Christian Europe. As the author of the Messianic Eclogue, he was the prophet of Christianity, and there developed legends about V. the magician. Chaucer admired him, Dante made him his guide in Hell and he exercised an influence on Milton and many others. Since the discovery of Homer in the late Middle Ages, V. somewhat lost his primary position but he has always remained at the core of the classical tradition in the Western culture. Texts and translations: A. Hirtzel (OCT), 1900; H. R. Fairclough (Loeb), 1919–1934; W. F. Jackson knight (*Aeneid*; Penguin Classics), 1956; E. V. Rein (*Bucolics*, Penguin Classics), 1949; B. Otis, *Virgil, A Study in Civilized Poetry*, 1963; M. C. J. Putnam, *The Poetry of the Aeneid*, 1965; U. Quinn, *Virgil's Aeneid*, 1968; L. P. Wilkinson, *The Georgics of Virgil*, 1969.

VITELLIUS (1), Lucius Roman senator and administrator, of an Equestrian family, began his career under Tiberius. He was governor of Syria in AD 35–7 and showed great skill and firmness in dealing with the Jews and the Parthians. He survived Caligula and became a close associate of the Emperor Claudius, though accused of adulation. He remained to govern Rome when Claudius went to participate in the invasion of Britain and was censor with him in 47. He probably died before Claudius.

VITELLIUS (2), Aulus Son of Vitellius (1), consul in 48 and later governor of Africa, lived AD 15–69. He was appointed commander of Lower Germany by Galba but his legates, *Caecina (2) Alienus and Fabius *Valens (1), induced the legions to proclaim him emperor (2 January 69). The western provinces supported him and his legates led the army to Italy; that *Otho had succeeded Galba did not make any difference to them. They defeated Otho and V. arrived in Rome in July 69. At that time *Vespasian became emperor in the East and won the allegiance of the Danubian army. Valens was ill, Caecina sought to desert to the other side and V. was good for nothing except gluttony. His army was routed at Cremona, and, in December, Rome was captured and V. executed. He was clearly the least suitable for the throne in the Year of the Four Emperors.
Suetonius, *Vitellius*.

VITRUVIUS Pollio Roman architect and writer, lived in the second part of the 1st century BC. The only building he is known to have built was the basilica at Fanum, but his work *De Architectura* is of prime importance in its field. The ten-book work — the only one on the subject to have survived — gives a comprehensive account of Greek and Roman architecture including town planning, the education of the architect, materials, temples, Orders, the various public buildings, private houses, water supply, decoration (frescoes, stucco, colouring), astronomy, geometry, time-measurement, and various machines for civil and military use. He also deals with proportions and setting of houses. V.'s work was abridged and known in the Middle Ages. It was published in 1485 and had great influence on architects and artists including Michelangelo, Bramante (St. Peter) and Leonardo da Vinci. The classical tradition in European architecture is due, to a great extent, to his influence.
F. Granger (Loeb), 1931–1934.

VOLATERRAE (modern Volterra) Etruscan city, one of the leading in the league of the twelve Etruscan cities, commanding the Caecina (modern Cecina) Valley. V. was a wealthy city and rich tombs have been discovered there. It fought Sulla in the Civil War and on part of its territory which was confiscated a colony of veterans was established.

Scullard, *Etruscan Cities*, 146ff;
W. V. Harris, *Rome in Etruria*, 1971 (s.v.).

VOLCANUS (VULCAN) The old Italian god of fire. He was associated with wild fire, such as that of volcanoes, and, for safety, his temple was always outside the city. His cult at Rome dates from the very beginning, and he had a festival, Volcanalia (23 August) and a flamen. He came to be identified with the Greek god *Hephaestus.

VOLOGESES I King of Parthia (AD 51–79) who contested Roman control over Armenia. He made his brother Tiridates king of Armenia (54); *Corbulo expelled him and enthroned Tigranes. But V. succeeded in forcing the governor of Cappadocia, Paetus, to surrender (*c.* 62). Finally a compromise was reached according to which Tiridates became king of Armenia but had to recognize Nero as suzereign, for which he went to Rome in 66. In contrast to former Parthian rulers, who tolerated or even encouraged Hellenism, V. pursued a national religious policy and supported Zoroastrianism.

N. C. Debevoise, *Political History of Parthia*, 1938, 174ff.

VOLSCI Italian people who expanded from central Italy in the late 6th century BC and occupied the region from the middle Liris to the Tyrrhenian coast. The Volscians lived in towns, among them *Tarracina, *Circei, *Antium, and *Arpinum, and their overall political organization is not clear. Allied with the *Aequi, they menaced Latium in the early 5th century BC which induced Rome to ally herself with the *Latins and *Hernici (493 and 486 respectively). The legend of *Coriolanus reflects the serious political situation in the 5th century. Even after Rome broke the power of the Aequi on the Algidus (431), the V. remained dangerous and it was only in the 4th century that a counter-offensive was launched against them. This was accompanied by the foundation of Latin colonies where the V. gave ground, for instance Circeii (393). Later, however, Volscian towns cooperated with the Latins against Rome and they were all defeated in the Latin War (340–338).

VOLSINII One of the leading Etruscan cities to be identified probably with modern Orvieto rather than Bolsena. The common sanctuary of the Etruscan cities, with an annual festival, was at V., the Forum Voltumnae. V. came under Roman control in the early 3rd century BC.

Scullard, *Etruscan Cities,* 126ff.; W. V. Harris, *Rome in Etruria,* 1971 (s.v.).

The Chimaera, an Etruscan work

Sculpture from the Nereid Monument at Xanthus

X

XANTHUS (1) Greek historian of the 5th century BC, a native of Lydia. He wrote a four-book *History of Lydia* of which only fragments survive. According to *Ephorus, he was used by Herodotus, and he apparently included folkloric material in his work.

L. Pearson, *Early Ionian Historians*, 1939.

XANTHUS (2) City of *Lycia which, like other Lycian cities, came under Greek influence. Finds of Attic vases show that it had close ties with Athens from the 6th century BC on. X. is known for the two monuments, called the Harpy Tomb and Nereid Tomb. The Xanthians were known for their love of freedom and in the Civil War after the death of Caesar they preferred to die rather than to surrender to *Brutus (2).

Jones, *Cities*² 95ff.

XENOCRATES Of Chalcedon, pupil of Plato and the third head of the Academy (339–314 BC). X. mainly concentrated on expounding loyally the philosophy of Plato, and sought to defend his master's system against criticism. In his works he was concerned with practical ethical questions and also with theological questions, including the relation of gods to the heavenly bodies.

XENOPHANES Greek philosopher, native of Colophon. He left Ionea at the age of 25, probably following the Persian conquest in 545 BC. He travelled much but spent most of his life in Sicily. He was still alive 67 years after he left his home country. X. composed poems of which survive fragments in hexameters and iambics and in which he expressed his philosophical views. An original thinker, he severely criticized the accepted anthropomorphic concepts of gods, notably as expressed in Homer and Hesiod. His argument that if horses had hands they would describe the gods in their shape has become famous. Instead he argued for a supreme, eternal one god, who governs the universe by reason, and is identical with it. He was interested in natural science and made observations of fossils. He also criticized conventional values. His influence on subsequent philosophers was great.

W. Jaeger, *The Theology of the Early Greek Philosophers*, 1947.

XENOPHON (1) Greek writer, historian and soldier, *c.* 428–*c.* 354 BC. Of a well-to-do Athenian family, X. lived in his youth in Athens and was an admirer of Socrates. He joined the service of *Cyrus (2) in 401 BC and took part in the expedition of the Persian prince against his brother. After the battle of *Cunaxa, and the treacherous execution of the Greek commanders, he became one of the commanders of the Greek force which was with Cyrus (the "Ten Thousand"). Despite the Persian attacks they safely arrived at the Black Sea (400 BC). Thereafter he served with Spartan commanders in Asia Minor including *Dercylidas and King *Agesilaus. A sentence of exile was passed against him in Athens and when Agesilaus returned to Greece he came with him and was at the Battle of Coronea. The Spartans gave him an estate at Scillus near Olympia. He lived there comfortably until expelled by Elis in 371. After his exile was repealed he returned to Athens where he lived for the rest of his life.

X. was a prolific writer and he wrote on a wide variety of subjects. His works include: 1) *Hellenica*, a seven-book history of Greece from 411 (where Thucydides breaks off) to 362 BC. The treatment of subjects is uneven, according to the sources which were at X.'s disposal at each period; 2) *Anabasis*, an account of the expedition of the Greek mercenaries in the service of Cyrus and the retreat to the Black Sea; 3) *Cynegeticus* deals with hunting which X. considers as important for military training; 4) *On Horsemanship*, the work of an expert on the subject; 5) *Hipparchicus*, a treatise on the duties of the cavalry officer; 6) *Oeconomicus*, an account of estate management written in the dialogue form; 7) *Apology*, a defence of Socrates which gives X.'s version of the trial; 8) *Memorabilia*, four books of memories about Socrates which deal with various subjects including education; 9) *Symposium*, an account of a conversation at a party with Socrates as a guest; 10) *Cyropaedia*, a biography of Cyrus I with an account of his education and the organization of the Persian Empire. In fact it is a historical novel; 11) *Hieron*, a dialogue between Hieron I of Syracuse and the poet Simonides, discussing the problems of the tyrant; 12) *Agesilaus*, an encomiastic biography of Agesilaus; 13) *Spartan Constitution*, a laudatory account of the Spartan education and institutions. Under Xenophon's name has come the *Constitution of Athens*, a political pamphlet which was written by an extreme oligarch at the beginning of the Peloponnesian War.

X. is neither a great historian nor a profound philosopher; but he writes clearly and simply and in an attractive way. His writings are of interest and in some subjects his knowledge is that of an expert. In religion he holds orthodox views and practices. His admiration for Sparta was later tempered by experience. Above all he presents the outlook of a conservative person with stress on traditional values, and always with attention to practice rather than theory.

W. Miller, *Cyropaedia* (Loeb), 1914;
C. L. Brownson and O. J. Todd, *Hellenica, Anabasis, Apology, Symposium* (Loeb), 1918—1922;
E. C. Marchant, *Memorabilia, Oeconomicus* (Loeb), 1923;
A. I. Anderson, *Xenophon*, 1974.

XENOPHON (2) EPHESIUS The author of a Greek novel called *Ephesiaca*. His date is not known but is not earlier than the 2nd century AD. The five-book novel describes the adventures of the young lovers Anthia and Habrocomes who after their marriage lost each other. After various ordeals, throughout which they remained faithful to each other, they were united and lived happily at Ephesus. The novel conforms to the genre and there is nothing exceptional about it.

XERXES I Son of Darius I and Atossa, king of Persia (486—465 BC). X. is mainly known for his invasion of Greece, which he received as an inheritance from his father after the Persian defeat at Marathon. X. mustered an enormous land and naval force, and advanced to Greece through the Hellespont which he ordered to lash three hundred times after a storm broke the bridge. But the Persian navy was routed at *Salamis and thereafter X. returned to Asia. In the following year the Persian land army was routed at Plataea and in the subsequent years the Greeks of Asia Minor were liberated. Herodotus gives a vivid account of X. He was murdered in 465.

A. T. Olmstead, *History of the Persian Empire*, 1923.
A. R. Burn, *Persia and the Greeks*, 1962.

Z

ZALEUCUS Reputedly the earliest of the Greek law-givers, lived in the 7th century BC. He provided Locri in south Italy with a code of laws, which was famous for its severity. His laws were adopted by many other Greek cities in Sicily and Magna Graecia. He was also known as a successful mediator in civil strifes.

ZAMA The location of Z., the famous battle in which *Hannibal was defeated by *Scipio (2) Africanus, is not known. This is because there were probably more than one town by the name of Z. in North Africa. Moreover, Z. was probably only a camp on the way of Hannibal to the battlefield, though not far from it.

ZENO (1) Greek philosopher, native of Elea, lived in the 5th century BC. Pupil of *Parmenides, he accompanied his leader on his voyage to Athens. In his one book Z. defended the theory of monism against critics of Parmenides. To disprove the views of the pluralists he showed that they resulted in absurd propositions and so presented his famous paradoxes which dealt with time, space and numbers. These included the one on Achilles and the tortoise and the flying arrow.

ZENO (2) A native of Citium in Cyprus, son of Mneses, a Greek philosopher, the founder of Stoicism, lived 335–263 BC. Z. went to Athens to study philosophy and was a pupil of Polemon, the head of the Academy, and then of the Cynic, Crates. He became attracted to the works of *Antisthenes and Socrates and finally opened a school of his own in the Stoa Poikile ("Painted Porch") at the Athenian Agora. Z.'s main concern was with ethics, that is, to determine rules of conduct and to demonstrate that they were right. But with this he developed a complete philosophical system with logic and physics and not only ethics. In his famous *Politeia* ("Republic"), Z. described a society of wise men the best society, one that could be practised. In this work he did away with all the conventional features of the Greek polis. He envisaged a community of property, including women, removal of political barriers between cities and the rule of reason. He wrote various works but only fragments survive. See *Stoa (with bibliography).

A. C. Pearson, *The Fragments of Zeno and Cleanthes*, 1891.

ZENOBIA Second wife of *Odaenathus who took control of Palmyra as guardian of her son after the murder of her

A terracotta of a war-elephant from Pompeii. Hannibal used elephants at Zama

husband (AD 267) in which she may have been involved. Unlike her dead husband, she launched on an expansionist policy against the Roman provinces in the East. Her armies occupied Syria, Egypt and most of Asia Minor (270) and in 271 she made her son Augustus. This caused the reaction of *Aurelianus. He himself conducted the campaign against her and after defeating her armies captured Palmyra and Z. The city was sacked (273) and Z. and her son led in triumph at Rome; their lives, however, were spared.

ZENODOTUS A Greek scholar, a native of Ephesus, lived c. 325–c. 234 BC, the first head of the Alexandrian Library (284). Under his direction began the edition of texts of Greek epic and lyric poets. He published a *Homeric Glossary*, and a recension of the *Iliad* and the *Odyssey*. He divided the two epics into twenty-four books, and aimed at reconstructing the original text by collecting manuscripts and making alterations according to his own understanding and instinct. He also prepared recensions of Hesiod, Pindar and Anacreon.

ZEPHYRUS In mythology, son of *Eos and Astraeus, the god of the west wind, father of the swift horses of Achilles. Occasionally he was said to be the husband of *Iris. It was Z. who — out of jealousy — killed *Hyacinthus.

ZEUGITAI The third class of Athenians under the reform of *Solon; those who had an annual income of 200–300 *medimnoi* of corn (or the equivalent thereof). Such a class of independent farmers had existed before Solon, but he used it for his timocratic organization of Athens. By a law of 487 BC, the Z. could be elected (by lot) as *Archontes. The Z. formed the main hoplite body in the Athenian army.

ZEUS The supreme Greek god in mythology, the son of *Kronos and Rhea. He was brought up in a cave by *Amalthea after his mother saved him from his father who used to swallow his sons. The *Curetes danced in order that Kronos should not hear him crying. Later he fought, together with his brothers, against Kronos and dethroned him. In the division of the world, Z. received the Sky, Poseidon the Seas and Hades the Underworld. He secured his power by conquering the Titans and the *Gigantes. Z. originally was — and did not lose this aspect — god of sky as the abode of weather phenomena. He had been an Indo-European god and his name meant "sky". His cult was introduced to Greece by the Greek invaders.

The war against the Titans is sometimes taken as a reflection of the replacement of the old, pre-Hellenic gods by those whom the conquerers brought with them. His primitive cult was on the tops of mountains. He was believed to dwell on Mount Olympus, and the other gods were related to him as a family. The old pre-Hellenic goddess became his wife and was called *Hera. He also had children: Apollo, Artemis, Athena, Hermes, Ares and Dionysus. He was "father of god and men", that is, all belonged to his family and he had absolute power over them. He was especially associated with the king and was the protector of his authority. The various epithets of Z. reveal his functions: god of the guests (*Xenios*), of the household (*Ktesios*), of the city (*Polieus*), saviour (*Soter*), of freedom (*Eleutherios*). He was often the supreme god of the city; but above all he became the supreme god of the universe. The Greeks used to identify him with great gods of other peoples and foreign cities. He was, of course, identified with *Jupiter. His most famous temple was in Olympia, and he had an important oracle at *Dodona. He was honoured by many festivals, including the Olympian and Nemean Games.

Z. was considered as the defender of law and right. As one who is responsible for justice he appears in Aeschylus. But in legends he is most immoral in his amorous affairs. His loves include *Europa, *Antiope, *Danaë, *Io, *Leda and *Semele and all bore him children. *Dione, *Themis, *Metis and *Mnemosyne were at some time his wives.

In art Z. is depicted with a beard, in a dignified position and with a dignified expression, in a robe or naked. His attributes are the sceptre or the thunderbolt and with him is often the eagle. The most famous statue of Z. was the one made of gold and ivory by *Phidias for the temple in Olympia.

A. B. Cook, *Zeus*, 1914–1940.

ZEUXIS Greek painter, a native of Heraclea in Lucania, probably of the late 5th century BC. He followed the shadowing technique of Apollodorus and introduced light and shade in contrast and gradation. The effect of his enlivened, realistic pictures was so great that birds were said to peck at his pictures of grapes. His other famous pictures were Helen, Eros with roses, the Centaur Family and Heracles in the Cradle. The Helen, commissioned for Croton, was composed of parts of several models — to achieve an ideal form.

MAPS

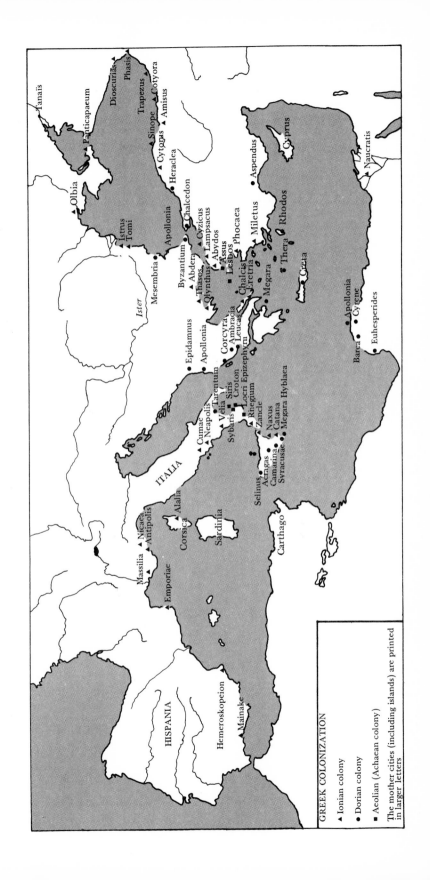

GREEK COLONIZATION

▲ Ionian colony

● Dorian colony

■ Aeolian (Achaean colony)

The mother cities (including islands) are printed
in larger letters

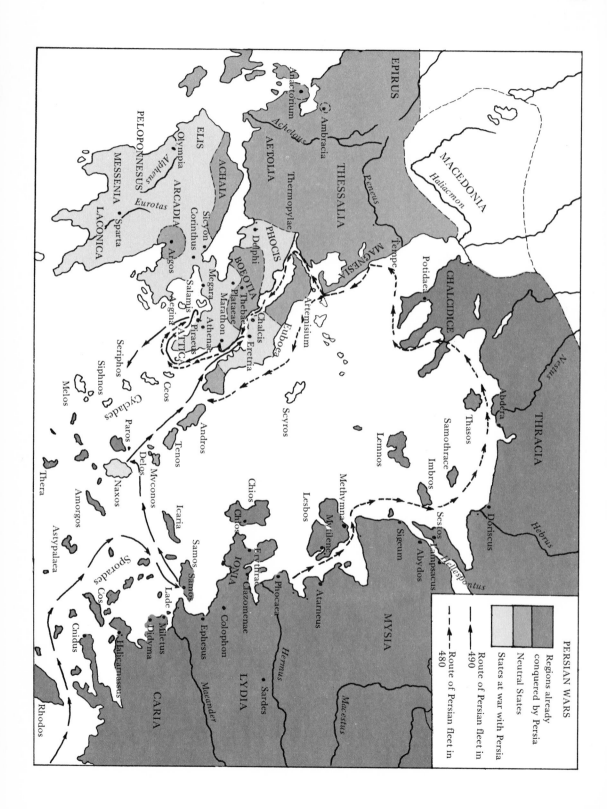

EPIRUS

Anactorium

Ambracia

Acheloüs

AETOLIA

PELOPONNESUS

ELIS

Olympia

Alpheus

ACHAIA

MESSENIA

ARCADIA

Eurotas

LACONICA

Sparta

Argos

Sicyon

Corinthus

THESSALIA

Peneus

Thermopylae

MAGNESIA

Tempe

MACEDONIA

Haliacmon

Potidaea

CHALCIDICE

DELPHI

PHOCIS

BOEOTIA

Thebae

Marathon

Plataeae

Megara

Salamis

Aegina

Piraeus

Athenae

ATTICA

Chalcis

Eretria

Euboea

Artemisium

Seriphos

Siphnos

Melos

Paros

Thera

Amorgos

Astypalaea

Naxos

Delos

Myconos

Cyclades

Ceos

Tenos

Andros

Scyros

Icaria

Sporades

Cos

Cnidus

Rhodos

Halicarnassus

Didyma

Miletus

Lade

Samos

Samos

IONIA

Erythrae

Chios

Chios

Lesbos

Methymna

Mytilene

Clazomenae

Colophon

Ephesus

CARIA

Maeander

LYDIA

Sardes

Hermus

Phocaea

Atarneus

Sigeum

Abydos

Lampsacus

Sestos

Hellespontus

MYSIA

Macestus

Lemnos

Imbros

Samothrace

Thasos

Abdera

Doriscus

THRACIA

Nestus

Hebrus

PERSIAN WARS

Regions already conquered by Persia

Neutral States

States at war with Persia

Route of Persian fleet in 490

Route of Persian fleet in 480

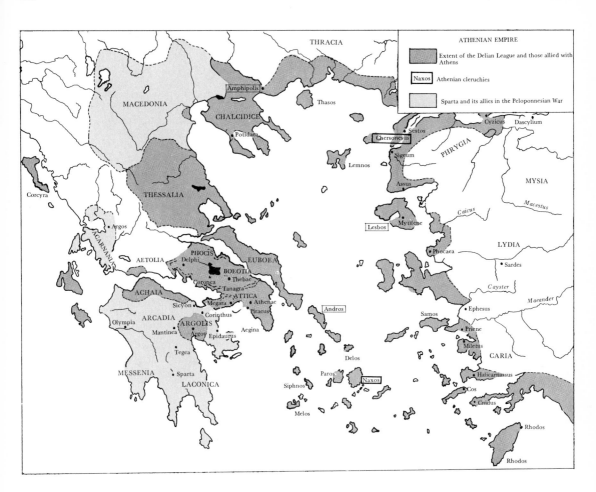

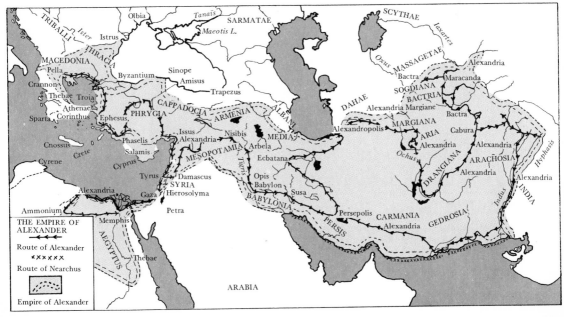

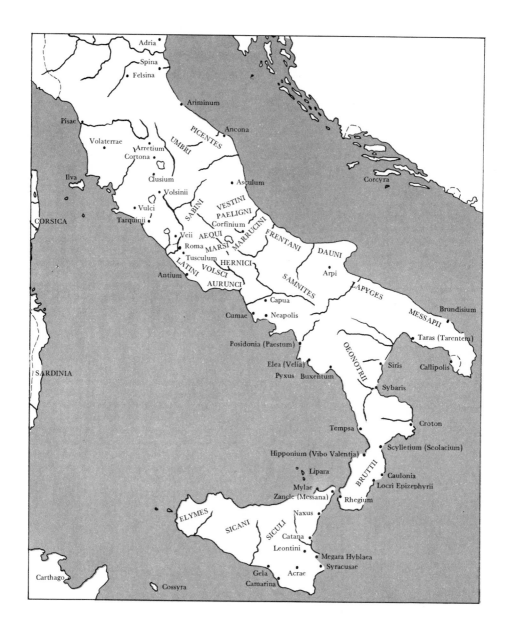

Adria

Spina

• Felsina

Ariminum

Pisae

PICENTES

Volaterrae

UMBRI

Ancona

Arretium

Cortona •

Clusium

• Asculum

Ilva

Volsinii

CORSICA

• Vulci

SABINI

Tarquinii

VESTINI

PAELIGNI

Corfinium

Veii

AEQUI

MARRUCINI

Roma •

MARSI

FRENTANI

Tusculum

HERNICI

DAUNI

LATINI

VOLSCI

Antium

AURUNCI

Arpi

SAMNITES

LAPYGES

Capua

MESSAPII

Brundisium

Cumae

Neapolis

Posidonia (Paestum)

Taras (Tarentem)

Elea (Velia)

OENOTRII

Siris

Callipolis

Pyxus Buxentum

SARDINIA

Sybaris

Tempsa

Croton

Hipponium (Vibo Valentia)

Scylletium (Scolacium)

Lipara

Caulonia

BRUTTII

Mylae

Locri Epizephyrii

Zancle (Messana)

Rhegium

Naxus

ELYMES

SICANI

SICULI

Catana

Leontini

Megara Hyblaea

Gela

Acrae

Syracusae

Carthago

Camarina

Cossyra

Corcyra

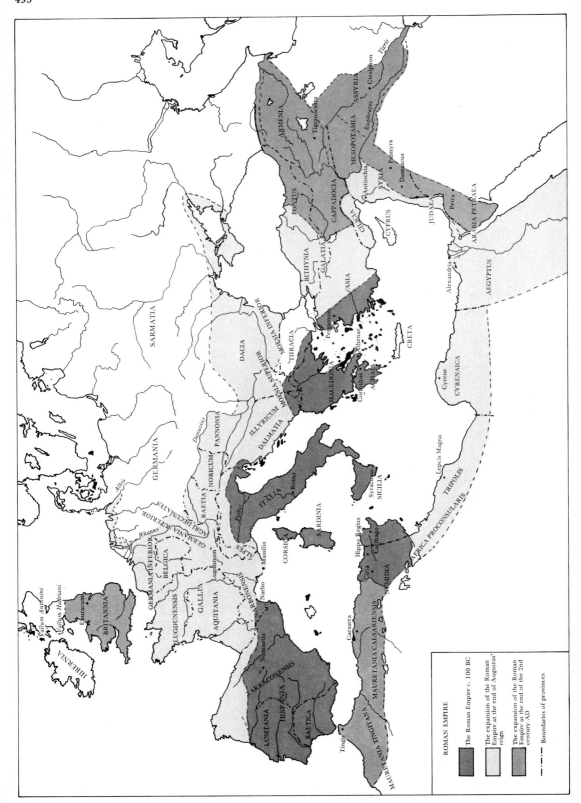

SARMATIA

GERMANIA

Albis

Rhenus

Danuvius

DACIA

ARMENIA

PONTUS

Tigranocerta

CAPPADOCIA

ASSYRIA

MESOPOTAMIA

Ctesiphon

Tigris

Euphrates

Palmyra

Damascus

SYRIA

Antiochia

CILICIA

JUDAEA

Petra

ARABIA PETRAEA

CYPRUS

Alexandria

AEGYPTUS

BITHYNIA

GALATIA

ASIA

Pergamum

CRETA

Athenae

ACHAIA

Corinthus

MACEDO

THRACIA

MOESIA INFERIOR

MOESIA SUPERIOR

ILLYRICUM

DALMATIA

PANNONIA

NORICUM

RAETIA

AGRI DECUMATES

GERMANIA SUPERIOR

GERMANIA INFERIOR

BELGICA

LUGDUNENSIS

GALLIA

AQUITANIA

NARBONENSIS

Narbo

Massilia

Lugdunum

Padus

ITALIA

Roma

Alpes

CORSICA

SARDINIA

SICILIA

Syracusae

Roma

Cyrene

CYRENAICA

Lepcis Magna

TRIPOLIS

AFRICA PROCONSULARIS

Carthago

Hippo Regius

NUMIDIA

Cirta

Caesarea

MAURETANIA CAESARIENSIS

MAURETANIA TINGITANA

Tingis

Numantia

TARRACONENSIS

HISPANIA

LUSITANIA

BAETICA

BRITANNIA

Eburacum

Vallum Antonini

Vallum Hadriani

HIBERNIA

ROMAN EMPIRE

The Roman Empire c. 100 BC

The expansion of the Roman Empire at the end of Augustus' reign

The expansion of the Roman Empire at the end of the 2nd century AD

Boundaries of provinces

TABLES

KINGS OF SPARTA*

AGIADS		EURYPONTIDS	
Leon	c. 590–560 BC	Hippocratides	c. 600–575 BC
Anaxandridas	c. 560–520	Agasicles	c. 575–550
Cleomenes I	c. 520–490	Ariston	c. 550–515
Leonidas I	490–480	Demaratus	c. 515–491
Pleistarchus	480–459	Leotychidas II	491–461
Pleistonax	459–409	Archidamus II	469–427
Pausanias	409–395	Agis II	427–399
Agesipolis I	395–380	Agesilaus II	399–360
Cleombrotus I	380–371	Archidamus III	368–338
Agesipolis II	371–370	Agis III	338–331
Cleomenes II	370–309	Eudamidas I	331–c. 305
Areus I	309–265	Archidamus IV	c. 305–275
Acrotatus	265–262	Eudamidas II	c. 275–244
Areus II	262–254	Agis IV	c. 244–241
Leonidas II	254–235	Eudamidas III	241–c. 228
Cleomenes III	235–222	Archidamus V	228–227
Agesipolis III	219–215	Eucleidas	227–221
		Lycurgus	219–c. 212
		Pelops	c. 212–c. 200

*The list of Spartan kings begins c. 900 BC but becomes more reliable in the 6th century BC.

KINGS OF MACEDON

Alexander I	c. 495–450 BC	Alexander II	370–369/8
Perdiccas II	C. 450–413	Ptolemaeus	369/8–365
Archelaus	413–399	Perdiccas III	365–359
Orestes	399–396	Philip II	359–336
Aeropus	396–393	Alexander HII	336–323
Amyntas II	393–392	Philip III Arrhidaeus	323–316
Pausanias	393–392	Alexander IV	316–311
Amyntas III	393–370		

PTOLEMIES

Ptolemy I Soter	323–282 BC (King from 301)
Ptolemy II Philadelphus	382–246
Ptolemy Euergetes I	246–222
Ptolemy IV Philopator	222–205
Ptolemy V Epiphanes	204–180
Ptolemy VI Philometer	180–145 (expelled 164–163).
Joint rule of Ptolemy VI, Ptolemy VIII and Cleopatra II	170–164
Ptolemy VII Neos Philopator	145–144 Joint-ruler
Ptolemy VIII Euergetes Physcon	145–116
Ptolemy IX Soter III Lathyrus and Cleopatra III	116–107
Ptolemy X Alexander and Cleopatra III	107–101
Ptolemy X Alexander I and Cleopatra Berenice	101–88
Ptolemy IX Soter II	88–81
Cleopatra Berenice and Ptolemy XI Alexander II	80
Ptolemy XII Auletes	80–58
Berenice IV	58–55
Ptolemy XII Auletes	55–51
Cleopatra VII and Ptolemy XIII	55–47
Cleopatra VII and Ptolemy XIV	47–44
Cleopatra VII and Ptolemy XV (Caesarion)	44–30

THE SELEUCIDS

Seleucus I Nicator	311–281 BC	Antiochus VI Epiphanes	145–129
Antiochus I Soter	281–261	Cleopatra Thea and Antiochus VIII Grypus	125–121
Antiochus II Theos	261–246	Antiochus VIII Grypus	121–96
Seleucus II Callinicus	246–225	Antiochus IX Cyzicenus	115–95
Seleucus III Soter	225–223	Seleucus VI Epiphanes	96–5
Antiochus III	223–187	Demetrius III Philopator	95–88
Seleucus IV Philopator	187–175	Antiochus X Eusebes	95–83
Antiochus IV Epiphanes	175–164	Antiochus XI Philadelphus	94
Antiochus V Eupator	163–162	Philip I Philadelphus	94–83
Demetrius I Soter	162–150	Antiochus XII Dionysus	87–84
Alexander Balas	150–145	Antiochus XIII Asiaticus	69–64
Demetrius II Nicator	145–140; 129–125	Philip II	65–64

ANTIGONIDS

Antigonus I Monophthalmus	306–301 BC
Demetrius I Poliorcetes	301–283
Antigonus II Gonatas	283–239
Demetrius II	239–229
Antigonus III Doson	229–221
Philip V	221–179
Perseus	179–168

THE ATTALIDS OF PERGAMUM

Philetairus	283–263 BC
Eumenes I	263–241
Attalus I Soter	241–197 (took the royal title)
Eumenes II Soter	197–160
Attalus II	160–139
Attalus III	139–133

KINGS OF PONTUS

Mithridates I	302/1–266/5 BC	Mithridates IV Philopator Philadelphus	c. 170–c. 150
Ariobarzanes	266/5–c. 255	Mithridates V Euergetes	c. 150–120
Mithridates II	c. 225–c. 220	Mithridates VI Eupator	120–63
Mithridates III	c. 220–c. 185		
Pharnaces I	c. 185–c. 170		

KINGS OF NUMIDIA

Masinissa	202–149 BC
Micipsa	149–118
Adherbal, Hiempsal, Jugurtha	118–116
Jugurtha	116–105
Gauda	105–?
Hiempsal II	c. 88–c. 50
Juba I	c. 50–46
Juba II	c. 30–c. 25 BC

KINGS OF BITHYNIA

Zipoetes	c. 315–c. 280 BC (king from 298)
Nicomedes I	c. 280–before 242
Ziadas	before 242–c. 230
Prusias I	c. 230–c. 182
Prusias II	c. 182–149
Nicomedes II Epiphanes	149–c. 127
Nicomedes III Euergetes	c. 127–c. 94
Nicomedes IV Philopator	c. 94–74

KINGS OF CAPPADOCIA

Ariarathes III	225–220 BC	Ariarathes VIII	c. 96
Ariarathes IV Eusebes	220–c. 162	Ariobarzanes I	c. 95–c. 62
Ariarathes V Eusebes Philopator	c. 162–c. 130	Ariobarzanes II Philopator	62–c. 54
Ariarathes VI Epiphanes Philopator	c. 130–c. 111	Ariobarzanes III Eusebes	c. 54–42
Ariarathes VII Philometer	c. 111–c. 100	Ariarathes IX	42–36
Ariarathes Eusebes Philpator (son of Mithridates VI of Pontus)	c. 100–c. 88 (expelled)	Archelaus	36–AD 17

THE HASMONAEANS AND HERODIANS

Jonathan	152–142	Antigonus	40–37
Simon	142–134	Herod I	37–4 BC
John Hyrcanus I	134–104	Archelaus (Judaea)	4 BC–AD 6
Aristobulus	104–103	Herod Antipas (Galilee)	4 BC –AD 39
Alexander Jannaeus	103–76	Philip	4 BC–AD 34
Salome	76–67	Herod Agrippa I	AD 37–44
Aristobulus II	67–63	Agrippa II	53–c. 96
Hyrcanus II	63–40		

ROMAN EMPERORS FROM AUGUSTUS TO THEODOSIUS I

Augustus	27 BC—AD 14	Gordian III	238—244
Tiberius	14—37	Philip the Arab	244—249
Gaius Caligula	37—41	Decius	249—251
Claudius	41—54	Trebonianus Gallus	251—253
Nero	54—68	Valerianus	253—260
Galba	68—69	Gallienus	253—268
Otho	69	Claudius Gothicus	268—270
Vitellius	69	Aurelian	270—275
Vespasian	69—79	Tacitus	276
Titus	79—81	Probus	276—282
Domitian	81—96	Carus	282—283
Nerva	96—98	Numerian	283—284
Trajan	98—117	Diocletian	284—305
Hadrian	117—138	Maximianus	286—305
Antoninus Pius	138—161	Constantius I Chlorus	293—306
Marcus Aurelius	161—180	Galerius	293—311
Commodus	180—192	Licinius	308—324
Pertinax	193	Constantinc	306—337
Didius Julianus	193	Constantius II	337—361
Septimius Severus	193—211	Constans	337—350
Pescennius Niger	193—194	Julian	361—363
Clodius Albinus	193—197	Jovian	363—364
Caracalla	211—217	Valentian I	363—375
Macrinus	217—218	Gratian	367—383
Elagabalus	218—222	Valentian II	375—392
Alexander Severus	222—235	Valens	364—378
Maximian	235—238	Theodosius I	378—395

MAIN GREEK COLONIES IN 8TH—5TH CENTURIES BC

Name	Year	Mother-city
Trapezus	756	Miletus
Cyzicus	756	Miletus
Ischia	c. 750	

Name	Year	Mother-city
Cumae	c. 750	Chalcis
Naxos (Sicily)	c. 734	Chalcis
Syracuse	c. 733	Corinth
Mende and Methone	c. 730	Eretria
Catana	c. 729	Naxos
Leontini	c. 729	Naxos
Megara Hyblaea	c. 728	Megara
Messana	c. 725	Cumae/Chalcis
Sybaris	c. 720	Achaea
Croton	c. 708	Achaea
Taras (Tarentum)	c. 706	Sparta
Posidonia (Paestum)	c. 700	Sybaris
Gela	c. 688	Rhodes and Creta
Chalcedon	685	Megara
Locri Epizyphyroi	c. 673	Locris
Byzantium	c. 660	Megara
Acanthus	c. 654	Andros
Lampsacus	c. 654	Phocaea
Abdera	c. 654	Clazomenae
Himera	649	Zancle
Cyrene	c. 630	Thera
Sinope	c. 629	Miletus
Selinus	c. 628	Megara Hyblaea
Epidamnus	c. 627	Corinth
Ambracia	625	Corinth
Anactorium	625	Corinth
Leucas	625	Corinth
Naucratis	c. 610	
Perinthus	c. 601	Samos
Massilia	c. 600	Phocaea
Potidaea and Apollonia	c. 600	Corinth
Panticapaeum	c. 600	Miletus
Camarina	c. 598	Syracuse
Acragas	c. 580	Gela
Alalia	c. 560	Phocaea
Thurii	443	Athens

ROMAN COLONIZATION UNTIL THE GRACCHI

LATIN COLONIES		ROMAN COLONIES
495 Signia	264 Firmum	338 Antium
494 Velitrae	258 Beneventum	329 Tarracina
492 Norba	253 Aesernia	296 Minturnae
442 Ardea	246 Brundisium	Sinuessa
393 Circeii	241 Spoletium	283 Sena Gallica
385 Satricum	218 Cremona	264 Castrum Novum (Etruria)
383 Sutrium	218 Placentia	247 Alsium
” Nepete	193 Copia (Thurii)	Aesis
382 Setia	192 Vibo Valentia	245 Fregenae
334 Cales	190 Placentia and Cremona	194 Volturnum
328 Fregellae	189 Bononia	Liternum
314 Luceria	181 Aquileia	Puteoli
313 Saticula	180 Lucca	Salernum
Suessa Aurunca		Buxentum
312 Interamna on the Liris		Sipontum
303 Sora		Tempsa
Alba Fucens		Croton
299 Narnia		184 Potentia (Picenum)
298 Carsioli		Pisaurum
291 Venusia		Auximum
c. 290 Castrum Novum		183 Mutina
Hadria		Parma
273 Cosa		Saturnia
Paestum		181 Graviscae
268 Ariminum		177 Luna

SELECT BIBLIOGRAPHY

HISTORY

Cambridge Ancient History I–XII (new edition of I–II in progress).

Greece
a. J. B. Bury and R. Meiggs, *A History of Greece*[4], 1975.
   M. I. Finley, *The Ancient Greeks*, 1966.
   N. G. L. Hammond, *A History of Greece to 322 BC*[2], 1966.
   – *Studies in Greek History*, 1973.
   A. J. Toynbee, *Some Problems in Greek History*, 1969.
b. *Archaic Greece*
   J. Boardman, *The Greeks Overseas*, 1964.
   A. R. Burn, *The Lyric Age of Greece*, 1960.
   M. I. Finley, *The World of Odysseus*, 1965.
   C. G. Starr, *The Origins of Greek Civilization*, 1962.
c. *Classical Greece*
   V. Ehrenberg, *From Solon to Socrates*, 1967.
   M. L. Laistner, *A History of the Greek World*, 479–323 BC[3], 1957.
   R. Meiggs, *The Athenian Empire*, 1972.
d. *Hellenistic World*
   M. Cary, *A History of the Greek World*, 323–146 BC[2], 1951.
   A. K. Narain, *The Indo-Greeks*, 1957.
   W. W. Tarn, *The Greeks in Bactria and India*, 1951.
   W. W. Tarn and G. T. Griffith, *Hellenistic Civilization*[2], 1952.

Rome
a. A. E. R. Boak and W. G. Sinnigen, *A History of Rome to AD 565*[5], 1965.
   M. Cary, *A History of Rome Down to the Reign of Constantine*[2], 1964.
   D. R. Dudley, *Civilization of Rome*[2], 1962.
   M. Grant, *The World of Rome*, 133 BC–AD 217[2], 1964.
   H. H. Scullard, *From the Gracchi to Nero*[2], 1963.
b. *Early Rome and the Republic*
   E. Badian, *Foreign Clientelae, 264–70 BC*, 1958.
   – *Roman Imperialism in the late Republic*[2], 1969.
   R. Bloch, *The Origins of Rome*, 1960.
   J. Heurgon, *The Rise of Rome*, 1974.
   F. B. Marsh, *A History of the Roman Worlds*, 146–30 BC[3], 1953.
   Th. Mommsen, *History of Rome* (Eng. Tr.).
   H. H. Scullard, *A History of the Roman World, 753–146*[3], 1961.
   A. J. Toynbee, *Hannibal's Legacy*, 1965.
c. *Empire*
   J. B. Bury, *History of the Later Roman Empire, AD 395–565*, 1923.
   A. H. M. Jones, *The Later Roman Empire, 284–602*, 1964.
   – *The Decline of the Ancient World*, 1966.
   F. Millar, *The Roman Empire and Its Neighbours*, 1967.
   H. M. D. Parker, *A History of the Roman World, AD 138–337*, 1935.
   E. P. Salmon, *A History of the Roman World, 30 BC–AD 138*[3], 1957.
   C. G. Starr, *Civilization and the Caesars*, 1954.
   R. Syme, *The Roman Revolution*, 1939.

CONSTITUTION AND GOVERNMENT

Greece

V. Ehrenberg, *The Greek State*², 1969.
G. Glotz, *The Greek City*, 1929.
C. Hignett, *A History of the Athenian Constitution*, 1952.
A. H. M. Jones, *The Greek City*, 1940.
— *Athenian Democracy*, 1957.
J. A. O. Larsen, *Representative Government in Greek and Roman History*, 1955.
— *Greek Federal States*, 1968.
P. J. Rhodes, *The Athenian Boule*, 1972.

Rome

F. F. Abbott and A. C. Johnson, *Municipal Administration in the Roman Empire*, 1926.
O. W. Botsford, *The Roman Assemblies*, 1909.
K. von Fritz, *The Theory of the Mixed Constitution in Antiquity*, 1954.
A. H. J. Greenidge, *Roman Public Life*, 1901.
H. F. Jolowicz, *Historical Introduction to the Study of Roman Law*³ (rev. by B. Nicholas), 1972.
L. R. Taylor, *The Voting Districts of the Roman Republic*, 1960.
— *Roman Voting Assemblies*, 1966.
Ch. Wirszubski, *Libertas as a Political Idea at Rome*, 1950.

ECONOMY AND SOCIETY

Greece

A. M. Andreades, *A History of Greek Public Finance*, 1933.
A. French, *The Growth of the Athenian Economy*, 1964.
J. Hasebroek, *Trade and Politics in Ancient Greece*, 1933.
H. Michell, *The Economics of Ancient Greece*², 1957.
M. I. Rostovzeff, *The Social and Economic History of the Hellenistic World*, 1941.

Rome

J. P. V. Balsdon, *Life and Leisure in Ancient Rome*, 1969.
P. A. Brunt, *Italian Manpower*, 1971.
M. P. Charlesworth, *The Trade Routes and Commerce of the Roman Empire*², 1926.
T. Frank (ed.), *An Economic Survey of Ancient Rome*, 1933–1940.
L. Friedländer, *Roman Life and Manners* (Eng. Tr.), 1908–1914.
R. MacMullen, *Enemies of the Roman Order*, 1963.
M. I. Rostovtzeff, *The Social and Economic History of the Roman Empire*², 1957.
R. E. M. Wheeler, *Rome Beyond the Imperial Frontiers*, 1954.

LITERATURE

R. A. Bolgar, *The Classical Heritage and Its Beneficieries*, 1954.
C. M. Bowra, *Landmarks in Greek Literature*, 1966.
J. W. Duff and A. M. Duff, *A Literary History of Rome to the Close of the Golden Age*², 1962.
— *A Literary History of Rome in the Silver Age*³, 1964.
A. W. Gomme, *The Greek Attitude to Poetry and History*, 1954.
G. M. A. Grube, *The Greeks and Roman Critics*, 1965.
J. Higginbotham (ed.), *Greek and Latin Literature*, 1969.
G. Highet, *The Classical Tradition, Greek and Roman Influence on Western Literature*, 1949.
A. Lesky, *A History of Greek Literature*, 1966.
R. M. Ogilvie, *Latin and Greek, A History of the Influence of the Classics on English Life 1600–1918*, 1964.
H. J. Rose, *A Handbook of Greek Literature*, 1934.
— *A Handbook of Latin Literature*³, 1954.
T. B. L. Webster, *Hellenistic Poetry and Art*, 1964.

PHILOSOPHY

A. H. Armstrong, *An Introduction to Ancient Philosophy*⁴, 1965.
A. H. Armstrong (ed.), *The Cambridge History of Later Greek and Early Mediaeval Philosophy*, 1967.
J. Burnet, *Early Greek Philosophy*⁴, 1930.
W. K. C. Guthrie, *A History of Greek Philosophy*, 1962.
B. Farrington, *Greek Science*, 1961.

SCIENCE

B. Farrington, *Greek Science*, 1961.
G. E. R. Lloyd, *Early Greek Science*, 1970.
– *Greek Science after Aristotle*, 1973.
O. Neugebauer, *The Exact Sciences in Antiquity*², 1957.
S. Sambursky, *The Physical World of the Greeks*, 1956.
– *The Physics of the Stoics*, 1959.
G. Sarton, *A History of Science*, 1953–1959.

RELIGION AND MYTHOLOGY

F. Altheim, *A History of Roman Religion*, 1938.
C. Bailey, *Phases in the Religion of Ancient Rome*, 1932.
E. R. Dodds, *The Greeks and the Irrational*, 1951.
A. J. Festugière, *Personal Religion among the Greeks*, 1954.
W. W. Fowler, *The Religious Experience of the Roman People*, 1911.
M. Grant, *Roman Myths*, 1971.
R. Graves, *The Greek Myth*², 1960.
W. K. C. Guthrie, *The Greeks and their Gods*², 1954.
C. Kerényi, *The Gods of the Greeks*, 1951.
– *The Heroes of the Greeks*, 1959.
H. J. Rose, *Ancient Greek Religion*, 1946.
– *Ancient Roman Religion*, 1949.
– *A Handbook of Greek Mythology*⁶, 1958.
L. R. Taylor, *The Divinity of the Roman Emperor*, 1931.

ART AND ARCHITECTURE

P. E. Arias, *A History of Greek Vase Painting*, 1962.
J. D. Beazley, *Attic Black-figure Vase Painters*, 1956.
– *Attic Red-figure Vase Painters*, 1963.
M. Bieber, *The Sculpture of the Hellenistic Age*², 1961.
R. Carpenter, *Greek Sculpture*, 1970.
R. M. Cook, *Greek Painted Pottery*², 1972.
P. Devambez, *Greek and Roman Painting*, 1962.
G. M. Hanfmann, *Roman Art*, 1964.
G. M. A. Richter, *A Handbook of Greek Art*⁷, 1974.
– *The Sculpture and Sculptors of the Greeks*², 1970.
D. S. Robertson, *A Handbook of Greek and Roman Architecture*, 1947.
A. Stenico, *Roman and Etruscan Painting*, 1963.
J. M. C. Toynbee, *The Art of the Romans*, 1965.
R. E. M. Wheeler, *Roman Art and Architecture*, 1965.

WORKS OF REFERENCES

Atlas of the Classical World, ed. F. Van den Meer and H. H. Scullard, 1958.
*A Companion to Greek Studies*⁴, ed. L. Whibley, 1931.
*A Companion to Roman Studies*³, ed. J. E. Sandys, 1929.
*Oxford Classical Dictionary*², 1970.

ABBREVIATIONS OF COMMON ROMAN PRAENOMINA

A.	Aulus	D.	Decimus	Q.	Quintus
Ap.	Appius	L.	Lucius	Sex.	Sextus
C.	Gaius	M.	Marcus	T.	Titus
Gn.	Gnaeus	P.	Publius	Ti.	Tiberius

INDEX

INDEX OF NAMES, TERMS AND SUBJECTS
WHICH ARE NOT TITLES OF ENTRIES IN THE ENCYCLOPAEDIA

A

Aachen → Aquae
Abas → Demeter
ab epistulis → Claudius (4)
abrogatio → Lex
Ab Urba Condita → Livy
Academus → Academia
Acamas → Demophon
Acis → Galatea
Acra → Jerusalem
Acrisius → Dana
Acrocorinth → Acropolis
Adgistis → Attis
Adrianopolis, battle of → Valens
adyton → Temple
Aeetes → Medea
Aegae → Edessa (1)
Aegates Islands, battle of → Carthage
Aegis → Athena
Aelia Capitolina → Jerusalem
Aenaria → Ischia
aes grave → Coinage, Roman
aes rude → Coinage, Roman
aes signatum → Coinage, Roman
Aethra → Theseus
Afer → Domitian
Afranius → Comedy, Roman
Agatharchus → Painting
Agave → Pentheus
ager Gallicus → Flaminius
Agii Apostoloi → Pella
Agonium → Janus
Agrigentum → Acragas
agrimensores → Gromatici
Agrius → Diomedes
Aigikoreis → Ion, Ionia
Aigion → Achaea
aisymnetes → Alcaeus (1); Pittacus
Aix-en-Provence → Aquae
alae → Atrium
Alathea → Meleager (1)

Alba Fucens → Aequi
Alciphon → Letters
Alcmaeon of Croton → Medicine
Alcyoneus → Gigantes
Alexander Helios → Cleopatra (2) VII
Alexandretta → Alexandria
Alfenus Varus → Digesta
Aloadae → Apollo
Ambrones → Cimbri
amici Caesaris → Consilium Principis
Ammonius Saccas → Neoplatonism
Amphissus → Apollo
Amphitheatrum Flavium → Colosseum
Amphitrite → Nereus; Poseidon
Amphora → Measures; Pottery
Ampurias → Emporium
Amulius → Romulus
Amycus → Dioscuri
Anagni → Anagnia
Anatomy → Medicine
Anaxarchus → Abdera
ancilia → Salii
Androcles → Ephesus
Androgenus → Minos
Anna → Dido
annales maximi → Annals
Antaeus → Heracles
Anthology → Anthologia Palatina
Antibes → Massalia
antidosis → Liturgy
Antiochus I of Commagene →
    Commagene
Antiope → Amazons
Antiphates → Laestrygenes
antoninianus → Coinage, Roman
Anxur → Tarracina
Anzio → Antium
Aphroditus → Hermaphroditus
apex → Salii
Apollonius Sophista → Apion
Apoxyomenus → Lysippus
Apple of Discord → Eris
apud iudicem → Law, Roman

Apulum → Dacia
aquae et ignis interdictio →
    Exilium
aquila → Signa Militaria
a rationibus → Claudius (4)
Arbogast → Eugenius
Archagathus → Medicine
Arcesilas → Cyrene
archagetai → Sparta
Archestratus → Ennius
Archytas → Medicine
Ardashir I → Artaxerxes (2)
Ardiaei → Illyricum
Ardys → Lydia
Arethusa → Alpheus
Arezzo → Arretium
Argadeis → Ion, Ionia
Argia → Adrastus
argentum Oscense → Coinage,
Roman
Aristides of Thebes → Painting
Arles → Arelate
Armour → Armies
Arpino → Arpinum
Arras → Atrebates
Arta → Ambracia
Artaxata → Armenia
Aryballos → Pottery
as → Coinage, Roman
Assianism → Rhetoric
Astarte → Aphrodite; Eryx
Astorga → Astures
Astrology → Astronomy
atarxia → Epicurus
Ateius Capito → Labeo
Atella → Atellana Fabula
Athenis → Hipponax
Atomic theory → Democritus
Atrium Vestae → Vesta
Atropos → Moira
auctoritas → Augustus
audax → Fimbria
Audin → Tralles

Aufidus → Cannae
Augsburg → Augusta Vindelicorum
Augst → Augusta Raurica
aureus → Coinage, Roman
Ausones → Italy
Autun → Augustudunum

B

Baal → Dolichenus, Jupiter
Baalbek → Heliopolis
Babrius → Aesop
Bacchiadae → Corinth
Baecula, battle of → Scipio (2)
Bagoas → Darius (3)
Balkesu → Aspendus
Banyas → Caesarea Philippi
Barcelona → Tarraco
Basilides → Gnosticism
Bath (Britain) → Aquae
Battus → Cyrene
Baucis → Philemon
Bedriacum, battle of → Othno
Beirut → Berytus
Bellum Africanum → Hirtius
Bellum Alexandrinum → Hirtius
Bellum Hispaniense → Hirtius
Bergama → Pergamum
biltu → Coinage, Greek
Biton → Clobis
Blossius of Cumae → Tiberius
    Gracchus (2)
Boeum → Doris
Bologna → Bononia
Bône → Hippo Regius
Bonifatius → Gaiseric
Bordeaux → Aquitania
Bostra → Nabataeans
Branchidae → Didyma
Brindizi → Brundisium
Briseis → Homer
Bupalus → Hipponax
Byzacium → Hadrumetum

C

Cadiz → Gades
Cadmea → Cadmus; Thebes
caduceus → Hermes
Caecilius Isidorus → Freedmen
Caelian → Rome (City)
Calaureia → Amphictionies
Calendar → Chronology; Fasti
Calabri → Messapia
Callicrates → Ictinus
Calleva → Atrebates
Callimachus → Polemarchos
Callinus → Elegiac Poetry
Callipus of Cyzicus → Astronomy
Callirhoe → Alcmaeon
Callisto → Artemis
Camirus → Rhodes
Canals → Aqueducts
Canopic canal → Aqueducts
cantica → Plautus
Capella → Amalthea
Cardia → Chersonesus (1)
Carsioli → Aequi
Cassiopea → Andromeda
Castor → Dioscuri

Catalepton → Appendix Vergiliana
Catamitus → Ganymedes
Campi Magni, battle of → Scipio (2)
catharsis → Tragedy
Catuvellauni → Verulamium
cavea → Theatre
celeres → Equites
Celeus → Demeter
cella → Temple
census → Censors
centuriatio → Gromatici
Centurion → Legion
Cepheus → Andromeda
Cerialia → Ceres
Chandragupta → Seleucus I
Chaones → Epirus
character → Coinage, Greek
Charondas → Catana; Law, Greek
Charybdis → Scylla
cheirotonia → Ekklesia
Chechel → Caesarea Iol
Chiliarch → Hephaestion
Chiusi → Clusium
Chloris → Flora
choliambos → Hipponax
choregia → Liturgy
choregos → Liturgy
Chrysaor → Geryon
Chryseis → Troilus
Chrysippus → Oedipus
Cimon of Cleonae → Painting
Cirencester → Dobunni
Ciris → Appendix Vergiliana
Cispius → Esquiline
Cithara → Music
Civita Castellana → Falerii
civitas sine suffragio → Municipium
civitates foederatae → Provincia
civitates liberae et immunes →
    Provincia
civitates stipendiariae → Provincia
Claros → Colophon
classis → Censors; Comitia
Claudius Nero, Tiberius → Tiberius
clavus angustus → Equites; Senate
clavus latus → Equites; Senate
Cleander → Commodus
Cleonides → Aristoxenus
Cleopatra Selene → Cleopatra (2)
    VII
Clermont Ferrand → Arverni
clipeus → Armies, Roman
Cloaea Maxima → Tarquinius (2)
Clotho → Moira
Clubs → Collegium
Cnossos → Crete; Minoan Civilization;
    Mycenaean Civilization
Cocalus → Daedalus
cognitio extra ordinem → Law,
    Roman
cognomen → Names
Colaeus → Samos
Colonization → Apoikia; Cleruchy;
    Colonia
Comaetho → Amphitryon
comes sacrarum largitionum → Con-
    sistorium
  comes rerum privatarum → Consis-
    torium
    comitatenses → Constantine (1);
    Legion
    commentarii senatus → Acta

comites → Provincia
compluvium → Atrium
concilium → Gallia
concordia ordinum → Cicero (1)
Conon (Astronomer) → Samos
Constatine (city) → Cirta
constitutio Antoniniana → Caracalla
Copa → Appendix Vergiliana
Corax → Rhetoric
Cordoba → Corduba
Core → Demeter; Persephone
Corfinio → Corfinium
Corfu → Corcyra
Corinthian War → Corinth
Corioli → Coriolanus
Cornelius Fuscus → Domitian
Corybantes → Curetes
Crates → Academy
Crates → Comedy, Greek
Crateuas → Botany
Cresida → Troilus
Crispina → Commodus
Crotone → Croton
Ctesiphon → Demosthenes (2)
Culex → Appendix Vergiliana
Cunaxa → Cyrus II
Cunctator → Fabius (3)
Cupid → Eros; Psyche
cura ludorum → Aediles
cura aquarum → Aediles
cura urbis → Aediles
curia Hostilia → Tullus Hotilius
Cydonia → Crete
Cynoscephalae, battle of → Philip V
Cytinum → Doris

D

Danai → Danaus
Danube → Danuvius
Dardanians → Dardanus
Dardanus, Peace of → Sulla
dareikos → Coinage, Greek
decretum → Law, Roman
Deiphyle → Tydeus
Delian League → Athens
Demes → Demoi
Demetrian War → Demetrius (2)
demiurgoi → Achaea
demiurgos → Plato
denarius → Coinage, Roman
deportatio → Exilium
deuteragonistes → Tragedy
Diakrioi → Megacles
diekplus → Navies
Dierna → Dacia
diolkos → Periander
Diophanes → Gracchus (3)
Dirae → Appendix Vergiliana
Dirge → Lyric Poetry
Discobolus → Myron
Divination → Augures; Auspicium;
    Delphi; Oracles
docena → Dioscuri
domi → Dictator
domus → Architecture
Doric Order → Architecture
Doryphorus → Polyclitus
drachma → Coinage, Greek
Drobeta → Dacia
Dryope → Apollo

Dumuzi → Adonis
Durazzo → Epidamnus
Dymanes → Dorians
Dyrrachium → Epidamnus

E

Echenais → Daphnis
Eclectus → Commodus
Edict of Milan → Constantine (1)
Edirne → Hadrian
eiren → Education, Greek
Electryon → Amphitryon
Electrum → Coinage, Greek
Elegiae in Maecenatem → Appendix
    Vergiliana
Elpinice → Cimon
Elymians → Segesta
Enceladus → Gigantes
Encomium → Lyric Poetry
Encyclopaedy → Cato (1); Cassiod-
    erus; Celsus (1); Festus; Isidor-
    us; Varro (2)
Endymion → Selene
Eneti → Veneti
enkyklema → Tragedy
Epaphus → Io
Ephesiaca → Xenophon (2)
Ephialtes → Gigantes
Epicaste → Oedipus
Epigoni → Seven against Thebes
Epimetheus → Pandora
Epinician → Lyric Poetry
epistates → Prytaneis
epoikia → Apoikia
Erato → Muses
Eratosthenes → Lysias
Erekli → Perinthus
Ergane → Athena
Erigone → Icarius
Erineus → Doris
Eriphyle → Amphiaraus
Eskihisar → Stratoniceia
Este → Ateste
Eudemus → Mathematics
Eumenides → Erinyes
Eumolpidae → Eumolpus
Eunomia → Horae
Eurotas → Laconia
Eurynome → Hephaestus
Eurytion → Geryones
Euterpe → Muses
euthynoi → Euthyna

F

Faliscans → Falerii
Favorinus → Dio (1)
Felsina → Bononia
Ferentinum → Hernici
feriae → Festivals
fescenini versus → Comedy,
Roman
fides → Cliens
Fiesole → Faesulae
Flavius Clemens → Domitian
Flavius Silva → Masada
Flood myth → Deucalion
Foedus Cassianum → Cassius (1)

formulae → Law, Roman
Fossa di Valca → Cremera
François Vase → Clithias
Fréjus → Forum (2)
Frascati → Tusculum

G

Gabiene → Eumenes (1)
Gaius → Caligula
galea → Armies, Roman
Gallipoli → Chersonesus (1)
Gaugamela, battle of → Alexander
    (4)
Gaul → Gallia
Ge → Gaia
Geleontes → Ion, Ionia
Geta → Caracalla
Gemini → Dioscuri
Gigantomachia → Gigantes
gladius → Armies, Roman
Glaucia → Saturninus (1)
gnomon → Anaximander; Chronol-
    ogy
Golden Fleece → Athamas
Golden House → Domus Aurea
Gordios → Gordium
Graces → Charites
grammaticus → Education, Roman
grammatistes → Education, Greek
Granicus, battle of → Alexander (4)
Gratiae → Charites
gymnasiarchos → Education, Greek
Gytheum → Laconia

H

Haemon → Creon (1)
Halia → Ekklesia
Halieia → Helios
Harran → Carrhae
Harmiona → Cadmus
Hasmonaeans → Judaea
hasta → Armies, Roman
hastati → Legion
Hecabe → Hecuba
Hecale → Theseus
Hecatompedon → Acropolis
Hecatoncheires → Gaia
Hedylus → Asclepiades
Heirate → Hamilcar
Helene → Adiabene
Helle → Athamas
Hellen → Hellenes
Hellanodikai → Olympian Games
Heracleites → Dion
Herat → Alexandria
Herma(e) → Hermes
Herondas → Herodas
Hesione → Heracles
Hierocles → Apollonius (4)
Hippocrates (tyrant) → Gela
Hippocrates of Chios → Mathematics
Hippodamia → Pelops
Hippomenes → Atalanta
Hirpini → Samnium
Hispania → Spain
Hissarlik → Troy
Homs → Emessa
Hopletes → Ion, Ionia

humiliores → Honestiores
hybris → Nemesis
Hydra → Pottery
Hylleis → Dorians
Hyllus → Heraclidae
Hymn → Lyric Poetry
Hypatia → Theon
Hyperion → Eos
Hypermestra → Danaids
hyporchema → Lyric Poetry
Hyppolyta → Amazons

I

Ialysus → Rhodes
Iasius → Demeter
Iconium → Lycaonia
Ida → Crete
Idus → Chronology
Idyll → Theocritus
Iguvine Tables → Umbrians
Ilipa → Scipio (2)
Ilium → Troy
immunitas → Munus
Inachus → Io
in iure → Law, Roman
Ino → Athamas; Leucothea
insula → Architecture
intercessio → Tribuni Plebis
Iobates → Bellerophon; Proetus
Iocasta → Oedipus
Iolcus → Jason (1)
Ionic Order → Architecture
Ionian Revolt → Persian Wars
Iphianassa → Iphigenia
Iphicles → Heracles
Isagoras → Cleisthenes (2)
Ischys → Coronis
Issus, battle of → Alexander (4)
iugerum → Measures
Iulus → Ascanius
ius auspiciorum → Auspicium
ius auxilii ferendi → Tribuni Plebis
ius edicendi → Edictum
ius honorarium → Edictum
ius naturale → Ius Gentium
Iznik → Nicaea

J

Jalapur → Bucephalus
Japyges → Messapia
Jarbas → Dido
Jebeil → Byblus
Jerash → Gerasha
Jonathan (Hasmonaean) → Judaea
Judas Maccabaeaus → Judaea
Junius Blaesus → Imperator
Justinus → Trogus, Pompeius

K

Kalendae → Chronology
Kantharos → Piraeus
Kerykeion → Hermes
kitharistes → Education, Greek
Knights → Equites
Köln → Colonia Agrippinensis
komos → Comedy, Greek

Kore → Sculpture, Greek
kosmetes → Epheboi
Kouros → Sculpture, Greek
Krater → Pottery
Kylix → Pottery

L

Labdacus → Oedipus
labrys → Labyrinth
Lachesis → Moira
Laco → Eurycles
Lacus Curtius → Curtius
Lade, battle of → Persian Wars
Ladon → Hesperides
Lago Averno → Avernus
Lambèse → Lambaesis
Lamian War → Lamia
Land → Ager Publicus; Colonus; Gromatici; Latifundia; Villa
Lanuvio → Lanuvium
Laodicea in Phoenicia → Berytus
Laomedes → Heracles; Poseidon
lapis niger → Romulus
Lapseki → Lampsacus
Laranda → Lycaonia
Lars Tolumnius → Cossus
Larunda → Acca Larentia
Latakia → Laodice (1)
Latin League → Latini; Latium
lauchme → Etruscans
Lausus → Mezentius
Lavinia → Latinus
lawagetas → Mycenaean civilization
Leagues → Achaea; Aetolia; Amphictionies; Boeotia; Peloponnesian League; Second Athenian League; Thessaly
Leander → Hero
Lebadeia → Trophonius
legatio libera → Senate
leges → Lex
legis actio → Law, Roman
legislatio → Lex
Lekythos → Pottery
Leleges → Caria
Lemuria → Manes
Lentini → Leontini
Lerida → Ilerda
Lesbia → Clodia
Leuce → Achilles
Leucippidae → Leucippus (2)
lex Aebutia → Law, Roman
Lex Menenia → Patrum Auctoritas
lex Porcia → Provocatio
lex Publilia → Patrum Auctoritas
lex Valeria → Provocatio
Liberalia → Liber
libri lintei → Macer
limitanei → Constantine (1); Legion
Lincoln → Lindum
Lindus → Rhodes
Linear A → Crete; Minoan Civilization
Linus → Music
litterator → Education, Roman
Longus → Daphnis and Chloe
Luceres → Tribus
Lucullus (consul 151 BC) → Felicitas
Lucumo → Etruscans

Lucus Feroniae → Feronia
Ludi Saeculares → Secular Games
Luperci → Lupercalia
Lycaon → Arcas
Lycambes → Archilochus
Lyceum → Peripatetic School
Lydiadas → Megalopolis
Lygdamis → Naxos (1)
Lynceus → Danaids; Idas
Lyon → Lugdunum
Lyre → Music

M

Maccabaeus → Judaea
Macedonian Wars → Philip V; Perseus (2)
Machaon → Medicine
Magas → Cyrene
magister officiorum → Consistorium
Magna Mater → Cybele
Magnetes → Magnesia
Mahon → Mago
Mainz → Mogontiacum
Malchus → Porphyry
manah → Coinage, Greek
Mandrocles → Samos
manipulus (maniple) → Armies, Roman; Legion
manumissio → Freedmen
Marcii → Coriolanus
Marcion → Gnosticism
Marica → Minturnae
Maroboduus → Marcomanni
Marpessa → Idas
Marsala → Lilybaeum
Marseilles → Massalia
mater castrorum → Faustina; Julia Domna
Mechane → Aeschylus; Tragedy
Medimnos → Measures
Medius → Medea
Medjerda → Carthage
Medusa → Gorgo
Megalesia → Cybele
megaloi theoi → Cabiri
Melanion → Atalanta
Melanippus → Tydeus
Melanthus → Codrus
Melpomene → Muses
Memmius → Lucretius
Memnon (historian) → Heraclea Pontica
Memnoneion → Memnon (1)
Menaechmus → Mathematics
Menoecus → Creon (1)
mensores → Gromatici
Merida → Augusta (2) Emerita
Merope → Orion
Merv → Antioch (1)
Mesogeia → Attica
Messina → Messana
Metaneira → Demeter
Metaurus, battle of → Hasdrubal (2)
Metellus Nepos, Q. → Didius
Meton → Astronomy
Metrocles → Diogenes (4)
Milan → Mediolanum
Milâs → Mylassa
militiae → Dictator; Pomerium
mimiambi → Herodas

mina → Coinage, Greek
Misenus → Misenum
Mithridates (Parthian) → Parthia
Mithridates Callinicus → Commagene
Mnemosyne → Muses
Mnesicles → Acropolis; Propylaea
Modena → Mutina
Modestinus → Herennius Modestinus
modius → Measures
Molon → Antiochus III
Molossus → Neoptolenus
Monte San Guiliano → Eryx
Motya → Libybaeum
Mulvian bridge, battle of → Maxentius
Murena → Mithridates VI
Myrrha → Adonis
Myrtilus → Poseidon

N

Naïos → Dodona
naos → Temple
Naples → Neapolis
Narbonne → Narbo
Narona → Dalmatia
Narses → Diocletian
Naulochus → Agrippa (1)
navicularii → Annona
Nectar → Ambrosia
Nemetacum → Atrebates
neoi → Education, Greek
neoteri → Catullus
Nephele → Athamas
nequia → Odysseus
Nereids → Nereus
Nesiotes → Critius
Nessus → Deianira; Heracles
Nice → Massalia
Nicaea → Bithynia
Nicopolis → Actium
Nîmes → Nemausus
nomen → Names
nomographoi → Achaea
Nomoi → Egypt
nomophylakia → Areopagus
Nomos → Lyric Poetry
Nonae → Chronology
Notium → Colophon
Numitor → Romulus
nundinae → Didius

O

Obols → Coinage, Greek; Measures
Octavianus → Augustus
Octavius → Augustus
Oenomaus → Pelops
Oenotri → Brutii; Italy
oikistes → Apoikia
Oenoche → Pottery
Oinophyta → Athens
Olorus → Miltiades; Thucydides (2)
Onchestos → Amphictionies
opisthodomos → Temple
Oppius → Esquiline
Oppius Sabinus, C. → Domitian
Orange → Arausio
Oratory → Rhetoric
Orders → Architecture

ordo equester → Equites
Oreithyia → Boreas
Orthagoras → Cleisthenes (1); Sicyon
Orthia → Artemis
Orthos → Geryon
Orthygia → Asteria; Delos
Orvieto → Volsinii
Ostrogoths → Goths

P

Pacorus → Orodes II
Padua → Patavium
Paetus → Corbulo
paidagogus → Education, Greek
paidonomos → Education, Greek
paidotribes → Education, Greek
palaestra → Gymnasium
Palermo → Panormus
Palestrina → Praeneste
Palladion → Athena
Pallas → Athena
Pallene → Chalcidice
Pamphyloi → Dorians
Panchaea → Euhemerus
Pantomime → Mimus
par potestas → Consul; Imperium
parabasis → Comedy, Greek
Paraetacene, battle of → Eumenes (1)
Paraloi → Megacles
Parcae → Moira
Parentalia → Manes
parhesia → Athens; Rhetoric
Paris → Lutetia Parisorum
Parni → Parthia
parodoi → Theatre
Parthenopaeus → Atalanta
Parthenos → Athena
Parysatis → Darius II
Pasion → Freedmen
Pasiphaë → Daedalus; Minos
Pasithea → Charites
pater patratus → Fetiales
patronus → Cliens
Pausias of Sicyon → Painting
pedarii → Senate
peleïades → Dodona
Pelias → Jason (1); Neleus
Pelike → Pottery
pentekonteres → Ships
Penthesilea → Amazons
Pentri → Samnium
Perennis → Commodus
Perge → Pamphylia
perioche → Livy
Periphetes → Theseus
peristylion → Temple
Perugia → Perusia
Perusine War → Fulvia; Perusia
Pessinus → Cybele
Peucetii → Messapia
Phaestus → Minoan Civilization
Phalanthus → Tarentum
phalera → Equites; Signa Militaria
Phalerum → Piraeus
Phanes → Orphism
Phasis → Colchis
Phegeus → Alcmaeon
Philadelphia → Decapolis
philippeioi → Coinage, Greek
Philippicae → Cicero (1)

Philomelus → Onomarchus
Philoxenus → Mosaics
Phoenice, Peace of → Hannibal;
    Philip V

Phryxis → Athamas
Phyllis → Demophon
pilum → Armies, Roman
Pinarii → Hercules
Pindus → Doris
Pithecusae → Ischia
plebiscitum Claudianum → Flaminius
Pleiades → Atlas
plethron → Measures
Plouton → Hades
Podalirius → Medicine
Podium → Temple
Pollux → Dioscuri
Polybotes → Gigantes
Polybus → Adrastus; Oedipus
Polydectes → Perseus
Polydeucus → Dioscuri
Polyhymnia → Muses
Polyphemus → Cyclopes
Polynices → Eteocles; Seven against
    Thebes
Polyzelus → Delphi; Hieron I
pompa → Gladiators; Triumph
populares → Optimates
Porphyrion → Gigantes
Portus → Ostia
Porus → Alexander (4)
Poseidonia → Paestum
Posidippus → Asclepiades
Potiti → Heracles
Pozzuoli → Puteoli
praeda → Manubiae
Praefectus Vigilum → Vigiles
praenomen → Names
praesides → Diocletian
Pratinas → Satyrs
Priapea → Priapus
princeps senatus → Senate
Principate → Princeps; Augustus
principes → Legion
probouleumata → Boule
Procne → Philomela
Proculiani → Sabinus
promulgatio → Lex
pronaos → Temple
Propraetor → Proconsul; Provincia
prorogatio imperii → Proconsul
Proserpina → Persephone
proskenion → Theatre
proskynesis → Alexander (4)
prosodion → Lyric Poetry
protagonistes → Tragedy
Psammetichus → Periander
psephismata → Ekklesia
Psykter → Pottery
Pterelaus → Amphitryon
Puglia → Apulia
Pylades → Iphigenia; Orestes
Pyrrhus → Neoptolenus
Pythius → Mausoleum
Pyxis → Pottery

Q

quadrans → Coinage, Roman
quadrigati → Coinage, Roman
Quadrium → Varro (2)

quaestor sacri palatii → Consis-
    torium; Quaestor
quinarius → Coinage, Roman
Quirinal → Rome (City)

R

Raphia, battle of → Antiochus III
Ramnes → Tribus
Rasena → Etruscans
Reate → Sabini
recognitio → Equites
Reggio → Rhegium
relegatio → Exilium
Remus → Romulus
Res Privata → Severus
Res Gestae → Monumentum Ancyranum
rescripta (sing. *rescriptum*) → Law,
    Roman
responsa → Jurisprudence
retiarius → Gladiators
Rex Nemorensis → Diana
Rhea → Kronos; Zeus
Rhea Silvia → Romulus
rhetor → Education, Roman
Rhome → Latinus
Rhython → Pottery
riciniata → Fabula
Rimini → Ariminum
Roads → Via (Aemilia, etc.)
rogatio → Lex
Roscius Amerinus → Cicero (1)
Rullus → Cicero (1)

S

Sabiniani → **Sabinus**
Sacred Wars → Amphictionies
sacrosanctitas → Tribuni Plebis
saeculum → Secular Games
Sagunto → Saguntum
St. Albans → Verulamium
Salagassus → Pisidia
Salamacis → Hermaphroditus
Salome, Alexandra → Judaea
Salona → Dalmatia
Salonika → Thessalonica
Samsun → Amisus
Samnite Wars → Samnium
Samos (king) → Commagene
Samsat → Samosata
Santorini → Thera
Sarmizegethusa → Dacia
Saturnalia → Saturnus
Satyr-play → Satyrs
Satyricon → Petronius
Sauroctonus → Praxiteles
Scaevola → Porsenna
Scamandrius → Astyanax
Scardona → Dalmatia
scazon → Hipponax
Scias → Theodorus
Scipio Serapio, P. → Gracchus (2)
Scipionic Circle → Scipio (5)
Scriptores Historiae Augustae → His-
    toria Augusta
scutum → Armies, Roman
Scylla → Nisus
Scyrus → Cimon; Theseus
Scythopolis → Decapolis

seisachtheia → Solon
Selge → Pisidia
Selinunte → Selinus
Sellasia, battle of → Cleomenes (2)
selloi → Dodona
semis → Coinage, Roman
Senators → Senate
sententiae → Seneca (1)
sestertius → Coinage, Roman
Sestos → Chersonesus (1)
Sevilla → Hipsalis
seviri Augustales → Augustales
sextans → Coinage, Roman
Sextius Lateranus, L. → Stolo
Side → Pamphylia
Sigeum → Troas
Sila (forrest) → Bruttium
Silchester → Atrebates
Simon (Hasmonaean) → Judaea
Simon Magnus → Gnosticism
Sinis → Theseus
Siphnos → Coinage, Greek
Sithonia → Chalcidice
skene → Theatre
Skyphos → Pottery
Smyrna → Cinyras
Social War → Bellum Sociale;
    Philip V
solidus → Coinage, Roman
Sophron → Mimus
sophronistai → Epheboi
Sphacteria → Cleon
Spoleto → Spoletium
Sousse → Hadrumetum
spolia opima → Cossus
Stamnos → Pottery
Stater → Coinage, Greek
Stoa Poicile → Athens
Strasbourg → Argentorate
Strato's Tower → Caesarea Maritima
suasoriae → Seneca (1)
Suez → Aqueducts and Canals
Symplegades → Argonauts
Sychaeus → Dido
Syrinx → Pan

T

tabulae novae → Catiline
Tactics → Armies
Tadmor → Palmyra
Talent → Coinage, Greek
Tammuz → Adonis
Taormina → Taurominium
Taras → Tarentum
Taranto → Tarentum
Tarchon → Tarquinii
Tarquinia → Tarquinii
Tarraconensis → Spain
Tarragona → Tarraco
Tauris → Iphigenia
Taxiles → Alexander (4)
Tebessa → Theveste

Tectosages → Galatia
Telamon, battle of → Boii
Telegones → Odysseus
Telesterion → Eleusis
temenos → Temple
Ten Thousand → Xenophon
Terentia → Cicero (1)
Teres → Thrace
Tereus → Philomela
Termessus → Pisidia
Terminalia → Terminus
Terpsichore → Muses
Terracina → Tarracina
terra sigillata → Pottery
Tetrarchy → Diocletian
Teutones → Cimbri
Thalia → Muses
Thamyris → Muses
Theodorus of Cyrene → Mathe-
    matics
Theseum → Athens
Thesproti → Epirus
Thisbe → Pyramus and Thisbe
Thoas → Hypsipyle
thracian → Gladiators
Thrasybulus → Miletus
Thrasymachus → Plato
Thyestes → Atreus and Thyestes
Thyone → Semele
Thyrsus → Maenads
Timarchus → Demosthenes (2)
Tiberias → Herod (2) Antipas
Time-reckoning → Chronology
Timesitheus → Gordian III
Tingi → Mauretania
Tiribazus → Conon
Tiridates III → Diocletian
Tisias → Rhetoric
Tities (Titienses) → Tribus
Titus Tatius → Romulus
Tivoli → Tibur
Tolistobogii → Galatia
Tolosa (Toulouse), Treasure of →
    Caepio
Torino → Augusta (3) Taurinorum
trabea → Equites; Salii
transvectio → Equites
Trapani → Drepana
Treasure of Atreus → Atreus and
    Thyestes
Treason → Perduellio; Maiestas
Trebia, battle of → Hannibal
Trebizond → Trapezus
Trebonius → Dolabella
tresviri → Triumivi
triarii → Legion
Tribunicean power → Tribuni Plebis
triens → Coinage, Roman
Triptolemus → Demeter
tritagonistes → Tragedy
Triumvirate (First, Second) →
    Triumviri
triumviri monetales → Coinage, Roman
Trivium → Varro (2)

U

Ulixes → Odysseus
Ummidius Quadratus → Commodus
uncia → Coinage, Roman
Urania → Muses
Urfa → Edessa (2)
Utique → Utica

V

Valentianus → Gnosticism
Valerio-Horatian Laws → Valerius
    (2) Potitus
Vase-Painting → Pottery
Velia → Elea
velites → Legion
venationes → Ludi
verbenarius → Fetiales
Vercellae, battle of → Catullus (1);
    Marius
vexillatio → Signa Militaria
vexillum → Signa Militaria
vicarii → Dioecesis
vici → vicomagistri
victoriatus → Coinage, Roman
Vienna → Vindobona
Viminal → Rome (City)
Visigoths → Goths
Vivarium → Cassiodorus
Volterra → Volaterrae
Vulcan → Volcanus

W

wanax → Mycenaean Civilization
Weights → Measures
Wiesbaden → Aquae

X

Xanthippe → Socrates
Xanthippus → Athens; Pericles
Xiphilinus → Dio (2) Cassius

Y

York → Eburacum

Z

Zagreus → Orphism
Zancle → Messana
Zea → Piraeus
Zethus → Amphion
Zilath → Etruscans
Zipoites → Bithynia
Zonaras → Dio (2) Cassius

ACKNOWLEDGMENTS

The Publishers wish to express their special thanks and appreciation to Elsevier Publishing Projects, Amsterdam, and to their Managing Director Drs. A. A. M. van der Heyden for allowing us to reproduce their pictures and for their kind help. Our thanks also goes to the following individuals for their help and advice: Hannah Livij, Felix Graber;

to the following for permission to reproduce illustrations: Fratelli Alinari S.p.A., Firenze (p. 12, 14, 15, 22, 26, 27, 30, 32, 38, 60, 88, 90, 94, 95, 104, 112, 120, 123, 124, 128, 133, 135, 136, 139, 152, 154, 158, 181, 192, 202, 203, 209, 212, 217, 222, 223, 230, 241, 257, 260, 261, 266, 267, 285–287, 301, 304, 308, 311, 313, 327, 330, 332, 335–337, 341, 342, 346, 358, 371, 374, 377, 399, 403, 413, 414, 416, 421, 426, 445, 446, 449–452, 455, 472, 475, 477, 483); Elsevier Publishing Projects, Amsterdam (p. 17, 49, 55, 62, 74, 76, 77, 82, 85–87, 91, 100, 109, 111, 118, 143, 186, 202, 221, 229, 239, 243, 250, 271, 295, 299, 333, 362, 364, 367, 383, 395, 431, 448, 464, 467, endpaper); Staatliche Museen zu Berlin (p. 18, 436); National Museum, Athens (p. 25, 423); Arnold Spaer Collections (p. 31, 45, 131); Frenkel Collections (p. 32); Department of Antiquities, Israel Ministry of Education and Culture, Jerusalem (p. 36, 309, 478); Photographie Giraudon, Paris (p. 40, 48, 63, 97, 101, 117, 214, 345, 350, 374); Museum Vaticani (p. 44, 246); David Harris, Jerusalem (p. 31, 32, 45, 57, 84, 106, 131, 248, 255); Fred Csasvnik (p. 65); Metropolitan Museum of Art, Rogers Fund 1919 (p. 75, 374, 439); Hirmer Fotoarchiv, München (p. 81, 113, 126, 129, 149, 151, 160, 184, 191, 195, 199, 215, 219, 249, 259, 282, 321, 374, 391, 410, 411, 454, 456, 478, 487); Ministry of Culture and Science, Athens, TAP Service (p. 85, 412, 423, 432, 447); Teddy Kollek Collection (p. 94); Hunting Aerosurveys Ltd., London (p. 145); The British Museum (p. 168, 374, 484); Chuseville (p. 198); Carta, Jerusalem (p. 254); Museum of Art, Boston (p. 279, 314, 316); Photo Custodia Terra Sancta (p. 351); National Museum, Naples (p. 385); The Oriental Institute, The University of Chicago (p. 437); Kunsthistorisches Museum, Wien (p. 455); Nelson Glueck (p. 470);

to the following for permission to reproduce colourprints: Holle Bildarchiv, Baden-Baden (p. 33, 34, 54, 169, 170, 187, 190, 207, 305, 323–326, 343, 344, 441, 442, 459, 460–61, 479, 480); David Harris (p. 51, 306); Fratelli Alinari S.p.A. (p. 52, 53, 71, 72); Biblioteca Ambrosiana, Milano (p. 188, 189); Elsevier Publishing Projects (p. 208); The British Museum (p. 462).

Maps: Haim Eitan, Ofra Levi.